lonely planet

Los Angeles,
San Diego & Southern California

Santa Barbara County
p390
Palm Springs & the Deserts
p337
Los Angeles
p56
Disneyland & Orange County
p218
San Diego
p272

THIS EDITION WRITTEN AN

Sara Ben

Andrew Bender, A

PLAN YOUR TRIP

Welcome to Southern California . . . 4

Southern California Map . . 6

Los Angeles, San Diego & Southern California's Top 25 . . . 8

Need to Know . . . 20

If You Like . . . 22

Month by Month . . . 25

Itineraries . . . 27

Southern California's Beaches . . . 33

The Great Outdoors . . . 37

Disneyland Trip Planner . . . 46

Travel with Children . . . 50

Regions at a Glance . . . 53

MARK READ / LONELY PLANET ©

DEATH VALLEY NATIONAL PARK P369

PREDRAG VUCKOVIC /GETTY IMAGES ©

VENICE BEACH P168

ON THE ROAD

LOS ANGELES . . . 56

Los Angeles Highlights . . . 66

Downtown Los Angeles . . . 68

Hollywood . . . 87

Los Angeles Neighborhoods . . . 94

Los Feliz & Griffith Park . . . 99

Silver Lake & Echo Park . . . 105

West Hollywood & Mid-City . . . 108

Culver City & Mar Vista . . . 127

Beverly Hills, Bel Air, Brentwood & Westwood . . . 131

Malibu & Pacific Palisades . . . 144

Santa Monica . . . 152

Southern California's Best Beaches . . . 162

Venice & Marina del Rey . . . 168

South Bay Beaches . . . 177

Manhattan Beach . . . 177

Hermosa Beach . . . 179

Redondo Beach & Torrance . . . 181

Palos Verdes Peninsula . . 182

Long Beach & San Pedro . . . 183

Burbank, Universal City & the San Fernando Valley . . . 189

Pasadena & the San Gabriel Valley . . . 193

Eagle Rock, Highland Park, Mt Washington & Lincoln Heights . . . 201

Boyle Heights & East Los Angeles . . . 202

Westlake & Koreatown . . 203

South Central & Exposition Park . . . 205

Around Los Angeles . . . 213

Catalina Island . . . 213

Six Flags Magic Mountain & Hurricane Harbor . . . 215

Palms to Pines . . . 216

Big Bear Lake . . . 216

DISNEYLAND & ORANGE COUNTY . . 218

Disneyland & Anaheim . . . 219

Around Disneyland . . . 236

Knott's Berry Farm . . . 236

Medieval Times Dinner & Tournament . . . 237

Discovery Science Center . . . 238

TY MILFORD /GETTY IMAGES ©

SURFING, HUNTINGTON BEACH P245

Contents

Bowers Museum & Kidseum.............238
Old Towne Orange......239
Christ Cathedral........240
Richard Nixon Library & Museum......240
Orange County Beaches..............240
Seal Beach.............241
Sunset Beach..........243
Huntington Beach......244
Newport Beach.........249
Around Newport Beach...257
Laguna Beach..........260
Around Laguna Beach...268
Dana Point.............269
San Clemente..........271

SAN DIEGO........272
La Jolla & North County Coast........317
La Jolla...............317
Del Mar................323
Solana Beach..........326
Cardiff-by-the-Sea.....327
Encinitas..............327
Carlsbad...............329
Oceanside.............332
Temecula Area.......334
Temecula..............334

PALM SPRINGS & THE DESERTS.....337
Palm Springs & the Coachella Valley......339
Joshua Tree National Park........350
Anza-Borrego Desert State Park.....358
Around Anza-Borrego..363
Salton Sea.............363
Julian..................363

Route 66............364
Barstow................365
Mojave National Preserve.............367
Around Mojave National Preserve.....369
Nipton.................369
Primm..................369
Death Valley National Park.........369
Around Death Valley National Park.........376
Beatty, Nevada.........376
Shoshone...............377
Tecopa.................377
Upper Mojave Desert..378
Lancaster-Palmdale.....378
Mojave.................378
Boron..................379
Ridgecrest.............379
Trona Pinnacles........380
Randsburg..............380
Las Vegas............380

SANTA BARBARA COUNTY...........390
Santa Barbara........392
Santa Barbara Wine Country........408
Los Olivos.............414
Solvang................415
Buellton...............418
Around Santa Barbara.............419
Montecito..............419
Summerland.............420
Carpinteria............420
Ojai...................421
Ventura................423
Channel Islands National Park..........425

UNDERSTAND

Southern California Today...............430
History...............432
The Lifestyle.........441
As Seen on TV (& Film)..............448
Music & the Arts.....453
SoCal Architecture....458
Flavors of SoCal......461
Wild Things..........466

SURVIVAL GUIDE

Directory A–Z........470
Transportation.......479
Index................488
Map Legend...........495

SPECIAL FEATURES

The Great Outdoors..........37
Disneyland Trip Planner.......46
Los Angeles Neighborhoods....94
Southern California's Best Beaches....162

Welcome to Southern California

Southern California, or SoCal as everyone calls it, is a land of sunsets over Pacific blue, coastal drives with the roof down, and authentic tacos with cold beers and friends. But you can dress up here too.

Pop Culture

Even though you won't find many real-life stars in Hollywood these days, you might spot A-list celebs shopping at LA's cutting-edge boutiques or walking along the beach in Malibu. Take a sneak peek behind the scenes of 'The Industry' on a movie studio tour or join a live TV audience. Round up the whole family for Southern California's theme parks; with cartoon characters and adventure rides, Disneyland and Disney California Adventure are classics. Or go for a walk on the wild side at the San Diego Zoo and Safari Park, where giraffes and zebras roam.

Beaches & Natural Beauty

Southern California may be best known for its artificial beauty (hello, Botox and silicone), but its beaches are really an ace in the hole. Whether you're a punk surfer, aspiring pro volleyball nut or new-agey bohemian, there's an idiosyncratic SoCal beach town just for you. Offshore, the Channel Islands are a jewel-like archipelago encompassing civilized Catalina and a wild national park. Escape to Big Bear Lake's cooler alpine climes or turn up the heat in SoCal's deserts with a getaway to the retro-modern resort of Palm Springs. In Death Valley, Joshua Tree and Anza-Borrego, dusty 4WD roads and hiking trails lead to hidden canyons and native fan-palm oases.

California Cuisine & Wine

Maybe your SoCal sojourn will be an epicurean quest. Finding the best fish tacos and craft beers in San Diego alone could take days. Meanwhile in LA, foodies passionately argue about where the best sushi bar or fusion food truck is. LA is also a melting pot of ethnic cooking, from the kitchens of Little Tokyo and Thai Town to the *taquerías* of East LA. Then cruise up the coast highway past Malibu, stopping at seafood shacks, before following back roads through Santa Barbara's wine country.

Arts & Architecture

LA is the creative capital of Southern California, with edgy art museums, historic movie palaces and post-modern landmarks jutting out of the cityscape. The same creativity that fuels 'The Industry' keeps lifeblood pumping through the city's buzzing theater, music and performing arts scenes. Naturally inspiring landscapes bring out SoCal's artistic side in Laguna Beach, a historic artists' colony in Orange County, and in Palm Springs, an icon of mid-20th-century modern architecture.

Why I Love Southern California

By Sara Benson, Coordinating Author

With 315 days of sunshine every year, SoCal is where I've chosen to make my home. I never get tired of exploring (or more truthfully, eating my way around) LA's modern mosaic of neighborhoods and driving coastal highways to hidden beaches. In winter, balmy San Diego is the place to be. Spring usually finds me escaping into SoCal's deserts to see spectacular wildflower blooms in Death Valley or for Modernism Week in Palm Springs. The vineyards of Santa Barbara are practically in my backyard, tempting me to play truant on any given weekday.

For more about our authors, see page 496

Above: Skateboarding, Venice Beach (p171)

Los Angeles, San Diego & Southern

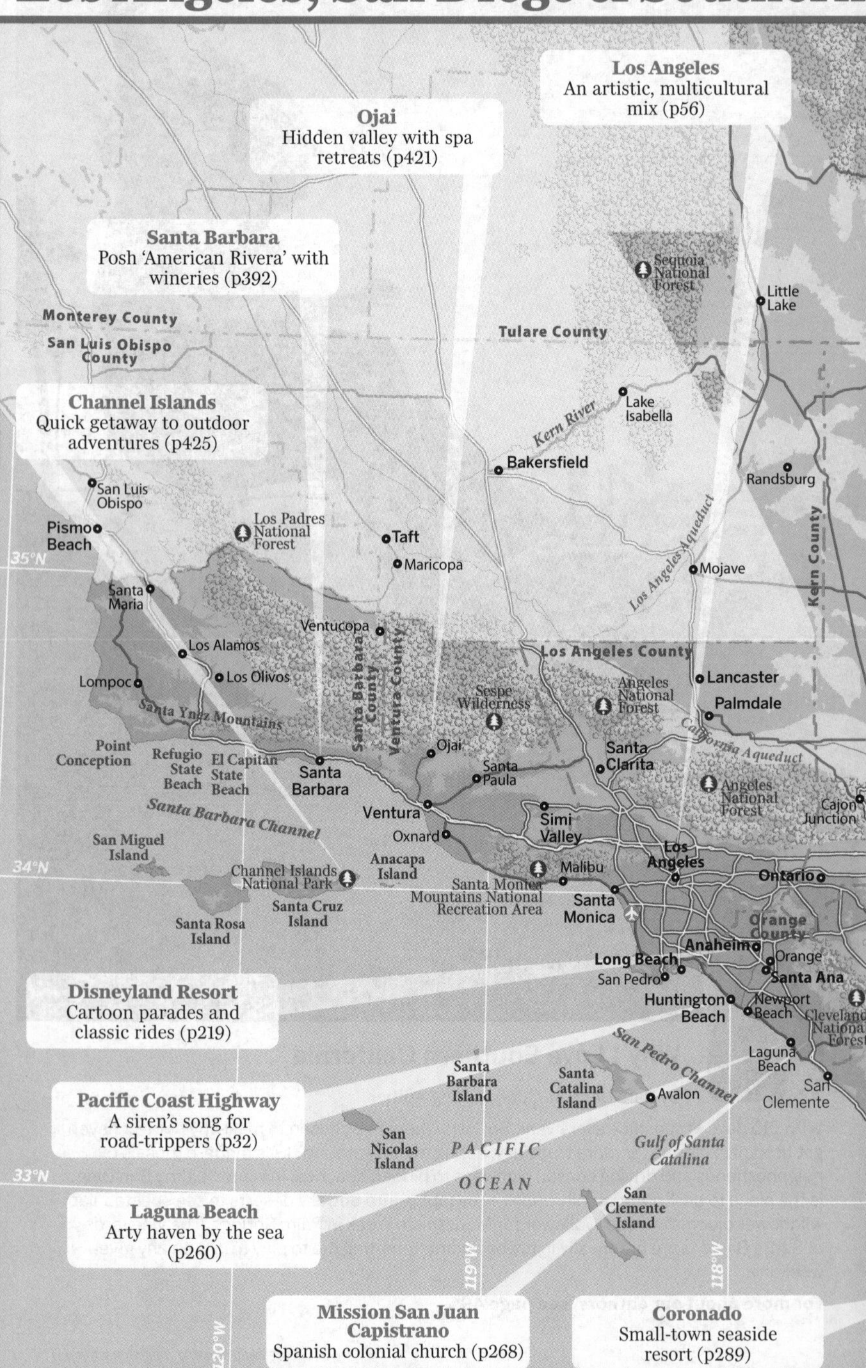

California

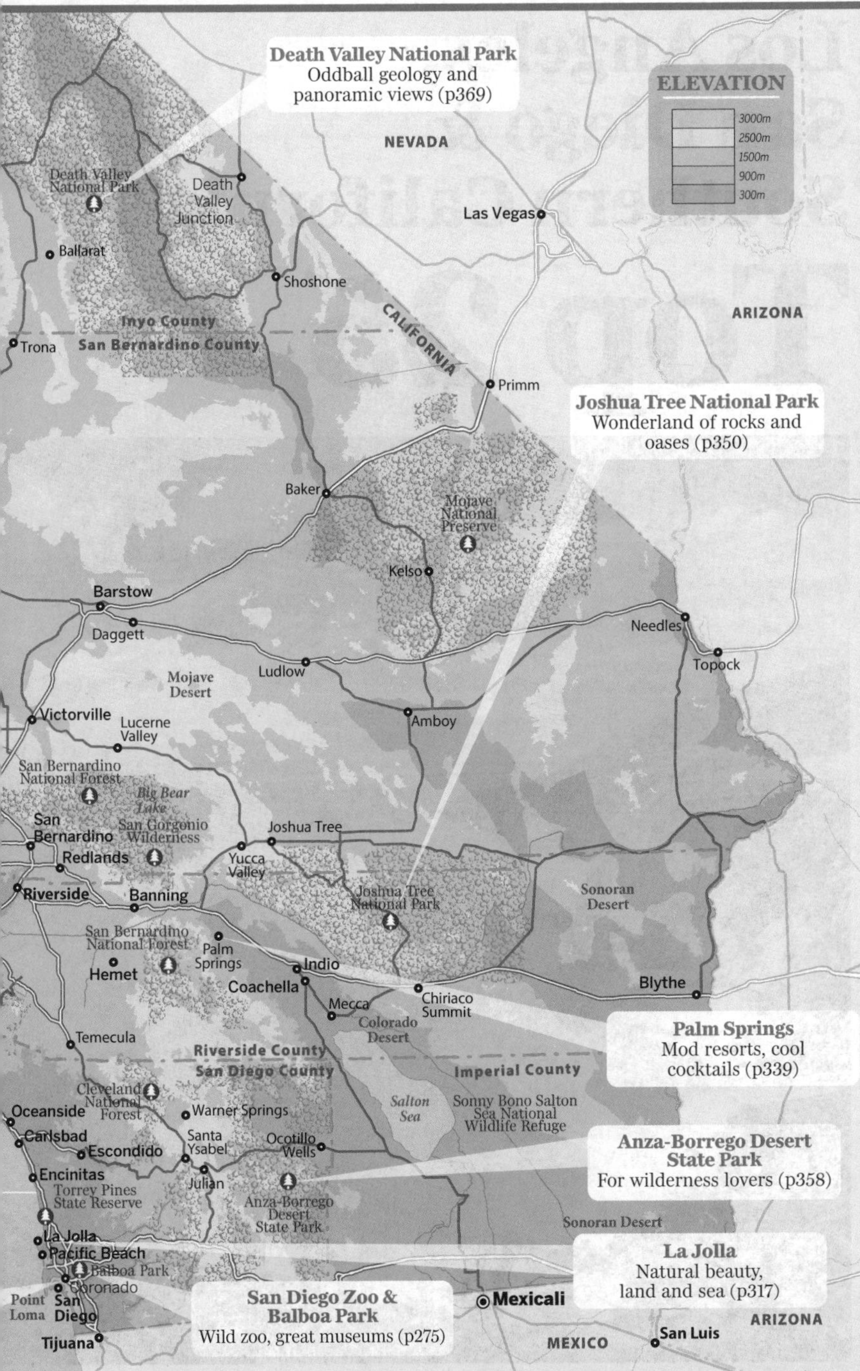

0 100 km
0 50 miles
Death Valley National Park
Oddball geology and panoramic views (p369)
ELEVATION
3000m
2500m
1500m
900m
300m
NEVADA
Las Vegas
Death Valley National Park
Death Valley Junction
Ballarat
Shoshone
ARIZONA
CALIFORNIA
Inyo County
San Bernardino County
Trona
Primm
Joshua Tree National Park
Wonderland of rocks and oases (p350)
Baker
Mojave National Preserve
Kelso
Barstow
Daggett
Needles
Topock
Ludlow
Mojave Desert
Victorville
Lucerne Valley
Amboy
San Bernardino National Forest
Big Bear Lake
San Gorgonio Wilderness
San Bernardino
Redlands
Joshua Tree
Yucca Valley
Riverside
Banning
Joshua Tree National Park
Sonoran Desert
San Bernardino National Forest
Palm Springs
Hemet
Indio
Coachella
Blythe
Mecca
Chiriaco Summit
Colorado Desert
Palm Springs
Mod resorts, cool cocktails (p339)
Temecula
Riverside County
San Diego County
Imperial County
Cleveland National Forest
Oceanside
Warner Springs
Salton Sea
Sonny Bono Salton Sea National Wildlife Refuge
Carlsbad
Escondido
Santa Ysabel
Ocotillo Wells
Anza-Borrego Desert State Park
For wilderness lovers (p358)
Encinitas
Torrey Pines State Reserve
Julian
Anza-Borrego Desert State Park
Sonoran Desert
La Jolla
Pacific Beach
Balboa Park
Coronado
La Jolla
Natural beauty, land and sea (p317)
Point Loma
San Diego
San Diego Zoo & Balboa Park
Wild zoo, great museums (p275)
Mexicali
ARIZONA
Tijuana
MEXICO
San Luis

Los Angeles, San Diego & Southern California's Top 25

1

Pacific Coast Highway

1 Make your escape from SoCal's tangled, traffic-jammed freeways and cruise in the coast's slow lanes. Legendary Hwy 1 (p32) snakes past sea cliffs and sunny beach towns, each with its own idiosyncratic personality, from offbeat bohemian to glamorously rich. In between, you'll uncover hidden beaches and coves, locals' fave surf breaks, rustic seafood shacks dishing up the day's freshest catch, and old-fashioned wooden piers where you can walk out and catch the sun setting over endless Pacific horizons.

Los Angeles

2 If you think you've already got LA figured out – celebrity culture, smog, gridlocked traffic, Botoxed babes and reality TV – think again. SoCal's biggest metropolis (p56) is made up of dozens of independent cities, where over 90 languages are spoken. Of course you'll want to join other star-struck sightseers in Hollywood and Beverly Hills, and beachgoers in Santa Monica and Venice, but also check out what else contemporary LA has to offer, especially Downtown: cutting-edge creative arts, high-minded cultural institutions, a melting pot of world cultures and postmodern architectural landmarks.

Frank Gehry's Walt Disney Concert Hall (p68)

BMINERP / GETTY IMAGES ©

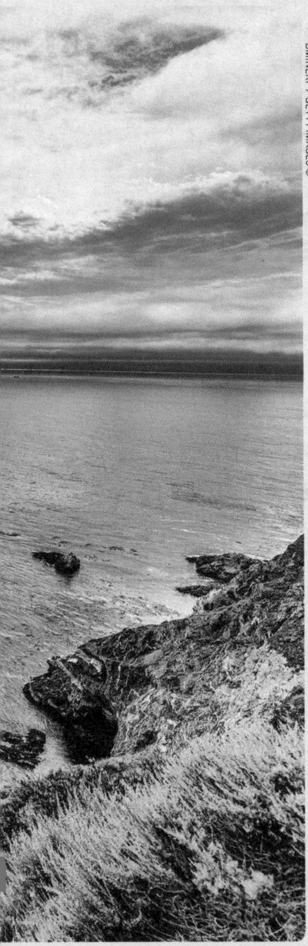

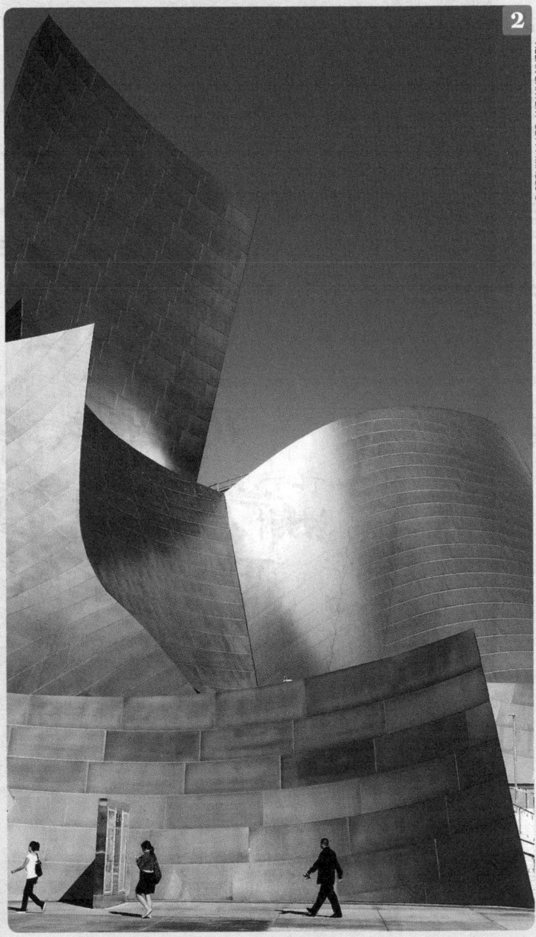

2

ALLAN BAXTER / GETTY IMAGES ©

3

ZSSD / GETTY IMAGES ©

4

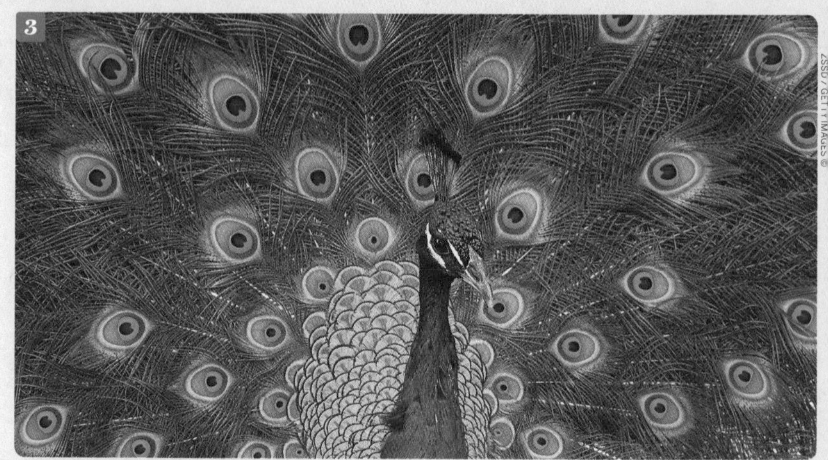

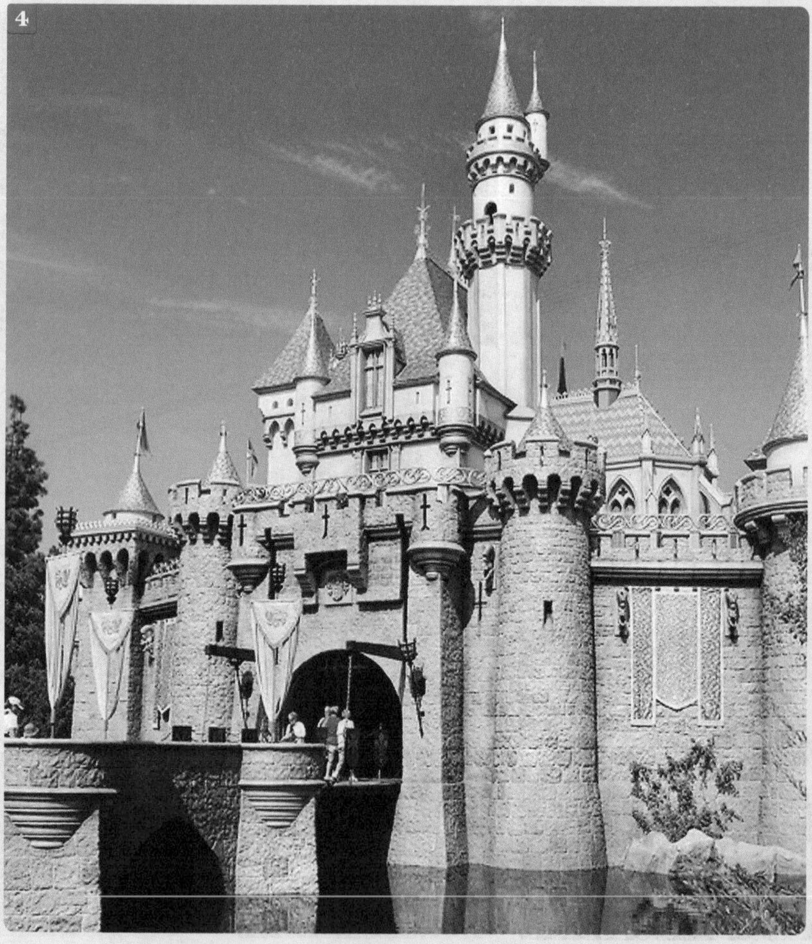

© DISNEY

ANDRIS OBORN / GETTY IMAGES ©

San Diego Zoo & Balboa Park

3 An enormous urban green space (an increasingly rare sight in SoCal), beautiful Balboa Park (p275) is where San Diegans come to play when they're not at the beach. Bring the whole family and spend the day immersed in over a dozen art, cultural and science museums, or marvel at the Spanish Colonial Revival architecture while sunning yourself along El Prado promenade. Glimpse exotic wildlife at the world-famous zoo (p276), or see a show at the Old Globe theater (p313), a faithful reconstruction of the Shakespearean original. Indian peafowl, San Diego Zoo (p276)

Disneyland Resort

4 Where orange groves and walnut trees once grew, there Walt Disney built his dream, throwing open the doors of his Magic Kingdom in 1955. Today, Disneyland (p221) is SoCal's most-visited tourist attraction, with beloved cartoon characters parading arm-in-arm down Main Street, USA and fireworks exploding over Sleeping Beauty Castle. If you're a kid, or just hopelessly young at heart, you'll also want to make time for next-door Disney California Adventure, a Golden State–themed amusement park with thrill rides, parades and a nighttime sound-and-lights spectacular. Sleeping Beauty Castle (p223)

Laguna Beach

5 In Orange County, Huntington Beach draws the hang-loose surfer crowd, while yachties play in the fantasyland of Newport Beach. But further south, Laguna Beach (p260) tempts with a more sophisticated blend of money, culture and natural beauty. Startling seascapes led an early-20th-century artists' colony to put down roots here, and Laguna's bohemian past peeks out in downtown art galleries, arts-and-crafts bungalows tucked among multimillion-dollar mansions and an annual Festival of Arts and Pageant of the Masters. Crescent Bay, Laguna Beach (p260)

Big Bear Lake

6 Let some of SoCal's best mountain scenery scroll past your windshield as you escape from LA to the cooler elevations and alpine scenery of Big Bear Lake (p216). The unforgettably twisting Rim of the World Scenic Byway, with its hairpin turns and jaw-dropping lookouts, is by far the best way to get to this family-friendly resort town encircled by woodsy holiday cabins. Once here, take a dip in the water and a hike on the lake's quieter north shore. Mountain biking, Big Bear Lake (p216)

Palm Springs

7 A star-studded oasis in the Mojave ever since the heyday of Frank Sinatra's Rat Pack, 'PS' (p337) is a retro-chic getaway for LA urbanites. Do like A-list stars and hipsters do: lounge by your mid-century modern hotel's swimming pool, go art-gallery hopping and vintage shopping, then drink cocktails after sunset. Feeling less loungey? Break a sweat on hiking trails that wind through desert canyons across Native American tribal lands, or scramble to a summit in the San Jacinto Mountains, reached via a head-spinning aerial tramway. A golf course with a view of the San Jacinto Mountains

6

MICHAEL SALAS / GETTY IMAGES ©

7

JENNIFERPHOTOGRAPHYIMAGING / GETTY IMAGES ©

JEFF DIEHL / GETTY IMAGES ©

BRENT WINEBRENNER / GETTY IMAGES ©

S. GREG PANOSIAN / GETTY IMAGES ©

Death Valley National Park

8 Just uttering the name brings up visions of broken-down pioneer wagon trains and parched lost souls crawling across desert sand dunes. Maybe the most surprising thing about Death Valley (p369) is how full of life it is. Spring wildflower blooms explode with a painter's palette of hues across camel-colored hillsides. Feeling adventurous? Twist your way up narrow canyons hiding geological oddities, stand atop volcanic craters formed by violent prehistoric explosions, or explore Wild West mining ghost towns where fortunes were made and lost. Mesquite Flat sand dunes, Stovepipe Wells (p372)

Foxen Canyon Wine Trail

9 Forget Northern California's chi-chi wine countries. SoCal beckons with the fog-kissed Santa Ynez and Santa Maria Valleys, aka *Sideways* wine country. Less than an hour's drive from Santa Barbara, you can wander through fields of grapes, tipple pinot noir and other prized varietals and live the good life all around. Start in the village of Los Olivos, overflowing with wine-tasting rooms and cafes. Then follow the Foxen Canyon Wine Trail (p411) along winding country roads where big-name vineyards rub shoulders with risk-taking boutique winemakers. Winery, Santa Maria Valley (p408)

Santa Barbara

10 Santa Barbara (p392) is so idyllic it actually lives up to its self-proclaimed 'American Riviera' nickname. Waving palm trees, powdery beaches, fishing boats clanking about in the harbor – it'd be a travel cliché if it wasn't the plain truth. California's 'Queen of the Missions' is a rare beauty, especially with its signature red-roofed, whitewashed adobe buildings. In fact, all of downtown was rebuilt harmoniously in Spanish colonial style after a devastating earthquake in 1925. Come escape LA for the day or a wine-soaked weekend in the country. Mission Santa Barbara (p392)

RICHARD CUMMINS / GETTY IMAGES ©

SF_FOODPHOTO / GETTY IMAGES ©

EDDIE BRADY / GETTY IMAGES ©

Gaslamp Quarter

11 If you can tear yourself away from San Diego's bodacious beaches after dark, it's time for restaurant-, club-, and bar-hopping in this revitalized downtown district (p308). Cobblestone streets and gas lamps evoke 19th-century nostalgia, but this rollickin' neighborhood's true historical legacy is long-gone gambling dens, saloons and bordellos. Nowadays the party scene spills out onto the sidewalk nightly, while bands, DJs, craft beers and cocktails wait indoors. The quarter takes all comers: you won't have to fight velvet-rope bouncers here.

Taquerías

12 *Taquerías* are a staple of the SoCal lifestyle, whether you're a beach-bum surfer or an actor rushing between auditions, or both. Taco shops are ubiquitous, particularly in San Diego where the Baja-style fish taco – a corn tortilla wrapped around fried or grilled fish on a bed of cabbage slathered with *pico de gallo* salsa and drizzled with a piquant white sauce – reigns supreme. In SoCal you'll see taco trucks parked by the side of the road almost wherever you go. Try 'em. We bet you'll like 'em. Quesadillas

La Jolla

13 On what some argue is the most beautiful stretch of San Diego's coastline, La Jolla (p317) is definitely not just another SoCal beach town. Atop rocky bluffs just a whisper's breath from the sea, its richly adorned downtown is crowded with boutiques and cafes. But what's right on the shoreline is even more of a treasure, especially the all-natural fish bowl of La Jolla Cove and windswept Torrey Pines State Natural Reserve, further north along the coast, where migratory whales swim by and hang-gliders fly. Wild seals, La Jolla coast (p317)

Joshua Tree National Park

14 With crooked arms reaching up toward heaven like a biblical prophet, Joshua trees are SoCal desert icons. Leave the windshield scenery behind for this park's (p350) network of hiking trails, which will take you up close to even more natural wonders, from native fan-palm oases that look airlifted straight out of Africa to vistas of the strange Salton Sea and snow-dusted San Bernardino Mountains. Kids love boulder-hopping in the park's Wonderland of Rocks, an outdoor playground for rock jocks. Boy Scout Trail (p354), Joshua Tree National Park

Channel Islands

15 Tossed like so many lost pearls off the coast, the Channel Islands are SoCal's last outpost of civilization. They've been that way for thousands of years, ever since seafaring Chumash tribespeople established villages on these remote rocks. The islands also support an abundance of marine life, from coral reefs to giant elephant seals. Get back to nature in rustic Channel Islands National Park (p425), a wildlife haven with fantastic sea kayaking and snorkeling, or make a posh getaway to Mediterranean-esque Catalina Island, with its harborfront hotels.

14

MARK NEWMAN / GETTY IMAGES ©

15

YENWEN LU / GETTY IMAGES ©

Route 66

16 The SoCal section of this beautifully lonely, world-famous heritage highway (p364) appears for a stretch in the Mojave Desert before being gobbled up by the interstate. You'll know you've succeeded in finding America's legendary Mother Road again though when you cruise by neon-lit diners, cool drive-ins, retro motels and kitschy roadside attractions that demand you stop for a photo op. Speed west through atmospheric ghost towns and sleep inside a 1940s faux wigwam before getting your final kicks with the waving palm trees and bustling pier at Santa Monica.

San Diego's North County

17 With dozens of miles of coastline and a nearly perfect climate year-round, it's tough to know where to start on the northern coast of San Diego County (p317). Maybe do what the locals do: grab a fish taco and a surfboard and hit the beach. Or avoid the hoi-polloi as you sit pretty in ritzy Del Mar; get in touch with your inner yogi in enlightened Encinitas; take the kids to Legoland in Carlsbad; or learn to surf by the pier in Oceanside. Surf beach, Encinitas (p327)

BILL DICKINSON / GETTY IMAGES ©

MATTHEW MICAH WRIGHT / GETTY IMAGES ©

18
RICHARD CUMMINS / GETTY IMAGES ©

19
WITOLD SKRYPCZAK / GETTY IMAGES ©

20
BARRY WINIKER / GETTY IMAGES ©

Mission San Juan Capistrano

18 When you visit SoCal, you can't help but follow in at least a few of the footsteps of early Spanish conquistadors and Catholic priests. Mission San Juan Capistrano (p268), nicknamed the 'Jewel of the Missions,' was founded by peripatetic priest Junípero Serra in 1776. Authentically restored, the mission today deserves its nickname, with gorgeous gardens, stone arcades and fountains, and a chapel adorned with spiritual frescoes. In mid-March the whole town celebrates the swallows' famous return from South America to nest in the mission's walls. Great Stone Church, Mission San Juan Capistrano (p268)

Anza-Borrego Desert State Park

19 When you start feeling crushed by SoCal's 22 million residents, head inland from San Diego until you can breathe easy again in the wide-open desert. California's largest state park (p358) is an incredible place to get lost. Follow 4WD roads or hiking trails to find hidden canyons, wind caves, cactus gardens and even herds of endangered bighorn sheep. In the middle of the park, the low-key town of Borrego Springs feels refreshingly far away from the urban rat race. Fish Creek, Split Mountain wind caves (p359)

Coronado

20 Who says you can't turn back time? Speed over the two-mile bay bridge or board the ferry from San Diego to seaside Coronado (p289), a civilized reminder of a more genteel era. Revel in the late-19th-century socialite atmosphere at the palatial 'Hotel Del' where royalty and presidents have bedded down and Marilyn Monroe cavorted in the 1950s screwball comedy *Some Like It Hot*. Then pedal past impossibly white beaches all the way down the peninsula's Silver Strand, stopping for ice cream and cotton candy. Hotel del Coronado (p289)

21
DANITA DELIMONT / GETTY IMAGES ©

22
RICH REID / GETTY IMAGES ©

23
RICHARD CUMMINS / GETTY IMAGES ©

Temecula

21 Make a weekend getaway from San Diego to this Old West–flavored town (p334), the jumping-off point for a wine-tasting tour through hilly vineyards. Luiseño tribespeople, who were present when Spanish missionaries first traipsed through in 1797, called this desert place *temecunga* (place of the sun). It became a ranching outpost for Mission San Luis Rey, and later a stop on the Butterfield stagecoach line and a railroad. Today, with ocean breezes and coastal fog cooling things down at night, it's a place where olive trees and grapes flourish, especially sun-seeking Mediterranean varietals.

Ojai

22 The scenery is so surreal that Frank Capra set the 1937 movie *Lost Horizon* about a mythical Shangri-La in this mountain valley, flush with orange orchards. Ojai (p421) has delighted generations of artists, bohemians and new-age mystics. Doing nothing much is the goal for most visitors, especially those on retreat at one of Ojai's spas, but you can happily spend an afternoon ambling around downtown's quaint shops or drop by the bountiful Sunday farmers market. And around sunset, catch a legendary 'pink moment,' when the mountains emanate a rosy glow. Citrus tour, Ojai (p421)

Julian

23 Winding through pine-covered mountains and tree-shaded valleys east of San Diego, you'll finally arrive at the one-horse town of Julian (p363). Settled by ex-Confederate soldiers after the US Civil War, flecks of gold were found in a creek here in 1869, sparking a short-lived burst of speculation. Today you can tour an underground 19th-century mine, then dig into homemade apple pie waiting in the windows of false-fronted shops on Main St. Show up for apple picking in the orchards during fall.

Santa Monica Mountains

24 Ready to get wild? LA's urban jungle has nothing on this national recreation area (p161), which stretches west from the Hollywood Hills all the way past Topanga Canyon and Malibu's beaches. Superb camping, hiking, mountain biking and horseback riding opportunities abound, or take a guided tour of the historic Paramount Ranch, used for filming Hollywood Westerns starting in the 1920s. Malibu Creek State Park is another famous TV and movie filming location, starring in *M*A*S*H** and *Planet of the Apes*.

Surfing

25 Even if you never set foot on a board – and we, like, totally recommend that you do, dude – there's no denying the influence of surfing on all aspects of SoCal life, from fashion to the way everyday people talk. With gnarly local waves, you won't need to jet over to Hawaii to experience the adrenaline rush for yourself. Pros ride world-class breaks off Malibu, San Diego, Huntington Beach (aka 'Surf City USA') and Santa Barbara, while newbies get schooled at 'surfari' camps along SoCal's sunny coastline. Surfing, Encinitas

24

25

Need to Know

For more information, see Survival Guide (p469)

Currency
US dollars ($)

Language
English

Visas
Generally not required for stays of 90 days or less for citizens of Visa Waiver Program (VWP) countries with ESTA approval (apply online at least 72 hours in advance).

Money
ATMs are widely available. Credit cards are usually required for reservations. Tipping is customary, not optional.

Cell Phones
Cell-phone coverage is spotty in deserts. The only foreign phones that will work in the USA are GSM multiband models. Buy prepaid SIM cards or cell phones locally.

Time
Pacific Standard Time (GMT/UTC minus eight hours). Clocks move one hour ahead during Daylight Saving Time (DST) from the second Sunday in March to the first Sunday in November.

When to Go

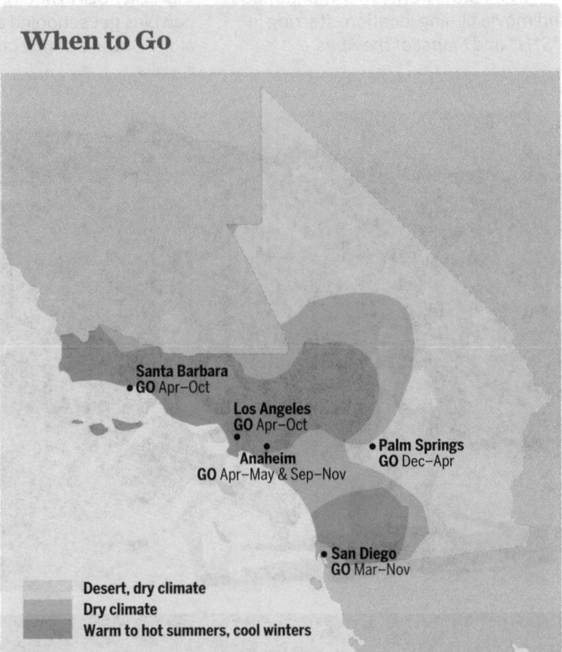

High Season (Jun–Aug)

- Accommodations prices up 50–100%
- Major holidays are even busier and more expensive
- Thick clouds may blanket the coast during 'June gloom'
- Coincides with low season in the desert

Shoulder (Apr–May & Sep–Nov)

- Crowds and prices drop off, especially along the coast
- Temperatures remain mild, with sunny, cloudless days in early autumn
- Weather typically wetter in spring, drier in autumn

Low Season (Dec–Mar)

- Accommodations rates drop near the coast, but not always in cities
- Chillier temperatures, more frequent rainstorms and mountain snow
- Coincides with peak season in the desert regions

Useful Websites

CalTrans (www.dot.ca.gov) Current highway conditions and construction updates.

California Tourism (www.visitcalifornia.com) Multilingual trip-planning guides.

LA Times Travel (www.latimes.com/travel) Daily news, SoCal travel deals and travel blogs.

Lonely Planet (www.lonelyplanet.com/usa/california) Destination info, hotel bookings, travelers' forums and more.

Theme Park Insider (www.themeparkinsider.com) Reviews, tips and discussion boards.

Important Numbers

All phone numbers have a three-digit area code followed by a seven-digit local number. For long-distance and toll-free calls, dial 1 plus all 10 digits.

Country code	☎1
International dialing code	☎011
Operator	☎0
Emergency (ambulance, fire & police)	☎911
Directory assistance (local)	☎411

Exchange Rates

Australia	A$1	$0.95
Canada	C$1	$0.93
China	Y10	$1.62
Euro zone	€1	$1.35
Japan	¥100	$0.98
Mexico	MXN10	$0.77
New Zealand	NZ$1	$0.86
UK	£1	$1.70

For current exchange rates see www.xe.com.

Daily Costs

Budget: Less than $75

- Dorm bed: $25–40
- Take-out meal: $6–10
- Beach parking: Free–$15

Midrange: $75–$200

- Two-star inland motel or hotel double room: $75–150
- Rental car per day, excluding insurance and gas: $30–75

Top End: More than $200

- Three-star beach hotel or resort double room: $150–275
- Three-course meal (excluding drinks) in top restaurant: $75–100

Opening Hours

Businesses, restaurants and shops may close earlier and for additional days during the off-season (usually winter; summer in the desert). Otherwise, standard opening hours are as follows:

Banks 9am–5pm Monday to Thursday, to 6pm Friday, some open 9am–2pm Saturday

Bars 5pm–2am daily

Business hours (general) 9am–5pm Monday to Friday

Nightclubs 10pm–4am Thursday to Saturday

Post offices 8:30am–4:30pm Monday to Friday, some 9am–noon Saturday

Restaurants 7:30am–10:30am, 11:30am–2:30pm and 5:30–10pm daily

Shops 10am–6pm Monday to Saturday, noon–5pm Sunday (malls open later)

Arriving in SoCal

Los Angeles International Airport (LAX; p210) Taxis around town ($30 to $50) take 30 minutes to one hour. Door-to-door shuttles ($16 to $27) operate 24 hours. The FlyAway bus ($8) runs to downtown LA. Free shuttles will get you to LAX City Bus Center & Metro Rail station.

San Diego International Airport (SA; p480) Taxis to downtown ($10 to $25) take 15 to 30 minutes. Door-to-door shuttles ($8 to $20) operate 24 hours. Bus No 992 ('the Flyer'; $2.25) runs to downtown San Diego every 15 to 30 minutes from 5am to 11pm.

Getting Around

Most people drive themselves around Southern California. Within cities, hop aboard city buses, light-rail trains or trolleys when distances are too far to walk, or grab a taxi.

Car Traffic in metro areas and along coast highways can be nightmarish, especially during weekday rush hours (7am to 10am and 3pm to 7pm) and on sunny weekends. Parking is an expensive hassle in LA.

Train Light-rail trains are a fast way to get around LA, but don't go everywhere (eg to Santa Monica). More expensive regional trains connect some coastal and inland destinations.

Trolley An alternative to buses in San Diego, with limited routes including to the Mexico border.

Bus Typically the cheapest and slowest option, but with the most extensive metro-area networks. Inter-city and regional routes are limited and pricier.

For much more on **getting around**, see p481

If You Like...

Theme Parks

If visiting Disney's 'happiest place on earth,' getting a thrill from Hollywood's movie magic or riding rad roller coasters is on your itinerary, you've definitely come to the right place.

Disneyland Topping almost every family's must-do fun list is Walt Disney's 'imagineered' theme park, with Disney California Adventure next door. (p221)

Universal Studios Hollywood Cinematic theme park with a studio backlot tram tour, tame rides and live-action, special-effects shows. (p190)

Six Flags Magic Mountain Hair-raising roller coasters will scare the bejeezus out of speed-crazed teens. (p215)

Legoland Low-key theme park made of those beloved building blocks for tots. (p329)

San Diego Zoo Safari Park Take a safari-style tram tour through an 'open-range' zoo. (p331)

Wine

Northern California's Napa and Sonoma Valleys may be more famous, but SoCal's wine countries hold their own. Just crack open a bottle from these sun-kissed vineyards and you'll become a believer.

Foxen Canyon Wine Trail Pastoral country roads wind past some of Santa Barbara's most famous vintners. (p411)

Los Olivos The poshest village in Santa Barbara's wine country, where quaint streets are lined by wine-tasting rooms. (p414)

Santa Rita Hills Independent innovators artfully crush grapes in the Santa Maria Valley, west of Hwy 101. (p412)

Temecula Stroll past Old West–style shops, then head out into San Diego's wine country. (p334)

Urban Wine Trail Amble on foot between wine bars and tasting rooms in Santa Barbara's 'Funk Zone'. (p404)

Ethnic Food

Especially around LA, celebrity restaurateurs have invaded many neighborhoods. But dollar for dollar, SoCal's flavorful cornucopia of mom-and-pop ethnic eateries is what will really satisfy your belly and soul.

Little Tokyo Settle into an *izakaya* (gastropub) and go nuts in downtown LA. (p76)

Koreatown The aromas of do-it-yourself barbecue grills will pull you in off LA's streets. (p203)

Thai Town East of Hollywood you'll find tastes as authentic as a Bangkok night market. (p87)

San Gabriel Valley Let the Chinese seafood feasts commence in LA's suburbs. (p193)

Little Saigon Orange County's mecca for Vietnamese cooking; *pho* (noodle soup) is just the beginning. (p242)

San Diego Just north of the border, Mexican *taquerias* – and the city's famous fish tacos – are serious business. (p302)

Freebies

Who says you need to throw around a lot of money to have a good time in SoCal? Many of the most beautiful beaches are free, just for starters.

El Pueblo de Los Angeles Get a feel for LA's earliest days along lively, adobe-building lined Olvera St. (p69)

Getty Center Arrive by public transportation, and stroll a multimillion-dollar art collection gratis. (p131)

Griffith Observatory Be amazed by family-friendly science demonstrations and sky-watching in Griffith Park. (p99)

Getty Villa Malibu's trove of ancient Greco-Roman art is another can't-miss freebie (but you'll have to pay for parking). (p145)

Hollywood Forever Cemetery DIY tours of the gobsmacking graves of bygone stars and free outdoor movies in summer. (p90)

Top: Mammoth skeleton, Page Museum & La Brea Tar Pits (p112)

Bottom: Salvation Mountain (p363), with artwork by Leonard Knight

Old Town San Diego A historic 19th-century Mexican and American *pueblo.* (p287)

Anza-Borrego Desert State Park Hike to hidden canyons, drive to jaw-dropping viewpoints and even pitch your tent for free. (p358)

Scenic Drives

Coastal highways always beckon, while even more detours await inland for adventure-seeking road trippers. So drop the convertible top and step on it!

Pacific Coast Hwy SoCal's most famous scenic drive delivers beautiful ocean vistas between beach towns. (p32)

Hwy 190 Deep inside Death Valley, horizons look boundless and roadside geology makes for epic scenery. (p369)

Rim of the World Scenic Byway Every hairpin turn will make you gasp on the way to Big Bear Lake. (p216)

Palms to Pines Scenic Byway Carved into the San Jacinto Mountains above Palm Springs, it leads to Idyllwild. (p216)

Mulholland Dr So famous David Lynch named a movie after it, LA's most twisted road winds past movie-star mansions. (p157)

Shopping

From vintage clothing shops and deeply discounted outlet malls to high-end boutiques where celebrities drop thousands of dollars, SoCal is a shoppers' dream.

Robertson Blvd Forget Rodeo Dr and Melrose Ave: LA's highest density of star-worthy boutiques per block is here. (p142)

It's a Wrap! Castoffs from real TV shows and movies hang on the racks of these unique resale shops in LA. (p193)

Abbot Kinney Blvd Browse an eclectic mix of indie boutiques by the beach in Venice. (p176)

Costa Mesa Skip power shopping at South Coast Plaza for The Camp and The Lab, offbeat 'anti-malls.' (p258)

Palm Springs Heaven for vintage fashion shoppers, antique hounds and outlet mall fans. (p349)

Celebrity Spotting

While no one can guarantee you'll run into Halle Berry or Matthew McConaughey being followed by paparazzi with giant zoom-lens cameras, it's more likely to happen in SoCal than anywhere else.

Malibu Millionaire movie stars love their privacy, but you can often glimpse them in Malibu's shopping plazas. (p151)

Beverly Hills Rodeo Dr designer shops and the classic Nate 'n Al delicatessen are good star-spotting bets. (p136)

Hollywood & WeHo Notice who's next to you at celeb-happy haunts such as Bar Marmont (p120) and Arclight Cinemas. (p98)

Join a live TV studio audience You never know who the special guest star will be at a sitcom or talk-show taping. (p91)

Weird Kitsch

SoCal's deserts rope in kooks and offbeat bohemian souls, but even metro areas such as loopy LA are jam-packed with just plain weird stuff you probably won't want to miss

Venice Boardwalk A human zoo of chainsaw-jugglers, Speedo-clad snake-charmers and a roller-skating Sikh minstrel. (p168)

Integratron With the help of aliens, this rejuvenation and time machine was built in the Mojave. (p354)

Salvation Mountain This monumental folk-art piece is a testament to one man's spiritual beliefs. (p363)

World's Biggest Dinosaurs Vintage roadside attraction now housing a museum of Christian creationism alleging dinos didn't exist. (p346)

Solvang Danish-flavored tourist trap spirited out of a Hans Christian Andersen fairy tale. (p415)

Museums

Who says SoCal only has pop culture? You could spend most of your trip immersed in multimillion-dollar art galleries, science exhibits and more.

Balboa Park Go all-day museum hopping in San Diego, taking in top-notch art, history and science exhibitions. (p275)

Getty Center & Villa Art museums that are as beautiful as their elevated settings, and ocean views in West LA and Malibu. (p131)

LA County Museum of Art More than 150,000 works of art span the ages and cross all borders. (p109)

Aquarium of the Pacific Meet SoCal's denizens of the deep in Long Beach. (p185)

Autry National Center Learn the true stories of cowboys and Native Americans in LA's Griffith Park. (p101)

Architecture

Whether you're admiring the intricate handiwork of arts-and-crafts bungalows, the stark angular lines of mid-century modernism or the groovy sculptural forms of postmodernism, SoCal has plenty to see.

Gamble House Where brothers Charles and Henry Greene created California's 'ultimate bungalows' in the early 20th century. (p196)

Palm Springs Mid-century modern playground in the desert, best visited in February during stylish Modernism Week.

Walt Disney Concert Hall Globe-trotting maverick Frank Gehry defies gravity in downtown LA – you won't be unmoved. (p68)

Getty Center Pritzker Prize winner Richard Meier's cutting-edge postmodern design perches over West LA. (p131)

Schindler House Rule-breaking modernist Rudolph Schindler's home and studio, now a living architectural center in LA. (p114)

Hollyhock House Not Frank Lloyd Wright's finest work, but still a singular experience. (p100)

History

Native American tribes, Spanish colonial presidios (forts), Catholic missions, Mexican pueblos (villages) and mining ghost towns have all left traces in SoCal.

Julian Pan for real gold in this historic mining town in the hills east of San Diego. (p363)

Old Town San Diego The site of California's first civilian Spanish colonial pueblo. (p287)

Mission Santa Barbara The 'queen of the missions' was the only one to survive secularization under Mexican rule. (p392)

La Brea Tar Pits Where prehistoric mammoths, sloths and saber-toothed cats once roamed around what is now LA. (p112)

Month by Month

TOP EVENTS

Rose Bowl & Parade, January

Modernism Week, February

Coachella Music & Arts Festival, April

Cinco de Mayo, May

Miramar Air Show & Fleet Week, September

January

Typically the wettest month in SoCal, January is a slow time for coastal travel. Mountain ski resorts are busy, as are desert destinations.

Rose Bowl & Parade

Held before the Tournament of Roses college football game, this New Year's Day parade of flower-festooned floats, marching bands and prancing equestrians draws over 700,000 spectators to Pasadena, outside LA.

Chinese New Year

Firecrackers, parades, lion dances and street food celebrate the lunar new year in late January or early February. SoCal's biggest celebrations are in LA.

February

Usually another rainy month for coastal California, but ski resorts stay busy. The low desert gets more visitors as wildflowers start blooming. Valentine's Day is booked solid at restaurants and resorts.

Modernism Week

Join other mid-century modern aficionados in mid-February for more than a week of architectural tours, art shows, film screenings, lectures and swingin' parties around Palm Springs.

Academy Awards

The red carpet gets rolled out for Hollywood's A-list stars on Oscar night at the Dolby Theatre in late February or early March.

March

The rain eases, so travelers head back to the SoCal coast, especially during spring break (dates vary). High season in the deserts. Ski season ends.

Festival of the Swallows

After wintering in South America, the swallows famously return to Mission San Juan Capistrano in Orange County around March 19. The historic mission town celebrates its Spanish and Mexican heritage with events all month.

April

Peak wildflower season in the high desert. Shoulder season in the mountains and on the coast means lower prices, except during spring break.

Coachella Music & Arts Festival

Indie no-name bands, cult DJs and superstar rock bands and rappers descend on Indio, outside Palm Springs, for a musical extravaganza held over two weekends in mid-April.

May

The weather starts to heat up, although some coastal areas are blanketed by fog (May grey). Kicking off summer, the Memorial Day weekend is one of the year's busiest travel times.

Cinco de Mayo

¡Viva México! Margaritas, music and merriment commemorate the victory of Mexican forces at the Battle of Puebla on May 5. LA and San Diego do it up in style.

June

Once school lets out for the summer, nearly everywhere in SoCal gets busier, from beaches to theme parks to mountain resorts. In the deserts, it's just too hot. Some coastal fog lingers (June gloom).

LA Pride

Out and proud, SoCal's biggest LGBT pride celebration takes place over a long weekend of partying with a parade in June.

July

Beach season gets into full swing on the coast. Theme parks are mobbed by vacationing families, as are mountain resorts, but the deserts are deserted. The July 4th holiday is summer's peak travel weekend.

Opening Day at Del Mar Racetrack

Horse racing returns in mid-July to Del Mar's elegant racetrack, built by Hollywood stars in the 1930s. It's worth going just to see the ladies' hats.

Festival of Arts

Exhibits by hundreds of artists and a pageant of masterpieces 're-created' using actors makes Laguna Beach a popular place during July and August.

Comic-Con International

The alt-nation's biggest annual convention of comic book geeks, sci-fi and animation lovers, and pop-culture memorabilia collectors brings out-of-this-world costumed madness to San Diego in late July.

August

Warm weather and water temperatures keep beaches busy. School summer vacations come to an end, but everywhere (except for the hot, hot deserts) stays packed. Travel slows slightly before Labor Day weekend.

Old Spanish Days Fiesta

Santa Barbara celebrates its early Spanish and Mexican *rancho* culture with parades, rodeo events, crafts exhibits and performances in early August.

September

Summer's last hurrah is the Labor Day holiday weekend, which is extremely busy almost everywhere (except the deserts). After kids go back to school, the beaches and cities get fewer visitors.

Miramar Air Show & Fleet Week

San Diego's military pride is on display during this week (or actually, more like a month) of land, air and sea events, including parades, concerts, ship-board tours and the USA's largest air show in late September or early October.

October

Shoulder season means things quieten down just about everywhere in SoCal, even though the weather is sunny and balmy. Travel deals abound along the coast, in cities and in the desert, where temperatures cool off.

West Hollywood Halloween Carnival

More than 200,000 revelers come out to LA's most established gay-and-lesbian 'hood for all-day partying, dancing and a street fair with over-the-top, often X-rated costumes.

November

Temperatures drop everywhere, with scattered winter rainstorms starting. Coastal beach areas, cities, theme parks and even the deserts are less busy, except around the Thanksgiving holiday. Ski season just barely begins.

Día de los Muertos

Mexican communities, including those in LA and San Diego, honor their deceased relatives on November 2 with costumed parades, sugar skulls, graveyard picnics, candlelight processions and fabulous altars.

December

Winter rains usually begin in coastal areas. Travel to typically sunny, drier desert regions picks up. Christmas and New Year's Eve are extremely crowded travel times, though there's usually a short-lived lull between them.

Christmas Boat Parade

Brightly illuminated and decorated boats, including multimillion-dollar yachts, float through Newport Beach's harbor during the week before Christmas.

Itineraries

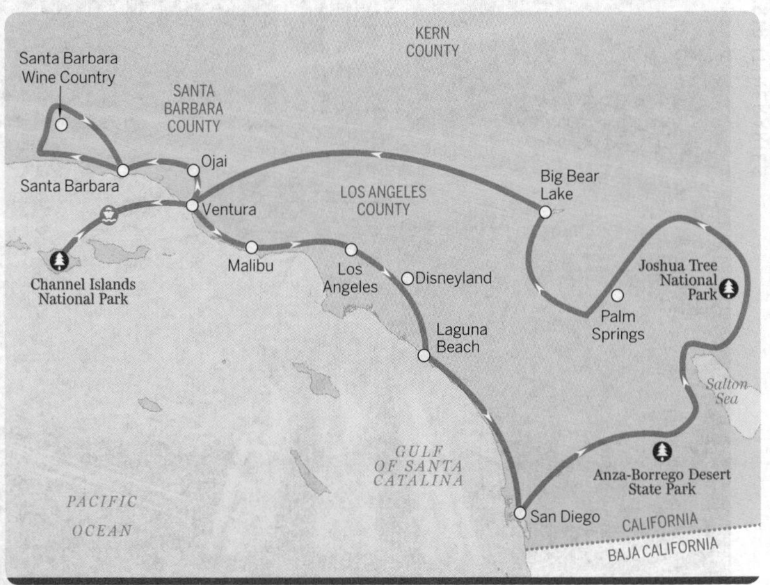

2 WEEKS SoCal Classics

Kick things off in **Los Angeles**, where top-notch sights, bodacious beaches and tasty food form an irresistible trifecta. Follow up with a date with Mickey at **Disneyland** or a day of sybaritic downtime in **Laguna Beach**, before heading south to **San Diego** for arts and culture in Balboa Park and a wild night out in the Gaslamp Quarter. Leaving civilization behind, head out to starkly beautiful **Anza-Borrego Desert State Park**. Cruise around the eerie **Salton Sea** and into **Joshua Tree National Park**, beckoning with its 'Wonderland of Rocks.' Squeeze in a day of margarita-sipping and lazing poolside in **Palm Springs** before heading to **Big Bear Lake** for hiking, biking, fishing and skiing. Wind west via the Rim of the World Scenic Byway to **Ventura** for a boat trip to **Channel Islands National Park**, then head inland to arty, alternative **Ojai** to catch a 'pink moment' at sunset. Take a breather in seaside **Santa Barbara**, with its gorgeous Spanish-Mediterranean downtown and offbeat Funk Zone. Before heading back to LA via star-studded **Malibu**, stock up on Pinot Noir in **Santa Barbara Wine Country**.

LOU JONES / GETTY IMAGES ©

Top: Carnival rides, Knott's Berry Farm (p236)

Bottom: Posing for photos on the Hollywood Walk of Fame (p89). *Hollywood TM and Hollywood Walk of FameTM & Design © 2014 HCC. All Rights Reserved*

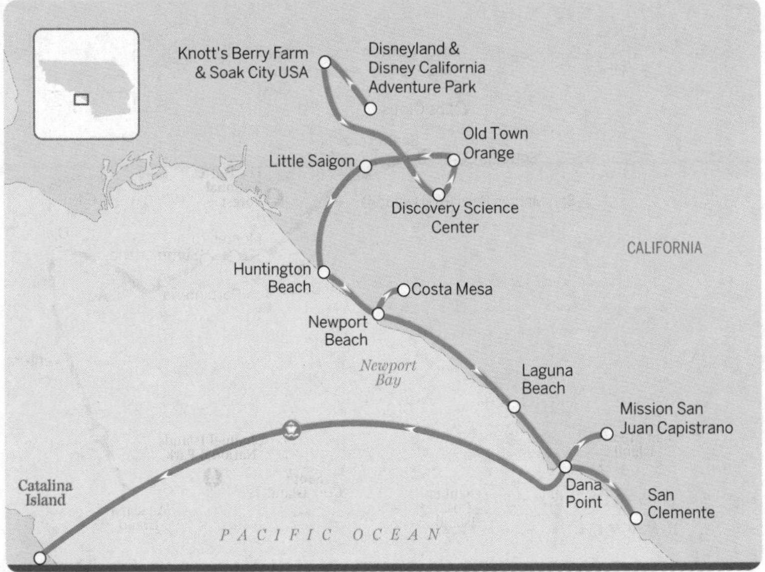

Disneyland & Orange County

It's no secret: many of SoCal's most popular attractions are in Orange County, famed for its cinematic beaches, sunny skies and cartoonish theme parks. But there's more to discover here, too, from high-tech museums to historic Spanish missions.

It will leave the kids thrilled and you exhausted, but there's no question an audience with Mickey at **Disneyland** is a quintessential SoCal experience. Skip down Main Street, USA or dive into **Disney California Adventure Park** next door. Then head to nearby **Knott's Berry Farm**, America's oldest theme park, which pairs Old Western cowboy themes with futuristic roller-coasters and classic fried-chicken dinners with boysenberry pie. If it's too darn hot, cool off at Knott's **Soak City USA** water park.

Just so you don't think SoCal is all about theme-park thrills, drop by the interactive **Discovery Science Center** in Santa Ana, where the whole family can virtually experience the shake, rattle 'n' roll of a 6.9-magnitude earthquake. Also near Anaheim, **Old Town Orange** is another break from Disneyfied magic, with its antique and vintage shops and eclectic restaurants. **Little Saigon** is not far away either, where you can trade those theme-park hot dogs for a steaming bowl of *pho* (Vietnamese noodle soup).

Cruise toward the OC's unbeatable beaches. Take a day off in **Huntington Beach**, aka 'Surf City USA'. Rent a board, play beach volleyball, build a bonfire around sunset – just kick back and chill, dude. The next day, roll south to **Newport Beach**, for soap-opera-worthy people-watching by the piers. Make a quick stop for power shopping or eclectic eats in **Costa Mesa**, then keep going south to **Laguna Beach**, a former artists' colony with more than two dozen public beaches to spoil you, as well as an art museum and chic downtown shopping and dining scenes.

From **Dana Point** you could catch a ferry to **Catalina Island**. Otherwise slingshot back toward the I-5, stopping off at **Mission San Juan Capistrano** for a small sampling of Spanish colonial and Mexican rancho history. Or keep the beach-bum attitude going by slacking south to **San Clemente**, near Trestles, a year-round surf break.

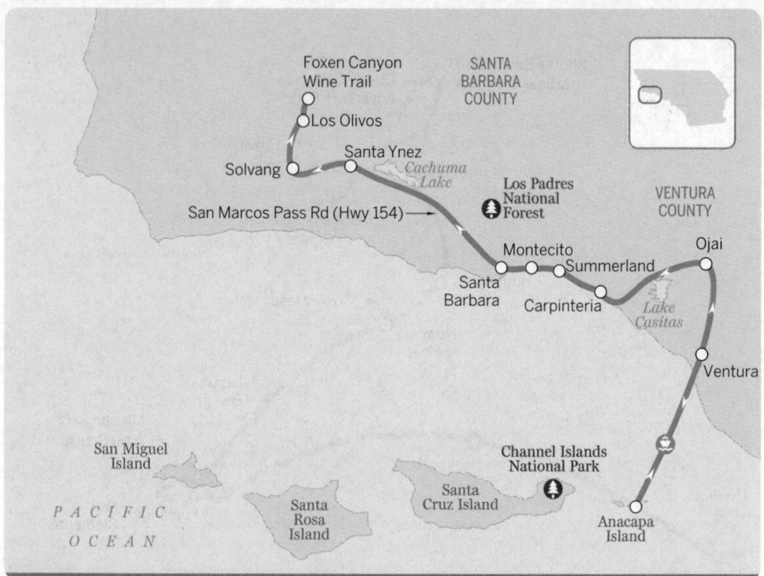

Santa Barbara & Wine Country

Leave behind star-struck LA and uncover the pacific charms of Santa Barbara and its vineyards. A sun-kissed Mediterranean climate earns this stretch of SoCal coast the nickname of the 'American Riviera,' and that's honestly not too far wrong.

If you crave a little solitude first, hop on a ferry from **Ventura** over to **Channel Islands National Park** and spend a day or two exploring 'California's Galapagos'. Back on dry land, oceanfront **Ventura** has a walkable downtown, plum full of vintage shops, bars and cafes. Mountainous **Ojai** is an inland Shangri-la with stunning scenery, artistic and spiritual vibes and unbeatable spa experiences.

It's less than an hour's drive from Ojai to Santa Barbara, but why rush? Once you hit the coast, drop by **Carpinteria** for a lazy afternoon at the beach and a plate of Mexican tacos or a burger, fries and a milkshake. Carpinteria's old-fashioned main street is lined with surf shacks and shops. Just up Hwy 101, **Summerland** and **Montecito** are more affluent Santa Barbara suburbs for antiques and boutique shoppers.

Ah, **Santa Barbara**. Strut down State St, with its sea of red-tile roofs, then climb to the top of the courthouse for bird's-eye vistas. Down at Stearns Wharf, dig into a bowl of chowder on the pier. Then join a pickup game of volleyball on East Beach, or take your sweetheart to romantic Butterfly Beach. Santa Barbara's 'Queen of the Missions' awaits inland, as do several petite museums, from art to maritime and Spanish colonial history. After dark, explore the restaurants, bars and wine-tasting rooms of the Funk Zone, down by the railroad tracks.

Take a scenic drive on **San Marcos Pass Rd (Hwy 154)** past **Los Padres National Forest** and **Cachuma Lake Recreation Area** up to Santa Barbara's wine country. Drive west to kitschy Danish **Solvang**, with its faux windmills and historical mission, then north to hoity-toity **Los Olivos**. The **Foxen Canyon Wine Trail** lazily winds along rural roads past wineries where you can tipple to your heart's content.

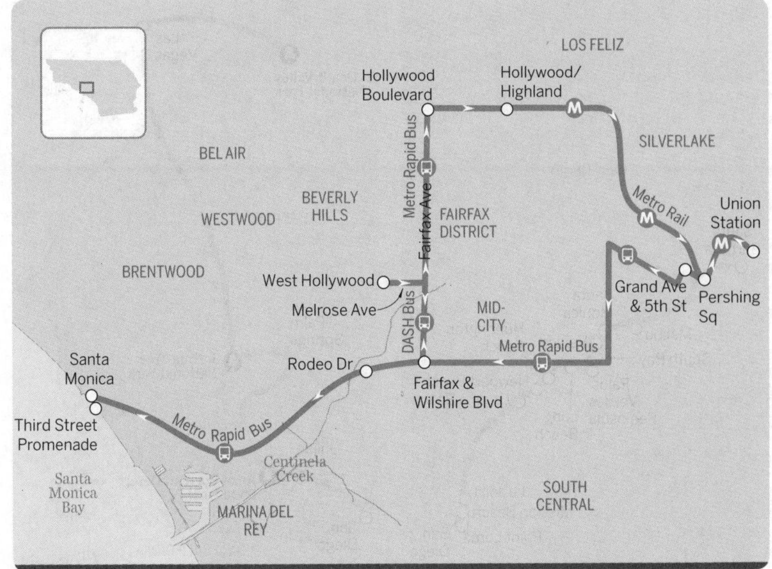

Los Angeles: No Car Required

Hollywood Walk of Fame. Walt Disney Concert Hall. Melrose Ave. Beverly Hills. The beaches. Yup, it can all be done in LA without a car, we promise. You'll just need patience, a good sense of direction and a couple of Metro day passes. Get an early start and know that most DASH buses don't run on Sundays. Double-check bus and subway route maps and timetables with **Metro** and **LADOT** before heading out.

Without further ado, may we present the logistics for three fun-filled carless days in LA, a city infamous for its traffic. **West Hollywood** makes a handy base of operation and puts you within walking distance – or a short DASH bus ride – of the Original Farmers Market and Grove mall, Mid-City's Museum Row, fashion-forward shopping on Melrose Ave, art galleries and hip restaurants and bars. Spend your first day exploring the local area.

On the morning of day two, catch the DASH bus east along Melrose Ave to Fairfax Ave, transferring to Metro bus 217 up to **Hollywood Boulevard**. Explore the famous star-studded Hollywood Walk of Fame, then at Hollywood/Highland board the Metro Rail Red Line toward Downtown LA. Get off at **Union Station** and spend the afternoon exploring Downtown's vibrant neighborhoods on foot. Return to Union Station before 5pm to take the Red Line to **Pershing Square**, then walk one block northwest to **Grand Ave & 5th St** and board Metro Rapid bus 720 west to **Fairfax Ave & Wilshire Blvd**, catching the last DASH Fairfax bus north at 6:30pm.

On day three, pack a swimsuit because you're headed to the beach. But first, Beverly Hills. Take the DASH bus east along Melrose Ave and south on Fairfax Ave, transferring at **Fairfax & Wilshire Blvd** to Metro Rapid bus 720 west. Get off at **Rodeo Dr** to gawk at the lifestyles of the rich and famous. Then it's back on the 720 and on to **Santa Monica**. Spend a couple of hours at the beach, check out the pier and squeeze in shopping along **Third Street Promenade**. Catch Metro Rapid 720 back east no later than 5pm, again transferring at Wilshire Blvd & Fairfax Ave to the last 6:30pm DASH north.

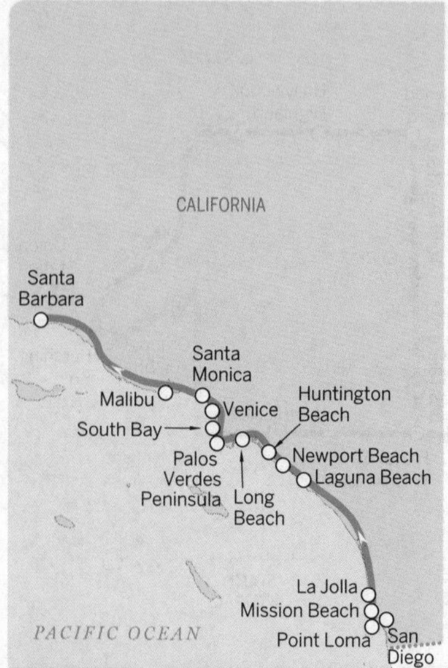

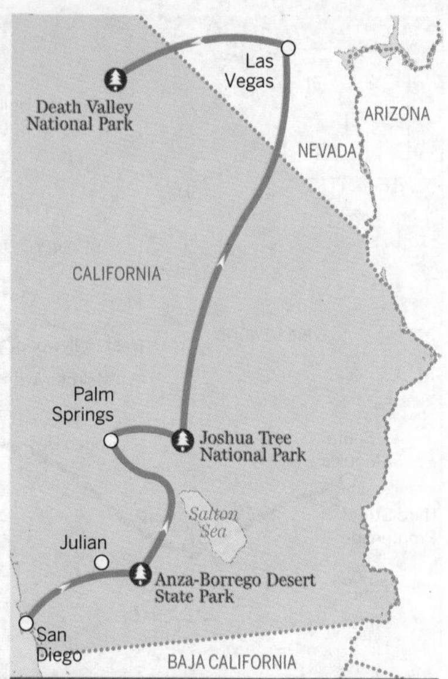

Pacific Coast Highway

Drop the convertible top, cue up 'California Girls' and step on it. This famous route starts in **San Diego** and hugs the Pacific throughout most of SoCal.

Before heading north, admire 360-degree views from **Point Loma**, buff surfers in **Mission Beach** and the underwater treasures of **La Jolla** in San Diego. Our vote for prettiest Orange County town is arty **Laguna Beach**, whose secluded coves and craggy cliffs enchant. Want ritzy? Plow on to **Newport Beach**, where bobbing yachts are tell-tale signs of the rich and famous. Officially 'Surf City USA', **Huntington Beach** is just up the road.

Head across the LA County line to **Long Beach**, where families find plenty of fun. Continue around beautiful **Palos Verdes Peninsula** before plunging into LA's **South Bay** beach towns. North of boho-chic **Venice**, **Santa Monica** beckons with a carnival pier and shopping.

The busy coast highway delivers surreal ocean vistas en route to **Malibu**, a celebrity hideaway. Wrap up your tour in **Santa Barbara**, a symphony of red-tile roofs, wineries and idyllic beaches.

1 WEEK

Desert Escapes

Start your trip in surfside **San Diego,** then head for the hills and **Julian**, an Old West mining town where you can pan for gold and gorge on apple pie. Drop into **Anza-Borrego Desert State Park**, where dirt roads and trails lead to hidden canyon oases, Native American petroglyphs and 19th-century stagecoach stops.

Gaze into the mirage-like Salton Sea, before heading north to retro-chic **Palm Springs**, the once-again hip resort hangout of Elvis and the Rat Pack. Then it's goodbye to poolside cocktails and off to mystical **Joshua Tree National Park**, whose twisted namesake trees have inspired artists and poets, while its desert-baked boulders challenge rock climbers.

By now, you're ready for a big-city fix: **Las Vegas**, baby. It's seductive, cheesy and absolutely outrageous. Where else can you climb the Eiffel Tower, make out in a gondola and witness an exploding volcano, all in the same day? Before you gamble away your life savings, drive west to **Death Valley National Park**, a jigsaw puzzle of sand dunes, sun-baked salt flats, volcanic cinder cones and ghost towns.

Plan Your Trip

Southern California's Beaches

With miles and miles of wide, sandy beaches, you'll find it hard to resist getting wet and wild in Southern California. Beach life and surf culture are part of the free-wheeling SoCal lifestyle, so play hooky any day of the week and go hit the waves like locals so often do.

Beaches & Swimming

Ocean temperatures for swimming become tolerable in SoCal by about May, peaking in July and August. During the hottest dog days of summer, another way to keep kids' temperatures cool is at water parks such as Six Flags Hurricane Harbor (p215) north of LA, Legoland (p329) north of San Diego, Soak City OC (p237) in Anaheim or Wet 'n' Wild Palm Springs. (p344)

Top 10 Swimming Beaches

Santa Monica (p156), Los Angeles

Coronado (p290), San Diego

Venice (p168), Los Angeles

Mission Beach (p293), San Diego

Balboa Peninsula (p249), Newport Beach

Pacific Beach (p293), San Diego

Main Beach (p260), Laguna Beach

Doheny State Beach (p269), Dana Point

San Buenaventura State Beach (p424), Ventura

El Capitán State Beach (p398), near Santa Barbara

SoCal's Best Beaches

Los Angeles County

Santa Monica & Venice Giant-sized sunsets and a cycling path.

Malibu Hidden strands of paradisiacal sand.

Orange County

Huntington Beach Officially, 'Surf City, USA' – 'nuff said.

Crystal Cove State Park Wild, rugged coastline pocked with tide pools.

San Diego County

Coronado Miles of white sand along the Silver Strand.

Mission & Pacific Beaches Surfing, amusement-park rides and beach bums.

Santa Barbara County

Leadbetter Beach Where local families picnic and swim.

East Beach Lazy sunbathing near a historic wharf.

Carpinteria State Beach Palm trees, sand dunes and swimming.

Southern California's Beaches

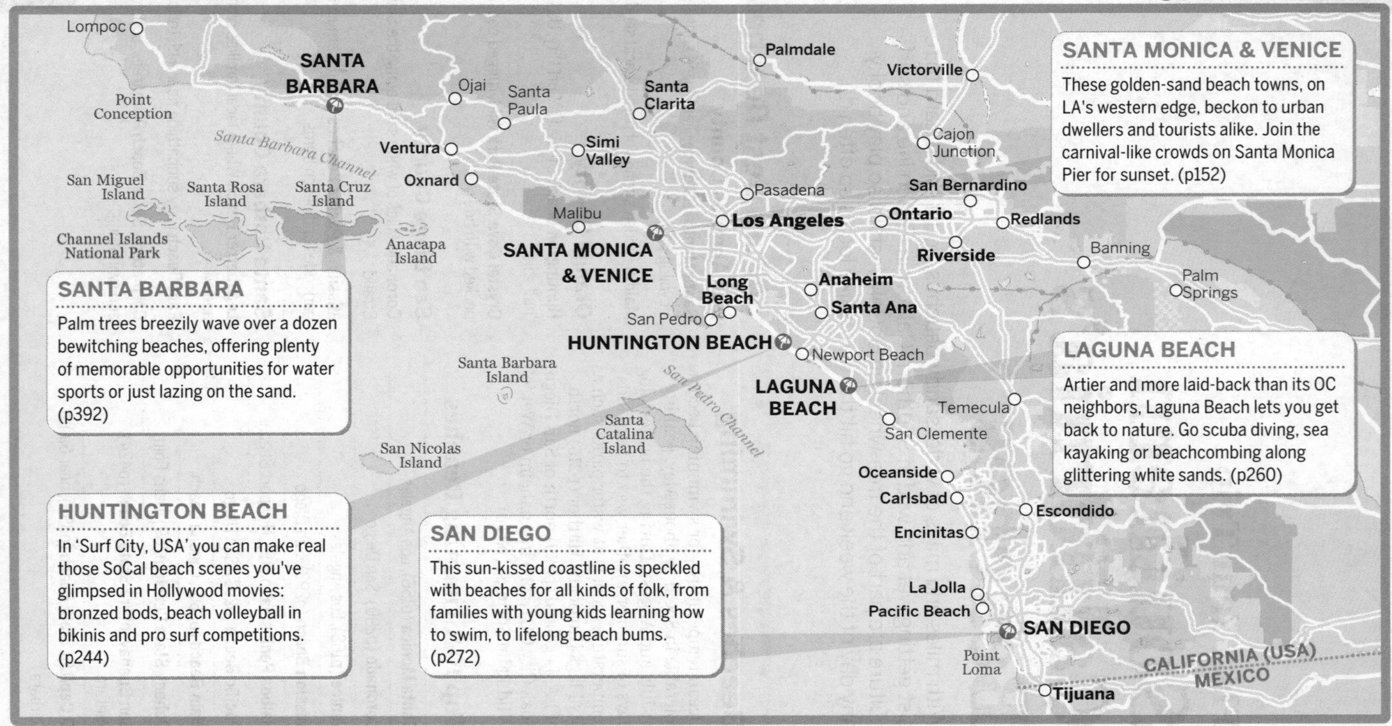

SANTA MONICA & VENICE

These golden-sand beach towns, on LA's western edge, beckon to urban dwellers and tourists alike. Join the carnival-like crowds on Santa Monica Pier for sunset. (p152)

SANTA BARBARA

Palm trees breezily wave over a dozen bewitching beaches, offering plenty of memorable opportunities for water sports or just lazing on the sand. (p392)

LAGUNA BEACH

Artier and more laid-back than its OC neighbors, Laguna Beach lets you get back to nature. Go scuba diving, sea kayaking or beachcombing along glittering white sands. (p260)

HUNTINGTON BEACH

In 'Surf City, USA' you can make real those SoCal beach scenes you've glimpsed in Hollywood movies: bronzed bods, beach volleyball in bikinis and pro surf competitions. (p244)

SAN DIEGO

This sun-kissed coastline is speckled with beaches for all kinds of folk, from families with young kids learning how to swim, to lifelong beach bums. (p272)

Best Family-Friendly Beaches

Silver Strand State Beach (p290), Coronado

Leo Carrillo State Beach (p158), Malibu

Balboa Peninsula (p249), Newport Beach

Carpinteria State Beach (p420), Santa Barbara County

Arroyo Burro Beach County Park (Hendry's; p396), Santa Barbara

Best Beach Volleyball

Manhattan Beach (p177), LA's South Bay

Hermosa Beach (p179), LA's South Bay

Huntington Beach (p244), Orange County

Ocean Beach (p291), San Diego

East Beach (p398), Santa Barbara

Beach Safety Tips

➡ Most beaches have flags to distinguish between surfer-only sections and sections for swimmers. Flags also alert beachgoers to dangerous water conditions.

➡ Popular beaches have lifeguards, but can still be dangerous places to swim. Obey all posted warning signs and ask about local conditions before venturing out.

➡ Stay out of the ocean for at least three days after a major rainstorm because of dangerously high levels of pollutants flushed out through storm drains.

➡ Water quality varies from beach to beach, and day to day. For current water-safety conditions and beach closures, check the **Beach Report Card** (http://brc.healthebay.org) issued by the nonprofit organization **Heal the Bay** (www.healthebay.org).

Books & Maps

The outstanding *California Coastal Access Guide* (University of California Press; www.ucpress.edu) has comprehensive maps of every public beach, reef, harbor, cover, overlook and coastal campground, with valuable information about parking, hiking trails, facilities and wheelchair access. It's especially helpful for finding secret pockets of uncrowded sand.

Surfing

Surf's up! Are you down? Even if you have never set foot on a board, there's no denying the influence of surfing on every aspect of SoCal beach life, from clothing to lingo. It's an obsession up and down the coast, particularly in San Diego and Orange Counties.

The most powerful swells arrive in late fall and winter, while May and June are generally the flattest months, although they do bring warmer water. Speaking of temperature, don't believe all those images of hot blonds surfing in skimpy swimsuits – without a wet suit, you'll likely freeze your butt off except at the height of summer.

Crowds can be a problem at many surf spots, as can overly territorial surfers. Befriend a local surfer for an introduction before hitting SoCal's most famous waves, such as Windansea or Trestles. Sharks do inhabit California waters but attacks are rare.

SoCal's Best Surf Spots for Pros

California comes fully loaded with easily accessible world-class surf spots, the lion's share of which are in SoCal – lucky you!

➡ Near San Clemente in Orange County, **Trestles** (p271) is a premier summer spot with big but forgiving waves, a fast ride, and both right and left breaks.

➡ **Huntington Beach** (p244) in Orange County may have the West Coast's most consistent waves, with miles of breaks centered on the pier.

➡ San Diego's **Windansea Beach** (p320) is a powerful reef break, while nearby **Big Rock** (p320) churns out gnarly tubes.

➡ Malibu's **Surfrider Beach** (p145) has a clean right break that just gets better with bigger winter waves.

➡ Santa Barbara County's **Rincon Point** (p420) in Carpinteria is a legendary right point-break that peels forever.

SoCal's Best Surf Breaks for Beginners

The best spots to learn to surf are at beach breaks at long, shallow bays where the waves are small and rolling. Popular places

Huntington Pier (p244)

for beginners in SoCal, where many surf schools offer lessons, include:

San Diego Mission Beach, Pacific Beach, La Jolla and Oceanside

Orange County Seal Beach, Huntington Beach, Newport Beach and Laguna Beach

Los Angeles Santa Monica and Malibu

Santa Barbara Leadbetter Beach and Carpinteria

Surf Lessons & Rentals

You'll find board rentals on just about every patch of sand where surfing is possible. Expect to pay from around $20 per half day for a board, with wetsuit rental another $10.

Two-hour group lessons for beginners start around $100 per person, while private, two-hour instruction costs over $125. If you're ready to jump in the deep end, many surf schools offer weekend surf clinics and weeklong 'surfari' camps.

Stand-up paddle boarding (SUP) is easier than learning how to board surf, and it's skyrocketing in popularity. You'll find similarly priced SUP rentals and lessons popping up all along the coast, from San Diego to Santa Barbara.

Online Resources

➡ Browse the comprehensive atlas, live webcams and surf reports at **Surfline** (www.surfline.com) for the lowdown from San Diego to Santa Barbara.

➡ Orange County–based **Surfer** (www.surfermag.com) magazine's website has travel reports, gear reviews, newsy blogs, forums and videos.

➡ Plan a coastal surfing adventure using **Surfline**, which covers seasonal conditions, water hazards and extended weather forecasts.

➡ If you're a kook, bone up on your surf-speak so the locals don't go aggro and give you the stinkeye. For translations, use the **Riptionary** (www.riptionary.com).

Books & Maps

➡ Water-resistant *Surfer Magazine's Guide to Southern California Surf Spots* (2006) is jam-packed with expert reviews, information, maps and photos.

Plan Your Trip

The Great Outdoors

Weather forecasters in Southern California probably have the easiest job in the world. 'Today it's...sunny. Tomorrow will be...sunny. And our extended forecast is...' You get the picture. With its Mediterranean climate, SoCal is an outdoor playground that will get your blood pumping in any season.

Snorkeling & Scuba Diving

Not surprisingly, Southern California has some excellent underwater snorkeling and diving spots – from rock reefs to shipwrecks to kelp forests – suited for all skill and experience levels. Just don't expect crystal-clear waters like those in Hawaii or the Caribbean, as local dive spots can be murky. Ocean waters are warmest between July and September. That said, wetsuits are recommended year-round.

SoCal's Best Places to Snorkel & Dive

Outstanding spots, especially for first-time divers, are **San Diego–La Jolla Underwater Park Ecological Reserve** (p320) and **Casino Point (Avalon Underwater Park;** p213) on Catalina Island. Accessible right from shore, both have fertile kelp beds teeming with critters close to the surface.

More experienced divers might want to steer towards **Orange County's Crystal Cove State Park** (p259) and **Divers Cove** (p261) around Laguna Beach, as well as **Wreck Alley**, near San Diego's Mission Bay, where you can explore sunken military aircraft and ships.

Best...

Time to Go

Swimming and beach volleyball July and August

Surfing and windsurfing September to November

Kayaking, snorkeling and diving June to October

Whale-watching January to March

Hiking April to May and September to October

Skiing and snowboarding December to March

Outdoor Experiences

Sea kayaking and whale-watching in the Channel Islands

Snorkeling or scuba diving at La Jolla

Cycling in LA's South Bay or Santa Barbara

Rock climbing or hiking in Joshua Tree National Park

Horseback riding in LA County's Santa Monica Mountains

Hang-gliding at Torrey Pines in La Jolla

Hot-air ballooning over Del Mar, north of San Diego

Skiing and snowboarding at Big Bear Lake

Many popular dive spots are also good for snorkeling, for example **Channel Islands National Park** (p425). Guided dive boats and combo kayaking-and-snorkeling trips to the park's islands leave from Ventura and Oxnard, between Santa Barbara and LA.

Rentals, Lessons & Tours

Local dive shops are your best resources for equipment, guides, instructors and dive-boat trips. To explore California's deep waters, you must have an open-water certificate from the Professional Association of Dive Instructors (PADI) or another recognized organization. If you already have your open-water certification, you can book boat dives for about $65 to $150 (reserve trips at least a day in advance).

If you just want to dabble in diving, look for outfitters offering beginner courses that include basic instruction, followed by a shallow beach or boat dive, for around $150. If you're serious about learning and have the time and money, sign up for a multi-day open-water certificate course, which costs from $250 to $600.

Snorkelers can rent a mask, snorkel, fins and even a wetsuit for about $20 to $45 per day from concessionaires at some beaches and in towns nearby snorkeling sites. If you're going to take the plunge more than once or twice, it's probably worth buying your own high-quality mask and fins. Remember not to touch anything while you're out snorkeling and don't snorkel alone.

Books, Magazines & Online Resources

- Lonely Planet's *Diving & Snorkeling Southern California & the Channel Islands* by David Krival is a hands-on guide to happy encounters with garibaldi, sheephead, calico bass and other offshore creatures in SoCal's waters.
- Although not updated regularly, **LA Diver** (www.ladiver.com) has many helpful links to dive sites and shops, certification programs, safety resources and weather conditions for LA, San Diego, Orange, Ventura and Santa Barbara Counties.
- **Scuba Diving** (www.scubadiving.com) and **Sport Diver** (www.sportdiver.com), both magazines published by PADI, have comprehensive websites dedicated to underwater adventures.

Kayaking

Few water-based sports are as accessible and fun for the whole gang as kayaking, and most people manage to get paddling along quickly with minimal instruction. Whether you're looking for adventure and exploring sea caves or just serenely paddling along coastal bluffs, opportunities abound along SoCal's coast.

SoCal's Best Places to Kayak

Sea kayaking is fabulous in **Channel Islands National Park** (p425), offshore

SOCAL'S DESTINATION SPA RESORTS & DAY SPAS

If the road has left you feeling frazzled and achy, an hour or more at a day spa may be just what the doctor ordered. There are literally hundreds of spas throughout SoCal, from simple storefronts in strip malls to luxurious oases in the hoity-toity zip codes of the rich and famous, such as **Palm Springs** (p344).

Every spa has its own 'treatment menu,' usually including a variety of massages such as Thai, shiatsu, deep-tissue, Swedish, tandem (two therapists equals four hands) and hot-stone. Beauty treatments range from classic facials and botanical wraps to exotic elixir baths and body cocktail scrubs.

For a treat, detour to **Glen Ivy Hot Spring**s (p238), aka 'Club Mud,' located in inland Orange County. Famous for its red-clay mud bath, Glen Ivy also offers clear mineral-water tubs and a large swimming pool. In the mountains north of Ventura, closer to LA, **Ojai Valley Inn & Spa** (p422) is another renowned retreat.

Wherever you go, massage sessions typically cost at least $80 for 50 minutes, while a facial will set you back $60 or more. By the time you've added a 20% tip, the final tab may be high enough to put that frown right back on your forehead.

from Ventura, and **Catalina Island** (p213), closer to LA. Both are ideal overnight getaways for experienced paddlers.

Day trips are equally rewarding, especially for beginners who launch their kayaks in the calm, protected waters of San Diego's **Mission Bay** (p291) and **Dana Point** (p269) or **Huntington Harbor** (p243) in Orange County.

You can explore sea caves while floating above the kelp forests and reefs of **San Diego–La Jolla Underwater Park Ecological Reserve.**

You'll find even more coastal kayaking in **Malibu** (p144), Orange County's **Laguna Beach** (260) and among the sea caves of **Gaviot**, west of Santa Barbara.

Rentals & Tours

Most kayaking outfitters offer a choice between sit-upon (open) kayaks and sit-in (closed-hull) ones; the latter usually require some training before you head out. Kayak rentals average $30 to $50 for a half day, and you'll usually have a choice between single and tandem kayaks. A reputable outfitter will make sure you're aware of the variable tide schedule and wind conditions for your proposed route.

Many kayaking outfitters lead half-day ($50 to $90) or full-day (starting over $100) coastal trips. Some offer kayak/hike combos or thrilling sunset or after-dark paddles. There's nothing quite like seeing the reflection of the moon and stars glittering on the water and hearing the gentle splash of water on your kayak's hull. Small group tours led by local guides with natural-history knowledge are best.

Whether you're taking a guided tour or renting kayaks, try to make reservations at least a day beforehand.

Online Resources

- For dozens of links to local kayaking outfitters, schools and organizations, plus handy advice for beginners to experts, visit **Kayak Online** (www.kayakonline.com).
- **California Kayak Friends** (www.ckf.org) hosts discussion forums about anything from popular paddling destinations and put-ins to recent trip reports and upcoming events.

AVOIDING SEASICKNESS

Choppy seas can be nauseating for some landlubbers. To avoid seasickness, sit outside on the boat's second level – not too close to the diesel fumes in back. Over-the-counter motion-sickness pills (eg Dramamine) are effective but will make you drowsy. Staring at the horizon works for some people, as does chewing ginger or wearing acupressure wristbands.

Whale-Watching

Every summer an estimated 20,000 gray whales feed in the Arctic waters between Alaska and Siberia, and every fall they start moving south down the west coast of Canada and the USA to sheltered lagoons in the Gulf of California off Baja California. In spring these whales turn around and head back to the Arctic. During their 12,000-mile round-trip, the whales pass just off the California coast, typically between late December and early April.

And it's not only gray whales that make appearances in SoCal. Blue, humpback and sperm whales as well as schools of dolphins can be seen swimming offshore throughout the summer and fall, but spotting these marine mammals is not quite as predictable.

On Land vs at Sea

You can try your luck whale-watching while staying ashore (eg at lighthouses) – it's free, but you're less likely to see whales and you'll be at a distance from all the action. **Point Vicente** (p183) on the Palos Verdes Peninsula in LA and San Diego's **Point Loma** are two well-known whale-watching spots, but you could get just as lucky somewhere else.

For bigger thrills, just about every SoCal port town worth its salt offers whale-watching boat tours, especially during winter. Don't forget your binoculars! Half-day whale-watching boat trips (from $25 to $90 per adult, usually discounted up to half for children) last from 2½ to four hours, and sometimes include snacks and drinks. Make reservations at least a day or two in advance.

Look for whale-watching boat tours that limit the number of people and have a trained naturalist or marine biologist on board. Some tour-boat companies will let you go again for free if you don't spot any whales on your first cruise.

Windsurfing & Kiteboarding

Experienced windsurfers tear up the waves along the coast, while newbies or those who want a mellower ride skim along calm bays and protected beaches. There's almost always a breeze, but the best winds blow from September through November. Wetsuits are a good idea year-round.

SoCal's Best Places to Windsurf & Kiteboard

Basically, any place that has good windsurfing also has good kiteboarding. Look for the people doing aerial acrobatics as their parachute-like kites yank them from the water. In wide open spaces devoid of obstacles such as piers and power lines, you won't have to worry about unexpected flights that could slam you into concrete.

➡ In San Diego, beginners should check out **Santa Clara Point** in Mission Bay.

➡ Santa Barbara's **Leadbetter Beach** (p398) is another good place for beginners to learn.

➡ In LA, you'll see lots of action off **Belmont Shore** (p185) near **Long Beach** and **Point Fermin** (p185) near San Pedro.

Rentals & Lessons

The learning curve in windsurfing is steeper than other board sports – imagine balancing on a fast-moving plank through choppy waters while trying to read the wind and angle the sail just so. At most windsurfing hot spots, you'll spend about $100 to $150 for an introductory lesson.

Although it's harder to get started kiteboarding, experts say it's easier to advance quickly once the basics are down. Beginner kiteboarding lessons start at over $200, usually taking place over a few days. The first lesson is spent learning kite control on the beach and the second lesson gets you into the water.

Windsurfing-gear rentals cost about $50 to $75 per half-day for a beginner's board and harness. Most windsurfing shops at least dabble in kiteboarding, but usually won't rent kiteboarding gear to people who aren't taking lessons from them.

Online Resources

➡ Wind reports, weather forecasts, live windcams and active discussion forums are available at www.iwindsurf.com.

➡ Aspiring and experienced kiteboarders should check out www.ikitesurf.com for prime locations, wind reports and more.

Hiking

Got wanderlust? With awesome scenery, Southern California is perfect for exploring on foot. That's true no matter whether you've got your heart set on peak-bagging 10,000-footers, trekking to palm-tree oases, hiking among fragrant pines or simply going for a wander on the beach beside the booming surf. During spring and early summer, a painter's palette's worth of wildflowers bloom on shaggy hillsides, in mountain meadows, on damp forest floors and, most famously, in desert sands.

SoCal's Best Places to Hike

No matter where you find yourself in Southern California, you're never far from a trail, even in the metropolitan areas. The best trails are often amid the jaw-dropping scenery of national and state parks, national forests, recreation areas and other public lands. You'll find the gamut of routes, from paved trails negotiable by wheelchairs and baby strollers to multiday backpacking routes through rugged wilderness.

➡ In Los Angeles you can hike for miles in **Griffith Park** (p103), one of America's largest urban parks.

➡ Outside LA, the **Santa Monica Mountains** (p161) and **Big Bear Lake** (p216) are both cooler escapes during summer.

➡ East of San Diego, **Cleveland National Forest** is another cool summer hiking place.

➡ The **Santa Ynez Mountains** (p413) and **Los Padres National Forest** (p409) beckon around Santa Barbara, especially during the more temperate spring and fall seasons.

➡ Offshore, more rugged trails crisscross **Channel Islands National Park** (p425) and **Catalina Island** (p213).

➡ Palm Springs has fantastic hiking in summer atop its aerial tramway inside **Mt San Jacinto State Park** (p343), and in winter at **Indian Canyon** (p343) and **Tahquitz Canyon** (p341).

➡ For spectacular spring wildflower displays, head deeper into the desert to **Anza-Borrego Desert State Park** (p358), **Death Valley National Park** (p369), the **Mojave National Preserve** (p367) and **Joshua Tree National Park** (p350).

➡ In San Diego and Orange Counties, you can hike along coastal bluffs, such as at **Torrey Pines State Natural Reserve** (p319) and **Crystal Cove State Park** (p259), or in the canyons above **Laguna Beach** (p260).

Hiking Safety Tips

➡ Pay attention on the trail and be aware of potential dangers. Even a minor injury such as a twisted ankle can be life-threatening, especially if you're alone or in inclement weather.

➡ Always let someone know where you're going and how long you plan to be gone. When available, use sign-in boards at trailheads or ranger stations.

➡ Always carry extra water, snack food and extra layers of clothing.

➡ Don't rely on your cell phone: service is spotty or nonexistent in many areas, especially in the forest, mountains, deserts and canyons.

➡ Weather can be unpredictable. Afternoon summer thunderstorms, for instance, are quite common in the deserts. Double-check the forecast before heading out.

SOCAL'S TOP 10 NATIONAL & STATE PARKLANDS

PARK	FEATURES	ACTIVITIES	BEST TIME TO VISIT
Anza-Borrego Desert State Park (p358)	Badlands, canyons, fan-palm oases, hot springs, caves; bighorn sheep, birds	4WD, stargazing, hiking, horseback riding, birding	Nov-Mar
Channel Islands National Park (p425)	Rocky islands with steep cliffs; elephant seals, sea lions, otters, foxes	Snorkeling, diving, kayaking, hiking, birding	Apr-Oct
Crystal Cove State Park (p259)	Beach, woodland, marine park, tide pools, historic cottages, wildflowers; bobcats	Swimming, diving, kayaking, hiking, mountain biking	Year-round
Death Valley National Park (p369)	Unique geology, sand dunes, canyons, volcanic craters, wildflowers; desert tortoise, bighorn sheep, bats	Hiking, 4WD, horseback riding, mountain biking, birding	Oct-Apr
Joshua Tree National Park (p350)	Rocky desert, fan-palm oases, Joshua trees, cacti, wildflowers; desert tortoise, bighorn sheep, coyotes, snakes	Rock climbing, hiking, 4WD, mountain biking, birding	Sep-May
Los Padres National Forest (p409)	Canyons, chaparral-covered foothills, mountains, forests, waterfalls, hot springs; California condors, mule deer, coyotes, black bears	Hiking, birding, wildlife-watching, mountain biking, swimming	Apr-Oct
Mt San Jacinto State Park (p343)	Alpine mountains, forests, meadows, aerial tramway, wildflowers; deer, mountain lions, foxes	Hiking, cross-country skiing, snowshoeing, birding	Year-round
Santa Monica Mountains National Recreation Area (p161)	Tree- and chaparral-covered coastal range, wildflowers; lizards, mountain lions, bobcats, snakes, raptors	Hiking, mountain biking, birding	Year-round
Torrey Pines State Natural Reserve (p319)	Coastal lagoon, beaches, salt marsh, pine trees, coastal sage; seals, sea lions, foxes, birds	Hiking, birding, tide pooling	Year-round
Upper Newport Bay Nature Preserve (p256)	Estuary, beach, salt marsh, mud flats, sand dunes, coastal scrub grasslands; birds	Birding, kayaking, cycling, horseback riding, hiking	Oct-Apr

Top: Matilija Creek, Los Padres National Forest (p409)

Bottom: Golf cart, Catalina Island (p213)

➡ Encounters with mountain lions and black bears are extremely rare but possible. Rattlesnakes and spiders also present potential dangers. Watch your step!

➡ Be aware of the warning signs and symptoms of heat exhaustion, heatstroke and hypothermia.

➡ See the Directory chapter for more information on health and safety (p473).

Fees

➡ Most California state parks charge a daily parking fee of $4 to $15, though there's often no charge for cyclists or those arriving on foot. Don't park on the road's shoulder outside a state park just to avoid paying the fee.

➡ National park entrance averages $15 to $20 per vehicle, and is usually good for seven consecutive days. There's no fee to enter **Channel Islands National Park** (p425).

➡ For unlimited admission to national parks, national forests and other federal recreation lands, buy the **'America the Beautiful' annual pass** (p472). They're sold at national park visitor centers and entry stations, as well as at most USFS ranger stations. Lifetime 'America the Beautiful' passes are free for US citizens (and permanent residents) with disabilities, and $10 for those aged 62 and over; these passes must be purchased in person or by mail.

➡ If you don't have an 'America the Beautiful' pass, you'll need a **National Forest Adventure Pass** (☎909-382-2623, 909-382-2622; www.fs.fed.us/r5/sanbernardino/ap/; per day $5, annual pass $30) to park in some recreational areas of the San Bernardino, Cleveland, Angeles or Los Padres National Forests. Buy passes from USFS ranger stations or local vendors (check the website for a current list), or order them online in advance.

Maps & Information

There are bulletin boards showing basic trail maps and other information at most major trailheads, some of which also have free trail brochure dispensers. Most national parks and forests, and some state parks, have a visitors center or ranger station with clued-in staff happy to offer trail tips and suggestions.

For short, well-established hikes in national or state parks, the free trail maps handed out at ranger stations and visitors centers are usually sufficient. Occasionally a more detailed topographical map may be necessary, depending on the length, difficulty and remoteness of your hike. The **USGS Store** (www.store.usgs.gov) offers its topographic maps as free downloadable PDFs, or you can order print copies online.

Books

➡ Former *Los Angeles Times* columnist John McKinney's excellent hiking guides include the *Day Hiker's Guide to California State Parks*, *Day Hiker's Guide to California Coastal Parks* and *Day Hiker's Guide to Southern California*.

➡ Jerry Schad's *Afoot & Afield: San Diego County*, *101 Hikes in Southern California* and *Top Trails: Los Angeles* detail many locals' favorite trails with insider tips.

Online Resources

➡ SoCal hiking guru Casey Schreiner's **Modern Hiker** (http://modernhiker.com) is a one-stop newsy blog, hikers' forum and virtual encyclopedia of hiking trails, especially in national forests and recreation areas around LA.

➡ Visit **Trails.com** (www.trails.com) to search for descriptions of myriad trails that explore SoCal's mountains, deserts and more; trail summary overviews are free.

➡ Learn how to minimize your impact on the environment while hiking and camping in the wilderness at the **Leave No Trace Center for Outdoor Ethics** (http://lnt.org) online.

WARNING: POISON OAK

Watch out for western poison oak in forests throughout California, especially in areas below 5000ft in elevation. Poison oak is a shrub most easily identified by its shiny reddish-green tripartite leaves, which turn crimson in the fall, and its white berries. In the winter months, when the plant has no leaves, it looks brown and twiggy, but can still cause a serious allergic reaction. If you brush against poison oak, remove any affected clothing and scrub the exposed area immediately with soap and cool water or an over-the-counter remedy such as Tecnu, a soap specially formulated to remove the plant's itchy urushiol oils.

Cycling & Mountain Biking

Strap on your helmet: Southern California is outstanding cycling territory, no matter whether you're off for a leisurely spin along the beach, an adrenaline-fueled mountain-bike ride or a multiday road-cycling tour along the coast. Avoid the mountains in winter (too much rain and snow at higher elevations) and the deserts in summer (too dang hot). Know your own skill and fitness levels, and plan accordingly.

SoCal's Best Places for Cycling & Mountain Biking

For the inside scoop on SoCal's cycling and mountain biking scenes, ask the knowledgeable staff at local bicycle shops.

➡ SoCal's cities are not terribly bike-friendly, but shining exceptions include **Palm Springs**, **Santa Barbara** and **Santa Monica** as well as several smaller beach towns.

➡ For photo-worthy scenery, paved oceanfront cycling routes include **LA's South Bay Trail** (p152); between **Huntington State Beach** (p252) and **Bolsa Chica State Beach** in Orange County; between **San Buenaventura State Beach** (p424) and **Emma Wood State Beach** in Ventura; along the harborfront in **Santa Barbara**; and between **El Capitán State Beach** (p398) and **Refugio State Beach** (p398), west of Santa Barbara.

➡ Mountain bikers can follow tracks in the **Santa Monica Mountains** outside LA; in Orange County at **Crystal Cove State Park** (p259) and **Aliso & Wood Canyons Park**, both near **Laguna Beach**; and at **Anza-Borrego Desert State Park** (p358), east of San Diego.

➡ Fat-tire speed freaks also sing the praises of Snow Summit park at **Big Bear Lake** (p216), in the San Bernardino Mountains outside LA.

Road Rules

➡ In national parks, bikes are usually limited to paved and dirt roads and are not allowed on trails or in designated wilderness areas.

➡ Most national forests and BLM lands are open to mountain bikers. Stay on already established tracks (don't create any new ones) and always yield to hikers and horseback riders.

BUT WAIT, THERE'S MORE!

ACTIVITY	LOCATION	DESCRIPTION
Fishing	Big Bear Lake	Catch trout in the mountains northeast of LA
	Dana Point	Popular departure point for sportfishing boats
	Malibu	Fish right from the pier, or take a sportfishing tour
	Marina del Rey	Lots of sportfishing trips, including to Catalina Island
	San Diego	Dangle a rod from public piers, or take a sportfishing trip
Hang-gliding & paragliding	Torrey Pines	Glide at SoCal's gliding capital, near La Jolla
	Santa Barbara	A good spot to soar by the coast
Horseback riding	Santa Monica Mountains	Canter where film stars once shot Hollywood Westerns on location
Hot-air ballooning	Del Mar	SoCal's ballooning capital, in northern San Diego County
Rock climbing	Joshua Tree	World-class, mostly short technical rock climbs, plus bouldering
Skiing & snowboarding	Big Bear Lake	This family-friendly sports resort is the closest powder to LA
	Mt San Jacinto State Park	Forested cross-country skiing and snowshoeing, high above Palm Springs
Yoga	Los Angeles	Indoor studios abound, from traditional Hatha and heated Bikram to power and martial-arts styles

Mountain biker, Big Bear Lake (p216)

➡ At California state parks, trails are off-limits to bikes unless otherwise posted, while paved and dirt roads are usually open to both cyclists and mountain bikers.

Maps & Online Resources

Local tourist offices can usually supply you with cycling route ideas, maps and advice.

Adventure Cycling Association (www.adventurecycling.org) sells long-distance cycling route guides and touring maps, for the entire Pacific Coast.

California Association of Bicycling Organizations (www.cabobike.org) provides freeway access info for bicyclists, printable e-guides and cycling maps, and links to partner organizations statewide.

Los Angeles Bicycle Coalition (http://la-bike.org) sponsors group rides and has free downloadable bicycle maps for LA, Santa Monica, Long Beach and Orange County.

MTBR.com (www.mtbr.com) and **SoCal Trail Riders** (www.socaltrailriders.org) host online forums and user reviews of mountain-biking trails.

Santa Barbara Bicycle Coalition (www.bike-santabarbara.org) offers downloadable do-it-yourself cycling tours, including of Santa Barbara's Wine Country, and links to bicycle rental shops, tour companies and bike-friendly accommodations.

Golf

The **Palm Springs** and **Coachella Valley** (p344) resort area is SoCal's undisputed golfing center, offering more than 100 courses. San Diego, LA and Orange Counties have many more places to get in a round, and even **Catalina Island** (p213) has a notably historic course to play.

Most cities and bigger towns in Southern California have public golf courses with reasonable greens fees, although many of the top-ranked courses are at private golf clubs, where you may have to be invited by a member or get a referral from the pro at your home club. Semiprivate clubs are open to nonmembers, except at peak times like weekend mornings.

Fees

Green fees vary hugely, from $15 to $250 or more for 18 holes, depending on the course, season and day of the week, and that usually doesn't include cart or club rental. Golfers can save money – sometimes as much as 50% – by booking twilight play, when desert courses also happen to be cooler. Book tee times well in advance.

Online Resources

For a searchable directory of golf courses throughout Southern California, as well as tee-time bookings, visit www.scga.org.

Handy regional golfing websites include:

City of Los Angeles Golf (http://golf.lacity.org)

Golf San Diego (www.golfsd.com)

Los Angeles County Golf Courses (http://parks.lacounty.gov)

Orange County: California's Golf Coast (www.occgolf.com)

Palm Springs Golf (http://palmspringsgolf.com)

Santa Barbara Golfing (www.santabarbara.com/activities/golf)

Plan Your Trip

Disneyland Trip Planner

Taking a trip to the Disneyland Resort (Disneyland, Disney California Adventure, and their surrounding hotel and shopping districts) may seem like a Herculean task. But really, it couldn't be easier. We've got advance-planning tips and strategies to help you out, including the best times to go (and when not to go), and we'll show you how to save money on tickets, hotels, restaurants and more.

The Best...

Times to Visit

Mid-April–mid-May Miss both spring-break and summer-vacation crowds, but still have a good chance of sunny weather.

Mid-September–late September Summer vacationers depart after Labor Day and temperatures cool down, but it's still sunny.

Late November–early December As visitation dips between Thanksgiving and Christmas, holiday decorations spruce up the parks.

Weekdays Year-round, they're less busy than weekends.

Tour Rides & Attractions

Disneyland Pirates of the Caribbean, Indiana Jones Adventure, Haunted Mansion, Space Mountain, Finding Nemo Submarine Voyage, it's a small world, Fantasmic! show

Disney California Adventure Radiator Springs Racers, Soarin' Over California, The Twilight Zone Tower of Terror, California Screamin', Grizzly River Run, Pixar Play Parade, World of Color show

For details on individual sites, see the Disneyland & Orange County chapter, p218.

Timing Your Visit

➡ Both Disneyland and Disney California Adventure (DCA) are open 365 days a year; hours vary. Check the **current schedule** (☎714-781-4565; www.disneyland.com) in advance.

➡ During peak summer season (roughly mid-June to early September), Disneyland's hours are usually 8am to midnight; the rest of the year, it's open from 10am to 8pm or 10pm. DCA closes at 10pm or 11pm in summer, earlier in the off-season.

➡ Opening hours may be extended during spring break (March/April) and the winter holidays, from a week before Christmas through New Year's Day.

➡ Off-season, some attractions and shows may not be running, including fireworks. Check the website in advance to avoid disappointment.

➡ Don't worry about getting stuck waiting for a ride or attraction at closing time. Parks stay open until the last guest in line has had their fun.

Busiest Times to Go

March/April Unless you love crowds and the chance of rain showers, don't visit when schools take their spring break vacation, especially the weeks before and after Easter.

July & August The hottest dog days of summer are the busiest time in the parks, with families taking summer vacations.

October Although the weather is balmy and summer crowds have vanished, Halloween celebrations make this a busy time, too.

Mid- to late November The week leading up to the Thanksgiving long weekend is crowded. Plus, there's a chance of rainfall, and not all of the holiday decorations are up yet.

Special events High schoolers take over the parks on 'Grad Nites' in late May and June. Unofficial, queer-friendly 'Gay Days' in early October.

Weekends Year-round, the parks are busiest on Saturdays and Sundays.

Beating the Crowds

➡ Arrive when parking lots and ticket booths open, an hour before the theme parks' official opening times.

➡ The parks are busiest between 11am and 4pm, go back to your hotel for a mid-day swim (and a nap!). Then return after dinner.

➡ Downtown Disney's restaurants and shops get crowded after 5pm. Visit around lunchtime for smaller crowds and cheaper menu prices.

➡ Disneyland and DCA's FASTPASS system can cut wait times significantly for some rides.

➡ Look for shorter, single-rider lines.

➡ Smartphone apps may also help you avoid long queues in the parks.

Buying Tickets

➡ Tickets never sell out, but buying them in advance will save you time waiting in ticket lines and probably some money.

➡ Ticket prices rise annually. Currently, one-day admission to *either* Disneyland or DCA theme park costs $92 for adults and $86 for children aged three to nine.

➡ 'Park Hopper' ticket (single day per adult/child $137/131) let you visit both parks in one day.

➡ Multi-day 'Park Hopper' tickets cost from $210/197 for two days to $300/279 for five days of admission within a two-week period.

➡ Some 'Park Hopper' tickets include one 'Magic Morning' early-bird admission to select attractions on certain days (arrive 75 minutes before the theme park opens to the general public).

➡ A Deluxe Annual Passport for unlimited theme-park entry on 315 pre-selected days of the year costs $499 per person, regardless of age; a Premium Annual Passport with no blackout dates costs $669, including parking (which otherwise costs $16 per day).

Discounts & Deals

➡ Look for specials online such as the five-day 'Park Hopper' tickets for the three-day price.

➡ Southern California residents (defined by zip code, extending as far north as San Luis Obispo County) may be eligible for discounted theme-park admission tickets and passports.

➡ Anyone can buy a **Southern California CityPass** (p472), covering three-day 'Park Hopper' admission to Disneyland and DCA, plus one-day admission to **SeaWorld San Diego** (p291) and **Universal Studios Hollywood** (p190). The CityPass price is at least $100 off the combined regular ticket prices.

DISNEYLAND TO-DO LIST

A Month or More in Advance

☐ Make area hotel reservations or book a Disneyland vacation package.

☐ Sign up online for Disney Fans Insider e-newsletters and resort updates.

A Week or Two Ahead

☐ Check the parks' opening hours and entertainment schedules online.

☐ Make reservations for restaurants or special meals with Disney characters.

☐ Buy tickets and passes online.

The Day Before

☐ Recheck the next day's opening hours and Anaheim Resort Transportation (ART) or hotel shuttle schedules.

☐ Pack a small day pack with sunscreen, hat, sunglasses, swimwear, change of clothes, jacket or hoodie and a lightweight poncho.

☐ Fully charge your electronic devices, including cameras and phones.

☐ Download a Disneyland app to your smartphone.

➡ **Walt Disney Travel Company** (☎714-520-5060, 800-225-2024; www.disneytravel.com) sells vacation packages, some steeply discounted, including air, hotel and theme-park tickets, plus perks like early-morning park admission and dining plans.

➡ For further information contact **Disneyland Resort** (☎recorded info 714-781-4565, live assistance ☎714-781-7290; www.disneyland.com)

Bringing the Kids

You're never too young or too old for Disneyland. You'll see huge families all enjoying the parks together, including: mothers with newborn babes in arms, young honeymooners and elderly great-grandparents.

Infants & Toddlers

➡ Stroller rentals are available but rental strollers can only be used in the theme parks, not Downtown Disney.

➡ Your own stroller will save time, money and a headache if the parks' rentals are all taken, especially during peak season or later in the day.

➡ Strollers are not allowed on escalators or the parking lot tram. Fold up strollers before bringing them on the monorail.

➡ Stroller parking areas are available outside most park rides and attractions.

➡ Baby centers, including diaper-changing and nursing facilities with comfy rocking chairs, are available at Disneyland (Main Street, USA) and DCA (Pacific Wharf).

➡ Day lockers are available.

➡ The 'rider swap' system lets two parents with babies or small children each ride without standing in line twice. Ask a staff member at any ride for a pass (both adults must be present).

Kids & Tweens

➡ Tell kids that if they get lost, contact the nearest Disney staff, who will escort them to a 'lost children' center (on Disneyland's Main Street, USA or at DCA's Pacific Wharf).

➡ Study online the minimum-height charts for rides and attractions in advance, to avoid whining and disappointment when you get to the park.

➡ If you've booked a Disneyland Resort vacation package, schedule a complimentary pre-trip phone call for your kids from Mickey, Minnie or Goofy.

➡ Every restaurant has a kids' menu.

➡ If you're here for a birthday, inquire about decorate-your-own-cake parties and personal-size cakes (at least 48 hours in advance), and stop by Disneyland's City Hall for a free 'It's My Birthday!' badge.

➡ Kids aged nine years and under may wear costumes inside the park (but no masks, toy weapons or other sharp objects). During Halloween time, preteens may wear costumes.

➡ For sensitive children: many kids' rides – including Roger Rabbit's Car Toon Spin and Mr Toad's Wild Ride – can be surprisingly scary.

Teens

➡ Tell your teens that if their cell phones don't work, they can leave a message for 'Lost Parents' at City Hall, just inside Disneyland's entrance.

DISNEYLAND DOS & DON'TS

Dos

☐ Designate a meeting place in case someone in your group gets lost.

☐ Drink plenty of fluids to avoid dehydration.

☐ Arrive early at the parks, then take a midday break back at your hotel.

☐ Use FASTPASS to skip long lines at select rides and attractions.

☐ Buy tickets in advance.

☐ Keep your ticket if you leave and re-enter.

☐ Leave pets at home, or board them for the day at Disneyland's kennels.

Don'ts

☐ Don't try to cram both theme parks into one day – allow two days minimum.

☐ Don't arrive at 11am – it's the busiest time to buy tickets and enter the parks.

☐ Don't bring soft-sided coolers bigger than a six-pack or any kind of wheels (eg rolling luggage, bikes, skateboards, even shoes with wheels!) into the parks.

☐ Don't show up without restaurant reservations if you want a sit-down meal.

☐ Don't walk up *and* down Downtown Disney – use the monorail as a one-way shortcut to/from Disneyland.

☐ Don't light up in the parks, except at specially designated smoking areas.

➡ Clothing or tattoos with language, graphics or designs deemed offensive are prohibited, as is displaying what Disneyland deems an 'excessive' amount of bare skin (eg bikini tops).

Visitors with Special Needs

The Disneyland Resort may be the most accessible place in all of Southern California for anyone with mobility issues or other disabilities. If you need something, just ask.

Mobility Support

➡ Rental wheelchairs and motorized scooters are available, but it's best to bring your own because rentals are only for use in the parks (not Downtown Disney). They may also sell out.

➡ Most rides are either fully accessible to those in wheelchairs or scooters or allow guests to board via a 'transfer access vehicle.'

➡ Companion restrooms are available at Disneyland and DCA; consult park maps.

Other Services

➡ Service animals (eg guide dogs) may accompany guests into the parks but must remain on a leash or harness at all times and are not allowed on some rides and attractions.

➡ Braille guides, digital audio tours, supplemental audio descriptions, assisted listening systems, captioning and sign-language interpretation services are all available free of charge but may require a same-day refundable deposit or advance notice.

Where to Sleep

At Disneyland Resort

➡ For the full-on Disneyland experience, stay in one of the resort's three **hotels** (☎reservations 714-956-6425, 800-225-2024; www.disneyland.com).

➡ Resort hotel guests usually get bonus perks, from early 'magic hour' admission to the parks' attractions to preferred seating for live shows and parades.

➡ Rates are expensive but fluctuate almost daily. Shop around if your schedule is flexible.

➡ You might save money by booking multi-night stays or vacation packages, including theme-park admission tickets and optional dining plans, with the Walt Disney Travel Company.

Outside the Parks

➡ Many Anaheim area motels and hotels offer packages combining lodging with theme-park tickets; most have family rooms or suites that sleep four to six people.

➡ Some local accommodations operate complimentary guest shuttles to Disneyland.

➡ Otherwise, consider staying within walking distance of the parks or along the public shuttle route operated by **Anaheim Resort Transportation** (p236).

Dining & Drinking

➡ Technically, you can't bring any food or drinks into the parks, but security-inspection staff usually look the other way at small water bottles and a few snacks.

➡ Store soft-sided coolers and other food in the all-day lockers outside the main entrance.

➡ Within the parks, reservations are recommended at top-end restaurants. If you haven't made reservations, plan on eating at off-peak times.

➡ Convenient (overpriced) fast food and carnival-style snacks are sold everywhere in the parks.

➡ Park maps indicate restaurants and cafes where you can find healthy-food options.

➡ For good-value eats and fresher menu options, exit the parks and walk to Downtown Disney (or ride the monorail).

➡ You can't buy any alcohol in Disneyland, but you can at DCA, in Downtown Disney and at the resort's hotel restaurants, bars and lounges.

➡ Drinking fountains are everywhere, so bring a refillable water bottle.

Reservations & Special Meals

➡ For sit-down dining in the parks or at resort hotels, reservations are essential.

➡ **Disney Dining** (☎714-781-3463; http://disneyland.disney.go.com/dining) handles reservations and can advise on dietary restrictions, character dining (meals during which Disney characters work the dining room and greet the kids), and dinner-and-a-show picnics.

➡ Available with Disneyland vacation packages, Disneyland Dining Plans (DDPs) may save you money if you are eating at least two meals a day in the parks.

Plan Your Trip

Travel with Children

Southern California is unquestionably one of the most child-friendly vacation spots on the planet. The kids will be begging to go to theme parks and teens to celebrity hotspots. Get those over with (you might enjoy them too), then introduce them to many other worlds, big and small.

Best Regions for Kids

Orange County

There's a reason Disneyland is the most popular attraction in Southern California. Generations of kids and the young-at-heart all love it. Teens will enjoy the thrill rides at Disney California Adventure park next door, and there's shopping and dining for everyone at Downtown Disney.

Los Angeles

See stars in Hollywood and get behind the movie magic at Universal Studios, then hit the beaches and Griffith Park for SoCal fun in the sun. What, it's raining? Dive into the city's many kid-friendly museums instead.

San Diego

From pandas to koalas, flamingos to elephants, San Diego Zoo is paws-down the best zoo in Southern California. Also make time for the zoo's safari park in Escondido, as well as the other family-oriented attractions in Balboa Park, maritime sites along downtown's Embarcadero and colorful Legoland in Carlsbad.

Southern California for Kids

SoCal's sunny skies and warm temperatures lend themselves to outdoor activities of all kinds. Here's a small sampling: swimming, surfing, snorkeling, bicycling, kayaking, hiking and horseback riding. Many outdoor outfitters and tour operators have dedicated kids' activities. On those rare cold, rainy days – or if you need a break from all that sun – you'll find top-notch museums and indoor entertainment galore.

Sometimes no organized activity is even needed. We've seen young kids thrill at catching their first glimpse of a palm tree, and teens with sophisticated palates bliss out over their first taste of heirloom tomatoes at a farmers market. The bottom line: if the kids are having a good time, you will be too.

Eating Out

Most restaurants in Southern California – not just fast-food places – are easygoing places to bring kids. A good measure is the noise level: the louder, the more kid-friendly. Casual eateries in well-trafficked neighborhoods typically have high chairs and children's menus, and some break out the paper placemats and crayons for drawing. Even restaurants without special kids' menus can usually whip up something your children will eat. Generally, dining earlier (say, before 6pm) is better for families with young ones.

Theme parks have dozens of ways to get the kids hopped-up on sugar and salt at expensive prices, and many don't permit picnics or food to be brought in. One way to get around this is to carry a cooler in the car and have a picnic in the parking lot (although be sure to get everyone's hand stamped for park re-entry afterward).

One place kids are generally *un*welcome is at high-end restaurants. Unless your children are exceptionally well behaved, properly dressed and old enough to appreciate the meal, neither the staff nor the other diners are likely be charmed.

If all else fails, supermarket chains such as Trader Joe's, Whole Foods and Gelson's have healthy takeout food. Baby food, infant formula, disposable diapers (nappies) and other necessities are also widely sold at supermarkets and pharmacies. Most women are discreet about breastfeeding in public.

Children's Highlights

Theme Parks

Disneyland (p221) Anaheim

Disney California Adventure (p221) Anaheim

Legoland (p329), San Diego

Universal Studios Hollywood (p190), Los Angeles

Six Flags Magic Mountain (p215), north of LA

Knott's Berry Farm (p236) **& Soak City USA** (p237), Buena Park (Orange County)

Aquariums & Zoos

San Diego Zoo (p276), Balboa Park (San Diego)

San Diego Zoo Safari Park (p331), Escondido

Aquarium of the Pacific (p185), Long Beach

Los Angeles Zoo (p101), Griffith Park (LA)

Living Desert Zoo & Gardens (p341), Palm Springs

Birch Aquarium (p319) La Jolla (San Diego)

Museums

Reuben H Fleet Science Center (p276), Balboa Park (San Diego)

San Diego Natural History Museum (p276), Balboa Park (San Diego)

California Science Center (p206), Exposition Park (LA)

Natural History Museum of Los Angeles (p206), Exposition Park (LA)

Page Museum at La Brea Tar Pits (p112), Los Angeles

USS Midway Museum (p288), San Diego

Discovery Science Center (p238), Santa Ana (Orange County)

Planning

A word of advice: don't pack your schedule too tightly. Traveling with kids always takes longer than expected, especially when navigating metro areas such as LA.

Children's discounts are available for everything from museum admission and movie tickets to bus fares. The definition of a 'child' varies from 'under 18' to age six.

At amusement parks, some rides may have minimum-height requirements, so let younger kids know about this in advance, to avoid disappointment – and tears.

Many public toilets have a baby-changing table. Bigger, private gender-neutral 'family' bathrooms may be available at airports, museums etc.

What to Pack

Sunscreen. Lots of sunscreen. And bringing sunscreen should remind you to bring hats, swimsuits, goggles and flip-flops. If you like beach umbrellas and sand chairs, pails and shovels, you'll probably want to bring your own or buy them at local supermarkets and pharmacies. At many beaches, you can rent bicycles and watersports gear (eg snorkel sets) for kids.

For mountain outings, bring broken-in hiking shoes, plenty of food and water, and your own camping equipment. Outdoor gear can be purchased or sometimes rented from local outdoor outfitters and sporting-goods shops. But remember that the best time to test out gear is before you take your trip. Murphy's Law dictates that wearing brand-new hiking shoes results in big blisters, and setting up a new tent in the dark ain't easy.

If you forget some critical piece of everyday equipment, **Traveling Baby Company** (%800-304-4866; www.travelingbaby.com) and **Baby's Away** (%800-571-0077; https://babysaway.com) rent cribs, portacots, strollers, car seats, high chairs, beach gear and more. Rates vary according to equipment, rental duration and delivery charges.

Accommodations

Rule one: if you're traveling with kids, always mention it when making reservations. At a few places, notably B&Bs, you may have a hard time if you show up with little ones. When booking, be sure to request the specific room type you want, although this is not often guaranteed.

Motels and hotels often have rooms with two beds or an extra sofabed. They may also have rollaway beds or cots available (request these when making reservations), typically for a surcharge. Some offer 'kids stay free' promotions, although this may apply only if no extra bedding is required; ask when booking. Some hotels provide free breakfast for the whole family too.

Bigger hotels and resorts may offer daytime activity programs for kids, especially during summer. Fees can be cheaper than babysitting and everyone may enjoy the change of pace. At some hotels, the front-desk staff or concierge can help you make babysitting arrangements. Ask whether babysitters are licensed and bonded, what they charge per hour per child, whether there's a minimum fee and if they charge extra for transportation and meals.

Transportation

Airlines usually allow infants (up to age two) to fly for free (bring proof of age). Older children require a seat of their own. Children do receive substantial discounts on Amtrak trains and Greyhound buses.

California law requires all passengers in private cars to wear seat belts. Any child under age six or weighing less than 60lb must be buckled up in the car's back seat in a child or infant safety seat. Most car-rental agencies rent these for about $10 per day, but you must book them in advance.

For better or for worse, being on the road is an essential part of the SoCal experience. So is traffic, especially in LA. From LA to all but the most remote destinations in the Southland, travel time is theoretically two hours or less, but can easily multiply in traffic, especially during peak times.

Plan some in-car distractions in case the kids get fidgety. On the road, rest stops on freeways are few and far between, and gas stations and fast-food bathrooms are frequently not very clean. However, you're usually never far from a shopping mall, which generally have well-kept restrooms.

Books & Online Resources

➡ Lonely Planet's *Travel with Children* is loaded with valuable tips and amusing anecdotes, especially for new parents and families who haven't traveled before.

➡ **Lonelyplanet.com** (www.lonelyplanet.com): ask questions and get advice from other travelers in the Thorn Tree's 'Kids to Go' and 'USA' forums.

➡ The state's official tourism website, **Visit California** (www.visitcalifornia.com), lists family-friendly attractions, activities and more – just search for 'Family Fun' and 'Events'.

SOCAL'S TOP FIVE PIERS FOR FAMILIES

Santa Monica Pier (p152) – LA's coastal gem, built in 1908, has its own amusement park on top, an aquarium underneath and summer twilight concerts.

Balboa Island (p253), Newport Beach – It's not one but two piers, plus a peanut-sized amusement park made famous on TV's *The OC*.

Stearns Wharf (p393), Santa Barbara – The West Coast's oldest continuously operating pier hosts the engaging Ty Warner Sea Center.

Crystal Pier (p302), Pacific Beach – If you're lucky enough to book the Crystal Pier Hotel, the surf lapping beneath your cottage on the pier is a natural lullaby.

Paradise Pier (p227), Disney California Adventure – Granted, it's not technically a pier (it's nowhere *near* the ocean), but who cares when the rides are so good?

Regions at a Glance

Los Angeles

Culture
Shopping
Beaches

Seeing Stars

Hollywood has its glittering restored movie palaces, the pink-starred Hollywood Walk of Fame and red-carpet movie premieres. Almost everywhere you go in LA, the cult of celebrity will follow, whether you're star-spotting with paparazzi in Malibu or joining a live studio audience.

Fashionista Alert

You don't need to see *Project Runway* to know that LA is a fashion capital on par with NYC, Paris and Tokyo. Hit cutting-edge boutiques on Melrose Ave and Robertson Blvd, then shop with A-list stars at revered Fred Segal and along Rodeo Dr in Beverly Hills.

Gold Coastin'

Follow any jammed freeway westbound and you'll eventually hit the beach. Ride the Ferris wheel on Santa Monica's pier, meet zany characters along Venice's boardwalk, mix with the South Bay's surfers and party animals, or take the whole family to Long Beach.

p56

Disneyland & Orange County

Family Fun
Beaches
Surfing

Theme Parks

Bring the kids, grandparents, cousins – heck, load up everyone in the minivan. Disneyland is just the start of your zany trip through SoCal's theme parks. Of course, the Magic Kingdom and Disney California Adventure might be reason enough for your whole trip.

'The OC'

You've gawked at Orange County's beautiful beaches and sunbathers in countless movies and TV shows. Now see the fantasy spring to life along this almost too-beautiful stretch of coastline between LA and San Diego.

Surf City USA

You'll find SoCal's hang-loose surf culture personified at Huntington Beach, though the OC's waves don't stop there. Earn your wave-riding chops with a learn-to-surf class or a wild weekend 'surfari' camp.

p218

San Diego

Beaches
Mexican Food
Museums

Cooling Off

Here it's almost always sunny and a perfect 68°F (20°C). Do like the locals do and just relax, bro. Take your pick of more than a dozen beach towns, each with its own eclectic personality, then join the buff, bronzed bods on golden sands.

Chow Town

It should be a crime to visit San Diego and not have at least one fish taco, or maybe six. With SoCal's best Mexican food dished up all over town, SD has more taco shops per capita than LA. You'll be addicted soon enough.

Culture Vultures

Dumb-blond surfer jokes aside, the city has a surprising wealth of arts and culture. Wander historic Old Town, then spend an afternoon in the museums of Balboa Park. Don't forget the world-famous zoo!

p272

Palm Springs & the Deserts

Shopping & Spas
Outdoors
Nightlife

Retro Modern

The mid-century modern hang out of Elvis, the Rat Pack and Hollywood celebs, PS is hip again. Tour the resort's architectural gems, fill your bags with vintage treasures or just soak up the sun by the pool at a hipster hideaway.

Desert Oases

It's not just PS' spas and hot springs that will rejuvenate you. SoCal's deserts are a nature-loving playground (except during summer – it's just too dang hot), from Joshua Tree's fan-palm oases to Anza-Borrego's hidden canyons to Death Valley's sand dunes and salt flats.

Dirty Weekends

When it comes to nightlife down in the deserts, nothing can compete with the neon-lit Strip in Las Vegas, just across the California–Nevada state line. We can't think of many reasons to ever leave SoCal, but 'Sin City' is one.

p337

Santa Barbara County

Wine
Beaches
History

Vineyards

Forget Napa. Even before the movie *Sideways,* Santa Barbara's wine country was beloved – and respected – for its pinot noir. Sip award-winning vintages with glam crowds from LA, or search out unpretentious tasting rooms on country back roads.

'American Riviera'

Honestly, that touristy tag line stretches the point only a little. Santa Barbara's sunny coast, with its white sands and waving palm trees, can compete with any of SoCal's best, whether you're a beach-bum surfer or want to chill at a luxe oceanfront hotel.

Spanish Views

Rebuilt in Spanish Colonial Revival style after an earthquake in 1925, Santa Barbara's downtown is awash in red-tiled roofs and white-stucco walls. Climb the *Vertigo*-esque county courthouse bell tower for cinematic vistas, then tour a gorgeous 18th-century Spanish mission.

p390

On the Road

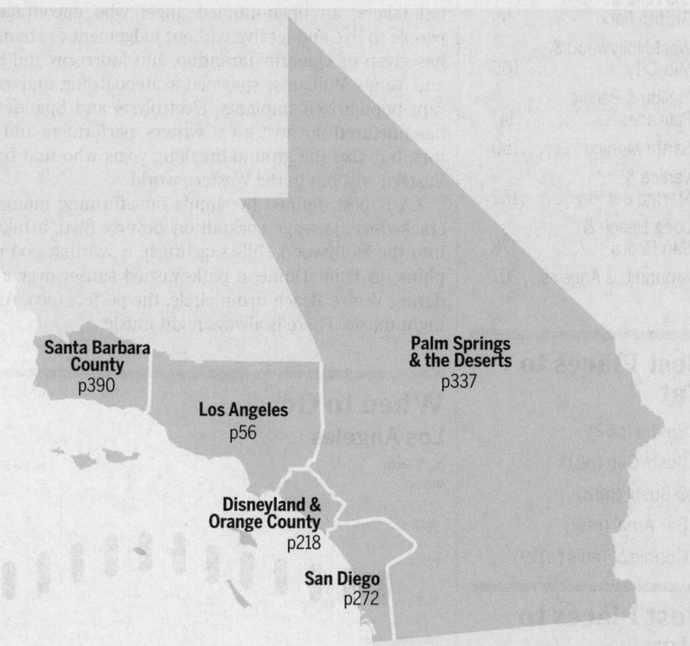

Santa Barbara County p390

Los Angeles p56

Palm Springs & the Deserts p337

Disneyland & Orange County p218

San Diego p272

Los Angeles

Includes ➡

Downtown LA 66
Hollywood 85
Los Feliz & Griffith Park 95
West Hollywood & Mid-City 105
Malibu & Pacific Palisades............141
Santa Monica 150
Venice & Marina del Rey 162
Long Beach & San Pedro 178
Around Los Angeles . . 207

Best Places to Eat

- Bestia (p82)
- Sushi Gen (p81)
- Q Sushi (p82)
- Bar Ama' (p82)
- Connie & Ted's (p119)

Best Places to Stay

- Line Hotel (p204)
- Palihouse (p159)
- Chateau Marmont (p115)
- Terranea Resort (p183)
- Petit Ermitage (p115)

Why Go?

LA runs deeper than her blonde beaches, rolling hills and beemers-for-days would have you believe. She's a myth. A beacon for countless small-town dreamers, rockers and risk-takers, an open-minded angel who encourages her people to live and let live without judgement or shame. She has given us Quentin Tarantino, Jim Morrison and Serena and Venus Williams; spawned skateboarding and gangsta rap; popularized implants, electrolysis and Spandex; and has nurtured not just great writers, performers and directors, but also the ground-breaking yogis who first brought Eastern wisdom to the Western world.

LA is best defined by simple life-affirming moments: a cracked-ice, jazz-age cocktail on Beverly Blvd, a hike high into the Hollywood Hills sagebrush, a swirling pod of dolphins off Point Dume, a pink-washed sunset over a thundering Venice Beach drum circle, the perfect taco. And her night music. There is always night music.

When to Go

Los Angeles

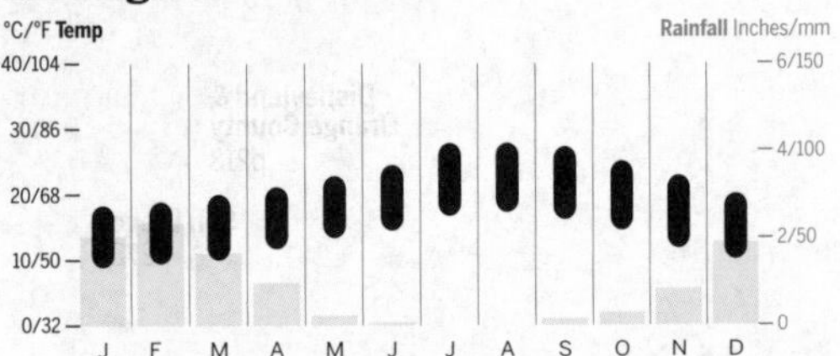

Feb The red carpet is rolled out for the Academy Awards. Prime time for celeb-spotting.

Apr & Sep Most tourists visit when the sun shines the brightest on LA's golden sands.

Oct–Nov & Jan–Mar The region's two distinct wet seasons.

LA Now

Now is an exciting time to visit LA. Downtown is booming, tech money has turned Santa Monica and Venice into Silicon Beach, and Echo Park and Highland Park bring Eastside cool. Recession nightmares are over, the economy is thriving, and an open and experimental climate energizes the art, architecture, music and fashion scenes, while LA's eclectic palate is challenged and sated by progressive chefs who source from local growers that flaunt their earthy goods at hundreds of weekly outdoor farmers markets throughout the city.

WORLD-CLASS MUSIC

The sheer abundance of world-class musicians within LA's orbit, paired with spectacular and historic venues, make it a minor tragedy to leave town without a concert in the memory files. The **Hollywood Bowl**, which aside from being the summer home of the LA Philharmonic, has hosted countless legends from Ella to Radiohead. Sitting beneath and among the stars, in a natural bowl tucked into the Hollywood Hills, while music washes over you, will make you feel all kinds of glamorous. A second, and only slightly less tasty, summertime venue is the **Greek Theatre** – another nature-cupped outdoor amphitheater, which hosts rock and pop acts from MGMT to Gary Clark Jr to Wilco.

The music doesn't stop when the weather turns. The **Walt Disney Concert Hall**, the winter base for the LA Phil, is an architectural masterwork and also hosts jazz giants such as Sonny Rollins and Keith Jarrett.

Crave the ass-shaking underground? Check into **TheLift**, our favorite house music throwdown, co-hosted by KCRW DJ Jeremy Sole. Acoustic troubadours hold pre-tour residencies at the Bootleg Theater (p108) in Silver Lake, and the recently renovated United Artists Theatre (p78), adjacent to uber-cool Ace Hotel Downtown, launched with a stirring show by Spiritualized.

LA's Best Beaches

- Westward Beach is often overshadowed by Zuma to the north, but this wide sweep of sand rambles all the way to Point Dume. Seals, sea lions and dolphins are frequently glimpsed beyond the break.
- El Matador State Beach is defined by sandstone rock spires that rise from the swirling azure sea, and its topless-optional ethos.
- Venice Beach offers boardwalk, bodybuilders, streetballers, skate rats and hippies old and new peddling goods bizarre, bland and beautiful. The Sunday drum circle is an institution.

DON'T MISS

On a balmy summer evening, there are few better places to find yourself than at mid-century mod Dodger Stadium (p107), where the sunsets are stunning, the beer cold, the crowd passionate and the ball club a consistent winner.

Fast Facts: LA County

- Population: 9,963,000
- Area: 4060 sq miles
- No of major movie studios: six
- No of unsold screenplays: countless

Planning your Trip

- Think about what you want to see and where you want to hang out, and book accommodations accordingly to minimize traffic masochism and maximize joy. We suggest moving around the city, staying for a few nights each in different neighborhoods.
- Book your accommodations at http://hotels.lonelyplanet.com.

Resources

- **LA Observed** (www.laobserved.com) offers a high-brow, independent and incisive perspective on the inner workings of the city – from arts to fashion to politics to dining.

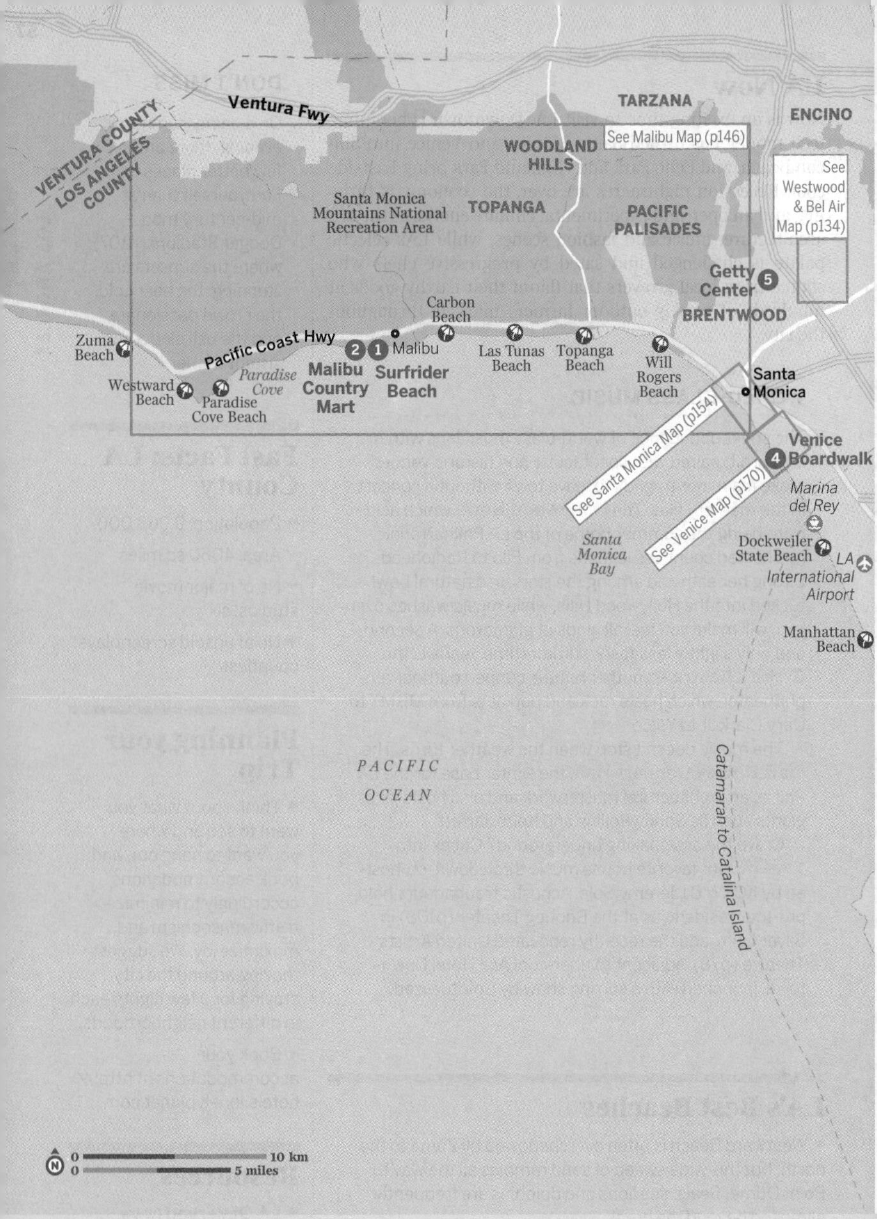

Los Angeles Highlights

1. Watching surfers carve waves at **Surfrider Beach** (p145) in Malibu.
2. Shopping like – and maybe spotting – a star at **Malibu Country Mart** (p152).
3. Swerving along breathtaking Palos Verdes Dr, then hunting for starfish and anemones in the tide pools of **Abalone Cove Shoreline Park** (p183).
4. Getting your freak on while milling with snake charmers and tarot readers on the **Venice Boardwalk** (p168).
5. Feeling your spirits soar surrounded by the fantastic

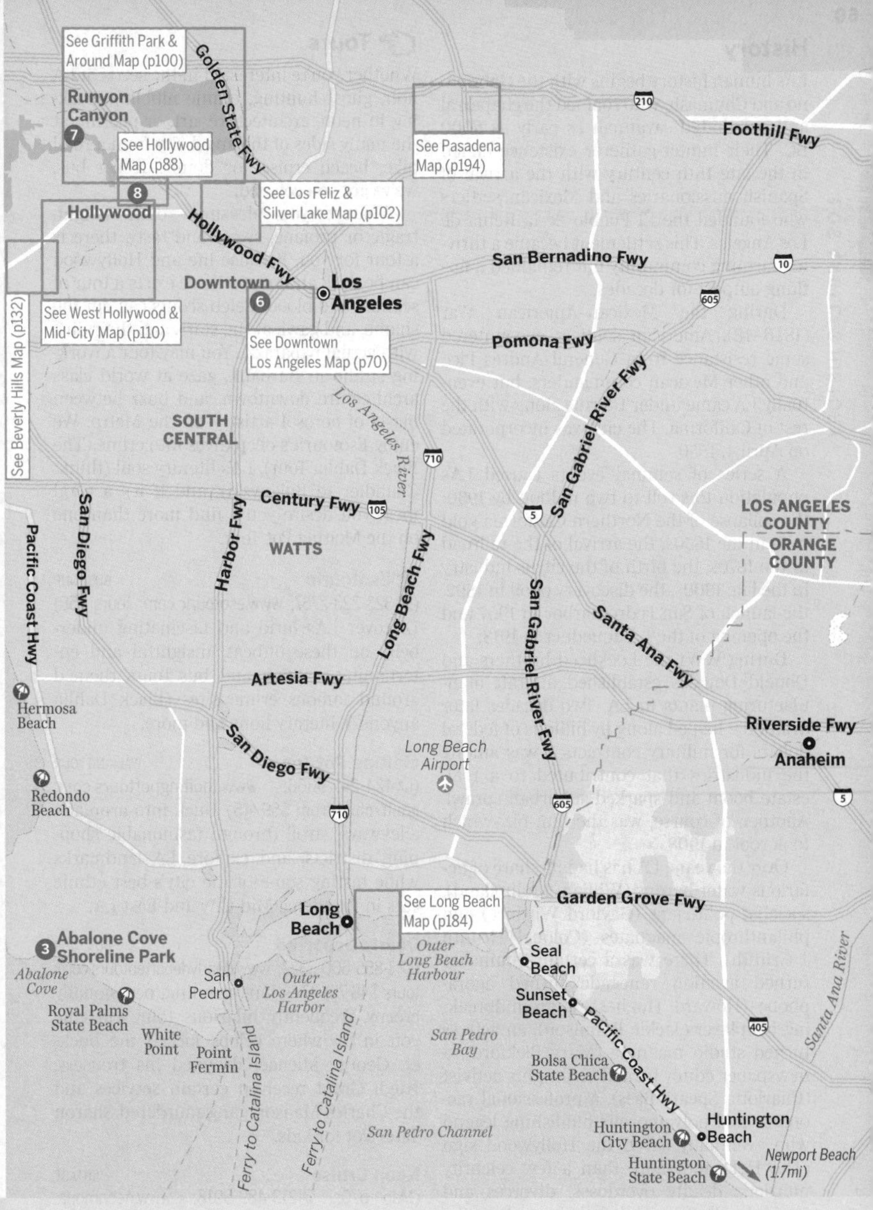

art, architecture, views and gardens of the **Getty Center** (p131).

6 Rubbing shoulders with fashionistas, sipping cocktails in sleek basement lounges and sampling world class cuisine **Downtown**.

7 Joining the buff, the famous and their canine companions on a hike through **Runyon Canyon** (p115).

8 Hitting the bars and clubs of **Hollywood** (p210) for a night of tabloid-worthy decadence and debauchery.

History

LA's human history begins with the Gabrielino and Chumash, who roamed the chaparral and oak-dotted savannah as early as 6000 BC. Their hunter-gatherer existence ended in the late 18th century with the arrival of Spanish missionaries and Mexican settlers who founded the El Pueblo de la Reina de Los Angeles. This settlement became a thriving farming community but remained a far-flung outpost for decades.

During the Mexican-American War (1846–48), American soldiers encountered some resistance from General Andrés Pico and other Mexican commanders, but eventually LA came under US rule along with the rest of California. The city was incorporated on April 4, 1850.

A series of seminal events caused LA's population to swell to two million by 1930: the collapse of the Northern California gold rush in the 1850s, the arrival of the railroad in the 1870s, the birth of the citrus industry in the late 1800s, the discovery of oil in 1892, the launch of San Pedro harbor in 1907 and the opening of the LA aqueduct in 1913.

During WWI the Lockheed brothers and Donald Douglas established aircraft manufacturing plants in LA. Two decades later aviation – helped along by billions of federal dollars for military contracts – was among the industries that contributed to a real-estate boom and sparked suburban sprawl. Another, of course, was the film biz, which took root in 1908.

Over the years, LA has had its share of nefarious water barons (William Mulholland), socialist politicians (Gaylord Wilshire) and philanthropic magnates (Colonel Griffith J Griffith). There was a certain filmmaker turned aviation renegade turned agoraphobe (Howard Hughes), a groundbreaking ballplayer (Jackie Robinson), an actress turned studio magnate (Mary Pickford), a newspaper editor turned civil rights activist (Charlotta Spears Bass), a professional raconteur and polyamorous publishing legend who eventually saved the Hollywood sign (The Hef) and more than a few celebrity murders, deadly overdoses, divorces and scandals, all of which left their mark on the city. But arguably the biggest impact was made by Detroit's big three automakers who bought, then dismantled the famed LA trolley system after WWII and built freeways – lots of them. While it certainly spurred a massive spike in sales, the insider move left a once congruous city carved up, and largely defined, by the automobile.

☞ Tours

Whether you're interested in the seeds of LA noir, ghost hunting, ethnic nibbling, soaking in neon, architecture, art, or peering at the many sides of the angel city from a road bike, beach cruiser or double-decker bus, we've got you covered.

Whatever your pleasure – dark or light, tragic or profane, sweet and tasty, there is a tour for you. Because life and Hollywood can be dark and tragic, there exists a tour of scandal and blood. Celeb scouts can cut the shame, and gawk at the stars, and their dirt, with actual paparazzi. You may tour a working studio in Burbank, gaze at world class architecture downtown, and buzz between blasts of aerosol artistry on the Metro. We enjoy Esotouric's deep dives into crime (The Black Dahlia Tour), LA's literary soul (think: Chandler to Bukowski), and if it's a good meal you desire you'll find more than one on the Melting Pot Tour.

★ Esotouric BUS TOUR

(☎323-223-2767; www.esotouric.com; tours $58) Discover LA's lurid and fascinating underbelly on these offbeat, insightful and entertaining walking and bus tours themed around famous crime sites (Black Dahlia anyone?), literary lions and more.

Melting Pot Tours WALKING TOUR

(☎424-247-9666; www.meltingpottours.com; adult/child from $59/45) Duck into aromatic alleyways, stroll through fashionable shopping districts, and explore LA landmarks while tasting some of the city's best ethnic eats in Pasadena, Mid-City and East LA.

Dearly Departed BUS TOUR

(☎1-855-600-3323; www.dearlydepartedtours.com; tours $48-75) This long-running, occasionally creepy, frequently hilarious tour will clue you in on where celebs kicked the bucket, George Michael dropped his trousers, Hugh Grant received certain services and the Charles Manson gang murdered Sharon Tate. Not for kids.

Neon Cruise VINTAGE

(Map p70; ☎213-489-9918; www.neonmona.org; 136 W 4th St, Downtown; tours $55; ⏲7:30-10:30pm select Sat) From movie marquees to hotel signs, vintage neon is hot. Start by touring the fabulous Los Angeles Theater, then see LA's best neon art from a genuine London double-decker bus. Tours depart from 4th & Main Downtown. Book early, tours often sell out.

Architecture Tours Los Angeles ARCHITECTURE
(☎323-464-7868; www.architecturetoursla.com; tours from $70; ⏲tours 9:30am & 1:30pm) If you think LA architecture begins with Frank Lloyd Wright and ends with Frank Gehry, these van tours, six of which focus on particular neighborhoods, will broaden your horizon, but cover the big guns too. Reservations required.

LA River Walks ECO-URBAN
(☎323-223-0585; www.folar.org; tours $50) Discover the history, mystery and ecology of the LA River as you follow it from Chinatown to Long Beach. Along the way find out why it's not just that ugly concrete channel you've been making jokes about.

Metro Rail Art Tours ART
(www.metro.net/about/art/art-tours; ⏲10am 1st Sat & Sun of month) FREE Some of LA's best contemporary art is not in a museum but in its metro stations. Discover works by Jonathan Borowsky and Gilbert 'Magu' Lujan, among others, on these two-hour tours leaving from the Hollywood/Highland station on Saturday, and from Union Station at 10am on Sunday. They also offer tours at 5:30pm on the first Thursday of the month in the springtime, leaving from Union Station.

Perry's Legends Beach Bike Tour CYCLING
(☎310-939-0000; www.perryscafe.com; adults/senior & studens/child under 12yr $45/40/25; ⏲May-Sep) The mysteries of Muscle Beach, Jim Morrison's house and Skateboard Mamma all feature on this leisurely two-hour bike tour of Santa Monica and Venice. The tour charge includes water, a helmet and an additional hour of bike rental for self-exploring. Reservations required.

Spirit Dinner Cruises CRUISE
(☎310-548-8080; www.spiritdinnercruises.com; cruises $15-60) A lovely way to experience LA on a warm day. Activities include harbor tours, dinner cruises, champagne brunch cruises and whale-watching excursions (January to March) from San Pedro and Long Beach.

Hornblower CRUISE
(☎310-301-6000; www.hornblower.com; Fisherman's Village) Dining and day cruises are available on a fun steamer that looks and feels as if it was airlifted out of Cape Cod. They offer a champagne brunch cruise ($63), starlight dinner cruise ($82 to $88) and a summertime day cruise ($33).

Los Angeles Conservancy WALKING TOUR
(☎info 213-430-4219, reservations 213-623-2489; www.laconservancy.org; adult/child $10/5) Downtown LA's intriguing historical and architectural gems – from an art-deco penthouse to a beaux-arts ballroom and a dazzling silent-movie theater – are revealed on 2½-hour walking tours operated by this nonprofit group. To see some of LA's grand historic movie theaters from the inside, the conservancy also offers the Last Remaining Seats film series, screening classic movies in a gilded theater. Check the schedule and book tickets online.

TMZ Tours HOLLYWOOD TOUR
(Map p88; ☎855-4TMZ-TOUR; www.tmz.com/tour; 6925 Hollywood Blvd; adult/child $55/45; ⏲approximately 10 tours daily) Cut the shame; do you really want to spot celebrities, glimpse their homes, and gawk and laugh at their dirt? Join this branded tour imagined by the paparazzi made famous. Tours are two

LOS ANGELES IN...

One Day

Fuel up at the **Square One** (p96), then go star-searching on the **Hollywood Walk of Fame** along **Hollywood Boulevard**. Up your chances of spotting celebs by hitting the fashion-forward boutiques on paparazzi-infested **Robertson Blvd** (p142) and having lunch at the **Ivy** (p141). Take a digestive stroll along **Rodeo Dr** (p136) before heading to the lofty **Getty Center** (p131). Wrap up with dinner and drinks at **Tasting Kitchen** (p174) on Abbot Kinney.

Two Days

On the second day, explore rapidly evolving Downtown LA, starting with its roots at **El Pueblo de Los Angeles** (p69), catching up with the present at the dramatic **Walt Disney Concert Hall** (p68), then grab lunch at **Bestia** (p82) in the emerging Arts District. Check out the boutiques in **Echo Park** and **Silver Lake**, begin the night early at **El Carmen** (p120), then catch a band at the **Fonda Theatre** (p97) or **El Rey** (p121), or fall by **Harvard & Stone** (p97) for a blast of whiskey drenched cool. Still feel like dancing? Hit the floor at **King King** (p98).

Greater Los Angeles

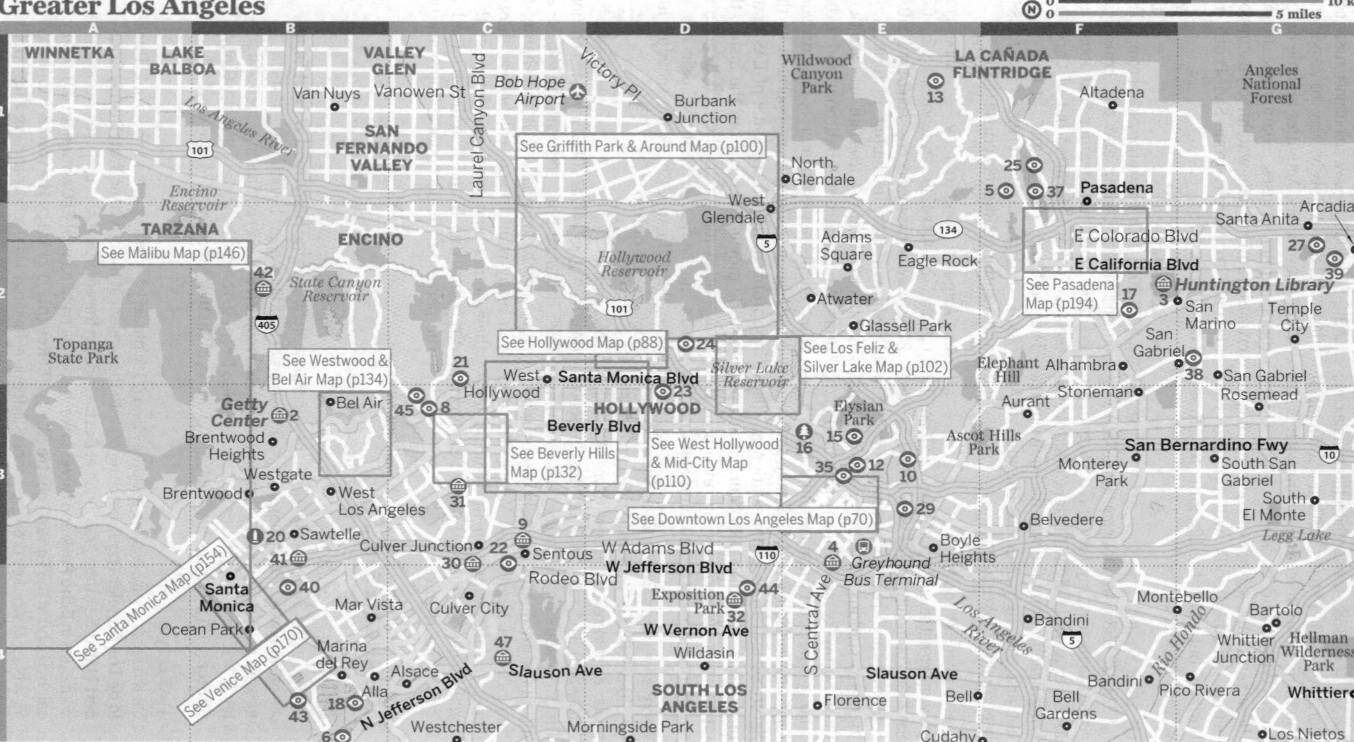

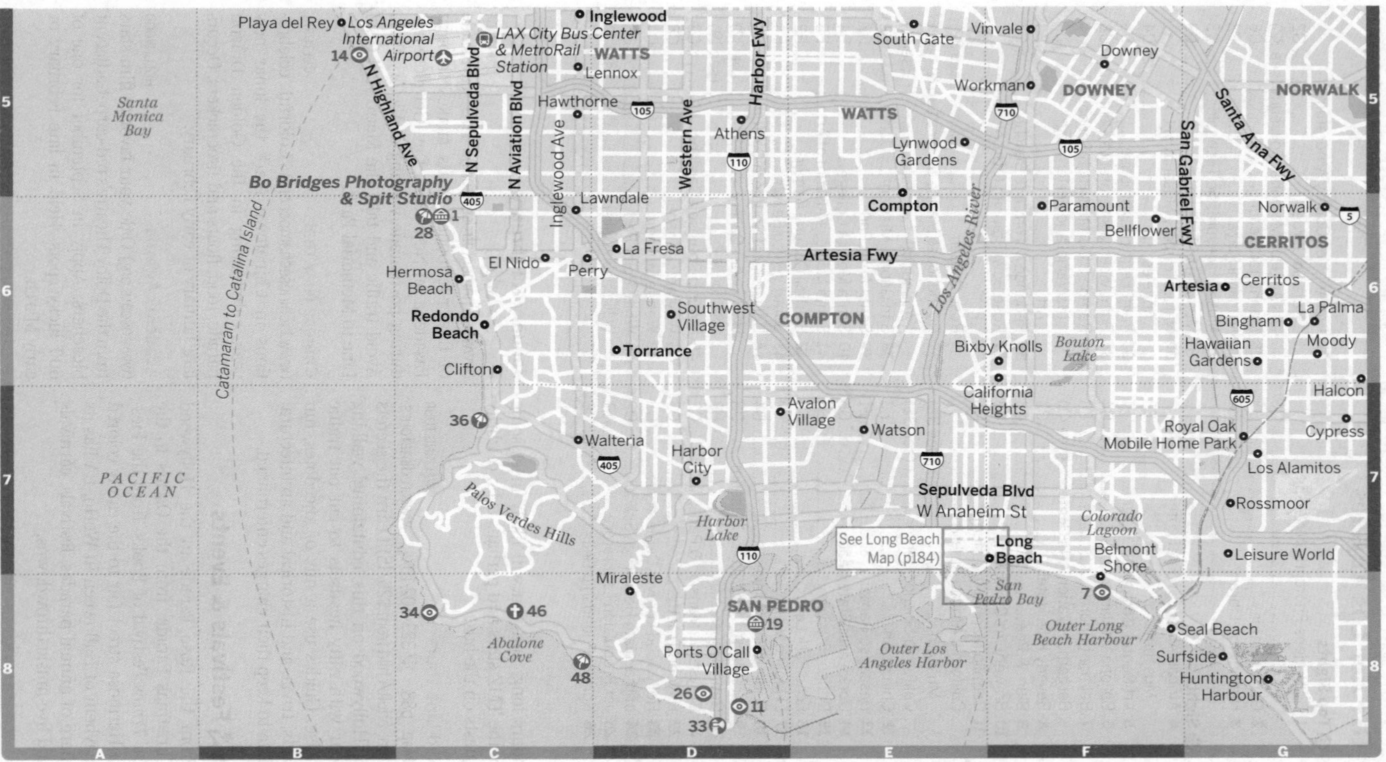
Playa del Rey
Los Angeles International Airport
14
N Highland Ave
LAX City Bus Center & MetroRail Station
Inglewood
WATTS
Lennox
N Sepulveda Blvd
N Aviation Blvd
Hawthorne
Inglewood Ave
Western Ave
Harbor Fwy
Athens
South Gate
Vinvale
Workman
Downey
DOWNEY
NORWALK
WATTS
Lynwood Gardens
Santa Ana Fwy
San Gabriel Fwy
Santa Monica Bay
Bo Bridges Photography & Spit Studio
1
28
Lawndale
Compton
Paramount
Bellflower
Norwalk
CERRITOS
Catamaran to Catalina Island
El Nido
Perry
La Fresa
Hermosa Beach
Artesia Fwy
Los Angeles River
Artesia
Cerritos
La Palma
Bingham
Moody
Hawaiian Gardens
Redondo Beach
Southwest Village
COMPTON
Torrance
Bixby Knolls
Bouton Lake
Clifton
California Heights
Halcon
Avalon Village
Watson
Royal Oak Mobile Home Park
Cypress
Los Alamitos
36
Walteria
Harbor City
PACIFIC OCEAN
Sepulveda Blvd
W Anaheim St
Rossmoor
Palos Verdes Hills
Harbor Lake
Colorado Lagoon
See Long Beach Map (p184)
Long Beach
Belmont Shore
Leisure World
Miraleste
San Pedro Bay
7
34
46
SAN PEDRO
19
Abalone Cove
Outer Long Beach Harbour
Seal Beach
Ports O'Call Village
Outer Los Angeles Harbor
Surfside
48
Huntington Harbour
26
11
33
A
B
C
D
E
F
G
5
6
7
8

Greater Los Angeles

Top Sights

1 Bo Bridges Photography & Spit Studio C6
2 Getty Center B3
3 Huntington Library F2

Sights

4 African American Firefighter Museum E3
5 Art Center College of Design F1
6 Ballona Wetlands B4
7 Belmont Shore F8
Bergamot Station Arts Center .... (see 41)
8 Beverly Hills Hotel C3
9 Blum & Poe C3
10 Brewery Art Complex E3
11 Cabrillo Marine Aquarium D8
California African American Museum .... (see 32)
California Science Center .... (see 32)
12 Chinatown E3
13 Descanso Gardens E1
14 Dockweiler State Beach B5
15 Dodger Stadium E3
16 Echo Park Lake E3
17 El Molino Viejo F2
18 Fisherman's Village B4
19 Fort MacArthur Military Museum D8
20 Gehry House B3
21 Greystone Mansion & Park C2
22 Hayden Tract C3
23 Hollywood Forever Cemetery D3
24 Immaculate Heart High School D2
25 Jet Propulsion Laboratory F1
26 Korean Friendship Bell D8
27 Los Angeles County Arboretum & Botanic Garden G2
Los Angeles Memorial Coliseum .... (see 32)
28 Manhattan Beach C6
29 Mariachi Plaza E3
30 Museum of Jurassic Technology C3
31 Museum of Tolerance C3
32 Natural History Museum of Los Angeles D4
33 Point Fermin Lighthouse D8
34 Point Vicente Interpretive Center C8
35 Ramón C Cortines High School for the Visual and Performing Arts E3
36 Redondo & Torrance Beaches C7
37 Rose Bowl Stadium & Brookside Park F1
Rose Garden .... (see 32)
Roundhouse Marine Studies Lab & Aquarium .... (see 1)
38 San Gabriel Mission G2
39 Santa Anita Park G2
40 Santa Monica College B4
41 Santa Monica Museum of Art B3
42 Skirball Cultural Center B2
43 South Venice Beach B4
44 University of Southern California D4
USC Fisher Gallery .... (see 32)
USS Iowa .... (see 19)
45 Virginia Robinson Gardens C3
46 Wayfarers Chapel C8
47 Wende Museum C4
48 White Point Park C8
Williamson Gallery .... (see 5)

hours long, and you will likely meet some of the TMZ stars and perhaps even celebrity guests on the bus!

Red Line Tours WALKING TOUR
(Map p88; ☎323-402-1074; www.redlinetours.com; adult/child from $25/15) Learn the secrets of Hollywood on this 'edutaining' walking tour with nifty headsets to cut out traffic noise. Guides use a mix of anecdotes, fun facts, trivia, and historical and architectural data to keep their charges entertained.

Festivals & Events

From the Rose Parade to the Hollywood Christmas Parade, from the Oscars to the *LA Times* Festival of Books, from the Fiesta Hermosa street fair to the candy colored mayhem of Halloween in WeHo, LA has its share of annual parades, festivals, carnivals and live-music throwdowns.

January & February

Rose Parade PARADE
(www.tournamentofroses.com) This cavalcade of flower-festooned floats snakes through Pasadena on New Year's Day. Get close-ups during postparade viewing at Victory Park. Avoid traffic and take the Metro Rail Gold Line to Memorial Park.

Chinese New Year CULTURAL
(www.lachinesechamber.org) Colorful celebrations in Chinatown mark the lunar new year, culminating in the Golden Dragon parade, food, floats and firecrackers. Occurs late January or early February.

Academy Awards HOLLYWOOD
(www.oscars.org) Ogle your favorite film stars from the Dolby Theatre's red-carpet-adjacent bleachers. Apply in September for one of 600 lucky spots. Held in late February or early March.

March

LA Marathon SPORTS

(www.lamarathon.com) Held in mid-March, this marathon is a 26.2-mile party through the city from Dodger Stadium to the Santa Monica Pier. Rally the 25,000 runners and wheelchair racers. Then wander performance stages and finish-line festivities.

April

Toyota Grand Prix of Long Beach SPORTS

(www.gplb.com) World-class drivers tear up city streets at this weeklong racing spectacle by the sea.

Los Angeles Times Festival of Books CULTURAL

(www.latimes.com/festivalofbooks) It's a bookworm's paradise for one long weekend of reveling in readings, discussions and storytelling at USC.

Fiesta Broadway STREET

(http://fiestabroadway.la) One of the world's largest Cinco de Mayo parties brings half a million folks to Downtown LA, although in 2014 they held it in late April. Check the website for details.

May

Cinco de Mayo CULTURAL

(www.olvera-street.com) Celebrates the Mexican victory over the French at the Battle of Puebla (1862); free festivities around Olvera St on May 5.

Topanga Banjo Fiddle Contest & Folk Festival MUSIC

(www.topangabanjofiddle.org) Tasty bluegrass tunes float through Paramount Ranch in the Santa Monica Mountains.

Fiesta Hermosa STREET

(www.fiestahermosa.com) A three-day festival where you can browse for arts and crafts, groove to surf music and tribute bands, and graze through an international food court. It's held every Memorial Day and Labor Day weekend.

June

LA Pride GAY PRIDE

(www.lapride.org) Running since 1970, this three-day festival held in mid-June includes music, exhibitions and a parade down Santa Monica Blvd.

Long Beach Bayou MUSIC

(www.longbeachfestival.com; tickets $30) A weekend of Cajun, zydeco and blues music against the backdrop of the *Queen Mary*.

July

Independence Day FIREWORKS

(www.rosebowlstadium.com) Take a seat for official Fourth of July fireworks extravaganzas held at the Rose Bowl, the Hollywood Bowl or in Marina del Rey. Alternatively, drive up to any hilltop and watch the skies explode.

Central Avenue Jazz Festival MUSIC

(www.centralavejazz.org) Veteran jazz players perform for free during this weekend festival, with music, food, arts and crafts, celebrating the pre-WWII era when Central Ave was a hotbed of West Coast jazz.

August

Nisei Week Japanese Festival CULTURAL

(www.niseiweek.org) This free nine-day festival takes over Little Tokyo with parades, *taiko* (drumming), tea ceremonies, karaoke, food, dancing and crafts.

Long Beach Jazz Festival MUSIC

(www.longbeachjazzfestival.com) This three-day festival features top talent and tickets often sell out, so book early.

September

Leimert Park African Art & Music Festival STREET

Historic Leimert Park becomes a Labor Day weekend street party with live music, food and exceptional African art and handicrafts.

LA County Fair FAIR

(www.lacountyfair.com) A month of horse and pig racing, wine tasting, culinary competitions, monster trucks and rock and roll.

Mexican Independence Festival CULTURAL

(www.olvera-street.com/html/fiestas) On Olvera St, a free mid-September celebration of Mexico's independence from Spain, with live performers and delicious food.

Abbot Kinney Festival STREET

(www.abbotkinney.org) Soak up the groovy Venice vibe at this annual celebration of local arts, crafts, food and eccentrics.

Watts Towers Day of the Drum & Jazz Festival ART, MUSIC

(http://wattstowers.org) Multicultural beats on Saturday followed by a day of jazz, gospel and blues. Late September.

October

LA Triathlon SPORTS

(www.latriathlon.com) It's swim, bike and run in an athletic tour de force that draws some top talent. Athletes start on Venice Beach and run through the tape at LA Live.

1

2

EDDIE BRADY / GETTY IMAGES ©

1. Griffith Observatory (p99) 2. Silver Lake nightlife (p107) 3. Los Angeles County Museum of Art (LACMA; p109), designed by William Pereira

Los Angeles Highlights

Griffith Observatory & Hollywood Sign

The crown atop LA's most beloved urban green space, the landmark 1935 observatory has had star turns in feature films and offers a nice vantage point for the iconic Hollywood sign.

LACMA

From stunning permanent collections to special exhibitions and live Friday night jazz in the summertime, there's a reason this is one of LA's favorite cultural oases.

Walt Disney Concert Hall

Frank Gehry's downtown masterpiece, which will pair nicely with the forthcoming Broad Museum, is an abstract, melting mass of brushed steel on the outside, and a wooden music box, blessed with perfect acoustics and top musicians, on the inside.

Explore the Eastside

Los Angeles culture and nightlife once revolved around the Sunset Strip and points west, but no longer. These days the hippest hoods – with prime dining, shopping, drinking and dancing – are in Los Feliz, Silver Lake, Echo Park and Downtown.

Westward Beach

A wide swath of golden sand on the open ocean side of Point Dume, with good surf, *beaucoup* bikinis, and crystal-clear waters that teem with wildlife.

Fairfax, La Brea & the Other Melrose

The stretch of shopping on Melrose between Fairfax and La Brea draws the crowds, but some of LA's best shopping lies on its outskirts. High-end fashion boutiques gather west of Fairfax on Melrose; La Brea is lined with alluring galleries; and Fairfax has become a funky mash-up of urban skate culture.

West Hollywood Halloween Carnaval STREET
(www.visitwesthollywood.com) This rambunctious street fair brings 350,000 revelers (many in over-the-top and/or X-rated costumes) out for a day of dancing, dishing and dating.

November

Día de los Muertos CULTURAL
(Day of the Dead; www.olvera-street.com) Honor beloved ancestors with dance, face painting, decorated altars and candlelight processions on Olvera St, at Hollywood Forever Cemetery, and in Boyle Heights. Held around November 1.

Hollywood Christmas Parade PARADE
(www.thehollywoodchristmasparade.com) Celebs ring in the season by waving at fans from flash floats rolling down Hollywood Boulevard. Easy access via the Metro Rail Red Line. Held the Sunday after Thanksgiving.

December

Marina del Rey Holiday Boat Parade PARADE
(www.mdrboatparade.org) Boats, decked out in twinkling holiday cheer, promenade for prizes in the marina. Check it out from Burton Chase Park.

Las Posadas CULTURAL
(www.olvera-street.com; 5:30-8:30pm Dec 16-24) Free candlelight processions that re-enact Mary and Joseph's journey to Bethlehem, followed by piñata-breaking and general merriment on Olvera St.

DOWNTOWN LOS ANGELES

Downtown Los Angeles is historical, multi-layered and fascinating, and it's become so cool so fast that the likes of *GQ* have called it America's best downtown. In reality, DTLA – as it's known – is a city within a city, and many of its gifts have long been available. We're talking about great architecture from 19th-century beaux arts to futuristic Frank Gehry, world-class music at the Walt Disney Concert Hall, top-notch art at the Museum of Contemporary Art and the forthcoming Broad Museum, superb dining from tiny taquerias to hip Brazilian kitchens to brassy gourmet restaurants. Downtown is both a power nexus housing City Hall, the courts and the hall of records, and an ethnic mosaic. Yet, just 15 years ago it was still a relative ghost town at night when it was abandoned to the skid-row tramps and addicts, and the ravers who braved the scene for a warehouse or loft party in rickety relics. Today its streets are fertile and alive.

Thousands of young professionals, designers and artists have snapped up stylish lofts in art-deco buildings, and the growing gallery district along Main and Spring Sts draws thousands to its monthly art walks. And speaking of art, the velocity of street art is everywhere. It's as if an entire city has something to say crammed within a handful of blocks. We love the JR piece on the outside of LA Cafe (p81).

If you arrive by car, you can save by parking at one of several lots south of 6th St on Main and Los Angeles, charging only $5 all day. An excellent way to get around is by DASH shuttle.

Sights

★Walt Disney Concert Hall BUILDING
(Map p70; info 213-972-7211, tickets 323-850-2000; www.laphil.org; 111 S Grand Ave; guided tours usually noon & 1pm Tue-Sat; P) FREE A molten blend of steel, music and psychedelic architecture, this iconic concert venue is the home base of the Los Angeles Philharmonic, but has also hosted contemporary bands such as Phoenix and classic jazz men like Sonny Rollins. Frank Gehry pulled out all the stops: the building is a gravity-defying sculpture of heaving and billowing stainless-steel.

The auditorium, meanwhile, feels like the inside of a finely crafted cello, clad in walls of smooth Douglas fir with terraced 'vineyard' seating wrapped around a central stage. Even seats below the giant pipe organ offer excellent sightlines. Forty-five-minute, free, self-guided audio tours are available most days, and there are guided tours available too, but they won't let you see the auditorium. The best way to experience the hall is to see a show.

Union Station LANDMARK
(Map p70; www.amtrak.com; 800 N Alameda St; P) Built on the site of LA's original Chinatown, the station opened in 1939 as America's last grand rail station. It's a glamorous exercise in Mission Revival with art-deco accents. The marble-floored main hall, with cathedral ceilings, original leather chairs and grand chandeliers, is breathtaking.

The tiled twin domes north of the station belong to the Terminal Annex, once LA's central post office before it was closed and later reopened as an active postal branch. This is where Charles Bukowski worked, inspiring his 1971 novel *Post Office*.

★**Museum of Contemporary Art** MUSEUM (MOCA; Map p70; ☎213-626-6222; www.moca.org; 250 S Grand Ave; adult/child $12/free, 5-8pm Thu free; ⌚11am-5pm Mon & Fri, to 8pm Thu, to 6pm Sat & Sun) A collection that arcs from the 1940s to the present and includes works by Mark Rothko, Dan Flavin, Joseph Cornell and other big-shot contemporary artists is housed in a postmodern building by Arata Isozaki. Galleries are below ground, yet sky-lit bright.

Don't forget to swing by the bookstore gift shop. Tickets are also good for same-day admission at Geffen Contemporary at MOCA (p76) in Little Tokyo, a quick DASH bus ride away; catch it at the corner of Grand Ave and 1st St.

El Pueblo de Los Angeles

Compact, colorful and car-free, this vibrant historic **district** (http://elpueblo.lacity.org; 👪) FREE, a short stroll northwest of Union Station, sits near the spot where LA's first colonists settled in 1781. It preserves the city's oldest buildings, some dating back to its

LOS ANGELES FOR CHILDREN

Los Angeles is often touted as kid-unfriendly, but that's a myth. Looking around Rodeo Dr, the Sunset Strip and Grand Ave, you might think that LA's children have been banished to a gingerbread cottage in the woods. But they're here, trust us – you've just gotta know where to look.

Sights & Activities

With miles of beaches, mountain trails, urban parks and museums dedicated to them, there are countless activities at your disposal and several restaurants fit the kid-friendly bill quite happily. As far as beaches go, Santa Monica, Zuma and Manhattan beaches are the best for kids, with wide sweeps of golden sand, and long shallows perfect for wading. Zuma can be a bit more treacherous than the others when the rip tides strike, however.

Pacific Park (p152) at the Santa Monica Pier was made for kids. With a carousel, roller coasters and old-school arcades, hours can be spent in hyper reverie.

At Griffith Park there's the Southern Railroad (p102) and the Observatory (p99), as well as horse stables, trails and shady fields where kids can run and spin and play while mom and dad picnic happily.

La Brea Tar Pits (p112) is a must for dino-philes, and what kid isn't in love with dinosaurs?

And the California Science Center (p206) and the **Zimmer Children's Museum** (Map p110; www.zimmermuseum.org; Suite 100, 6505 Wilshire Blvd; adult/child 5-12yr $8/5; ⌚10am-5pm Tue-Thu, 10am-4pm Fri, 12:30-5pm Sun; 🅿👪) are educational diversions disguised as fun.

Then there's the Santa Monica Mountains. All the trails in the Santa Monicas are suitable for and doable with kids – even the trail to Sandstone Peak. We're not saying they won't whine, but kids do love searching for critters, sniffing sage and spotting wildflowers in the chaparral-draped mountains that define the city.

Best Shops & Restaurants

The city's best shops catering to kids include the following:

Puzzle Zoo (p167)

Whimsic Alley (p127)

American Girl Place (p127)

Lola Et Moi (Map p132; www.lolaetmoi.com; 238½ S Beverly Dr)

For a meal the whole family will enjoy, try these eateries:

Bob's Big Boy (p192) San Fernando Valley

Farmers Market (p109) Mid-City

Mama D's (p178) Manhattan Beach

San Pedro Fish Market & Restaurant (p188) San Pedro

Uncle Bill's Pancake House (p178) Manhattan Beach

Downtown Los Angeles

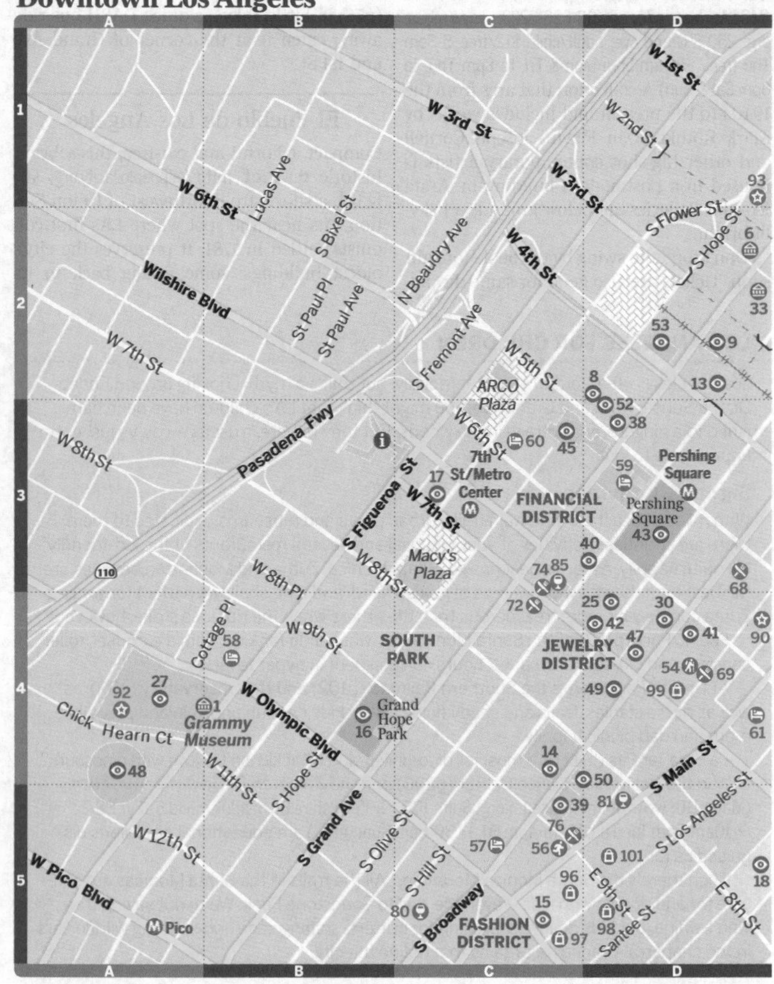

days as a dusty, lawless outpost. More than anything, though, El Pueblo is a microcosm of LA's multi-ethnic heritage and the contributions made by immigrants from Mexico, France, Italy and China. To learn more join a free guided tour leaving from the Old Plaza Firehouse at 10am, 11am and noon Tuesday to Saturday. Or you can pick up a free self-guided tour pamphlet at the El Pueblo Visitors Center.

Olvera Street LANDMARK

(Map p70; www.calleolvera.com;) A festive Mexican marketplace, with gaudy decorations and souvenir stalls that scream 'tourist trap,' you can still find authentic experiences here. You can shop for Chicano art, slurp thick, Mexican-style hot chocolate or pick up handmade candles and candy. At lunchtime, construction workers and cubicle drones swarm the little eateries for tacos, *tortas* (sandwiches) and burritos.

Avila Adobe MUSEUM

(Map p70; 213-628-1274; http://elpueblo.lacity.org; Olvera St; 9am-4pm) FREE The oldest surviving house in LA was built in 1818 by a wealthy ranchero and one-time LA mayor,

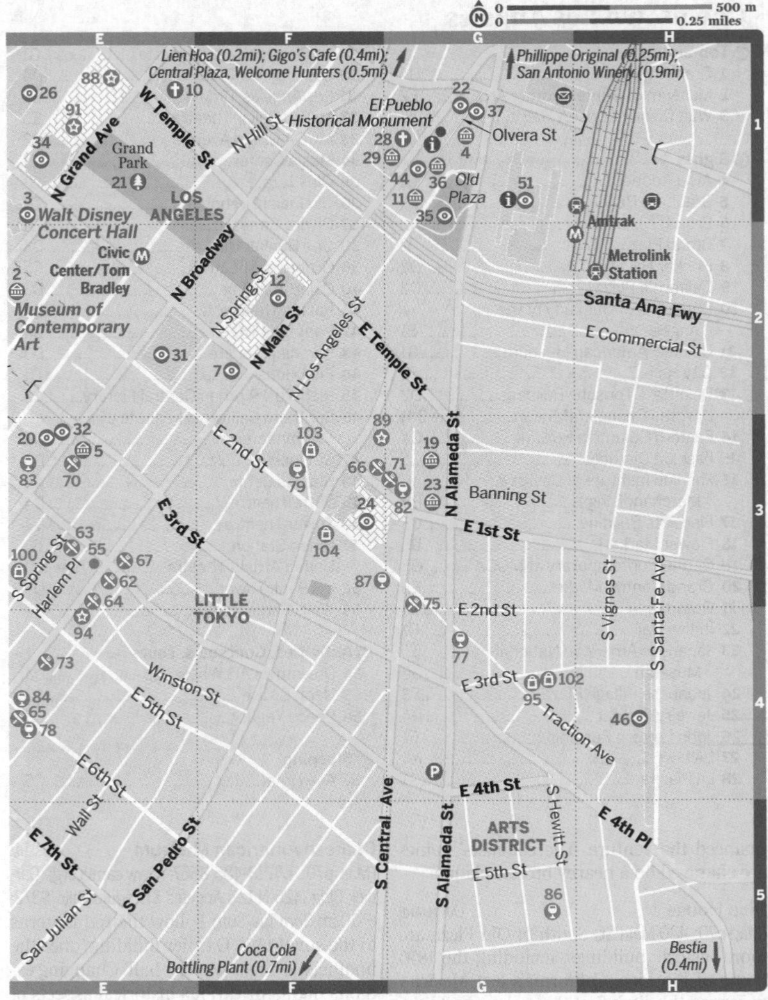

and later became a boarding house and restaurant. Restored and furnished in heavy oak, it's open for self-guided tours and provides a look at life in the early 19th century.

Italian Hall LANDMARK

(Map p70; 644-1/2 Main St) A sight notable for its rare rooftop mural called *América Tropical* by David Alfaro Siqueiros, one of Mexico's great early-20th-century muralists. The 1932 work shows a crucified Native American in front of a Mayan pyramid and was so controversial that city fathers ordered it whitewashed immediately. The Getty Conservation Institute rehabilitated it.

Old Plaza LANDMARK

(Map p70; Olvera St) El Pueblo's central, magnolia-shaded square is crowned by a pretty wrought-iron gazebo. Sleepy during the week, it often turns into a full-blown fiesta zone on Saturdays and Sundays, drawing mariachis, costumed dancers, kissing couples and strolling families.

The best time to visit is for one of the many Mexican festivals, such as Cinco de Mayo or Día de los Muertos. Dotted around the plaza are statues of such key historical figures as Felipe de Neve, who led the first group of settlers, and King Carlos III of Spain, who

Downtown Los Angeles

Top Sights

1 Grammy Museum ... B4
2 Museum of Contemporary Art ... E2
3 Walt Disney Concert Hall ... E1

Sights

4 Avila Adobe ... G1
5 Bradbury Building ... E3
6 Broad ... D2
7 Broad Plaza ... F2
8 Bunker Hill Steps ... D2
9 California Plaza ... D2
10 Cathedral of Our Lady of the Angels ... E1
11 Chinese American Museum ... G1
12 City Hall ... F2
13 Deloitte & Tousche Building ... D2
Dorothy Chandler Pavilion ... (see 34)
14 Eastern Columbia Building ... C4
15 Fashion District ... C5
16 Fashion Institute of Design & Merchandising ... B4
17 Fine Arts Building ... C3
18 Flower Market ... D5
19 Geffen Contemporary at MOCA ... G3
20 Grand Central Market ... E3
21 Grand Park ... E1
22 Italian Hall ... G1
23 Japanese American National Museum ... G3
24 Japanese Village Plaza ... F3
25 Jewelry District ... D4
26 John Ferraro Building ... E1
27 LA Live ... A4
28 La Placita ... G1
29 La Plaza de Cultura y Artes ... G1
30 Los Angeles Theatre ... D4
31 Los Angeles Times ... E2
32 Million Dollar Theatre ... E3
33 MOCA Grand Avenue ... D2
34 Music Center ... E1
35 Old Plaza ... G1
36 Old Plaza Firehouse ... G1
37 Olvera Street ... G1
38 One Bunker Hill ... D3
39 Orpheum Theatre ... C5
40 Oviatt Building ... D3
41 Palace Theatre ... D4
42 Pantages Theatre ... D4
43 Pershing Square ... D3
44 Pico House ... G1
45 Richard J Riordan Central Library ... C3
46 Southern California Institute of Architecture ... H4
47 St Vincent Court ... D4
48 Staples Center ... A4
49 State Theatre ... D4
50 Tower Theatre ... D4
51 Union Station ... G1
United Artists Theatre ... (see 57)
52 US Bank Tower ... D3
53 Wells Fargo Center ... D2

Activities, Courses & Tours

54 Downtown Art Walks ... D4
55 Neon Cruise ... E3
56 Peace Yoga ... C5

Sleeping

57 Ace Hotel ... C5

financed the venture. The colonists' names are engraved on a nearby bronze plaque.

Pico House LANDMARK
(Map p70; 430 Main St) South of Old Plaza are more historic buildings, including the 1870 home of Pio Pico, California's last Mexican governor, the city's first three-story building, and later a glamorous hotel with 21 parlors.

Old Plaza Firehouse MUSEUM
(Map p70; 134 Paseo de la Plaza; 10am-3pm Tue-Sun) FREE The city's oldest fire station (1884) is now a one-room museum filled with dusty old fire-fighting equipment and photographs. Tours are free.

La Placita CHURCH
(Map p70; www.laplacita.org; 535 N Main St) Founded as Iglesia Nuestra Senora Reina De Los Angeles (Our Lady Queen of Angels Church) in 1781, and now affectionately known as 'Little Plaza.' Peek inside for a look at the gilded altar and painted ceiling.

Chinese American Museum MUSEUM
(Map p70; 213-485-8567; www.camla.org; Garnier Bldg, 425 N Los Angeles St; adult/child $3/2; 10am-3pm Tue-Sun) Follow the red lanterns to the small 1890 Garnier Building, once the unofficial Chinatown 'city hall'. Changing exhibits highlight various historical aspects of the Chinese American experience.

La Plaza de Cultura y Artes MUSEUM
(Map p70; 213-542-6200; www.lapca.org; 501 N Main St; noon-5pm Mon, Wed & Thu, to 6pm Fri-Sun) FREE This museum chronicles the Mexican-American experience in Los Angeles, from the Mexican–American War when the border crossed the original pueblo, to the Zoot Suit Riots to Cesar Chavez and the Chicana movement.

South Park & Fashion District

This is where fashionistas in minis, knee-high boots and new school cardigans, flaunt-

58 Figueroa Hotel...B4
59 Millennium Biltmore Hotel...................D3
60 Standard Downtown LA......................C3
61 Stay..D4

Eating
62 Baco Mercat...E3
63 Bar Ama'..E3
64 Blossom...E3
Cafe Dulce.................................(see 24)
65 Cole's...E4
66 Daikokuya...F3
67 Dr. J's...E3
Eggslut......................................(see 20)
68 Gorbals...D3
69 LA Cafe...D4
70 Maccheroni Republic..........................E3
71 Marugame Monzo...............................G3
72 Mo-Chica..C4
73 Nickel Diner...E4
Orsa & Winston.........................(see 63)
74 Q Sushi...C3
Shabu Shabu House...................(see 24)
75 Sushi Gen..G3
Thai Street Food........................(see 20)
Valerie..(see 20)
76 Woodspoon...C5

Drinking & Nightlife
77 Angel City Brewery..............................G4
78 Association..E4
79 Blue Whale...F3
80 Club Mayan..C5
81 Crane's Bar...D5
82 Far Bar..G3
83 La Cita..E3
84 Las Perlas..E4
85 Seven Grand..C3
Varnish.......................................(see 65)
86 Villains Tavern...G5
87 Wolf & Crane..F3

Entertainment
88 Ahmanson Theatre..................................E1
89 East West Players...................................F3
90 Los Angeles Theater Center.................D4
91 Mark Taper Forum.................................E1
92 Nokia Theatre..A4
Orpheum Theatre........................(see 39)
93 Red Cat...D1
94 Regent Theater...E4
Staples Center..............................(see 48)
United Artists Theatre...............(see 57)

Shopping
95 Apolis..G4
96 California Market Center......................C5
97 Cooper Design Space.............................C5
98 Gerry Building..D5
99 Hive..D4
Jewelry District............................(see 25)
100 Last Bookstore in Los Angeles..........E3
101 New Mart...D5
102 Poketo..G4
103 Q Pop..F3
104 Raggedy Threads....................................F3
RIF.LA..(see 104)

ing just enough sass to make you look twice, wander among crack heads and drunks in neck tattoos and a perma-haze. Here you'll scope fresh-sprayed graffiti art, meet east-side artists and foul-mouthed yogis, among the looming graystone edifices.

LA Live BUILDING
(Map p70; www.lalive.com; 800 W Olympic Blvd) Across the street from the Staples Center and LA Convention Center is this corporate entertainment hub which includes the 7100-seat Nokia Theatre (p85). There's also a mega-plex **cinema**, a dozen restaurants, ESPN's LA headquarters, and a 54-story hotel tower shared by Marriott and the Ritz-Carlton.

★**Grammy Museum** MUSEUM
(Map p70; www.grammymuseum.org; 800 W Olympic Blvd; adult/child $13/11, after 6pm $8; 11:30am-7:30pm Mon-Fri, from 10am Sat & Sun;) The highlight of LA Live. Music lovers will get lost in interactive exhibits, which define, differentiate and link musical genres, while live footage strobes. You can glimpse such things as GnR's bass drum, Lester Young's tenor, Yo Yo Ma's cello and Michael's glove (though exhibits and collections do rotate).

Interactive sound chambers allow you and your friends to try your hand at mixing and remixing, singing and rapping. The 2nd floor tends to focus on one band or musician. We saw the Ringo exhibit, and we didn't want to leave.

Staples Center STAIDUM
(Map p70; 213-742-7340; www.staplescenter.com; 1111 S Figueroa St; P) South Park got its first jolt in 1999 with the opening of this saucer-shaped sports and entertainment arena. It's home court for the Los Angeles Lakers, Clippers and Sparks basketball teams, and home ice for the LA Kings. When major headliners – like, say, Beyonce – are in town, they'll most likely perform at the Staples. Parking costs $20.

Fashion Institute of Design & Merchandising FASHION

(FIDM; Map p70; www.fidm.edu; 919 S Grand Ave; ⏲10am-4pm Tue-Sat) A private college with an international student body. The gallery has some interesting rotating exhibits, including costumes worn by actors in Academy Award–nominated movies. Bargain hunters should check out the FIDM Scholarship Store, where you can get new but slightly damaged contemporary clothing donated by department stores for just a few dollars.

Fashion District FASHION

(Map p70; www.fashiondistrict.org) FIDM graduates often go on to launch their own brands or work for established labels in this 90-block nirvana for shopaholics. Bounded by Main and Wall Sts and 7th St and Pico Blvd, the district's prices are lowest in bazaar-like **Santee Alley**, but the styles are grooviest in the **Gerry and Cooper buildings**.

Flower Market MARKET

(Map p70; www.laflowerdistrict.com; Wall St; admission Mon-Fri $2, Sat $1; ⏲8am-noon Mon & Wed, 6-11am Tue, 6am-noon Thu, 8am-2pm Fri, 6am-2pm Sat) Cut flowers at cut-rate prices are the lure here, where a few dollars gets you armloads of Hawaiian ginger or sweet roses, a potted plant or elegant orchid. The market is busiest in the wee hours when florists stock up. Bring cash. It's located in between 7th and 8th Sts.

Financial District & Jewelry District

Richard J Riordan Central Library LANDMARK

(Map p70; ☎213-228-7000; www.lapl.org/central; 630 W Fifth St; ⏲10am-8pm Mon-Thu, to 5:30pm Fri & Sat, 1-5pm Sun) The Egyptian-flavored 1922 central library was designed by Bertram Goodhue and named for a former mayor. Sphinxes greet you at the 5th St entrance, a colorful 1933 mural showing milestones in LA history swathes a grand rotunda on the 2nd floor, and it's crowned with a stunning Mesoamerican mosaic of the sun.

In the modern Tom Bradley wing, escalators cascade down four glass-walled floors through a whimsically decorated glass atrium. Besides 2.1 million books, the library also holds a prized archive of historical photographs, art exhibits, and keeps a dynamic events schedule. One of the best is the **Aloud LA** (www.lfla.org/aloud) series, often featuring major movers and shakers in arts, literature and politics. Recent speakers have included Stephen King, Walter Kirn and Sebastian Junger. It's free but popular, so make online reservations. There are also free tours at 12:30pm on weekdays, and 11am and 2pm on Saturday.

US Bank Tower & Bunker Hills Steps LANDMARK

FREE At 1018ft, the **US Bank Tower** (Map p70; 633 W 5th St) is the tallest building between Chicago and Taiwan. For now. The new 73-story Wilshire Grand Tower will take the title when it opens in 2017. Still, film buffs might remember this one was attacked by an alien spaceship in *Independence Day*. Of course, the **Deloitte & Tousche Building** (Map p70) nearby is more stunning.

The tower abuts the **Bunker Hill Steps** (Map p70), a cheesy set-piece staircase that links 5th St with the **Wells Fargo Center** (Map p70) and other hilltop office complexes. At the top is a small fountain featuring a female nude by Robert Graham.

Pershing Square LANDMARK

(Map p70; www.laparks.org; 532 S Olive St) The hub of Downtown's historic core, Pershing Sq was LA's first public park in 1866 and is now a postmodern concrete patch enlivened by public art, summer concerts, a holiday-season ice rink and the hulking 1923 Millennium Biltmore Hotel (p80).

LA's most illustrious defender of the grand-hotel tradition, it has hosted presidents, kings and celebrities, plus the 1960 Democratic National Convention and eight Academy Awards ceremonies. Its sumptuous interior boasts carved and gilded ceilings, marble floors, grand staircases and palatial ballrooms decorated by White House muralist Giovanni Smeraldi.

Jewelry District NEIGHBORHOOD

(Map p70; www.lajd.net; Hill St) South of Pershing Sq (between 6th and 8th Sts) is the country's second-largest jewelry district after New York. Gold and diamonds are the main currency. One of the marts occupies the historic **Pantages Theatre** (Map p70; 401-21 W 7th St), a vaudeville venue in the 1920s.

Between Hill St and Broadway, on 7th St, is one of Downtown's oddities, **St Vincent Court** (Map p70). The recently restored alleyway is supposed to look like a quaint Parisian street, and is lined with Middle Eastern cafes where clusters of men sip minty tea, and hipsters chow gyro. Broadway is home to legions of discount jewelers.

Eastern Columbia Building THEATER
(Map p70; www.easterncolumbialofts.com; 849 S Broadway) Across the street from the Orpheum, this strikingly turquoise art-deco tower (1929) originally housed a clothing store and was recently converted into luxury lofts. Note the gilded sunburst pattern above the entrance and on the tower's clock face. One-bedroom lofts rent for upwards of $3000 a month; Johnny Depp allegedly bought the penthouse for a cool $2.1 million.

Around the Music Center

City Hall LANDMARK
(Map p70; 213-978-1995; www.lacity.org; 200 N Spring St; 9am-5pm Mon-Fri) FREE Until 1966 no LA building stood taller than the 1928 City Hall, which appeared in the *Superman* TV series and 1953 sci-fi thriller *War of the Worlds*. On clear days you'll have views of the city, the mountains and several decades of Downtown growth from the observation deck.

Also check out the grand domed rotunda on the 3rd level with a marble floor as intricate as those found in Italian cathedrals. Free 30- to 40-minute guided tours are available from 9am to noon on weekdays, but reservations must be made at least seven days in advance. The public entrance is on Main St.

Los Angeles Times NEWSPAPER
(Map p70; 213-237-5757; www.latimes.com; 202 W 1st St; tours 11am & 1:30pm last Tue & Thu of month; P) FREE News junkies can get their fix on a free tour of the *Los Angeles Times* building. Explore either the print works or the editorial offices, learn the paper's history and the publishing process just don't ask about the dark and murky future of newspapers. Kids under 10 can't come and reservations must be made weeks in advance.

A BROAD COLLECTION

Move over LACMA and MOCA, and you too Getty, there's a new museum in town, and it cannot be ignored. Under construction at research time, the forthcoming museum, the **Broad** (Map p70; www.thebroad.org; 221 S Grand Ave) FREE promises to be both an architectural marvel and a deep and nourishing well of modern art. After all, its namesake, Eli Broad (pronounced like road), an eighty-year-old billionaire entrepreneur turned philanthropist and the only man ever to found two Fortune 500 companies in different industries, has long been a noted art collector. He owns 200,000 works of art, much of it locked away in vaults when not on loan to various museums of the world – including LACMA and MOCA. Stand-outs from his collection include 42 works by Jasper Johns, 20 of Gregory Crewdson's exquisitely lit photographs, and several pieces from Neo Rauch, an artist who merges social realism with surrealism. He also has pop art by Roy Lichtenstein and Andy Warhol, works by Jeff Koontz and Christopher Wool, canvasses by Jackson Pollock, photography by Cindy Sherman, and mixed media pieces by Damien Hirst. And that doesn't even scratch the surface.

His collection has been critiqued as being, pardon the pun, too broad. Some have said he's been swayed too often by the size or volume of a piece. And it's true that he owns the largest Wool, Koontz and Sherman pieces they've ever done, but such criticism ignores the gift of what he's gathered. Precisely because he's bought so many pieces from the same artist, works created decades apart, his collection offers the rare chance to see how an artist has evolved over a period of 20, 30 or even 40 years.

The building itself is a modern, mind-melding marvel that will be perfectly at home down the block from the Disney Concert Hall. Designed by Liz Diller of the firm Diller Sconfidio + Renfro, who also designed the wonderful High Line Park in New York, the $140 million project was built on city land, and wrapped in a mesh veil, cut with a higher hemline on either corner. Diller has described it 'as a lady lifting just so much of her skirt to tempt you.'

Visitors will be tempted inside through the glass gateway and into a lobby with some 15,000 sq ft of gallery space. Then they'll take an escalator, through a narrow tunnel, and emerge into the 34,000 sq ft 3rd-floor gallery, home to the permanent collection. Also here, hidden deep within the bowels of the edifice, is an art vault, where the entire Broad collection can be stored in one place for the very first time. Scheduled to open in 2015 as his gift to a city he has long called home, the Broad will be free of charge to all comers.

Broad Plaza LANDMARK
(Map p70; www.dot.ca.gov; 100 S Main St) FREE OK, maybe Caltrans didn't earn their new $150-million digs based on performance, but that doesn't change the fact that this floating steel-mesh-and-glass-skinned monstrosity is worthy of praise. Its 2nd St steps have become a vortex for Downtown's skate punks.

Music Center ARTS CENTER
(Map p70; www.musiccenter.org; 135 N Grand Ave; tours depart 10:30am & 12:30pm Tue & Sat; P) FREE Disney hall is part of a cultural complex known as the Music Center. Aside from the LA Phil's old home, the **Dorothy Chandler Pavilion** (Map p70), it encompasses the **Mark Taper Forum**, the **Ahmanson Theatre** and a fountain plaza. Guided 90-minute tours through the four theaters make a brief stop in the Disney hall lobby.

Grand Park PARK
(Map p70; www.grandparkla.org; 227 N Spring St) Everything from free yoga to spectacular free concerts and DJ sets to long days of lounging and people-watching happen at this new park that cascades from the Music Center down to City Hall, with gushing fountains, a manicured lawn and plenty of benches on each tier. It even has wi-fi.

John Ferraro Building LANDMARK
(Map p70; 111 N Hope St) Home to the Los Angeles Department of Water & Power, this Ferraro-designed classic isn't LA's biggest, tallest or flashiest, but it's an architectural gem, surrounded by a reflection pond. At night it positively glows. The parking lot's shade structure is a solar farm.

Cathedral of Our Lady of the Angels CHURCH
(Map p70; 213-680-5200; www.olacathedral.org; 555 W Temple St; 6:30am-6pm Mon-Fri, from 9am Sat, from 7am Sun; P) FREE José Rafael Moneo mixed Gothic proportions with contemporary design for his 2002 Cathedral of Our Lady of the Angels, which exudes a calming serenity achieved by soft light filtering through its alabaster panes. Wall-sized tapestries as detailed as a Michelangelo fresco festoon the main nave.

They depict 135 saints whose gaze is directed toward the main altar, a massive yet simple slab of red marble. Gregory Peck is buried in the beehive-like subterranean mausoleum. Favorite times to visit the cathedral include the 1pm weekday tours and popular organ recitals at 12:45pm on Wednesday.

Little Tokyo & Around

Little Tokyo swirls with outdoor shopping malls, Buddhist temples, public art, traditional gardens and some of the most authentic sushi bars, *izakayas* (taverns) and *shabu-shabu* parlors in town. The community can trace its roots back to the 1880s, but only a few historic buildings survive along E 1st St. Stop by the Little Tokyo Koban for maps and information.

It's easily accessible by Metro and DASH.

Japanese American National Museum MUSEUM
(Map p70; 213-625-0414; www.janm.org; 100 N Central Ave; adult/child $9/5; 11am-5pm Tue-Wed & Fri-Sun, noon-8pm Thu) A great first stop in Little Tokyo, this is the country's first museum dedicated to the Japanese immigrant experience. You'll be moved by galleries dealing with the painful chapter of the WWII internment camps. Afterward relax in the tranquil garden, and browse the well-stocked gift shop. Admission is free on Thursdays from 5pm to 8pm, and all day on the third Thursday of each month.

Geffen Contemporary at MOCA GALLERY
(Map p70; 213-626-6222; www.moca.org; 152 N Central Ave; adult/student/child 12 & under $12/7/free; 11am-5pm Mon & Fri, to 8pm Thu, to 6pm Sat & Sun) Arty types can pop into Geffen Contemporary to peruse the cutting-edge conceptual exhibits and installations at this MOCA branch converted from a police garage by Frank Gehry.

Japanese Village Plaza PLAZA
(Map p70; btwn 1st & 2nd Sts) The funny-looking tower is a *yagura*, a traditional fire-lookout tower typically found in rural Japan. It's the gateway to this kitschy outdoor mall with gift shops, a couple of noteworthy eateries and good people-watching.

Grand Central Market & Around

Grand Central Market MARKET
(Map p70; www.grandcentralsquare.com; 317 S Broadway; 9am-6pm) On the ground floor of a 1905 beaux-arts building where architect Frank Lloyd Wright once kept an office, stroll along the sawdust-sprinkled aisles beneath old-timey ceiling fans and neon signs, past stalls piled high with mangoes, peppers and jicamas, and glass bins filled with dried chilies and nuts.

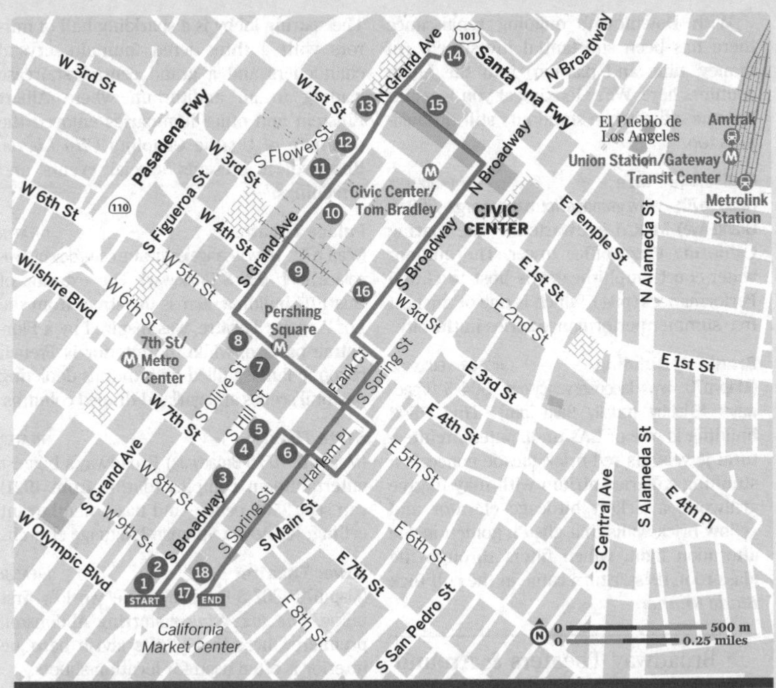

Walking Tour Downtown

START UNITED ARTISTS THEATRE
END WOODSPOON
LENGTH 2.5 MILES

Start at the 1 **United Artists Theatre** (p78), grab a coffee at the 2 **Ace Hotel** (p80) next door, then head north on Broadway through the old theater district. This heady mixture of beaux-arts architecture, discount jewelers and new bars, restaurants and shops sums up the Downtown renaissance in just a few short blocks. Take note of the 3 **State Theatre** (p78) and 4 **St Vincent Court** (p74), 5 **Los Angeles Theatre** (p78) and the 6 **Palace Theatre** (p78).

Turn right at 6th St, continue along for two blocks, then turn left onto Main, where you'll see a flowering of new restaurants and bars at nearly every turn. Turn left on 5th St and continue for six blocks, passing 7 **Pershing Square** (p74) and glimpsing the 8 **Biltmore Hotel** (p80). At Grand Ave turn right and walk past the 9 **Deloitte & Tousche building** (p74), then bisect 10 **MOCA** (p69) on one side and the 11 **Broad** (p75) on the other, continuing until you reach the stunning 12 **Walt Disney Concert Hall** (p68) and the 13 **Music Center** (p76). You'll see the 14 **Cathedral of Our Lady of Angels** (p76) beckoning. Duck inside then follow the traffic down the steps of 15 **Grand Park** (p76) until you reach Broadway once more.

Make a right on Broadway, and grab lunch at the 16 **Grand Central Market** (p76). Afterward, walk another block south, turn left on 4th St, and then right on lively Spring St, which is dotted with still more cafes and bars. Enjoy the street life and the people-watching until Spring dead ends at Main St, just above 9th St. Say hello to the Cheri Rae at 17 **Peace Yoga** (p79) (you kind of have to meet her), and hang a right on 9th to Broadway. If you're hungry for dinner by now, grab a table at 18 **Woodspoon** (p81).

With Downtown's ongoing renaissance there has been substantial investment (of money, time and passion) into the lunch counters here. We're looking at you Eggslut! But the old ceviche standouts still do business too.

California Plaza LANDMARK

(Map p70; www.grandperformances.org; 350 S Grand Ave) MOCA is dwarfed by the soaring California Plaza office tower. The outdoor water-court amphitheater is host to Grand Performances (p84), which is one of the best free summer performance series in the city.

Bradbury Building HISTORIC BUILDING

(Map p70; www.laconservancy.org; 304 S Broadway; ⊙lobby usually 9am-5pm) This 1893 building is one of LA's undisputed architectural jewels. Its red-brick facade conceals a stunning galleried atrium with inky filigree grillwork, a rickety birdcage elevator and yellow-brick walls that glisten golden in the afternoon light, which filters through the glass roof. Its star turn came in the cult flick *Blade Runner*.

Broadway Theaters & Around

Until eclipsed by Hollywood in the mid-1920s, Broadway was LA's entertainment hub with no fewer than a dozen theaters built in a riot of styles, from beaux arts to east Indian to Spanish Gothic. Their architectural and historic significance even earned them a spot on the National Register of Historic Places.

However, since this area is still only partly gentrified, and packed with cut-rate retail and more than a pinch of gritty urban action, they're usually closed to the public. The best way to see them is by joining one of the excellent tours offered by the Los Angeles Conservancy (p61).

Million Dollar Theatre THEATER

(Map p70; www.milliondollar.la; 307 S Broadway) This was the first theater built by Sid Grauman of Chinese Theatre and Egyptian Theatre fame. Big bands played here in the '40s and, a decade later, it became the first Broadway venue to cater to Spanish speakers. Briefly a church, it's now rented out for film shoots.

Los Angeles Theatre THEATER

(Map p70; ☎213-629-2939; www.losangelestheatre.com; 615 S Broadway) This 1931 theater is the most lavish movie palace on the strip. The soaring lobby is a sparkling hall of mirrors with a three-tiered fountain, crystal chandeliers and a grand central staircase leading to an auditorium where Albert Einstein and other luminaries enjoyed the premiere of Charlie Chaplin's *City Lights*. Restored, it presents special events and screenings.

Palace Theatre THEATER

(Map p70; www.losangelestheatre.com/downtown-palace.html; 630 S Broadway) The exterior of this 1911 building, across the street from the Los Angeles Theatre, was inspired by a Florentine palazzo, while the interior is French baroque fantasy filled with murals depicting pastoral scenes and garland-draped columns.

State Theatre THEATER

(Map p70; 703 S Broadway) Broadway's biggest entertainment complex (dating from 1921) can seat 2500 people and has a flamboyant ceiling; it's now a Spanish-language church.

Tower Theatre THEATER

(Map p70; 802 S Broadway) The world's first talkie, *The Jazz Singer* starring Al Jonson, premiered here in 1927. Its lavish baroque interior is often used for location shoots.

Orpheum Theatre THEATER

(Map p70; www.laorpheum.com; 842 S Broadway) This 1926 theater was built for vaudeville and has hosted such entertainers as Judy Garland, George Burns and Nat King Cole. It's a truly sumptuous place with silk tapestries, a gilded, coffered ceiling, still-functioning Wurlitzer organ and an old brass box office. Fully restored, it offers a rich entertainment calendar. See a show here if you can.

United Artists Theatre THEATER

(Map p70; ☎213-623-3233; www.acehotel.com/losangeles/theatre; 929 S Broadway) This gorgeous Spanish Gothic theater, with ornate stone work and stained glass, and grand, yet intricate murals, was built in 1927 and bankrolled by bygone heavyweights Mary Pickford, Douglas Fairbanks and Charlie Chaplin. They'd tired of the studio stronghold on filmmaking and distribution (back then studios owned the movie houses too), so they joined forces as United Artists.

Once the second-tallest building in the city next to City Hall, some thought it was too far south on Broadway, and too separate from the rest of the theater district to thrive, and it has lived a checkered life. Only moderately successful as a movie theater, it turned to Vaudeville through the depression, then went back to the movies until it closed in the 1950s, opening only for the odd rock-and-roll show. From 1962 to 1989 it played Spanish-language films and catered to LA's immigrant community until the old cable preacher Dr Gene Scott bought it and televangelized from the pulpit of Chaplin and Christ. The Scott family earned praise from architecture buffs when they refused to sell it after Dr Gene passed, until they found the Ace Hotel who restored it with passionate attention to detail and now use it to host modern dance shows and rock concerts.

Arts District

In the gritty, industrial section southeast of Little Tokyo is an increasingly lively and gentrifying arts district, thanks to a young, adventurous and spirited crowd of people who live and work in studios and upscale lofts above warehouses and small factories wrapped in sensational graffiti. There's also a growing number of cafes, restaurants and shops.

Most of the action can be found between 3rd and 6th, east of Alameda and West of Santa Fe, with swaths of skid row grit mixed in.

Southern California Institute of Architecture BUILDING

(Sci-Arc; Map p70; www.sciarc.edu; 960 E 3rd St; gallery admission free; ⏲gallery 10am-6pm) The surrounding area got a nod of respectability when this institute moved into the former Santa Fe Freight Yard in 2001. It's a progressive laboratory with faculty and students that continually push the envelope in architectural design. You can see some of the results in the **gallery** or attend a lecture or film screening; see the website for upcoming events.

Elsewhere in Downtown LA

Chinatown NEIGHBORHOOD

(Map p62; www.chinatownla.com) Walk north from El Pueblo and you'll breach the dragon gates. After being forced to make room for Union Station, the Chinese resettled a few blocks north along Hill St and Broadway. Chinatown is still the community's traditional hub, even though most Chinese Americans now live in the San Gabriel Valley.

There are no essential sights here, but the area, a stop on Metro Gold Line, is fun for an aimless wander. Restaurants beckon with dim sum and crispy duck, while shops overflow with curios, ancient herbal remedies and lucky bamboo.

Brewery Art Complex ARTS CENTER

(Map p62; www.labrewery.com; 2100 N Main St; P) Across the LA River is LA's largest artist colony, housed in a former brewery. Most lofts and studios are generally closed to the public except during the biannual **Artwalks** (usually in spring and fall; check the website for details), though you can wander around to examine the large installations – usually works in progress – scattered throughout.

Activities

★Peace Yoga YOGA

(Map p70; www.peaceyogagallery.com; 903 S Main St; per class $10-20) A 4000-sq-ft underground studio space all banged together by one badass, eternally creative Ashtanga yogi named Cheri Rae. The bathroom features reclaimed sinks from barber shops, there are exposed brick walls, DJ decks, massage grottos and more concrete floor space than any other yoga studio in the city.

Friday evening classes include live sitar accompaniment. And we haven't even mentioned the raw-food kitchen (dishes $6 to $15). Come for yoga, stay for lunch, or dinner, and definitely dessert!

Downtown Art Walks WALKING TOUR

(Map p70; www.downtownartwalk.org; ⏲noon-9pm 2nd Thu of month) FREE A mad swirl of art lovers invades Downtown once a month for self-guided, liberally lubricated art walks that link more than 40 galleries and museums across the Downtown grid. You'll find most between 3rd and 9th and Broadway and Main. The scene often surpasses the art.

LA Gun Club SHOOTING RANGE

(☎213-612-0931; www.thelosangelesgunclub.com; 1375 E 6th St; gun rental $5-10, ammunition $14-17; ⏲3-11pm Mon-Thu, from 11am Fri-Sun) An indoor shooting range in the Arts District, where you can pick and choose among magnums, .38 specials and assault rifles, then grab a target and start shooting. They'll give you a modicum training, and a swift background check, then it's all about the shooting. Valentine's Day is their busiest of the year. Um, yeah.

Sleeping

Stay HOTEL, HOSTEL $

(Map p70; ☎213-213-7829; www.stayhotels.com; 640 S Main St; dm with shared bath $39, r 89; P@📶🚭) Formerly the Hotel Cecil, Stay has marble floors, retro furnishings and bedspreads, iPod docks and accent walls. Gleaming shared bathrooms serve just two dorm rooms each and include showers hewn from marble. Rooms have private bathrooms.

Figueroa Hotel HISTORIC HOTEL **$$**
(Map p70; ☎800-421-9092, 213-627-8971; www.figueroahotel.com; 939 S Figueroa St; r $148-184, ste $225-265; P❄@🛜≋🐾) It's hard not to be charmed by this rambling owner-operated oasis a basketball toss from LA Live. Global-chic rooms blend Moroccan mirrors, Iraqi quilts and Kurdish grain-sack floor cushions with paper lanterns from Chinatown. Prince (he's got an all-purple room named for him) is a repeat visitor. Parking costs $8.

Millennium Biltmore Hotel HOTEL **$$**
(Map p70; ☎213-624-1011; www.thebiltmore.com; 506 S Grand Ave; r $133-300; P@🛜≋) Drenched in tradition and gold leaf, Downtown's grand dame has bedded stars, presidents and royalty in modestly sized, gold-and-blue-hued rooms with all the trappings. The gorgeous art-deco health club is the good kind of old school. Parking is $40.

Ace Hotel HOTEL **$$$**
(Map p70; ☎213-623-3233; www.acehotel.com/losangeles; 929 S Broadway Ave; r from $250, ste from $400) Either lovingly cool, a bit too hip or a touch self-conscious depending upon your purview, there is no denying that Downtown's newest hotel opened to universal acclaim. And the minds behind it care deeply about their product. Some rooms are cubby-box small, but the 'medium' rooms are doable.

Some have cool record players set up with a stack of vinyl or a guitar at the ready. There are molded concrete ceilings and queen beds, deco tile in the shower, and marble wash basins. Suites are a step up in size and price. The pool and fabulous bar are on the rooftop, along with magnificent views.

Standard Downtown LA BOUTIQUE HOTEL **$$$**
(Map p70; ☎213-892-8080; www.standardhotels.com/downtown-la; 550 S Flower St; r $220-315, ste from $340; P❄@🛜≋🐾) This design-savvy hotel in a converted oil-company building was a big hit when it first opened years ago, and still appeals to a young, hip-ish crowd. Rooms are mod and minimalist. Hit the rooftop bar for fun with a view. Their black-lit ping-pong bar on the mezzanine is fabulous too. Parking costs $36.

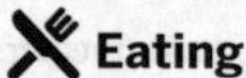

Eating

Marugame Monzo JAPANESE **$**
(Map p70; www.facebook.com/marugamemonzo; 329 E 1st St; mains $7-12; ⏲11:30am-2:30pm & 5-10pm daily) If you care to step up from ramen to udon, come to this special dark-wood udon emporium where they make their noodles fresh in the open kitchen. Appetizers include tempura-fried chicken skin and raw, sliced scallops dolloped with flying-fish roe. But the udon is what draws the raves.

Daikokuya JAPANESE **$**
(Map p70; ☎213-626-1680; www.daikoku-ten.com/locations/littletokyo/; 327 E 1st St; dishes $5-14; ⏲11am-midnight Mon-Fri, to 1am Sat, to 11pm Sun) If you are partial to Japanese noodles, follow your nose to this funky Little Tokyo diner. You can smell the scallions and bubbling broth from the sidewalk, where many line up to grab a red vinyl booth or bar stool. They serve rice bowls, but ramen is king.

Thai Street Food THAI **$**
(Map p70; 317 S Broadway; meals $9-10; ⏲11am-6pm) Well-prepared Thai street food is crafted from organic and free-range ingredients and quality oils in Downtown's fabulous Grand Central Market. They always do three set meals: a BBQ chicken served with sticky rice and *som tom* (green papaya salad), a Hainan chicken served with garlic rice and chicken soup, and a beef panang with coconut rice.

They also have three rotating specials on offer, and usually prepare dishes that are hard to find in most other Thai restaurants in town. If it's available, try the northern Thai sausage.

Eggslut DINER **$**
(Map p70; www.eggslut.com; Grand Central Market, 317 S Broadway; dishes $6-10; ⏲8am-4pm) A classic breakfast counter has been brought back to life by local foodie punks who, among other things, stuff housemade turkey sausage, eggs and mustard aioli in brioche, and make a dish known only as 'the slut': a coddled egg nestled on top of potato purée poached in a glass jar and served with a toasted crostini.

Cole's BAR & GRILL **$**
(Map p70; www.213nightlife.com/colesfrenchdip; 118 E 6th St; sandwiches $6-9; ⏲11am-10pm Sun-Wed, to 11pm Thu, to 1am Fri & Sat) A funky old basement tavern known for originating the French Dip sandwich way back in 1908, when those things cost a nickel. You know

the drill – french bread piled with sliced lamb, beef, turkey, pork or pastrami, dipped once or twice in au jus.

Enjoy yours in a vintage vinyl booth beneath twirling fans with jazz humming from the hi-fi. It offers happy hour on Tuesdays. The bar stays open until 2am Thursday through Saturday.

Gigo's Cafe VIETNAMESE $

(213-229-8889; 853 Broadway Ave; pho $5.50-6.50; 9am-7pm) A basic, tile-floored *pho* joint infused with the aroma of garlic and thinly sliced rare beef in a bowl of noodles that are sought after by locals on this stretch of Broadway. It has chicken and veggie *pho* too). High-school kids love the boba teas!

Dr. J's VEGAN $

(Map p70; 213-537-0905; www.drjsvibrantcafe.com; 334 S Main St; mains $8-12; 11am-9pm) Set in a Main St new building this devout vegan cafe stuffs bowls with grilled tofu, curried potatoes, tossed kale salad (of course) and they even make a vegan chicken sandwich that looks pretty good. There's a juice bar too. Order at the counter and sit among the healthy and fashionable in the spacious, modern yet comfy dining hall.

Cafe Dulce CAFE $

(Map p70; 213-346-9910; www.cafedulce.co; 134 Japanese Village Plaza; pastries & coffee drinks $3-5) Among the best diversions in the Japanese Village Plaza is this terrific donut-shop-turned-gourmet-cafe serving blueberry mocha and green-tea roti (Malaysian sweet buns stuffed with cream), bacon donuts, green-tea donuts and spirulina churros, as well as chewy tapioca rolls. And they pour damn good coffee.

Valerie CAFE $

(Map p70; www.valerieconfections.com; 317 S Broadway; pastries & dishes $4-7; 8am-4pm) This new French bakery and cafe in the Grand Central Market does salted caramel bread pudding, kale hand pies and jars of chocolate pudding (!), as well as entree salads and cold fried chicken sandwiches that get high marks. The coffee is terrific.

LA Cafe CAFE $

(Map p70; 213-612-3000; www.thelacafe.com; 639 S Spring St; mains $7-11; 24hr;) Even back when DTLA was still more dodgy than hip, this cafe was bringing the goodness 24 hours a day. The coffee is tasty, the pastries made fresh, and the lobster grilled cheese is a superfood. Not nutritionally speaking, but order it anyway.

Blossom VIETNAMESE $

(Map p70; 213-623-1973; 426 S Main St; dishes $5-17; noon-4pm & 5:30-11pm) This stylish kitchen churns out fresh and tasty Vietnamese food on the cheap. Start with the *goi cuon* (shrimp and pork spring rolls), and follow it with spicy *pho* (noodle soup) paired with a Southeast Asian pilsner.

Lien Hoa CHINESE $

(721 N Broadway St; dishes under $10; 8am-7pm) As funky and flavorful as Chinatown gets, this broke-down deli is deadly serious about its whole, quartered Peking duck and tangy spareribs, which are chopped, weighed and wrapped for carry out.

★Sushi Gen JAPANESE $$

(Map p70; 213-617-0552; www.sushigen.org; 422 E 2nd St; sushi $11-21; 11:15am-2pm & 5:30-9:45pm) Come early to grab a table, and know that they don't do the uber-creative 'look at me' kind of rolls. In this Japanese classic sushi spot, seven chefs stand behind the blonde wood bar, carving thick slabs of melt-in-your-mouth salmon, buttery toro and a wonderful Japanese snapper, among other staples. Their sashimi special at lunch ($18) is a steal. It's set in the Honda Plaza.

Woodspoon BRAZILIAN $$

(Map p70; 213-629-1765; www.woodspoonla.com; 107 W 9th St; mains $11-20; 11am-2:45pm & 5-10pm Tue-Fri, noon-3pm & 6-11pm Sat, closed Sun) We love it all: the hand-picked china, the vintage pyrex pots of black beans and rice, and the Brazilian owner-operator who still chefs it up in the back. Her pork ribs fall off the bone in a bath of grits and gravy. Her take on steak frites, subs wedges of fried yucca for fries and her pot pie put this place on the map.

Maccheroni Republic ITALIAN $$

(Map p70; 213-346-9725; 332 S Broadway Ave; mains $10-14; 11:30am-3pm & 5:30-10pm Mon-Fri, 5:30-10pm Sat, 4:30-9pm Sun) Tucked away on a still ungentrified corner is this gem with a lovely heated patio and tremendous Italian slow-cooked food. Don't miss the *polpettine di gamberi* (flattened ground shrimp cakes fried in olive oil), and their range of delicious housemade pastas. They don't have beer or wine but you're welcome to bring your own.

You can find them on Facebook; just search Maccheroni Republic Los Angeles.

Gorbals EASTERN EUROPEAN $$
(Map p70; ☎213-488-3408; www.thegorbalsla.com; 216 5th St; dishes $6-30; ⏲lunch & dinner) An Eastern European tapas joint set in the old Alexandria Hotel lobby. Menu mainstays include duck latkes with apple sauce, bacon-wrapped matzo balls served with pink-hot horseradish mayo, and boneless lamb neck roasted with Ethiopian spices.

Shabu Shabu House JAPANESE $$
(Map p70; ☎213-680-3890; 127 Japanese Village Plaza; meals $13-19; ⏲11:30am-2pm & 5:30-9:30pm) It's a humble joint with limited seating around a horseshoe bar illuminated with florescent lights and lined with industrial carpeting. Yet, it's always packed, and those table-top pots are always steaming. This was allegedly the very first ever Shabu restaurant in the US.

Nickel Diner DINER $$
(Map p70; ☎213-623-8301; www.nickeldiner.com; 524 S Main St; mains $7-14; ⏲8am-3:30pm Tue-Sun, 6-10pm Tue-Sat) Named for the intersection of 5th and Main, termed 'the Nickel' by nearby skid-row residents who used to come to this corner for their daily meds, this kitschy red-vinyl joint re-imagines American diner fare. Avocados are stuffed with quinoa salad, burgers are piled with poblano chilies, and don't sleep on the maple-glazed bacon donut.

Mo-Chica PERUVIAN $$
(Map p70; ☎213-622-3744; www.mo-chica.com; 514 W 7th St; dishes $9-16; ⏲11:30am-10pm Mon-Thu, to 11pm Fri & Sat) An acclaimed chef dishes up *arroz con pollo* (grilled chicken with cilantro rice), Peruvian paella and great ceviche in mod, concrete-floor environs. Dishes are mostly small plates. They offer lunch specials ($15) mid-week.

★**Bar Ama'** MEXICAN FUSION $$$
(Map p70; ☎213-687-8002; www.bar-ama.com; 118 W 4th St; dishes $8-25, dinners $32-36; ⏲11:30am-2:30pm & 5:30-11pm Mon-Thu, 11:30am-3pm & 5:30pm-midnight Fri, 11:30am-midnight Sat, to 10pm Sun) One of three exquisite Downtown restaurants with profound Mexican influences offered by Josef Centeno. This one fries pig ears, braises short rib, and smothers enchiladas with mole sauce. Brussel sprouts are garnished with pickled red onions, and the roasted cauliflower and cilantro pesto, served with cashew and pine nuts, is a tremendous veggie choice.

If it's a family-style dinner you crave, order the lamb birria, two pounds of chicken mole or the whole roasted dorado which come with sides and are served family style. Oh, and the drinks list is sublime.

★**Q Sushi** SUSHI $$$
(Map p70; ☎213-225-6285; www.qsushila.com; 521 W 7th St; per person lunch/dinner $75/165) A slender wedge of exquisite sushi. This stunning dark and blonde wood sushi bar is all *omakase* all the time. At dinner there will be 20 courses (lunch about half that) all created by Japanese sushi savant Hiro Naruke, who lost his business in the post tsunami aftermath. Two LA lawyers, who've done business in Tokyo for years and have always loved his food, bankrolled his move.

Expect blow-torched toro with chili paste made with rice that's been fermented for one month, oysters with Bonita sauce, cold jellyfish and cucumber salad with gomae dressing, and a tender octopus that's been braised in sake and brown sugar for two to three hours. They even brew their own soy sauce.

★**Bestia** ITALIAN $$$
(☎213-514-5724; www.bestia.com; 2121 7th Pl; dishes $10-29; ⏲6-11pm Sun-Thu, to midnight Fri & Sat) The most sought-after reservation in town can be found at this new and splashy Italian kitchen in the Arts District. The antipasti ranges from crispy lamb pancetta to sea urchin crudo to veal tartare crostino. Did we mention the lamb's heart? Yeah, you may have to leave the vegan at home.

There are tasty pizzas and pastas, squid-ink risotto stuffed with chunks of lobster, mussels, clams and calamari; they roast chops and whole fish, as well. A worthy splurge indeed.

Baco Mercat FUSION $$$
(Map p70; ☎213-687-8808; www.bacomercat.com; 408 S Main St; dishes $9-25, dinners $29-58) At lunch it's an upscale *torta* (Mexican sandwich) joint (think beef tongue schnitzel or lamb meatballs), at dinner it's a Mexican-Asian fusion dynamo. Seafood dishes include squid stuffed with shrimp and pine nuts, and a popular yellowtail collar. They also do intriguing veggie dishes, including a crispy eggplant and baby yellow beet salad.

Orsa & Winston ASIAN FUSION $$$
(Map p70; ☎213-687-0300; www.orsaandwinston.com; 122 W 4th St; 5-course/8-course tasting menu per person $60/85; ⏲6-11pm Tue-Sat) The newest Josef Centeno kitchen is also the snoot-

iest, and with good reason. The food, the presentation and the flair are all unapologetically upscale and modern. Although there is a slender à-la-carte menu for solo diners, couples and groups dine *omakase* style from a rotating menu that is served in five or eight courses.

Meals include a crudo fish course, a rice or noodle dish (the one with uni and pecorino cream sounds tasty), and roast meat (say pork loin with chicken-liver mousse garnish), and come with optional wine pairings.

Drinking & Nightlife

Las Perlas BAR

(Map p70; 107 E 6th St; ⏲7pm-2am Mon-Sat, 8pm-2am Sun) With an Old Mexico whimsy, a chalkboard menu of over 80 tequilas and mescals, and friendly barkeeps who mix ingredients such as egg whites, blackberries and port syrup into new-school takes on the classic margarita, there's a reason we love Downtown's best tequila bar. But if you truly want to dig tequila, select a highland variety and sip it neat.

You can find them on Facebook; search Las Perlas Los Angeles.

Varnish BAR

(Map p70; ☎213-622-9999; www.213nightlife.com/thevarnish; 118 E 6th St; ⏲7am-2pm) Tucked into the back of Cole's is this cubbyhole-sized speakeasy, where good live jazz burns Sunday through Tuesday.

Association BAR

(Map p70; www.theassociation-la.com; 110 E 6th St; ⏲7pm-2am) This hip basement bar flashes old-school glamour with leather bar stools and lounges tucked into intimate coves. But the bar is the thing. We're talking dozens of whiskeys, ryes, rums and tequilas.

Wolf & Crane BAR

(Map p70; ☎213-935-8249; www.wolfandcranebar.com; 366 E 2nd St; ⏲5pm-2am Mon-Fri, 3pm-2am Sat & Sun; 📶) A fun, new Little Tokyo bar with waxed concrete floors, a blonde-wood slab bar, common tables and built-in bench seating. They have flat screens for the ball games, Japanese art on the walls, and nine locally crafted draft beers. But we prefer the house special, Wolf & Crane: a shot of Johnnie Red, and a Sapporo.

Blue Whale JAZZ

(Map p70; ☎213-620-0908; www.bluewhalemusic.com; 123 Onizuka St 301) An intimate space on the top floor of Weller Court in Little Tokyo. There's concrete floors, a bandstand dedicated to live jazz and a heated patio. When Charlie Hunter rolls through town, he plays here.

Crane's Bar DIVE BAR

(Map p70; ☎323-787-7966; www.facebook.com/CranesDowntown; 810 S Spring St; ⏲5pm-late) From the graffed up concrete floor, to the butcher-block bar (carved from a 130-year-old Douglas fir) to the red vinyl booth to the underground, bank vault location (yes, this was a vault in another life), we love everything about DTLA's newest, sweetest and hottest dive.

Seven Grand BAR

(Map p70; ☎213-614-0737; www.sevengrandbars.com; 2nd fl, 515 W 7th St; ⏲5pm-2am Mon-Wed, from 4pm Thu & Fri, from 7pm Sat) At this dusky whiskey bar with tongue-in-cheek hunting decor there are 175 varieties of amber to explore. DJs and smoking patio, too.

Far Bar PUB

(Map p70; ☎213-617-9990; www.farbarla.com; 347 E 1st St; ⏲11am-2am Mon-Fri, from 10am Sat & Sun) A vintage Asian bar with old-school funk, groovy tunes on the stereo, sports on five strobing flat screens and fusion bites. They do everything from wild boar and Mongolian lamb burgers to sushi. So grab a stool at the refurbished bar or a seat at the common table and order something alcoholic.

Angel City Brewery BREWERY

(Map p70; ☎213-622-1261; www.angelcitybrewery.com; 216 S Alameda St; ⏲4-10pm Mon-Thu, to midnight Fri, noon-midnight Sat, noon-10pm Sun) This wonderful microbrewer of fine beers and ales is the only one of its kind in Downtown LA. Located on the edge of the Arts District, tours are available on weekends, but you can always stop by their Public House to drink beer, listen to occasional live music, and patronize the food trucks that descend with welcome flavor.

Villains Tavern PUB

(Map p70; ☎213-613-0766; www.villainstavern.com; 1356 Palmetto St; ⏲5:30pm-2am Tue-Sat) Restaurateur and interior designer Dana Hollister has turned a run-down deli in the Arts District into a dark-wood and iron den of bluesy cool. There's a salvaged bar top, church-pew seating, high ceilings dangling with vintage chandeliers and a 1600-sq-ft open-air patio where live blues rocks the stage.

La Cita CLUB

(Map p70; www.lacitabar.com; 336 S Hill St; ⏲10am-2am Mon-Fri, from 11am Sat & Sun) The perfect setting for an afternoon that lasts until midnight or a wild, soul-infused dance party, this red-vinyl, Mexican dive bar alternates between a dance club, music venue for Downtown hipsters, and a live-band salsa party. DJs whip the crowd into a frenzy with hip-hop, soul, punk and whatever else gets people moving.

Club Mayan CLUB

(Map p70; www.clubmayan.com; 1038 S Hill St; cover $10-25; ⏲9pm-3am Fri & Sat, varies Sun-Thu) Kick up your heels during Saturday's Tropical Nights when a salsa band turns the heat up against the faux Mayan temple backdrop. Don't know how? Come early for lessons, but there is a dress code. On Fridays it's house and hip-hop, and the club also hosts its share of wrestling events, indie bands and DJs with a following.

☆ Entertainment

Orpheum Theatre THEATER

(Map p70; ☎877-677-4386; www.laorpheum.com; 842 S Broadway) In the early 20th century, cacophonous Broadway was a glamorous shopping and theater strip, where megastars such as Charlie Chaplin leapt from limos to attend premieres at lavish movie palaces. Some – such as the Orpheum Theatre – have been restored and again host screenings and parties. Jam band Gods, Widespread Panic and MGMT played here recently.

United Artists Theatre PERFORMING ARTS

(Map p70; ☎213-623-3233; www.acehotel.com/losangeles/theatre; 929 S Broadway) A historic gem of a theater restored by the Ace Hotel, who curate the calendar. It's homebase for LA's best modern dance company, and stages indie and up-and-coming bands as well.

Regent Theater LIVE MUSIC

(Map p70; 448 Main St) This historic theater originally opened in 1914 as the National Theater, and became the Regent in 1917. In 2014 it opened as Downtown's newest historic live-music venue, seating about 1000 people.

Red Cat THEATER

(Map p70; www.redcat.org; 631 W 2nd St) Downtown's most avant-garde performance laboratory where theater, dance, music, poetry and film merge into impressive exhibitions presented in their own theater and gallery within the Walt Disney Concert Hall complex. The curious name is an acronym for Roy and Edna Disney/Cal Arts Theater. Admission to the gallery is free, theater ticket prices vary.

Mark Taper Forum THEATER

(Map p70; www.centertheatergroup.org; 135 N Grand Ave) Part of the Music Center, the Mark Taper is one of the three venues used by the Center Theatre Group, SoCal's leading resident ensemble and producer of Tony-, Pulitzer- and Emmy-winning plays. It's an intimate space with only 15 rows of seats arranged around a thrust stage, so you can see every sweat pearl on the actors' faces.

Ahmanson Theatre THEATER

(Map p70; www.centertheatregroup.org; 135 N Grand Ave) This grand space is a Center Theatre Group venue in the Music Center,

FREE SOUNDS OF SUMMER

Summer is a great time to visit LA, not in the least because of the free concert series that are offered all over town. Most take place weekly. Check the websites listed here for details.

Some of the biggest crowds come out for the **Twilight Dance Series** (www.santamonicapier.org/twilight; ⏲Thu). The eclectic, multicultural lineup turns the Santa Monica Pier, and adjacent beaches, into a dance party. In 2013 performers included Nick Waterhouse, Trombone Shorty and Jimmy Cliff.

In keeping with its overall renaissance, Downtown has become a hot spot for concerts. Pershing Sq (p74) hosts live acts on Saturday and Thursday nights. In the Financial District, **Grand Performances** (www.grandperformances.org) brings international music, dance and theater acts to California Plaza on Friday and Saturday nights.

Museums also get into the music game. At Los Angeles County Museum of Art, art and jazz prove an irresistible mix during **Friday Night Jazz** (www.lacma.org), which runs from April to November, and the Getty's **Saturdays Off the 405** (www.getty.edu; ⏲6-9pm Sat May-Oct) FREE offers some of the best acts in the bunch.

used primarily for big-time musicals on their way to or from Broadway.

Staples Center SPECTATOR SPORTS
(Map p70; 213-742-7340; www.staplescenter.com; 1111 S Figueroa St;) The **LA Lakers** (213-742-7340; www.nba.com/lakers; tickets $50-250) were down on their luck as of this writing, but the NBA's most successful organization still packs all 19,000 seats on a regular basis. Floor seats, like those filled by the ubiquitous Jack Nicholson, cost in excess of $5000 per game.

Staples is also the home base for the city's other NBA team, the once mismanaged and now high-flying LA Clippers, a legitimate championship contender thanks to Doc Rivers, Chris Paul and Blake Griffin. Unfortunately, their 2014 playoff run was derailed by the scandalous Donald Sterling, whose surreptitiously recorded hate speech was well-publicized and reviled far and wide. The WNBA LA Sparks season (late May to August) follows the regular men's NBA season (October to April). Tickets are sold online and at the Staples Center box office. Parking at the Staples Center costs $20.

Los Angeles Theater Center THEATER
(Map p70; 213-489-0994; www.thelatc.org; 514 S Spring St; admission $5-20; gallery noon-6pm Tue-Sat) Housed in the Old Pacific Stock Exchange building, built in 1915, the downstairs gallery rotates exhibitions curated by the Latino Museum of Art, while the excellent stage shows, produced by the Latino Theater Company, explore culturally diverse material and often feature emerging playwrights.

Nokia Theatre LIVE MUSIC
(Map p70; 213-763-6030; www.nokiatheatrelive.com; 777 Chick Hearn Ct) This 7100-seat theater was christened by the Eagles and the Dixie Chicks when it opened in 2007, and has also hosted Neil Young, Anita Baker and Ricky Gervais. Check its website for info on upcoming shows; admission prices vary.

East West Players THEATER
(Map p70; www.eastwestplayers.org; 120 N Judge John Aiso St) Founded in 1965, this pioneering Asian-American ensemble seeks to build a bridge between Eastern and Western theatrical styles. Its repertoire of Broadway to modern classics takes a backseat to acclaimed premieres by local playwrights. Alumni have gone on to win Tony, Emmy and Academy awards.

DON'T MISS

GET LIFTED

Once a month word leaks out about a dance party or live music event hosted beneath a massive mirror ball. **TheLIFT** is the brainchild of KCRW DJ Jeremy Sole and DJ Wiseacre, but they aren't the only ones spinning records. They recruit the world's best DJs to pump tunes 'without boundaries' through a top-level sound system. Think: Gilles Peterson, Bonobo, Moodymann, Gaslamp Killer, Psychemagik and Mr. Scruff. Their theLIFT (Live) series brings unheralded yet masterful, genre-bending live performances to intimate and sensational venues. Regardless of the venue and musical format, the crowd is always packed with multiculti party people who dance and howl deep into the night. Keep your ear tuned into Jeremy Sole (www.kcrw.com/music/programs/bh or Twitter: @jeremysole), and when you hear the whispers, RSVP or buy tickets in advance.

Shopping

★Raggedy Threads VINTAGE
(Map p70; 213-620-1188; www.raggedythreads.com; 330 E 2nd St; noon-8pm Mon-Sat, to 6pm Sun) A tremendous vintage Americana store just off the main Little Tokyo strip. There's plenty of beautifully raggedy denim and overalls, soft T-shirts, a few Victorian dresses, and a wonderful turquoise collection at great prices. The owner also collects sensational glasses frames and watches.

Last Bookstore in Los Angeles BOOKS
(Map p70; www.lastbookstorela.com; 453 S Spring St; 10am-10pm Mon-Thu, to 11pm Fri & Sat, to 6pm Sun) Who said the inky page is dead? What started as a one-man operation out of a Main St storefront is now nearly an entire ground floor of an old bank building, and it's stuffed with used books of all stripes as well as a terrific vinyl collection for musicologists.

There are arm chairs for reading downstairs, and a delicious crime novel den in the upstairs vault. There's also a book tunnel, a flying typewriter and a few art galleries too. Yeah, books are still cool.

Apolis FASHION
(Map p70; 213-613-9626; www.apolisglobal.com; 806 E 3rd St) A tremendous, but not cheap,

mens-wear brand that creates tailored chinos, jeans, T-shirts and blazers. Owned by two Santa Barbarian brothers, the line fits comfortably between J Crew and James Perse. They're all about fair trade, and prove it with development projects in American inner cities, Peruvian and Ugandan villages, as well as Bangladesh.

In fact, the brand is most famous for their Bangladeshi farmers market bags, the manufacturing of which directly employs 70 women. They've been based in the Arts District since it was much more gritty and dangerous, and now sell in 200 stores worldwide.

Poketo BOUTIQUE

(Map p70; www.poketo.com; 820 E 3rd St; ⌚noon-7pm Mon-Fri, from 11am Sat & Sun) A cute clothing and gifts boutique in the Arts District where you can find everything from Linus bikes and Poler bags to groovy tea sets, glassware, beauty products and art books.

Jewelry District JEWELRY

(Map p70; www.lajd.net; Hill St) For bargain bling head to this bustling Downtown district, between 6th and 8th Sts, where you can snap up watches, gold, silver and gemstones at up to 70% off retail prices. The mostly traditional designs are unlikely to be seen on the red carpet, but the selection is unquestionably huge. Quality varies, however.

Hive ART GALLERY

(Map p70; www.thehivegallery.com; 729 S Spring St; ⌚1-6pm Wed-Sat) Nestled in a decided-

LA'S FASHION DISTRICT DEMYSTIFIED

Bargain hunters love the frantic, 90-block warren of fashion in southwestern Downtown that is the Fashion District. Deals can be amazing, but first-timers are often bewildered by the district's size and immense selection. For orientation, check out www.fashiondistrict.org, where you can download a free app and a map of the area. Basically, the area is subdivided into several distinct retail areas:

Women Los Angeles St between Olympic and Pico Blvds; 11th St between Los Angeles and San Julian Sts

Children Wall St between 12th St and Pico Blvd

Men and bridal Los Angeles St between 7th and 9th Sts

Textiles 9th St between Santee and Wall Sts

Jewelry and accessories Santee St between Olympic Blvd and 13th St

Designer knockoffs Santee Alley and New Alley (enter on 11th St between Maple Ave and Santee St)

Shops are generally open from 10am to 5pm daily, with Saturday being the busiest day because that's when many wholesalers open up to the public. Cash is king and haggling may get you 10% or 20% off, especially when buying multiple items. Refunds or exchanges are a no-no, so choose carefully and make sure items are in good condition. Most stores don't have dressing rooms.

Sample Sales

Every last Friday of the month, clued-in fashionistas descend upon the corner of 9th St and Los Angeles St armed with cash and an attitude to catfight it out for designer clothes priced below wholesale. Their destination: the hip showrooms at the **Gerry Building** (Map p70; www.gerrybuilding.com; 910 S Los Angeles St), **Cooper Design Space** (Map p70; ☎213-627-3754; www.cooperdesignspace.com; 860 S Los Angeles St) and the **New Mart** (Map p70; ☎213-627-0671; www.newmart.net; 127 E 9th St). They each specialize in contemporary and young fashions – though the Cooper and the Gerry are considered the hippest of the bunch. The **California Market Center** (Map p70; ☎213-630-3600; www.californiamarketcenter.com; 110 E 9th St) has a great fashion bookstore on the ground floor, among make-up and fragrance retailers, and houses both clothing and home-furnishing wholesalers. Open from 9am to 3pm, this is the only time the general public is allowed in these trade-only buildings. Come early and leave your modesty at home, as you'll either be trying things on in front of others or not at all. During the Christmas season there are often several sales each week. Check the websites for dates and participating showrooms.

ly not-yet-gentrified stretch of Spring is a seemingly small, but surprisingly deep, artist-owned gallery, where the art always delivers and its openings rock.

RIF.LA SHOES

(Map p70; www.rif.la; 334 E 2nd St; ⏲noon-7pm) Your one-stop shop for new and used limited edition, imported and old-school sneakers. T-shirts and hats are available in their annex two doors down.

Q Pop BOUTIQUE

(Map p70; ☎213-687-7767; www.qpopshop.com; 128 S Onizuka St; ⏲noon-10pm) If you dig Japanese anime and steampunk action figures, art, t-shirts and stuffed toys, you'll love this colorfully funky droplet of noise and peace. Groovy it is.

HOLLYWOOD

Dear sweet Hollywood, the nexus of the global entertainment industry, has some backstory. First, there was the Golden Age, the dawn of the movie industry, when industry strongmen ruled and owned it all. Its very name synonymous with the entire movie industry. Then the '70s happened and the studios fled in search of more space in Burbank and Studio City. Soon the only 'stars' left were embedded in the sidewalk. Worse, you had to hopscotch around runaways and addicts to see them.

In the late '90s the momentum began to shift, and over the next 10 years, big, intelligent dollars, along with a touch of smart design, flooded the area. Shiny new clubs, trendy restaurants and luxe boutiques appeared, supplanting some (not all) of the tacky souvenir shops, tattoo parlors and stripper-supply stores. And the celebs were back. Buying up homes in nearby Los Feliz, attending premieres at Grauman's Chinese Theater and the Oscars at the Dolby Theater, being interviewed by Jimmy Kimmel at his own theater on Hollywood Boulevard, and ducking into hole-in-the-wall Thai joints in Thai Town – a 12-block stretch of Hollywood and Sunset Blvds.

If you're relying on public transport, central Hollywood is a convenient base. The Metro Red Line whisks you to Los Feliz, Downtown and Universal Studios in minutes, and DASH buses provide easy links east along Hollywood Boulevard and west to the Sunset Strip and Melrose Ave. Parking at Hollywood & Highland costs just $2 for four hours with validation from any merchant or the Hollywood visitors center.

Sights

★Hollywood Bowl LANDMARK

(Map p100; www.hollywoodbowl.com; 2301 Highland Ave; rehearsals free, performance costs vary; ⏲Apr-Sep; P) Summers in LA just wouldn't be the same without this chill spot for music under the stars, from symphonies to big-name acts such as Baaba Maal, Sigur Ros, Radiohead and Paul McCartney. A huge natural amphitheater, the Hollywood Bowl has been around since 1922 and has great sound.

Big projection screens give even the folks in the 'nosebleed' sections (tickets $1 to $14) close-ups of the performers. Come early to claim a table in the park-like grounds for a pre-show picnic (alcohol permitted). There are food stands if you don't want to lug your own grub.

The bowl is the summer home of the LA Philharmonic and the Hollywood Bowl Orchestra. Eavesdrop on free rehearsals usually held from 9am to noon on Tuesday, Wednesday and Friday during the season.

Parking is free during the day, but expensive and limited on performance nights. Save yourself the headache and take a shuttle, such as the one running from Hollywood & Highland (p91), which costs $5 per person round-trip.

Hollywood Bowl Museum MUSEUM

(Map p100; www.hollywoodbowl.com/event/museum.cfm; ⏲10am-showtime Mon-Sat, 4pm-showtime Sun Jun-Sep, 10am-5pm Tue-Fri Oct-May) FREE The Bowl, as it's affectionately known around town, enjoys a glamorous history, and this is where you can literally listen to it, and watch it. Classic Bowl moments are yours thanks to audio and video footage of folks like the Beatles, the Stones and Mr James Hendrix.

Hollywood Sign LANDMARK

(Map p100) LA's most famous landmark first appeared in the hills in 1923 as an advertising gimmick for a real-estate development called 'Hollywoodland.' Each letter is 50ft tall and made of sheet metal. Once aglow with 4000 light bulbs, the sign even had its own caretaker who lived behind the 'L' until 1939.

Hollywood

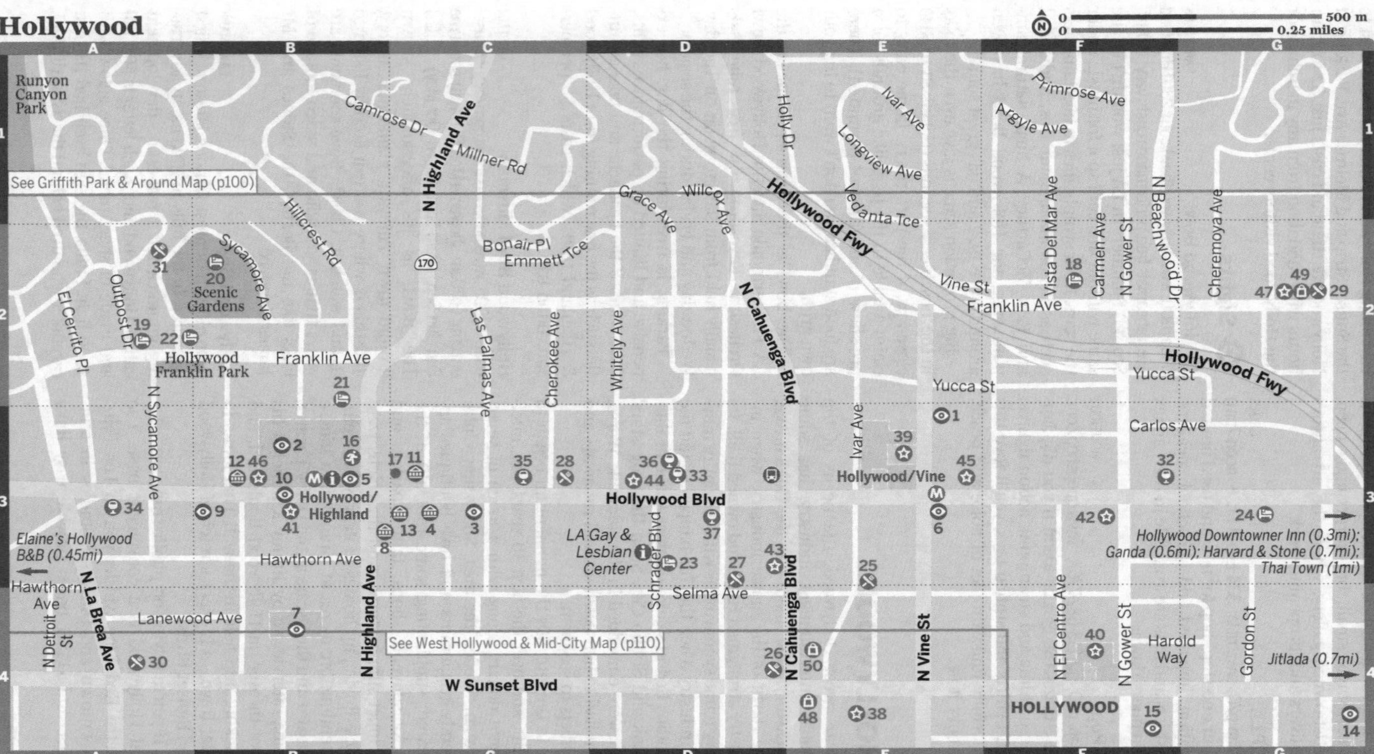
0 500 m
0 0.25 miles
Runyon Canyon Park
See Griffith Park & Around Map (p100)
Camrose Dr
Millner Rd
N Highland Ave
Hillcrest Rd
Sycamore Ave
Scenic Gardens
Outpost Dr
El Cerrito Pl
Hollywood Franklin Park
Franklin Ave
N Sycamore Ave
Las Palmas Ave
Cherokee Ave
Whitely Ave
Bonair Pl
Emmett Tce
Grace Ave
Wilcox Ave
Hollywood Fwy
Holly Dr
Ivar Ave
Longview Ave
Vedanta Tce
Primrose Ave
Argyle Ave
Vista Del Mar Ave
Carmen Ave
N Gower St
N Beachwood Dr
Cheremoya Ave
Vine St
N Cahuenga Blvd
Yucca St
Carlos Ave
Hollywood/Vine
Hollywood/Highland
Hollywood Blvd
Elaine's Hollywood B&B (0.45mi)
Hawthorn Ave
LA Gay & Lesbian Center
Schrader Blvd
Selma Ave
N La Brea Ave
Lanewood Ave
N Detroit St
See West Hollywood & Mid-City Map (p110)
W Sunset Blvd
N Vine St
N El Centro Ave
Harold Way
Gordon St
HOLLYWOOD
Hollywood Downtowner Inn (0.3mi); Ganda (0.6mi); Harvard & Stone (0.7mi); Thai Town (1mi)
Jitlada (0.7mi)

Hollywood

Sights

1 Capitol Records Tower ... E3
2 Dolby Theatre ... B3
3 Egyptian Theatre ... C3
El Capitan Theatre ... (see 41)
4 Guinness World Records Museum ... C3
5 Hollywood & Highland ... B3
6 Hollywood & Vine ... E3
7 Hollywood High School ... B4
8 Hollywood Museum ... B3
9 Hollywood Roosevelt Hotel ... B3
10 Hollywood Walk of Fame ... B3
11 Hollywood Wax Museum ... C3
12 Madame Tussaud's ... B3
13 Ripley's Believe It or Not! ... C3
14 Sunset Bronson Studios ... G4
15 Sunset Gower Studios ... F4
TCL Chinese Theatre ... (see 46)

Activities, Courses & Tours

16 Lucky Strike ... B3
17 Red Line Tours ... C3
TMZ Tours ... (see 46)

Sleeping

18 Best Western Hollywood Hills Hotel ... F2
19 Highland Gardens Hotel ... A2
20 Hollywood Hills Hotel & Apartments ... B2
Hollywood Roosevelt Hotel ... (see 9)
21 Loew's Hollywood ... B2
22 Magic Castle Hotel ... A2
23 USA Hostels Hollywood ... D3
24 Vibe Hotel ... G3
W Hollywood ... (see 6)

Eating

25 Hollywood Farmers Market ... E3
26 Life Food Organic ... D4
27 Little Fork ... D3
28 Loteria ... C3
29 Oaks Gourmet ... G2
30 Pa Ord ... A4
31 Yamashiro Farmers Market ... A2

Drinking & Nightlife

32 Create ... F3
33 Dirty Laundry ... D3
34 Emerson Theatre ... A3
35 Musso & Frank Grill ... C3
36 No Vacancy ... D3
37 Sayers Club ... D3

Entertainment

American Cinematheque ... (see 3)
38 Arclight Cinemas ... E4
39 Bardot ... E3
40 CBS ... F4
41 El Capitan Theatre ... B3
42 Fonda Theatre ... F3
43 Hotel Cafe ... D3
44 King King ... D3
45 Pantages Theater ... E3
46 TCL Chinese Theatre ... B3
47 Upright Citizens Brigade Theatre ... G2

Shopping

48 Amoeba Music ... E4
49 Counterpoint ... G2
50 Space 1520 ... E4

In 1932 a struggling young actress named Peggy Entwistle leapt her way into local lore from the letter 'H'.

The last four letters were lopped off in the '40s as the sign started to crumble. In the late '70s Alice Cooper and Hugh Hefner joined forces with fans to save the famous symbol, and Hef was back at it again in 2010 when the hills behind the sign became slated for a housing development. The venerable Playboy donated the last $900,000 of the necessary $12.5 million it took to buy and preserve the land.

Technically, it's illegal to hike up to the sign, but viewing spots are plentiful, including Hollywood & Highland (p91), the top of Beachwood Dr and the Griffith Observatory (p99).

Hollywood Walk of Fame LANDMARK

(Map p88; www.walkoffame.com; Hollywood Blvd)

Big Bird, Bob Hope, Marilyn Monroe and Aretha Franklin are among the stars being sought out, worshipped, photographed and stepped on along the Hollywood Walk of Fame. Since 1960 more than 2400 performers – from legends to bit-part players – have been honored with a pink-marble sidewalk star.

But don't expect any Kardashian stars any time soon; so far, reality stars have been shunned from the galaxy that glitters along Hollywood Boulevard between La Brea Ave and Gower St, and along Vine St between Yucca St and Sunset Blvd. Check the website for upcoming ceremonies, usually held once or twice monthly.

TCL Chinese Theatre LANDMARK

(Map p88; ☎323-463-9576; www.tclchinesetheatres.com; 6925 Hollywood Blvd; tours & movie tickets adult/child/senior $13.50/6.50/11.50)

Ever wondered what it's like to be in George Clooney's shoes? Just find his footprints in the forecourt of this world-famous movie palace. Formerly Grauman's Chinese Theatre, this exotic pagoda theater – complete with temple bells and stone heaven dogs from China – has shown movies since 1927 when Cecil B DeMille's *The King of Kings* first flickered across the screen.

To see the inside, buy a movie ticket or join a half-hour guided tour offered throughout the day (check in at the gift shop). Of course, most Tinseltown tourists are content to find out how big Arnold's feet really are or to search for Betty Grable's legs or Whoopi Goldberg's braids.

Hollywood Roosevelt Hotel — LANDMARK

(Map p88; www.hollywoodroosevelt.com; 7000 Hollywood Blvd; ⊙24hr; P) FREE Great architecture, rich history and delicious gossip rendezvous at this venerable hotel, where the first Academy Awards ceremony was held in 1929. After a renovation, it briefly became the new millennium's poolside Hollywood hot spot as tabloid regulars were frequently spotted misbehaving at the pool bar.

Back in her day, glamazon Marilyn Monroe shot her first print ad (for suntan lotion) posing on the diving board of said pool, the bottom of which was later decorated with squiggles by artist David Hockney. And while we're name-dropping: actor Montgomery Clift, who stayed in room 928 while filming *From Here to Eternity*, apparently never checked out; his ghost can still be heard playing the bugle.

El Capitan Theatre — LANDMARK

(Map p88; www.elcapitan.go.com; 6838 Hollywood Blvd) Spanish Colonial meets East Indian at the flamboyant El Capitan movie palace built for live performances in 1926 and now run by Disney. The first flick to show here was *Citizen Kane* in 1941 and it's still a fine place to catch a movie, which is often accompanied by a live show.

Before or after, peruse the museum-style exhibits in the lobby related to the current release. Kids love the colorful Disney Soda Fountain downstairs.

Egyptian Theatre — LANDMARK

(Map p88; www.egyptiantheatre.com; 6712 Hollywood Blvd) The Egyptian, the first of the grand movie palaces on Hollywood Boulevard, premiered *Robin Hood* in 1922. The theater's lavish getup – complete with hieroglyphs and sphinx heads – dovetailed nicely with the craze for all things Egyptian sparked by the discoveries of archaeologist Howard Carter.

In its heyday, it had live caged monkeys and usherettes dressed like Cleopatra. These days it's a shrine to serious cinema thanks to the nonprofit American Cinematheque.

Hollywood & Vine — LANDMARK

(Map p88) If you turned on the radio in the 1920s and '30s, chances were you'd hear a broadcast 'brought to you from Hollywood and Vine', and thanks to a mega-development splurge, including a W hotel and a Metro stop, and occasional block parties hosted by Jimmy Kimmel Live, this revitalized corner is taking a bow once more.

Capitol Records Tower — LANDMARK

(Map p88; 1750 N Vine St) FREE You'll recognize this iconic 1956 tower, one of LA's great modern-era buildings. Designed by Welton Becket, it resembles a stack of records topped by a stylus blinking out 'Hollywood' in Morse code. Garth Brooks and John Lennon have their stars outside.

Hollywood Museum — MUSEUM

(Map p88; ☎323-464-7776; www.thehollywoodmuseum.com; 1660 N Highland Ave; adult/child $15/5; ⊙10am-5pm Wed-Sun) We quite like this musty temple to the stars, crammed with kitsch posters, costumes and rotating props. The museum is housed inside the handsome 1914 art-deco Max Factor Building, where the make-up pioneer once worked his magic on Marilyn Monroe and Judy Garland.

The make-up rooms, complete with custom lighting to complement the ladies' complexion and hair color, and Marilyn's pill bottles, are still located on the ground floor, along with a wall of Factor's most glamorous clients and the 1965 Silver Cloud Rolls Royce once owned by Cary Grant.

Hollywood Forever Cemetery — CEMETERY

(Map p62; ☎323-469-1181; www.hollywoodforever.com; 6000 Santa Monica Blvd; ⊙8am-5pm; P) Next to Paramount, Hollywood Forever boasts lavish landscaping, over-the-top tombstones, epic mausoleums and a roll call of departed superstars. Residents include Cecil B DeMille, Rudolph Valentino, femme fatale Jayne Mansfield and punk-rock icons Johnny and Dee Dee Ramone. For a full list of residents, pick up a map ($5) at the flower shop (9am to 5pm).

But these hallowed grounds are anything but dead. Summer brings outdoor movie screenings and Shakespeare in the Cemetery, while in November the gates open for Día de los Muertos (Day of the Dead).

Dolby Theatre — THEATER

(Map p88; www.dolbytheatre.com; 6801 Hollywood Blvd; tours adult/child, senior & student $17/12; ⊙10:30am-4pm) The Academy Awards are handed out at the Dolby Theatre, which has also hosted the American Idol finale, the ESPY awards, the Miss USA pageant and a recent Neil Young residency. On the tour you get to sniff around the auditorium, admire a VIP room and see Oscar up close.

Hollywood & Highland PLAZA

(Map p88; www.hollywoodandhighland.com; 6801 Hollywood Blvd; ⏲10am-10pm Mon-Sat, to 7pm Sun) FREE It's apropos that a Disney-fied shopping mall would be the spark for Hollywood Boulevard's rebirth. A marriage of kitsch and commerce, the main showpiece is a triumphal arch inspired by DW Griffith's 1916 movie *Intolerance*, which frames the Hollywood sign.

Sunset Gower & Sunset Bronson Studios LANDMARK

(www.sgsandsbs.com) Two intersections with a ton of cinematic history. When Nestor Film Company moved to the corner of Sunset and Gower in 1911 it became the Sunset Gower Studios (Map p88; cnr Sunset Blvd & Gower Ave), which birthed Columbia Pictures when the Cohn brothers took it over and signed Frank Capra as their star auteur. Jack Warner founded Sunset Bronson (Map p88; cnr Sunset Blvd & Bronson Ave). He built his studio on old farmland.

In fact, it was here after Warner and Zanuck's 1924 success with *Rin Tin Tin*, shot on the lot, that the Warner Brothers franchise was born. Both studios thrived in the 'Golden Age' of cinema then languished as their parent companies moved off the lots. Gene Autry bought Sunset Bronson in 1964 and turned it into indie production space. Sunset Gower languished and became rock rehearsal spaces for guys like Frank Zappa and John Lennon, as well as indoor tennis courts. These days, the two studios are fused and once again offering stage and office space to big-game productions.

Ripley's Believe It or Not! MUSEUM

(Map p88; www.ripleys.com/hollywood/; 6780 Hollywood Blvd; adult/child $17/9; ⏲10am-midnight) Life's pretty strange and it'll feel stranger still after you've visited Ripley's, where exhibits range from the gross to the grotesque. If shrunken heads, a sculpture of Marilyn Monroe made from shredded $1 bills and a human-hair bikini capture your imagination, this is your place.

Guinness World Records Museum MUSEUM

(Map p88; www.guinnessmuseumhollywood.com; 6764 Hollywood Blvd; adult/child/senior $17/9/15; ⏲10am-midnight;) You know the drill: the

YOUR 15 MINUTES OF FAME

Come on, haven't you always dreamed of seeing your silly mug on TV or in the movies? Well, LA has a way of making dreams come true, but you have to do your homework before coming to town.

Be in a Studio Audience

Sitcoms and game shows usually tape between August and March before live audiences. To nab free tickets, check with TV Tickets (www.tvtix.com) or Audiences Unlimited (☎818-260-0041; www.tvtickets.com). CBS (Map p88; ☎323-575-2624; www.cbs.com; 7800 Beverly Blvd; ⏲9am-5pm Mon-Fri) handles its own ticketing; the office is off Fairfax past the open green gate. Tickets to *Jimmy Kimmel Live*, which conveniently tapes at its namesake theater, are available via 1iota.com. If you don't have tickets, you may still be able to sneak in just before the 6pm taping. Just ask one of the ushers outside the theater (if they don't ask you first!). Most shows have a minimum age of 18.

Become an Extra

If you'd like to see yourself on screen, check with Be In a Movie (www.beinamovie.com) on how to become an extra in a big crowd scene at major film shoots. There's no money in it, but the behind-the-scenes experience and chance of seeing a big star live and in person should make you a hit back home at the office water cooler.

Become a Game Show Contestant

Jeopardy and *Wheel of Fortune* are among the game shows that tape in LA, but the chances of actually becoming a contestant are greatest on *The Price is Right*, taped at CBS. Check www.on-camera-audiences.com/shows/The_Price_is_Right for details.

Guinness is all about the fastest, tallest, biggest, fattest and other superlatives.

Hollywood Wax Museum MUSEUM
(Map p88; ☎323-462-5991; www.hollywoodwax.com; 6767 Hollywood Blvd; adult/child/senior $17/9/15; ⏲10am-midnight; 👪) Starved for celeb sightings? Don't fret: at this museum Angelina Jolie, Halle Berry and other red-carpet royalty will stand still – very still – for your camera. This retro haven of kitsch and camp has been around for over 40 years.

Madame Tussaud's MUSEUM
(Map p88; www.madametussauds.com; 6933 Hollywood Blvd; adult/child $27/20; ⏲10am-9pm Mon-Fri, to 10pm Sat & Sun; 👪) A rich woman's wax museum. Here you can find motionless movie stars (Salma Hayek, Samuel L Jackson, Messrs Depp and Washington), icons (Clark Gable, Audrey Hepburn etc), movie characters like Hugh's Wolverine from *X-Men,* legendary pop stars and all-time great directors.

Activities

Golden Bridge Yoga YOGA
(Map p110; ☎323-936-4172; www.goldenbridgeyoga.com; 1357 N Highland Ave; per person per class $20) Gurmukh, Kundalini yogi to the stars, was an early student of Yogi Bhajan's. She built her Golden Bridge brand on the strength of her unparalleled prenatal yoga classes based on Bhajan's teachings. Her Hollywood center offers 100 classes a week, workshops, a cafe and wellness center.

Sunset Ranch Hollywood OUTDOORS
(Map p100; ☎323-469-5450; www.sunsetranchhollywood.com; 3400 Beachwood Dr; 1/2hr rides $25/40; 👪) Rides through Griffith Park, plus famous sunset rides, and dinner rides to a Mexican restaurant in Burbank. Advanced reservations are highly recommended. Families will appreciate its '2-for-1 Tuesdays.' Download the coupon from its website. Lessons (Western or English riding) start at $85 per hour.

Lucky Strike BOWLING
(Map p88; ☎323-467-7776; www.bowlluckystrike.com; 6801 Hollywood Blvd; ⏲noon-1am Mon-Wed, noon-2am Thu & Fri, 11am-2am Sat & Sun) These 12 lanes are as stylish as bowling gets. There's a DJ booth, projection screens, bottle service and leather seating.

Sleeping

Vibe Hotel HOSTEL $
(Bungalow; Map p88; ☎323-469-8600; www.vibehotel.com; 5920 Hollywood Blvd; dm $22-25, r $85-95; P@令) A funky motel turned hostel with both co-ed and female-only dorms – each with a flat screen and kitchenette, and several recently redone private rooms that sleep three. You'll share space with a happening international crowd.

USA Hostels Hollywood HOSTEL $
(Map p88; ☎323-462-3777, 800-524-6783; www.usahostels.com; 1624 Schrader Blvd; dm $30-40, r w shared bath $81-104; ❄@令) This sociable hostel puts you within steps of the Hollywood party circuit. Private rooms are a bit cramped, but making new friends is easy during staff-organized barbecues, comedy nights and $25 all-you-can-drink limo tours. Freebies include a cook-your-own-pancake breakfast. They have cushy lounge seating on the front porch and free beach shuttles too.

Hollywood Downtowner Inn MOTEL $
(☎323-464-7191; www.hollywooddowntowner.com; 5601 Hollywood Blvd; r from $84; P@令≋) You'll dig the bougainvillea on the railings, and the historic neon sign. Rooms are spacious and spotless with exposed-brick walls, sponged walls and high ceilings; some have a kitchenette. Built in the late 1950s, this is the last standing Melrose-style building in Hollywood.

★**Magic Castle Hotel** HOTEL $$
(Map p88; ☎323-851-0800; http://magiccastlehotel.com; 7025 Franklin Ave; r incl breakfast from $174; P❄@令≋) Walls at this perennial pleaser are a bit thin, but otherwise it's a charming base of operation with large, modern rooms, exceptional staff and a petite courtyard pool where days start with fresh pastries and gourmet coffee. Enquire about access to the Magic Castle, a fabled members-only magic club in an adjacent Victorian mansion. Parking costs $10.

Elaine's Hollywood B&B B&B $$
(☎323-850-0766; www.elaineshollywoodbedandbreakfast.com; 1616 N Sierra Bonita Ave; r $100-120; 令) This B&B offers four rooms in a lovingly restored 1910 bungalow on a quiet street. Your outgoing hosts speak several languages, make a mean breakfast and will happily help you plan your day. Cash only.

Best Western Hollywood Hills Hotel MOTEL $$

(Map p88; ☎323-464-5181; www.bestwestern-california.com; 6141 Franklin Ave; r from $162; P@令≋) Not all rooms are created equal at this family-run hotel with colorful retro touches. For more space and quiet get one in back facing the sparkling pool. Self-caterers will welcome the refrigerator and microwave, although the on-site coffee shop serves some pretty good comfort food and is open late; service, though, can be glacial.

Highland Gardens Hotel HOTEL $$

(Map p88; ☎323-850-0536; www.highlandgardenshotel.com; 7047 Franklin Ave; r $129-370; P@≋) This '50s residential-style motel is retro without even trying, but the lobby is more glamorous than the rooms. Brad Pitt stayed here when he first arrived in Hollywood and wore a chicken suit for nearby El Pollo Loco. Janis Joplin overdosed in room 105.

Hollywood Hills Hotel & Apartments HOTEL $$

(Map p88; ☎800-741-4915, 323-850-1909; www.hollywoodhillshotel.com; 1999 N Sycamore Ave; r $144-174; P≋) Breathtaking city views, a curvy pool guarded by a pagoda, and roomy digs with balcony and kitchen are among the assets at this older but well-kept property, perched high in the hills. Check in at the Magic Castle Hotel (p92). Parking costs $10. No children allowed.

Hollywood Roosevelt Hotel HOTEL $$$

(Map p88; ☎800-950-7667, 323-466-7000; www.hollywoodroosevelt.com; 7000 Hollywood Blvd; r from $339; P❄@令≋) The pool still draws plenty of eye-candy with attitude, and the cabanas are the way to go if you're looking for a splurge. Parking is $30.

W Hollywood HOTEL $$$

(Map p88; ☎323-798-1300; www.whollywoodhotel.com; 6250 Hollywood Blvd; r $379-619; P@令) Corner Suites have circular white leather sofas, and triangular glass bedrooms. The more basic Marvelous Suites are just big hotel rooms with a sexy lace curtain separating the bed from the sofa. No matter the category, marble bathrooms are huge with rain showers and soaker tubs.

Loew's Hollywood HOTEL $$$

(Map p88; ☎323-856-1200; www.loewshotels.com; 1755 N Highland Ave; r from $249) This tower hotel adjacent to the Hollywood & Highland shopping center was recently redone, giving it up-to-the-minute, four-star appeal. The location is terrific.

Eating

Hollywood Farmers Market MARKET $

(Map p88; www.farmernet.com; cnr Ivar & Selma Ave; ⏰8am-1pm Sun; 👪) On the shortlist for the city's best farmers market. This Sunday-morning sprawl offers organic and specialty produce from over 90 farmers, as well as 30 vendors selling tasty prepared food, from smoothies to tamales to crepes to grilled sausages. It's great for the family.

Pa Ord THAI $

(Map p88; ☎323-461-3945; www.paordnoodle.com; 5301 Sunset Blvd; dishes $7-15) A delightful mini-mall Thai diner where the noodles are savory, veggie options plentiful and the lunch specials are a steal. Known for their authentic Thai noodle dishes, their most popular is the Boat Noodle soup, which comes with ground and barbecued pork, pork ball and liver as well as dried shrimp. Authentic flavor deluxe!

Life Food Organic ORGANIC $

(Map p88; www.lifefoodorganic.com; 1507 N Cahuenga Ave; dishes $4-14; ⏰7:30am-9pm) 🌿 This place serves the healthiest fast-food around. Have a chocolate shake made with almond milk, a veggie chili burger with a sesame seaweed salad on the side, and a chocolate cream pie for dessert. None of it cooked! You can dine in, but most take it away.

Yamashiro Farmers Market MARKET $

(Map p88; www.yamashirorestaurant.com; 1999 N Sycamore Ave; ⏰5-9pm Thu May-Sep; P) The best farmers market views in LA are yours from Yamashiro's spectacular perch. In addition to organic produce, expect tasty prepared food and live music. There's also a wine-tasting bar. It's held every Thursday from late May through Labor Day.

Ganda THAI $

(5269 Hollywood Blvd; dishes $6-8; ⏰11am-2am Sun-Thu, to 3am Sat & Sun; P) Get a whiff of real Thai street food. Its pick-and-mix steam table has the same selection of stewed, fried and broiled seafood, chicken and veggie dishes as you'd find in any Bangkok night market.

Los Angeles Neighborhoods

Los Angeles, the nation's second-biggest metro area, is a quilt of self-contained neighborhoods. These are our favorites.

1. Downtown
A gleaming nightlife beacon with an arty, funky population of dreamers.

2. Hollywood
Not just about the glitterati – we love Hollywood for LA's beloved Thai Town and its nocturnal hot spots.

Hollywood TM and Hollywood Walk of FameTM & Design © 2014 HCC. All Rights Reserved

3. Los Feliz & Griffith Park
Laid-back, hip and tasteful, with cafes, landmark architecture and LA's signature green space.

4. Silver Lake & Echo Park
Silver Lake's kitchens and shops are tip top. Echo Park and its fountain lake are for the young, freaky and funky.

5. West Hollywood & Mid-City
The set-piece Sunset Strip, terrific shopping, the hub of Gay LA and some of the city's best museums and galleries are all here.

6. Culver City & Mar Vista
Art galleries, cutting-edge architecture, stucco subdivisions, East German inspired museums and more hipster communities (Westside edition) all converge just inland from Venice Beach.

7. Bel Air, Brentwood & Westwood
Celebrity mansions in Bel Air, the Getty Center in Brentwood, and the wonderful Hammer Museum in Westwood.
Getty Center, designed by Richard Meier

8. Malibu & Pacific Palisades
Stop by the Getty Villa on your way to epic beaches and an underrated coastal mountain range laced with trails.

9. Santa Monica
LA's most beloved beach city, for countless reasons.

10. Venice & Marina del Rey
Venice retains its status as LA's bohemian dream incarnate, despite now being flush with high-tech cash. Marina del Rey is awash with pricey sailboats.

11. South Bay Beaches
Looking for the archetypal golden-sun, small-town beach dream in a big city? Come here.

12. Burbank, Universal City & San Fernando Valley
Tour Universal Studios and dine on Sushi Row.

1

4

7

10

2

ERIC SCHAKENBERG / GETTY IMAGES ©

3

BRENT WINEBRENNER / GETTY IMAGES ©

5

DEEDEE DEGELIA / GETTY IMAGES ©

6

PANORAMIC IMAGES / GETTY IMAGES ©

8

JOAO CANZIANI / GETTY IMAGES ©

9

GEOFFREY GEORGE / GETTY IMAGES ©

11

LEE PETTET / GETTY IMAGES ©

12

RICHARD CUMMINS / GETTY IMAGES ©

Oaks Gourmet DELI $
(Map p88; ☎323-871-8894; www.theoaksgourmet.com; 1915 N Bronson Ave; mains $8.95-11.95; ⏲7am-midnight; P) A hipster deli and wine shop with a devoted following, its ultimate BLT combines heirloom tomato, creamy Camembert cheese, avocado and black-forest bacon on toasted sourdough; specialty nights feature grilled sausages, grilled cheese and tacos. The breakfast burrito is special.

Jitlada THAI $$
(☎323-667-9809; jitladala.com; 5233 West Sunset Blvd; appetizers $5-10, mains $11-30; ⏲lunch & dinner; P) A transporting taste of southern Thailand. The crab curry and *fried som tum* (fried papaya salad) are fantastic, regulars dream about the Thai-style burger between visits, and the vivacious owner-operator counts Ryan Gosling and Natalie Portman among her loyal, mostly *farang* (European American) customers. Look for the wall of fame near the bathrooms.

Pikey GASTROPUB $$
(Map p110; ☎323-850-5400; www.thepikeyla.com; 7617 W Sunset Blvd; dishes $12-28; ⏲noon-2am Mon-Fri, from 11am Sat & Sun) A tasteful kitchen that began life as Coach & Horses, one of Hollywood's favorite dives before it was reimagined into a place where you can get broccoli roasted with bacon, arctic char crudo with grapefruit and jalapeños, seared squid with curried chickpeas, and a slow roasted duck leg. The cocktails rock.

Loteria MEXICAN $$
(Map p88; ☎323-465-2500; www.loteriagrill.com; 6627 Hollywood Blvd; tacos $3-9, appetizers $6-12, mains $16-23; ⏲11am-11pm Mon-Thu, to midnight Fri & Sat, 9am-11pm Sun; P) Spawned from the long-running, widely loved, farmers-market taco stand of the same name, this version offers elegant ambience and a ceviche bar. The kitchen turns out a range of classic Mexican mains and the barmen pour over 80 premium tequilas.

Square One DINER $$
(Map p102; ☎323-661-1109; www.squareonedining.com; 4854 Fountain Ave; mains $9-14; ⏲8:30am-3pm) In the shadows of the sprawling Scientology campus you'll find this adorable breakfast and lunch spot where they braise mustard and collard greens to serve with baked eggs and grits. Tacos are filled with scrambled eggs, jalapeños and chorizo, and they serve a range of gourmet salads and sandwiches too.

★ **Pizzeria & Osteria Mozza** ITALIAN $$$
(Map p110; ☎323-297-0100; www.mozza-la.com; 6602 Melrose Ave; pizzas $11-19, dinner mains $27-38; ⏲pizzeria noon-midnight daily, osteria 5:30-11pm Mon-Fri, 5-11pm Sat, 5-10pm Sun) Osteria Mozza is all about fine cuisine crafted from market fresh, seasonal ingredients; but being a Mario Batali joint, you can expect adventure (squid-ink chitarra freddi with Dungeness crab, sea urchin and jalapeño) and consistent excellence. Reservations are recommended.

Pizzeria Mozza next door is (much) more laid-back and less expensive. Thin-crust pies come with squash blossoms and mozzarella, eggs and bacon, and fennel sausage and pancetta, among other delights.

Providence MODERN AMERICAN $$$
(Map p110; ☎323-460-4170; www.providencela.com; 5955 Melrose Ave; appetizers $6-26, mains $40-49; ⏲noon-2pm Fri, 6-10pm Mon-Fri, 5:30-10pm Sat, to 9:30pm Sun; P) Blinged out with two Michelin stars, this has long been one of LA's finest restaurants. Dishes include scallop tartare, veal sweetbreads, and lobster with roasted porcini mushrooms and spiced hazelnuts. To truly sample the goods, splurge for the nine-course tasting menu.

Little Fork MODERN SOUTHERN $$$
(Map p88; ☎323-465-3675; www.littleforkla.com; 1600 Wilcox Ave; dishes $9-28; ⏲11am-3pm Sat & Sun, 5-10pm Sun-Thu, to midnight Fri & Sat; P) A converted studio, the stucco exterior is a horror show, but inside all is dark and moody, and the kitchen churns out plates of house-smoked trout, brick-roasted chicken, potato gnocchi cooked in bacon lard, tarragon and cream, and a one-pound lobster roll.

Drinking & Nightlife

La Descarga LOUNGE
(☎323-466-1324; www.ladescargala.com; 1159 N Western Ave; ⏲8pm-2am Wed-Sat) This tastefully frayed, sublimely sweaty, rum and cigar lounge is a revelation. Behind the marble bar are over 100 types of rum from Haiti, Guyana, Guatemala and Venezuela.

The bartenders mix and muddle specialty cocktails, but you'd do well to order something aged, and sip it neat as you enjoy the mambo and *son* sounds bouncing off the walls, and the burlesque ballerina on the catwalk. Reservations are mandatory, and there's a dress code too. Guys, wear smart shoes and shirts. No jeans. Ladies, wear a dress and heels.

★No Vacancy BAR

(Map p88; ☎323-465-1902; www.novacancyla.com; 1727 N Hudson Ave; ⏲8pm-2am) An old, shingled Victorian has been converted into LA's hottest night out. Even the entrance is theatrical: you'll follow a rickety staircase into a narrow hall and enter the room of a would-be madame, dressed in fishnet and hospitality who will soon press a button to reveal another staircase down into the living room and out into a courtyard.

There are bars in nearly every corner. The barkeeps work wonders and there's even burlesque dancers and a tightrope walker to entertain the droves of party people. There's a velvet rope, however, so it helps to gather a group and book a table to ensure entry.

Dirty Laundry BAR

(Map p88; ☎323-462-6531; dirtylaundrybarla.com; 1725 N Hudson Ave; ⏲10pm-2am) Under a cotton-candy pink apartment block of no particular import, is a funky den of musty odor and great times, low ceilings, exposed pipes, good whiskey behind the bar, groovy funk on the turntables and plenty of pretty people with low inhibitions. There are velvet rope politics at work here, so reserve a table to make sure you slip through.

Harvard & Stone BAR

(www.harvardandstone.com; 5221 Hollywood Blvd; ⏲8pm-2am) Here, the craftsman whiskey, bourbon and cocktail specials rotate daily. It lures hipsters with live bands, burlesque troops and solid DJs – especially on Sunday when a rockabilly theme and the sexy crowd will make you twist and, possibly, shout.

Emerson Theatre CLUB

(Map p88; ☎323-525-2453; www.sbe.com/nightlife/brands/emersontheatre; 7080 Hollywood Blvd) A mash-up of prohibition cocktails, scantily clad burlesque dancers, hip-hop, velvet ropes and VIP sections. The pretty people who enjoy their LA glitz party here.

Sayers Club CLUB

(Map p88; ☎323-871-8416; www.sbe.com/nightlife/locations/thesayersclub-hollywood; 1645 Wilcox Ave; cover varies; ⏲8pm-2am Tue, Thu & Fri) When rock royalty such as Prince, established stars such as the Black Keys, and even movie stars such as Joseph Gordon-Levitt decide to play secret shows in intimate environs, they come to the back room at this brickhouse Hollywood nightspot, where the booths are leather, the lighting moody and the music always satisfies.

Create CLUB

(Map p88; ☎323-463-3331; www.sbe.com/nightlife/brands/createnightclub/; 6021 Hollywood Blvd; ⏲10pm-4am Fri & Sat) If you enjoy the glitz and glam of big-city nightclubs, but are more partial to EDM than hip-hop and pop, find your way to this new offering from LA nightlife empresarios, SBE. There will be a list and a rope.

Musso & Frank Grill BAR

(Map p88; www.mussoandfrankgrill.com; 6667 Hollywood Blvd) Hollywood history hangs in the thick air at Musso & Frank Grill, Tinseltown's oldest eatery (since 1919). Charlie Chaplin used to knock back vodka gimlets at the bar and Raymond Chandler penned scripts in the high-backed booths.

☆ Entertainment

★Upright Citizens Brigade Theatre COMEDY

(Map p88; ☎323-908-8702; www.losangeles.ucbtheatre.com; 5919 Franklin Ave; tickets $5-10) Founded in New York by *SNL* alums Amy Poehler and Ian Roberts along with Matt Besser and Matt Walsh, this sketch-comedy group cloned itself in Hollywood in 2005 and is arguably the best improv theater in town. Most shows are $5 or $8 but Sunday's 'Assssscat' is freeeee.

Pantages Theater THEATER

(Map p88; www.pantages-theater.com; 6233 Hollywood Blvd) The splendidly restored Pantages Theater is an art-deco survivor from the Golden Age and a fabulous place to catch a play or Broadway musical. Oscars were handed out here between 1949 and 1959, when Howard Hughes owned the building. The uber-noir Frolic Room bar next door was featured in *LA Confidential*. Recent shows include *Book of Mormon*.

Fonda Theatre CONCERT VENUE

(Map p88; ☎323-464-6269; www.fondatheatre.com; 6126 Hollywood Blvd) The old Henry Fonda theatre has been restored, and remains one of Hollywood's best venues for live music. It's an intimate, general-admission space with an open dance floor and balcony seating. It books progressive rock bands (Mumford & Sons and Broken Bells), groove masters such as Chromeo and can lure all-time greats like Tom Petty for intimate residencies.

MOVIES UNDER THE STARS

Angelenos love their movies and their fine weather, so it's only logical they combine the two. Screenings under the stars are a popular summer tradition. Come early to stake out a good spot and bring pillows, blankets and snacks.

Cinespia (323-221-3343; www.cemeteryscreenings.com; tickets $14; Sat May-Oct) has a 'to-die-for' location at Hollywood Forever Cemetery, *the* place of perpetual slumber for a galaxy of old-time movie stars. Classics by Milos Forman, Robert Altman and Alfred Hitchcock are projected onto a mausoleum wall around 9pm, but the hipster crowd starts lining up long before gates open at 7:30pm for picnics and cocktails (yes, alcohol is allowed!) while a DJ spins smooth soundtracks.

If that's too morbid for you, catch the Pacific sea breeze while camping out on the Santa Monica Pier where the **Front Porch Cinema at the Pier** (www.santamonicapier.org/frontporchcinema) FREE presents populist faves every Friday night from late September through October. Tickets are free but must be picked up at the Santa Monica Visitors Center.

El Floridita LATIN

(Map p110; 323-871-8612; www.elfloridita.com; 1253 N Vine St; cover $10, with dinner free; Mon, Wed, Fri & Sat) *The* place for grown-up *salseros*. Order a mojito and watch the beautiful dancers do their thing (or join in if you feel you've got the moves). The Monday night jams led by Johnny Polanco y su Orquesta Amistad are legendary; make reservations at least a week in advance.

Arclight Cinemas CINEMA

(Map p88; 323-464-1478; www.arclightcinemas.com; 6360 W Sunset Blvd; tickets $14-16) Assigned seats and exceptional celeb-sighting potential make this 14-screen multiplex the best around. If your taste dovetails with its schedule, the awesome 1963 geodesic Cinerama Dome is a must. Bonuses: age 21-plus screenings where you can booze it up, and Q&As with directors, writers and actors. Parking is $3 for four hours.

Hotel Cafe LIVE MUSIC

(Map p88; 323-461-2040; www.hotelcafe.com; 1623 N Cahuenga Blvd; tickets $10-20) An anomaly on glittery Cahuenga Corridor, this intimate venue is the place for handmade music by message-minded singer-songwriters. Big names such as Suzanne Vega show up on occasion, but mostly it's a stepping stone for newbie balladeers. Get there early and enter from the alley.

King King CLUB

(Map p88; 323-960-9234; www.kingkinghollywood.com; 6555 Hollywood Blvd; cover $10-20; 10pm-4am) This brickhouse club attracts known DJs such as Mark Farina and local master Warques Wyatt, who spin ass-shaking house music into the wee hours. No attitude, all groove.

American Cinematheque CINEMA

(Map p88; www.americancinematheque.com; 6712 Hollywood Blvd; adult/senior & student $11/9) A nonprofit screening tributes, retrospectives and foreign films in the Egyptian Theatre (p90). Directors, screenwriters and actors often swing by for post-show Q&As.

El Capitan Theatre CINEMA

(Map p88; 800-347-6396; elcapitan.go.com; 6838 Hollywood Blvd; VIP $25, general admission adult/senior & child $15/12;) Disney rolls out family-friendly blockbusters at this movie palace, often with costumed characters putting on the Ritz in live preshow routines. The best seats are on the balcony in the middle of the front row. VIP tickets ($20) allow you to reserve a seat and include popcorn and a beverage.

Grauman's Chinese Theatre CINEMA

(Map p88; www.manntheatres.com/chinese; 6925 Hollywood Blvd; adult $11.75-15.75, child & senior $9-12) Nowhere in the world are movie premieres as glitzy as at this industry favorite. Make sure you buy tickets for the glam historic theater, not the ho-hum Mann Chinese six-multiplex next door.

Bardot CLUB

(Map p88; www.bardothollywood.com; 1735 N Vine St; Mon-Sat) On Monday Nights, KCRW's Chris Douridas brings **School Night** (www.itsaschoolnight.com), a free live music club featuring buzz-worthy talent to the atmospheric top floor of the old Avalon theater. There is no exclusivity here, but you do have to RSVP and show up early enough to get in prior to max capacity.

Shopping

Amoeba Music MUSIC

(Map p88; ☎323-245-6400; www.amoeba.com; 6400 W Sunset Blvd; ⏲10:30am-11pm Mon-Sat, 11am-9pm Sun) When a record store not only survives but thrives in this techno age, you know they're doing something right. Flip through half-a-million new and used CDs, DVDs, videos and vinyl at this granddaddy of music stores. Handy listening stations and its outstanding *Music We Like* booklet keep you from buying lemons.

Check the website for free in-store live performances by touring bands.

Meltdown Comics & Collectibles COLLECTIBLES

(Map p110; www.meltcomics.com; 7522 Sunset Blvd; ⏲11am-9pm Thu-Tue, 10am-10pm Wed; 🐾) LA's coolest comics store beckons with indie and mainstream books, from Japanese manga to graphic novels. Also here is the kid-oriented, store-within-a-store **Baby Melt**, with a great selection of offbeat books, clothing and toys.

Counterpoint MUSIC, BOOKS

(Map p88; www.counterpointrecordsandbooks.com; 5911 Franklin Ave; ⏲11am-11pm) Woodblock stacks are packed high with used fiction, while crude plywood bins are stuffed with vinyl soul, classical and jazz. The real gems (the rare first editions and vintage rock posters) are in the collectible wing next door.

Space 1520 MALL

(Map p88; www.space1520.com; 1520 N Cahuenga Blvd; ⏲11am-9pm Mon-Fri, 10am-10pm Sat, to 9pm Sun) The hippest minimall in Hollywood, this designer construct of brick, wood, concrete and glass is home to classic and trend-setting mini-chains such as Umami Burger, Hennesy & Ingalls and Free People.

LOS FELIZ & GRIFFITH PARK

Twenty years ago, when *Swingers* mania tore through LA like a proto-hipster storm, Los Feliz, (mis)pronounced *Fee*-liz by the hordes, emerged as LA's next great neighborhood. For it was here, north and a touch east of Hollywood, on the clean-swept, tree-lined streets in the shadow of Griffith Park, that packs of aspiring actors and writers lived in one-room apartments housed in old Hollywood relics, and gathered in bars and coffeehouses cracking wise, and dreaming and flirting big. What gave it depth was the fact that Los Feliz has history.

This whole area was once one enormous ranch, called Rancho Los Feliz. In fact, the adobe ranch house, built in the 1830s, still stands. In 1882 Colonel Griffith Jenkins Griffith bought the majority of the ranch and later bequeathed it to the city of LA, forming what became Griffith Park, LA's largest municipal open space. Early movie studios sprouted in the flats, along with mansions in the hills. These days, however, the hipster hub has migrated east to Echo Park and into Downtown, and Los Feliz is still way too cool to care.

Sights

Griffith Park PARK

(Map p100; ☎323-913-4688; www.laparks.org/dos/parks/griffithpk; 4730 Crystal Springs Dr; ⏲5am-10:30pm, trails sunrise-sunset; P 👪) FREE A gift to the city in 1896 by mining mogul Griffith J Griffith, and five times the size of New York's Central Park, Griffith Park is one of the country's largest urban green spaces. It contains a major outdoor theater, the city zoo, an observatory, two museums, golf courses, playgrounds, 53 miles of hiking trails, Batman's caves and the Hollywood sign.

Access to the park is easiest via the Griffith Park Dr or Zoo Dr exits off I-5 (Golden State Fwy). Parking is plentiful and free. For information and maps stop by the **Griffith Park Ranger Station** (Map p100; ☎323-665-5188; 4730 Crystal Springs Dr).

★**Griffith Observatory** MUSEUM

(Map p100; ☎213-473-0800; www.griffithobservatory.org; 2800 E Observatory Rd; admission free, planetarium shows adult/child $7/3; ⏲noon-10pm Tue-Fri, from 10am Sat & Sun; P 👪) FREE This landmark 1935 observatory opens a window onto the universe from its perch on the southern slopes of Mt Hollywood. Its planetarium boasts the world's most advanced star projector, and astronomical touch displays on the evolution of the telescope, and the ultraviolet x-rays used to map our solar system. We loved the camera obscura on the main floor.

The public is welcome to peer into the Zeist Telescope on the east side of the roof where sweeping views of the Hollywood Hills and the gleaming city below are spectacular, especially at sunset. After dark, staff wheel additional telescopes out to the front lawn for stargazing.

Griffith Park & Around

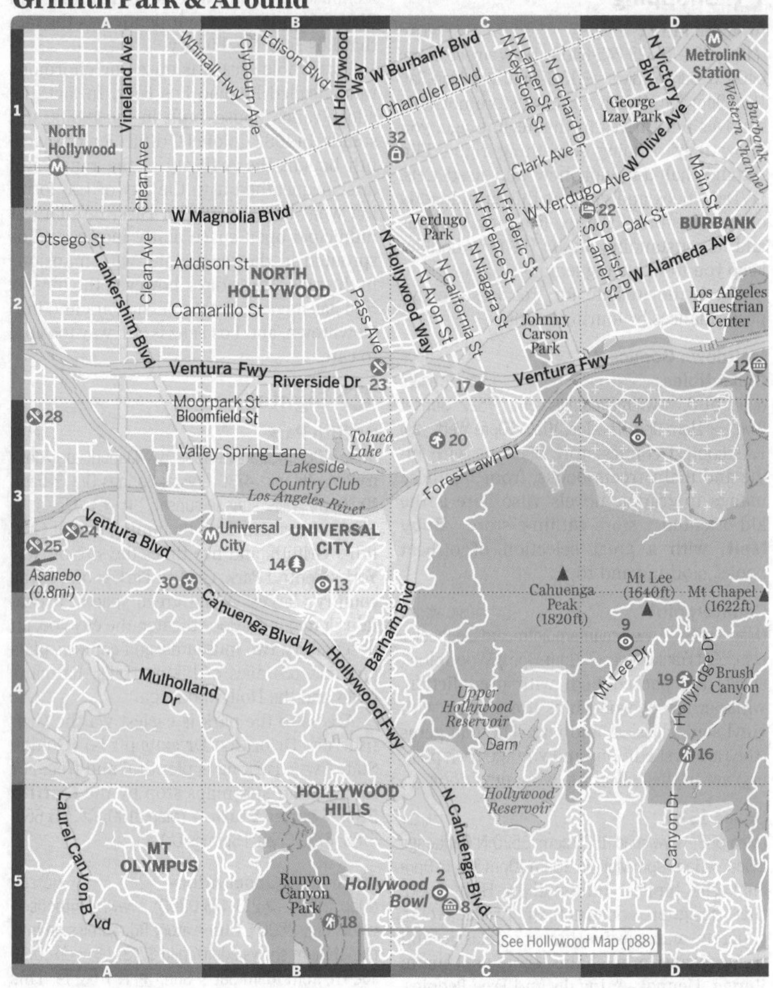

You'll definitely want to grab a seat in the Planetarium – the aluminum-domed ceiling becomes a massive screen where lasers are projected to offer a tour of the cosmos, while another laser-projection show allows you to search for water, and life, beyond earth.

The observatory has starred in many movies, most famously *Rebel Without a Cause* with James Dean. Outside, have your picture snapped beside the actor's bust with the Hollywood sign caught neatly in the background. The carless can hop on the LADOT Observatory Shuttle (35 minutes, 50c) from the Red Line station on Vermont and Sunset Blvd.

Barnsdall Art Park LANDMARK

(Map p102; www.barnsdallartpark.com; 4800 Hollywood Blvd) This promontory of a park, with views northwest to the Hollywood sign and northeast to the Griffith Observatory, makes a fine urban sunbathing spot. But the crown jewel is Frank Lloyd Wright's **Hollyhock House** (Map p102; ☎323-644-6269; www.hollyhockhouse.net; 4800 Hollywood Blvd; adult/student/child $7/3/free; ⏰tours hourly 12:30-3:30pm Wed-Sun; Ⓟ), a prime example of Wright's California Romanza style.

Commissioned in 1919 by oil heiress and art nut Aline Barnsdall, its walls, carpets

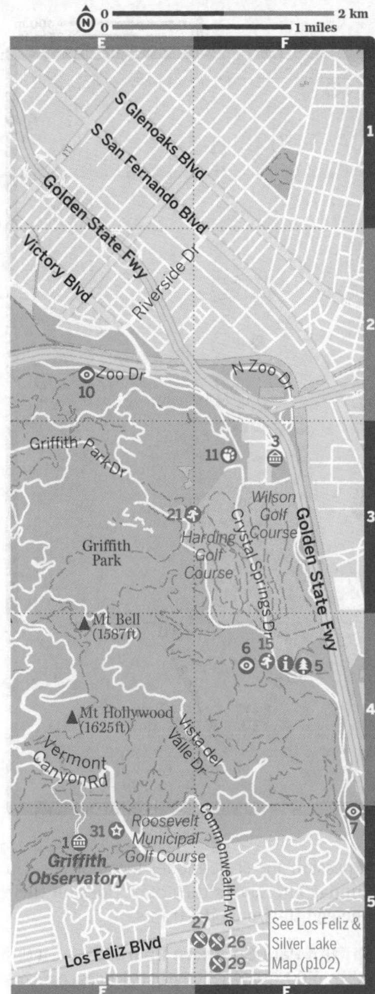

Griffith Park & Around

Top Sights

1 Griffith Observatory E5
2 Hollywood Bowl C5

Sights

3 Autry National Center F3
4 Forest Lawn Memorial Park – Hollywood Hills D3
5 Griffith Park F4
6 Griffith Park Merry-Go-Round F4
7 Griffith Park Southern Railroad F5
8 Hollywood Bowl Museum C5
9 Hollywood Sign D4
10 Los Angeles Live Steamers E2
11 Los Angeles Zoo & Botanical Gardens F3
12 Travel Town D2
13 Universal City Walk B3
14 Universal Studios Hollywood B3

Activities, Courses & Tours

15 Bike-rental Concession F4
16 Bronson Canyon D4
17 New York Film Academy C2
18 Runyon Canyon B5
19 Sunset Ranch Hollywood D4
20 Warner Bros Studios C3
21 Wilson Harding Golf Complex E3

Sleeping

22 Safari Inn D2

Eating

Aroma Coffee & Tea .... (see 28)
23 Bob's Big Boy B2
Caitoti Pizza Cafe .... (see 28)
Community .... (see 29)
24 Daichan A3
25 Kazu Sushi A3
26 Little Dom's F5
27 Mess Hall F5
28 Suck It A3
29 Yuca's F5

Entertainment

30 Baked Potato A3
31 Greek Theatre E5

Shopping

32 It's a Wrap! C1

and furniture are awash in abstract hollyhocks, her favorite flower.

Barnsdall donated the house and grounds to the city of LA with the proviso that they become a public park. There is a Municipal Art Gallery with a sculpture garden and a theater. It also sells Hollyhock House tour tickets. The gallery rotates up to 800 pieces of local art at a time and is free.

Los Angeles Zoo & Botanical Gardens ZOO
(Map p100; 323-644-4200; www.lazoo.org; 5333 Zoo Dr; adult/senior/child $18/15/13; 10am-5pm, closed Christmas; P) The Los Angeles Zoo, with its 1100 finned, feathered and furry friends from over 250 species, rarely fails to enthrall the little ones. What began in 1912 as a refuge for retired circus animals now brings in over a million visitors each year.

Autry National Center MUSEUM
(Map p100; 323-667-2000; www.autrynational-center.org; 4700 Western Heritage Way; adult/senior & student/child $10/6/4, 2nd Tue each month free; 10am-4pm Tue-Fri, to 5pm Sat & Sun; P) Want

Los Feliz & Silver Lake

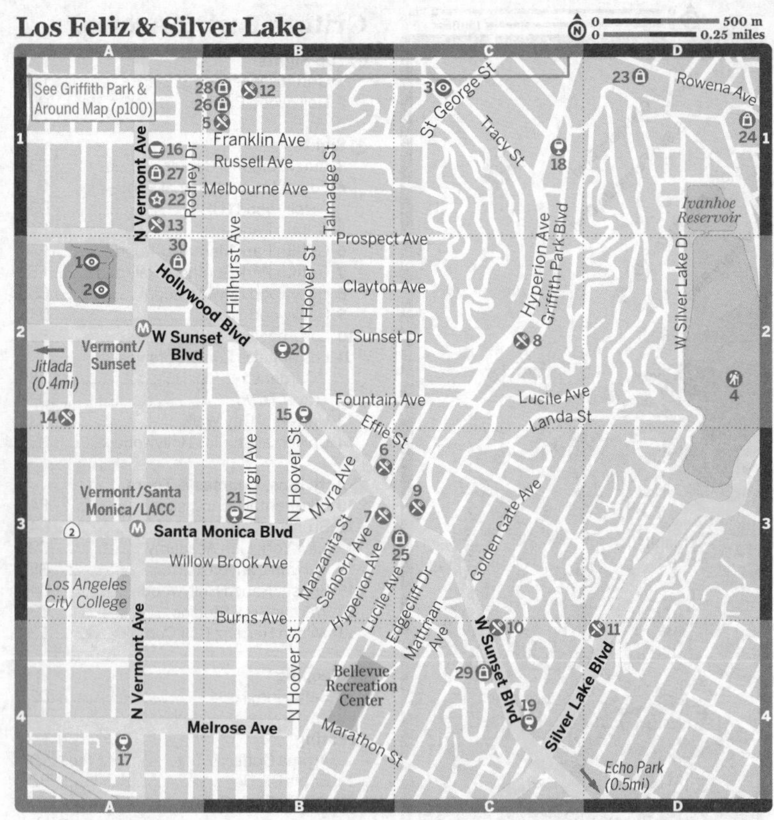

to know how the West was really won? Then mosey over to this excellent museum – its exhibits on the good, the bad and the ugly of America's westward expansion rope in even the most reluctant cowpokes. Kids can pan for gold and explore a stagecoach. Year-round gallery talks, symposia, film screenings and other cultural events spur the intellect.

Travel Town MUSEUM

(Map p100; www.traveltown.org; 5200 W Zoo Dr; 10am-4pm Mon-Fri, to 5pm Sat & Sun; P) FREE This delightful rail yard displays dozens of vintage railcars and locomotives, the oldest from 1864. Kids are all smiles imagining themselves as engineers, clambering around the iron horses.

Los Angeles Live Steamers TRAINS

(Map p100; www.lals.org; 5202 Zoo Dr; suggested donation $3; 11am-3pm Sun; P) Just east of Travel Town is this group of local folks with a passion for scale-model locomotives. On Sunday afternoons they offer rides on their one-eighth-size model trains.

Griffith Park Southern Railroad TRAINS

(Map p100; www.griffithparktrainrides.com/content/griffith-park-southern-railroad; 4400 Crystal Springs Dr; adult & child/senior $2.75/2.25; 10am-4:15pm Mon-Fri, to 4:45pm Sat & Sun; P) This fleet of miniature trains has ferried generations of children around a 1-mile loop past pony rides, a Native-American village and an old Western town since 1948.

Forest Lawn Memorial Park – Hollywood Hills CEMETERY

(Map p100; www.forestlawn.com; 6300 Forest Lawn Dr; 8am-5pm; P) FREE Pathos, art and patriotism rule at this humongous cemetery next to Griffith Park. A fine catalog of old-time celebrities – including Lucille Ball, Bette Davis and Stan Laurel – rests within

Los Feliz & Silver Lake

Sights
1 Barnsdall Art Park...A2
2 Hollyhock House...A2
3 John Marshall High School...C1

Activities, Courses & Tours
4 Silver Lake Reservoir...D2

Eating
5 Alcove...B1
6 Blossom...B3
Café Stella...(see 7)
7 Casbah Cafe...B3
8 Casita del Campo...C2
9 Forage...C3
10 Heywood...C4
11 L&E Oyster Bar...D4
12 Lucifer's...B1
13 Ramekin...A1
14 Square One...A2

Drinking & Nightlife
15 Akbar...B2
16 Bru...A1
17 Faultline...A4
Intelligentsia...(see 7)
18 Other Side...C1
19 Thirsty Crow...C4
20 Tiki-Ti...B2
21 Virgil...B3

Entertainment
Cavern Club Theater...(see 8)
22 Dresden...A1
Rockwell...(see 13)

Shopping
Bar Keeper...(see 7)
23 Broome Street General Store...D1
Bucks & Does...(see 7)
24 Clover...D1
25 Matrushka Construction...C3
26 Meowdy...B1
Ragg Mopp Vintage...(see 25)
27 Skylight Books...A1
28 Spitfire Girl...B1
29 Sumi's...C4
Una Mae's...(see 22)
30 Wacko...A2

the manicured grounds strewn with paeans to early North American history.

Staff aren't helpful in locating stars' graves, but you can download guides online at www.seeing-stars.com. More dead stars are at the original Forest Lawn in nearby Glendale.

Griffith Park Merry-Go-Round CAROUSEL
(Map p100; www.laparks.org/DOS/parks/griffithPK/mgr.htm; Griffith Park center; rides $2; 11am-5pm daily May-Sep, Sat & Sun Oct-Apr;) The richly festooned 1926 amusement park ride was brought to its current home in 1937. It has 68 carved and painted horses sporting real horsehair tails.

Activities

There is plenty to keep even the most active busy in Griffith Park.

Directly adjacent to the Crystal Springs picnic area, close to a baseball diamond and the freeway, is the park's only **bike-rental concession** (Map p100; 323-662-6573; www.laparks.org; 4730 Crystal Springs Rd; bikes per hr/day $8/25; 2-6pm Mon-Fri, 10:30am-dusk Sat & Sun).

The **Wilson Harding golf complex** (Map p100; 323-663-2555; www.laparks.org/DOS/parks/griffithPK/golf.htm; 4730 Crystal Springs Dr; greens fees $35-39; dawn-dusk) is actually two 18-hole courses with electric golf carts ($24) available for rent. Or play a short round at the nine-hole **Roosevelt Municipal Golf Course** (323-665-2011; www.laparks.org/DOS/parks/griffithPK/golf.htm; greens fees $17.50-20; dawn-dusk), which slopes down the mountain on the other side of the park. Golf clubs are available for rent at the Wilson Harding pro shop.

Bronson Canyon HIKING
(Map p100; www.laparks.org; 3200 Canyon Dr; 5am-dusk) Although most of the pretty people prefer to do their running, walking and hiking in Runyon Canyon, we always preferred Bronson. A wide fire road rises to a lookout point and links to the Hollywood sign, Griffith Park, and the famed **Bronson Caves** – where scenes from the old *Batman* and *The Lone Ranger* series were shot.

Head north on Canyon Dr and park in the last lot before the locked gate at Hollywoodland Camp. Walk back south, then turn left and head past a gate and up the fire road. For the Bronson Caves, turn left when the trail forks and the caves will be right there. The trail continues on the other side of the caves.

Eating

Ramekin DESSERTS $
(Map p102; 323-667-9627; www.ramekinla.com; 1726 N Vermont Ave; dishes $5-8) A sweet addition to Vermont Ave, Ramekin specializes

in made-to-order desserts such as pumpkin cheesecake, persimmon tarts, passionfruit panna cota, berry cobbler, chocolate bread pudding and strawberry brick toast. They also offer homemade ice creams and some tasty sandwiches, if you're in a savory mood.

Yuca's MEXICAN **$**

(Map p100; 323-662-1214; www.yucasla.com; 2056 Hillhurst Ave; items $4-10; 11am-6pm Mon-Sat) Location, location, location…is definitely not what lures people to this parking-lot snack shack. It's the tacos! And the *tortas,* burritos and other Mexi faves that earned the Herrera family the coveted James Beard Award in 2005.

★Mess Hall GASTROPUB **$$**

(Map p100; 323-660-6377; www.messhallkitchen.com; 4500 Los Feliz Blvd; mains $15-31; 11:30am-3pm & 4-11pm Mon-Thu, to midnight Fri, 10am-3pm & 5pm-midnight Sat, 10am-3pm & 4-11pm Sun) Formerly The Derby, a swing dance spot made famous by the film *Swingers,* which was shot in the area, it is now a gastropub where you'll find $1 oysters and $5 beers on Tuesdays. It's been written up for having one of the best burgers in LA, and they also do a pulled-pork sandwich and a kale Caesar.

Little Dom's ITALIAN **$$**

(Map p100; 323-661-0055; www.littledoms.com; 2128 Hillhurst Ave; pizza $11, mains $15-41; 8am-3pm & 5:30-11pm Mon-Thu, to midnight Fri, 8am-midnight Sat, to 11pm Sun; P) An understated, yet stylish Italian deli and restaurant with deep booths, marble tables and wood floors. It does a dynamite kale salad and good thin-crust pizza. But it's beloved for its antipasti and sandwiches – especially the fried oyster po'boy. If you don't want full service, pop into the deli next door.

Alcove CAFE **$$**

(Map p102; 323-644-0100; www.thealcovecafe.com; 1929 Hillhurst Ave; mains $10-17; 6am-midnight; P) Hillhurst's choice breakfast hangout, this sunny cafe spills onto a multi-level, streetside brick patio. It's housed in a restored 1897 Spanish-style duplex, and the food is quite good. There's crab cake Benedict, bison chili omelettes, and crepes stuffed with espresso-infused cream.

There's a full bar serving tasty cocktails too. And if you sit there (first come, first served), you don't have to wait in that long line to order at the counter.

Lucifer's PIZZERIA **$$**

(Map p102; 323-906-8603; www.luciferspizza.com; 1958 Hillhurst Ave; pizzas $10-20; 11am-11pm) These hard-rocking devils, toss and fire a terrific pizza pie. Gluten-free crust is an option and the Greek lamb, kalamata olive and feta pizza rocks. With just a tiny seating area inside, it's best as a take out option.

Community DELI **$$**

(Map p100; 323-913-0478; www.epicureanumbrella.com; 2044 Hillhurst Ave; mains $11-19; 11:30am-5pm Tue-Thu, to 4pm Fri, 5:30-9pm Fri-Sun) A storefront diner with reclaimed wood floors, artsy photos and a rather spare menu of burgers, sandwiches (Philly cheesesteaks, turkey Reubens and Cajun whitefish) plus a few mains at dinner including a house special fried chicken on Sundays.

Drinking & Nightlife

Tiki-Ti BAR

(Map p102; 323-669-9381; www.tiki-ti.com; 4427 W Sunset Blvd; 6pm-1am Wed & Thu, 6am-2am Fri & Sat) This garage-sized tropical tavern packs in grizzled old-timers and young cuties for sweet and wickedly strong drinks (try a Rae's Mistake, named for the bar's founder). The under-the-sea decor is surreal. Cash only.

Bru CAFE

(Map p102; 323-664-7500; www.brucoffeebar.com; 1866 N Vermont Ave; coffee drinks $3-5; 7am-8pm Mon-Sat, from 8am Sun;) Los Feliz's ubercool coffee bar comes with naturally lit loft environs, exposed rafters, rotating local art on the walls, and a marble slab common table where locals camp out, suck down coffee and tap their feet to indie rock. There's also free wi-fi.

Entertainment

★Greek Theatre LIVE MUSIC

(Map p100; 323-665-5857; www.greektheatrela.com; 2700 N Vermont Ave; May-Oct) A more intimate version of the Hollywood Bowl, this 5800-seat outdoor amphitheater tucked into a woodsy hillside of Griffith Park is much beloved for its vibe and variety – Los Lobos to MGMT to Willie Nelson. Parking is stacked, so plan on a post-show wait.

Dresden JAZZ

(Map p102; 323-665-4294; www.thedresden.com; 1760 Vermont Ave; 8pm-1am) Marty and Elayne have been a Los Feliz fixture since 1982 when they first brought their quirky Sinatra style to the Dresden's lounge. He rumbles on the drums and the upright bass. She tickles the ivories and plays the flute. Both sing. Their fame peaked when they made a brief appearance in the film *Swingers*.

Rockwell LIVE MUSIC
(Map p102; ☎323-669-1550; www.rockwell-la.com; 1714 N Vermont Ave) If you like to be entertained while you chew, come to this table and stage where artists such as Jeff Goldblum and his Mildred Snitzer Orchestra perform.

Shopping

Spitfire Girl GIFTS
(Map p102; www.spitfiregirl.com; 1939 Hillhurst Ave) One of our favorite (and perhaps the city's quirkiest) gift boutiques trades gift and photography books, its own stuffed-gnome and throw-pillow line (that's how the business launched), and organic and aromatic candles and soaps.

Wacko COLLECTIBLES
(Map p102; ☎323-663-0122; www.soapplant.com; 4633 Hollywood Blvd; ⊙11am-7pm Mon-Wed, to 9pm Thu-Sat, noon-6pm Sun) Billy Shire's giftorium of camp and kitsch has been a fun browse for over three decades. Pick up a dashboard Jesus, or a Frida Kahlo mesh bag. It has a great selection of comics and books by LA authors such as Ray Bradbury and Philip K Dick. Out back is La Luz de Jesus, one of LA's top lowbrow art galleries.

Meowdy VINTAGE
(Map p102; www.meowdy.com; 1939 Hillhurst Ave; ⊙11am-7pm) With American Vintage out of business, this is now the go-to shop for vintage on Hillhurst. They have handbags, shoes and boots, denim jackets and hats for women, some choice vintage glassware, and lots of cat purses. Um, yeah.

Una Mae's FASHION
(Map p102; ☎323-662-6137; www.unamaesclothing.com; 1768 N Vermont Ave; ⊙11am-7pm Mon-Thu, noon-8pm Fri & Sun, 11am-8pm Sat) One of our favorite shops on Vermont. Designer labels such as Kill City and limited edition Tom's shoes are set alongside old vintage flannels and plaids, suede and leather jackets, and some period baby doll dresses too. The jewelry collection is excellent.

Skylight Books BOOKS
(Map p102; ☎323-660-1175; www.skylightbooks.com; 1818 N Vermont Ave; ⊙10am-10pm) Like moths, bookworms (and God bless them) are drawn to this skylight: a loft-like, indie bookstore focusing on local, nontraditional and foreign authors. It also hosts several book groups and runs meet-the-author events.

SILVER LAKE & ECHO PARK

For decades devout Eastsiders have maintained the coolest, hippest place to be in Los Angeles is Silver Lake, and when Beck burst onto the Spaceland stage with his quirky take on hip-hop, funk and vintage sportscoats in the '90s, Silver Lake's cultural capital crystallized. Hipsters and artists poured into a neighborhood that was then mostly Latino, frequently smoggy and often crime-blanched. Eventually the Silver Lake ideal – revitalized modernist homes, groovy bistros, coffeehouses and boutiques patronized by a real community of upwardly mobile, progressive creatives – began to take hold. Which is to say Silver Lake gentrified faster than you can say Beck is so not cool anymore. Rents soared, working-class Latino families were pushed out and yuppie babies came along with gaggles of Eastside soccer moms pushing jogger strollers around the reservoir. Silver Lake's terrific shopping and dining are still worthy of praise. But gone is the grit, and gone is the funk.

Which is exactly why, if you dig the uneasy interface of edgy urban art and music and culture in multi-ethnic neighborhoods, and if you like your rent cheap and historic homes somewhat rickety, you'll enjoy Echo Park. One of LA's oldest neighborhoods is punctuated by a serene lake featured in Polanski's *Chinatown*, and for decades has been home to poor, working-class Latinos. Well, the artists and hipsters have arrived, but not in Silver Lake numbers. The *panaderias* and *cevicherias*, swap-meet shopping and lively streets are still here.

Sights

Dodger Stadium LANDMARK
(Map p62; ☎866-363-4377; http://losangeles.dodgers.mlb.com/la/ballpark/tours.jsp; 1000 Elysian Park Ave; tours adult/child 4-14yr & senior $15/10; ⊙10am & 11:30am; P) Built in 1962, and one of Major League Baseball's classic ballparks, Dodger Stadium offers behind-the-scenes tours of the historic stadium.

Your 90 minutes will cover the press box (basecamp of the legendary Vin Scully), the Dodger dugout, the Dugout Club, the field and the Tommy Lasorda Training Center. Reservations are strongly advised.

During the season (April to October), tours are held almost daily – except on game days. In the off-season they are less frequent. The best way to experience the stadium is to go to the ol' ballgame with MLB's most dedicated fan base. LA does love its Dodgers.

Echo Park Lake PARK

(Map p62; www.laparks.org; 751 Echo Park Ave; P) Surrounded by shingled craftsmen homes that rise with the steep streets and looming hills to the north, and blessed with keyhole Downtown views to the south, this fountain lake park is patronized by cool rockers, laid-back vatos, flocks of ducks and crows, and home to wild, wind-rustled palms.

When Jack Nicholson's Gittis was on the tail of Mr Mulray and his young lover in *Chinatown*, he snapped incriminating photos from a canoe on this very lake. The paddleboat and canoe concession is back up and running, so you can make like Jack if you like. On sunny summer days, when the geyser of a fountain gushes to the sky, and the lotus flowers are in bloom, the lake glimmers with beauty undeniable.

Activities

Echo Park Boathouse PEDAL BOATS

(213-481-8577; www.facebook.com/EchoParkLakePedalBoatsCanoeGondola; 751 N Echo Park Ave; pedal boats per hr adult/child $10/5, canoe rides adult/child $10/5, gondola rides per couple $50; 9am-7pm) Find the endearing boathouse cafe, run by Square One (p96), and you'll find the docks where you can pedal your own boat by the hour, hop in a canoe, or get romantic during a 30-minute gondola ride, a la Venezia. The kids love it!

Silver Lake Reservoir WALKING

(Map p102; www.silverlakereservoirs.org; Silver Lake Blvd) Silver Lake's wind-kissed namesake shimmers in the late-afternoon sun, when walkers, joggers and cyclists circle it. And even though you can't touch the shore, you will enjoy the views as the lake sits on a plateau surrounded by hills dotted with midcentury modern homes, with keyhole vistas of the Angeles Crest on clear days.

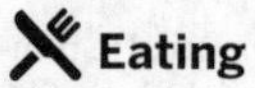

Eating

Celaya BAKERY $

(1630 Sunset Blvd; baked goods $1; 6am-8pm) A proper *panaderia* (Mexican bakery) is always a beautiful thing. Get your warm pan *dulce* (sweet bread), *panales* (pastries stuffed with flavored cream cheese), *pasteles* (cakes), donuts and some special tamales.

Sage VEGAN $

(310-456-1492; www.sageveganbistro.com; 1700 W Sunset Blvd; mains $10-14; 11am-10pm Mon-Wed, to 11pm Thu & Fri, 9am-4pm & 5-11pm Sat, to 10pm Sun;) Sage is an organic vegan kitchen with sandwiches and veggie burgers, and tacos stuffed with jackfruit or butternut squash – all served in heaping portions. And the menu is only the second-best thing here. The best? That would be Kind Kreme's good-for-you, raw ice cream. Taste to believe.

Casbah Cafe CAFE $

(Map p102; 323-664-7000; www.casbahcafe.com; 3900 Sunset Blvd; dishes $5-10; 6am-11pm Mon-Sat, from 7am Sun) A groovy, very popular and affordable habitat serving everything from Syrian pastries to empanadas to chicken-salad sandwiches and goat-cheese baguettes, not to mention great coffee. The tables are almost always full.

Heywood SANDWICHES $$

(Map p102; www.heywoodgrilledcheese.com; 3337 W Sunset Blvd; sandwiches $10-12; 11am-10pm Sun-Wed, to 3am Thu-Sat) If you enjoy that good ol' American staple, the grilled cheese sandwich, then stop at this popular concrete-floor cafe where they do 'em all gourmet like. Try the house special, Heywood: it comes with aged English cheddar and caramelized onion confit on fresh sourdough. Bonus fact: they stay open until 3am on party nights!

★ **Elf Cafe** VEGETARIAN $$

(213-484-6829; www.elfcafe.com; 2135 Sunset Blvd; mains $12-20) One of the best – if not the very best – vegetarian (not vegan) restaurants in LA. Start with feta wrapped in grape leaves and some spiced olives and almonds, then move onto a kale salad dressed with citrus, wild mushroom risotto and a fantastic kebab of seared oyster mushrooms.

Blossom VIETNAMESE $$

(Map p102; 323-953-8345; www.blossomrestaurant.com; 4019 W Sunset Blvd; mains $9-12; noon-4pm & 5:30-11pm;) The Silverlake edition of the Downtown favorite, Blossom serves *pho* with your choice of rare steak, brisket, tendon, tripe, chicken, shrimp or tofu. They also simmer a handful of curries and stir-fry vermicelli noodles. Seafood lovers should consider the crab noodle soup: dungeness crab and Manila clams, eggs, vermicelli noodles and red cabbage in tomato broth.

Forage CAFE **$$**
(Map p102; www.foragela.com; 3823 W Sunset Blvd; meals $10-15; ⏲11:30am-3pm & 5:30-9:30pm Tue-Fri, 11:30am-4pm & 5:30-9:30pm Sat) A gourmet market cafe serving everything from bread pudding to pear-and-frangipani galettes dusted with powdered sugar, to tossed arugula salads. They have daily quiche and pork belly sandwiches too, or you could opt for a pick-and-mix plate lunch.

Masa PIZZERIA **$$**
(www.masaofechopark.com; 1800 W Sunset Blvd; mains $13-17; ⏲11am-11pm Mon-Thu, to midnight Fri, 8am-midnight Sat, to 11pm Sun; P) Chicago deep-dish pizza (where the locally sourced toppings are piled high in a cradle of hand-rolled, house-baked dough, then hidden beneath a layer of cheese) served in whimsical environs that recall the wild, colorful swirl of New Orleans, right down to the swing music. They do brunch on weekends.

★L&E Oyster Bar SEAFOOD **$$$**
(Map p102; ☎323-660-2255; www.leoysterbar.com; 1637 Silver Lake Blvd; mains $17-28; ⏲5-10pm Mon-Thu, to 11pm Fri & Sat) Silver Lake's seafood house opened to rave reviews in 2012, and is still a neighborhood darling. Locals and celebs claim tables in the intimate dining room and heated porch to feast on raw and grilled oysters, smoked mussels and whole roasted fish dressed in miso, pickled ginger, chili and garlic.

They have a nice collection of salads and sides, and a raw bar upstairs that serves all the shellfish, along with beer and wine.

Café Stella FRENCH **$$$**
(Map p102; ☎323-666-0265; www.cafestella.com; 3932 W Sunset Blvd; mains $10-36; ⏲9am-3pm & 6-11pm Tue-Sat, to 10pm Sun; P) As charming as it gets, Café Stella is a cloud of clinking glasses, red wine, good jazz and classic French bistro cuisine under a tented patio that rambles into an antiquated dining room. Artful and inviting, it bustles at lunch and is packed for dinner.

Drinking & Nightlife

Thirsty Crow BAR
(Map p102; www.thirstycrowbar.com; 2939 W Sunset Blvd; ⏲5pm-late Mon-Fri, from 2pm Sat & Sun) A divey whiskey bar on Sunset where bourbon is the preferred poison and you can park your own damn car.

Intelligentsia COFFEE
(Map p102; www.intelligentsiacoffee.com; 3920 W Sunset Blvd; ⏲6am-8pm Sun-Wed, to 11pm Thu-Sat; 📶) LA's original overly intellectual coffee house (and there are a number of them now) offers an island bar inside where you can sit with your laptop, and a pleasant patio where you'll sip outstanding fair-trade coffee pulled and steamed expertly by occasionally snobby yet charming baristas.

Short Stop CLUB
(☎213-482-4942; 1455 W Sunset Blvd; ⏲5pm-2am Mon-Fri, from 2pm Sat & Sun) Echo Park's beloved and deceptively sprawling dive has a dance floor in one room, a bar strobing ballgames on flat screens in another, and a pool table and pinball machines in still another section. Longtime Echo Park locals and new-breed hipsters bump shoulders and more here. Especially on Motown Mondays, when vintage jams fill the room with joy.

Virgil BAR
(Map p102; www.thevirgil.com; 4519 Santa Monica Blvd; ⏲7pm-close) A local joint serving craftsman cocktails. A stocked calendar of entertainment from live comedy to bands and DJs takes it from feeling like a neighborhood spot early in the evening to something wilder late at night.

Entertainment

★Echo CLUB
(www.attheecho.com; 1822 W Sunset Blvd; cover varies) Eastsiders hungry for an eclectic alchemy of sounds pack this funky-town dive that's basically a sweaty bar with a stage and a smoking patio. It books indie bands, and also has regular club nights. Their Funky Sole party every Saturday is always a blast.

Dodger Stadium SPECTATOR SPORTS
(☎866-363-4377; www.dodgers.com; 1000 Elysian Park Ave; ⏲Apr-Sep) Few baseball clubs can match the Dodgers when it comes to history (Jackie Robinson, Sandy Koufax, Kirk Gibson and Vin Scully), success and fan loyalty. The club's newest owners bought the organization for roughly two billion dollars, an American team sports record.

LA Laker-great Magic Johnson is among an ownership group that has re-invigorated the team with talent and lured baseball's most dedicated fan base back to the ballpark. The season lasts from April to October. Parking costs $15.

Bootleg Theater PERFORMING ARTS
(www.bootlegtheater.org; 2220 Beverly Blvd) Part progressive-rock and folk venue, part theater space, part multidisciplinary arts foundation and laboratory. This restored 1930s warehouse hosts one-off shows and long-term residencies for edgy indie bands and up-and-comers. It also supports spoken word, dance and dramatic artists pushing boundaries.

Shopping

★Matrushka Construction FASHION
(Map p102; www.matrushka.com; 3822 W Sunset Blvd) Who says fashion has to be superficial? Lara Howe crafts her sublime, tailored designs from remnant fabrics personally and locally sourced by the owner-operator. The fabrics are still top-notch – they are simply either vintage or discarded by large corporate manufacturers.

Stories BOOKS
(www.storiesla.com; 1716 W Sunset Blvd; 8:30am-9pm Mon-Thu, to 10pm Fri, 10am-10pm Sat, to 8pm Sun;) Bob your head to dub on the hi-fi while you wander through a maze of new and used literature. It has an LA section, plays, short stories, graphic novels and Carl Jung. Brainy types congregate in the back-end cafe.

Ragg Mopp Vintage VINTAGE
(Map p102; 323-666-0550; www.raggmoppvintage.net; 3816 W Sunset Blvd; noon-7pm Mon-Fri, to 6pm Sat & Sun) A fantastic little vintage shop with an excellent collection of T-shirts, frocks, hats, belts and leather goods, not to mention groovy tunes on the stereo.

Bucks & Does FASHION
(Map p102; 323-515-7385; www.bucksanddoes.com; 3906 W Sunset Blvd) They keep it simple but fun here, with Steve McQueen specs, Nudie jeans, designer tees, summery blouses and dresses. Everything is well-made and fitted.

Broome Street General Store BOUTIQUE
(Map p102; www.broomestgeneral.com; 2912 Rowena Ave; 8am-7pm Mon-Sat, 9am-5pm Sun) Locals love this cozy boutique-cum-cafe set in a converted house for its generous, leafy front patio, designer denim, wool sweaters and upmarket organic beauty products. And caffeine. Mostly they're here for caffeine.

Sumi's BOUTIQUE
(Map p102; sumisinsilverlake.com; 3204 Sunset Blvd; 11am-7pm Mon-Sat, to 6pm Sun) An artful boutique with everything from groovy messenger bags to hippie-chic jewelry to sew-yourself stuffed animals (and the Wool Buddies are damn cute), to a smidge of fine art.

Clover GIFTS
(Map p102; www.cloversilverlake.com; 2756 Rowena Ave; 11am-7pm) This store has everything from cuddly stuffed toys to designer waste baskets, bamboo salad bowls, alluring fragrances and designer jeans made downtown for mom and dad. There is also outstanding, locally designed gold and silver jewelry. It's one big blast of hippie-chic groovy.

Bar Keeper DRINK
(Map p102; www.barkeepersilverlake.com; 3910 W Sunset Blvd; 11am-6pm Sun-Thu, to 7pm Fri & Sat) Eastside mixologists now have their dream habitat. Here you'll find all manner of stemware, absinthe fountains, shakers, mixers and vessels needed to pour fine cocktails. They also sell the very (very) good stuff, and have a tasting bar to prove it.

WEST HOLLYWOOD & MID-CITY

Upscale and low-rent (but not that low), gay fabulous and Russian-ghetto chic, this is a bastion of LA's fashionista best and home to some of the trashiest shops you'll ever see. Here you can find raw kitchens, bright market cafes and dark-edged tequila bars. Rainbow flags fly proudly over Santa Monica Blvd, and Sunset Strip, with its classic rock clubs and iconic hotels overlooking a sea of twinkling lights, still attracts Hollywood glitterati wannabes, especially on weekends when the boulevard swells with suburbanites. When real stars come here to rave, they're usually hidden away in a house party high in the hills. Welcome to West Hollywood (WeHo), an independent city that packs more personality (some might say, frivolity) into its 1.9-sq-mile frame than LA's larger barrios.

To the south and east of WeHo is an amorphous area we call Mid-City. It encompasses the groovy Fairfax District with the farmers market, Miracle Mile with Museum Row, and old-money Hancock Park with its grand mansions.

Street parking codes in West Hollywood can only be described as fascist, but you'll find two hours of free parking at 8383 Santa Monica Blvd. Mid-City areas usually have plenty of street parking. DASH buses serve the area on the Fairfax Route and the Hollywood/West Hollywood Route.

Sights

★Farmers Market & Around MARKET

(Map p110; www.farmersmarketla.com; 6333 W 3rd St, Fairfax District; 9am-9pm Mon-Fri, to 8pm Sat, 10am-7pm Sun; P) FREE Long before the city was flooded with farmers markets, there was the Farmers Market. Fresh produce, roasted nuts, donuts, cheeses, blinis – you'll find them all at this 1934 landmark. Casual and kid-friendly, it's a fun place for a browse, snack or for people-watching.

From late May to mid-September it holds the Summer Music Series (7pm to 9pm). On Thursday nights it's all jazz, and on Fridays the bands can range from zydeco to pop.

★Los Angeles County Museum of Art MUSEUM

(LACMA; Map p110; 323-857-6000; www.lacma.org; 5905 Wilshire Blvd; adult/child $15/free; 11am-5pm Mon, Tue & Thu, to 9pm Fri, 10am-7pm Sat & Sun; P) LA's premier art museum, LACMA's galleries are stuffed with all the major players – Rembrandt, Cézanne, Magritte, Mary Cassat, Ansel Adams, to name a few – plus several millennia worth of ceramics from China, woodblock prints from Japan, pre-Columbian art, and ancient sculpture from Greece, Rome and Egypt.

The depth and wealth of the collection is stunning, and the Renzo Piano 'Transformation' finally brought a sense of design to the 20-acre LACMA campus worthy of the art it contains.

It includes a surreal light-post entry pavilion and the **Broad Contemporary Art Museum**, presenting part of the personal collection of developer Eli Broad, including seminal works by Jasper Johns, Roy Lichtenstein and Andy Warhol. How much will remain once the Broad (p75) museum opens is unknown.

LACMA also hosts headlining touring exhibits (the James Turrell one was special) and frequent movie screenings, readings and other events, including a popular Friday-night jazz series.

Grove PLAZA

(Map p110; www.thegrovela.com; 189 The Grove Dr) Next door to the Farmers Market is a faux-European, yet attractive outdoor, and rather corporate, shopping mall built around a central plaza with a musical fountain (nicest after dark, almost magical at Christmas time). Little known secret: the city and Hollywood Hills views from the top floor of the parking structure are stunning, especially at sunset.

CBS Television City TV STUDIO

(Map p110; www.cbs.com; 7800 Beverly Blvd) North of the Farmers Market is CBS, where game shows, talk shows, soap operas and other programs are taped, often before a live audience.

Melrose Avenue STREET

(Map p110; Melrose Ave) A popular shopping strip as famous for its epic people-watching as it is for its consumer fruits. You'll see hair (and people) of all shades and styles, and everything from gothic jewels to custom sneakers to medical marijuana to stuffed porcupines available for a price. The strip is located between Fairfax and La Brea.

Sunset Strip NEIGHBORHOOD

(Map p110; Sunset Blvd) A visual cacophony of billboards, giant ad banners and neon signs, the sinuous stretch of Sunset Blvd running between Laurel Canyon and Doheny Dr has been nightlife central since the 1920s.

Mobster Bugsy Siegel and his posse hung out at clubs such as Ciro's (now the Comedy Store); Marilyn Monroe had her first date with Joe DiMaggio at the Rainbow Bar & Grill, which later became the preferred late-night hub of Guns N' Roses. The Whisky A Go-Go gave birth to both the Doors and go-go dancing, and Led Zeppelin raced motorcycles in the Andaz Hotel, formerly the Hyatt, and henceforth known as the 'Riot House.' Then, in the late '90s, the strip recaptured the limelight with the House of Blues (HOB), the ultraposh Sky Bar at the Mondrian hotel and the sexy Standard Hollywood.

These days, though, it seems to be coasting on its fabled legacy. The young, hip and fickle have moved west to Abbot Kinney and east to Downtown, leaving the Strip to the

st Hollywood & Mid-City

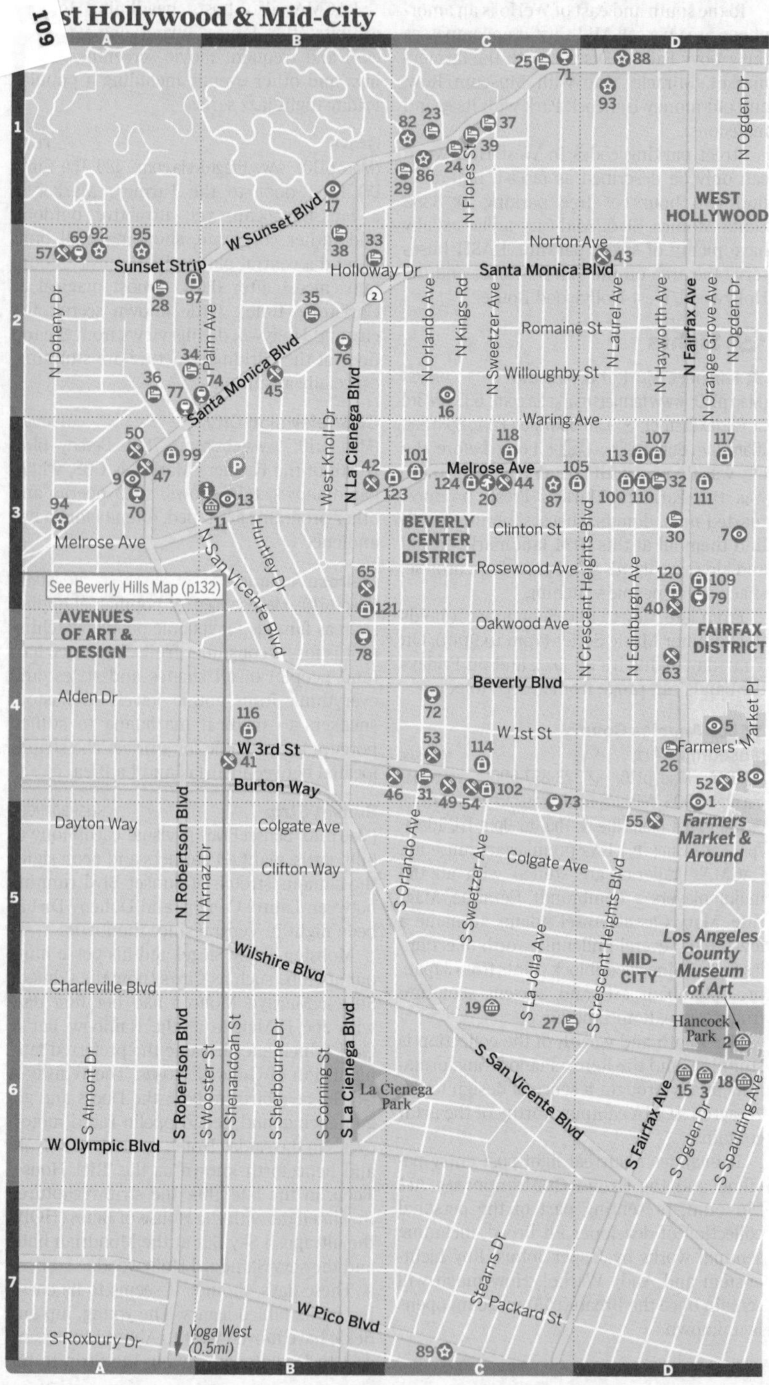

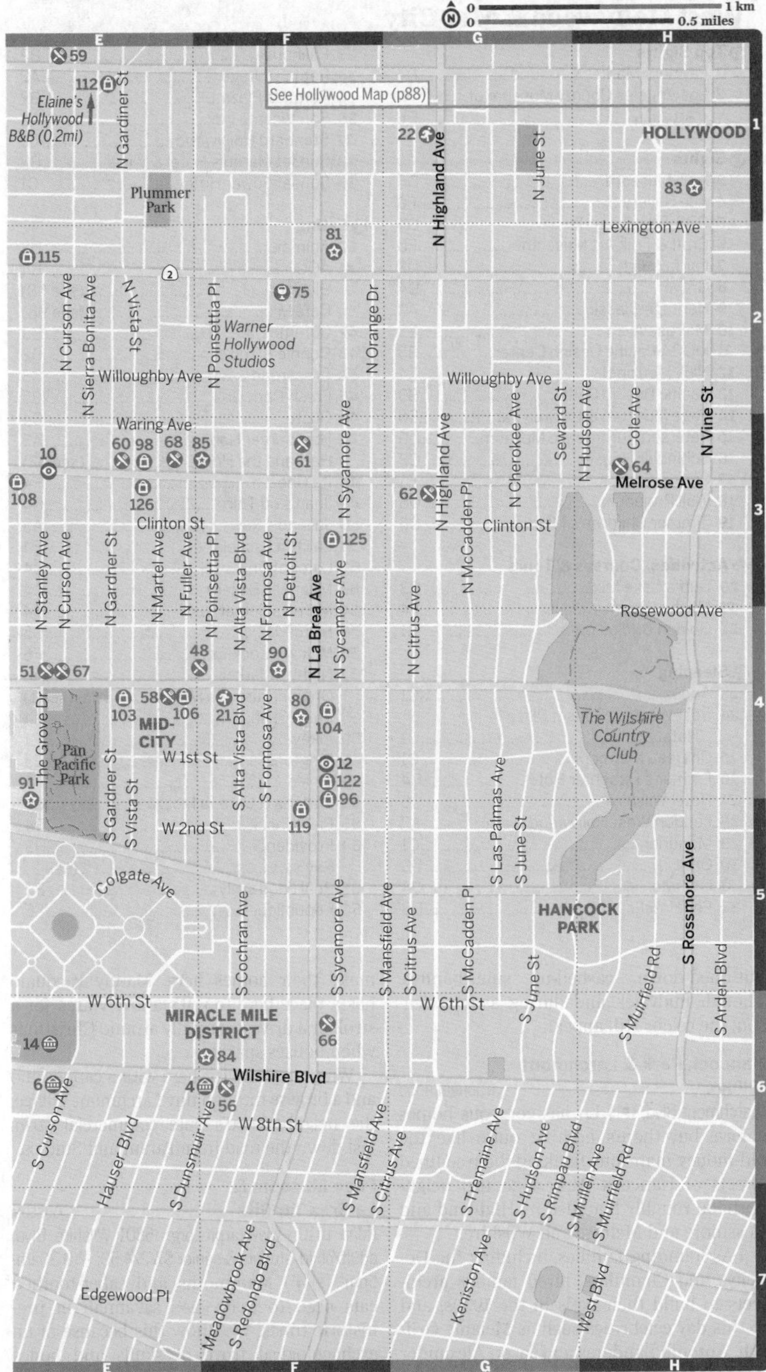

0
1 km
0
0.5 miles
E
F
G
H
1
2
3
4
5
6
7
See Hollywood Map (p88)
Elaine's Hollywood B&B (0.2mi)
HOLLYWOOD
Plummer Park
Lexington Ave
N Gardiner St
N Highland Ave
N June St
N Curson Ave
N Sierra Bonita Ave
N Vista St
N Poinsettia Pl
Warner Hollywood Studios
N Orange Dr
Willoughby Ave
Waring Ave
N Sycamore Ave
N Highland Ave
N McCadden Pl
N Cherokee Ave
Seward St
N Hudson Ave
Cole Ave
N Vine St
Melrose Ave
Clinton St
N Stanley Ave
N Gardner St
N Martel Ave
N Fuller Ave
N Alta Vista Blvd
N Formosa Ave
N Detroit St
N La Brea Ave
N Citrus Ave
Rosewood Ave
The Wilshire Country Club
MID-CITY
W 1st St
The Grove Dr
Pan Pacific Park
S Gardner St
S Vista St
S Alta Vista Blvd
S Formosa Ave
W 2nd St
S Las Palmas Ave
S June St
S Rossmore Ave
Colgate Ave
S Cochran Ave
S Sycamore Ave
S Mansfield Ave
S Citrus Ave
S McCadden Pl
HANCOCK PARK
S Muirfield Rd
S Arden Blvd
W 6th St
MIRACLE MILE DISTRICT
Wilshire Blvd
S Curson Ave
Hauser Blvd
S Dunsmuir Ave
W 8th St
S Tremaine Ave
S Hudson Ave
S Rimpau Blvd
S Mullen Ave
Meadowbrook Ave
S Redondo Blvd
Keniston Ave
West Blvd
Edgewood Pl
59
112
22
83
81
115
75
10
60
98
68
85
61
64
108
126
62
125
48
90
51
67
103
58
106
21
80
104
12
122
96
91
119
14
84
66
6
4
56

West Hollywood & Mid-City

Top Sights
1 Farmers Market & Around....D4
2 Los Angeles County Museum of Art....D6

Sights
3 A+D Museum....D6
4 Ace Gallery....F6
5 CBS Television City....D4
6 Craft & Folk Art Museum....E6
7 Fairfax High....D3
8 Grove....D4
9 Heritage Classics....A3
10 Melrose Ave....E3
11 MOCA Pacific Design Center....B3
12 Nick Metropolis....F4
13 Pacific Design Center....B3
14 Page Museum & La Brea Tar Pits....E6
15 Petersen Automotive Museum....D6
16 Schindler House....C2
17 Sunset Strip....B1
18 Wall Project....D6
19 Zimmer Children's Museum....C6

Activities, Courses & Tours
20 Duff's Cake Mix....C3
21 Fly the Dream....F4
22 Golden Bridge Yoga....G1

Sleeping
23 Andaz....C1
24 Best Western Sunset Plaza Hotel....C1
25 Chateau Marmont....C1
26 Farmer's Daughter Hotel....D4
27 Hotel Wilshire....C6
28 London West Hollywood....A2
29 Mondrian....C1
30 Orbit....D3
31 Orlando....C4
32 Pali Hotel....D3
33 Palihouse....B2
34 Petit Ermitage....A2
35 Ramada Plaza....B2
36 San Vicente Inn....A2
37 Standard Hollywood....C1
38 Sunset Marquis Hotel & Villas....B2
39 Sunset Tower Hotel....C1

Eating
40 Animal....D3
41 AOC....B4
Blu Jam....(see 68)
Café Midi....(see 96)
42 Comme Ca....B3
43 Connie & Ted's....D2
44 Crossroads....C3
45 Fresh Corn Grill....B2
46 Gusto....C4
47 Hamburger Habit....A3
Hart and the Hunter....(see 32)
48 Ita Cho....F4
49 Joan's on Third....C4
50 Juliano's Raw....A3
51 La Otra Escuela....E4
52 Lotería! Grill....D4
53 Magnolia Bakery....C4
54 Mama's Secret....C4
55 Mercado....D5
56 Milk Jar Cookies....F6
57 Night + Market....A2
Original Farmers Market....(see 1)
58 Petty Cash....E4
59 Pikey....E1
60 Pingtung....E3
61 Pink's....F3
62 Pizzeria & Osteria Mozza....G3
63 Plan Check....D4
64 Providence....H3
Ray's....(see 2)
65 Real Food Daily....B3
66 Republique....F6

buttoned-down, cashed-up suburbanites. Though midweek and during awards season, the celebs still appear.

Hancock Park & Larchmont Village NEIGHBORHOOD

(Larchmont Blvd; P) LA has gorgeous homes galore, but there's nothing quite like the old-money mansions flanking the tree-lined streets of Hancock Park, a genteel neighborhood roughly bounded by Highland and Rossmore and Melrose and Wilshire.

LA's founding families, including the Dohenys and Chandlers, hired famous architects to build their pads in the 1920s, and to this day celebrities such as Melanie Griffith, Antonio Banderas and Jason Alexander make their homes here. Manny Pacquaio has a place here too. It's a lovely area for a stroll or a drive, especially around Christmas when houses sparkle.

Wrap up your visit here with a cappuccino and a browse through tiny Larchmont Village, the neighborhood's cute commercial strip, just down the road from Paramount Studios.

Page Museum & La Brea Tar Pits MUSEUM

(Map p110; www.tarpits.org; 5801 Wilshire Blvd; adult/child/student & senior $7/2/4.50; 9:30am-5pm; P) Mammoths and saber-toothed cats used to roam LA's savannah in prehistoric times. We know this because of an archaeological trove of skulls and bones

Son of a Gun .... (see 31)
67 Terroni E4
68 Village Idiot E3
Yuko Kitchen .... (see 56)

Drinking & Nightlife
69 1 Oak A2
70 Abbey A3
71 Bar Marmont C1
72 Beverly Hills Juice Club C4
Churchill .... (see 31)
73 El Carmen C4
74 Eleven B2
Fiesta Cantina .... (see 77)
75 Formosa Cafe F2
76 Greystone Manor B2
Juice Served Here .... (see 31)
77 Micky's A2
78 Roger Room B4
79 Rosewood Tavern D3
Trunks .... (see 74)

Entertainment
80 Acme Comedy Theatre F4
81 Celebration Theatre F2
82 Comedy Store C1
83 El Floridita H1
84 El Rey F6
85 Groundlings F3
86 House of Blues C1
87 Improv C3
Largo at the Coronet .... (see 78)
88 Laugh Factory D1
89 Mint C7
90 New Beverly Cinema F4
91 Pacific Theatres at the Grove E4
92 Roxy A2
93 Sundance Sunset Cinema D1
94 Troubadour A3
95 Whisky-a-Go-Go A2

Shopping
Agent Provocateur .... (see 107)
American Girl Place .... (see 8)
96 American Rag Cie F4
97 Book Soup A2
98 Brooklyn Projects E3
99 Chi Chi Larue's A3
100 Chucks Vintage D3
Creatures of Comfort .... (see 113)
101 Diane von Furstenberg C3
102 DL Rhein C4
103 Espionage E4
104 Fahey/Klein Gallery F4
105 Fred Segal C3
106 Gibson E4
107 Great Frog D3
108 Joyrich E3
109 Kayo D3
110 Kidrobot D3
Le Labo .... (see 53)
Lotta Boutique .... (see 31)
111 Melrose Trading Post D3
112 Meltdown Comics & Collectibles E1
Mystery Pier Books .... (see 97)
113 Nudie Jeans D3
114 OK C4
115 Pleasure Chest E2
116 Polkadots & Moonbeams B4
117 Record Collector D3
118 Reformation C3
119 Shelter Half F5
120 Supreme D3
121 Trashy Lingerie B3
Traveler's Bookcase .... (see 53)
122 Undefeated F4
123 Vera Wang C3
124 Vivienne Westwood C3
125 Voila! F3
126 Wasteland E3
Whimsic Alley .... (see 56)

unearthed at La Brea Tar Pits, one of the world's most fecund and famous fossil sites.

Thousands of Ice Age critters met their maker between 40,000 and 10,000 years ago in gooey crude oil bubbling up from deep below Wilshire Blvd. Animals wading into the sticky muck became trapped and were condemned to a slow death by starvation or suffocation. A life-size drama of a mammoth family outside the museum dramatizes such a cruel fate. Parking costs $6.

Petersen Automotive Museum MUSEUM
(Map p110; www.petersen.org; 6060 Wilshire Blvd; adult/senior & student/child $15/10/5; 10am-6pm Tue-Sun; P) A four-story ode to the auto, the Petersen Automotive Museum is a treat even for those who can't tell a piston from a carburetor. Start by ambling along a fun streetscape that reveals LA as the birthplace of gas stations, billboards, strip malls, drive-in restaurants and drive-in movie theaters. Then head upstairs to the hot rods, movie cars and celebrity-owned rarities, presented in rotating exhibits.

Sadly, in 1997, the great gangsta rapper Notorious B.I.G. was gunned down in his car outside the museum after leaving a Soul Train Music Awards party.

Heritage Classics MUSEUM
(Map p110; www.heritageclassics.com; 8980 Santa Monica Blvd; 9am-6pm Mon-Fri, 10am-5pm Sat) Motorcar eye candy is yours at this

showroom of rare and restored gems from newish Bentleys to classic Corvettes and Porsches, to old muscle cars and wood-paneled surf wagons.

Pacific Design Center LANDMARK

(PDC; Map p110; www.pacificdesigncenter.com; 8687 Melrose Ave; 9am-5pm Mon-Fri) Interior design is big in WeHo, with over 120 trade-only showrooms at the Pacific Design Center and dozens more in the surrounding **Avenues of Art & Design** (Beverly Blvd, Robertson Blvd & Melrose Ave). PDC showrooms generally sell only to design pros, but often you can get items at a mark-up through the Buying Program.

The PDC itself is an architectural landmark designed by Cesar Pelli of Petronas Twin Towers (Kuala Lumpur) fame. Best viewed from a Runyon Canyon trail or a hotel rooftop, the three glass buildings, one each in race-car red, forest green and cobalt blue, bear a rather striking footprint.

MOCA Pacific Design Center GALLERY

(Map p110; 213-621-1741; www.moca.org; 8687 Melrose Ave; 11am-5pm Tue-Fri, to 6pm Sat & Sun) FREE Standing a bit forlorn amid the glassy behemoths is the small satellite branch of Downtown's Museum of Contemporary Art (p69). Exhibits usually have an architectural or design theme.

Ace Gallery GALLERY

(Map p110; www.acegallery.net; 5514 Wilshire Blvd; 10am-6pm Tue-Sat) An amazing gallery sprawls the entire 2nd floor of the Desmond building (c 1927). The art is all modern edged, including minimalist canvasses, strobing video installations, plexiglass orbs and rusted coils of steel. Bernar Venet, Gary Lang, Gisele Colon and Peter Alexander are among the artists represented here.

Schindler House ARCHITECTURE

(Map p110; 323-651-1510; www.makcenter.org; 835 N Kings Rd; adult/senior & student/child under 12yr $7/6/free, 4-6pm Fri free; 11am-6pm Wed-Sun) The former home and studio of Vienna-born architect Rudolph Schindler (1887–1953) offers a fine primer on the modernist elements that so greatly influenced mid-century California architecture. The open floor plan, a flat roof and glass sliding doors, while considered avant-garde back in the 1920s, all of which became design staples after WWII.

Today Schindler's old pad houses the **MAK Center for Art and Architecture**, which runs tours on weekends.

Nick Metropolis ANTIQUES

(Map p110; www.nickmetropolis.com; 100 S La Brea; 10am-7pm Mon-Sat, from 11am Sun) There's nothing quite like this street corner occupied with a pack rat's extravagance. Not to mention more than a few Instagram photo ops.

Craft & Folk Art Museum MUSEUM

(Map p110; www.cafam.org; 5814 Wilshire Blvd; adult/student & senior/under 12yr $7/5/free, 1st Wed of month free; 11am-5pm Tue-Fri, noon-6pm Sat & Sun;) Zulu ceramics, Japanese *katagami* paper art, Palestinian embroidery – cultural creativity takes infinite forms at this well-respected museum where exhibits change every few months. Also check for upcoming kid-oriented workshops and storytelling sessions, usually held on Saturdays. The gift store is one of the best in town.

Wall Project MUSEUM

(Map p110; www.wallproject.org; 5900 Wilshire Blvd) FREE Slabs of the old Berlin Wall – augmented by known street artists – are on display on the lawn of a Wilshire high-rise across the street from LACMA as part of the global Wall Project, curated by the fabulous Wende Museum in Culver City.

A+D Museum MUSEUM

(Map p110; www.aplusd.org; 6032 Wilshire Blvd; adult/senior & student $5/2.50; 11am-5pm Tue-Fri, noon-6pm Sat & Sun) A small Getty-sponsored space that keeps its finger on the pulse of emerging trends, people and products in the design and architecture community from its base near the Petersen Automotive Museum. There was a Ray Eames exhibit on when we came through.

Activities

Duff's Cake Mix CAKE DECORATING

(Map p110; 323-650-5555; duffscakemix.com; 8302 Melrose Ave; cupcakes $3.50, jars $4-8, cakes $32-57; 11am-6:30pm Mon-Thu, to 8pm Fri, 10am-8pm Sat, to 6:30pm Sun) Cake lovers, rejoice! Your sweet tooth will lead to artistic breakthroughs (or not) at this glass-box bakery where you choose your cake from the menu and compile your own cake kit from a selection of fillings, frosting and decorations. It's a good time, but if you just want to get to the eating, you can munch a cupcake.

Fly the Dream FLIGHT SIMULATOR
(Map p110; ☎323-965-2222; www.flythedream.com; 7270 Beverly Blvd; per person $89; ⊙varies) Don a flight suit (you may as well), and strap into one of seven F-16 flight simulators. Take the 10-minute lesson then engage in a kill-or-be-killed dogfight against your friends and competitors. Don't worry, you can restart after every crash. They offer up to five flight times per day, and you must reserve in advance.

Runyon Canyon HIKING
(Map p100; www.lamountains.com; 2000 N Fuller Ave; ⊙dawn-dusk) A chaparral-draped cut in the Hollywood Hills, this 130-acre public park is as famous for its beautiful, bronzed and buff runners as it is for the panoramic views from the upper ridge. Follow the wide, partially paved fire road up, then take the smaller track down to the canyon, where you'll pass the remains of the Runyon estate.

Sleeping

Orbit HOSTEL $
(Banana Bungalow; Map p110; ☎323-655-1510; www.orbithotels.com; 603 N Fairfax Ave; dm $22-25, r $69-79) This popular, well-run hostel occupies a converted art-deco nursing home. Translation: the local bubbies are gone and the global hipsters have moved in. Private rooms all have their own baths, TV and mini-fridge and there are six- to 12-bed dorms, which may only be booked online via the Hostel World website.

San Vicente Inn GUESTHOUSE $
(Map p110; ☎323-854-6915; www.thesanvicenteinn.com; 845 N San Vicente Blvd; r $99-200; P ☎ ≋) There's no boys-only rule, but it feels like it's raining men at this WeHo party-people compound. It doesn't look like much from the front, but you'll soon discover charming and clean rooms and cottages, which spill onto a pool, hot tub and tropical garden.

★**Pali Hotel** BOUTIQUE HOTEL $$
(Map p110; ☎323-272-4588; www.pali-hotel.com; 7950 Melrose Ave; r from $179; P @ ☎) We love the rustic wood-paneled exterior, the polished-concrete floor in the lobby, the Thai massage spa (just $35 for 30 minutes), and the 32 contemporary rooms with two-tone paint jobs, wall-mounted, flat-screen TV, and enough room for a sofa. Some have terraces. Terrific all-around value.

Best Western Sunset Plaza Hotel HOTEL $$
(Map p110; ☎323-654-0750; www.sunsetplazahotel.com; 8400 W Sunset Blvd; r $188-229; P ☎ ≋) There's more elegance and class at this Mediterranean-inspired chateau than one would expect from the brand. Rooms have crown moldings, rambling bougainvillea twisting around the wrought-iron window treatments, iPod docks and flat-screen TVs. Nothing hip about it, but it's nice value.

Orlando BOUTIQUE HOTEL $$
(Map p110; ☎323-658-6600; www.theorlando.com; 8384 W 3rd St; r from $196; P @ ☎ ≋) Smack-dab in the W 3rd St shopping district and just a five-minute walk from the Beverly Center mall. Natural woods, earth tones and votive candles provide a soothing antidote to an exhausting shopping spree, as do the heated saltwater pool and pocket-sized gym. Nearby chic eateries abound.

Ramada Plaza HOTEL $$
(Map p110; ☎310-652-6400; www.ramadaweho.com; 8585 Santa Monica Blvd; r $169-461; P @ ☎ ≋) Yes, it's a chain, but it's also a simple, clean, three-star choice with amenities in the heart of the action.

★**Petit Ermitage** BOUTIQUE HOTEL $$$
(Map p110; ☎310-854-1114; www.petitermitage.com; 8822 Cynthia St; ste from $350; P ❄ @ ☎ ≋) If you're drawn to bohemian-chic environs with Turkish rugs, old-world antiques, rooftop bars and fine booze, then these suites may be for you. This intimate boutique hotel offers suites with a wet bar and kitchenette, featuring Venetian-style plaster walls. And the rooftop pool, surrounded by the Hollywood Hills, will make you smile.

★**Chateau Marmont** HOTEL $$$
(Map p110; ☎323-656-1010; www.chateaumarmont.com; 8221 W Sunset Blvd; r $435, ste from $550; P ☎ ≋) The French-flavored indulgence may look dated, but this faux castle has long lured A-listers with its five-star mystique and legendary discretion. Howard Hughes used to spy on bikini beauties from the same balcony suite that became the favorite of U2's Bono.

The garden cottages are the most romantic, but the superstitious might want to steer clear of No 2 where John Belushi set his final speedball in 1982.

Sunset Tower Hotel BOUTIQUE HOTEL $$$
(Map p110; ☎323-654-7100; www.sunsettowerhotel.com; 8358 W Sunset Blvd; r $325-365, ste $415-2500; P@) Connect to the magic of yesteryear, when Errol Flynn, Truman Capote and Marilyn Monroe resided at this art-deco marvel. Recently renovated, this classy boutique hotel with a historic pedigree invokes romance in soothing rooms, a flirty bar (in Bugsy Siegel's former apartment) and a top-notch spa with Turkish hammam (steam bath).

Hotel Wilshire HOTEL $$$
(Map p110; ☎323-852-6000; www.hotelwilshire.com; 6317 Wilshire Blvd; r from $255) A fashionable hotel in the heart of the mid-Wilshire district, ideally located close to several of the city's best museums and blessed with a wonderful rooftop bar. It's a Kimpton hotel which means it's relatively eco- and pet-friendly.

London West Hollywood LUXURY HOTEL $$$
(Map p110; ☎866-282-4560; www.thelondonwesthollywood.com; 1020 N San Vicente Blvd; ste incl breakfast from $379; P@) A sleek, grand all-suite property on the doorstep of the Sunset Strip is favored by the young, hip and upwardly optimistic. The lobby's pearl-toned mosaic motif migrates to guestrooms where there's Berber carpeting, marble desks, silver washbasins and fleur-de-lis wallpaper. South-facing views are massive.

Mondrian HOTEL $$$
(Map p110; ☎310-650-8999, reservations 800-606-6090; www.mondrianhotel.com; 8440 W Sunset Blvd; r from $252, ste from $396; P@) Like *Anchorman's* Ron Burgundy, this elegant tower is staying classy. The lobby is still sleek and billowy white. Rooms have wood floors, dangling chandeliers, rain showers and down duvets. And the new restaurant is trying to rekindle its late-'90s heyday, when its attached Sky Bar was *the* place to be.

Sunset Marquis Hotel & Villas HOTEL $$$
(Map p110; ☎310-657-1333; www.sunsetmarquishotel.com; 1200 N Alta Loma Rd; r from $295, ste from $330; P@) 'Rock-and-roll retreat' may sound like an oxymoron, but not at this quiet, secluded, tropical-garden hideaway that often hosts visiting music royalty, including Mick Jagger and Eric Clapton. There's even a recording studio on-site.

Standard Hollywood HOTEL $$$
(Map p110; ☎323-650-9090; www.standardhotel.com; 8300 Sunset Blvd; r from $235, ste from $335; @) Kind of yesterday's news but still a good standby, this Sunset Strip haunt has you shacking up in sizable shagadelic rooms with beanbag chairs, orange-tiled bathrooms and Warhol poppy-print curtains. South-facing rooms have the views.

Andaz HOTEL $$$
(Map p110; ☎323-656-1234; www.westhollywood.andaz.hyatt.com; 8401 W Sunset Blvd; r from $265; P@) The famed Hollywood Hyatt House (aka Riot House) is now an Andaz, Hyatt's mod urban brand. The rooms have flat-screen TVs, marble baths, and complimentary snacks and nonalcoholic drinks. The infamous John Bonham party tore up the 6th floor.

Farmer's Daughter Hotel MOTEL $$$
(Map p110; ☎800-334-1658, 323-937-3930; www.farmersdaughterhotel.com; 115 S Fairfax Ave; r from $209; P@) Denim bedspreads and rocking chairs lend this flirty motel a farmhouse vibe. Long before the renovation, a young Charlize Theron stayed here with mom when they were hunting for a Hollywood career. Adventurous lovers should ask about the No Tell Room, which has mirrored headboards and another on the ceiling.

Palihouse BOUTIQUE HOTEL $$$
(Map p110; ☎323-656-4100; www.palihouse.com; 8465 Holloway Dr; r from $309; P@) One of two Palihouse hotels in the city (the other is in Santa Monica), and associated with the Pali Hotel on Melrose, this cool spot offers 36 studio, one- and two-bedroom suites, and apartments nestled between Santa Monica Blvd and the Sunset Strip. Decor is modern with raw bulb lighting, marble counters and wash basins, but there's no pool.

Eating

Original Farmers Market MARKET $
(Map p110; www.farmersmarketla.com; 6333 W 3rd St; mains $6-12; 9am-9pm Mon-Fri, to 8pm Sat, 10am-7pm Sun; P) The Farmers Market is a great spot for a casual meal any time of day, especially if the rug rats are tagging along. There are lots of options here, from gumbo to Singapore-style noodles to tacos.

Pingtung ASIAN $
(Map p110; ☎323-866-1866; www.pingtungla.com; 7455 Melrose Ave; dishes $6-12; 11:30am-10:30pm;) Our new favorite place to eat

on Melrose is this Pan-Asian market cafe where the dim sum (wild crab dumplings), seaweed and green papaya salads, and rice bowls piled with curried chicken and BBQ beef are all worthy of praise. They have an inviting back patio with ample seating, wi-fi and good beer on tap.

Lotería! Grill MEXICAN $

(Map p110; ☎323-930-2211; http://loteriagrill.com/; 6333 W 3rd St; tacos $3, sopes $5, tostadas $7, burritos $9; ⏲8am-9pm Mon-Fri, to 8pm Sat, to 7pm Sun) Back-to-basics, authentic, regional Mexican food, which makes it gourmet.

Mama's Secret TURKISH $

(Map p110; ☎323-424-3482; www.mamassecretbakery.com; 8314 W 3rd St; mezzes $5-8, mains $10-14; ⏲8am-8pm Mon-Sat, to 6pm Sun) A delightful Turkish cafe where tables spill from a cheery interior onto the sidewalk. The gyro is wrapped in freshly baked lavash, the burger is made with a Mediterranean meatball patty, and *gozleme* (flat breads) are filled with spinach and feta or spicy *soujouk* and ground beef. They do all the typical *mezzes* (hummus, tabbouleh etc) too.

Milk Jar Cookies COOKIES $

(Map p110; www.milkjarcookies.com; 5466 Wilshire Blvd; cookies $3; ⏲11am-8pm Tue-Thu, to 11pm Fri & Sat, noon-5pm Sun) Once you get over the heavenly scent of freshly baked cookies (it takes a moment) you can get around to the business of choosing a chocolate chip, rocky road, banana split, chocolate pecan caramel or white chocolate raspberry cookie. Pair it with milk, coffee or salted caramel ice cream.

Magnolia Bakery BAKERY $

(Map p110; www.magnoliabakery.com; 8389 W 3rd St; desserts $4-6.50; ⏲8am-8pm Mon-Wed, to 10pm Thu-Sat, 10am-9pm Sun) A buttery and delightfully aromatic cake shop doing a brisk business in mini red-velvet cheesecakes, banana cake smothered with chocolate buttercream, and hummingbird cupcakes (which combine the flavors of pineapple, pecans and bananas). They do classic lemon-vanilla bundt and mini flourless chocolate cakes too.

Pink's FAST FOOD $

(Map p110; ☎323-931-4223; www.pinkshollywood.com; 709 N La Brea Ave; dishes $4-8; ⏲9:30am-2am Sun-Thu, to 3am Fri & Sat) Landmark doggeria with glacially moving lines thanks to the droves who descend for garlicky, all-beef frankfurters, painted with mustard or drenched in chili.

Mercado MEXICAN $$

(Map p110; ☎323-944-0947; www.mercadorestaurant.com; 7910 W 3rd St; ⏲5-10pm Mon-Wed, to 11pm Thu & Fri, 4-11pm Sat, 10am-3pm & 4-10pm Sun) Terrific *nuovo*-Mexican food served in white washed brick environs, with dangling bird-cage chandeliers and a terrific marble tequila bar. The slow-cooked carnitas melt in your mouth. They also spit-roast beef, grill sweet corn, and fold tasty tacos and enchiladas. Their *hora feliz* (happy hour) is among the best in the city.

Yuko Kitchen JAPANESE $$

(Map p110; ☎323-933-4020; www.yukokitchen.com; 5484 Wilshire Blvd; mains $10-15; ⏲11am-9:30pm Mon-Sat) This adorable Japanese cafe just off Wilshire Blvd serves sashimi salads, udon, and rice bowls piled with taco-seasoned ground beef, grilled tofu, spicy salmon and smelt eggs, or albacore sashimi. They also make terrific desserts. Staff are lovely; there is seating inside and out.

Joan's on Third CAFE $$

(Map p110; ☎323-655-2285; www.joansonthird.com; 8350 W 3rd St; mains $10-16; ⏲8am-8pm Mon-Sat, to 7pm Sun;) One of the first market cafes in the LA area, Joan's on Third is still one of the best. The coffee and pastries are absurdly good, and the deli churns out tasty gourmet sandwiches and salads. Hence all the happy people eating alfresco on buzzy 3rd St.

Terroni ITALIAN $$

(Map p110; ☎323-954-0300; www.terroni.ca; 7605 Beverly Blvd; mains $10-20; ⏲11:30am-10:30pm Sun-Thu, to 11:30pm Fri & Sat) Traditional southern Italian cuisine, by way of, um…Toronto? Facts is facts, and you will love the *carpaccio di tonno,* the thin-crust *pizze* and exquisite *pasta al limone.* Just don't expect pizza cutters or substitutions. Terroni doesn't change nuthin' for nobody! But do demand the awesome, vinegary, fiery red chilies.

Ita Cho JAPANESE $$

(Map p110; ☎323-938-9009; www.itachorestaurant.com; 7311 Beverly Blvd; dishes $6-20; ⏲11:30am-2:30pm & 5:30-10:30pm Mon-Fri, from 6pm Sat, 5-10pm Sun; P) Simply put, this is some of the best Japanese food available in Los Angeles. Order any of their small plates, but don't miss the *nasu miso* (eggplant coated in sweet miso sauce), the buttery *enoki,* the broiled *unagi* and anything sashimi. Celeb sightings happen here.

Plan Check PUB $$

(Map p110; ☎323-288-6500; www.plancheck.com; 351 N Fairfax Ave; mains $9-15; ⏰11:30am-11pm Sun-Thu, to 1am Fri & Sat) Modern American comfort food is their jam – portobello mushrooms stuffed with crispy kale, salmon pastrami, short-rib pot roast and damn good fried chicken. The burgers rock too. Check the blackboards for specials before you order. That's also where you'll find the current beer list. Eight of their taps are taken over by a single buzz-worthy microbrew each month.

Fresh Corn Grill GRILL $$

(Map p110; ☎310-855-9592; www.freshcorngrill.com; 8714 Santa Monica Blvd; mains $10-13; ⏰11:30am-10pm; 📶) A fantastic, fresh, all-natural joint with affordable grilled veggie salads, semi-authentic tacos, home-baked desserts and good coffee. It's a perfect choice for quick healthy eats, and the side of grilled corn is fantastic.

Night + Market THAI $$

(Map p110; ☎310-275-9724; www.nightmarketla.com; 9041 W Sunset Blvd; dishes $7-12; ⏰6-10:30pm Tue-Sun) Set behind Talesai, a long-running Thai joint on the strip, this related kitchen is dedicated to authentic Thai street food and Thai-inspired fusion (we're thinking of you, catfish tamale!). Start with the pork satay or *larb lanna* (a chopped pork salad), then move onto the *tom yum; chiengrei* herb sausage is a winner too.

Do not skip the ice-cream sandwich, made from coconut ice cream and sticky rice.

Real Food Daily VEGAN $$

(Map p110; ☎310-289-9910; www.realfood.com; 414 N La Cienega Blvd; mains $13-15; ⏰11am-10pm Mon-Fri, from 10am Sat & Sun; 🖉) 🌿 Once the one-and-only tasty option for vegans, Ann Gentry's famous kitchen on La Cienega still satisfies even devout carnivores. And she's been doing it since 1993.

Petty Cash MEXICAN $$

(Map p110; ☎323-933-5300; pettycashtaqueria.com; 7360 Beverly Blvd; ⏰5-10pm Mon, to 11pm Tue-Sat, noon-10pm Sun) A big, funky, reimagined taco joint with raw light-bulb chandeliers, a pounded metal bar and bright pink-paper menu. Pulled pork-shoulder tacos come folded with pickled red-onion *habanero* and black beans. The grilled octopus taco is garnished with *chile de arbol*, peanuts, jack cheese and avocado.

They serve authentic *al pastor* and pork belly carnitas too, but the grilled maitake mushroom taco is our favorite. Oily, flavorful and nestled on a bed of spinach, you'll probably want another. Their cocktails are creative, but they keep them on tap, which we don't love. Order one of their 35 tequilas and sip it neat.

Café Midi CAFE $$

(Map p110; www.cafemidi.com; 148 S La Brea Ave; mains $13.50-16; ⏰10am-7pm Mon-Sat, from noon Sun; 🅿) Let the bossa nova grooves flow at this ever-so-cute French cafe set in the American Rag complex. There are tables on the sidewalk, but we like the sofa lounges and throwback vibe inside. Pouty model types tend to gather to eat quiche and sip espresso off-peak hours.

Village Idiot PUB $$

(Map p110; ☎323-655-3331; www.villageidiotla.com; 7383 Melrose Ave; mains $12-23; ⏰11:30am-2am Mon-Fri, 10am-2am Sat & Sun; 🅿) Fantastic pub fare with recommended fish-and-chips and other comfort food in a habitat that lures a smart, but plenty boisterous, crowd. The kitchen stays open until midnight. Drinks flow until 2am, and it has all the football matches on the TV.

Blu Jam CAFE $$

(Map p110; www.blujamcafe.com; 7371 Melrose Ave; mains $7-15; ⏰8am-4pm; 🅿🖉👪) Yes, it serves lunch, but you should come for the all-day breakfast with organic coffee and tea. There are two pages of mains that include four kinds of Benedict and a popular Corn Flakes–crusted 'crunchy French toast.'

Crossroads VEGETARIAN $$

(Map p110; ☎323-782-9245; www.crossroadskitchen.com; 8284 Melrose Ave; dishes $9-20; ⏰11:30am-2:30pm & 5pm-midnight Mon-Wed, 11:30am-2:30pm & 5pm-1am Thu & Fri, 5pm-1am Sat, 5pm-10pm Sun) Dark and moody with plush booths and a full bar, this is not some Birkenstock-ian vegan joint. Here, you may start with a kale Caesar, or a beet and citrus salad, then move onto small plates such as calamari made from hearts of palm, a pistachio and kalamata flat bread, wood-roasted mushrooms or a pappardelle bolognese (made with faux-meat, of course).

La Otra Escuela MEXICAN $$

(Map p110; ☎323-932-6178; escuelataqueria.com; 7615 Beverly Blvd; ⏰11am-11pm Sun-Thu, to midnight Fri & Sat) An upscale, new-school *taqueria*. Vegetarians may opt for the roasted *poblano* and jack cheese; fish heads will dig the branzino, shrimp or lobster (hell yes!). They also serve carnitas, and the crispy beef and pickle is their answer to a burger in taco clothing. The salsa can use a pinch more chili and they don't serve beer, but you can bring your own for $4.

Juliano's Raw RAW $$
(Map p110; ☎310-288-0989; www.planetraw.com; 8951 Santa Monica Blvd; mains $9-25; ⏰9am-midnight) Chef Juliano closed Santa Monica's first raw kitchen and moved to this location, where he still serves his brand of all raw, veggie organic cuisine (and the best smoothies on earth) that have earned him rave reviews and a spot on *Oprah*. Sit by the fountain on the patio or in the cozy, glass-box dining room.

★Ray's NEW AMERICAN $$$
(Map p110; ☎323-857-6180; www.raysandstarkbar.com; 5905 Wilshire Blvd; dishes $11-27; ⏰11:30am-3pm & 5-10pm Mon-Fri, from 10am Sat & Sun; 🚌MTA 20) They change the menu twice daily, but if they offer it, order the shrimp and grits: it's rich and buttery, with chunks of andouille sausage, okra and two king prawns. Their burrata melts with tang, the yellow-tail collar is crisp and moist, and the bacon-wrapped rabbit sausage will wow you.

They even have a water list, which would normally be worthy of ridicule, but it's actually kind of amazing. In LA, seldom does a restaurant blessed with as golden a location as this one – on the plaza of LA's best museum – live up to the address. Ray's does.

★Connie & Ted's SEAFOOD $$$
(Map p110; ☎323-848-2722; www.connieandteds.com; 8171 Santa Monica Blvd; mains $12-26; ⏰5-11pm Mon & Tue, noon-11pm Wed-Sun) The design is an instant classic, and there are always up to a dozen oyster varieties at the stocked raw bar. Fresh fish is pan-fried or grilled to order. The lobster roll can be served cold with mayo or hot with drawn butter, and the shellfish marinara is a sacred thing.

Pair your choice with a craftsman beer or something crisp and dry from the wine list.

Son of a Gun SEAFOOD $$$
(Map p110; ☎323-782-9033; www.sonofagunrestaurant.com; 8370 W 3rd St; dishes $8-27; ⏰11:30am-2:30pm Mon-Fri, 6-11pm Sun-Thu, to midnight Fri & Sat) If you love seafood, head straight for this creative kitchen where they glaze and grill kampachi collars, sear octopus with chili, make a mean lobster roll, a terrific linguine and clams, and plate their burrata with uni.

Republique CONTINENTAL $$$
(Map p110; ☎310-362-6115; www.republiquela.com; 624 S La Brea; mains $18-32; ⏰8am-4pm Mon-Sat, 6-10pm Mon-Wed, to 11pm Thu-Sat) A design gem with the gourmet ambition to match. The old Campaline interior is still an atrium restaurant with stone arches, a brightly lit front end scattered with butcher-block tables, and a marble bar peering into an open kitchen; there are tables in the darker, oakier back room too.

The menu changes daily but may include a pumpkin agnolotti, crab risotto, pig's head and lentils, and braised short rib. There's always a delicious bakery, raw bar and a selection of charcuterie.

Gusto ITALIAN $$$
(Map p110; ☎323-782-1778; www.gusto-la.com; 8432 W 3rd St; mains $19-31; ⏰6-11pm Mon-Thu, to 11:30pm Fri & Sat, to 10pm Sun) This neighborhood Italian joint feels like it's belonged here since forever, though it opened in 2012. That's when it was named one of *Esquire's* best new restaurants. We suggest you start with the octopus with heirloom cannellini beans. Then move onto black spaghetti with anchovy and chili or bucatini carbonara.

Comme Ca FRENCH $$$
(Map p110; ☎310-782-1178; www.commecarestaurant.com; 8479 Melrose Ave; mains $18-29; ⏰6-10pm Tue-Thu, to 11pm Fri, 11am-2:30pm & 6-11pm Sat, 11am-2:30pm Sun; 🅿) The dining is French bistro classic. Think: steak or moules frites, braised short rib, roasted beet salads and bouillabaisse, all served to white-leather booths as jazz wafts over you. The burger earns rave reviews (it better, for $18), and that bar – cocktails do not get much better.

AOC ITALIAN $$$
(Map p110; ☎323-653-6359; www.aocwinebar.com; 8700 W 3rd St; small plates $9-17, mains $28-40; ⏰11:30am-11pm Mon-Fri, from 10am Sat, 10am-10pm Sun; 🅿) It's moved slightly west, but the small plates and terrific wines (over 50 of which can be ordered by the glass) are all here. Expect such gifts as artisanal cheeses, homemade terrines, and roast clams with green garlic. They even roast whole chickens ($42) and racks of lamb ($70), that serve two or more.

Animal MEAT $$$

(Map p110; ☎323-782-9225; www.animalrestaurant.com; 435 N Fairfax Ave; dishes $3-68; ⏰6-11pm Sun-Thu, to midnight Fri & Sat) Begin with chicken liver toast or spicy beef tendons (which may be dipped in a *pho* sauce), then get the gnocchi drenched in six-hour, slow-cooked bolognese, or crispy pig's head, veal tongue or rabbit legs. We know it sounds intimidating, but carnivorous foodies do pray at the Animal altar.

Hart and the Hunter SOUTHERN $$$

(Map p110; ☎323-424-3055; www.thehartandthehunter.com; 7950 Melrose Ave; mains $10-32; ⏰7am-10pm Tue-Thu, to 11pm Fri & Sat, to 9pm Sun) This spare, Southern-inspired kitchen with a small, rotating menu is based at one of our favorite new hotels, the Pali (p115). The shrimp and grits awash in a bacon vinaigrette is a staple at lunch and brunch, but they also serve a kale salad and smoked trout on toast; the biscuits are legit too.

Dinner gets serious with oysters barbecued with chili butter, steamed clams, hangar steaks, and a low country shrimp boil that looks amazing. There aren't many tables, so book ahead.

Drinking & Nightlife

Roger Room BAR

(Map p110; www.therogerroom.com; 370 N La Cienega Blvd; ⏰6pm-2am Mon-Fri, 7pm-2am Sat, 8pm-2am Sun) Cramped but cool; too cool even to have a sign out front. When handcrafted, throwback cocktails first migrated west and south from New York and San Fran, they landed here.

El Carmen BAR

(Map p110; 8138 W 3rd St; ⏰5pm-2am Mon-Fri, from 7pm Sat & Sun) A pair of mounted bull heads and *lucha libre* (Mexican wrestling) masks create an over-the-top, 'Tijuana North' look and pull in an industry-heavy crowd at LA's ultimate tequila and mezcal tavern (over a hundred to choose from).

Bar Marmont BAR

(Map p110; ☎323-650-0575; www.chateaumarmont.com/barmarmont.php; 8171 Sunset Blvd; ⏰6pm-2am) Elegant, but not stuck up; been around, yet still cherished. With high ceilings, molded walls and terrific martinis, the famous, and wish-they-weres, still flock here. If you time it right you might see Thom Yorke, or perhaps Lindsay Lohan? Come midweek. Weekends are for amateurs.

Formosa Cafe BAR

(Map p110; ☎323-850-9050; 7156 Santa Monica Blvd; ⏰4pm-2am Mon-Fri, 6pm-2am Sat & Sun) Humphrey Bogart and Clark Gable used to knock'em back at this dark railcar of a watering hole so authentically noir that scenes from *LA Confidential* were filmed here. Skip the Chinese food.

Beverly Hills Juice Club JUICE BAR

(Map p110; www.beverlyhillsjuice.com; 8382 Beverly Blvd; ⏰7am-6pm Mon-Fri, 9am-6pm Sat) This hippie classic – the first on the LA health-food, raw-power bandwagon – started out on Sunset when Tom Waits and Rickie Lee Jones used to stumble in between shows. It still attracts an in-the-know crowd craving wheatgrass shots and banana-manna shakes. Get yours with a shot of algae. No, seriously.

Juice Served Here JUICE

(Map p110; www.juiceservedhere.com; 8366 W 3rd St; juices $8-10; ⏰7:30am-7pm Mon-Sat, 8am-6pm Sun) Are there too many juice bars in LA? Yes, yes there are, but you could still make the argument that there should be more of this particular juice bar brand, which is replicating itself across the city. At this branch, there's a tiny, sunny back porch, a wide marble bar, and their concoctions are creative, healthy (of course) and come bottled in glass.

Greystone Manor CLUB

(Map p110; ☎310-652-2012; www.greystonemanorla.com; 643 N La Cienega Blvd; ⏰10pm-2am Wed, Sat & Sun) A favorite for those who like to dress up fine and dance in big rooms dripping with chandeliers and throbbing with bass. DJs get good marks. Drinks aren't cheap, and the velvet rope won't rise for just anyone, so book ahead if you can.

1 Oak CLUB

(Map p110; www.1oakla.com; 9039 W Sunset Blvd; ⏰10pm-2am Thu & Sat) The brand-new LA shingle of a club brand that rocks NYC, Vegas and Mexico City, 1 Oak runs over two stories, with sizable tables and a sumptuous VIP section. The 2014 Golden Globes party was held here, which gave the place some buzz. It can get crowded though and the music, we hear, often trends toward pop.

Churchill PUB

(Map p110; ☎323-655-8384; www.the-churchill.com; 8384 W 3rd St; ⏰7am-midnight Sun-Thu, to 2am Fri & Sat; 📶) Set on the ground floor of the Orlando hotel, this fun pub has an inviting outdoor patio, seating upstairs and down, and they pour craftsman suds and cocktails. The food is a slight step above pub grub, and it can catch a fun crowd day or night.

Rosewood Tavern PUB

(Map p110; ☎323-944-0980; rosewoodtavern.com; 448 N Fairfax Ave; ⏲5pm-2am Mon-Fri, noon-2am Sat & Sun) Beloved by the neighborhood locals who reside in the Spanish-style duplexes that dominate the streets east of Fairfax, this concrete floor, brick-wall pub serves craftsman beers and whiskeys, and decent food on small and large plates.

☆ Entertainment

Largo at the Coronet PERFORMING ARTS & MUSIC

(Map p110; ☎310-855-0530; www.largo-la.com; 366 N La Cienega Blvd) Ever since its early days on Fairfax Ave, Largo has been progenitor of high-minded pop culture (it nurtured Zach Galifinakis to stardom). Now part of the Coronet Theatre complex, it features edgy comedy, such as Sarah Silverman and Jon Hodgman, and nourishing night music from Brad Meldau and his jazz piano to Andrew Bird's acoustic ballads.

El Rey CONCERT VENUE

(Map p110; www.theelrey.com; 5515 Wilshire Blvd; cover varies) An old art-deco dance hall decked out in red velvet and chandeliers and flaunting an awesome sound system and excellent sightlines. Although it can hold 800 people, it feels quite small. Performance-wise, it's popular with indie acts such as Black Joe Lewis and the Honeybears, and the rockers who love them.

Mint CONCERT VENUE

(Map p110; www.themintla.com; 6010 W Pico Blvd; cover $5-25) Built in 1937, Mint is an intimate, historic venue. Legends such as Ray Charles and Stevie Wonder played here on the way up, and axe-man Ben Harper got his start here, too. Expect a packed slate of terrific jazz, blues and rock shows, sensational sound, and you'll never be more than 30ft from the performance stage.

Troubadour LIVE MUSIC

(Map p110; www.troubadour.com; 9081 Santa Monica Blvd) The celebrated 1957 rock hall launched a thousand careers, including those of James Taylor and Tom Waits, and was central to John Lennon's 'Lost Weekend in 1973'. It's still a great spot for catching tomorrow's headliners and appeals to beer-drinking music aficionados who keep attitude to a minimum. Come early to snag a seat on the balcony. No age limit.

Groundlings COMEDY

(Map p110; ☎323-934-4747; www.groundlings.com; 7307 Melrose Ave; tickets $10-20) This improv school and company launched Lisa Kudrow, Will Ferrell, Maya Rudolph and other top talent. Their sketch comedy and improv can be belly-achingly funny, especially on Thursdays when the main company, alumni and surprise guests get to riff together in 'Cookin' with Gas.'

Roxy CONCERT VENUE

(Map p110; ☎310-276-2222; www.theroxyonsunset.com; 9009 W Sunset Blvd) A Sunset fixture since 1973, the Roxy has presented everyone from Miles Davis to David Bowie to Jane's Addiction, and still occasionally manages to book music that matters today. It's a small venue, so you'll be up close and personal with the bands.

House of Blues LIVE MUSIC

(Map p110; ☎323-848-5100; www.hob.com; 8430 W Sunset Blvd) Frankly, there ain't much blues playing these days at this faux Mississippi Delta shack, but at least its small size and imaginative decor make it a neat place to catch bands of all stripes: headliners and up-and-comers, rock, reggae or hip-hop.

Comedy Store COMEDY

(Map p110; www.thecomedystore.com; 8433 W Sunset Blvd) There's no comedy club in the city with more street cred than Sammy and Mitzi Shore's Comedy Store on the strip. Sammy launched the club, but Mitzi was the one who brought in hot young comics such as Richard Pryor, George Carlin, Eddie Murphy, Robin Williams and David Letterman. These days her son, Pauly, runs it.

Improv COMEDY

(Map p110; www.improv.com; 8162 Melrose Ave; tickets $10-25; ⏲Thu-Sat) The launch pad for countless stand-up comics from Richard Pryor to Jerry Seinfeld to Ellen DeGeneres to Dave Chapelle. Improv still gets the odd headliner, but it's mostly up-and-comers these days. Tuesday evenings at 5pm anyone can grab the open mic.

Laugh Factory COMEDY

(Map p110; ☎323-656-1336; www.laughfactory.com; 8001 W Sunset Blvd) The Marx Brothers used to keep offices at this long-standing club. It still gets some big names from time to time.

GAY & LESBIAN LOS ANGELES

LA is one of the country's gayest cities, and has made a number of contributions to gay culture. Your gaydar may well be pinging throughout the county, but the rainbow flag flies especially proudly in Boystown, along Santa Monica Blvd in West Hollywood (WeHo), flanked by dozens of high-energy bars, cafes, restaurants, gyms and clubs. Most cater to gay men, although there's plenty for lesbians and mixed audiences. Thursday through Sunday nights are prime time.

Beauty reigns supreme among the buff, bronzed and styled of Boystown. Elsewhere, the scene is considerably more laid-back and less body-conscious. The crowd in Silver Lake runs from cute hipsters to leather-and-Levi's and an older contingent. Venice and Long Beach have the most relaxed, neighborly scenes.

If nightlife isn't your scene, there are plenty of other ways to meet, greet and engage. Outdoor activities include the **Frontrunners** (www.lafrontrunners.com) running club and the **Great Outdoors** (www.greatoutdoorsla.org) hiking club. They offer a Gay LA walking historical tour of Downtown, as well. There's gay theater all over town, but the **Celebration Theatre** (Map p110; www.celebrationtheatre.com; 7051 Santa Monica Blvd, West Hollywood) ranks among the nation's leading stages for LGBT plays. The **Cavern Club Theater** (Map p102; www.cavernclubtheater.com; 1920 Hyperion Ave, Silver Lake) pushes the envelope, particularly with uproarious drag performers including Julie Brown's Homecoming Queens and Jackie Beat; it's downstairs from Casita del Campo restaurant. If you are lucky enough to be in town when the **Gay Men's Chorus of Los Angeles** (www.gmcla.org) is performing, don't miss out: this amazing group has been doing it for 35 years. For more ideas, check www.fronteirsla.com, which contains up-to-date listings and news about the community and gay-friendly establishments around town. The website www.westhollywood.com is another good source.

The **LA Gay & Lesbian Center** (Map p88; ☎323-993-7400; www.laglc.org; 1625 Schrader Blvd, Hollywood; ⏰9am-8pm Mon-Fri, to 1pm Sat) is a one-stop service and health agency, and its affiliated **Village at Ed Gould Plaza** (www.laglc.org; 1125 N McCadden Pl, Hollywood; ⏰6-10pm Mon-Fri, 9am-5pm Sat) offers art exhibits and theater programs around a leafy courtyard.

The festival season kicks off in mid to late May with the **Long Beach Pride Celebration** (www.longbeachpride.com) and continues with the three-day LA Pride (p65) in early June with a parade down Santa Monica Blvd. On **Halloween** (October 31), the same street brings out 350,000 outrageously costumed revelers of all persuasions.

WeHo

Abbey (Map p110; www.abbeyfoodandbar.com; 692 N Robertson Blvd; mains $9-13; ⏰11am-2am Mon-Thu, from 10am Fri, from 9am Sat & Sun) Once a humble coffee house, the Abbey has developed into WeHo's bar/club/restaurant of record. Always cool and fun, it has so many different flavored martinis and mojitos that you'd think they were invented here, plus a full menu. Match your mood to the many different spaces, from outdoor patio to goth lounge to chill room. On weekends, they're all busy.

Whisky-a-Go-Go LIVE MUSIC
(Map p110; ☎310-652-4202; www.whiskyagogo.com; 8901 W Sunset Blvd) Like other aging Sunset Strip venues, the Whisky coasts more on its legend status than current relevance. Yup, this was where the Doors were the house band and go-go dancing was invented back in the '60s. These days the stage usually belongs to long-shot hard rockers.

Sundance Sunset Cinema CINEMA
(Map p110; ☎323-654-2217; www.sundancecinemas.com; 8000 W Sunset Blvd; tickets $11-14) First there was a festival, then a channel, and now there is a bourgeoning art-house cinema chain bearing the name of Redford's most famous character. Here you may have a glass of wine and beer while you take in the latest un-blockbuster. Hence, screenings are all 21 and over.

Micky's (Map p110; www.mickys.com; 8857 Santa Monica Blvd; ⏲5pm-2am Sun-Thu, to 4am Fri & Sat) A two-story, quintessential WeHo dance club, with go-go boys, expensive drinks, attitude and plenty of eye-candy. There is a marble circle bar, exposed steel girders and doors that open all the way to the street. Check online for special events.

Eleven (Map p110; www.eleven.la; 8811 Santa Monica Blvd; ⏲5pm-2am Mon-Thu, to 3am Fri, noon-3am Sat, 11am-2am Sun) This glam spot occupies a historic building, and offers different theme nights from Musical Mondays to high-energy dance parties; check the website for event listings. They serve decent food.

Trunks (Map p110; www.trunksbar.com; 8809 Santa Monica Blvd; ⏲1pm-2am) With pool tables and sports on the flat-screen TVs, this brick house, low-lit dive is a long-running boulevard staple that is less fabulous and more down to earth than most in WeHo. And that can be a very good thing.

Hamburger Habit (Map p110; ☎310-659-8774; 8954 Santa Monica Blvd; mains $5-8; ⏲10am-midnight) The greasy burgers are middling at best, but the after-sundown scene, which may include restaurant sing-alongs and topless men dancing on tables, can be as unique as it is wonderful. If you time it right.

Fiesta Cantina (Map p110; www.fiestacantina.net; 8865 Santa Monica Blvd) Extra-long happy hours, reasonably priced nachos and a busy sidewalk patio are the draw for a vibrant crowd of 20-something revelers. Nothing fancy, but always busy.

Beyond WeHo

Akbar (Map p102; www.akbarsilverlake.com; 4356 W Sunset Blvd; ⏲4pm-2am) Best jukebox in town, Casbah-style atmosphere, and a great mix of people that's been known to change from hour to hour – gay, straight, on the fence or just hip, but not too hip for you.

Casita del Campo (Map p102; www.casitadelcampo.net; 1920 Hyperion Ave; mains lunch $8, dinner $14-17; ⏲11am-11pm Sun-Wed, to midnight Thu, to 2am Fri & Sat; P) What's not to love about this Mexican cantina? It's cozy, it's fun, and you might even catch a drag show in the tiny Cavern Club Theater (p122).

Faultline (Map p102; www.faultlinebar.com; 4216 Melrose Ave; ⏲5pm-2am Wed-Fri, 2pm-2am Sat & Sun) Indoor-outdoor venue that's party central for manly men. Take off your shirt and join the Sunday-afternoon beer bust (it's an institution), but get there early or expect a long wait.

Other Side (Map p102; www.flyingleapcafe.com; 2538 Hyperion Ave; ⏲4pm-2am Mon-Thu, from noon Fri-Sun) Old-school piano bar where the crowd skews older and you can hear yourself talk. Friday nights tend to be rowdiest; otherwise it's pretty mellow. Prices are reasonable.

Roosterfish (Map p170; www.roosterfishbar.com; 1302 Abbot Kinney Blvd; ⏲11am-2am) The Westside's last gay bar standing has a bit of a locals only attitude but power through that veneer and you'll feel at home. Go on Friday for the busiest night, or go for the laid-back Sunday-afternoon barbecue.

Acme Comedy Theatre COMEDY
(Map p110; www.acmecomedy.com; 135 N La Brea Ave; tickets $15-30; ⏲Thu-Sat) Not the most famous sketch-comedy theater, but big names such as Adam Corolla, Joel McHale and Russell Brand have appeared on stage.

New Beverly Cinema CINEMA
(Map p110; www.newbevcinema.com; 7165 W Beverly Blvd; adult/senior & child $8/6) Serious filmophiles and megaplex foes put up with the worn seats and musty smell of this beloved double-feature revival house that started out as a vaudeville theater in the '20s and went porno in the '70s.

In 2007 Quentin Tarantino, who has been coming to this cinema since 1982, held the world premiere of *Grindhouse* here, shortly before the cinema's longtime owner passed away suddenly. Then, with the cinema on the verge of closure, Tarantino bought it just to keep the doors open. 'It was going to be turned into a Super Cuts,' he said.

Pacific Theatres at the Grove CINEMA
(Map p110; www.pacifictheatres.com; 189 The Grove Dr; adult/senior/child $13/9/9.50;) This is a fancy all-stadium, 14-screen multiplex with comfy reclining seats, wall-to-wall screens and superb sound. The Monday Morning Mommy Movies series (11am) gives the diaper-bag brigade a chance to catch a flick with their tot but without hostile stares from nonbreeders.

Shopping

This is by far the best and most diverse shopping territory in a city that often feels like it's been built by and for shopaholics. Melrose Ave, between La Brea and Fairfax, gets most of the buzz, thanks to the boutiques stuck together in block-long hedgerows. Most of their gear is rather low-brow and low end, however. If you want the good stuff, make your way west of Fairfax on Melrose or 3rd St. Both Beverly Blvd and La Brea Ave are stocked with gorgeous interiors showrooms and galleries, with the odd fashion boutique mixed in. And Fairfax Ave between Beverly and Melrose is where hip-hop and skate culture collide.

★**Reformation** FASHION
(Map p110; www.thereformation.com; 8253 Melrose Ave; 11am-7pm) Here's classic, retro-inspired, fashionable outer wear that's eco-conscious without the granola. Its tagline is 'change the world without changing your style'. They get it done by using only pre-existing materials, which means no additional dyeing of fabrics and half the water use of other fashion brands, and everything is made locally Downtown.

Fahey/Klein Gallery ARTWORK
(Map p110; www.faheykleingallery.com; 148 S La Brea Ave; 10am-6pm Tue-Sat) The best in vintage and contemporary fine-art photography by icons such as Annie Leibovitz, Bruce Weber and the late, great rock 'n' roll shutterbug, Jim Marshall. It even has his lesser-known civil-rights catalog in its vast archives.

Espionage VINTAGE, INTERIORS
(Map p110; 323-272-4942; www.espionagela.com; 7456 Beverly Blvd; 11am-6pm Mon, to 7pm Tue-Fri, 10:30am-7pm Sat, to 6pm Sun) A fabulous boutique blessed with a tasteful melange of new and vintage goods. Their jewelry is fantastic, as are the chunky vintage perfume bottles and ash trays. The leather chairs work perfectly with the brass-and-glass end tables, and they offer a collection of vintage couture clothing sold on consignment.

Supreme FASHION
(Map p110; 323-655-6205; supremenewyork.com; 439 N Fairfax Ave) When we rolled by, this beloved skate/punk/hip-hop mashup of a label had just re-opened their doors with fans lined up for half a block to get a taste of the new line. So, yes, it's a thing. Also, they have a half pipe in the store, and that's maybe the best of things.

Kayo FASHION
(Map p110; www.thekayostore.com; 464 N Fairfax Ave; 11am-7pm Mon-Sat, from noon Sun) This hip-hop skater retailer on Fairfax is set in a converted bank building and they have the vault to prove it. They deal in labels such as Organika and have some of the best and most interesting T-shirt designs on the block. They also hock decks, trucks and wheels if you need a ride.

Nudie Jeans DENIM
(Map p110; www.nudiejeans.com; 710 N Edinburgh Ave; 11am-7pm Mon-Sat, noon-6pm Sun) This is the only branded shop in North America from the Swedish-owned Nudie denim line. Jeans come in a variety of colors and range in price from $180 to $310, including free hemming and repair. The shop itself is a converted house outfitted with blackboard walls, one of which offers suggestions on when to wash your new denim. Short answer: every five to six months. Seriously.

Chucks Vintage VINTAGE
(Map p110; 323-653-5386; www.chucksvintage.com; 8012 Melrose Ave; noon-6pm Mon-Sat) Easily the coolest – not cheapest – vintage shop on Melrose. The hand-picked selection here is less about quantity and all about quality, from soft cotton tees to tasteful flannel and lace dresses to rugged denim and leather. The vintage signage on the walls is dope too.

Diane von Furstenberg FASHION
(Map p110; 323-951-1947; www.dvf.com; 8407 Melrose Ave; 11am-7pm Mon-Sat, noon-6pm Sun) The LA flagship of the great and grand dame of fashion. Belgian born, von Furstenberg married into German royalty, divorced it, and became an American fashion icon thanks to – among other imagineerings – her signature wrap dress. If you be a fashion slave or spy, it's worth a wander.

Gibson VINTAGE, INTERIORS
(Map p110; ☎323-934-4248; www.garygibson.com; 7350 Beverly Blvd; ⏰9am-6pm Mon-Fri, 11am-5pm Sat) If you love vintage interiors, step into this gem of a gallery, where (almost) everything from vintage baseball bats to arm chairs and desks to the art on the walls was birthed in another era (or reproduced to look that way). It's owned and operated by noted designer Gary Gibson, who operates his interior-design studio out back.

Vera Wang FASHION
(Map p110; www.verawang.com; 8445 Melrose Ave; ⏰11am-7pm Mon-Sat, noon-6pm Sun) An American fashion icon, and former figure skater, Vera Wang is best known for her haute-couture wedding gowns and bridesmaid collections. She dresses the best – whether it's for Olympic figure-skating competitions or the red carpet. Better for a browse than a buy, unless you brought your black card.

Voila! ARTWORK
(Map p110; www.voilagallery.com; 518 N La Brea Ave; ⏰10am-5pm Mon-Fri, noon-7pm Sat) This La Brea gallery has eye-popping contemporary photography, paintings and mixed-media work, but it also sells rare decorative collectibles, such as French clock-tower faces, glove molds and antique print work. It's a fascinating place to burn some time.

Great Frog JEWELRY
(Map p110; ☎323-879-9100; www.thegreatfroglondon.com; 7955 Melrose Ave; ⏰11am-7pm Mon-Sat, noon-6pm Sun) A sterling-silver jewelry company known for their skulls, Great Frog started in London, have a shop in NYC, and this is their latest offering. They cast in gold as well, and sell leather jackets too. We loved the vintage motorcycle engines in the jewelry case and the stunning 1941 Indian in the window.

Vivienne Westwood FASHION
(Map p110; www.viviennewestwood.co.uk; 8320 Melrose Ave; ⏰11am-7pm Mon-Sat, noon-6pm Sun) Freaky, funky Vivienne Westwood is the UK designer credited with mainstreaming punk and new-wave fashion, then building it into an empire. This is her LA flagship store and it's ultra high-end, darlings.

Kidrobot ANIME
(Map p110; www.kidrobotla.com; 7972 Melrose Ave; ⏰11am-7pm Mon-Sat, noon-6pm Sun) A den of freaky, lovely animation action figures. It's a mash-up of Kidrobot's own characters and those featured in Marvel comics, *Family Guy, Futurama* and *The Simpsons*.

Creatures of Comfort FASHION
(Map p110; ☎323-655-7855; www.creaturesofcomfort.us; 7971 Melrose Ave; ⏰11am-7pm Mon-Sat, noon-6pm Sun) Upscale lady shoppers should pop into this inviting space stocked with classic dresses and Repetto shoes. They have their own linen and denim lines, and cotton blouses, most of it soft and flowing.

Shelter Half FASHION, OUTDOOR EQUIPMENT
(Map p110; www.shelterhalf.com; 161 La Brea Ave; ⏰11am-7pm Mon-Sat, to 6pm Sun) If you like surf, adventure and the gear that helps you look good doing it, this store will make you smile. It's stocked with Stormy Monday denim, Kletterwerks backpacks and climbing ropes, Almond shirts and long boards, and some excellent sofas made from reclaimed military tents (hence the name).

Joyrich FASHION
(Map p110; www.joyrich.com; 7700 Melrose Ave; ⏰11am-8pm Mon-Sat, to 7pm Sun) A bright and funky boutique selling sportswear – blinged up and fashion-forward. There's Simpsons gear, leather shirts and jackets, reimagined football jerseys for girls, and cool handbags, clutches and backpacks.

Record Collector MUSIC
(Map p110; ☎323-655-6653; www.therecordcollector.net; 7809 Melrose Ave) If you dig vinyl – specifically jazz and classical on vinyl – you must check out this record trader. It's stuffed floor to ceiling and staffed with a shopkeeper who would love to help you hunt down the gems. They've been doing it since 1974.

Wasteland VINTAGE
(Map p110; www.shopwasteland.com; 7428 Melrose Ave; ⏰11am-8pm Mon-Sat, noon-7pm Sun) A popular and rather polished vintage boutique with racks packed with skirts and tops, fur-collared jackets and Pendleton wool shirts.

Melrose Trading Post FLEA MARKET
(Map p110; http://melrosetradingpost.org; Fairfax High School, 7850 Melrose Ave; admission $2; ⏰9am-5pm Sun) Here you'll find threads, jewelry, housewares and other offbeat items proffered by over 100 purveyors. It's held in the Fairfax High parking lot and proceeds help fund school programs.

Fred Segal FASHION

(Map p110; ☎323-651-4129; www.fredsegal.com; 8100 Melrose Ave; ⊙10am-7pm Mon-Sat, noon-6pm Sun) Celebs and beautiful people circle for the very latest from Babakul, Aviator Nation and Robbi & Nikki at this warren of high-end boutiques under one impossibly chic but slightly snooty roof. The only time you'll see bargains (sort of) is during the two-week blowout sale in September.

OK GIFTS

(Map p110; www.okthestore.com; 8303 W 3rd St; ⊙11am-6:30pm Mon-Sat, noon-6pm Sun) A concrete-floor emporium of quirky cool, OK has art and cookbooks, bar kits and paper lanterns, glass radiometers (measures light), pens and notebooks. But you might enjoy the jewelry and glassware most of all.

DL Rhein ANTIQUES

(Map p110; ☎323-653-5590; www.dlrhein.com; 8300½ W 3rd St; ⊙10am-6pm Mon-Fri, 11am-6pm Sat, to 5pm Sun) A cluttered den of interior delights from antique glass to furniture, including very special limited-edition pieces. There's silver and crystal, scented candles and baking trays stuffed with jewelry. The entire shop, owned by a noted interior designer, is a terrific browse.

Book Soup BOOKS

(Map p110; ☎310-659-3110; www.booksoup.com; 8818 W Sunset Blvd; ⊙9am-10pm Mon-Sat, to 7pm Sun) A bibliophile's indie gem, sprawling and packed with entertainment, travel, feminist and queer studies, eclectic and LA-based fiction, plus appearances by big-name authors.

Polkadots & Moonbeams BOOKS

(Map p110; ☎323-655-3880; www.polkadotsandmoonbeams.com; 8367 W 3rd St; ⊙11am-7pm Mon-Sat, noon-6pm Sun) Like a burst of sunlight on a cloudy day, enjoy this whimsical, yet exceptional, vintage womenswear shop, stocked with affordable designer dresses, shades, scarves and hats. There's another branch with some new labels a few doors down, but the vintage shop is where it's at.

American Rag Cie VINTAGE

(Map p110; ☎323-935-3154; www.amrag.com; 150 S La Brea; ⊙10am-9pm Mon-Sat, noon-7pm Sun) This industrial-flavored, warehouse-sized space has kept trend-hungry stylistas looking fabulous since 1985. Join the vintage vultures in their hunt for second hand leather, denim, T-shirts and shoes. It also has some new gear. It's not cheap, but it is one hell of a browse. We particularly enjoyed the period homewares in the Maison Midi wing.

Lotta Boutique FASHION

(Map p110; www.lottanyc.com; 8372 W 3rd St; ⊙11am-7pm Mon-Sat, noon-5pm Sun) Boho-chic style is served at this single label shop where you'll find handmade Lotta Stensson gowns and baby doll dresses, unique jewelry and hats popular among such glitterati as Beyonce.

Le Labo PERFUMERY

(Map p110; ☎323-782-0411; www.lelabofragrances.com; 8385 W 3rd St; ⊙11am-7pm Mon-Sat, to 5pm Sun) The West Hollywood branch of this noted fragrance lab based in New York offers 14 fragrances, including one you may only purchase here. All are alchemized with natural oils such as patchouli, vetiver, iris and ylang ylang. Simply pick the one you like and they'll make a bottle fresh for you. They have addictive shower gel, body lotion, massage oil and balm too.

Undefeated SHOES

(Map p110; ☎310-399-4195; www.undftd.com; 112½ S La Brea Ave; ⊙11am-7pm) The Mid-City branch of LA's top limited-edition and imported sneaker store offers the smoothest kicks this side of Tokyo.

Trashy Lingerie LINGERIE

(Map p110; www.trashy.com; 402 N La Cienega Blvd; ⊙10am-7pm Mon-Sat, noon-5pm Sun) Those who worship at the altar of hedonism should check into this cluttered store, stocked with burlesque-inspired corsets, cat masks, school-girl outfits and whatever else girls and boys with imagination might need for a night of naughtiness. To keep out lookyloos, you must pay $5 for an 'annual membership' at the door.

Pleasure Chest EROTICA

(Map p110; ☎323-650-1022; www.thepleasurechest.com; 7733 Santa Monica Blvd; ⊙10am-midnight Sun-Wed, to 1am Thu, to 2am Fri & Sat) LA's kingdom of kinkiness is filled with sexual hardware catering to every conceivable fantasy and fetish. Please, who doesn't need a penis beaker and a blow-up doll? Yeah, there's more naughty than nice.

Chi Chi Larue's EROTICA

(Map p110; ☎800-997-9072; www.chichilarues.com; 8932 Santa Monica Blvd; ⊙10am-midnight Sun-Wed, to 2am Thu-Sat) If other erotica stores are too tame or hetero-friendly for you, make your way here, where you can size up in the manhood department; pick up aromas, oils and films to spark the mood; grab some assless chaps; and otherwise combine your love of retail with the joy of sex.

Agent Provocateur LINGERIE
(Map p110; www.agentprovocateur.com; 7961 Melrose Ave; ⌚11am-7pm Mon-Sat, noon-6pm Sun) As sexy as it is expensive (read: very, very), you'll love the sweet and naughty burlesque sheers, lace and silks that will work quite well with the thigh-highs or the slender pumps, and could potentially coexist with the sharp, studded bustier if, you know, the occasion calls for it.

Mystery Pier Books BOOKS
(Map p110; www.mysterypierbooks.com; 8826 W Sunset Blvd; ⌚11am-7pm Mon-Sat, noon-5pm Sun) An intimate, hidden-away courtyard shop that specializes in selling signed shooting scripts from past blockbusters, and first editions from Shakespeare ($2500 to $4000), Salinger ($21,000) and JK Rowling ($30,000 and up).

Traveler's Bookcase BOOKS
(Map p110; ☎323-655-0575; www.travelers-bookcase.com; 8375 W 3rd St; ⌚11am-5pm Mon, 10:15am-7pm Tue-Fri, 10am-7pm Sat, noon-6pm Sun) It's cool to support indie booksellers, especially ones catering to unrepentant nomads. Maps, travel guides, fiction and photography books are geared to whet the appetite of wanderlust.

Brooklyn Projects FASHION
(Map p110; www.brooklynprojects.com; 7427 Melrose Ave; ⌚noon-8pm) Hip-hop fashion has always been a staple on Melrose and this spot combines that with a skate/punk mash-up that works. Grab a deck, some limited edition sneakers, glasses, T-shirts, hoodies and flannels. They even have tricked out BMX bikes for sale.

Whimsic Alley CHILDREN
(Map p110; ☎310-453-2370; www.whimsicalley.com; 5464 Wilshire Blvd; ⌚11am-6pm Mon-Fri, from 10am Sat & Sun; 👪) Muggles love LA's own Diagon Alley, where Harry Potter and friends seem to wait just one portkey away. Flip through Hogwarts sweaters and capes at Haber & Dasher, find your favorite wand at Phoenix Wands, or poke around nooks overflowing with Harry Potter memorabilia and like-minded literature on piratology, dragons and wand making.

American Girl Place CHILDREN
(Map p110; www.americangirl.com; 189 The Grove Dr, Grove Mall; ⌚9am-9pm Mon-Sat, to 7pm Sun; 👪) Little girls go gaga for this make-believe toyland where they can take their plastic friends to lunch or afternoon tea at the cafe or a revue-style show, get photographed for a mock *American Girl* magazine cover at the photo studio or give them a makeover in the doll hair salon.

CULVER CITY & MAR VISTA

A decade or so ago, Culver City bloomed from its bland, semi-suburban, studio-town roots into a stylish, yet unpretentious destination for fans of art, culture and food. Local media raved. Then the recession happened, and Culver City (like so many other parts of town) took a hit. Some galleries couldn't make it through. The Jazz Bakery – a horn-blowing, Helms Bakery institution – closed its doors. Layoffs hit Sony Pictures, which tightened the belts of local eateries, and optimism waned.

But as the economy regained its footing and LA surged once again, Culver City's groovy roots sprouted anew, resulting in even more terrific restaurants and galleries. The wonderful Kirk Douglas Theatre and Actor's Gang are still here, as is the venerable Culver Hotel, where the Munchkins from *The Wizard of Oz* once slept within the city limits. And they still make motion pictures here too.

Then there's Mar Vista: a flowering of laid-back Venice cool and Culver City charm can be found on Venice Boulevard, something of an asphalt bridge between the two.

Sights

Arts District GALLERY
(www.ccgalleryguide.com; La Cienega Blvd) The Helms complex marks the beginning of Culver City's vital arts district, which runs east along Washington to La Cienega and up one block to Venice Blvd. In 2003 art-world movers and shakers Blum & Poe relocated their gallery here from Santa Monica, drawn by cheap rents and airy, malleable spaces in old warehouses.

Since then, more than two dozen galleries have piggybacked on their success. The best of the bunch are on La Cienega.

Museum of Jurassic Technology MUSEUM
(MJT; Map p62; ☎310-836-6131; www.mjt.org; 9341 Venice Blvd; suggested donation adult/student & senior/under 12yr $5/3/free; ⏲2-8pm Thu, noon-6pm Fri-Sun) This is one of LA's most intriguing exhibition spaces. Nope, it has nothing to do with dinosaurs and even less to do with technology. Instead, you'll find madness nibbling at your synapses as you try to read meaning into displays about Cameroonian stink ants, a tribute to trailer parks and a sculpture of the Pope squished into the eye of a needle.

It may all be a mind-bending spoof, an elaborate hoax or a complete exercise in ironic near-hysteria by founder David Wilson. Maybe. For an entertaining read about the place, pick up *Mr Wilson's Cabinet of Wonder* by ex–*New Yorker* staff writer Lawrence Weschler.

Blum & Poe GALLERY
(Map p62; www.blumandpoe.com; 2727 S La Cienega Blvd; ⏲10am-6pm Tue-Sat) Major player and juggernaut of the Culver City arts district, Blum & Poe represents such international stars as Takashi Murakami, Sam Durant and Sharon Lockhart. When we came through both floors were consumed by a phenomenal Yoshitomo Mara show.

Hayden Tract ARCHITECTURE
(Map p62; 3500 block of Hayden Ave) Architecture fans gravitate to the block where Eric Owen Moss has turned a worn-out industrial compound into eye-popping offices. The Samitaur building at 3529 Hayden looks like an alien spacecraft made of concrete steel and glass. Imagine your office building were a Transformer. Just as cool is the melting parking structure behind it.

The bizarre, rusted-steel and glass tower on the corner of National and Hayden is just a roped off staircase to nowhere, but they do project light on some of the exterior screens which can be a cool sight from down below at night. 3535 Hayden is a collection of studio spaces with some interesting contours.

Activities

Massage Garage WELLNESS
(☎310-202-0082; www.themassagegarage.com; 3812 Main St; massages 30/60/90min $32/48/74, facials from $45; ⏲10am-9pm) Feeling as rundown as your '97 Honda? Why not pull in

DON'T MISS

THE OPEN SOURCE MUSEUM

Even given Culver City's artistic lean, the **Wende Museum** (Map p62; ☎310-216-1600; www.wendemuseum.org; 5741 Buckingham Pkwy; ⏲10am-5pm Fri) FREE stands out – both for its vast, yet niche collection, and how widely and weirdly they share it.

German for 'in between', Wende collects anything and everything made, bought, sold and created in East Germany during the Cold War, from the end of WWII to the fall of the Berlin Wall. It's the brainchild of Harvard grad Justin TK, who has traveled to and lived in Germany several times, saving countless films, photographs and artifacts from incinerators and garbage dumps to reveal how typical Germans lived behind the wall.

If that sounds dry to you, don't worry, it's anything but. He's revealed the strange world of the East German hippie, now owns the largest East German film archive on earth, and has over 100,000 pieces all told, including a wonderful Lenin bust painted pink and turquoise by a 1980s street artist. Yet he's still collecting, and his team of young archivists are always processing storage containers full of new material in the Culver City office headquarters.

Most museums typically share 10% of their collection at a time, while the rest remains archived, and that's what makes Wende so different. They strive to share and show 90% of their collection all the time. They do it by inviting known artists to use their collection as fodder for installations in galleries and museums around the world. For example, they invited Shephard Ferry (of Andre the Giant Obey fame) to adorn a slab of the Berlin Wall that now sits across from LACMA.

Soon, though, much of it will be shown at their newly expanded museum space. Wende has recently won a long-term lease of an old, abandoned armory – which, during the Cold War, was to be a shelter in the event of a nuclear strike. It will anchor a newly planned art zone filled in over the next 10 years with public sculpture and galleries. The new Wende will be open for tours by 2015, and it should not be missed.

for a 'test drive' (30 minutes), a 'tune-up' (60 minutes) or an 'overhaul' (90 minutes) at this industrial-flavored, yet comfortable day spa? Choose from five massage treatments, including shiatsu and Swedish massage.

Sleeping

Rodeway Inn MOTEL $
(310-398-1651; www.rodewayinn.com; 11933 W Washington Blvd; r $74-89; P@) Rooms have granite washbasins, fridge and microwave. Some have flat-screen TVs. There's no pool, but hummingbirds love the adobe-style fountain gushing on their patch of grass out front. You're closer to Venice than Culver's main drag. A satisfying budget motel.

Culver Hotel HOTEL $$$
(310-558-9400; www.culverhotel.com; 9400 Culver Blvd; r $249-269; P@) The Munchkins bunked in this 1924 heritage hotel in downtown Culver City while filming *The Wizard of Oz*. A mahogany-paneled lobby gives way to rooms with antique furnishings and marble bathrooms but surprisingly few amenities.

Eating

Versailles CUBAN $
(310-289-0392; www.versaillescuban.com; 10319 Venice Blvd; mains $8-18; 11am-10pm Sun-Thu, to 11pm Fri & Sat; P) We'll always have a soft spot for the Cuban-style roast lemon chicken and succulent roast pork doled out to everyone from college kids to grizzled grips. Plates are served with beans, rice, fries and salad, and the service is impeccable. The lunch specials are a steal.

Earl's Gourmet Grub SANDWICHES $
(www.earlsgourmetgrub.com; 12226 Venice Blvd; dishes $10-12; 8am-4pm) Where sandwiches go gourmet. Whether you order sushi grade ahi, avocado and Asian slaw on brioche; the prosciutto, fig and blue cheese on walnut bread; or a Greek-themed spinach wrap named by Ron Burgundy (you figure it out), you'll have a whole new appreciation for sandwiches and sandwich makers by the last bite.

Curious Palate CAFE $
(310-437-0144; www.thecuriouspalate.com; 12034 Venice Blvd; dishes $8-14; 7:30am-8pm Mon-Sat, to 3pm Sun) A humble, but special Mar Vista kitchen cafe where the chalkboard menu features sinful sandwiches such as the mouth-melting miso shortrib wrap. They cure their own pastrami, make fresh soups, sell organic chocolates, and toss tasty, fresh and filling salads.

Samosa House INDIAN $
(www.samosahouse.net; 10700 W Washington Blvd; dishes $3.50, meals $9; 10:30am-9:30pm;) A family-owned, vegetarian steam table serving, among other things, charcoal-smoked cauliflower daal, *aloo* curry, *chana masala*, and samosas, of course. The modern glass-box interior and breezy patio are inviting.

Akasha MODERN AMERICAN $$
(310-845-1700; www.akasharestaurant.com; 9543 Culver Blvd; mains $8-22; 11:30am-2:30pm & 5:30-9:30pm Mon-Thu, to 10:30pm Fri & Sat, 10:30am-2:30pm & 5-9pm Sun;) The classic building was restored to its original steel, concrete and brick arches with a modern flair. The kitchen takes all-natural ingredients and turns them into tasty small plates such as tandoori-spiced chicken wings, and big plates such anise-braised short rib.

LYFE CAFE $$
(310-507-7955; www.lyfekitchen.com; 9540 W Washington Blvd; mains $7-16; 7am-9pm Mon & Tue, to 10pm Wed-Fri, 8am-10pm Sat, to 9pm Sun) You may forgive an acronym that translates into the rather clunky Love Your Food Everyday, when it leads to such a healthy, omnivore eatery. We love the kale Caesar salad, which comes with chunks of steamed broccoli and cherry tomatoes. They also do a 'gardein' sausage and mozzarella ravioli, fish tacos and char grass-fed steaks.

Father's Office PUB $$
(310-736-2224; www.fathersoffice.com; 3229 Helms Ave; dishes $6-13; 5pm-1am Mon-Thu, noon-2am Fri & Sat, noon-midnight Sun) In contrast to the musty old confines of the Santa Monica original, this airy, modern space spills onto an outdoor patio, where you can sip any of their 36 craft beers, munch on smoked eel, spread roasted bone marrow on toast and devour the beloved burger, topped with Gruyère and Maytag blue cheese. No substitutions tolerated.

Wild Craft PIZZERIA $$
(310-815-8100; www.wildcraftpizza.com; 9725 Culver Blvd; mains $11-16; noon-9pm Sun & Mon, to 10pm Tue-Thu, to 11pm Fri & Sat) There's a lot to love at this sourdough-crusted pizza joint, from the slab marble bar to the craft beer and wine list to the artsy stenciled walls and the wood-fired pies. Popular choices include

the pork and beef meatballs, roasted tomato and smoked mozzarella, or the spicy fennel sausage. Salads are huge.

Public School PUB $$
(☎310-558-0414; www.publicschool310.com; 9411 Culver Blvd; mains $11-15; ⊙11:30am-midnight) The menus are composition-book mock-ups, and the food is gastro-pub deluxe with roasted chicken tacos, shrimp and cheddar grits, a range of burgers and a nice *jidori* chicken and white bean ragout. The beer and wine are craft quality.

★**Waterloo & City** GATSROPUB $$$
(☎310-391-4222; www.waterlooandcity.com; 12517 Washington Blvd; small plates $12-15, mains $20-29; ⊙5-11pm Sun & Mon, to midnight Tue-Thu, to 1am Fri & Sat) At the forefront of LA's gastropub movement, Waterloo & City remains one of the city's best – if not the undisputed champ – thanks to pork shank ravioli served with grilled apples, grilled octopus, shishito peppers and squid-ink aioli, and a beef Wellington that will make you cry tears of joy. The sticky toffee pudding is a must.

Lukshon SOUTHEAST ASIAN $$$
(☎310-202-6808; www.lukshon.com; 3239 Helms Ave; dishes $9-31; ⊙noon-3pm & 5:30-10pm Tue-Thu, to 10:30pm Fri & Sat) Upscale Southeast Asian cuisine in a modern, naturally lit space with soothing wooden walls, spacious booths, a fine wood-block bar, and terrific patio out front. Mains include Hawaiian butterfish with pickled watermelon radish and daikon garnish, crab fritters with chili jam, and pork ribs slathered in chicory coffee BBQ sauce.

Drinking & Nightlife

Blind Barber BAR
(www.blindbarber.com; 10797 Washington Blvd; ⊙noon-midnight Mon & Tue, to 2am Wed-Sat, to 6pm Sun) Literally a barber shop, you enter through the hair trimmings into a dimly lit back bar thrumming with good music and usually packed with a fun, ironically shaggy crowd. But you can get your hair cut too, or a shave, if you must.

Venice Grind COFFEE SHOP
(www.venicegrind.com; 12224 Venice Blvd; ⊙6am-10pm; 📶) The sound of classic roots reggae blends with the steam-engine whir of a top-end espresso machine and mingles with the aroma of the locally roasted, world's favorite caffeine-delivery system. Industrial but still inviting. They have outdoor seating too.

El Baron CLUB
(8641 Washington Blvd; cover $10; ⊙9am-11pm Mon-Fri, 8am-late Sat & Sun) This stucco-cottage nightclub has tasty tequila at good prices, a wide dance floor and a bandstand featuring DJs and live acts playing the pan-Latin spectrum for a fun-loving, working-class Latino crowd. The food gets mixed reviews.

☆ Entertainment

Kirk Douglas Theatre THEATER
(www.centertheatergroup.org; 9820 Washington Blvd) An old-timey movie house has been recast as a 300-seat theater, thanks to a major cash infusion from the Douglas family. Since its opening in 2004, it's become an integral part of Culver City's growing arts scene. It's primarily a showcase for terrific new plays by local playwrights.

Actors' Gang Theater THEATER
(www.theactorsgang.com; 9070 Venice Blvd, Culver City) The 'Gang' was founded in 1981 by Tim Robbins and other renegade UCLA acting-school grads. Its daring and offbeat reinterpretations of classics have a loyal following.

Shopping

Gregg Fleishman Studio GALLERY
(www.greggfleishman.com; 3850 Main St; ⊙11am-7pm Wed-Sat) Like Eames on acid, Fleishman puts the 'fun' in functional with his ingenious, solid-birch plywood furniture bent, carved and spiraled into springy forms. Lumbar support never looked or felt so... mind opening. And if you think the modular playhouses are cool, dig the automobile. It, and the artist, have done some time at Burning Man.

Helms Bakery District FURNITURE
(www.helmsbakerydistrict.com; 8800 Venice Blvd) From points north, this charming 1932 art-deco former bakery complex is the gateway to Culver City. These days the warehouses and studios are packed with one of the most stylish collections of furniture galleries in the city. There are a few restaurants here too, including a Culver City branch of Santa Monica's beloved Father's Office (p129).

Soaptopia SOAP
(www.soaptopia.com; 12228 Venice Blvd; ⊙10am-6pm Mon-Fri, to 5pm Sat, to 3pm Sun) Part soap factory, part showroom, they make bars and bottles of bubbly-smell goods from all natural ingredients and they don't take themselves too seriously. Bars have names

like Sudweiser (it's made with hops, beer and lemon) and Miami Vice (orange blossom and key lime). They do perfumes, body scrubs and oils too.

Arcana BOOKS
(www.arcanabooks.com; 8675 W Washington Blvd; ⌚11am-7pm Tue-Sun) Set in the Helms Complex, Arcana is the city's best art-book depot. The sheer breadth is overwhelming. Photography books feature Saul Bass, Led Zeppelin, *The Godfather,* and Billy Wilder's *Some Like It Hot* stills. Any artist or architect you can imagine has a tome stocked here, and the loft-like space with alternative rock soundtrack attracts artsy bookworms.

BEVERLY HILLS, BEL AIR, BRENTWOOD & WESTWOOD

With its reputation for old-Hollywood glamour, top-end couture and posh dining still circulating in the collective consciousness, Beverly Hills remains impressive to those who stroll Beverly Blvd and Rodeo Dr for the first time. But if you take a closer look, you might see some slippage. Most, if not all, of the downtown Beverly Hills shopping is of the corporate variety. The names are here – Prada, Gucci – but most of it is designer in label only (the best shopping is actually on N Robertson and further east in West Hollywood). Still, the new, blue glass MGM building has helped refresh the local skyline and there remain more Ferraris per capita here than anywhere else.

Downtown, several city-owned garages offer two hours of free parking, including one at 9510 Brighton Way. For two hours of free valet parking, head to the garage underneath Two Rodeo (enter from Dayton Way).

West of Beverly Hills, past the mini-downtown of Century City (a commercial district created and named for the 20th Century Fox Studio), is a college town plopped into the middle of a big city. Westwood is practically synonymous with UCLA. The huge campus is hemmed in by Sunset Blvd and Westwood Village. The village is pedestrian-friendly but it's increasingly vacant these days as the charming, but aging, movie theaters continue to lose traffic to nearby multiplexes, and LA nightlife pulls students out into the wider world. A farmers market along Weyburn Ave livens things up on Thursday afternoons, and the Hammer Museum is a must. You can snag an hour of free parking in the public garage at 1036 Broxton Ave.

North of Westwood, Bel Air is a favorite hideaway of stars whose sybaritic homes are generally hidden behind security gates and dense foliage, among them the great Quincy Jones' estate and Hef's Playboy Mansion.

Brentwood, west of the I-405 (San Diego Fwy), is almost as exclusive as Bel Air and is home to one of LA's big attractions, the hilltop Getty Center. Despite a high celeb quotient (Spielberg lives here), it's pretty low-key, and young professionals like the location, close to Santa Monica and only 20 minutes from the Sunset Strip. Marilyn Monroe died in her home at 12305 Helena Dr, and decades later Brentwood made global headlines again when Nicole Simpson and her friend Ron Goldman were murdered at 875 Bundy Dr. In the subsequent criminal trial, her husband OJ Simpson was (in)famously acquitted.

Sights

★Getty Center MUSEUM
(Map p62; ☎310-440-7300; www.getty.edu; 1200 Getty Center Dr, off I-405 Fwy; ⌚10am-5:30pm Tue-Fri & Sun, to 9pm Sat; P) FREE In its billion-dollar, in-the-clouds perch, high above the city grit and grime, the Getty Center presents triple delights: a stellar art collection (everything from renaissance artists to David Hockney), Richard Meier's cutting-edge architecture, and the visual splendor of seasonally changing gardens.

On clear days, you can add breathtaking views of the city and ocean to the list. A great time to visit is in the late afternoon after the crowds have thinned. Sunsets create a remarkable alchemy of light and shadow and are especially magical in winter.

Even getting up to the 110-acre 'campus' aboard a driverless tram is fun. From the sprawling arrival plaza a natural flow of walkways, stairs, fountains and courtyards encourages a leisurely wander between galleries, gardens and outdoor cafes. Five buildings hold collections of manuscripts, drawings, photographs, furniture, decorative arts and a strong assortment of pre-20th-century European paintings. Must-sees include Van Gogh's *Irises,* Monet's *Wheatstacks,* Rembrandt's *The Abduction of Europa* and Titian's *Venus and Adonis.* Don't miss the lovely Cactus Garden on the remote South Promontory for amazing city views.

Beverly Hills

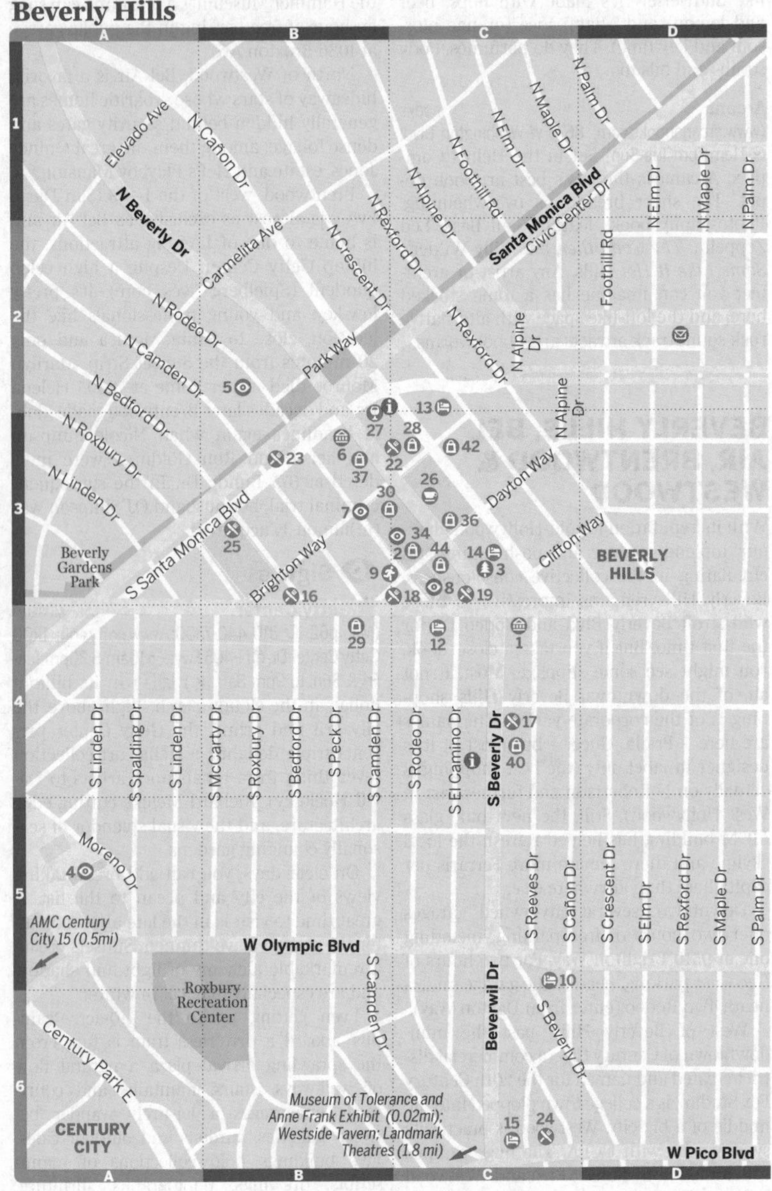

Tours, lectures and interactive technology (including audioguides; $3) help make the art accessible to all. Children can take a Family Tour, visit the interactive Family Room, borrow a kid-oriented audioguide or browse the special kid bookstore. They even host garden concerts for kids.

Concerts, lectures, films and other cultural events for grown-ups keep the space buzzing with locals. Most are free but some require reservations (or try standby). The

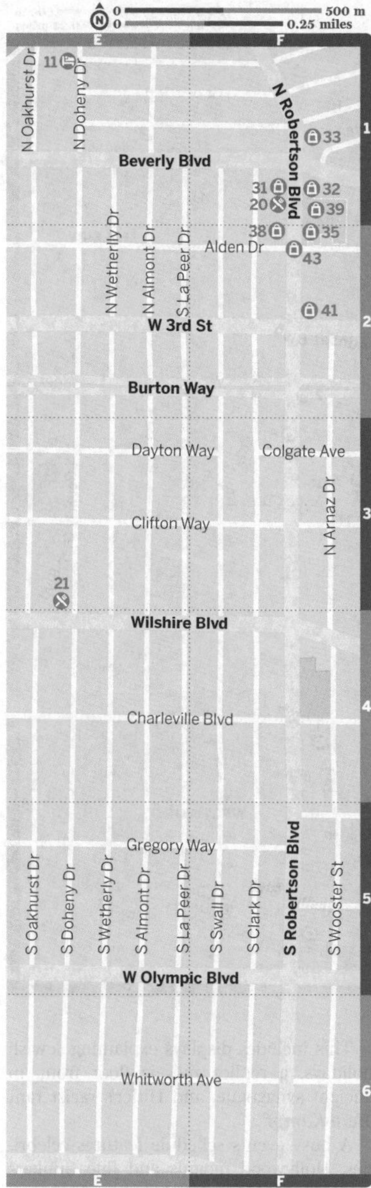

free (almost weekly) summertime Saturday-evening concert series, 'Off the 405', brings some tremendous progressive pop and world music acts to the Getty gardens.

Admission is free, but parking is $15 ($10 after 5pm); Metro Bus 761 stops at the Getty.

Beverly Hills

Sights
1 Ace Gallery C4
2 Anderton Court C3
3 Beverly Canon Gardens C3
4 Beverly Hills High School A5
5 O'Neill House B2
6 Paley Center for Media B3
7 Rodeo Drive B3
8 Via Rodeo C3

Activities, Courses & Tours
9 Beverly Hills Trolley B3

Sleeping
10 Avalon Hotel C5
11 Beverly Terrace Hotel E1
12 Beverly Wilshire C4
13 Crescent C2
14 Montage C3
15 Mr C C6

Eating
16 Bedford & Burns B3
Bouchon .... (see 14)
17 Cabbage Patch C4
18 Grill on the Alley C3
19 Hakkasan C3
20 Ivy F1
21 Kate Mantilini E3
22 Nate'n Al C3
23 Papa Jakes B3
24 Picca C6
25 Sayuri Sushi B3

Drinking & Nightlife
26 Nespresso C3
27 Nic's Beverly Hills B3

Shopping
28 American Tea Room C3
29 Barneys New York B4
30 Cartier B3
31 Chanel F1
32 Curve F1
33 Guy Hepner Gallery F1
34 Harry Winston C3
35 Iijin F2
36 Jigsaw C3
37 K Soho B3
38 Kitson F2
39 Kitson Men F1
40 Lola Et Moi C4
41 Madison F2
42 Marimekko C3
43 Robertson Boulevard F2
44 Scoop C3
Tiffany .... (see 8)
Wall Street Gallery .... (see 33)

Westwood & Bel Air

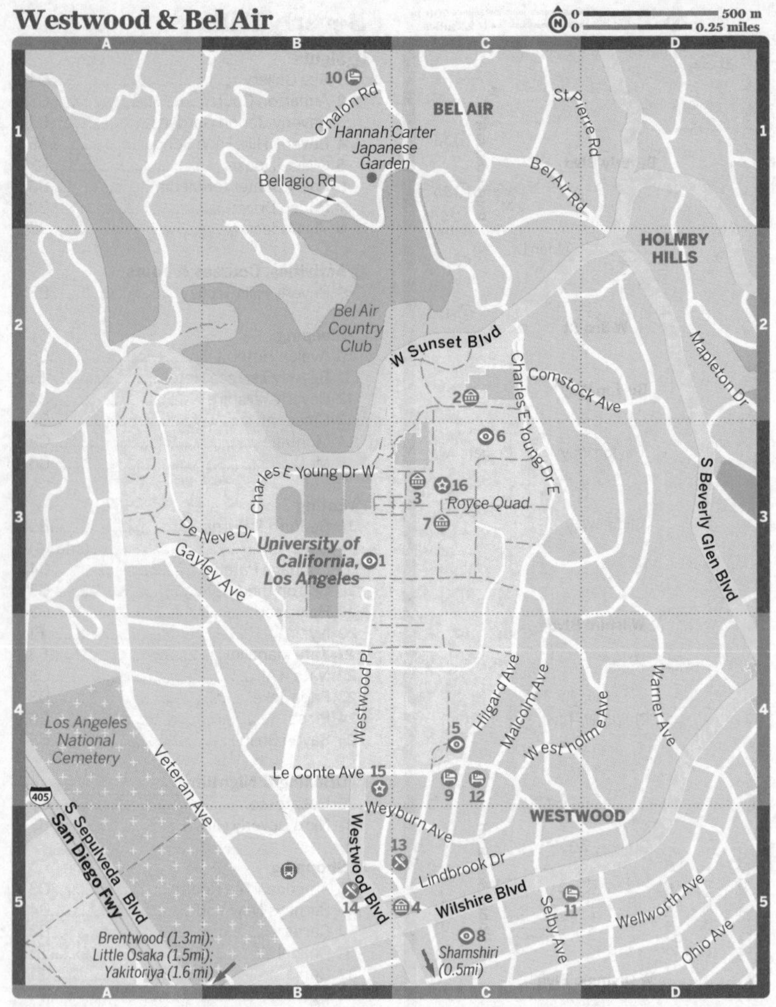

Skirball Cultural Center MUSEUM

(Map p62; ☎310-440-4500; www.skirball.org; 2701 N Sepulveda Blvd; adult/under 12yr/student & senior $10/5/7, Thu free; ⊗noon-5pm Tue-Fri, 10am-5pm Sat & Sun; 👪) Although it is, technically speaking, the country's largest Jewish museum and cultural center, the Skirball has something for all. The preschool set can board a gigantic wooden **Noah's Ark** while grown-ups gravitate to the permanent exhibit, an engagingly presented romp through 4000 years of history, traditions, trials and triumphs of the Jewish people.

This includes displays explaining Jewish holidays, a replica mosaic floor from an ancient synagogue, and Hitler's racist rant *Mein Kampf*.

A busy events schedule features celebrities, Hollywood moguls and fine thinkers in panel discussions, lectures, readings and performances. And while you may be less interested in some of the rotating exhibits, such as the quirky 'Jews on Vinyl,' it does lure world-music acts for the occasional summer concert.

Westwood & Bel Air

Top Sights

1 University of California, Los Angeles ... B3

Sights

2 Broad Art Center ... C2
3 Fowler Museum at UCLA ... C3
4 Hammer Museum ... C5
5 Mildred E Mathias Botanical Garden ... C4
6 Murphy Sculpture Garden ... C3
Powell Library ... (see 1)
7 UCLA Film and TV Archive ... C3
8 Westwood Village Memorial Park ... C5

Sleeping

9 Hilgard House Hotel ... C4
10 Hotel Bel-Air ... B1
11 Hotel Palomar ... C5
12 W ... C4

Eating

13 Napa Valley Grille ... C5
14 Native Foods ... B5

Entertainment

15 Geffen Playhouse ... B4
16 Royce Hall ... C3

University of California, Los Angeles UNIVERSITY

(UCLA; Map p134; www.ucla.edu; P) Founded in 1919, the alma mater of Jim Morrison, Kareem Abdul Jabbar and Jackie Robinson ranks among the nation's top universities. The campus is vast: walking briskly from one end to the other takes at least 30 minutes; free tours (reservations required) are offered at 10:30am and 1:30pm.

The grounds make for a lovely saunter along manicured, sycamore-shaded lawns, through profuse gardens and past replicas of Italian renaissance churches on historic Royce Quad. One of them, the **Powell Library** (Map p134), harbors the **UCLA Film and TV Archive** (Map p134; www.cinema.ucla.edu; 9am-5pm Mon-Fri) FREE, the country's second-largest after the Library of Congress, with more than 220,000 movies and TV shows. It's only open to researchers, but regular screenings take place at the state-of-the-art Billy Wilder Theater in the Hammer Museum.

Garden retreats include the **Murphy Sculpture Garden** (Map p134) northeast of Royce Quad, with more than 70 stunning works by Rodin, Moore, Calder and other American and European artists set amid jacaranda and coral trees. We're partial to the giant, torqued ellipse by Richard Serra in the plaza of the **Broad Art Center** (Map p134). Designed by Richard Meier, it houses the UCLA visual-arts programs and an MFA student gallery.

In the campus' southeastern corner, the **Mildred E Mathias Botanical Garden** (Map p134; www.botgard.ucla.edu/bg-home.htm; 8am-5pm Mon-Fri, to 4pm Sat) FREE has more than 5000 native and exotic plants and flowers. Enter on Tiverton Ave. On winter weekdays gates close an hour earlier. It's only open by reservation for self-guided, 50-minute tours.

Fowler Museum at UCLA MUSEUM

(Map p134; www.fowler.ucla.edu; noon-5pm Wed & Fri-Sun, to 8pm Thu) FREE Near the Film & Television Archive in UCLA, this museum presents sometimes intriguing, and sometimes baffling, ethno-exhibits. A recent one featured paintings, sculpture and digital works inspired by the saints, sinners and folklore from Mexico, the Caribbean, South America and New Orleans. Another displayed the Yaqui masks of Carlos Castaneda, the author of a series of books on shamanism.

Hammer Museum MUSEUM

(Map p134; http://hammer.ucla.edu; 10899 Wilshire Blvd; 11am-8pm Tue-Fri, to 5pm Sat & Sun) FREE Once a vanity project of the late oil tycoon Armand Hammer, his eponymous museum has become a widely respected art space. Selections from Hammer's personal collection include relatively minor works by Monet, Van Gogh and Mary Cassat, but the museum really shines when it comes to cutting-edge contemporary exhibits featuring local, under-represented and controversial artists. Best of all, it's free.

As an intellectual forum, it presents diverse, high-caliber (and often free) readings, lunchtime art talks, screenings, happenings, discussions, lectures and concerts. Their annual K.A.M.P. program links 50 to 60 former artists in residence with children ($125 to $150 per child) for four hours of sculpting, sticker making and painting workshops. The courtyard is a great place to hang and is wired with wi-fi, and the museum store is the best in LA. Parking costs $3.

Ace Gallery GALLERY

(Map p132; 310-858-9090; www.acegallery.net; 9430 Wilshire Blvd; 10am-6pm Tue-Sat) Two floors of top-level, modern, large-format art in an iconic converted bank building. Expect everything from postmodern, almost steam punk, pen-and-ink drawings by Laurie Lipton, to flat, circular spirals of color and mayhem from Gary Lang. The sculpture is amazing too.

Rodeo Drive NEIGHBORHOOD
(Map p132; btwn Wilshire & Santa Monica Blvds) It's pricey and pretentious, but no trip to LA would be complete without a saunter along glittery Rodeo Dr, the famous three-block ribbon of style where sample-size fembots browse for Escada and Prada.

Most people gravitate to Euro-flavored **Via Rodeo** (Map p132; cnr Rodeo Dr & Wilshire Blvd), a cobbled lane lined with outdoor cafes for primo people-watching.

For Frank Lloyd Wright fans, there's the 1953 **Anderton Court** (Map p132; 322 N Rodeo Dr), a zany zigzag construction, although clearly not his best work. Also check out the 1988 **O'Neill House** (Map p132; 507 N Rodeo Dr), a few blocks north. It doesn't have a famous architect, but the free-form, art-nouveau design in the tradition of Catalan master Antonio Gaudí is definitely one of the more imaginative structures in the area.

Paley Center for Media MUSEUM
(Map p132; ☎310-786-1000; www.paleycenter.org; 465 N Beverly Dr; suggested donation adult/child $10/5; ⏲noon-5pm Wed-Sun; P) The main lure here is the mind-boggling archive of TV and radio broadcasts dating to 1918. The Beatles' US debut on the *Ed Sullivan Show*? The moon landing? The *All In The Family* pilot? All here. Plus, two theaters for screenings and discussions with the casts of shows such as the great *Key & Peele* and *How I Met Your Mother*.

Getty Center architect Richard Meier designed the crisp, gleaming-white building.

Beverly Hills Hotel LANDMARK
(Map p62; www.beverlyhillshotel.com; 9641 Sunset Blvd) Affectionately known as the 'Pink Palace,' the Beverly Hills Hotel has served as unofficial hobnobbing headquarters for the industry elite since 1912. In the 1930s, its Polo Lounge was a notorious hangout of Darryl F Zanuck, Spencer Tracy, Will Rogers and other lords of the polo crowd.

Marlene Dietrich had her very own 7ft-by-8ft bed installed in Bungalow 11, and Howard Hughes, the billionaire recluse, went progressively off his nut during 30 years of delusional semiresidence. Elizabeth Taylor bedded six of her eight husbands in various bungalows. While filming *Let's Make Love,* Yves Montand and Marilyn Monroe were probably doing just that; Marilyn is also reported to have 'bungalowed' both JFK and RFK here.

Virginia Robinson Gardens GARDENS
(Map p62; ☎tour reservations 310-550-2087; www.robinsongardens.org; 1008 Elden Way; tour adult/5-12yr/student & senior $11/4/6; ⏲10am & 1pm Tue-Fri) Beverly Hills' ultimate 'secret' garden is tucked among the manicured estates north of Sunset Blvd. Virginia Robinson, wife of department-store mogul Harry Robinson, had a passion for plants and devoted much of her life to creating this sloping, 6-acre symphony of trees and flowers that can only be experienced on guided tours.

You'll also get to peek inside the Robinsons' magnificent beaux-arts mansion, where Fred Astaire, Ronald Reagan and other Hollywood royalty used to pop by for a game of bridge and a stiff whiskey. Make reservations at least two weeks in advance, and even further ahead in spring.

Museum of Tolerance MUSEUM
(Map p62; ☎info 310-553-8403, reservations 310-772-2505; www.museumoftolerance.com; 9786 W Pico Blvd; adult/senior/student $15.50/12.50/11.50, Anne Frank Exhibit adults/senior/student $15.50/13.50/12.50; ⏲10am-6:30pm Sun-Wed, to 9:30pm Thu, 10am-5pm Fri; P) Run by the Simon Wiesenthal Center, this museum uses interactive technology to engage visitors in discussion and contemplation around racism and bigotry, with particular focus given to the Holocaust. You can study various Nazi-era memorabilia, including bunk beds from the Majdanek camp and Göring's dress-uniform cap.

Their goal is for visitors – mostly groups of school children – to learn and absorb the hard lessons of the past so they aren't repeated. Diversity is discussed, intolerances that we all carry are exposed, and champions of rights in America are celebrated. The last entry is 1½ hours before closing, and reservations are highly recommended due to stiff security protocol and school-tour scheduling. Reservations make your entry more seamless and swift. The new Anne Frank exhibit (p137) costs extra and takes more time, but is it ever worth it.

There's a gorgeous new theater which hosted, among other events, the global premieres of multiple Academy Award winners, *12 Years A Slave* and *Dallas Buyers Club*.

DON'T MISS

MEET ANNE FRANK

The Museum of Tolerance (p136) recently unveiled a jaw-dropping, $2.5 million **Anne Frank Exhibit** (www.museumoftolerance.com; adult/senior/student $15.50/13.50/12.50). You'll learn that she was born in Frankfurt, harbored Hollywood dreams – which offers a credible link to LA – and that her father, Otto, was an officer in the German army during WWI. When he landed a job in Amsterdam just ahead of the Holocaust, Otto chose to resettle the family there because it was as neutral as Switzerland and was considered a safe haven for Jews. Then the Nazis steamrolled into the Netherlands and the Franks went into hiding.

Throughout the exhibit, where the halls are lined with recovered concentration camp prison robes, you will see Anne's words, and hear them through the sound system. They come from her diaries and from her original letters to an Iowa pen pal, which you'll see. You'll listen and watch tasteful re-enactments as her perspective shifts from cute, childish and dreamy to insightful, profound and inspiring. And you'll spend time in a mock-up attic, like the one that sheltered her family for years.

They almost made it too. The Franks were discovered on August 4, 1944. The family was divided and Anne and her big sister, Margot, died of typhus together in Bergen-Belsen just weeks before that camp was liberated. Otto was the only survivor, and it was he who published Anne's diary, which has since been translated into 70 languages and is among the most widely read books of all time.

At the exhibit's end, you will greet an interactive station and be invited to make a pledge and express your feelings, which you can either Tweet out or simply send to a digital Tree of Life on the screen above. You may be choking back tears at the same time. The exhibit is that powerful.

Greystone Mansion & Park HISTORIC BUILDING
(Map p62; ☎310-550-4654; www.greystonemansion.org; 905 Loma Vista Dr; ⏰10am-6pm Apr-Oct, to 5pm Nov-Mar; P) Gloomy and gothic, this 1928 castle-like mansion seems better suited to foggy Scottish moors than shiny Beverly Hills. In 1929 its owner, oil-heir Ned Doheny, was found with a bullet in his head along with his male secretary in an alleged murder-suicide – a mystery that remains unsolved to this day.

Nobody's lived here since, but the mansion has appeared in countless movies and TV shows, including *Spider-Man 3*, *Indecent Proposal* and *Alias*. It's empty and closed except for special events, but you're free to peer through the dusty windows and explore the surrounding park, which has an odd melancholic air about it. Views from the top are quite impressive (drive up to the parking lot).

Beverly Canon Gardens PARK
(Map p132; 241 N Cañon Dr; 👪) More chill spot than park, this lovely courtyard garden connects Beverly Dr with Cañon and was built by the developers of the Montage to create more public usage of the choice property. At lunch the picnic tables beside a gushing fountain are full and the people-watching is fabulous; the park even has wi-fi.

Westwood Village Memorial Park CEMETERY
(Map p134; www.dignitymemorial.com; 1218 Glendon Ave; ⏰8am-dusk) This little cemetery packs more old-Hollywood star power per square foot than any other in town. Best of all, the staff are happy to have you here and will even help you locate your favorite six-foot-under resident. Lipstick prints usually decorate Marilyn Monroe's crypt next to one reserved for Hugh Hefner.

Activities

Yoga West WELLNESS
(www.yogawestla.com; 1535 S Robertson Blvd; classes $17; ⏰9am-9pm Mon & Thu, to 9:30pm Tue & Wed, 7am-8:30pm Fri, 8:30am-2pm Sat, 10am-6:30pm Sun) Yogi Bhajan began teaching Kundalini yoga in a dusty antique shop on Robertson. Eventually, he found a permanent location and Yoga West was born. One of his first students, Guru Singh – part of a community of American Sikhs which originated right here – teaches two to three classes most weeks, and there's no better teacher in all of LA.

Beverly Hills Trolley TOUR

(Map p132; cnr Rodeo Dr & Dayton Way; adult/under 12yr $5/1; ⏲11am-4pm Tue-Sun Jul, Aug & Dec, Sat & Sun Jan-Jun, Sep-Nov) A 40-minute, narrated spin around Beverly Hills aboard an open-air trolley.

Sleeping

Beverly Terrace Hotel HOTEL $$

(Map p132; ☎310-274-8141; www.hotelbeverlyterrace.com; 469 N Doheny Dr; r from $199; P 🛜 ≋) This older, but high-value, Euro-style property dances on the border with West Hollywood and puts you close to the Santa Monica Blvd fun zone. Rooms aren't huge but are decorated in mid-century style with soothing greens, crisp blues and bright reds. The rooftop sundeck is blessed with beautiful views of the Hollywood Hills. Parking is $10.

Hilgard House Hotel HOTEL $$

(Map p134; ☎310-208-3945; www.hilgardhouse.com; 927 Hilgard Ave, Westwood; r $164-209; P 🛜) This 55-room, Euro-style hotel near UCLA is an unflashy, unpretentious abode. Rooms are smallish but the high ceilings make them feel airy, and the marble entryways and antiques offer a classy kiss. Ask for the UCLA rate ($164).

★**Mr C** HOTEL $$$

(Map p132; ☎877-334-5623; www.mrchotels.com; 1224 Beverwil Dr; r from $320) This long-standing tower hotel has been redesigned by the Cipprioni brothers, who have been so involved in their passion project, they've designed everything down to the furniture in the rooms. Rooms on even floors offer white decor, odd floors are brown, and both varieties include marble baths, leather sofas and lounges. North-facing rooms have spectacular views.

Hotel Bel-Air HOTEL $$$

(Map p134; ☎310-472-1211; www.hotelbelair.com; 701 N Stone Canyon Rd, Bel Air; r from $495; P @ 🛜 ≋) One of LA's iconic properties, this Bel Air hideaway favored by royalty – Hollywood and otherwise – is a classy Spanish Colonial estate where white swans preen in romantic gardens and pink stucco rooms come with private entrances and French furnishings. If you can't afford to stay, do have a drink in the dark, leathery bar.

Avalon Hotel HOTEL $$$

(Map p132; ☎800-670-6183, 310-277-5221; www.viceroyhotelgroup.com/avalon; 9400 W Olympic Blvd; r from $200; ❄ @ 🛜 ≋ 🐾) Mid-century modern gets a 21st-century spin at this fashion-crowd fave, which was Marilyn Monroe's old pad in its days as an apartment building. Funky retro rooms are all unique, but most have arced walls, marble slab desks and night stands, and fun art and sculpture. There's also a sexy hourglass-shaped pool. Call it affordable glamour.

Crescent HOTEL $$$

(Map p132; ☎310-247-0505; www.crescentbh.com; 403 N Crescent Dr; r from $217; P @ 🛜) The buzzy fireside lounge out front attracts a crowd from time to time, and though the rooms are more minimalist than fancy, they do feel good. Single rooms are a tight squeeze, but queen rooms are spacious and good value. They have jazz in the lounge every Thursday night.

Hotel Palomar HOTEL $$$

(Map p134; ☎310-475-8711; www.hotelpalomar-lawestwood.com; 10740 Wilshire Blvd; r from $250; P 🛜 ≋ 🐾) 🍃 Hip and eco-conscious (they compost, recycle and use nontoxic cleaners exclusively), such earnest leanings have no bearing on the stylish rooms with faux-snakeskin dressers, floating day beds and 42in plasma TVs. Pets are welcome. The entire 16th floor is hypoallergenic. South-facing nests have views of the Mormon Temple and beyond.

W HOTEL $$$

(Map p134; ☎310-208-8765; www.wlosangeles.com; 930 Hilgard Ave; r $339-1348; P @ 🛜) Like all Ws, public spaces are infused with ambient and modern rock music, and most rooms are suites and blessed with mod furnishings. Their smooth poolside cabanas are the Westside spot for sun-drenched weekend brunches and midweek power lunches.

Beverly Wilshire HOTEL $$$

(Map p132; ☎310-275-5200; www.fourseasons.com/beverlywilshire; 9500 Wilshire Blvd; r $515-640, ste $780-1330; ❄ @ 🛜 ≋) Now part of Four Seasons, the Beverly Wilshire has corked Rodeo Dr since 1928. The rooms in both the original Italian renaissance wing and in the newer addition have been updated. And yes, this is the very hotel from which Julia Roberts first stumbled then strutted in *Pretty Woman,* where Eddie Murphy sourced bananas for the tailpipe in *Beverly Hills Cop,* and where Warren Beatty kept a suite for 10 years.

Beverly Hills Hotel LUXURY HOTEL $$$

(310-276-2251; www.beverlyhillshotel.com; 9641 Sunset Blvd; r from $395;) If the powdery pink walls of this belle hotel could talk, the tales would make you laugh, blush, cry and cringe. Staying here means dwelling in the utmost, old-school luxury.

Montage HOTEL $$$

(Map p132; 310-860-7800; www.montage-beverlyhills.com; 225 N Cañon Dr; r from $515, ste from $803;) New-build Italian renaissance style is yours at the Montage, featuring spacious and elegant rooms with marble foyer, leather martini shakers, sofas and mountain views from the upper reaches. The lobby sprawls with plenty of nooks to relax into, and there's a rooftop pool. Of course, the real attraction is Thomas Keller's new restaurant, Bouchon (p141), across the plaza.

Eating

Native Foods VEGAN $

(Map p134; 310-209-1055; www.nativefoods.com; 1114 Gayley Ave, Westwood; dishes $8-10; 11am-10pm;) Pizzas, burgers, sandwiches, salads – the menu reads like those at your typical diner with one notable difference: no animal products will ever find their way into this vegan haven. Don't come for ambience but do try the Classic Deli Ruben and Native Chili.

Papa Jakes SANDWICHES $

(Map p132; www.papajakes.com; Santa Monica Blvd; mains $6-10; 11am-4pm Mon-Sat) This greasy hole-in-the-wall is a longtime Beverly Hills classic, famous for its Philly-cheese steaks made with thinly sliced rib eye or, if you must, chicken breast. Papa Jakes promises 'the best 12-inches you'll ever put in your mouth.' Um, yeah.

Shamshiri PERSIAN $$

(www.shamshiri.com; 1712 Westwood Blvd, Westwood; appetizers $4-16, mains $13-22; 11:30am-10pm Mon-Thu, to 11pm Fri & Sat, noon-10pm Sun;) One of a string of Persian kitchens, these guys bake their own pita which they use to wrap chicken, beef and lamb shawarma, kebabs and falafel served with a green, *shirazi* or tabbouleh salad. They also do broiled lamb and seafood platters, and vegan stews. Come for one of their great-value lunch specials ($8 to $10).

Cabbage Patch CAFE $$

(Map p132; www.cabbagepatchla.com; 214 S Beverly Dr; mains $9-16; 11am-9pm Mon-Fri, to 4pm Sat) Affordable, fresh and tasty salads, sandwiches and sides are served at this South Beverly storefront. They make custom salads from a kale or wild arugula base, and plate proteins such as soy-marinated salmon or grass-fed steak.

Sayuri Sushi SUSHI $$

(Map p132; 310-246-9031; 456 N Bedford Dr; dishes $5-22; 11:30am-9pm Mon-Sat) This intimate sushi bar bustles at lunch. They do a wonderful snapper sushi and a tasty toro hand roll for just $9. We also liked the *miu roll:* albacore sashimi layered over a spicy tuna roll with jalapeño crispy onion and a garlic *ponzu.*

Nate 'n Al DELI $$

(Map p132; 310-274-0101; www.natenal.com; 414 N Beverly Dr; dishes $6.50-13; 7am-9pm;) Dapper seniors, chatty girlfriends, busy execs and even Larry King have kept this New York–style nosh spot busy since 1945. The huge menu brims with corned beef, lox and other old-school favorites, but we're partial to the pastrami, made fresh on-site.

Westside Tavern GASTROPUB $$

(www.westsidetavernla.com; 10850 W Pico Blvd, Westwood; mains $14-24; 11:30am-10pm Sun-Thu, to 11pm Fri & Sat;) Set in the ground floor of the Westside Pavilion shopping mall, this gastropub sports clean lines and gets creative in the kitchen. Think: pulled pork and leek flatbreads, a tri-tip sandwich piled with arugula and brushed with mustard-horseradish sauce. The most popular dish, the one folks order to go, after they've eaten? Hummus.

Coral Tree Cafe CAFE $$

(www.coraltreecafe.com; 11645 San Vicente Blvd, Brentwood; salads, sandwiches & pasta $10-15; 7am-11pm;) Probably the most popular lunch spot in Brentwood, where spinach salads are served in deep bowls and grilled portobello burgers are devoured in the open, wood-floor interior or on the shady patio. They pour organic coffee and teas, and mix mimosas ($6).

Kate Mantilini AMERICAN $$

(Map p132; www.katemantilinirestaurant.com; 9101 Wilshire Blvd; mains $9-29; 8am-10pm Mon, to

FAMOUS ALUMNI

They may not be like the rest of us, but even celebs once studied math and science. Our list shows you who went where.

Beverly Hills High School (Map p132; 241 S Moreno Dr, Beverly Hills) Nicolas Cage, Jamie Lee Curtis, Angelina Jolie, Lenny Kravitz, Rob Reiner, David Schwimmer and Alicia Silverstone.

Buckley School (3900 Stansbury Ave, Sherman Oaks) This illustrious private school nurtured Laura Dern, Paris Hilton, Alyssa Milano, Matthew Perry and Nicole Richie.

Fairfax High (Map p110; 7850 Melrose Ave, Mid-City) Home to the cool Melrose Trading Post (p125) flea market at the weekend, this school taught algebra to David Arquette, Flea, Anthony Kiedis and all of the original Red Hot Chili Peppers, James Elroy, Al Franken, Demi Moore and Slash.

Hollywood High School (Map p88; 1521 N Highland Ave, Hollywood) Brandy, Carol Burnett, Laurence Fishburne, Judy Garland and Lana Turner are alumni depicted in the big mural on Highland Ave, but there are literally hundreds more, including James Garner and Sharon Tate.

Immaculate Heart High School (Map p62; 5515 Franklin Ave, Hollywood) No boys are allowed at this Catholic school once attended by Tyra Banks, Natalie Cole and Mary Tyler Moore.

John Marshall High School (Map p102; www.johnmarshallhs.org; 3939 Tracy St) Leonardo DiCaprio's alma mater doubled as Sunnydale High in the 1992 big-screen version of *Buffy the Vampire Slayer*.

Notre Dame High School (13645 Riverside Dr, Sherman Oaks) Rachel Bilson, Kirsten Dunst and Dave Navarro.

Polytechnic High (1600 Atlantic Ave, Long Beach) Cameron Diaz, Snoop Dogg, Marilyn Horne and Spike Lee.

Santa Monica College (Map p62; 1900 Pico Blvd, Santa Monica) Arnold Schwarzenegger studied English, and Dustin Hoffman honed his acting chops at this community college that also counts Buzz Aldrin, James Dean and Hillary Swank as alumni.

Santa Monica High School (601 Pico Blvd, Santa Monica) Robert Downey Jr, Rob Lowe, Sean Penn, Emilio Estevez and Charlie Sheen undoubtedly caused trouble at this public school near the beach.

University High School (11800 Texas Ave, near Santa Monica) Marilyn Monroe dropped out; Jeff Bridges, James Brolin, Bridget Fonda, Nancy Sinatra and Elizabeth Taylor graduated.

University of California, Los Angeles (UCLA; 405 Hilgard Ave, Westwood) Carol Burnett, James Dean, Francis Ford Coppola, Heather Locklear, Jim Morrison, Tim Robbins, Kareem Abdul Jabbar, Bill Walton and Jackie Robinson.

University of Southern California (USC; 3535 S Figueroa St, Downtown) Neil Armstrong, Frank Gehry, Ron Howard, George Lucas, Tom Selleck, OJ Simpson, John Wayne and Robert Zemeckis.

10:30pm Tue-Thu, to 11:30pm Fri, 11am-11:30pm Sat, 10am-10pm Sun; 👪) Restaurants that vacillate from deli to pasta to roast chicken and seafood rarely get anything right. This classic LA spot, a stylish glass box named for the world's first female boxing promoter, is the exception. It bustles best at lunch and during happy hour, but breakfast rocks too and the kitchen stays open late.

Picca PERUVIAN **$$$**
(Map p132; ☎310-277-0133; www.piccaperu.com; 9575 W Pico Blvd; dishes $8-28; ⏲6-11pm) Start with a crispy chicken tail, move onto a skirt steak topped with a fried egg and served with fried bananas and chickpeas, then finish with a vanilla-bean pisco flan. Or better yet, dive deep and wide into their spectacular raw bar – filled with a variety of ceviche, sashimi and other succulent seafood concoctions.

Hakkasan CHINESE FUSION $$$

(Map p132; ☎310-888-8661; www.hakkasan.com; 233 N Beverly Dr; mains $26-68; ⏰noon-2:30pm & 5-11pm Mon-Thu, to midnight Fri & Sat) Beverly Hills' fancy new Chinese spot in the ground floor of the MGM building serves wok-fried tenderloin and lobster, clay-pot chicken, truffle-braised noodles, and jasmine tea-smoked short rib. It's pricey but an experience.

The decor, from the marble hostess bar to the leather booths paired off by labyrinthine Chinese screens, to the glowing bar, exudes swanky sexy.

Bedford & Burns CONTINENTAL $$$

(Map p132; ☎310-273-8585; www.bedfordandburns.com; 369 N Bedford Dr; mains $15-28; ⏰11am-10:30pm Mon-Sat) A sumptuous bistro with classic decor, booths on the street-side patio, and a seasonal menu that includes oysters, pan-roasted trout, steak frites, an egg-white frittata with goat cheese, and wood-roasted chicken. Popular at lunch, they have good happy-hour deals too.

Bouchon FRENCH $$$

(Map p132; ☎310-279-9910; www.bouchonbistro.com; 235 N Cañon Dr; mains $17-59; ⏰11:30am-9pm Mon, to 10:30pm Tue-Fri, 11am-10:30pm Sat, to 9pm Sun; P) Quiche and salad, oysters on the half-shell, mussels steamed open in white-wine sauce, steak frites, and roast leg of lamb with artichoke – Thomas Keller's Bouchon empire brings you classic French bistro cuisine in classy, but not stuffy, environs. You can taste the goods at a discount at Bar Bouchon downstairs.

Ivy CALIFORNIAN $$$

(Map p132; ☎310-274-8303; www.theivyrestaurants.com; 113 N Robertson Blvd; mains $22-97; ⏰8am-11pm) With a long history of celebrity power lunches, this is where Southern comfort food (such as fried chicken and crab cakes) has been elevated to haute cuisine. Service is refined and impeccable, and paparazzi etiquette (among one another and their prey) is a fluid, dynamic beast.

Napa Valley Grille CALIFORNIAN $$$

(Map p134; ☎310-824-3322; www.napavalleygrille.com; 1100 Glendon Ave, Westwood; dishes $7-32; ⏰11:30am-3pm Mon-Fri, 5:30-9:30pm Mon-Thu, 5-11pm Fri & Sat, 5-9pm Sun; P 👪) Preppy, but not stuffy, this is the spot for good, honest California cuisine: grilled Sonoma lamb, Catalina Island swordfish, and pan-roasted diver scallops. The grilled salmon club on sourdough is also a great choice. Pair your meal with a glass of wine from the all-Californian wine list.

Grill on the Alley CONTINENTAL $$$

(Map p132; ☎310-276-0615; www.thegrill.com; 9560 Dayton Way; mains $16-39; ⏰11:30am-9pm Mon, to 10pm Tue-Thu, to 10:30pm Fri & Sat, 5-9pm Sun) A back-alley marble, oak and leather steak house where Hollywood heavyweights – who flock here from nearby agencies – slug it out over lunch. They're known for their steaks but the grilled ahi, salmon and whitefish are all divine, and they do a terrific Joe's special if you'd rather have brunch.

Farmshop MODERN AMERICAN $$$

(☎310-566-2400; www.farmshopca.com; 225 26th St; mains $15-30; ⏰7:30-11am, 11:30am-2:30pm & 5:30-9:30pm Mon-Fri, 8am-2pm & 5:30-9:30pm Sat, to 9pm Sun) This farm-to-table kitchen with attached market cafe (where you can grab something tasty for the Getty) is in the Brentwood Country Mart. They cure their own pastrami, sear scallops, do a tasty dungeness-crab-cake sandwich, but are best known for their special fried-chicken dinners on Sunday nights.

🍷 Drinking & Nightlife

★Nic's Beverly Hills BAR

(Map p132; ☎310-550-5707; www.nicsbeverlyhills.com; 453 N Cañon Dr; ⏰4pm-midnight Mon-Wed, to 2am Thu-Sat) Martinis for every palate lure the cocktail crowd to upscale, but fun-loving, Nic's, the only decent watering hole in all of Beverly Hills, where the libations and crowd range from the colorful and sassy to the no-frills and classy.

Polo Lounge LOUNGE

(www.beverlyhillshotel.com; 9641 Sunset Blvd; ⏰7am-1:30am) With its mix of tennis whites, business suits and chichi dresses, this swanky, wood-paneled watering hole has the feel of a Hollywood country club. From Isaac Mizrahi to George Hamilton to David Arquette, you never know who you'll see murmuring in the perpetually reserved, dark booths. It's part of the Beverly Hills Hotel.

Nespresso CAFE

(Map p132; www.nespresso-us.com; 320 N Beverly Dr; ⏰9am-7pm) A monument to postmodern coffee, disposable plastic containers and the overseas-only George Clooney advertising model. You can buy the fancy machines here, drink fancy coffee and eat fancy grilled cheese (with truffles no less) among the fancy people and/or wannabes.

When we came through, the salesman told a story about how when he visited the West Bank the only ad he saw was a giant picture of Clooney sipping a Nespresso. This happened in Jericho. Yet here, in the gleaming American flagship of a brand he helped re-invent, in a city in which he lives, there are no shots of Clooney.

Oh, and if you pretend you might buy a machine they'll make you a cup for free.

☆ Entertainment

UCLA Basketball SPECTATOR SPORTS

(www.uclabruins.com; tickets $15-150; ⏲ Nov-Feb) In all of American sports, it would be hard to find a more dominant team than the UCLA squads under the late, great John Wooden. A mastermind of team basketball, the coach known as 'the wizard of Westwood' cultivated the genius of Kareem Abdul Jabbar (then Lew Alcindor) and Bill Walton.

He led his teams to 10 national titles in 12 years (including seven straight), and once owned an 88-game winning streak. The Bruins, who play on campus in the Pauley Pavilion, where Wooden has a statue, remain a competitive bunch feeding studs such as Oklahoma City's Russell Westbrook and Minnesota's Kevin Love into the NBA.

Royce Hall PERFORMING ARTS

(Map p134; www.uclalive.org; UCLA; tickets from $22) An exceptional theater housed in UCLA's historic heart. The brick building reeks of academia, but **UCLA Live** have been known to bring in authors such as David Sedaris and Anthony Bourdain for lively readings, as well as spectacular musicians such as piano man Chick Corea, and the Philip Glass ensemble.

Geffen Playhouse THEATER

(Map p134; ☎ 310-208-5454; www.geffenplayhouse.com; 10886 Le Conte Ave, Westwood; tickets $37-67) David Geffen forked over $17 million to get his Mediterranean-style playhouse back into shape. The 2014 season included a run of *Ruth Draper's Monologues,* performed and directed by Annette Bening.

Nuart Theatre CINEMA

(www.landmarktheaters.com; 11272 Santa Monica Blvd, Westwood; adult/senior & child $11/9) This dank, but still hip art and revival house presents the best in offbeat and cult flicks, including a highly interactive screening of *The Rocky Horror Picture Show* supported by an outrageous live cast at midnight on Saturdays. Bring glow sticks and toilet paper.

Landmark Theatres CINEMA

(www.landmarktheatres.com; 10850 W Pico Blvd, Westwood; adult/child & senior $13.50/10.50) 'Art house' and blockbuster 'multiplex' in the same breath? That's the cocktail at the sleek Landmark with its dozen deluxe, stadium-style screening rooms, making this the go-to cinema for Westsiders. The supremely comfortable leather chairs, gourmet snack menu, wine bar and free parking don't hurt either.

Shopping

While downtown Beverly Hills and Rodeo Dr still get most of the shopping hype, the best boutiques are hidden in plain sight on **Robertson** (Map p132; btwn Beverly Blvd & 3rd St), between Beverly Blvd and Burton Way.

You're guaranteed superior quality, with corresponding price tags, at any of the jewelry shops on Rodeo Dr in Beverly Hills. For those of us who failed to triple our net worth during that Vegas side trip, even a pair of tiny diamond stud earrings may remain elusive at $4000. But, hey, there's no cost for oohing and aahing at the trio of treasure chests of **Tiffany** (Map p132; www.tiffany.com; 210 N Rodeo Dr), **Cartier** (Map p132; www.cartier.us; 370 N Rodeo Dr) and **Harry Winston** (Map p132; ☎ 310-271-8554; www.harrywinston.com; 310 N Rodeo Dr).

K Soho KOREAN GOODS

(Map p132; www.ksohobh.com; 425 N Beverly Dr; ⏲ 11am-6pm Mon-Sat, 11am-5pm Sun) A small but unique department store featuring the top brands from Korea including a high-end handbag line depicting anime characters, and Hormiga bags, manufactured by the same folks using the same leather as Hermes. And they have useful gadgets such as high-end nail clippers, LED lights for your bike, trekking poles, mini laptop desks and more.

Marimekko FASHION, TEXTILES

(Map p132; ☎ 310-299-2528; www.marimekko.com; 370 N Cañon Dr; ⏲ 10am-6pm Mon-Sat, noon-5pm Sun) A Finnish brand, new to the US, has set up shop in Beverly Hills. Here, you can make your own beanbag chairs from a collection of coated cottons dyed with fun love. They sell terrific backpacks and shoulder bags, sheets and towels, offer a wonderful kids' selection, and a quirky, cute line of dresses.

Barneys New York DEPARTMENT STORE
(Map p132; ☎310-276-4400; www.barneys.com; 9570 Wilshire Blvd; ⏲10am-7pm Mon-Wed, Fri & Sat, to 8pm Thu, noon-6pm Sun) Four floors of straight-up chic. Prices are steep, so keep an eye out for one of its twice-annual warehouse sales for some cheap threads. There's a deli on the top floor that's worth trying.

Scoop FASHION
(Map p132; ☎310-362-6100; www.scoopnyc.com; 265 N Beverly Dr; ⏲10am-7pm Mon-Sat, 11am-6pm Sun) A grab bag of designer denim and limited-edition sneakers, funky belts and designer camo jackets. Their women's line is more chic than sporty, sprinkled with gorgeous dresses, handbags and heels. It's set in the ground floor of the fabulous new MGM building.

Brentwood Country Mart BOUTIQUES
(www.brentwoodcountrymart.com; 225 26th St; ⏲7am-10pm) A long-running, barn-red complex filled with high-end boutiques such as **Space.nk Apothecary**, **James Perse**, **Diesel Bookstore**, and some tasty eats too.

Guy Hepner Gallery ARTWORK
(Map p132; www.guyhepner.com; 300 N Robertson Blvd) Fans of high-fashion photography, pop and street art will love the eye-popping, glittering canvasses and photography on display at this small, sleek and groovy gallery. There was a distinct street aesthetic happening here when we popped in.

Wall Street Gallery ARTWORK
(Map p132; ☎424-279-9404; www.wall-streetgallery.com; 302 N Robertson Blvd; ⏲noon-6pm & by appointment) This new gallery is the domain of Mr Brainwash of *Exit Through the Gift Shop* fame. Whatever you may think of Banksy, Mr Brainwash or the film, it's worth stopping in to take a look for yourself.

Jigsaw FASHION
(Map p132; ☎310-271-7988; www.jigsaw-london.com; 314 N Beverly Dr; ⏲10am-6pm Mon-Sat, from 11am Sun) One of the least stuffy stores on this strip of Beverly Dr comes from London. A single label boutique, one of just four in the US, it defines smart casual. Jigsaw goods include pastel-dyed denim, cute sundresses and hats, blouses and beaded jewelry. It's not crazy pricey either.

Kitson FASHION
(Map p132; ☎310-859-2652; www.shopkitson.com; 115 S Robertson Blvd; ⏲10am-7:30pm Mon-Sat, 11am-7pm Sun) Paris and her crew made it famous, and high-energy tunes keep the girls fast-flipping through up-to-the-second hoodies, purses, shoes and jeans. Guys should check the goods at **Kitson Men** (Map p132; 146 N Robertson Blvd).

American Tea Room DRINKS
(Map p132; www.americantearoom.com; 401 N Cañon Dr) If you consider fine tea one of life's great pleasures, you'll find kindred spirits at this exquisite boutique. Friendly staff will gladly help you find a new favorite from among the 250 varieties of quality teas from the Amazon to north China, each with its own distinctive character.

Madison FASHION
(Map p132; ☎310-275-1930; www.madisonlosangeles.com; 8745 W 3rd St; ⏲11am-7pm) An essential shopping destination for LA women who move seamlessly from casual days to glitzy nights. They stock denim from Current/Elliott and Rag and Bone, dresses by ALC and Alexander Wang, and handbags and heels by Valentino.

Chanel FASHION
(Map p132; ☎310-278-5505; www.chanel.com; 125 N Robertson Blvd; ⏲11am-7pm Mon-Sat, noon-5pm Sun) Upscale bags and bathing suits, sun hats and wallets, pearls and leather gloves, suit jackets and dresses, all of which would make Audrey Hepburn blush. Even after all these years, Chanel remains the most popular label on most blocks. This one included.

Curve FASHION
(Map p132; ☎310-360-8008; www.shopcurve.com; 154 N Robertson Blvd; ⏲11am-7pm Mon-Sat, noon-6pm Sun) A funky fashion boutique that isn't as stiff as some of the other players on Robertson. They offer Acne denim, Rona Pfeiffer jewelry, and a range of funky trenches, spiked heels, sexy minis, leather vests, baby doll dresses and some wonderful leather high tops from Maison Martin Margiela.

Iijin FASHION
(Map p132; ☎310-888-8015; www.iijin.com; 116 N Roberston Blvd; ⏲11am-7pm Mon-Sat, to 6pm Sun) An upscale, quirky and colorful shop full of sweats and T-shirts blessed with anime characters, as well as sparkly and patterned trainers, high tops and boots. They have several stores in Hong Kong, where the brand originated, but this is the first in the US.

MALIBU & PACIFIC PALISADES

Malibu enjoys near-mythical status thanks to its large celebrity population, and the incredible beauty of its coastal mountains, pristine coves, wide sweeps of golden sand and epic waves. Stretched out for 27 miles, there are several small commercial strips, but the heart of town is at the foot of Pepperdine, where you'll find the Malibu Country Mart and the Malibu Civic Center.

Malibu has been celebrity central since the 1930s, when money troubles forced landowner May Rindge to lease out property to her famous Hollywood buds. Clara Bow and Barbara Stanwyck were the first to stake out their turf in what would become the Malibu Colony. Privacy-seeking A-listers, including Leo, Jen Aniston and many others, are or have been residents, owning or renting houses for as much as $25,000 per month. While it's impossible to get past the gate without a personal invitation from a resident, you could always join the paparazzi on the beach – just stay below the high-tide mark. For photogenic bird's-eye views of the colony, head up the coast to **Malibu Bluffs Park**.

Despite its wealth and star quotient, the best way to appreciate Malibu is through its natural assets, so grab your sunscreen and a towel and head to the beach. Westward Beach, Zuma and El Matador are especially nice and teem with tight bods on summer weekends. You may strike gold and find free parking on the Pacific Coast Hwy (check signs for restrictions), but otherwise lots charge between $6 and $10. On summer weekends they often fill up by midday.

During the cooler months, hitting the trails of the Santa Monica Mountains National Recreation Area, including Malibu Creek, Sycamore Canyon and La Jolla Canyon State Parks, is a ticket to sanity for many locals.

East of Malibu, Pacific Palisades, founded by Methodists in the 1920s, is another upscale neighborhood with a small-town feel and high celebrity quotient, as well as the spectacular Getty Villa. Strolling along Sunset Blvd and its side streets, you may spot local residents such as Tom Hanks or Dustin Hoffman. Though the architecture is dated (and not in a good way), and retail and dining options are limited, Rick Caruso, one of the developers behind The Grove in mid-city, is hoping to change that. He and his partners have acquired most of the real estate in the Palisades commercial corridor. It may take some time, but big changes are coming.

Sights

El Matador State Beach BEACH

(32215 Pacific Coast Hwy; parking $8; P) Arguably Malibu's most stunning beach, where you park on the bluffs and stroll down a trail to sandstone rock towers that rise from emerald coves. Topless sunbathers meander through the tides, and dolphins breech the surface beyond the waves. It's been impacted by coastal erosion, but you can still find a sliver of dry sand tucked against the bluffs.

Zuma & Westward Beach BEACH

Zuma is easy to find, and thanks to the wide sweep of blonde sand that has been attracting valley kids to the shore since the 1970s, it gets busy on weekends and summer afternoons. But we prefer Westward Beach. That same wide stretch of sand winds south of Zuma and wraps halfway around hulking Point Dume.

Here the surf thunders and rip currents can be strong, but the water is crystal clear, and sea lions, seals and dolphins are frequent visitors. You can even glimpse

MALIBU BEACHES FOR ALL

Malibu's locals, famous for their love of privacy, don't want you to know this, but you're actually free to be on any beach as long as you stay below the high-tide line. That means you can walk, swim and beach-comb on Carbon Beach, Broad Beach, Little Dume and wherever the famous like to frolic. You may get nasty looks from security guards, but there's nothing they can legally do to stop you from being there. Driving along Pacific Coast Hwy, keep an eye out for the brown Coastal Access signs. Locals have been known to take them down and put up 'Private Beach' or 'No Trespassing' signs; don't be deterred. For the full scoop and 'secret' access points, download the handy map and guide from www.laurbanrangers.org/site/malibu or get the free **Our Malibu Beaches** app for your smart phone, developed by a local environmental writer and beachcombing populist, Jenny Price

whales in the winter. If you get here early you should find free parking on Westward Rd. Point Dume State Beach begins once you pass through the parking gate south of the Sunset restaurant. Keep walking down the beach and navigate a short trail to semi-private Pirate's Cove.

Surfrider Beach BEACH
(26000 Pacific Coast Hwy; P) Surf punks descend on this cove that shapes some of the best waves in Southern California. There are several breaks here: the first is well formed for beginners and long boarders, the second and third breaks demand short boards and advanced-level skills. Whichever way you ride, know your etiquette before paddling out.

★Getty Villa MUSEUM
(☎310-430-7300; www.getty.edu; 17985 Pacific Coast Hwy; ⏰10am-5pm Wed-Mon; P) FREE Although self-described as the Getty Villa Malibu, this famous museum in a replica 1st-century Roman villa is actually in Pacific Palisades. It's a stunning 64-acre showcase for exquisite Greek, Roman and Etruscan antiquities amassed by oil tycoon J Paul Getty.

When it reopened in 2006 after a seven-year renovation, the institution immediately found egg on its face when allegations of illegally obtained treasures surfaced. Although dozens of items have since been returned to Italy, there's plenty left. You'll see wine goblets, beads and pendants culled from Partha tombs, and cut, blown and colored glass from the 1st century. The geometric configurations in the **Hall of Colored Marble** will bend your brain. Then there's the **Temple of Herakles**, and who doesn't love an action hero? The upper balcony has the best view of the lovely courtyard garden surrounding a reflecting pool.

Admission is theoretically free, and available by timed ticket, which can be reserved online, but parking costs $15, and there are no drop-offs or walk-ins allowed unless you arrive by public bus and ask the driver to hole-punch your villa ticket.

Self-Realization Fellowship Lake Shrine GARDENS
(www.lakeshrine.org; 17190 Sunset Blvd; ⏰9am-4:30pm Tue-Sat, 12:30-4:30pm Sun; P) FREE No matter your religious persuasion, any negative vibes seem to disappear while strolling through these uplifting meditation gardens. Paths meander around a spring-fed, artificial lake and past clumps of flowers and swaying palms to the **Windmill Chapel** where George Harrison's memorial was held, and to a shrine containing some of the ashes of Mahatma Gandhi.

Sprinkled throughout are quotes from Hindu and Christian saints. The gold-lotus peaked sanctuary situated on the hillside is where meditation services and lectures are held by resident monks and nuns on Thursday evenings at 8pm and Sunday mornings at 9am and 11am, and are open to the public. The fellowship was founded in 1925 by charismatic yogi Paramahansa Yogananda, one of the first yogis to come to the West from India. His teachings blend traditions and stories from the five major religions.

Malibu Pier LANDMARK
(www.malibupiersportfishing.com) The pier marks the beginning of Malibu's commercial heart. It's open for strolling and license-free fishing and delivers fine views of surfers riding waves off Surfrider Beach. The restaurant at the end caters to tourists. You can rent a rod and reel ($14 for two hours), and buy bait ($5) here too.

Adamson House & Malibu Lagoon Museum LANDMARK
(☎310-456-8432; www.adamsonhouse.org; 23200 Pacific Coast Hwy; adult/child $7/2; ⏰11am-3pm Wed-Sat; P) Up on a bluff overlooking Surfrider Beach is this gorgeous Spanish-style villa, which used to belong to the Rindge family and is awash in locally made, hand-painted tiles. Check out the 'Persian rug' in the entryway and the tiled dog bath outside.

To learn more about Malibu's arc of history (Chumash to glamourtown) pop into the adjacent Malibu Lagoon Museum. The last tour leaves at 2pm. From here it's a pleasant stroll through the marsh to Surfrider Beach.

Malibu Hindu Temple TEMPLE
(www.malibuhindutemple.org; 1600 Las Virgenes Canyon Rd; ⏰9am-noon & 5-8pm Mon-Fri, to 7pm Nov-Mar, 8am-7pm Sat & Sun; P) FREE This house (or, more precisely, these houses) of Hindu gods sneaks up on you as you drive up Malibu Canyon, but you won't miss the ivory towers located 6.5 miles north of Pepperdine. Temple grounds are shaped and dappled like a big blissful sandcastle and include a series of shrines to various deities.

Visitors are welcome any time, but it's best to visit on a Hindu holiday, when colorfully robed flocks descend with fruit, flowers and smoldering incense in hand. Kick your shoes off at the entrance.

Malibu

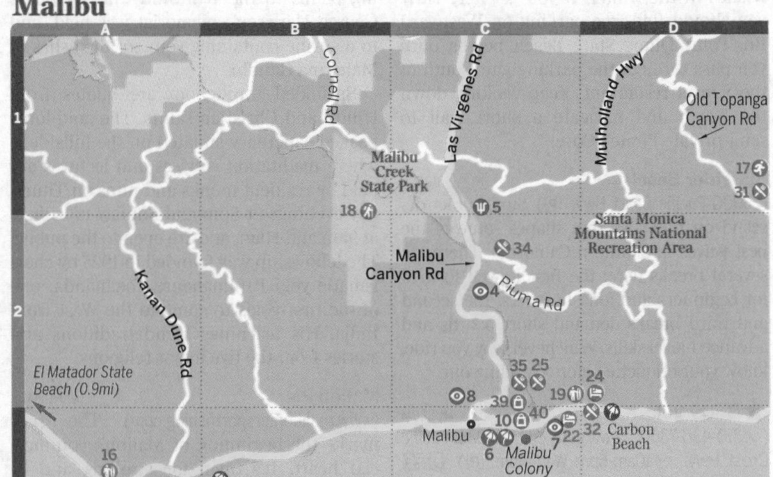

Malibu

Top Sights
1 Getty Villa....E2

Sights
Adamson House & Malibu Lagoon Museum....(see 7)
2 Eames House & Studio....F3
Frederick R Weisman Museum of Art....(see 8)
3 Inspiration Point....F2
4 Malibu Canyon....C2
5 Malibu Hindu Temple....C1
6 Malibu Lagoon State Beach....C3
7 Malibu Pier....C3
8 Pepperdine University....C2
9 Self-Realization Fellowship Lake Shrine....E2
10 Surfrider Beach....C3
11 Topanga Canyon....E2
12 Villa Aurora....E2
Will Rogers Ranch House....(see 13)
13 Will Rogers State Historic Park....F2
14 Zuma & Westward Beach....A3

Activities, Courses & Tours
15 Annenberg Community Beach House....F3
16 Clout....A3
17 Los Angeles Horseback Riding....D1
18 Malibu Creek State Park....B1
19 Malibu Surf Shack....C2
20 Topanga Canyon State Park....E1

Sleeping
21 Channel Road Inn B&B....F3
22 Malibu Beach Inn....C3
23 Malibu Country Inn....A3
24 Malibu Motel....D2

Eating
25 Café Habana....C2
26 Canyon Bistro....E1
27 Duck Dive....A3
28 Farmshop....F2
29 Father's Office....F3
30 Fresh....E1
31 Inn of the Seventh Ray....D1
John's Garden....(see 40)
Kreation....(see 29)

Malibu Lagoon State Beach BEACH
(www.parks.ca.gov; P) This salty marsh is where Malibu Creek meets the ocean, attracting migratory birds and their human admirers. Which is why it was undergoing a major native species restoration at research time. About 50,000 individual plants of roughly a dozen native marsh species have

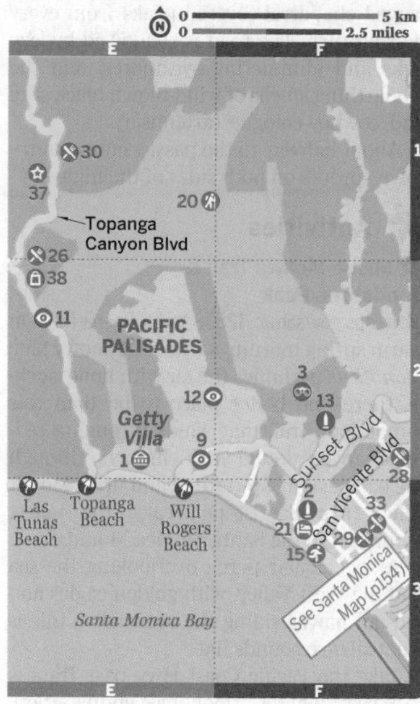

32 Nobu Malibu D3
33 R&D Kitchen F3
34 Saddle Peak Lodge C2
Taverna Tony .... (see 40)
35 Tra Di Noi C2

Drinking & Nightlife
Cafecito Organico .... (see 27)
Sunlife Organics .... (see 27)
36 Sunset A3

Entertainment
Aero Theater .... (see 33)
37 Will Geer's Theatricum Botanicum E1

Shopping
Blues Jean Bar .... (see 33)
Brentwood Country Mart .... (see 28)
38 Hidden Treasures E2
39 Lumberyard C2
40 Malibu Country Mart C3
Planet Blue .... (see 33)
Ten Women .... (see 29)

been planted, temporary drip irrigation installed and weeds hand removed.

Once the restoration is complete this will be the kind of place to bring a picnic and binoculars and grab a spot in the sand or at a picnic table near Malibu Creek Bridge. However, given that this is where the creek meets the sea, water quality tends to be low. Swimmers and surfers should push further north.

Pepperdine University UNIVERSITY
(www.pepperdine.edu; 24255 Pacific Coast Hwy; P) FREE Self-assuredly holding court atop a grassy slope where deer graze at sundown, this private institution has views of the Pacific and the mountains, and is one of California's most beautiful campuses.

Ken Starr, the independent investigator who revealed to the world where Bill Clinton put his cigars, was the dean of the law school here from 2004 to 2010. Art fans should check out the latest show at the university's **Frederick R Weisman Museum of Art** (www.pepperdine.edu/arts/museum; 11am-5pm Tue-Sun; P) FREE, which rotates edgy works created by contemporary American artists.

Will Rogers State Historic Park MONUMENT, PARK
(www.parks.ca.gov; 1501 Will Rogers State Park Rd; 8am-sunset, ranch house tours 11am, 1pm & 2pm Thu & Fri, hourly 10am-4pm Sat & Sun; P) This park sprawls across ranch land once owned by Will Rogers (1875–1935), an Oklahoma-born cowboy turned humorist, radio-show host and movie star (in the early 1930s he was the highest-paid actor in Hollywood). In the late '20s he traded his Beverly Hills manse for a 31-room **ranch house** and lived here until his tragic 1935 death by plane crash.

Free guided tours allow you to nose around the western art, and Native American rugs and baskets, and marvel at the porch swing right in the living room. Parking costs $12.

The park's chaparral-cloaked hills, where Rogers used to ride his horses, are laced with trails and offer an easy escape from the LA hubbub. The best time for a ramble is late in the day when the setting sun delivers golden views of the mountains, city and ocean from **Inspiration Point**. They're yours after an easy-to-moderate 1.5-mile trek. Trails continue along the Backbone Trail into Topanga State Park.

A big polo fan, Will Rogers built his own field to battle such famous buddies as Spencer Tracy, Gary Cooper and Walt Disney. The **Will Rogers Polo Club** (www.willrogerspolo.org; 2pm Sat, 10am Sun late Apr–early Oct) FREE still plays in the park on what is the city's only remaining polo field.

Eames House & Studio MONUMENT

(☎310-459-9663; www.eamesfoundation.org; 203 Chautauqua Blvd; adult/child $10/free; ⊙10am-4pm Mon & Tue, Thu-Sat; P) The striking Eames House & Studio, built in 1949 by Charles and Ray Eames, resembles a Mondrian painting in 3D. It's still used by the Eames family, but with at least 48-hour advance reservations you can study the exterior, walk around the garden, which was a natural meadow preserved by the Eameses, and peek through the window into the kitchen and living room.

Visitors are allowed inside the home if they become members of the Eames Foundation.

While here also have a look at the adjacent 1949 **Entenza House**. Termite infested, torn down and rebuilt almost exactly as it was designed by Charles Eames and Eero Saarinen, it can be seen peeking elegantly behind the modern monstrosity. The best view is across the wall from the Eames House garden. Richard Neutra designed the nearby **Bailey House**, which was built from 1946 to 1948.

Villa Aurora CULTURAL BUILDING

(☎310-454-4231; www.villa-aurora.org; Paseo Miramar) FREE High in the hills above Sunset Blvd, Lion Feuchtwanger's old home, complete with a 1927 pipe organ (yes, there is an organ room), thick timber-beamed ceilings and miraculous sea views, was once a gathering place for European artists and intellectuals in exile.

Folks like Bertholt Brecht, Charles Chaplin and Thomas Mann were part of Feuchtwanger's loose network and buzz-worthy salons. It stands to reason then that it is now a German-American art and cultural center hosting visiting artists, musicians, filmmakers and writers in residence. It hosts occasional concerts, screenings and events here too. Tours are free but must be arranged in advance.

Malibu Canyon SCENIC DRIVE

(Malibu Canyon Rd) One of the most beautiful drives through the Santa Monica Mountains starts right next to Pepperdine on Malibu Canyon Rd, which cuts through Malibu Creek State Park, bisects Mulholland Hwy (beyond which it's called Las Virgenes Rd) and joins with the 101 (Ventura Fwy) near Agoura Hills.

Topanga Canyon SCENIC DRIVE

(Topanga Canyon Rd) Take this sinuous road from the sea and climb into a primordial cut deep in the Santa Monica Mountains, one that lays bare naked boulders and reveals jagged chaparral-covered peaks from every hairpin turn. The road is shadowed by lazy oaks and glimmering sycamores, and the whole thing smells of wind-blown black sage and 'cowboy cologne' (artemisia).

About halfway to the pass, a cute country town sprouts on both sides of the highway.

Activities

★Mishe Mokwa Trail & Sandstone Peak HIKING

(www.nps.gov/samo; 12896 Yerba Buena Rd) On warm spring mornings when the snowy blue *ceonothus* perfumes the air with honeysuckle, there's no better place to be than this 6-mile loop trail that winds through a red-rock canyon dotted with climbers, through the oak oasis at **Split Rock** and up to Mount Allen (aka Sandstone Peak), the tallest mountain in the Santa Monica Mountains.

A spectacular perch overlooking the sea and the West Valley, with golden eagles and red-tail hawks riding the thermals – this is what silence sounds like.

Take the Pacific Coast Hwy past Trancas to Yerba Buena Rd (look for Neptune's Net). Make a right on Yerba Buena and follow it to the ranger station at Circle X Ranch. Maps and trail conditions are available at the ranger station, but it's usually only staffed on weekends. You can also download a map online. The trailhead is actually a mile past the station on the left. Hike for 800m up the fire road (spoiler alert – this steep yet wide trail leads directly to the peak in 1.5 miles) before verging onto the Mishe Mokwa connector trail, a spur that will lead you to the gorgeous Mishe Mokwa trail. Picnic beneath the oaks, then keep humping up to the peak – you won't be able to miss it. After enjoying the view, don't double back on Mishe Mokwa; keep hiking down the fire road all the way to the parking lot. It gets crowded on weekends.

Topanga Canyon State Park HIKING

(www.parks.ca.gov; Entrada Rd; per vehicle $10; ⊙8am-dusk) There are 36 miles of trails in this scenic 11,529-acre state park that wind through grass savannah and aromatic chaparral, duck beneath shady live oaks, reach peaks, and skirt cliffs with ocean views.

Most link with the Santa Monica Mountains' contiguous **Backbone Trail**, which means you can hike north and south from here to other canyons and parks. A quick day hike from park headquarters leads 2.2 miles south to a seasonal waterfall along the **Santa Ynez Trail**. The **Eagle Rock Trail**

(2 miles) leads to a picnic area surrounded by contoured ridges.

Pt Mugu State Park HIKING, BIKING
(www.parks.ca.gov; 9000 Pacific Coast Hwy; per vehicle $12) With 70 miles of trails connecting two canyons, shaded by hulking oak and sycamores, laced with seasonal creeks and blanketed with blooming chaparral in the upper reaches, there is plenty of excellent hiking and mountain biking to be had in Pt Mugu State Park. The park has 5 miles of coastline too, but the beaches are better elsewhere.

It's set just past the Ventura County border, and a popular surf spot called **County Line**, which is not for beginners. The fire road that borders the campsites in Sycamore Canyon leads for 7.4 miles to Rancho Serra Vista, high in the hills and is popular with mountain bikers.

Malibu Creek State Park HIKING, SWIMMING
(www.parks.ca.gov; Las Virgenes/Malibu Canyon Rd) A beautiful spot in the Santa Monica Mountains, *M*A*S*H* and *Planet of the Apes* were shot here. Laced by a creek with swimming holes in the spring, this park has excellent hiking, with trails leading past craggy oaks and stately sycamores. The park is about 5 miles north of the Pacific Coast Hwy via Malibu Canyon Rd.

Malibu Surf Shack SURFING
(www.malibusurfshack.com; 22935 Pacific Coast Hwy; kayaks per day $30, surfboards per day $20-35, SUP per hr/day $45/75, wetsuits per day $10-15, surf/SUP lessons per person $125/100; ⏲10am-6pm) This barefoot surf shop rents (and sells) kayaks, SUP kits and surfboards. Surf and SUP lessons take place on Surfrider Beach, last 90 minutes and include a full day's rental of the board and wetsuit. The paddling between here and Point Dume is excellent, with frequent dolphin and sea lion sightings.

Clout SURFING
(☎310-457-1511; 29575 Pacific Coast Hwy; per day surfboards $35, wetsuits $15, bodyboards $15, fins $15, SUP $65) A surf and skate shop in the mini-mall across from Zuma beach. They rent SUP, surf and kite gear and do lessons too.

Malibu Long Boards SURFING
(☎310-467-6898; www.malibulongboards.com; 2hr surf/SUP $99/120) Private lessons in Malibu given by college-level surf and SUP instructors.

Los Angeles Horseback Riding HORSE RIDING
(☎818-591-2032; www.losangeleshorsebackriding.com; 2623 Old Topanga Canyon Rd, Topanga Canyon; 1hr ride per couple $125, sunset rides per couple $205, plus mandatory gratuity) Day and full-moon rides along the Santa Monica Mountains Backbone Trail with fabulous views all around, and beach rides on the Ventura county coast (four to five hours total travel time). Western-style only, group size limited to six people, reservations required.

Sleeping

Pt Mugu State Park Campground CAMPGROUND $
(☎800-444-7275; www.reserveamerica.com; 9000 Pacific Coast Hwy; campsite $45, day use $12; Ⓟ) You have two choices here: the creekside campsites shaded by gnarled, native sycamore and oak, or the windswept beachside spots that are visible (and well within earshot) of the highway. All are within walking distance of flush toilets and coin-operated hot showers.

Leo Carrillo State Park Campground CAMPGROUND $
(☎800-444-7275; www.reserveamerica.com; 35000 W Pacific Coast Hwy; campsite $45, day use $12; 📶) This kid-friendly campground sits on a famous 1.5-mile stretch of beach. Offshore kelp beds, caves, tide pools, plus the wilderness of the Santa Monica Mountains create a natural playground. There are 140 flat, tree-shaded sites, flush toilets and coin-operated hot showers. Bookings for summer weekends should be made months in advance.

★**Malibu Country Inn** INN $$
(☎310-457-9622; www.malibucountryinn.com; 6506 Westward Beach Rd; r $160-275; Ⓟ📶) Perched above the highway and overlooking Westward Beach is this humble shingled inn with an array of fairly large rooms drenched in corny florals. But they all have sun patios and some have massive sea views.

Malibu Motel MOTEL $$
(☎310-456-6169; www.themalibumotel.com; 22541 Pacific Coast Hwy; r $189-219; Ⓟ📶🏊) This 18-room motel offers comfy beds draped in crisp linen, and slate floors in the bathrooms, but few amenities. Light sleepers should gear up with earplugs to combat Pacific Coast Hwy traffic noise. Still, not bad value for the area and the beach is just across the highway. Third-floor rooms have ocean views.

Malibu Beach Inn INN $$$
(☎310-456-6444; www.malibubeachinn.com; 22878 Pacific Coast Hwy; r $300-675; P 📶) Hollywood mogul David Geffen has given this intimate hacienda the four-star treatment. It has 47 ocean-facing rooms sheathed in soothing browns and outfitted with fireplaces and plush linens. First-floor oceanfront rooms have a deck so close to the beach you can almost touch the rocks

Eating

Howdy's MEXICAN $
(www.howdysmalibu.com; 3835 Cross Creek Rd; mains $8-15; ⏲9am-9pm Mon-Wed, 8am-10pm Thu-Sun) The best *taqueria* in Malibu. They do chicken, steak, veggie, ahi and wild salmon tacos and burritos, tasty breakfast burritos, and some damn good ceviche too. Service is swift and friendly.

Fresh MARKET CAFE $
(www.topangafreshmarket.com; 1704 N Topanga Canyon Rd; dishes $3-10; ⏲10am-7pm Tue-Sun; 🌿) A canary yellow roadside market near the Topanga Canyon pass, where the juices and smoothies, wonderful deli salads and soups (they offer five daily) are all organic, vegetarian and fresh. The ice cream is all natural; so are the dark chocolate truffles. It's a perfect place to grab lunch for a Topanga Canyon State Park picnic.

Grom ICE CREAM $
(3886 Cross Creek Rd; small/medium/large $5.25/6.25/7.25; ⏲11am-10pm) The name is surf-speak for kid, as in bring the groms to the gelato bar. Set in the Cross Creek shopping center they do nothing but all-natural creams and sorbets. The flavors aren't wildly creative, but it is creamy, rich and delicious. You may combine two to three flavors in one cup.

John's Garden DELI $
(www.johnsgardenmalibu.com; 3835 Cross Creek Rd; salads & sandwiches $7-12; ⏲10am-6pm; P) At Malibu's favorite lunch counter you can order fresh daily soups such as curry tomato lentil and Louisiana gumbo, salads culled from the gardens of Greece, Italy, Cape Cod and Korea, and tasty sandwiches, such as the Woody (corned beef and swiss on rye) or the Surfer Princess (turkey and avocado).

Tra Di Noi ITALIAN $$
(☎310-456-0169; www.tradinoimalibu.com; 3835 Cross Creek Rd; mains $10-29; ⏲noon-10pm) A dependably good, classic Italian kitchen in the heart of Cross Creek, with ample patio seating, good wines and pastas, and almost always a full house. But we're actually partial to the Tra Di Noi Express window at lunch, where you can order a range of entree salads, panini, pastas and pizzas on the cheap.

Canyon Bistro CAFE $$
(☎310-455-7800; www.canyonbistrotopanga.com; 120 N Topanga Canyon Blvd; mains $10-20; ⏲11am-9pm Mon-Fri, to 10pm Sat, 5-9pm Sun) Tucked away in the Pine Tree Circle complex, they make a gorgeous warm goat-cheese salad (the cheese is breaded with Panko and baked), a popular yellowfin tartare, crab empanadas, and a seared-tuna sandwich topped with two thick slices of bacon, avocado and smoked jalapeño aioli served open face on grilled ciabatta.

Café Habana MEXICAN, CUBAN $$
(☎310-317-0300; www.habana-malibu.com; 3939 Cross Creek Rd; mains $14-22; ⏲11am-11pm Sun-Wed, to 1am Thu-Sat; P 👪) A Mexican joint disguised as a Cuban joint with terrific margaritas, sumptuous booths on the heated patio, salsa on the sound system and two dishes that prevail above all else: the shrimp and the *carne asada* tacos. Both come piled with either chili and lime sautéed rock shrimp, or cubes of ancho-rubbed and grilled steak. Ask for one of each.

Oh, and it's owned by Randy Gerber, which means the tequila is Casamigos.

Duck Dive GASTROPUB $$
(☎310-589-2200; www.duckdivegastropub.com; 29169 Heathercliff Rd; small plates $5-13, mains $9-32; ⏲11:30am-10pm Sun-Thu, to late Fri & Sat)

SIMMERING IN THE SUN

For over three decades the Malibu branch of the Kiwanis club has sponsored a Labor Day **Chili Cook-off** (www.malibukiwanischilicookoff.com; 23789 Stuart Ranch Rd; ⏲Labor Day weekend) that takes over downtown Malibu with booths, rides, games and a bandstand. While Fourth of July is Malibu's wildest holiday, the cook-off is its signature festival, and the chili competition is the thing. It lures chefs – both amateur and professional – into one bubbling vat of fun. Some use pulled pork, others sirloin, beef and pork shoulder or prime rib. Tastings are offered, bowls bought and consumed, but there can only be one chili champ.

This fantastic little concrete-floor pub has a stainless-steel bar and patio seating. They pour craftsman draft brews, hand cut and sizzle their fries in duck fat, and they do a smoked mac and cheese that can be ramped up with jalapeños and pork belly upon request. They also offer a house-made veggie burger and hearty meat ones too.

Nobu Malibu JAPANESE $$$
(310-317-9140; www.noburestaurants.com; 22706 Pacific Coast Hwy; dishes $8-46; 11am-3pm & 5:30pm-late; P) South of the pier and born again in landmark quality digs, Nobu Malibu is a cavernous, modern wood chalet with a long sushi bar on the back wall and a dining room that spills onto a patio overlooking the swirling sea. Remember, it's the cooked food that built the brand.

Taverna Tony GREEK $$$
(310-317-9667; www.tavernatony.com; 23410 Civic Center Way; appetizers $8-18, mains $13-40; lunch & dinner; P) This lively spot fronted by a flowery terrace feeds both the soul and the belly. At lunchtime the baby lamb sandwich is divine, but for a serious indulgence loosen your belt and order the Greek Feast ($40 per person; two-person minimum), and indulge in 15 different dishes. Dinner reservations are advised.

Inn of the Seventh Ray ORGANIC $$$
(310-455-1311; www.innoftheseventhray.com; 128 Old Topanga Canyon Rd; mains $20-44; 11:30am-3pm & 5:30-10pm Mon-Fri, from 10:30am Sat, from 9:30am Sun; P) If you lived through the '60s, you might experience flashbacks at this New-Agey hideaway in an impossibly idyllic setting in Topanga Canyon. They grill hangar steaks and roast lamb belly, but they also bubble soba noodles and make a nice squid-ink pasta.

Saddle Peak Lodge AMERICAN $$$
(818-222-3888; www.saddlepeaklodge.com; 419 Cold Canyon Rd; appetizers $14-32, mains $35-54; 6-9pm Wed-Fri, 5-10pm Sat, 10:30am-2pm & 5-9pm Sun; P) Rustic as a Colorado mountain lodge, and tucked into the Santa Monica Mountains with a creek running beneath, Saddle Peak Lodge serves up elk, venison, buffalo and other game in a setting watched over by mounted versions of the same. Though the furnishings are all rustic timber, this is fine dining so don't come here after a day on the trail.

Drinking & Nightlife

Sunset BAR
(www.thesunsetrestaurant.com; 6800 Westward Rd; noon-10pm) A converted white washed beach house with tasty flatbreads and a popular weekend brunch. But we consider it to be the perfectly strange oasis after a day at the beach – mostly because the happy hour crowd gets weird. Like rich, celebrity, plastic surgery, comb-over weird. We do love us some Malibu.

Cafecito Organico CAFE
(www.cafecitoorganico.com; 29169 Heathercliff Rd; drinks $3-5; 6am-7pm Mon-Thu, to 8pm Fri, 7am-8pm Sat, 7am-7pm Sun) A terrific, indie-owned Point Dume coffee bar that shares a shingle with a bookstore. They do all the espresso drinks with fair-trade beans, and have house-made almond milk which they use to make their *cortado*. Think 1.5oz almond milk and 1.5oz of espresso. Delish.

Sunlife Organics JUICE BAR
(www.sunlifeorganicsmalibu.com; 29169 Heathercliff Rd; smoothies & juices $6-8; 7am-7pm Mon-Fri, from 8am Sat, 9am-6pm Sun) The place to come for everything from organic cat food (we wish we were kidding) to wild honey, organic chocolate, supplements galore, and their raison d'être – a fabulous juice bar where they blend kale; berries; bananas; coconut oil, meat and water; Madagascar vanilla bean and even coffee in creative concoctions that cultivate a regular following.

Entertainment

Will Geer's Theatricum Botanicum THEATER
(310-455-3723; www.theatricum.com; 1419 N Topanga Canyon Blvd, Topanga; tickets $25-40) TV's Grandpa Walton founded this beloved theater as a refuge for blacklisted actors like himself during the McCarthy years. The woodsy setting is a perfect backdrop for such classic crowd-pleasers as Shakespeare's *A Midsummer Night's Dream* and Bram Stoker's *Dracula*.

The season runs from June to early October. To get there, head north on Pacific Coast Hwy, turn inland on Topanga Canyon Blvd and proceed for 6 miles; the theater will be on your left.

Shopping

★ **Hidden Treasures** VINTAGE
(www.facebook.com/hiddentreasurestopanga; 154 N Topanga Canyon Blvd; 10am-6pm) This

one-of-a-kind store pops from the Topanga Canyon roadside, thanks to skeletons and mannequins dressed like Egyptian eunuchs and Viking warriors, standing sentry among the old wagons and totem poles out front. Inside it's a sprawling vintage boutique of sweaters and coats, sweatshirts and Pendleton wool flannels, denim jackets and leather bombers.

And it's stuffed with fun knickknacks too, such as antique lanterns, clocks and...is that a giant rubber octopus?

Malibu Country Mart SHOPPING CENTER
(www.malibucountrymart.com; 3835 Cross Creek Rd) Across from Surfrider Beach, this mall spans both sides of Cross Creek Rd. Which is why it's affectionately known as Cross Creek by the sweet, sexy, sun-kissed local beach girls and boys who gather on this high-end outdoor shopping mall to flirt, grub and shop.

There are some stunning, creative and casual designer boutiques such as **Madison** (madisonlosangeles.com; 3835 Cross Creek Rd; ⏲10am-6pm Mon-Sat, 11am-5pm Sun) and **Planet Blue** (www.shopplanetblue.com; 3835 Cross Creek Rd; ⏲10am-6pm), and you may glimpse a celebrity soccer mom or dad as they sip coffee or watch their toddlers scramble around the courtyard playground. There's a cinema here too.

Lumberyard MALL
(www.themalibulumber.com; 3939 Cross Creek Rd; 📶) Steps west of the Malibu Country Mart is the sleekest and newest shopping center in town, set on the site of Malibu's longtime lumber yard. The highlights here are the refined longboard of a boutique that is **James Perse** (www.jamesperse.com), and the pretty, powerful sophisticate that is **Intermix** (www.intermixonline.com; 3939 Cross Creek Rd; ⏲10am-7pm Mon-Sat, from 11am Sun).

SANTA MONICA

Here's a place where real-life Lebowskis sip white Russians next to martini-swilling Hollywood producers, celebrity chefs dine at family-owned *taquerias,* and soccer moms and career bachelors shop shoulder to shoulder at abundant farmers markets. It's a small city with forward-thinking social and environmental ideals and fascist parking codes. Here, you'll navigate a landscape of surf rats, skate punks, string bikinis, yoga freaks, psychics, street performers and a prodigious homeless population. Most, if not all, of which can be found along a stretch of sublime coastline that cradles the city to the west, and laps at the heels of an undulating mountain range that defines the entire LA area to the north. This is Santa Monica – LA's cute, alluring, hippie-chic little sister, its karmic counterbalance and, to many, its salvation.

Well within the Hollywood sphere of influence, production houses, post-production studios and, more recently, a thundering herd of tech companies, lend it a certain buzz. Shoppers patrol three distinct shopping districts, rummage through thrift stores and dress up in refined boutiques. At night you can choose from sprawling outdoor cafes, chic hotel lounges, dance clubs and casual wine bars. There's live blues, salsa and world music almost every night of the week, and Santa Monica cuisine spans the globe with something for every wallet. As the sun drops, however, there is really only one place you'll want to be. That's the wide golden beach that put Santa Monica on the map in the first place.

Sights

Santa Monica Pier WATERFRONT
(☎310-458-8900; www.santamonicapier.org; 👪) Once the very end of the mythical Route 66, and still the object of a tourist love affair, the Santa Monica Pier dates back to 1908, and is the city's most compelling landmark. There are arcades, carnival games, a vintage carousel, a Ferris wheel, a roller coaster and an aquarium, and the pier comes alive with free concerts (Twilight Dance Series) and outdoor movies in the summertime.

There are also a number of bars and restaurants, but the thing here is the view: extending almost a quarter mile over the Pacific, you can stroll to the edge, hang out among the motley anglers, and lose yourself in the rolling, blue-green sea.

Kids get their kicks at **Pacific Park** (☎310-260-8744; www.pacpark.com; ⏲11am-9pm Sun-Thu, to midnight Fri & Sat Jun-Aug, shorter hours Sep-May; 👪), a small amusement park with a solar-powered Ferris wheel, kiddy rides, midway games and food stands. Rides cost between $3 and $5 each; a day of unlimited spins costs $21.95/15.95 (over/under 42in tall); check the website for discount coupons.

Near the pier entrance, nostalgic souls and their offspring can giddy up the beautifully hand-painted horses of the 1922 **carousel** featured in the movie *The Sting*.

Peer under the pier – just below the carousel – for Heal the Bay's **Santa Monica Pier Aquarium** (☎310-393-6149; www.healthebay.org; 1600 Ocean Front Walk; adult/child $5/free; ⏲2-5pm Tue-Fri, 12:30-5pm Sat & Sun; 👪). Sea stars, crabs, sea urchins and other critters and crustaceans scooped from the bay stand by to be petted – ever so gently, please – in their adopted touch-tank homes.

South of the pier is the **Original Muscle Beach**, where the Southern California exercise craze began in the mid-20th century, and new equipment now draws a new generation of fitness fanatics. Close by, the search for the next Bobby Fischer is on at the **International Chess Park**. Anyone can join in. Following the **South Bay Bicycle Trail**, a paved bike and walking path, south for about 1.5 miles takes you straight to Venice Beach. Bike or in-line skates are available to rent on the pier and at beachside kiosks.

California Heritage Museum MUSEUM
(www.californiaheritagemuseum.org; 2612 Main St; adult/student & senior/under 12yr $10/5/free; ⏲11am-4pm Wed-Sun; Ⓟ) For a trip back in time, check out the latest exhibit at this museum housed in one of Santa Monica's few surviving grand Victorian mansions – this one built in 1894. Curators do a wonderful job presenting pottery, colorful tiles, craftsman furniture, folk art, vintage surfboards and other fine collectibles in as dynamic a fashion as possible.

WORTH A TRIP

LITTLE OSAKA

Though it's called Little Osaka, West LA's Asian bloom, which runs on Sawtelle for about two blocks north from Olympic Blvd to La Grange Ave, is not exclusively Japanese. Among the karaoke bars, grocers, cafes and boutiques are restaurants devoted to ramen and Korean-style tofu, *shabu shabu,* macaroons, dim sum, *pho* and *yakitori*.

Buttercup (www.thebuttercupla.com; 11301 West Olympic Blvd; 2pc $4, 6pc $11; ⏲noon-10pm Sun-Thu, to 11pm Fri & Sat) Owned and operated by a young couple, this macaroon shop offers transporting flavors invented by the Vietnamese-born, Paris-trained chef, such as vanilla bean and coconut, chocolate and passion fruit, earl grey, sea-salt caramel, lavender and rose petal. They even have durian and taro. The colors are just as appealing.

Yakitoriya (☎310-479-5400; 11301 W Olympic Blvd; dishes $2.50-27; ⏲6-10:30pm Mon, Wed-Sun; 👪) Simple and real, this chef-owned and family-operated *yakitori* (Japanese grilled chicken) joint crafts the most tender and savory skewers you can imagine. We love the wings, neck, chicken skin, meatballs and the minced chicken bowl topped with quail egg.

Tsujita LA (☎310-231-7373; tsujita-la.com; 2057 Sawtelle Blvd; ramen $9-14) This artisan noodle joint is known for their ramen with pork, which they only serve at lunch. They serve decent Japanese cooked food at dinner, but demand for their ramen was so great, they were compelled to build an annex caddy corner, where noodles are served all day and night.

Coffee Tomo (www.coffeetomo.com; 11309 Mississippi Ave; ⏲7:30am-10pm Mon-Thu, to 10:30pm Fri, 9am-10:30pm Sat, to 9pm Sun; 📶) An excellent coffee roaster that also pours a mean latte and bakes exquisite… pretzels? Yes, pretzels. There's a reason so many huddle on their wooden tables, over their laptops, for hours on end.

Black Market (www.blackmarketla.com; 2023 Sawtelle Blvd; ⏲11am-9pm Sun-Fri, to 10pm Sat) The best fashion boutique in the district, Black Market sells Nudie jeans, Manhattan Portage bags and Pop Killer socks. They even have shoes, stationery and beauty products, not to mention a killer soundtrack, and sweet, helpful staff.

Rimo (www.rimolosangeles.com; 2008 Sawtelle Blvd; ⏲noon-9pm Mon-Sat, to 8pm Sun) The LA link in a small Hawaiian chain, here's a charming contemporary boutique with flowy blouses and charming handbags, decent denim and cute jewelry; none of it too pricey.

Giant Robot (☎310-478-1819; www.giantrobot.com; 2015 Sawtelle Blvd; ⏲11:30am-8pm Mon-Sat, noon-7pm Sun) Fans of anime will want to riffle through the T-shirts, action figures, stuffed creatures, throw pillows and books, at this ode to weird, ugly cute.

Santa Monica

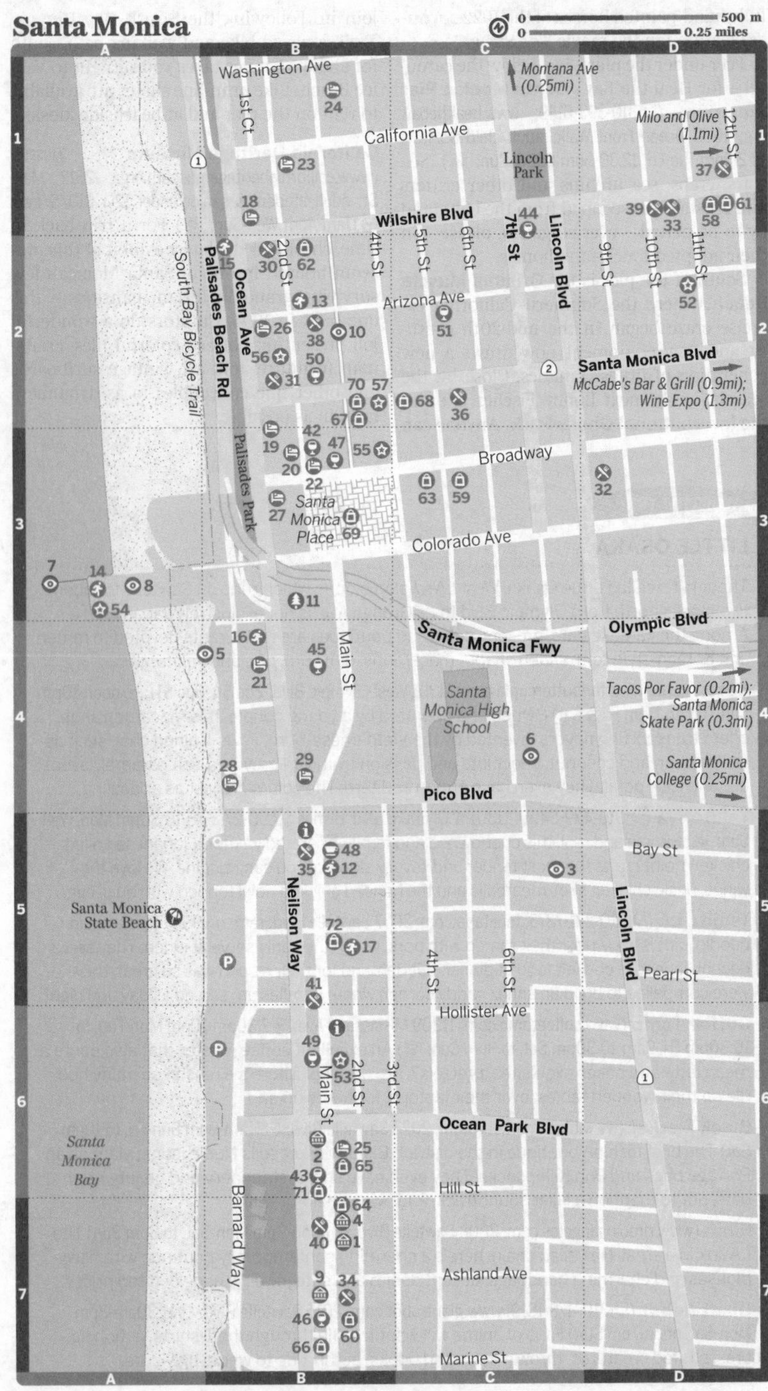

Santa Monica

Sights

1	Axiom Gallery	B7
2	California Heritage Museum	B6
	Carousel	(see 7)
3	Green Street	C5
	International Chess Park	(see 5)
4	Jadis	B7
5	Original Muscle Beach	B4
6	Santa Monica High School	C4
7	Santa Monica Pier	A3
8	Santa Monica Pier Aquarium	A3
9	Streetcraft LA	B7
10	Third Street Promenade	B2
11	Tongva Park	B3

Activities, Courses & Tours

12	Alchemie	B5
13	Bhakti Yoga Shala	B2
	Bike Attack	(see 41)
	IZip	(see 1)
14	Pacific Park	A3
15	Perry's Café & Rentals	B2
16	Poseidon	B4
	Soul Cycle	(see 30)
	Trapeze School New York	(see 7)
17	Yoga Works	B5

Sleeping

18	Fairmont Miramar	B1
19	Georgian Hotel	B3
20	HI Los Angeles-Santa Monica	B3
21	Hotel California	B4
22	Hotel Carmel	B3
23	Huntley	B1
24	Palihouse	B1
25	Sea Shore Motel	B6
26	Shangri-La	B2
27	Shore Hotel	B3
28	Shutters	B4
29	Viceroy	B4

Eating

30	800 Degrees	B2
31	Bar Pintxo	B2
32	Bay Cities	D3
	Curious Palate	(see 69)
	Fig	(see 18)
33	Huckleberry	D1
34	Library Alehouse	B7
35	M Street Kitchen	B5
	M.A.K.E.	(see 69)
36	Real Food Daily	C2
37	Rustic Canyon	D1
38	Santa Monica Farmers Markets	B2
39	Santa Monica Seafood	D1
40	Sunny Blue	B7
41	Thai Vegan	B5

Drinking & Nightlife

42	Bar Chloe	B3
43	Basement Tavern	B6
44	Bungalow	C1
45	Chez Jay	B4
46	Circle Bar	B7
47	Copa d'Oro	B3
48	Dogtown Coffee	B5
49	Galley	B6
50	Misfit	B2
	Rick's Tavern	(see 34)
51	Zanzibar	C2

Entertainment

52	Broad Stage	D2
53	Edgemar Center for the Arts	B6
54	Front Porch Cinema at the Pier	A3
55	Harvelle's	B3
56	Laemmle's Monica 4	B2
57	Magicopolis	B2

Shopping

58	Address Boutique	D1
	Aura Shop	(see 9)
59	Fred Segal	C3
60	Free People	B7
61	Great Labels	D1
62	Hennessey & Ingalls	B2
63	Hundreds	C3
64	Mindfulnest	B7
65	Paris 1900	B6
66	Planet Blue	B7
67	Puzzle Zoo	B2
68	REI	C2
69	Santa Monica Place	B3
70	Supra	B2
71	Undefeated	B6
72	Vital Hemp	B5

To see locals at play, come during the Sunday morning farmers market in the museum's parking lot.

Streetcraft LA GALLERY

(www.streetcraftla.com; 2912 Main St) A cooperative of street artists, Streetcraft LA started as a nonprofit taking vandal artists and teaching them the skills to beome working artists. They do occasional art openings, live graffiti demos, and offer **street art tours** (per person $40) of Santa Monica and Venice.

They even have some small pieces for sale, perfect for packing a piece of LA-inspired street art in your bag before you leave town.

Jadis MUSEUM

(2701 Main St; per person $1; noon-5pm Sun) Don't miss this homespun, steam-punk paradise. It's a museum grinding with old gears and spare-part robots, antique clocks,

ANNENBERG COMMUNITY BEACH HOUSE

Like a beach club for the rest of us, this sleek and attractive public **beach club** (www.beachhouse.smgov.net; 400 Pacific Coast Hwy; parking $3, swimming pool adult/senior/child $10/5/4; 8:30am-5:30pm Nov-Mar, to 6:30pm Apr & Oct, to 8:30pm Jun-Sep) built on actress Marion Davies' estate (she had a thing with William Randolph Hearst), has a lap pool, lounge chairs, yoga classes, beach volleyball, a fitness room, photo exhibits and even poetry readings. There's a cafe nearby, and it's set on a sweet stretch of Santa Monica Beach.

concept planes and cars, old globes and lanterns – most of which were old film props. The prized piece is the robot from the famed 1927 film *Metropolis*.

Third Street Promenade PLAZA
Stretching for three long blocks sprawled between Broadway and Wilshire Blvd, Third Street Promenade is a case study in how to morph a dilapidated, dying main street into a dynamic and happening strip. It offers carefree and car-free strolling accompanied by the sound of flamenco guitar or hip-hop acrobatics courtesy of street performers.

You can grab a bite to eat, catch a movie and browse the Gap or Zara. And every Wednesday and Saturday, hobby cooks and professional chefs jostle for the freshest foods at the farmers market.

Santa Monica Museum of Art MUSEUM
(Map p62; www.smmoa.org; 2525 Michigan Ave; donation adult/senior & student $5/3; 11am-6pm Tue-Sat) A saucy and irreverent home of edgy art, this small museum gives exposure to both local and national artists working with new and experimental media. It's part of the **Bergamot Station Arts Center** (Map p62; www.bergamotstation.com; 2525 Michigan Ave; 10am-6pm Tue-Fri, 11am-5:30pm Sat; P), a cluster of galleries, studios and shops set in a former railyard.

Gehry House MONUMENT
(Map p62; 1002 22nd St) In his creative life before the Walt Disney Concert Hall, Frank Gehry was primarily known as that crazy guy who sculpted houses from chain-link fencing, plywood and corrugated aluminum. A great place to see the 'early Gehry' is his 1979 private home, a deconstructivist post-modern collage that architecture-critic Paul Heyer called a 'collision of parts.'

Axiom Gallery GALLERY
(www.axiomcontemporary.com; 2801 Main St; 11am-6pm Mon-Thu, to 7pm Fri & Sat) FREE This spacious, contemporary art gallery featuring sculpture and canvasses spread over two rooms always makes for a fun wander.

Tongva Park PARK
(1615 Ocean Ave; 6am-11pm) A brand-new and meticulously designed green space that connects Ocean Ave to the Santa Monica Civic Center area. Well-lit and maintained, there are palms and agave groves, cascading fountains and amphitheater seating, trim lawns and an adorable, ergonomic playground for tots.

Activities

What's the number one activity destination in Santa Monica? That would be that loamy, quarter-mile deep, 5-mile stretch of golden sand lapped by the Pacific. Water temperatures become tolerable by late spring and are highest (about 67°F/20°C) in September. Water quality varies; for updated conditions check the **Beach Report Card** (www.healthebay.org).

The waves in Santa Monica are gentle and well shaped for beginner surfers, as well as bodyboarders and bodysurfers. The best swimming beaches are Will Rogers State Beach on the border of Pacific Palisades, and the beach south of the pier.

South Bay Bicycle Trail BIKING
Dodge the in-line skaters, power walkers, lollygaggers, surfers and volleyballs as you pedal the South Bay Bicycle Trail, which parallels the sand for most of the 22 miles between Will Rogers Beach near Santa Monica and Torrance Beach. Weekends get jammed and there are sections where you might have to push your bike.

Bike Attack BICYCLE RENTAL
(www.bikeattack.com; 2400 Main St; cruisers per hr/day $15/30, mountain bikes per day $50; 9:30am-5:30pm) A terrific resource for mountain bikers, this laid-back shop rents the best beach cruisers and mountain bikes in Santa Monica. They know the top mountain-bike trails in Southern California, and can repair your bike if necessary.

Trapeze School New York TRAPEZE

(www.trapezeschool.com; 370 Santa Monica Pier; 2hr classes $47-65; ⏲ classes 10:45am & 1:15pm) Ever wanted to learn how to fly on the trapeze? In a cordoned-off and netted area on the Santa Monica Pier, you'll get your chance. So chalk up, and leave your fear of heights and your inhibitions at the door. The public is watching.

Perry's Café & Rentals GEAR RENTAL

(☎310-939-0000; www.perryscafe.com; Ocean Front Walk; mountain bikes & Rollerblades per hr/day $10/30, bodyboards per hr/day $7/17; ⏲9:30am-5:30pm) With several locations on the bike path, they rent bikes and skates – or perhaps you'll grab a bodyboard and ride the foaming rollers in the wide Santa Monica Bay? They offer a unique beach butler service too, but only accept cash.

Santa Monica Skate Park SKATING

(www.socalskateparks.com; cnr 14th St & Olympic Blvd; daily pass adult/child $6.50/5) Skate rats will love the 20,000 sq ft of vert, street and tranny terrain in Memorial Park.

Yoga Works YOGA

(☎310-272-5641; www.yogaworks.com; 2215 Main St; per class $22; ⏲7am-9pm) Part of a yoga chain, they offer dozens of classes per week, for all levels of expertise, plus one- and two-day intro courses. If you're new to Yoga Works you're eligible for a $30 two-week pass which offers unlimited classes at any of their Southern and Northern California studios. A good deal for a rambling yogi. There's also a branch at 1426 Montana Ave.

Poseidon WATER SPORTS

(☎310-694-8428; www.poseidonstandup.com; 1654 Ocean Ave; SUP rentals per 1hr/2hr/day $35/50/70, surfboards per 2hr/day $25/35, lessons $90-120; ⏲10am-6pm) Ever wonder what it feels like to be one of those bad-asses paddling the long board beyond the break and then riding the swell? Then find this little nook of a shop south of the pier. They sell and rent SUP boards – the sport Laird Hamilton helped make famous – and can set you up with lessons too.

Bhakti Yoga Shala YOGA

(www.bhaktiyogashala.com; 207 Arizona Ave; suggested donation $10-15; ⏲5-8 classes daily) Donation-based yoga and meditation classes offered in a simple space near the promenade. You won't feel like om-ing cattle here.

IZip ELECTRIC BIKES

(☎424-272-1153, 310-310-8846; www.active-movement.com; 2803 Main St; per 1hr/2hr/day $20/35/75; ⏲10am-6pm Mon-Sat, 9am-5pm Sun) An electric-bike showroom that offers rentals and helps arrange two-hour tours ($65).

MULHOLLAND DRIVE DRIVING TOUR

What to See

If you found David Lynch's 2001 movie *Mulholland Drive* a tad bizarre, perhaps a drive along the road itself will clear things up. The legendary road winds and dips for 24 miles through the **Santa Monica Mountains** (www.nps.gov/samo/planyourvisit/parksites), skirting the mansions of the rich and famous (Jack Nicholson's is at No 12850, Warren Beatty's at No 13671) and delivering iconic views of Downtown, Hollywood and the San Fernando Valley at each bend. Named for its creator, California aqueduct engineer William Mulholland, it's especially pretty just before sunset (go west to east, though, to avoid driving into the setting sun) and on clear winter days when the panorama opens up from the snowcapped **San Gabriel Mountains** to the shimmering Pacific Ocean.

At the very least, drive up to the **Hollywood Bowl Overlook** for classic views of the Hollywood sign and the beehive-shaped bowl below. Other pullouts offer hiking-trail access, for instance to Runyon Canyon (p115) and **Fryman Canyon**. Note that pulling over after sunset is verboten and may result in a traffic ticket.

Time & Route

Driving the entire route takes about an hour, but even a shorter spin is worth it. Mulholland Dr runs from the US-101 Fwy (Hollywood Fwy; take the Cahuenga exit, then follow signs) to about 2 miles west of the I-405 (San Diego Fwy). About 8 miles of dirt road, closed to vehicles but not to hikers and cyclists, links it with Mulholland Hwy, which continues a serpentine route through the mountains for another 23 miles as far as Leo Carrillo State Beach.

Soul Cycle SPINNING
(☎310-622-7685; www.soul-cycle.com; 120 Wilshire Blvd; 1st class $20, thereafter $34; ⏲classes 7am-8:30pm) A spin class mashed up with aerobics and turned up to hyper speed has made addicts out of (mostly) women, young and old. At this, the first LA location of a New York transplant, they have lockers, showers, drinking water and the special shoes. When you aren't heaving and trying not to die, it's fun.

Alchemie SPA
(☎310-310-8880; www.alchemiespa.com; 2021 Main St; massage $85; ⏲10:30am-8pm) Spa seekers rejoice, for here is an attractive, chilled-out day spa with blonde-wood floors, aromatherapy in the air and a menu of beauty and body treatments. Massages come in many flavors including deep tissue, Thai, Esalen and hot stone. The 2½-hour Signature Retreat ($199) includes a custom body scrub, mini facial, aromatherapy massage and pedicure.

Learn to Surf LA SURFING
(☎310-663-2479; www.learntosurfla.com; per lesson per person $90-120) Great for beginners, Learn to Surf LA guarantees you'll get up on the board on your first lesson. Lessons last one hour and 45 minutes.

Sleeping

HI Los Angeles-Santa Monica HOSTEL $
(☎310-393-9913; www.hilosangeles.org; 1436 2nd St; dm $38-49, r $99-159; ❄@📶) Near the beach and Promenade, this hostel has an

TOP 10 LA BEACHES

Long before the Beach Boys brought surf culture to the masses, Southern California was an American dream destination for one reason: the beach. With miles of golden sand, swaying palms, wide beaches hemmed in by ragged, towering bluffs, and gentle, rolling surf that serves beginners but can get big enough to charge up even old sea dogs, LA remains an epic beach destination. The following beaches are listed north to south.

Leo Carrillo Families love this summer-camp-style beach with enough stimulating tide pools, cliff caves, nature trails and great swimming and surfing to tire out even the most hyperactive kids.

El Matador This small, remote hideaway is a popular filming location thanks to battered rock cliffs and giant boulders, but the surf is wild and clothing is optional.

Westward Beach Around the bend from Point Dume and just south of Zuma, Malibu locals favor this wide, blonde beach for crystal water, resident dolphin pods and sea lion colonies. The shallows aren't made for kiddies though.

Zuma Two miles of pearly sand. Mellow swells make for perfect body surfing. Come early on weekends to snag parking.

Paradise Cove The site of a kitschy restaurant and an upscale mobile-home park (only in Malibu), the beach is close enough to Point Dume to get set-piece rock formations and mellow waves. Eating at the restaurant cuts the $25 parking fee down to $5.

Santa Monica Wide slab of sand where beach-umbrella-toting families descend like butterfly swarms on weekends to escape the inland heat. Water quality is poor right by the pier but OK a few hundred yards south.

Venice Beach Get your freak on at the Venice Boardwalk. During Sunday's drum circle, the bongos crescendo and dancers turn to silhouettes as the sun dips into the ocean. Plus, the wide beaches south of the Venice Pier are an oft-ignored gem with excellent bodysurfing.

Manhattan Beach Brassy SoCal beach with a high flirt factor and hard-core surfers hanging by the pier.

Hermosa Beach LA's libidinous, seemingly never-ending beach party with hormone-crazed hard bodies getting their game on over beach volleyball and in the raucous pubs along Pier Ave. If you have nothing happening on July 4, come here.

Malaga Cove This crescent-shaped, cliff-backed shoreline is the only sandy Palos Verdes beach easily accessible by the hoi polloi. It blends into rocky tide pools and has excellent rolling waves for surfers (at Haggerty's), but no lifeguards.

enviable location on the cheap. Its 200 beds in single-sex dorms and bed-in-a-box doubles with shared bathrooms are clean and safe, and there are plenty of public spaces to lounge and surf, but those looking to party are better off in Venice or Hollywood.

Sea Shore Motel MOTEL $$
(☎310-392-2787; www.seashoremotel.com; 2637 Main St; r from $140; P ❄ 📶) These friendly, family-run lodgings put you just a Frisbee toss from the beach on happening Main St (expect some street noise). The tiled rooms are basic, but families can stretch out comfortably in the modern suites with kitchen and balcony in a nearby building.

Hotel Carmel BOUTIQUE HOTEL $$
(☎310-451-2469; www.hotelcarmel.com; 201 Broadway Ave; r from $179; P 📶) Charming historic facade aside, there's nothing fancy about this aging boutique hotel around the corner from the Promenade. Despite the weathered carpeting, rooms are fairly bright and have ceiling fans, wood furnishings and new mattresses; some have sea views. There's only one elevator, but management is fastidious, in a good way.

Channel Road Inn B&B B&B $$
(☎310-459-1920; www.channelroadinn.com; 219 W Channel Rd; r $195-395; P @ 📶) This frilly home in leafy Santa Monica Canyon mixes Cape Cod colonial with West Coast craftsman and has romantic rooms facing the ocean or the lovely garden. Breakfast is a gourmet affair. There are also convivial afternoon teas, evening wine receptions with fellow guests, and a Jacuzzi out back. Free bike rentals.

★ **Palihouse** BOUTIQUE HOTEL $$$
(☎310-394-1279; www.palihousesantamonica.com; 1001 3rd St; r $279-319, studios $319-379; P ❄ @ 📶) LA's grooviest new hotel brand (not named Ace) has taken over the 36 rooms, studios and one-bedroom apartments of the historic Embassy Hotel (c 1927). Expect a lobby with terra-cotta floors, beamed ceilings and coffee bar, plus booths and leather sofas.

The hotel rooms are updated with period tile and are plenty comfortable; spacious studios have slightly sunken floor plans and each has a unique design, including picnic table desks and a full kitchen. Service could not be better, which is probably why some guests stay for months. You do get a discount for longer stays.

Huntley BOUTIQUE HOTEL $$$
(☎310-394-5454; www.thehuntleyhotel.com; 1111 2nd St; r from $399; @ 📶 🏊) A stylish boutique nest offering olive-green rooms with chocolate-wood furnishings, lush linens and designer suites with mid-century style seating, a window-side daybed and two flat-screen TVs. The cool factor follows you from the lobby to the rooftop restaurant, **The Penthouse**, where you marvel at the Santa Monica Mountains tumbling into the sea.

Shutters HOTEL $$$
(☎310-458-0030; www.shuttersonthebeach.com; 1 Pico Blvd; r $525; P @ 📶) Bringing classic Cape Cod charm to the Pacific Coast, the best rooms have a beach-cottage feel with marble baths, wood floors, spectacular ocean views and white washed shutters, of course. The in-house seafood cafe is charming and tasty, and the upstairs restaurant draws rave reviews, as well. This is as upscale as Santa Monica nests get.

Viceroy BOUTIQUE HOTEL $$$
(☎800-622-8711, 310-260-7500; www.viceroysantamonica.com; 1819 Ocean Ave; r from $323; P ❄ @ 📶 🏊 🐾) Starving for some LA glam by the sea? With porcelain hounds at the door, frosted glass and white-vinyl lounges in the lobby, and shag carpet in the library, the mod-meets-regency design works. Rooms are so slick even the marble bathroom is hip. Ambient electronic music infuses public spaces, there's a flashy bar scene, and it's a block from the beach.

Hotel California INN $$$
(☎310-393-2363; www.hotelca.com/losangeles/; 1670 Ocean Ave; r $219-319; P) A converted apartment complex, covered tastefully in ivy, offers sunny rooms and studios with kitchenette, and vintage surf rocker decor, walking distance to the promenade, the beach and Main St.

Shangri-La HOTEL $$$
(☎310-394-2791; www.shangrila-hotel.com; 1301 Ocean Ave; r from $305; @ 📶 🏊) Stylish enough to be alluring but not too stuck up or intimidating, this art-deco classic, built across the avenue from the bluffs in 1932, sports suites and apartments with funky paint jobs and wallpaper, marble baths, wood floors and kitchenettes. They all have at least a sliver of a sea view.

Georgian Hotel HOTEL $$$

(☎310-395-9945, 800-538-8147; www.georgianhotel.com; 1415 Ocean Ave; r $319-439; P @ wi-fi) This eye-catching, art-deco landmark has a snug verandah for breakfast and sunset lounging, and decor so *Great Gatsby*-esque that wearing a straw boater wouldn't feel out of place. The rooms, in soothing earth tones, are surprisingly modern, and we love the parlor-like bath tile.

Shore Hotel HOTEL $$$

(☎310-458-1515; www.shorehotel.com; 1515 Ocean Ave; r from $309) Massive and modern with clean lines, this is one of the newest hotels on Ocean Ave, and the only gold LEED certified hotel in Santa Monica, which means they have a reasonably light footprint. Case in point: the lovely back garden is seeded with drought tolerant plants. The wood-and-glass rooms each have private terraces.

Fairmont Miramar HOTEL $$$

(☎310-576-7777; www.fairmont.com/santa-monica/; 101 Wilshire Blvd; r from $342; P ⊖ ❄ @ wi-fi ≋) Santa Monica's original grand dame of hotels, Fairmont Miramar is a block from the bluffs and the promenade, shaded by gorgeous old trees, and home to a fabulous restaurant and one of Santa Monica's best nightspots. The rooms are four-star comfortable, if a touch stodgy.

Eating

★Santa Monica Farmers Markets MARKET $

(www.smgov.net/portals/farmersmarket; Arizona Ave, btwn 2nd & 3rd Sts; ⏲8:30am-1:30pm Wed, to 1pm Sat; 👪) 🌿 You haven't really experienced Santa Monica until you've explored one of its weekly outdoor farmers markets stocked with organic fruits, vegetables, flowers, baked goods and freshly shucked oysters.

The Wednesday market begins on 3rd and Arizona and winds along three blocks – it's the biggest and arguably the best for fresh produce, which is why it's so often patrolled by local chefs. The Sunday morning market on Main St has more of a community scene. There's live music, pony rides, and a half-dozen stalls cooking up omelettes, tamales, crepes and grilled corn. Just hand your bicycle to the valet (um, yes, we know, but it is free), and relax with the locals on the lawn.

Bay Cities DELI $

(www.baycitiesitaliandeli.com; 1517 Lincoln Blvd; sandwiches $5-9; ⏲9am-7pm Tue-Sat, to 6pm Sun) Not just the best Italian deli in LA, this is arguably the best deli, period. They have sloppy, spicy godmothers (piled with salami, mortadella, coppacola, ham, prosciutto, provolone and pepper salad), house-roasted tritip, tangy salads, imported meats, cheeses, breads, oils and extras. Get your sandwich with the works. And, yes, it's worth the wait.

Tacos Por Favor MEXICAN $

(www.tacosporfavor.net; 1406 Olympic Blvd; dishes $4.50-11; ⏲8am-8pm) This is a no-nonsense taco joint – a dingy hole-in-the-wall that's smoky, hot and crowded. It also happens to serve the best shrimp, chicken and *carne asada* tacos and burritos in town. Hence, the lunchtime crush.

Sunny Blue JAPANESE $

(☎310-399-9030; www.sunnyblueinc.com; 2728 Main St; omusubi from $3) A new *omusubi* joint, and the first of its kind in LA. What is *omusubi* you ask? It's a Japanese sandwich cum handroll where fillings such as chicken curry, or albacore with diced cucumber, or miso beef are stuffed in rice balls wrapped in seaweed. Sides include *edamame* (soybean snack), *sunomono* and *kim chee*. They also serve tasty frozen yogurt, featuring flavors such as black sesame!

Thai Vegan THAI $

(www.thaivegansm.com; 2400 Main St; dishes $6-8; ⏲11am-midnight; ✍) Part vegan Thai joint, part juice bar, they do meatless *massaman* and *panang* curries, veggie dumplings and, of course, pad Thai. The food is good, not great, but it is cheap, healthy and they're open late.

★Milo and Olive ITALIAN $$

(☎310-453-6776; www.miloandolive.com; 2723 Wilshire Blvd; dishes $7-20; ⏲7am-11pm daily) We love them for their small batch wines, incredible pizzas, terrific breakfasts (creamy polenta and poached eggs anyone?), breads and pastries, all of which you may enjoy at the marble bar or shoulder to shoulder with new friends at one of two common tables. It's a cozy, neighborhood joint so they don't take reservations.

★Bar Pintxo SPANISH $$

(☎310-458-2012; www.barpintxo.com; 109 Santa Monica Blvd; tapas $4-16, paella $30; ⏲4-10pm Mon-Wed, to 11pm Thu, to midnight Fri, noon-midnight Sat, to 10pm Sun) Conceived by Joe Miller, from the great Joe's restaurant (p175) on Abbot Kinney, is this Barcelona-inspired tapas bar. It's small, it's cramped, it's a bit

DON'T MISS

HIKING LA

If hiking doesn't feel like an indigenous LA activity to you, you need to reassess. This town is hemmed in and defined by two mountain ranges and countless canyons. In the **San Gabriel range**, trails wind from Mt Wilson into granite peak wilderness, once the domain of the Gabrielino people and the setting for California's last grizzly-bear sighting. The Chumash roamed the **Santa Monicas**, which are smaller, but still offer spectacular views of chaparral-draped mountains with stark drops into the Pacific. The **Backbone Trail** spans the range, but our favorite hike is to Sandstone Peak. Day hikes in Topanga Canyon, Malibu Canyon, Point Mugu and Leo Carrillo State Parks are also recommended. And if you only have an hour or two, check out Runyon or Bronson Canyons in Hollywood. For more advice about trails in and around Southern California check out www.trails.com, or buy these two tomes: *Top Trails: Los Angeles* (Wilderness Press) and *60 Hikes Within 60 Miles* (Menasha Ridge Press; 2009).

loud and it's a lot of fun. Tapas include pork belly braised in duck fat, filet mignon skewers, lamb meatballs and a tremendous seared calamari.

And the paella can't be missed. It's served in a tapas size ($9) on Tuesdays, but the full pan (which can serve four comfortably) comes with two sangria on Sunday and Monday nights. If it's warm enough they may even make it on the patio.

Huckleberry CAFE **$$**

(www.huckleberrycafe.com; 1014 Wilshire Blvd; mains $10-14; ⏲8am-8pm Mon-Fri, to 5pm Sat & Sun) The second in a growing epicurean family from the couple behind Rustic Canyon (p164), and arguably its most popular offering, at Huckleberry Zoe Nathan devises some of the most exquisite pastries available in the city. Think: crostatas bursting with blueberries, maple bacon biscuits, and pumpkin and ginger tea cakes.

Later in the day the crowds keep coming for the turkey meatball sandwich, the much-loved brisket plate or any number of deli salads. We call it yuppie soul food.

Santa Monica Seafood SEAFOOD **$$**

(www.santamonicaseafood.com; 1000 Wilshire Blvd; appetizers $3-15, mains $13-21; ⏲9am-9pm Mon-Sat, to 8pm Sun) The best seafood market in Southern California offers a tasty oyster bar and market cafe, where you can sample delicious chowder, salmon burgers, albacore melts, oysters on the half shell, and pan-roasted halibut.

M.A.K.E. VEGAN **$$**

(☎310-394-7046; www.matthewkenneycuisine.com; 395 Santa Monica Pl; dishes $10-18; ⏲11am-9pm Sun-Thu, to 10pm Fri & Sat; 🖉) This upscale raw, vegan eatery dreamt up by raw chef and author Matthew Kenney is set in The Market section of the Santa Monica Place's Dining Deck. They feature beet ravioli, and a raw lasagna with heirloom tomatoes, macadamia and pistachio nuts. Dine at the marble bar or at the butcher-block common table.

Curious Palate ARTISAN FOODS **$$**

(www.thecuriouspalate.com; 395 Santa Monica Place; mains $8-22; ⏲9am-9pm Sun-Thu, to 10pm Fri & Sat) The dominant force of The Market, a special market hall on the Santa Monica Place Dining Deck. They make sandwiches and salads, as well as a range of reasonably priced mains you can munch on marble table tops. They also have a cheese shop and a coffee bar down the hall.

M Street Kitchen CALIFORNIAN **$$**

(☎310-396-9145; www.mstreetkitchen.com; 2000 Main St; mains $7-21; ⏲8am-10pm Sun-Thu, to 11pm Fri & Sat; P) This wildly popular breakfast and lunch choice, with abundant sunshine patio seating, conjures farmers market produce and all-natural ingredients into comfortable creations such as pulled chicken nachos, terrific fried-egg sandwiches at breakfast, house-made veggie burgers at lunch and soft taco platters that have their own devout cult following.

Real Food Daily VEGAN **$$**

(☎310-451-7544; www.realfood.com; 514 Santa Monica Blvd; appetizers $9-11, mains $12-15; ⏲lunch & dinner; 🖉) Vegan-cooking guru Ann Gentry gives meat and dairy substitutes an interesting inflection. The lentil-walnut pâté is a complex starter and classics such as the Salisbury seitan (a wheat gluten-based dish) and tempeh tacos feed the body and soul.

Southern California's Best Beaches

Hundreds of miles of Pacific beaches edge SoCal's golden coast – which makes choosing just one to visit almost impossible. Take your pick depending on what you prefer doing: launching your surfboard onto a world-famous break; snapping on a snorkel mask and peeking at colorful marine life; or just lazing on the sand.

1

3

4

1. Santa Monica (p152)
A carnival pier with a solar-powered Ferris wheel and a tiny aquarium for the kiddos sits atop this idyllic, 3-mile long strand, where LA comes to play.

2. Malibu (p144)
Celebrity residents aren't keen to share their paradisaical pocket beaches, but with persistence and some insider tips, you too can share these million-dollar views.

3. Huntington Beach (p244)
Officially 'Surf City, USA,' Huntington Beach is everything you imagined SoCal beach life to be, from surfing by the pier to sunset bonfires on the sand.

4. Mission Beach (p293)
A day trip to San Diego's most fun-crazed beach should begin with a ride on the Giant Dipper wooden roller coaster and end with sunset along Ocean Front Walk.

5. Crystal Cove State Park (p259)
Tired of manicured beaches filled with bikini babes? Escape instead to this wilder, undeveloped Orange County gem for beachcombing and scuba diving.

6. Coronado (p289)
Pedal a beach cruiser along the Silver Strand, or frolic like Marilyn Monroe did on the golden sand fronting San Diego's landmark Hotel Del.

7. East Beach (p398)
Next to historic Stearns Wharf, where Santa Barbara meets the sea, this easy-access beach fills in summer with swimmers, volleyball players and even sea kayakers.

8. Carpinteria State Beach (p420)
Even tots can get their feet wet or poke around the tide pools at this Santa Barbara County classic, where palm trees wave above soft sands.

2

DENISE TAYLOR / GETTY IMAGES ©

5

LAYLAND MASUDA / GETTY IMAGES ©

6

MACIEJ TOPOROWICZ / GETTY IMAGES ©

7

GERI LAVROV / GETTY IMAGES ©

8

VENTURE MEDIA GROUP / GETTY IMAGES ©

Father's Office PUB $$
(☎310-736-2224; www.fathersoffice.com; 1018 Montana Ave; dishes $5-15; ⌚5-10pm Mon-Wed, 5-11pm Thu, 4-11pm Fri, noon-11pm Sat, noon-10pm Sun) This elbow-to-elbow gastropub is famous for its burger: a dry-aged-beef number dressed in smoky bacon, sweet caramelized onion and an ingenious combo of Gruyère and blue cheese. Pair it with fries served in a mini shopping cart and a mug of handcrafted brew chosen from the three dozen on tap. No substitutions tolerated.

800 Degrees PIZZERIA $$
(☎310-566-0801; www.800degreespizza.com; 120 Wilshire Blvd; salads $4-7, pizzas $8-13; ⌚11am-1:30am Sun-Wed, to 2am Thu-Sat) The name refers to the temperature of their wood-fired pizza oven. Your job: follow the line into the big, splashy, marble-floored environs and create your own Neopolitan-style pizza.

First, pick your base: margherita, marinara, bianca (white) or verde (pesto), and watch as they pound and spin the dough in front of you. Then build your pie from a toppings bar stocked with fresh ingredients. The concept is cool, the servings are huge, and they stay open late.

R&D Kitchen CONTINENTAL $$
(☎310-395-3314; www.rd-kitchen.com; 1323 Montana Ave; dishes $13-29; ⌚11:30am-10pm Mon-Wed, to 11pm Thu & Fri, 11am-11pm Sat, to 10pm Sun; P 🚼) The sceniest spot on Montana Ave, this bar-restaurant's clean lines and chestnut interior open wonderfully onto the street attracting the yuppies from all corners for its tasty burgers, salads, steaks and pastas...and the full bar, of course.

Kreation CAFE $$
(☎310-458-4880; www.kreationkafe.net; 1023 Montana Ave; ⌚7am-10pm) The original, in what is now a growing local chain, is a combination of juicery and cafe. The juice bar blends coconut milk and blueberries, blood orange with carrots and turmeric, and all the greens. The cafe has a rustic Persian twist. They offer fresh poached salmon, tasty frittatas, and organic chicken and beef kebabs.

Library Alehouse PUB $$
(☎310-314-4855; www.libraryalehouse.com; 2911 Main St; mains $8-19; ⌚11:30am- midnight) Locals gather for the food as much as the beer at this wood-paneled gastropub with a cozy outdoor patio in the back. Angus burgers, fish tacos and hearty salads sate the 30-something, postwork regulars while 29 handcrafted microbrews keep 'em hanging around till midnight.

Rustic Canyon CALIFORNIAN $$$
(☎310-393-7050; www.rusticcanyonwinebar.com; 1119 Wilshire Blvd; dishes $12-33; ⌚5:30-10:30pm Sun-Thu, to 11pm Fri & Sat) Almost all the ingredients come from local organic producers, which means the menu shifts with availability, but count on two handmade pasta dishes, and an assortment of stunning small plates. Think: burrata with broccoli and a grilled lamb heart with crispy wild rice.

Or just get the burger: a world-class mound of mouth-melting meat on a buttered bun. Pair it with a California burgundy from the superb cellar.

Fig BISTRO $$$
(☎310-319-3111; www.figsantamonica.com; 101 Wilshire Blvd; mains lunch $13-24, dinner $18-34; ⌚7am-2pm daily, 5-10pm Tue-Sat) Set poolside at the historic Miramar hotel, and conceived with a coastal organic ethos, Fig leans heavily on local growers – most of what is served here is sourced from the twice-weekly farmers market down the street. We love the corn and kale veggie burger, and the BLT (with quarter-inch thick slab of bacon) at lunch.

For dinner they chop ceviche, steam mussels and serve a divine short rib and pancetta meatloaf.

Drinking & Nightlife

★Basement Tavern BAR
(www.basementtavern.com; 2640 Main St; ⌚5pm-2am) A creative speakeasy, housed in the basement of the Victorian, and our favorite well in Santa Monica. We love it for its crafted cocktails, cozy booths, island bar, and nightly live-music calendar that features blues, jazz, bluegrass and rock bands. It gets way too busy on weekends for our taste, but weeknights can be special.

Copa d'Oro BAR
(www.copadoro.com; 217 Broadway Ave; ⌚5:30pm-midnight Mon-Wed, to 2am Thu-Sat) The cocktail menu was created by the talented Vincenzo Marianella – a man who knows his spirits, and has trained his team to concoct addictive cocktails from a well of top-end spirits and a produce bin of fresh herbs, fruits, juices and a few veggies too. The rock tunes and the smooth, dark ambience don't hurt.

Misfit LOUNGE
(☎310-656-9800; www.themisfitbar.com; 225 Santa Monica Blvd; ⊙noon-late Mon-Fri, from 11am Sat & Sun) This darkly lit emporium of food, drink and fun is notable for the decent – not great – menu, and phenomenal cocktails made from craftsman spirits. Set in a historic building decked out with a retro interior, it's busy from brunch to last call.

Bar Chloe LOUNGE
(www.barchloe.com; 1449 2nd St; ⊙6pm-midnight Mon, to 1am Tue, to 2am Wed-Fri, 7pm-2am Sat) Cozy, dark and elegant with dangling chandeliers, twinkling candles, intimate booths, crisp white tablecloths, and a chamomile mai tai that has earned rave reviews. We wouldn't know, we ordered a whiskey neat. The tapas and sliders are decent too.

Rick's Tavern BAR
(☎310-392-2772; 2907 Main St; ⊙11am-2am) When everywhere else on Main is dead, this reasonably priced, friendly sports bar has a pulse. Late night? Midday? There's usually a fun vibe, a ballgame on the flat-screen TV, and it serves a mean bar burger too.

Bungalow LOUNGE
(www.thebungalowsm.com; 101 Wilshire Blvd; ⊙5pm-2am Mon-Fri, 2pm-2am Sat, 2-10pm Sun) A Brent Bolthouse nightspot, the indoor-outdoor lounge at the Fairmont Miramar was one of the hottest nights out in LA when it burst onto the scene a couple of years ago. It's since settled down, and like most Westside spots can be too dude-centric late in the evening, but the setting is elegant, and there is still beautiful mischief to be found here.

Dogtown Coffee CAFE
(www.dogtowncoffee.com; 2003 Main St; ⊙5:30am-5pm Mon-Fri, from 6:30am Sat & Sun) Set in the old Zephyr surf shop headquarters, where skateboarding was invented during a 1970s drought that emptied pools across LA, they brew great coffee and make a mean breakfast burrito, the preferred nutritional supplement of surfers the world over. And they're open for dawn patrol.

Galley STEAKHOUSE
(www.thegalleyrestaurant.net; 2442 Main St; ⊙5-11pm Mon-Sat, to 1am Sun) This long-running, much beloved steak and seafood house has occupied this boat-themed restaurant since 1934 and we love the bar here. It's strung with Christmas lights, staffed by no-nonsense, but fun barkeeps, and is almost always packed with regulars. This is old Santa Monica, folks.

Circle Bar BAR
(www.thecirclebar.com; 2926 Main St; ⊙9pm-2am) A long-running 'meet market.' Strong drinks, loud music and seductive red-on-black decor further loosen inhibitions, but waiting in line to get past the bouncers can be a turnoff.

Zanzibar CLUB
(www.zanzibarlive.com; 1301 5th St; cover $5-10; ⊙9pm-2am Tue-Sun) Beat freaks will be in heaven at this groovetastic den dressed in a sensuous Indian-African vibe. A shape-shifting, global DJ line-up spans Arabic to Latin to African, depending on the night. The crowd is just as multicultural.

Chez Jay BAR
(www.chezjays.com; 1657 Ocean Ave; ⊙2pm-midnight Mon, 11:30am-2am Tue-Fri, 9am-2am Sat & Sun) Rocking since 1959, this nautical-themed dive is dark and dank and all the more glorious for it. The food's not bad either.

☆ Entertainment

★Harvelle's BLUES
(☎310-395-1676; www.harvelles.com; 1432 4th St; cover $5-15) This dark blues grotto has been packing 'em in since 1931 but somehow still manages to feel like a well-kept secret. There are no big-name acts here, but the quality is usually high. Sunday's Toledo Show mixes soul, jazz and cabaret, and Wednesday night brings the always funky House of Vibe All-Stars.

McCabe's Guitar Shop LIVE MUSIC
(☎310-828-4497; www.mccabes.com; 3101 Pico Blvd; tickets $15-30) Sure, this mecca of musicianship sells guitars and other instruments, but you want to come for concerts in the back room or at their nearby **bar & grill** (2455 Santa Monica Blvd; ⊙11am-2am), where the likes of Jackson Browne, Charlie Hunter and Liz Phair have performed.

Laemmle's Monica 4 CINEMA
(www.laemmle.com; 1332 2nd St; adult/child $11/8; ⊙11am-1am) Art-house films are screened in old-school multiplex environs that could use a once-over. Still, the screens are good-sized and the cinema current and tasteful.

Aero Theater CINEMA
(www.americancinematheque.com; 1328 Montana Ave) Santa Monica's original movie theater

(c 1940) is now operated by **American Cinematheque**, where they screen old and neo classics, and offer Q&A sessions with bigwigs from time to time. Check their online calendar for upcoming shows.

Broad Stage THEATER
(www.thebroadstage.com; 1310 11th St) A 499-seat, state-of-the-art theater is the anchor of SMC's striking, modernist performing-arts complex, which is a satellite campus on its own. It features new interpretations of classic Shakespeare, one-man shows, and classical and world music performances.

Magicopolis MAGIC
(☎310-451-2241; www.magicopolis.com; 1418 4th St; tickets $24-34; ⏲8pm Fri & Sat, 2pm Sat & Sun; 👪) Aspiring Harry Potters won't be the only ones who enjoy the comedy-laced sleight-of-hand, levitation and other illusions performed by Steve Spills and cohorts in this intimate space. Escapes from reality last about 90 minutes, and there's even a small shop for all your wizard supplies.

Edgemar Center for the Arts THEATER
(www.edgemarcenter.org; 2437 Main St) With two stages and a gallery, the Edgemar also provides a platform for crossover collaborations between playwrights, musicians, actors, dancers and performance artists. It also has an acting school.

Shopping

For big chains like Anthropologie, the flagship Apple, Guess and Converse (where you can build your own shoes), make your way to the Third Street Promenade (p156). **Santa Monica Place** (www.santamonicaplace.com; 395 Santa Monica Pl; ⏲10am-9pm Mon-Thu, to 10pm Fri & Sat, 11am-8pm Sun) offers more upscale, corporate consumption. For more indie-minded boutiques, head to Montana Ave and Main St.

★**Paris 1900** VINTAGE
(www.paris1900.com; 2703 Main St) An exquisite collection of vintage French fashion from 1900 to 1930, and a few new vintage-inspired garments. Expect the finest jewelry and lace, with an emphasis on period bridal. Look for the Montmartre-inspired art-nouveau entry.

Planet Blue FASHION
(www.shopplanetblue.com; 2940 Main St; ⏲10am-6pm) Everyone from moneyed hipsters to soccer moms to Hollywood royalty peruses the racks at this expansive and stylish boutique stocked with tremendous denim and contemporary casual collections, as well as high-end beauty essentials and some sexy silver too. Men's gear can be found on **Montana Ave** (www.shopplanetblue.com; 800 14th St; ⏲10am-6pm).

Blues Jean Bar DENIM
(☎855-341-0073; www.thebluesjeanbar.com; 1409 Montana Ave; ⏲10am-6pm Mon-Sat, 11am-5pm Sun) Belly up to the rustic wood bar and order yours by style (boot cut, skinny or straight), size and wash (dark, light, medium or distressed), and they'll find you something from their well of denim, which includes the likes of Henry and Bell, Fidelity, Hudson and more. Jeans range from $150 to $250.

Vital Hemp FASHION
(☎310-450-2260; www.vitalhemp.com; 2305 Main St; ⏲10am-7pm) A boutique stocked with designer hemp goods made in Downtown LA. They have fitted tees, chinos, hoodies and more.

Mindfulnest ARTWORK, GIFTS
(www.mindfulnest.com; 2711 Main St; ⏲11:30am-8pm Mon-Thu, 11am-8:30pm Fri & Sat, 11am-7pm Sun) An endearing shop, named one of the best in LA by *Los Angeles Magazine*, stocked with pop art and handmade games, leather bracelets and earrings. Most of it has been crafted by local artists, including Jeff Clarence who creates fun graphic art printed on wood.

Ten Women ARTWORK
(www.tenwomengallery.com; 1128 Montana Ave; ⏲10am-6pm) They recently moved from Abbot Kinney to their new Montana Ave digs, but the ethos at this gallery hasn't changed. They sell the art, folk art and crafts from a cooperative of 21 (they used to be 10) female artists.

Supra SHOES
(☎310-458-6200; www.suprafootwear.com; 304 Santa Monica Blvd; ⏲10am-9pm Mon-Thu, to 10pm Fri & Sat, 11am-7pm Sun) For those who crave high-end high tops, this branded store delivers fit and style.

Great Labels FASHION
(www.greatlabels.com; 1126 Wilshire Blvd; ⏲10am-6pm Mon-Sat, 11am-5pm Sun) Sensational secondhand couture and designer hand-me-downs from celebrity consigners. There's

Oscar and Golden Globe gowns, elegant handbags, shoes and accessories from Pucci, Prada, Jimmy Choo and Dior. If you've ever wanted to pay $250 for a four-figure dress, come here.

Free People FASHION
(www.freepeople.com; 2925 Main St; ⏲11am-7pm Mon-Sat, noon-6pm Sun) Hippie-chic women's gear with a dash of retro cool. Santa Monica's pretty, pouty, upscale flower children get dressed here.

Hundreds CLOTHING
(www.thehundreds.com; 416 Broadway Ave; ⏲11am-7pm Mon-Sat, noon-6pm Sun) A decade-old, LA-based, urban-skate-culture- and hip-hop-inspired label with tailored T-shirts, hoodies, sweaters and jackets. It's all stylish and affordable. Lately they've collaborated with the artist, James Jean, whose work graces some of their tees and skateboards. The boards are especially cool. They'll fully construct any of their skates for $135.

Wine Expo DRINKS
(www.wineexpo.com; 2933 Santa Monica Blvd) LA's best nightlife generally sprouts at house parties. When you get your invitation, stop here to grab wine, champagne, whiskey or tequila from the best small producers and distilleries in the world. There are always sweet deals to be had. Ask the knowledgeable staff for guidance. They have an attached tasting room, if you need a drink, like now.

Fred Segal FASHION, JEWELRY
(www.fredsegal.com; 500 Broadway; ⏲10am-7pm Mon-Sat, noon-6pm Sun) Celebs and beautiful people circle this impossibly chic, but slightly snooty, warren of high-end boutiques that straddles 5th St and dominates an entire block.

REI OUTDOOR EQUIPMENT
(www.rei.com; 402 Santa Monica Blvd; ⏲10am-9pm Mon-Sat, 11am-7pm Sun) This 'cathedral to outdoor gear' makes it easy to stock up on everything from wool socks to speed-dry underwear, rolling backpacks to Everest-capable sleeping bags. The staff are friendly and knowledgeable. REI also rents camping equipment.

Undefeated SHOES
(www.undeftd.com; 2654b Main St; ⏲10am-7pm Mon-Sat, 11am-6pm Sun) Get your kicks at this slammin' sneaker store specializing in vintage and limited editions, hand selected from the manufacturer by the manager. When new shipments arrive, expect sidewalk campouts.

Puzzle Zoo GAMES
(☎310-393-9201; www.puzzlezoo.com; 1413 Third St Promenade; ⏲10am-9pm Sun-Thu, to 11pm Fri & Sat; 👪) Those searching galaxy-wide for the caped Lando Calrissian action figure, look no more. Puzzle Zoo stocks every imaginable Star Wars figurine this side of Endor. There's also an encyclopedic selection of puzzles, board games and toys. Kids adore it.

LOCAL KNOWLEDGE

ANDY LIPKIS: ENVIRONMENTALIST

For over 30 years TreePeople founder Andy Lipkis and his team have been leading tree plantings in neighborhoods, on school campuses and in the mountains around LA. These days he's focused on solving LA's massive water problem.

Biggest Success

We convinced the county to invest $250,000 into the Sun Valley watershed, instead of spending $50,000 on a storm drain. Now floodwaters, which pour past auto yards and were carrying pollutants to the sea, filter through permeable asphalt, soil and gravel and back into the water table.

Most Visible Project

We developed a **Green Street** (Bicknell St, btwn Main & Pacific) 🍃 with the city of Santa Monica. We ripped out asphalt and replaced it with permeable concrete, doubled the parkway and now rainwater, which was pooling in the street, flows into mulched swails and filters directly to the roots of nearby palms.

Favorite Leafy Street

I love Pasadena's live oaks, and the way the camphors on Maple Dr in Beverly Hills form a canopy over the street. They are huge, sculptural, beautiful.

Aura Shop NEW AGE
(www.aurashop.com; 2914 Main St; ⏲11am-6pm Mon-Sat, to 5pm Sun) Well, you *are* in California. You may as well get your aura read. Yes, auras do exist (it's that heat energy radiating off your skin) and the color trails they leave behind signify…something, or so we're told. Just get the aura photo and the reading and believe it or not. Also sells books, candles and crystals.

Address Boutique FASHION
(www.theaddressboutique.com; 1116 Wilshire Blvd; ⏲10am-6pm Mon-Sat, noon-5pm Sun) A consignment boutique on Wilshire, Address Boutique offers couture from the likes of Chanel, Alexander McQueen, Chloe and Burberry, some of which were once draped on Meg Ryan, Salma Hayak and Sharon Stone.

Hennessey & Ingalls BOOKS
(☎310-458-9074; www.hennesseyingalls.com; 214 Wilshire Blvd; ⏲10am-8pm) LA's best art and architecture bookstore features works on Matisse, Renzo Piano and all the giants of architecture, as well as lesser known volumes on sustainable design and graffiti. All in a cavernous and stylishly spare warehouse space with exposed beams patrolled by staff who have forgotten more about design than most will ever know.

VENICE & MARINA DEL REY

If you were born too late, and have always been a little jealous of the hippie heyday, come down to the Boardwalk and inhale an incense-scented whiff of Venice, a boho beach town and longtime haven for artists, new agers, road-weary tramps, freaks and free spirits. This is where Jim Morrison and the Doors lit their fire, where Arnold Schwarzenegger pumped himself to stardom, and the place the late Dennis Hopper once called home.

SoCal's quintessential bohemian playground is the legacy of Abbot Kinney (1850–1920). A tobacco mogul by trade and a dreamer at heart, Kinney dug canals and turned fetid swampland into a cultural and recreational resort he dubbed the 'Venice of America.' For nearly two decades, crowds thronged to this 'Coney Island on the Pacific' to be poled around by imported gondoliers, walk among Renaissance-style arcaded buildings and listen to Benny Goodman tooting his horn in clubs. But time was not kind to Kinney's vision.

Most of the canals were filled and paved over in 1929 and Venice plunged into a steep decline until its cheap rents and mellow vibe drew first the beatniks, then hippies in the '50s and '60s. A decade later Venice turned 'Dogtown' as modern skateboarding hit the big time. These days, tech and entertainment dollars have fueled a hard-charging gentrification that is changing this once low-key enclave with a strong sense of community. Still there are more indie boutiques and cafes than chains (though in LA that's an increasingly blurry line too), and there's plenty of innovative architecture and public art. The Boardwalk, the bike path and the beach are the traditional attractions here, but the whole area's worth a wander. Abbot Kinney Blvd has street parking, Ivy League baristas, jihadi-bearded tech millionaires, and pretension to spare, but you must experience it. Parking lots on and near the beach charge between $6 and $12.

Follow the coast south of Venice and you'll come to Marina del Rey, which has nearly as many boats as residents. Some 5300 vessels bob in what is one of the largest artificial small-craft harbors in the country. Wrested from coastal wetlands in the '60s, the surrounding neighborhood consists mostly of generic concrete towers and has the disjointed, sterile feel typical of urban planning during the modernist era. As an architectural case study, the Marina has its appeal, but most visitors are really here to get active in what is truly an aquatic playground.

South of the Marina is the laid-back beach enclave of Playa Del Rey, where the beach is loamy, wide and piled into dunes, beachside fire pits are legal and the last swath of the Ballona wetlands still blooms.

Sights

★Venice Boardwalk WATERFRONT
(Ocean Front Walk; Map p170; Venice Pier to Rose Ave; ⏲24hr) Life in Venice moves to a different rhythm and nowhere more so than on the famous Venice Boardwalk, officially known as Ocean Front Walk. It's a freak show, a human zoo and a wacky carnival alive with hoola-hoop magicians, old-timey jazz combos, solo distorted garage rockers and artists (good and bad) – as far as LA experiences go, it's a must.

The Sunday-afternoon drum circle draws hundreds of revelers for tribal jamming and spontaneous dancing on the grassy mounds (sometimes beats migrate to the sand, as well). If the noise doesn't show you the way there, just follow your nose toward skunky cigarettes, which are sold over the counter at several cannabis clubs. And don't miss the tagged up towers and the free-standing concrete wall, forever open to aerosol Picassos.

Venice Canals NEIGHBORHOOD
(Map p170) Even many Angelenos have no idea that just a couple of blocks away from the Boardwalk madness is an idyllic neighborhood that preserves 3 miles of Kinney's canals. The **Venice Canal Walk** threads past eclectic homes, over bridges and waterways where ducks preen and locals lollygag in little rowboats. It's best accessed from either Venice or Washington Blvds.

Abbot Kinney Boulevard STREET
(Map p170) Kinney would probably be delighted to find that one of Venice's best-loved streets bears his name. Sort of a seaside Melrose with a Venetian flavor, the mile-long stretch of Abbot Kinney Blvd between Venice Blvd and Main St is full of upscale boutiques, galleries, lofts and sensational restaurants.

In late September, the **Abbot Kinney Festival** draws thousands of revelers, as does the now-institutionalized **First Friday** art walk, when the galleries and shops stay open late and you'll roam all night with the tramps, hippies, weirdos, fashionistas, yuppies and squares.

LA Louver GALLERY
(Map p170; www.lalouver.com; 45 N Venice Blvd; ⌚10am-6pm Tue-Sat) FREE The best art gallery in Venice, and arguably the best in all of LA, LA Louver was established by Peter Gouls in 1975, and since 1994 has been housed in a landmark building designed by Frederick Fisher. It's a modern and contemporary art gallery featuring rotating, museum-quality exhibitions that show for five to six weeks.

We saw a mind-bending exhibit of German furnishings from the 1970s in the downstairs gallery, which included Nazi distributed Volksenfanger radios and strange interactive twists. Upstairs there was work by Boyle Heights–street-artist-turned-fine-artist Gajin Fujita. They also represent David Hockney. All are welcome.

Fisherman's Village NEIGHBORHOOD
(Map p62; www.visitmarinadelrey.com; 13755 Fiji Way) Most boats, including a seasonal ferry

VENICE ART WALK

Who needs galleries when you've got great outdoor art? Venice has plenty of both, so keep your eyes open as you stroll around town (and let us know your favorite finds!). A leisurely tour might start at the corner of Rose Ave and Main St where Jonathan Borofsky's 30ft-tutu-clad **Ballerina Clown** (Map p170) (1989) offers up a surreal presence. One block south, Frank Gehry's **Chiat/Day building** (Map p170) is fronted by massive binoculars by Claes Oldenburg and Coosje van Bruggen.

But Venice's real strength is its murals. Fine specimens along the Venice Boardwalk include **Chagall Returns to Venice Beach** (Map p170; 201 Ocean Front Walk at Ozone Ave) by Christina Schlesinger, and **Venice Reconstituted** (Map p170; 25 Windward Ave) by Rip Cronk. The latter is a parody of Botticelli's *Venus in the Halfshell* containing a cacophony of figures, many of them real Venetians. As you walk around, you'll find many more Cronk murals. His **Homage to a Starry Night** (Map p170; Ocean Front Walk at Wavecrest Ave) was inspired by the Van Gogh original. The same artist also created the epic 30ft-high portraits of one-time Venice resident **Jim Morrison** (Morning Shot; Map p170; 1881 Speedway) and of city founder **Abbot Kinney** (Map p170; N Venice at Pacific Ave).

With such a strong mural tradition, it only makes sense that the nonprofit **Social & Public Art Resource Center** (SPARC; Map p170; www.sparcmurals.org; 685 N Venice Blvd; ⌚10am-5pm Mon-Fri) FREE, which promotes, preserves and produces public murals throughout LA, is based in Venice. They have a gallery here too.

Each May the Venice Family Clinic sponsors an art auction and studio tour also known as the **Venice Art Walk** (www.theveniceartwalk.org; tickets $50) to help raise funds for the clinic, which brings health care to 24,000 underserved men, women and children each year. With the ticket, you receive a map and pass that grants entry into over 50 local studios featuring hundreds of original pieces, whether you plan on bidding or not.

Venice

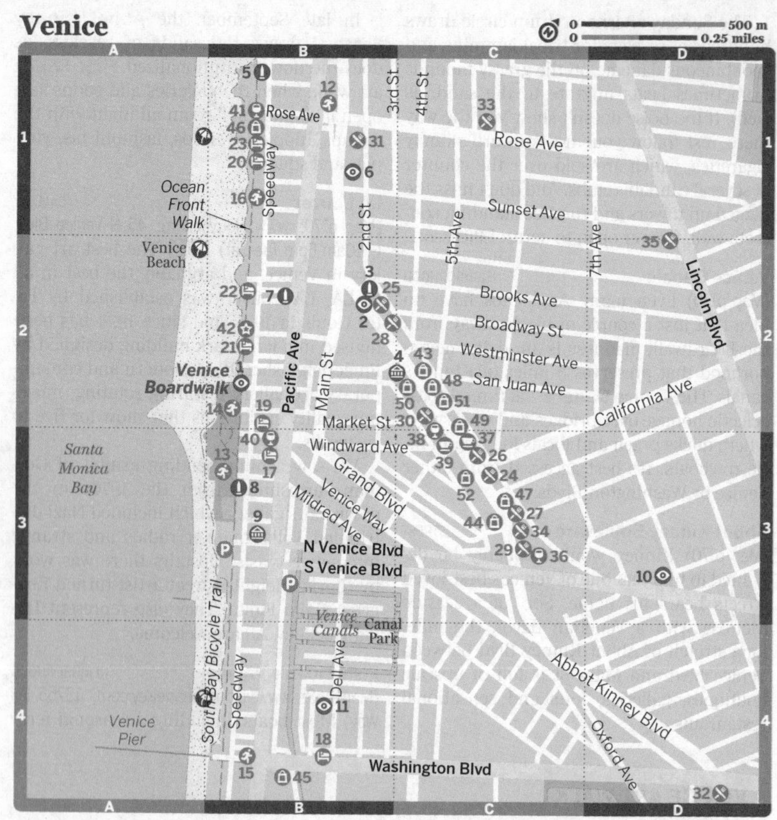

to Catalina Island, party fishing boats and winter whale-watching tours leave from this kitschy strip of candy-colored cottages filled with tacky gift shops and restaurants.

North of here, the small **Burton Chace Park** is a good spot for a picnic, flipping a Frisbee, flying a kite or watching the parade of boats sailing through the Main Channel. In July and August there's a weekend concert series in the evenings. The same months also see the Water Bus in operation. It makes six strategic stops, including at Fisherman's Village and the park, and costs $1 per boarding or $5 for a day pass.

Ballona Wetlands OUTDOORS

(Map p62) Wetlands are the unsung heroes of the natural world. They clean silty rivers before the water trickles into the sea, provide shelter and hatcheries for birds and fish, and are extremely difficult to restore and protect in an increasingly urbanized world.

These last remaining wetlands in LA County are home to at least 200 migrating and resident bird species, including the great blue heron. Their habitat, however, has shrunk significantly since Playa Vista, a much-debated custom-planned luxury community for about 11,000 residents, took root across Lincoln. But the developers, via the **Friends of the Ballona Wetlands** (www.ballonafriends.org), get points for restoring and expanding the healthiest intact marsh, which has seen increasing bird activity.

Dockweiler State Beach OUTDOORS

(Map p62) With jumbo jets soaring overhead, sailboats bobbing beyond the rolling surf, bonfires raging in the pit, and a waxing moon rising high, summer nights on Dockweiler – a 3.5-mile stretch of open beach – are always a good time.

Venice

Top Sights
1 Venice Boardwalk B2

Sights
2 Abbot Kinney Boulevard B2
3 Abbot Kinney Mural B2
Ballerina Clown .... (see 12)
4 C.A.V.E. C2
5 Chagall Returns to Venice Beach B1
6 Chiat/Day Building B1
7 Homage to a Starry Night B2
8 Jim Morrison Mural B3
9 LA Louver B3
10 Social & Public Art Resource Center D3
11 Venice Canals B4
Venice Reconstituted .... (see 19)

Activities, Courses & Tours
12 Exhale B1
13 Muscle Beach B3
14 Venice Beach Skate Park B2
15 Venice Bike & Skate B4
16 Venice Boardwalk Bike Rental B1

Sleeping
17 Hotel Erwin B3
18 Inn at Venice Beach B4
19 Samesun B2
20 Su Casa B1
21 Venice Beach Inn & Suites B2
22 Venice Breeze Suites B2
23 Venice Suites B1

Eating
24 Abbot's Pizza Company C3
25 Axe B2
26 Casa Linda C3
Fig Tree's Café .... (see 20)
27 Gjelina C3
28 Joe's B2
29 Lemonade C3
Oscar's Cerveteca .... (see 33)
30 Pork Belly's C2
31 Rose Café B1
32 Scopa D4
33 Superba C1
34 Tasting Kitchen C3
35 Wurstkuche D2

Drinking & Nightlife
36 Brig C3
37 Intelligentsia Coffeebar C3
38 Roosterfish C3
39 Tom's C3
40 Townhouse & Delmonte Speakeasy B3
41 Venice Beach Ale House B1
Venice Beach Wines .... (see 33)

Entertainment
42 Venice Beach Freakshow B2

Shopping
43 A + R Store C2
44 Alexis Bittar C3
Alternative .... (see 26)
45 Arbor B4
46 Arbor B1
Bountiful .... (see 26)
47 Firefly C3
48 Nightcap C2
49 Principessa C2
50 Strange Invisible C2
51 Warakuku C2
52 Will C3

South Venice Beach OUTDOORS
(Map p62) South of Washington Blvd, the throng dissipates, and the golden sands unfurl in a more pristine manner. Waves roll in consistently and are ideal for bodysurfing. Volleyball games erupt at a moment's notice. Parking is an issue, which makes it a mostly local scene. Bike and crash it.

C.A.V.E. GALLERY
(Map p170; www.cavegallery.net; 1108 Abbot Kinney Blvd; noon-6pm Wed-Sun) One of our favorite galleries on Abbot Kinney, they specialize in single artist exhibitions. When we passed they hosted the works of Ralph Ziman, a South African–born artist who hung traditionally beaded machine guns to publicize the effects of conflict across Africa. He called it 'Ghosts.'

Activities

Venice Boardwalk Bike Rental CYCLING, SKATING
(Map p170; 310-396-2453; 517 Ocean Front Walk; per hr/2hr/day bikes $7/12/20, surfboards $10/20/30, skates $7/12/20) Located in the Gingerbread Court complex, which was built by Charlie Chaplin, these days there are a few shops, a cafe, some apartments above, and this reliable Venice outfitter.

Venice Bike & Skate BIKES, BLADES
(Map p170; 310-301-4011; 21 Washington Blvd; per hr/day cruisers $6/21, rollerblades & skates $5/20; 9:30am-5pm Mon-Fri, from 8:30am Sat & Sun) Get outfitted for a day on the bike path.

Venice Beach Skate Park SKATE PARK
(Map p170; 1800 Ocean Front Walk; dawn-dusk) Long the destination of local skate punks,

the concrete at this skate park has now been molded and steel-fringed into 17,000 sq ft of vert, tranny and street terrain with unbroken ocean views. The old-school-style skate run and the world-class pool are most popular for high flyers and gawking spectators.

Exhale WELLNESS
(Map p170; www.exhalespa.com; 245 S Main St; per class $22, community class $11; ⏲7am-9:30pm Mon-Fri, 7:15am-8pm Sat, 8:45am-8pm Sun) Just over the border from Venice, and part of a national yoga and spa chain, Exhale has two spacious studios, a gifted teacher roster, and a loyal dogtown crowd. They generally offer one community class on each weekday.

Muscle Beach GYM
(Map p170; www.musclebeach.net; 1800 Ocean Front Walk; per day $10; ⏲8am-7pm May-Sep, to 6pm Oct-Apr) Gym rats with an exhibitionist streak can get a tan and a workout at this famous outdoor gym right on the Venice Boardwalk where Arnold and Franco Columbo once bulked up.

Marina Del Rey Parasailing PARASAILING, BOATING
(☎310-306-2222; www.marinadelreyparasailing.com; flights from $75; ⏲10:30am-sunset Mon-Fri, from 9:30am Sat & Sun) Set in Fisherman's Village behind **El Torito**, Marina Del Rey Parasailing will harness you in and make you fly up to 500ft high. For $10 more you can fly 800ft. It's a quick thrill. Flights last eight to 12 minutes.

You may also rent a variety of vessels here, including sail boats (per hour $80), motor boats (per hour $75), kayaks (per hour $15 to $25) and SUP kits (per hour $25).

Sleeping

Samesun HOSTEL $
(Map p170; ☎310-399-7649, reservations 888-718-8287; www.samesun.com; 25 Windward Ave; dm $35-41, r with shared/private bath $95/115) Venice's newest hostel is a refurbished version of an old standby, but it's well located on Windward Ave, has spectacular rooftop views of Venice Beach, and four- to

IT'S A FREAK SHOW

When Todd Ray was a young buck growing up in South Carolina he was into magic. One day he went to a carnival sideshow featuring a man whose limbs were ossified. Ray watched as this man, who couldn't move his arms or legs, rolled a cigarette with his lips, tongue and shoulders. He even managed to light it. Afterwards, Todd approached the man who told him, 'If I can do that in my condition then you can do anything you've ever dreamed of.'

That encounter may explain why Ray went on to enjoy a wildly successful music career. He produced records for LA favorite, Ozomatli and the legendary Santana. He even won three Grammy Awards. But it may also explain why he has a soft spot for the unique, challenged and odd among us. And we're not just talking about humans.

Disenchanted with the music business, Ray opened the **Venice Beach Freakshow** (Map p170; ☎310-314-1808; www.venicebeachfreakshow.com; 909 Ocean Front Walk; admission $5; ⏲10am-6pm Sat & Sun) in 2008. He started small. One day he found a two-headed turtle. On another he re-connected with an old neighbor who swallowed swords. He sought out the weird and weirder and rented a small storefront on the boardwalk that he's since expanded into nearly the entire ground floor of the same building.

'This is where the lost children go,' he said. 'I have a guy with 2000-some piercings in his face and forty-some in his mouth. He has trouble getting apartments.' Ray co-signed a lease for that fellow, and he counsels his bearded lady. He's also a pastor, and officiated over the ceremony of The Littlest Married Couple in the World and is their defacto marriage counselor. 'I have to make sure they don't break up,' he said.

What it all amounts to is a circus-style sideshow, including a live 20-minute performance where you'll watch a fire eater, a Rubber Girl and an Electric Lady who gets shot up with 100,000 volts of electricity with no drama at all. Her secret? She survived a lightning strike. There's also a gallery where you can observe 60 of the strangest creatures on earth, including 10 two-headed animals.

Perhaps there was something special about that encounter he had years ago, could be his charm and generosity, or maybe Todd Ray is just a gifted soul, but everything he touches seems to flourish. Even his freak show, the behind-the-scenes workings of which are now a reality television series on AMC.

eight-person dorms, as well as some private rooms with either en suite or shared baths. Service won't win any awards, but it's still a popular choice.

Venice Beach Inn & Suites BOUTIQUE HOTEL $$
(Map p170; ☎310-396-4559; www.venicebeachsuites.com; 1305 Ocean Front Walk; r from $159; P) This good-value place right on the Boardwalk scores big for its bend-over-backwards staff, and bevy of beach toys for rent. There are exposed-brick walls, kitchenettes, wood floors and built-in closets. It's ideal for long stays. Kitchen suites are big enough for dinner parties.

Inn at Venice Beach MOTEL $$
(Map p170; ☎310-821-2557; www.innatvenicebeach.com; 327 Washington Blvd; r from $199; P) Close to the beach, the Venice canals, bars and restaurants, this Oaxacan-themed motel sports brightly hued rooms with a good range of amenities. All wrap around a central courtyard perfect for munching your free breakfast in the morning.

Inn at Playa del Rey INN $$$
(☎310-574-1920; www.innatplayadelrey.com; Culver Blvd; r $205-385; P @) A rambling cottage turned impeccably run inn overlooks the state-protected Ballona Wetlands. They have pastel brushed rooms with a contemporary feel all with bathtubs, iPod docks, and some with balcony or fireplaces (get room 207 if you can). There's free bike rental, wine hour, freshly baked chocolate chip cookies and sensational breakfasts too.

Venice Breeze Suites BOUTIQUE HOTEL $$$
(Map p170; ☎310-566-2222; www.venicesuites.com; 2 Breeze Ave; r $200-270; P) A classy beachfront property with stylish studios and suites boasting wood floors, exposed-brick walls, floating beds, rain showers, frosted-glass desks and wall-mounted, flat-screen TVs. Suites have full-sized kitchens and there's a communal barbecue area on the rooftop. Parking is included.

Hotel Erwin BOUTIQUE HOTEL $$$
(Map p170; ☎800-786-7789; www.hotelerwin.com; 1697 Pacific Ave; r from $263; P ❄ @) This old motor inn has been dressed up, colored and otherwise funkified in retro style. Think: eye-popping oranges, yellows and greens, framed photos of graffiti art, flat-screen TVs, and ergo sofas in the spacious rooms. Book online for the best deals. Whether you stay here or not, the rooftop lounge is a wonderful place for a sundowner.

Venice Suites INN $$$
(Map p170; ☎310-566-5224; www.venicesuites.com; 417 Ocean Front Walk; studios from $160, 1-bedroom ste from $270; P ❄) Tasty one-bedroom suites and studios right on the beach with hardwood floors, flat-screen TVs, kitchenettes, marble trim in the baths and a special rooftop deck where the views are magnificent. Expect a discount for extended stays.

Su Casa BOUTIQUE HOTEL $$$
(Map p170; ☎310-452-9700; www.sucasavenice.com; 431 Ocean Front Walk; r from $209; P) Set in the string of boho boardwalk studio and apartment hotels overlooking the Boardwalk, rooms here are fairly large with new wood floors, wall-mounted flat-screen TVs, humidifiers and air-con, and framed black-and-white photos of old-school surfers.

Eating

Wurstkuche SAUSAGE $
(Map p170; www.wurstkuche.com; 625 Lincoln Blvd; dishes $4-8; 11am-midnight, bar to 2am) Set in a brick-house loft, but sealed off from the on-rushing madness of Lincoln Blvd, this German sausage and beer *haus* specializes in three things: gourmet and classic grilled sausages; fine Belgian, German and North American beers; and Belgian fries with ample dipping sauces. Highly recommended.

Pork Belly's BARBECUE $
(Map p170; ☎424-777-8875; www.porkbellysla.com; 1146 Abbot Kinney Blvd; mains $9-14; 11am-9pm) This place has always been a BBQ joint, but it's been re-imagined as the kind of place that serves new-school chopped chicken and brisket sandwiches, and slow-smoked pork belly topped with BBQ sauce served up on a plate or in a stripped down BLT sandwich on sourdough with aioli. They also fry pickles and serve sweet-potato tots.

Abbot's Pizza Company PIZZERIA $
(Map p170; ☎310-396-7334; www.abbotspizzaco.com; 1407 Abbot Kinney Blvd; slices $3-5, pizzas $12-29; 11am-11pm Sun-Thu, to midnight Fri & Sat;) Join the flip-flop crowd at this shoebox-sized pizza kitchen for habit-forming bagel-crust pies tastily decorated with tequila-lime chicken, portobello mushrooms, goats cheese and other gourmet morsels served up at tummy-grumbling speed.

Lemonade CALIFORNIAN $
(Map p170; http://lemonadela.com; 1661 Abbot Kinney Blvd; meals $8-13; ⏲11am-9pm) The first incarnation of an imaginative, local market cafe with a line-up of tasty salads (watermelon radish and chili or tamarind pork and spicy carrots), and stockpots bubbling with lamb and stewed figs or miso-braised short ribs. It has six kinds of lemonade augmented with blueberries and mint or watermelon and rosemary. Yummy sweets too.

Señor G's MEXICAN $
(☎310-822-7733; www.senorgs.com; 343 Culver Blvd; mains $4-12; ⏲7am-8:30pm) A beloved laid-back Mexican joint packed with Playa Vista business types at lunch and locals at dinner. They do massive burritos filled with chunks of beef simmered in red sauce (chile Colorado) and tender pork bubbled in tomatillo sauce (chili verde); veggie types may enjoy the cactus burrito.

They also do tacos, enchiladas, tostadas, some terrific Mexican breakfasts and fresh-pressed juices.

Casa Linda MEXICAN $
(Map p170; www.casalindamexicangrill.com; 1357 Abbot Kinney Blvd; mains $6-10; ⏲11:30am-9:30pm) Consider the chicken *mole* plate, contemplate the tacos and tamales, then order an authentic *torta* (Mexican sandwich) smeared with black-bean paste, and piled with avocado, onions and your choice of chicken, pork or tongue. The best part: it's affordable, which is saying something on this bougie-hippie boulevard.

Shack PUB $
(185 Culver Blvd; dishes $5.25-9.25; ⏲11am-10pm; P) A Playa Del Rey classic, with a knotted-wood bar, flat-screen TVs strobing sports and porthole windows inside, as well as a sunshine patio out back. But the crowds are here for the famed Shack Burger (a beef patty topped with a butterflied Louisiana sausage); it's a slightly intimidating, spicy, savory thing of artery-clogging beauty.

Axe ASIAN FUSION $$
(Map p170; ☎310-664-9787; www.axerestaurant.com; 1009 Abbot Kinney Blvd; mains $12-24; ⏲9-11am & 11:30am-3pm Wed-Fri, 6-10pm Wed & Thu, 6-10:30pm Fri & Sat, 6-9:30pm Sun; P) One of our favorite kitchens in Venice offers light, healthy and tasty Asian fusion. At lunch get the basic bowl, which combines brown rice, marinated cucumber, sprouts and other veggies with grilled chicken, salmon or tofu. At dinner they do a range of seafood mains, braised rabbit and delicious house-made pork sausage served in chic, minimalist environs.

Superba MODERN AMERICAN $$
(Map p170; ☎310-399-6400; www.superbasnackbar.com; 533 Rose Ave; dishes $8-19; ⏲10:30am-2:30pm Fri-Sun, 6-10:30pm Sun-Thu, 6-11:30pm Fri & Sat) A sleek glass box of culinary goodness, this is where you order plentiful small plates and pastas, and dine family-style. Start with one of their toasts – braised bacon and tomato marmalade perhaps? Move onto fried chicken in a red-wine vinegar glaze or the ocean trout crudo, and finish with pasta.

We loved the *wakame spaghetini* with crab and uni tossed in miso butter.

Rose Café CAFE $$
(Map p170; www.rosecafe.com; 220 Rose Ave; mains $12-15; ⏲7am-5pm Mon-Fri, from 8am Sat & Sun; P 👪) Laptop-toting writers, tech geeks and beefcakes from nearby Gold's Gym dig this Euro-style cafe-bakery with two hedge-framed patios on which to slurp your latte or scarf up tasty salads and frittatas. Order at the market counter, or head for the hostess stand. Before leaving, browse the unique knickknacks in the quirky, fun gift shop.

Oscar's Cerveteca MEXICAN FUSION $$
(Map p170; www.cervetecala.com; 523 Rose Ave; mains $12-21; ⏲5-11pm Mon-Thu, 5pm-midnight Fri, 2pm-midnight Sat, 2-11pm Sun) A gourmet Mexican kitchen with fusion digressions (such as the chorizo burger and the mac-n-cheese with bacon). The patio is inviting, but so is the stylish interior, with a wide marble bar, craftsman drafts (this is a *cerveteca,* or beer bar, after all) and global tunes on the sound system.

Fig Tree's Café CALIFORNIAN $$
(Map p170; www.figtreescafe.com; 429 Ocean Front Walk; appetizers $8-11, mains $12-16; ⏲8am-8pm; 🖉) The best eats on the boardwalk. Here you can munch shiitake omelettes made with organic eggs, ginger noodles, or a pesto-brushed, arugula-dressed salmon sandwich. The veg-heads will appreciate the spinach nut burger. Meals come with complimentary sea views.

Tasting Kitchen ITALIAN $$$
(Map p170; ☎310-392-6644; www.thetastingkitchen.com; 1633 Abbot Kinney Blvd; mains $16-40; ⏲10:30am-2pm Sat & Sun, 6pm-late daily) From the salt-roasted branzino to the

SILICON BEACH

Get your head out of the gutter! As shallow as LA can seem at times – and we admit there is plenty of work for the plastic surgeon union here – LA isn't exactly South Beach. What earned Venice and Santa Monica the moniker of Silicon Beach has more to do with algorithms and artificial intelligence than augmented anatomy. Anchored in the north by Google, who landed a satellite pod in Santa Monica years ago, and have since expanded their SoCal operations into splashy new quarters near Abbot Kinney in Venice, and Elon Musk's Space X and Tesla compound to the south, is a bubbling brew of start-up entrepreneurs, venture capital, tech-entertainment crossover brands, idea incubators and hackers. All after that elusive thing that will disrupt the old guard and make it rain money. According to www.siliconbeachla.com, there were upwards of 875 tech start-ups in LA in 2014, the lion's share occupying office space in Venice and Santa Monica. Four of them, Auction.com, Snapchat, Beats Music and Space X have been valued at over $1 billion, and Tinder is knocking on the door. Those kind of numbers explain why real-estate development in Venice is at an all-time high, and why there are so many Teslas un-idling on Abbot Kinney.

porcini-crusted hangar steak to the burger and the quail, it's all very good here. Especially the pastas (that bucatini is a gift from the gods), and the cocktails, of course. Which is why it's almost always packed. Book ahead.

★Gjelina ITALIAN **$$$**

(Map p170; ☎310-450-1429; www.gjelina.com; 1429 Abbot Kinney Blvd; dishes $8-26; ⊙11:30am-midnight Mon-Fri, from 9am Sat & Sun; 👪) Carve out a slip on the communal table between the hipsters and yuppies, or get your own slab of wood on the elegant, tented, stone terrace, and dine on imaginative small plates (raw yellowtail spiced with chili and mint and drenched in olive oil and blood orange) and sensational thin-crust, wood-fired pizza. They serve food until midnight.

Many of their pizzas, blackened fish plates, an assortment of deli salads, pork meatball subs and a brisket *bahn mi* are available at **GTA** (Gjelina Take Away) next door. Order at the counter and grab a seat on the bench or the milk crate on the stone patio attached. Seriously. Sit on the damn milk crate!

Joe's CALIFORNIAN, FRENCH **$$$**

(Map p170; ☎310-399-5811; www.joesrestaurant.com; 1023 Abbot Kinney Blvd; mains $10-32; ⊙noon-2:30pm & 6-10pm Tue-Fri, from 11am Sat & Sun; P) Joe's was one of the first restaurants on Abbot Kinney's restaurant row and, like a fine wine, only seems to get better with age. It's casual yet stylish, with gimmick-free Californian-French food. The best deal here is the three-course, prix-fixe lunch for $19. No cell phones allowed!

Scopa ITALIAN **$$$**

(Map p170; ☎310-821-1100; www.scopaitalianroots.com; 2905 Washington Blvd; dishes $6-49; ⊙5pm-2am daily) Venice cool has leaked into the Marina del Rey border regions with wonderful results. This place is big and open with polished concrete floors and an expansive marble L-shaped bar. The crudo bar serves scallops and steak tartare, four varieties of oysters, uni and mussels, while mains include a whole roasted branzino and a 24oz T-bone.

Drinking & Nightlife

Brig BAR

(Map p170; www.thebrig.com; 1515 Abbot Kinney Blvd; ⊙6pm-2am) Old-timers remember this place as a divey pool hall owned by ex-boxer Babe Brandelli (that's him and his wife on the outside mural). Now it's a bit sleeker, and attracts a trendy mix of grown-up beach bums, arty professionals and professional artists. On First Fridays, the parking lot attracts a fleet of LA's famed food trucks.

Venice Beach Wines WINE BAR

(Map p170; www.venicebeachwines.com; 529 Rose Ave; ⊙4-11pm Mon-Thu, to midnight Fri, 10:30am-midnight Sat, to 11pm Sun) A sweet and cozy hideaway with louvered benches and tables so close together you will commune with strangers. Here, you may sip international wines by the glass or bottle (including a complex and invigorating French syrah) and munch charcuterie, *pizzettas* and the like. For dessert try the *pot de crème:* it's 75% cacao and 100% orgasmic.

Intelligentsia Coffeebar CAFE

(Map p170; www.intelligentsiacoffee.com; 1331 Abbot Kinney Blvd; 6am-8pm Mon-Wed, 6am-11pm Thu & Fri, 7am-11pm Sat, 7am-8pm Sun;) In this hip, industrial, minimalist monument to the coffee gods, skilled baristas – who roam the circle bar and command more steaming machines than seems reasonable – never short you on foam or caffeine, and the Cake Monkey scones and muffins are addictive.

Tom's CAFE

(Map p170; www.toms.com; 1344 Abbot Kinney Blvd; 6am-8pm Mon-Fri, 7am-9pm Sat, 7am-8pm Sun;) You know Tom, the 1:1 entrepreneur who made his name selling fun, slip-on canvass shoes and giving a pair away to underprivileged kids overseas for each one he sells in the US. Now he's doing the same with shades and coffee, which translate into optometry and water projects in needy communities.

This is his flagship store, and it includes a wonderful back patio area with a lawn, fireplace, shared tables and lounge seating in the sun and shade, and it's wired with wi-fi. A great hang.

Venice Beach Ale House PUB

(Map p170; www.venicealehouse.com; 2 Rose Ave; 10am-10pm) A fun pub right on the boardwalk, blessed with ample patio seating for sunset people-watching, long boards suspended from the rafters, rock on the sound system, and plenty of local brews on tap. Beer flights are served in a drilled-out skate deck, and the pub grub works.

Townhouse & Delmonte Speakeasy BAR

(Map p170; www.townhousevenice.com; 52 Windward Ave; 5pm-2am Mon-Thu, noon-2am Fri-Sun) Upstairs is a cool, dark and perfectly dingy bar with pool tables, booths and good booze. Downstairs is the speakeasy, where DJs spin pop, funk and electronic music, comics take the mic, and jazz players set up and jam. It's a reliably good time almost any night.

Shopping

Strange Invisible APOTHECARY

(Map p170; 310-314-1505; www.siperfumes.com; 1138 Abbot Kinney Blvd; 11am-7pm Mon-Sat, noon-6pm Sun) Organic, intoxicating perfumes crafted from wild and natural ingredients, with names like Aquarian Rose and Fair Verona, although some are gender neutral. Also sells dark chocolate.

Principessa FASHION

(Map p170; www.principessavenice.com; 1323 Abbot Kinney Blvd; 11am-7pm) An affordable and worthy boutique with sporty denim and skirts, jewelry and droopy hats, baby doll dresses, scarves, Native American–style leather boots and purses, and some cute bikinis and negligees.

Alexis Bittar JEWELRY

(Map p170; 310-452-6901; www.alexisbittar.com; 1612 Abbot Kinney Blvd; 11am-7pm Mon-Sat, noon-6pm Sun) High-end jewelry known for Bittar's use of lucite, which is hand-carved and painted in his Brooklyn studio. Some of it looks like stone. He started by selling it on the streets in Manhattan where he was picked up by the MOMA store.

Now he's a stylist for major magazine shoots and offers a nice collection of vintage jewelry, some of which dates back to the 1780s! That piece will cost you $2200.

Will LEATHER GOODS

(Map p170; www.willleathergoods.com; 1360 Abbot Kinney Blvd; 10am-8pm) A terrific leather goods store out of Portland, and one of just three nationwide. They sell fine leather bags, briefcases, backpacks, belts, wallets and sandals for men and women. Our favorite was the bike messenger bag inlaid with colorful remnant Oaxacan wool.

Since Abbot Kinney is the man-purse capital of America, you'll be pleased to know that they do carry handbags for men (and women).

Alternative CLOTHING

(Map p170; www.alternativeapparel.com; 1337 Abbot Kinney Blvd; 11am-7pm) Alternative built its name on organic cotton and recycled poly hoodies and tees, but has expanded its collection to include beachy, hip flannels, cardigans, skirts and slacks.

Firefly GIFTS

(Map p170; www.shopfirefly.com; 1409 Abbot Kinney Blvd; 11am-7pm Mon-Sat, to 6pm Sun) One of our favorite shops on Abbot Kinney, Firefly deals in quality aromatherapy candles, art books, a smattering of boho chic attire for ladies, fair-trade beach bags from India, and beaded jewelry. They serve tots at the kids' store two doors down.

A + R Store GIFTS

(Map p170; 800-913-0071; www.aplusrstore.com; 1121 Abbot Kinney Blvd; 11am-7pm Tue-Sun) This is top-end industrial design and a great browse, with interesting ceramic speakers, ergonomic headphones, chairs, wooden toys and strange-yet-alluring high-format cameras.

Bountiful ANTIQUES, GIFTS
(Map p170; ☎310-450-3620; www.bountifulhome.com; 1335 Abbot Kinney Blvd; ⊙9am-6pm) On all too hip and self-important Abbot Kinney, this joyful store is a hodgepodge of new and cheap gifts, like Angry Bird confetti balls, martini glass cufflinks, vintage cap guns and Mr Potato Heads. There's lots of terrific vintage glassware too.

Warakuku SHOES, FASHION
(Map p170; www.warakukuusa.com; 1225 Abbot Kinney Blvd; ⊙10am-7pm) Warakuku is a compact, Japanese-owned shop for shoe lovers. It blends Far East couture with mainstream street brands such as Puma and Converse. Some 60% of the shoes are imported from Japan, the rest are domestic limited editions.

Nightcap LACE
(Map p170; https://nightcapclothing.com; 1225 Abbot Kinney Blvd; ⊙11am-6pm Tue-Sat, from noon Sun) This locally designed and made label is known for their stretch lace, a material sourced from French and Italian textiles. They started with lounge wear and then transitioned into a full ready-to-wear line. Every girl needs a nice black dress and they have a lace variety that is special.

Arbor SKATEBOARDS
(Map p170; www.arborcollective.com; 305 Ocean Front Walk; ⊙11am-7pm) A Venice homegrown label since 1995, Arbor started on Lincoln Blvd as a snowboard shop. The snowboards have since moved to a new **shop** (Map p170; www.arborcollective.com; 102 Washington Blvd; ⊙11am-7pm) south of the Venice pier; this skate shop is on the north end. In addition to decks they sell chinos, hoodies and T-shirts.

SOUTH BAY BEACHES

When you've had all the Hollywood ambition, artsy pretension, velvet ropes and mind-numbing traffic you can take, head south of the airport, where this string of beach towns will soothe that mess from your psyche in one sunset. It all starts with Manhattan Beach, just 15 minutes from the airport. An upmarket town with its share of high-end shopping and dining, homes are stacked high on the steep streets above a sublime stretch of sand and sea.

USC frat boys and sorority girls, financially challenged surfers and the beautiful people who love them, all call Hermosa Beach home. The rents are lower here, and the scene trashier, but that's part of the charm. And if you prefer a cool, casual distance from the Pier Ave fracas, just belly up to one of the town's epic dives.

As the coast winds to the south end of Santa Monica Bay you can follow it to diverse Redondo Beach, which bleeds into Torrance, which leads to the stunning Palos Verdes Peninsula.

Manhattan Beach

A bastion of surf music and the birthplace of beach volleyball, Manhattan Beach has gone chic. Its downtown area along Manhattan Beach Blvd has seen an explosion of trendy restaurants, boutiques and hotels. Yet, even with this Hollywood-ification, it remains a serene seaside enclave with prime surf on either side of the pier.

There's a Friday **farmers market** (⊙noon-4pm Fri) near city hall, metered parking at the base of the pier and a public parking garage on Valley Dr between Manhattan Beach Blvd and 13th St.

Sights & Activities

★Bo Bridges Photography & Spit Studio GALLERY
(Map p62; ☎310-937-3764; www.bobridgesgallery.com; 112 Manhattan Ave; ⊙11am-5pm Sat & Sun, varies Mon-Fri) Bridges made his name as a surf photographer then branched into general sport, commercial and pop art work. Check out dramatic shots of glacier surfers in Alaska, Kelly Slater barreling Pipeline, and portraits of Derek Jeter, Kobe Bryant, Bono and Shaun White. He also does fun water and landscape shots printed on aluminum for more shine.

Manhattan Beach Open VOLLEYBALL
(www.themanhattanbeachopen.com) Every August thousands of bad-ass babes take to the sand during the world's oldest and most prestigious volleyball tournament (played since 1960). Hit the beach courts near Marine Ave to see the players practice year-round.

Roundhouse Marine Studies Lab & Aquarium AQUARIUM
(Map p62; ☎310-379-8117; www.roundhouseaquarium.org; suggested donation $2; ⊙3pm-sunset Mon-Fri, 10am-sunset Sat & Sun; 👪) A compact

aquarium at the end of the 928ft-long pier that has seen better days. Still, you can pet a slimy sea cucumber, check out the deep-ocean tank with its anemones, baby sharks and sunflower starfish, and see eels...lots and lots of eels.

Nikau Kai SURF & SUP
(☎310-545-7007; www.nikaukai.com; 1300 Highland Ave; lessons private $90-95, semi-private $70-75, group lessons $55-60, surfboard rentals per hr/day $15/35, SUP rentals per hr/day $35/65, wetsuit rentals $15; ⊙9am-6pm) Just across the street from Uncle Bill's, you'll find this terrific new surf shop with board shorts and tees, flip-flops and boards. They run SUP and surf rentals and lessons, which are an hour long. Book them a day in advance.

Sleeping

★**Sea View Inn** MOTEL $$
(☎310-545-1504; www.seaview-inn.com; 3400 N Highland Ave; r $130-295; P) This one-time motel turned boutique spans all four corners of Highland Ave and 34th St with luxurious, ocean-facing rooms on the west side, and nicely appointed rooms on the east side. All of them are just uphill from the beach, and they offer free bikes, beach chairs and boogie-board rentals.

Shade Hotel BOUTIQUE HOTEL $$$
(☎310-546-4995; www.shadehotel.com; 1221 N Valley Dr; r from $350; P@) All rooms have spa tubs big enough for two and private terraces. Downstairs rooms have daybeds, top-floor rooms have fireplaces. The beach is just three blocks away and the Zinc Lounge bar is buzzy.

Eating

Manhattan Beach Creamery ICE CREAM $
(www.mbcreamery.com; 1120 Manhattan Ave; ice creams $4-6; ⊙10am-10pm Sun-Thu, to 11pm Fri & Sat) Gourmet, house-made ice creams come served in cones or pressed between two chocolate-chip cookies if you're in the mood for a Cream'wich. The line is so worth it.

Mama D's ITALIAN $
(☎310-456-1492; www.mamadsrestaurant.com; 1125 Manhattan Ave; dishes $5-15; ⊙5pm-late Mon-Fri, from noon Sat & Sun;) This neighborhood Italian joint fits like a well-worn shoe. The thin-crust pizzas, homemade ravioli, tangy *cioppino* and freshly baked bread, all served with a smile, keep regulars coming back for more.

Uncle Bill's Pancake House DINER $
(☎310-545-5177; www.unclebills.net; 1305 N Highland Ave; dishes $8-15; ⊙6am-3pm Mon-Fri, from 7am Sat & Sun;) Grab a stool, a booth or, better yet, an ocean-view table at this greet-the-day South Bay institution. Sexy surfers, tottering toddlers and gabbing girlfriends – everybody's here for the famous pancakes and big fat omelettes (try the 'Istanbul' made with turkey). Put your name on the list – the wait's worth it.

★**Fishing with Dynamite** SEAFOOD $$
(☎310-893-6299; www.eatfwd.com; 1148 Manhattan Ave; oysters from $2.25, dishes $9-19; ⊙11:30am-10pm Sun-Wed, to 10:30pm Thu-Sat) You'll love this place for their oysters and raw bar, the miso black cod, the serrano scallops seared and garnished with uni, and for their fried oyster po'boy, which is soul stirring. The menu is constantly rotating, but trust us, if you like binge eating on fine seafood, starve yourself for a day, then come here. And have a cocktail. They rock, and the bar stays open late.

Petros GREEK $$
(☎310-545-4100; www.petrosrestaurant.com; 451 Manhattan Beach Blvd; mains $12-25; ⊙11am-11pm Sun-Thu, to midnight Fri & Sat; P) Finally, a Greek restaurant for the 21st century. There's a feta-encrusted rack of lamb, a smoky eggplant and walnut dip, and people cross town for their *avgolemono* soup (lemon chicken and rice). Grab a seat on the people-watching patio or lose the baseball cap for a dress-code-worthy experience indoors.

Fishbar SEAFOOD $$
(☎310-796-0200; www.fishbarmb.com; 3801 Highland Ave; mains $12-30; ⊙11am-midnight Mon-Thu, to 2am Fri, 9am-2am Sat, to midnight Sun) Aficionados of old-school fish houses will enjoy this divey joint decked out with rattan furnishings, aquariums and flat-screen TVs. The menu includes truffle mac-n-cheese, seared tuna and lobster tacos (cheap on Taco Tuesday), and they do 10 varieties of mesquite grilled fish too. It's popular for weekend brunch.

Simmzy's Pub PUB $$
(www.simmzys.com; 229 Manhattan Beach Blvd; mains $10-14; ⊙11am-1am) A terrific gastropub with a popular bacon blue burger, topped with blue cheese and caramelized bacon. The spice-and-vinegar pulled pork is another staple, as is The Sammy – wood-fired grilled salmon, avocado and buttermilk sauce on a brioche bun. They have 24 craft beers on tap.

MB Post ASIAN FUSION $$$

(☎310-545-5405; www.eatmbpost.com; 1142 Manhattan Ave; small plates $9-13, mains $11-39; ⏲5-10pm Mon-Thu, 11:30am-10:30pm Fri, 10am-10:30pm Sat, 10am-10pm Sun; 👪) There's a lot to love here, from the reclaimed wood-paneled exterior to the exposed rafters and wood-block common tables where you'll munch pomegranate couscous with lavender feta, house-cured charcuterie, oak-grilled squid, Vietnamese pork jowl with *som tom*, and barbecued lamb belly with Japanese eggplant. Did we mention the chef earned a Michelin star?

Circa ASIAN FUSION $$$

(☎310-374-4422; www.circamb.com; 903 Manhattan Ave; dishes $6-36; ⏲5pm-midnight Tue-Thu, 5pm-2am Fri & Sat, 5pm-late Sun) This gourmet joint with Asian-fusion chops has a strong local following. They steam mussels in Thai curry, make duck confit tacos, char octopus with chorizo and wood-grill prawns. They mix pre-prohibition cocktails too.

Strand House FUSION $$$

(☎310-545-7470; www.thestrandhousemb.com; 117 Manhattan Beach Blvd; mains $24-44; ⏲5pm-late Mon, 11:30am-3pm & 5pm-late Tue-Fri, 10am-late Sat & Sun) A splashy new place perched a block from the sand with three floors dedicated to dining and drinking, and floor-to-ceiling windows revealing the Pacific. Start with a Korean pork belly with kimchi, and finish with branzino with black truffle risotto or a New York strip and creamed broccolini. It's ambitious and packed on weekends.

Drinking

Ercole's DIVE BAR

(☎310-372-1997; 1101 Manhattan Ave; ⏲10am-2am) A nice counterpoint to the HD-inundated, design-heavy sports bars on Manhattan Beach Blvd. This hole is dark and well irrigated. The tile is chipped and faded, and the barn door has been open to everyone from salty barflies to yuppie pub crawlers to volleyball stars and wobbly coeds since 1927.

Hermosa Beach

Strolling down Hermosa Beach's **Pier Avenue** on a summer weekend, you're immediately struck by two things: everybody's wearing flip-flops, tiny tees and a tan, and they all seem to be having way too much fun. The short, car-free strip is party central in a small town (within a big town) that's always lived the easy life. Once home to long-haired hippies and underground punk bands such as Black Flag, it's now solidly ruled by hormone-crazed surfer dudes and the chicks that dig 'em. The beach is indeed *muy hermosa* (Spanish for 'beautiful') – long, flat and dotted with permanent volleyball nets. Go to 16th St to see local pros bump, set and spike in preparation for the **AVP Hermosa Open** (www.avp.com; ⏲early Aug).

Every Memorial Day and Labor Day weekend Hermosa's three-day Fiesta Hermosa (p65), with music, food, kiddy rides and a huge arts-and-crafts fair, attracts throngs of revelers.

Activities

Pier Surf SURF & SUP

(☎310-372-2012; 21 Pier Ave; surf lessons private $110, group $70-80, rental per hr surfboard $7-15, SUP $17; ⏲9am-8pm) Surf and SUP rentals and lessons are yours on the Pier St walking strip. A three-hour rental covers the whole day, and you can get weekly rates too. Boards are in good condition and lessons should be booked in advance if possible.

They have a roster of 30 instructors and ask you to fill out a questionnaire so they can match you with a like mind.

Hermosa Cyclery BIKE RENTALS

(www.hermosacyclery.com; 20 13th St; ⏲10am-5pm; 👪) Get your cruisers, six-speeds, boogie boards and beach chairs by the hour or day. Rates are competitive and the quality is high.

Sleeping

Surf City Hostel HOSTEL $

(☎310-798-2323; www.surfcityhostel.com; 26 Pier Ave; dm/r $27/70; @📶) Steps from the sand, the halls of this convivial, yet aging, hostel offer mostly co-ed four- and six-person dorms; even the private rooms have shared baths. If you're looking to spend your days beaching and your nights partying, this is your place.

Sea Sprite Motel MOTEL $$

(☎310-376-6933; www.seaspritemotel.com; 1016 The Strand; r $119-279; P📶🏊) The rooms here aren't fancy, but they come with minifridge, microwaves and wood furnishings, and the location – right on the beach, overlooking the bustling Strand – could not be better.

Grand View Inn HOTEL $$

(☎310-374-8981; www.gvinn.com; 55 14th St; r $149-300) This new, three-star choice feels like a retrofitted apartment block, but it works because rooms are huge, with Berber carpet, queen beds, terraces, wall-mounted flat-screen TVs and mother of pearl baths. Choice views cost more.

Beach House at Hermosa Beach BOUTIQUE HOTEL $$$
(☎374-3001, 888-895-4559; www.beach-house.com; 1300 The Strand; r from $259; MTA buses 130, 439) This sparkling beachfront inn epitomizes California's laid-back lifestyle. Open the balcony door of your lofty ocean-view suite to let in the ocean breezes, soak in a deep, warm tub or fall asleep to the soft crackling of a wood-burning fireplace. The paved bikeway is right outside and restaurants and nightlife are a quick stroll away. No kids allowed.

Eating

As you will no doubt grasp, Hermosa Beach has to be considered the world capital of the gastropub. There are plenty of choices on the **Pier Street** walking strip.

Martha's 22nd St Grill DINER $
(☎310-376-7786; 25 22nd St; dishes $6.50-13; 7am-3pm;) Locals swear by the eggs at this unassuming beachside patio joint. It does sandwiches and salads too, but the eight varieties of Benedict eggs and omelettes stuffed with veggies, havarti, avocado, bacon, cheddar, hummus, sundried tomatoes and goats cheese, are the draw.

★ **Abigaile** GASTROPUB $$
(☎310-798-8227; www.abigailerestaurant.com; 1301 Manhattan Ave; mains $10-30; 5pm-late Mon-Fri, from 11am Sat & Sun) Hermosa's gastropub duxe. Sandwiches include the 'dirty bird' – a fried chicken number garnished with pickles and maple syrup. They get healthy with *pho* and soba noodles, and go all out at breakfast too. One wall is tagged with anarchy, the bar is stainless steel and there's ample seating at wooden tables scattered throughout the hardwood interior and on a sunny patio.

Dia De Campo MEXICAN $$$
(☎310-379-1829; www.diadecampohb.com; 1238 Hermosa Ave; dishes $8-28; 5-10pm Mon-Wed, to 12:30am Thu, 3pm-1am Fri, noon-1am Sat, noon-9pm Sun) Without a doubt the most refined joint in Hermosa, this upscale Mexican kitchen does *mole* scallops, braised lamb nachos and chorizo-stuffed dates, and has a full raw bar including eight varieties of ceviche – try the hamachi and uni version if they have it. The interior is classy with red leather bar stools and mod picnic table booths.

Drinking

★ **Mermaid** DIVE BAR
(☎310-374-9344; 11 Pier Ave; 10am-10:30pm) The bad old granddad of the Hermosa strand, this divey classic with black-vinyl booths and a circle bar patrolled by grizzled vets who make a mean martini, is the perfect antidote to the varying degrees of fromage found beyond its grimy windows, which do open on occasion to reveal ocean views.

Barnacle's DIVE BAR
(www.facebook.com/barnaclesbarandgrill; 837 Hermosa Ave; 9am-2am) Nestled thankfully off the Pier Ave crush, this decidedly grungy neighborhood joint has friendly (not bubbly) blondes behind the bar, boards (snow, skate, surf) in the rafters, Credence on the stereo and ball games on the flat-screen TVs, but you may as well wander outside to the sun patio to gaze at the big blue sea.

Entertainment

Saint Rocke's CONCERT VENUE
(www.saintrocke.com; 142 Pacific Coast Hwy; from 5pm Mon-Fri, from 6pm Sat & Sun) The South Bay's best live-music venue lies within this dated brick house with nightly live bands ranging from cabaret (think: Rita Wilson) to the up-and-coming (Sea Wolf) to the past-their-prime and still doing it well (Young Dubliners).

Comedy & Magic Club LOUNGE
(www.comedyandmagicclub.com; 1018 Hermosa Ave; 5:30pm-1am Mon-Fri, from 2pm Sat & Sun) Live music and comedy right on the Hermosa strip. It has something going almost every night, but Sunday means Jay Leno live and up close. He's their big draw.

Shopping

★ **Stars Antique Market** ANTIQUES
(www.starsantiquemarket.com; 526 Pier Ave; 11am-6pm Mon-Sat, to 5pm Sun) If you dig old stuff, weird stuff and weird old stuff, stop by this old barn crammed with Brunswick record players and Hammond typewriters. There are vintage watches, china, glassware, signage, furniture, lanterns and chandeliers. It's a terrific browse.

Turquoise BOUTIQUE
(www.turquoise-shop.com; 321 Pier Ave; 10:30am-7pm) A cute beachy boutique selling Toms

shoes, organic beauty products, colorful beach bags, flip-flops, terry-cloth boy shorts, cut offs, blousey throws, towels, sunglasses and more.

Redondo Beach & Torrance

Redondo Beach is a working-class beach town; it's also the largest in the South Bay, and the most ethnically diverse, as it wanders inland and bleeds into neighboring Torrance. Its heart is at King's Harbor, where the dated pier is still an excursion-worthy detour on your way south to an absurdly beautiful coastline.

Sights

Redondo Beach Pier LANDMARK

Arching from the bottom of Torrance Blvd all the way to **King's Harbor**, this classic 1960s multilevel beast is the Redondo hub with a weekly Thursday **farmers market** (7am to 1pm), and plenty of pierside anglers, restaurants and watering holes to keep you entertained. It's also the end point of the bike path, 20 miles from Santa Monica.

Redondo & Torrance Beaches BEACH

(Map p62) These beaches, which technically join in one contiguous stretch of sand, have their beauty and charms, but the middle section thins out, exposing drain pipes and breakwaters at low tide. It's best to stick to the northern stretch of Redondo (which is actually south of the pier), and the southern edge of Torrance Beach.

Activities

Marina Bike Rentals CYCLING

(☎310-318-2453; marinabikerentals.com; 505 Harbor Dr, Redondo Beach; bike rental per hr $8-15, day $24-45; ⊙10am-6:30pm Mon-Fri, from 9am Sat & Sun; 👪) Can you really contemplate that winding concrete bike path stretching north from King's Harbor through Hermosa and Manhattan Beach and not rent a cruiser?

Seaside Lagoon POOL

(www.redondo.org/seasidelagoon; 200 Portofino Way at Harbor Dr, Redondo Beach; adult/child $6/5; ⊙10am-5:45pm late May–early Sep; 👪) Geared toward the little ones, this large, shallow, saltwater outdoor pool with a slide and cascading fountain usually teems with an ethnic potpourri of families frolicking in the sand or picnicking in the grass. Parking costs $3 with validation.

Redondo Special SPORTFISHING

(☎310-372-2111; www.redondospecialsportfishing.com; 233 North Harbor Dr, Redondo Beach; adult/senior & child $40/35; ⊙trips at 7:30am & 1pm) Redondo Special run the only fully outfitted half-day fishing trips out of King's Harbor, a working fishing marina off the Redondo Pier.

Smog City Brewing Co. BREWERY

(www.smogcitybrewing.com; 1901 Del Amo Blvd, Torrance; ⊙tap room & tours 4-9pm Fri, noon-8pm Sat, noon-6pm Sun) This family-run craft brewery got its start in 2011 and is already making waves in the LA culinary scene. Based in Torrance, they have a tap room where you can taste experimental and unreleased brews and they offer tours too.

Sleeping

Redondo Inn & Suites MOTEL $

(☎310-540-1888; www.redondoinnandsuites.com; 711 S Pacific Coast Hwy, Redondo Beach; r $84-129; P 📶) Rooms aren't huge at this humble motor hotel, but the carpet is fresh, the bathroom tiles sparkling, and there's a mini-fridge and microwave. It's just two blocks from the beach.

Miyako Hybrid Hotel BOUTIQUE HOTEL $$

(☎310-212-5111; www.miyakohybridhotel.com; 21381 S Western Ave, Torrance; r from $119; P 📶) A slice of Tokyo in downtown Torrance. The location near Honda and Toyota's US headquarters attracts suits midweek, but it deserves mention because of its sustainable ethos (recycled wallpaper, recyclable carpeting and solar power), as well as the only-in-Japan touches such as deep-soaking tubs and robo-toilets. You can score deals on weekends.

Portofino Hotel & Yacht Club HOTEL $$

(☎310-379-8481; www.hotelportofino.com; 260 Portofino Way, Redondo Beach; r $189-259; P @ 📶 🏊) This '60s oceanfront property next to the Redondo Pier blends urban sophistication with nautical lightheartedness. Get an ocean-view room with a balcony for watching the sunset and an adorable sea lion colony. Marina-facing views overlook not only boats, but also a power plant, partially hidden behind a Wyland whale mural.

Eating

The Redondo Beach Pier offers plenty of family-run, Chinese-inflected seafood joints serving live prawns and crabs.

★ Standing Room FUSION BURGERS $

(☎310-374-7575; www.facebook.com/thestandingroomRB; 144 N Catalina Ave, Redondo Beach; burgers & sandwiches $7-14, plates $13-20; ⏰11am-9:30pm Mon-Sat, noon-8pm Sun) South Bay heads who know descend onto this tiny takeout grill, built into the back of a liquor store, where they do a range of burgers and reimagine other greasy spoon delights. Burgers are topped with scallions, a sesame leaf and a fried egg, or bacon, shishito peppers, cheddar and hoisin BBQ sauce.

They also do soft-shell crab, miso-glazed salmon, and braised short-rib sandwiches, fried chicken and pork belly plates. Don't whiff on the skunky truffle fries, which can be dipped in one of 11 house sauces. There can be a long wait.

El Indio MEXICAN $

(☎310-370-0038; 2523 Artesia Blvd, Torrance; dishes $4-10; ⏰9am-8:30pm; P 👪) Family-owned and -operated since 1960, El Indio loyalists venture into Torrance for *carne asada* burritos, carnitas tacos and especially for its unparalleled tamales. Sweet and spicy, they come in one flavor: pork. Just like in old Mexico.

Green Temple VEGAN $

(www.greentemple.net; 1700 S Catalina Ave, Redondo Beach; appetizers $6-10, mains $8-13; ⏰11am-4pm & 5-9pm Tue-Thu, to 10pm Fri & Sat, 9am-4pm & 5-9pm Sun; 🖉) 🍃 Sit in the flowery courtyard or amid funky Asian artwork at this sanctuary where meat is a no-no and organic, local produce is plentiful. Salads, including the tasty Sproutada, come with a slice of homemade bread.

Quality Seafood SEAFOOD $$

(www.qualityseafood.net; 130 International Boardwalk, Redondo Beach; meals $10-20; ⏰10:30am-6:30pm Mon-Thu, to 7:30pm Fri-Sun) They've been doing their thing on the north end of the Redondo pier since 1953. Pick your crab – they've been caught by those crab traps stacked by the trawlers in the harbor, so you know it's fresh. They'll steam it live and give you a hammer so you can get down to business.

Ask them to pop the top off a few urchins while you're at it, then devour your grub over a spread of newsprint, paired with one of two dozen beers on tap.

Hudson House GASTROPUB $$

(☎310-798-9183; www.hudsonhousebar.com; 514 N Pacific Coast Hwy, Redondo Beach; dishes $5-16; ⏰5pm-1am Mon-Thu, from 3pm Fri & Sat, 3pm-midnight Sun) A fun, laid-back gastropub that's low lit and neighborhoody at its best. They do craftsman cocktails, steamed little neck clams, a grilled albacore Niçoise, mac-n-goat-cheese, fried chicken, and waffles. The striped bass comes with fresh corn grits.

Christine FUSION $$$

(☎310-373-1952; www.restaurantchristine.com; 24530 Hawthorne Blvd, Torrance; mains $16-33; ⏰11:30am-2pm Mon-Fri, 5pm-late daily; P) Chef Christine finds inspiration in the feisty flavors of Provence, Tuscany and the Pacific Rim, all expertly woven together in such dishes as orange zest–crusted scallops plated with miso BBQ shortrib. On Mondays there are special seafood and wine dinners served family-style (per person $68 including wine pairings).

🍷 Drinking & Entertainment

Old Tony's BAR

(www.oldtonys.com; 210 Fishermans Wharf, Redondo Beach; ⏰11:30am-10pm Sun-Thu, to 11pm Fri & Sat) This holdover from 1952 is as cool as the Redondo Pier gets, with its classic neon sign, glass octagonal lounge upstairs and long, terra-cotta bar downstairs. Both have gas fireplaces roaring and local barflies buzzing. The food is whatever. Have a beverage.

Redondo Fun Factory ARCADE

(www.redondofunfactory.com; 123 International Boardwalk, Redondo Beach; ⏰2-10pm Mon-Fri, 10am-midnight Sat, 10am-10pm Sun) Families shouldn't miss this dated fun factory, flashing and blinging with old-fashioned arcade games and rides. You can win prizes at carnival games such as ski-ball and pop-a-shot, and play your early onset gaming favorites with the kiddies. It opens at 10am on all nonschool days.

Palos Verdes Peninsula

Drive the coastal highway and enjoy a revelation of sand-swept silver bays and Catalina shadows whispering through a fog rising from cold Pacific blue. Long, elegant and perfectly manicured lawns front sprawling mansions, and to the north, south and east there's nothing but layered jade hills forming the headland that cradles the southernmost reach of the great Santa Monica Bay. You're not in Malibu. You've landed on the lesser known PV, aka the Palos Verdes Peninsula.

Sights

Wayfarers Chapel CHURCH

(Map p62; 310-377-1650; www.wayfarerschapel.org; 5755 Palos Verdes Dr S; 10am-5pm; P) The most stunning non-natural attraction on Palos Verdes was built by Lloyd Wright (son of Frank) in 1951, and no matter where you stand among the great saints, this place will touch your soul. It's a glass church cradled by soaring redwood trees. Not surprisingly, it's a popular spot to tie the knot, so avoid coming on weekends.

Abalone Cove Shoreline Park PARK

(www.palosverdes.com; Palos Verdes Dr; entry per vehicle $5; 9am-4pm; P) The best place to hunt for starfish, anemones and other tidepool critters is in and around this rock-strewn eco-preserve. The walk down to the beach gets pretty steep in some sections, so watch your footing.

Point Vicente Lighthouse LANDMARK

(www.palosverdes.com/pvlight; P) FREE Watch the earth curve and the sea crash on the Point Vicente bluffs while leaning against the gleaming-white 1926 lighthouse, which was staffed until 1971. These days electronic sensors activate the foghorn, which you can hear bellow on the wings of the wind.

You can only access this end of the bluffs and explore the lighthouse itself from 10am to 3pm on the second Saturday of the month.

Point Vicente Interpretive Center VIEWPOINT

(Map p62; 310-377-5370; 31501 Palos Verdes Dr W; donations appreciated; 10am-5pm; P) FREE Binocular-toting whale-watchers gather north of the adjacent lighthouse between December and April when the Pacific gray whales embark on their fascinating and arduous migration from Alaska to Mexico. Inside are fun exhibits for boning up on the specifics. You'll also glimpse giant mako shark fossils, and Tongva ceramics and arrowheads. Picnic beneath palm trees and stroll along the blufftop trail.

Year 2014 was a particularly good year for baleen types. According to the American Cetacean Society – an organization that tracks whale migrations – over 2000 whales were tracked migrating up and down the Southern California coast between December 2013 and April 2014. Most were gray whales, but they spotted some humpbacks and sperm whales, and orcas too.

South Coast Botanic Garden GARDENS

(www.southcoastbotanicgarden.org; 26300 Crenshaw Blvd; adult/5-12yr/student $9/4/6; 9am-5pm; P) It's hard to believe that this flowering and fruiting, sprouting and sprawling blast of life (we're talking around 2000 species of life) was reclaimed from a former landfill. Plant shows and sales take place year-round. Admission is cash only.

PV Peninsula SCENIC DRIVE

(Palos Verdes Dr, Palos Verdes;) For awesome eyefuls of stunning shoreline, take a scenic drive. Start at Point Fermin Park in San Pedro, and cruise north along Palos Verdes Dr at sunset. Steep cliffs tumble to rocky shores and secluded coves as the roadway ribbons past rambling multi-million-dollar mansions. Catalina Island looms across the sparkling Pacific.

Sleeping

★**Terranea** RESORT $$$

(310-265-2800; www.terranea.com; 100 Terranea Way, Palos Verdes; r $350-500, ste $655-2150; P@) Once the domain of trick sea mammals, the old Marineland property is now LA's best five-star beach resort. Rooms are flooded with natural light, and have been designed in classic California style. Some 92% of them have ocean views.

Trails wrap the property, skirt the wild coast and are open to the public, as are the five restaurants and nine-hole golf course. Parking and access to the beach is free and guests have free access to kayaks, mountain bikes and paddleboards.

LONG BEACH & SAN PEDRO

Long Beach has come a long way since its working-class oil and navy days. Over the past two decades, LA's southernmost seaside enclave has quietly reinvented its gritty downtown, making it an attractive place to live and party. On any Saturday night the restaurants, clubs and bars along lower **Pine Avenue** and the **Promenade**, a new upscale loft district, are abuzz with everyone from buttoned-down conventioneers to hipsters to the testosterone-fueled frat pack. Additional eateries line **Shoreline Village**, the departure point for boat cruises.

Long Beach

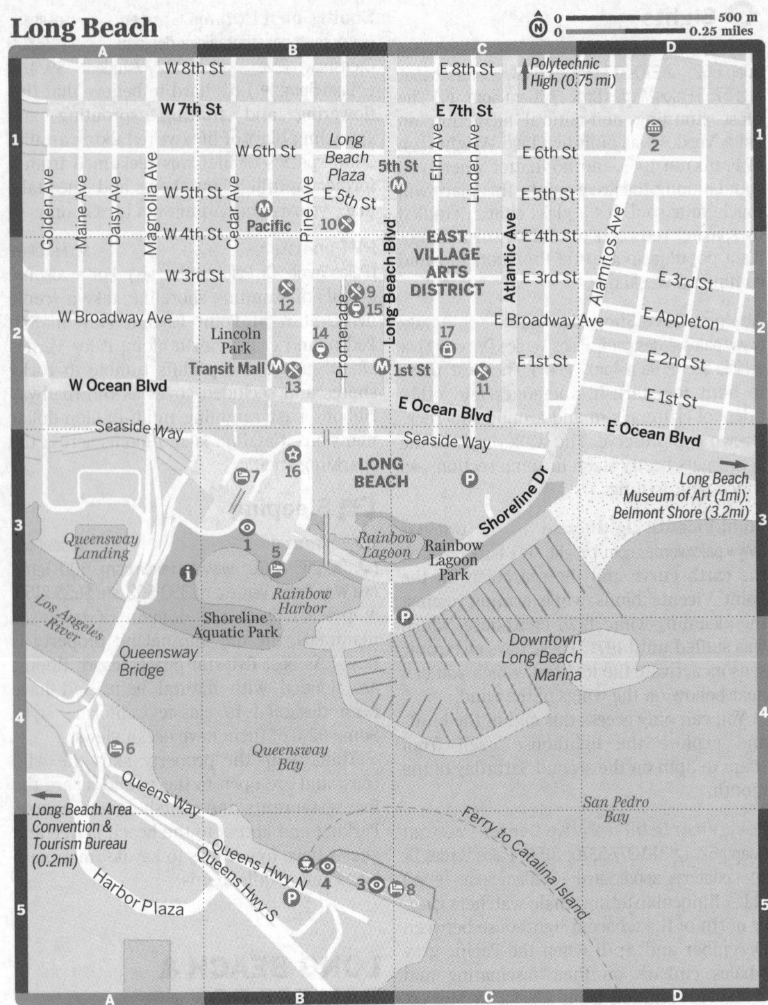

Despite the name, the beach isn't a big draw here. In fact, the water is rather polluted thanks to the proximity of the giant Port of Los Angeles, the country's busiest (it ranks 16th worldwide). And those palm-studded mini-islands you see offshore? They're actually disguised oil rigs. If you want to hit the water locally, do it in Belmont Shore, about 2 miles east of downtown.

The stress-free way to get to Long Beach is by riding the air-conditioned Metro Rail Blue Line. Once downtown you can walk or catch the red Passport buses, which swing by all the museums and other points of interest, including Belmont Shore ($1.25; exact change required). From June to mid-September, the AquaBus ($1) links the aquarium and the Queen Mary, as does the high-speed AquaLink ($5), which also goes out to Alamitos Bay (Naples).

Just northwest of Long Beach, the port town of San Pedro (San *Pee*-dro) is a working-class harbor town and commuter town, charming and just rough enough to be real without losing its sweetness. Expect old wooden homes, wind-ravaged bluffs, and cold, salty blasts of sea. The Pedro time warp is so pervasive that many of the dive bars where Charles Bukowski probably ruined his liver are still open. LA's late, great, bad-boy poet now rests in plot 875 in **Green Hills Memorial Park** (www.greenhillsmemorial.com; 27501 S Western Ave, Ocean View; P).

'San Pedro is real quiet,' Bukowski once observed. That's still true today, except for the distant clanging of containers being hoisted on and off gigantic cargo vessels. LA's own 'Golden Gate', the 1500ft-long suspended Vincent Thomas Bridge, links San Pedro with Terminal Island.

Sights

Aquarium of the Pacific AQUARIUM

(tickets 562-590-3100; www.aquariumofpacific.org; 100 Aquarium Way, Long Beach; adult/senior/child $29/26/15; 9am-6pm;) Long Beach's most mesmerizing experience, the Aquarium of the Pacific is a vast, high-tech indoor ocean where sharks dart, jellyfish dance and sea lions frolic. More than 12,000 creatures inhabit four re-created habitats: the bays and lagoons of Baja California, the frigid northern Pacific, the coral reefs of the tropics, and local kelp forests. Parking costs $8.

Among the many not-to-be-missed exhibits is the Shark Lagoon, where you can pet young sharks in a touch pool and go nose-to-nose – through a window – with their adult-sized cousins patrolling a larger tank. The teeth on the bull shark are the stuff of nightmares. The best time to be here is during the daily feeding sessions (check the schedule online or in the lobby).

Elsewhere, you'll be entertained by the antics of sea otters, spooked by football-sized crabs with spiny 3ft-long arms, and charmed by Seussian-looking sea dragons. It's a wondrous world that'll easily keep you enthralled for a couple of hours. On weekdays, avoid the field-trip frenzy by arriving around 2pm; on weekends beat the crowd by getting here as early as possible. For an extra fee, the aquarium offers behind-the-scenes tours and, from late May to early September, ocean boat trips.

Point Fermin Park & Around PARK

(San Pedro) Locals come to this grassy community park on the bluffs to jog, picnic, watch wind- and kitesurfers, cool off in the shade of spreading magnolias, wonder at never-ending waves pounding a rugged crescent coastline or enjoy live jazz on balmy summer Sundays.

Ostensibly the main visitor attraction is the restored 1874 Victorian **Point Fermin Lighthouse** (Map p62; www.pointferminlighthouse.org; 807 Paseo Del Mar, San Pedro; 1-4pm Tue-Sun), one of the oldest in the West. The first keepers of the light were trailblazing sisters Mary and Ellen Smith. After the tour stop by the geriatric biker bar, Walker Cafe.

Just north of Point Fermin, in Angels Gate Park, is the **Fort MacArthur Military Museum** (Map p62; www.ftmac.org; 3601 S Gaffey St, San Pedro; admission $10; noon-5pm Tue, Thu, Sat & Sun), an LA harbor defensive post until 1945. Bring the kids to this outdoor museum to scale the gun batteries and search for secret tunnels. Even more impressive is the newly restored **Korean Friendship Bell** (Map p62; www.kccla.org; 3601 S Gaffey St, San Pedro; 10am-6pm; P). A gift from South Korea to the US government, this huge, cast-iron, low-slung oval chime and its green-tiled pagoda dominates the hillside and makes for a fantastic lookout point.

Belmont Shore & Naples NEIGHBORHOOD

If downtown Long Beach feels urban and corporate, Belmont Shore exudes a quintessential SoCal laid-back air. It has a fine beach with a pier for fishing and watching

Long Beach

Sights

1 Aquarium of the Pacific B3
2 Museum of Latin American Art....D1
3 Queen Mary B5
4 Scorpion....B5

Sleeping

5 Dockside Boat & Bed B3
6 Hotel Maya....A4
7 Pike B3
8 Queen Mary Hotel....C5

Eating

9 Beachwood....B2
10 Downtown Long Beach Farmers Market B1
11 James Republic....C2
12 Omelette Inn....B2
13 Pier 76 ....B2

Drinking & Nightlife

Congregation Ale House....(see 15)
14 Federal Bar B2
15 Harvelle's B2

Entertainment

16 Laugh Factory Long Beach....B3

Shopping

17 Academy C2

SWAMIS, HIPPIES & HOLLYWOOD

Los Angeles enjoys one of the richest and deepest yoga traditions in the West, because this was where the gurus first brought forth their peaceful warrior wisdom from the ashrams of India. Parmanahansa Yogananda was one of the first to make the Stateside sojourn, when he came straight from Ranchi, India to address a religious conference in 1920. He could barely speak English. Three years later the *Los Angeles Times* reported on 'the extraordinary spectacle of thousands…being turned away an hour before the advertised opening of [his] lecture with the 3,000-seat LA Philharmonic Hall filled to its utmost capacity.' In October 1925 he established the Self Realization Fellowship at a vacant Mt Washington hotel. Yogananda felt his success lay in the fact that he offered something the religious establishment did not, a physical experience of God. In his *Autobiography of a Yogi* he wrote, 'The universal appeal of yoga is its approach to God through a daily usable scientific method, rather than a devotional fervor that, for the average man, is beyond his emotional scope.'

Another powerful guru, Yogi Bhajan, a devout Sikh, arrived here during the second wave, when the American streets were alive with revolution and free love. He showed up with next to no money, and began teaching immediately. His classes filled up quickly, especially those at a dusty antique shop on Robertson Blvd, where every night 80 to 90 hippies emerged from packed vans to take his class. Yogi Bhajan told his obviously experimental students, 'Do Kundalini yoga. You can get higher, it's legal and there are no side effects.' Two of his original students, Guru Singh and Gurmukh still teach in town at Yoga West (p137) and Golden Bridge Yoga (p92). Yogi Bhajan went on to found Yogi Teas and Peace Cereals, and taught until his death in 2004.

But it's Hatha yoga that keeps most of LA om-ing and sweating in studios from Long Beach to the Valley, from Santa Monica to Pasadena. LA's original Hatha pioneer was the Russian-born, India-educated Indra Devi. She opened her Hollywood studio in 1947, and taught the first in a long line of celebrities how to down dog properly.

sunsets, and keeps it real along a buzzy, four-block strip of boutiques, cafes and bars filled with surfers and students.

Naples, just south of here, is Long Beach's most exclusive neighborhood. It's a canal-laced borough, created in 1903 by Arthur Parsons, not coincidentally, a contemporary of Venice's Abbot Kinney. It's best explored on a gondola.

White Point Park BEACH

(Map p62; 628 Alamitos Ave, San Pedro) There's a baseball field up top, and wind-blasted pebble shoals down below, where daredevil kitesurfers ride gales and catch air along the bluffs as gulls ride the thermals. It's also the high-school hangout. Low tide leaves small pools between the rocks south of the lifeguard tower.

East Village Arts District NEIGHBORHOOD

(www.eastvillagelive.com; East Long Beach) Don't get overly excited just because the words East Village and Arts happen to appear in the same sentence. Still, this rather small corner of Long Beach (between Ocean Blvd and 7th St) does have a funky feel with some groovy cafes, restaurants and boutiques to explore.

Queen Mary BOAT

(www.queenmary.com; 1126 Queens Hwy, Long Beach; tours adult/child from $26/15; ⌚10am-6:30pm; P) Long Beach's 'flagship' attraction is this grand and supposedly haunted British luxury liner. Larger and more luxurious than even the *Titanic,* she transported royals, dignitaries, immigrants, WWII troops and vacationers between 1936 and 1964. Sure, it's a tourist trap, but study the memorabilia, and you may envision dapper gents escorting ladies in gowns to the art-deco lounge for cocktails or the sumptuous Grand Salon for dinner.

Basic admission, aka the Queen Mary Passport, includes the hokey **Ghosts & Legends** special-effects tour, which features strange apparitions in the 1st-class swimming pool and the boiler room. Various other tours and packages are also available; combination tickets with the aquarium cost $42/19 per adult/child. Parking costs $10, and opening hours can vary according to the season; check the website for times before you visit.

The Cold War–era Soviet submarine **Scorpion** (adult/child $13/11) is moored alongside the Queen. As you scramble around, imagine how 78 crew shared 27 bunks and two bathrooms, often for months at a time; definitely not for the claustrophobic.

Museum of Latin American Art MUSEUM
(www.molaa.org; 628 Alamitos Ave, Long Beach; adult/senior & student/child $9/6/free, Sun free; 11am-5pm Wed, Thu, Sat & Sun, to 9pm Fri; P) This gem of a museum presents a rare survey of Latin American art created since 1945. Cecilia Míguez' whimsical bronze statuettes, Eduardo Kingman's wrenching portraits of indigenous people and Arnaldo Roche Rabel's intensely spiritual abstracts are among the many outstanding pieces in the permanent collection.

Long Beach Museum of Art MUSEUM
(www.lbma.org; 2300 E Ocean Blvd, Long Beach; adult/senior & student/child $7/6/free; 11am-5pm Fri-Sun, to 8pm Thu) The beachfront location is breathtaking, and the restaurant in a nicely detailed 1912 craftsman mansion serves tasty lunches, but exhibits in the adjacent two-room pavilion can be a bit hit-and-miss. The museum's permanent collections boast pop art, mid-century pieces and some contemporary work.

Most of the work is by regional artists.

Cabrillo Marine Aquarium AQUARIUM
(Map p62; www.cabrillomarineaquarium.org; 3720 Stephen White Dr, San Pedro; suggested donation adult/child $5/1; noon-5pm Tue-Fri, 10am-5pm Sat & Sun; P) This city-owned aquarium is the smaller, older, low-tech cousin of Long Beach's Aquarium of the Pacific. It's also a lot lighter on your wallet and less overwhelming for small children. Spiky urchins, slippery sea cucumbers, magical jellyfish and other local denizens will bring smiles to even the most iPad-jaded youngster.

Naturalists lead rambles around the rocky tide-pools and salt marshes, and organize all sorts of other educational programs, including grunion watches (April to July). The curvaceous rocky breakwater, swatch of golden sand, and deep, green sea out front aren't bad either.

Los Angeles Maritime Museum & Around MUSEUM
(www.lamaritimemuseum.org; Berth 84, San Pedro; adult/child & senior $3/1; 10am-5pm Tue-Sun; P) Galleries set up in a historic ferry building tell the story of LA's relationship with the sea and display enough ship models (including an 18ft cutaway of the *Titanic*), figureheads and navigational equipment to keep your imagination afloat for an hour or so.

If you enjoy clambering around old ships, head a mile north to the **SS Lane Victory** (www.lanevictory.org; Berth 94, San Pedro; adult/child $3/1; 9am-3pm), a museum vessel that sailed the seven seas from 1945 to 1971. Self-guided tours take in the engine room and the cargo holds. See the website for directions.

Further south, you'll be besieged by shrieking gulls and excited children at **Ports O'Call Village** (Berth 77, San Pedro; 11am-10pm) FREE. Skip the trinket stores and fill up on fresh fish and shrimp at the raucous San Pedro Fish Market & Restaurant. Afterwards, hop on a port cruise or join a whale-watching trip (January to March).

Activities

LA Harbor Sportfishing BOATING
(310-547-9916; www.laharborsportfishing.com; 1150 Nagoya Way, Berth 79, San Pedro; whale-watching adult/child $30/15, sportfishing adult/child $65/50, harbor tours adult/under 11yr $15/free;) Whether you love dropping a line or making like Melville and spotting the biggest mammal of them all, this humble shop is your gateway to the blue Pacific. Trips head out from the harbor about 6 to 7 miles into the open ocean. The best time to spot blue and humpback whales is between October and April.

Open boat fishing trips are available year-round. It does 45-minute harbor tours too.

SS Lane Victory Catalina Cruise AQUATIC
(310-519-9545; www.lanevictory.org; Berth 94, San Pedro; adult/child $135/80) It's one thing to clamor around this old warship, but it's quite another to ride a retired WWII merchant vessel on the open sea. Five times each summer, the old girl makes the day-long haul to Catalina.

On the way back into harbor you'll receive a fireboat escort and have to duck as vintage planes dive and attack, just like in (great) granddad's day.

Sleeping

Queen Mary Hotel SHIP $
(562-435-3511; www.queenmary.com; 1126 Queens Hwy, Long Beach; r from $99;) There's an irresistible romance to ocean liners such as the *Queen Mary*, a nostalgic retreat that time-warps you to a long-gone, slower-paced era. The rooms are small, but the 1st-class staterooms are nicely refurbished

with original art-deco details. Avoid the cheapest cabins on the inside – claustrophobic!

Hotel Maya BOUTIQUE HOTEL $$
(☎562-435-7676; www.hotelmayalongbeach.com; 700 Queens Way, Long Beach; r from $179; P@🛜🏊) West of the *Queen Mary*, this once boutique property now associated with Double Tree hits you with hip immediately upon entering the rusted-steel and glass lobby. The feel continues in the rooms (coral tile, river-rock headboards), which are set in four 1970s-era hexagons with views of downtown Long Beach. The floating poolside cabanas aren't bad either.

Pike HOTEL $$$
(☎562-432-1234; www.thepikelongbeach.hyatt.com; 285 Bay St, Long Beach; r from $229; P@🛜🏊) This sleek hotel in the Pike Center complex was recently rebranded as a Hyatt. It's a short walk from the aquarium, rooms have modern furnishings, flat-screen TVs and small sitting areas.

Dockside Boat & Bed B&B $$
(☎562-436-3111, 800-436-2574; www.boatandbed.com; Rainbow Harbor, Dock 5, 316 E Shoreline Dr, Long Beach; r from $175; P🛜) Get rocked to sleep by the waves aboard your own private yacht with retro '70s charm, galley kitchens and high-tech entertainment centers. Boats are moored right along the newly expanded waterfront fun zone in downtown Long Beach, so expect some noise. Breakfast is delivered to your vessel.

Eating

Downtown Long Beach Farmers Market MARKET $
(City Place Center, N Promenade & E 4th St, Long Beach; ⏲10am-3pm Fri; P👪) One of the two best markets in south LA gets points for its 21 farmers selling fresh, mostly organic produce. Crowds swell for the vendors who deal in smoked ribs and chicken, pecan pie and pralines, and sweet corn – roasted or kettle popped.

Omelette Inn DINER $
(www.omeletteinn.com; 318 Pine Ave, Long Beach; dishes $6-10; ⏲7am-2:30pm; 👪) From clerks to cops to city-council members, *everybody's* got a soft spot for this unassuming joint where breakfasts and sandwiches are served in belt-loosening portions. Build your own omelettes from more than 40 ingredients or pick from tried-and-true menu favorites such as the Sicilian or Grecian Formula.

Pier 76 SEAFOOD $$
(☎562-983-1776; www.pier76fishgrill.com; 95 Pine Ave, Long Beach; mains $8-19; ⏲11am-9pm) A terrific, affordable seafood house in downtown Long Beach. Step to the counter and order yellowtail, salmon, trout, mahi mahi or halibut glazed and grilled, and served with two sides. The fries and kale salad are both good. They have fish tacos, sandwiches, poke and ceviche too. They even have a $19 lobster.

Beachwood BARBECUE $$
(☎562-436-4020; www.beachwoodbbq.com; 210 E 3rd St, Long Beach; mains $9-20; ⏲11:30am-midnight) They do two things well, barbecue – brisket, pulled pork, smoked chicken, and ribs – and beer, which they brew themselves. Grab a seat at the bar or on the sunny patio fronting the promenade. House sauces will be jarred and waiting for you at your table. The kitchen closes at 9:30pm.

James Republic MODERN AMERICAN $$
(☎562-901-0235; www.jamesrepublic.com; 500 E 1st St, Long Beach; mains $11-26; ⏲7-10:30am & 11:30am-2:30pm Mon-Fri, 10:30am-3pm Sat & Sun, 6-10pm Mon-Sat, 6-9pm Sun) The best new restaurant in Long Beach offers farm-to-table New American eating, though some dishes have a South Asian twist. They grill cauliflower and hangar steaks, spoon a rabbit bucatini, make grass-fed burgers, a pastrami sandwich with Gruyère and beer mustard, and a wonderful roast chicken.

The modern space is lit by raw bulb lanterns, and has glass doors that open wide to the patio and the street. Brunch is special, and they're slammed on weekend nights. Book ahead.

Simmzy's GATSROPUB $$
(☎562-439-5590; www.simmzys.com; 5271 E 2nd St, Belmont Shore; mains $10-17; ⏲11am-11pm Mon-Thu, 11am-midnight Fri, 10am-midnight Sat, 10am-11pm Sun) The Belmont Shore branch of the Manhattan Beach favorite. They serve tasty burgers, a terrific salmon sandwich and wood-fired pizzas, and the design here is special too. The doors roll up completely to the street, there are butcher-block common tables, a marble bar, and a chalkboard scrawled with craft brews of the day.

San Pedro Fish Market & Restaurant SEAFOOD $$
(www.sanpedrofishmarket.com; 1190 Nagoya Way, San Pedro; meals $13-18; ⏲8am-8pm; P👪) Seafood feasts don't get more decadent than the ones at this family-run, harbor-view institu-

tion. Pick from the day's catch, have it spiced and cooked to order with potatoes, tomatoes and peppers, lug your tray to a picnic table, fold up your sleeves and devour meaty crabs, plump shrimp, slimy oysters, melty yellowtail and tender halibut.

Don't forget to order some buttery garlic bread and a pile of extra napkins. You can save a buck or two next door at **Crusty Crab**, doing the same exact work.

Drinking & Entertainment

★Federal Bar BAR

(www.lb.thefederalbar.com; 102 Pine Ave, Long Beach; ⏲11:30am-11pm) This converted, historic bank with its weighty granite bar, crystal chandeliers and burly wooden columns offers craft beers and booze behind the bar. They also have a venue downstairs where they host DJs and local bands, including nationally known stand-outs like Dengue Fever.

Harvelle's BAR

(☎562-239-3700; www.longbeach.harvelles.com; 201 E Broadway, Long Beach; cover varies; ⏲from 8pm Mon-Sat) A Long Beach shingle of the venerable Santa Monica spot, they host regular blues bands, burlesque dancers, and the famed Toledo Show on Thursdays.

Congregation Ale House PUB

(201 E Broadway Ave, Long Beach; ⏲11:30am-1am Mon-Thu, to 2am Fri & Sat, to midnight Sun) A popular pub on the Promenade in the ground floor of a historic building, Congregation Ale House has nearly 30 craft beers on tap and a nice patio out front. They have decent pub grub too.

Riley's SPORTS BAR

(5331 E 2nd St, Belmont Shore; ⏲11am-midnight Sun-Thu, to 2am Fri & Sat) Local sports freaks and sun worshippers collide at Riley's for big games. Ice-cold beer is poured into massive goblets, the pub grub is decent and the outdoor patio is usually populated.

Walker Cafe BAR

(700 Paseo del Mar, San Pedro; ⏲10am-9pm) Bessie Walker started selling sandwiches at this biker bar in 1943 and the place has hardly changed a lick. Great Americana, greasy burgers, cold beers, and it was featured in *Chinatown*.

Laugh Factory Long Beach COMEDY

(www.laughfactory.com; 151 S Pine Ave, Long Beach; ⏲8pm & 10pm Wed-Sat) The Long Beach shingle of Hollywood's comedy classic features both stand-up veterans and up-and-comers.

Shopping

★Academy MEN'S CLOTHING

(www.theacademylb.com; 429 E 1st St, Long Beach; ⏲noon-7pm) A wonderful local brand, based in the Arts District, selling active wear with travelers in mind. Conceived by two Cambodian brothers who were wartime refugees, they do chinos in four colors, and denim made for cycling. You pick the buttons and they'll customize them.

Their 'world peace' floral print shirt features every country's national flower. The best part? It's all affordable and sewn locally.

Long Beach Outdoor Antique & Collectible Market FLEA MARKET

(www.longbeachantiquemarket.com; Veteran's Memorial Stadium, 4901 E Conant St, Long Beach; admission $5; ⏲6:30am-3pm 3rd Sun of month) Bargains abound at this sprawling market with over 800 stalls hawking everything from vintage postcards to pottery, and fur to furniture near the Long Beach Airport.

BURBANK, UNIVERSAL CITY & THE SAN FERNANDO VALLEY

Home to most of LA's major movie studios – including Warner Bros, Disney and Universal – 'the Valley' is an exercise in sprawl. It also has the dubious distinction of being the original world capital of porn, memorably captured in Paul Thomas Anderson's 1997 *Boogie Nights*. Car culture was also basically invented in the Valley, which claims to have given birth to the minimall, the drive-in movie theater, the drive-in bank and the drive-in restaurant.

Attractions are few and scattered about; Burbank has the studios, and North Hollywood, west of here, is home to a growing arts scene. Studio City, west of Universal, has some superb sushi on Ventura Blvd. At last count there were 21 sushi bars within a six-block radius, which is why some call it LA's Sushi Row. Studio City's grooviest shopping and cafe strip can be found on leafy Tujunga Blvd, which is also where you'll find Vitello's restaurant, where Robert Blake's wife was killed by a gunshot wound in 2001.

Note that temperatures here are usually 20°F (11°C) higher – and pollution levels worse – than in areas further south. But it's not all bad. In fact, with lower-cost housing and the lack of congestion, the Valley is more laid-back and down to earth than elsewhere in the city. This is where LA gets real.

Sights

Universal Studios Hollywood THEME PARK

(Map p100; www.universalstudioshollywood.com; 100 Universal City Plaza, Universal City; admission from $87, under 3yr free; open daily, hours vary; P) One of the world's oldest continuously operating movie studios, Universal presents an entertaining mix of fairly tame – and sometimes dated – thrills, live-action shows and a tram ride. It is a working studio, but the chances of seeing any action, let alone a star, are slim to none.

Try to budget a full day, especially in summer. To beat the crowds, get there before the gates open or invest in the Front of Line Pass ($139) or the deluxe guided VIP Experience ($349). Some rides have minimum height requirements. Buying online tickets usually yields discounts and coupons.

First-timers should head straight for the 45-minute narrated **Studio Tour** aboard a rickety tram that drives around the sound stages in the front lot, then heads to the back lot past the crash site from *War of the Worlds,* vehicles from *Jurassic Park,* and the spooky Bates Motel from *Psycho.* Also prepare to brave a flash flood, survive a shark attack, a spitting dino and an 8.3-magnitude earthquake, before facing down King Kong in a new 3D exhibit created by Peter Jackson. It's a bit hokey, but fun.

The most popular thrill ride is **Jurassic Park**, a gentle float through a prehistoric jungle with a rather 'raptor-ous' ending. **Revenge of the Mummy** is a short, but thrilling, indoor roller-coaster romp through 'Imhotep's Tomb,' that at one point has you going backwards and hits speeds of up to 45mph. A ride based on **The Simpsons** sends guests rocketing along with the Simpson family to experience a side of Springfield previously unexplored. You can also get a flight-simulated thrill on the new **3D Transformers** ride. Another 3D ride certain to get the kids smiling is the delightful **Despicable Me Minion Mayhem**.

In late 2013 the park launched a $1.6 billion expansion that has already inflicted collateral damage. The Gibson Amphitheater, a 40-year-old live-music institution, which hosted countless sold-out shows and had a particularly strong connection to Latin Pop, was shut down in favor of a coming Wizarding World of Harry Potter attraction.

Snack food and drinks, including beer and margaritas, are available throughout the park, although you'll have more choices at the adjacent Universal CityWalk, a promenade of restaurants, shops, bars and entertainment venues. Be sure to get your hand stamped for re-entry. Parking costs $10 to $16. Opening hours vary by season.

Forest Lawn Memorial Park – Glendale CEMETERY

(www.forestlawn.com; 1712 S Glendale Ave; 9am-5pm; P) FREE The final home of such Golden Age superstars as Clara Bow, Humphrey Bogart and Jimmy Stewart. Alas, many of their graves are in mausoleums and are off-limits to the public. It doesn't help that cemetery staff strongly discourage star seekers.

You can download maps from the internet (for example www.seeing-stars.com), but be discreet or risk having them confiscated.

Americana at Brand PLAZA

(www.americanaatbrand.com; 889 Americana Way, Glendale) If you dig The Grove (p109) in Mid-City, then you'll enjoy this narrow, set-piece shopping mall, developed by the same folks, that feels like an extended walking street. There's an 18-screen multiplex, 19 restaurants, and some very good, albeit very corporate, shopping, including an affordable Barney's Co-op.

Sleeping

Sportsmen's Lodge HOTEL $$

(818-769-4700; www.sportsmenslodge.com; 12825 Ventura Blvd, Studio City; r from $149) This valley classic had a renovation and is back on the radar. Ok it's still a glorified motel, but much more inviting. The spacious rooms have orange and lime-green disco sheets, wall-mounted flat-screen TVs and two-tone walls. There's a sexy pool area too. You'll find the best deals online.

Hotel Amarano BOUTIQUE HOTEL $$

(818-842-8887; www.hotelamarano.com; 322 N Pass Ave, Burbank; r weekend/midweek from $179/235; P @) A boutique business hotel where even the basic superior rooms are large and sunny, with fresh Berber carpeting, stylish blonde-wood furnishings, soft bedding and a slate-blue accent wall. Step up in class and you can have a kitchenette and a huge flat-screen TV.

Embassy Suites HOTEL $$
(☎818-550-0828; www.embassysuites.com; 800 N Central Ave, Glendale; r from $179; P@📶🏊) Ignore the oh-so-corporate moniker. This tower hotel with a frosted-glass facade has class and value. All rooms are suites, there's a lap pool on the 2nd-floor ledge, a full fitness center, and a free full breakfast for up to four people. It's set in downtown Glendale and within walking distance of the Americana mall.

Safari Inn MOTEL $$
(Map p100; ☎818-845-8586; www.safariburbank.com; 1911 W Olive Ave, Burbank; r $120-150; P📶🏊) This 1950s motel boasts a vintage neon sign, beds are draped in animal print bedspreads, and framed poster art adds charm to rooms that are otherwise on the small and darkish side. The pool is nice, the staff professional, and you'll be close to the studios.

BLVD Hotel HOTEL $$
(☎818-623-9100; www.theblvdhotel.com; 10730 Ventura Blvd, Studio City; r from $139; P🏊) A fun, great-value boutique property on Ventura Blvd with 69 spacious, Ikea-chic rooms with wood floors, wet bar, rain showers, high ceilings and plush linens. Amenities include a heated indoor pool, covered parking and a lobby bar.

Eating & Drinking

Suck It FROZEN DESSERTS $
(Map p100; ☎818-980-7825; www.suckitsweets.com; 4361 1/2 Tujunga Ave, Studio City; desserts $4; ⏰1-8pm) Don't you dare call them popsicles! These are frozen desserts on a stick. The key-lime-pie flavor really is pie frozen on a stick. Same goes for coconut cream, Mexican hot chocolate and strawberry cheesecake. Everything is made in house and by the millennial owner and 'chief suckologist' (her words!).

She hops farmers markets for ingredients and disembowels anybody who utters the p-word in her presence. No, not really, but you may get a stern tongue lashing.

Baklava Factory MIDDLE EASTERN $
(https://baklavafactory.com/; 17540 Ventura Blvd, Encino; ⏰9am-8pm Mon-Fri, to 8:30pm Sat, to 7:30pm Sun) Hidden in the Encino sprawl, it's easy to miss this tiny pastry shop, but if you enjoy sweet, light, nutty, syrupy, crunchy

BEHIND THE CURTAIN: MOVIE MAGIC UNMASKED

Did you know it takes a week to shoot a half-hour sitcom? Or that you rarely see ceilings on shows because the space is filled with lights and lamps? You'll learn these and other fascinating nuggets of information about the make-believe world of film and TV while touring a working studio. Star-sighting potential is better than average, except during 'hiatus' (May to August) when studios are deserted. Reservations are required and so is photo ID.

Paramount (☎323-956-1777; www.paramountstudiotour.com; 5555 Melrose Ave; tours from $53; ⏰tours 9:30am-2pm Mon-Fri, hours vary Sat & Sun) *Star Trek, Indiana Jones* and *Shrek* are among the blockbusters that originated at Paramount, the longest operating movie studio and the only one still in Hollywood proper. Two-hour tours through the back lots and sound stages are available year-round and are led by passionate, knowledgeable guides.

Sony (☎310-244-8687; www.sonypicturesstudiostours.com; 10202 W Washington Blvd; tour $38; ⏰tours usually 9:30am, 10:30am, 1:30pm & 2:30pm Mon-Fri) This two-hour tour includes visits to the sound stages where *Men in Black, Spider-Man* and *Charlie's Angels* were filmed. Munchkins hopped along the Yellow Brick Road in *The Wizard of Oz*, filmed when this was still the venerable MGM studio.

Warner Bros (Map p100; ☎818-972-8687, 877-492-8687; www.wbstudiotour.com; 3400 W Riverside Dr, Burbank; tours from $54; ⏰8:15am-4pm Mon-Sat, hours vary Sun) This tour offers the most fun, yet authentic, look behind the scenes of a major movie studio. The 2¼-hour romp kicks off with a video of WB's greatest film hits (*Rebel Without a Cause, Harry Potter* etc) before a tram whisks you to sound stages, back-lot sets and technical departments, including props, costumes and the paint shop. Tours conclude at the studio museum, a treasure trove of props and memorabilia, including Hogwarts' famous Sorting Hat. Tours leave every half hour.

desserts, you shouldn't overlook it. These folks do baklava right: all-natural with pistachios and walnuts, some rolled, others sliced into squares. You can buy it by the pound or by the piece. Just…wow!

Bob's Big Boy DINER $

(Map p100; ☎818-843-9334; www.bigboy.com; 4211 Riverside Dr, Burbank; burgers & sandwiches $7-10; ⏲24hr; P ♿) Bob, that cheeky pompadoured kid in red-checkered pants, hasn't aged a lick since serving his first double-decker in 1936. This Wayne McAllister–designed, Googie-style 1950s coffee shop is the oldest remaining Big Boy's in America. On Friday at about 4pm hot-rods roar into the parking lot and stay all night, while the weekend car-hop service (5pm to 10pm Saturday and Sunday) brings in families and love doves.

★ **Phoenicia** LEBANESE $$

(☎818-956-7800; www.phoeniciala.com; 343 N Central Ave, Glendale; appetizers $5-8, meals $11-23; ⏲11:30am-11pm Sun-Thu, to midnight Fri & Sat) OK, the design lacks charm, but this is where local Lebanese and Armenian families land on Sunday nights for homeland delicacies such as *soujouk* (a spicy Armenian beef sausage, dried, sliced and sautéed with onion and tomato), *maanek* (Lebanese beef sausage with a lemon glaze), *lessanat* (lamb tongue sliced thin) and *nekhat* (lamb brains cooked in olive oil, lemon juice and garlic, served cold).

Don't worry, they do falafel, kebabs, shwarma, hummus, tabbouleh, and a mouth-melting lamb shank too. Meals come with broiled tomato, pita, salad, hummus and choice of rice or fries. Pair yours with an Almaza, Lebanon's favorite beer, and finish it off with a hit from the shisha pipe ($22).

★ **Daichan** JAPANESE $$

(11288 Ventura Blvd, Studio City; mains $8.50-19; ⏲11:30am-3pm & 5:30-9pm Mon-Sat; P) Stuffed with knickknacks, pasted with posters and staffed by the sunny and sweet owner-operator, this offbeat Japanese diner offers the best (and one of the tastiest) deals on sushi row. The fried seaweed tofu *gyoza* are divine and so are the bowls – especially the *negitoro* bowl, where fatty tuna is served over rice, lettuce and seaweed.

Aroma Coffee & Tea CAFE $$

(Map p100; ☎818-508-7377; www.aromacoffeeandtea.com; 4360 Tujunga Ave, Studio City; mains $9-14; ⏲6am-11pm Mon-Sat, from 7am Sun) This popular cafe is set in a converted house where wood tables crowd heated patios and the line runs out the door. Meals include goat-cheese and walnut salads, popular turkey burgers, and breakfasts such as chilaquiles and breakfast enchiladas, and a spinach puff pastry topped with scrambled eggs.

Caitoti Pizza Cafe ITALIAN $$

(Map p100; ☎818-761-3588; www.caiotipizzacafe.com; 4346 Tujunga Ave, Studio City; mains $9-14; ⏲11am-10pm Mon-Thu, to 11pm Fri, 9am-11pm Sat, to 10pm Sun) Once set in Laurel Canyon this longtime, long-loved Italian cafe serves salads, bison burgers and Italian sausage sandwiches, as well as some terrific pizzas and pastas. All served in an attractive concrete-floor cafe where it can be tough to get a table at dinnertime.

Kazu Sushi JAPANESE $$$

(☎818-763-4836; 11440 Ventura Blvd, Studio City; dishes $10-19; ⏲noon-2pm & 6-10pm Mon-Sat; P) Stuck in a cramped and otherwise nondescript, split-level minimall that's easy to miss, is one of the best-kept secrets among LA's sushi aficionados. Kazu Sushi is Michelin-rated, very high-end, has a terrific sake selection, and is worth the splurge.

Asanebo SUSHI $$$

(☎818-760-3348; www.asanebo-restaurant.com; 11941 Ventura Blvd, Studio City; dishes $3-21; ⏲noon-2pm & 6-10:30pm Tue-Fri, 6-10:30pm Sat, to 10pm Sun) Asanebo is a Michelin-star standout thanks to dishes such as halibut sashimi with fresh truffle, and *kanpachi* with miso and serrano chilies.

Laurel Tavern PUB

(www.laureltavern.com; 11938 Ventura Blvd, Studio City; ⏲noon-2am) This new, tastefully modern pub with wood floors, wood-slab bar and brick walls has an extensive craftsman beer and wine list on the chalkboard. They have sports on the flat-screen TV, enticing pub grub and a full bar.

☆ Entertainment

The NoHo, aka North Hollywood, arts district is sprinkled with theaters and venues offering plays and stand-up comedy. The **Anateus Company** (☎818-506-5436; www.antaeus.org; 5112 Lankershim Blvd, North Hollywood; tickets $30-34) is among the better reviewed in LA. They operate out of their own theater on Lankershim. The **Acme Comedy Theatre** (www.acmecomedy.com; 5124 Lankershim Blvd, North Hollywood), an improv troupe, has a branch here too.

Baked Potato JAZZ, BLUES

(Map p100; www.thebakedpotato.com; 3787 Cahuenga Blvd, Studio City; cover $10-25, plus 2 drinks; 7pm-2am) Near Universal Studios a dancing spud beckons you to come inside this diminutive jazz-and-blues hall where the schedule mixes no-names with big-timers. Drinks are stiff, and actual baked potatoes (priced from $6.50 to $15) are optional.

Noho Arts Center Ensemble THEATER

(www.thenohoartscenter.com; 11136 Magnolia Blvd, North Hollywood; tickets $25; shows 8pm Fri & Sat, 3pm Sun) The crown jewel of North Hollywood's budding theater scene offers reimagined classic and new cutting-edge theater.

Pacific 18 CINEMA

(www.pacifictheatres.com; 322 Americana Way, Glendale; adult/senior/child $13/11.25/10.25; shows 10:30am-10:30pm) Cushy seats, an amphitheater arrangement, leg room for days, and Monday Morning Mommy Movies at 11am.

Shopping

Psychic Eye NEW AGE

(818-906-8263; www.pebooks.com; 13435 Ventura Blvd, Sherman Oaks; readings 15/30/60min $20/30/50; 10am-10pm Mon-Sat, to 8pm Sun) A longtime pipeline of psychics, astrologers, amulets, idols, pentacles, books, candles and potions. If there's a spell you'd like to cast or break, if you need intuitive advice or would otherwise like to peer into the past or the future, find this strange vortex of the occult.

It's a Wrap! VINTAGE

(Map p100; www.itsawraphollywood.com; 3315 W Magnolia Blvd, Burbank; 10am-8pm Mon-Fri, 11am-6pm Sat & Sun) Here are fashionable, post-production wares worn by TV and film stars. What that means to you is great prices on mainstream designer labels, including racks of casual and formal gear worn on such shows as *Nurse Jackie, The Office* and *Scandal*. The suits are a steal, and so is the denim. New arrivals are racked by show affiliation.

PASADENA & THE SAN GABRIEL VALLEY

One could argue that there is more blue-blood, meat-eating, robust Americana in Pasadena than in all other LA neighborhoods combined. Here you'll find a community with a preppy old soul, a historical perspective, an appreciation for art and jazz, and a slightly progressive undercurrent. The Rose Parade and Rose Bowl football game may have given Pasadena its long-lasting fame, but it's the spirit of this genteel city and its location beneath the lofty San Gabriel Mountains that make it a charming and attractive place to visit year-round. Its immaculate streets are shaded by gnarled, native oaks and lined with grand old craftsman mansions and mid-century modern apartment buildings. There are museums and gardens, as well as lively Old Pasadena, a bustling 20-block shopping and entertainment district set up in historic brick buildings along Colorado Blvd west of Arroyo Pkwy.

South Pasadena is Main Street USA meets Southern California – a land where free parking still exists (hell, it's encouraged), old brick and wood edifices still stand, people-moving trains still roll through downtown, and shoppers and neighbors still smile at one another when crossing paths.

The San Gabriel Valley, where you'll find the San Gabriel Mission, actually predates the city of LA. Though it boasts the art-deco Santa Anita race track and the LA County Arboretum, these days it's best known for thousands of native Chinese residents who have turned this string of communities into one of the great dim-sum destinations.

Pasadena is served by the Metro Rail Gold Line from Downtown LA. Pasadena ARTS buses (fare 75¢) plow around the city on seven different routes.

Sights

Rose Bowl Stadium & Brookside Park LANDMARK

(Map p62; 626-577-3100; www.rosebowlstadium.com; 1001 Rose Bowl Dr, Pasadena) One of LA's most venerable landmarks, the 1922 Rose Bowl Stadium can seat up to 93,000 spectators and has its moment in the sun every New Year's Day when it hosts the famous Rose Bowl post-season college football game. At other times, the UCLA Bruins play their home games here, and the occasional concert or special event also brings in the masses. As does a monthly flea market.

The Rose Bowl is surrounded by **Brookside Park**, which is a nice spot for hiking, cycling and picnicking. Families should check out the excellent **Kidspace Children's Museum** (Map p194; www.kidspacemuseum.org; 480 N Arroyo Blvd; admission $11;

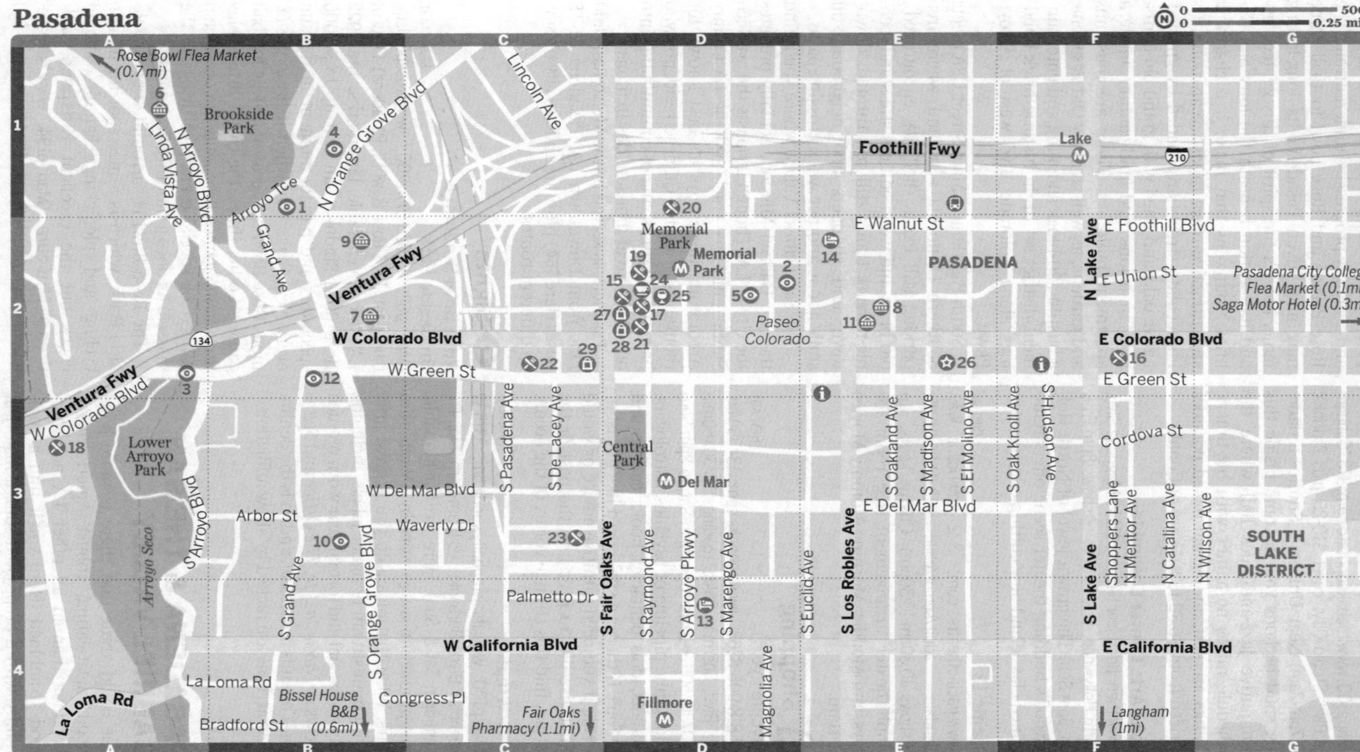
Pasadena
500 m
0.25 miles
Rose Bowl Flea Market (0.7 mi)
Brookside Park
Linda Vista Ave
N Arroyo Blvd
N Orange Grove Blvd
Arroyo Tce
Grand Ave
Lincoln Ave
Foothill Fwy
Lake
210
Ventura Fwy
134
W Colorado Blvd
W Green St
E Walnut St
E Foothill Blvd
N Lake Ave
PASADENA
E Union St
Pasadena City College Flea Market (0.1mi); Saga Motor Hotel (0.3mi)
Memorial Park
Paseo Colorado
E Colorado Blvd
E Green St
Lower Arroyo Park
Arroyo Seco
S Arroyo Blvd
S Pasadena Ave
S De Lacey Ave
Central Park
Del Mar
W Del Mar Blvd
E Del Mar Blvd
Arbor St
Waverly Dr
S Fair Oaks Ave
S Raymond Ave
S Arroyo Pkwy
S Marengo Ave
S Euclid Ave
S Los Robles Ave
S Oakland Ave
S Madison Ave
S El Molino Ave
S Oak Knoll Ave
S Hudson Ave
Cordova St
S Lake Ave
Shoppers Lane
N Mentor Ave
N Catalina Ave
N Wilson Ave
SOUTH LAKE DISTRICT
Palmetto Dr
S Grand Ave
S Orange Grove Blvd
W California Blvd
E California Blvd
Magnolia Ave
La Loma Rd
Bissel House B&B (0.6mi)
Congress Pl
Bradford St
Fair Oaks Pharmacy (1.1mi)
Fillmore
Langham (1mi)

Pasadena

Sights

1 Charles Greene's Former Private Residence B1
2 City Hall D2
3 Colorado St Bridge A2
4 Gamble House B1
5 Jackie & Mack Robinson Memorial D2
6 Kidspace Children's Museum A1
7 Norton Simon Museum B2
8 Pasadena Museum of California Art E2
9 Pasadena Museum of History B2
10 Tournament House & Wrigley Gardens B3
11 USC Pacific Asia Museum E2
12 Vista del Arroyo Hotel B2

Sleeping

13 Pasadena Inn D4
14 Westin E2

Eating

15 Akbar D2
16 Bistro 45 .... F2
17 Kal's D2
18 Little Flower A3
19 Market on Holly D2
20 Marston's D1
21 Mi Piace D2
22 Racio'n C2
23 Saladang Song C3

Drinking & Nightlife

24 Chado Tea Room D2
25 Vertical Wine Bistro D2

Entertainment

26 Pasadena Playhouse E2
Red White & Bluezz .... (see 26)

Shopping

27 Gold Bug D2
28 Neo 39 .... D2
29 Rocket Fizz C2

9:30am-5pm Tue-Fri, from 10am Sat & Sun, 9:30am-5pm Mon Jun-Aug only; P), and architecture nuts should look for the palatial 1903 **Vista del Arroyo Hotel** (Map p194; 125 S Grand Ave), now home to the Ninth Circuit Court of Appeals. It's open to the public, and worth stepping into the law library to see the old, stopped Chicago clock on the south wall and sensational views of the gracefully arched 1913 **Colorado St Bridge** (Map p194).

★Huntington Library — MUSEUM, GARDENS

(Map p62; 626-405-2100; www.huntington.org; 1151 Oxford Rd, San Marino; adult weekday/weekend & holidays $20/23, child $8, 1st Thu each month free; 10:30am-4:30pm Wed-Mon Jun-Aug, noon-4:30pm Mon & Wed-Fri, from 10:30am Sat, Sun & hol idaysSep-May; P) Unwind in the Zen-like tranquility of a Japanese garden. Study the jaunty pose of Thomas Gainsborough's *The Blue Boy*. Linger over the illuminated vellum of a 1455 Gutenberg *Bible*. It's hard to know where to start exploring this genteel country estate, the legacy of railroad tycoon Henry Huntington, and one of the most delightful and inspirational spots in LA.

El Molino Viejo — HISTORIC MILL

(Old Mill; Map p62; www.old-mill.org; 1120 Old Mill Rd, San Marino; 1-4pm Tue-Sun; P) While in the Huntington Library area, make a quick detour to this transporting brick-and-adobe structure with creaky wood floors and exposed timbers in the rafters. It houses Southern California's first water-powered gristmill, built in 1816 for the San Gabriel Mission. The displays here are nothing special, but the building is worth the trip.

Norton Simon Museum — MUSEUM

(Map p194; www.nortonsimon.org; 411 W Colorado Blvd, Pasadena; adult/child $10/free; noon-6pm Wed-Mon, to 9pm Fri; P) Rodin's *The Thinker* is only a mind-teasing overture to the full symphony of art in store at this exquisite museum. Norton Simon (1907–93) was an entrepreneur with a Midas touch and a passion for art who parlayed his millions into a respectable collection of Western art and Asian sculpture.

The accessible, user-friendly galleries teem with choice works by Rembrandt, Renoir, Raphael, Van Gogh, Botticelli and Picasso, as well as an outstanding array of paintings and sculpture by Degas. Asian sculpture is in the basement, while Western sculpture graces the gorgeous garden inspired by Monet's garden at Giverny, France.

Angeles National Forest — OUTDOORS

(www.fs.fed.us/r5/angeles) The San Gabriel mountain range that hems in the northern edge of Pasadena, and all of urban LA, is part of the Angeles Crest. Its creeks, canyons and campgrounds provide quick city getaways year-round. It's particularly pretty during the spring wildflower season and gets lovely fall color.

Note that visiting the Angeles National Forest requires a National Forest Adventure

Pass which you can buy online. Visit the USFS website for more details.

Mt Wilson Observatory LANDMARK

(www.mtwilson.edu; Red Box Rd, Mt Wilson; 10am-5pm Apr-Nov) FREE As you drive into the Angeles National Forest take the Red Box Rd turn-off which, 5 miles later, dead-ends atop 5715ft Mt Wilson. Operating since 1904, this was the world's top astronomical research facility in the early 20th century and is still in use today.

You can walk around the grounds (download a handy self-guided tour from the website) and visit the museum. Free guided tours run at 1pm on Saturdays and Sundays. The website also has details on how to schedule a viewing session using the 1908 60-inch telescope (half-/full night $900/1700 for groups of up to 25 people). It's closed in bad weather.

Gamble House ARCHITECTURE

(Map p194; info 626-793-3334, tickets 800-979-3370; www.gamblehouse.org; 4 Westmoreland Pl, Pasadena; tours adult/child from $12.50/free; tours noon-3pm Thu-Sun, gift shop 10am-5pm Tue-Sat, 11:30am-5pm Sun; P) It's the exquisite attention to detail that impresses most at the Gamble House, a 1908 masterpiece of craftsman architecture built by Charles and Henry Greene for Procter & Gamble-heir David Gamble. The entire home is a work of art, its foundation, furniture and fixtures all united by a common design and theme inspired by its Southern California environs.

Note sleeping porches, iridescent stained glass and subtle appearances of the Gamble family's rose and crane crest.

Other Greene and Greene homes, including **Charles Greene's former private residence** (Map p194; 368 Arroyo Tce), line nearby Arroyo Tce and Grand Ave. Pick up a self-guided walking-tour pamphlet at the Gamble House bookstore.

Descanso Gardens GARDENS

(Map p62; www.descansogardens.org; 1418 Descanso Dr, La Cañada Flintridge; adult/5-12yr/student & senior $9/4/6; 9am-5pm; P) The lovely Descanso botanical gardens put on a dazzling show all year, but especially in January and February when some 34,000 camellias brighten the LA winter, some as tall as 20ft. In spring lilacs perfume the air, followed by roses in summer. It's easy to spend a whole day amid the greenery, waterways and bird sanctuary.

The gardens are in La Cañada Flintridge, about 6 miles northwest of Pasadena at the foot of the Angeles Crest Scenic Byway.

Art Center College of Design COLLEGE

(Map p62; tour reservations 626-396-2373; www.artcenter.edu; 1700 Lida St, Pasadena) FREE Overlooking the Arroyo Seco from its ridge-top perch is this world-renowned arts campus. Free tours for prospective students are offered during the school year at 2pm Monday to Friday; reservations are required. To see what students and alumni have been up to, check out the latest exhibit at the **Williamson Gallery** (Map p62; www.artcenter.edu/williamson; noon-5pm Tue-Sun, to 9pm Fri).

California Institute of Technology UNIVERSITY

(Caltech; tours 626-395-6341; www.caltech.edu; 551 S Hill Ave, Pasadena; tours 11:15am year-round, 2:15pm Mar, Apr, Jul & Aug) FREE With 31 Nobel laureates among its faculty and alumni, it's no surprise that Caltech is regarded with awe in academic circles. Earthquake studies were essentially pioneered here in the 1920s with the inventions of the seismograph and the Richter scale, and to this day Caltech scientists are usually the first experts to be consulted whenever a shaker strikes.

The hallowed campus is dotted with century-old stone buildings and shady old oaks mixed in with new mind-bending steel and glass structures such as the **Cahill Center for Astronomy and Astrophysics**. Free student-led tours depart from the **Office of Undergraduate Admissions** (355 S Holliston, Pasadena). Alternatively, pick up a self-guided tour booklet at the office or download one from the website.

Caltech also operates the **Jet Propulsion Laboratory** (JPL; Map p62; tours 818-354-9319; www.jpl.nasa.gov; 4800 Oak Grove Dr, Pasadena), NASA's main center for robotic exploration of the solar system, about 3.5 miles north of campus. It's possible to visit JPL during public lectures in the annual open house (usually in May) or by requesting a free tour well in advance.

San Gabriel Mission LANDMARK

(Map p62; www.sangabrielmission.org; 428 S Mission Dr, San Gabriel; adult/6-17yr $5/3; 9am-4:30pm Mon-Sat, 10am-4pm Sun; P) In 1781, settlers departed from this mission to found El Pueblo de Los Angeles in today's Downtown area. Set about 3 miles southeast of Pasadena in the city of San Gabriel, it's the fourth in the chain of 21 missions in California and is one of the prettiest.

Its church boasts Spanish Moorish flourishes, a copper baptismal font, carved statues of saints and a 1790 altar made in Mexico City. The mission surroundings are also well worth a quick stroll. Following Mission Dr takes you past the 1927 Civic Auditorium, the Civic Center, a historical museum and galleries.

Los Angeles County Arboretum & Botanic Garden GARDENS
(Map p62; www.arboretum.org; 301 N Baldwin Ave, Arcadia; adult/5-12yr/student & senior $9/4/6, 3rd Tue of month free; ⏲9am-4:30pm) It's easy to spend hours amid the global vegetation, waterfalls, spring-fed lake and historic buildings of this fantastic, rambling park. Originally the private estate of real-estate tycoon Elias 'Lucky' Baldwin, it's so huge there's even a tram to haul those who are foot-weary.

The grounds are often used in filming, for instance standing in for the African jungle in *African Queen* and as Central Park in *End of Days*. It's in Arcadia, about 5 miles east of central Pasadena, right by the Santa Anita Park racetrack.

Santa Anita Park SPORT
(Map p62; ☎tickets 626-574-6366; www.santaanita.com; 285 W Huntington Dr, Arcadia; admission general $5, clubhouse $10, under 17yr free; ⏲racing season Christmas–mid-Apr, late Sep-early Nov, tram tours 8:30am & 9:45am Sat & Sun) Home of the legendary Seabiscuit, this stunning, art-deco thoroughbred racetrack is the oldest and one of the most prestigious in Southern California. Free **tram tours** take you to Seabiscuit's barn, the jockey's room and other sights during racing season.

The track opened in 1934 and pioneered the use of the automated starting gate, the photo finish and the electrical timer. Stars who kept and raced their horses here have ranged from Bing Crosby and Errol Flynn to Mark McGrath (of Sugar Ray), Alex Trebek and Burt Bacharach. The only stain on its legacy happened during WWII when it served as a Japanese-American detention camp.

Pasadena Civic Center Area LANDMARK
Pasadena's Civic Center, built in the 1920s, is a reflection of the great wealth and local pride that have governed the city since its early days. Highlights include the Spanish Renaissance–style **City Hall** (Map p194; 100 N Garfield Ave, Pasadena) and the **Central Library** (285 E Walnut St, Pasadena). Nearby, the **Jackie & Mack Robinson Memorial** (Map p194; cnr Garfield & Union Sts, Pasadena) honors the Georgia-born, but Pasadena-reared athletic brothers.

The often overshadowed Matthew 'Mack' Robinson was a former world-record holder who won an Olympic silver medal in the 200m sprint in the 1936 Olympics in Berlin (he finished 0.4 seconds behind Jesse Owens). In 1945 his youngest brother, Jackie, became the first African American to be signed to a major-league baseball team. He became a perennial all-star, World Series champion, and hall-of-famer for the Brooklyn (now LA) Dodgers.

USC Pacific Asia Museum MUSEUM
(Map p194; ☎626-449-2742; www.pacificasiamuseum.org; 46 N Los Robles Ave, Pasadena; adult/student & senior $10/7; ⏲10am-6pm Wed-Sun; P) A block east of the Civic Center, a re-created Chinese palace that was once the home of local art dealer and Asia-phile Grace Nicholson now houses nine galleries, which rotate ancient and contemporary art and artifacts from Asia and the Pacific Islands. From Himalayan Buddhas to Chinese porcelain and Japanese costumes, the quality and range of Nicholson's collection is stellar.

Pasadena Museum of California Art MUSEUM
(Map p194; www.pmcaonline.org; 490 E Union St, Pasadena; adult/student & senior/child $7/5/free, 1st Fri of month free; ⏲noon-5pm Wed-Sun; P) This progressive gallery is dedicated to art, architecture and design created by California artists since 1850. Shows change every few months and have included masterpieces by Maynard Dixon, collages by beatnik artist Jess, and vinyl toys by Gary Basemen. Also swing by the **Kosmic Kavern**, which is what this former garage has become thanks to spray-mural pop artist Kenny Scharf.

Tournament House & Wrigley Gardens LANDMARK
(Map p194; www.tournamentofroses.com; 391 S Orange Grove Blvd, Pasadena; ⏲2pm & 3pm Thu Feb-Aug) Chewing-gum magnate William Wrigley spent his winters in the elegant Italian Renaissance–style mansion where the Tournament of Roses Association now masterminds the annual Rose Parade. When they're not busy, you can tour the rich

interior and inspect Rose Queen crowns and related memorabilia. Feel free to nose around the rose garden any time.

Pasadena Museum of History MUSEUM
(Map p194; www.pasadenahistory.org; 470 W Walnut St, Pasadena; adult/senior & student $7/6, tours $15; ⏲noon-5pm Wed-Sun, tours 12:15pm Fri-Sun; P) A palatial beaux-arts mansion that once housed the Finnish consulate, this interesting museum now presents changing exhibits on some facets of the culture, history and art of Pasadena and its neighboring communities. If you want to see the precious antiques and furnishings of the house itself, you'll need to join a tour.

Angeles Crest SCENIC DRIVE
(www.byways.org/explore/byways/10245/travel.html; Hwy 2) The two-lane Angeles Crest Scenic Byway treats you to fabulous views of big-shouldered mountains, the Mojave Desert and deep valleys on its 55-mile meander from La Cañada to the resort town of Wrightwood. The road skirts LA County's tallest mountain, officially called **Mt San Antonio** (10,064ft), but better known as Old Baldy for its treeless top.

You'll pass ranger stations along the way, but the main **Chilao Visitors Center** (www.fs.fed.us; ⏲8am-4pm Sat & Sun mid-Apr–mid-Oct) has natural exhibits and trails and is about 27 miles from the turnoff.

Activities

Kenyon Devore Trail HIKING
(www.fs.fed.us; Mt Wilson Observatory, Red Box Rd, Mt Wilson) Named after a longtime San Gabriel Mountain man, this trail begins a quarter mile from the Mt Wilson summit on Red Box Rd and drops down the mountain for 3000ft through stunning oak and pine habitat, meandering on both sides of the year-round Strayns Creek.

It's stunning countryside, especially in the spring – when wildflowers pop – and the fall when valley and black oaks turn gold and drop their spinning leaves. Follow the trail for about 4 miles to West Fork Campground, before turning back. It's a strenuous 9-mile round-trip. You can also cross Strayns Canyon Creek and make a right at the Gabrielino Trail which leads back up the mountain in a 10.5-mile loop. Whatever your game plan, be sure to pick up a good map and carry plenty of water.

Switzer Falls HIKING
(www.fs.fed.us; Switzer Picnic Area, Hwy 2) This easy 4-mile round-trip leaves from the Switzer Picnic Area (signposted 10.5 miles from La Cañada on Hwy 2). Follow the trail down the canyon, boulder hopping along the way.

When you reach Switzer Trail Camp follow the trail as it climbs out of the canyon (do not follow the stream below the camp – there's a steep vertical and rocky drop), and make a left at the unmarked junction with the Arroyo Seco Trail (if you go right, you'll be hiking to the Rose Bowl), dropping back into the gorge. When you reach the creek, follow it back upstream for a quarter mile to reach the falls.

Sleeping

Saga Motor Hotel MOTEL $
(☎800-793-7242, 626-795-0431; www.thesagamotorhotel.com; 1633 E Colorado Blvd, Pasadena; r incl breakfast from $85; P❄@🛜) This peach-tinted, palm-shaded motel isn't fancy or as cool as the sign makes it look, but even if some of the beds are saggy and the carpet faded, rooms are clean, have tubs and showers, and some homey touches – such as shutters on the window and books on the shelves.

Pasadena Inn MOTEL $
(Map p194; ☎626-795-8401; www.oldpasadenainn.com; 400 S Arroyo Pkwy, Pasadena; r $99-109; P@🛜🏊) This older property won't be featured in the pages of *House Beautiful*, but it offers shut-eye at a modest tariff. In the morning drag your coffee and Danish out to the pool area. At night the adjacent Thai restaurant makes a decent curry if you don't feel like hoofing it to Old Pasadena, a 15-minute walk away.

★**Bissell House B&B** BED & BREAKFAST $$
(☎626-441-3535; www.bissellhouse.com; 201 S Orange Grove Blvd, Pasadena; r $159-259; P🛜🏊) Antiques, hardwood floors and a crackling fireplace make this secluded Victorian B&B on 'Millionaire's Row' a bastion of warmth and romance. The hedge-framed garden feels like a sanctuary, and there's a pool for cooling off on hot summer days. The Prince Albert room has gorgeous wallpaper and a claw-foot tub. All seven rooms have private baths.

Anna Bissel, the original owner, was the heir to the man who invented the first carpet sweeper – a predecessor to the vaccum cleaner. She became a philanthropist and Albert Einstein once sat at her dining room table. The very one where you'll have breakfast. You'll see at least one vintage sweeper if you look close.

Langham RESORT $$$
(☎626-568-3900; www.pasadena.langhamhotels.com; 1401 S Oak Knoll Ave, Pasadena; r from $230; P@) Opened as the Huntington Hotel in 1906, it spent the last several decades as the Ritz Carlton before recently donning the robes of Langham. But some things don't change and this incredible 23-acre, palm-dappled, beaux-arts country estate – complete with rambling gardens, giant swimming pool and covered picture bridge – has still got it. Rates are reasonable.

Westin HOTEL $$$
(Map p194; ☎626-792-2727; www.westin.com; 191 N Los Robles Ave, Pasadena; r from $249; P@) Pasadena's slickest sleep is a large, modern, Spanish-style complex with comfortable rooms and all the amenities in a central old-town location. A nice, four-star choice.

Eating

★Little Flower CAFE $
(Map p194; ☎626-304-4800; www.littleflowercandyco.com; 1424 W Colorado Blvd, Pasadena; mains $8-15; ⊙7am-7pm Mon-Sat, 9am-4pm Sun) An adorable, locally loved cafe set just a mile over the Colorado Bridge from Old Town. They make *banh mi* sandwiches with chicken, roast beef or tempeh, as well as bowls stuffed with such things as dahl, raita, curried eggplant and steamed spinach, or salmon, shredded carrots, daikon, micro greens and ponzu.

You'd better save room for dessert. They are famous for their candies and exquisite pastries.

Yum Cha Café CHINESE $
(www.yumchacafe.com; 1635 S San Gabriel Blvd, San Gabriel; dim sum $1-4, pork & duck plates $5-9; ⊙8:30am-8pm; P) Set in a minimall, this classic Cantonese cheapie is where roast duck and slabs of roast pork are chopped and wrapped to go. It also does a tremendous noodle soup with barbecued pork and various concoctions of *congee* (rice porridge) with ingredients such as pork blood, intestine or preserved egg.

Market on Holly CAFE $
(Map p194; www.themarketonholly.com; 57 E Holly St, Pasadena; mains $7-13; ⊙8am-4pm Mon-Fri, 9am-2pm Sat & Sun) A cute, concrete-floor market cafe with a handful of marble and wood common tables. Salads include an unchopped version of a chopped salad and a salmon salad with black-bean relish. They also make a balsamic-glazed chicken sandwich, garnished with feta and kalamata olives. Their weekend brunch is popular and affordable.

Marston's DINER $$
(Map p194; www.marstonsrestaurant.com; 151 E Walnut St, Pasadena; mains $8-16; ⊙7am-2:30pm Mon-Fri, 8am-2:30pm Sat & Sun; P) Marston's serves lunch, but it's the prospect of the scrumptious all-American breakfasts that helps us get out of bed. But no matter when you get there, this diminutive cottage with its sunny porch is likely to be packed. It has been for 25 years.

Sea Harbour CHINESE $$
(☎626-288-3939; 3939 Rosemead Blvd, Rosemead; dishes $10-30; ⊙10:30am-2:30pm & 5-10pm; P) When Chinese foodies crave dim sum, they come here, where classic dumplings have been modernized. Not that a novice would notice. Because when we see shredded pork wrapped in sticky rice and a lotus leaf, or shrimp folded into thick flat noodles and soaked in sweet soy, all we do is eat.

Akbar INDIAN $$
(Map p194; www.akbarcuisineofindia.com; 44 N Fair Oaks Ave, Pasadena; mains $10-16; ⊙11:30am-2:30pm & 5-10pm Mon-Thu, to 11pm Fri, 10am-11pm Sat, 11:30am-10pm Sun) Cozy without being cramped, this tiny saffron-scented dining room with an open kitchen bakes bread, broils meat in a tandoori oven, and stirs up all the curries too.

Kal's GREEK $$
(Map p194; ☎626-440-0100; www.kalsbistro.com; 43 E Union Ave, Pasadena; mains $12-20; ⊙11:30am-3pm & 5-11pm Tue-Thu, to midnight Fri, 11:30am-midnight Sat, 11:30am-11pm Sun) An old-school Greek bar and grill where they serve affordable steaks, shwarma and lamb burgers, and a mixed grill that would feed three.

Saladang Song THAI $$
(Map p194; ☎626-793-5200; www.facebook.com/SaladangSong/info; 383 S Fair Oaks Ave, Pasadena; dishes $10-18; ⊙7:30am-9:30pm; P) Traditional Thai is served in contemporary environs at this pseudo-industrial outpost hemmed in by artfully rendered concrete walls. It serves simple curries, vermicelli with fish balls steamed in green curry, and

real-deal Thai breakfasts (rice porridge and muddy coffee), which are often hard to find this side of Bangkok.

Mi Piace ITALIAN $$
(Map p194; www.mipiace.com; 25 E Colorado Blvd, Pasadena; mains $12-21; 8am-midnight Sun & Mon, to 11:30pm Tue & Wed, to 1am Thu-Sat; P) This midrange Italian kitchen gets packed with Pasadena's business crowd on weekdays, and shoppers on weekends. There's a shady sidewalk patio, a Sinatra soundtrack and popular thin-crust pizza.

Mike & Anne's MODERN AMERICAN $$
(626-799-7199; www.mikeandannes.com; 1040 Mission St, South Pasadena; mains $7-24; 8am-2:30pm & 5-9pm Sun & Tue-Thu, to 10pm Fri & Sat; P) Right on the Mission St drag in South Pasadena, Mike & Anne's is popular for their inviting patio, lemon and ricotta pancakes with caramelized blueberry compote at breakfast, and entree salads and sandwiches ranging from pulled pork to grilled eggplant to meatloaf and cheese at lunch.

Racio'n SPANISH $$$
(Map p194; 626-396-3090; www.racionrestaurant.com; 119 W Green St, Pasadena; dishes $5-45; 6-10pm Mon, 11:30am-3pm & 6-10pm Tue-Thu, to 11pm Fri & Sat, 5:30-10pm Sun) This Basque-inspired restaurant offers tapas such as duck sausage, stuffed squid, beer-braised octopus and seared prawns in salsa verde. They house cure yellowfin tuna in anchovy vinegrette, and offer larger plates *(raciones)* ranging from a wild market fish with heirloom beans to slow-braised lamb belly.

Bistro 45 CONTINENTAL $$$
(Map p194; 626-795-2478; www.bistro45.com; 45 Mentor Ave, Pasadena; mains $23-40; 5-9pm Tue-Thu, 11am-2pm & 5-10pm Fri & Sat, 5-8:30pm Sun; P) Touted as the best fine-dining in the 'dena, this pink-and-green, art-deco dining room is elegant, yet not stiff. It's the kind of place top Central Californian winemakers choose if they're hosting a dinner for potential buyers. The seafood, steaks and chops are all seriously good.

Crossings MODERN AMERICAN $$$
(626-799-7001; www.crossings-restaurant.com; 1010 Mission St, South Pasadena; mains $16-34; 5:30-9:30pm Sun-Thu, to 10pm Fri & Sat) If you land in South Pasadena at dinnertime, consider this chic space near the tracks. They do a crunchy, spicy ahi poke with jalapeño and toasted rice, as well as roast lamb, pork chops, bass and salmon. The surf-and-turf burger with a beef patty topped with crayfish is indulgent and divine.

OUR FAVORITE FLEA MARKETS

Flea markets are like urban archaeology: you'll need plenty of patience and luck when sifting through other people's trash and detritus, but oh, the thrill when you finally unearth a piece of treasure! Arrive early, bring small bills, wear walking shoes and get ready to haggle. These are the best of the best:

Rose Bowl Flea Market (p201)

Pasadena City College Flea Market (p201)

Melrose Trading Post (p125)

Drinking

Vertical Wine Bistro WINE BAR
(Map p194; www.verticalwinebistro.com; 70 N Raymond Ave, Pasadena; 4pm-midnight Tue-Thu & Sun, to 1:45am Fri & Sat) Although it's a sophisticated wine bar dressed in cocoa and candlelight, don't worry if you can't tell your pinot noir from your pinot grigio. Tapas come with a wine recommendation and you can sample 2oz tastes from most of the over 400 bottles in the cellar.

Chado Tea Room TEAHOUSE
(Map p194; 626-431-2832; www.chadotea.com; 79 N Raymond Ave, Pasadena; full tea service per person $18; 11:30am-7pm) This Indian-owned emporium serves teas from all over the globe. They have 350 in all, from milky oolong to white teas. They even have a green Darjeeling. Sensible ladies descend for affordable afternoon tea service.

Entertainment

Red White & Bluezz JAZZ
(Map p194; 626-792-4441; www.redwhitebluezz.com; 37 S El Molino Ave, Pasadena; 10:30am-9pm Sun, from 11am Mon-Wed, 11am-11pm Thu, to midnight Fri & Sat) Just off the Pasadena playhouse courtyard, the bandstand is in the dining room, which is blessed with wood floors, exposed fixtures, silk-screened photos of musical legends on the wall, and live jazz nightly.

Pasadena Playhouse THEATER
(Map p194; www.pasadenaplayhouse.org; 39 S Molino Ave, Pasadena) Since 1917 actors good and

bad, the well-known and the lesser-known, have infused this attractive, adobe-style complex with drama (and some musical comedy too). Check the website for current shows.

Shopping

★Gold Bug ARTWORK

(Map p194; ☎626-744-9963; www.goldbugpasadena.com; 22 E Union St, Pasadena; ⊙10am-5pm Mon, 10am-6pm Tue-Sat, noon-5pm Sun) An amazing boutique with a steampunk vibe, Gold Bug shows work and collections created (or curated) by 100 area artists. We saw a robotic, metallic Cheshire Cat; exquisite vintage jewelry and lamps; raw crystals and selenite; and a terrific art book collection.

Rose Bowl Flea Market FLEA MARKET

(www.rgcshows.com; 1001 Rose Bowl Dr, Pasadena; admission from $8; ⊙9am-4:30pm 2nd Sun each month, last entry 3pm) California's Marketplace of Unusual Items descends upon the Rose Bowl football field bringing forth the rummaging hordes. There are over 2500 vendors and 15,000 buyers here every month, and it's always a great time.

Rocket Fizz CANDY

(Map p194; www.rocketfizz.com; 111 W Green St, Pasadena; ⊙11am-9pm Mon-Thu, to 11pm Fri & Sat, to 8pm Sun) If you're a fan of sugary chews and fizzy drinks, not to mention rock-and-roll posters and catchy tunes from yesteryear, step into this brick house of fun and questionable dental choices. It will make you smile.

Pasadena City College Flea Market VINTAGE, GIFTS

(www.pasadena.edu; 57 E Colorado Blvd, Pasadena; ⊙7am-3pm first Sun of each month) A Pasadena rummage blooms on the 1st Sunday of every month, on this decidedly stylish and spare art-deco campus. There are about 450 vendors here, with some particularly good vinyl music to be discovered. Proceeds help fund scholarships and student activities.

Neo 39 SHOES

(Map p194; www.neo39.com; 39 E Colorado Blvd, Pasadena; ⊙10am-9pm Sun-Thu, to 10pm Fri, to 11pm Sat) In the thick of the Old Town Pasadena shopping district is this smart sneaker depot sporting rare, imported and generally colorful and stylish high tops, low tops and skate shoes.

EAGLE ROCK, HIGHLAND PARK, MT WASHINGTON & LINCOLN HEIGHTS

Once you cross the picturesque Colorado St Bridge, the conservative, old California vibration that permeates Pasadena fades into a groovy nook of working-class LA. There are some renovated and downright stylish Spanish-style homes and California bungalows tucked into a bowl that rests between the last gasp of the Santa Monicas and the stark rise of the San Gabriel foothills, but for the most part Eagle Rock is about left-leaning Occidental college, and the regular Dodger-loving, Laker-rooting masses. Tough yet laid-back, cool in a completely unpretentious way, Eagle Rock is low on sights but worth checking out if you're doing the Pasadena museum disco.

Jonathan Gold, LA's erstwhile, Pultizer Prize–winning restaurant critic swears by the square-cut pizza at **Casa Bianca** (☎323-256-9617; www.casabiancapizza.com; 1650 Colorado Blvd, Eagle Rock; pizzas $6-20; ⊙4pm-midnight Tue-Thu, to 1am Fri & Sat; 👪), and it's frequently packed. Gold suggests ordering yours topped with fried eggplant and sweet-and-spicy homemade sausage. **Little Beast** (☎323-341-5899; www.littlebeastrestaurant.com; 1496 Colorado Blvd, Eagle Rock; small plates $6-13, mains $15-25; ⊙5pm-close Tue-Sun), however, eats better. Set in a fun converted cottage glowing with red light, they serve small and large plates crafted from local organic ingredients.

Mt Washington and Highland Park wrap around the Arroyo Seco, a rocky riverbed running from the San Gabriel Mountains to Downtown LA. It was flooded with artists and architects in the early 20th century, but lost its idyllic setting with the arrival of the I-110 (Pasadena Fwy) in 1940. Of late, though, there's been an artistic revival and the area is slowly becoming the go-to place for creative types thriving on relatively low rents and the largely Latino, community feel. About two-dozen galleries now belong to the **Northeast Los Angeles Arts Organization** (NELAart; www.nelaart.com). They keep their doors open late during Gallery Night every second Saturday of the month. Galleries are too scattered to be explored on foot, so plan on driving or hop on a bicycle for the free **Spoke(n) Art Tour** (http://bikeoven.com/spokenart) FREE. Highland Park's main drag

WORTH A TRIP

MISSION SAN FERNANDO REY DE ESPAÑA

It's a long drive out to the northern San Fernando Valley, but history and architecture buffs will likely enjoy this haunting old **Spanish mission** (www.missiontour.org; 15151 San Fernando Mission Rd, Mission Hills; adult/7-15yr & senior $4/3; ⏲9am-4:30pm; P), the 17th of 21 missions built in California. And so will fans of Bob Hope who, in 2003, was buried in a special garden adjacent to the main building. Singer Richie 'La Bamba' Valens, who died in the 1959 plane crash that also killed Buddy Holly, rests in the cemetery behind the mission.

is the wonderful York Ave. It's dotted with many of the aforementioned galleries, some tasty bites, fun bars and a sweet cafe. When it comes to ice cream, **Scoops** (5105 York St, Highland Park; scoops $3, pints $7; ⏲2-9pm Mon-Sat) is one of our favorites thanks to flavors such as Gouda melon or pistachio, rose and honey, almond and nutmeg, and salty chocolate. **Cafe de Leche** (www.cafedeleche.net; 5000 York Blvd, Highland Park; ⏲7am-6pm Sun-Thu, to 7pm Fri & Sat) may be the perfect coffee house. It's hip and sunshiny with rotating art on the walls, an adorable children's coloring corner and ergonomic seating. And the coffee rocks.

Mt Washington's brightest beacon is the original **Self Realization Fellowship** (www.yogananda-srf.org; 3880 San Rafael Ave; ⏲9am-5pm; P 🚻). When Parmanhansa Yogananda first came to LA from India in the 1920s to spread his yoga love (p186), he set up shop at this beautiful estate, which remains a working monastery, with plenty of sitting areas in the garden, offering stunning views of the downtown skyline. The house doors are also open. Peek into the library where you'll find a number of books by 'yogiji' (as he's affectionately called), as well as his letter opener, his robes and locks of his hair. You'll also find tomes from great philosophers and poets from Plato and Dostoevsky to Gandhi (one of his contemporaries). It is said that if you sit in an area where Yogananda sat for a prolonged period, you may feel his calming vibration. Word is that every night before bed he sipped tea on the sofa by the fireplace.

Lincoln Heights is another historically working-class neighborhood wedged on either side of the LA River north of Chinatown, with a main drag on Broadway. These days it's best known for the collective of experimental DJs who are bridging the gap between improvisational jazz and psychedelic dubstep at the weekly **Low End Theory** (www.lowendtheoryclub.com; 2419 N Broadway Ave, Lincoln Heights; 18 & over cover $10; ⏲10pm-2am Wed) club at the Airliner. But don't expect jazzanova remixes of late, great horn blowers. Here, jazz is an idea, a mode of thought, a way of mashing industrial and harmonic sounds. The club was founded by resident DJs Daddy Kev and Gaslamp Killer, and gained notoriety for launching the great Flying Lotus into the international limelight. Special guests such as Q-Tip from Tribe Called Quest have been known to roll through and spin.

BOYLE HEIGHTS & EAST LOS ANGELES

The Los Angeles River is a bit like the US-Mexican border without the wall and the Minutemen. Beyond the concrete gulch lies the oldest and largest Mexican community outside of Mexico. It's been the breeding ground for musicians such as Los Lobos, athletes such as boxer Oscar de la Hoya, and actors such as Anthony Quinn.

Life in the barrio is tough but lively. Stroller-pushing moms stop for *pan dulce* (sweet bread), gossip at local *panaderías* (bakeries), and pick up dinner at the *carnicería* (butcher shop), and fresh tortillas straight from the factory. On summer nights, makeshift grills pop up at street corners, *taquerias* (taco shops) get packed with families, and laborers chill with a cold *cerveza* (beer) after another hard day's work. Street art blooms from all corners.

But there's more than Mexican-American roots beneath the concrete. Developer Andrew Boyle purchased the river bluffs in 1858. Within 40 years the suburb had water and sewage services and became known as the Ellis Island of Los Angeles, when newly arrived immigrants from Europe flocked here after reading of clear blue skies and river views while suffering in Chicago and New York tenements. By 1939 Boyle Heights was predominantly Jewish, but along with the original Canter's Deli, there were also several Japanese stores and Buddhist temples in the mix.

Even a quick drive or stroll east of downtown, augmented by a bite in one of several excellent restaurants, will deepen your understanding of Los Angeles. Access has been made much easier since the completion of the Metro Rail Gold Line extension, and there is an ongoing blossoming of cool out here without the reek of gentrification.

Step off at **Mariachi Plaza** (Map p62; cnr Boyle Ave & 1st St), where traditional Mexican musicians in fanciful suits and wide-brimmed hats troll for work in the old-school *zócalo* (public square) on one side, while out the front of the futuristic Metro station on the other side, B-boys and skate punks gather and grind. Within a block or two of the plaza you'll find **Espacio 1839** (www.facebook.com/Espacio1839; 1839 E 1st St; ⏲noon-8pm Tue-Thu, to 9pm Fri & Sat, to 6pm Sun), a concrete-floor boutique and cooperative of four artists/entrepreneurs. It's part bookstore (curated by the resident bookworm); part record store (curated by the world-music buyer for Amoeba in Hollywood); the headquarters for **Radio Sombra**, an online radio feed; and the T-shirts and art are mostly designed by the graphic artist who did the mural. They have terrific children's books, and host live events and art openings. Just down the block **LA First St Taqueria** (1843 1/2 1st St; tacos $1.75, burgers $5.50; ⏲11am-11pm Sun-Thu, to midnight Fri & Sat) is an aromatic greasebomb of goodness. Foodies swear by **Guisados** (www.guisados.co; 2100 E Cesar Chavez Ave; tacos $2-5; ⏲10:30am-8pm Mon-Sat, 10:30am-5pm Sun), another *taqueria* a short jaunt away on Cesar Chavez; they get a little more creative with their flavors, make their tortillas in house and serve gourmet coffee too. **Eastside Luv** (www.eastsideluv.com; 1835 E 1st St; ⏲8pm-2am Wed-Sat) is a wine bar across from the plaza with frequent live bands and DJs.

East of here, a nondescript building houses the **Hollenbeck Youth Center** (www.hollenbeckpbc.org; 2015 E 1st St), where Oscar 'Golden Boy' de la Hoya punched himself into shape for his 1992 Olympic gold medal. Further on, and set in an otherwise bland urban corridor, is a gem of a kitchen, **Mi India Bonita** (4731 Olympic Blvd; burritos $5.50, mains $9.50-10.50; ⏲8am-5pm). Order their Serafin Special: an *arracherra* steak, sliced thin and served in a chile sauce with whole pinto beans, rice and a wedge of avocado. If you're still hungry, get a *barbacoa* taco. If it's seafood you want, find the greatest shrimp taco of your life at **Mariscos 4 Vientos** (3000 E Olympic Blvd; dishes $3-9; ⏲9am-6:30pm Mon-Thu, to 7pm Fri & Sun, to 8:30pm Sat). Order from the truck (if you're in a hurry) or grab a table inside their packed dining room. Either way, expect corn tortillas folded and stuffed with shrimp, then fried and smothered in *pico de gallo*. They also do a searing *aguachile* (shrimp cured in lime juice and chile). It's no frills, all soul here.

We never need an excuse to come to East Los, as it's affectionately known, aside from shrimp tacos, that is. But if you do, the Southland's best **Día de Los Muertos** (Day of the Dead) celebration is held here. It lasts for three days, peaking on the day itself, November 1.

WESTLAKE & KOREATOWN

Until relatively recently, historic Westlake, just west of Downtown, was the go-to zone for scoring rock cocaine or a fake driver's license. Slowly, though, the area is cleaning up its act and even toying with gentrification. Crime is down and families have returned to **MacArthur Park** (cnr Wilshire Blvd & Alvarado St) for picnics and paddling around a spring-fed lake, at least in the daylight hours. So have the skaters (they grind in benign packs) and the world beats. The restored Levitt Pavilion band shell is the place for the park's **summer concert series** (www.levittla.org). And yes, this is the park that 'melts in the dark' in the eponymous Jimmy Webb song made famous by Donna Summer. The park is at its best north of Wilshire. It's gets gritty south of the lake. Though still largely a working-class, Latino neighborhood, artists, hipsters and young professionals are trickling into the neighborhood with bars, eateries and cultural spaces following in their tracks. Get off at the Wilshire/MacArthur Park stop of the Red Line subway and see for yourself.

Westlake spills seamlessly into Koreatown, a vast area that can feel more like Seoul than LA. Korean immigrants began settling here in the 1960s and formed a tight-knit community. Many signs are in Korean and some shopkeepers and servers speak only a few words of English. All this makes for an interesting experience, especially when it comes to food and day spas. Koreatown's nightlife is thriving too. The new Line Hotel has a buzzy lobby bar, with a speakeasy from LA's best nocturnal designers – the Houston Brothers (La Descarga, No Vacancy etc) – to come.

Wilshire Blvd is the most attractive thoroughfare, lined with historic churches and towers harkening back to a time when this area was a wealthy business and residential district known as Wilshire Center.

Sights & Activities

Bullocks Wilshire ARCHITECTURE
(www.swlaw.edu/bullockswilshire; 3050 Wilshire Blvd) This 1929 art-deco gem was the country's first department store designed for shoppers arriving by car. Unfortunately, it closed in 1992 and is now a law school rarely open to the public.

Century Sports Club & Day Spa SPA
(www.centurydayspa.com; 4120 W Olympic Blvd; 24hr) If you want to do some serious spa time you'll need to find this place, where for just $20 you can get a deep steam in wet and dry, clay, wood and marble saunas, enjoy a belching vichy, dip into some seriously hot tubs and get your sinuses clear with a cold plunge.

It offers a range of massage treatments (including Korean-style shiatsu) and has golf and fitness facilities, as well.

Beverly Hot Springs SPA
(www.beverlyhotsprings.com; 308 N Oxford Ave; per person Mon-Thu $30, Fri-Sun $40; 9am-9pm) If you want less marble and more grotto, you'll do your soaking at this place where the water is geothermically heated 2200ft below the city streets.

Sleeping

★**Line Hotel** HOTEL $$
(213-381-7411; www.thelinehotel.com; 3515 Wilshire Blvd; r from $199) Line Hotel is the latest venture from Roy Choi, the man who sparked the LA food truck revolution and became a celebrity chef. Now he's a hotelier, and this nest does not disappoint: walls are polished concrete, floor-to-ceiling windows overlook the city. Desks sport built-in USB and HDMI connections so you can blip your media to the wall-mounted flat-screen TV.

They have their own line of bikes that are complimentary for guest use, and include helmet, locks and lights. The art and photography is first-rate, and so are the lobby bar and Choi's newest restaurant, **Pot**.

Eating

Ma Dang Gook Soo NOODLES $
(213-487-6008; 869 S Western Ave; dishes $6-9; 9am-10pm) A groovy little noodle spot known for its house-made, knife-cut noodles and wonderful house-made chili sauce. Portions are huge.

Oh Ma Ni KOREAN $
(807 Ardmore; dishes $7-13; 8am-9pm Mon-Sat) A tucked away little find, cheery Yun Li is the house mother and she'll recommend the chicken noodle soup – her specialty. She makes the noodles in house, and also does a mean blood sausage. It's soft and mild, stuffed with blood and rice and not an acquired taste. All comes with kimchi and assorted pickled vegetables.

Buil Sam Gye Tang KOREAN $$
(4204 W 3rd St; mains $13-21; 11am-9:30pm Mon-Fri, to 9pm Sat, closed sun; P) Who doesn't love a chicken in a pot? Of course, you can opt for deer antler or abalone instead, but we're partial to the chicken in our bubbling pot of ginseng broth teeming with herbs, and swirling with rice. It may need salt, but it's healing.

Chosun Galbee KOREAN BARBECUE $$
(323-734-3330; www.chosungalbee.com; 3330 W Olympic Blvd; meals $10-30; 11am-11pm) An ideal K Town BBQ habitat, one with both class and charm, thanks to superb heated patio seating. Grills are built into the tables of course, and aside from the paper-thin rib eye, which you'll cook yourself, they do a nice *bibimbap,* and black cod stew. Says one local in the know, 'the fish is like butter.'

BCD Tofu House KOREAN $$
(www.bcdtofu.com; 3575 Wilshire Blvd; dishes $9-18; 24hr; P) Sure, it's called the Tofu House, but it still serves 'small intestine of cattle.' More to the point, these worn wooden floors are patrolled by no-nonsense Korean maidens and madams who herd diners with absolute authority and serve steaming tofu soup, curry, spicy raw crab and sizzling skillets of thinly sliced beef all night long.

Jun Won KOREAN $$
(323-731-0509; 3100 Olympic Blvd; dishes $11-26; 11am-2:30pm & 5:30-9pm Mon-Sat) They steam pollock and cod, but we love the pan-fried mackerel: crispy skin, tender morsels

of fish flesh and an array of sides that will occupy nearly your entire table, including greens drizzled in rice vinegar, fried tofu topped with chili, and spicy pickled cabbage. It's cozy, so you may need to wait a while, but it's worth it.

Drinking

R Bar LOUNGE

(☎213-387-7227; www.myspace/4rbar.com; 3331 8th St; ⏲7pm-2am) The jukebox is stocked with classics and neo-classics, and you have to know the password to get past the gate keeper. Seriously. Call or log-on to their Facebook page for the password, as it's always changing. They have karaoke and movie nights, and many more themes depending upon the evening.

Beer Belly PUB

(www.beerbellyla.com; 532 S Western Ave; ⏲5-11pm Mon & Tue, to midnight Wed & Thu, to 1am Fri, noon-1am Sat, to 11pm Sun; 📶) Tucked off the western strip is this funky wood-paneled barrel of craft beer and creative pub grub, which is written in colorful script on the chalkboard behind the bar. Expect pilsner from Berkeley, an IPA from El Segundo, and far darker, funkier concoctions where the alcohol content rises to 10%.

Eats can be wild too. They deep-fry duck livers, Oreos and Twinkies!

Prince BAR

(3198 W 7th St; ⏲4pm-midnight) In the movie *Chinatown,* Faye Dunaway meets with Jack Nicholson at this campy joint that defies any categorization. It's a former hotel lounge with colonial-era, British-pub looks (check out the wacky soldier lamps), and *soju* and Hite beer on the menu. The crowd is a potpourri of ethnicities united by a penchant for stiff drinks at civilized prices.

Taylor's BAR, STEAKHOUSE

(www.taylorssteakhouse.com; 3361 8th St; ⏲11:30am-3pm Mon-Fri, 4-9:30pm Mon-Thu & Sun, to 10pm Fri & Sat) Some consider it an LA institution for the decent steaks at affordable prices. We like the dark-leather booths, the dim lights, and the oak bar, which holds up a martini glass just fine.

Boba Time CAFE

(www.itsbobatime.com; 701 S Vermont Ave; drinks $3-5; ⏲8am-midnight Mon-Sat, from 8:30am Sun) A corner coffee shop in a mini-mall with an assortment of slushies, smoothies and teas, the best of which is the wonderful taro slushie with boba balls. It tastes velvety and smooth and as purple as it looks. It's not too overpowering with the sweet and those balls are chewy and delightful. There's a reason locals mob this joint.

☆ Entertainment

Wiltern Theatre THEATER

(www.wiltern.com; 3790 Wilshire Blvd) This 1931 movie theater (*West Side Story* premiered here) turned epic concert venue struts its stuff in a glorious turquoise mantle at the intersection of Wilshire and Western Blvds (get it?). Neil Young, Bob Dylan, the National and Portugal the Man are among the artists who've played here recently.

If you find a show you like, do not miss it. This stage has a way about bringing out the best in a performer.

SOUTH CENTRAL & EXPOSITION PARK

South Central LA burst into global consciousness with the rat-a-tat-tat rhythm and rhyme of some of hip-hop's greatest pioneers. With infectious beats and sharp tongues, folks like Ice T, Ice Cube, Eazy E, Dr Dre and, later, Tupac Shakur brought gangsta life to the suburbs and beyond. The notoriety was a double-edged blade: in one sense, awareness is the first step to healing; on the other hand, South Central was suddenly defined by its gangs, drugs, poverty, crime and drive-by shootings, which, though not entirely undeserved, never told the whole story.

After WWII over five million African Americans left what was, at the time, a violently racist South and moved to northern cities such as Chicago, Philadelphia and NYC to work in manufacturing jobs, in what has been called the Second Great Migration (nearly two million moved in the first migration, which took place between 1910 and 1930). Some of those families moved west, from Mississippi, Louisiana and Texas to Los Angeles. They found manufacturing jobs, bought property and built fully functioning, working-class neighborhoods south of downtown. They also brought a thriving Central Ave jazz scene with them and, though life wasn't perfect, it was a step up.

Fast-forward 30 years and suddenly the high-wage manufacturing jobs dried up, drug addiction soared, families fell apart, guns became accessible, gang violence bloomed and South Central began to earn its reputation. But recent investments of time, money and vision from the likes of Magic Johnson and Ted Watkins, along with an expanded rail service and fantastic Exposition Park museum complex, have helped turn the tide somewhat. Sure, much of South Central still feels bleak and foreboding, but there's also a lot of spirit here, especially in the thriving cultural hub of Leimert Park, and around the Watts Towers, which are not to be missed. And lest we forget, this is the neighborhood of the University of Southern California, where the Trojans play football, George Lucas studied film, and Will Ferrell became, well, Will Ferrell.

Sights

Leimert Park CULTURAL DISTRICT

(Degnan Blvd & 43rd St) The soft lilt of a saxophone purrs from a storefront. Excited chatter streams from a coffee house. The savory aroma of barbecue wafts into the steamy noontime air. Welcome to Leimert *(luh-mert)* Park, the cultural hub of LA's African-American community.

About 2.5 miles west of Exposition Park, the mostly residential neighborhood was designed by the Olmsted brothers of New York Central Park fame, and was nicknamed 'the black Greenwich Village' by filmmaker and local resident John Singleton *(Boyz n the Hood)*. Here, bongo freaks gather in the park for Sunday afternoon drum circles. Nearby, the World Stage is a destination for jazz aficionados. Check out the **Sankofa Passage** (Leimert Park's walk of fame) paying homage to local figures such as LA jazz legends Horace Tapscott, Dexter Gordon and Buddy Collette.

Natural History Museum of Los Angeles MUSEUM

(Map p62; ☎213-763-3466; www.nhm.org; 900 Exposition Blvd; adult/student & senior/child $12/9/5; ⏲9:30am-5pm; 👪) Dinos to diamonds, bears to beetles, hissing roaches to African elephants – this museum will take you around the world and back, across millions of years in time. It's all housed in a beautiful 1913 Renaissance-style building that stood in for Columbia University in the first Toby McGuire *Spider-Man* movie – yup, this was where Peter Parker was bitten by the radioactive arachnid.

The special exhibits usually draw the biggest crowds, but don't miss out on a spin around the permanent halls to see such trophy displays as the **Dinosaur Hall**, featuring the world-first T. rex Growth series. Historical exhibits include prized Navajo textiles, baskets and jewelry in the **Hall of Native American Cultures**. If diamonds are your best friend, head to the **Gem & Mineral Hall** with its walk-through gem tunnel and a Fort Knox–worthy gold collection.

Kids will have plenty of 'ooh' and 'aah' moments in the spruced-up **Discovery Center**, where they can make friends with Cecil the iguana and Peace, a 9ft boa; dig for dinosaur fossils; handle bones, antlers and minerals; and get close to tarantulas, scorpions and other creepy-crawlies.

For grown-ups, the museum turns up the volume during its **First Fridays** event series, which combines brainy lectures, live music and KCRW DJs in the African Mammal Hall, two bars and late-night access to the exhibits, which are all bathed in nocturnal light. Check the website for upcoming dates.

California Science Center MUSEUM

(Map p62; ☎film schedule 213-744-2109, info 323-724-3623; www.californiasciencecenter.org; 700 Exposition Park Dr; IMAX movie adult/child $8.25/5; ⏲10am-5pm; 👪) FREE A simulated earthquake, baby chicks hatching and a giant techno-doll named Tess bring out the kid in all of us at this multimedia museum with plenty of buttons to push, lights to switch on and knobs to pull.

The enormous space is divided into themed areas. Upstairs on the left, **World of Life** focuses mostly on the human body. You can 'hop on' a red blood cell for a computer fly-through of the circulatory system, ask Gertie how long your colon really is, watch open-heart surgery, and learn about homeostasis from Tess, billed as '50ft of brains, beauty and biology.' Tots may have trouble understanding the science, but they will remember Tess.

Creative World is all about the ingenious ways humans have devised to communicate with each other, transport things and build structures. Meet a family of crash-test dummies, fly a virtual hovercraft and get all shook up during a fake earthquake. **Ecosystems** takes visitors through a variety of habitats: desert, river, island, urban and forest.

Aircraft and space travel take center stage in the **Sketch Foundation Gallery**, in an adjacent Frank Gehry building (yes, he's everywhere). Spirits will soar at the sight of a pioneering 1902 Wright glider; the original

Gemini X1 capsule flown by US astronauts in 1996; and a replica Soviet Sputnik, the first human-made object to orbit the earth in 1957. The Science Center is also home to **Space Shuttle Endeavor** – you may remember its much ballyhooed fly over the city, followed by it being towed through the city streets in the dead of night. It's new permanent home will be in a new gallery called the **Samuel Oschin Air and Space Center**, but while that's under construction you can see the beast in the Samuel Oschin Pavillion.

Exposition Park LANDMARK

(www.expositionpark.org; 700 Exposition Park Dr) A quick jaunt south of Downtown LA by DASH bus, the family-friendly Exposition Park began as an agricultural fairground in 1872, then devolved into a magnet for the down-and-out, and finally emerged as a patch of public greenery in 1913. It contains three quality museums, a robust and rambling **Rose Garden** (Map p62; www.laparks.org; 701 State Dr; ⏲9am-sunset Mar 15–Dec 31) FREE, and the 1923 **Los Angeles Memorial Coliseum** (Map p62; www.lacoliseum.com; 3939 S Figueroa St).

The latter hosted the 1932 and 1984 Summer Olympic Games, the 1959 baseball World Series and two Super Bowls, and is the home stadium for USC Trojans (American) football team. The adjacent indoor Los Angeles Memorial Sports Arena dates from 1959 and is still used for the rare rock concert.

University of Southern California UNIVERSITY

(USC; Map p62; ☎213-740-6605; www.usc.edu; Exposition Blvd & Figueroa St) FREE George Lucas, John Wayne and Neil Armstrong are among the famous alumni of this well-respected private university, founded in 1880, just north of Exposition Park. Free 50-minute, student-led tours touch on campus history, architecture and student life and leave on the hour from the Admissions Center midweek. Reservations are strongly recommended.

Harris Hall is the home of **USC Fisher Gallery** (Map p62; www.fisher.usc.edu; 823 Exposition Blvd; ⏲noon-5pm Mon-Fri) FREE, which presents changing selections from its ever-expanding collection of American landscapes, British portraits, French Barbizon School paintings and modern Mexican masters such as Salomón Huerta and Gronk (Glugio Nicandro). They offer an annual student exhibition timed to commencement ceremonies each May.

Watts Labor Community Action Committee COMMUNITY CENTER

(WLCAC; ☎323-563-5639; www.wlcac.org; 10950 S Central Ave; tours adult/child $5/free; ⏲8:30am-5pm) Watts was the epicenter of two sets of LA riots – 1965 and 1992 – when this vibrant community and cultural center was burned to the ground. The neighborhood is still teeming with large numbers of kids growing up poor and angry, but there are pockets of improvements thanks in part to such groups as this.

Founded by Ted Watkins and run by his son, Timothy, their headquarters doubles as a cultural theme park. A huge bronze sculpture of a black woman called *Mother of Humanity* dominates the campus, and the **Cecil Ferguson Gallery** rotates exhibits of LA's best African-American artists such as Willie Middlebrook and Michael Massenburg. The most powerful exhibit, though, is the **Civil Rights Museum**, only available by guided tours that must be booked at least a day in advance. Guides take you through the hull of the *Amistad* (the actual facade used in the Spielberg film), a body-filled slave ship, and along the Mississippi Delta Rd to displays about Martin Luther King, the Black Panther Party and the 1960s Civil Rights Movement. There's also a wonderful new skate park (open 8am to dusk) here where South Central's growing crew of skaters freelance and grind with incredible skill.

★**Watts Towers** LANDMARK

(www.wattstowers.us; 1761-1765 E 107th St; adult/under 12yr/teen & senior $7/free/$3; ⏲11am-3pm Fri, 10:30am-3pm Sat, 12:30-3pm Sun; P) The fabulous Watts Towers rank among the world's greatest monuments of folk art. In 1921 Italian immigrant Simon Rodia set out 'to make something big' and then spent 33 years cobbling together this whimsical free-form sculpture from a motley assortment of found objects – from green 7-Up bottles to sea shells, and rocks to pottery.

You can admire it from beyond the fencing any time, but to get inside you must pay and take the tour. The adjacent **Watts Towers Art Center** sponsors workshops, performances and classes for the community, hosts art exhibits and organizes the acclaimed **Watts Towers Day of the Drum and Jazz Festival** in September.

Central Avenue HISTORIC DISTRICT

From the 1920s to the 1950s, Central Ave was the lifeblood of LA's African-American community, not by choice but because segregation laws kept black people out of other neighborhoods. It was also a hotbed of jazz and R&B, a legacy commemorated every July with the **Central Avenue Jazz Festival** (www.centralavejazz.org; late Jul) held outside the 1928 **Dunbar Hotel** (4225 S Central Ave).

Duke Ellington once maintained a suite at what was LA's only 1st-class hotel for African Americans. It's now a low-income seniors center, but has been renovated and the facade faithfully restored. It's worth a peek.

African American Firefighter Museum MUSEUM
(Map p62; www.aaffmuseum.org; 1401 S Central Ave; 10am-2pm Tue & Thu, 1-4pm Sun) FREE This museum has the usual assortment of vintage engines and uniforms, as well as an 1890 hose wagon. It's set in a restored 1913 fire station that, until 1955, was one of only two in town that employed black firefighters.

California African American Museum MUSEUM
(Map p62; 213-744-7432; www.caamuseum.org; 600 State Dr; 10am-5pm Tue-Sat, from 11am Sun) FREE This museum does an excellent job of showcasing African-American artists, such as the great John T Scott, whose woodblock prints are full of expression and shadow. There's an old bill of sale from the slavery days, photos of Tom Bradley and Ella Fitzgerald, and you'll learn that blacks made up over half the population of the original pueblo.

Eating & Drinking

Phillips Barbecue BARBECUE $
(4307 Leimert Blvd; sandwiches $4-10, platters $11.50-18; 11am-10pm Tue-Thu, to 11pm Fri & Sat, to 6pm Sun; P) The pork and beef ribs are fall-off-the-bone tender and the sauce is smoky at this soulful hole-in-the-wall that perfumes the whole block. The sauce comes with various degrees of heat, so go easy. The 7-Up cake makes for an unusual finish. Cash only.

Ackee Bamboo JAMAICAN $$
(323-295-7275; www.ackeebamboojacuisine.com; 4305 Degnan Blvd; meals $9-19; 8am-9pm Mon-Sat) They do all the authentic Jamaican favorites: saltfish and ackee at breakfast; curry goat, jerk chicken and oxtails at lunch. Their brown stew chicken is popular, as is their fish soup, which they serve on Friday and Saturday only.

Entertainment

LA is a movie town, of course, so a fun time to visit South Central is during the annual **Pan African Film Festival** (www.paff.org; Feb). Filmmakers from across the African diaspora congregate for two weeks each February to show their films at the **Rave Theaters** (www.baldwinhillscrenshawplaza.com; 3650 W Martin Luther King Jr Blvd; adult/child $14/7) in the Baldwin Hills Crenshaw Plaza. A wonderful arts and handicrafts bazaar takes over both floors of the shopping center, as well.

World Stage JAZZ
(www.theworldstage.org; 4344 Degnan Blvd) Founded by the late hard-bop drummer Billy Higgins, this place doesn't serve food or drink, just good music from some of the best emerging talents in jazz. The Thursday jam session has people grooving until 2am. And on Sundays, the open Sisters of Jazz (women-only performers) jam hums till midnight. There are drum, writing and vocal workshops too.

Downtown Comedy Club COMEDY
(213-841-3940; www.downtowncomedyclub.com; 4305 Degnan Blvd; cover $20; 8pm Sat) *Saturday Night Live* alumnus Garrett Morris, one of the original cast members, takes the stage weekly at the new Barbara Morrison Performing Arts Center in Leimert Park, along with up-and-coming stars and a rocking blues band led by Morrison herself.

Shopping

The vibrant Leimert Park district is full of antique and art galleries, and its momentum is building. Nearby, the **Baldwin Hills Crenshaw Plaza** (www.baldwinhillscrenshawplaza.com; 3650 W Martin Luther King Jr Blvd; 10am-9pm) offers a fun South Central shopping scene every day and night. They have movie theaters too.

★ **Sika** FOLK ART
(4330 Degnan Blvd; noon-6pm) It would be hard to find a better collection of antiques, masks, clothes and jewelry outside of West Africa than those found in this owner-operated treasure chest. It co-sponsors a three-day **Labor Day Music, Food & Art Festival** in the lot next door.

Eso Won Books BOOKS (www.esowonbookstore.com; 4331 Degnan Blvd; ⏲10am-7pm Mon-Sat, noon-5pm Sun) Nearly 30 years in business and still doing it in an Amazon world, this store focuses on African-American literature, fiction and nonfiction. Luminaries such as Maya Angelou, BB King and Kareem Abdul-Jabbar have held book signings here, and Bill Clinton and President Obama have both stopped by.

Information

EMERGENCY

Police, Fire, Ambulance (911) For police, fire or ambulance service.

Police (877-275-5273; www.lapdonline.org) For nonemergencies within the city of LA.

Rape & Battering Hotline (310-392-8381, 213-626-3393; ⏲24hr)

INTERNET ACCESS

Internet cafes in LA seem to have the lifespan of a fruit fly, but dozens of cafes and restaurants around town offer free wi-fi.

LIBRARIES

There are public libraries everywhere. All of them offer free internet and wi-fi access, carry international periodicals, have special reading rooms for kids, and host readings and cultural events.

Beverly Hills Library (www.bhpl.org; 444 N Rexford Dr, Beverly Hills; ⏲9:30am-9:30pm Mon-Thu, 10am-6pm Fri & Sat, noon-5pm Sun; wi-fi)

Hollywood Library (323-856-8260; www.lapl.org; 1623 Ivar Ave, Hollywood; ⏲10am-8pm Mon & Wed, from 12:30pm Tue & Thu, 10am-5:30pm Fri & Sat, 1-5pm Sun; wi-fi)

Richard Riordan Central Library (www.lapl.org; 630 W 5th St, Downtown; ⏲10am-8pm Mon-Thu, to 5:30pm Fri & Sat, 1-5pm Sun; wi-fi)

Santa Monica Public Library (310-458-8600; www.smpl.org; 601 Santa Monica Blvd, Santa Monica; ⏲10am-9pm Mon-Thu, to 5:30pm Fri & Sat, 1-5pm Sun; wi-fi)

MEDIA

KCRW 89.9 FM (www.kcrw.com) LA's cultural pulse, the best radio station in the city beams National Public Radio (NPR); eclectic and indie music, intelligent talk, and hosts shows and events throughout Southern California.

KPFK 90.7 FM (www.kpfk.org) Part of the Pacifica radio network; news and progressive talk.

La Opinión (www.laopinion.com) Spanish-language daily newspaper.

LA Weekly (www.laweekly.com) Free alternative news, live music and entertainment listings.

Los Angeles Downtown News (www.downtownnews.com) The finger on the cultural, political and economic pulse of the booming Downtown district.

Los Angeles Magazine (www.losangelesmagazine.com) Glossy lifestyle monthly magazine with a useful restaurant guide and some tremendous feature stories.

Los Angeles Sentinel (www.losangelessentinel.com) African-American weekly.

Los Angeles Times (www.latimes.com) Major daily newspaper.

MEDICAL SERVICES

Cedars-Sinai Medical Center (310-423-3277; http://cedars-sinai.edu; 8700 Beverly Blvd, West Hollywood) 24-hour emergency room.

Keck Medicine of USC (323-226-2622; www.doctorsofusc.com; 1200 N State St, Downtown; ⏲24hr emergency room)

Rite Aid Pharmacies (800-748-3243; www.riteaid.com)

Ronald Reagan UCLA Medical Center (310-825-9111; www.uclahealth.org; 757 Westwood Plaza, Westwood; ⏲24hr emergency room)

Venice Family Clinic (310-392-8636; www.venicefamilyclinic.org; 604 Rose Ave, Venice) Good for general health concerns, with payment on a sliding scale according to your means.

Women's Clinic (310-203-8899; www.womens-clinic.org; Suite 500, Century City, 9911 W Pico Blvd) Fees are calculated on a sliding scale according to your capacity to pay.

MONEY

Travelex Santa Monica (310-260-9219; www.travelex.com; 201 Santa Monica Blvd, Suite 101, Santa Monica; ⏲9am-5pm Mon-Thu, to 6pm Fri); West Hollywood (310-659-6093; www.travelex.com; US Bank, 8901 Santa Monica Blvd, West Hollywood; ⏲9:30am-5pm Mon-Thu, 9am-6pm Fri, 9am-1pm Sat)

POST

Call 800-275-8777 for the nearest post office branch.

TOURIST INFORMATION

Beverly Hills Tourist Information (Map p132; www.lovebeverlyhills.com; 9400 S Santa Monica Blvd, Beverly Hills; ⏲9am-5pm Mon-Fri, from 10am Sat & Sun)

Downtown LA Visitor Center (Map p70; www.discoverlosangeles.com; 800 N Alameda St, Downtown; ⏲8:30am-5pm Mon-Fri)

El Pueblo Visitors Center (Map p70; www.lasangelitas.org; 622 N Main St, Sepulveda House, Downtown; ⏲10am-3pm)

Hollywood Visitor Information Center (Map p88; ☎323-467-6412; http://discoverlosangeles.com; Hollywood & Highland complex, 6801 Hollywood Blvd, Hollywood; ⏰10am-10pm Mon-Sat, to 7pm Sun) In the Dolby Theatre walkway.

Long Beach Area Convention & Tourism Bureau (☎562-628-8850; www.visitlongbeach.com; 3rd fl, One World Trade Center, 301 E Ocean Blvd, Long Beach; ⏰11am-7pm Sun-Thu, 11:30am-7:30pm Fri & Sat Jun-Sep, 10am-4pm Fri-Sun Oct-May)

Marina del Rey (www.visitthemarina.com; 4701 Admiralty Way, Marina el Rey; ⏰9am-5pm Mon-Fri, 10am-4pm Sat & Sun)

Pasadena (Map p194; www.visitpasadena.com; 300 E Green St, Pasadena; ⏰8am-5pm Mon-Fri, 10am-4pm Sat)

Santa Monica (☎800-544-5319; www.santamonica.com; 2427 Main St, Santa Monica) Roving information officers patrol the promenade on Segways!

West Hollywood (www.visitwesthollywood.com; Suite M38, Pacific Design Center blue bldg, 8687 Melrose Ave, West Hollywood; ⏰8:30am-5:30pm Mon-Fri)

WEBSITES

www.blacknla.com Online directory for LA's African-American community.

www.discoverlosangeles.com Official Convention and Visitors' Bureau website.

www.experiencela.com Excellent cultural calendar packed with useful public transportation maps and trips.

www.hiddenla.com A quirky blog with a Facebook page where LA locals post their favorite hidden jewels.

www.kcrw.com LA's public-radio beacon of good taste, real news and great music. It hosts several local live shows and events each month.

www.la.com Solid guide to shopping, dining, nightlife and events.

www.la.curbed.com Delicious bites of history, neighborhood esoterica, shopping and dining tips.

www.laist.com Hip lists of the city's bests, from dive bars to trails to french fries to spas.

www.laalmanac.com All the facts and figures at your fingertips.

www.latinola.com Plugs you right into the Latino arts and entertainment scene.

www.laobserved.com An incisive perspective on the inner workings of the city – from arts to fashion to politics to dining.

www.laweekly.com LA's longtime alternative news source, and the most comprehensive arts and entertainment listings available.

www.lonelyplanet.com/usa/los-angeles Lonely Planet's dedicated Los Angeles page offers lots of links and inspiration.

www.thefoodiegirls.com NYC transplants comb the city for culinary gems in a series of short video and written reviews.

Getting There & Away

AIR

The main LA gateway is **Los Angeles International Airport** (LAX; ☎310-646-5252; www.lawa.org/lax; 1 World Way; 📶), a U-shaped, bilevel complex with nine terminals linked by the free **Shuttle A** leaving from the lower (arrival) level. Cabs, and hotel and car-rental shuttles, stop here as well. A free minibus for travelers with disabilities can be ordered by calling ☎310-646-6402. Ticketing and check-in are on the upper (departure) level. The hub for most international airlines is the Tom Bradley International Terminal.

BEDDING DOWN BEFORE TAKEOFF

If you get into LAX late or have to catch an early flight, you'll probably want to stay near the airport. But how to avoid generic, beige-box blandness? We've cased the area and found some stylish shut-eye zones. All have free shuttle buses to the airport.

Custom Hotel (☎310-645-0400; www.customhotel.com; 8639 Lincoln Blvd; r $139-225; P@📶🏊) A mid-century tower by Welton Beckett (who also drafted the crafty Capital Records Tower in Hollywood) that radiates just enough urban posh to appeal to the style patrol.

Sheraton Gateway (☎310-642-1111, 800-325-3535; www.sheratonlosangeles.com; 6101 W Century Blvd; r from $159; P@📶) It has tempting design, and more intimate, boutique-style service than you'd expect from an airport hotel.

Belamar Hotel (☎310-750-0300; www.thebelamar.com; 3501 Sepulveda Blvd; r from $187; P📶🏊) Five minutes from Manhattan Beach and 10 minutes from the airport, the Belamar Hotel is a bit off the beaten track, so it's often overlooked. Still, a decent rate buys stylish digs, and easy access to a nature trail to the beach for jogging off your jet lag.

Domestic flights operated by Alaska, American, Southwest, United and other major US airlines also arrive at Bob Hope/Burbank Airport (p480), which is handy if you're headed for Hollywood, Downtown or Pasadena.

To the south, on the border with Orange County, the small Long Beach Airport (p480) is convenient for Disneyland and is served by Alaska, US Airways and Jet Blue.

BUS

The main bus terminal for **Greyhound** (Map p62; ☎213-629-8401; www.greyhound.com; 1716 E 7th St) is in a grimy part of Downtown, so try not to arrive after dark. Take bus 18 to the 7th St subway station or bus 66 to Pershing Square Station, then hop on the Metro Rail Red Line to Hollywood or Union Station with onward service around town. Some Greyhound buses go directly to the terminal in **Hollywood** (1715 N Cahuenga Blvd) and a few also pass through **Pasadena** (645 E Walnut St) and **Long Beach** (1498 Long Beach Blvd).

CAR & MOTORCYCLE

If you're driving into LA, there are several routes by which you might enter the metropolitan area.

From San Francisco and Northern California, the fastest route to LA is on I-5 through the San Joaquin Valley. Hwy 101 is slower but more picturesque, while the most scenic – and slowest – route is via Hwy 1 (Pacific Coast Hwy, or PCH).

From San Diego and other points south, I-5 is the obvious route. Near Irvine, I-405 branches off I-5 and takes a westerly route to Long Beach and Santa Monica, bypassing Downtown LA entirely and rejoining I-5 near San Fernando.

From Las Vegas or the Grand Canyon, take I-15 south to I-10, then head west into LA. I-10 is the main east–west artery through LA and continues on to Santa Monica.

TRAIN

Amtrak trains roll into Downtown's historic **Union Station** (☎800-872-7245; www.amtrak.com; 800 N Alameda St). Interstate trains stopping in LA are the *Coast Starlight* to Seattle, the *Southwest Chief* to Chicago and the *Sunset Limited* to New Orleans. The *Pacific Surfliner* travels daily between San Diego, Santa Barbara and San Luis Obispo via LA.

ℹ Getting Around

TO/FROM THE AIRPORT

All services mentioned below leave from the lower terminal level of Los Angeles International Airport. Practically all airport-area hotels have arrangements with shuttle companies for free or discounted pick-ups. Door-to-door shuttles, such as those operated by **Prime Time** (☎800-733-8267; www.primetimeshuttle.com) and **Super Shuttle** (☎800-258-3826; www.supershuttle.com) charge $21, $27 and $16 for trips to Santa Monica, Hollywood or Downtown, respectively.

Curbside dispatchers will be on hand to summon a taxi for you. The flat rate to Downtown LA is $47, while going to Santa Monica costs $30 to $35, to West Hollywood around $40, to Hollywood $50 and to Disneyland $90.

Public transportation has become a lot easier since the arrival of **LAX FlyAway** (☎866-435-9529; www.lawa.org; one-way $8). These buses travel nonstop to Downtown's Union Station ($8, 45 minutes), Van Nuys ($8, 45 minutes), Westwood Village near UCLA ($10, 30 minutes), and to the Expo Line Light Rail station at La Brea and Exposition Blvd ($7, 1¼ hours) for connections to South Central, Hollywood and Union Station.

For Santa Monica or Venice, catch the free Shuttle C bus to the **LAX City Bus Center & MetroRail Station** (Map p62; 96th St & Sepulveda Blvd), then change to the Santa Monica Rapid 3 ($1, one hour). The center is the hub for buses serving all of LA. If you're headed for Culver City, catch Culver City bus 6 ($1, 20 minutes). For Manhattan or Hermosa Beach, hop aboard Beach Cities Transit 109 ($1), which also stops at Lot G. For Redondo Beach head to Lot C and hop the Metro Local 232 ($1.50). Trip-planning help is available at www.metro.net.

The **Disneyland Resort Express** (☎714-978-8855; http://graylineanaheim.com; ⏲7:30am-10:30pm) travels hourly or half-hourly from LAX to the main Disneyland resorts (adult/child one way $30/20, round-trip $48/35).

BICYCLE

Most buses have bike racks, and bikes ride for free, although you must securely load and unload them yourself. Bicycles are also allowed on Metro Rail trains except during rush hour (6:30am to 8:30am and 4:30pm to 6:30pm Monday to Friday).

CAR & MOTORCYCLE

Unless time is no factor – or money is extremely tight – you're going to want to spend some time behind the wheel, although this means contending with some of the worst traffic in the country. Avoid rush hour (7am to 9am and 3:30pm to 6pm).

Parking at motels and cheaper hotels is usually free, while fancier ones charge anywhere from $8 to $40 for the privilege. Valet parking at nicer restaurants and hotels is commonplace with rates ranging from $3.50 to $10.

The usual international car-rental agencies have branches at LAX and throughout LA, and there are also a couple of companies renting hybrid vehicles. If you don't have a prebooking, use the courtesy phones in the arrival areas at LAX. Offices and lots are outside the airport, but each company has free shuttles leaving from the lower level.

For Harley rentals, go to Route 66 (p483). Rates start from $99 to $139 per day, and there are discounts for longer rentals.

PUBLIC TRANSPORTATION

Most public transportation is handled by **Metro** (☎ 323-466-3876; www.metro.net), which offers trip-planning help through its website.

The regular base fare is $1.75 per boarding or $7 for a day pass with unlimited rides. Weekly passes are $25 and are valid from Sunday to Saturday. Monthly passes are $100 and valid for 30 days.

Single tickets and day passes are available from bus drivers and vending machines at each train station. Weekly and monthly passes must be bought at one of 650 locations around town, including Ralphs, Vons and Pavilions supermarkets (call or see the website for the one nearest to you).

Metro Buses

Metro operates about 200 bus lines, most of them local routes stopping every few blocks. Metro Rapid buses stop less frequently and have special sensors that keep traffic lights green when a bus approaches. Commuter-oriented express buses connect communities with Downtown LA and other business districts and usually travel via the city's freeways.

Metro Rail

The Metro Rail network consists of six light-rail lines and two subway lines, with five of them converging in Downtown.

Red Line The most useful for visitors! It's a subway linking Downtown's Union Station to North Hollywood (San Fernando Valley) via central Hollywood and Universal City; connects with the Blue Line at the 7th St/Metro Center station in Downtown and the Metro Orange Line express bus at North Hollywood.

Blue Line Downtown to Long Beach; connects with the Red Line at 7th St/Metro Center station and the Green Line at the Imperial/Wilmington stop.

Gold Line East LA to Little Tokyo, Chinatown and Pasadena via Union Station, Mt Washington and Highland Park; connects with the Red Line at Union Station.

Green Line Norwalk to Redondo Beach; connects with the Blue Line at Imperial/Wilmington.

Purple Line Subway between Downtown LA and Koreatown; shares six stations with the Red Line.

Orange Line Links Downtown and Hollywood with the west San Fernando Valley; connects with the Red Line in North Hollywood.

Expo Line Links USC and Exposition Park with Culver City to the west and Downtown LA to the northeast, where it connects with the Red Line at Union Station. Construction is well under way on the Santa Monica extension.

Municipal Buses

Santa Monica–based Big Blue Bus burns clean fuel and serves much of western LA, including Santa Monica, Venice, Westwood and LAX ($1). Its express bus 10 runs from Santa Monica to Downtown ($2, one hour).

The Culver CityBus provides service throughout Culver City and the Westside, including LAX ($1). Long Beach Transit serves Long Beach and surrounding communities.

DASH Buses

These small, clean-fuel shuttle buses, run by the **LA Department of Transportation** (LADOT; www.ladottransit.com), operate along 33 routes serving local communities (50¢ per boarding), but only until 7pm and with limited services on weekends. Many lines connect with other DASH routes; see the website for details. Here are some of the most useful lines:

Beachwood Canyon Route (Monday to Saturday) Useful for close-ups of the Hollywood sign; runs from Hollywood Boulevard and Vine St up Beachwood Dr.

Downtown Routes (daily) Six separate routes hit all the hot spots, including Chinatown, City Hall, Little Tokyo and the Financial District.

FREEWAY LOGIC

Angelenos live and die by their freeways and sooner or later you too will end up part of this metal cavalcade. It helps to know that most freeways have both a number and a name, which corresponds to where they're headed. However, to add to the confusion, freeways passing through Downtown LA usually have two names. The I-10, for instance, is called the Santa Monica Fwy west of the central city and the San Bernardino Fwy east of it. The I-5 heading north is the Golden State Fwy, heading south it's the Santa Ana Fwy. And the I-110 is both the Pasadena Fwy and the Harbor Fwy. Generally, freeways going east–west have even numbers, those running north–south have odd numbers. Except for the 110 that is. Hmmm...

Fairfax Route (Monday to Saturday) Makes a handy loop past the Beverly Center mall, the Pacific Design Center, western Melrose Ave, the Farmers Market/Grove and Museum Row.

Hollywood Route (daily) Covers Hollywood east of Highland Ave and links with the short Los Feliz Route (daily) at Franklin Ave and Vermont Ave.

TAXI

Because of LA's size and its traffic, getting around by cab will cost you. Cabs are best organized over the phone, though some prowl the streets late at night, and they are always lined up at airports, train stations, bus stations and major hotels. Fares are metered and vary depending upon the company and the city they're registered in. **Uber** and **UberX** is extremely popular for cheap and more luxurious rides in LA. Download the Uber app if you haven't already. In the city of LA, rates are $2.85 at flagfall plus about $2.70 per mile. Cabs leaving from LAX charge a $4 airport fee. For details, check www.taxicabsla.org.

Beverly Hills Cab (800-273-6611; www.beverlyhillscabco.com) A solid, dependable company, with good rates to the airport and a wide service area.

Taxi Taxi (310-444-4444; www.santamonicataxi.com) Easily the best and most professional fleet available. They'll drive you anywhere, but can only pick up in Santa Monica.

Yellow Cab (877-733-3305; www.layellowcab.com) If all else fails.

AROUND LOS ANGELES

Make like Jack Kerouac, ditch the congestion, crowds and smog, and use LA as a hub to all the natural glory of California. Get an early start to beat the commuter traffic (or catch a ferry, Greyhound bus or ride the Amtrak rails), and point the compass across the ocean, up into the mountains or into the vast and imposing desert.

Catalina Island

Mediterranean-flavored Catalina Island is a popular getaway for harried Angelenos, but sinks under the weight of day-trippers in summer. Stay overnight, though, and feel the ambience go from frantic to romantic. Catalina has a unique ecosystem and has gone through stints as a hangout for seaotter poachers, smugglers and Union soldiers. It was snapped up by chewing-gum magnate William Wrigley Jr (1861–1932) in 1919, and for years he sent his Chicago Cubs baseball team here for spring training. Today most of it is owned by the Santa Catalina Island Conservancy. Commercial activity is concentrated in Avalon, which is small enough to be explored in an hour or two, so there's plenty of time for hiking, swimming and touring.

The only other settlement, even tinier than Avalon, is Two Harbors on the remote west coast, which has a general store, a dive and kayak center, a snack bar and a lodge.

Sights & Activities

It's a nice stroll along the waterfront to the 1929 art-deco **Casino** (1 Casino Way), which has well-done murals, a movie theater with a twinkling ceiling and a fabulous upstairs ballroom; the last can only be seen on guided one-hour tours ($23). Tickets also include admission to the modest but insightful **Catalina Island Museum** (www.catalinamuseum.org; adult/senior/child $5/4/free; 10am-5pm) in the same building. Construction of a new, larger museum building is under way and is scheduled to open in 2015. Continuing past the casino takes you to the privately owned **Descanso Beach**, where you can fork over $70 to lie on a chaise lounge or $400 to buy out a cabana. If an upscale beach club vibe is your thing, look into it. There's good snorkeling at **Lovers' Cove** and at **Casino Point (Avalon Underwater Park)**, a marine reserve that's also the best shore dive. Another way to escape the throngs is by kayaking to the quiet coves along Catalina's rocky coastline. **Descanso Beach Ocean Sports** (www.kayakcatalinaisland.com; kayak rentals per hr/day from $22/52, SUP rentals per hr/day $24/60) rents snorkeling gear, SUP kits and kayaks, and also runs guided kayaking tours and kayak camping trips.

About 1.5 miles inland from Avalon harbor is the peaceful **Wrigley Memorial & Botanical Gardens** (310-510-2595; 1400 Avalon Canyon Rd; adult/senior/child $7/5/free; 8am-5pm), where you'll enjoy sweeping garden views from a monument awash in colorful local tile. Wrap up the day with a luxuriant massage, facial or mud wrap at **A Touch of Heaven** (800-300-8528; www.hotel-metropole.com; massages from $50).

To get into the protected backcountry, hop on the **Safari Bus** (310-510-2800; tickets $10-32; mid-Jun–early Sep), which goes all the way to Two Harbors. You must book in advance and get a permit (and maps) from the **Catalina Conservancy** (310-510-2595;

www.catalinaconservancy.org; 125 Claressa Ave, Avalon; biking/hiking $35/free) if you're going to be hiking or mountain biking. Mountain bikers must also pay the annual membership to the conservancy for a Freewheeler Bike Pass. Hiking permits are free. There are 200 miles of scenic trails (including the 37.2-mile Trans-Catalina trail, which can be done in three days), but very little shade, so bring a hat, sunscreen and plenty of water. The best hiking and mountain-biking maps and trip planning tools can be found via the conservancy's smart phone app ($5), a worthy investment if you plan on heading into the backcountry.

Alternatively, you could just hop on an air-conditioned tour bus and let someone else show you around. Both **Catalina Adventure Tours** (☎877-510-2888; www.catalinaadventuretours.com; Green Pier, Avalon; adult/senior/child $39/34/30) and **Discovery Tours** (www.visitcatalina.com; tours $14-79) operate historical Avalon itineraries, and jaunts further out with memorable views of the rugged coast, deep canyons and sandy coves, and possible encounters with eagles and a herd of bison left behind after a 1924 movie shoot. Discovery Tours also offers a Zip Line Eco Tour (two hours, per person $109 to $120), leading you from an altitude of 500ft down to sea level in five zips – including a 1045ft line that will have you humming at 45mph.

Certified scuba divers should find **Catalina Dive Shop** (www.catalinadiveshop.com; Lovers Cove; per trip $99-129) to glimpse local shipwrecks and kelp forests. It rents snorkel gear here too. **Two Harbors Dive and Recreation Center** (www.visitcatalinaisland.com; guided dive trips $100-140) accesses pristine dive sites off the island's less-developed coast.

Sleeping

Rates soar on weekends and between May and September, and are about 30% to 60% lower at other times. For camping information, see www.visitcatalinaisland.com/avalon/camping.php.

Hotel Atwater HOTEL $

(☎877-778-8322; www.visitcatalinaisland.com/hotels-packages/avalon/hotel-atwater; 120 Sumner Ave; r from $98) This historic hotel is a block inland from the beach in central Avalon. There are 91 basic, carpeted, clean rooms with varying degrees of natural light. You'll pay more for good views. Nothing fabulous, but it is about as economical as Catalina gets, unless you're camping.

★ **Banning House Lodge** BE&B $$

(☎877-778-8322; www.visitcatalinaisland.com/hotels-packages/two-harbors/banning-house-lodge; 1 Banning House Rd; r from $129) Set in Two Harbors and built in 1910 by the Banning brothers, who owned the island at the time, this classic craftsman has been converted into an inviting bed and breakfast. All 12 rooms are uniquely decorated and have private baths. Sip wine by the fire in the living room and enjoy breakfast on a lanai (verandah) with spectacular mountain and sea views.

Pavilion Hotel HOTEL $$

(☎877-778-8322; www.visitcatalinaisland.com/hotels-packages/avalon/pavilion-hotel; 513 Crescent Ave; r from $185) At this low-slung, sweet but not swanky beach resort rooms have attractive wood furninshings and private lanai overlooking the water. A nice choice.

Hotel Metropole BOUTIQUE HOTEL $$$

(☎800-300-8528; www.hotel-metropole.com; 205 Crescent Ave; r from $175) Ocean Front rooms

WORTH A TRIP

RONALD REAGAN LIBRARY & MUSEUM

No matter how you feel about Ronald Reagan (1911–2004), his **presidential library** (www.reaganlibrary.com; 40 Presidential Dr; adult/teen/senior $16/9/13; ⏰10am-5pm; Ⓟ) is really quite fascinating. Galleries cover the arc of the man's life from his childhood in Dixon, Illinois, through his early days in radio and acting, to his years as governor of California, although the focus is obviously on his stint as president (1980–88) in the waning years of the Cold War. The museum features re-creations of the Oval Office and the Cabinet Room, Reagan family memorabilia, gifts from heads of state, a nuclear cruise missile and even a graffiti-covered chunk of the Berlin Wall. His grave is on the grounds as well. Get there via the I-405 (San Diego Fwy) north to the 118 (Ronald Reagan Fwy) west; exit at Madera Rd South, turn right on Madera and continue straight for 3 miles to Presidential Dr.

are huge with wood floors, fireplaces, soaker tubs and spectacular sea views. The design is more classic California than edgy, and that works perfectly on this island.

Eating & Drinking

Sandtrap MEXICAN $
(www.catalinasandtrap.com; 501 Avalon Canyon Rd; mains $4-11; 8am-3pm) Set next to the botanical gardens, this is a perfect place to stop for lunch after a long slog to the Wrigley monument. They serve authentic Mexican food at lunch – the tacos are particularly good.

Eric's on the Pier BURGERS $
(310-510-0894; On The Pier 4; mains $6-11; 9am-10pm) If you're in Avalon and are hungry for a burger, this is your place.

Casino Dock Café CAFE $
(www.casinodockcafe.com; 1 Casino Way; mains $4-10; 8am-3pm) A casual, local's waterfront hangout. Good for a beer, a greasy spoon breakfast or both.

Bluewater Grill SEAFOOD $$$
(310-510-3474; www.bluewatergrill.com; 306 Crescent Ave; mains $19-39; 11am-10pm) The most popular restaurant on the island, Bluewater Grill serves glazed cod with miso, grilled salmon over cedar, seasoned mahi mahi with lemon pepper, grilled steaks and shrimp, and steamed lobster and crab.

CC Gallagher CAFE
(www.ccgallagher.com; 523 Crescent Ave; 7am-midnight Sun-Thu, to 1am Fri & Sat) Part wine shop, part cafe, part deli, part sushi bar? They do it all, but you should find them because they serve the best coffee in Avalon, and have a decent deli if you need a packed lunch for the trail.

Information

Tourist Office (www.catalina.com) On the Green Pier.

Getting There & Around

A few companies operate ferries to Avalon and Two Harbors. Reservations are recommended in the summer.

The use of cars on Catalina is restricted, so there are no vehicle ferry services.

Catalina Express (www.catalinaexpress.com; round-trip adult/child $75/60) Ferries to Avalon from San Pedro, Long Beach and Dana Point in Orange County, and to Two Harbors from San Pedro. It takes one to 1½ hours, with up to three ferries daily. You'll ride free on your birthday. True story.

Catalina Flyer (800-830-7744; www.catalinaferries.com; round-trip adult/senior/under 12yr $70/65/53) Catamaran to Avalon and Two Harbors from Balboa Harbor in Newport Beach (one to 1½ hours).

Six Flags Magic Mountain & Hurricane Harbor

About 30 miles north of LA, right off the I-5 (Golden State Fwy), velocity is king at **Six Flags Magic Mountain** (661-255-4111; www.sixflags.com/parks/magicmountain; 26101 Magic Mountain Pkwy, Valencia; adult/child under 4ft & seniors $68/43;), a daredevil roller-coaster park that has had its financial ups and downs and almost got sold off to land developers in 2006. Fortunately, operators decided to hang on to it, so for now you can still go up, down and inside out faster and in more baffling ways than anywhere else besides a space shuttle. Parking is $20.

Teens and college kids get their jollies on the 16 bone-chilling roller coasters, including the aptly named **Scream**, which goes through seven loops, including a zero-gravity roll and a dive loop, with you sitting in a floorless chair. If you've got a stomach of steel, don't miss **X2**, where you ride in cars that spin 360 degrees while hurtling forward and plummeting all at once. You can also ride the classic wooden **Colossus** and the new-school **Batman**, where your seats dangle from a track above, backwards. Note that many rides have height restrictions ranging from 36in to 58in. However, families need not worry as there are plenty of tamer rides for the elementary-school set, plus shows, parades and concerts to keep everyone entertained.

Still, on hot summer days, little ones might be more in their element next door at **Six Flags Hurricane Harbor** (www.sixflags.com/parks/hurricaneharborla; 26101 Magic Mountain Pkwy; adult/child under 4ft & senior $40/32;), a jungle-themed, 22-acre water park where you can chill in a tropical lagoon, brave churning wave pools and plunge down wicked high-speed slides with names like **Banzai Pipeline** and **Taboo Tower**.

Check the website for packages, discounts and opening hours, which vary throughout the year. If you don't have your own vehicle, look for flyers for organized tours in your hotel or hostel.

Palms to Pines

The **Palms to Pines Scenic Byway** takes you from the desert floor to cedar-scented mountain ridges in just a couple of hours. And if you depart from Santa Monica in the morning during winter, you'll be able to touch the sea and the snow in one day. To surf then ski has long been a SoCal cliché, and that's because it's possible here, unlike almost anywhere else.

Of course, this scenic drive actually starts from Palm Desert. Take Hwy 74 into the **Santa Rosa Wilderness** and the **Santa Rosa & San Jacinto Mountains National Monument BLM Visitor Center**. Here, native fan palms form an oasis, and big horn sheep are known to scramble along the craggy high desert floor, as the great San Jacinto Mountain looms. If you have your hiking boots, join the **Pacific Crest Trail** for a stretch. Part of that 2650-mile-long trail can be accessed from a trailhead along the highway. This is where it climbs out of the Sonora Desert and up the San Jacinto before rambling onward to Canada. Swerve past **Lake Hemet** and glimpse eagles and falcons overhead as you enter the arty town of **Idylwild**, our favorite mountain village in all of Southern California. The Cahuilla people once camped here during the summers to escape the stifling heat of the Coachella Valley. Today their example is followed faithfully by legions of retirees. Hippies rediscovered homesteading in Idylwild back in the 1960s, when LSD guru Timothy Leary owned a ranch nearby. These days it's best known for its arts scene and live music, especially its outdoor art shows and the **Jazz in the Pines** festival in late August. When you're ready to head back toward sea level, no need to backtrack. Continue northeast on Hwy 243, over the Banning Pass, which meets I-10 west of Palm Springs.

Big Bear Lake

Big Bear Lake is a low-key, family-friendly mountain resort (elevation 6750ft) about 110 miles northeast of LA. Snowy winters lure scores of ski bunnies and boarders to its two mountains, while summer brings hikers, mountain bikers and water-sports enthusiasts wishing to escape the stifling heat down in the basin. Even getting here via the spectacular, curvy, panorama-filled **Rim of the World Scenic Byway** (Hwy 18) is a treat.

Activities

Big Bear's two ski mountains are jointly managed by **Big Bear Mountain Resorts** (www.bigbearmountainresorts.com; adult/child lift ticket $56/46). The higher of the two, **Bear Mountain** (8805ft) is nirvana for freestyle freaks with over 150 jumps, 80 jibs and two pipes, including a 580ft in-ground superpipe. **Snow Summit** (8200ft) is more focused on traditional downhill and has trails for everyone. Altogether the mountains are served by 26 lifts and criss-crossed by over 55 runs. Ski and boot rentals are about $30. After a day on the slopes, prevent muscle fatigue with an expert massage by **Mountain Mobile Massage** (909-800-8103; www.bigbearmassage.com; 30/60min $55/85); a therapist will come to you.

In summer Snow Summit issues its siren call to mountain bikers. Several pro and amateur races take place here each year. The 9-mile **Grandview Loop** is great for getting your feet in gear. The **Scenic Sky Chair** (one-way/day $12/25; May-start of ski season) provides easy access to the top. Maps, tickets and bike rentals are available from **Bear Valley Bikes** (www.bvbikes.com; 40298 Big Bear Blvd; bikes per hr incl helmet $10-20, per day $40-70). It charges higher rates for full suspension, and has fat bikes too. Hiking is another major summer activity, as are swimming, jet skiing, kayaking, boating and fishing. Boating rentals are available along the lakeshore.

To get off the beaten track, take your car for an off-road spin along the **Gold Fever Trail**, a 20-mile self-guided romp on a graded dirt road around an old gold-mining area. If you prefer to let someone else do the driving, contact **Big Bear Off-Road Adventures** (909-585-1036; www.offroadadventure.com) for its tour schedule.

Sleeping

Big Bear Hostel HOSTEL $
(909-866-8900; www.adventurehostel.com; 527 Knickerbocker Rd; r $20-40; P @) This clean and friendly hostel on the edge of the village is run by people happy to provide advice about the best trails, runs and all things extreme. Linens are provided, but BYO towel.

Bear Creek Resort MOTEL, CABIN $$
(877-428-9335; http://bearcreek-resort.com; 40210 Big Bear Blvd/Hwy 18; r $109-169, cabins $209-309; @) Right off the highway (expect some traffic noise), the tidy, renovated studio cabins have wood-burning

fireplaces and kitchenettes. The sister property, Wolf Creek Resort, is closer to the ski resorts.

Switzerland Haus B&B $$
(800-335-3729, 909-866-3729; www.switzerlandhaus.com; 41829 Switzerland Dr; r incl breakfast $125-249;) King sleigh beds, private mountain-view patios and a Nordic sauna on the deck are among the perks at this friendly, well-kept, five-room inn. Snow Summit ski resort is next door.

Castlewood Theme Cottages CABIN $$
(909-866-2720; www.castlewoodcottages.com; 547 Main St; cabins from $114;) Bored with bland motel rooms? Your fantasies can go wild in these well-crafted, clean and amazingly detailed cabins, complete with Jacuzzi tubs and costumes. Let your inner Tarzan roar, fancy yourselves Robin and Marian or Antony and Cleopatra, or cavort among woodland fairy-folk or an indoor waterfall. It's cheesy, wacky and, oddly, fun. Kids are not allowed.

Knickerbocker Mansion B&B $$
(909-878-9190, 877-423-1180; www.knickerbockermansion.com; 869 Knickerbocker Rd; r from $125;) A classy, ornate B&B in a handbuilt 1920s log home, secluded from the tourist fray. It has great breakfasts, tasty Friday- and Saturday-night dinners, and asks a two-night minimum stay on weekends.

Eating

Himalayan SOUTH ASIAN $
(www.himalayanbigbear.com; 672 Pine Knot Ave; mains $8-17; 11am-9pm Sun-Tue, to 10pm Fri & Sat;) In the busy village, this kitchen cooks up authentic Nepali and Indian dishes, including flaming-hot tandoori grills and mellow *momo* (Tibetan dumplings). Standoffish, but quick service.

North Shore Café AMERICAN $
(909-866-5879; www.dininginbigbear.com; 39226 North Shore Dr/Hwy 38, Fawnskin; breakfast & lunch mains $6-12; 8am-4pm Wed-Thu, 8am-9pm Fri, 7am-9pm Sat, 7am-6pm Sun Oct-Apr, also 8am-4pm Mon May-Sep;) This homey north-shore cabin is a heart-warming breakfast or brunch stop for homemade corned-beef hash, custardy French toast and fluffy pancakes.

Peppercorn Grille AMERICAN $$
(909-866-5405; www.peppercorngrille.com; 553 Pine Knot Ave; mains $8.95-15.95; 11am-9pm Sun-Thu, to 10pm Fri & Sat) Locals and visitors alike swear by the Italian-inspired American fare for a fancy meal in the village.

Information

Big Bear Blvd (Hwy 18), the main road, runs south of the lake, skirting the pedestrian-friendly village with cutesy shops, galleries, restaurants and the **visitors center** (www.bigbear.com; 630 Bartlett Rd; 8am-5pm Mon-Fri, 9am-5pm Sat & Sun). The ski resorts are east of the village. Quiet N Shore Dr (Hwy 38) provides access to campgrounds and trails.

If you're driving, pick up a National Forest Adventure Pass, available at the **Big Bear Discovery Center** (909-382-2790; www.bigbeardiscoverycenter.com; 40971 N Shore Dr, Fawnskin; 8am-4:30pm, closed Wed & Thu mid-Sep–mid-May) on the North Shore.

Getting There & Away

Big Bear is on Hwy 18, an offshoot of Hwy 30 in San Bernardino. A quicker approach is via Hwy 330, which starts in Highland and intersects with Hwy 18 in Running Springs. If you don't like serpentine mountain roads, pick up Hwy 38 near Redlands, which is longer, but easier on the queasy. **Mountain Area Regional Transit Authority** (Marta; 909-878-5200; www.marta.cc) buses connect Big Bear with the Greyhound and Metrolink stations in San Bernardino ($2.50, 1¼ hours).

RIM OF THE WORLD

While most folks are in a hurry to head to the mountains, which means picking up Hwy 30 in San Bernardino, consider taking the slow road, blessed with hair-raising cliff drop-offs and postcard canyon views. The Rim of the World drive is one of America's Scenic Byways, and with good reason. We suggest diverging from the trodden path early, and visiting the sculpted sandstone of **Mormon Rocks**. From there take Hwy 138 past **Silverwood Lake** and **Lake Gregory**, then climb Hwy 18 into quaint **Blue Jay** and **Lake Arrowhead**. This is where the vistas get serious and the hairpins exciting. Lake Arrowhead's fashionable mall and ski resort makes a nice respite from the road. Once back on the highway, the most jaw-dropping stretch of road takes you into **Big Bear Lake**.

Disneyland & Orange County

Includes ➡

Disneyland & Anaheim............219
Around Disneyland.........236
Orange County Beaches...........240
Seal Beach..........241
Sunset Beach......243
Huntington Beach..244
Newport Beach.....249
Laguna Beach......260

Best Places to Stay

- ➡ Shorebreak Hotel (p246)
- ➡ Grand Californian Hotel & Spa (p227)
- ➡ Montage (p264)
- ➡ Crystal Cove beach cottages (p259)
- ➡ Casa Tropicana (p271)

Best Places to Eat

- ➡ Walt's Wharf (p242)
- ➡ Napa Rose (p231)
- ➡ 242 Cafe Fusion Sushi (p265)
- ➡ Bear Flag Fish Company (p255)
- ➡ Ramos House Café (p268)

Why Go?

LA and Orange County may be the closest of neighbors, but in some ways they could hardly be more different. If LA is about stars, the OC is about surfers. LA: ever more urban, OC: proudly *sub*urban. If LA is SoCal's seat of liberal thinking, the OC's heritage is of mega-churches and ultra-conservative firebrands. If LA is Hollywood glam, the OC is *Real Housewives.*

Chances are the OC has seeped into your consciousness even if you've never been here. Beyond Mickey Mouse and friends, TV series from *Laguna Beach* and *The OC* to *Arrested Development* have all been set here, taking the county image from humdrum to hip, a place of mythically (gl)amorous teens, gorgeous beaches and socialite cat fights.

While there's some truth to those stereotypes – big, boxy mansions, fortress-like shopping malls, conservatives tossing Happy Meal detritus out of their Humvees – this diverse county's 789 sq miles, 34 cities and 3 million people create deep pockets of individuality, beauty and different ways of thinking, keepin' the OC 'real,' no matter one's reality.

When to Go

Anaheim

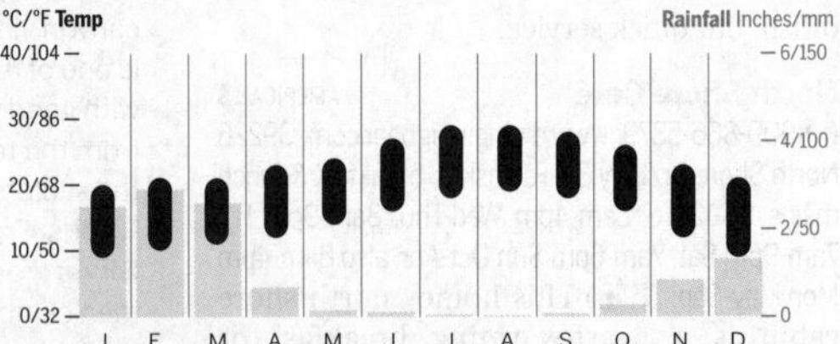

May Visitation dips from spring break to Memorial Day. Mostly sunny, balmy temperatures.

July & Aug Summer vacation and beach season peak. Surfing and art festivals by the coast.

Sep Blue skies, cooler temperatures inland, fewer crowds. Tall Ships Festival at Dana Point.

DISNEYLAND & ANAHEIM

POP 343,250 (ANAHEIM)

Mickey is one lucky mouse. Created by animator Walt Disney in 1928, this irrepressible mouse caught a ride on a multimedia juggernaut (film, TV, publishing, music, merchandising and theme parks) that rocketed him into a global stratosphere of recognition, money and influence. Plus, he lives in the 'Happiest Place on Earth,' an 'imagineered' hyper-reality where the streets are always clean, the employees – called 'cast

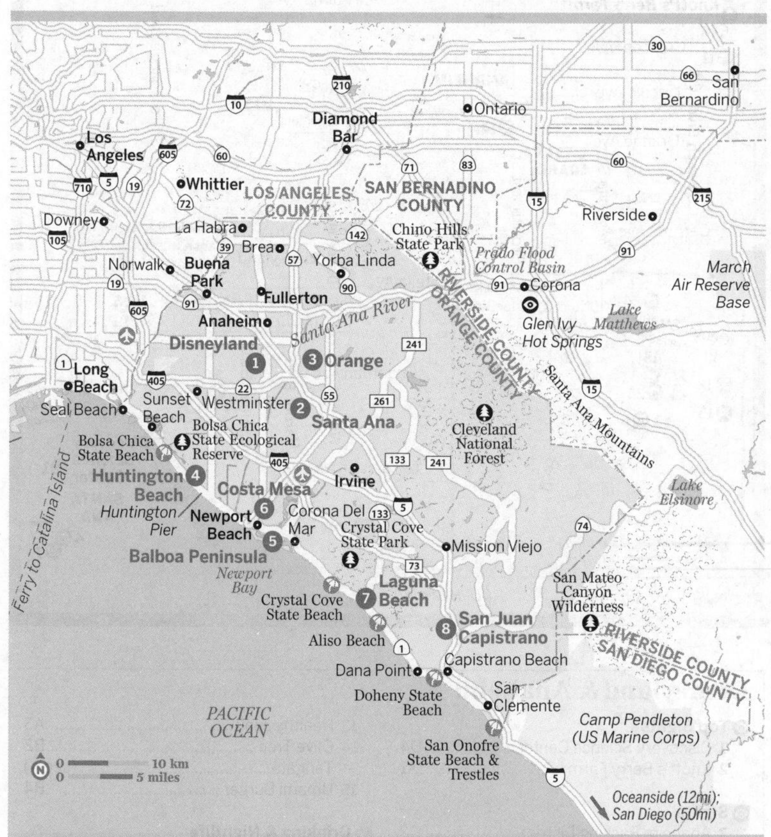

Disneyland & Orange County Highlights

1. Meeting Mickey and screaming your head off on Space Mountain at **Disneyland**, then catching the fireworks show (p232).
2. Fighting outrageous bed hair inside the eye of a hurricane at the **Discovery Science Center** (p238) in **Santa Ana**.
3. Shopping for vintage treasures and slurping milkshakes from a soda fountain in **Old Towne Orange** (p239).
4. Building a beach bonfire after a day of surfing killer waves at **Huntington Beach** (p244).
5. Cycling past the as-seen-on-TV sands of Newport Beach's **Balboa Peninsula** (p249).
6. Discovering Orange County's alternative side (yes, there is one) at **The Lab** (p258) and **The Camp** (p258) 'anti-malls' in **Costa Mesa** (p257).
7. Watching the sun dip below the horizon from the bluff-tops of art-filled **Laguna Beach** (p260).
8. Being awed by the Spanish colonial history and beauty of **Mission San Juan Capistrano** (p268).

Disneyland & Anaheim

Disneyland & Anaheim

Top Sights

1 Discovery Science Center D4
2 Knott's Berry Farm A1

Sights

3 Anaheim Packing District C2
4 Bowers Museum D4
5 Center Street Anaheim A3
6 Christ Cathedral C3
7 Kidseum D4

Activities, Courses & Tours

8 Soak City OC A1

Sleeping

9 Ayres Hotel Anaheim D3
10 Hotel Menage C2
11 Knott's Berry Farm Hotel A2

Eating

12 118 Degrees A3
13 Healthy Junk A3
14 Olive Tree B2
Tangata .... (see 4)
15 Umami Burger B4

Drinking & Nightlife

16 Anaheim Brewery B4
17 Barbeer A3
18 Ink & Bean A3

Entertainment

19 Angel Stadium D3
20 Block at Orange D3
21 City National Grove of Anaheim D3
22 Honda Center D3
23 Medieval Times A1

Shopping

24 Good A3
25 Look A3

members' – are always upbeat and there are parades every day of the year.

It would be easy to hate the guy, but since opening his Disneyland home in 1955, he has been a pretty thoughtful host to millions of guests. There are a few potholes on Main St – every ride seems to end in a gift store, prices are sky-high and there are grumblings that management could do more about affordable housing and health insurance for employees – but even the most determined grouch should find something to warrant a grin. For the more than 14 million kids, grandparents, honeymooners and international tourists who visit every year, Disneyland remains a magical experience.

History

When Walt Disney opened Disneyland on July 17, 1955, he declared it the 'Happiest Place on Earth.' Nearly 60 years later, it's hard to argue.

Carved out of orange and walnut groves in the city of Anaheim, the construction of the 'theme park' (another Disney term) took just one year. Disneyland's opening day was a disaster, however. Temperatures over 100°F (38°C) melted asphalt underfoot, leaving women's high heels stuck in the tar. There were plumbing problems: all of the drinking fountains quit working. Hollywood stars didn't show up on time, and more than twice the number of expected guests – some 28,000 by day's end – crowded through the gates, some holding counterfeit tickets. But none of this kept eager Disney fans away for long, as more than 50 million tourists visited in its first decade alone.

During the 1990s, Anaheim undertook a staggering $4.2 billion revamp and expansion, cleaning up rundown stretches and establishing the first tourist police force in the US. In 2001, a second theme park, Disney California Adventure (DCA), was added, designed to salute the state's most famous natural landmarks and cultural history. More recently added was Downtown Disney, an outdoor pedestrian mall. The ensemble is called the Disneyland Resort.

Meanwhile, Anaheim continues to fill in with malls like Anaheim GardenWalk (2008) to the Packing District (2013), plus improved roads and transit.

Sights

The Disneyland Resort is open 365 days a year. During peak summer season, Disneyland's hours are usually 8am to midnight; the rest of the year, 10am to 8pm or 10pm. DCA closes at 10pm or 11pm in summer, earlier in the off-season.

One-day admission to *either* Disneyland or DCA currently costs $96 for adults and $90 for children aged three to nine. To visit *both* parks in one day costs $150/144 per adult/child on a 'Park Hopper' ticket. Multi-day Park Hopper tickets cost from $217/204 for two days up to $300/279 for five days of admission within a two-week period. A ticket covers all of the parks' rides and attractions.

Disneyland Park

It's hard to deny the change in atmosphere as you're whisked by tram from the parking lot into the heart of the resort. Wide-eyed children lean forward with anticipation while stressed-out parents sit back, finally relaxing. Uncle Walt's in charge, and he's taken care of every possible detail.

Walk through the gates of **Disneyland** (Map p222; ☎714-781-4565; disneyland.disney.go.com; 1313 Disneyland Dr; adult/child $96/90, both parks daypass adult/child $150/144; 👪) and along the red-brick path – suggestive of a red carpet – and a floral Mickey Mouse blooms before you. A sign above the nearby archway reads 'Here you leave today and enter the world of yesterday, tomorrow and fantasy.' It's an apt but slightly skewed greeting that's indicative of the upbeat, slightly skewed 'reality' of the park itself – and the

FLYING SOLO

If you're here alone, ask the staff at the entrance to park rides if a single-rider line is available, where you wait in a separate, shorter line. Availability may depend on the size of the crowd – and also on how that particular cast member is feeling that day, so be nice! Disneyland's single-rider attractions include the ever-popular Indiana Jones Adventure (p224) and Splash Mountain (p225). At DCA, look for single-rider lines at Soarin' Over California (p226), California Screamin' (p227), Goofy's Sky School (p227), Grizzly River Run (p227) and Radiator Springs Racers (p227).

Disneyland Resort

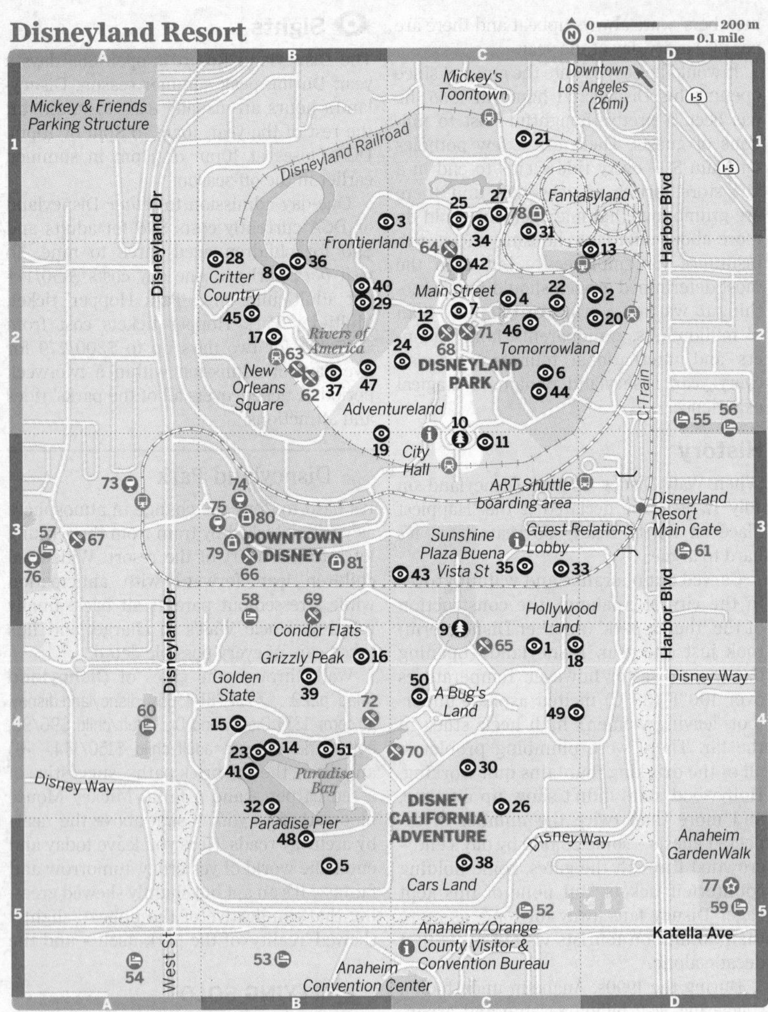

undeniable delight to the millions of children who visit every year. This is their park, but adults who can willingly suspend disbelief and give in to the 'magic of Disney' may have just as much fun.

Main Street, USA RIDES, ATTRACTIONS

Fashioned after Walt's hometown of Marceline, Missouri, bustling Main St, USA resembles the classic turn-of-the-20th-century, all-American town. It's an idyllic, relentlessly upbeat representation, complete with barbershop quartet, penny arcades, ice-cream shops and a steam train. The music playing in the background is from American musicals, and there's a flag-retreat ceremony every afternoon.

The Disneyland Story presenting **Great Moments with Mr Lincoln**, a 15-minute Audio-Animatronics presentation on Honest Abe, sits inside the fascinating **Disneyland Story** exhibit. Oh, and it's air-conditioned. While you wait, comedian Steve Martin narrates Disneyland's history with vintage film footage. Nearby, kids love seeing old-school Disney cartoons like *Steamboat Willie* inside **Main Street Cinema**.

Disneyland Resort

Sights

1 Animation Building C4
2 Autopia D2
3 Big Thunder Mountain Railroad B1
4 Buzz Lightyear's Astro Blaster C2
5 California Screamin' B5
6 Captain EO C2
7 Central Plaza C2
8 Davy Crockett's Explorer Canoes B2
9 Disney California Adventure C4
10 Disneyland Park C3
11 Disneyland Story C3
12 Enchanted Tiki Room C2
13 Finding Nemo Submarine Voyage D2
14 Golden Zephyr B4
15 Goofy's Sky School B4
Great Moments with Mr Lincoln ... (see 11)
16 Grizzly River Run B4
17 Haunted Mansion B2
18 Hyperion Theater C4
19 Indiana Jones Adventure B3
20 Innoventions D2
21 it's a small world C1
22 Jedi Training Academy C2
23 Jumpin' Jellyfish B4
24 Jungle Cruise C2
25 King Arthur Carrousel C1
26 Luigi's Flying Tires C4
27 Mad Tea Party C1
28 Many Adventures of Winnie the Pooh B2
29 Mark Twain Riverboat B2
30 Mater's Junkyard Jamboree C4
31 Matterhorn Bobsleds C1
32 Mickey's Fun Wheel B4
33 Monsters, Inc: Mike & Sulley to the Rescue! C3
34 Mr Toad's Wild Ride C1
35 Muppet Vision 3D theater C3
36 Pirate's Lair on Tom Sawyer Island B2
37 Pirates of the Caribbean B2
38 Radiator Springs Racers C5
39 Redwood Creek Challenge Trail B4
40 Sailing Ship Columbia B2
41 Silly Symphony Swings B4
42 Sleeping Beauty Castle C2
43 Soarin' Over California C3
44 Space Mountain C2
45 Splash Mountain B2
46 Star Tours–The Adventure Continues C2
47 Tarzan's Treehouse B2
48 Toy Story Midway Mania B5
49 Twilight Zone Tower of Terror C4
50 Walt Disney Imagineering Blue Sky Cellar C4
51 World of Color B4

Sleeping

52 Alpine Inn C5
53 Anabella B5
54 Best Western Plus Stovall's Inn A5
55 Camelot Inn & Suites D2
56 Carousel Inn & Suites D2
57 Disneyland Hotel A3
58 Grand Californian Hotel & Spa B3
59 Hotel Indigo Anaheim Main Gate D5
60 Paradise Pier Hotel A4
61 Park Vue Inn D3

Eating

62 Blue Bayou B2
63 Café Orleans B2
64 Carnation Cafe C2
65 Carthay Circle C4
66 Catal Restaurant & Uva Bar B3
67 Earl of Sandwich A3
68 Jolly Holiday Bakery & Cafe C2
69 Napa Rose B3
70 Pacific Wharf Cafe C4
71 Plaza Inn C2
Steakhouse 55 .... (see 57)
72 Wine Country Terrace B4

Drinking & Nightlife

73 ESPN Zone A3
Golden Vine Winery .... (see 72)
74 House of Blues B3
Napa Rose Lounge .... (see 69)
75 Ralph Brennan's New Orleans Jazz Kitchen B3
76 Trader Sam's Enchanted Tiki Lounge A3
Uva Bar .... (see 66)

Entertainment

77 Anaheim GardenWalk D5

Shopping

78 Bibbidi Bobbidi Boutique C1
D Street .... (see 75)
79 Disney Vault 28 .... B3
80 Ridemakerz B3
81 World of Disney B3

Main St ends in the **Central Plaza** Lording over the plaza is **Sleeping Beauty Castle**, the castle featured on the Disney logo. Inside the iconic structure (fashioned after a real 19th-century Bavarian castle), dolls and big books tell the story of Sleeping Beauty. As if you didn't know it already.

Tomorrowland RIDES, ATTRACTIONS

How did 1950s imagineers envision the future? As a galaxy-minded community filled with monorails, rockets and Googie-style

> **DETAILS, DETAILS, DETAILS**
>
> For lots of practical tips for managing your Disney Resort vacation, see our Disneyland Trip Planner on p46.

architecture, apparently. In 1998 this 'land' was revamped to honor three timeless futurists – Jules Verne, HG Wells, and Leonardo da Vinci – while major corporations like Microsoft, Honda, Siemens and HP sponsor futuristic robot shows and interactive exhibits in the **Innoventions pavilion**.

The retro high-tech **monorail** glides to a stop in Tomorrowland, its rubber tires traveling a 13-minute, 2.5-mile round-trip route to Downtown Disney. Just outside Tomorrowland station, kiddies will want to shoot laser beams on **Buzz Lightyear's Astro Blaster** adventure and drive their own miniature cars in the classic **Autopia** ride (don't worry, they're on tracks – drive too slowly, and you may get bumped from behind!). Then jump aboard the **Finding Nemo Submarine Voyage** to look for the world's most famous clownfish from within a refurbished submarine and rumble through an underwater volcanic eruption.

Star Tours – The Adventure Continues clamps you into a Starspeeder shuttle for a wild and bumpy 3D ride through the desert canyons of Tatooine on a space mission with several alternate storylines, so you can ride it again and again. **Space Mountain**, Tomorrowland's signature attraction and one of the USA's best roller coasters, hurtles you into complete darkness at frightening speed. Another classic is **Captain EO**, a special-effects tribute film, starring none other than Michael Jackson.

Fantasyland RIDES, ATTRACTIONS

(Map p222) Behind Sleeping Beauty Castle, Fantasyland is filled with the characters of classic children's stories. If you only see one attraction in Fantasyland, visit **it's a small world** , a boat ride past hundreds of creepy Audio-Animatronics children from different cultures all singing the annoying theme song in an astounding variety of languages, now joined by Disney characters. Another classic, the **Matterhorn Bobsleds** is a steel-frame roller coaster that mimics a bobsled ride down a mountain. Fans of old-school attractions will also get a kick out of the *Wind in the Willows*–inspired **Mr Toad's Wild Ride**, a loopy jaunt in an open-air jalopy through London. Younger kids love whirling around the **Mad Tea Party** teacup ride and **King Arthur Carrousel**, then cavorting with characters in nearby **Mickey's Toontown**, a topsy-turvy mini-metropolis where kiddos can traipse through Mickey and Minnie's houses and dozens of storefronts.

Frontierland RIDES, ATTRACTIONS

(Map p222) Arrgh matey! Captain Jack Sparrow and his pirate crew have hijacked an American classic. Frontierland's Tom Sawyer Island – the only attraction in the park personally designed by Uncle Walt – has been reimagined in the wake of the *Pirates of the Caribbean* movies. Renamed the **Pirate's Lair on Tom Sawyer Island**), the island now honors Tom in name only. After a raft ride to the island, wander among roving pirates, cannibal cages, ghostly apparitions and buried treasure. Or just cruise around the island on the **Mark Twain Riverboat**, a Mississippi-style paddle-wheel boat, or the 18th-century replica **Sailing Ship Columbia**. The rest of Frontierland gives a nod to the rip-roarin' Old West with a shooting gallery and **Big Thunder Mountain Railroad**, a mining-themed roller coaster.

Adventureland RIDES, ATTRACTIONS

(Map p222) Adventureland loosely derives its jungle theme from Southeast Asia and Africa. The hands-down highlight is the safari-style **Indiana Jones™ Adventure**. Enormous Humvee-type vehicles lurch and jerk their way through the wild for spine-tingling encounters with creepy crawlies and scary skulls in re-creations of stunts from the famous film trilogy. Nearby, little ones love climbing the stairways of **Tarzan's Treehouse™**. Cool down with a **Jungle Cruise**, as exotic Audio-Animatronic animals from the Amazon, Ganges, Nile and Irrawaddy Rivers jump out and challenge your boat's skipper. Even if you don't stay for the South Seas show, at least walk into the vintage **Enchanted Tiki Room** to look at the carvings of Hawaiian gods and goddesses.

New Orleans Square RIDES, ATTRACTIONS

(Map p222) Adjacent to Adventureland, New Orleans Square has all the charm of the French Quarter but none of the marauding drunks. New Orleans was Walt's and his wife Lillian's favorite city, and Walt paid tribute to it by building this stunning square. **Pirates of the Caribbean** is the longest ride in Disneyland (17 minutes) and provided 'inspiration' for the popular movies. You'll float through the subterranean haunts of tawdry pirates, where dead buccaneers perch atop their mounds of booty and Jack Sparrow pops up occasionally. Over at the **Haunted Mansion**, 999 'happy haunts' – spirits, goblins, shades and ghosts – appear and evanesce while you ride in a cocoonlike 'Doom Buggy' through web-covered graveyards of dancing skeletons.

Critter Country RIDES, ATTRACTIONS

(Map p222) Tucked behind the Haunted Mansion, Critter Country's main attraction is **Splash Mountain**, a flume ride that transports you through the story of Brer Rabbit and Brer Bear, based on the controversial 1946 film *Song of the South*. Right at the big descent, a camera snaps your picture. Some visitors lift their shirts, earning the ride the nickname 'Flash Mountain,' though R-rated pics are destroyed. Just past Splash Mountain, hop in a mobile beehive on **The Many Adventures of Winnie the Pooh**, Nearby on the Rivers of America, you can paddle **Davy Crockett's Explorer Canoes** on summer weekends.

Disney California Adventure

Across the plaza from Disneyland's monument to fantasy and make-believe is **Disney California Adventure** (DCA; 714-781-4400, 714-781-4565; www.disneyland.com; 1313 Harbor Blvd, Anaheim; 1-day pass Disneyland Park or DCA adult/child 3-9yr $80/74, both parks $105/99;), an ode to California's geography, history and culture – or at least a sanitized G-rated version. DCA, which opened in 2001, covers more acres than Disneyland and feels less crowded, and it has more modern rides and attractions.

DCA's entrance was designed to look like an old-fashioned painted-collage postcard. After passing under the Golden Gate Bridge, you'll arrive at a homage to a 1920s Los Angeles streetscape, complete with a red trolley running down the street.

Hollywood Land RIDES, ATTRACTIONS

(Map p222) California's biggest factory of dreams is presented here in miniature, with soundstages, movable props, and – of course – a studio store. If you arrive early in the day, you'll have an unobstructed look at the forced-perspective **mural** at the end of the street, a sky-and-land backdrop that looks, at least in photographs, like the street keeps going. Very cool.

The big attraction is **The Twilight Zone Tower of Terror**, a 13-story drop down

DISNEYLAND & ANAHEIM IN...

One Day

Get to **Disneyland** early. Stroll **Main Street, USA** toward Sleeping Beauty Castle. Enter **Tomorrowland** to ride Space Mountain. In **Fantasyland** don't miss the classic it's a small world ride. Race down the Matterhorn Bobsleds or take tots to **Mickey's Toontown**. Grab a FASTPASS for the Indiana Jones Adventure or Pirates of the Caribbean before lunching in **New Orleans Square**. Plummet down Splash Mountain, then visit the Haunted Mansion before the **fireworks** and **Fantasmic!** shows begin.

Two Days

At **Disney California Adventure**, take a virtual hang-gliding ride on **Soarin' Over California** and let kids tackle the **Redwood Creek Challenge Trail** before having fun at **Paradise Pier**, with its roller coaster, Ferris wheel and carnival games. Watch the **Pixar Play Parade**, then explore **Cars Land** or cool off on the **Grizzly River Run**. After dark, drop by **The Twilight Zone Tower of Terror** and **World of Color** show.

Three Days

Escape the mouse house for more thrills-a-minute at **Knott's Berry Farm** theme park or educational family fun at the **Discovery Science Center** Sans kids, take a spa day at **Glen Ivy Hot Springs**, aka Club Mud, then go vintage shopping in **Old Towne Orange**, appreciate art at the **Bowers Museum** or eat your way through **Little Saigon**. Spend the evening exploring Anaheim's hip side, on **Center Street** and the **Packing District**.

an elevator chute situated in a haunted hotel – one eerily resembling the historic Hollywood Roosevelt Hotel (p90) in Los Angeles. From the upper floors of the tower, you'll have views of the Santa Ana mountains, if only for a few heart-pounding seconds. Less brave children can navigate a taxicab through 'Monstropolis' on the **Monsters, Inc: Mike & Sulley to the Rescue!** ride heading back toward the street's beginning.

Hot enough for ya? Slip into the cool, air-conditioned **Muppet Vision 3D theater** for a special-effects film. Then learn how to draw like Disney in the **Animation Academy**, discover how cartoon artwork becomes 3D at the **Character Close-Up** or simply be amazed by the interactive **Sorcerer's Workshop**, all housed inside the **Animation Building**.

Golden State RIDES, ATTRACTIONS

(Map p222) Just off Sunshine Plaza, Golden State is broken into sections highlighting California's natural and human achievements. **Condor Flats** recognizes the aerospace industry. Its main attraction, **Soarin' Over California** , is a virtual hang-gliding

FASTPASS

Disneyland and DCA's FASTPASS system can significantly cut your wait times.

- Walk up to a FASTPASS ticket machine – located near the entrance to select theme park rides – and insert your park entrance ticket or annual passport. You'll receive a slip of paper showing the 'return time' for boarding (it's always at least 40 minutes later).
- Show up within the window of time on the ticket and join the ride's FASTPASS line. There'll still be a wait, but it's shorter (typically 15 minutes or less). Hang on to your FASTPASS ticket until you board the ride.
- If you're running late and miss the time window printed on your FASTPASS ticket, you can still try joining the FASTPASS line, although showing up before your FASTPASS time window is a no-no.

You're thinking, what's the catch, right? When you get a FASTPASS, you will have to wait at least two hours before getting another one (check the 'next available' time printed at the bottom of your ticket).

So, make it count. Before getting a FASTPASS, check the display above the machine, which will tell you what the 'return time' for boarding is. If it's much later in the day, or doesn't fit your schedule, a FASTPASS may not be worth it. Ditto if the ride's current wait time is just 15 to 30 minutes.

DCA FASTPASS Attractions

California Screamin' (p227), Paradise Pier

Goofy's Sky School (p227), Paradise Pier

Grizzly River Run (p227), Golden State

Soarin' Over California (p226), Golden State

Twilight Zone Tower of Terror (p225), Hollywood Land

Radiator Springs Racers (p227), Cars Land

World of Color (p230), Paradise Pier

Disneyland FASTPASS Attractions

Autopia (p224), Tomorrowland

Big Thunder Mountain Railroad (p224), Frontierland

Indiana Jones Adventure (p224), Adventureland

Roger Rabbit's Car Toon Spin, Mickey's Toontown (p224)

Space Mountain (p224), Tomorrowland

Splash Mountain (p225), Critter Country

Star Tours (p224), Tomorrowland

ride using Omnimax technology that 'flies' you over landmarks such as the Golden Gate Bridge, Yosemite Falls, Lake Tahoe, Malibu and, of course, Disneyland itself. Enjoy the light breeze as you soar, keeping your nostrils open for the smell of the sea, orange groves and pine forests blowing in the wind. **Grizzly River Run** takes you 'rafting' down a faux Sierra Nevada river – you *will* get wet, so come when it's warm. While fake flat-hatted park rangers look on, kids can tackle the **Redwood Creek Challenge Trail**, with its 'Big Sir' redwoods, wooden towers and lookouts, and rock slide and climbing traverses. Get a behind-the-scenes looks at what's in the works next for Disneyland's theme parks inside **Walt Disney Imagineering Blue Sky Cellar**.

Paradise Pier RIDES, ATTRACTIONS

(Map p222) If you like carnival rides, you'll love Paradise Pier, designed to look like a combination of all the beachside amusement piers in California. The state-of-the-art **California Screamin'** roller coaster resembles an old wooden coaster, but it's got a smooth-as-silk steel track: it feels like you're being shot out of a cannon. Awesome. Just as popular is **Toy Story Midway Mania** , a 4D ride where you earn points by shooting at targets while your carnival car swivels and careens through an oversize, old-fashioned game arcade. Want a bird's-eye view of the park? Head to **Mickey's Fun Wheel** a 15-story Ferris wheel where gondolas pitch and yaw in little loops as well as the big one (unless you've requested one of the stationary ones). Nearby, **Silly Symphony Swings** is a hybrid carousel with tornado-like chair swings; the pre-school set can ride a more sedate version on the **Golden Zephyr** and bounce along on the **Jumpin' Jellyfish** **Goofy's Sky School** is a cute and relatively tame cartoon-themed coaster ride. Cool your jets or get a pick-me up at the **Boudin Bakery** or the **Ghirardelli Soda Fountain and Chocolate Shop**.

Cars Land RIDES, ATTRACTIONS

(Map p222) DCA's newest land, based on the popular Disney Pixar movie *Cars,* opened in 2012 and became an instant hit. Top billing goes to the wacky **Radiator Springs Racers**, a race-car ride that bumps and jumps around a track painstakingly decked out like the Great American West. Tractor-towed trailers swing their way around the 'dance floor' at **Mater's Junkyard Jamboree**.

THE WHAMMY

Have you gotten the Disneyland whammy yet? Don't worry, it's not a hex that cast members put on you for cutting in line. It's what fanatics call riding all three of Disneyland's 'mountain' rides – Splash Mountain, Space Mountain and the Big Thunder Mountain Railroad – in one day. Over-achievers can jump on the Matterhorn Bobsleds for extra credit.

Steer your bumper car (well, bumper tire, to be exact) through **Luigi's Flying Tires** (enter via the Casa Della Tires shop) or ride along with Route 66–themed gift shops; diners like the tepee-style **Cozy Cone Motel** will take on that special glow of nostalgia underneath neon lights in the evening.

Sleeping

Disneyland Resort

Each of the resort's **hotels** (☎800-225-2024, reservations 714-956-6425; www.disneyland.com) has a swimming pool with a waterslide, kids' activity programs, fitness center, restaurants and bars, business center, and valet or complimentary self-parking for registered guests. Every standard room can accommodate up to five guests and has a mini-fridge and a coffeemaker. Staying at one of Disney's resort hotels may also get you early admission to the parks. Lodging and admission-ticket packages can save money.

★**Grand Californian Hotel & Spa** LUXURY HOTEL **$$$**

(Map p222; ☎info 714-635-2300, reservations 714-956-6425; disneyland.disney.go.com/grand-californian-hotel; 1600 S Disneyland Dr; d from $360; P❄@📶🏊) Soaring timber beams rise above the cathedral-like lobby of the six-story Grand Californian, Disney's homage to the Arts and Crafts architectural movement. Cushy rooms have triple-sheeted beds, down pillows, bathrobes and all-custom furnishings. Outside there's a faux-redwood waterslide into the pool. At night, kids wind down with bedtime stories by the lobby's giant stone hearth. For a little adult pampering, your coconut rub and milk ritual wrap awaits at the Mandara Spa.

Even if you're not staying here, a brief respite in the astounding lobby is a must (and totally acceptable). Enter from DCA or Downtown Disney.

Paradise Pier Hotel HOTEL $$$
(Map p222; ☎ info 714-999-0990, reservations 714-956-6425; http://disneyland.disney.go.com/paradise-pier-hotel; 1717 S Disneyland Dr; d from $240; P ❄ @ ☞ ≋) Sunbursts, surfboards and a giant superslide are all on deck at the Paradise Pier Hotel, the smallest (472 rooms), cheapest and maybe the most fun of the Disney hotel trio. Kids will love the beachy decor and game arcade, not to mention the roof deck pool and the tiny-tot video room filled with mini Adirondack chairs.

Rooms are just as spotlessly kept as at the other hotels and are decorated with colorful fabrics and custom furniture. The hotel connects directly to DCA. It also has the best views of the parks – request a room with a partial view of Paradise Bay's World of Color (p230) show – you can stream the soundtrack on your in-room TV.

Disneyland Hotel HOTEL $$$
(Map p222; ☎ 714-778-6600; www.disneyland.com; 1150 Magic Way; r $210-395; P @ ☞ ≋) Built in 1955, the year Disneyland opened, the park's original hotel had grown a little rundown but has just been rejuvenated with a dash of bibbidi-bobbidi-boo. There are three towers with themed lobbies (adventure, fantasy and frontier), and the 972 good-sized rooms now boast Mickey-hand wall sconces and headboards lit like the fireworks over Sleeping Beauty Castle. It also has the best swimming pool of the three Disney hotels (amoeba shaped with water slides and kiddie pools), plus cartoon-character-themed Signature Suites.

It sits at the entrance to Downtown Disney, a short walk from the Monorail.

TOP RIDES FOR TEENS

For the adventure seekers in your brood, try the following rides:

Indiana Jones Adventure (p224), Adventureland

Space Mountain (p224), Tomorrowland

Twilight Zone Tower of Terror (p225), Hollywood Land, DCA

Splash Mountain (p225), Critter Country

California Screamin' (p227), Paradise Pier, DCA

Soarin' Over California (p226), Golden State, DCA

Big Thunder Mountain Railroad (p224), Frontierland

Anaheim

Apart from Disneyland tourism, Anaheim is a year-round convention destination. Room rates spike accordingly, so listed rates fluctuate. Most motels and hotels offer packages including tickets to Disneyland or other local attractions. Ask about family-friendly suites that sleep five or more people. Some hotels offer free Disneyland shuttles, or you can ride frequent shuttles from many area hotels, operated by Anaheim Resort Transportation (p236).

HI Fullerton HOSTEL $
(☎ 714-738-3721; www.hihostels.com; 1700 N Harbor Blvd, Fullerton; dm $24-27, r per person $46-56; ⊙ mid-Jun–mid-Sep; P ⊖ ❄ @ ☞) On a former dairy farm in Brea Dam State Park, 6 miles north of Disneyland, this two-story hacienda houses 20 beds in three dorm types (male, female, mixed), and the usual youth-hostel amenities. Rates include continental breakfast and parking. By bus from Disneyland, walk to Harbor Blvd and Ball Rd to catch OCTA bus No 43 ($2, about one hour).

★ **Anabella** HOTEL $$
(Map p222; ☎ 800-863-4888, 714-905-1050; www.anabellahotel.com; 1030 W Katella Ave; r $89-199, ste $109-199; P @ ☞ ≋) Formerly three separate motels, this 7-acre complex has the feel of a laid-back country club, complete with trams that carry guests effortlessly from the lobby to their buildings. Large rooms have wooden floors and a whisper of Spanish Colonial style, with extras like mini-fridges and TV entertainment systems. Bunk-bedded kids' suites have Disney-inspired decor.

Grab a 'Tangerita' cocktail on the poolside patio. Parking is $15.

Hotel Indigo Anaheim Main Gate BOUTIQUE HOTEL $$
(Map p222; ☎ 714-772-7755; 435 W Katella Ave; r $159-279; P ⊖ @ ☞ ≋ 🐾) New for 2013, this 104-room hotel has a clean, mid-century modernist look and a dancing fountain out front. There's a fitness center and pool, plus guest laundry. Mosaic murals are modeled af-

ter the walnut trees that once bloomed here. It's about 20 minutes' walk or a quick drive to Disneyland's main gate. Free parking.

Best Western Plus Stovall's Inn MOTEL $$
(Map p222; ☎800-854-8175, ext 3, 714-778-1880; www.bestwestern.com; 1110 W Katella Ave; r incl breakfast $90-170; P ❄ @ ☎ ≋) This motel's 290 remodeled sleek and sophisticated design motel rooms sparkle; all have air-con, a microwave and minifridge, and there's a hot breakfast included. Walk to Disneyland in 15 minutes. Parking is $10. Another Best Western motel nearby, the Pavilions, is cheaper, but it's slightly further away from Disneyland.

Hotel Menage HOTEL $$
(Map p220; ☎888-462-7275, 714-758-0900; www.hotelmenage.com; 1221 S Harbor Blvd; r $85-159; P @ ☎ ≋ 🐾) This stylish hotel pulls off a sophisticated vibe that's perfect after a day of running around the mouse house, bedecked with earth-tone sofas, black-stone flooring, leather headboards, plasma TVs, fridges and sunflower showerheads and a nice fitness center.

Splurge on high-ceilinged 'studio loft' rooms and a poolside cabana, or have drinks at the lanai-style Palapa bar. The hum of traffic noise from the nearby freeway is omnipresent around the pool but barely noticeable inside rooms. Parking is $10.

Alpine Inn MOTEL $$
(Map p222; ☎714-772-4422; www.alpineinnanaheim.com; 715 W Katella Ave; r incl breakfast $60-190; P ⊖ ❄ @ ☎ ≋) Connoisseurs of kitsch will hug their Hummels over this 42-room, snow-covered chalet sporting an A-frame exterior and icicle-covered roofs – framed by palm trees, of course. Right on the border of DCA, the inn also has Ferris wheel views. It's circa 1958, and air-con rooms are aging but clean. Simple continental breakfast served in the lobby.

Ayres Hotel Anaheim HOTEL $$
(Map p220; ☎800-595-5692, 714-634-2106; www.ayreshotels.com/anaheim; 2550 E Katella Ave; r incl breakfast $120-150; P ⊖ ❄ @ ☎ ≋) Orange County's minichain of business hotels delivers solid-gold value. Rooms possess a modicum of French regency style, with velvet curtains, mahogany furnishings, carved headboards, fridge, wet bar and pillowtop mattresses, and rates include a full breakfast. It's about a 10-minute drive east of Disneyland, near the train station and sports stadiums. Look for social hours Monday to Thursday with wine and snacks.

TOP FIVE THEME-PARK AREAS FOR YOUNG KIDS

Fantasyland (p224), Disneyland

Mickey's Toontown (p224), Disneyland

Critter Country (p225), Disneyland

Paradise Pier (p227), DCA

Cars Land (p227), DCA

Camelot Inn & Suites MOTEL $$
(Map p222; ☎714-635-7275, 800-828-4898; www.camelotanaheim.com; 1520 S Harbor Blvd; r $99-179, ste $190-269; P @ ☎ ≋) This five-story, 200-room motel with accents of English Tudor style has mini-fridges and microwaves in every room, plus on-site laundry, a pool and hot tub. You can walk to Disneyland in 10 minutes. The pool deck and some top-floor rooms have fireworks views. Parking is $9.

Carousel Inn & Suites MOTEL $$
(Map p222; ☎714-758-0444, 800-854-6767; www.carouselinnandsuites.com; 1530 S Harbor Blvd; r $89-149; P @ ☎ ≋) Just over the wall from Disneyland, this four-story motel makes an effort to look good, with upgraded furnishings, pillowtop mattresses, plantation shutters and flowerpots hanging from the exterior corridors' wrought-iron railings. The rooftop pool has great views of Disneyland's fireworks. Parking costs $10.

Park Vue Inn MOTEL $$
(Map p222; ☎714-772-3691, 800-334-7021; www.parkvueinn.com; 1570 S Harbor Blvd; r $105-163; P ❄ @ ☎ ≋) This two-story, 86-room motel gets rotating hordes of families, but well-scrubbed, contemporary-style rooms come with air-con, microwaves and minifridges, and downstairs there's an outdoor pool and hot tub. It's almost opposite Disneyland's main gate.

Eating

From stroll-and-eat Mickey-shaped pretzels ($4) and jumbo turkey legs ($10) to deluxe, gourmet dinners (sky's the limit), there's no shortage of eating options inside the Disney parks, though mostly pretty expensive and targeted to mainstream tastes. Phone **Disney Dining** (%714-781-3463) to make reservations up to 60 days in advance.

DON'T MISS

DCA SHOWS & PARADES

DCA's premier show is **World of Color** (Map p222), a dazzling nighttime display of lasers, lights and animation projected over Paradise Bay. It's so popular, you'll need a FASTPASS ticket. Otherwise, reserved seating (714-781-4400, per person $15) includes a picnic meal; make reservations up to 30 days in advance. Tip: if you're here in summer and have a park-hopper ticket, see World of Color first, then head over to Disneyland for the fireworks and to catch the later show or Fantasmic!

During the day, don't miss the **Pixar Play Parade**, led by hot-rodder Lightning McQueen from *Cars* and featuring energetic, even acrobatic appearances by characters from other popular animated movies like *Monsters, Inc*, *The Incredibles*, *Ratatouille*, *Finding Nemo* and *Toy Story*. Be prepared to get squirted by aliens wielding water hoses.

DCA's other live entertainment includes mini-musical extravaganzas like *Aladdin* and *Toy Story*, based on the movies. Check out what's playing at the **Hyperion Theater** (Map p222) in Hollywood Land. Arrive 30 to 60 minutes early to get good seats.

Outside the park, the offerings and price points expand considerably by driving just a couple of miles or so – to retro Old Towne Orange (p239) or the newly hipster Packing District (p236) on the other side of Anaheim. Ethnic enclaves include Little Saigon (p242) in Garden Grove and Westminster and Anaheim's own Little Arabia, about 2.2 miles west of Disneyland.

Disneyland Park

In the park, each 'land' has several places to eat, mostly fast-food stands and family-style restaurants. Almost all are overpriced compared to outside the park, jam-packed and carry just a few dishes whose quality rarely rises above average. Within the Disney Resort, restaurant hours vary seasonally and sometimes daily. Check http://disneyland.disney.go.com/dining for same-day hours.

Jolly Holiday Bakery & Cafe RESTAURANT, BAKERY **$**
(Map p222; Main Street, USA; mains $7-10; breakfast, lunch & dinner) At this Mary Poppins–themed restaurant, the Jolly Holiday combo (grilled cheese and tomato basil soup for $9) is a decent deal and very satisfying. The cafe does other sandwiches on the sophisticated side, like the mozzarella *caprese* or turkey on ciabatta. Great people watching from outdoor seating.

Café Orleans CAJUN, CREOLE **$$**
(Map p222; New Orleans Square; mains $16-20; seasonal hours vary;) The next best thing to Blue Bayou is this Southern-flavored restaurant, which is famous for its Monte Cristo sandwiches at lunch. Breakfast served seasonally.

Plaza Inn AMERICAN **$$**
(Map p222; Main Street, USA; mains $12-17, breakfast buffet adult/child 3-9yr $27/13; breakfast, lunch & dinner) Finger-lickin' good fried chicken platter and pot roast come with mashed potatoes, buttermilk biscuits and veggies at this 1950s original. There's a fun breakfast buffet with Disney characters. The rest of the day, if you can snag an outdoor table you'll also get great people-watching here, at the crossroads of Main Street, USA.

Carnation Cafe AMERICAN **$$**
(Map p222; Main Street, USA; mains $9-16; breakfast, lunch & dinner) Near the Disneyland entrance, this wood-built spot serves baked potato soup, meatloaf and gravy and fried chicken and Mickey-shaped breakfast waffles. Next door, the ice-cream parlor serves a dizzying selection of desserty decadence.

Blue Bayou SOUTHERN **$$$**
(Map p222; 714-781-3463; New Orleans Square; mains lunch $26-40, dinner $30-46; lunch & dinner) Surrounded by the 'bayou' inside the Pirates of the Caribbean attraction, this is the top choice for sit-down dining in Disneyland Park and is famous for its Creole and Cajun specialties at dinner. Order fresh-baked pecan pie topped by a piratey souvenir for dessert.

Disney California Adventure

Though you'll find easy, high-priced theme park food here too, DCA has stepped up the options recently.

★**Carthay Circle** AMERICAN **$$**
(Map p222; Buena Vista St; mains lunch $20-30, dinner $25-44; lunch & dinner) Decked out

like a Hollywood country club, new Carthay Circle is the best dining in either park, with steaks, seafood, pasta, smart service and a good wine list. Your table needs at least one order of fried biscuits, stuffed with white cheddar, bacon and jalapeño, and served with apricot honey butter. Inquire about special packages including dinner and the World of Color (p230) show.

Wine Country Terrace CALIFORNIAN $$
(Map p222; Golden State; mains $13-17; ⏲ lunch & dinner) If you can't quite swing the Napa Rose or Carthay Circle, this sunny Cal-Italian terrace restaurant is a fine backup. Fork into Italian pastas, salads or veggie paninis. Decent wine list.

Pacific Wharf Cafe AMERICAN $$
(Map p222; Golden State; mains $9-12; ⏲ breakfast, lunch & dinner) At least the hearty soups in sourdough bread bowls, farmers-market salads and deli sandwiches are pretty filling.

Downtown Disney & Disneyland Resort

Downtown Disney is often packed, but the restaurant selection is better than inside the parks.

Earl of Sandwich SANDWICHES $
(Map p222; ☎ 714-817-7476; Downtown Disney; mains $4-7; ⏲ 8am-11pm Sun-Thu, 8am-midnight Fri & Sat) This counter-service spot near the Disneyland Hotel serves grilled sandwiches that are both kid- and adult-friendly. The 'original 1762' is roast beef, cheddar and horseradish, or look for chipotle chicken with avocado or holiday turkey. There are also pizza, salad and breakfast options.

★**Napa Rose** CALIFORNIAN $$$
(Map p222; ☎ 714-300-7170; Grand Californian Hotel & Spa; mains $39-45, 4-course prix-fixe dinner from $90; ⏲ 5:30-10pm; 👪) Soaring windows, high-back Arts and Crafts–style chairs, leaded-glass windows and towering ceilings befit the Disneyland Resort's top-drawer restaurant. On the plate, seasonal 'California Wine Country' (read: NorCal) cuisine is as impeccably crafted as Sleeping Beauty Castle. Kids' menu available. Reservations essential. Enter the hotel from DCA or Downtown Disney.

Steakhouse 55 AMERICAN $$$
(Map p222; ☎ 714-781-3463; 1150 Magic Way, Disneyland Hotel; mains breakfast $8-12, dinner $30-40, 3-course prix-fixe menu $40; ⏲ breakfast & dinner) Nothing at Disneyland is exactly a secret, but this grown-up hideaway comes pretty darn close. Dry-rubbed, bone-in rib eye, Australian lobster tail, heirloom potatoes and green beans with applewood-smoked bacon uphold a respectable chophouse menu. Kids' menu available. Good wine list.

Catal Restaurant & Uva Bar MEDITERRANEAN $$$
(Map p222; ☎ 714-774-4442; www.patinagroup.com/catal; Downtown Disney; mains breakfast $10-15, dinner $24-41; ⏲ 8am-10pm; 👪) The chef cooks up a fusion of Californian and Mediterranean cuisines (squid-ink pasta with lobster, grilled ahi with curry sauce) at this airy two-story restaurant decorated in a sunny Mediterranean-Provençal style with exposed beams and lemon-colored walls. Sit on the balcony.

Anaheim

Most restaurants on the streets surrounding Disneyland are chains, albeit Anaheim GardenWalk (p233) has some upscale ones (California Pizza Kitchen, McCormick & Schmick's, Johnny Rocket's, etc). The mall may be a long walk from Disneyland with little ones, so take the ART shuttle (p236).

More adventurous palates can head further afield to Little Saigon or Little Arabia.

★**Olive Tree** MIDDLE EASTERN $$
(Map p220; ☎ 714-535-2878; 512 S Brookhurst St; mains $8-16; ⏲ 9am-9pm) In Little Arabia, this simple restaurant in a nondescript strip mall ringed by flags of Arab nations has earned accolades from local papers to *Saveur* magazine. You *could* get standards like falafel and kebabs, but daily specials are

> **TIRED TOOTSIES?**
>
> The miniature bio-diesel **Disneyland Railroad** chugs in a clockwise circle around Disneyland, stopping at Main Street, USA, New Orleans Square, Mickey's Toon Town and Tomorrowland, taking about 20 minutes to make a full loop. Between the Tomorrowland and Main Street, USA stations, look out for **dioramas** of the Grand Canyon and a Jurassic-style 'Primeval World.' From Tomorrowland, you can catch the zero-emissions monorail directly to Downtown Disney.

where it's at; Saturday's *kabseh* is righteous, fall-off-the-bone lamb shank over spiced rice with currants and onions.

Afterwards, stop for baklava at the bakery a few doors down.

Umami Burger HAMURGERS **$$**
(Map p220; ☎714-991-8626; www.umamiburger.com; 338 S Anaheim Blvd; mains $11-15; ⏰11am-11pm Sun-Thu, to midnight Fri & Sat) The Anaheim outpost of this LA-based mini-chain sets the right tone for the Packing District. Burgers span classic to truffled and the Hatch burger with roasted green chilies. Get 'em with deep-fried 'smushed' potatoes with house-made ketchup, and top it off with a salted chocolate ice cream sandwich. Good beer selection too.

The rusted license plates on the wall were discovered during excavations of this former Packard dealership.

Drinking & Nightlife

You can't buy alcohol in Disneyland, but you can at DCA, Downtown Disney and Disney's trio of resort hotels. Downtown Disney offers bars, live music, a 12-screen cinema and more.

★Trader Sam's Enchanted Tiki Lounge TIKI BAR
(Map p222; 1150 Magic Way, Disneyland Hotel) It's tiki to the max and good, clean fun inside this faux-grass shack in the Disneyland Hotel's courtyard. Look for strong, sweet cocktails like the Shrunken Zombie Head and Hippopotamai-tai served with ice cubes that light up. Order the right drink, and the walls might start moving. No, really.

Uva Bar WINE BAR
(Map p222; www.patinagroup.com; Downtown Disney) *Uva* is Italian for grape, and this bar resembling a Paris Metro station is Downtown Disney's best outdoor spot to tipple wine, nibble Cal-Mediterranean tapas and people-watch. There are 40 wines available by the glass. Come for happy hour.

ESPN Zone SPORTS BAR
(Map p222; www.espnzone.com; Downtown Disney) Show up early and score a personal leather recliner at this sports and drinking emporium with 175 TVs – flat-screens even hang above the men's-room urinals. Ball-park food and couch-potato classics make up an all-American menu. Families gravitate toward the virtual-reality and video-game arcade upstairs.

House of Blues CLUB
(Map p222; ☎714-778-2583; www.houseofblues.com; Downtown Disney) HOB occasionally gets some heavy-hitting rock, pop, jazz and blues concerts. Call or check online for showtimes and tickets. Make reservations for Sunday's fun gospel brunch. But come for the music, not the food.

Golden Vine Winery BAR
(Map p222; Disney California Adventure) Centrally located terrace is a great place for relaxing and regrouping in DCA. Nearby at Pacific Wharf, walk-up window **Rita's Margaritas** whips up frozen cocktails.

Napa Rose Lounge LOUNGE
(Map p222; Grand Californian Hotel & Spa) Raise a glass to Napa as you nosh on pizzettas, artisan cheese plates and Scharffen Berger chocolate truffle cake.

DISNEYLAND FIREWORKS, PARADES & SHOWS

The fireworks spectacular above Sleeping Beauty Castle, **Remember – Dreams Come True**, happens nightly around 9:25pm in summer. (In winter, artificial snow falls on Main Street, USA after the fireworks.) In **Mickey's Soundsational Parade**, floats glide down Main Street, USA with bands playing a variety of music from Latin to Bollywood, accompanying costumed characters.

At the **Princess Fantasy Faire** in Fantasyland, your little princesses and knights can join the Royal Court and meet some Disney princesses. Storytelling and coronation ceremonies happen throughout the day in summer. Younglings can learn to harness 'The Force' at **Jedi Training Academy** (Map p222), which accepts Padawans several times daily in peak season, at Tomorrowland Terrace.

The outdoor extravaganza on Disneyland's Rivers of America, **Fantasmic!**, may be the best show of all, with its full-size ships, lasers and pyrotechnics, pink elephants, princesses and an evil queen. Arrive early to scope a spot – the best are down front by the water – or reserve balcony seats in New Orleans Square. Book reserved seating (☎714-781-7469, adult/child $60/50) up to 30 days in advance.

Ralph Brennan's New Orleans Jazz Kitchen BAR
(Map p222; http://rbjazzkitchen.com; Downtown Disney) Hear live jazz combos on the weekends and piano weeknights at this resto-bar. Food quality is erratic.

Anaheim Brewery BEER
(Map p220; www.anaheimbrew.com; 336 S Anaheim Blvd; ⌚5-9pm Tue-Thu, 4-9pm Fri, 11am-9pm Sat, 11am-6pm Sun) Try the surprisingly good local brew at this simple tasting room in a renovated warehouse in the Packing District. Standouts include the Hefeweizen Red and Coast to Coast IPA with nice citrus notes. Six-glass tastings for $11.

☆ Entertainment

City National Grove of Anaheim CONCERT VENUE
(Map p220; ☎714-712-2700; www.thegroveofanaheim.com; 2200 E Katella Ave) At this indoor 5000-seat venue, headliners from the Magnetic Zeros to Last Comic Standing appear, plus 'locally grown' rock bands. Sightlines are great. Call or check online for showtimes and tickets. Parking is $10.

Honda Center STADIUM
(Map p220; ☎800-745-3000; www.hondacenter.com; 2695 E Katella Ave) The 2007 Stanley Cup–winning Anaheim Ducks play hockey from October to April at this indoor venue. Professional rodeo events, fight nights and megaconcerts round out the schedule. Tickets prices vary. Parking is $15 to $20.

Angel Stadium STADIUM
(Map p220; ☎714-940-2000, 888-796-4256; www.angelsbaseball.com; 2000 Gene Autry Way) The controversially (and oh-so-awkwardly) named Los Angeles Angels of Anaheim play major-league baseball here from May to October. Single-game tickets start at $6 for nosebleed sections. Parking is $10.

Anaheim GardenWalk CINEMA, PLAZA
(Map p222; www.anaheimgardenwalk.com; 321 W Katella Ave; ⌚11am-9pm) This dining, shopping and entertainment complex just east of Disneyland (take the ART shuttle; p236), has a family-friendly bowling alley, cineplex and adults-only wine bar.

Block at Orange CINEMA, PLAZA
(Map p220; ☎714-769-4001; www.simon.com; 20 City Blvd W, Orange; 📶) Another megamall with a cineplex, Dave & Buster's video game arcade, Vans skate park and cool Lucky Strike Lanes for a round of beers, bowling and billiards.

DON'T MISS

IS IT A SMALL WORLD AFTER ALL?

Pay attention to the cool optical illusion along Main Street, USA. As you look from the entrance up the street toward Sleeping Beauty Castle, everything seems far away and bigger-than-life. When you're at the castle looking back, everything seems closer and smaller – a technique known as forced perspective, a trick used on Hollywood sets where buildings are constructed at a decreasing scale to create an illusion of height or depth. Welcome to Disneyland.

Shopping

Disneyland Park & Disney California Adventure

Each 'land' has its own shopping, appropriate to its particular theme, whether the Old West, Route 66 or a seaside amusement park. The biggest theme-park stores – Disneyland's **Emporium** (Main Street, USA) and **Greetings from California** (DCA) have a mind-boggling variety of souvenirs, clothing and Disneyana, from T-shirts to mouse ears. Girls go wild at the **Bibbidi Bobbidi Boutique** (Map p222; ☎reservations 714-781-7895; Fantasyland), where princess makeovers – including hairstyle, makeup and gown – don't come cheap. For collectors, **Disney Gallery** (Main Street, USA) and **Off the Page** (DCA) sell high-end art and collectibles like original sketches and vintage reproduction prints.

You don't have to carry your purchases around all day; store them at the Newsstand (Main Street, USA), Star Trader (Tomorrowland), Pioneer Mercantile (Frontierland) or Engine Ear Toys (DCA). If you're staying at Disneyland, have packages sent directly to your hotel.

Downtown Disney

Downtown Disney is a triumph of marketing – once inside one of the shops here (not just Disney stuff either), it may be hard to extract yourself. Most shops here open and close with the parks.

Disney Vault 28 CLOTHING, GIFTS
(Map p222; Downtown Disney) From distressed T-shirts with edgy Cinderella prints to black

YOU SAY IT'S YOUR BIRTHDAY

If you're visiting on a special day and want to embrace the Disney experience whole-mouse, stop by Main Street, USA's City Hall to pick up some ornamental flair in the form of oversize buttons celebrating birthdays, anniversaries, 'Just Married', your first visit to Disneyland and more.

tank tops patterned with white skulls, the hipster inventory is discombobulating. They stock a few familiar brands like Harajuku Lovers and Betsey Johnson, but it's the Disney-only boutique lines – like Disney Couture, by top designers – that really intrigue.

Ridemakerz TOY CARS

(Map p222; Downtown Disney) Why should clothes hounds have all the fun? This shop lets you custom build your own toy racecar *(duuuuude!)*. Select a chassis, body, tires (monster tires, should you want them), remote control or not etc, and the staff will help you put it together.

D Street CLOTHING, GIFTS

(Map p222; Downtown Disney) Even wannabe gangstas, skate rats and surfers get their own store at Disney. If you've got tweens or teens, resistance is futile. Retro comic-book hero, Japanimation-style and Star Wars–inspired Ts and toys hang on the racks next to urbanized Western wear and rockabilly dresses.

World of Disney SOUVENIRS

(Map p222; Downtown Disney) Pirates and princesses are hot at this mini-metropolis of mouse-related merchandising. Don't miss the special room dedicated to Disney's villains – gotcha, Evil Queen! Grab last-minute must-haves here.

Information

Before you arrive, consult our Disneyland Trip Planner. For more help and up-to-date information about the parks, contact the **Disneyland Resort** (live assistance 714-781-7290, recorded info 714-781-4565; www.disneyland.com)

INTERNET ACCESS

There's no internet access inside the theme parks.

FedEx Office (714-703-2250; 700 W Convention Way, Anaheim Marriott; per min 40¢; 7am-10pm Mon-Fri, 9am-5pm Sat & Sun) Self-service online computer workstations.

INTERNET RESOURCES & MOBILE APPS

MousePlanet (www.mouseplanet.com) One-stop fansite for all things Disney, with news updates, podcasts, trip reports, reviews and discussion boards.

Lonely Planet (www.lonelyplanet.com/usa/california/disneyland-and-anaheim) For planning advice, author recommendations, traveler reviews and insider tips.

Theme Park Insider (www.themeparkinsider.com) Newsy blog, travel tips and user reviews of Disneyland rides, attractions and lodging.

ScreamScape (www.screamscape.com) Independent views on theme-park news, developments and rumors.

MouseWait (www.mousewait.com) This free iPhone app offers up-to-the-minute updates on ride wait times and what's happening in the parks.

Disneyland Explorer Free official Disney-released app for iPhone and iPad.

Disneyland Wait Times Free unofficial app for iPhone with details of expected waits at Disneyland and DCA attractions.

KENNELS

Disneyland Kennel Club (714-781-7290; per animal per day $20; 30min before park opening to 30min after park closing) Pets are not permitted in the parks or some hotels, but just outside the theme parks' main entrance, Disney offers indoor day-boarding (no overnights) for cats and dogs with proof of vaccinations.

LOCKERS

Self-service lockers with in-and-out privileges cost $7 to $15 per day. You'll find them on Main Street, USA (Disneyland), in Sunshine Plaza (DCA) and at the picnic area just outside the theme park's main entrance, near Downtown Disney.

LOST & FOUND

Lost and Found (714-817-2166) Look for the office steps just east of DCA's main entrance.

MEDICAL SERVICES

You'll find first-aid facilities at Disneyland (Main Street, USA), DCA (Pacific Wharf) and Downtown Disney (next to Ralph Brennan's Jazz Kitchen).

Anaheim Urgent Care (714-533-2273; 2146 E Lincoln Ave, Anaheim; 8am-8pm Mon-Fri, 10am-6pm Sat & Sun) Walk-in nonemergency medical clinic.

Western Medical Center (WMC; 714-533-6220; 1025 S Anaheim Blvd, Anaheim; 24hr) Hospital emergency room.

MONEY

Disneyland's City Hall offers foreign-currency exchange. In DCA, head to the guest relations lobby. Multiple ATMs are found in both theme parks and at Downtown Disney.

Travelex (☎714-502-0811; Downtown Disney; ⊙10am-4pm Mon-Fri) Also exchanges foreign currency.

POST

Holiday Station (Map p220; www.usps.com; 1180 W Ball Rd, Anaheim; ⊙9am-5pm Mon-Fri) Full-service post office.

SMOKING

Check theme-park maps for specially designated smoking areas, which are few and far between. At Downtown Disney, smoking is allowed outdoors.

STROLLERS & WHEELCHAIRS

Rental strollers and wheelchairs may be used in the theme parks, but not Downtown Disney. Strollers cost $15 per day. Nonmotorized wheelchairs rent for $12 per day; an Electronic Convenience Vehicle (ECV) costs $50. Rentals may be sold out during busy times, so it's better to bring your own.

TOURIST INFORMATION

For information or help inside the parks, just ask any cast member or visit Disneyland's City Hall (Map p222) or DCA's guest relations lobby (Map p222).

Anaheim/Orange County Visitor & Convention Bureau (Map p222; ☎855-405-5020; www.anaheimoc.org; Anaheim Convention Center) Offers information on countywide lodging, dining and transportation. Convention Center parking is $15.

Getting There & Away

AIR

Most international travelers arrive at Los Angeles International Airport (LAX) or San Diego (SAN), but for easy-in, easy-out domestic travel, nothing beats the easily navigated John Wayne Airport (p480) in Santa Ana, served by all major US airlines and Canada's WestJet. The airport is about 14 miles south of Disneyland, near the junction of Hwy 55 and I-405 (San Diego Fwy).

If you do arrive at LAX, it's probably not worth your time to change planes, as it's barely an hour by road. Super Shuttle (www.supershuttle.com) offers one-way fares of $16 per person from LAX to Disneyland area hotels.

BUS

Southern California Gray Line/Coach America (☎714-978-8855, 800-828-6699; www.graylineanaheim.com) runs Disneyland Resort Express buses from LAX and SNA to Disneyland-area hotels every 30 minutes to one hour from 7:30am until 10pm. Fares are $35/48 adult one-way/round trip from LAX, $20/35 from SNA. It's free for up to three children up to age 11. Reservations aren't required, except if you want to take advantage of money-saving family passes.

Greyhound (Map p220; ☎714-999-1256, 800-231-222; www.greyhound.com; 100 W Winston Rd, Anaheim) has several daily buses to/from Downtown LA ($12, 40 minutes) and San Diego ($18, 2¼ hours). The bus station is a half mile east of the Disneyland Resort, accessible via taxi or the ART shuttle.

The **Orange County Transportation Authority** (☎714-560-6282; www.octa.net; ride/day pass $2/5) operates buses serving towns throughout the county. Both types of tickets are sold on board (cash only, exact change).

CAR & MOTORCYCLE

Disneyland Resort is just off I-5 (Santa Ana Fwy), about 30 miles southeast of Downtown LA.

Arriving at Disneyland and DCA is like arriving at an airport. Giant, easy-to-read overhead signs indicate which ramps you need to take for the theme parks, hotels or Anaheim's streets.

TRAIN

All trains stop at the newly opened **Anaheim Regional Transit Intermodal Center** (ARTIC) next to Angel Stadium, a quick ART shuttle or taxi ride east of Disneyland. **Amtrak** (☎714-385-1448; www.amtrak.com; 2150 E Katella Ave) has almost a dozen daily trains to/from LA's Union Station ($15, 40 minutes) and San Diego ($28, two hours). Less frequent **Metrolink** (☎800-371-5465; www.metrolinktrains.com; 2150 E Katella Ave) commuter trains connect Anaheim to LA's Union Station ($9, 50 minutes), Orange ($5.25, five minutes), San Juan Capistrano ($8.75, 40 minutes) and San Clemente ($10, 50 minutes).

> **GET SMART**
>
> If you've got a smartphone, make sure you bring it with you to Disneyland fully charged (with an extra battery and a plastic bag to keep it dry on water rides). The fierce market for Disney-specific smartphone apps means that you can easily download all the details you need – restaurant menus, insider 'Hidden Mickey' tips, live webcams, park opening hours and show schedules and, most importantly, current wait times at rides and attractions – into your handheld mobile device. Some of the best apps are free, so check out app user reviews before spending any money.

WORTH A TRIP

ANAHEIM PACKING DISTRICT & CENTER STREET

With all the hype of the Mouse House, it's sometimes easy to forget that there's a whole other Anaheim outside the gates. New developments are changing that. Case in point: the **Anaheim Packing District** (Map p220; anaheimpackingdistrict.com; S Anaheim Bl), around a long-shuttered 1925 car dealership and 1919 orange-packing house a couple miles from Disneyland, near the city's actual downtown. It relaunched in 2013–14 with chic new restaurants like Umami Burger (p232), the Anaheim Brewery (p233), an evolving collection of shops and a park for events.

About 0.3 miles away is **Center Street** (Map p220; www.centerstreetanaheim.com; W Center St), a quietly splashy redeveloped neighborhood with an ice rink designed by starchitect Frank Gehry and a couple of blocks packed with hipster-friendly shops like the **Good** (Map p220; 161 W Center St Promenade), for men's clothing, the **Look** (Map p220; 201 Center St Promenade), for women's, **Barbeer** (Map p220; 165 Center St Promenade), where you can get a shave, haircut and brewski, and the writerly **Ink & Bean** (Map p220; www.inkandbeancoffee.com; 115 W Center St Promenade) coffee saloon. Dining offerings include **118 Degrees** (Map p220; 185 W Center St;), dedicated to the raw diet and **Good Food**, a mini food court where you might indulge in healthy junk at **Healthy Junk** (Map p220; www.healthyjunk.com; 201 Center St Promenade).

Getting Around

CAR & MOTORCYCLE

All-day parking costs $16 ($20 for oversize vehicles). Enter the 'Mickey & Friends' parking structure from southbound Disneyland Dr, off Ball Rd. Walk outside and follow the signs to board the free tram to Downtown Disney. The parking garage opens one hour before the parks do.

Downtown Disney parking is reserved for diners, shoppers and movie-goers and the first three hours are free. Downtown Disney also offers drive-up valet parking in the evenings for an additional $6 plus tip (cash only).

SHUTTLE

Anaheim Resort Transportation (ART; 714-563-5287; www.rideart.org; single ride $3, day pass adult/child $5/2) operates some 20 shuttle routes between Disneyland and area hotels, convention centers, malls, stadiums and the transit center, saving traffic jams and parking headaches. Shuttles typically start running an hour before Disneyland opens, operating from 7am to midnight daily during summer. Departures are typically two to three times per hour, depending on the route. Purchase single or multiday ART passes at kiosks near ART shuttle stops or online in advance.

Many hotels and motels offer their own free shuttles to Disneyland and other area attractions; ask when booking.

TRAM & MONORAIL

With an admission ticket to Disneyland, you can ride the monorail between Tomorrowland and the far end of Downtown Disney, near the Disneyland Hotel. It sure beats walking both ways along crowded Downtown Disney.

AROUND DISNEYLAND

Disneyland's not the only game in town. Within 10 easy miles of the Mouse House you'll find a big scoopful of sights and attractions worth a visit in their own right. Anaheim's streets are laid out in an easy-to-navigate grid. So get out, explore, expand your horizons. It *is* a small world, after all.

Knott's Berry Farm

They bring 'em in by the busload to America's oldest **theme park** (Map p220; 714-220-5200; www.knotts.com; 8039 Beach Blvd, Buena Park; adult/child $62/33; from 10am, closing time varies 6-11pm;). Knott's is smaller and less frenetic than Disneyland, but it can be more fun, especially for thrill-seeking teens, roller-coaster fanatics and younger kids who love the *Peanuts* gang.

The park opened in 1932, when Walter Knott's boysenberries (a blackberry-raspberry hybrid) and his wife Cordelia's fried-chicken dinners attracted crowds of local farmhands. Mr Knott built an imitation ghost town to keep them entertained, and eventually hired local carnival rides and charged admission. Mrs Knott kept frying the chicken, but the rides and Old West buildings became the main attraction.

Today Knott's keeps the Old West theme alive and thriving with a variety of shows and demonstrations at **Ghost Town**, but it's the thrill rides that draw the big crowds. The **Sierra Sidewinder** roller coaster rips through banks and turns while rotating on its axis. Nearby, the suspended, inverted **Silver Bullet** screams through a corkscrew, a double spiral and an outside loop. From the ground, look up to see the dirty socks and bare feet of suspended riders who've removed their shoes just for fun. **Xcelerator** is a 1950s-themed roller coaster that blasts you, as if from a cannon, from 0mph to 82mph in under 2½ seconds; there's a hair-raising twist at the top. For tamer rides, **Camp Snoopy** is a kiddy wonderland populated by the *Peanuts* characters.

If it's too darn hot, the park's **Perilous Plunge** whooshes at 75mph down a 75-degree angled water chute that's almost as tall as Niagara Falls.

Opening hours vary seasonally, so call ahead, and check the website for discounts and deals: online savings can be substantial (eg buying print-at-home tickets). Manual/motorized wheelchair rentals cost $15/45 per day. Minimum height restrictions apply for many rides and attractions, so check the theme park's website in advance to avoid disappointment.

Next door to Knott's Berry Farm is the affiliated water park **Soak City OC** (Map p220; ☎714-220-5200; www.soakcityoc.com; 8039 Beach Blvd, Buena Park; adult/child 3-11yr $36/26; ⊙10am-5pm, 6pm or 7pm mid-May–mid-Sep), boasting a 750,000-gallon wave pool and dozens of high-speed slides, tubes and flumes. You must have a bathing suit without rivets or metal pieces to go on some slides. Bring a beach towel and a change of dry clothes.

The park is open from Memorial Day (end May) to Labor Day (start of September), plus additional May and September weekends. Look online for often significant discounts off the full admission. Rental lockers ($7 to $22 per day) and private cabanas (from $99) are available.

Sleeping & Eating

Conveniently adjacent to the theme park, **Knott's Berry Farm Resort Hotel** (Map p220; ☎714-995-1111, 866-752-2444; www.knottshotel.com; 7675 Crescent Ave, Buena Park; r $79-169; @🛜🏊) is a contemporary high-rise with an outdoor pool, fitness center and tennis and basketball courts. Rooms are mostly bland, but for young Charlie Brown fans, ask about Camp Snoopy rooms, where kids will be treated to *Peanuts*-themed decor (dog house headboards? Awesome!), telephone bedtime stories and a goodnight 'tuck-in' visit from Snoopy himself. Shuttle service to Disneyland is complimentary. Overnight parking costs $7.

You're only allowed to bring small bottles of water and sports drinks, plus soft-sided shoulder coolers with baby food, into the theme park. The park has plenty of carnival-quality fast food, but the classic meal is the button-busting fried chicken and mashed potato dinner at the nuthin'-fancy **Mrs Knott's Chicken Dinner Restaurant** (☎714-220-5055; 8039 Beach Blvd, Buena Park; mains $7-17, chicken dinner $17; ⊙8am-8:30pm Mon-Thu, 7am-9pm Fri, 7am-9:30pm Sat, 7am-8:30pm Sun). In a hurry? Grab a bucket from **Chicken-to-Go** (meals/buckets from $9/29) and slices of pie from **Knott's Berry Farm Bakery** (pie slice $4). All three eateries are open daily (hours vary) in the California Marketplace, a shopping center outside the park's main gate.

Getting There & Away

Knott's Berry Farm is about 6 miles northwest of Disneyland, off the I-5 Fwy or Hwy 91 (Artesia Fwy). All-day parking costs $12. There's free three-hour parking for California Marketplace visitors only.

Medieval Times Dinner & Tournament

Hear ye, hear ye! All those who have sired knights-to-be and future princesses, gather ye clans and proceed forthwith to **Medieval Times** (Map p220; ☎714-523-1100, 866-543-9637; www.medievaltimes.com; 7662 Beach Blvd, Buena Park; adult/under 12yr $60/37; 👪) for an evening-long medieval feast and performance. Yep, it's completely over-the-top but in a harmless, party-like-it's-1099 sort of way. Dinner guests root for various knights as they joust, fence and show off

DON'T MISS

KNOTT'S SCARY FARM

Every year, Knott's Berry Farm puts on SoCal's scariest Halloween party. On select days from late September through October 31, the park closes and reopens at night as **Knott's Scary Farm**. Horror-minded thrills include a dozen creepy mazes, monster-themed shows and a thousand employees trying to scare the bejeezus out of you in 'scare zones'. Boo!

their horsemanship on real Andalusian horses to protect the honor of the kingdom and the beautiful princess. The food is all right – roast chicken and spare ribs that you eat with your hands (vegetarian options available) – but the show's the thing. Make reservations, show up 90 minutes early (seating is not guaranteed, even with reservations) and accept that you'll be wearing a cardboard crown for the evening. The mock castle is about a half mile north of Knott's Berry Farm. Buy discounted tickets online.

Discovery Science Center

Follow the giant 10-story cube – balanced on one of its points – to the doors of the best educational kiddie attraction in town, the **Discovery Science Center** (Map p220; ☎714-542-2823; www.discoverycube.org; 2500 N Main St, Santa Ana; adult/child 3-14yr & senior $16/13, 4D movies $2 extra; ⏰10am-5pm; 👪), about 5 miles southeast of Disneyland via the I-5. More than 100 interactive displays await in exhibit areas with names such as Discovery Theater (playing 4-D movies), Dino Quest and more. Step into the eye of a hurricane – your hair will get mussed – or grab a seat in the Shake Shack to virtually experience a magnitude 6.4 quake. Warning: parents may be tempted to nudge their kids aside for a turn at many of the interactive displays. Special science-themed exhibits, like 'Grossology' or adventures in archaeology inspired by Indiana Jones, are fun too.

Bowers Museum & Kidseum

The should-be-better-known **Bowers Museum** (Map p220; ☎714-567-3600, 877-250-8999; www.bowers.org; 2002 N Main St, Santa Ana; adult/child 6-17yr & senior $13/10 Tue-Fri, $15/12 Sat & Sun, special-exhibit surcharge varies; ⏰10am-4pm Tue-Sun) explodes on to the scene every year or two with remarkable exhibits that remind LA-centric museum-goers that the Bowers is a power player on the local and national scenes too. Permanent exhibits are impressive too, with a rich collection of pre-Columbian, African, Oceanic and Native American art. Docent-guided gallery tours are given every afternoon. For lunch, the atmospheric cafe **Tangata** (Map p220; mains $10-20; ⏰11am-3pm Tue-Sun) serves fresh soups, salads and sandwiches, as well as California wines by the glass.

General admission tickets to the Bowers Museum include entry to the family-focused **Kidseum** (Map p220; ☎714-480-1520; 1802 N Main St, Santa Ana; admission $3, child under 3yr free; ⏰10am-3pm Tue-Fri, 11am-3pm Sat & Sun; 👪), two blocks further south. Hands-on arts and cultural exhibits will keep the preschool and early-elementary school set entertained.

The museums are 6 miles southeast of Disneyland, off I-5 in Santa Ana. Admission is free on the first Sunday of each month. Public parking in nearby lots costs $2.

DON'T MISS

CLUB MUD

Nicknamed 'Club Mud' for its famous red-clay mineral mud bath, **Glen Ivy Hot Springs** (☎888-453-6489; www.glenivy.com; 25000 Glen Ivy Rd, Corona; admission Mon-Thu $46, Fri-Sun & holidays $64; ⏰9:30am-5pm, to 6pm May-Oct) has no fewer than 19 pools and spas filled with naturally heated mineral water, surrounded by acres of bougainvillea blooms, eucalyptus and palm trees.

You can wallow in the water, lounge in the saunas or steam rooms, take an aqua-aerobics class, swim laps in a swimming pool or treat yourself to a massage (for an extra fee). The minimum age for entry is 16. It gets busy in summer, so arrive early if you want a chair.

For lunch, try a fresh salad, panini or stuffed calzone at the spa's **Café Solé** (mains $7-14) or head back toward the freeway to stock up on fresh fruits, artisan cheeses and old-fashioned candy at **Tom's Market** (☎951-277-4422; www.tomsfarms.com; 23900 Temescal Canyon Rd, Corona), which also serves tasty tacos at **Senor Tom's** (mains $6-18).

Glen Ivy is in Corona, in Riverside County just east of Orange County. To get here, exit off I-15 at Temescal Canyon Rd, turn right on Trilogy Rd and left on Warm Springs Rd to Glen Ivy Rd, then take another right and go straight to the end. If traffic isn't too bad, it's about a 45-minute drive from Old Towne Orange.

Old Towne Orange

Settlers began arriving en masse in Orange County after the Civil War, responding to the lure of cheap land and fertile fields. Rumor had it that almost anything could be grown in the rich soil, and many crops (such as oranges, apricots, corn, lemons, pumpkins, peaches and walnuts) did indeed thrive despite occasional irrigation and drought issues. Today the city of Orange, 7 miles southeast of Disneyland, retains its charming historical center. It was originally laid out by Alfred Chapman and Andrew Glassell, who in 1869 received the 1-sq-mile piece of real estate in lieu of legal fees. It became California's only city laid out around a central plaza, making it pleasantly walkable, even in the 21st century. Nowadays it's still where locals go, and visitors will find it well worth the detour for antiques and vintage clothing shops, smart restaurants and pure SoCal nostalgia.

Eating

Stroll around Old Towne Orange's traffic circle, then north along Glassell St to take your pick of more than a dozen cafes, restaurants, wine bars and brewpubs.

★Filling Station DINER $

(www.fillingstationcafe.com; 201 N Glassell St; mains $7-14; 6:30am-9pm, to 10pm Fri & Sat;) For breakfast, nothing beats this former vintage gas station now serving haute pancakes, chorizo eggs, Cobb salads and patty melts instead of unleaded. Check out the vintage SoCal photographs on the walls. Sit on the outdoor patio (which is dog-friendly), or grab a shiny counter stool or booth inside. Breakfast is served all day, lunch from 11am.

Front Porch Pops FROZEN DESSERTS $

(714-614-0857; www.frontporchpops.com; 120 E Chapman Ave; pops $3; noon-6pm Tue-Thu, to 7pm Fri & Sat, to 5pm Sum) Attached to Watson Drug is this adorable storefront selling outre flavors of ice pops and ice-cream bars. Think cranberry orange meringue to dark-chocolate sea salt.

Citrus City Grille BISTRO $

(714-639-9600; www.citruscitygrille.com; 122 N Glassell St; mains lunch $10-18, dinner $11-35; 11am-10pm Mon-Thu, to 11pm Fri & Sat, 9:30am-10pm Sun) Sophisticated yet casual Cal-American bistro cooking creative modern classics like wild-mushroom meatloaf, bacon-wrapped blue cheese dates and Chilean sea bass with asparagus risotto. House-made rosemary bread, yum. Famous for brunch.

Rutabegorz CALIFORNIAN $$

(www.rutabegorz.com/orange; 264 N Glassell St; mains $7-12; 10:30am-9pm Mon-Sat;) Known by locals as just 'Ruta's,' this flowering cottage north of the plaza puts a healthy spin on breakfast or lunch. Cal-Mexican, vegetarian and Middle Eastern snacks all jostle on the tables alongside comfort-food sandwiches, wraps, salads, soups and fruit smoothies. Kids' menu available.

Watson Drug DINER $$

(www.watsonsdrugs.com; 116 E Chapman Ave; mains $6-15; 7am-9pm Mon-Sat, 8am-6pm Sun) Old-fashioned soda-fountain treats such as malts, milkshakes and sundaes, as well as burgers and all-day breakfast burritos, set inside an 1899 pharmacy with vintage lunch counter.

Felix Continental Cafe LATIN AMERICAN $$$

(714-633-5842; www.felixcontinentalcafe.com; 36 Plaza Sq; mains $8-17; 11am-10pm Mon-Fri, 8am-10pm Sat & Sun) Longtime downtown favorite serves spiced-just-right Caribbean, Cuban and Spanish dishes, most accompanied by a hefty serving of plantains, black beans and rice. Paella is the house specialty, and the roast pork is popular too. Scope out a patio table if you can. Lunch is served until 5pm.

Shopping

Shops line up primarily north and south but also east and west of Old Towne's **plaza** (cnr Chapman Ave & Glassell St), where you can find the OC's most concentrated collection of antiques, collectibles, and vintage and consignment shops. It's fun to browse, but real bargains are rare and unscrupulous dealers may try to pass off fakes as authentic.

Woody's Antiques ANTIQUES

(173 N Glassell St) Unlike stuffier antiques minimalls, indie Woody's Antiques feels like walking on to a *Mad Men* set, with mid-century modern and art-deco furnishings and accent pieces galore.

Elsewhere Vintage VINTAGE CLOTHING

(www.elsewherevintage.com; 131 W Chapman Ave) A hipsters' love affair, this store hangs sundresses next to hats, leather handbags and fabulous costume jewelry.

Joy Ride VINTAGE CLOTHING
(133 W Chapman Ave) Elsewhere Vintage's brother shop, Joy Ride, does the same job for men's clothing: 1950s bowling shirts to immaculately maintained wool blazers.

Dragonfly Shops & Gardens GIFTS
(www.dragonflyshopsandgardens.com; 260 N Glassell St) Whimsical Dragonfly Shops & Gardens sells native California plants, garden-minded gifts and beaded jewelry inside a white-picketed cottage.

Getting There & Away

The drive from Anaheim takes under 20 minutes: take I-5 south to Hwy 22 east, then drive north on Grand Ave, which becomes Glassell St, for just over a mile. Both **Amtrak** (800-872-7245; www.amtrak.com) and **Metrolink** (800-371-5465; www.metrolinktrains.com) commuter trains stop at Orange's **train station** (191 N Atchison St), a few blocks west of the plaza.

Christ Cathedral

About 3 miles southeast of Disneyland and currently under renovation, this wondrous glass **cathedral** (Map p220; www.christcathedralcalifornia.org; 12141 Lewis St, Garden Grove) was built in the shape of a four-pointed star and boasts 10,661 windows, seating capacity for 3000 and an organ with 16,000 pipes. Originally known as Crystal Cathedral, it was constructed in 1981 by 20th-century architectural great Philip Johnson for the televangelist Robert Schuller, but after Schuller's Crystal Cathedral Ministries went bankrupt, the building was bought by the Roman Catholic Diocese of Orange. Expected completion: 2016.

Richard Nixon Library & Museum

About 10 miles northeast of Anaheim, the **Richard Nixon Presidential Library & Museum** (714-993-5075; www.nixonfoundation.org; 18001 Yorba Linda Blvd, Yorba Linda; adult/child 7-11yr/student/senior $12/5/7/8.50; 10am-5pm Mon-Sat, 11am-5pm Sun) offers a fascinating walk though America's modern history and that of this controversial native son of Orange County. Noteworthy exhibits include excerpts from the Nixon and Kennedy debates, a full-size replica of the White House's East Room, audiotapes of conversations with Apollo 11 astronauts while on the moon and access to the ex-presidential helicopter, complete with wet bar and ashtrays.

That said, it's the exhibits about Watergate, the infamous scandal that ultimately brought down Nixon's administration, that rightfully garner the most attention. The museum's original Watergate exhibit called it a 'coup' instigated by Nixon's rivals and provided favorably edited White House tapes. That changed when the library was transferred to federal control in 2007, with oversight by the National Archives. The old exhibit was completely torn out, and now the story unfolds from many perspectives, like a spy thriller. It was a bold move, considering that 'Tricky Dick' and First Lady Pat Nixon lie buried just outside.

To get here, take Hwy 57 north and exit east on Yorba Linda Blvd, then continue straight and follow the signs.

ORANGE COUNTY BEACHES

It's true you'll find gorgeous sunsets, prime surfing and just-off-the-boat seafood when traveling the OC's sun-kissed coast. But it's also the unexpected, serendipitous discoveries you'll remember long after you've left this blissful 42 miles of surf and sand behind. Whether you're learning to surf the waves in Seal Beach, playing Frisbee with your pooch in the surf at Huntington Dog Beach, piloting your own boat around Newport Harbor, wandering around eclectic art displays on a bluff-top trail in Laguna Beach, or spotting whales on a cruise out of yacht-filled Dana Point harbor – you'll discover that each beach town has its own brand of quirky charm.

Your mission, should you choose to accept it, is to find out which beach town suits your personality best. Starting near the LA County line, Seal Beach is the OC's northernmost beach town. From there, you can crawl along Route 1, aka the Pacific Coast Hwy (PCH), south along the ocean for more than 40 miles, passing through Sunset Beach, Huntington Beach, Newport Beach, Laguna Beach, Dana Point and San Clemente just before reaching San Diego County. The drive takes at least an hour, but with bumper-to-bumper beachfront traffic, especially on summer weekends, expect it to take two or three times that long. But don't worry: it's almost always worth it.

Seal Beach

POP 24,664

In the SoCal beauty pageant for pint-size beach towns, the first beach town in from LA County enjoys an unfair advantage over the competition: 1.5 miles of pristine beach sparkling like a crown. And that's without mentioning three-block Main St, a stoplight-free zone with mom-and-pop restaurants and indie shops that are low on 'tude and high on charisma. Seal Beach's lasting small-town allure may owe a debt to Leisure World ('Seizure World' to the non-PC), a sprawling retirement community looming north of town, and the huge US Naval Weapons Station (look for grass-covered bunkers) crouching to the east. Thoughts of shuffleboard and apocalypse aside, Seal Beach is one of the last great California beach towns and a refreshing alternative to the more crowded coast further south.

Sights & Activities

In the morning or afternoon, amble **Main Street** and check out the laid-back local scene – barefoot surfers trotting toward the beach, friendly shopkeepers opening their doors and silver-haired foxes scoping the way-too-young beach bunnies. Where Main St ends, walk out onto **Seal Beach Pier**, extending 1865ft over the ocean. The 1906 original fell victim to winter storms in the 1930s and has since been rebuilt three times with a wooden boardwalk. It's splintery in places, so wear shoes (no heels!). Snap a picture of the playful bronze seal standing guard at the pier's east entrance – he may be the only one you see.

On the **beach**, which faces south here, families spread out on blankets, build sand castles and play in the water. Though there's a hideous oil derrick just offshore, if you put on dark sunglasses and focus on what's immediately in front of you, it's lovely. The gentle waves make it a great place to learn to surf. Newbies should stick close to the pier. Surfers and boogie boarders are segregated; read the signs or ask a lifeguard. For surf conditions, look for the sign on the sand between the parking lots. The ocean here is also popular with stingrays, attracted to the warm water flowing in with the San Gabriel River from the north.

M&M Surfing School SURFING
(☎714-846-7873; www.surfingschool.com; 802 Ocean Ave; 3hr group lesson from $72, wetsuit/surfboard rental $15/25;) Offers five-day surf intensives, or three-hour group lessons which include surfboard and wet suit rental. Look for their van in the parking lot just north of the pier, off Ocean Ave at 8th St.

Sleeping

There are no budget accommodations in Seal Beach. Either head inland or south along the Pacific Coast Hwy.

Pacific Inn MOTEL $$
(☎562-493-7501, 866-466-0300; www.pacificinn-sb.com; 600 Marina Dr; r $150-180;) The only motel that's within walking distance of Main St and the beach has recently renovated rooms with extras such as down comforters and comfy mattresses. We don't love the open garage on the ground floor, but a sunny central pool and hot tub, a workout room, free wi-fi and complimentary guest shuttle around town make up for that. Bicycle rentals available. Pet fee $50.

Eating

Crema Café BAKERY, CAFE $
(☎562-493-2501; cremacafe.com; 322 Main St; mains $5-13; 6:30am-3pm Mon-Fri, 7am-4pm Sat & Sun) Service can be harried at this breezy, open-air cafe, but all is forgiven after a bite of their 'simple' French crepe covered with cinnamon sugar, whipped cream and caramel sauce. Add strawberries and bananas for an extra splash of flavor. In a hurry? Made-from-scratch pastries and muffins are fab, as are garden-fresh salads and toasted panini sandwiches.

Nick's Deli DELI $
(223 Main St; mains $5-8; 7am-7pm Mon-Fri, to 4pm Sat & Sun) Don't be fooled by the extensive hand-scrawled menu hanging over the counter at Nick's, a local joint where traditional deli fare is served alongside Mexican

CHEAP(ER) SLEEPS

In summer the OC's beach accommodations get booked out far in advance, room rates rise, and some places require minimum two- or three-night stays. You can often save money by staying multiple nights in one beach town and just taking day trips to the others. Otherwise, look inland to chain motels and hotels closer to I-405 and I-5 Fwys – for example, in Costa Mesa, Santa Ana or Irvine.

specialties. The crowds flock here for one thing: the mad breakfast tortilla stuffed with scrambled eggs, chorizo, bacon, potatoes and cheese – basically, a heart attack on a plate. Ask for it toasted.

Beachwood BBQ BARBECUE **$$**
(☎562-493-4500; www.beachwoodbbq.com; 131 1/2 Main St; mains $9-20; ⊙11:30am-11pm Tue-Sun) Downtown's barbecue hut ropes in regulars with fried pickles, buffalo sloppy joe sandwiches, applewood-smoked beef brisket with blue-cheese grits on the side, and a cool selection of microbrews (check out the website's 'Hop Cam'). For beach picnics, order takeout.

★ **Walt's Wharf** SEAFOOD, STEAKHOUSE **$$$**
(☎562-598-4433; www.waltswharf.com; 201 Main St; mains lunch $11-23, dinner $20-45; ⊙11am-3:30pm & 4-9pm) Everybody's favorite for fresh fish (some drive in from LA), Walt's packs them in on weekends. You can't make reservations for dinner (though they're accepted for lunch), but it's worth the wait for the oak-fire-grilled seafood and steaks in the many-windowed ground floor or upstairs in captain's chairs. Otherwise, eat at the bar.

Don't be overwhelmed by the long menu or the huge selection of wines by the glass – knowledgeable waitstaff are happy to share their expertise.

Mahé SUSHI, FUSION **$$$**
(☎562-431-3022; www.eatatmahe.com; 1400 Pacific Coast Hwy; mains lunch $13-16, dinner $19-39; ⊙11:30am-9:30pm Mon & Tue, to 10pm Wed-Sat, to 9pm Sun, bar to 1am) Raw-fish fans gather barside at this surfboard-chic sushi bar with live bands some nights. Baked scallop parmesan, albacore jalapeño sushi and sliders of Kobe beef, short ribs and mahi-mahi all hang out on the Cal-Japanese menu. A new lunch menu adds sandwiches with a similar fusion twist.

Drinking & Nightlife

Bogart's Coffee House CAFE
(www.bogartscoffee.com; 905 Ocean Ave; ⊙6am-9pm Mon-Thu, to 10pm Fri, 7am-10pm Sat, 7am-9pm Sun; 📶) Sip espresso on the leopard-print sofa and play Scrabble by the beach view as you watch the surf roll in. Bogart's sometimes hosts live music, psychic readings, book clubs and morning meditations by the sea.

WORTH A TRIP

LITTLE SAIGON

Ready for a break from big-eared mice and boysenberry pie? Head to Little Saigon in suburban Westminster, about 7 miles southwest of Anaheim. The strip-mall neighborhood lies south of Hwy 22 (Garden Grove Fwy) and east of the I-405 (San Diego Fwy). Vietnamese immigrants began arriving here after the end of the Vietnam War in the early 1970s, carving out their own vibrant commercial district, starting around the intersection of Bolsa Ave and Brookhurst St. A short drive further west takes you to the **Asian Garden Mall** (9200 Bolsa Ave; 📶), a behemoth of a structure packed with scores of food shops, boutiques, herbalists, silver jewelers and *anime*-inspired clothing and goods.

The best reason to visit Little Saigon is the food. Newbies can start at the mall's **Lee's Sandwiches** (www.leessandwiches.com; 9200 Bolsa Ave, Suite 305; sandwiches from $4; ⊙8am-7pm; 📶) or just west of the mall at **Ba Le** (9152 Bolsa Ave; sandwiches from $3; ⊙6am-6pm Mon-Sat, 7am-6pm Sun), both fast-growing chains serving budget-friendly Vietnamese sandwiches on French baguette rolls. The traditional toppings on these belly-fillers provide a delish, not-too-spicy kick – try the pork. Another great, inexpensive casual eatery at the Asian Garden Mall is **Pho 79** (9200 Bolsa Ave, Suite 117; mains from $6; ⊙8am-7:30pm), which dishes up a variety of noodle and vegetable dishes. The *pho ga* (chicken noodle soup) has a hearty broth.

For a real treat visit **Brodard** (☎714-530-1744; www.brodard.net; 9892 Westminster Ave; mains $5-14; ⊙8am-9pm Wed-Mon), known for its *nem nuong cuon* – rice-paper spring rolls wrapped tightly around Spam-like grilled pork patties and served with a tangy sauce. It's oddly addictive.

Cheat sheet: *pho* is soup, *ga* is chicken, *tom* is shrimp and *bo* is beef. Enjoy.

Wait, you're vegetarian? **Thien Dang** (☎714-531-1888; 13253 Brookhurst St, Garden Grove; mains $6-7; ⊙7am-7pm Fri-Wed) makes fresh salads, noodle soups, rice bowls, clay pots and more with vegan mock meats like seitan. Although service sure ain't flowery and the surroundings are kinda drab, the savory flavors are right on.

Entertainment

Jazz, folk and bluegrass bands play by the pier at the foot of Main St from 6pm to 8pm every Wednesday during July and August for the annual **Summer Concerts in the Park**.

Shopping

Be sure to walk the full three blocks of Main St and browse the eclectic shops.

Harbour Surfboards OUTDOORS
(www.harboursurfboards.com; 329 Main St) It's not just about computer-designed boards, but also the surf-and-skate lifestyle, man. Eavesdrop on local surfers talking about their wax as you pillage the racks of hoodies, wet suits, beach Ts and beanie hats. Across the street, **Alternative Surf** (330 Main St) is bodyboarding central.

Endless Summer CLOTHING
(124 Main St) Teenie Wahine, Roxy and Billabong jostle for attention at this bustling store for girly tweens to college-age beach babes. It's packed to the rafters with bikinis, beach bags, shades and loads more.

Up, Up & Away GIFTS
(http://upupandawaykites.com; 139 1/2 Main St) In addition to kites in every color of the rainbow, you'll find tons of decorative flags. Lighthouses, sailboats, frogs wearing sunglasses – if you want it waving in front of your house, there's a flag for it. Badass beach kites are at the back.

Knock Knock Toy Store TOYS
(www.knockknocktoystore.com; 219 1/2 Main St) Thoughtfully chosen, fun and educational toys line the shelves here, from name brands to quirky one-off products like wind-up space robots.

Information

Mary Wilson Library (www.ocpl.org; 707 Electric Ave; ⏲noon-8pm Mon & Tue, 10am-6pm Wed & Thu, 10am-5pm Sat) Free one-hour walk-in guest internet access.

Post Office (221 Main St; ⏲9am-5pm Mon-Fri) Three blocks inland from the beach.

Getting There & Around

OCTA (☎714-560-6282; www.octa.net) bus 1 connects Seal Beach with the OC's other beach towns and LA's Long Beach every hour; the one-way fare is $2 (exact change).

There's two-hour free parking along Main St between downtown Seal Beach and the pier, but it's difficult to find a spot in summer. Public parking lots by the pier cost $3 per two hours, $6 all day. Free parking along residential side streets is subject to posted restrictions.

Sunset Beach

A 1-mile strip of coastal real estate south of genteelly retro Seal Beach, Sunset Beach is actually part of Huntington Beach but doesn't feel like it, or the rest of the OC for that matter. With a high concentration of dive bars, ratty motels and beach bum 'tude, it's a great place to surf, kayak and drink, but you might not want to, um, live here.

Activities

Kayak the calm waters of **Huntington Harbor** for an up-close look at ritzy homes and tricked-out yachts.

OEX Sunset Beach SURFING
(☎562-592-0800; www.oexsunsetbeach.com; 16910 Pacific Coast Hwy) Rents kayaks (single/double $15/25 for two hours) and stand-up paddle (SUP) surfboard sets (per hour/half day $15/35) and offers lessons and tours.

Bruce Jones Surfboards SURFING
(☎562-592-2314; www.brucejones.com; 16927 Pacific Coast Hwy) Surfers can rent hard and soft boards here from $20 per half day (wet suit $10 to $15).

Katin Surf Shop SURF GEAR
(☎562-592-2052; www.katinsurf.com; 16250 Pacific Coast Hwy) A local icon since 1959, Katin Surf Shop is known for their handmade canvas board shorts, but nowadays they sell all kinds of surfwear, swimsuits and beach gear.

Sleeping & Eating

Best Western Harbour Inn & Suites MOTEL $$
(☎562-592-4770, 800-546-4770; www.bestwestern.com; 16912 Pacific Coast Hwy; r $139-199; P⊖❄@📶) This reliable roadside chain boasts a workout room. Spacious, spic-and-span rooms have a dash of tropical flair, some with lime-green accent walls and aloha-print comforter covers. No pool, but the ocean's *right there*.

★**Harbor House Café** AMERICAN $$
(www.harborhousecafe.com; 16341 Pacific Coast Hwy; mains $6-20; ⏲24hr; 👪) High-school skaters, 30-something beach bums and old-timers mix easily under ramshackle

walls slathered with movie posters at this classic neon-lit roadside diner from 1939. The menu is long, portions huge and waitstaff downright friendly. Breakfast is served around the clock, but cheese fries are your best bet after midnight.

Romano Cucina ITALIAN **$$**
(☎ 562-592-5552; www.romanocucina.com; 16595 Pacific Coast Hwy; mains $13-18; ⊙ 5-10pm) For hearty Italian fare, follow the twinkling lights to this trattoria, known as much for its thick slices of bruschetta, baked meatball mozzarella and huge pasta bowls as for the ripped waiters serving the food. Weekday specials include $5 Martini Thursdays.

Drinking & Nightlife

Sunset Beach is the unofficial capital of SoCal dive bars.

Turc's BAR
(16321 Pacific Coast Hwy) For a wood-paneled, trapped-in-the-captain's-hold vibe, try Turc's; it's the ivy-covered building at the corner of PCH and Anderson St in the shadows of the water-tower-like house.

Mother's Tavern BAR
(16701 Pacific Coast Hwy) Tiny but raucous biker bar Mother's Tavern is in the red building with Harleys out front, just past the barber shop. On a lazy Sunday, you might catch a rockabilly band there. Gals will be invited to tack their bra to the wall or ceiling, so look out.

Don the Beachcomber BAR
(16278 Pacific Coast Hwy) This seriously kitschy tiki bar will knock you over the head with its 'Vicious Virgin' and 'Missionary's Downfall' drinks. Zombie cocktail limit: two.

Brix NY Deli BAR
(16635 Pacific Coast Hwy; ⊙ noon-8pm Sun-Tue, to 9pm Wed, to 10pm Thu-Sat) For low-key pours, drop by the bar here, which has more than 20 craft beers on tap plus West Coast wine flights.

Huntington Beach

POP 194,700

Hawaiian-Irish surfing star George Freeth, after being hired by railroad magnate and real-estate developer Henry Huntington, gave demonstrations in Huntington Beach (HB) in 1914, and the city has been a surf destination ever since. In recent years, its surfing image has been heavily marketed, city politicos even getting legally aggressive in ensuring HB's exclusive rights to their now-trademarked nickname 'Surf City, USA' (Santa Cruz lost that fight, sorry). The sport is big business, with buyers for major retailers coming here to see what surfers are wearing, then marketing the look.

At times HB can seem like a teenager with growing pains. Long considered a low-key, not-quite-fashionable beach community, recent development along Main St has left downtown with a vaguely antiseptic, prefab feel – except for sidewalk-surfing skate rats and hollering late-night barflies. Still, HB remains a quintessential spot to celebrate the hang-loose SoCal coastal lifestyle. With consistently good waves, surf shops, a surf museum, bonfires on the sand, a canine-friendly beach and a sprinkling of hotels and restaurants with killer views, it's an awesome place for sun, surf and sand.

Sights

Huntington Pier HISTORIC SITE
(⊙ 5am-midnight) The 1853ft-long Huntington Pier has been here – in one form or another – since 1904. The mighty Pacific has damaged giant sections or completely demolished it multiple times since then, though. The current concrete structure was built in 1983 to withstand 31ft waves or a 7.0 magnitude earthquake, whichever hits HB first. On the pier you can rent a fishing pole from **Let's Go Fishin'** (☎ 714-960-1392; 21 Main St; ⊙ hours vary seasonally) a bait and tackle shop.

Huntington City Beach BEACH
(⊙ 5am-midnight) One of SoCal's best beaches, the sand surrounding the pier at the foot of Main St gets packed on summer weekends with surfers, volleyball players, swimmers and families. Bathrooms and showers are located north of the pier at the back of the snack-bar complex.

In the evening, volleyball games give way to beach bonfires. If you want to build one or have a barbecue, stake out one of the 1000 cement fire rings early in the day, especially on holiday weekends, when you should plan to arrive when the beach opens. To indicate that it's taken, surround the ring with your gear. You can buy firewood from concessionaires on the beach.

International Surfing Museum MUSEUM
(www.surfingmuseum.org; 411 Olive Ave; donations welcome; ⊙ noon-5pm Mon-Fri, 11am-6pm Sat &

Sun) One of the few of its kind in California, this small museum is an entertaining stop for surf-culture enthusiasts. Exhibits chronicle the sport's history with photos, vintage surfboards, movie memorabilia and surf music. For the best historical tidbits, spend a minute chatting with the all-volunteer staff.

Activities

If you forgot to pack beach gear, you can rent umbrellas, beach chairs, volleyballs and other essentials from Zack's or **Zach's Two** (☎714-536-2696; 21579 Pacific Coast Hwy). Just south of the pier on the Strand, friendly Dwight's Beach Concession, around since 1932, rents bikes, boogies boards, umbrellas and chairs.

Surfing

Surfing in HB is competitive. Control your longboard or draw ire from local dudes who pride themselves on being 'aggro.' If you're a novice (or need a bodyguard), it's a good idea to take lessons. Surf north of the pier.

Zack's SURFING
(☎714-536-0215; www.zackshb.com; 405 Pacific Coast Hwy) Offers one-hour lessons ($75 to $100) at the beach that include all-day board and wet-suit rental. For board rentals, you'll pay $12/35 per hour/day, plus $5/15 each for bodyboards and wet suits.

Dwight's Beach Concession SURFING
(201 Pacific Coast Hwy) Rents surfboards, bodyboards and wet suits at competitive rates.

Huntington Surf & Sport SURFING
(☎714-841-4000; www.hsssurf.com; 300 Pacific Coast Hwy) Megastore at the corner of PCH and Main St rents surfboards for $10/30 per hour/day (wet suits $8/15).

Cycling & Skating

Explore the coast while cycling or skating along the 8.5-mile **paved recreational path** running from Huntington State Beach in the south to Bolsa Chica State Beach. Rent beach cruisers ($10/30 per hour/day) or tandem bikes ($18/50) at Zack's. Dwight's Beach Concession also rents cruiser bikes at similar rates – ask for a copy of the owner's hand-drawn map of the bike path showing distances from the pier.

Frisbee

Huntington Beach Disc Golf Course FRISBEE
(Huntington Central Park, 18381 Goldenwest St; admission $1-2) Throw a disc back and forth for hours on the beach, or test your skills at the Huntington Beach Disc Golf Course. Aim for baskets at this scenic 18-hole course, downhill from the sports complex. Newbies and seasoned players welcome. The on-site pro shop sells discs.

Festivals & Events

Every Tuesday brings **Surf City Nights** (www.surfcitynights.com; 1st 3 blocks Main St, Huntington Beach; ⏲5pm-9pm Tue), a street fair with a petting zoo and bounce house for the kids, crafts, sidewalk sales for the grown-ups and live music and farmers market goodies for everyone.

Car buffs, get up early on Saturday mornings for the **Donut Derelicts Car Show** (www.donutderelicts.com), a weekly gathering of woodies, beach cruisers and pimped-out street rods at the corner of Magnolia St and Adams Ave, 2.5 miles inland from PCH.

4th of July PARADE
(www.hb4thofjuly.org) Expect big crowds when the city closes sections of Main St and PCH for its Independence Day parade. The day-long celebration ends with evening fireworks over the pier.

US Open of Surfing SURFING
(www.usopenofsurfing.com; ⏲late Jul & early Aug) This six-star competition lasts several days and draws more than 600 world-class surfers. Festivities include beach concerts, motocross shows and skateboard jams.

Huntington Harbor Cruise of Lights CHRISTMAS
(www.cruiseoflights.org; ⏲Dec) If you're here for the Christmas holidays, don't miss the evening boat tour past harborside homes

GIMME MORE!

Want even more surf and sand? Further south of the pier, **Huntington State Beach** (www.parks.ca.gov; ⏲6am-10pm; P) extends 2 miles from Beach Blvd (Hwy 39) to the Santa Ana River and Newport Beach boundary. All-day parking costs $15. Meanwhile, dogs can romp in the surf at **Huntington Dog Beach** (www.dogbeach.org; ⏲5am-10pm; P), between Goldenwest St and Seapoint Ave, north of Huntington City Beach. Nearly a mile long, it's a postcard-perfect place to play with your pooch. Parking meters cost 25¢ every 10 minutes.

twinkling with holiday lights. Ticket sales support nonprofit school programs.

Sleeping

There aren't many budget options in HB, especially during summer beach season. Head inland along mind-numbing Hwy 39 toward the I-405 (San Diego Fwy) to find cheaper cookie-cutter motels and hotels.

Huntington Surf Inn MOTEL $$
(714-536-2444; www.huntingtonsurfinn.com; 720 Pacific Coast Hwy; r $159-209; P) You're paying for location at this two-story motel just south of Main St and across from the beach. Nine of its rooms were recently redesigned by surf company Hurley in conjunction with surfers – cool, brah. There's a small common deck area with a beach view.

★ **Shorebreak Hotel** BOUTIQUE HOTEL $$$
(714-861-4470; www.shorebreakhotel.com; 500 Pacific Coast Hwy; r $189-495; P@) Stow your surfboard (lockers provided) as you head inside HB's hippest hotel, a stone's throw from the pier. The Shorebreak has a surf concierge, a fitness center and yoga studio, bean-bag chairs in the lobby and rattan and hardwood furniture in geometric-patterned air-con rooms (some pet-friendly). Have sunset cocktails on the upstairs deck at Zimzala restaurant. Parking is $27.

Hilton Waterfront Beach Resort RESORT $$$
(714-845-8000, 800-445-8667; www.waterfrontbeachresort.hilton.com; 21100 Pacific Coast Hwy; r $279-390; P@) The sprawling, lounge-filled poolside is reminiscent of Vegas, but then you see the backdrop: miles and miles of gorgeous deep-blue sea. This 100% nonsmoking hotel has a giant tower that stands in blatant disregard of the town's low rooflines, but every room has an angled balcony for ocean view. Rooms are plush but tempered with earth tones. Bicycle rentals available. Parking $30.

Hyatt Regency Huntington Beach Resort & Spa RESORT $$$
(714-698-1234, 800-492-8804; www.huntingtonbeach.hyatt.com; 21500 Pacific Coast Hwy; r $320-400; P@) This 517-room property with conference center hulks like an ersatz Spanish-style condo complex, but rooms are inviting and recently renovated and have balconies and dermotologist-designed bath products. Look for two outdoor saltwater swimming pools, splash pool with slides, a 20,000-sq-ft day spa and direct access to the beach via a pedestrian bridge, plus Camp Hyatt activities for kids.

Parking $34.

HUNTINGTON BEACH FOR CHILDREN

If you want a break from the beach scene, **Huntington Central Park** (www.ci.huntington-beach.ca.us; 18000 Goldenwest St;), 3 miles north of downtown, is a green suburban retreat with a disc-golf course (p245), down-and-dirty adventure playground featuring rope bridge and cable slide, and two little lakes with walking paths. For a thoughtful examination of local flora and fauna, including abundant bird life, stop by **Shipley Nature Center** (www.shipleynature.org; 17851 Goldenwest St; 9am-1pm Mon-Sat;), which has kid-friendly exhibits on conservation efforts and a self-guided wetlands nature trail.

Eating

Sancho's Tacos MEXICAN $
(714-536-8226; www.sanchostacos.com; 602 Pacific Coast Hwy; mains $3-10; 8am-9pm Mon-Sat, to 8pm Sun) There's no shortage of taco stands in HB, but locals are fiercely dedicated to Sancho's, across from the beach. This two-room shack with patio grills flounder, shrimp and tri-tip to order. Trippy Mexican-meets-skater art.

Sugar Shack CAFE $
(www.hbsugarshack.com; 213 1/2 Main St; mains $4-10; 6am-4pm Mon-Tue & Thu, to 8pm Wed, to 5pm Fri-Sun;) Expect a wait at this HB institution, or get here early to see surfer dudes don their wet suits. Breakfast is served all day on the bustling Main St patio and inside, where you can grab a spot at the counter or a two-top. Photos of surf legends plastering the walls raise this place almost to shrine status.

Park Bench Cafe AMERICAN $
(www.parkbenchcafe.com; 17732 Goldenwest St; mains $8-11; 7:30am-2pm Tue-Fri, to 3pm Sat & Sun;) Sometimes Fido likes to order too. In a dog-friendly setting with shady outdoor picnic tables, try this casual outdoor restaurant in Huntington Central Park. Order an avocado-topped omelette or BLT sandwich

for yourself and a juicy 'Hound Dog Heaven' beef patty for your four-legged friend.

Mother's Market & Kitchen ORGANIC $
(19770 Beach Blvd; mains $5-10; 8am-10pm;) Get your organic, health-conscious groceries here. A deli and take-out cafe caters to all diets (eg vegetarian, vegan, gluten-free, nondairy). Juice bar open till 8pm daily.

Bodhi Tree VEGETARIAN $$
(www.bodhitreehb.com; 501 Main St; mains $8-16; 11am-10pm;) Just north of downtown, this 100% vegetarian and vegan pan-Asian joint has a huge and varied menu, including mock-meat delights like *pho* noodle soup and Thai curries with fake 'chicken' and 'beef.' Vietnamese baguette sandwiches and wok-fried garlic 'shrimp' are also tasty.

Duke's SEAFOOD, HAWAIIAN $$
(714-374-6446; www.dukeshuntington.com; 317 Pacific Coast Hwy; mains lunch $7-16, dinner $19-32; 11:30am-2:30pm Tue-Fri, 10am-2pm Sun, 5-9pm Tue-Sun) It may be touristy, but this Hawaiian-themed restaurant – named after surfing legend Duke Kahanamoku – is a kick. With unbeatable views of the beach, a long list of fresh fish and a healthy selection of sassy cocktails, it's a primo spot to relax and show off your tan. For just drinks and appetizers, step into the Barefoot Bar (open from 3:30pm daily).

Sandy's CALIFORNIAN $$
(714-374-7273; www.sandyshb.com; 315 Pacific Coast Hwy; mains lunch $10-17, dinner $11-32; 11:30am-8:30pm Mon, to 9:30pm Tue-Fri, 9am-9:30pm Sat, 9am-8:30pm Sun) If Duke's is Hawaii, new Sandy's is California. It's downstairs from Duke's, right at beach-volleyball level with a generous beachside deck, easy-breezy dining room and dishes from breakfast pizza and short rib breakfast burrito for weekend brunch, to pecan-crusted seabass with shrimp couscous, or the jalapeño-date burger. Happy hour is 3:30pm to 5:30pm daily.

Cucina Alessá ITALIAN $$
(714-969-2148; www.cucinaalessa.com; 520 Main St; mains lunch $9-13, dinner $12-25; 11am-10pm Mon-Thu, to 11pm Fri & Sat, 10am-10pm Sun) Every beach town needs its favorite go-to Italian kitchen. Alessa wins hearts and stomachs with classics like Neopolitan lasagna, butternut squash ravioli and chicken marsala. Lunch brings out panini, while weekend breakfasts include frittata and 'famous' French toast. Get sidewalk seating, or sit behind big glass windows.

Spark Woodfire Grill CALIFORNIAN, BARBECUE $$
(714-960-0996; www.sparkwoodfiregrill.com; 300 Pacific Coast Hwy, 2nd fl; mains $8-29; 5-10pm Mon-Fri, 11am-11pm Sat, 10am-2pm & 4-9pm Sun) Come before dark to this 2nd-floor Cal-Mediterranean restaurant and watch the sun set over the water while forking into fire-grilled steaks, chops and seafood or crispy-thin pizzas from the wood-burning oven. An over-30 crowd habituates at the bar with tasty appetites.

DON'T MISS

WALK LIKE A SURF STAR

You'll find Huntington Beach's official **Surfing Walk of Fame** (www.hsssurf.com/shof), which immortalizes local legends, on the corner of PCH and Main St, not far from the pier. Recent hall-of-fame inductees include Bruce Brown, surf film pioneer, and Pat O'Connell, co-star of *Endless Summer II*.

Drinking & Nightlife

It's easy to find a bar in HB: just walk up Main St. For dives, look inland along Beach Blvd.

Hurricanes Bar & Grill BAR
(www.hurricanesbargrill.com; 2nd fl, 200 Main St) Two words: meat market. But then again, any strip of beach bars worth its margarita salt needs at least one. DJs nightly, ocean-view patios, a laser-light dance floor, 22 beer taps and loads of special cocktails – if you're not slurping body shots by midnight, you have no one to blame but yourself.

Killarney Pub & Grill BAR
(www.killarneypubandgrill.com; 209 Main St) It bills itself as an Irish pub, but the profusion of plasma TV screens makes it more like a sports bar with leprechaun-green-painted walls. Rollicking good fun for beer-drinking Wii Sports fans. DJs and dancing, live bands or howlin' karaoke after dark.

Huntington Beach Beer Co BAR
(www.hbbeerco.com; 2nd fl, 201 Main St; from 11am;) Two-decade-old, cavernous brewpub with a big balcony, specializing in ales brewed in a half dozen giant, stainless-steel kettles on site, like the HB Blonde, Brickshot

Red and seasonal beers flavored with sage to cherry. Try the sampler. DJs and dancing Thursday to Saturday nights.

Main Street Wine Company WINE BAR (www.mainstreetwinecompany.com; 301 Main St, Suite 105; ⏲noon-9pm Tue-Thu, 11am-10pm Fri, 1-10pm Sat, 1-8pm Sun) Boutique California-wine shop with a sleek bar, generous pours and meet-your-(wine)maker nights.

Zimzala LOUNGE (www.restaurantzimzala.com; Shorebreak Hotel, 2nd fl, 500 Pacific Coast Hwy; ⏲11am-11pm Mon-Thu, 10am-midnight Fri & Sat, 10am-11pm Sun) With a long, lazy afternoon happy hour, this happening hotel lounge has 2nd-floor ocean-view perches surrounding fire pits. Sexy cocktails, microbrews and California wines.

Shopping

About halfway up Huntington Beach Pier, you'll find two tiny stores. **Surf City HB** is the only shop in town officially licensed to use the name 'Surf City' on its merchandise – pick up a beach hoodie or T-shirt. Across the way, **Kite Connection** vends single-line and deluxe spinner kites.

Huntington Surf & Sport SPORTS, CLOTHING (www.hsssurf.com; 300 Pacific Coast Hwy) Towering behind the statue of surf hero Duke Kahanamoku at the corner of PCH and Main St, this massive store supports the Surf City vibe with vintage surf photos, concrete handprints of surf legends and lots of tiki-themed decor. You'll also find rows of surfboards, beachwear and surfing accessories. It also does test-marketing for OC-based Hurley.

Born Punk CHILDREN'S CLOTHING (www.bornpunk.com; 326 Main St) Get your little rock stars started on the right (?) foot with biker- and punk-inspired clothing, furniture and accessories: motorbike-shaped rockers, tiny skirts adorned with skulls and punk band T-shirts for the pre-school set.

American Vintage Clothing CLOTHING (201c Main St) Thrift and vintage hounds check out this small but jam-packed store. Boots, Jim Morrison T-shirts, earrings and loads of dresses arranged by decade. Enter off Walnut Ave.

Information

There's internet access and free wi-fi at **Central Library** (www.hbpl.org; 7111 Talbert Ave; internet per hr $5; ⏲1-9pm Mon, 9am-9pm Tue-Thu, 9am-5pm Fri & Sat; wi-fi) and **Main St Library** (www.hbpl.org; 525 Main St; internet per hr $5; ⏲10am-7pm Tue-Fri, 9am-5pm Sat; wi-fi).

Beach Center Post Office (316 Olive Ave; ⏲9am-5pm Mon-Fri)

Huntington Beach Hospital (☎714-843-5000; www.hbhospital.com; 17772 Beach Blvd; ⏲24hr)

Visitors Bureau (☎800-729-6232; www.surfcityusa.com) Hard-to-spot upstairs office on Main St (☎714-969-3492; 2nd fl, 301 Main St; ⏲9am-5pm) provides maps and information,

WORTH A TRIP

BOLSA CHICA STATE BEACH

A 3-mile-long strip of sand favored by surfers, volleyball players and fishers, **Bolsa Chica State Beach** (www.parks.ca.gov; Pacific Coast Hwy, btwn Seapoint & Warner Aves; parking $15; ⏲6am-10pm; P) stretches alongside PCH between Huntington Dog Beach to the south and Sunset Beach to the north. Even though it faces a monstrous offshore oil rig, Bolsa Chica (meaning 'little pocket' in Spanish) gets mobbed on summer weekends. You'll find picnic tables, fire rings and beach showers, plus a bike path running north to Anderson Ave in Sunset Beach and south to Huntington State Beach.

At the park's small **visitors center** you can check out the views through telescopes pointed at the beach or inland at **Bolsa Chica Ecological Reserve** (http://bolsachica.org; ⏲sunrise-sunset), on the other side of PCH. The reserve may look desolate, but its restored salt marsh is an environmental success story and teems with more than 200 species of birds. Over 1200 acres were saved by a band of determined locals from numerous development projects over the years. Sadly, it's also one of the last remaining coastal wetlands in SoCal – over 90% have already succumbed to development. A 1.5-mile loop trail starts from the footbridge near the south parking lot right on PCH. A mile north, the **Bolsa Chica Wetlands Interpretative Center** (www.bolsachica.org; 3842 Warner Ave, Huntington Beach; ⏲9am-4pm) sits in the north parking lot, near other walking trails.

but the Pier Plaza booth (Pier Plaza; ⏰11am-7pm) is more convenient.

Getting There & Around

Pacific Coast Hwy runs alongside the beach. Main St intersects PCH at the pier. Heading inland, Main St ends at Hwy 39 (Beach Blvd), which connects north to I-405.

Public parking lots by the pier and beach – when you can even get a spot – are 'pay and display' for $1.50 per hour, $15 daily maximum. Self-service ticket booths scattered across the parking lot take notes or coins. More municipal lots alongside PCH and around downtown cost at least $15 per day in summer, typically with an evening flat rate of $5 after 5pm. On-street parking meters cost $1 per 40 minutes.

OCTA (☎714-560-6282; www.octa.net) bus 1 connects HB with the rest of OC's beach towns every hour; one-way/day pass $2/5, payable on board (exact change). At press time, a free **Surf City Downtown Shuttle** (☎714-536-5542) operates from 10am until 8pm on weekends during summer, making a 3.5-mile loop around downtown to the pier, starting from the free public parking lot at **City Hall** (2000 N Main St).

TOP FIVE CHEAPO BREAKFASTS BY THE BEACH

Sugar Shack (p246), Huntington Beach

Harbor House Café (p243), Sunset Beach

Cappy's Café (p254), Newport Beach

Orange Inn (p265), Laguna Beach

El Campeon (p268), San Juan Capistrano

Newport Beach

POP 87,028

Remember the primetime soap *The OC*? Well, it wasn't quite accurate and kinda was. There are really three Newport Beaches: a paradise for wealthy Bentley- and Porsche-driving yachtsmen and their trophy wives; the surfers and stoners who populate the beachside dives and live for the perfect wave; and the rest of the folk, trying to live the day-to-day, chow down on seafood and enjoy the glorious sunsets. Somehow, these diverse communities all seem to live – mostly – harmoniously.

For visitors, the pleasures are many: just-off-the-boat seafood, boogie-boarding the human-eating waves at the Wedge, and the ballet of yachts in the harbor. Just inland, more lifestyles of the rich and famous revolve around Fashion Island, a posh outdoor mall and one of the OC's biggest shopping centers.

Sights

Four miles long but less than a half mile wide, the **Balboa Peninsula** has a white-sand beach on its ocean side and countless stylish homes, including the 1926 **Lovell Beach House** (1242 W Ocean Front). Designed by Rudolph Schindler, one of SoCal's most prominent modernist architects, it was built using site-cast concrete frames shaped like figure eights. It's just inland from the paved beachfront **recreational path**, across from a small **playground**.

Hotels, restaurants and bars cluster around the peninsula's two famous piers: **Newport Pier** near the western end and **Balboa Pier** at the eastern end. The 2-mile oceanfront strip between them teems with beachgoers, and people-watching is great. Near Newport Pier, several shops rent umbrellas, beach chairs, volleyballs and other necessities. For swimming, families will find a more relaxed atmosphere and calmer waves at 10th St and 18th St. The latter beach, also known as **Mothers Beach**, has a lifeguard, restrooms and a shower.

At the very tip of Balboa Peninsula, by the West Jetty, the **Wedge** is a bodysurfing, bodyboarding and knee-boarding spot famous for its perfectly hollow waves that can swell up to 30ft high. The waves are shore-breakers that crest on the sand, not out to sea, so you can easily slam your head. There's usually a small crowd watching the action. This is not a good place for learning how to handle the currents. Newcomers should head a few blocks west. Park on Channel Rd or E Ocean Blvd and walk through tiny **West Jetty View Park**.

ExplorOcean MUSEUM
(☎949-675-8915; www.explorocean.org; 600 E Bay Ave, Balboa Fun Zone; adult/child 4-12yr $5/3; ⏰11am-3:30pm Mon-Thu, to 6pm Fri & Sat, to 5pm Sun) In the Balboa Fun Zone (p250), this newly refurbished museum calls itself an 'ocean literacy center' with critter-filled touch tanks, remotely operated vehicles, the rowboat used by adventurer Roz Savage on her five-year, round-the-world solo voyage, and an innovation lab.

Newport Beach & Around

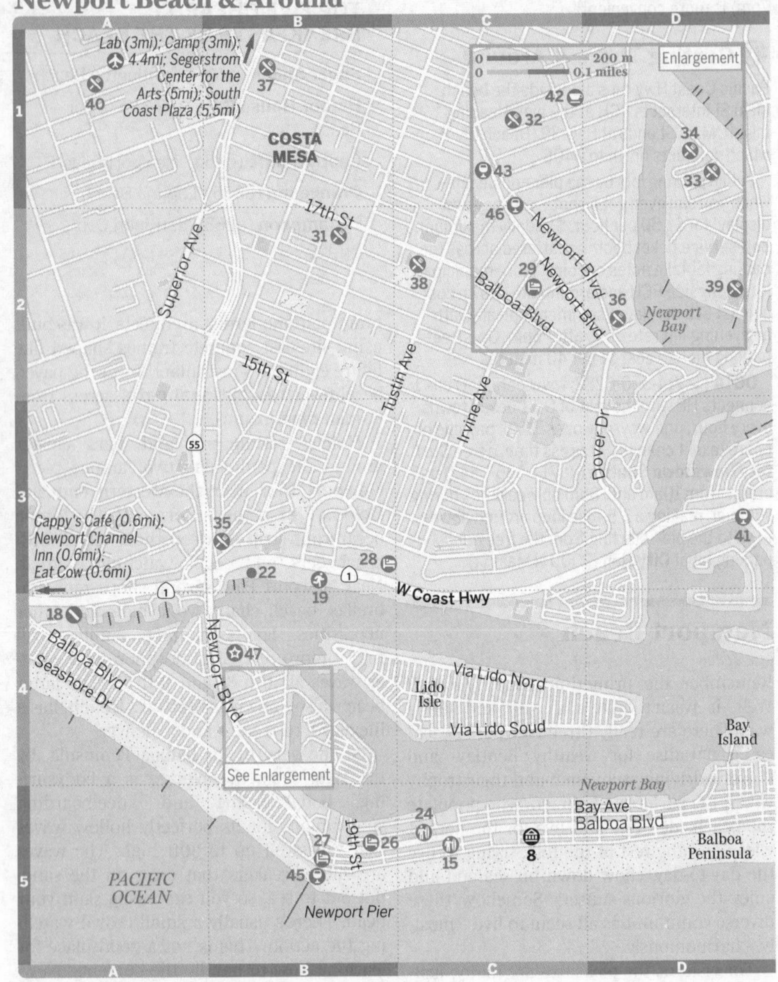

★**Orange County Museum of Art** MUSEUM
(☎949-759-1122; www.ocma.net; 850 San Clemente Dr; adult/student/child under 12yr $10/8/free; ⊙11am-5pm Wed-Sun, to 8pm Thu) Less than a half mile from Fashion Island, this museum highlights California art and cutting-edge contemporary artists, with exhibitions rotating through two large spaces. Recent exhibitions have included 'Birth of the Cool: Art, Design and Culture at Midcentury' and '15 Minutes of Fame: Portraits from Ansel Adams to Andy Warhol.' There's also a sculpture garden, eclectic gift shop and a theater screening classic, foreign and art-related films.

On the third Thursday of the month, stop by for behind-the-scenes gallery tours, films and videos, and even live music and DJs.

Activities

Balboa Fun Zone AMUSEMENT PARK
(www.thebalboafunzone.com; 600 E Bay Ave; ⊙Ferris wheel 11am-8pm Sun-Thu, to 9pm Fri, to 10pm Sat) On the harbor side of Balboa Peninsula, the Fun Zone has delighted locals and visitors since 1936. There's a small Ferris wheel ($4 per ride, where Ryan and Marissa shared their first kiss on *The OC*), arcade games, touristy shops and restaurants, and

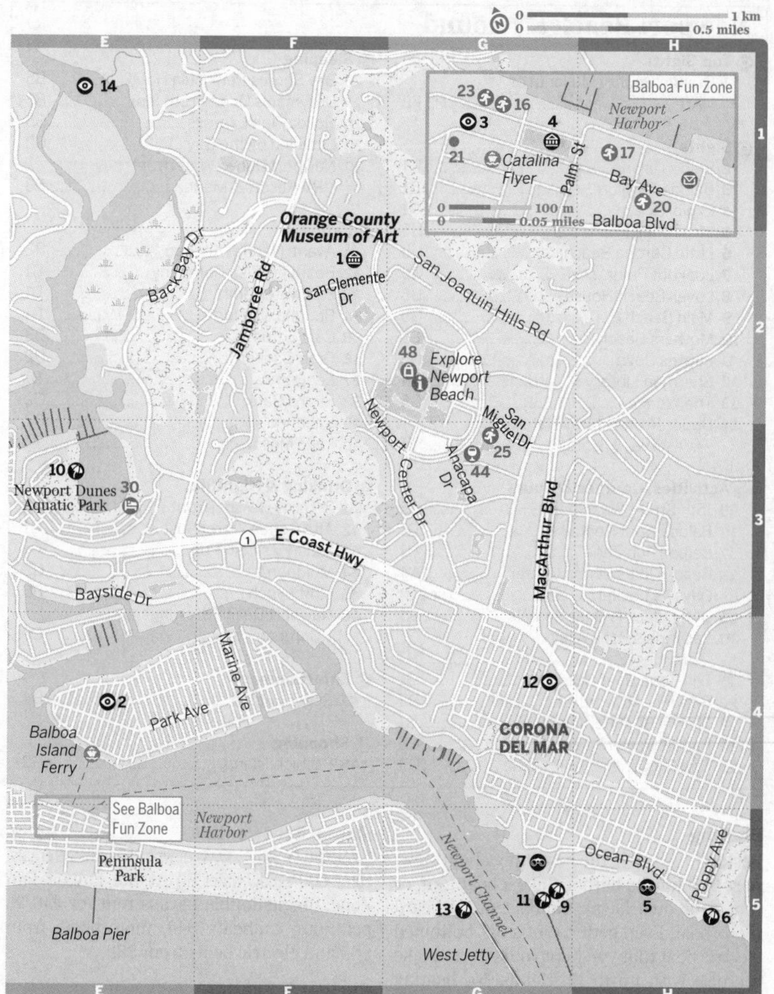

frozen banana stands (just like the one in the TV sit-com *Arrested Development*). Nearby the landmark 1905 **Balboa Pavilion** is beautifully illuminated at night. The Fun Zone is also the place to catch a harbor cruise, fishing or whale-watching excursion, or the ferry to Balboa Island (p253) just across the channel.

Surfing

Surfers flock to the breaks at the small jetties surrounding the Newport Pier between 18th and 56th streets. Word of warning: locals can be territorial. For lessons, try Huntington Beach or Laguna Beach instead.

15th Street Surf Shop SURFING
(☎949-673-5810; www.15thstreetsurfshop.com; 103 15th St; boogie boards per hour/day $2.50/8, surfboards $6/20) Rent a full compliment of boogie boards, surfboards and accessories from wet suits to umbrellas. Prices may fluctuate and shop hours are variable, so call ahead to check.

Paddle Power SURF GEAR
(☎949-675-1215; www.paddlepowerh2o.com; 1500 W Balboa Blvd) Near Newport Pier, this place rents stand-up paddle boards ($20/75 per hour/day) and kayaks ($14/55) and offers 90-minute SUP lessons (from $45).

Newport Beach & Around

Top Sights
1 Orange County Museum of Art F2

Sights
2 Balboa Island E4
3 Balboa Pavilion G1
4 ExplorOcean G1
5 Inspiration Point H5
6 Little Corona Beach H5
7 Lookout Point G5
8 Lovell Beach House C5
9 Main Beach G5
10 Mothers Beach E3
11 Pirates Cove G5
12 Sherman Library & Gardens G4
13 The Wedge G5
14 Upper Newport Bay Nature Preserve E1

Activities, Courses & Tours
15 15th Street Surf Shop C5
16 Balboa Boat Rentals G1
17 Balboa Fun Zone H1
18 Beach Cities Scuba Center A4
Davey's Locker .... (see 3)
19 Duffy Electric Boat Rentals B3
20 Easyride's Back Alley Bicycles H1
21 Fun Zone Boat Co G1
22 Gondola Adventures B3
23 Marina Boat Rentals G1
24 Paddle Power C5
25 Spa Gregorie's G3

Sleeping
26 Bay Shores Peninsula Hotel B5
27 Doryman's Oceanfront Inn B5
28 Holiday Inn Express B3
29 Little Inn by the Bay C2
30 Newport Dunes Waterfront RV Resort & Marina E3

Eating
31 Avanti Natural Kitchen B2
32 Bear Flag Fish Company C1
33 Bluewater Grill D1
34 Buddha's Favorite D1
35 Cafe Lotus B3
36 Crab Cooker D2
37 Eat Chow B1
38 Plums Café C2
39 Sabatino's D2
40 Taco Mesa A1

Drinking & Nightlife
41 3-Thirty-3 Waterfront D3
42 Alta Coffee Warehouse C1
43 Malarky's Irish Pub C1
44 Muldoon's G3
45 Mutt Lynch B5
46 Newport Beach Brewing Company C2

Entertainment
47 Regency Lido B4

Shopping
48 Fashion Island G2

Boating

Besides the beach, the best thing about Newport Beach is its harbor. Take a boat tour, or rent your own kayak, sailboat or outboard motorboat. Even better, rent a flat-bottomed electric boat that you pilot yourself, and take a cruise with up to 12 friends. No boating experience required; maps provided. Paddle Power (p251) also rents kayaks.

Duffy Electric Boat Rentals BOATING
(☎949-645-6812; www.duffyofnewportbeach.com; 2001 W Pacific Coast Hwy; per hr weekday/weekend $85/100; ⏰10am-8pm) Advance reservations recommended for heated electric boats with canopies. Bring CDs, food and drinks for a fun evening.

Balboa Boat Rentals BOATING
(☎949-673-7200; http://boats4rent.com; 510 E Edgewater Pl; kayaks per hr from $15, sailboats $45, powerboats from $70, electric boats from $75) By the Balboa Fun Zone.

Marina Boat Rentals BOATING
(☎949-673-3372; www.newportbeachboatrentals.com; 600 E Edgewater Pl) At the Balboa Fun Zone. Single/double kayaks rent for $18/25 per hour, sailboats $49, motorboats from $69 and electric boats from $89.

Cycling & Skating

To experience fabulous ocean views, ride a bike along the paved **recreational path** that encircles almost the entire Balboa Peninsula. Inland cyclists like the paved **scenic loop** around Upper Newport Bay Nature Preserve (p256).

There are many places to rent bikes near Newport and Balboa Piers.

Easyride's Back Alley Bicycles BICYCLE RENTAL
(☎949-566-9850; www.easyridebackalleybikes.com; 204 Washington St; beach cruisers per day $20, tandem bicycles per hr/day $15/30, surreys per hr from $25) On the boardwalk, near Balboa Fun Zone. Think twice before renting a surrey (with the fringe on top) and pedaling

the pier-flanked bike path, as locals have been known to bombard surreys with water balloons!

Diving

There's terrific diving just south of Newport Beach at the underwater park at Crystal Cove State Park (p259), where divers can check out reefs, anchors and an old military plane-crash site.

Beach Cities Scuba Center DIVING

(949-650-5440; www.beachcitiesscuba.com; 4537 W Coast Hwy) For dive-boat trips, stop by Beach Cities Scuba Center, where full equipment rental costs $60 per day.

Spa

Spa Gregorie's SPA

(949-644-6672; www.spagregories.com; 200 Newport Center Dr, ste 100) After power shopping at Fashion Island, indulge yourself at Spa Gregorie's. After you've been rejuvenated by the quiet room, a one-hour massage starts around $100 or unwind with a 75-minute signature facial from $119, plus tip.

Tours

Several companies offer narrated tours of glitzy Newport Harbor, departing near the Balboa Fun Zone (p250) and Balboa Pavilion (p251). Reserve ahead for the Christmas Boat Parade, when boat tours cost about $26 per adult, less for seniors and children.

Fun Zone Boat Co BOAT

(949-673-0240; www.funzoneboats.com; 600 Edgewater Pl; 45min cruise per adult/senior/child 5-11yr from $14/7/11) Sea lion–watching and celebrity home tours depart beneath the Ferris wheel in the Fun Zone.

Davey's Locker BOAT

(949-673-1434; www.daveyslocker.com; 400 Main St; 2½hr whale-watching cruise per adult/child 3-12yr & senior from $32/26, half-day sportfishing $41.50/34) At Balboa Pavilion; offers whale-watching and sportfishing trips.

Gondola Adventures BOAT

(949-646-2067, 888-446-6365; www.gondola.com; 3101 W Coast Hwy; 1hr cruise per couple from $135) Totally cheesy Venetian-esque gondola rides with chocolates and sparkling cider for your sweetie.

Festivals & Events

Newport Beach Film Festival FILM

(www.newportbeachfilmfest.com; mid-Apr) Roll out the red carpet for screenings of over 350 mostly new independent and foreign films, along with occasional major-studio premieres such as *Crash* and anniversary showings of classics like *Sunset Boulevard*.

Newport Beach Wine and Food Festival FOOD, WINE

(newportwineandfood.com; mid-Sep) Flashy food-and-wine fest shows off local restaurateurs, top chefs, prestigious winemakers and brewmasters with live rock concerts staged near Fashion Island.

Christmas Boat Parade CHRISTMAS

(www.christmasboatparade.com; Dec) The week before Christmas brings thousands of spectators to Newport Harbor to watch a tradition dating back over a century. The 2½-hour parade of up to 150 boats, including some fancy multimillion-dollar yachts all decked out with Christmas lights and holiday cheer, begins at 6:30pm. You can watch for free from the Fun Zone or Balboa Island, or book ahead for a harbor boat tour.

DON'T MISS

BALBOA ISLAND

For a quick pleasure trip across Newport Harbor, the **Balboa Island Ferry** (www.balboaislandferry.com; 410 S Bay Front; adult/child $1/50¢, car incl driver $2; 6:30am-midnight Sun-Thu, to 2am Fri & Sat) leaves from the Balboa Fun Zone about every 10 minutes. It's tiny, holding just three cars packed single file between open-air seats. The distance covered is only 800ft, and the trip lasts less than five minutes.

The ferry lands at Agate Ave, a half mile west of Marine Ave, the main drag on **Balboa Island** (www.balboa-island.net). It's lined with beachy boutique shops, cafes and restaurants, and old-fashioned ice-cream shops vending Balboa bars (vanilla ice cream dipped in chocolate, peanuts, sprinkles and crushed Oreo cookies on a stick).

For close-ups of the island's beautiful, well-maintained homes, take a stroll along its shoreline. It's only about 1.5 miles around. Then catch the ferry back. You can also drive south of PCH along Jamboree Rd to Marine Ave. But what fun is that?

Sleeping

A Newport stay ain't cheap, but outside of the peak season rates often drop 40% or more. Otherwise, to save some dough, you'll find chain hotels and motels further inland, especially around John Wayne Airport and the triangle junction of Hwy 55 (Costa Mesa Fwy), toll road Hwy 73 and I-405 (San Diego Fwy).

Newport Channel Inn MOTEL **$$**
(☎800-255-8614, 949-642-3030; www.newportchannelinn.com; 6030 W Coast Hwy; r $129-199; P) The ocean is just across PCH from this spotless 30-room, two-story 1960s-era motel. Other perks include large rooms with microwaves and mini-fridges, a big common sundeck, beach equipment for loan and genuinely friendly owners with lots of local knowledge. Enjoy a vacation-lodge vibe under the A-frame roof of room 219, which sleeps up to seven.

Newport Dunes Waterfront RV Resort & Marina CABINS, CAMPGROUND **$$**
(☎949-729-3863, 800-765-7661; www.newportdunes.com; 1131 Back Bay Dr; campsites from $55, studios/cottages from $150/200; P@) RVs and tents aren't required for a stay at this upscale campground: two dozen tiny A-frame studios and one-bedroom cottages are available, all within view of Newport Bay. A fitness center and walking trails, kayak rentals, board games, family bingo, ice-cream socials, horseshoe and volleyball tournaments, an outdoor pool and playground, and summertime movies on the beach await. Wheelchair-accessible.

Holiday Inn Express MOTEL **$$**
(☎800-633-3199, 949-722-2999; www.hienewportbeach.com; 2300 W Coast Hwy; r incl breakfast $199-259; P@) The 83 spacious rooms here have up-to-date furnishings and extras like microwaves, mini-fridges and work desks. Centrally located on a busy stretch of PCH, between major attractions. There's a coin-op laundry and cardio equipment. Rates include hot and cold breakfast buffet.

Little Inn by the Bay MOTEL **$$**
(☎949-673-8800, 800-438-4466; www.littleinnbythebay.com; 2627 Newport Blvd; r from $195; P@) If you're not bothered by street noise, you can walk to the beach from this mid-century motel. Recently upgraded rooms feature contemporary style, with microwave, fridge, iron and coffee maker, and some have Jacuzzis. Beach gear and bikes to borrow.

Resort at Pelican Hill RESORT **$$$**
(☎949-467-6800, 800-315-8214; www.pelicanhill.com; 22701 Pelican Hill Rd S; r from $495; P@) At this Tuscan-themed resort secluded in the Newport Coast hills, mature trees and Palladian columns line the way to over 300 deluxe air-con bungalows and villas. Pleasures include a circular mosaic-inlaid swimming pool (diameter: 136ft), two 18-hole championship golf courses, a soothing spa, top-notch Northern Italian fare at Andrea restaurant and multilingual concierge staff who define solicitous. Rates: sky high. Pampering: priceless.

Bay Shores Peninsula Hotel HOTEL **$$$**
(☎800-222-6675, 949-675-3463; www.thebestinn.com; 1800 W Balboa Blvd; r incl breakfast $190-300; P@) This three-story, reimagined motel is ready to flex some surf-themed muscle. From *Endless Summer* surfing murals and complimentary fresh-baked cookies, free rental movies and a 360-degree-view sun deck, Bay Shores is beachy, casual and customer-focused. Its location close to Newport Pier partially explains the steep rates. Complimentary parking, beach gear and breakfast buffet. Coin-op laundry available.

Doryman's Oceanfront Inn B&B **$$$**
(☎949-675-7300; www.dorymansinn.com; 2102 W Oceanfront; r incl breakfast $269-399; P) This 2nd-floor oceanfront B&B was built in 1891 and retains that Victorian country style. Each of the 11 rooms is unique, and some boast ocean views, fireplaces and deep soaking tubs. It has a great location by Newport Pier (view it from the roof deck), although it can get loud. Parking and breakfast (quiche, bagels, etc) included.

Eating

Newport has some of the OC's best restaurants. Don't overlook some tasty finds in prefab strip malls, especially in adjacent Costa Mesa (p257).

Cappy's Café AMERICAN **$**
(www.cappyscafe.com; 5930 W Coast Hwy; mains $6-12; ⏰6am-3pm Mon-Fri, to 4pm Sat & Sun) This bright-blue diner by the ocean serves monster omelettes, crispy bacon, country fried steak, stuffed French toast and other classic blue-plate breakfasts. Not the place for lunch, though.

Cafe Lotus VIETNAMESE **$**
(☎949-574-2479; 325 Old Newport Blvd; mains $5-11; ⏰10am-8pm Mon-Sat;) In the shadow of

Hwy 55, this small, simple, family-run spot serves crunchy Vietnamese baguette sandwiches, BBQ-shrimp steamed buns, chicken *pho, poulet roti* (roast chicken), rich iced coffee and more.

★Bear Flag Fish Company SEAFOOD $$
(☎949-673-3434; www.bearflagfishco.com; 407 31st St, Newport Beach; mains $8-15; ⏰11am-9pm Tue-Sat, to 8pm Sun & Mon; 👪) This squat glass box is *the* place for generously sized, grilled and panko-breaded fish tacos, ahi burritos, spankin' fresh ceviche and oysters. Pick out what you want from the ice-cold display cases, then grab a picnic-table seat. About the only way this seafood could be any fresher is if you caught and hauled it off the boat yourself!

Eat Chow CALIFORNIAN $$
(☎949-423-7080; www.eatchownow.com; 211 62nd St; mains $8-15; ⏰8am-9pm Mon-Thu, to 10pm Fri, 7am-10pm Sat, 7am-9pm Sun) Hidden a block off W Coast Hwy, the crowd is equal parts tatted hipsters and ladies who lunch, which makes it very Newport indeed. They all queue happily for big salads like ribeye Thai beef salad, grilled salmon tacos with curry slaw, and bodacious burgers like the Chow BBQ burger with home-made barbecue sauce, smoked gouda, crispy onions and more. Groovy indie-rock soundtrack.

Crab Cooker SEAFOOD $$
(☎949-673-0100; www.crabcooker.com; 2200 Newport Blvd; mains $12-23, lobster $40; ⏰11am-9pm Sun-Thu, to 10pm Fri & Sat; 👪) Expect a wait at this always-busy joint, a landmark since 1951. It serves great seafood and fresh crab on paper plates to an appreciative crowd wearing flip-flops and jeans. Don't miss the delish chowder – it's loaded with clams. If you're in a hurry, saunter up to the fish market counter inside and order your seafood to go.

Buddha's Favorite JAPANESE $$
(☎949-723-4203; www.buddhasfavorite.com; 634 Lido Park Dr; mains $4-16; ⏰5:30pm-10pm Mon-Thu, to 10:30pm Fri & Sat, to 9:30pm Sun) Who are we to disagree with the Enlightened One? This sushi joint's Yokohama-born chef has a hipster following for creative hot and cold appetizers like sashimi 'candy,' a tuna tower and deep-fried halibut with eel sauce. Snag a table outside on the heated deck and enjoy the twinkling harbor lights.

If you're not a fan of raw fish, try tempura, soba or udon noodles, or heaping *donburi* rice bowls.

Bluewater Grill SEAFOOD $$
(☎949-675-3474; www.bluewatergrill.com; 630 Lido Park Dr; mains $10-39; ⏰11am-10pm Mon-Thu, to 11pm Fri & Sat, 10am-10pm Sun) Sit on the wooden deck and watch the boats at this polished harborside restaurant and oyster bar that serves incredibly fresh fish. Great for Bloody Marys and a leisurely lunch – maybe swordfish tacos and coleslaw, beer-battered fish and chips or seared ahi with white-bean hummus. Happy hour and small-plates menu available from 3:30pm to 6:30pm weekdays.

Sabatino's ITALIAN $$
(☎949-723-0621; www.sabatinoschicagosausage.com; 251 Shipyard Way, Cabin D; mains $9-23; ⏰8am-10pm) The claim to fame of this authentic Italian place in the dockyards is its handmade sausage, blended with Sicilian goat cheese for that cholesterol double-whammy. Family-size deli sandwiches, shrimp scampi and stuffed and baked pastas keep the locals coming back for more. It's hard to find – when you get lost, just call.

🍷 Drinking & Nightlife

Alta Coffee Warehouse COFFEE SHOP
(www.altacoffeeshop.com; 506 31st St; ⏰6am-10:30pm Mon-Thu, 7am-11pm Fri & Sat, 7am-10:30pm Sun) Hidden on a side street, this cozy coffeehouse in a beach bungalow with a covered patio lures locals with live music and poetry readings, art on the brick walls and honest baristas who dish the lowdown on the day's desserts and baked goods. No coffee or food service after 9pm weekdays, 10pm weekends.

Malarky's Irish Pub BAR
(www.malarkyspub.com; 3011 Newport Blvd; ⏰7:30am-2am) After sunset at the beach, follow the laughing leprechaun to this Balboa Peninsula bar where hunky lifeguard bartenders pour pints for sorority girls and their frat-boy suitors from USC. Bring ID – you *will* get carded – and show up early, or wait in line.

Newport Beach Brewing Company BREWPUB
(www.newportbeachbrewingcompany.com; 2920 Newport Blvd; ⏰11:30am-11pm Sun-Thu, to 1am Fri & Sat; 📶) The town's only microbrewery (try their signature Newport Beach Blonde or Bisbee's ESB), 'Brewco' is a laid-back place to catch the big game or just kick it over burgers, pizzas and fried fare with your buds after a day at the beach.

WORTH A TRIP

NEWPORT BAY ECOLOGICAL RESERVE

Inland from the harbor, where runoff from the San Bernardino Mountains meets the sea, the brackish water of 752-acre **Newport Bay Ecological Reserve** (from $20 per person) supports nearly 200 bird species. As this is one of SoCal's few estuaries that has been preserved, it's an important stopover on the migratory Pacific Flyway, as well as for nature lovers in Orange County. It's also under the flyway for planes taking off from John Wayne Airport, but this annoyance doesn't overly detract from the wildlife viewing.

Inside the boundaries of the reserve is the **Upper Newport Bay Nature Preserve**. Stop by the **Muth Interpretive Center** (949-923-2290; www.ocparks.com/unbic; 2301 University Dr, off Irvine Ave; 10am-4pm Tue-Sun;), made from sustainable and renewable materials. Built right into the hillside, it's not visible from the parking lot. Walk past the information kiosk and down a short hill to the center. Inside, you can wander around the kid-friendly exhibits, which explain how the bay is like an egg beater and a sponge, among other scientific fun facts. Before heading out, grab a trail map.

Muldoon's BAR
(www.muldoonspub.com; 202 Newport Center Dr; closed Mon) At upscale, upbeat Muldoon's, choose from indoor, outdoor (under a leafy tree) and bar seating and enjoy decent, if pricey, Irish pub grub, 10 beers on tap and live acoustic sounds Friday and Saturday nights and most Sunday afternoons. It anchors an office park across the street from Fashion Island.

Mutt Lynch BEACH BAR
(www.muttlynchs.com; 2301 W Oceanfront; 7am-midnight) Rowdy dive by the beach offers pool tables, schooners filled with dozens of beers on tap and martinis made with *soju* (Korean vodka). Food is in large portions, especially at breakfast. It's Best on 'Sunday Fundays.'

3-Thirty-3 Waterfront LOUNGE
(www.3thirty3nb.com; 333 Bayside Dr) Sip cocktails with Newport's in-crowd at this upscale lounge with killer views of the yacht-filled harbor. With leopard-spotted lampshades, can you say 'Cougartown'?

Entertainment

Regency Lido CINEMA
(949-673-8350; www.regencymovies.com; 3459 Via Lido) Showing movies since 1938, the Lido screens mostly mainstream Hollywood fare, but some indie flicks too. Fully restored, it has a red-velvet waterfall curtain and Italian tile work. It's at the corner of Newport Blvd, just over the bridge on the Balboa Peninsula.

Shopping

On Balboa Island, **Marine Ave** is lined with darling shops in an old-fashioned village atmosphere, a good place to pick up something for the kids, unique gifts and beachy souvenirs, or jewelry, art and antiques for yourself.

Fashion Island PLAZA
(949-721-2000; 550 Newport Center Dr; 10am-9pm Mon-Fri, 11am-7pm Sat, 11am-6pm Sun) A chic outdoor mall that opened in 1967, Fashion Island sits in the middle of a traffic loop known as Newport Center Dr. Anchored by Bloomingdales, Macy's and Neiman Marcus, the mall's breezy, Mediterranean-style walkways are lined with more than 200 specialty stores, upscale kiosks, 40 chain restaurants, two multiplex cinemas and the occasional koi pond or burbling fountain. The miniature train will keep the kiddies amused.

Information

Balboa Post Office (www.usps.com; 204 Main St; 9am-4pm Mon-Fri) Close to the beach.

Explore Newport Beach (www.visitnewportbeach.com; 401 Newport Center Dr, Fashion Island, Atrium Court, 2nd fl; 10am-9pm Mon-Fri, to 7pm Sat, to 6pm Sun) The city's official visitor center hands out free brochures and maps.

FedEx Office (949-760-1595; www.fedexoffice.com; 230 Newport Center Dr; per min 30¢, wi-fi free; 7am-11pm Mon-Fri, 8am-9pm Sat, 9am-9pm Sun) Internet access at self-service computer workstations.

Hoag Memorial Hospital Presbyterian (949-764-4624; www.hoaghospital.org; 1 Hoag Dr; 24hr)

Marque Medical (949-760-9222; www.marquemedical.com; 2075 San Joaquin Hills Rd; 8am-8pm Mon-Fri, 9am-5pm Sat & Sun) Nonemergency urgent-care clinic, across from Fashion Island.

Getting There & Around

BUS

OCTA (☎714-560-6282; www.octa.net) bus 1 connects Newport Beach and Fashion Island mall with the OC's other beach towns, including Corona del Mar just east, every 30 minutes to one hour. From the intersection of Newport Blvd and PCH, bus 71 heads south along the Balboa Peninsula to Main Ave every hour or so. On all routes, the one-way fare is $2 (exact change).

BOAT

The West Coast's largest passenger catamaran, the **Catalina Flyer** (☎800-830-7744; www.catalinainfo.com; 400 Main St; round-trip adult/child 3-12yr/senior $70/53/65, per bicycle $7), makes a daily round-trip to Catalina Island, taking 75 minutes each way. It leaves Balboa Pavilion around 9am and returns before 6pm; check online for discounts.

CAR & MOTORCYCLE

Frequently jammed from dawn till dusk, Hwy 55 (Newport Blvd) is the main access road from I-405 (San Diego Fwy); it intersects with the Pacific Coast Hwy near the shore. In town, PCH is called W Coast Hwy or E Coast Hwy, both in mailing addresses and conversationally by locals.

The municipal lot beside Balboa Pier costs 50¢ per 20 minutes, or $15 per day. Street parking meters on the Balboa Peninsula cost 50¢ to $1 per hour. Free parking on residential streets, just a block or two from the sand, is time-limited and subject to other restrictions. In summer, expect to circle like a hawk for a space.

Around Newport Beach

Costa Mesa

Costa Mesa at first glance looks like just another landlocked suburb transected by the I-405, but two top venues attract some 24 million visitors each year. South Coast Plaza is SoCal's largest mall – properly termed a 'shopping resort', and Orange County's cultural heart is steps away in the performing arts venues Segerstrom Center for the Arts and South Coast Repertory.

If that all sounds rather hoity-toity, a pair of 'anti-malls' called The Lab and The Camp brings hipster cool to the shopping scene, while strip malls reveal surprisingly tasty cafes, ethnic food holes-in-the-wall, bars and clubs. Costa Mesa's chain hotels and motels can be bargains compared with Newport Beach's.

Eating

Browse Costa Mesa's outer reaches for some surprisingly authentic, unpretentious restaurants. There's also a branch of **Eat Chow** (☎949-650-2469; 1802 Newport Blvd) here.

Mentatsu Ramen JAPANESE $
(☎714-979-2755; 688 Baker St; mains $7-10; ⏲lunch & dinner) If you've been missing those true-blue Tokyo noodle houses, look no further. This top-rated ramen shop, at the corner of Bristol St, is a casual affair, with piping-hot bowls of *negi-miso* ramen with green onions and succulent sliced pork, or *mabo* ramen with chili sauce, maybe with steaming hot *gyōza* (pot stickers). Add a bottle of Sapporo or Kirin and you're in hog heaven. Wait for a table, or grab a seat at the counter.

Avanti Natural Kitchen VEGETARIAN $
(www.avantinatural.com; 259 E 17th St; mains $8-11; ⏲11am-10pm Mon-Fri, 10:30am-10pm Sat, 10:30am-8pm Sun; 🖉) 🌿 A mom-and-pop vegetarian cafe that's so good, even carnivores will leave feeling sated. It looks like just another strip-mall storefront, but step inside for the creative chef duo's magic with pizzas, roasted stuffed portobello mushrooms and the hot-taco brunch. The menu features organic produce from local farms.

Taco Mesa MEXICAN $
(www.tacomesa.net; 647 W 19th St; mains $2-10; ⏲7am-11pm) This healthy Mexican hot spot with a salsa bar is a consistent local favorite.

Native Foods CAFE $
(www.nativefoods.com; the Camp, 2937 Bristol St; mains $8-10; ⏲11am-10pm; 🖉👪) Lunch in a yurt? In Orange County? Them's the digs at this vegan spot serving organic salads, veggie burgers, rice bowls and ooey-gooey desserts.

Plums Café CALIFORNIAN $$
(☎949-722-7586; www.plumscafe.com; 369 E 17th St; mains $10-25; ⏲8am-3pm, dinner from 5pm) Raise your breakfast game at this gourmet caterer's bistro tucked in the corner of a cookie-cutter strip mall. With its exposed brick walls and sleek designs, Plums will have you feeling oh-so-chic as you nibble Dutch baby pancakes with Oregon pepper bacon, or alderwood smoked-salmon hash. Breakfast served until 11:30am weekdays, brunch till 3pm on weekends.

Breakfast cocktails incorporate fun ingredients like cucumber-mint or blood orange.

Habana LATIN AMERICAN **$$**
(☎714-556-0176; The Lab, 2930 Bristol St; mains lunch $6-13, dinner $15-36; ⏰11:30am-4pm & 5-11pm Sun-Thu, to midnight Fri & Sat) With its flickering votive candles, ivy-covered courtyard and spicy Cuban, Mexican and Jamaican specialties, this sultry cantina whispers rendezvous. Paella, *ropa vieja* (shredded flank steak in tomato sauce) and salmon *al parilla* (grilled) come with plantains and black beans on the side. On weekends, the bar gets jumpin' late-night.

Memphis Café Bar SOUTHERN **$$**
(☎714-432-7685; http://memphiscafe.com; 22701 Pelican Hill Rd S; 2920 Bristol St; mains lunch $7-12, dinner $12-22; ⏰8am-10pm Mon-Wed, to 10:30pm Thu-Sat, 8am-3pm & 5-9:30pm Sun) Inside a vintage mid-century modern building, this fashionable eatery is all about down-home flavor – think pulled-pork sandwiches, popcorn shrimp, gumbo and buttermilk-battered fried chicken. Happy hour at the bar is best.

Drinking & Nightlife

Milk + Honey CAFE
(The Camp, 2981 Bristol St; ⏰8am-10pm Mon-Thu, to 11pm Fri & Sat, 10am-10pm Sun; 📶) Fair-trade, shade-grown and organic coffee, chai tea and strong espresso drinks, plus fruit smoothies, seasonal fro-yo flavors and Japanese-style shave ice with flavors like strawberry, red bean and almond.

Wine Lab WINE BAR
(www.winelabcamp.com; The Camp, 2937 Bristol St, Suite A101B; ⏰noon-10pm Tue-Thu, to 11pm Fri & Sat, to 9pm Sun, 4-9pm Mon) This friendly wine shop offers New World wine and craft-beer tasting flights, plus small plates of artisan cheeses and charcuterie.

Entertainment

Segerstrom Center for the Arts THEATER, CONCERT HALL
(☎714-556-2787; www.scfta.org; 600 Town Center Dr) The county's main performance venue is home to the Pacific Symphony, Philharmonic Society of Orange County and Pacific Chorale and draws international performing-arts luminaries and Broadway shows, in three main theaters. Check the website for the wide-ranging calendar.

South Coast Repertory THEATER
(☎714-708-5555; www.scr.org; 655 Town Center Dr) Next to Segerstrom Center, South Coast Rep was started by a band of plucky theater grads in the 1960s and has evolved into a multiple-Tony Award–winning company. It's managed to hold true to its mission to 'explore the most urgent human and social issues of our time' with groundbreaking, original plays from fall through to spring.

Shopping

South Coast Plaza MALL
(www.southcoastplaza.com; 3333 Bristol St; ⏰10am-9pm Mon-Fri, to 8pm Sat, 11am-6:30pm Sun) The stats at SoCal's premier luxury shopping destination speak for themselves. About $2 billion in annual sales, nearly 300 luxury brand and chain shops, five department stores, five valet stations and 12,750 parking spaces. Grab a map from a concierge booth. South Coast Plaza offers thrice-daily shuttles from Anaheim hotels (☎888-288-5823).

The Lab MALL
(www.thelab.com; 2930 Bristol St) This outdoor, ivy-covered 'anti-mall,' is an in-your-face alternative to South Coast Plaza. Indie-minded shoppers can sift through vintage clothing, unique sneakers and trendy duds for teens, tweens and 20-somethings. For short attention spans, contemporary-art exhibitions are displayed in the walk-through trailers of the community **ARTery Gallery**.

The Camp MALL
(www.thecampsite.com; 2937 Bristol St) 🍃 Vegans, tree-huggers and rock climbers, lend me your ears. The Camp offers one-stop shopping for all your outdoor and natural-living needs. Active Ride Shop, fair-trade Seed People's Market and the toxin-free nail salon Lollipop are among the stores clustered along a leafy outdoor walkway. The parking lot is painted with inspirational quotes like 'Show Up for Life.'

Information

Travelex (South Coast Plaza, 1st fl, 3333 Bristol St; ⏰10am-9pm Mon-Fri, to 8pm Sat, 11am-6:30pm Sun) Foreign-currency exchange inside the mall, between Sears and Bloomingdale's.

Getting There & Around

Costa Mesa starts immediately inland from Newport Beach via Hwy 55. South Coast Plaza is off Bristol St, north of the intersection of I-405, toll-road Hwy 73 and Hwy 55, about 6 miles northeast of PCH.

Several **OCTA** (☎714-560-6282; www.octa.net) routes converge on South Coast Plaza, including bus 57 running along Bristol Ave south to Newport Beach's Fashion Island ($2, 20 minutes, every half hour).

Corona del Mar

Savor some of SoCal's most celebrated ocean views from the bluffs of Corona del Mar, a chichi community stretching along PCH and hugging the eastern flank of Newport Channel. In addition to stellar lookouts, several postcard-perfect beaches, rocky coves and child-friendly tide pools beckon along this idyllic stretch of coast.

A half mile long, **Main Beach** (Corona del Mar State Beach; 949-644-3151; 6am-10pm; P) lies at the foot of rocky cliffs. There are restrooms, fire rings (arrive early to snag one) and volleyball courts. All-day parking costs $15, but spaces fill by 9am on weekends. If you're lucky, you may find free parking atop the cliffs behind the beach along Ocean Blvd.

Above the west end of Main Beach, **Lookout Point** (Ocean Blvd) is near Heliotrope Ave. Conceal your chardonnay: technically you can't drink here, though many people do. In fact, some people practically throw cocktail parties, mostly because of the fantastic views overlooking the harbor. Take the nearby stairs off the north end of the Main Beach parking lot down to hideaway **Pirates Cove**, a waveless beach that's great for families. Scenes from the classic TV show *Gilligan's Island* were shot here.

Kids also love the tide pools at **Little Corona Beach** just east of Main Beach, but be aware that the pools are being loved to death. Don't yank anything from the rocks and tread lightly; light, oxygen and heavy footsteps can kill the critters. Because there's no parking lot here, crowds may be lighter. Look for street parking on Ocean Blvd near Poppy Ave. Further west near the intersection of Ocean Blvd with Orchid Ave is **Inspiration Point**, where the views of surf, sand and sea are impressive.

Downtown along PCH at the **Sherman Library & Gardens** (949-673-2261; www.slgardens.org; 2647 E Pacific Coast Hwy; adult/child 12-16yr/under 12 $3/1/free, Mon free; 10:30am-4pm, library closed Sat & Sun), profuse orchids, a rose garden, a koi pond and even a desert garden are worth a wander. The small, noncirculating research library holds a wealth of historical documents from California, Arizona, Nevada and Baja.

Crystal Cove State Park

With 3.5 miles of open beach and over 2300 acres of undeveloped woodland, this **state beach** (949-494-3539; www.parks.ca.gov; 8471 N Coast Hwy; per car $15, campsites $25-75) lets you forget you're in a crowded metropolitan area, at least once you get past the parking lot and stake out a place on the sand. Many visitors don't know it, but Crystal Cove is also an underwater park. Scuba enthusiasts can check out two historic anchors dating from the 1800s as well as the crash site of a Navy plane that went down in the 1940s. Alternatively you can just go tide pooling, fishing, kayaking and surfing along the undeveloped shoreline. On the park's inland side, miles of hiking and mountain biking trails await.

Sleeping & Eating

In the park's historic district, you can rent your own little **cottage** (reservations 800-444-7275; www.crystalcovebeachcottages.com; 35 Crystal Cove, Newport Beach; r with shared bath $42-127, cottages $162-249; check-in 4-9pm) on the beach. Competition is so fierce that you'll usually need to book on the first day of the month six months before your intended stay, unless you get very lucky with a last-minute cancellation. You can reserve cottages and campsites by contacting **ReserveAmerica** (800-444-7275; www.reserveamerica.com; campsites $25, cottages shared $60-170, private $125-360). Campsites are environmentally friendly and undeveloped (no drinking water or toilets) and are only accessible via a strenuous 3-mile hike.

Ruby's Crystal Cove Shake Shack DINER $
(www.rubys.com; 7703 E Coast Hwy; shakes $5; 6:30am-9pm, to 10pm Fri & Sat) South Carolina has South of the Border, South Dakota has Wall Drug and SoCal has Ruby's Crystal Cove Shake Shack. Although this been-here-forever wooden shake stand is now owned by the Ruby's Diner chain, at least the ocean views are as good as ever. Don't fear the date shake, it's delish. The shack is just east of the Crystal Cove/Los Trancos entrance to the state park's historic district.

Beachcomber Café AMERICAN $$
(949-376-6900; www.thebeachcombercafe.com; 15 Crystal Cove; mains breakfast $9-18, lunch $13-21, dinner $23-36; 7am-9:30pm; P) The atmospheric Beachcomber Café lets you soak up the vintage 1950s beach vibe as you

tuck into macadamia-nut pancakes, roasted turkey club sandwiches or more serious surf-and-turf. Sunset is the magic hour for Polynesian tiki drinks by the sea. Validated parking with purchase over $15.

Laguna Beach

POP 23,176

It's easy to love Laguna: secluded coves, romantic cliffs, azure waves and waterfront parks imbue the city with a Riviera-like feel. But nature isn't the only draw. From public sculptures and art festivals to free summer shuttles, the city has taken thoughtful steps to promote tourism while discreetly maintaining its moneyed quality of life (MTV's racy reality show *Laguna Beach* being one drunken, shameless exception).

One of the earliest incorporated cities in California, Laguna has a strong tradition in the arts, starting with the 'plein air' impressionists who lived and worked here in the early 1900s. Today it's the home of renowned arts festivals, several dozen galleries, a well-known museum and exquisitely preserved Arts and Crafts cottages and bungalows that come as a relief after seeing endless miles of suburban beige-box architecture. It's also the OC's most prominent gay enclave.

Separated from the inland flatlands by a long steep canyon, Laguna stretches about 7 miles along PCH. Shops, restaurants and bars are concentrated along a short walkable stretch of downtown's 'village,' along three parallel streets: Broadway, Ocean Ave and Forest Ave. Downtown swells with tourists on summer weekends, but away from the downtown village (also the central business district) and Main Beach (where the downtown village meets the shore), there's plenty of uncrowded sand and open water.

Sights

With 30 public beaches sprawling along 7 miles of coastline, Laguna Beach is perfect for do-it-yourself exploring. There's always another stunning view or hidden cove just around the bend. Although many of the coves are blocked from street view by multimillion-dollar homes, a good local map or sharp eye will take you to stairways leading from PCH down to the beach. Just look for the 'beach access' signs, and be prepared to pass through people's backyards to reach the sand. Unlike its neighbors to the north, Laguna doesn't impose a beach curfew. You can rent beach chairs, umbrellas and boogie boards from **Main Beach Toys** (☎949-494-8808; 150 Laguna Ave; chairs/umbrellas/boards per day $10/10/15; ⏰9am-9pm), opposite Main Beach on the corner of South Coast Hwy.

★ Laguna Art Museum MUSEUM
(☎949-494-8971; www.lagunaartmuseum.org; 307 Cliff Dr; adult/student & senior/child $7/5/free, 1st Thu of month free; ⏰11am-5pm Fri-Tue, to 9pm Thu) This breezy museum has changing exhibitions featuring contemporary Californian artists, and a permanent collection heavy on Californian landscapes, vintage photographs and works by early Laguna bohemians. Free guided tours are usually given at 11am Tuesday, Thursday and Saturday, and there's a unique gift shop. Hours may be extended during some exhibitions.

Pacific Marine Mammal Center ANIMAL SHELTER
(☎949-494-3050; www.pacificmmc.org; 20612 Laguna Canyon Rd; admission by donation; ⏰10am-4pm) A nonprofit organization dedicated to rescuing and rehabilitating injured or ill marine mammals, this center northeast of town has a small staff and many volunteers who help nurse rescued pinnipeds – mostly sea lions and seals – before releasing them back into the wild. There are several outside pools and holding pens – but remember, this is a rescue center, not SeaWorld. Still, it's educational and heart-warming. Admission is by donation, and anything you buy in the gift shop (say, a stuffed animal) helps.

Central Beaches BEACHES
Near downtown's village, **Main Beach** has volleyball and basketball courts, a playground and restrooms. It's Laguna's best beach for swimming. Just north at **Picnic Beach**, it's too rocky to surf; tide pooling is best. Pick up a tide table at the visitors bureau. (Tide pool etiquette: tread lightly on dry rocks only and don't pick anything up that you find living in the water or on the rocks.)

Above Picnic Beach, the grassy, bluff-top **Heisler Park** offers vistas of craggy coves and deep-blue sea. Bring your camera – with its palm trees and bougainvillea-dotted bluffs, the scene is definitely one for posterity. Drop down below to Divers Cove, a deep, protected inlet popular with snorkelers and, of course, divers. A scenic walkway also connects Heisler Park to Main Beach.

North of downtown, **Crescent Bay** has big hollow waves good for bodysurfing, but parking is difficult; try the bluffs atop the

DON'T MISS

FESTIVALS & THE CITY

With a dramatic canyon backdrop, Laguna's **Festival of Arts** (www.foapom.com; 650 Laguna Canyon Rd; admission $7-10; usually 10am-11:30pm Jul & Aug) is a two-month celebration of original artwork in almost all its forms. About 140 exhibitors display artwork ranging from paintings and handcrafted furniture to scrimshaw. Begun in the 1930s by local artists who needed to drum up buyers, the festival now attracts international patrons. In addition to the art show, there are kid-friendly art workshops and live music and entertainment daily. Across the road, look for the slightly more independent-minded **Sawdust Festival** (949-494-3030; www.sawdustartfestival.org; 935 Laguna Canyon Rd; adult/child 6-12yr/senior $8.50/4/7; 10am-10pm late Jun-early Aug, to 6pm Sat & Sun late Nov–mid-Dec), which also hosts a more limited festival in late autumn.

The most thrilling part of the main festival, an experience that will leave you rubbing your eyes in disbelief, is the **Pageant of the Masters** (800-487-3378; www.foapom.com; 650 Laguna Canyon Rd; tickets from $15; 8:30pm daily mid-Jul–Aug) where human models blend seamlessly into re-creations of famous paintings. Tickets are hard to get, unless you order them more than six months in advance, but you may be able to snag last-minute cancellations at the gate.

beach; the views here are reminiscent of the Amalfi Coast. Off Cliff Dr north of Heisler Park before reaching Crescent Bay, **Shaw's Cove** provides the best tide pooling around. Volunteers are often on duty to answer questions and give you tide pooling tips.

Southern Beaches BEACHES

About 1 mile south of downtown, secluded **Victoria Beach** has volleyball courts and **La Tour**, a Rapunzel's-tower-like structure from 1926. Skimboarding (at the south end) and scuba diving are popular here. Take the stairs down Victoria Dr; there's limited parking along PCH.

Further south, **Aliso Beach County Park** (www.ocparks.com/alisobeach; 31131 S Pacific Coast Hwy; parking per hr $1; 6am-10pm) is popular with surfers, boogie boarders and skimboarders. With picnic tables, fire pits and a play area, it's also good for families. Pay-and-display parking costs $1 per hour. Or drive south and park on PCH for free.

Jealously guarded by locals, **Thousand Steps Beach** is hidden about 1 mile south of Aliso Beach. Just past Mission Hospital, park along PCH or residential side streets. At the south end of 9th St, more than 200 steps (way less than 1000) lead down to the sand. Though rocky, the beach is great for sunbathing, surfing and bodysurfing.

Activities

Diving & Snorkeling

With its coves, reefs and rocky outcroppings, Laguna is one of the best SoCal beaches for diving and snorkeling. One of the most famous spots is **Divers Cove** just below Heisler Park. It's part of the **Glenn E Vedder Ecological Reserve**, an underwater park stretching to the northern border of Main Beach. Also popular is **Shaw's Cove**. Check weather and surf conditions (949-494-6573) beforehand, as drownings have happened. The visitors bureau has tide charts.

Laguna Sea Sports DIVING

(949-494-6965; www.beachcitiesscuba.com; 925 N Coast Hwy; 10am-6pm Mon-Thu, to 7pm Fri, 7am-7pm Sat, 8am-5pm Sun) For rentals or to rinse your gear, stop by Laguna Sea Sports near Shaw's Cove. Check out its website for more info about local dive spots and diving etiquette, as well as classes.

Surfing

Because of Laguna's coves, the surfing here isn't as stellar as it is further north. If you must, try the beaches at Thalia St, Brooks St or St Ann's Dr (but beware of rocks).

CA Surf Shop WATER SPORTS

(949-497-1423; www.casurfshop.com; 689 S Coast Hwy; lessons group/private $75/95) Rents surfboards ($30), wet suits ($20) and bodyboards or skimboards ($15) and offers one-hour lessons in surfing and paddleboarding.

Stand Up Paddle Company WATER SPORTS

(949-715-9730; www.supcompany.com; 1103 S Coast Hwy; group/private lessons from $45/90, rental per 3hr/day $50/70) C'mon, everybody's doing it! It's time to learn to stand-up paddle surf. This shop's conveniently located to Oak St Beach.

Laguna Beach

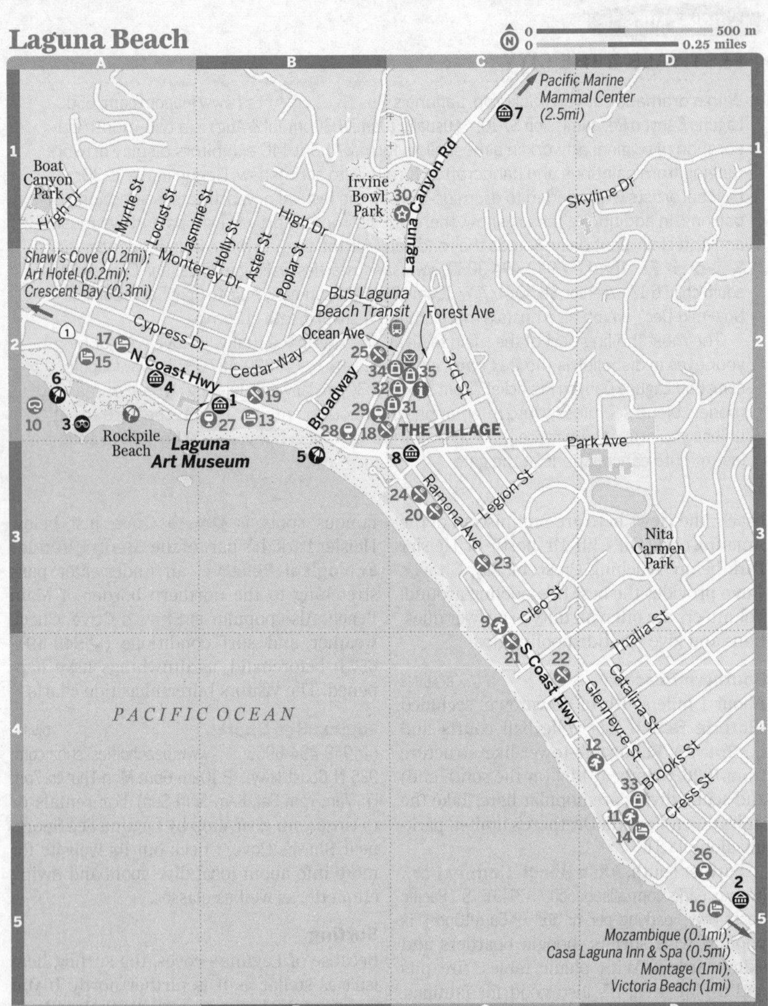

Kayaking

La Vida Laguna WATER SPORTS
(☎949-275-7544; www.lavidalaguna.com; 1257 S Coast Hwy; 2hr guided tour $95) Take a guided kayaking tour of the craggy coves of Laguna's coast and you might just see a colony of sea lions. Make reservations at least a day in advance.

Cycling & Mountain Biking

Laguna Beach isn't the greatest for road biking. Drivers along always-busy PCH are distracted by the view, so you must pay attention if you head out on that road. Up in the hills, you can have a blast mountain biking. Crystal Cove State Park and **Aliso & Wood Canyons Wilderness Park** (www.ocparks.com/alisoandwoodcanyons; 28373 Alicia Pkwy, Laguna Niguel) are rated highly by locals.

Laguna Cyclery BICYCLE RENTAL
(☎949-494-1522; www.lagunabeachcyclery.com; 240 Thalia St; ⌚9am-7pm Mon-Fri, to 6pm Sat, 10am-5pm Sat & Sun) Get trail info here; 24-hour road bike rental costs $65, mountain bikes $50 to $85.

Rainbow Bicycle Co BICYCLE RENTAL
(☎949-494-5806; www.teamrain.com; 485 N Coast Hwy; ⌚1-6pm Mon, 10am-6pm Tue-Thu,

Laguna Beach

Top Sights

1 Laguna Art Museum B2

Sights

2 Bluebird Gallery D5
3 Heisler Park A2
4 Laguna North Gallery A2
5 Main Beach B3
6 Picnic Beach A2
7 seven-degrees C1
8 Studio 7 Gallery C3

Activities, Courses & Tours

9 CA Surf Shop C3
10 Divers Cove A2
11 La Vida Laguna D4
Laguna Cyclery ..... (see 22)
Rainbow Bicycle Co ..... (see 15)
12 Stand Up Paddle Company D4

Sleeping

13 Inn at Laguna Beach B2
14 La Casa del Camino D5
15 Laguna Cliffs Inn A2
16 Surf & Sand Resort D5
17 Tides A2

Eating

18 230 Forest Avenue B2
19 242 Cafe Fusion Sushi B2
20 House of Big Fish & Cold Beer C3
21 Orange Inn C4
22 Stand C4
23 Taco Loco C3
24 Watermarc C3
25 Zinc Cafe & Market B2

Drinking & Nightlife

26 Bounce D5
Koffee Klatsch ..... (see 26)
27 Las Brisas B2
28 Marine Room Tavern B2
29 Ocean Brewing Company B2
Rooftop Lounge ..... (see 14)

Entertainment

30 Laguna Playhouse C1

Shopping

31 Art for the Soul C2
32 Hobie Surf Shop C2
33 Laguna Beach Books D4
34 Laguna Supply C2
35 Muse Boutique C2
Pacific Gallery ..... (see 18)

noon-4pm Fri-Sun) Just north of downtown, 24-hour rentals of road bikes cost $35, full-suspension mountain bikes $40 (helmets included).

Hiking

Surrounded by a green belt – a rarity in SoCal – Laguna has great nature trails for hikes. If you love panoramic views, take the short, scenic drive to **Alta Laguna Park**, a locals-only park, up-canyon from town. There, the moderate **Park Avenue Nature Trail**, a 1.25-mile one-way hike, takes you through fields of spring wildflowers. Open to hikers and mountain bikers, the 2.5-mile **West Ridge Trail** follows the ridgeline of the hills above Laguna. Both trails are in-and-out trips, not loops. To reach the trailheads, take Park Ave from town to its end at Alta Laguna Blvd then turn left to the park, which has restrooms and a drinking fountain.

Tours

Stop by the visitors bureau to pick up brochures detailing self-guided tours on foot and by public bus. The *Heritage Walking Companion* is a tour of the town's architecture with an emphasis on Laguna's many bungalows and cottages, most dating from the 1920s and '30s. Laguna also overflows with public art, from well-placed murals to freestanding sculptures in unlikely locations. The free *Public Art Brochure* has color photos of all of Laguna's public-art pieces and a map to help you navigate. Or you can just swing by Heisler Park to see almost a dozen sculptures.

Sleeping

Most lodging in Laguna is on busy PCH, so expect traffic noise; bring earplugs or ask for a room away from the road. For cheaper motels and hotels, head about 10 miles inland to the I-405 (San Diego Fwy) around Irvine.

★Tides MOTEL **$$**

(☎888-777-2107, 949-494-2494; www.tideslaguna.com; 460 N Coast Hwy; r $175-285; P❄📶🏊🐾)
A bargain for Laguna, especially considering its convenient location just three long blocks north of the village. It feels rather upscale from plush bedding to beachy-keen decor and inspirational quotes painted into each room. Each room is different; some have kitchenettes. Shared facilities include saltwater pool, barbecue grill and a fireplace for toasting marshmallows. Pet fee $25 to $40.

La Casa del Camino HISTORIC HOTEL $$
(☎855-634-5736, 949-497-2446; www.lacasadelcamino.com; 1289 S Coast Hwy; r from $159; P ⊖ ❄ @ ≋) Built 1929, this Spanish-style hotel has 36 rooms and the awesome Rooftop Lounge bar. No two rooms are the same and Casa Surf Suites feature hip design by local surf-gear companies. A $12 'resort fee' covers breakfast, wi-fi, parking, beach setup and access to a nearby gym.

Art Hotel MOTEL $$
(☎949-494-6464, 877-363-7229; www.arthotellagunabeach.com; 1404 N Coast Hwy; r $154-194; P ❄ @ ≋ ≈ 🐾) A mile northwest of the village, this easygoing, better-than-average shingled motel charges bargain rates, at least for Laguna. In keeping with the theme, colorful murals adorn the public spaces, and works of a different artist hang in each of the 28 rooms. Take the shuttle downtown.

★ **Montage** RESORT $$$
(☎949-715-6000, 866-271-6953; www.montagelagunabeach.com; 30801 S Coast Hwy; d from $525; @ ≋ ≈) You'll find nowhere more indulgent on the OC's coast than this over-the-top luxury waterside resort, especially if you hide away with your lover in a secluded bungalow. Even if you're not staying, come for a spa treatment or a cocktail and check out the lobby art and the spectacular sunburst-inlaid swimming pool.

Inn at Laguna Beach HOTEL $$$
(☎949-497-9722, 800-544-4479; www.innatlagunabeach.com; 211 N Coast Hwy; r $210-600; P ❄ ≋ ≈ 🐾) Pride of place goes to this three-story white concrete hotel, at the north end of Main Beach. Its 70 keen rooms were recently renovated with rattan furniture, blond woods, marble, French blinds and thick featherbeds. Some have balconies overlooking the water. Extras include DVD and CD players, bathrobes, beach gear to borrow and nightly ocean-view wine and beer reception. Parking costs $29.

Casa Laguna Inn & Spa B&B $$$
(☎949-494-2996, 800-233-0449; www.casalaguna.com; 2510 S Coast Hwy; r $159-389, ste from $279; P ❄ @ ≋ 🐾) Laguna's most romantic B&B is built around a historic 1920s mission revival house surrounded by flowering gardens. Smallish rooms include those inside former artists' bungalows from the 1930s and '40s. All have fluffy beds and some have Jacuzzis. There's also a full chef-prepared breakfast made with local, organic ingredients and evening wine-and-cheese reception. Some pets OK (fee $25).

Laguna Cliffs Inn HOTEL $$$
(☎800-297-0007, 949-497-6645; www.lagunacliffsinn.com; 475 N Coast Hwy; r $165-325; P ❄ @ ≋ ≈) Be it good feng shui, friendly staff or proximity to the beach, something just feels right at this renovated 36-room courtyard inn. From the big earth-tone pillows and hardwood floors to air-con and flat-screen TVs, the decor is contemporary, comfy and clean. Settle into the outdoor heated Jacuzzi with a glass of wine as the sun drops over the ocean.

Surf & Sand Resort HOTEL $$$
(☎888-869-7569, 949-497-4477; www.surfandsandresort.com; 1555 S Coast Hwy; r from $560; P ❄ @ ≋ ≈) Be lulled to sleep by crashing waves at this sparkling seaside hotel. Full-on ocean-view rooms have ultracomfy beds, flat-screen TVs, an iPod dock with speakers and soothing natural color schemes. There's a full-service spa, and the Splashes beach bar is the closest you can get to the Pacific without getting sand in your Manolos. Overnight parking is $30.

DIY GALLERY WALK

Laguna has three distinct gallery districts: **Gallery Row**, along the 300 to 500 blocks of N Coast Hwy; in **downtown's village**, along Forest Ave and PCH; and further south on **S Coast Hwy** between Oak St and Bluebird Canyon Dr. Pick up an art-walk map at the visitors bureau.

Laguna North Gallery (www.lagunanorthgallery.com; 376 N Coast Hwy; ⊙11am-4:30pm), **Studio 7 Gallery** (www.studio7gallery.com; 384b N Coast Hwy; ⊙11am-5pm) and off-the-beaten-path **seven-degrees** (www.seven-degrees.com; 891 Laguna Canyon Rd; ⊙10am-5pm Mon-Fri) further inland are all artists' cooperative galleries. South of downtown, **Bluebird Gallery** (www.bluebirdgallery.net; 1540 S Coast Hwy; ⊙11am-5pm Wed-Sun) exhibits California landscape paintings in Laguna's impressionist plein-air style. On First Thursdays (p265), most participating galleries stay open until 9pm.

Eating

Laguna's dining scene will tickle foodies' fancies. Vegetarians will be happy, too, especially at the weekly **farmers market** (384 Forest Ave; 8am-noon Sat) in the Lumberyard parking lot, near City Hall.

Taco Loco MEXICAN $
(http://tacoloco.net; 640 S Coast Hwy; mains $3-14; 11am-midnight Sun-Thu, to 2am Fri & Sat;) Throw back Coronas with the surfers while watching the passersby on PCH at this Mexican sidewalk cafe. Taco, quesadilla and nacho options seem endless: blackened calamari or tofu, swordfish, veggie (potato, mushroom, tofu) and shrimp to name a few. For dessert: hemp brownies. Order at the counter, dude.

Zinc Cafe & Market CAFE $
(www.zinccafe.com; 350 Ocean Ave, Laguna Beach; mains $6-11; market 7am-6pm, cafe to 4pm;) Ground zero for Laguna's see-and-be-seen vegetarians, this gourmet market has a hedge-enclosed patio where you can munch on tasty vegetarian and vegan meals such as garden-fresh salads and pizzas. If you've been hesitant to order oatmeal at a restaurant, resist no more: Zinc's fresh fruit-covered version is delish. Strong espresso too.

Stand CAFE $
(238 Thalia St; mains $6-10; 7am-7pm;) With its friendly, indie-spirited vibe comes this tiny tribute to healthy cuisine. From hummus and guac sandwiches to sunflower sprout salads and black-beans-and-rice burritos, the menu is varied and all of it soul-satisfying. Try a smoothie or an all-natural shake. Order at the counter in the red mini-barn, then cross your fingers for an outdoor patio table.

Orange Inn DINER $
(949-494-6085; www.orangeinnlagunabeach.com; 703 S Coast Hwy; mains $5-10; 6:30am-5pm, to 7pm Sat & Sun) Surfers fuel up before hitting the waves, at this little shop from 1931, which is credited in the *Guinness Book of Records* for inventing the smoothie. Also look for date shakes, big breakfasts, homemade muffins and deli sandwiches on wholewheat or sourdough bread.

House of Big Fish & Cold Beer SEAFOOD $$
(949-715-4500; www.houseofbigfish.com; 540 S Coast Hwy; mains $7-15; 11:30am-10:30pm) The name says it all (what else do you need?): Hawaii-style *poke* (marinated raw fish), Baja-style fish tacos, coconut shrimp and the fresh catch o' the day. Fish are sustainably raised, and there are dozens of beers including about one-third from California. Make reservations, or wait, like, forever.

DON'T MISS

FIRST THURSDAYS

On the first Thursday of the month, downtown Laguna Beach gets festive during the **First Thursdays Gallery Art Walk** (949-683-6871; www.firstthursdaysartwalk.com; 6pm-9pm 1st Thu of month) FREE. You can make the rounds of 40 local galleries and the Laguna Art Museum (p260) via free shuttles circling Laguna's art gallery districts.

★ **242 Cafe Fusion Sushi** JAPANESE $$$
(www.fusionart.us; 242 N Coast Hwy; mains $18-45; 4:30-10pm Sun-Thu, to 10:30pm Fri & Sat) One of the only female sushi chefs in Orange County, Miki Izumisawa slices and rolls organic rice into Laguna's best sushi, artfully presented. The place seats maybe two dozen people at a time, so expect a wait or come early. The 'sexy' handroll – spicy ahi and scallops with mint, cilantro, avocado and crispy potato – is date-enhancing.

Watermarc MODERN AMERICAN $$$
(949-376-6272; www.watermarcrestaurant.com; 448 S Coast Hwy; dinner mains $24-34; 11am-10pm Sun-Thu, 11am-11pm Fri & Sat) At this stylish purveyor of New American cuisine, the small-plates menu ($7 to $14) ranges from filet mignon pot pie and clams casino to sizzling garlic shrimp and *chilies fritas*. In fact, appetizers are so good, and the cocktail list so inventive (blueberry-coconut mojito, anyone?), you might decide to skip the classic surf-and-turf dinners. The sleek, not stuffy dining room has glass front doors thrown open to the sidewalk and sea breezes.

230 Forest Avenue CALIFORNIAN $$$
(949-494-2545; www.230forestavenue.com; 230 Forest Ave; mains $16-30; lunch from 11am, dinner from 5pm) Sleek, contemporary and chatty bistro in the heart of downtown's village is always bustling – not just for its martini bar but more importantly for its fresh seafood like buttermilk calamari, 'bang-bang' rock shrimp, five-spice ahi sashimi or garlic-lemongrass soup with clams and mussels. It may look haute, but you can get away with a dressy swimsuit cover-up at lunch.

Mozambique AFRICAN FUSION **$$$**
(☎949-715-7777; www.mozambiqueoc.com; 1740 S Coast Hwy; dinner mains $14-69; ⏰11am-11pm Sun-Thu, to midnight Fri & Sat) Macaws and toucans welcome you to this trendy, sophisticated, three-level ode to exotically spiced dishes from southern Africa – peri-peri prawns to soaring steaks and seafood, in small plates to pricey surf and turf. Who knows, you might see a *Real Housewives* cast member hiding out in the rooftop bar, which has live music on weekends.

Drinking & Nightlife

There are almost as many watering holes in downtown's village as there are art galleries. Most cluster along S Coast Hwy and Ocean Ave. If you drink, don't drive; local cops take DUIs very seriously.

Although Laguna has one of SoCal's largest gay populations, the once-thriving gay nightlife has vanished. As we went to press, the only remaining gay bar in town, **Bounce** (1460 S Coast Hwy), was rather dull, but new management promises improvements.

Rooftop Lounge BAR
(www.rooftoplagunabeach.com; 1289 S Coast Hwy) Perched atop La Casa del Camino, this bar, with 270-degree coastal views and a friendly vibe, has locals singing hallelujahs. Follow the fashionable crowds through the hotel's lobby and take the elevator to the top. Mango and wild berry mojitos add some spice to the cocktail menu, and you can snack on plates such as meatballs in guava barbecue sauce.

Marine Room Tavern DIVE BAR
(214 Ocean Ave) The party's always rockin' at this lively tavern in downtown's village where the Harley-loving crowd isn't afraid to whoop it up, sometimes right on the sidewalk. Although you won't find food or many marines, there are pool tables and pinball. Live music most nights.

Ocean Brewing Company BREWPUB
(www.oceanbrewing.com; 237 Ocean Ave) For pub grub and microbrews after a day of surfing. This place lines up copper vats behind the bar and has different DJs and live acoustic acts almost nightly (except when there's karaoke). Kick back on the outdoor patio for primo people-watching.

Las Brisas BAR
(www.lasbrisaslagunabeach.com; 361 Cliff Dr) Locals roll their eyes at the mere mention of this tourist-heavy resto, but out-of-towners flock here for a reason: the view. You won't soon forget the image of crashing waves as you sip margaritas on the glassed-in patio on the bluff. Cocktail hour gets packed. Don't come if it's dark outside.

Koffee Klatsch COFFEE SHOP
(1440 S Coast Hwy; ⏰7am-11pm Sun-Thu, to midnight Fri & Sat) About a mile south of downtown, this cozy coffee shop draws a mixed gay/straight/hipster crowd for coffees, breakfasts, salads and ginormous cakes.

☆ Entertainment

Laguna Playhouse THEATER
(☎949-497-2787; www.lagunaplayhouse.com; 606 Laguna Canyon Rd) Orange County's oldest continuously operating community theater stages lighter plays in summer, more serious works in winter.

Shopping

Downtown's village is a shopper's paradise, with hidden courtyards and eclectic little bungalows that beg further exploration. Forest Ave has the highest concentration of chic boutiques, but south of downtown, PCH has its fair share of fashionable, eclectic and arty shops where you can balance your chakras or buy vintage rock albums and posters.

Hobie Surf Shop SPORTS, CLOTHING
(www.hobie.com; 294 Forest Ave) Hobart 'Hobie' Alter started his internationally known surf line in his parents' Laguna Beach garage in 1950. Today, this is one of only a handful of logo retail shops where you can stock up on surfboards and beachwear for both babes and dudes.

Laguna Supply CLOTHING
(210 Beach St) This earth-toned corner shop hits that right pitch for an effortless girlfriends' weekend beach getaway, somewhere in between urban chic and beach preppy, with distressed denim, boyfriend shirts and breezy woven scarves.

Muse Boutique CLOTHING
(www.myspace.com/museboutiquelagunabeach; 300 Forest Ave) Fans of MTV's *Laguna Beach* will recognize this upbeat gallery where women's beach-chic couture, handbags and jewelry glitter under a sky-blue ceiling dotted with wispy clouds. You'll faint after glimpsing the price tags.

Art for the Soul GIFTS
(www.art4thesoul.com; 272 Forest Ave) Decorated in big, bold colors, this offbeat craft gallery is the place to fill your bags with surf 'woody' wagon night lights, painted pint glasses, art-glass jewelry and starfish wind chimes.

Pacific Gallery GIFTS
(www.pacificgallery.net; 228 Forest Ave) Here you'll find art that's whimsical and sometimes irresistible, but no bargains. All of the pieces are handmade – from sculptures and paintings to welded metal and mosaics – some by Laguna artists.

Laguna Beach Books BOOKS
(www.lagunabeachbooks.com; Old Pottery Place, 1200 S Coast Hwy #105; 10am-8pm) Friendly indie bookshop stocks everything, including surf culture and SoCal local-interest titles.

Information

Visit Laguna Beach Visitor Center, it has free wi-fi and internet terminal access.

Green Laguna Beach (http://greenlagunabeach.com) Website with green travel ideas, garden tours, hiking trails, eco-events and more tips.

Laguna Beach Coastline Pilot (www.coastlinepilot.com) Newspaper covering the dining, arts and culture scenes, with an up-to-date calendar online.

Mission Hospital Laguna Beach (949-499-1311; www.missionforhealth.com; 31872 Coast Hwy; 24hr) Four miles south of downtown along PCH.

OC Weekly (www.ocweekly.com) Free alternative tabloid and website reviewing nightlife, restaurants and the arts, plus a current events calendar.

Post Office (www.usps.com; 350 Forest Ave; 9am-5pm Mon-Fri)

Sleepy Hollow Medical Group (949-494-3740; www.andersonwmcmd.com; 364 Ocean Ave; 8am-6pm Mon-Sat, 9am-1pm Sun) Walk-in nonemergency clinic.

Visit Laguna Beach Visitors Center (949-497-9229; www.lagunabeachinfo.com; 381 Forest Ave; 10am-5pm;) Helpful staff, bus schedules, restaurant menus and free brochures on everything from hiking trails to self-guided walking tours.

Getting There & Away

From I-405, take Hwy 133 (Laguna Canyon Rd) southwest. Hwy 1 goes by several names in Laguna Beach: south of Broadway, downtown's main street, it's called South Coast Hwy; north of Broadway it's North Coast Hwy. Locals also call it Pacific Coast Hwy or just PCH.

OCTA (714-560-6282; www.octa.net) bus 1 heading along the coast connects Laguna Beach with Orange County's other beach towns, including Dana Point heading south, every 30 to 60 minutes. The one-way fare is $2 (exact change).

FIRE!

Forest fires are an ever-present danger all over Southern California – a truth Laguna Beach knows too well, due to fires large and small over the years. The canyons act like chimneys and small grass fires can quickly become infernos. Use extreme caution when lighting matches and don't just toss your cigarette butts – extinguish them with water or dirt, and once they're completely out, dispose of them properly.

Getting Around

BUS

Laguna Beach Transit (www.lagunabeachcity.net; 375 Broadway) has its central bus depot in downtown's village. Buses operate on three routes at hourly intervals (no service from 12:30pm to 1:30pm or on Sundays or public holidays). Routes are color-coded and are easy to follow. For tourists, the most important bus route is the red route that runs south of downtown along PCH. Rides cost 75c (exact change). All routes are free during July and August. You can pick up an information brochure and bus schedule at the visitors bureau.

CAR & MOTORCYCLE

Through town, PCH moves slowly in summer, especially on weekends.

Parking lots in downtown's village charge between $10 and $20 per entry; they fill up early in the day during summer. Street parking can be hard to find near the beaches during summer, especially in the afternoons and on weekends – arrive early. Coin- and credit-card-operated meters cost from $1 per hour and pay-and-display lots cost $2 per hour. Alternatively, you can park for free in residential areas, but obey time limits and posted restrictions, or you'll be towed. If you can't find parking downtown, drive to the north or south ends of town by the beach, then ride the bus.

SHUTTLE

To alleviate summer traffic, free trolley shuttles travel between downtown and popular Festival of Arts sites in Laguna Canyon and north–south along PCH. These trolleys make continuous loops every 20 to 30 minutes between 9:30am and 11:30pm daily from late June until late August.

Around Laguna Beach

San Juan Capistrano

Famous for its swallows that fly back to town every year on March 19 (though sometimes they're just a bit early), San Juan Capistrano is also home to the 'jewel of the California missions.' It's a little town, about 11 miles south and inland of Laguna Beach, but there's enough history and charm here to make almost a day of it.

Sights & Activities

★Mission San Juan Capistrano CHURCH
(☎949-234-1300; www.missionsjc.com; 26801 Ortega Hwy, San Juan Capistrano; adult/child $9/6; ⏲9am-5pm) Plan on spending at least an hour poking around the sprawling mission's tiled roofs, covered arches, lush gardens, fountains and courtyards – including the padre's quarters, soldiers' barracks and the cemetery. Particularly moving are the towering remains of the **Great Stone Church**, almost completely destroyed by a powerful earthquake on December 8, 1812. The **Serra Chapel** – whitewashed outside with restored frescoes inside – is believed to be the oldest existing building in California (1778). It's certainly the only one still standing in which Junípero Serra gave Mass. Serra founded the mission on November 1, 1776, and tended it personally for many years.

Admission includes a worthwhile free audio tour with interesting stories narrated by locals. The Mission is at the corner of Camino Capistrano.

Los Rios Historic District HISTORIC BUILDINGS
One block southwest of the Mission, next to the Capistrano train depot, this peaceful assemblage of a few dozen historic cottages and adobes now mostly houses cafes and gift shops. To see 1880s-era furnishings and decor, as well as vintage photographs, stop by the tiny **O'Neill Museum** (31831 Los Rios St; adult/child $1/50c; ⏲9am-noon & 1-4pm Tue-Fri, noon-3pm Sat & Sun) in a board and batten construction home. You can pick up a free walking-tour guide of historic San Juan Capistrano at the volunteer-staffed **information kiosk** off Verdugo St, by the railroad tracks.

> DON'T MISS
>
> **FIESTA DE LA GOLONDRINAS**
>
> The famous swallows return to nest in the walls of Mission San Juan Capistrano every year around March 19, the feast of Saint Joseph, after wintering in South America. Their flight covers about 7500 miles each way. The highlight of the town's month-long **Festival of the Swallows** (www.swallowsparade.com) is a big parade and outdoor *mercado* (market), held on a Saturday in mid-March.

Eating & Drinking

There are a lot of restaurants within walking distance of the Mission.

★El Campeon MEXICAN $
(31921 Camino Capistrano; $2-9; ⏲6:30am-9pm; 👪) For real-deal Mexican food, in a strip mall south of the Mission, try this multi-room counter-service restaurant, *panadería* (bakery) and *mercado* (grocery store). Look for tacos, tostadas and burritos in freshly made tortillas, *aguas frescas* (fruit drinks) in flavors like watermelon, strawberry and grapefruit, and breads and pastries starting at just 59¢.

Farmers Market MARKET $
(cnr Camino Capistrano & Yorba St; ⏲3-6pm Wed, to 7pm Apr-Oct) Sample local fruits, veggies and specialty foods at downtown's weekly farmers market.

★Ramos House Café CALIFORNIAN $$
(www.ramoshouse.com; 31752 Los Rios St; mains $15-20; ⏲8:30am-3pm Tue-Sun) The best spot for breakfast or lunch near the Mission, this Old West–flavored, wood-built house from 1881 is famous for organically raised comfort food flavored with herbs grown onsite. To find it, walk across the railroad tracks at the end of Verdugo St and turn right. Promptly reward yourself with apple-cinnamon beignets, basil-cured salmon lox or pulled-pork sandwiches.

El Adobe de Capistrano MEXICAN $$
(www.eladobedecapistrano.com; 31891 Camino Capistrano; mains lunch $11-21, dinner $11-34; ⏲11am-9pm Mon-Thu, to 10pm Fri & Sat, 10am-9pm Sun) In a building that traces its origins to 1797, this sprawling, beamed-ceilinged restaurant and bar does a big business in the standards (enchiladas, fajitas) through to blackened fish or lobster tacos and grilled steaks. It was a favorite of President Nixon who lived in nearby San Clemente.

Coach House CLUB
(☎949-496-8930; www.thecoachhouse.com; 33157 Camino Capistrano) Long-running live-music venue features a roster of local and national rock, indie, alternative and retro bands; expect a cover charge of $15 to $40, depending on who's playing. Recent performers include classic rockers like Marshall Tucker and the late Johnny Winter, plus tribute bands and comedy shows like the *Funniest Housewives of Orange County*.

Getting There & Away

From Laguna Beach, ride **OCTA** (☎714-560-6282; www.octa.net) bus 1 south to Dana Point. At the intersection of PCH and Del Obispo St, catch bus 91 northbound toward Mission Viejo, which drops you near the Mission. Buses run every 30 to 60 minutes. The trip takes about an hour. You'll have to pay the one-way fare ($2, exact change) twice.

Drivers should take I-5 exit 82 (Ortega Hwy), then head west about 0.25 miles. There's free three-hour parking on streets and in municipal lots.

The **Amtrak** (☎800-872-7245; www.amtrak.com; 26701 Verdugo St) depot is one block south and west of the Mission. You could arrive by train from LA ($21, 75 minutes) or San Diego ($22, 90 minutes) in time for lunch, visit the mission and be back in the city for dinner. A few daily **Metrolink** (☎800-371-5465; www.metrolinktrains.com) commuter trains link San Juan Capistrano to Orange ($8, 45 minutes), with limited connections to Anaheim.

Dana Point

POP 34,048

Dana Point was once called 'the only romantic spot on the coast.' Too bad that quote dates from seafarer Richard Dana's voyage here in the 1830s. Its built-up, parking-lotted harbor detracts from the charm of its neighbors have, but it still gets a lot of visitors for its lovely beaches and its port for whale watching, sport fishing and the like.

Sights

Most attractions cluster in and around artificial Dana Point Harbor, at the foot of Golden Lantern St, just south of PCH off Dana Point Harbor Dr.

Doheny State Beach BEACH
(☎949-496-6172; www.dohenystatebeach.org; entry per vehicle $15; ⏲6am-10pm, to 8pm Nov-Feb; P 👪) Adjacent to the southern border of Dana Point Harbor, this mile-long beach is great for swimmers, surfers, surf fishers and tide-poolers. You'll also find picnic tables with grills, volleyball courts and a butterfly exhibit at the 62-acre coastal park. All-day parking costs $15. Stop by the parks' **visitors center** to check out the five aquariums, mounted birds and 500-gallon simulated tide pool. Free wi-fi at the snack bar.

Ocean Institute MUSEUM
(☎949-496-2274; www.ocean-institute.org; 24200 Dana Pt Harbor Dr; adult/child $6.50/4.50; ⏲10am-3pm Sat & Sun; 👪) This child-friendly educational center encompasses four separate ocean-centric 'adventures.' On Sundays, admission includes the opportunity to discover what life was like aboard an early 19th-century tall ship, the brig **Pilgrim**. Guided tours of this full-size replica of the ship sailed by Richard Dana during his journey around Cape Horn to California are offered hourly.

The **Ocean Education Center** is reserved for school groups on weekdays, but on weekends families are welcome to enjoy the interactive marine-focused exhibits. You can also board the **R/V Sea Explorer** (adult/child four to 12 from $35/22), a 70ft-long floating lab, for a science-focused snorkeling cruise or blue-whale safari, or join a 'pyrate' adventure or gray-whale-watching cruise on the **Spirit of Dana Point** (adult/child four to 12 $40/23), a replica of an American Revolution–era tall ship. Make reservations.

Salt Creek Beach BEACH
(www.ocparks.com/saltcreekbeach; 33333 S Pacific Coast Hwy, off Ritz Carlton Dr; ⏲5am-midnight; P) Just south of the Laguna Beach boundary, this 18-acre county-run park is popular with surfers, sunbathers, bodysurfers and tide-poolers. Families make the most of the park's picnic tables, grills, restrooms and showers – all sprawling beneath the elegant bluff-top Ritz Carlton resort. Open in summer, a beach concession stand rents boogie boards, beach chairs and umbrellas. Pay-and-display parking costs $1 per hour. Call ahead to check the center's opening times, which are subject to change.

Activities

Rent bicycles at **Wheel Fun Rentals** (☎949-496-7433; www.wheelfunrentals.com; 25300 Dana Point Harbor Dr; cruiser rental per hr/day $10/28; ⏲9am-sunset daily late May-early Sep, Sat & Sun early Sep-late May), just south of the picnic area at Doheny State Beach. Off Dana Point Harbor Dr, **Capo Beach Watercraft Rentals** (☎949-661-1690; www.capobeachwatercraft.com; 34512 Embarcadero Pl) and **Dana Point Jet Ski & Kayak Center** (☎949-661-4947; www.danapointjetski.com; 34671 Puerto Pl) both rent kayaks for harbor paddling. For scuba rentals and dive-boat trips (from $115), try **Beach Cities Scuba** (☎949-443-3858; www.beachcitiescsuba.com; 34283 Pacific Coast Hwy).

Tours

In Mariner's Village off Dana Point Harbor Dr, Dana Wharf is the starting point for most boat tours and trips to Catalina Island. For more kid-friendly whale-watching tours and coastal cruises, book ahead with the Ocean Institute.

Capt Dave's Dolphin & Whale Safari BOAT
(☎949-488-2828; www.dolphinsafari.com; 34451 Ensenada Pl; adult/child 3-12yr from $59/39) Year-round dolphin- and whale-watching trips on a catamaran equipped with underwater viewing windows, plasma TV screens and stereophonic headphones.

Dana Wharf Sportfishing BOAT
(☎949-496-5794, 888-224-0603; www.danawharf.com; 34675 Golden Lantern St; sportfishing trips adult/child 3-12yr from $46/29, whale-watching tours from $45/25) Half-day sportfishing trips are best for beginners. Whale-watching tours for families operate both winter and summer.

Festivals & Events

Festival of Whales SEA
(www.dpfestivalofwhales.com; ⌚early–mid-Mar) For two weekends, a parade, street fair, nature walks and talks, canoe races, surfing clinics, art exhibitions, live music, and surf 'woody' wagon and hot-rod show make up the merriment.

Doheny Blues Festival MUSIC
(www.omegaevents.com/dohenyblues; ⌚mid-May) Blues legends such as Buddy Guy and Keb Mo perform alongside up-and-comers over a weekend of funky live music performances and family fun at Doheny State Beach.

Tall Ships Festival SEA
(www.tallshipsfestival.com; ⌚early Sep) The Ocean Institute hosts the West Coast's largest gathering of tall ships, with living-history encampments, scrimshaw carving demonstrations and lots more family-friendly marine-themed activities.

Sleeping & Eating

Mostly chain midrange motels and luxury resorts are what you'll find along PCH. The latter include the oceanfront **Ritz-Carlton Laguna Niguel** (☎949-240-2000; www.ritzcarlton.com; 1 Ritz-Carlton Dr; r from $420; @🛜🏊), well-positioned for catching sunsets at Salt Creek Beach. For budget motels, head inland along I-405 (San Diego Fwy) back toward Irvine.

Those hankering for straight-off-the-boat seafood can fill their bellies at pierside seafood restaurants around Dana Point Harbor. Take a wander and see what looks fresh and what tickles your fancy.

Doheny State Beach CAMPGROUND $
(☎800-444-7275; www.reserveamerica.com; 25300 Dana Point Harbor Dr; inland/beachfront campsites $35/60) Regularly voted the county's best campground, Doheny State Beach offers picnic tables, fire rings, restrooms and showers, but little shade.

Turk's BAR & GRILL $$
(☎949-496-9028; 34683 Golden Lantern St; mains $5-16; ⌚8am-2am, shorter hours winter) At Dana Wharf, Turk's dive bar is so dark it feels like you're drinking while jailed in the brig of a ship, but never mind. There's plenty of good pub grub (including burgers and fish-and-chips), Bloody Marys and beers, a mellow crowd and a groovy jukebox.

Information

Visitors Center (☎949-248-3501; www.danapoint.org; ⌚9am-4pm Fri-Sun late May-early Sep) Stop at this tiny booth at the corner of Golden Lantern St and Dana Point Harbor Dr for tourist brochures and maps. Gung-ho volunteers sure love their city.

Getting There & Around

From the harbor, **Catalina Express** (☎800-481-3470; www.catalinaexpress.com; 34675 Golden Lantern St; round-trip adult/child 2-11yr/senior $76.50/70/61) makes daily round-trips to Catalina Island, taking 90 minutes each way.

OCTA (☎714-560-6282; www.octa.net) bus 1 connects Dana Point with the OC's other beach towns every 30 to 60 minutes. The one-way fare is $2 (exact change).

Four-hour public parking at the harbor is free, or pay $5 per day (overnight $10).

San Clemente

POP 64,882

Just before reaching San Diego County, PCH slows down and rolls past the laid-back surf town of San Clemente. Home to surfing legends, top-notch surfboard companies and *Surfing* magazine, this unpretentious enclave may be one of the last spots in the OC where you can authentically live the surf lifestyle. Right on, brah.

A quick detour inland, the **Surfing Heritage Foundation** (☎949-388-0313; www.surfingheritage.org; 101 Calle Iglesia; adult/student/child under 12yr $5/4/free; ⏲11am-5pm Mon-Sat) tells the history of the sport by exhibiting surfboards ridden by the greats, from Duke Kahanmoku to Kelly Slater. Call for directions.

Otherwise, turn south off PCH and follow **Avenida del Mar** as it winds south through San Clemente's retro downtown district, where antiques and vintage shops, eclectic boutiques, cafes, restaurants and bars line the main drag. Keep curving downhill toward the ocean until you hit **San Clemente City Beach**, stretching beside the historic 1296ft-long **San Clemente Pier** (611 Avenida Victoria; ⏲4am-midnight), where Prohibition-era bootleggers once brought liquor ashore. Surfers go north of the pier, while swimmers and bodysurfers take the south side. Further south along the coast, at the foot of Trafalgar Street, **T-Street** is another popular surf break.

DON'T MISS

TRESTLES

Surfers won't want to miss world-renowned Trestles, just southeast of San Clemente. It's famous for its natural surf break that consistently churns out perfect waves, even in summer. It's also endangered; surfers and environmentalists have for years been fighting the extension of a nearby toll road that they contend would negatively affect the waves. Trestles lies inside protected **San Onofre State Beach** (www.parks.ca.gov; parking $15 per day), which has rugged bluff-top walking trails, swimming beaches and a developed inland **campground** (☎800-444-7275; www.reserveamerica.com; sites $35-60). To get here, exit I-5 at Basilone Rd or Los Christianos Rd (for the campground), then hoof to Trestles along the nature trail.

Sleeping & Eating

★Casa Tropicana BOUTIQUE HOTEL **$$$**
(☎949-492-1234, 800-492-1245; www.casatropicana.com; 610 Avenida Victoria; r incl breakfast from $275; @ 📶) The breezy B&B rooms at this delightful boutique hotel all have contemporary beachy design, private Jacuzzi baths, fireplace and ocean-view decks, right across from the pier for amazing sunsets. Rates include a nice breakfast basket and snacks and coffee in the 2nd-floor lounge.

La Galette Creperie FRENCH **$**
(www.lagalettecreperie.com; 612 Avenida Victoria; mains $7-12; ⏲7:30am-2pm Mon-Fri, to 3pm Sat & Sun) Near the pier is this brunch spot for sweet and savory crepes – try the molten chocolate or chicken with maple barbecue sauce.

Pipes Cafe DINER **$**
(☎949-498-5002; www.pipescafe.com; 2017 S El Camino Real; mains $4-8; ⏲7am-2pm Mon-Thu, to 3pm Fri-Sun) Surfers grab their breakfast burritos and eggy seaside scramblers inland at Pipes Cafe, which also has a coffee bar.

Bagel Shack BREAKFAST **$**
(☎949-388-0745; www.thebagelshack.com; 777 S El Camino Real; mains $4-8; ⏲5:30am-2:30pm) You'll find more wet-suit-clad crowds at the tiki-style Bagel Shack, which mixes fruit smoothies too. It's directly uphill from T-Street.

Riders Club Cafe BURGERS **$**
(www.ridersclubcafe.com; 1701 N El Camino Real; mains $7-9; ⏲11:30am-9pm Tue-Sun) Just off the I-5 (San Diego Fwy), where chain motels and hotels cluster, this little roadhouse grills juicy, top-quality burgers (beef to quinoa) and carnitas sandwiches on challah buns and has microbrewed beers on tap.

Getting There & Around

OCTA (☎714-560-6282; www.octa.net) bus 1 heads south from Dana Point every 30 to 60 minutes. At San Clemente's **Metrolink station** (☎800-371-5465; www.metrolinktrains.com), transfer to OCTA bus 191, which runs hourly to San Clemente Pier. Unless you have a bus pass, you'll need to pay the one-way fare ($2, exact change) twice.

At least two daily **Amtrak** (☎800-872-7245; www.amtrak.com) trains between San Diego ($21, 75 minutes) and LA ($23, 90 minutes), via San Juan Capistrano and Anaheim, stop at San Clemente Pier.

San Clemente is about 6 miles southeast of Dana Point via PCH. Pay-and-display parking at the pier costs $1 per hour.

San Diego

POP 1,338,348

Includes ➡

La Jolla & North County Coast 317
La Jolla.............317
Del Mar............ 323
Solana Beach 326
Cardiff-by-the-Sea...327
Encinitas 327
Carlsbad 329
Oceanside 332
Temecula 334

Best Places to Eat

- Cucina Urbana (p304)
- Puesto at the Headquarters (p306)
- Urban Solace (p304)
- Fish 101 (p329)
- Las Olas (p327)

Best Places to Stay

- Hotel del Coronado (p300)
- US Grant Hotel (p299)
- Hotel Solamar (p297)
- Legoland Hotel (p331)
- Lodge at Torrey Pines (p321)

Why Go?

New York has its cabbie, Chicago its bluesman and Seattle its coffee-drinking boho. San Diego, meanwhile, has the valet guy in a polo shirt, khaki shorts and crisp new sneakers. With his perfectly tousled hair, great tan and gentle enthusiasm, he looks like he's on a perennial spring break, and when he wishes you welcome, he really means it.

This may sound pejorative, but our intention is the opposite. San Diego calls itself 'America's Finest City' and its breezy confidence and sunny countenance filter down even to folks you encounter every day on the street. It's the nation's eighth-largest city, yet we're hard-pressed to think of a place of any size that's more laid-back.

What's not to love? San Diego bursts with world-famous attractions for the entire family, including the zoo, Legoland, the museums of Balboa Park and SeaWorld, plus a bubbling downtown and beaches ranging from ritzy to raucous – and America's most perfect weather.

When to Go

San Diego

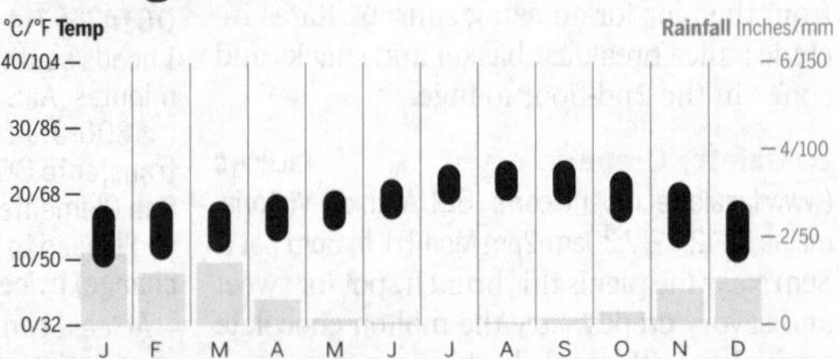

Jun–Aug High season; temperatures and hotel rates are highest

Sep–Oct, Mar–May Shoulder seasons; moderate rates.

Nov–Feb Low season while most of America escapes the cold.

History

Evidence of human habitation in the region goes back to at least 18,000 BC, in the form of middens (ancient refuse heaps). When Spanish explorer Juan Rodríguez Cabrillo became the first European to sail into San Diego Bay in 1542, the region was divided peaceably between the native Kumeyaay and Luiseño/Juaneño peoples. Their way of life continued undisturbed until Catholic missionary Father Junípero Serra and Gaspar de Portolá arrived in 1769. These newcomers founded the first permanent European settlement in California – a mission and fort on the hill now known as the Presidio.

When the United States took California from Mexico after the Mexican-American War of the 1840s, San Diego was little more

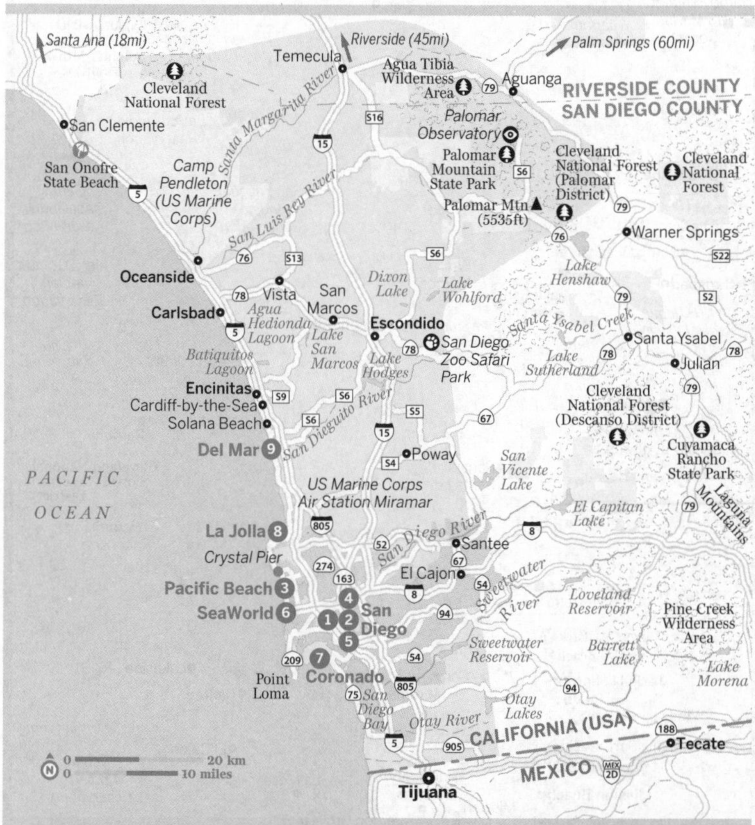

San Diego Highlights

1. Cooing at koalas and pandering to pandas at the **San Diego Zoo** (p276)
2. Museum-hopping in **Balboa Park** (p281), then sampling fish tacos or the next great taste in **Hillcrest and North Park** (p285)
3. Sunning and skating seaside in **Pacific Beach** (p294)
4. Swilling margaritas in **Old Town** (p310)
5. Pub-crawling Downtown's **Gaslamp Quarter** (p308)
6. Cheering for Shamu at **SeaWorld** (p291)
7. Marveling at the history and architecture of the **Hotel del Coronado** (p289)
8. Hang gliding, kayaking or giving your credit card a workout in **La Jolla** (p317)
9. Mingling with the hoi polloi at **Del Mar Racetrack** (p323)

San Diego & Around

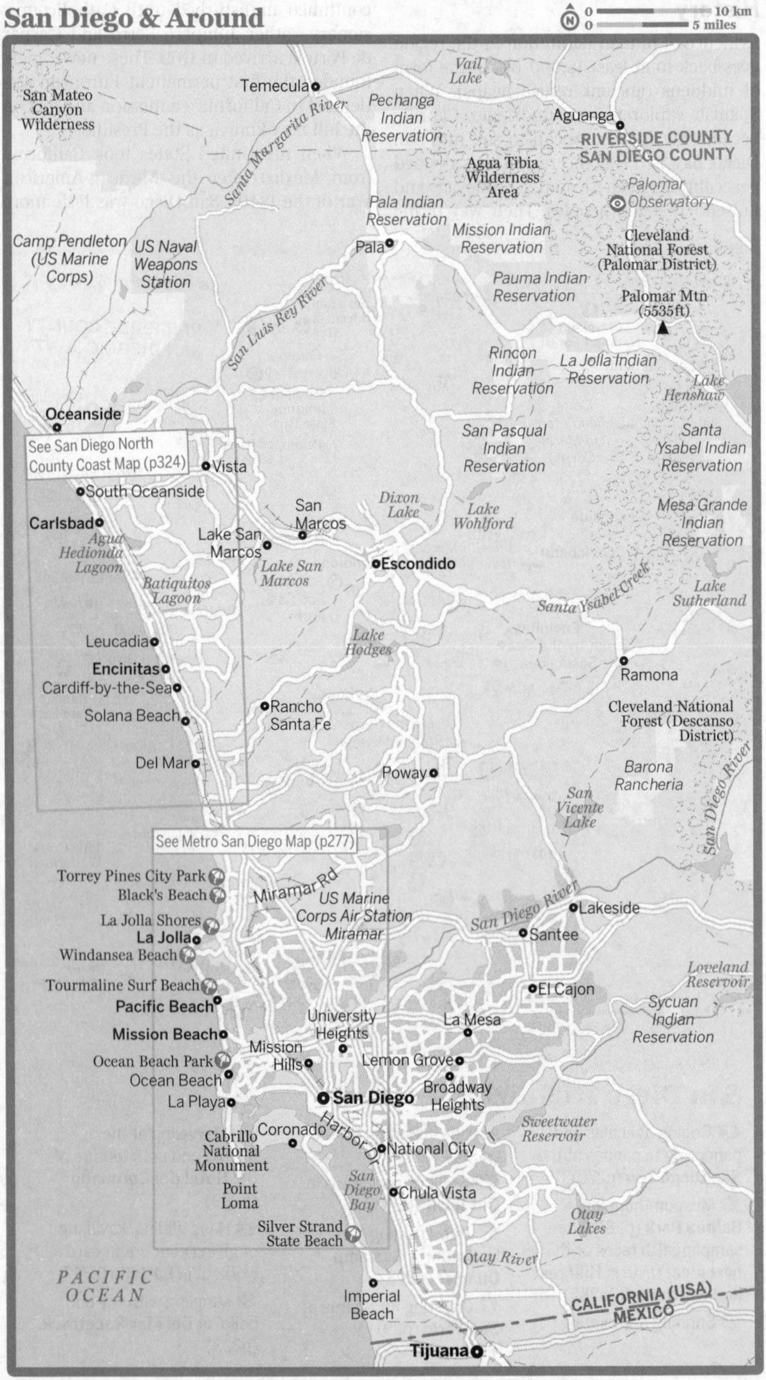

than a ramshackle village. But San Francisco property speculator William Heath Davis saw a fortune to be made. In the 1850s he bought 160 acres of bayfront property and erected homes, a wharf and warehouses. 'Davis' Folly' eventually went bust, but just a decade later another San Francisco speculator, Alonzo E Horton, acquired 960 acres of waterfront land and promoted it as 'New Town.' This time the idea stuck.

Gold was discovered in the hills east of San Diego in 1869, and the ensuing rush resulted in the construction of the railroad in 1884. It also led to a classic Wild West culture, with saloons, gambling houses and brothels behind the respectable Victorian facades of the present-day Gaslamp Quarter. But when gold played out, the economy took a nosedive and the city's population plummeted by as much as 50%.

Spurred by San Francisco's international exhibition of 1914, San Diego staged the Panama-California Exposition (1915–16), aiming to attract investment to the city with its deepwater port, railroad hub and perfect climate. Boosters built exhibition halls in the romantic Spanish Colonial style that still defines much of the city today.

However, it was the 1941 bombing of Pearl Harbor that permanently made San Diego. Top brass quickly chose San Diego, with its excellent, protected port, as home of the US Pacific Fleet. The military literally reshaped the city, dredging the harbor, building landfill islands and constructing vast tracts of instant housing.

The opening of a University of California campus in the 1960s heralded a new era as students and faculty slowly drove a liberal wedge into the city's homogenous, flag-and-family culture. The university, especially strong in the sciences, has also become a biotech incubator. The 2012 county census (3.2 million people) has continued the trend of the non-white population surpassing the white population (47.6%).

Sights

Whoosh – here comes a skateboarder. And there goes a wet-suited surfer toting his board to the break, while a Chanel-clad lady lifts a coffee cup off a porcelain saucer. Downtown San Diego and its nearby coastal communities offer all that and more.

San Diego's Downtown is the region's main business, financial and convention district. Whatever intense urban energy Downtown generally lacks, it makes up in spirited shopping, dining and nightlife in the historic Gaslamp Quarter, while the East Village and North Park are hipster havens. The waterfront Embarcadero is good for a stroll, and in the northwestern corner of Downtown, vibrant Little Italy is full of good eats, and Old Town is the seat of local history.

The city of Coronado, with its landmark 1888 Hotel del Coronado and top-rated beach, sits across San Diego Bay from Downtown. At the entrance to the bay, Point Loma has sweeping views across sea and city from the Cabrillo National Monument. Mission Bay, northwest of Downtown, has lagoons, parks and recreation from waterskiing to camping and the world-famous SeaWorld. The nearby coast – Ocean, Mission and Pacific Beaches – epitomizes the SoCal beach scene.

San Diego Zoo & Balboa Park

San Diego's zoo is a highlight of any trip to California and should be a high priority for first-time visitors. The zoo occupies some prime real estate in Balboa Park, which itself is packed with museums and gardens. To visit all the sights would take days; plan your trip at the **Balboa Park Visitors Center** (619-239-0512; www.balboapark.org; House of Hospitality, 1549 El Prado; 9:30am-4:30pm). Pick up a park map (suggested donation $1) and the latest opening schedule.

Discount admission coupons are widely available in local publications and at hotels and information-center kiosks. The **San Diego 3-for-1 Pass** covers unlimited admission for up to seven days to the San Diego Zoo Safari Park and SeaWorld, for $149/119 per adult/child.

If you plan to visit a lot of museums, you'll save money with admission passes including the **Passport to Balboa Park** (good for one-time entry to 14 museums within one week, adult/child $53/29), a **Stay for the Day** pass (five museums for $43) and the **Combo Pass** (Passport plus zoo admission adult/child $89/52). The **Balboa Park Explorer** (adult/child/family $129/99/199) covers admission to all the park's 17 museums for one year, though not the zoo.

Free tours depart the Visitors Center to uncover the park's architectural heritage (9:30am on the first Wednesday of the month) and nature and history, led by rangers (1pm Tuesday and Sunday).

Balboa Park is easily reached from Downtown on bus 7 along Park Blvd. By car, Park Blvd provides easy access to free parking. El Prado is an extension of Laurel St, which crosses Cabrillo Bridge with the Cabrillo Fwy (CA163) 120ft below; hanging greenery here makes it look like a rainforest gorge.

The free Balboa Park Tram bus makes a continuous loop; however, it's easiest and most enjoyable to walk.

★San Diego Zoo ZOO

(☎619-231-1515; www.sandiegozoo.org; 2920 Zoo Dr; 1-day pass adult/child from $46/36; 2-visit pass to Zoo and/or Safari Park adult/child $82/64; ⏲9am-9pm mid-Jun–early Sep, to 5pm or 6pm early Sep–mid-Jun; P 👪) This justifiably famous zoo is one of SoCal's biggest attractions, showing more than 3000 animals representing over 800 species in a beautifully landscaped setting, typically in enclosures that replicate their natural habitats. Its sister park is San Diego Zoo Safari Park (p331) in northern San Diego County.

Arrive early, as many of the animals are most active in the morning – though many perk up again in the afternoon. Pick up a map at the entrance to the zoo to find your own favorite exhibits.

The guided **double-decker bus tour** gives a good overview of the zoo with informative commentary: sitting downstairs puts you closer to the animals. Once you've made the loop, your ticket remains good for an express bus service in the park, a big help if you're unable to walk far. The **Skyfari** cable car goes right across the park and can save you some walking time, though there may be a line to get on it. Either way, you're going to do a lot of walking: carry quarters for the electric foot-massagers located around the park. Inquire about facilities for disabled visitors.

The **koalas** are so popular that Australians may be surprised to find them a sort of unofficial symbol of San Diego (they're featured in a new **Aussie Outback** exhibit), and the giant pandas run a close second. The **Komodo dragon**, an Indonesian lizard that can grow up to 10ft long, looks fearsome and strides menacingly around the reptile house.

Other bioclimatic environments include the 7.5-acre **Elephant Odyssey**; **Tiger River**, a re-created Asian rainforest; **Gorilla Tropics**, an African rainforest; and the **Sun Bear Forest**, where the Asian bears are famously playful.

Absolutely Apes is devoted to the apes of Indonesia, including orangutans and siamangs climbing in lush forests. The large, impressive **Scripps Aviary** and **Rainforest Aviary** have well-placed feeders to allow some close-up viewing. And you can walk right beneath 100 species of winged creatures inside the **Owens Aviary**. Finally, don't miss the **African Rock Kopje** (outcrop), where klipspringers (small antelopes) demonstrate their rock-climbing abilities.

The **zoo gardens** are renowned and some of the plants are used for the specialized food requirements of particular animals. Pick up a brochure for the self-guided botanical gardens tour.

And of course the zoo is made for kids, from **animal shows** to a **children's zoo** exhibit (where youngsters can pet small critters). Both children and adults will enjoy the **animal nursery**, where you can see the zoo's newest arrivals. Babies are born every spring and summer.

Reuben H Fleet Science Center MUSEUM

(☎619-238-1233; www.rhfleet.org; 1875 El Prado; adult/child $13/11, incl Giant Dome Theater $17/14; ⏲10am-5pm Mon-Thu, to 6pm Fri-Sun; 👪) One of Balboa Park's most popular venues, this hands-on science museum features interactive displays and a toddler room. Look out for opportunities to build gigantic structures with Keva planks and visit the **Gallery of Illusions and Perceptions**. The biggest drawcard is the **Giant Dome Theater** ($7 if purchased separately), which screens several different films each day. The hemispherical, wraparound screen and 152-speaker state-of-the-art sound system create sensations ranging from pretty cool to mind-blowing.

San Diego Natural History Museum MUSEUM

(☎619-232-3821; www.sdnhm.org; 1788 El Prado; adult/child $17/11; ⏲10am-5pm; 👪) The 'Nat' houses 7.5 million specimens, including rocks, fossils and taxidermied animals, as well as an impressive dinosaur skeleton and a California fault-line exhibit, all in beautiful spaces. Kids love the movies about the natural world in the giant-screen cinema; the selections change frequently. Children's programs are held most weekends. Special exhibits (some with an extra charge) span pirates to King Tut. The museum also arranges field trips and nature walks in Balboa Park and further afield.

Metro San Diego

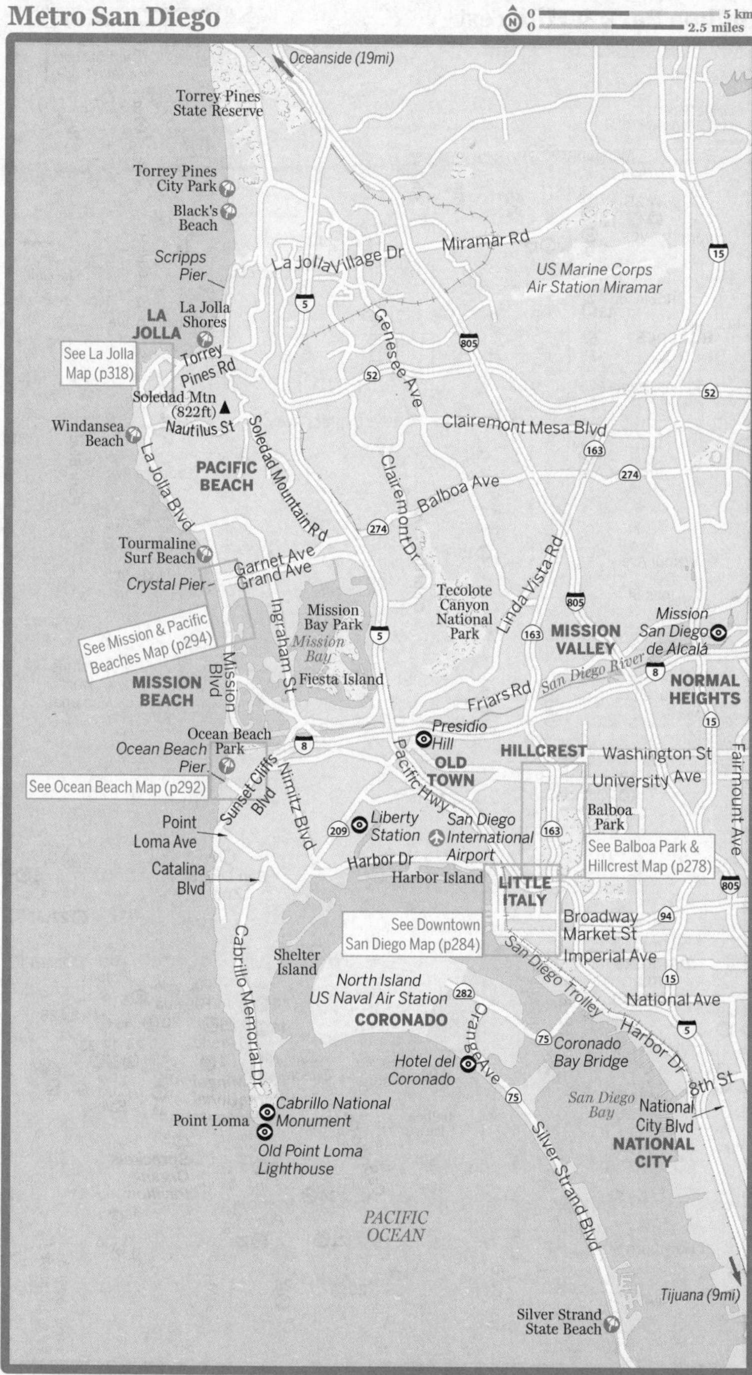

Balboa Park & Hillcrest

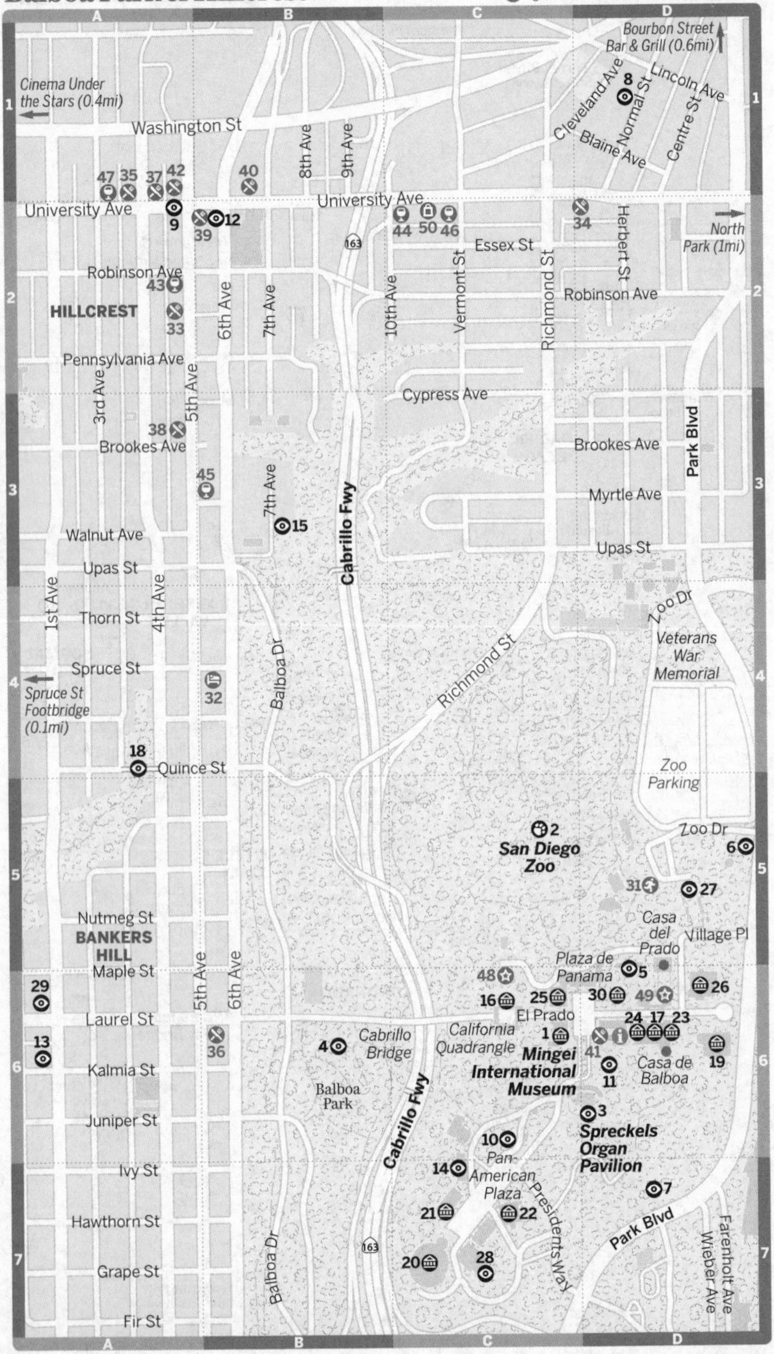

Balboa Park & Hillcrest

Top Sights
1 Mingei International Museum ... C6
2 San Diego Zoo ... C5
3 Spreckels Organ Pavilion ... D6

Sights
4 Balboa Park Gardens ... B6
5 Botanical Building ... D6
6 Carousel ... D5
7 Centro Cultural de la Raza ... D7
8 Farmers Market (Hillcrest) ... D1
9 Hillcrest Gateway ... A2
10 House of Pacific Relations ... C6
11 Japanese Friendship Garden ... D6
12 Kahn Building ... B2
13 Long-Waterman House ... A6
14 Marie Hitchcock Puppet Theater ... C7
15 Marston House ... B3
16 Museum of Man ... C6
17 Museum of Photographic Arts ... D6
18 Quince St Bridge ... A4
19 Reuben H Fleet Science Center ... D6
20 San Diego Air & Space Museum ... C7
21 San Diego Automotive Museum ... C7
22 San Diego Hall of Champions Sports Museum ... C7
23 San Diego History Center ... D6
24 San Diego Model Railroad Museum ... D6
25 San Diego Museum of Art ... C6
26 San Diego Natural History Museum ... D6
27 Spanish Village Art Center Artist Colony ... D5
28 Starlight Bowl ... C7
29 Timken House ... A6
30 Timken Museum of Art ... D6

Activities, Courses & Tours
31 Miniature Railroad ... D5

Sleeping
32 Inn at the Park ... B4

Eating
33 Babycakes ... A2
34 Baja Betty's ... D2
35 Bread & Cie ... A1
36 Cucina Urbana ... B6
37 East Village Asian Diner ... A1
38 Hash House a Go Go ... A3
39 Khyber Pass ... B2
40 Porkyland ... B1
41 Prado ... D6
42 Saigon on Fifth ... A1

Drinking & Nightlife
43 Brass Rail ... A2
44 Flicks ... C2
45 Nunu's Cocktail Lounge ... B3
46 Rich's ... C2
47 Urban Mo's ... A1

Entertainment
48 Old Globe Theaters ... C6
49 San Diego Junior Theatre ... D6

Shopping
50 Obelisk Mercantile ... C2

Spanish Village Art Center Artist Colony ARTIST COLONY

(11am-4pm) FREE Behind the Natural History Museum is a grassy square with a magnificent Moreton Bay fig tree (sorry, climbing is prohibited). Opposite the square stand there's an enclave of small tiled cottages (billed by park authorities as 'an authentic reproduction of an ancient village in Spain') that are rented out as artists' studios, where you can watch potters, jewelers, glass blowers, painters and sculptors churn out their crafts.

By Spanish Village and the zoo entrance there's a 1910 **carousel** (2920 Zoo Dr; tickets $2.50; 11am-5pm Sat, Sun & school holidays;) with most of the original hand-painted animals, and a **miniature railroad** (619-239-4748; 1800 Zoo Pl; tickets $3; 11am-4:30pm Sat, Sun & school holidays;) offering three-minute, half-mile rides.

Museum of Photographic Arts MUSEUM

(619-238-7559; www.mopa.org; Casa de Balboa, 1649 El Prado; adult/student/child $8/6/free; 10am-5pm Tue-Sun, to 9pm Thu late May–Aug) Some 7000 photos make up its permanent collection, tracing the history of photography, and the museum offers special exhibits from crowd-pleasing landscapes by Ansel Adams to avant-garde cell-phone photography.

San Diego Model Railroad Museum MUSEUM

(619-696-0199; www.sdmrm.org; Casa de Balboa, 1649 El Prado; adult/child under 6yr $8/free; 11am-4pm Tue-Fri, to 5pm Sat & Sun;) Your (inner) four-year-old boy will love this railroad museum. One of the largest indoor railroad museums in the world, it has some 27,000 sq ft of amazingly landscaped working models of actual Southern California railroads, both historical and contemporary.

San Diego History Center MUSEUM
(☎619-232-6203; www.sandiegohistory.org; 1649 El Prado, Suite 3; adult/child/student & senior $8/4/6; ⏱10am-5pm Tue-Sun) The San Diego Historical Society operates this center, with permanent and temporary exhibitions on city history. Through 2016, the Place of Promise exhibition covers the region from the Kumeyaay peoples through first European contact in 1542 and the collective influence of Spanish, Mexican and American cultures.

Botanical Building CONSERVATORY
(⏱Fri-Wed) FREE The Botanical Building looks lovely from El Prado, where you can see it reflected in the large lily pond that was used for hydrotherapy in WWII when the navy took over the park. The building's central dome and two wings are covered with redwood lathes, which let filtered sunlight into the collection of tropical plants and ferns. The planting changes every season; in December there's a particularly beautiful poinsettia display.

Timken Museum of Art MUSEUM
(☎619-239-5548; www.timkenmuseum.org; 1500 El Prado; ⏱10am-4:30pm Tue-Sat, from 1:30pm Sun) FREE Don't skip the Timken, home of the Putnam collection, a small but impressive group of paintings, including works by Rembrandt, Rubens, El Greco, Cézanne and Pissarro, plus a wonderful selection of Russian icons. Built in 1965, the building stands out for *not* being in imitation Spanish style.

San Diego Museum of Art MUSEUM
(SDMA; ☎619-232-7931; www.sdmart.org; 1450 El Prado; adult/child $12/4.50; ⏱10am-5pm Mon-Tue & Thu-Sat, from noon Sun, also 5-9pm Thu Jun-Sep) The SDMA is the city's largest art museum. The permanent collection has works by a number of European masters from the renaissance to the modernist eras (though no renowned pieces), American landscape paintings and several fantastic pieces in the Asian galleries, and there are often important traveling exhibits. The **Sculpture Garden** has works by Alexander Calder and Henry Moore.

Built in 1924, it was designed by San Diego architect William Templeton Johnson, and the ornate facade depicts Spanish artists, most of whom have pieces inside the museum.

★**Mingei International Museum** MUSEUM
(☎619-239-0003; www.mingei.org; 1439 El Prado; adult/child $8/5; ⏱10am-5pm Tue-Sun; 👪) A rare New Zealand kauri tree (a fragrant evergreen with flat leaves) marks the entrance to this diverse collection of folk art, costumes, toys, jewelry, utensils and other handmade objects from traditional cultures from around the world, plus changing exhibitions covering beads to surfboards. Check the website to find out what's on.

Museum of Man MUSEUM
(☎619-239-2001; www.museumofman.org; Plaza de California, 1350 El Prado; adult/student/child $12.50/8/5; ⏱10am-5pm) This is the county's only anthropological museum, with exhibits spanning ancient Egypt, the Mayans and local native Kumeyaay people, human evolution and the human life cycle. Recent temporary exhibits have covered everything from women's empowerment to beer. The basket and pottery collections are especially fine. The museum shop sells handicrafts from Central America and elsewhere.

It sits just north of where El Prado passes under an **archway**, which marked the main entrance for the 1915 exposition. Figures on either side of the arch represent the Atlantic and Pacific Oceans, while the arch itself symbolizes the Panama Canal.

★**Spreckels Organ Pavilion** MUSIC
(www.sosorgan.com) Going south from Plaza de Panama, you can't miss the circle of seating and the curved colonnade in front of the band shell housing the organ said to be the world's largest outdoor musical instrument. Donated by the Spreckels family of sugar fortune and fame, the pipe organ came with the stipulation that San Diego must always have an official organist. Make a point of attending the free **concerts**, held throughout the year at 2pm Sundays.

House of Pacific Relations ARCHITECTURE
(☎619-234-0739; www.sdhpr.org; 2191 W Pan American Rd; ⏱noon-4pm Sun; 👪) FREE Here are 15 cottages from the 1915 exposition, inside which you will find furnishings and displays from various countries, plus about as many built since. During opening hours, they often have crafts and food for sale.

Marie Hitchcock Puppet Theater THEATER
(☎619-685-5990; www.balboaparkpuppets.com; Balboa Park; admission $5.50; ⏱11am, 1pm & 2:30pm Wed-Sun late May-early Sep, shorter hr early Sep-late May; 👪) This theater in the Palisades Building puts on terrific hand- and rod-puppet and marionette shows for the little ones. There have been puppet shows here since the 1940s.

SAN DIEGO IN...

It's easy to spend most of a week in San Diego, but if your time is limited, here's a whirlwind itinerary. Things will go more smoothly if you've got access to a car, but public transportation can work if you plan ahead.

One Day

Rub elbows with the locals over breakfast in the **Gaslamp Quarter** (p302), then ramble around **Old Town State Historic Park** (p287) for a bit of history before a Mexican lunch. Devote the afternoon to the **San Diego Zoo** (p276), which is among the world's best, and if time permits visit some of the museums or gardens in graceful **Balboa Park** (p281). For dinner and a night out on the town, head to the hip **East Village** (p303) or back to the Gaslamp Quarter, where many restaurants have terrace seating for people-watching, and the partying ranges from posh to raucous.

Two Days

Take the ferry to Coronado for a sea-view breakfast at the **Hotel del Coronado** (p289), then enjoy the California beach scene at **Mission** and **Pacific Beaches** (p293). **La Jolla** (p317) beckons this afternoon: explore **Torrey Pines State Reserve** (p319), **Birch Aquarium at Scripps** (p319), kayak the sea caves, try a glider ride or head to **La Jolla Village** to browse the 1920s Spanish-revival landmarks and boutiques. As the sun begins its descent over the ocean, head to **Del Mar** (p323), where you can cheer or snuggle from one of the restaurants on the roof of **Del Mar Plaza** (p323) as the sky turns brilliant orange and fades to black.

San Diego Automotive Museum MUSEUM

(☎619-231-2886; www.sdautomuseum.org; 2080 Pan American Plaza; adult/child $8.50/4; ⏰10am-5pm) This museum has a permanent collection of dozens of cars and motorcycles, perfectly restored and well displayed, with classics from a 1909 International Harvester to a 1991 De Lorean, plus a collection of Harley Davidson and Indian motorcycles. Special exhibits change quarterly.

San Diego Hall of Champions Sports Museum MUSEUM

(www.sdhoc.com; 2131 Pan American Plaza; adult/child $8/5; ⏰10am-4:30pm; 👪) Permanent and temporary exhibits at the 'Hall of Champs' – principally local sports legends – cover themes as wide-ranging as Ted Williams, skateboarder Tony Hawk and the World Series of Poker. There's also a media center, in which kids can call the commentary on a game. Look for it in the building covered with Mayan-style carvings.

San Diego Air & Space Museum MUSEUM

(☎619-234-8291; www.sandiegoairandspace.org 2001 Pan American Plaza; adult/child $18/7; ⏰10am-5:30pm Jun-Aug, to 4:30pm Sep-May; 👪) The round building at the southern end of the plaza houses an excellent museum with extensive displays of aircraft throughout history – originals, replicas, models – plus memorabilia from legendary aviators including Charles Lindbergh and astronaut John Glenn. Catch films in the new 3D/4D theater.

Starlight Bowl PERFORMANCE VENUE

(www.starlighttheatre.org; 2005 Pan American Plaza) A huge variety of musicals and light opera is presented at this amphitheater each summer.

Centro Cultural de la Raza MEXICAN & INDIGENOUS ART

(☎619-235-6135; www.centroculturaldelaraza.com; 2004 Park Blvd; suggested donation $5; ⏰noon-4pm Tue-Sun) The center hosts powerful exhibitions of Mexican and Native American art, including temporary exhibits of contemporary indigenous artwork, dance, theater and musical performances. The round, steel building, originally a water tank, is impressively painted with 240 feet of murals. It's on the edge of the main museum area.

Balboa Park Gardens GARDENS

Balboa Park includes a number of gardens, reflecting different horticultural styles and environments, including **Alcazar Garden**, a formal, Spanish-style garden; **Palm Canyon**, with more than 50 species of palms; **Japanese Friendship Garden** (www.niwa.org; adult/senior/child under 6yr $6/4/free; ⏰10am-4:30pm except major holidays); **Australian Garden**; **Rose Garden**; and **Desert**

Garden (best in spring). **Florida Canyon** gives an idea of the San Diego landscape before Spanish settlement. Free weekly **Offshoot tours** (www.balboapark.org/info/tours.php; 10am Sat mid-Jan–Thanksgiving) depart from the Balboa Park visitors center (p275) and cover a rotating selection of themes including history and botany.

Marston House ARCHITECTURE
(www.sohosandiego.org; 3525 Seventh Ave; adult/child/senior $10/7/4; 10am-5pm Thu-Mon mid-Jun–early Sep, 10am-4pm Fri-Mon early Sep–mid-Jun) In the far northwestern corner of Balboa Park is the former home of George Marston, philanthropist and founder of the San Diego Historical Society. Built in 1905, Marston House was designed by noted San Diego architects William Hebbard and Irving Gill and is a fine example of the American Arts and Crafts style. Admission is by tour only.

Downtown San Diego

When Alonzo Horton established New Town San Diego in 1867, 5th Ave was its main street, lined with saloons, gambling joints, bordellos and opium dens; it became notoriously known as the Stingaree. By the 1960s it had declined to a skid row of flophouses and bars. In the early 1980s, when developers started thinking about demolition, protests from preservationists saved the area.

Good thing. The central Downtown area, now known as the Gaslamp Quarter, is now prime real estate. Handsomely restored 1870s to 1920s buildings house restaurants, bars, galleries and theaters amid wrought-iron, 19th-century-style street lamps, trees and brick sidewalks. This 16-block area, south of Broadway between 4th and 6th Aves, is designated a National Historic District. There's still a bit of sleaze though, with a few 'adult entertainment' shops, and a fair number of homeless folks, but we'll say that all lends texture.

If the Gaslamp Quarter is the center of Downtown, the Financial District is to the west, while east of the Gaslamp is the East Village, an up-and-coming enclave for local hipsters with worldly restaurants and fun nightspots. Southwest of the Gaslamp spreads the waterfront and large hotels serving the convention center.

Museum of Contemporary Art MUSEUM
(MCASD Downtown; Map p284; 858-454-3541; www.mcasd.org; 1001 Kettner Blvd; adult/child under 25yr/senior $10/free/$5, free 5-7pm 3rd Thu each month; 11am-5pm Thu-Tue, to 7pm 3rd Thu each month) This Financial District museum has brought an ever-changing variety of innovative artwork to San Diegans since the 1960s here in the downtown location and La Jolla branch (p317); check the website for exhibits. Across from the main building, a slickly renovated section of San Diego's train station houses permanent works by Jenny Holzer and Richard Serra. Tickets are valid for seven days in all locations.

About that train station building: San Diego's Santa Fe Depot (aka Union Station) looks a lot like a piece from a model railway, with Spanish-style tilework and a historic Santa Fe Railway sign on top. It was built in conjunction with the 1915 exposition in the hopes that the Santa Fe Railway would make San Diego its terminus; that designation eventually went to Los Angeles.

★**New Children's Museum** MUSEUM
(Map p284; www.thinkplaycreate.org; 200 W Island Ave; admission $10; noon-4pm Sun, 1am-4pm Mon & Wed-Sat;) This interactive children's museum is new both chronologically (opened 2008) and conceptually, in that it's interactive art meant for kids. Installations are designed by artists, so tykes can learn principles of movement and physics while simultaneously being exposed to art and working out the ants in their pants. Exhibits change every 18 months or so, so there's always something new.

If you need to get the kids outdoors, there's a futuristic **playground** across the street, and for a more traditional children's museum (with science exhibits and such), visit the Reuben H Fleet Science Center (p276).

San Diego Chinese Historical Museum MUSEUM
(Map p284; 404 3rd Ave; 10:30am-4pm Tue-Sun) FREE The historic heart of San Diego's Chinese community is 3rd Ave. Immigrants were once taught English and religion in the Chinese Mission Building, built in the 1920s. Displays include Chinese-American artifacts and local art objects, and the small, white stucco structure boasts decorative red tiles, hardwood floors, and an inviting backyard.

Gaslamp Museum & William Heath Davis House
MUSEUM

(Map p284; www.gaslampquarter.org; 410 Island Ave; adult/senior & student $5/4, walking tour $10/8; 10am-6pm Tue-Sat, 9am-3pm Sun, walking tour 11am Sat) This house, a pre-fab affair brought from Maine in 1850, contains a small museum with 19th-century furnishings. From here, the Gaslamp Quarter Historical Foundation leads a weekly two-hour **walking tour** of the neighborhood, which includes admission to the house.

Petco Park
STADIUM

(Map p284; 619-795-5011; www.padres.com; 100 Park Blvd; tours adult/child/senior $12/8/9; 10:30am & 12:30pm Sun-Fri, 10:30am, 12:30pm & 3pm off season;) A quick stroll southeast of the Gaslamp is one of the newest stadiums in baseball, home of the San Diego Padres (p313). It's also one of the most beautiful, with brick construction and skyscraper views over the outfield. If you can't attend a game, take an 80-minute behind-the-scenes tour which might include bullpen, press box and luxury suite. Call for tour schedules in season (April to early October).

★San Diego Main Library
LIBRARY

(Map p284; 619-236-5800; www.sandiego.gov/public-library; 330 Park Blvd; noon-8pm Mon, Wed & Fri, 9:30am-5:30pm Tue & Thu, 9:30am-2:30pm Sat, 1-5pm Sun) FREE A couple blocks east of Petco Park, the city's newest landmark (2013) is a beauty. Crowned by a steel and mesh dome, the futuristic nine-story library features art-filled public spaces and plenty of learning opportunities. The roof deck offers one-of-a-kind views, clear to Mexico weather permitting. Guided and self-guided tours are available, or just wander. Architects: Rob Wellington Quigley, who also designed the New Children's Museum (p282), and Tucker Sadler & Associates.

US Grant Hotel
HOTEL

(Map p284; 619-232-3121; 326 Broadway) No hotel in the region can compare to the Hotel del Coronado (p289) for history, but US Grant, built in 1910, comes close. It's on the National Register of Historic Places for a past including celebrity guests, magnificent ballrooms, a one-time Turkish bath and a speakeasy. Visitors can take a free tour with advance reservation by calling the concierge desk.

BALBOA PARK HISTORY

Early plans for San Diego included a 1400-acre City Park at the northeastern corner of what was to become downtown, in what was all bare hilltops, chaparral and deep arroyos. Enter Kate O Sessions, a UC Berkeley botany graduate who in 1892 started a nursery on the site to landscape fashionable gardens for the city's emerging elite. The city granted her 30 acres of land in return for planting 100 trees a year in the park and donating 300 more for placement throughout the city. By the early 20th century, Balboa Park (named for the Spanish conquistador believed to be the first European to sight the Pacific Ocean) had become a well-loved part of San Diego.

In 1915–16, Balboa Park hosted much of the grand Panama-California Exposition. New Yorkers Bertram Goodhue and Carlton Winslow designed the expo's pavilions in a romantic, Spanish Colonial style with beaux-arts and baroque flourishes. The pavilions were meant to be temporary – constructed largely of stucco, chicken wire, plaster, hemp and horsehair – but they proved so popular that many were later replaced with durable concrete structures in the same style. These buildings now house the museums along El Prado, the main pedestrian thoroughfare in the park.

The zoo originated with the Panama-California Exposition of 1915–16, which featured an assortment of animals in cages along Park Blvd. Local legend has it that one Dr Harry Wegeforth, hearing the roar of one of the caged lions, exclaimed, 'Wouldn't it be wonderful to have a zoo in San Diego? I believe I'll build one!' Balboa Park canyons helped to separate different species and prevent the spread of disease. By the end of WWII the San Diego Zoo had a strong worldwide reputation, and helped to rebuild collections of European zoos that had been devastated by the war.

Another expo, the 1935 Pacific-California Exposition, brought new buildings southwest of El Prado around the Pan-American Plaza. The Spanish Colonial architectural theme was expanded to include the whole New World, from indigenous styles including Pueblo and Mayan.

Downtown San Diego

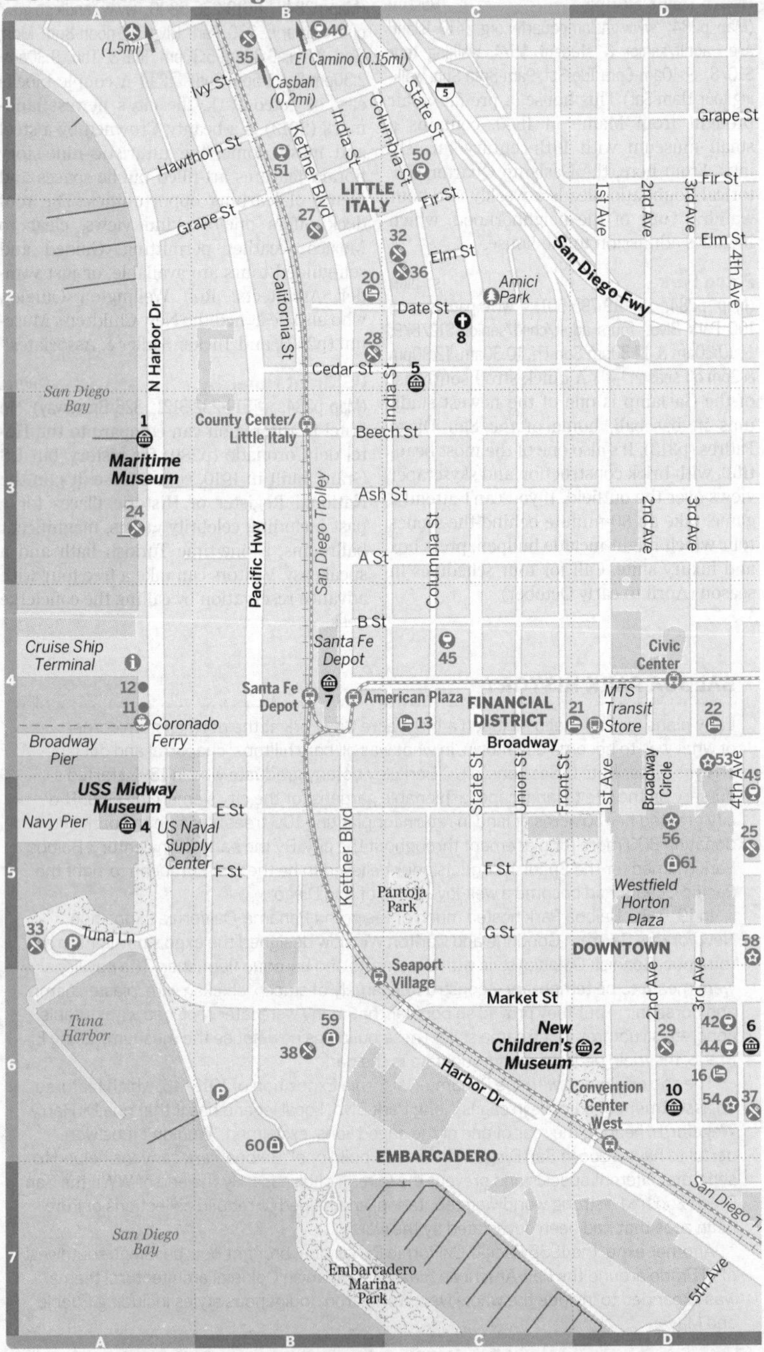
(1.5mi)
35
40
El Camino (0.15mi)
Casbah (0.2mi)
Ivy St
Hawthorn St
Grape St
Kettner Blvd
India St
Columbia St
State St
51
50
LITTLE ITALY
Fir St
27
32
36
Elm St
20
California St
Amici Park
Date St
8
San Diego Fwy
1st Ave
2nd Ave
3rd Ave
Grape St
Fir St
Elm St
4th Ave
28
Cedar St
5
India St
N Harbor Dr
San Diego Bay
1
Maritime Museum
County Center/ Little Italy
Beech St
San Diego Trolley
Ash St
24
Pacific Hwy
A St
Columbia St
2nd Ave
3rd Ave
B St
Santa Fe Depot
45
Cruise Ship Terminal
12
11
Santa Fe Depot
7
American Plaza
FINANCIAL DISTRICT
21
MTS Transit Store
Civic Center
22
Coronado Ferry
13
Broadway
Broadway Pier
State St
Union St
Front St
1st Ave
Broadway Circle
53
4th Ave
49
USS Midway Museum
Navy Pier
4
US Naval Supply Center
E St
Kettner Blvd
56
25
F St
F St
61
Westfield Horton Plaza
Pantoja Park
33
Tuna Ln
G St
DOWNTOWN
58
2nd Ave
3rd Ave
Seaport Village
Tuna Harbor
Market St
59
New Children's Museum
2
29
42
6
44
38
Harbor Dr
16
Convention Center West
10
54
37
60
EMBARCADERO
San Diego Tr
San Diego Bay
Embarcadero Marina Park
5th Ave
A
B
C
D
1
2
3
4
5
6
7

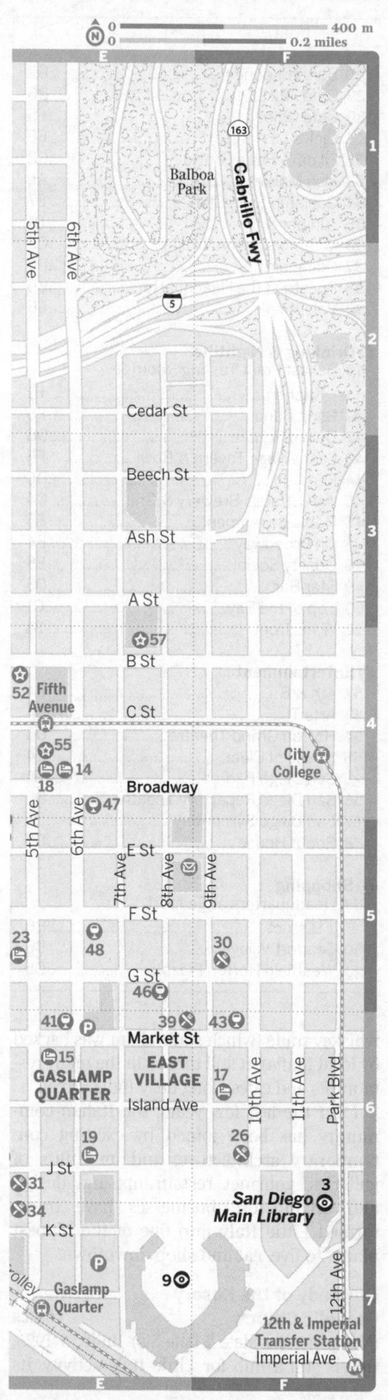

Uptown: Bankers Hill, Hillcrest & North Park

Uptown is roughly a triangle north of Downtown, east of Old Town and south of Mission Valley. There aren't any big-ticket sights here, but this string of neighborhoods is a good place to see some Victorian and art deco architecture and observe day-to-day life. Hillcrest, particularly, is one of San Diego's most diverse and desirable neighborhoods.

In the late 19th century it was fashionable to live in the hills north of Downtown, since only those who owned a horse-drawn carriage could afford it. Called **Bankers Hill** after some of the wealthy residents – or Pill Hill because of the many doctors there – the upscale heights had unobstructed views of the bay and Point Loma before I-5 was built.

Among the Victorian mansions, the 1889 **Long-Waterman House** (2408 1st Ave) is easily recognized by its towers, gables, bay windows and verandah; it was once the home of former California governor Robert Waterman. Also notable is the **Timken House** (2508 1st Ave), one block north. The 375ft **Spruce St Footbridge** (btwn Front & Brant Sts) hangs over a deep canyon and the **Quince St Bridge** (btwn 3rd & 4th Aves) is a wood-trestle bridge built in 1905 and refurbished in 1988 after community activists protested its slated demolition. In **Mission Hills**, a 1970s shingled complex at the corner of Washington and India Sts houses mostly eateries.

The heart of Uptown is **Hillcrest**, the first suburban real-estate development in San Diego. Driving around, you'll see the work of many of San Diego's best-known early-20th-century architects, including Irving Gill and William Templeton Johnson, alongside Mediterranean, Spanish Mission and Arts and Crafts styles. But Hillcrest's chief attraction is its lively street life, due largely to its status as the center of San Diego's gay and lesbian community.

Begin at the **Hillcrest Gateway**, an illuminated electric sign that arches over University Ave at 5th Ave. East on University Ave at No 535, look for the 1928 **Kahn Building**, an original commercial building with architectural elements that border on kitsch. Hillcrest's **farmers market** (cnr Normal St & Lincoln Ave; 9am-1pm Sun) is considered the best in town, great for watching fresh faces acquiring fresh produce.

East of Hillcrest is the hipster neighborhood of **North Park**, centered on 30th and

Downtown San Diego

Top Sights
1 Maritime Museum A3
2 New Children's Museum D6
3 San Diego Main Library F6
4 USS Midway Museum A5

Sights
5 Firehouse Museum C2
6 Gaslamp Museum & William Heath Davis House D6
7 Museum of Contemporary Art B4
8 Our Lady of the Rosary Catholic Church C2
9 Petco Park E7
10 San Diego Chinese Historical Museum D6
US Grant Hotel .... (see 22)

Activities, Courses & Tours
11 Flagship Cruises A4
12 Hornblower Cruises A4
Seal Tour .... (see 60)

Sleeping
13 500 West Hotel C4
14 Courtyard by Marriott San Diego Downtown E4
15 HI San Diego Downtown Hostel E6
16 Horton Grand Hotel D6
17 Hotel Indigo F6
18 Hotel Palomar San Diego E4
19 Hotel Solamar E6
20 La Pensione Hotel B2
21 Sofia Hotel D4
22 US Grant Hotel D4
23 USA Hostels San Diego E5

Eating
24 Anthony's Fish Grotto & Fishette A3
25 Bandar D5
26 Basic F6
27 Bencotto B2
28 Burger Lounge B2
29 Café 222 .... D6
30 Café Chloe F5
31 Dick's Last Resort E6
32 Filippi's Pizza Grotto C2
33 Fish Market A5
34 Gaslamp Strip Club E7
35 Juniper & Ivy B1
36 Mimmo's Italian Village C2
37 Oceanaire D6
38 Puesto at the Headquarters B6
39 Valentine's E6

Drinking & Nightlife
40 Ballast Point Tasting Room & Kitchen B1
41 Bang Bang E6
42 Dublin Square D6
43 East Village Tavern & Bowl F6
44 Fluxx D6
45 Karl Strauss Brewery & Grill C4
46 Noble Experiment E5
47 On Broadway E4
48 Quality Social E5
49 Star Bar D5
50 Top of the Bay C1
51 Waterfront B1

Entertainment
52 4th & B E4
53 Arts Tix D4
54 Horton Grand Theatre D6
55 House of Blues E4
San Diego Padres .... (see 9)
56 San Diego Repertory Theatre D5
57 San Diego Symphony E4
58 Shout House D5

Shopping
59 Headquarters at Seaport District B6
60 Seaport Village B6
61 Westfield Horton Plaza D5

University Aves. Around this area is a growing center of art in small studios and galleries around Ray St, a low-key gourmet scene, some cool bars and an inordinate number of hair salons.

Little Italy

Bounded by Hawthorn and Ash Sts on the north and south, and Front St and the waterfront on the east and west, Little Italy was settled in the mid-19th century by Italian immigrants, mostly fishermen and their families, who created a cohesive and thriving community based on a booming fish industry and whiskey trade (which some claim was backed by local Mafia). It still thrives in the many restaurants and cafes along busy India Street.

Over the last few years, the Italian community has been joined by exciting contemporary architecture, and an influx of galleries, gourmet restaurants and design and architecture businesses have transformed Little Italy into one of the hippest places to live, eat and shop downtown.

Our Lady of the Rosary Catholic Church — CHURCH

(Map p284; cnr State & Date Sts) Built in 1925, this is still a hub for Little Italy activity. Its rich ceiling murals, painted by an Italian who was flown over to do the work, are among San Diego's best pieces of religious art. Across the street in **Amici Park**, locals play bocce, an Italian form of outdoor bowling.

Firehouse Museum MUSEUM

(Map p284; ☎619-232-3473; www.sandiegofirehousemuseum.com; 1572 Columbia St at Cedar St; adult/child $3/2; ⏲10am-2pm Thu & Fri, to 4pm Sat & Sun; P) This museum preserves a historic collection of fire-fighting equipment and has exhibits depicting some of San Diego's 'hottest' moments from the late 1800s.

Old Town

Under the Mexican government, which took power in 1821, any settlement with a population of 500 or more was entitled to become a 'pueblo,' and the area below the Presidio became the first official civilian Mexican settlement in California – the *Pueblo de San Diego*. A plaza was laid out around Casa Estudillo, home of the pueblo's commandant, and within 10 years it was surrounded by about 40 huts and several houses. This square mile of land (roughly 10 times what remains today) was also the center of American San Diego until the fire of 1872, after which the city's main body moved to what's now Downtown (then called New Town).

John Spreckels built a trolley line from New Town to Old Town in the 1920s and, to attract passengers, began restoring the old district. In 1968 the area was named Old Town State Historic Park, archaeological work began, and the few surviving original buildings were restored. Now it's a pedestrian district of shade trees, a large open plaza, and shops and restaurants.

Old Town Transit Center (4009 Taylor St) is an important transit hub for the *Coaster* commuter train, the San Diego Trolley and buses. Old Town Trolley tour (p295) stop southeast of the plaza on Twiggs St. There is free parking in lots and on streets around Old Town.

★Old Town State Historic Park HISTORIC SITE

(☎619-220-5422; www.parks.ca.gov; 4002 Wallace St; ⏲visitor center & museums 10am-4pm Oct-Apr, to 5pm May-Sep; P 👪) FREE This park has an excellent history museum in the **Robinson-Rose House** at the southern end of the plaza. You'll also find a diorama depicting the original pueblo and the park's **visitors center**, where you can pick up a copy of the *Old Town San Diego State Historic Park Tour Guide & Brief History* ($3), or take a guided tour (free) at 11am and 2pm daily.

Across from the visitors center, the restored **Casa de Estudillo** is filled with authentic period furniture. Other buildings around the plaza include a blacksmith shop, print shop and a candle-dipping shop (hours vary).

Fiesta de Reyes, just off the plaza's northwestern corner, is a colorful collection of import shops and restaurants – great for Mexican souvenirs without the trip to Tijuana. Along San Diego Ave, on the southern side of the plaza, small, historical-looking buildings (only one is authentic) house more souvenir and gift shops.

WORTH A TRIP

MISSION SAN DIEGO DE ALCALÁ

Although the site of the first California mission (1769) was on Presidio Hill by present-day Old Town, in 1774 Padre Junípero Serra moved it about 7 miles upriver, closer to water and more arable land, now the **Mission Basilica San Diego de Alcalá** (☎619-281-8449; www.missionsandiego.com; 10818 San Diego Mission Rd; adult/child $3/1; ⏲9am-4:30pm; P). In 1784 missionaries built a solid adobe-and-timber church, which was destroyed by an earthquake in 1803. The church was promptly rebuilt, and at least some of it still stands on a slope overlooking Mission Valley.

With the end of the mission system in the 1830s, the buildings were turned over to the Mexican government and fell into disrepair. Some accounts say that they were reduced to a facade and a few crumbling walls by the 1920s. Extensive restoration began in 1931. The pretty white church and buildings you see now are the fruits of that work.

The mission sits north of an unlovely stretch of shopping centers and hotels along I-8 (take the Mission Gorge Rd exit); or take the San Diego Trolley Green Line to Mission San Diego, cutting through a scenic corridor not seen from the freeway.

Whaley House HISTORIC BUILDING
(☎619-297-7511; www.whaleyhouse.org; 2476 San Diego Ave; adult/child before 5pm $6/4, after 5pm $10/5; ⏰10am-10pm late May-early Sep, 10am-5pm Mon-Tue, to 10pm Thu-Sat early Sep-late May) Two blocks from the Old Town perimeter sits the city's oldest brick building (circa 1856), officially certified as haunted by the US Department of Commerce. Check out the collection of period furniture and clothing from when the house served as a courthouse, theater and private residence. After 5pm, admission is by tour only.

El Campo Santo CEMETERY
(San Diego Ave btwn Arista & Conde Sts) Continuing east, after San Diego Ave forks right at Conde St, you'll find this cemetery which dates from 1849. It is the resting place of some 20 souls, a simple dirt yard with the biographies of the deceased on signage above the graves.

Casa de Carillo ARCHITECTURE
(cnr Juan St & Wallace St) Just north of Old Town, this house dates from about 1820 and is said to be the oldest house in San Diego. It is now the pro shop for the public 18-hole **Presidio Hills Golf Course** (www.presidiohills-golf.com; greens fee $10).

Presidio Hill HISTORIC SITE
In 1769 Padre Junípero Serra and Gaspar de Portolá established the first Spanish settlement in California, overlooking the valley of the San Diego River. Walk up from Old Town along Mason St for excellent views of San Diego Bay and Mission Valley. Atop the hill, **Presidio Park** has several walking trails and shaded benches. A large cross, made with tiles from the original mission, commemorates Padre Serra.

A flagpole, a cannon, some plaques and earth walls now form the **Fort Stockton Memorial**, commemorating the fort built when American forces occupied the hill in 1846 during the Mexican-American War. The nearby **El Charro Statue**, a bicentennial gift to the city from Mexico, depicts a Mexican cowboy on horseback. Nothing remains of the original Presidio structures, and the mission (p287) was moved up river.

Junípero Serra Museum MUSEUM
(☎619-297-3258; www.sandiegohistory.org; 2727 Presidio Dr; adult/child $6/3; ⏰10am-4pm Sat & Sun mid-Sep–mid-May, to 5pm Sat & Sun mid-May–mid-Sep; P 👪) Located in one of the most important historical buildings in the city, this small but interesting collection of artifacts and pictures is from the Mission and rancho periods, and it gives a good sense of the earliest days of European settlement up to 1929 when the museum was founded.

Embarcadero & the Waterfront

South and west of the Gaslamp Quarter, San Diego's well-manicured waterfront promenades stretch along Harbor Dr, and are perfect for strolling or jogging (or watching well-built members of the US Navy doing same, if that's your thing!). Southwest of the ship museums, the convention center (1989), with its sail-inspired roof stretches for a half mile, while the newest gathering place is the former police headquarters (p313), turned into a shopping center.

★**Maritime Museum** MUSEUM
(Map p284; ☎619-234-9153; www.sdmaritime.org; 1492 N Harbor Dr; adult/child $16/8; ⏰9am-9pm late May-early Sep, to 8pm early Sep-late May; 👪) This museum is easy to find: look for the 100ft-high masts of the iron-hulled square-rigger *Star of India*. Built on the Isle of Man and launched in 1863, the tall ship plied the England–India trade route, carried immigrants to New Zealand, became a trading ship based in Hawaii and, finally, ferried cargo in Alaska. It's a handsome vessel, but don't expect anything romantic or glamorous on board.

The seven vessels moored here include submarines, the *California*, California's official tall ship, and the *America* of America's Cup fame. The latter two go out on excursions from a few hours to overnight, from $20 per person for the shorter cruises. The 1914 *Pilot*, which took harbor pilots to their merchant ships, has narrated rides that last 45 minutes and cost $5.

★**USS Midway Museum** MUSEUM
(Map p284; ☎619-544-9600; www.midway.org; 910 N Harbor Dr; adult/child $20/10; ⏰10am-5pm, last entry 4pm; P 👪) The giant aircraft carrier USS *Midway* was one of the navy's flagships from 1945 to 1991, last playing a combat role in the first Gulf War. On the flight deck of the hulking vessel, walk right up to some 25 restored aircraft including an F-14 Tomcat and F-4 Phantom jet fighter. Admission includes an audio tour, along the narrow confines of the upper decks to the bridge, admiral's war room, brig and

SAN DIEGO FOR KIDS

Tiny hands down, San Diego is one of America's best destinations for family travel. Here are some highlights to jump start your vacation.

Do the zoo (p276); it's everything they say and more, and while you're there spend another day enjoying the rest of Balboa Park (p275), one of the nation's best collections of museums. The Reuben H Fleet Science Center (p276), Model Railroad Museum (p279) and Natural History Museum (p276) are all tailor-made for kids, and the plazas, fountains and gardens offer plenty of space for them to let off steam.

Kids elementary school age and older will appreciate Old Town State Historic Park (p287) and the Mexican restaurants nearby.

Along the coast, SeaWorld (p291) is another national landmark (look for specials and combo tickets to keep costs down). Coronado is a calming getaway for the Hotel Del Coronado (p289) and the kid-friendly **public library** (☎619-522-7390; www.coronado.ca.us/library; 640 Orange Ave; ⏲10am-9pm Mon-Thu, to 6pm Fri & Sat, 1-5pm Sun; 📶 👪). Views from Cabrillo National Monument (p291) inspire awe, and a museum tells of the Spanish explorers key to local history.

Teens will be in their element among the surfers, bikers and bladers in Mission and Pacific Beaches (p293), while up the coast in La Jolla the Birch Aquarium (p319) entertains as it teaches. More active kids can go snorkeling off La Jolla Cove (p319).

In northern San Diego County, Legoland (p329) is the place for the 12-and-under set (and their parents will thrill at the workmanship of the millions of little bricks). Inland, the San Diego Zoo Safari Park (p331) will have the kids roaring.

'pri-fly' (primary flight control; the carrier's equivalent of a control tower).

If lines are long, docents are there to illuminate and enliven. There are also three flight simulators (phone for rates and reservations). Some inside areas get stuffy on warm summer days: come early to avoid midday heat and crowds. Allow at least two to four hours on board. Parking costs $10.

Coronado

Across the bay from Downtown San Diego, Coronado is a civilized escape from the jumble of the city and the chaos of the beaches. After crossing the bay by ferry or via the elegantly curved 2.12-mile-long Coronado Bay Bridge, follow the tree-lined, manicured median strip of Orange Ave a mile or so toward the commercial center, Coronado Village. Then park your car; you won't need it again until you leave.

The story of Coronado is in many ways the story of the Hotel del Coronado, opened in 1888 by John D Spreckels, the millionaire who bankrolled the first rail line to San Diego, took over Coronado and turned the island into one of the West Coast's most fashionable getaways.

As an alternative to ferries, water taxis and bike rentals, bus 901 from Downtown San Diego runs along Orange Ave to the Hotel del Coronado. The Old Town Trolley tour (p295) stops in front of Mc P's Irish Pub (p310).

★Hotel del Coronado HOTEL

(☎800-582-2595, 619-435-6611; www.hoteldel.com; 1500 Orange Ave; 👪) Few hotels in the world are as easily recognized or as much loved as 'The Del.' The world's largest resort (p300) when it was built, the all-timber, whitewashed main building offers conical towers, cupolas, turrets, balconies, dormer windows and cavernous public spaces typical of their designers, railroad-depot architects James and Merritt Reed. Acres of polished wood give the interior a warm, old-fashioned feel that conjures daydreams of Panama hats and linen suits.

The hotel achieved its widest exposure when it was featured in the 1959 movie *Some Like It Hot*, which earned it a lasting association with Marilyn Monroe. Other guests have included 11 US presidents and world royalty whose pictures and mementos adorn the hotel's history gallery. There's speculation that Edward (then Prince of Wales) first met Mrs Simpson (then Mrs Spencer) when he visited in 1920, though the two did not become an item until years later. There's an interesting resident ghost story, too, about a jilted woman who haunts the hotel; some claim she silently appears in hallways and on the TV screen in the room where she had her heart broken.

For a taste of the Del without a stay, enjoy breakfast or lunch at the beach-view Sheerwater restaurant or splurge on Sunday brunch under the grand dome of the spectacular Crown Room, under chandeliers designed by L Frank Baum, who wrote *The Wonderful Wizard of Oz*.

Coronado Municipal Beach BEACH
(parking up to $8;) Just beyond the 'Hotel Del,' this beach is consistently ranked in America's top 10. Four-and-a-half miles south of Coronado Village is the white-sand **Silver Strand State Beach** (619-435-5184; www.parks.ca.gov; 5000 Hwy 75; per car $10-15;). Both have warm, calm water, perfect for swimming and good for families. Silver Strand, a long, narrow sand spit, continues south to **Imperial Beach** and connects Coronado to the mainland, though people still call it 'Coronado Island.'

Visitors Center ART & TOURS
(619-437-8788, 866-599-7242; www.coronadovisitorcenter.com; 1100 Orange Ave; walking tour $15; 9am-5pm Mon-Fri, 10am-5pm Sat & Sun, walking tours 10:30am Mon, Wed & Fri, 2pm Sat & Sun) Coronado's visitors center doubles as the **Coronado Museum of History and Art** FREE and offers 90-minute historical **walking tours**.

Point Loma Area

On maps Point Loma looks like an elephant's trunk guarding the entrance to San Diego Bay. Highlights are the Cabrillo National Monument (at the end of the trunk), the shopping and dining of Liberty Station (at its base) and seafood meals around **Shelter Island**.

There's plenty of history here too. San Diego's first fishing boats were based at Point Loma, and in the 19th century whalers dragged whale carcasses here from faraway oceans to extract the precious and useful oil. Chinese fishermen settled on the harbor side of the point in the 1860s but were forced off in 1888 when the US Congress passed the Scott Act, prohibiting anyone without citizenship papers from entering the area. Portuguese fishing families arrived approximately 50 years later, around the same time that Italian immigrants settled in present-day Little Italy.

In 1927, Charles Lindbergh tested his *Spirit of St Louis* airplane on the tidal flats of **Loma Portal**, where Point Loma joins the mainland (at the elephant's neck). The following year an airport was established at his airstrip and named Lindbergh Field, now San Diego International Airport.

By WWII, the San Diego Naval Training Center by the bay had reached its peak population of around 33,000. It was decommissioned as a training center in 1997 and

TOP BEACHES IN SAN DIEGO

Choosing San Diego's best beaches is like comparing jewels at Tiffany. Coronado Municipal Beach (p290) has appeared on just about every Top 10 list; others depend on what you're looking for.

Bodysurfing Pacific Beach (p293) and La Jolla Shores (p319). Experienced bodysurfers can head to La Jolla for the big swells of Boomer Beach near La Jolla Cove, or the *whomp* (forceful tubes that break directly onshore) at Windansea (p320) or the beach at the end of Sea Lane.

Family friendly Shell Beach (La Jolla), 15th St Beach (Del Mar), Moonlight Beach (Encinitas).

Nude beach Black's Beach (p320).

Surf breaks, from south to north Imperial Beach (p290), best in winter; Point Loma (p290) for reef breaks, less accessible but less crowded, best during winter; Sunset Cliffs (p291) in Ocean Beach; Pacific Beach; in La Jolla: Big Rock (p320), California's Pipeline, Windansea (p320), hot reef break, best at medium to low tide, La Jolla Shores (p319), beach break, best in winter, and Black's Beach (p320), a fast, powerful wave; Cardiff State Beach (p327); San Elijo State Beach (p327) in Cardiff; Swami's (p327) in Encinitas; Carlsbad State Beach (p330) and Oceanside (p332).

Teen scene Mission Beach, Pacific Beach.

nowadays the attractive, 361-acre grounds and stately Spanish-style buildings, renamed Liberty Station (p314), are a mixed use complex of restaurants, shops and galleries.

Cabrillo National Monument MONUMENT
(☎619-557-5450; www.nps.gov/cabr; 1800 Cabrillo Memorial Dr; per car/person walk-in $5/3, good for 7 days; ⏲9am-5pm; P) Atop a steep hill at the tip of the peninsula, this is San Diego's finest locale for history, views and nature walks. It's also the best place in town to see the gray-whale migration (January to March) from land. You may forget you're in a major metropolitan area.

The **visitors center** has a comprehensive, old-school presentation on Portuguese explorer Juan Rodríguez Cabrillo's 1542 voyage up the California coast, plus good exhibits on native inhabitants and the area's natural history.

The 1854 **Old Point Loma Lighthouse**, atop the point, is furnished with late-19th-century period furniture, including lamps and picture frames hand-covered with hundreds of shells – testimony to the long, lonely nights endured by lighthouse keepers. The 1.8 mile **Bayside Trail** has about a 300ft elevation and interpretive signs about local plant life. On the ocean side, drive the steep mile down to the **tide pools** to look for anemones, starfish, crabs, limpets and dead man's fingers (thin, tubular seaweed), best seen in low tide in winter.

If you're not driving, the monument can be reached by the hourly bus 84 from Old Town Transit Center (p287).

Ocean Beach

San Diego's most bohemian seaside community is a place of seriously scruffy haircuts, facial hair and body art. You can get tattooed, shop for antiques and walk into a restaurant barefoot and shirtless without anyone batting an eye. Newport Ave, the main drag, runs perpendicular to the beach through a compact business district of bars, surf shops, music stores, used-clothing stores and antiques consignment stores.

Ocean Beach Pier PIER
(Map p292; ⏲bait & tackle shop 7am-9pm Mon-Fri, to 10pm Sat & Sun) This half-mile-long pier has all the architectural allure of a freeway ramp, but at its end you'll have a great perspective on the coast. There's also a **bait and tackle shop** where you can rent fishing poles ($17 per day) to fish off the pier.

Ocean Beach Coast BEACHES
Just north of the pier, near the end of Newport Ave, is the beach scene's epicenter, with volleyball courts and sunset barbecues. Further north on **Dog Beach** (Map p292) pups chase birds around the marshy area where the San Diego River meets the sea. Head a few blocks south of the pier to **Sunset Cliffs Park**, where surfing and sunsets are the main attractions.

There are good surf breaks at the cliffs and, to the south, off Point Loma. Under the pier, skillful surfers slalom the pilings, but the rips and currents can be deadly unless you know what you're doing.

Ocean Beach Farmers Market MARKET
(Map p292; 4900 Block of Newport Ave; ⏲4-7pm Wed Oct-May, to 8pm Wed Jun-Sep) If you're here on Wednesday afternoon, stop by the farmers market to see street performers and sample fresh food.

Mission Bay, Mission & Pacific Beaches

The big-ticket attraction around Mission Bay is SeaWorld, while the nearby beaches are the SoCal of the movies: buffed surfers and bronzed bohemians pack the 3-mile-long stretch of beach. For a cruise of the area try Bahia Belle (p296).

SeaWorld San Diego THEME PARK
(☎800-257-4268; www.seaworldsandiego.com; 500 SeaWorld Dr; adult/child 3-9yr $84/78; ⏲daily; P 👪) SeaWorld opened in San Diego in 1964 and remains one of California's most popular theme parks. Many visitors spend the whole day here, shuttling between shows, rides and exhibits – you can pick up a map at the entrance to plan your day around scheduled events.

The attraction is best known for the live shows featuring trained dolphins, sea lions and killer whales. **One Ocean** is the most visually impressive, a 30-minute show featuring the famous Shamu and other killer whales gliding through the water while interacting with each other, their trainers and the audience.

There are numerous other installations where you can see and learn about aquatic life: in **Penguin Encounter** several penguin species share a habitat that simulates Antarctic living conditions; while **Shark Encounter** offers the chance to see different species of shark as you walk through a 57ft

Ocean Beach

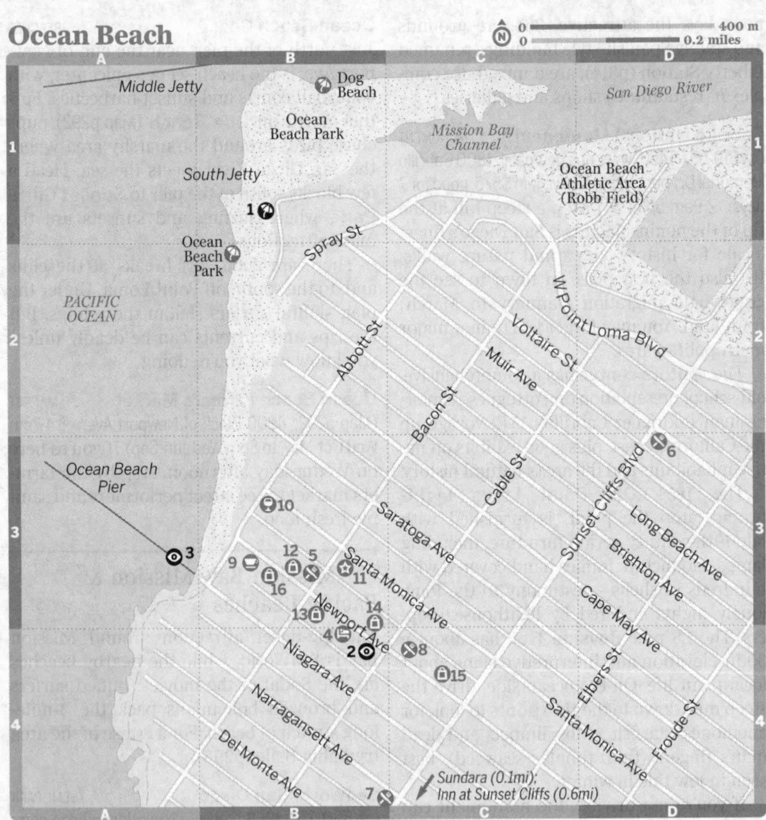

Ocean Beach

Sights

1 Dog Beach........B1
2 Ocean Beach Farmers Market........B4
3 Ocean Beach Pier........A3

Sleeping

4 Ocean Beach International Hostel........B4

Eating

5 Hodad's........B3
6 Ocean Beach People's Market........D3
7 Olive Tree Marketplace........B4
8 Ortega's Cocina........C4

Drinking & Nightlife

9 Jungle Java........B3
10 Shades........B3

Entertainment

11 Winston's........B3

Shopping

12 Cow........B3
13 Galactic........B3
14 Mallory's........B3
15 Newport Avenue Antique Center........C4
16 South Coast Longboards........B3

acrylic tunnel. Several amusement-park-style rides are also available. The new **Manta Ray** roller coaster swoops across the park at up to 43mph; **Journey to Atlantis** is a combination flume ride and roller coaster; and **Wild Arctic** is a simulated helicopter flight followed by a walk past beluga whales and polar bears. Expect long waits for rides, shows and exhibits during peak seasons.

Theme parks like SeaWorld have begun to attract controversy in recent years. While the park maintains that it does its share of animal conservation, rescue, rehabilitation, breeding and research, animal welfare groups disagree, questioning the whole idea of places like SeaWorld, and criticizing them for keeping the marine life in captivity, arguing that the conditions and treatment of the animals are harmful and stressful, and that all of this is exacerbated further by human interaction. A bill in the California state legislature in 2014 proposed to do away with killer whale shows; it was sent back for further study.

SeaWorld can also be an expensive day out, what with loud advertisements as you wait in line and omnipresent corporate logos and gift shops (mostly designed with young visitors in mind) encouraging additional souvenir spending. That said, good deals are often available for multiday or combination tickets with other parks, including San Diego Zoo and Wild Animal Park, Universal Studios Hollywood and/or Disneyland. Inquire at tourist offices and hotels. To save on food, all-you-can-eat passes to multiple SeaWorld restaurants are available seasonally, or keep a cooler in the car and picnic at tables outside the gates – be sure to get a hand-stamp for re-entry.

To get here by car, take SeaWorld Dr off I-5 less than a mile north of where it intersects with I-8. Parking costs $15. Check with Metropolitan Transit System (p315) for public transit. Some hotels offer shuttles.

Mission Bay OUTDOOR ACTIVITIES

Just east of Mission and Pacific Beaches is this 7-sq-mile playground, with 27 miles of shoreline and 90 acres of parks on islands, coves and peninsulas. Sailing, windsurfing and kayaking dominate northwest Mission Bay, while waterskiers zip around **Fiesta Island**. Kite flying is popular in **Mission Bay Park**, beach volleyball is big on Fiesta Island, and there's delightful cycling and inline skating on the miles of bike paths. Although hotels, boat yards and other businesses dot about one-quarter of the land, it feels wide open.

Fun fact: the Spanish called this expanse at the mouth of the San Diego River 'False Bay' – it formed a shallow bay when the river flowed and a marshy swamp when it didn't. After WWII, a combination of civic vision and coastal engineering turned it into a recreational area.

Mission & Pacific Beaches BEACHES

FREE Central San Diego's best beach scene is concentrated in a narrow strip of land between the ocean and Mission Bay. There's amazing people-watching on the **Ocean Front Walk**, the boardwalk that connects the two beaches. From South Mission Jetty to Pacific Beach Point, it's crowded with joggers, inline skaters and cyclists anytime of the year. On warm summer weekends, oiled bodies, packed like sardines, cover the beach from end to end and cheer the setting sun.

While there's lots to do here, perhaps the best use of an afternoon is to walk along the boardwalk, spread a blanket or kick back over cocktails and take in the scenery.

A block off Mission Beach, Mission Blvd (the main north–south road), is lined with surf, smoke and swimwear shops. Cheap Rentals (p316) rents bikes and skates and surfboards.

In Pacific Beach, to the north, activity extends inland, particularly along Garnet (say gar-*net*) Ave, lined with bars, restaurants and used-clothing stores, mostly targeted at a 20-something crowd. At the ocean end of Garnet Ave, Crystal Pier is a mellow place to fish or gaze out to sea.

At peak times these beaches can get so crowded that the police simply close them down, and parking around noon is just not gonna happen.

Belmont Park AMUSEMENT PARK

(☎858-458-1549; www.belmontpark.com; 3146 Mission Blvd; per ride $2-6, all-day pass adult/child $27/16; ⏲from 11am daily, closing time varies; P)

This old-style family amusement park at the southern end of Mission Beach has been here since 1925, and when it was threatened with demolition in the mid-1990s, community action saved it. Now there's a large indoor pool, known as the **Plunge**, and the **Giant Dipper**, a classic wooden roller coaster that'll shake the teeth right outta your mouth, plus bumper cars, a tilt-a-whirl, carousel and other classics.

More modern attractions include wave machines like **Flowrider** (wave-riding per hr $30) FREE, for simulated surfing. Even if it sits on dry land, it's pretty much to San Diego what the Santa Monica Pier amusement park is to LA.

Activities

Surfing

A good number of San Diegans moved here for the surfing, and boy is it good. Even beginners will understand why it's so popular.

Fall brings strong swells and offshore Santa Ana winds. In summer swells come from

Mission & Pacific Beaches

Activities, Courses & Tours
1 Bob's Mission Surf A2
2 Cheap Rentals A4
3 Mission Bay Sportcenter B4
4 Pacific Beach Surf Shop A2
Resort Watersports .... (see 7)

Sleeping
5 Banana Bungalow A2
6 Beach Cottages A2
7 Catamaran Resort Hotel B3
8 Crystal Pier Hotel & Cottages A1
9 Tower 23 .... A1

Eating
10 Green Flash A2
JRDN .... (see 9)
11 Kono's Surf Club A1
12 World Famous A2

Drinking & Nightlife
13 Bub's Dive B1
14 Café 976 .... B1
15 Pacific Beach Ale House A2
16 Society Billiard Cafe B1

Entertainment
17 710 Beach Club A1

Shopping
18 Buffalo Exchange B1
19 Pangaea Outpost B1
20 Pilar's Beachwear A4
21 South Coast Wahines A1

the south and southwest, and in winter from the west and northwest. Spring brings more frequent onshore winds, but the surfing can still be good. For the latest beach, weather and surf reports, call San Diego County Lifeguard Services at ☎619-221-8824.

Beginners should head to Mission or Pacific Beaches (p293), where the waves are gentle. North of Crystal Pier, Tourmaline Surf Beach is an especially good place to take your first strokes.

Rental rates vary depending on the quality of the equipment, but figure on soft boards from $15/45 per hour/full day; wet suits cost $7/28. Packages are available.

Pacific Beach Surf Shop SURFING
(☎858-373-1138; www.pbsurfshop.com; 4150 Mission Blvd; ⏲store 9am-7pm, lessons hourly until 4pm) This shop provides instruction through its Pacific Beach Surf School. It has friendly service, and also rents wetsuits and both soft (foam) and hard (fiberglass) boards. Call ahead for lessons.

Bob's Mission Surf SURF EQUIPMENT
(☎858-483-8837; www.missionsurf.com; 4320 Mission Blvd, Pacific Beach) Rents stand-up paddleboards and bikes in addition to surf equipment.

Diving & Snorkeling

Off the coast of San Diego County, divers will find kelp beds, shipwrecks (including the *Yukon*, a WWII destroyer sunk off Mission Beach in 2000) and canyons deep enough to host bat rays, octopuses and squid. For current conditions, call San Diego County Lifeguard Services at ☎619-221-8824.

Fishing

The most popular public fishing piers are Imperial Beach Pier, Embarcadero Fishing Pier, Shelter Island Fishing Pier, Ocean Beach Pier and Crystal Pier at Pacific Beach. Generally the best pier fishing is from April to October, and no license is required. For offshore fishing, catches can include barracuda, bass and yellowtail and, in summer, albacore. A state fishing license is required for people over 16 for offshore fishing – one day/two day/calendar year costs $15/23/46, available from operators that run daily fishing trips (from about $46/36 per adult/child for a near-shore, half-day trip), including these around Mission Bay and Point Loma.

H&M Landing FISHING CHARTER
(☎619-222-1144; www.hmlanding.com; 2803 Emerson St, Point Loma)

Point Loma Sport Fishing FISHING CHARTER
(☎619-223-1627; www.pointlomasportfishing.com; 1403 Scott St, Point Loma)

Seaforth Sportfishing FISHING CHARTER
(☎619-224-3383; www.seaforthlanding.com; 1717 Quivira Rd, Mission Bay)

Boating

You can rent powerboats (from $125 per hour), sailboats (from $24 per hour), and kayaks (from $13 per hour) and canoes on Mission Bay. Ocean kayaking is a good way to view sea life, and explore cliffs and caves inaccessible from land.

Family Kayak KAYAK RENTAL
(☎619-282-3520; www.familykayak.com; adult/child from $44/18; 👪) Guided tours and lessons. Inquire about longer tours. Locations vary, check the website.

Mission Bay Sportcenter BOAT RENTAL
(☎858-488-1004; www.missionbaysportcenter.com; 1010 Santa Clara Pl)

Resort Watersports BOAT RENTAL
(☎858-488-2582; www.resortwatersports.com) Located at the Bahia and Catamaran (p301) resort hotels.

Sailing

Experienced sailors are able to charter boats ranging from catamarans to yachts. Prices start at about $135 for four hours and rise steeply. Charter operators can be found around Shelter and Harbor Islands (on the west side of San Diego Bay near the airport).

Harbor Sailboats SAILING
(☎619-291-9568, 800-854-6625; www.harborsailboats.com; Suite 104, 2040 Harbor Island Dr)

Harbor Yacht Clubs SAILING
(☎800-553-7245; www.harboryc.com; 1880 Harbor Island Dr)

Whale-Watching

Gray whales pass from mid-December to late February on their way south to Baja California, and again in mid-March on their way back up to Alaskan waters. Their 12,000-mile round-trip journey is the longest migration of any mammal on earth.

Cabrillo National Monument (p291) is the best place to see the whales from land, where you'll also find exhibits, whale-related ranger programs and a shelter from which to watch the whales breach (bring binoculars).

Half-day whale-watching boat trips are offered by all of the companies that run daily fishing trips. The trips generally cost $20/15 per adult/child for a three-hour excursion, with a guaranteed sighting or a free ticket. Look for coupons and special offers at tourist kiosks and online.

Tours

Look for discounts in tourist literature or online.

Old Town Trolley Tours & Seal Tours TROLLEY TOUR
(☎888-910-8687; www.trolleytours.com; adult/child $39/19) Not to be confused with the municipal San Diego Trolley, this outfit operates hop-on-hop-off, open-air buses decorated like old-style streetcars, looping around the main attractions of Downtown and Coronado in about two hours, every 30 minutes or so. The main trolley stand is in Old Town, but you can start or stop at any of the well-marked trolley-tour stops. It also operates 90-minute amphibious **Seal Tours** (Map p284) which depart from Seaport Village (p314) and tour the bay via Shelter Island.

Taste of San Diego FOOD TOUR
(www.atasteof-sandiego.com; from $50) Walking tours showcase the city's gastronomic treasures from Downtown to diners and dives, with enthusiastic native San Diegan guides.

San Diego Scenic Tours BUS TOUR
(www.sandiegoscenictours.com; adult/child from $38/19) Half- and full-day bus tours around San Diego and Tijuana, some of which build in time to shop and dine. You can combine some tours with a harbor cruise.

Flagship Cruises BOAT TOUR
(Map p284; ☎619-234-4111; www.flagshipsd.com; 990 N Harbor Dr; tours adult/child from $23/11.50; 👪) Harbor tours and seasonal whale-watching cruises from the Embarcadero, from one to several hours long.

Hornblower Cruises BOAT TOUR
(Map p284; ☎888-467-6256; www.hornblower.com; 970 N Harbor Dr; adult/child from $24/12;) In addition to sightseeing cruises, Hornblower specializes in catered cruises with drinks, dinner or brunch (from $62 plus tax, service and drinks; departing from 1800 N Harbor Dr).

Bahia Belle CRUISES
(www.sternwheelers.com; 998 W Mission Bay Dr; adult/child $10/3) For a lovely time without adrenaline overload, board this floating bar disguised as a stern-wheeler paddleboat. It offers 30-minute cruises between two resort hotels, the Catamaran and the Bahia, on Friday and Saturday evenings January to May and September to November; Wednesday to Saturday in June; and daily in July and August. Cruises start at 6:30pm; call for exact departure times.

Festivals & Events

March

Ocean Beach Kite Festival OUTDOORS
(www.oceanbeachkiwanis.org; 1st Sat in Mar;) Kite making, decorating and flying, as well as competitions.

San Diego Crew Classic SPORTING EVENT
(www.crewclassic.org; late Mar/early Apr) The national college rowing regatta takes places in Mission Bay.

June

Rock 'n' Roll Marathon SPORTING EVENT
(www.runrocknroll.competitor.com; early Jun) Live bands perform at each mile mark of this 26.2-mile race, with a big concert at the finish line.

San Diego County Fair COUNTY FAIR
(www.sdfair.com; Del Mar Fairgrounds; early Jun-early Jul) Well over a million people watch headline acts, enjoy hundreds of carnival rides and shows and pig out on 'fair fare'.

July

Opening Day at Del Mar Racetrack SPORTING EVENT
(www.dmtc.com; mid-late Jul) Outrageous hats, cocktails and general merriment kicks off the horseracing season, 'where the turf meets the surf.' Racing through early September.

San Diego LGBT Pride COMMUNITY FESTIVAL
(www.sdpride.org; late Jul) The city's gay community celebrates in Hillcrest and Balboa Park at the month's end, with parades, parties, performances, art shows and more.

Comic-Con International CONVENTION
(www.comic-con.org; San Diego Convention Center; late Jul) America's largest event for collectors of comic, pop culture and movie memorabilia has gone from geek chic to trendmaker.

September

Bayfair SPORTING EVENT
(www.sandiegobayfair.org; mid-Sep) Some of the world's fastest speedboats compete on Mission Bay.

San Diego Film Festival ARTS
(www.sdff.org; late Sep-early Oct) The silver screen takes center stage in the Gaslamp Quarter and La Jolla, with screenings, panel discussions, parties and a good chance of star sightings.

Fleet Week MILITARY
(www.fleetweeksandiego.org; mid-Sep–early Oct) Actually more like 'Fleet Month.' The US military shows its pride in events including a sea and air parade, special tours of ships, the Miramar Air Show (the world's largest) and the Coronado Speed Festival featuring vintage cars.

October

Little Italy Festa FOOD, CULTURE
(www.littleitalysd.com; mid-Oct) Come for the tastes and aromas of old Italia, and stay for Gesso Italiano, chalk-art drawn directly onto the streets.

December

December Nights HOLIDAY FESTIVAL
(www.balboapark.org/decembernights; early Dec) This festival in Balboa Park includes crafts, carols and a candlelight parade.

Harbor Parade of Lights HOLIDAY FESTIVAL
(www.sdparadeoflights.org) Dozens of decorated, illuminated boats float in procession on the harbor on two Sunday evenings in December.

Las Posadas HOLIDAY FESTIVAL
(www.parks.ca.gov) This traditional Latin Christmas celebration in Old Town re-enacts Mary and Joseph seeking shelter.

Sleeping

We list high-season (summer) rates for single- or double-occupancy rooms. Prices drop significantly between September and

June. Whatever time of year, ask about specials, suites and package deals.

San Diego Tourism runs a **Room Reservation Line** (800-350-6205; www.sandiego.org).

For camping try Campland on the Bay (p302) or **KOA** (619-427-3601, 800-562-9877; www.sandiegokoa.com; 111 N 2nd Ave, Chula Vista; tent sites $40-61, RV sites $48-89, cabins $70-120, deluxe cabins $115-250; P @), about 8 miles south, with good camping facilities for families like a pool and bike rental, plus a Jacuzzi for mom and dad and off-leash dog park for Fido; new deluxe cabins include linens, private bathrooms and pots and pans.

Downtown San Diego

Downtown is San Diego's most convenient place to stay, for its wealth of restaurants and hotels and easy access to transit.

★USA Hostels San Diego HOSTEL $

(Map p284; 619-232-3100, 800-438-8622; www.usahostels.com; 726 5th Ave; dm/r with shared bath incl breakfast from $33/79; @) Lots of charm and color at this convivial hostel in a former Victorian-era hotel. Look for cheerful rooms, a full kitchen, a communal lounge for chilling and in-house parties and beach barbecues. Rates include linens, lockers and pancakes for breakfast. And it's smack-dab in the middle of Gaslamp nightlife. No air-con.

500 West Hotel HOTEL $

(Map p284; 619-234-5252, 866-500-7533; www.500westhotelsd.com; 500 W Broadway; s/d with shared bath from $59/79; @) Rooms are shoebox-sized and many bathrooms are down the hallway in this updated 1920s YMCA building, but hipsters on a budget love the bright decor, tiny flat-screen TVs, communal kitchen (or diner-style restaurant), gym at the Y ($10) and easy access to trolleys and long-distance buses. No air-con.

HI San Diego Downtown Hostel HOSTEL $

(Map p284; 619-525-1531; www.sandiegohostels.org; 521 Market St; 10-/4-bed dm with shared bath incl breakfast from $22/30, d from $75; @) Location, location, location. This Gaslamp Quarter HI facility is steps from public transportation restaurants and big-city fun, and it has a wide range of rooms including some with private bath. If the local nightlife doesn't suffice, there are movie nights and group dinners to join. Twenty-four-hour access.

★Hotel Indigo BOUTIQUE HOTEL $$

(Map p284; 619-727-4000; www.hotelinsd.com; 509 9th Ave; r from $189; P @) San Diego's first hotel to be certified green (opened 2009), the Indigo proves that enviro can still be comfy, with green roofs, sustainable construction, windows that open and cheery design motifs inspired by local waters and California poppies. Bonus: when the Padres are playing, watch the game from some rooms or the Level 9 rooftop bar. Parking is $41.

★La Pensione Hotel BOUTIQUE HOTEL $$

(Map p284; www.lapensionehotel.com; 606 W Date St; r $110-159; P ; 5, Pacific Hwy & W Cedar St) Despite the name, Little Italy's la Pensione isn't a pension but an intimate, friendly, recently renovated hotel of 68 rooms with queen-size beds and private bathrooms. It's set around a frescoed courtyard and it's just steps to the neighborhood's dining, cafes and galleries, and walking distance to most Downtown attractions. There's an attractive cafe downstairs. Parking is $15.

★Hotel Solamar BOUTIQUE, CONTEMPORARY $$

(Map p284; 877-230-0300, 619-531-8740; www.hotelsolamar.com; 435 6th Ave; r $169-299; P @) A great compromise in the Gaslamp: hip style that needn't break the bank. Lounge beats animate your view of skyscrapers from the pool deck and bar, and rooms have sleek lines and nautical blue and neo-rococo accents for a touch of fun. There's a fitness center, in-room yoga kit, loaner bikes and a nightly complimentary wine hour. Parking costs $41.

Hotel Palomar San Diego CONTEMPORARY $$

(Map p284; 619-515-3000; www.hotelpalomar-sandiego.com; 1047 5th Ave; r from $249; P @) Hollywood glam in San Diego. A 9000lb bronze front door pivots to reveal Nepalese carpets and multitextured surfaces: wooden blocks to sand-dollar-shaped ceramics, stingray skin to woven leather. There's doting service, a chic restaurant, lovely spa, nightly wine hour and coffee and tea in the morning. Parking is $39.

Sofia Hotel BOUTIQUE HOTEL $$

(Map p284; 800-826-0009, 619-234-9200; www.thesofiahotel.com; 150 W Broadway; r from $159; P @) Across from Westfield Horton Plaza, the historic Sofia has 211 rooms with fashionable darkwood furniture and sprightly printed fabrics. There are also

TRAVELING TO TJ

Just beyond the most crossed border in the world, **Tijuana, Mexico** (population around 2 million) was for decades a cheap, convivial escape for hard-partying San Diegans, Angelenos, sailors and college kids. Around 2008 a double-whammy of drug-related violence and global recession turned once-bustling tourist areas into ghost towns, but Tijuanenses (as the locals call themselves) have been slowly but surely reclaiming their city. The difference from squeaky-clean San Diego is palpable from the moment you cross the border, but so are signs of new life for those who knew TJ in the bad old days.

Avenida Revolución ('La Revo') is the main tourist drag, though its charm is marred by cheap clothing and souvenir stores, strip joints, pharmacies selling bargain-priced medications to Americans, and touts best rebuffed with a firm 'no'. It's a lot more appealing just beyond La Revo, toward and around Avenida Constitución, where sightseeing highlights include **Catedral de Nuestra Señora de Guadalupe** (Cathedral of our Lady of Guadalupe; cnr Av Niños Héroes & Calle 2a), Tijuana's oldest church, **Mercado El Popo** (cnr Calle 2a & Av Constitución), an atmospheric market hall selling needs from tamarind pods to religious iconography, and **Pasaje Rodríguez** (btwn Avenida Revolución & Avenida Constitución, Calle 3 & Calle 4), an arcade newly filled with youthful art galleries, bars and trendsetters.

A short ride away, **Museo de las Californias** (Museum of the Californias; from US 011-52-664-687-9600; www.cecut.gob.mx; cnr Paseo de los Héroes & Av Independencia; adult/child under 12yr M$20/free; 10am-6pm Tue-Sun;), inside the architecturally daring **Centro Cultural Tijuana** (CECUT; from US 011-52-664-687-9600; www.cecut.gob.mx; cnr Paseo de los Héroes & Av Independencia; 9am-7pm Mon-Fri, 10am-7pm Sat & Sun;), aka El Cubo (the Cube), offers an excellent history of the border region from prehistory to the present; there's signage in English. If you're in town on a Friday night, check out a **lucha libre** (from US 011-52-664-250-9015; Blvd Díaz Ordaz 12421, Auditorio Municipal Fausto Gutierrez Moreno; admission US$8-35) match, Mexican wrestling by oversized men in gaudy masks.

Tijuana's culinary claim to fame is the Caesar salad, invented at the **Hotel Caesar** (from US 011-52-664-685-1606; Av Revolución 827; Caesar salad $6; 9am-midnight) and now prepared tableside with panache in the elegant dining room lined with sepia pics. Ernest Hemingway and Anthony Quinn are among the illustrious patrons to dine at **Chiki Jai** (from US 011-52-664-685-4955; Av Revolución 1388; mains M$100-150; 11am-10pm Mon-Sat), here since the 1940s; it still serves Spanish specialties including paella, stuffed calamari and that 'other' *tortilla* (potato-based omelette) in the simple, tiled dining room. Tijuana's also a hotbed of chef-driven contemporary Mexican cuisine. Chef Javier Plascencia has a number of spots around town including the fun storefront **Erizo** (from US 011-52-686-3895; 3808 Avenida Sonora; tacos M$18-45, ceviches $62-180, ramen $90-120) for innovative takes on tacos, ceviche and even ramen, worth the 10-minute taxi ride from La Revo.

Turista Libre (www.turistalibre.com) runs a variety of public and private tours in English, led by an American expat with endless enthusiasm for the city and its lesser-known nooks and crannies.

A passport is required for the border crossing. By public transportation from San Diego, the **San Diego Trolley** (www.sdmts.com) runs from Downtown to San Ysidro, at the border. By car, take I-5 south and look for signs for the last US exit. Park at one of the many lots in the area (around $8 for up to 24 hours). Cross the border on foot, and pick up a map at the border station for the approximately 20-minute walk to La Revo; follow signs reading 'Centro Downtown.' If traveling by taxi from the Mexican side of the border, be sure to take a taxi with a meter.

Driving into Mexico is not recommended: directions can be difficult, nighttime smash-and-grab theft is common, separate Mexican auto insurance is required (purchase at shops on the US side of the border crossing for $15 to $25 per day depending on the value of vehicle and length of stay in Mexico) and the waits to cross back into the US can seem eternal.

For further information, head to shop.lonelyplanet.com to purchase a downloadable PDF of the Baja California chapter from Lonely Planet's *Mexico* guide.

in-room spa services, concierge, complimentary guided walks around the Gaslamp Quarter (Saturday and Sunday) and a fitness and yoga studio. There are three restaurants including branches of SoCal chains Coffee Bean and Tender Greens. Parking costs $30.

Courtyard by Marriott San Diego Downtown HERITAGE **$$**
(Map p284; ☎619-446-3000; www.marriott.com/sancd; 530 Broadway; r from $139; P ❄ @ 📶) Yeah, we know, Courtyard is better known for bland rooms in suburban office parks, but this Courtyard is cool because it's in a beautifully updated 1928 bank tower. Spacious, recently renovated rooms occupy the former offices, connected by hallways of vintage marble. Some have views to the harbor and Coronado Bay Bridge. Play in the fitness center and billiard room. Green retrofits include low-wattage bulbs, digital thermostats and motion sensors. Parking is $36.

★US Grant Hotel LUXURY **$$$**
(Map p284; ☎619-232-3121, 800-237-5029; www.starwood.com; 326 Broadway; r from $249; P ❄ @ 📶) This 1910 hotel was built as the fancy city counterpart to the Hotel del Coronado and hosted everyone from Albert Einstein to Harry Truman. Today's quietly flashy lobby combines chocolate-brown and ocean-blue accents, and rooms boast original artwork on the headboards. It's owned by members of the Sycuan tribe of Native Americans. Parking costs $39.

Horton Grand Hotel HISTORIC HOTEL **$$$**
(Map p284; ☎800-542-1886, 619-544-1886; www.hortongrand.com; 311 Island Ave; r from $199; 🚌5, 🚊2nd Ave & J St) At the edge of the Gaslamp, rooms in this brick hotel from 1886 are individually decorated in Victoriana and have gas fireplaces. If you're facing the street you may get a wrought-iron balcony but also street noise from nearby theaters and clubs; rooms facing the inner courtyard are the quietest. Parking costs $25.

Uptown: Bankers Hill, Hillcrest & North Park

Inn at the Park HOTEL, GAY-FRIENDLY **$$**
(☎619-291-0999; www.shellhospitality.com/inn-at-the-park; 525 Spruce St; r $129-299; P 🚭 ❄ @ 📶) This 82-room place, facing Balboa Park and a reasonable walk to central Hillcrest, used to be an apartment building, meaning mostly large rooms with kitchens, vast closets and Hollywood art deco–style decor. Green initiatives include a recycling program and efficient lighting. Parking is $15.

Old Town

Best Western Hacienda Hotel HOTEL **$$**
(☎619-298-4707, 800-888-1991; www.hacienda-hotel-oldtown.com; 4041 Harney St; r $189-239; P ❄ @ 📶 🏊) On four well-landscaped acres on the hillside above Old Town's restaurant row, the Hacienda has 200 rooms over eight buildings, neatly decorated in Mission style, some with pull-out sofas. Add in a workout room and Jacuzzi. Off-season rates start at around $100. Parking costs $14.

Cosmopolitan Hotel HISTORIC B&B **$$**
(☎619-297-1874; www.oldtowncosmopolitan.com; 2660 Calhoun St; r incl breakfast $150-250; ⊙front desk 9am-9pm; P 🚭 📶) Right in Old Town State Park, this creaky, 10-room hotel from 1870 has oodles of charm, antique furnishings, a possible haunting (!) and a restaurant downstairs for lunch and dinner. Don't go expecting modern conveniences like phones and TV, though there's free wi-fi. Breakfast is a simple affair centered around coffee and scones. Free parking.

Coronado

A stay in Coronado Village (around the Hotel del Coronado) puts you close to the beach, shops and restaurants. The northern end is an easy walk to the ferry. The lower the building number, the closer to the ferry.

Crown City Inn MOTEL **$$**
(☎619-435-3116, 800-422-1173; www.crowncityinn.com; 520 Orange Ave; r from $129; ste from $199; P ❄ @ 📶 🏊) This two-story, family-owned motel is an excellent value, set around a small parking area with a little pool. It offers loaner bikes for easy getaways and cookies and iced tea in the lobby. If its floral-accented rooms were beachside, they would start at $200 per night. The bistro onsite is a local fave.

El Cordova Hotel HISTORIC **$$**
(☎619-435-4131, 800-229-2032; www.elcordovahotel.com; 1351 Orange Ave; r from $199; ❄ @ 📶 🏊) This exceedingly cozy Spanish-style former mansion from 1902 has rooms and suites around an outdoor courtyard of shops, restaurants, pool, hot tub and barbecue grills. Rooms are charming in an antiquey sort of way, though nothing fancy.

MISSION VALLEY HOTELS

Downtown rates got you down? Beach booked? A couple dozen mostly chain hotels and motels along I-8 in Mission Valley offer in quantity and price what their neighborhood lacks in charm – they're popular for conventions, family vacations and shopping excursions. Outside of the summer peak, weekday rates are occasionally as low as $80.

Handlery Hotel (☎619-298-0511, 800-843-4343; www.handlery.com; 950 Hotel Circle N; r $139-179; P @ 🛜 🏊) The Handlery has attractive furnishings (wooden armoires and writing desks) and a complimentary shuttle to area attractions. Parking costs $12.

Crowne Plaza San Diego (☎619-297-1101; www.cp-sandiego.com; 2270 Hotel Circle N; r from $129; P @ 🛜 🏊) Leafy convention-class hotel with a Polynesian theme (koi ponds and waterfalls) and rooms with super-comfy mattresses. Parking costs $12.

Town & Country Hotel (☎619-291-7131, 800-772-8527; www.towncountry.com; 500 Hotel Circle N; r from $195; P @ 🛜 🏊) This property is so big that golf carts shuttle around four swimming pools, rose bushes, palms and a 10-story tower. There's a trolley stop and bridge to Fashion Valley shopping center (p314). Parking costs $14.

Glorietta Bay Inn HISTORIC $$
(☎619-435-3101, 800-283-9383; www.gloriettabayinn.com; 1630 Glorietta Blvd; r incl breakfast from $219; P ❄ @ 🛜 🏊) Overshadowed by the neighboring Hotel Del, the Glorietta is built in and around the neoclassical 1908 Spreckels Mansion – (11 rooms in the mansion, 89 in boxier two-story buildings). Rooms have handsome furnishings and extras such as triple-sheeted beds and high-end bath products. Mansion rooms are more expensive and have even more luxe amenities. Rates include continental breakfast.

Stop in and see the gorgeous music room, even if you're not staying here. Parking is $10.

Coronado Inn MOTEL $$
(☎619-435-4121, 800-598-6624; www.coronadoinn.com; 266 Orange Ave; r incl breakfast from $149, with kitchen from $199; P @ 🛜 🏊 🐾) This good midrange choice near the ferry is a wood-shingled affair decked with palms, little wooden gazebos, barbecue grills and deck chairs around the pool. Continental breakfast and all-day coffee and tea are served.

★**Hotel del Coronado** LUXURY HOTEL $$$
(Hotel Del; ☎619-435-6611, 800-468-3533; www.hoteldel.com; 1500 Orange Ave; r from $289; P ⊖ ❄ @ 🛜 🏊 🐾) San Diego's iconic hotel provides the essential Coronado experience: over a century of history (p289), a pool, full-service spa, shops, restaurants, manicured grounds, a white-sand beach and an ice-skating rink in winter. Even the basic rooms have luxurious marbled bathrooms. Note: half the accommodations are not in the main Victorian-era hotel (368 rooms) but in an adjacent seven-story building constructed in the 1970s. For a sense of place, book a room in the original hotel. Parking is $37.

Loews Coronado Bay Resort RESORT $$$
(☎619-424-4000, 800-235-6397; www.loewshotels.com; 4000 Coronado Bay Rd; r $229-299; P ❄ @ 🛜 🏊) Way down Silver Strand (complimentary shuttle to Coronado Village), the 439-room Loews is reached by a causeway and has its own private marina with boat rentals. Rooms boast sea hues and rattans, the lobby is all sunny yellows and sea blues, and there are three outdoor pools, plenty of kids' programs and romantic views from the chic, Mediterranean-inspired Mistral restaurant. Parking is $28.

Point Loma Area

Although it's a bit out of the way, Point Loma boasts some fun accommodations. Head to Shelter Island for tiki-style hotels.

HI San Diego Point Loma Hostel HOSTEL $
(☎619-223-4778; www.sandiegohostels.org; 3790 Udall St; dm/r per person with shared bath incl breakfast from $19/33; @ 🛜) It's a 20-minute walk from central Ocean Beach to this little red hostel, in a largely residential area close to a market and library. Cheery private rooms are a great deal. There are often cheap dinners, movie nights and free excursions around town and to Tijuana. Bus 923 runs along nearby Voltaire St. No lock-out times. No air-con.

Pearl MOTEL $$

(☎ 619-226-6100, 877-732-7574; www.thepearlsd.com; 1410 Rosecrans St; r $129-169; P ❄ 📶 ≋) The midcentury modern Pearl feels more Palm Springs than San Diego. The 23 rooms in its 1959 shell have soothing blue hues, trippy surf motifs and betas in fishbowls. There's a lively pool scene (including 'dive-in' movies on Wednesday nights), or play Jenga or Parcheesi in the groovy, shag-carpeted lobby. Light sleepers: request a room away from busy street traffic.

On-site parking is limited and costs $10.

Humphrey's Half Moon Inn & Suites POLYNESIAN $$

(☎ 619-224-3411, 800-345-9995; www.halfmoon-inn.com; 2303 Shelter Island Dr; r $150-229, ste $190-269; P @ 📶 ≋) Fans of boating, jazz and Polynesian style will feel at home in this harborside resort. Its 182 rooms and suites are clustered amid koi ponds, paddling mallards, palms and flower beds, in wooden shingle-roofed buildings like Hawaiian *lanais*. Some have balconies and views of yachts on the harbor. There's a good jazz club on site. Parking is $10.

Best Western Island Palms POLYNESIAN $$

(☎ 619-222-0561, 800-922-2336; www.islandpalms.com; 2051 Shelter Island Dr; r from $169; P ❄ @ 📶 ≋) Namesake palms adorn the lobby and grounds around this archipelago of three Polynesian-style buildings housing the resort's 174 rooms, pools and hot tubs. It has comfortable, well-maintained, upper-end-chain-motel-style rooms, plus free bike rentals. Parking is $10.

Ocean Beach

Ocean Beach (OB) is under the outbound flight path of San Diego airport, which won't be a problem if you rise at 6am. Light or late sleepers should stay elsewhere or bring earplugs.

Ocean Beach International Hostel HOSTEL $

(Map p292; ☎ 619-223-7873, 800-339-7263; www.sandiegohostel.us; 4961 Newport Ave; dm $15-40) Central OB's cheapest option is only a couple of blocks from the ocean; it's a simple but friendly and fun place reserved for international travelers and educators, with barbecues, music nights, bonfires and more. Free transfer from airport, bus or train station on arrival. No air-con. Prices depend on availability.

Inn at Sunset Cliffs BEACHSIDE INN $$$

(☎ 619-222-7901, 866-786-2453; www.innatsunsetcliffs.com; 1370 Sunset Cliffs Blvd; r/ste from $175/289; P ❄ @ 📶 ≋) At the south end of Ocean Beach, wake up to the sound of surf crashing onto the rocky shore. This low-key 1965 charmer wraps around a flower-bedecked courtyard with small heated pool. Its 24 breezy rooms are compact, but most have attractive stone and tile bathrooms, and some suites have full kitchens. Even if the ocean air occasionally takes its toll on exterior surfaces, it's hard not to love this place. Free parking.

Pacific Beach

Banana Bungalow HOSTEL $

(☎ 858-273-3060; www.bananabungalowsandiego.com; 707 Reed Ave; dm/d $35/100; 📶; 🚌 30) Right on Pacific Beach, the Bungalow has a top location, a beach-party atmosphere and is reasonably clean, but it's very basic and gets crowded. Shared rooms are mixed-gender. The communal patio fronts right on the boardwalk; it's a great place for people-watching and beer drinking. No air-con. Look for cheaper off-season rates.

Catamaran Resort Hotel POLYNESIAN $$

(☎ 858-488-1081, 800-422-8386; www.catamaranresort.com; 3999 Mission Blvd; r from $159; P @ 📶 ≋) Tropical landscaping and tiki decor fill this resort backing onto Mission Bay (there's a luau on some summer evenings!). A plethora of activities make it a perfect place for families (sailing, kayaking, tennis, biking, skating, spa-ing, etc), or board the Bahia Belle (p296) from here. Rooms are in low-rise buildings or in a 14-story tower; some have views and full kitchens.

Staff is warm and helpful. Parking costs $17/22 self/valet.

Beach Cottages MOTEL, COTTAGES $$

(☎ 858-483-7440; www.beachcottages.com; 4255 Ocean Blvd; r $160-355; 🚌 30, 34) Family owned and operated, Beach Cottages has everything from plain motel rooms to cozy 1940s cottages, just across the bike path from the sand. Sure, they're nothing fancy, but there's a loveable throwback feel to the clapboard construction, ping-pong, shuffleboard and rattan furniture. Larger rooms can be a real bargain if you're travelling in a group. No air-con.

Tower 23 BOUTIQUE HOTEL $$$
(☎858-270-2323, 866-869-3723; www.t23hotel.com; 723 Felspar St; r from $249; P ❄ @ ≋ 🐾) If you like your oceanfront stay with contemporary cool style, this modernist show place has an awesome location, minimalist decor, lots of teals and mint blues, water features and a sense of humor. There's no pool, but dude, you're right on the beach. Parking is $20.

Crystal Pier Hotel & Cottages COTTAGE $$$
(☎858-483-6983, 800-748-5894; www.crystalpier.com; 4500 Ocean Blvd; d $185-525; P ≋) Charming, wonderful and unlike anyplace else in San Diego, Crystal Pier has cottages built right on the pier above the water. Almost all 29 cottages have full ocean views and kitchens; most date from 1936. Newer, larger cottages sleep up to six. Book eight to 11 months in advance for summer reservations. Minimum-stay requirements vary by season. No air-con. Rates include parking.

Mission Bay

Just south of Mission Beach, Mission Bay has waterfront lodging at lower prices than on the ocean.

Campland on the Bay CAMPGROUND $
(☎858-581-4260, 800-422-9386; www.campland.com; 2211 Pacific Beach Dr; RV & campsites $45-238, beachfront from $194; P ≋ ≈) On more than 40 acres fronting Mission Bay, amenities include a restaurant, two pools, boat rentals, full RV hookups and outdoor activities from skateboarding to singalongs. Price varies depending on proximity to the water; reservations are recommended. Off-season discounts.

Paradise Point Resort RESORT $$$
(☎858-274-4630, 800-344-2626; www.paradisepoint.com; 1404 Vacation Rd; r from $149-359; P @ ≋ ≈ 🐾) The grounds are so lush and dotted with so many palms that you'll feel like you're in Hawaii at this upper-end resort, whose 462 rooms are in small ground-floor bungalows. Features for kids include a putting green and summer movies in one of the five swimming pools. Full-service spa. Parking costs $34.

Eating

Despite its border location, San Diego's food scene doesn't have the ethnic breadth of LA's, but there's a growing locavore and gourmet scene, especially in North Park, and some of the less-expensive options are fun and satisfying. Reservations are recommended, especially on weekends.

Balboa Park

★**Prado** CALIFORNIAN $$$
(☎619-557-9441; www.pradobalboa.com; House of Hospitality, 1549 El Prado; mains lunch $12-21, dinner $22-35; ⊙11:30am-3pm Mon-Fri, from 11am Sat & Sun, 5-9pm Sun & Tue-Thu, to 10pm Fri & Sat) In one of San Diego's most beautiful dining rooms, feast on Cal-eclectic cooking by one of San Diego's most renowned chefs: bakery sandwiches, chicken and *orecchiette* pasta, and pork prime rib. Go for a civilized lunch on the verandah or for afternoon cocktails and appetizers in the bar.

Gaslamp Quarter

There are some 100 restaurants in the Gaslamp, many of them very good. Some have bar scenes too.

Café 222 BREAKFAST $
(Map p284; ☎619-236-9902; www.cafe222.com; 222 Island Ave; mains $7-11; ⊙7am-1:30pm) Downtown's favorite breakfast place serves renowned peanut butter and banana French toast; buttermilk, orange-pecan or granola pancakes; and eggs in scrambles or benedicts. They also sell lunchtime sandwiches and salads, but we always go for breakfast (available until closing).

Gaslamp Strip Club STEAKHOUSE $$
(Map p284; ☎619-231-3140; www.gaslampsteak.com; 340 5th Ave; mains $14-24; ⊙5-10pm Sun-Thu, to midnight Fri & Sat) Pull your own bottle from the wine vault, then char your own favorite cut of steak, chicken or fish on the open grills in the retro-Vegas dining room at Downtown's best bargain for steak, salad and grill-your-own garlic bread. No bottle costs more than $36, no steak more than $25. Fab, creative martinis and 'pin-up' art by Alberto Vargas. Tons of fun. No one under 21 allowed.

Dick's Last Resort PUB $$
(Map p284; ☎619-231-9100; www.dickslastresort.com; 345 5th Ave; mains lunch $9-20, dinner $12-24; ⊙11am-1:30am) At Dick's, a legendary indoor-outdoor bar and grill with a riotously fun atmosphere, you can carry on in full voice while guzzling beer and chowing down

on burgers, pork ribs, fried chicken and fish, while the staff makes you a giant dunce cap out of table paper. None of the other revelers will care a whit.

Bandar MIDDLE EASTERN $$
(Map p284; ☎619-238-0101; www.bandarrestaurant.com; 825 4th Ave; mains lunch $12-20, dinner $19-29) Exotic spices and fragrant cooking make this white-tablecloth Persian–Middle Eastern a favorite for giant kebabs and salads that zing with flavor. Come hungry: portions are huge.

Oceanaire SEAFOOD $$$
(Map p284; ☎619-858-2277; www.theoceanaire.com; 400 J St; mains $23-52; ⏰5-10pm Sun-Thu, to 11pm Fri & Sat) The look is art-deco ocean liner, and the service is just as elegant, with an oyster bar and creations like Maryland blue-crab cakes and horseradish-crusted Alaskan halibut. If you don't feel like a total splurge, happy hour features bargain-priced oysters and fish tacos in the bar (times vary).

East Village

Basic PIZZERIA $
(Map p284; ☎619-531-8869; www.barbasic.com; 410 10th Ave; small/large pizzas from $9/14; ⏰11:30am-2am) East Village hipsters feast on fragrant New Haven–style, thin-crust, brick-oven-baked pizzas under Basic's high-ceilinged roof (it's in a former warehouse). Small pizzas have a large footprint but are pretty light. Toppings span the usual to the newfangled, like the mashed pie with mozzarella, mashed potatoes and bacon. Wash them down with beers (craft, naturally) or one of several mule cocktails.

The only other menu item, the basic salad ($8), is anything but, with sliced pears, candied walnuts, etc. Some nights are theme nights – art, DJs and more – it can get pretty loud.

Valentine's MEXICAN $
(Map p284; ☎619-234-8256; 844 Market St; mains $3.50-8; ⏰8am-midnight Sun-Thu, to 3am Fri & Sat) There's nothing urbane about this home-style Mexican joint, but it's a local institution. Apart from the usual tacos and burritos, the *carne asada* fries (French fries topped like nachos with grilled beef, sour cream, guacamole and such) are messy, coronary-inducing and oh so *bueno*. Late weekend hours mean it's great after a rager.

TOP FIVE CHEAP EATS

- Bread & Cie (p303)
- Café 222 (p302)
- Porkyland (p321)
- Saffron (p305)
- Zinc Café (p326)

Café Chloe FRENCH $$
(Map p284; ☎619-232-3242; www.cafechloe.com; 721 9th Ave; mains breakfast $7-12, lunch $11-17, dinner $20-29; ⏰7:30am-10pm Mon-Fri, 8:30am-10:30pm Sat, 8:30am-9:30pm Sun) This delightful corner French bistro has a simple style and gets the standards perfect, and everything else as well. Mac 'n' cheese transforms into macaroni, pancetta and French blue gratin, and the steak frites is served with herb butter and salad. Wonderful egg dishes for weekend brunch.

Uptown: Bankers Hill, Hillcrest & North Park

San Diego's restaurant scene is booming here. Bankers Hill and Hillcrest are well established, and North Park is a hub of innovation. Also look for a branch of the popular, cheap burrito joint, **Porkyland** (☎619-233-5139; 646 University Ave, Hillcrest; mains $4-9; ⏰10am-9pm Mon-Thu, to 10pm Fri & Sat, 11am-7pm Sun).

Bread & Cie BAKERY, CAFE $
(www.breadandcie.com; 350 University Ave, Hillcrest; mains $6-11; ⏰7am-7pm Mon-Fri, to 6pm Sat, 8am-6pm Sun; P) Aside from crafting some of San Diego's best breads (including anise and fig, kalamata black olive and three-raisin), this wide-open bakery-deli makes fabulous sandwiches with fillings such as curried-chicken salad and Black Forest ham. Boxed lunches cost $11. Great pastries, too.

Sipz VEGAN $
(☎619-795-2889; www.sipz.com; 3914 30th St, North Park; mains lunch $7.75, dinner $9.25; ⏰10:30am-9pm; ✎) Finally, a vegan place that doesn't feel like you're slumming it. The modern decor with clean lines and bold graphics is your first clue, and the menu, from Vietnamese pho to spicy basil with mock chicken or tofu and orange mock chicken have made believers out of North

DON'T MISS

SOUTH PARK'S KITCHEN

Heart and soul of the funky South Park neighborhood (south of North Park and east of Balboa Park) is **Big Kitchen** (☎619-234-5789; www.bigkitchencafe.com; 3003 Grape St, South Park; mains $5-13.50; ⏰8am-2pm; 👪). All are welcome (though credit cards are not) at this friendly enclave of food, art, music and civic bonhomie. Omelettes and challah French toast are stupendous, and breakfast combos are named for regulars including Whoopi Goldberg, who used to wait tables here.

Park. Desserts span sweet rice with fresh mango to vegan cheesecake.

San Diego Chicken Pie Shop PIES $
(☎619-295-0156; 2633 El Cajon Blvd, North Park; pies from $2.60, mains $5-14; ⏰8am-8pm) It's out of the way and looks like it hasn't been redecorated since the Carter administration, but local foodies love the namesake chicken pies, which don't muck up the chicken and creamy gravy with vegetables. Other mains include bacon and eggs for breakfast, and fish and steaks the rest of the day.

★ **Urban Solace** CALIFORNIAN $$
(☎619-295-6464; www.urbansolace.net; 3823 30th St, North Park; mains lunch $10-23, dinner $17-27; ⏰11:30am-10pm Mon-Thu, to 11pm Fri, 5-11pm Sat, 5-9pm Sun) North Park's young hip gourmets revel in creative comfort food here: bluegrass burger; 'not your mama's' meatloaf of ground lamb, fig, pine nuts and feta; 'duckaroni' (mac 'n' cheese with duck confit); and chicken and dumplings. The setting's surprisingly chill for such great eats; maybe it's the cocktails like mojitos made with bourbon.

★ **Cucina Urbana** CALIFORNIA-ITALIAN $$
(☎619-239-2222; 505 Laurel St, Bankers Hill; mains lunch $10-23, dinner $12-28; ⏰11:30am-2pm Tue-Fri, 5-9pm Sun & Mon, 5-10pm Tue-Thu, 5pm-midnight Fri & Sat) In this corner place with modern rustic ambience, business gets done, celebrations get celebrated and friends hug and kiss over refined yet affordable Cal-Ital cooking. Look for short rib pappardelle, pizzas like foraged mushroom with taleggio cheese and braised leeks, and smart cocktails and local 'brewskies'. Reservations recommended.

Waypoint Public GASTROPUB $$
(☎619-255-8778; www.waypointpublic.com; 3794 30th St, North Park; mains $9-21; ⏰4pm-1am Mon-Fri, from 10am Sat & Sun) Chef-driven Waypoint's comfort food menu is meant to pair craft beers with dishes from smoked tomato minestrone with grilled cheese to a burger with mozzarella, pulled pork, tomatillo salsa, fried egg and spicy pickled vegetables. Walls are attractively done up in reclaimed wood, and glass garage doors roll up to the outside, all the better for hipster-watching in busy North Park.

Hash House a Go Go AMERICAN $$
(☎619-298-4646; www.hashhouseagogo.com; 3628 5th Ave, Hillcrest; mains breakfast $9-18, dinner $15-29; ⏰7.30am-2pm Mon-Fri, to 2:30pm Sat & Sun, plus 5:30-9pm Tue-Thu, to 9:30pm Fri-Sun; 👪) This buzzing bungalow makes biscuits and gravy straight outta Indiana, towering benedicts, large-as-your-head pancakes and – wait for it – hash seven different ways. Eat your whole breakfast, and you won't need to eat for the rest of the day. It's worth coming back for the equally massive burgers, sage fried chicken and award-winning meatloaf sandwich. No wonder it's called 'twisted farm food.'

Saigon on Fifth VIETNAMESE $$
(☎619-220-8828; www.saigononfifth.menutoeat.com; 3900 5th Ave, Hillcrest; mains $7-16; ⏰11am-3am; Ⓟ) This Vietnamese place tries hard and succeeds, with dishes like fresh spring rolls, fish of Hue (with garlic, ginger and lemongrass) and rockin' 'spicy noodles.' Staff dress nicely and the room is elegant but not overbearing.

East Village Asian Diner ASIAN FUSION $$
(☎619-220-4900; www.eateastvillage.com; 406 University Ave, Hillcrest; mains $9-14; ⏰11:30am-2:30pm Mon-Fri, 5-10pm Mon-Wed, to midnight Fri, 11:30am-midnight Sat, 11:30am-10pm Sun) This den of modernist cool fuses mostly Korean cooking with Western and other Asian influences (witness the 'super awesome' beef-and-kimchi burrito). Try noodle dishes (Thai peanut, beef and broccoli, etc), or build your own 'monk's stone pot,' a super-heated rice bowl to which you can add ingredients from pulled pork to salmon. Sauces are made in-house.

Khyber Pass AFGHAN-INDIAN $$
(☎619-294-7579; www.sandiegokhyberpass.com; 523 University Ave, Hillcrest; mains $13-18; ⏰11:30am-10pm) Moody photos and Afghan

tapestries set the atmosphere in this tall-ceilinged space, with adventuresome Afghan cooking. If you've never had it, it's kind of like Indian meets Middle Eastern: yogurt curries, kabobs, stews and more. A few high-end dishes (eg filet mignon or rack of lamb kabob) are up to $30.

Baja Betty's MEXICAN **$$**
(☎619-269-8510; bajabettyssd.com; 1421 University Ave, Hillcrest; mains $6-15; ⊙11am-midnight Mon-Fri, 10am-1am Sat, 10am-midnight Sun) Gay-owned and straight-friendly, this restaurant-bar is always a party with a just-back-from-Margaritaville vibe (and dozens of tequilas to take you back there) alongside dishes like Mexi Queen queso dip, You Go Grill swordfish tacos and Fire in the Hole fajitas. Daily specials include Tostada Tuesdays and Margarita Madness on Sundays.

Little Italy

Little Italy is – surprise! – happy hunting ground for Italian cooking and cafes on India St and around Date St, and some non-Italian newcomers are rounding out the scene. Ballast Point Tasting Room (p310) also does some great vittles.

Burger Lounge BURGERS **$**
(Map p284; ☎619-237-7878; 1608 India St; burgers $8-11; ⊙10:30am-10pm Sun-Thu, to midnight Fri & Sat; 👪) This swingin' local chain serves chic comfort food. There's just a simple menu, but what they do with it! Plump burgers (grass-fed beef, turkey, veggie, albacore or elk), crisp fries, great salads, shakes and brownies for dessert!

Mimmo's Italian Village ITALIAN **$**
(Map p284; ☎619-239-3710; 1743 India St; meals under $10; ⊙8am-4pm Mon-Sat; 👪) In a tall-ceilinged space decorated like (wait for it) an Italian village complete with mini Ponte Vecchio, Mimmo's deli serves salads, hot and cold sandwiches, and lunch specials such as lasagna and eggplant parmigiana.

Bencotto ITALIAN **$$**
(Map p284; ☎619-450-4786; www.lovebencotto.com; 750 W Fir St; mains $14-26; ⊙11:30am-9:30pm Sun-Thu, to 10:30pm Fri & Sat; P) Bencotto melds the old with the new of Little Italy – contemporary, angular, multistory, architect-designed, arty and green – and the food is great too, from fresh-sliced prosciutto to pasta *a modo tuo* (your way), with a over 100 potential combos of fresh pasta and sauce.

Filippi's Pizza Grotto PIZZERIA, DELI **$$**
(Map p284; ☎619-232-5094; 1747 India St; dishes $6-20; ⊙9am-10pm Sun & Mon, to 10:30pm Tue-Thu, to 11:30pm Fri & Sat; 👪) There are often lines out the door for Filippi's old-school Italian cooking (pizza, spaghetti and ravioli) served on red-and-white-checked tablecloths in the dining room festooned with murals of *la bella Italia*. The front of the shop is an excellent Italian deli.

★ **Juniper & Ivy** CONTEMPORARY CALIFORNIAN **$$$**
(Map p284; ☎619-269-9036; www.juniperandivy.com; 2228 Kettner Bl; small plates $9-17, mains $19-36; ⊙4-10pm Sun-Thu, to 11pm Fri & Sat) Chef Richard Blais has opened San Diego's restaurant of the moment. The menu changes daily, but if we mention molecular gastronomic takes on prawn and pork rigatoni; artisan-farmed strip steak with smoked potato, porcini onion rings and kimchi ketchup; and homemade yodel snack cakes for dessert, do you get the idea? It's in a rockin' refurbished warehouse.

Reserve well in advance, or try for a seat at the always-busy bar (great cocktails too).

Mission Hills

Mission Hills is the neighborhood north of Little Italy and west of Hillcrest. On India St, where it meets Washington St, there's a block of well-regarded eateries.

Saffron THAI **$**
(☎619-574-0177; www.saffronsandiego.com; 3731 India St; mains $7-10; ⊙10:30am-9pm Mon-Sat, 11am-8pm Sun) This multi-award-winning, hole-in-the-wall is actually two shops – Saffron Thai Grilled Chicken and Noodles & Saté, but you can get both at either shop and enjoy it in the noodle shop. Chicken is cooked over a charcoal-grill and comes with a choice of sauces, salad, jasmine rice and a menu of finger foods.

Culinary fans over the years have included Julia Child and Martha Stewart.

El Indio MEXICAN **$**
(☎619-299-0333; www.el-indio.com; 3695 India St; dishes $3-9; ⊙8am-9pm; P 👪) Counter-service shop famous since 1940 for its taquitos, *mordiditas* (tiny taquitos), tamales and excellent breakfast burritos. Eat in a rudimentary dining room or at picnic tables under metal umbrellas across the street.

Shakespeare Pub & Grille BRITISH PUB $$
(619-299-0230; www.shakespearepub.com; 3701 India St; dishes $5-15; 10:30am-midnight Mon-Thu, to 1am Fri, 8am-1am Sat, 8am-midnight Sun) One of San Diego's most authentic English ale houses, Shakespeare is the place for darts, soccer by satellite, beer on tap and pub grub, including fish and chips and bangers and mash. One thing they don't have in Britain: a great sundeck. On weekends, load up with a British breakfast: bacon, mushrooms, black-and-white pudding and more.

Old Town

At the Mexican eateries all along San Diego Ave, hard-working ladies churn out an estimated 210,000 fresh tortillas per month, and most have great bar scenes too. Choose your setting: party, local or sublime.

Old Town Mexican Café MEXICAN $$
(619-297-4330; www.oldtownmexcafe.com; 2489 San Diego Ave; mains $4-16; 7am-2am;) Other restaurants come and go, but this place has been in this busy adobe with hardwood booths since the 1970s. While you wait to be seated, watch the staff turn out tortillas. Then enjoy *machacas* (shredded pork with onions and peppers), *carnitas* (grilled pork) and *posole* (hominy stew). For breakfast: *chilaquiles* (tortilla chips salsa or mole, broiled or grilled with cheese).

If the carpet has seen better days, that only lends authenticity.

Fred's MEXICAN $$
(619-858-8226; 2470 San Diego Ave; mains $9-15; 11am-11pm Sun, Mon, Wed & Thu, to midnight Tue, Fri & Sat) Every night, party people on a budget crowd into raucous Fred's, especially on bargain 'Taco-licious Tuesday.' The straight-down-the-middle enchiladas, burritos and tacos won't set standards, but it's hard not to love the colorful interior and rangy patio.

El Agave MEXICAN $$$
(619-220-0692; www.elagave.com; 2304 San Diego Ave; lunch mains $12-20; dinner mains $22-40; 11am-10pm; P) Candlelight flickers in this romantic 2nd-floor, white-tablecloth, high-end place catering to cognoscenti. The mole is superb (there are 10 types to choose from), and there are a whopping 1500 different tequilas covering just about every bit of wall space and in racks overhead, enough that it calls itself a tequila museum.

Embarcadero & the Waterfront

Anthony's Fish Grotto & Fishette SEAFOOD $
(Map p284; www.gofishanthony's.com; 1360 N Harbor Dr; dinner mains $14-29, lunch specials $10-15;) Next to the Maritime Museum, this pair of restaurants serves seafood and chowders with views of the tall ships on the harbor. The sit-down **Grotto** (619-232-5105; Grotto; mains lunch $8-15, dinner $12-25; 11am-9:30pm Sun-Thu, to 10pm Sat & Sun) has an old-style nautical theme (ahoy, mateys!), while the counter at the **Fishette** (619-232-2175; Fishette; mains $10-15; 10am-9pm Mon-Fri, 8am-9pm Sat & Sun) serves a more limited menu (think fish and chips or sandwiches) that you eat out on the deck.

★**Puesto at the Headquarters** MEXICAN $$
(Map p284; 610-233-8800; www.eatpuesto.com; 789 W Harbor Dr, The Headquarters; mains $11-19; 11am-10pm) This upscale eatery serves Mexican street food that knocked our *zapatos* off: innovative takes on traditional tacos like chicken (with hibsicus, chipotle, pineapple and avocado) and some out-there fillings like potato-soy chorizo. Other highlights: crab guacamole, *barbacoa* short ribs (braised in chile sauce) and Mexican street bowl (tropical fruits with chili, sea salt and lime).

Bonus: cocktails by the bottle! The art on the tall walls is almost as interesting as what's on the plate, and upstairs or outdoor seating offers great people watching.

Fish Market SEAFOOD $$$
(Map p284; 619-232-3474; 750 N Harbor Dr; mains lunch $10-28, dinner $13-35; 11am-10pm) For a daily market menu of sushi to smoked fish, chowder to the raw bar, steamers to cioppino and grilled fish, all with harbor views in a snappy dining room, walk to Tuna Harbor, opposite the port side of the USS *Midway*. Snag a window table if you can.

Coronado

Clayton's Coffee Shop DINER $
(619-435-5425; 979 Orange Ave; mains $8-12; 6am-9pm Sun-Thu, to 10pm Fri & Sat;) Some diners only *look* old-fashioned. This one is the real deal from the 1940s, with red leatherette swivel stools and booths with mini-jukeboxes. It does famous all-American breakfasts and some Mexican specialties like *machaca* (spiced meat) with eggs and

cheese, and it's not above panini and croque monsieur sandwiches. For dessert: mile-high pie from the counter.

Boney's Bayside Market MARKET $

(155 Orange Ave; sandwiches $5-7; 8:30am-9pm) For picnics, stop by this market near the ferry for fantastic, (mostly) healthy sandwiches and an extensive assortment of salads and organic products.

★1500 Ocean CALIFORNIAN $$$

(619-435-6611; www.hoteldel.com/1500-ocean; Hotel del Coronado, 1500 Orange Ave; mains $33-45; 5:30-10pm Tue-Sat, plus Sun summer; P) It's hard to beat the romance of supping at the Hotel del Coronado, especially at a table overlooking the sea from the verandah of its 1st-class dining room, where silver service and coastal cuisine with local ingredients set the perfect tone for popping the question or fêting an important anniversary.

Other dining experiences at the Del (p289) include the casual, beachside Sheerwater and fancy Sunday brunch in the Crown Room.

Primavera ITALIAN $$$

(619-435-0454; 932 Orange Ave; mains $19-39; 5-10pm) A subdued, romantic setting for subdued, romantic, Italian fare and a great wine list, presented by black-tied waiters. It's known for steaks, seafood dishes like shrimp in mushroom and champagne sauce over pasta, and a veal chop so big two can share it. Prices are high but worth it.

Point Loma Area

There's a great restaurant at the Pearl hotel (p301).

Corvette Diner DINER $

(619-542-1476; 2965 Historic Decatur Rd; mains $8-11.50; 11:30am-9pm Sun-Thu, to 11pm Fri & Sat;) Your kids will be your BFFs for bringing them to this over-the-top '50s-themed diner in Liberty Station. DJs spin rock-and-roll classics, waitresses wear poodle skirts and bouffant wigs, waiters dance in the aisles, and kids wear drinking straws in their hair, and there's a huge game arcade. (Oh, and the food is good, too. Try the meatloaf.)

★Stone Brewing World Bistro & Gardens BEER HALL $$

(www.stonelibertystation.com; Liberty Station, 2816 Historic Decatur Rd #116; mains lunch $14-21, dinner $15-29; 11:30am-10pm Mon-Sat, 11am-9pm Sun; P) Local brewer Stone has transformed the former mess hall of the naval training center at Liberty Station into a temple to local craft beer. Tuck into standard-setting, spin-the-globe dishes (yellowfin *poke* tacos, chicken schnitzel, beef *ssambap* – Korean-style lettuce cups – etc) at long tables or comfy booths under its tall beamed ceiling, or beneath twinkling lights in its courtyard.

The bistro's multiple rooms feature a *looooong* bar, brewing tanks, tasting room and huge stone slabs from a nearby quarry; outside, play bocce or watch the stars come out at night.

★Point Loma Seafoods SEAFOOD $$

(www.pointlomaseafoods.com; 2805 Emerson St; mains $7-16; 9am-7pm Mon-Sat, 10am-7pm Sun; P) For off-the-boat-fresh seafood sandwiches, salads, fried dishes and icy-cold beer, order at the counter at this fish-market-cum-deli and grab a seat at a picnic table on the upstairs, harbor-view deck. In the Shelter Island Marina, it's a San Diego institution dating back to Portuguese fisherman days. It also does great sushi and takeout dishes from ceviche to clam chowder.

Bali Hai POLYNESIAN $$

(619-222-1181; www.balihairestaurant.com; 2230 Shelter Island Dr; mains lunch $13-19, dinner $17-31, Sun brunch adult/child $35/17; 11:30am-9pm Mon-Thu, to 10pm Fri & Sat, 9:30am-2pm & 4-9pm Sun; P) Near the tiki-themed hotels of Point Loma, this longtime, special-occasion restaurant serves Hawaiian-themed meals like tuna *poke, pupus* (small plates), chicken of the gods (with tangy orange and cream sauces) and a massive Sunday champagne brunch buffet. The best part: views clear across San Diego Bay through its circular wall of windows.

Brigantine SEAFOOD $$

(mains lunch $9-15, dinner $14-32; 11:30am-10:30pm Mon-Thu, to 11pm Fri & Sat, 4-10:30pm Sun) At this respected local seafood chain, lunch is heavy on sandwiches and famous fish tacos, while dinners are fancier with dishes like marinated swordfish and macadamia-crusted mahi. The **Shelter Island Dr branch** (619-224-2871; 2725 Shelter Island Dr) has a balcony where you can peek through palm fronds to the harbor. Awesome happy hours. There are also branches in **Coronado** (619-435-4166; 1333 Orange Ave) and **Del Mar** (858-481-1166; 3263 Camino del Mar).

Ocean Beach

★Hodad's BURGERS $
(Map p292; ☎619-224-4623; www.hodadies.com; 5010 Newport Ave; dishes $4-13; ⏰11am-9pm Sun-Thu, to 10pm Fri & Sat) Since the flower-power days of 1969, OB's legendary burger joint has served great shakes, massive baskets of onion rings and succulent hamburgers wrapped in paper. The walls are covered in license plates, grunge/surf-rock plays (loud!) and your bearded, tattooed server might sidle in to your booth to take your order. No shirt, no shoes, no problem, dude.

Ortega's Cocina CAFE $
(Map p292; ☎619-222-4205; 4888 Newport Ave; mains $4-15; ⏰8am-10pm Mon-Sat, to 9pm Sun) Tiny, family-run Ortega's is so popular that people often queue for a spot at the counter (there are indoor and sidewalk tables too). Seafood, moles, *tortas* (sandwiches) and handmade tamales are the specialties, but all its dishes are soulful and classic.

Ocean Beach People's Market VEGETARIAN $
(Map p292; ☎619-224-1387; 4765 Voltaire St; dishes $8, per pound from $7.50; ⏰8am-9pm; 🖉) For strictly vegetarian groceries and fabulous prepared meals and salads north of central Ocean Beach, this organic cooperative does bulk foods, and excellent counter-service soups, sandwiches, salads and wraps.

Olive Tree Marketplace MARKET $
(Map p292; ☎619-224-0443; 4805 Narragansett Ave; sandwiches $7-8; ⏰8am-9pm) This neighborhood shop helps keep your beach picnic local with San Diego specialties like tortilla chips from El Indio (p305), baked goods from Bread & Cie (p303) and pies from Julian, plus a big menu of to-go sandwiches and local craft beers to wash them all down.

Sundara INDIAN $$
(☎619-889-0639; www.sundaracuisine.com; 1774 Sunset Cliffs Bl; mains $10; ⏰4-10pm Mon, Wed & Thu; noon-10pm Fri-Sun; 🖉) This little, modern, neat-as-a-pin place has a tiny but well-chosen menu of curries and tandoori chicken, and a longer menu of craft and bottled beers from as far as India. It's adorned with simple black-and-white photos of Indian street scenes.

Pacific Beach

Kono's Surf Club CAFE, BREAKFAST $
(☎858-483-1669; 704 Garnet Ave; mains $3-6; ⏰7am-3pm Mon-Fri, to 4pm Sat & Sun; 👪) This place makes four kinds of breakfast burritos that you eat out of a basket in view of Crystal Pier (patio seating available) alongside pancakes, eggs and Kono potatoes. It's always crowded but well worth the wait. Cash only.

Green Flash CAFE $$
(☎619-270-7715; www.greenflashrestaurant.com; 701 Thomas Ave; mains breakfast & lunch $5-15, dinner $11-29; ⏰8am-10pm) A terrific casual, beach-view breakfast or lunch spot for eggs, meaty burgers, big salads and triple-decker clubs, the Flash also has weekday sunset special meals ($11; 4:30pm to 6pm Sunday to Thursday), with happy hour until 7pm Monday through Friday. Score a table outside on the patio.

World Famous SEAFOOD $$$
(☎858-272-3100; www.worldfamouspb.com; 711 Pacific Beach Dr; mains breakfast & lunch $9-16, dinner $15-25; ⏰7am-midnight) Watch the surf while enjoying 'California coastal cuisine,' an ever-changing all-day menu of inventive dishes from the sea (lobster Benedict for breakfast or lunch; banana rum mahi-mahi), plus steaks, salads and lunchtime sandwiches and burgers and occasional specials like fish or lobster taco night. There's a great bar too.

JRDN CALIFORNIA $$$
(Jordan; ☎858-270-5736; Tower 23 Hotel, 723 Felspar St; mains breakfast & lunch $9-14, dinner $26-46; ⏰9am-9pm Sun-Thu, to 9:30pm Sat & Sun) A big heaping dose of chic amid PB's congenital laid-back feel. There's both an ocean view and a futuristic interior (and most excellent bar scene). Sustainably farmed meats and seafood join local veggies to create festivals on the plate. Try the lobster BLT, or 'build your own' steak with green onion 'creamers' (aka mashed potatoes).

Drinking & Nightlife

San Diego may not have the swinging nightlife scene of LA, but in the Gaslamp Quarter it's hard to tell.

Gaslamp Quarter

The Gaslamp has the city's highest concentration of nightlife venues. Many do double (even triple) duty as restaurants, bars and clubs.

★Bang Bang BAR,
(Map p284; www.bangbangsd.com; 526 Market St; ⏰closed Mon) Beneath lantern-light, the Gaslamp's hottest new spot gigs in local and world-known DJs and serves sushi

and Asian small plates like dumplings and panko-crusted shrimp to nurse the imaginative cocktails (some in giant goblets meant for sharing with your posse). Plus, the bathrooms are shrines to Ryan Gosling and Hello Kitty: in a word, awesome.

Fluxx DANCE CLUB
(Map p284; www.fluxxsd.com; 500 4th Ave; ⏲ Thu-Sat) Think Vegas in the Gaslamp. San Diego's hottest dance club has amazing design with rotating themes (jellyfish and mermaids, anyone?), DJs spinning electronic dance music and the occasional celeb sighting. Even a crowded dance floor, expensive cocktails ($17 vodka and Red Bull) and sometimes steep cover charges can't stop this place from being jam-packed.

On Broadway DANCE CLUB
(Map p284; www.obec.tv; 615 Broadway; cover $20; ⏲ Fri & Sat) Sprawling double-decker dance spot where DJs mix it up on – count them – five dancefloors. Dress to impress, or forget about making it past the velvet-rope goons.

Dublin Square IRISH PUB
(Map p284; www.dublinsquareirishpub.com; 544 4th Ave) Guinness? Check. Corned beef? Check. But what sets this rambling pub apart is its selection of nightly music. Try to go when the band Fooks is playing – check the website for the schedule. Meals are served from 11:30am to 10:30pm daily, and from 8am Saturday and Sunday.

Quality Social DIVE BAR
(Map p284; www.qualitysocial.com; 789 6th Ave) It sounds like an oxymoron, but this is an upscale dive bar. This concrete box has big windows out to the street, loud music and lots of beers, but you can snack on charcuterie and artisanal cheeses. Look also for $6 shots and cocktails like 'Not Your Grandma's Gin & Tonic.' Check the website for special events.

Star Bar BAR
(Map p284; 423 E St) When you've had it with gentrified style and you're looking for a historic dive, head to this old-school bar decorated year-round with Christmas lights for the cheapest drinks in the Gaslamp.

East Village

While out-of-towners frolic happily in the Gaslamp Quarter, locals and hipsters instead head east to these more insider-y bars.

SURF & SUDS

The beer that made San Diego famous' may not quite roll off the tongue, but never mind: America's Finest City is home to some of America's finest brew pubs. The **San Diego Brewers Guild** (www.sandiegobrewersguild.org) counts some 40 member establishments. Hop over to the guild's website (get it?) or pick up one of their pamphlets around town. To leave the driving to someone else, **Brewery Tours of San Diego** (☎619-961-7999; www.brewerytoursofsandiego.com; per person $65-95) offers bus tours to different breweries for a variety of tastes. Tour price varies by timing and whether a meal is served.

Check our recommendations to get you started, and see also Stone Brewing Company (p307) and Ballast Point Tasting Room & Kitchen (p310).

Coronado Brewing Co (www.coronadobrewingcompany.com; 170 Orange Ave, Coronado; ⏲ from 11am) Delicious Coronado Golden house brew goes well with pizzas, pastas, sandwiches and fries; near the ferry terminal.

Pacific Beach Ale House (www.pbalehouse.com; 721 Grand Ave, Pacific Beach; mains $9-25; ⏲ 11am-2am) Contempo-cool setting and a huge menu including lobster mac 'n' cheese, steamed clams and bistro meatloaf.

Pizza Port (☎760-720-7007; www.pizzaport.com; 571 Carlsbad Village Dr; mains $8-20; ⏲ 11am-10pm Sun-Thu, to midnight Fri & Sat; 👪) Rockin' and raucous local pizza chain with surf art, rock music and 'anti-wimpy' pizzas to go with the signature 'sharkbite red' brew. Multiple locations.

Karl Strauss Brewery & Grill (Map p284; ☎619-234-2739, 858-551-2739; 1157 Columbia St, cnr Wall St & Herschel Ave; ⏲ hours vary) Local microbrewery serving surprisingly decent pub grub (most mains $10 to $19). Pints cost $3.50 and pitchers are $12.95 during happy hour (4pm to 6:30pm Monday to Friday).

East Village Tavern & Bowl BAR, BOWLING

(Map p284; 930 Market St; 11:30am-1am, from 10am Sat & Sun) This large sports bar a few blocks from Petco Park has six bowling lanes (thankfully, behind a wall for effective soundproofing). Pub menu (dishes $6–11; pulled-pork sliders, applewood BLT) is served all day.

Noble Experiment BAR

(Map p284; 619-888-4713; http://nobleexperimentsd.com; 777 G St; 7pm-2am Tue-Sun) This place is literally a find. Open a secret door and enter a contemporary speakeasy with miniature gold skulls on the walls, classical paintings on the ceilings and some 400 cocktails on the list (from $12). The hard part: getting in. Text for a reservation, and they'll tell you if your requested time is available and how to find it.

Uptown: Bankers Hill, Hillcrest & North Park

Nightlife in Uptown's neighborhoods reflects their varied scenes. Hillcrest has the greatest concentration of bars, particularly gay spots, while North Park has a cool, hipster vibe.

★ **Polite Provisions** COCKTAIL BAR

(www.politeprovisions.com; 4696 30th St, North Park; 11:30am-1:30am) A mile north of central North Park, this swanky new cocktail bar is special from its glass ceiling to wood-paneled walls and tiled floors. They make their own syrups, sodas and infusions and pour a daily-changing selection of wine, cocktails and beers from taps. For vittles, the 'soda and swine' menu features meatballs and dozens of ways to eat them.

Coin-Op Game Room BAR, GAME ROOM

(619-255-8523; www.coinopsd.com; 3926 30th St, North Park; 4pm-1am) Dozens of classic arcade games – pinball to Mortal Kombat, Big Buck Safari to the Claw – line the walls of the hipster bar in North Park. All the better to quaff craft beers and cocktails like the Kentucky Tippler (grapefruit-infused bourbon with honey, lemon and sarsparilla bitters) and chow on Cuban croquette and sliders of pork, yellowtail and falafel.

Nunu's Cocktail Lounge COCKTAIL BAR

(www.nunuscocktails.com; 3537 5th Ave, Hillcrest) Dark and divey, this hipster haven started pouring when JFK was president and still looks the part with its curvy booths, big bar and lovably kitsch decor. Smoking patio.

Little Italy

Ballast Point Tasting Room & Kitchen BREWERY

(Map p284; 619-255-7213; www.ballastpoint.com; 2215 India St; dishes $7-14; 11am-11pm Mon-Sat, to 9pm Sun) Opened in 2013, this is the newest and funnest location from this San Diego–based brewery, and it does a lot of R&D for the rest of the company. Three 4oz tasters of their beers for just $5 is the best deal in town. Enjoy them with a full menu including house-made pretzels, beer-steamed mussels, salads and grilled dishes.

El Camino LOUNGE

(2400 India St) We're not sure what it means that this buzzy watering hole has a Dia de los Muertos (Mexican Day of the Dead holiday) theme in the flight path of San Diego Airport – watch planes land from the outdoor patio – but whatever, dude. The clientele is cool, design mod, the drinks strong and the Mexican vittles *fabuloso*.

Waterfront BAR

(Map p284; 2044 Kettner Blvd) San Diego's first liquor license was granted to this place in the 1930s (it was on the waterfront until the harbor was filled and the airport built). A room full of historic bric-a-brac, big windows looking onto the street and the spirits of those who went before make this a wonderful place to spend the afternoon or evening.

Old Town

Nightlife in Uptown's neighborhoods reflects their varied scenes. Hillcrest has the greatest concentration of bars, particularly gay spots, while North Park has a cool, hipster vibe.

Harney Sushi HIPSTER

(3964 Harney St) Yes, it's a sushi bar (dishes $4 to $15), but the *bar* bar takes over late at night as a rotation of DJs spins music from reggae to house to techno for a hip, younger crowd.

Old Town Saloon DIVE BAR

(2495 San Diego Ave) This one's for the locals, so be cool. Swill a Bud Light, and play pool at one of four tables.

Coronado

Mc P's Irish Pub PUB

(www.mcpspub.com; 1107 Orange Ave, Coronado) Dyed-in-the-wool Irish pub that's been here for a generation. Pints o' Guinness complement down-home Irish fare – corned beef, stew, meatloaf – as you listen to nightly live music from rock to Irish folk. Indoor and patio seating.

Ocean Beach

Jungle Java COFFEE HOUSE
(Map p292; 5047 Newport Ave, Ocean Beach; ⏲7am-6pm Mon, Tue & Thu, to 8pm Wed & Fri-Sun) Funky-dunky, canopy-covered cafe and plant shop, also crammed with crafts and art treasures.

Shades BEACH BAR
(Map p292; www.shadesOB.com; 5083 Santa Monica Ave, Ocean Beach; ⏲6:30am-9pm) For all your day-drinking needs, beachfront Shades has a huge ocean-view dining room (serving popular burgers, tortilla soup and big breakfasts), or just grab a beer or cocktail to watch the sunset over the ocean.

GAY & LESBIAN SAN DIEGO

Historians trace the roots of San Diego's thriving gay community to WWII. Amid the enforced intimacy of military life, gay men from around the US were suddenly able to create strong, if clandestine, social networks. Postwar, many of these new friends stayed.

In the late 1960s, a newly politicized gay community made its unofficial headquarters in Hillcrest, which still has the highest concentration of LGBT bars, restaurants, cafes and shops. The scene is generally more casual and friendly than in San Francisco or LA. For current events, visit the *San Diego Gay and Lesbian News* (www.sdgln.com).

Obelisk Mercantile (1037 University Ave; ⏲11am-9pm Sun-Thu, to 10pm Fri & Sat) Obelisk has morphed from San Diego's gay bookstore to one-stop shopping from books to T-shirts and sassy cards, many with local themes. Look for the giant original Hillcrest sign that used to hang over the street.

Babycakes (☎619-296-4173; www.babycakessandiego.com; 3766 5th Ave; ⏲9am-midnight Sun-Thu, to 1am Fri & Sat; 📶) Hillcrest location, a dozen-plus flavors of famously decadent cupcakes ($3.50), wi-fi, a full bar and a front yard festooned with smiley faces. What more could you ask for?

Bourbon Street Bar & Grill (☎619-291-4043; www.bourbonstreetsd.com; 4612 Park Blvd; ⏲4pm-2am Tue-Sun, from 11am Sun) In University Heights, away from Hillcrest's central strip, this bar's layout of rooms and courtyards, bar and dancefloor, makes for easy mingling during karaoke, club nights and ladies nights, over beers or tap or during happy hours (until 9pm nightly).

Top of the Bay (Map p284; www.glassdoorsd.com; 1835 Columbia St; ⏲5-10pm Fri) Start your weekend off big with after-work cocktails surrounded by a veritable gaggle of gays in the bayview penthouse restaurant of the Porto Vista Hotel in Little Italy.

The Hole (www.thehole.com; 2820 Lytton St; ⏲4pm-2am Mon, Thu & Sat, 2pm-2am Fri, noon-2am Sun) Literally underground, this uber-dive was one of the first openly gay bars in the country, across from the old naval training center. The surrounding auto repair shops no doubt made for good camo back in the day. Nowadays, it's all good fun and cheap drinks on the patio where manly men enjoy Sunday beer busts and barbecues, wet-underwear contests and more.

Urban Mo's (☎619-491-0400; www.urbanmos.com; 308 University Ave; ⏲9am-2am) Equal parts bar and restaurant, Urban Mo's is a Hillcrest institution for thumping beats, casual vibe, dance floor, decent grub and happy hours.

Rich's (www.richssandiego.com; 1051 University Ave; ⏲10pm-2am Wed-Sun) In the heart of Hillcrest, DJs shower the crowd with Latin, techno, pop and house at San Diego's biggest gay dance clubs, plus the popular #LEZ ladies party on Thursdays.

Brass Rail (thebrassrailsd.com; 3796 5th Ave) The city's oldest gay bar has a different theme nightly, from Latin to African, Top 40 to Ladies' Night. It also gets its share of straight folk and has lots of games to play, including pinball, pool and darts.

Flicks (www.sdflicks.com; 1017 University Ave) Video bar dominated by big screens, plus trivia, karaoke and more. Fun place to hang out and nurse a drink, or go for Sunday beer bust.

Mission & Pacific Beaches

PB is party central on the coast, with mostly 20-somethings on a beach bar bender (drivers: watch for tipsy pedestrians). If you've been there/done that, you might prefer one of the quieter coffee houses or restaurant bars.

Coaster Saloon DIVE BAR
(858-488-4438; 744 Ventura Pl, Mission Beach) Old-fashioned neighborhood dive bar with front-row views of the Belmont Park roller coaster. It draws an unpretentious crowd for events like Wii-bowling. Good margaritas too.

Bub's Dive DIVE BAR
(1030 Garnet Ave, Pacific Beach) Frat party atmosphere over tater tots and wings, at this rowdy spot where you might find yourself playing giant Connect Four or belting out 'Build me up, Buttercup' with a passel of new buds.

Society Billiard Cafe BILLIARDS
(1051 Garnet Ave, Pacific Beach; noon-2pm) Why settle for a beat-up pool table in the back of a dark bar when you can visit San Diego's plushest pool hall? The billiard room has about a dozen full-sized tables, snacks and a bar.

Café 976 COFFEE HOUSE
(976 Felspar St, Pacific Beach; 7am-11pm) Not everyone in PB spends the days surfing or the nights partying; some drink coffee and read books at this delightful sidestreet cafe in a converted old wooden house ensconced in rose bushes and flowering trees.

☆ Entertainment

Check out the San Diego *City Beat* or *UT San Diego* for the latest movies, theater, galleries and music gigs around town. **Arts Tix** (Map p284; 858-381-5595; www.sdartstix.com; Lyceum Theatre, 79 Horton Plaza), in a kiosk near Westfield Horton Plaza, has half-price tickets for same-day evening or next-day matinee performances and offers discounted tickets to other events. **Ticketmaster** (619-220-8497; www.ticketmaster.com) and House of Blues (p312) sell tickets to other gigs around the city.

Live Music

4th & B CLUB
(Map p284; www.4thandB.com; 345 B St) This midsized venue has music lovers head-bobbing with performances from an eclectic mix of talent and club nights, from unsigned hopefuls to the Psychedelic Furs, Snoop Dogg and the Last Comic Standing tour. Rest your feet – and eardrums – in the lounge. There's often a cover charge.

Casbah LIVE MUSIC
(619-232-4355; www.casbahmusic.com; 2501 Kettner Blvd; tickets $5-45) Bands from Smashing Pumpkins to Death Cab for Cutie all rocked the Casbah on their way up the charts and it's still a good place to catch tomorrow's headliners.

Shout House LIVE MUSIC
(Map p284; 619-231-6700; 655 4th Ave; cover free-$10) Good, clean fun at this cavernous Gaslamp bar with dueling pianos. Talented players have an amazing repertoire: standards, rock and more. We once heard Justin Timberlake's 'D*ck in a Box' (OK, maybe it's not so clean). The crowd ranges from college-age to conventioneers.

House of Blues BLUES, R&B
(Map p284; www.hob.com; 1055 5th Ave) You know what this is.

Winston's LIVE MUSIC
(Map p292; www.winstonsob.com; 1921 Bacon St, Ocean Beach) Bands play most nights, and each night has a different happening: open mic, karaoke, comedy, cover bands for the Grateful Dead and Red Hot Chili Peppers, local artists, game day etc.

710 Beach Club LIVE MUSIC
(www.710beachclub.com; 710 Garnet Ave, Pacific Beach) PB's main venue for live music books a solid lineup of rock, karaoke and comedy.

Classical Music

San Diego Symphony CLASSICAL
(Map p284; www.sandiegosymphony.com; 750 B St, Jacobs Music Center) This accomplished orchestra presents classical and family concerts at **Jacobs Music Center**. Look for Summer Pops concerts at Embarcadero Marina Park South.

Cinemas

Current movies fill multiplexes at big malls and in Hillcrest. Check local papers or visit www.moviefone.com. Also check the Pearl (p301), which has swim-up movies around its pool on Wednesdays.

Cinema Under the Stars OUTDOOR CINEMA
(www.topspresents.com; 4040 Goldfinch St; tickets $13.50) This unique venue screens mostly

classic American films on a heated patio in Mission Hills, a few nights a week from March to November.

Theater

Theater thrives in San Diego and is one of the city's greatest cultural attractions. There's also the La Jolla Playhouse (p322) and keep an eye out for the **San Diego Junior Theatre** (www.juniortheatre.com; Casa del Prado, Balboa Park) and the **San Diego Repertory Theatre** (Map p284; www.sdrep.org; Lyceum Theater, 79 Horton Plaza). Book tickets at the box office or online.

Old Globe Theaters THEATER
(www.theoldglobe.org; Balboa Park) Balboa Park's Old Globe Theaters date from the 1935 Exposition, and in the 1970s the main stage was rebuilt in the style of the original 17th-century Globe in England, where Shakespeare's works were originally performed. Between the three stages here – **Old Globe**, **Cassius Carter Stage** and the outdoor **Lowell Davies Festival Theater** – there are performances most days, including non-Shakespearean works.

Lamb's Players Theater THEATER
(www.lambsplayers.org; 1142 Orange Ave, Coronado) This well regarded company in Coronado also manages the **Horton Grand** (Map p284; www.lambsplayers.org; 444 4th Ave, Gaslamp Quarter).

National Comedy Theatre COMEDY
(www.nationalcomedy.com; 3717 India St, Mission Hills) Performances and improv classes in Mission Hills.

Spectator Sports

San Diego Padres BASEBALL
(Map p284; www.padres.com; Petco Park, 100 Park Blvd; tickets $11-91; ⏲ season Apr-early Oct) San Diego's Major League Baseball team plays in the handsome Petco Park (p283) stadium in the East Village. Tickets are usually available at the gate unless it's crucial to the standings or the LA Dodgers are in town.

San Diego Chargers FOOTBALL
(www.chargers.com; Qualcomm Stadium, 9449 Friars Rd; tickets from $52; ⏲ season Aug-Jan) The San Diego Chargers, SoCal's only National Football League team, play at this stadium in Mission Valley (there's a trolley stop right in front).

Shopping

Souvenir hunters will find stuffed Shamus at SeaWorld (p291), realistic-looking rubber snakes at the zoo (p276), or reprinted historical photos at the San Diego History Center (p280). The Spanish Village Art Center (p279) in Balboa Park is a good place to find paintings (mostly watercolors) of local scenes.

Given that adventure-sports gods Tony Hawk and Shawn White are San Diegans, surf and skate clothing are natural purchases here. There's a strip of stores, including Quicksilver and Oakley in the Gaslamp Quarter, on 5th Ave between J St and Island Ave.

Adams Avenue (www.adamsaveonline.com) is San Diego's main 'antique row,' with dozens of shops selling furniture, art and antiques from around the world, and cuts across some of San Diego's less-visited neighborhoods. You'll find the greatest concentration of shops around Normal Heights between the I-805 and I-15.

Most of coastal San Diego's shopping is limited to surf shops and bikini boutiques. A notable exception: Newport Ave in Ocean Beach, where a dozen antiques consignment shops line the main drag. **Newport Avenue Antique Center** (Map p292; 4864 Newport Ave) and **Mallory's** (Map p292; 4916 Newport Ave) are good places to start. **Cow** (Map p292; 5040 Newport Ave) gives the same treatment to music, and **Galactic** (Map p292; 4981 Newport Ave) to comics and video. Thrift shoppers should head to Garnet Ave in Pacific Beach for vintage and recycled drag. Most stores buy, sell and trade.

Downtown San Diego

Headquarters at Seaport District SHOPPING CENTER
(Map p284; www.theheadquarters.com; 789 W Harbor Dr) San Diego's newest shopping center (opened 2013) is also one of its oldest buildings, the 1939 former police headquarters now turned into some 30 shopping, dining and entertainment options. There's a small exhibit of vintage handcuffs, helmets, badges and jail cells for you and up to 15 of your friends.

Westfield Horton Plaza MALL
(Map p284; www.westfield.com/hortonplaza) At the edge of the Gaslamp, this five-story, seven-block shopping mall features shops big and small, including Norsdrom, Bebe and Coach. Los Angeles–based architect Jon

Jerde – who also designed **Universal City Walk** (Map p100) – gave it colorful, toy-town arches and postmodernist balconies making it feel slightly like an MC Escher drawing. Free three-hour parking with validation.

Seaport Village SHOPPING DISTRICT
(Map p284; www.seaportvillage.com; ⏲10am-10pm; 👪) Neither seaport nor village, this 14-acre collection of novelty shops and restaurants has a faux New England theme. It's touristy and twee but good for souvenir shopping and casual eats.

Mission Valley

Fashion Valley MALL
(www.simon.com; 7007 Friars Rd; ⏲10am-9pm Mon-Sat, 11am-7pm Sun) Premier shops here include Tiffany & Co, Burberry, James Perse, Ted Baker and Restoration Hardware, and department stores Neiman Marcus, Macy's and Nordstrom.

Westfield Mission Valley MALL
(www.westfield.com/missionvalley; 1640 Camino del Rio N; ⏲10am-9pm Mon-Sat, 11am-6pm Sun) This mall is quite casual with shops like Target and Hot Topic.

Hazard Center MALL
(www.hazardcenter.com; 7510-7610 Hazard Center Dr) The smallest of the three malls.

Point Loma Area

Liberty Station SHOPPING CENTER
(www.libertystation.com; 2640 Historic Decatur Rd) Between downtown and Point Loma, the former offices, barracks and mess halls of the decommissioned Naval Training Center are gradually being converted to shopping and dining. Look for fishing and outdoor gear and top restaurants including Corvette Diner (p307) and Stone Brewing Co (p307).

Kobey's Swap Meet FLEA MARKET
(www.kobeyswap.com; 3500 Sports Arena Blvd; admission Fri 50¢, Sat & Sun $1; ⏲7am-3pm Fri-Sun) The depth and breadth is awesome at the weekly flea market in the parking lot of the San Diego Sports Arena, and often the bargains are too. Look for all sorts of new and used items including sunglasses, clothing, jewelry, produce, flowers and plants, tools and furniture.

Mission & Pacific Beaches

Pangaea Outpost FASHION
(909 Garnet Ave, Pacific Beach) Like a mini-world unto themselves, the 70-plus merchants here offer a supremely eclectic selection of clothing, jewelry, wraps, handbags and semi-precious stones (just for starters!) from all around the world.

Buffalo Exchange FASHION
(1007 Garnet Ave, Pacific Beach) If you need something to wear to dinner, this store carries a good selection of contemporary and vintage fashions, including designer labels.

Pilar's Beachwear SWIMWEAR
(3745 Mission Blvd, Mission Beach) For swimwear, women should head to this shop, which has all the latest styles in all sizes.

South Coast Wahines SURFWEAR
(4500 Ocean Blvd, Pacific Beach) At the foot of Garnet Ave at Crystal Pier, this store carries spiffy surf apparel for women.

Ocean Beach

South Coast Longboards SURF SHOP
(Map p292; 5023 Newport Ave, Ocean Beach) Apathetic surfer dudes staff the counter at this beach-apparel and surf-gear shop that carries a good selection of Quiksilver, Hurley, Billabong and O'Neill for men and women. Oh yes, you can buy a surfboard here too.

Information

INTERNET ACCESS

All public libraries and most coffeehouses and hotel lobbies offer free wi-fi. Libraries also offer computer terminals for access.

MEDIA

Free listings magazines Tabloid-sized magazines, *Citybeat* (www.sdcitybeat.com) and *San Diego Reader* (www.sdreader.com), cover the active music, art and theater scenes. Find them in shops and cafes.

KPBS 89.5 FM (www.kpbs.org) National Public Radio station.

San Diego Magazine (www.sandiegomagazine.com) Glossy monthly.

UT San Diego (www.utsandiego.com) The city's major daily.

MEDICAL SERVICES

Scripps Mercy Hospital (☎619-294-8111; www.scripps.org; 4077 5th Ave) Has a 24-hour emergency room.

MONEY

You'll find ATMs throughout San Diego.

TravelEx (☎858-457-2412; www.travelex.com; University Towne Centre, 4417 La Jolla Village Dr; ⊙10am-7pm Mon-Fri, to 6pm Sat, 11am-4pm Sun) For foreign-currency exchange.

POST

For post office locations, call ☎800-275-8777 or log on to www.usps.com.

Downtown Post Office (Map p284; 815 E St; ⊙9am-5pm Mon-Fri)

Coronado Post Office (1320 Ynez Pl; ⊙8:30am-5pm Mon-Fri, 9am-noon Sat)

TOURIST INFORMATION

International Visitor Information Center (Map p284; ☎619-236-1212; www.sandiego.org; 1140 N Harbor Dr; ⊙9am-5pm Jun-Sep, to 4pm Oct-May) Across from the B St Cruise Ship Terminal, helpful staff offer very detailed neighborhood maps, sell discounted tickets to attractions and maintain a hotel reservation hotline.

Coronado Visitors Center (☎619-437-8788, 866-599-7242; www.coronadovisitorcenter.com; 1100 Orange Ave; ⊙9am-5pm Mon-Fri, 10am-5pm Sat & Sun)

USEFUL WEBSITES

Lonely Planet (www.lonelyplanet.com/usa/san-diego) Planning advice, author recommendations, traveler reviews and insider tips.

San Diego Tourism (www.sandiego.org) Search hotels, sights, dining, rental cars and more, and make reservations.

Getting There & Away

AIR

Most flights to San Diego International Airport-Lindbergh Field (p480) are domestic. The airfield sits just 3 miles west of Downtown; plane-spotters will thrill watching jets come in over Balboa Park for landing. Coming from overseas, you'll likely change flights – and clear US customs – at one of the major US gateway airports, such as LA, San Francisco, Chicago, New York or Miami.

The standard one-way fare between LA and San Diego is about $100 and takes about 35 minutes; unless you're connecting through LA, you're usually better off driving or taking the train.

To/from other US cities, flights to San Diego are generally up to about $120 more expensive than those to LA. All major US airlines serve San Diego, plus Air Canada, British Airways, Japan Airlines, Mexico's Volaris and the Canadian carrier WestJet.

BUS

Greyhound (☎619-515-1100, 800-231-2222; www.greyhound.com; 1313 National Ave) serves San Diego from cities across North America from its new location in East Village. Inquire about discounts and special fares, many available only online.

Buses depart frequently for LA; the standard one-way/round-trip fare is $18/36 and the trip takes 2½ to four hours. There are several daily departures to Anaheim ($18/36, about 2¼ hours).

Buses to San Francisco (one-way/round trip $86/172, 12 hours, about eight daily) require a transfer in Los Angeles; round-trip airfares often cost about the same. Most buses to Las Vegas (one-way/round-trip $55/83, eight to nine hours, about nine daily) require a transfer in LA or San Bernardino.

CAR & MOTORCYCLE

Allow two hours from LA in non-peak traffic. With traffic, it's anybody's guess.

TRAIN

Amtrak (☎800-872-7245; www.amtrak.com) runs the *Pacific Surfliner* several times daily to Anaheim ($28, two hours), Los Angeles ($37, 2¾ hours) and Santa Barbara ($42, 6½ hours) from the historic **Union Station** (Santa Fe Depot; 1055 Kettner Blvd).

Getting Around

TO/FROM THE AIRPORT

Bus 992 (the *Flyer*, $2.25) operates at 10- to 15-minute intervals between the airport and

> **BUS & TROLLEY TICKETS**
>
> While most people get around by car, it's possible to have an entire San Diego vacation using municipal buses and trolleys run by the **Metropolitan Transit System** (MTS; ☎619-557-4555; www.sdmts.com) and your own two feet. Most buses/trolleys cost $2.25/2.50 per ride. Transfers are not available, so purchase a day pass if you're going to be taking more than two rides in a day; a refillable **Compass Card** ($2 one-time purchase) will save hassles. The **Transit Store** (Map p284; ☎619-234-1060; 102 Broadway; ⊙9am-5pm Mon-Fri) is one-stop shopping for route maps, tickets and one-/two-/three-/four-day passes ($5/9/12/15). Same-day passes are also available from bus drivers. At trolley stations, purchase tickets from vending machines.

FREE RIDE

On Saturdays and Sundays, up to two children can ride the trolley for free with each fare-paying adult.

Downtown, with stops along Broadway. Taxis between Downtown and the airport typically cost between $10 and $16. Airport shuttle services (from about $13 per person to Downtown, more to other destinations) include **Super Shuttle** (800-258-3826; www.supershuttle.com) but these travel at their own pace and may drop off several others before your stop; call to reserve a day or two ahead.

BICYCLE

Mostly flat Pacific Beach, Mission Beach, Mission Bay and Coronado are all great places to ride a bike. Visit **icommute** (www.icommutesd.com) for maps and information about biking in the region. Public buses are equipped with bike racks.

A few outfits rent bicycles, from mountain and road bikes to kids' bikes and cruisers. In general, expect to pay about $8 per hour, $15–22 per half-day (four hours) and $25–30 per day.

Bikes & Beyond (619-435-7180; www.bikes-and-beyond.com; 1201 1st St, Coronado; per hr/day from $8/30; 9am-sunset) At the Coronado Ferry Landing

Cheap Rentals (858-488-9070, 800-941-7761; 3689 Mission Blvd, Pacific Beach; 9am-7pm, shorter hr autumn-spring) Rents bikes and skates ($5/12 per hour/day), plus surfboards ($15 per day) and wetsuits ($10 per day) at Pacific Beach. It also takes reservations for rentals.

Holland's Bicycles (619-435-3153; www.hollandsbicycles.com; 977 Orange Ave, Coronado) In Coronado.

BOAT

Flagship Cruises (p295) operates the hourly **Coronado Ferry** (Map p284; 619-234-4111; www.flagshipsd.com; tickets $4.25; 9am-10pm; 15 minutes) shuttling between the **Broadway Pier** (1050 N Harbor Dr) on the Embarcadero and the ferry landing at the foot of B Ave in Coronado, two blocks south of Orange Ave. Bikes are permitted on board at no extra charge. Flagship also operates a water taxi, serving mostly Downtown and Coronado.

BUS

MTS (p315) covers most of the metropolitan area, North County, La Jolla and the beaches. It's most convenient if you're based Downtown and not staying out late.

For route and fare information, call 619-233-3004 or 800-266-6883; operators are available 5:30am to 8:30pm Monday to Friday, and 8am to 5pm Saturday and Sunday (note that the 800 number works only within San Diego). For 24-hour automated information, call 619-685-4900.

Useful routes to/from Downtown:

No 3 Balboa Park, Hillcrest, UCSD Medical Center

No 7 Balboa Park, Zoo, Hillcrest, North Park

No 8/9 Old Town to Pacific Beach, SeaWorld

No 30 Old Town, Pacific Beach, La Jolla, University Towne Centre

No 35 Old Town to Ocean Beach

No 901 Coronado

CAR

All the big-name car-rental companies have desks at the airport, and lesser-known ones may be cheaper. Shop around – prices vary widely, even from day to day within the same company. The airport has free direct phones to a number of car-rental companies. Rental rates tend to be comparable to LA ($40 to $80 per day). Smaller agencies include **West Coast Rent a Car** (619-544-0606; www.sandiegoautos.org; 834 W Grape St; 9am-6pm Mon-Sat, to 5pm Sun), in Little Italy.

TAXI & RIDE SHARE

Taxi fares vary, but plan on about $2.40 to start, plus $2.60 for each additional mile. Established companies include **Orange Cab** (619-223-5555; www.orangecabsandiego.com) and **Yellow Cab** (619-444-4444; www.driveu.com). Recently app-based ride-share companies such as **Uber** (uber.com) and **Sidecar** (side.cr) have entered the market with lower fares.

TROLLEY

Municipal trolleys, not to be confused with Old Town Trolley tourist buses (p295), operate on three main lines. From the transit center across from the Santa Fe Depot, **Blue Line** trolleys go south to San Ysidro (Mexico border) and north to Old Town Transit Center (p287). The **Green Line** runs from Old Town east through Mission Valley. The **Orange Line** connects the Convention Center and Seaport Village with Downtown, but otherwise it's less useful for visitors.

Trolleys run between about 4:15am and 1am daily at 15-minute intervals during the day, and every 30 minutes in the evening. The Blue Line continues a limited all-night service on Saturday. Fares are $2.50 per ride, valid for two hours from the time of purchase at vending machines on the station platforms.

LA JOLLA & NORTH COUNTY COAST

Immaculately landscaped parks, white-sand coves, upscale boutiques, top restaurants, and cliffs above deep, clear blue waters make it easy to understand why 'La Jolla' translates from Spanish as 'the jewel' – say la-*hoy*-yah, if you please.

Northward from La Jolla, small beach towns extend like pearls on a strand. 'North County,' as locals call it, begins with pretty Del Mar and continues through low-key Solana Beach, Encinitas and Carlsbad (home of Legoland), before hitting Oceanside, largely a bedroom community for Camp Pendleton Marine Base.

North County's coast evokes the San Diego of 40 years ago, even if inland development, east of I-5, has created giant bedroom communities for San Diego and Orange Counties. The beaches are terrific, and the small seaside towns are great for days of soaking up the laid-back SoCal scene, working on your tan and catching up on your reading while watching the California sun glisten on the Pacific.

All that, and only about a half-hour's drive from Downtown San Diego.

Getting There & Away

North County Transit District (NCTD; ☎760-966-6500; www.gonctd.com) Breeze Bus 101 departs from University Towne Centre (p323) and follows the coastal road to Oceanside. NCTD also operates the *Coaster* commuter train from San Diego, stopping in Solana Beach, Encinitas, Carlsbad and Oceanside. There are 11 daily trains in each direction Monday to Friday and six/four trains on Saturday/Sunday. NCTD buses and trains have bike racks. A few Amtrak (p315) *Pacific Surfliner* trains stop here daily.

Greyhound (p315) buses stop at Oceanside and San Diego, but nowhere in between.

La Jolla

The name La Jolla may actually date from Native Americans who inhabited the area from 10,000 years ago to the mid-19th century, who called the place 'mut la hoya, la hoya' – the place of many caves. Whether your interest is jewels or caves, you'll feel at home in this lovely enclave.

Sights

La Jolla Village

La Jolla Village sits atop cliffs with the ocean on three sides. The main crossroads, Girard Ave and Prospect St, are the *x* and *y* axes of some of San Diego's best restaurants and certainly its best boutique shopping.

★Museum of Contemporary Art San Diego – La Jolla ART MUSEUM
(MCASD; ☎858-454-3541; www.mcasd.org; 700 Prospect St; adult/child $10/free, free 5-7pm 3rd Thu each month; ⏰11am-5pm Thu-Tue, to 7pm 3rd Thu each month) La Jolla's branch of this museum gets changing, world-class exhibitions. Originally designed by Irving Gill in 1916 as the home of newspaper heiress **Ellen Browning Scripps**, who basically created modern La Jolla circa 1897, the building was renovated by Philadelphia's postmodern architect Robert Venturi and has an Andy Goldsworthy sculpture out the front; tickets are good for one week at all three of the museum's locations (p282).

Athenaeum LIBRARY
(☎858-454-5872; www.ljathenaeum.org; 1008 Wall St; ⏰10am-5:30pm Tue-Sat, to 8:30pm Wed) Housed in a graceful Spanish renaissance structure, this space is devoted exclusively to art and music. Its reading room is a lovely place to relax and read, and it hosts a series of concerts from chamber music to jazz.

La Jolla Historical Society MUSEUM
(780 Prospect St; ⏰noon-4pm Thu & Fri) This place has vintage photos and beach memorabilia (think old bathing costumes and lifeguard buoys). For more historical structures, head southwest on Prospect St to **St James Episcopal Church**, the **La Jolla Recreation Center** and the **Bishop's School** (cnr Prospect St & La Jolla Blvd), all built in the early 20th century.

La Jolla Coast

A wonderful walking path skirts the shoreline for half a mile. At the west it begins at **Children's Pool** (Coast Blvd), where a jetty protects the beach from big waves. Originally intended to give La Jolla's youth a safe place to frolic, this beach is now given over to sea lions, which you can view up close as they lounge on the shore.

La Jolla

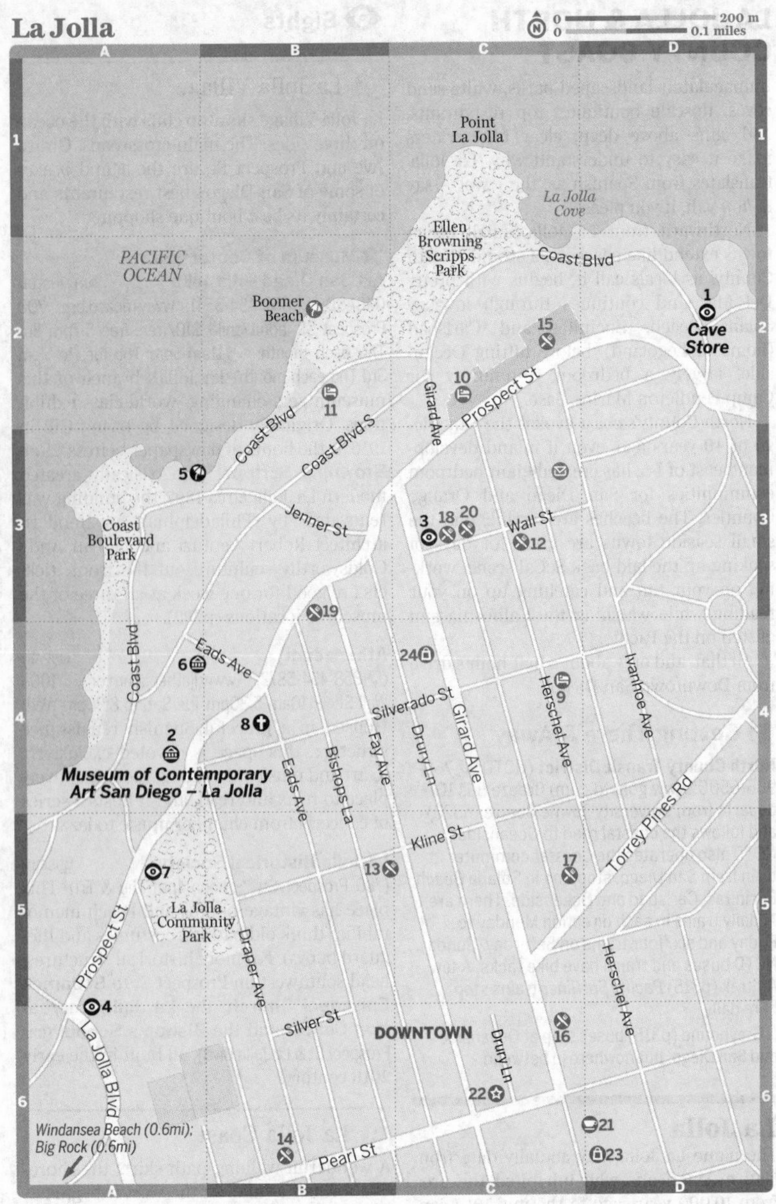

Atop **Point La Jolla**, at the path's eastern end, **Ellen Browning Scripps Park** is a tidy expanse of green lawns and palm trees, with **La Jolla Cove** to the north. The cove's gem of a beach provides access to some of the best snorkeling around; it's also popular with rough-water swimmers.

Look for the white buoys offshore from Point La Jolla to Scripps Pier (visible to the north) that mark the **San Diego-La Jolla Underwater Park Ecological Reserve**, a

La Jolla

Top Sights
1 Cave Store D2
2 Museum of Contemporary Art San Diego – La Jolla A4

Sights
3 Athenaeum C3
4 Bishop's School A6
5 Children's Pool A3
6 La Jolla Historical Society A4
7 La Jolla Recreation Center A5
8 St James Episcopal Church B4

Sleeping
9 La Jolla Village Lodge C4
10 La Valencia C2
11 Pantai Inn B2

Eating
12 Burger Lounge C3
13 Cottage B5
14 El Pescador B6
15 George's at the Cove C2
16 Harry's Coffee Shop C6
17 Porkyland C5
18 Puesto La Jolla C3
19 Roppongi B3
20 Whisknladle C3

Drinking & Nightlife
21 Pannikin D6

Entertainment
22 Comedy Store C6

Shopping
23 DG Wills D6
24 Warwick's C4

protected zone with a variety of marine life, kelp forests, reefs and canyons.

★ Cave Store CAVES
(☎858-459-0746; www.cavestore.com; 1325 Coast Rd; adult/child $4/3; ⊙10am-5pm;) Waves have carved a series of caves into the sandstone cliffs east of La Jolla Cove. The largest is called **Sunny Jim Cave**, which you can access via this store. Taller visitors, watch your head as you descend the 145 steps.

La Jolla Shores

Called simply 'the Shores,' this primarily residential area northeast of La Jolla Cove is where La Jolla's cliffs meet the wide, sandy beaches. Waves here are gentle enough for beginner surfers, and kayakers can launch from the shore without much problem. Take La Jolla Shores Dr north from Torrey Pines Rd, and turn west onto Ave de la Playa.

Birch Aquarium at Scripps AQUARIUM
(☎858-534-3474; www.aquarium.ucsd.edu; 2300 Exhibition Way, La Jolla; adult/child $17/12.50; ⊙9am-5pm; P) Marine scientists were working at the Birch Aquarium at Scripps Institution of Oceanography (SIO) as early as 1910 and, helped by donations from the ever-generous Scripps family, the institute has grown to be one of the world's largest marine research institutions. It is now a part of UCSD. Off N Torrey Pines Rd, the aquarium has brilliant displays. The **Hall of Fishes** has more than 30 fish tanks, simulating marine environments from the Pacific Northwest to tropical seas.

Salk Institute ARCHITECTURE
(☎858-453-4100, ext 1287; www.salk.edu; 10010 N Torrey Pines Rd; tours $15; ⊙tours by reservation 11:45am Mon-Fri; P) In 1960 Jonas Salk, the polio-prevention pioneer, founded the Salk Institute for biological and biomedical research. San Diego County donated 27 acres of land, the March of Dimes provided financial support and renowned architect Louis Kahn designed the building, completed in 1965. It is regarded as a modern masterpiece, with its classically proportioned travertine marble plaza and cubist, mirror-glass laboratory blocks framing a perfect view of the Pacific, and the fountain in the courtyard symbolizing the River of Life. The Salk Institute attracts the best scientists to work in a research-only environment. The original buildings were expanded with new laboratories designed by Jack McAllister, a follower of Kahn's work.

Torrey Pines State Natural Reserve PARK
(☎858-755-2063; www.torreypine.org; 12600 N Torrey Pines Rd, La Jolla; ⊙7:15am-dusk, visitor center 10am-4pm Oct-Apr, 9am-6pm May-Sep; P) Between N Torrey Pines Rd and the ocean, and from the Torrey Pines Gliderport (p321) to Del Mar, this reserve preserves the last mainland stands of the Torrey pine *(Pinus torreyana)*, a species adapted to sparse rainfall and sandy, stony soils. Steep sandstone gullies have eroded into wonderfully

textured surfaces, and the views over the ocean and north, including whale-watching, are superb. Rangers lead nature walks on weekends and holidays. Several walking trails wind through the reserve and down to the beach. Parking fees per car vary from $4 per hour to $15 per day.

University of California, San Diego UNIVERSITY
(UCSD; ucsd.edu; 9500 Gilman Dr) UCSD was established in 1960 and now has more than 18,000 students and a strong reputation, particularly for mathematics and science. It lies on rolling coastal hills in a parklike setting, surrounded by tall, fragrant eucalyptus. Its most distinctive structure is the **Geisel Library**, an upside-down pyramid named for children's author Theodor Geisel, aka Dr Seuss of *Cat in the Hat* fame; there's a collection of his drawings and books. Download a map of UCSD's excellent collection of public art at stuartcollection.ucsd.edu.

Activities

La Jolla Beaches BEACHES
Some of the county's best beaches are north of the Shores in **Torrey Pines City Park**, betweeen the Salk Institute and Torrey Pines State Reserve. Hang-gliders and paragliders launch into the sea breezes rising over the cliffs at Torrey Pines Gliderport (p321), at the end of Torrey Pines Scenic Dr. It's a beautiful sight – tandem flights are available if you can't resist trying it.

SEALS VS SWIMMERS

La Jolla's Children's Pool (p317) was created in the early 1930s when the state deeded the area to the city as a public park and children's pool. Then came the seals, drawing tourists but gradually nudging out swimmers completely by 1997. Animal rights groups and swimmers duked it out in court to protect the cove as a rookery while swimmers and divers wanted the seals – whose presence raises bacterial levels in the waters to unsafe levels – removed. State and federal courts have consistently ruled that the seals must go, but Mother Nature may be the final authority. For now the seals remain, surrounded by a simple rope barrier to keep humans at bay.

Down below, **Black's Beach** is one of America's most storied clothing-optional venues – though bathing suits are technically required, most folks here don't seem to know that; there's a gay section at the far (north) end.

At extreme low tides (about twice per year), you can walk from the Shores north to Del Mar along the beach.

San Diego-La Jolla Underwater Park SNORKELING, DIVING
Some of California's best and most accessible diving is in this reserve, accessible from La Jolla Cove. With an average depth of 20ft, the 6000 acres of look-but-don't-touch underwater real estate is great for snorkeling, too. Ever-present are the spectacular, bright orange Garibaldi fish – California's official state fish and a protected species (there's a $500 fine for poaching one). Further out you'll see forests of giant California kelp (which can increase its length by up to 3ft per day) and the 100ft-deep **La Jolla Canyon**.

A number of commercial outfits conduct scuba-diving courses, sell or rent equipment, fill tanks, and conduct boat trips to nearby wrecks and islands. The Cave Store (p319) and other outfitters rent snorkel and fin sets (about $20 for two hours).

Windansea Beach SURFING
Experienced surfers can head to this beach, 2 miles south of downtown (take La Jolla Blvd south and turn west on Nautilus St); the surf's consistent peak (a powerful reef break that's not for beginners) works best at medium to low tide. However, some of the locals can be unfriendly toward outsiders.

Big Rock SURFING
You'll find a pleasant welcome immediately south of Windansea Beach, at the foot of Palomar Ave. Big Rock is California's version of Hawaii's Pipeline, which has steep, hollow, gnarly tubes. The name comes from the large chunk of reef protruding just offshore – a great spot for **tide-pooling** at low tide. La Jolla Shores and Black's Beach are also popular surfing spots.

Surf Diva SURFING
(☎858-454-8273; www.surfdiva.com; 2160 Avenida de la Playa; ⏲store 8:30am-6pm, varies seasonally) The wonderful women here offer surf classes from $75 and rent boards and wetsuits.

Torrey Pines Gliderport HANG GLIDING
(☎858-452-9858; www.flytorrey.com; 2800 Torrey Pines Scenic Dr; 20min paragliding $150, hang gliding tandem flight per person $200) Conditions permitting, glider riders hang at this world-famous gliding location. It's also one of the best gliding schools in the country. Experienced pilots can join in if they have a USHGA Hang 4 (paragliders need a P3 rating) and take out an associate membership of the Torrey Pines Hang Glider Association.

Sleeping

Lodging in central La Jolla ain't cheap. We've given summer high-season (June to August) rack rates. Inquire about specials and packages, and lower rates at other times of year.

La Jolla Village Lodge MOTEL $$
(☎858-551-2001, 877-551-2001; www.lajollavillagelodge.com; 1141 Silverado St; r incl breakfast $100-200; P) At the edge of downtown La Jolla, this 30-room 1950s-era motel was recently restored in period mid-century style with custom-built tables and chairs, teak headboards and new mattresses. Flat-screen TVs are a concession to the 21st century. A roof deck gives long-distance views.

★**Lodge at Torrey Pines** CRAFTSMAN, GOLF $$$
(☎800-995-4507, 858-453-4420; www.lodgetorreypines.com; 11480 N Torrey Pines Rd; r from $350; P@) Inspired by the architecture of Greene & Greene, the turn-of-the-20th-century Arts and Crafts masters who designed the Gamble House (p196) in Pasadena, the Lodge's discreetly luxurious rooms have Mission oak-and-leather furniture à la Stickley, Tiffany-style lamps, plein-air paintings and basket-weave bathroom-floor tiling in marble. There's a stellar full-service spa and a croquet lawn. Parking costs $25.

Pantai Inn B&B, SUITES $$$
(☎858-224-7600, 855-287-2682; www.pantaiinn.com; 1003 Coast Blvd; r from $295; P@) About as close as you can stay to the beach and Scripps Park, colorful banners mark the perimeter of this new, Balinese-style inn. Rooms vary in size, but all have kitchens and sitting areas, and suites are filled with Balinese art and antiques. Continental breakfast is served in the Gathering Room; enjoy it on multiple ocean-view decks.

La Valencia HISTORIC HOTEL $$$
(☎858-454-0771, 800-451-0772; www.lavalencia.com; 1132 Prospect St; r from $385; P@) Publicity stills of Lon Cheney, Lillian Gish and Greta Garbo line the hallways of this 1926 landmark: pink-walled, Mediterranean-style and designed by William Templeton Johnson. Among its 112 rooms, the ones in the main building are rather compact (befitting the era), but villas are spacious and in any case the property wins for Old Hollywood romance. Even if you don't stay, consider lifting a toast – and a pinkie – to the sunset from its Spanish Revival lounge, La Sala. Parking is $29.

Estancia La Jolla Hotel & Spa LUXURY RESORT $$$
(☎877-437-8262, 858-550-1000; www.estancialajolla.com; 9700 N Torrey Pines Rd; r $199-349; P@) North of the village, this rambling rancho-style resort with its pathways, patios and lush gardens is down-to-earth, romantic and cushy all at once. Unwind by the heated, saltwater pool, during an expert massage at the spa, or while sipping killer margaritas by the outdoor fireplace. Rooms feature custom furniture, luxurious linens and big bathrooms. Two restaurants. Parking costs $25.

Eating

Look for locations of **Puesto** (☎858-454-1260; www.eatpuesto.com; 1026 Wall St; ⊙11am-9pm) and **Burger Lounge** (☎858-456-0196; 1101 Wall St) in La Jolla Village.

Porkyland MEXICAN $
(☎858-459-1708; 1030 Torrey Pines Rd; dishes $4-9; ⊙9am-7pm) This tiny Mexican joint in a corner shopping center on the edge of La Jolla Village has only simple indoor-outdoor seating, but the burritos and fish tacos have a devoted following. The *verde carnitas burrito* ($6) will make your taste buds roar (in a good way) and still leave you money for beer.

Harry's Coffee Shop DINER $
(☎858-454-7381; 7545 Girard Ave; dishes $5-13; ⊙6am-3pm;) This classic 1960 coffee shop has a posse of regulars from blue-haired socialites to sports celebs. The food is standard-issue American – pancakes, tuna melts, burgers (and a local concession, breakfast burritos) – but it's the aura of the place that makes it special.

Whisknladle CALIFORNIAN $$
(☎858-551-7575; www.wnlhosp.com; 1044 Wall St; lunch mains $14-21, dinner $15-36; ⊙11:30am-9pm Mon-Thu, to 10pm Fri, 10am-10pm Sat,

10am-9:30pm Sun) Gourmets and gourmands alike love Whisknladle's 'slow food' preparations of local, farm-fresh ingredients, served on a breezy covered patio and meant for sharing. Every minute preparation from curing to pickling and macerating is done in-house. The menu changes daily, but it's always clever. So are the cocktails (the London's Burning mixes gin and jalapeño water).

El Pescador SEAFOOD $$
(☎858-456-2526; www.elpescadorfishmarket.com; 634 Pearl St; mains $7-20; ⏰10am-8pm) You could pay three times as much for seafood with the tourists at fancier restaurants in town; meanwhile locals will be at this fish market and restaurant, just moved to spanking new digs on the edge of La Jolla Village. Order your catch from refrigerator cases, and it'll be prepared into sandwich, salad or plate.

Roppongi ASIAN FUSION $$
(☎858-551-5252; 875 Prospect St; most dishes $10-25; ⏰11:30am-9:30pm Sun-Thu, to 10:30pm Fri & Sat) Asian tapas-style dishes shine at this gorgeous eatery with clever lighting that makes everyone look good. The Polynesian crab stack, piled high and tossed at table, is a killer choice and the ahi tuna with watermelon a surprising flavor bomb. Great wines and sakes, too.

Cottage MODERN AMERICAN $$
(☎858-454-8409; 7702 Fay Ave; mains breakfast $9-12, lunch $10-19, dinner $11-26; ⏰7:30am-9pm) Shhh! Don't tell anybody that the stuffed French toast, eggs La Jolla (with Canadian bacon, mushrooms, spinach and garlic and balsamic vinegar), fish tacos and granola-crusted mahi mahi make this place a local favorite. It's crowded enough as it is, especially on weekends for brunch. Expect a wait if you arrive much after 8:30am.

★George's at the Cove CALIFORNIAN $$$
(☎858-454-4244; www.georgesatthecove.com; 1250 Prospect St; mains $13-50; ⏰11am-10pm Mon-Thu, to 11pm Fri-Sun) If you've got the urge to splurge, the Euro-Cal cooking is as dramatic as the oceanfront location thanks to the bottomless imagination of chef Trey Foshée. George's has graced just about every list of top restaurants in California, and indeed the USA. Three venues allow you to enjoy it at different price points: Ocean Terrace, George's Bar and George's California Modern.

Marine Room MODERN AMERICAN $$$
(☎858-459-7222; 2000 Spindrift Dr; mains $26-46; ⏰6-10pm) Yet another only-in-La Jolla experience. When money is no object and you want high-drama cooking and views, book a sunset table at this clubby dining room outside the town center. You'll feast on highly stylized contemporary-fusion meats and seafood, while waves splash against the window at high tide (April–August).

The 34-page wine and cocktail menu is dizzying. Lounge menu too (4pm to 6pm Sunday to Friday).

Drinking & Entertainment

La Jolla has a cluster of bars around Prospect St and Girard Ave.

Pannikin CAFE
(pannikincoffeeandtea.com; 7467 Girard Ave; ⏰6am-6pm Mon-Fri, 6:30am-6pm Sat & Sun; 📶) A few blocks from the water, this clapboard shack of a cafe with a generous balcony is popular for its organic coffees, Italian espresso and Mexican chocolate, and occasional live music. Like all the Pannikins, it's a North County institution.

Comedy Store COMEDY
(☎858-454-9176; www.comedystorelajolla.com; 916 Pearl St) One of the area's most established comedy venues, the Comedy Store also serves meals, drinks and barrels of laughs. Expect a cover charge ($15 to $20 on weekends with a two-drink minimum), and some of tomorrow's big names.

La Jolla Symphony & Chorus CLASSICAL MUSIC
(☎858-534-4637; www.lajollasymphony.com; UCSD) Come here for quality concerts at UCSD's Mandeville Auditorium running from October to June.

La Jolla Playhouse THEATER
(☎858-550-1010; www.lajollaplayhouse.org; 2910 La Jolla Village Dr, Mandell Weiss Center for the Performing Arts) This theater has sent dozens of productions to Broadway including *Jersey Boys, Peter and the Startcatcher* and 2010 Tony winner *Memphis*.

Shopping

La Jolla's skirt-and-sweater crowd pays retail for cashmere sweaters and expensive tchotchkes downtown: paintings, sculpture and decorative items, and small boutiques fill the gaps between Talbot's, Banana Republic, Ralph Lauren, Jos A Bank and Armani Exchange.

DG Wills (7461 Girard Ave) and **Warwick's** (7812 Girard Ave) have good book selections and host readings and author events.

Westfield University Towne Centre MALL
(UTC; 4545 La Jolla Village Dr) Mall shoppers: make a beeline for this large mall out of downtown La Jolla and east of I-5; anchor stores include Nordstrom, Macy's and Sears, and for non-shoppers there are movies and an indoor ice-skating rink, **Icetown** (☎858-452-9110; www.icetown.com); call for opening hours. It's also the transit hub for La Jolla. There's also a branch of **Travelex** (University Towne Centre; ⊙10am-7pm Mon-Fri, to 6pm Sat, 11am-4pm Sun) foreign currency exchange.

Getting There & Away

Via I-5 from Downtown San Diego, take the La Jolla Pkwy exit and head west toward Torrey Pines Rd, from where it's a right turn onto Prospect St.

Del Mar

POP 4250

The ritziest of North County's seaside suburbs, with a Tudor aesthetic that somehow doesn't feel out of place, Del Mar boasts good (if pricey) restaurants, unique galleries, high-end boutiques and, north of town, the west coast's most renowned horse-racing track, also the site of the annual county fair. Downtown Del Mar (sometimes called 'the village') extends for about a mile along Camino del Mar. At its hub, where 15th St crosses Camino del Mar, the tastefully designed **Del Mar Plaza** (1555 Camino Del Mar) shopping center has restaurants, boutiques and upper-level terraces that look out to sea.

Sights & Activities

Del Mar Racetrack & Fairgrounds RACETRACK
(☎858-755-1141; www.dmtc.com; admission from $6; ⊙race season mid-Jul–early Sep) Del Mar's biggest draw was founded in 1937 by a prestigious group including Bing Crosby and Jimmy Durante. It's worth trying to brave the crowds on opening day, if nothing else to see the amazing spectacle of ladies wearing over-the-top hats. Driving here on opening day… just don't. The racetrack runs free double-decker shuttle buses to and from the train station in Solana Beach. The rest of the season, you'll have to be satisfied with the mere visual perfection of the track's lush gardens and pink, Mediterranean-style architecture.

Seagrove Park PARK
At the end of 15th St, this park abuts the beach and overlooks the ocean. This little stretch of well-groomed lawn is a community hub and perfect for a picnic.

California Dreamin' BALLOONING
(☎800-373-3359; www.californiadreamin.com; per person from $288) Brightly colored hot-air balloons are a trademark of the skies above Del Mar, on the northern fringe of the metropolitan area. For flights, contact California Dreamin', which also serves Temecula.

Sleeping

In summer, especially around opening day at Del Mar Racetrack, rooms in Del Mar fill up and rates soar. Discounts may be available midweek. Most choices are in the town center; there are less expensive chain properties out of town, near the I-5.

Les Artistes Inn BOUTIQUE HOTEL **$$**
(☎858-755-4646; www.lesartistesinn.com; 944 Camino Del Mar; r $165-250; P ❄ @ ☜ 🐾) Behind the eclectic Craftsman-style facade of this inn set back from Camino del Mar, each of the 12 spacious rooms is meticulously furnished in the style of an artist or art movement: Botero through O'Keefe to van Gogh, even Zen.

Clarion Del Mar Inn MOTEL **$$**
(☎800-451-4515, 858-755-9765; www.delmarinn.com; 720 Camino Del Mar; r incl breakfast $119-229; P ⊖ @ ☜ ≋) This well-kept, 80-room upscale motel tries hard to please with helpful staff, pool and large-ish rooms (many with balconies and kitchens or bathroom vanities with granite countertops), all recently updated with beachy pale blues and sages. There's a library lounge and indoor-outdoor bistro.

L'Auberge Del Mar Resort & Spa LUXURY **$$$**
(☎800-553-1336, 858-259-1515; www.laubergedelmar.com; 1540 Camino Del Mar; r $350-540; P ❄ @ ☜ ≋ 🐾) Rebuilt in the 1990s on the grounds of the historic Hotel del Mar, where 1920s Hollywood celebrities once frolicked, L'Auberge continues a tradition of European-style elegance with luxurious linens, a spa and lovely grounds. It feels so intimate and the service is so individual, you'd never know there are 120 rooms. Parking is $25.

San Diego North County Coast

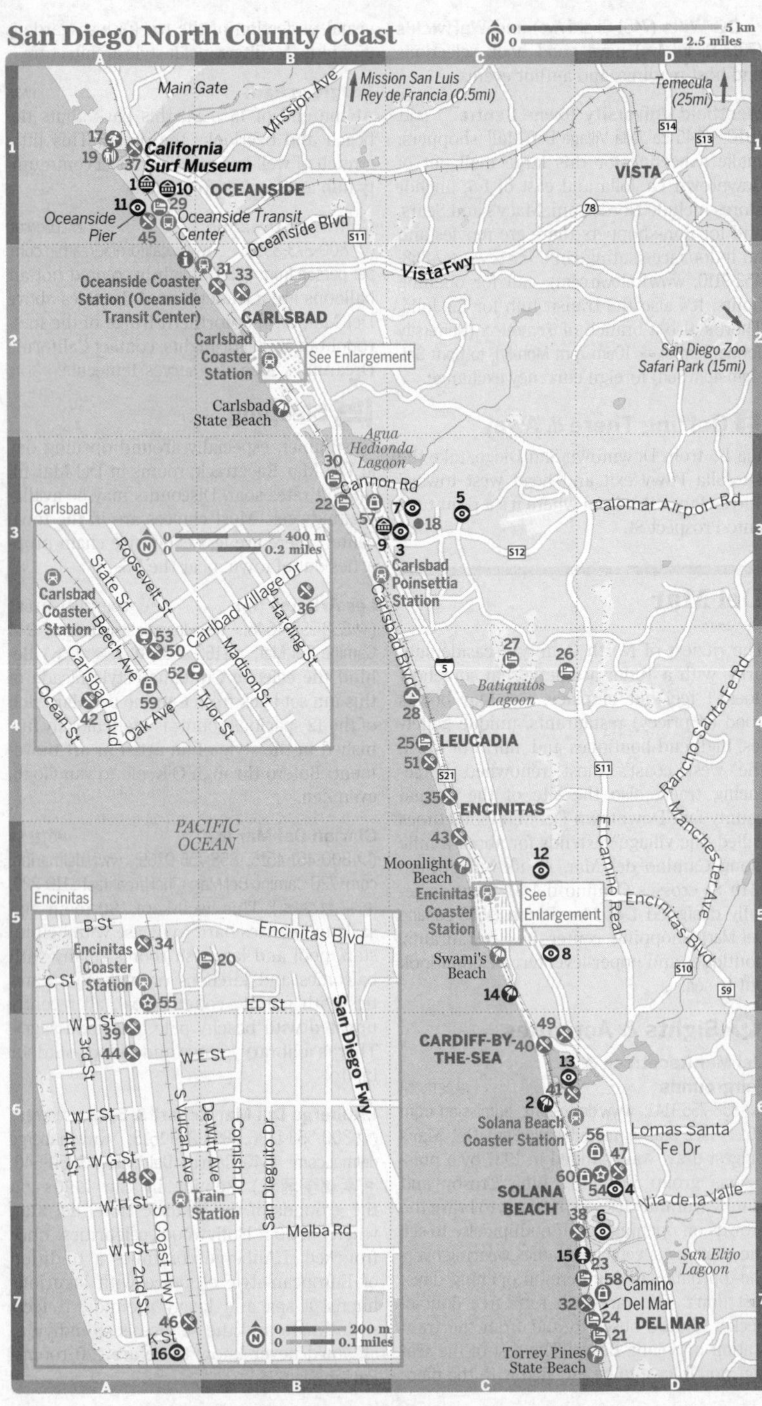

San Diego North County Coast

Top Sights

- 1 California Surf Museum A1

Sights

- 2 Cardiff State Beach C6
- 3 Carlsbad Ranch Flower Fields C3
- 4 Cedros Design District D6
- 5 Crossings at Carlsbad C3
- 6 Del Mar Racetrack & Fairgrounds D7
- 7 Legoland C3
- 8 Lux Art Institute C5
- 9 Museum of Making Music B3
- 10 Oceanside Museum of Art A1
- 11 Oceanside Pier A1
- 12 San Diego Botanic Garden C5
- 13 San Elijo Lagoon C6
- 14 San Elijo State Beach C5
- 15 Seagrove Park D7
- 16 Self-Realization Fellowship Retreat A7

Activities, Courses & Tours

- Asylum Surf .... (see 10)
- Chopra Center .... (see 26)
- 17 Helgren's A1
- 18 K1 Speed C3
- 19 Surfcamps USA A1

Sleeping

- 20 Best Western Encinitas Inn & Suites B5
- 21 Clarion Del Mar Inn D7
- 22 Hilton Carlsbad Oceanfront Resort & Spa B3
- Hotel Indigo San Diego Del Mar .... (see 21)
- 23 L'Auberge Del Mar Resort & Spa D7
- Legoland Hotel .... (see 7)
- 24 Les Artistes Inn D7
- 25 Leucadia Beach Inn C4
- 26 Omni La Costa Resort & Spa C4
- 27 Park Hyatt Aviara Resort C4
- San Elijo State Beach Campground .... (see 14)
- 28 South Carlsbad State Park Campground C4
- 29 Springhill Suites Oceanside Downtown A1
- 30 West Inn & Suites B3

Eating

- 31 101 Café B2
- 32 Americana D7
- 33 Beach Break Café B2
- 34 El Callejon A5
- En Fuego .... (see 32)
- 35 Fish 101 .... C4
- 36 French Pastry Cafe B3
- 37 Harbor Fish & Chips A1
- Hello Betty Fish House .... (see 29)
- Il Fornaio .... (see 58)
- 38 Jake's Del Mar C7
- 39 Kealani's A6
- 40 Ki's Restaurant C6
- 41 Las Olas C6
- 42 Las Olas A4
- Pacifica Del Mar .... (see 58)
- 43 Pannikin Coffee & Tea C5
- 44 Q'ero A6
- Rendezvous .... (see 58)
- 45 Ruby's Diner A1
- 46 Swami's Café A7
- That Boy Good .... (see 29)
- 47 Tony's Jacal D6
- 48 Trattoria I Trulli A6
- 49 Trattoria Positano C6
- 50 Vigilucci's Cucina Italiana A4
- Wild Note Café .... (see 54)
- 51 Yumeya Sake House C4
- Zel's .... (see 58)
- Zinc Café .... (see 54)

Drinking & Nightlife

- Daley Double .... (see 39)
- 52 Pizza Port A4
- 53 Relm A4

Entertainment

- 54 Belly Up D6
- 55 La Paloma Theatre A5

Shopping

- 56 Adventure 16 .... D6
- 57 Carlsbad Premium Outlets B3
- 58 Del Mar Plaza D7
- 59 Farenheit 451 .... A4
- 60 Leaping Lotus D6
- Solo .... (see 54)

Hotel Indigo San Diego Del Mar BOUTIQUE HOTEL $$$

(☎858-755-1501; www.hotelindigosddelmar.com; 710 Camino Del Mar; r from $199;) This collection of white-washed buildings with gray clay-tiled roofs, two pools, a spa and new fitness and business centers received a tip-to-toe renovation for 2014. Rooms boast hardwood floors, mosaic tile accents and horserace- and beach-inspired motifs. Some units have kitchenettes and distant ocean views, and Ocean View Bar & Grill serves breakfast, lunch and dinner.

Eating

Del Mar Village has a dozen-plus restaurants from historic to chef-driven along Camino del Mar. Or head to Del Mar Plaza (p323) to check out the rooftop patio and its upscale restaurants for North County's best vantage points, especially at sunset **Il Fornaio** (☎858-755-8876; mains lunch $11-19, dinner $13-27; ⏰11:30am-10pm Sun-Thu, to 11pm Fri & Sat) for pizzas, pastas, salads and steak; the futuristic **Pacifica Del Mar** (☎858-792-0476; mains lunch $11-18, dinner $19-35) with fresh seafood and inventive preparations (arrive by 6pm for two-course prix-fixe menu, $22); and **Rendezvous** (☎858-755-2669; mains lunch $8-12, dinner $12-17; ⏰11:30am-3pm daily, plus 4-9:30pm Sun-Thu, 4-10pm Fri & Sat), which despite the French name serves popular Chinese and Asian fusion dishes including pricey filet mignon ($28).

En Fuego MEXICAN **$$**

(☎858-792-6551; www.enfuegocantina.com; 1342 Camino Del Mar; mains $6-16; ⏰11:30am-midnight Sun-Thu, to 1am Fri & Sat) On the site of Del Mar's first restaurant, this airy, multilevel Nuevo Mexicano spot is both restaurant and bar. Specialties on the forward-thinking menu include *borracho* shrimp (sautéed in tequila), filet mignon rancheros and honey habanero chicken (in a sweet spicy glaze), with lots of indoor-outdoor space to enjoy them.

Zel's CALIFORNIAN **$$**

(☎858-755-0076; www.zelsdelmar.com; 1247 Camino Del Mar; mains lunch $9-15, dinner $9-24; ⏰11am-10pm Mon-Thu, 9am-midnight Sat, 9am-10pm Sun) Zel was a longstanding local merchant, and his grandson continues the family tradition of welcoming locals and visitors, over excellent flatbread pizzas (like chicken with asparagus, truffle oil, arugula and avocado), burgers of bison, quinoa or locally-raised beef, and lots of craft beers. Live music Thursday to Sunday.

Americana MODERN AMERICAN **$$**

(☎858-794-6838; 1454 Camino del Mar; mains breakfast & lunch $7-14, dinner $14-21; ⏰7am-3pm Sun & Mon, to 10pm Tue-Sat) This quietly chichi and much-loved local landmark serves a diverse lineup of regional American cuisine: cheese grits to chicken Reubens, sesame salmon on succotash to seared duck breast with Israeli couscous, plus artisan cocktails, all amid checkerboard linoleum floors, giant windows and homey wainscoting.

Jake's Del Mar SEAFOOD **$$$**

(☎858-755-2002; www.jakesdelmar.com; 1660 Coast Blvd; mains lunch $11-26, dinner $16-36; ⏰4-9pm Mon, 11:30am-9pm Tue-Fri, 11:30am-9:30pm Sat, 8am-9pm Sun) Head to this beachside classic for ocean-view drinks and half-price appetizers from 4pm to 6pm weekdays and 2:30pm to 4:30pm on Saturday. The view's great, the atmosphere chic and the food imaginative, like burrata and heirloom tomato salad, ahi tartare tacos and 'surfing steak' with herb grilled jumbo shrimp, sweet corn cream, sauteed spinach and truffle mash potatoes.

ℹ Getting There & Away

N Torrey Pines Rd from La Jolla is the most scenic approach from the south. Heading north, the road (S21) changes its name from Camino del Mar to Coast Hwy 101 to Old Hwy 101. If you're in a hurry or headed out of town, the faster I-5 parallels it to the east. Traffic can snarl everywhere during rush hour and race or fair season.

Solana Beach

POP 13,150

Solana Beach is the next town north from Del Mar – it's not as posh, but it has good beaches and lots of contemporary style, particularly in the **Cedros Avenue Design District** (Cedros Ave), four blocks where interior designers from all over the region come for inspiration and merchandise from buttons to bathrooms, paint to photographs and even garden supplies. Over 100 merchants fill **Leaping Lotus** (www.leapinglotus.com; 240 S Cedros Ave; ⏰10am-6pm Mon-Sat, 11am-6pm Sun), and the cavernous **Solo** (309 S Cedros Ave) sells design books, trinkets, furniture and accessories and has a design office. Other offerings include antiques shops, handcrafted-clothing boutiques, and camping and travel gear at **Adventure 16** (143 S Cedros Ave, Suite M)

The **Belly Up Tavern** (☎858-481-8140; www.bellyup.com; 143 S Cedros Ave, Solana Beach; tickets $10-45) is a converted warehouse and bar that consistently books good bands from jazz to funk, and big names like Aimee Mann to Merle Haggard and tribute bands. Its **Wild Note Café** (☎858-259-7310; 143 S Cedros Ave; mains lunch $9-16, dinner $13-25; ⏰11am-3pm Mon, to 9pm Tue-Thu, to 10pm Fri & Sat) serves upscale pub food and fancier fare such as Dijon-herb crusted salmon and brie burgers.

Across the street, order at the counter and sit outside at the minimalist, all-veg **Zinc Café** (☎858-793-5436; www.zinccafe.com; 132 S Cedros Ave; mains $6-11; ⏰7am-5pm; 🌱), which serves breakfasts, salads, burritos, quesadillas and pizza good enough to satisfy all but the most hardcore carnivores.

A short drive from the town center, **Tony's Jacal** (☎858-755-2274; www.tonys-jacal.com; 621 Valley Ave; mains $6-17; ⊙lunch & dinner, Wed-Mon), in business since 1946 (current building from the '60s), has rough-hewn wood beams, dark wood paneling, icy-delicious margaritas and some of North County's best traditional Mexican. Make reservations for dinner. (Valley Ave goes north of Via de la Valle, just west of I-5.)

Cardiff-by-the-Sea

POP 12,000

Beachy Cardiff is good for surfing and popular with a laid-back crowd. The town center has the perfunctory supermarkets and everyday shops along San Elijo Ave, about 0.25 miles from the ocean and across the railroad tracks, but the real action is the miles of restaurants and surf shops along Hwy 101.

San Elijo Lagoon OUTDOORS
(☎760-623-3026; www.sanelijo.org; 2710 Manchester Ave; ⊙nature center 9am-5pm) FREE One of the town's main draws is this 1000-acre ecological preserve popular with bird-watchers for its herons, coots, terns, ducks, egrets and more than 250 other species. A 7-mile network of trails leads through the area.

Cardiff State Beach BEACH
(www.parks.ca.gov; ⊙7am-sunset; P) Just south of Cardiff-by-the-Sea, the surf break on the reef here is mostly popular with long boarders, but it gets very good at low tide with a big north swell. Parking costs $10.

San Elijo State Beach BEACH
A little north of Cardiff State Beach, San Elijo State Beach has good winter waves and $10 parking.

Sleeping & Eating

San Elijo State Beach Campground CAMPGROUND $
(☎760-753-5091, reservations 800-444-7275; www.parks.ca.gov; 2050 S Coast Hwy 101; summer tent/RV sites from $35/55) Overlooks the surf at the end of Birmingham Dr.

★**Las Olas** MEXICAN $$
(☎760-942-1860; www.lasolasmex.com; 2655 S Coast Hwy 101, Cardiff-by-the-Sea; mains $9-19; ⊙11am-9pm Mon-Thu, to 9:30pm Fri, 10am-9:30pm Sat, 10am-9pm Sun;) For fish tacos with a sea view, Las Olas is so popular it has its own traffic light, right across the street from the beach. Lobster is served in the style of the legendary Baja lobster village Puerto Nuevo. House cocktails include pineapple and chili margaritas and drinks made with RIP (rum infused with pineapple). Happy hour until 6pm daily.

Ki's Restaurant CALIFORNIAN $$
(☎760-436-5236; 2591 S Coast Hwy 101; mains breakfast $5-9, lunch $7-14, dinner $13-22; ⊙8am-8:30pm Sun-Thu, to 10pm Fri, 9pm Sat; P) Across from the beach, Ki's is an organic cafe-restaurant and a hub of local activity. At the juice bar on the first floor are awesome smoothies, healthy burgers, salads, tacos and butternut squash and corn enchiladas. Upstairs there's a great ocean view from the sit-down restaurant and bar, where from 4:30pm daily fancier dishes like Jidori chicken or macadamia-coated mahimahi with Thai peanut sauce are served with ingredients from nearby family farms.

Trattoria Positano ITALIAN $$$
(☎760-632-0111; 2171 San Elijo Ave; mains $16-34; ⊙lunch Mon-Sat, dinner daily) Its streetside storefront looks rather plain from the outside, but inside this shop run by three sisters is awash with warm tones and white-tablecloth service. The garlicky tomato sauce for your bread is addictive, as is *caterinelli* pasta with Kobe beef and porcini mushrooms.

Encinitas

POP 61,000

Peaceful Encinitas has a decidedly down-to-earth vibe and a laid-back, beach-town main street, perfect for a relaxing day trip or weekend escape. North of central Encinitas, yet still part of the city, is **Leucadia**, a leafy stretch of N Hwy 101 with a hippie vibe of used clothing stores and taco shops.

Sights & Activities

Self-Realization Fellowship Retreat RETREAT
(☎760-753-1811; www.yogananda-srf.org; 215 K St; ⊙meditation garden 9am-5pm Tue-Sat, 11am-5pm Sun) FREE Yogi Paramahansa Yogananda founded his center here in 1937, and the town has been a magnet for holistic healers and natural-lifestyle seekers ever since. The gold lotus domes of the hermitage – conspicuous on South Coast Hwy 101 – mark the southern end of Encinitas and the turn-out for **Swami's Beach**, a powerful reef break

surfed by territorial locals. The fellowship's compact but lovely **Meditation Garden** has wonderful ocean vistas, a stream and koi pond. If you're interested in more detailed exploration of meditation and the religion's principles, visit the website.

San Diego Botanic Garden GARDEN
(www.sdbgarden.org; 230 Quail Gardens Drive; adult/child/senior $14/8/10; 9am-5pm;) This 30-acre garden has a large collection of California native plants and flora of different regions of the world, including Australia and Central America. There are special activities in the children's garden (10am Tuesday to Thursday); check the website for a schedule. From I-5, go east on Encinitas Blvd to turn left on Quail Gardens Dr.

Lux Art Institute ART CENTER
(www.luxartinstitute.org; 1550 S El Camino Real; 2-visit admission $5; 1-5pm Thu & Fri, 11am-5pm Sat;) A few miles east of central Encinitas, this new institute lets spectators be present at the creation of art. A changing lineup of artists in residence take turns crafting major pieces, from concept to construction, while spectators watch in the 'green' studio building. Creative types will want to make a beeline. From Encinitas, take Encinitas Blvd east and turn right onto S El Camino Real, for about 1.3 miles.

Sleeping & Eating

Central Encinitas

Best Western Encinitas Inn & Suites MOTEL $$
(760-942-7455, 866-236-4648; www.bwencinitas.com; 85 Encinitas Blvd; r incl breakfast from $169;) Atop a hill between the freeway, shopping center and Coast Hwy is this hexagonal hotel, a few minutes on foot from the sand. Design is nothing fancy, but it's well kept, all rooms have balconies and suites have kitchenettes and sleep sofas. Some rooms have ocean or park views.

Kealani's HAWAIIAN $
(760-942-5642; 137 W D St; mains $5-8; 11am-6pm Mon & Wed, to 8pm Tue & Thu-Sat) Traditional Hawaiian plate lunches such as *kalbi* ribs, *kalua* pig, teriyaki chicken and grilled mahimahi (get the side of macaroni salad!) are the thing in this cheery storefront with booths like little grass shacks and tables decorated with glossaries of Hawaiian slang.

Swami's Café CAFE $
(760-944-0612; 1163 S Coast Hwy 101; mains $5-10; 7am-5pm;) This local institution can't be beat for breakfast burritos, multigrain pancakes, stir-fries, salads, smoothies and three-egg *ohm*-lettes (sorry, we couldn't resist). Vegetarians will be satisfied too. Most of the seating is out on an umbrella-covered patio. It's across from the Self-Realization Fellowship.

El Callejon MEXICAN $$
(760-634-2793; www.el-callejon.com; 345 S Coast Hwy 101; mains $9-22; 11am-9pm Mon-Thu, to 11pm Fri, 10am-11pm Sat, 10am-9pm Sun;) A raucous, fun, local favorite, this indoor-outdoor candy-colored cantina is at the north end of the town center. The menu is as long as the phone book of a small village, and it would take you over two years of trying a different tequila every day to go through their tequila list.

★**Trattoria I Trulli** ITALIAN $$
(760-943-6800; www.trattoriaitrullisd.com; 830 S Coast Hwy 101; mains lunch $13-21, dinner $14-26; 11:30am-2:30pm daily, 5-10pm Sun-Thu, to 10:30pm Fri & Sat) Country-style seating indoors and great people-watching on the sidewalk. Just one taste of the homemade gnocchi, ravioli or lasagna, salmon in brandy mustard sauce or *pollo uno zero uno* (101; chicken stuffed with cheese, spinach and artichokes in mushroom sauce) and you'll know why this mom-and-pop Italian trattoria is always packed. Reservations recommended.

Q'ero PERUVIAN $$
(760-753-9050; 540 S Coast Hwy 101; mains lunch $6-18, dinner $19-26; 11am-3pm & 5-9pm Mon-Thu, to 10pm Fri, 11:30am-11pm Sat) The flavors of Peru tempt from this tiny, atmospheric storefront festooned with Peruvian art and iconography. Try small plates like ceviche or *papa rellena* (potato inside ground beef), or mains like *lomo saltado* of Kobe beef or *aji gallina* (chicken in toasted walnut and chili sauce). Reservations recommended at dinner.

North Encinitas & Leucadia

Leucadia Beach Inn MOTEL $
(760-943-7461; www.leucadiabeachinn.org; 1322 N Coast Hwy; r $85-145;) All the sparkling-clean rooms in this charming 1920s courtyard motel have tile floors and bright paint jobs, and many have kitchenettes. The beach is a few blocks' walk. No phones or

internet access from rooms. It's across Hwy 101 from the train tracks, so light sleepers should take earplugs or look elsewhere.

Pannikin Coffee & Tea CAFE $
(760-436-0033; mains $4-8; 6am-6pm) In a sunny-yellow wooden building that used to be the Encinitas train station (transported from its original site), Pannikin is an adorable sprawl of nooks, crannies, balconies and lawns. Muffins and coffees are wonderful, natch, and bagel and lox with steamed scrambled eggs is very attractive indeed. The kitchen closes at 3pm weekdays, 4pm weekends.

★**Fish 101** SEAFOOD $$
(760-634-6221; www.fish101restaurant.com; 1468 N Coast Hwy 101; mains $10-19) In this roadside shack all growed up, order at the counter, sidle into a butcher block or picnic table, sip craft beer, wine or Mexican Coke from a Mason jar and use paper towels to wipe your face. Simple grilling techniques allow the fresh catch's natural flavors to show through, and healthy rice-bran oil is used for deep frying.

Yumeya Sake House JAPANESE $$
(760-633-4288; 1246 N Coast Hwy 101; dishes $3-11; from 5:30pm Tue-Sat) This simple stucco and bamboo box of an *izakaya* (Japanese pub) has loyal fans thanks to its large assortment of small plates: tempura, *kushi-katsu* (fried meats on skewers), udon noodles and small plates like black cod with miso and bay scallops with *shimeji* mushrooms. There's a great sake selection, Japanese beers and *shochu* (Japanese distilled spirit), all with a cheery reggae soundtrack.

Drinking & Nightlife

Daley Double DIVE BAR
(546 S Coast Hwy 101) Once Encinitas' most notorious dive bar, it's now Encinitas' hippest dive bar. Fantastic Old West saloon-style murals make a great backdrop for good old-fashioned sipping and flirting. Expect a line out the door on weekends.

Entertainment

La Paloma Theatre THEATER
(760-436-7469; www.lapalomatheatre.com; 471 S Coast Hwy 101) Built in 1928, this landmark (and central Encinitas' main venue) shows arthouse movies nightly and *Rocky Horror* on Fridays at midnight, and stages occasional concerts.

Carlsbad

POP 109,000

Most visitors come to Carlsbad for Legoland and head right back out, and that's too bad because they've missed the charming, intimate Carlsbad Village with shopping, dining and beaching nearby. It's bordered by I-5 and Carlsbad Blvd, which run north–south and are connected by Carlsbad Village Dr running east–west.

Carlsbad came into being with the railroad in the 1880s. John Frazier, an early homesteader, sank a well and found water that had a high mineral content, supposedly identical to that of spa water in Karlsbad, Bohemia (now in the Czech Republic). He built a grand Queen Anne–style spa hotel, which prospered until the 1930s and is now a local landmark.

If you've come looking for Carlsbad Caverns, you're outta luck. Those are in New Mexico.

Sights & Activities

Carlsbad has a number of attractions outside the village and Legoland areas. You pretty much need a car to reach them, and it's best to phone for directions since they can be hard to find.

Legoland THEME PARK
(760-918-5346; http://california.legoland.com; 1 Legoland Dr, Carlsbad; adult/child from $83/73; daily mid-Mar–Aug, Wed-Sun Sep–mid-Mar; P) A fantasy environment built largely of those little colored plastic blocks from Denmark. Many rides and attractions are targeted to elementary schoolers: a junior 'driving school', a jungle cruise lined with Lego animals, wacky 'sky cruiser' pedal cars on a track, and fairytale, princess, pirate, adventurer and dino-themed escapades. If you have budding scientists (age 10 and over) with you, sign them up on arrival at the park for an appointment for **Mindstorms**, where they can make computerized Lego robots. There are also lots of low-thrill activities like face-painting and princess-meeting.

The whole family will probably get a kick out of **Miniland**, recreating the skylines of New York, Washington, DC, San Francisco and Las Vegas entirely of Lego blocks, alongside many world monuments. New York's 25ft Freedom Tower (to replace the World Trade Center) was built according to the real winning design, years before the actual building will be complete. Adjacent are amazing *Star Wars* models.

Compared with some of the bigger, flashier theme parks such as Disneyland and SeaWorld, Legoland is rather low-key and far less commercial – though there are plenty of opportunities to buy Lego. At least it sparks creativity.

One could easily spend an entire day at Legoland (not least because of long lines to get into some of the more popular attractions); a second day of admission costs $20. Just adjacent are the **Sea Life Aquarium** (in which real sea creatures swim among Lego creations) and **Legoland Water Park**. A new **Chima Water Park**, themed after the Cartoon Network's Legends of Chima collaboration with Lego, was set to open as we went to press, with rides and waterways evoking the characters.

There are many ways to visit Legoland parks, each at a different price point. The most expensive two-day 'Resort Hopper' combination ticket (adult/child $127/117) gives two-day admission for all three main attractions. Check the website and tourist kiosks for other discount opportunities, extended summer peak hours and occasional closures September to May.

From I-5, take the Legoland/Cannon Rd exit and follow the signage. Parking is $15. By public transit, take the *Coaster* commuter train to Carlsbad Village Station; from here bus 321 operated by **North County Transit District** (www.gonctd.com; ticket $2, 20 mins; 7:55am, 8:55am & 9:55am Mon-Fri) stops at the park.

Carlsbad Coast BEACHES

Carlsbad's long, sandy beaches are great for walking and searching for seashells. Good access is from Carlsbad Blvd, two blocks south of Carlsbad Village Dr, where there's a boardwalk, rest rooms and free parking.

Carlsbad Ranch Flower Fields GARDEN

(760-431-0352; www.theflowerfields.com; 5704 Paseo del Norte; adult/child $12/6; usually 9am-6pm Mar–mid-May; P) The 50-acre flower fields of Carlsbad Ranch are ablaze in a sea of the carmine, saffron and snow-white blossoms of ranunculuses. Take the Palomar Airport Rd exit off of I-5, head east and turn left on Paseo del Norte. Outside of the official season, there are some rose gardens on the site which, depending on the condition of the blooms, may be accessed via the Armstrong Garden Center next door.

Batiquitos Lagoon NATURE PARK

(760-931-0800; www.batiquitosfoundation.org; 7380 Gabbiano Ln; nature center 9am-12:30pm Mon-Fri, to 3pm Sat & Sun) One of the last remaining tidal wetlands in California, Batiquitos Lagoon separates Carlsbad from Encinitas. A self-guided tour lets you explore area plants, including the prickly pear cactus, coastal sage scrub and eucalyptus trees, as well as lagoon birds such as the great heron and the snowy egret. One artificial island in the lagoon is a nesting site for the endangered terns and plovers. You can hike the reserve anytime, but stop by the Nature Center if it's open.

Museum of Making Music MUSEUM

(www.museumofmakingmusic.com; 5790 Armada Dr; adult/child & senior $8/5; 10am-5pm Tue-Sun) Historical exhibits and listening stations of 450 instruments from the 1890s to the present, from manufacturing to the distribution of popular music.

Crossings at Carlsbad GOLF

(www.thecrossingsatcarlsbad.com; 5800 the Crossings Dr) Carlsbad is an important center for golf; some major equipment manufacturers are based here including Titleist and Taylor Made. This course is a 6850-yard municipal course, and the Park Hyatt Aviara and La Costa resorts both have landmark golf courses.

Chopra Center MIND-BODY CENTER

(www.chopra.com; 2013 Costa del Mar Rd, Omni La Costa Resort & Spa) Slow down with alternative-health guru Deepak Chopra, who leads seminars on mind-body medicine, complemented by specialized spa treatments, at this center at Omni La Costa Resort & Spa (p331).

K1 Speed INDOOR KARTING

(www.k1speed.com; Corte Del Abeto; 14-lap race $20; noon-10pm Mon-Thu, 11am-11pm Fri, 10am-11pm Sat, 10am-8pm Sun) To pick up the pace, this place fills your need for speed with indoor karting (electric drag racing). They supply all the necessary equipment including helmet and 'head socks;' first-timers must purchase a special license ($6 extra) It's in an office park east of I-5; inquire about midweek discounts.

Sleeping

If you're looking for a budget stay, there are numerous motels near the freeway.

WORTH A TRIP

SAN DIEGO ZOO SAFARI PARK

Since the early 1960s, the San Diego Zoological Society has been developing this 1800-acre **open-range zoo** (☎760-747-8702; www.sdzsafaripark.org; 15500 San Pasqual Valley Rd; adult/child from $44/34, 2-day ticket incl San Diego Zoo $79/61; ⏰9am-7pm late Jun–mid-Aug, to 5pm or 6pm mid-Aug–late Jun; P), where herds of giraffes, zebras, rhinos and other animals roam the open valley floor. For an instant safari feel, board the **Africa Tram** ride, which tours you around the second-largest continent in under half an hour.

Elsewhere, animals are in enclosures so naturalistic it's as if the humans are guests, and there's a petting krall and animal shows; pick up a map and schedule. Additional 'safaris,' like zip-lining, a chance to observe a cheetah whiz by while chasing a mechanical rabbit, and even sleepovers (yowza!) are available with reservations and additional payment (from $45).

The park's just north of Hwy 78, 5 miles east of I-15 from the Via Rancho Pkwy exit. Parking is $10. Plan on 45 minutes transit by car from San Diego, except in rush hour when that figure can double. For bus information contact **North San Diego County Transit District** (☎619-233-3004, from North County 800-266-6883; www.gonctd.com).

South Carlsbad State Park Campground CAMPGROUND $
(☎760-438-3143, reservations 800-444-7275; www.reserveamerica.com; 7201 Carlsbad Blvd; ocean-/street-side campsites $50/35; P) Three miles south of town and sandwiched between Carlsbad Blvd and the beach, this campground has over 200 tent and RV sites.

★ **Legoland Hotel** HOTEL $$$
(☎877-534-6526, 760-918-5346; california.legoland.com/legoland-hotel; 5885 the Crossings Dr; r incl breakfast from $369; P) Lego designers were let loose on this hotel, just outside Legoland's main gate, and boy is it fun: 3500 Lego models (dragons to surfers) populate the property, and the elevator turns into a disco between floors. Each floor has its own theme (pirate, adventure, kingdom), down to the rooms' wallpaper, props (Lego cannonballs – cool!), even the shower curtains.

It's tailor-made for little ones, from kid-size bunk beds and junior level peepholes in the doors, to bedtime stories in the lobby and bin after bin of the bricks to play with. Meanwhile, there's a nice bar for moms and dads. The breakfast buffet includes healthy options. Rates cover parking.

Hilton Carlsbad Oceanfront Resort & Spa RESORT HOTEL $$$
(☎760-602-0800; www.carlsbadoceanfrontresortandspa.hilton.com; 1 Ponto Rd; r from $249; P) Most of Carlsbad's top lodgings are inland, but this swanky new spot (opened 2012) is an easy walk to the ocean across Hwy 101. Pools, spa, business and fitness centers will keep you busy on land. Chandler's restaurant serves three squares, including creative dinners like falafel crabcakes and diver scallops with artichokes and smoked almonds. Parking costs $19.

It's about 4 miles south of Carlsbad Village and west of Legoland, separated from the ocean by the campground.

Omni La Costa Resort & Spa RESORT $$$
(☎760-438-9111, 800-854-5000; www.lacosta.com; 2100 Costa Del Mar Rd; r from $300; P) Splurge-worthy La Costa offers a 400-acre, whitewashed 600-room campus overlooking Batiquitos Lagoon. It's got two PGA golf courses, excellent children's programs including pools with multiple slides, nursery and educational programming. Venues for grownups include the stunning spa and Chopra Center, lovely restaurants and a touch of Hollywood history. Check for discounted packages. Free self-parking.

West Inn & Suites HOTEL $$$
(☎866-431-9378, 760-448-4500; www.westinnandsuites.com; 4970 Avenida Encinas; r incl breakfast $159-359; P) About halfway between Legoland and Carlsbad Village, this hyper-friendly independently run, 86-room inn caters to both business travelers (note business and fitness centers) and vacationing families (note the sparkling pool, beach and Legoland shuttle service and nightly milk and cookies). You'd think you'd be paying a lot more as you enjoy your king-size bed, fresh orchids, Aveda bath products and 30in flat-screen TV. Free parking.

Park Hyatt Aviara Resort RESORT $$$
(760-603-6800; www.parkhyattaviara.com; 7100 Aviara Resort Dr; r from $249;) From the marble bathrooms in sumptuous suites to the luxurious fitness center and the Aviara Kids Academy programs, this tippy-top resort offers superb service and top-flight amenities, golf, tennis, the 15,000 Aviara Spa and more. The Argyle steakhouse is worth a trip by itself. Aviara looks out over Batiquitos Lagoon and offers discounted packages. Parking costs $35.

Eating & Drinking

State St just north of Carlsbad Village Dr is Carlsbad's most charming stretch, with a number of restaurants worth browsing.

For a luxury experience, also check out the restaurants at Omni La Costa Resort & Spa and Park Hyatt Aviara Resort. At the other end of the scale are the brew pub Pizza Port (p309), and the local branch of **Las Olas** (760-434-5850; 2939 Carlsbad Blvd).

French Pastry Cafe BAKERY, CAFE $
(760-729-2241; 1005 Carlsbad Village Dr; mains $6; 7am-6pm;) Its location may be in a drab-looking shopping center just off I-5, but it's the real deal for croissants and brioches baked daily and kick-start espresso, plus omelettes, salads and sandwiches until 2:30pm.

Vigilucci's Cucina Italiana ITALIAN $$
(760-434-2500; 2943 State St; mains lunch $8-18, dinner $15-32; 11am-10pm) There's white-tablecloth service and a lovely sidewalk terrace at this State St institution. For lunch try pastas or panini (the one with parma ham and portobello mushrooms is a fave), while dinner might be pappardelle with field mushrooms and seared diver scallops in white truffle and brandy cream sauce, or linguine alla Luciana (with baby calamari, garlic and tomato sauce).

Relm WINE BAR
(760-434-9463; www.thewinerelm.com; 2917 State St; from 4pm Tue-Sun) This cozy, modernist storefront pours from over 60 bottles (wine flights $12) and serves cheeseboards and flatbreads to go with them. When they have live music, it's irresistible.

Shopping

Carlsbad Premium Outlets OUTLET SHOPPING
(www.premiumoutlets.com; Paseo del Norte; 10am-8pm) Big-name retailers such as Calvin Klein and Coach and purveyors of cookware to fashion blue jeans have off-price boutiques among the 90 shops here. It's less than 1 mile southeast of the Cannon Rd exit off I-5.

Farenheit 451 BOOKS
(www.farenheit451books.com; 325 Carlsbad Village Dr) This is an honest-to-goodness, old-style bookshop, selling mainly used books, including rare and first editions in plastic sleeves. They even have a no-cell-phone policy; bless their hearts.

Information

Carlsbad Visitors Center (760-434-6093; www.visitcarlsbad.com; 400 Carlsbad Village Dr) Housed in the original 1887 Santa Fe train depot.

Oceanside

POP 171,000

The largest North County town, Oceanside is home to many who work at giant Camp Pendleton Marine Base just to the north. The huge military presence mixes with an attractive natural setting, surf shops and head shops and a downtown that's slowly revitalizing.

Little remains from the 1880s streetscape, when the new Santa Fe coastal railway came through Oceanside, but a few buildings designed by Irving Gill and Julia Morgan still stand. The Welcome Center has a pamphlet describing a self-guided history walk.

Sights & Activities

Oceanside Pier PIER
This wooden pier extends more than 1900ft out to sea. Bait-and-tackle shops rent poles (per hr/day $5/15) to the many anglers who line its wooden fences. Two major surf competitions – the West Coast Pro-Am and the National Scholastic Surf Association (NSSA) – take place near the pier each June.

★**California Surf Museum** MUSEUM
(www.surfmuseum.org; 312 Pier View Way; adult/student/child $5/3/free, Tue free; 10am-4pm Fri-Wed, to 8pm Thu) It's easy to spend an hour in this heartfelt museum of surf artifacts, from a timeline of surfing history to surf-themed art and a radical collection of boards, including the one chomped by a shark when it ate the arm of surfer Bethany Hamilton. Special exhibits change frequently along different themes (eg women of surfing).

Oceanside Museum of Art MUSEUM
(www.oma-online.org; 704 Pier View Way; adult/senior/student $8/5/3; ⏲10am-4pm Tue-Sat, 1-4pm Sun) This museum underwent a recent revamp and it now stands at an impressive 16,000 sq ft in a modernist, white shell. There are about 10 rotating exhibits a year, with an emphasis on SoCal artists (especially from the San Diego region) and local cultures.

Mission San Luis Rey de Francia MISSION
(www.sanluisrey.org; 4050 Mission Ave; adult/child/senior $5/4/4; ⏲10am-4pm) About 4.5 miles inland from central Oceanside, this was the largest California mission and the most successful in recruiting Native American converts. At one point some 3000 neophytes lived and worked here. After the Mexican government secularized the missions, San Luis fell into ruin; the adobe walls of the church, from 1811, are the only original parts left. Inside are displays on work and life in the mission, with some original religious art and artifacts.

Helgren's BOAT CHARTERS
(☎760-722-2133; www.helgrensportfishing.com; 315 Harbor Dr S) At the northern end of town, Oceanside's extensive harbor is home to hundreds of boats. This outfit leads a variety of charter trips for sportfishing (from $55 per half-day) and whale-watching (adult/child $35/20). Phone ahead for details and reservations.

Asylum Surf SURF HIRE
(www.asylumboardshop.com; 310 Mission Ave; surfboards 3hr/full day $20/30, wetsuits $10/15) Surfers can rent equipment here.

Surfcamps USA SURFING
(www.surfcampsusa.com; 1202 N Pacific St; lessons per person from $55; 🚸) Newbies and not-so-newbies can take two-hour private or group lessons from this popular operator. All equipment is included.

Sleeping & Eating

★Springhill Suites Oceanside Downtown HOTEL $$$
(☎760-722-1003; www.shsoceanside.com; 110 N Myers St; r incl breakfast $219-279; P ⊖ @ ≋ ≋) Brand new for 2014, this modern, six-story, ocean-view hotel is awash in summery yellows and sea blues in the lobby. Rooms have crisp lines and distressed-wood headboards, and ocean- and pier-view rooms have balconies or patios. Best views are from the pool and hot tub on the top floor, where there's also a fitness center. Hot breakfast buffet included. Parking is $24.

Harbor Fish & Chips SEAFOOD $
(☎760-722-4977; 276 Harbor Dr S; mains $7-13; ⏲11am-9pm Sun-Thu, to 10pm Fri & Sat; P 🚸) Nuthin' fancy about this harborside chippie from the '60s, but when the fish is fried to a deep crackle and you eat it at a picnic table on the dock while classic pop tunes play on the radio, you still feel pretty good. There's a large local following and taxidermied catches on the walls.

Beach Break Café CAFE $
(☎760-439-6355; 1802 S Coast Hwy; mains $7-12; ⏲7am-2pm; P 🚸) Fuel up before surfing on omelettes, scrambles and pancakes, or afterwards on sandwiches, tacos and salads at this surfers' diner on the east side of the road. A second location by the harbor (280 Harbor Dr) serves the same menu in a stellar setting.

101 Café DINER $
(☎760-722-5220; 631 S Coast Hwy; mains $6-10; ⏲7am-2pm; P 🚸) This tiny 1928 streamline moderne diner serves the classics: omelettes, burgers etc. If you're lucky, you'll catch the owner and can quiz him about local history.

Ruby's Diner DINER $
(☎760-433-7829; 1 Oceanside Pier; mains $8-14; ⏲7am-9pm Sun-Thu, to 10pm Fri & Sat; 🚸) This midpriced '50s-style diner has good burgers and milkshakes, big breakfasts and a full bar. Yes, it's a chain, but it's right at the end of the pier.

Hello Betty Fish House SEAFOOD $$
(☎760-722-1008; www.hellobettyoceanside.com; 211 Mission Ave; mains $10-24; ⏲11am-10pm Sun-Thu, to 11pm Fri & Sat) This new beachfront spot opened in 2014 and locals already love its Baja stone crab and cheese dip, fried and grilled tacos (from $4.50) and salmon burger with Asian slaw and wasabi aioli. Grilled fish platters and other large plates run up to $24. Not to mention O'side's best views from the bar and deck.

That Boy Good BARBECUE $$
(TBG; ☎760-433-4227; www.tbgbbq.com; 207 N Coast Hwy; mains $9-25; ⏲from 4pm Mon, 11am Tue-Sun) This new shrine to the Mississippi Delta serves belly-busting portions of fried chicken and waffles, pork ribs and the Crossroads Cup (baked beans, mac 'n' cheese and coleslaw topped with your choice

of meat). Wash it all down with a craft or canned beer or the BBQ Bloody Mary, topped with a rib.

Walls are hewn from salvaged wood, there are sofas for lounging and the game on TV.

Information

California Welcome Center (☎760-721-1101, 800-350-7873; www.visitoceanside.org; 928 N Coast Hwy; ⏰9am-5pm) Helpful, informative staff dispense coupons for local attractions, as well as maps and information for the San Diego area and the entire state, and can book lodging in Oceanside. It's just off the freeway exit.

Getting There & Away

Oceanside Transit Center (235 S Tremont St) Buses and trains all stop here.

TEMECULA AREA

Temecula

POP 100, 097

Temecula has become a popular short-break destination for its Old West Americana main street, nearly two dozen wineries, and California's largest casino, Pechanga.

Temecula means 'Place of the Sun' in the language of the native Luiseño people, who were present when Fr Fermin Lasuen became the first Spanish missionary to visit in 1797. In the 1820s the area became a ranching outpost for the Mission San Luis Rey, in present-day Oceanside. Later, Temecula became a stop on the Butterfield stagecoach line (1858–61) and the California Southern railroad.

But it's Temecula's late-20th-century growth that's been most astonishing, from 2700 people in 1970 – the city didn't get its first traffic light until 1984 – to some 100,000 residents today. Between Old Town and the wineries is an off-putting, 3 mile buffer zone of suburban housing developments and shopping centers. Ignore that and you'll do fine.

Temecula is in the southeast corner of Riverside County, near San Diego and Orange Counties. The five-block Old Town Front St, heart of Old Town Temecula, is a minute's drive from the I-15 Freeway. From here, Rancho California Rd is the main route into wine country.

Sights & Activities

Front St HISTORIC DISTRICT

Old Town Front St's turn-of-the-last-century storefronts and wooden sidewalks make for an attractive stroll – pick up the *Historic Old Town Temecula* leaflet with building descriptions. En route, sample local agricultural bounty at shops like **Temecula Olive Oil Company** (www.temeculaoliveoil.com; 28653 Old Town Front St; ⏰9:30am-6pm) and **Front Street Jerky** (www.frontstreetjerky.com; 28655 Old Town Front St). The latter offers ostrich, buffalo, venison and more traditional beasties. Hundreds of **antique dealers** populate the neighborhood, most agglomerated into large antique halls.

Temecula Valley Museum MUSEUM

(☎909-694-6450; 28314 Mercedes St; admission $2; ⏰10am-4pm Tue-Sat, 1-4pm Sun; Ⓟ) Just off Old Town Front St, this one-room museum tells the history of the region from the Luiseño people through the Spanish period (look for the ancient bible and folk-art cross) and stagecoach times, plus a scale model of the Mission San Luis Rey (p333).

Wine Country

Wine tasting is big in the rolling hills east of Old Town, about 10 minutes' drive away. The newness of the wineries and the preponderance of large gift shops make them less quaint than elsewhere in California, but you can find award-winning and creative wines.

Wilson Creek WINERY

(www.wilsoncreekwinery.com; 35960 Rancho California Rd; tasting Mon-Fri $15, Sat & Sun $20; ⏰10am-5pm) This place makes almond champagne (infused with almond oil in the fermentation process) and a chocolate-infused port.

Longshadow Ranch WINERY

(www.longshadowranchwinery.com; 39847 Calle Contento; tasting $15; ⏰noon-5pm Mon-Fri, 10am-5pm Sat & Sun; 👪) A nice stop if you've got children in tow; the kids can look at Clydesdales while mommy and daddy sip.

Leonesse Cellars WINERY

(www.leonessecellars.com; 38311 De Portola Rd; tasting $15; ⏰11am-5pm) Further afield, this place offers award-winning viognier and melange des reves, plus sweeping views from its sort-of-Teutonic tower.

WORTH A TRIP

PALOMAR OBSERVATORY

High on Palomar Mountain, at an elevation of 5500ft to avoid light pollution, the **Palomar Observatory** (760-742-2119; www.astro.caltech.edu/palomar; 35899 Canfield Rd; 9am-4pm, to 3pm early Nov–mid-Mar; P) FREE is simply spectacular – as large as Rome's Pantheon, with a classic design dating from the 1930s. Run by Pasadena's prestigious California Institute of Technology (p196), it houses five telescopes including the 200in Hale Telescope, once the world's largest. On weekends, visitors can take guided tours. Bring a fleece jacket – temperatures inside the observatory hover just above freezing during cooler months.

The observatory is between Temecula and Julian. From San Diego/Temecula, take the I-15 north/south to the Pala exit, and turn into Hwy 76 eastbound. After about 20 miles, turn left onto County Rd S6, aka South Grade Rd, which climbs 11.5 miles up Palomar Mountain. Call ahead to check road conditions and opening hours before making the long, winding drive here.

Grapeline Temecula TRANSPORTATION, TOURS
(888-894-6379; www.gogrape.com; shuttle service/tours from $69/89) To leave the driving to someone else, this outfit offers day-long wine shuttles and tours among the vineyards by minivan, with pickup at many of the area's lodgings.

California Dreamin' HOT-AIR BALLOONING
(800-373-3359; www.californiadreamin.com; per person from $148) To see the region from the air, contact this outfit which operates hot-air balloon rides.

Sleeping

Palomar Inn Hotel HISTORIC $
(951-676-6503; www.palomarinntemecula.com; 28522 Old Town Front St; r weekday/weekend from $65/99; P) In the heart of Old Town, this 1927 10-room hostelry feels like a rooming house in the Old West. Eight of the rooms have shared bathrooms, and the other two have private bath and kitchenette. Rooms sleep up to four, and the location is primo.

Temecula Creek Inn RESORT, GOLF $$
(888-976-3404; www.temeculacreekinn.com; 44501 Rainbow Canyon Rd; r Sun-Thu from $119, Fri & Sat from $189; P) Wake up to a view of the 27-hole golf course at this lush, green campus-style resort a few miles from Old Town. The Corkfire Kitchen restaurant sources from local farms for its new American dishes (*huevos* Benedict for breakfast, with chorizo and corn bread) and has an extensive whisky program, plus wines of course. Even breakfast syrup is aged in bourbon barrels.

South Coast Winery Resort & Spa HOTEL $$$
(951-587-9463; www.wineresort.com; 34843 Rancho California Rd; r $199-329, plus resort fee per room $18; P) A very Temecula way to stay – 76 villa rooms dot the edge of the vineyards, around a spa, fitness facility and new 50-suite hotel (opened 2013). Your room key comes with a wine glossary, and rates include a bottle of wine. Tastings are $15/20 weekdays/weekends.

Eating & Drinking

Mad Madeline's Grill BURGERS, BARBECUE $
(951-669-3776; www.madmadelinesgrill.com; 28495 Old Town Front St; mains $8-13; 11am-5pm Mon-Thu, to 9pm Fri & Sat, to 7pm Sun; P) Award-winning burgers (served about 20 ways) are the thing in this cheerful red-and-white wooden roadhouse in the center of Old Town, plus onion rings worth breaking your diet for. On Fridays nights, look for smoked baby-back ribs too.

Bank of Mexican Food MEXICAN $
(951-676-6160; 28645 Old Town Front St; mains $7-13; 11am-9pm Mon-Thu, to midnight Fri, 8am-10am Sat & Sun) In this handsome former bank (c 1913), try mahi tacos, huevos rancheros or anything with the righteous Mexican rice. A patio bar stays open until late.

Swing Inn Cafe DINER $$
(951 676 2321; www.swinginncafe.com; 28676 Old Town Front St; mains $7-13; 5am-9pm) A proud local institution since 1927, with red leatherette seating and windows to watch the world go by. The Swing Inn serves three square meals, but everyone goes for

breakfast (to $11.50) – luckily it's served all day. The biscuits and gravy are renowned.

Vineyard Rose CALIFORNIAN $$$
(☎951-587-9463; 34843 Rancho California Rd; lunch mains $14-23, dinner $26-40; ⏰7am-10:45am & 11:30am-3pm Mon-Fri, 7am-3:30pm Sat & Sun, plus 5:30-9pm; P) South Coast Winery's gracious main restaurant has a Craftsman-style barn feel and vineyard views from the balcony. Salads and pizzas are popular at lunch, or lobster ravioli and rib-eye at dinner. Plus, wine pairing recommendations, naturally. At breakfast, the bananas Foster pancake with vanilla-bean sauce may make your head spin.

Crush & Brew BAR & GRILL
(☎951-693-4567; www.crushnbrew.com; 28544 Front St, Suite 103; ⏰11:30am-10pm Sun-Thu, to midnight Fri & Sat) This attractive new place pays tribute to the local wine industry with wines supplied by local producers and over 30 craft beers on tap. For food: a great selection of salads and sandwiches and dishes like lobster mac 'n' cheese.

☆ Entertainment

Many wineries offer entertainment, from guitar soloists to chamber concerts. Check at the visitors center or www.temeculacvb.com for upcoming events.

Pechanga Resort & Casino CASINO
(www.pechanga.com; 45000 Pechanga Pkwy) This Native American–owned casino-hotel offers plenty of slots, blackjack and roulette. Entertainment includes stand-up acts in its comedy club, and the 1200-seat **Pechanga Theater** hosts the likes of John Legend and Barenaked Ladies.

ℹ Information

Visitors Center (☎951-491-6085, 888-363-2852; www.temeculacvb.com; 28690 Mercedes St; ⏰9am-5pm Mon-Sat) Cheery center operated by Temecula Valley Convention & Visitors Bureau.

ℹ Getting There & Away

Temecula is just off the I-15 freeway, which begins in San Diego. Either of the Rancho California Rd or Rte 79 exits will take you to Old Town Front St. Allow 45 minutes from San Diego, 55 from Anaheim, 75 from Palm Springs or 80 from LA.

Greyhound Stop (☎800-231-2222, 951-676-9768; www.greyhound.com; 28464 Old Town Front St) Sells tickets for twice-daily buses heading to San Diego (from $21.25 when purchased online).

Palm Springs & the Deserts

Includes ➡

Palm Springs & the Coachella Valley . . 339
Joshua Tree National Park 350
Anza-Borrego Desert State Park. . . 358
Salton Sea 363
Route 66 364
Barstow 365
Mojave National Preserve. 367
Death Valley National Park 369
Las Vegas. 380

Best Places to Eat

- Trio (p347)
- Cheeky's (p347)
- Inn at Furnace Creek (p375)
- Pastels Bistro (p378)

Best Places to Stay

- Riviera Palm Springs (p346)
- El Morocco Inn & Spa (p346)
- La Casa del Zorro (p362)
- Sacred Sands (p356)
- Mandalay Bay (p385)

Why Go?

There's something undeniably artistic in the way the landscape unfolds in the California desert. Weathered volcanic peaks stand sentinel over singing sand dunes and mountains shimmering in hues from mustard yellow to vibrant pink. Hot mineral water spurts from the earth's belly to feed palm oases and soothe aching muscles in stylish spas. Tiny wildflowers push up from the hard-baked soil to celebrate springtime.

The riches of the desert soil have lured prospectors and miners, while its beauty and spirituality have tugged at the hearts of artists, visionaries and wanderers. Eccentrics, misfits and the military are drawn by its vastness and solitude. Hipsters and celebs come for the climate and retro flair. Through it all threads iconic Route 66, lined with moodily rusting roadside relics. No matter what your trail, the desert will creep into your consciousness and never fully leave.

When to Go

Palm Springs

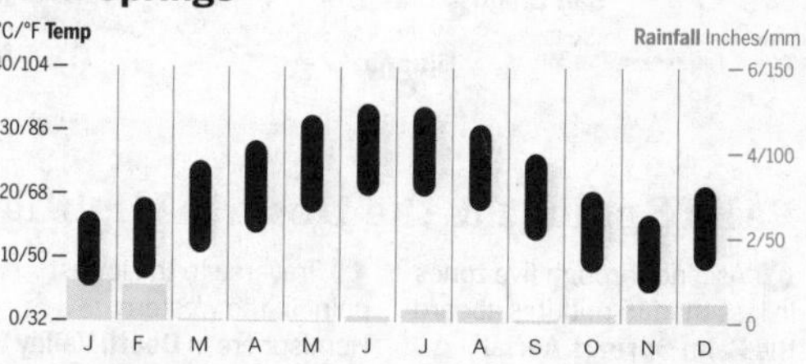

Dec-Apr Moderate temperatures lure in 'snowbirds' and LA weekend trippers.

May–mid-Jun, mid-Sep–Nov Crowds thin out as temperatures arc during shoulder season.

Jun-Sep Some inns and restaurants close in summer's heat; many of the rest offer great deals.

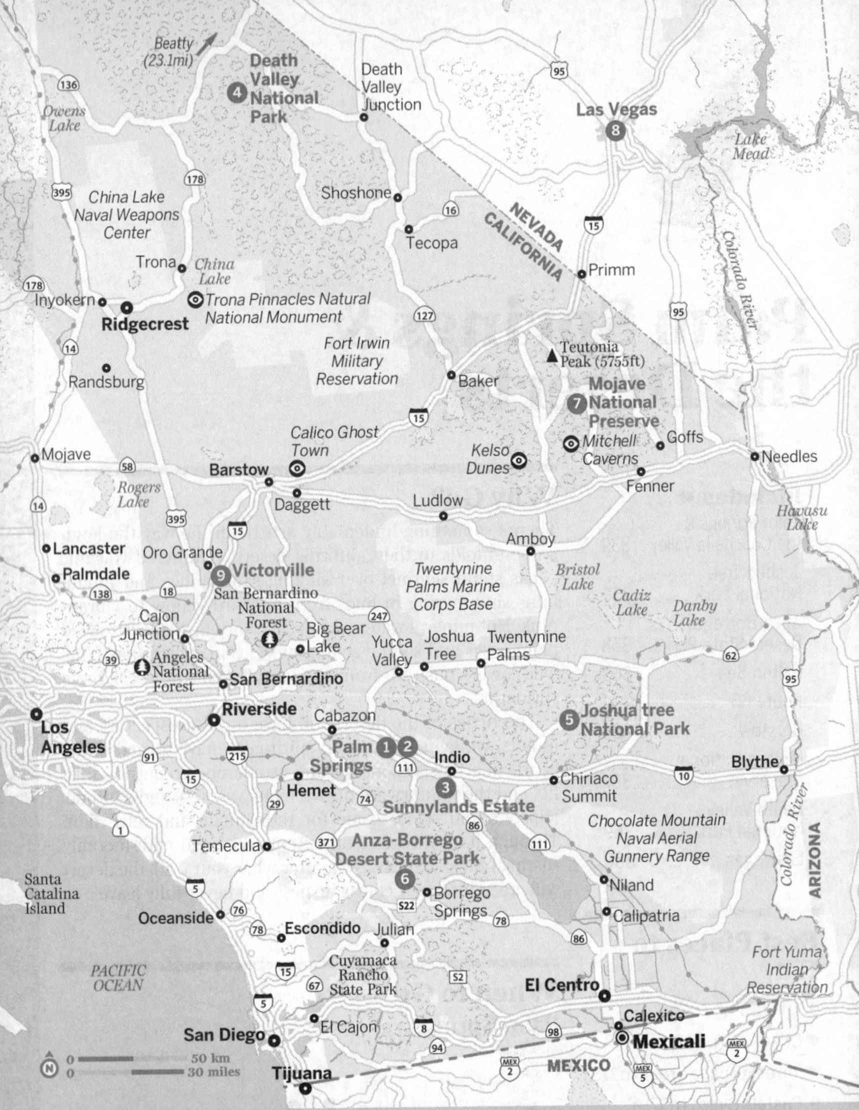

Palm Springs & the Deserts Highlights

1 Ascend through five zones in less than 15 minutes aboard the **Palm Springs Aerial Tramway** (p339).

2 Stretch out next to a kidney-shaped pool in a mid-century modern hotel in **Palm Springs**.

3 Walk in the footsteps of presidents and royalty at **Sunnylands Estate** (p347) .

4 Traverse to the lowest point in the Western Hemisphere in **Death Valley National Park** (p369)

5 Navigate smooth boulders in the **Hidden Valley** (p351) at **Joshua Tree National Park**.

6 Scramble around the wind caves of vast **Anza-Borrego Desert State Park** (p358).

7 Hide out at **Hole-in-the-Wall** (p368) in the forgotten **Mojave National Preserve**.

8 Lose yourself (but hopefully not your money) on the **Las Vegas Strip** (p380).

9 Revel in the mythology of the Mother Road at the California Route 66 Museum (p365) in **Victorville**.

PALM SPRINGS & THE COACHELLA VALLEY

The Rat Pack is back, baby, or at least its hangout is. In the 1950s and '60s, Palm Springs, some 100 miles east of LA, was the swinging getaway of Sinatra, Elvis and dozens of other stars, partying the night away in fancy modernist homes. Once the Rat Pack packed it in, though, the 300-sq-mile Coachella Valley surrendered to retirees in golf clothing. That is, until the mid-1990s, when a new generation fell in love with the city's retro-chic charms: steel-and-glass bungalows designed by famous architects, boutique hotels with vintage decor and kidney-shaped pools, and hushed piano bars serving the perfect martini. In today's Palm Springs, retirees and snowbirds mix comfortably with hipsters, hikers and a significant gay and lesbian contingent, on weekend getaways from LA or from clear across the globe.

Palm Springs is the principal city of the Coachella Valley, a string of desert towns ranging from ho-hum Cathedral City to glamtastic Palm Desert and America's date capital of Indio, all linked by Hwy 111. North of Palm Springs, Desert Hot Springs is garnering its share of visitors thanks to a slew of chic boutique hotels built on top of those soothing springs.

History

Cahuilla (ka-*wee*-ya) tribespeople have lived in the canyons on the southwest edge of the Coachella Valley for over 1000 years. Early Spanish explorers called the hot springs beneath Palm Springs *agua caliente* (hot water), which later became the name of the local Cahuilla band.

In 1876 the federal government carved the valley into a checkerboard of various interests. The Southern Pacific Railroad received odd-numbered sections, while the Agua Caliente were given even-numbered sections as their reservation. Casinos have made the tribes actually quite wealthy today.

In the town of Indio, about 20 miles southeast of Palm Springs, date palms were imported from French-held Algeria in 1890 and have become the valley's major crop, along with citrus and table grapes.

FAST FACTS

Population of Palm Springs 45,900

Population of Las Vegas 596,425

Los Angeles to Palm Springs 110 miles, two to three hours

San Diego to Borrego Springs 95 miles, 1½ to two hours

Los Angeles to Las Vegas 280 miles, four to five hours

Sights

In Palm Springs' compact downtown, Hwy 111 runs south as Palm Canyon Dr, paralleled by northbound Indian Canyon Dr. Tahquitz Canyon Way, dividing addresses north from south, heads east to Palm Springs' airport.

Some of the area's attractions are spread out across the Coachella Valley, also called 'Down Valley', as you head southeast from Palm Springs. Travel on Hwy 111 links the towns, but can be extremely slow thanks to dozens of traffic lights. Depending on where in the valley you're headed, it may be quicker to take I-10.

Notable buildings around town include the **1884 McCallum Adobe**, 1946 international-style **Kaufmann House**, and the E Stewart Williams–designed **Chase Bank**.

Palm Springs

★**Palm Springs Aerial Tramway** CABLE CAR

(☎888-515-8726; www.pstramway.com; 1 Tram Way; adult/child $24/17; ⏲from 10am Mon-Fri, 8am Sat & Sun, last tram up 8pm, last tram down 9:45pm daily) North of downtown, this rotating cable car is a highlight of any Palm Springs trip. It climbs nearly 6000 vertical feet through five different vegetation zones, from the Sonoran desert floor to the San Jacinto Mountains, in less than 15 minutes. The 2.5-mile ascent is said to be the temperature equivalent of driving from Mexico to Canada. It's 30°F to 40°F (up to 22°C) cooler as you step out into pine forests at the top, so bring warm clothing.

Snow is not uncommon, even in the spring and fall.

The **Mountain Station** (8516ft), at the top of the tramway, has a bar, restaurant, observation area and theater showing documentary films. Beyond here sprawls the wilderness of **Mt San Jacinto State Park**, which is criss-crossed by hiking trails.

The turnoff for the tram is about 3 miles north of downtown Palm Springs.

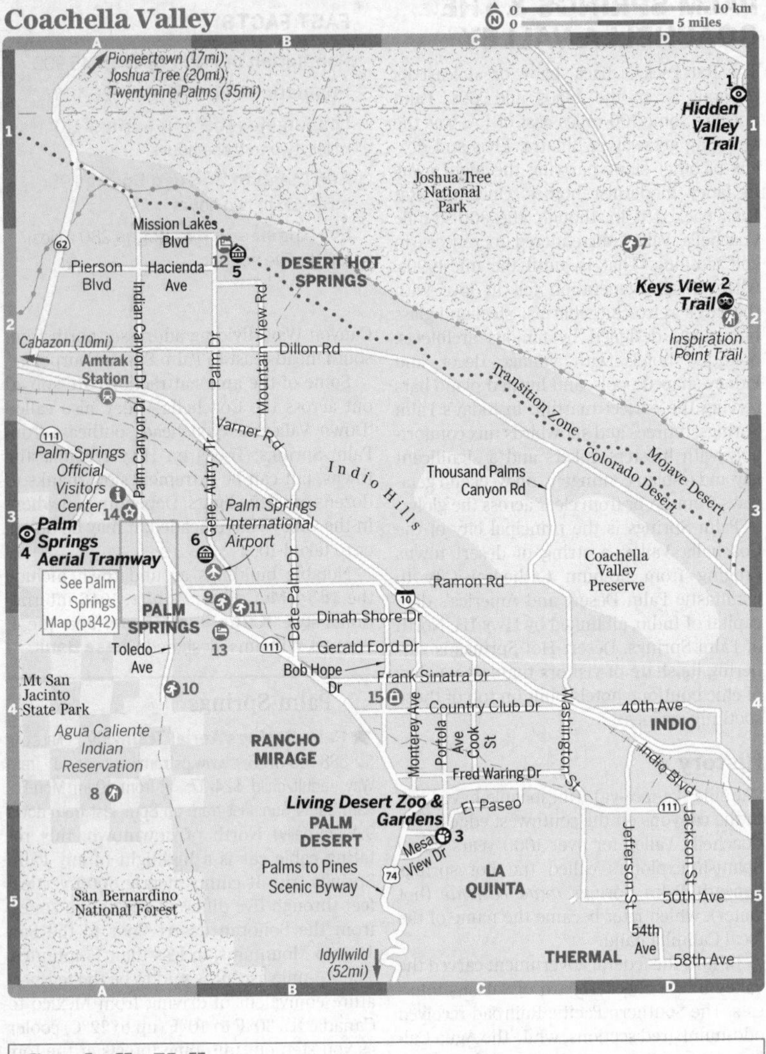

Coachella Valley

Top Sights
1 Hidden Valley Trail D1
2 Keys View Trail D2
3 Living Desert Zoo & Gardens C5
4 Palm Springs Aerial Tramway A3

Sights
5 Cabot's Pueblo Museum B2
6 Palm Springs Air Museum B3

Activities, Courses & Tours
7 Covington Flats D2
8 Indian Canyons A4
9 Palm Springs Yacht Club B3
10 Smoke Tree Stables A4
11 Wet 'n' Wild Palm Springs B3

Sleeping
12 El Morocco Inn & Spa B2
13 Parker Palm Springs B4

Entertainment
14 Toucan's Tiki Lounge A3

Shopping
15 Collectors Corner C4

★**Palm Springs Art Museum** MUSEUM

(☎760-322-4800; www.psmuseum.org; 101 Museum Dr; adult/child $12.50/free, 4-8pm Thu free; ⏰10am-5pm Tue-Wed & Fri-Sun, noon-8pm Thu) See the evolution of American painting, sculpture, photography and glass art over the past century. Alongside well-curated temporary exhibitions, the permanent collection is especially strong in modern painting and sculpture, with works by Henry Moore, Ed Ruscha, Mark di Suvero and other heavy hitters. There's also stunning glass art by Dale Chihuly and William Morris and a collection of pre-Columbian figurines.

The museum recently renovated an iconic 1961 mid-century modern bank building into its **Architecture and Design Center** (300 S Palm Canyon Dr), at the southern edge of downtown. Designed to pay tribute to the region's signature style, it opened in late 2014 and is the first free-standing architecture and design museum housed in a modern building.

Agua Caliente Cultural Museum MUSEUM

(☎760-323-0151; www.accmuseum.org; 219 S Palm Canyon Dr, Village Green Heritage Center; ⏰10am-5pm Wed-Sat, noon-5pm Sun) FREE The largest of the museums in the Village Green Heritage Center, this museum showcases the history and culture of the Agua Caliente band of Cahuilla peoples through permanent and changing exhibits and special events.

Palm Springs Historical Society MUSEUM

(www.pshistoricalsociety.org; 221 S Palm Canyon Dr; adult/child $1/free; ⏰10am-4pm Wed-Sat, noon-3pm Sun Oct-May) Palm Springs Historical Society delves into a rich past in a small, but classy exhibit of photos and memorabilia in the town's oldest building, the 1884 McCallum Adobe.

Ruddy's General Store HISTORIC SITE

(www.palmsprings.com/points/heritage/ruddy.html; 221 S Palm Canyon Dr; adult/child 95¢/free; ⏰10am-4pm Thu-Sun Oct-Jun, 10am-4pm Sat & Sun Jul-Sep) This reproduction of a 1930s general store shows amazingly preserved original products from groceries to medicines, beauty aids to clothing and hardware, with period showcases and signage.

Moorten Botanical Gardens GARDENS

(☎760-327-6555; www.moortenbotanicalgarden.com; 1701 S Palm Canyon Dr; adult/child $4/2; ⏰10am-4pm Thu-Tue, Fri-Sun only in summer) Chester 'Cactus Slim' Moorten, one of the original Keystone Cops, and his wife Patricia channeled their passion for plants into this compact garden founded in 1938. Today, it's an enchanting symphony of cacti, succulents and other desert flora.

Palm Springs Air Museum MUSEUM

(☎760-778-6262; www.palmspringsairmuseum.org; 745 N Gene Autry Trail; adult/child $15/8; ⏰10am-5pm) Adjacent to the airport, this museum has an exceptional collection of WWII aircraft and flight memorabilia, a movie theater and occasional flight demonstrations.

Around Palm Springs

★**Living Desert Zoo & Gardens** ZOO

(☎760-346-5694; www.livingdesert.org; 47900 Portola Ave, Palm Desert, off Hwy 111; adult/child $17.25/8.75; ⏰9am-5pm Oct-May, 8am-1:30pm Jun-Sep; 👪) This amazing zoo exhibits a variety of desert plants and animals, alongside exhibits on desert geology and Native American culture. Highlights include a walk-through wildlife hospital and an African-themed village with a fair-trade market and storytelling grove. Camel rides, a spin on the endangered species carousel, and a hop-on, hop-off shuttle cost extra. It's educational fun and worth the 30-minute (15 mile) drive down-valley.

Cabot's Pueblo Museum MUSEUM

(☎760-329-7610; www.cabotsmuseum.org; 67616 E Desert Ave, Desert Hot Springs; tour adult/child $11/9; ⏰tours 9:30am, 10:30am, 11:30am, 1:30pm & 2:30pm Tue-Sun Oct-May, 9:30am, 10:30am & 11:30am Wed-Sun Jun-Sep) Cabot Yerxa, a wealthy East Coaster who traded high society for desert solitude, hand built this rambling 1913 adobe from reclaimed and found objects, including telephone poles and wagon parts. Today it's a quirky museum displaying Native American basketry and pottery, as well as a photo collection from Cabot's turn-of-the-century travels to Alaska. Call ahead to confirm tour availability. It's about 13 miles north of central Palm Springs.

Activities

Tahquitz Canyon HIKING

(☎760-416-7044; www.tahquitzcanyon.com; 500 W Mesquite Ave; adult/child $12.50/6; ⏰7:30am-5pm Oct-Jun, Fri-Sun only Jul-Sep) A historic and sacred centerpiece for the Agua Caliente people, this canyon featured in the 1937 Frank Capra movie *Lost Horizon*. In the 1960s it was taken over by teenage squatters and

Palm Springs

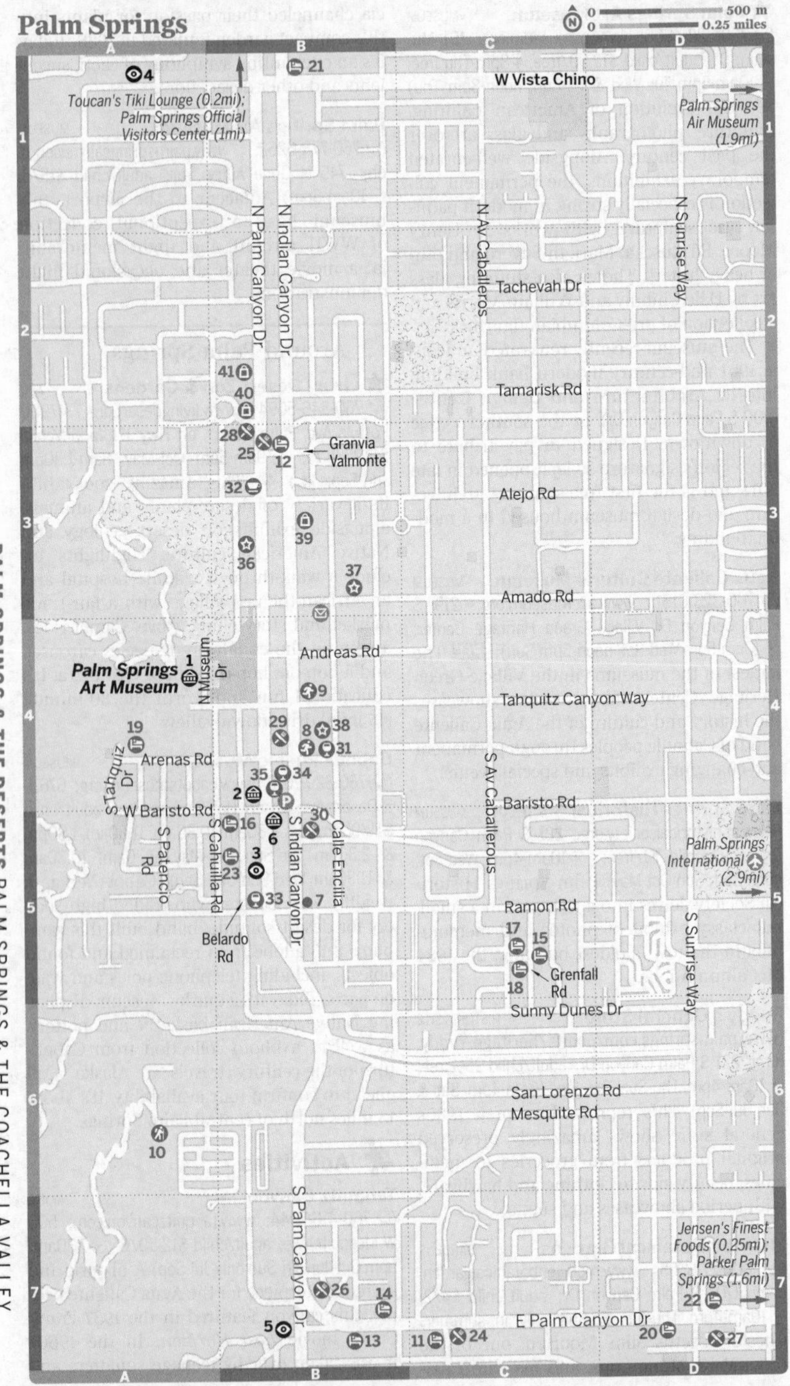

Palm Springs

Top Sights

1 Palm Springs Art Museum A4

Sights

2 Agua Caliente Cultural Museum B4
3 Chase Bank B5
4 Kaufmann House A1
McCallum Adobe .... (see 2)
5 Moorten Botanical Gardens B7
6 Palm Springs Art Museum Architecture and Design Center B5
Palm Springs Historical Society .... (see 2)
Ruddy's General Store .... (see 2)

Activities, Courses & Tours

7 Best of the Best Tours B5
8 Bike Palm Springs B4
Estrella Spa at Viceroy Palm Springs .... (see 23)
Feel Good Spa at Ace Hotel & Swim Club .... (see 11)
9 Spa Resort Casino B4
10 Tahquitz Canyon A6

Sleeping

11 Ace Hotel & Swim Club C7
12 Alcazar B3
13 Caliente Tropics B7
14 Casitas Laquita B7
15 Century Palm Springs C5
16 Del Marcos Hotel B5
17 Hacienda at Warm Sands C5
18 Inndulge C5
19 Orbit In A4
20 Queen of Hearts D7
21 Riviera Palm Springs B1
22 Saguaro D7
23 Viceroy B5

Eating

24 Appetito C7
25 Cheeky's B3
26 El Mirasol B7
King's Highway .... (see 11)
27 Native Foods D7
28 Trio B3
29 Tyler's Burgers B4
30 Wang's in the Desert B5

Drinking & Nightlife

Birba .... (see 25)
31 Hunters B4
32 Koffi B3
33 Melvyn's B5
34 Shanghai Red's B4
35 Village Pub B4

Entertainment

Annenberg Theater .... (see 1)
36 Azul B3
37 Spa Resort Casino B3
38 Streetbar B4

Shopping

39 Angel View B3
40 Modern Way B2
41 Trina Turk B2

soon became a point of contention between tribespeople, law-enforcement agencies and squatters in its rock alcoves and caves. After the squatters were booted out, it took the tribe years to haul out trash, erase graffiti and restore the canyon to its natural state.

The visitors center has natural and cultural history exhibits and shows a video about the legend of Tahquitz, a shaman of the Cahuilla people. Rangers lead educational 2-mile, 2½-hour hikes; reserve in advance. Self-guided hiking is available until 3:25pm.

Indian Canyons HIKING

(☎760-323-6018; www.indian-canyons.com; 38520 S Palm Canyon Dr; adult/child $9/5, 90min guided hike $3/2; ⏱8am-5pm Oct-Jun, Fri-Sun only Jul-Sep) Streams flowing from the San Jacinto Mountains sustain a rich variety of plants in oases around Palm Springs. Home to Native American communities for hundreds of years and now part of the Agua Caliente Indian Reservation, these canyons, shaded by fan palms and surrounded by towering cliffs, are a delight for hikers.

Ask for directions to canyons with picnic areas, bird watching, Native American mortar holes, and possibly a bighorn sheep sighting.

From downtown Palm Springs, head south on Palm Canyon Dr (continue straight when the main road turns east) for about 2 miles to the reservation entrance. From here, it's 3 miles up to the Trading Post, which sells hats, maps, water and knickknacks.

Mt San Jacinto State Park HIKING

(☎951-659-2607; www.parks.ca.gov) The wilderness beyond the Palm Springs Aerial Tramway mountain station is criss-crossed by 54 miles of hiking trails, including a non-technical route up Mt San Jacinto (10,834ft). If you're heading into the backcountry (even just for a few hours of hiking), you must self-register for a wilderness permit at the ranger station.

Winter Adventure Center SKIING, SNOWSHOEING

(☎general info 760-325-1449; www.pstramway.com/winter-adventure-center.html; snowshoe/skis rental per day $18/21; ⊙open seasonally 10am-4pm Thu-Fri & Mon, from 9am Sat & Sun, last rentals 2:30pm) Outside the Palm Springs Aerial Tramway mountain station, this outfit gets you into the snowy backcountry on snowshoes and cross-country skis, available on a first-come, first-served basis.

Smoke Tree Stables HORSEBACK RIDING

(☎760-327-1372; www.smoketreestables.com; 2500 S Toledo Ave; 1-/2hr guided ride $50/100) Near the Indian Canyons, this outfit arranges trail rides ranging from one-hour outings to all-day treks, for both novice and experienced riders. Reservations required.

Wet 'n' Wild Palm Springs WATER PARK

(☎760-327-0499; www.wetnwildpalmsprings.com; 1500 S Gene Autry Trail; adult/child & senior $37/27; ⊙mid-Mar–mid-Oct) To keep cool on hot days, Wet 'n' Wild boasts a massive wave pool, thunderous water slides and tube rides, and 'dive-in' movies on Fridays in midsummer. Parking costs $14. Call or check the website for current opening hours.

Stand By Golf GOLF

(☎760-321-2665; www.standbygolf.com) Golf is huge here, with more than 100 public, semi-private, private and resort golf courses scattered around the valley. This outfit books tee times for discounted same-day or next-day play at a few dozen local courses.

Tours

Pick up self-guided tour brochures at the visitors center (p350): public art and historic sites (free), modernism ($5) and stars' homes ($5). For guided tours, reservations are a must.

Best of the Best Tours GENERAL INTEREST

(☎760-320-1365; www.thebestofthebesttours.com; 490 S Indian Canyon Dr; tours from $35) Extensive program includes windmill tours and bus tours of celebrity homes.

Desert Adventures 4WD

(☎760-340-2345; www.red-jeep.com; tours $59-135) Four-wheel-drive tours cover a diverse lineup from gay icons of Palm Springs to an eco-tour to canyons of the San Andreas Fault.

Historic Walking Tours WALKING

(☎760-323-8297; www.pshistoricalsociety.org; tours $15) Just what it says: a variety of tours covering architecture, Hollywood stars and more. Organized by the Palm Springs Historical Society.

Palm Springs Modern Tours DESIGN

(☎760-318-6118; www.palmspringsmoderntours.com; tours $75) Three-hour minivan tour of mid-century modern architectural jewels by such masters as Albert Frey, Richard Neutra and John Lautner.

Festivals & Events

During festivals, especially the Coachella Music & Arts Festival, expect hotel rooms to be scarce and costly. Book early.

Every Thursday night locals and visitors alike flock to Palm Canyon Dr in downtown Palm Springs for **Villagefest**, with a farmers market, food stalls, craft vendors and street performers.

Palm Springs International Film Festival FILM

(www.psfilmfest.org) Early January brings a Hollywood-star-studded film festival, showing more than 200 films from over 60 countries. A short-film festival follows in June.

TOP FIVE SPAS

Get your stressed-out self to these pampering shrines to work out the kinks and turn your body into a glowing lump of tranquility. Reservations are de rigueur.

Estrella Spa at Viceroy Palm Springs (p346) Stylish boutique-hotel spa for massages in poolside cabanas.

Feel Good Spa at Ace Hotel & Swim Club (p345) At Palm Springs' newest hipster spa you can get a treatment inside a yurt.

Spa Resort Casino (☎760-778-1772; www.sparesortcasino.com; 100 N Indian Canyon Dr) Try a five-step 'taking of the waters' course through the valley's original hot springs.

Spa Terre at Riviera Palm Springs (p346) The ultimate in swanky pampering, with Watsu pool and exotic spa rituals.

Palm Springs Yacht Club (p346) This newly renovated spa is again the ritzy, glitzy fave of celebs and society ladies.

Modernism Week CULTURAL
(www.modernismweek.com) Ten-day celebration of all things mid-century modern: architecture and home tours, films, lectures, design show and lots of parties. Held in mid-February.

Coachella Music & Arts Festival MUSIC
(www.coachella.com; 1-/3-day pass around $100/300) Held at Indio's Empire Polo Club over two weekends in April, this is one of the hottest indie-music festivals of its kind. Get tickets early or forget about it.

Stagecoach Festival MUSIC
(www.stagecoachfestival.com; 1-/3-day pass from $100/250) The weekend after Coachella, also held at Indio's Empire Polo Club, this festival celebrates new and established country-music artists.

Restaurant Week FOOD
(www.palmspringsrestaurantweek.com) Discounted prix-fixe menus at top restaurants throughout the valley. Held in June.

DON'T MISS

ELVIS' LOVE NEST

One of the most spectacular mid-century modern houses in Palm Springs was designed in the early 1960s by local developer Robert Alexander for his wife, Helene. It consists of four circular rooms built on three levels, accented with glass and stone. *Look* magazine called it the 'House of Tomorrow' and featured it in an eight-page spread, making the Alexanders national celebrities. Sadly the entire family died in a plane crash in 1965, but the estate gained even greater fame a year later when Elvis Presley moved in. On May 1, 1967 he carried his new bride Priscilla over the threshold to begin their honeymoon. The **Elvis Honeymoon Hideaway** (760-322-1192; www.elvis-honeymoon.com; 1350 Ladera Circle; per person $30; tours 1pm & 3:30pm daily or by appointment) has been authentically restored and can be visited on daily tours (reservations recommended).

Sleeping

Palm Springs and the Coachella Valley offer an astonishing variety of lodging options, including fine vintage-flair boutique hotels, full-on luxury resorts, and chain motels. We quote high-season (November to April) rack rates; summer savings can be significant. Campers should head to Joshua Tree National Park or Mt San Jacinto State Park.

Palm Springs

Caliente Tropics MOTEL $
(760-327-1391, 800-658-6034; www.calientetropics.com; 411 E Palm Canyon Dr; r weekday/weekend from $54/109; P) Elvis once frolicked poolside at this premier budget pick, a nicely kept 1964 tiki-style motor lodge. Drift off to dreamland on quality mattresses in rooms that are spacious and dressed in warm colors.

★**Orbit In** BOUTIQUE HOTEL $$
(760-323-3585, 877-966-7248; www.orbitin.com; 562 W Arenas Rd; r incl breakfast from $149; P) Swing back to the '50s – pinkie raised and all – during the 'Orbitini' happy hour at this fabulously retro property, with high-end mid-century modern furniture (Eames, Noguchi et al) in rooms set around a quiet saline pool with a Jacuzzi and fire pit. The long list of freebies includes bike rentals and daytime sodas and snacks.

★**Ace Hotel & Swim Club** HOTEL $$
(760-325-9900; www.acehotel.com/palmspings; 701 E Palm Canyon Dr; r from $200; P@) Palm Springs goes Hollywood – with all the sass, but sans the attitude – at this former Howard Johnson motel turned hipster hangout. Rooms (many with patio) sport a glorified tent-cabin look and are crammed with lifestyle essentials (big flat-screen TVs, MP3 plugs). Happening pool scene and the **Feel Good Spa** (760-329-8791; www.acehotel.com/palmsprings/spa; 701 E Palm Canyon Dr), on-site restaurant and bar to boot.

Saguaro HOTEL $$
(760-323-1711, 877-808-2439; www.thesaguaro.com; 1800 E Palm Canyon Dr; r from $159; P@) The hot colors of a desert blooming with wildflowers animate this newly updated mid-century hotel. Three stories of rooms look over a generous pool deck. The main restaurant, Tinto, serves tapas and Spanish-inspired cooking by Iron Chef Jose Garces, and his El Jefe bar does great tacos and tequilas.

Del Marcos Hotel BOUTIQUE HOTEL $$
(760-325-6902, 800-676-1214; www.delmarcoshotel.com; 225 W Baristo Rd; r incl breakfast $139-269;) At this 1947 gem, designed by William F Cody, groovy lobby tunes usher

you to a saltwater pool and ineffably chic rooms. And it's steps from the shops and eats of downtown Palm Springs' village.

Alcazar BOUTIQUE HOTEL $$
(760-318-9850; www.alcazarpalmsprings.com; 622 N Palm Canyon Dr; r incl breakfast from $149;) At the edge of Uptown, a fashionable (but not party) crowd makes new friends poolside before retiring to one of the 34 rooms around a pool. Some have Jacuzzi tubs, patios, fireplaces or all three. Gleaming white floors lead to equally minimalist walls and bed linens. Look for loaner bikes and pastries from Cheeky's (p347).

★**Riviera Palm Springs** LUXURY HOTEL $$$
(760-327-8311; www.psriviera.com; 1600 Indian Canyon Dr; r $240-260, ste $290-540;) This Rat Pack playground now sparkles brighter than ever. Expect the full range of fancy mod-cons amid luscious gardens, three amoeba-shaped pools, 17 (count 'em) fire pits, the **Spa Terre** (760-778-6690; www.psriviera.com; 1600 N Indian Canyon Dr), and '60s accents such as shag rugs, classy-campy crystal chandeliers and Warhol art. **Circa 59** indoor-outdoor restaurant and lounge makes you and your sweetie look good.

It's about a mile to downtown Palm Springs; shuttle service available.

★**Parker Palm Springs** RESORT $$$
(760-770-5000; www.theparkerpalmsprings.com; 4200 E Palm Canyon Dr; r from $300;) Featured in the Bravo TV series *Welcome to the Parker*, this posh resort highlights whimsical decor by Jonathan Adler. Drop by for a cocktail at Mister Parker's or a posh brunch at Norma's five-star coffee shop. The grounds boast hammocks, *boules* (lawn bowling) and a fabulous spa. The $30 resort charge covers parking, wi-fi, and access to the **Palm Springs Yacht Club spa** (760-770-5000; www.theparkerpalmsprings.com/spa; Parker Palm Springs, 4200 E Palm Canyon Dr).

WHAT THE...?

West of Palm Springs, you may do a double take when you see the **World's Biggest Dinosaurs** (951-922-0076; www.cabazondinosaurs.com; 50770 Seminole Dr, Cabazon; adult/child $8/7; 10am-5:30pm Mon-Fri, 10am-6:30pm Sat & Sun). Claude K Bell, a sculptor for Knott's Berry Farm, spent over a decade crafting these concrete behemoths, now owned by Christian creationists who contend that God created the original dinosaurs in one day, along with the other animals. In the gift shop, alongside the sort of dino-swag you might find at science museums, you can read about the alleged hoaxes and fallacies of evolution and Darwinism.

Viceroy BOUTIQUE HOTEL $$$
(760-320-4117; www.viceroypalmsprings.com; 415 S Belardo Rd; r from $300;) Wear a Pucci dress and blend right in at *Top Design*'s Kelly Wearstler's 1960s-chic miniresort done up in black, white and lemon-yellow (think Austin Powers meets Givenchy). There's the **Estrella** (760-320-4117; www.viceroypalmsprings.com; 415 S Belardo Rd) spa, a fab but pricey Cal-French restaurant for a white-linen luncheon or swanky supper, and free town-cruiser bikes to borrow.

Desert Hot Springs

★**El Morocco Inn & Spa** BOUTIQUE HOTEL $$
(888-288-9905, 760-288-2527; www.elmoroccoinn.com; 66814 4th St, Desert Hot Springs; r incl breakfast $179-219;) Heed the call of the casbah at this drop-dead gorgeous hideaway where the scene is set for romance. Twelve exotically furnished rooms wrap around a pool deck where your enthusiastic host serves free 'Moroccotinis' during happy hour. Other perks: on-site spa, huge DVD library and delicious homemade mint iced tea.

Spring BOUTIQUE HOTEL $$
(760-251-6700; www.the-spring.com; 12699 Reposo Way; r incl breakfast $179-279;) Splash out in this humble 1950s motel that's morphed into a chic, whisper-quiet spa retreat where natural hot mineral water feeds three pools. The 13 rooms are minimalist in design but not in amenities (rich duvets, fluffy robes, small kitchens). Achieve a state of bliss while enjoying a treatment or simply calming valley and mountain views.

Eating

Tyler's Burgers BURGERS $
(www.tylersburgers.com; 149 S Indian Canyon Dr; dishes $3-9; 11am-4pm Mon-Sat;) This tiny shack in the center of downtown Palm Springs serves the best burgers in town, bar none. Waits are practically inevitable, which is presumably why there's an amazingly well-stocked magazine rack. Cash only.

DON'T MISS

SUNNY LIVING AT SUNNYLANDS

Sunnylands (760-328-2829; www.sunnylands.org; 37977 Bob Hope Dr, Rancho Mirage; admission free, house tour $35; 9am-4pm Thu-Sun, closed Jul & Aug) is the retro-glam, mid-century modern estate of Walter and Leonore Annenberg, one of America's 'first families'. Walter (1908–2002) was an American publisher, ambassador and philanthropist, and 'Lee' (1918–2009) was Chief of Protocol under President Ronald Reagan. At their winter estate in Rancho Mirage, designed by A Quincy Jones and surrounded by grounds incorporating a nine-hole golf course, the Annenbergs entertained seven US presidents, royalty, and Hollywood and international celebrities. These days Sunnylands is nicknamed the 'West Coast Camp David' for summits between President Obama and world leaders including Chinese president Xi Jinping and King Abdullah of Jordan.

Now the rest of us can visit too. A new visitor center and museum screen a film and show changing exhibits about the estate. Just beyond is a magnificent desert garden. Reserve as early as possible for tours of the stunning house with its art collection, architecture and furniture. Tickets go on sale online on the 1st and 15th of each month for the period beginning two weeks onward.

Native Foods VEGAN $
(760-416-0070; www.nativefoods.com; Smoke Tree Village, 1775 E Palm Canyon Dr; mains $8-11; 11am-9:30pm Mon-Sat;) Vegan cooking guru Tanya Petrovna does an amazing job at injecting complex flavors into meat and dairy substitutes. The creative sandwiches, southwestern salads, sizzling-hot rice bowls, and tasty pizzas and burgers feed both body and soul.

★Cheeky's CALIFORNIAN $$
(760-327-7595; www.cheekysps.com; 622 N Palm Canyon Dr; mains $8-13; 8am-2pm Wed-Mon, last seating 1:30pm) Waits can be long and service only so-so, but the farm-to-table menu dazzles with witty inventiveness. Dishes change weekly, but custardy scrambled eggs, arugula pesto frittata and bacon bar 'flights' keep making appearances.

El Mirasol MEXICAN $$
(760-323-0721; www.elmirasolrestaurants.com; 140 E Palm Canyon Dr; mains $10-19; 11am-10pm) There are showier Mexican places around town, but everyone ends up back at El Mirasol, with its earthy decor, generous margaritas and snappy dishes. The chicken in mole or in *pipián* sauce (made from ground pumpkin seeds and chilis) are menu stars.

King's Highway AMERICAN $$
(760-325-9900; www.acehotel.com; Ace Hotel & Swim Club, 701 E Palm Canyon Dr; mains $8-30; 7am-11pm Sun-Thu, to 3am Fri & Sat;) A fine case of creative recycling, this former Denny's is now a diner for the 21st century where the tagliatelle is handmade, the sea bass wild-caught, the beef grass-fed, the vegetables organic and the cheeses artisanal. Great breakfast, too.

Wang's in the Desert CHINESE $$
(760-325-9264; www.wangsinthedesert.com; 424 S Indian Canyon Dr; mains $12-20; 5-9:30pm Sun-Thu, to 10:30 Fri & Sat) This mood-lit local fave with indoor koi pond delivers creatively crafted Chinese classics and has a busy daily happy hour – it's a huge gay scene on Fridays.

Appetito ITALIAN, DELI $$
(760-327-1929; www.appetitodeli.com; 1700 S Camino Real; mains $8-20; 11am-10pm Sun-Thu, until 11pm Fri & Sat) This newcomer dishes up paninis such as porchetta, broccoli rabe, provolone and chili aioli; pastas like pillowy ricotta gnocchi with kale pesto, walnuts and lemon; and tiramisu profiteroles, to spirited crowds hanging out in the tall, minimalist room or on the enclosed terrace.

★Trio CALIFORNIAN $$$
(760-864-8746; www.triopalmsprings.com; 707 N Palm Canyon Dr; mains lunch $11-26, dinner $14-29; 11am-10pm Sun-Thu, until 11pm Fri & Sat) The winning formula in this '60s modernist space: updated American comfort food (awesome Yankee pot roast!), eye-catching artwork and picture windows. The $19 prix-fixe three-course dinner (served until 6pm) is a steal.

Drinking & Nightlife

Many restaurants have hugely popular happy hours, and there are happening hotel bars at the Parker, Riviera, Ace and Saguaro.

GAY & LESBIAN PALM SPRINGS

Nicknamed 'Provincetown in the Desert' and 'Key West of the West,' Palm Springs is one of America's great gay destinations.

In early April, **Dinah Shore Weekend** (www.thedinah.com) hosts lesbian comedy, pool parties, mixers and more during the Kraft Nabisco (ex-Dinah Shore) LPGA golf tournament. Over Easter weekend, the **White Party** (www.jeffreysanker.com) is one of the USA's biggest gay dance events. Show up in early November for **Palm Springs Pride** (www.pspride.org).

Accommodations

Most men's hotels are concentrated in the Warm Sands neighborhood, just southeast of downtown Palm Springs, and are clothing-optional. Lesbian resorts (fewer in number) are scattered throughout town. As with other lodging in the desert, rates fall steeply in summer (roughly mid-June to mid-September) and shoulder seasons.

Hacienda at Warm Sands (☎760-327-8111; www.thehacienda.com; 586 Warm Sands Dr; r incl breakfast & lunch $250-400; P ❄ @ ≋) With Indonesian teak and bamboo furnishings, the Hacienda raises the bar for luxury gay men's lodging and has genial innkeepers who are never intrusive but always available.

Inndulge (☎760 327 1408, 800 833 5675; www.inndulge.com; 601 Grenfall Rd; r incl breakfast from $195; P ❄ @ ≋) Don't let the randy name fool you; this is a solid midrange choice for gay men. It gets plenty of repeat customers for its 1950s shell and variety of up-to-date rooms and suites (some have kitchens). The nightly social hour, pool and hot tub encourage mingling.

Century Palm Springs (☎760-323-9966; www.centurypalmsprings.com; 598 Grenfall Rd; r incl breakfast $180-300; P ❄ @ ≋) At the small gay-oriented Century, designed by William Alexander in 1955, rooms are hued in cheerful orange and olive and are furnished with plush bedding and pieces by Starck, Eames and Noguchi. Soak up cocktails and serene mountain views from the minimalist pool deck.

Casitas Laquita (☎760-416-9999; www.casitaslaquita.com; 450 E Palm Canyon Dr; r $155-195; P ❄ ≋) This newly made-over, southwest-flavored compound for lesbians has rooms and suites with kitchens; some even have kiva-style fireplaces. Afternoon tapas and drinks are complimentary, as is continental breakfast.

Queen of Hearts (☎760-322-5793; www.queenofheartsps.com; 435 Avenida Olancha; r incl breakfast $120-145; P ❄ ≋) Palm Springs' original lesbian hotel counts many regulars among its guests, thanks, in large part, to its super-friendly owner, Michelle. It's in a quiet neighborhood with nine rooms encircling a swimming pool and patios framed by fruit trees.

Drinking & Entertainment

The city's main 'gayborhood' is the block of Arenas Rd east of S Indian Canyon Dr, with about a dozen gay-themed bars, cafes and shops. Other venues are scattered throughout town. The bars at Azul (p349) and Wang's in the Desert (p347) are also buzzy stops on the gay party circuit.

Hunters (www.huntersnightclubs.com; 302 E Arenas Rd; ⏰10am-2am) Wildly diverse male clientele, lots of TV screens, a cruisy dance scene and pool tables.

Streetbar (www.psstreetbar.com; 224 E Arenas Rd) Congenial mix of locals, long-time visitors and occasional drag performers. There's a cozy streetside patio for watching the crowds saunter by.

Toucan's Tiki Lounge (www.toucanstikilounge.com; 2100 N Palm Canyon Dr; ⏰noon-2am) North of town, this locals' hangout has something for everyone: tropical froufrou, trivia, karaoke, drag revues, smoking patio and dance floor. Packed on weekends.

Birba BAR
(www.birbaps.com; 622 N Palm Canyon Dr; ⏰5-11pm Sun & Wed-Thu, to midnight Fri & Sat) It's cocktails and pizza at this fabulous indoor-outdoor space where floor-to-ceiling sliding glass doors separate the long marble bar from a hedge-fringed patio with sunken fire pits.

Shanghai Red's BAR
(www.fishermans.com; 235 S Indian Canyon Dr; ⏲4pm-late Mon-Sat, from noon Sun) This bar has a busy courtyard, an inter-generational crowd and live blues on Friday and Saturday nights.

Melvyn's BAR
(www.inglesideinn.com; Ingleside Inn, 200 W Ramon Rd) Join the Bentley pack for stiff martinis and quiet jazz at this former Sinatra haunt at the Ingleside Inn. Sunday afternoon jazz is a long-standing tradition. Shine your shoes.

Koffi COFFEE SHOP
(www.kofficoffee.com; 515 N Palm Canyon Dr; snacks & drinks $3-6; ⏲5:30am-7pm; 📶) Tucked among the art galleries on N Palm Canyon Dr, this coolly minimalist, indie java bar serves strong organic coffee. There's a second Palm Springs location at 1700 S Camino Real, near the Ace Hotel.

Village Pub PUB
(www.palmspringsvillagepub.com; 266 S Palm Canyon Dr; 📶) This casual dive is perfect for kicking back with your posse over beers, darts, loud music and the occasional live band.

☆ Entertainment

Azul MUSIC
(☎760-325-5533; www.azultapaslounge.com; 369 N Palm Canyon Dr; mains $11-24, Judy Show incl dinner $35; ⏲11am-late) Popular with gays and their friends, the Azul restaurant has almost nightly entertainment in its piano bar, plus the wickedly funny **Judy Show** (www.thejudyshow.com) on Sundays, starring impersonator Michael Holmes as Judy Garland, Mae West and other campy legends of yore.

Annenberg Theater PERFORMING ARTS
(☎760-325-4490; www.psmuseum.org; 101 Museum Dr) This intimate theater at the Palm Springs Art Museum presents an eclectic schedule of films, lectures, theater, ballet and music performances.

Spa Resort Casino CASINO
(www.sparesortcasino.com; 401 E Amado Rd; ⏲24hr) There's this perfectly legal Native American–owned den of vice right in the heart of downtown Palm Springs, as well as other gambling halls off I-10. Vegas they ain't.

Shopping

Central Palm Springs has two main shopping districts along N Palm Canyon Dr, divided by Alejo Rd. North of Alejo, Uptown is more for art and design(-inspired) shops, while Downtown (south of Alejo) is ground zero for souvenirs and fun clothing. Given the city's demographic, vintage clothing stores flourish here like few other places. West of town is a destination outlet mall.

Trina Turk CLOTHING, HOMEWARES
(☎760-416-2856; www.trinaturk.com; 891 N Palm Canyon Dr; ⏲10am-5pm Mon-Fri, to 6pm Sat, noon-5pm Sun) Trina makes form-flattering 'California-chic' fashions that are beautifully presented amid shag carpeting and floral foil wallpaper in her original boutique in a 1960s Albert Frey building. Her Mr Turk menswear line is also available here.

Modern Way FURNITURE
(www.psmodernway.com; 745 N Palm Canyon Dr) The oldest and most stylin' consignment shop for collectors of modern furniture.

Angel View THRIFT SHOP
(☎760-320-1733; www.angelview.org; 462 N Indian Canyon Dr; ⏲9am-6pm Mon-Sat, 10am-5pm Sun) At this well-established thrift store, today's hipsters can shop for clothes and accessories as cool as when they were first worn a generation or two ago.

Collectors Corner VINTAGE
(71280 Hwy 111, Rancho Mirage; ⏲9:30am-4:15pm Mon-Sat) It's a trek from central Palm Springs (about 12 miles), but this two-story shop is oh so worth it for large collections of antiques, vintage clothing, jewelry and furniture.

El Paseo MALL
(www.elpaseo.com; El Paseo, Palm Desert) For serious shopping, head to Palm Desert where the elegant El Paseo shopping strip has been dubbed the 'Rodeo Drive of the Desert'. It's one block south of and parallel to Hwy 111, 14 miles southeast of Palm Springs.

Desert Hills Premium Outlets MALL
(www.premiumoutlets.com; 48400 Seminole Dr, Cabazon; ⏲10am-8pm Sun-Thu, to 9pm Fri, 9am-9pm Sat) Bargain hunters, make a beeline for dozens of outlet stores: Gap to Gucci, Polo to Prada, Off 5th to Barneys New York. Wear comfortable shoes – this mall is huge! It's off I-10 (exit at Fields Rd), 20 minutes west of Palm Springs. If you've got energy to spare, the smaller Cabazon Outlets mall is next door.

ℹ Information

High season is October to April, but Palm Springs (elevation 487ft) stays reasonably busy even in summer, when hotel rates drop and temperatures spike above 100°F (37°C). Between June and August many businesses keep shorter hours or even close, so call ahead to check.

Palm Springs Official Visitors Center (☎760-778-8418; www.visitpalmsprings.com; 2901 N Palm Canyon Dr; ⏲9am-5pm) Well-stocked and well-staffed visitors center 3 miles north of downtown, in a 1965 Albert Frey–designed gas station at the tramway turnoff.

Desert Regional Medical Center (☎760-323-6511; www.desertregional.com; 1150 N Indian Canyon Dr; ⏲24hr) Emergency room and physician referral.

Palm Springs Police (☎760-323-8116) For nonemergency situations. In case of emergency, dial 911.

Post Office (333 E Amado Rd; ⏲8am-5pm Mon-Fri, 9am-3pm Sat)

Palm Springs Library (www.palmspringsca.gov; 300 S Sunrise Way; ⏲10am-5pm Wed-Sat, to 7pm Tue; 📶) Free wi-fi and internet terminals.

ℹ Getting There & Away

AIR

A 10-minute drive northeast of downtown, Palm Springs International Airport (p480) is served year-round by Alaska, Allegiant, American, Delta, Horizon, United, US Airways and Westjet, and seasonally by Frontier, Sun Country and Virgin America.

BUS

Greyhound (www.greyhound.com) operates a few daily buses to/from LA ($28, three hours). The terminus is at Palm Springs train station.

CAR & MOTORCYCLE

From LA, the trip to Palm Springs and the Coachella Valley takes about two to three hours via I-10 with no traffic. With traffic, it's anybody's guess.

TRAIN

Amtrak (www.amtrak.com) serves the unstaffed and kinda-creepy – it's deserted and in the middle of nowhere – North Palm Springs station, 5 miles north of downtown Palm Springs. Trains run to/from LA ($41, 2½ hours) a few days per week and are often late.

ℹ Getting Around

TO/FROM THE AIRPORT

Many downtown Palm Springs hotels provide free airport transfers. Otherwise, a taxi to downtown Palm Springs costs about $12 to $15. If you're staying in another Coachella Valley town, rides on shared shuttle vans, such as **Skycap Shuttle** (☎760-272-5988; www.skycapshuttle.com), will likely be more economical. Fares depend on distance and reservations are advised. SunLine bus 24 stops by the airport and goes most of (though, frustratingly, not all of) the way to downtown Palm Springs.

BICYCLE

Central Palm Springs is pancake-flat, and more bike lanes are being built all the time. Many hotels have loaner bicycles.

Bike Palm Springs (☎760-832-8912; www.bikepsrentals.com; 194 S Indian Canyon Dr; standard/kids/electric/tandem bikes half-day from $20/12/30/40, full day $25/15/50/50) Great for tooling around central Palm Springs.

Funseekers (☎760-340-3861; www.palmdesertbikerentals.com; 73-865 Hwy 111, Palm Desert; bicycles per 24hr/3 day/week from $25/50/65, delivery & pick up $30) Outside of central Palm Springs, this outlet rents and sells bikes, mopeds and Segways for city and nature excursions.

BUS

Alternative-fuel–powered **SunLine** (www.sunline.org; fare/day pass $1/3; ⏲around 5am-10pm) buses travel around the valley, albeit slowly. Bus 111 links Palm Springs with Palm Desert (one hour) and Indio (1½ hours) via Hwy 111. Buses have air-con, wheelchair lifts and a bicycle rack. Cash only (bring exact change).

CAR & MOTORCYCLE

Though you can walk to most sights in downtown Palm Springs, you'll need a car to get around the valley. Major rental-car companies have airport desks. **Scoot Palm Springs** (☎760-413-2883; www.scootpalmsprings.com; 701 East Palm Canyon Dr; half day scooter rentals from $65) rents scooters. For motorcycles try **Eaglerider** (☎877-736-8243; www.eaglerider.com), whose rates start at $99 per day.

JOSHUA TREE NATIONAL PARK

Taking a page from a Dr Seuss book, the whimsical Joshua trees (actually tree-sized yuccas) welcome visitors to this 794,000-acre **park** (☎760-367-5500; www.nps.gov/jotr; 7-day entry per car $15) at the convergence of the Colorado and Mojave Deserts. It was Mormon settlers who named the trees because the branches stretching up toward heaven reminded them of the Biblical prophet Joshua pointing the way to the promised land.

Rock climbers know 'JT' as the best place to climb in California, but kids and the young at heart also welcome the chance to scramble up, down and around the giant boulders. Hikers seek out hidden, shady, desert-fan-palm oases fed by natural springs and small streams, while mountain bikers are hypnotized by the desert vistas.

In springtime, the Joshua trees send up a huge single cream-colored flower, and the octopus-like tentacles of the ocotillo cactus shoot out crimson flowers. The mystical quality of this stark, boulder-strewn landscape has inspired many artists, most famously the band U2, who named their 1987 album *The Joshua Tree*.

Unless you plan on day-tripping from Palm Springs, base yourself in the desert communities linked by Twentynine Palms Hwy (Hwy 62) along the park's northern perimeter.

Sights & Activities

Joshua Tree has three park entrances. Access the west entrance from the town of Joshua Tree, the north entrance from Twentynine Palms and the south entrance from I-10. The park's northern half harbors most of the attractions, including all of the Joshua trees.

★Hidden Valley Trail NATURAL LANDSCAPE

Some 8 miles south of the West Entrance, this whimsically dramatic cluster of rocks is a rock climbers' mecca, but just about anyone can enjoy a clamber on the giant boulders. An easy 1-mile trail loops through it and back to the parking lot and picnic area.

★Keys View Trail LOOKOUT

From Park Blvd, it's an easy 20-minute drive up to Keys View (5185ft), where breathtaking views take in the entire Coachella Valley and extend as far as the Salton Sea and – on a good day – Mexico. Looming in front of you are Mt San Jacinto (10,834ft) and Mt San Gorgonio (11,500ft), two of Southern California's highest peaks, while down below you can spot a section of the San Andreas Fault.

Desert Queen Ranch HISTORIC SITE

(☎reservations 760-367-5555; tour adult/child $5/2.50; ⊙tours 10am & 1pm daily year-round, 7pm Tue & Thu-Sat Oct-May) Anyone interested in local history and lore should take the 90-minute guided tour of this ranch that's also known as Keys Ranch after its builder, Russian immigrant William Keys. He built a homestead here on 160 acres in 1917 and over the next 60 years turned it into a full working ranch, school, store and workshop. The buildings stand much as they did when Keys died in 1969.

Tour reservations are highly recommended; remaining tickets may be available one day in advance at the Cottonwood, Joshua Tree and Oasis park visitors centers.

The ranch is about 2 miles northeast of Hidden Valley Campground, up a dirt road.

THE PERFECT DATE

The Coachella Valley is the ideal place to find the date of your dreams – the kind that grows on trees, that is. Some 90% of US date production happens here, with dozens of permutations of shape, size and juiciness, and species with exotic-sounding names such as halawy, deglet noor and golden zahidi.

Date orchards let you sample different varieties for free, an act of shameless but delicious self-promotion. Another signature taste is the date shake: crushed dates mixed into a vanilla milkshake (about $4). They're much richer than they look!

Shields Date Gardens (www.shieldsdategarden.com; 80-225 Hwy 111, Indio; ⊙9am-5pm) In business since 1924 this is where you can watch *The Romance and Sex Life of the Date*, with the chirpy feel of a 1950s educational film.

Oasis Date Gardens (www.oasisdate.com; 59-111 Grapefruit Blvd, Thermal; ⊙9am-4pm) En route to the Salton Sea, this certified-organic date garden is handy for picking up gift boxes and yummy date shakes.

Hadley Fruit Orchards (☎888-854-5655; www.hadleyfruitorchards.com; 48980 Seminole Dr, Cabazon; ⊙9am-7pm Mon-Thu, 8am-8pm Fri-Sun) This landmark claims to have invented trail mix and makes a good grab-and-go stop on your way to or from LA.

National Date Festival (www.datefest.org; Riverside County Fairgrounds, 82-503 Hwy 111, Indio; adult/child $8/6; 👪) For old-fashioned carnival fun, come in February for outrageous camel and ostrich races. From I-10, exit at Monroe St.

Joshua Tree National Park

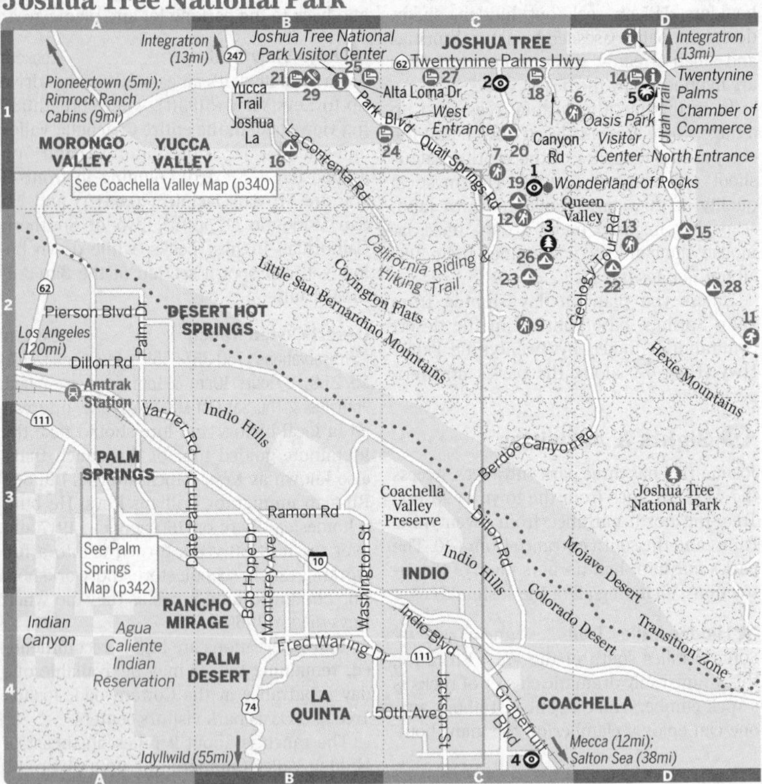

Joshua Tree National Park

Sights

1 Desert Queen Ranch C1
2 Indian Cove C1
3 Joshua Tree National Park C2
4 Oasis Date Gardens C4
5 Oasis of Mara D1

Activities, Courses & Tours

6 49 Palms Oasis Trail D1
7 Boy Scout Trail C1
8 Cholla Cactus Garden Trail E2
9 Lost Horse Mine Trail C2
10 Lost Palms Oasis Trail E4
11 Pinto Basin Road D2
12 Ryan Mountain Trail C2
13 Skull Rock Trail D2

Sleeping

14 29 Palms Inn D1
15 Belle Campground D2
16 Black Rock Canyon Campground B1
17 Cottonwood Campground E4
18 Harmony Motel C1
19 Hidden Valley Campground C1
20 Indian Cove Campground C1
21 Joshua Tree Inn B1
22 Jumbo Rocks Campground D2
23 Ryan Campground C2
24 Sacred Sands C1
25 Safari Motor Inn B1
26 Sheep Pass Campground C2
27 Spin & Margie's Desert Hide-a-Way C1
28 White Tank Campground D2

Eating

29 Crossroads Cafe B1

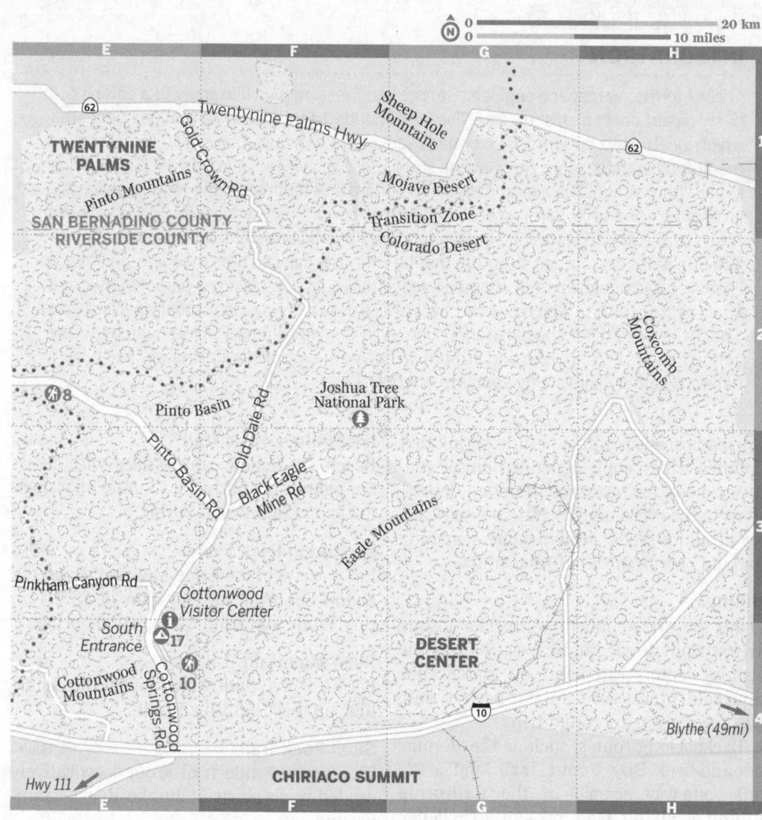

Drive as far as the locked gate where your guide will meet you.

Oasis of Mara OASIS

Behind the Oasis visitors center in Twentynine Palms, this natural oasis encompasses the original 29 palm trees for which the town is named. They were planted by members of the Serrano tribe, who named this 'the place of little springs and much grass.' The Pinto Mountain Fault, a small branch of the San Andreas, runs through the oasis, as does a 0.5-mile, wheelchair-accessible nature trail with labeled desert plants.

Geology Tour Road DRIVING TOUR

East of Hidden Valley, travelers with 4WD vehicles or mountain bikes can take this 18-mile field trip into and around Pleasant Valley, where the forces of erosion, earthquakes and ancient volcanoes have played out in stunning splendor. Before setting out, pick up a self-guided tour brochure and an update on road conditions at any park visitors center.

Covington Flats DRIVING TOUR

Joshua trees grow throughout the northern section of the park, including right along Park Blvd, but some of the biggest trees are found in this area accessed via La Contenta Rd, which runs south off Hwy 62 between the towns of Yucca Valley and Joshua Tree. For photogenic views, follow the dirt road 3.8 miles up Eureka Peak (5516ft) from the picnic area.

Pinto Basin Road DRIVING TOUR

To see the natural transition from the high Mojave Desert to the low Colorado Desert, wind down to Cottonwood Spring, a 30-mile drive from Hidden Valley. Stop at **Cholla Cactus Garden**, where a 0.25-mile loop leads around waving ocotillo plants and jumping 'teddy bear' cholla. Near the Cottonwood visitors center, **Cottonwood**

OFF THE BEATEN TRACK

INTEGRATRON

In 1947 former aerospace engineer George van Tassel moved his family to a patch of dusty desert north of Joshua Tree. The land included a free-standing boulder, beneath which local desert rat Frank Critzer had excavated a series of rooms. Van Tassel started meditating in these rooms and, as the story goes, was visited in August 1953 by a flying saucer from Venus. The aliens invited him aboard and taught him the technique for rejuvenating living cells. Van Tassel used his otherworldly knowledge to build the **Integratron** (☎760-364-3126; www.integratron.com; 2477 Belfield Boulevard, Landers; sound baths $20-80), a wooden domed structure that he variously called a time machine, an antigravity device and a rejuvenation chamber. Judge for yourself by taking a personal tour or a sonic healing bath, in which crystal bowls are struck under the acoustically perfect dome. Check the website for special events such as UFO symposiums. Public sound baths are conducted at 11:45am, 1pm and 2:15pm on two weekends a month (the website has dates). All other visits are by appointment only.

Spring is an oasis with a natural spring that Cahuilla tribespeople depended on for centuries. Look for *morteros,* rounded depressions in the rocks used by Native Americans for grinding seeds. Miners came searching for gold here in the late 19th century.

Hiking

Leave the car behind to appreciate Joshua Tree's trippy lunar landscapes. Staff at the visitors centers can help you match your time and fitness level to the perfect trail. Distances given are round-trip.

Backpacking routes, such as the 16-mile, out-and-back **Boy Scout Trail**, and a 35-mile one-way stretch of the **California Riding & Hiking Trail**, present a challenge because of the need to carry gallons of water per person per day. No open fires are allowed in the park, so you'll also have to bring a camping stove and fuel. Overnight backcountry hikers must register (to aid in census-taking, fire safety and rescue efforts) at one of 13 backcountry boards located at trailhead parking lots throughout the park. Unregistered vehicles left overnight may be cited or towed.

49 Palms Oasis Trail HIKING

Escape the crowds on this 3-mile, up-and-down trail starting near **Indian Cove**.

Barker Dam Trail HIKING

A 1.1-mile loop that passes a little lake and a rock incised with Native American petroglyphs; starts at Barker Dam parking lot.

Lost Horse Mine Trail HIKING

A strenuous 4-mile climb that visits the remains of an authentic Old West silver and gold mine, in operation until 1931.

Lost Palms Oasis Trail HIKING

Reach this remote canyon filled with desert fan palms on a fairly flat 7.2-mile hike starting from Cottonwood Spring.

Mastodon Peak Trail HIKING

Enjoy views of the Eagle Mountains and the Salton Sea from an elevation of 3371ft on this 3-mile hike from Cottonwood Spring.

Ryan Mountain Trail HIKING

For bird's-eye park views, tackle the 3-mile hike up this 5458ft-high peak.

Skull Rock Trail HIKING

This easy 1.7-mile trail around evocatively eroded rocks starts at Jumbo Rocks campground.

Cycling

Popular riding routes include challenging **Pinkham Canyon Rd**, starting from the Cottonwood visitors center, and the long-distance **Black Eagle Mine Rd**, which starts 6.5 miles further north. **Queen Valley** has a gentler set of trails with bike racks found along the way, so people can lock up their bikes and go hiking, but it's busy with cars, as is the bumpy, sandy and steep Geology Tour Rd (p353). There's a wide-open network of dirt roads at Covington Flats (p353).

Cycling is only permitted on paved and dirt public roads; bikes are not allowed on hiking trails.

Rock Climbing

JT's rocks are famous for their rough, high-friction surfaces; from boulders to cracks to multipitch faces, there are more than 8000 established routes. Some of the most popular climbs are in the Hidden Valley area.

Shops catering to climbers with quality gear, advice and tours include **Joshua Tree Outfitters** (☎760-366-1848; www.joshuatreeoutfitters.com; 61707 Hwy 62), **Nomad Ventures** (☎760-366-4684; www.nomadventures.com; 61795 Twentynine Palms Hwy, Joshua Tree; ⏲8am-6pm Mon-Thu, to 8pm Fri & Sat, to 7pm Sun Oct-Apr, 9am-7pm daily May-Sep) and **Coyote Corner** (☎760-366-9683; www.joshuatreevillage.com/546/546.htm; 6535 Park Blvd, Joshua Tree; ⏲9am-7pm).

Joshua Tree Rock Climbing School (☎760-366-4745; www.joshuatreerockclimbing.com), **Vertical Adventures** (☎949-854-6250; www.verticaladventures.com) and **Uprising Adventure** (☎888-254-6266; www.uprising.com) offer guided climbs and climbing instruction starting at $135 for a one-day introduction.

Festivals & Events

National Park Art Festival ART
(www.joshuatree.org/art-festival) This nonprofit festival shows desert-themed paintings, sculpture, photography, ceramics and jewelry in early April.

Joshua Tree Music Festival MUSIC
(www.joshuatreemusicfestival.com; day pass $20-80, weekend pass $140) Over a long weekend in May, this family-friendly, indie-music fest grooves out at Joshua Tree Lake Campground. It's followed by a soulful roots celebration in mid-October. No dogs.

Pioneer Days CULTURAL
(www.visit29.org) Twentynine Palms' Old West–themed carnival on the third October weekend has a parade, an arm-wrestling competition and a chili dinner.

Hwy 62 Art Tours ART
(www.hwy62art.org) Tour artists' studios, galleries and workshops over two weekends in October and/or November.

Sleeping

Inside the park there are only campgrounds, but there are plenty of lodging options along Hwy 62. Twentynine Palms has the biggest selection of accommodations, including national chain motels. Pads in Joshua Tree have more character and charm.

Joshua Tree Inn MOTEL $
(☎760-366-1188; www.joshuatreeinn.com; 61259 Twentynine Palms Hwy, Joshua Tree; r/ste incl breakfast from $89/159; ⏲reception 3pm to 8pm;) This funky-cool, rock 'n' roll-infused, wisteria-strewn motel has 11 spacious rooms behind turquoise doors leading off from a desert-garden courtyard with great views. It gained notoriety in 1973 when rock legend Gram Parsons overdosed in Room 8, now decorated in tribute. Other famous guests have included John Wayne, Donovan and Emmylou Harris.

The communal area features a rock fireplace, where coffee, tea and granola bars are served.

Safari Motor Inn MOTEL $
(☎760-366-1113; www.joshuatreemotel.com; 61959 Twentynine Palms Hwy, Joshua Tree; r from $49; P) This basic, 12-room motel around a simple courtyard is a good option for modern nomads not keen on dropping bunches of cash for a roof over their heads. Most of the well-worn rooms have microwaves and mini refrigerators. It's a short walk to eateries and outdoor outfitters. Pool opens in summer only.

Harmony Motel MOTEL $
(☎760-367-3351; www.harmonymotel.com; 71161 Twentynine Palms Hwy, Twentynine Palms; r $75-85; P@) This 1950s motel, where U2 stayed while working on the *Joshua Tree* album, has a small pool and large, cheerfully painted rooms; some have kitchenettes.

Hicksville Trailer Palace MOTEL $$
(☎310-584-1086; www.hicksville.com; d $100-250;) Fancy sleeping among glowing wigs, in a haunted house, or in a horse stall? Check in at Hicksville, where 'rooms' are eight outlandishly decorated vintage trailers set around a kidney-shaped, saltwater swimming pool. The vision of LA writer and director Morgan Higby Night, each offers a journey into a unique, surreal and slightly wicked world. All but two share facilities. To keep out looky-loos, you'll only be given directions after making reservations.

Spin & Margie's Desert Hide-a-Way INN $$
(☎760-366-9124; www.deserthideaway.com; 64491 Hwy 62; ste $145-175;) This handsome hacienda-style inn is perfect for restoring calm after a long day on the road. The five boldly colored suites are an eccentric symphony of corrugated tin, old license plates and cartoon art. Each has its own kitchen and flat-screen TV with DVD and CD player. Knowledgeable, gregarious owners ensure a relaxed visit. It's down the dirt Sunkist Rd, about 3 miles east of downtown Joshua Tree.

★Sacred Sands B&B $$$

(☎760-424-6407; www.sacredsands.com; 63155 Quail Springs Rd, Joshua Tree; d incl breakfast $299-329;) In an isolated, pin-drop-quiet spot, these two desert-chic suites, each with a private outdoor shower, hot tub, sundeck, 2ft-thick walls and sleeping terrace under the stars, are the ultimate romantic retreat. There are astounding views across the desert hills and into the National Park. Owners Scott and Steve are gracious hosts and killer breakfast cooks.

It's four miles south of Twentynine Palms Hwy (via Park Bl), one mile west of the park entrance.

29 Palms Inn HOTEL $$$

(☎760-367-3505; www.29palmsinn.com; 73950 Inn Ave, Twentynine Palms; r & cottages incl breakfast $100-300;) History oozes from every nook and cranny in these old-timey adobe- and wood-built cabins dotted around a palm oasis.

Camping

Of the park's nine **campgrounds** (www.nps.gov/jotr; camping & RV sites $10-15;), only **Cottonwood** and **Black Rock** have potable water, flush toilets and dump stations. **Indian Cove** and Black Rock accept **reservations** (☎877-444-6777, 518-885-3639; www.recreation.gov). The others are first-come, first-served and have pit toilets, picnic tables and fire grates. None have showers, but there are some at Coyote Corner in Joshua Tree, which charges $4. During the springtime wildflower bloom, campsites fill by noon, if not earlier.

Backcountry camping (no campfires) is allowed 1 mile from any trailhead or road and 100ft from water sources; free self-registration is required at the park's 13 staging areas. Joshua Tree Outfitters (p355) rents and sells quality camping gear.

Along Park Blvd, **Jumbo Rocks** has sheltered rock alcoves that act as perfect sunset- and sunrise-viewing platforms. **Belle** and **White Tank** also have boulder-embracing views. **Hidden Valley** is always busy. **Sheep Pass** and **Ryan** are also centrally located campgrounds.

Family-friendly Black Rock is good for camping novices; more remote Indian Cove also has 100-plus sites. Cottonwood, near the park's southern entrance, is popular with RVs.

Eating & Drinking

Yucca Valley has several large supermarkets, as well as the tiny **Earth Wise Organic Farms**, a co-op that sells produce grown by local farmers; it's at the turnoff to Pioneertown Rd. On Saturday mornings, locals gather for gossip and groceries at the **farmers market** in a parking lot just west of Park Blvd in Joshua Tree. For drinking, check out Pappy & Harriet's (p357) in Pioneertown.

JT's Country Kitchen BREAKFAST, ASIAN $

(☎760-366-8988; 61768 Twentynine Palms Hwy, Joshua Tree; mains $4-10; ⏲6:30am-3pm Wed-Mon) This roadside shack serves all-day breakfasts of down-home cookin': eggs, pancakes, biscuits with gravy, sandwiches and… what's this? Cambodian noodles and salads? Delish.

Crossroads Cafe AMERICAN $

(☎760-366-5414; 61715 Twentynine Palms Hwy, Joshua Tree; mains $5-12; ⏲7am-9pm daily;) The much-loved Crossroads is the go-to place for carbo-loaded breakfasts, fresh sandwiches and dragged-through-the-garden salads that make both omnivores (burgers, Reuben sandwich) and vegans (spinach salad) happy.

Restaurant at 29 Palms Inn AMERICAN, ORGANIC $$

(☎760-367-3505; www.29spalmsinn.com; 73950 Inn Ave, Twentynine Palms; mains lunch $7-15, dinner $12-28; ⏲11am-2pm Mon-Sat, 9am-2pm Sun, 5-9pm Sun-Thu, 5pm-9:30pm Fri & Sat;) This well-respected restaurant has its own organic garden and does burgers and salads at lunchtime, and grilled meats and toothsome pastas for dinner.

Pie for the People PIZZERIA $$

(☎760-366-0400; www.pieforthepeople.com; 61740 Hwy 62, Joshua Tree; pizzas $11-25; ⏲11am-9pm Mon-Thu, to 10pm Fri & Sat, to 8pm Sun;) Thin-crust pizzas for takeout and delivery. Flavors span standards to the David Bowie: white pizza with mozzarella, Guinness caramelized onions, jalapenos, pineapple, bacon, and sweet plum sauce. Enjoy yours under the exposed rafters in the wood and corrugated metal dining room, or under the tree on the back patio.

Joshua Tree Saloon BAR

(www.thejoshuatreesaloon.com; 61835 Twentynine Palms Hwy; ⏲8am-2am;) This watering hole with jukebox, pool tables and cowboy flair serves bar food along with rib-sticking burgers and steaks. Most people come here for the nightly entertainment, such as open-mic Tuesdays, karaoke Wednesdays and DJ Fridays. Over 21 only.

Shopping

In arty Joshua Tree, look for a cluster of galleries on Twentynine Palms Hwy within a couple blocks of the park entrance. Opening hours and works vary.

Wind Walkers CRAFTS
(http://windwalkershoppe.com; 61731 Twentynine Palms Hwy, Joshua Tree; ⏲9am-4pm Thu-Tue) This neat place has an entire courtyard with pottery large and small, as well as a hand-picked selection of Native American crafts, silver jewelry, blankets and knickknacks.

Ricochet Vintage Wears VINTAGE
(61705 Twentynine Palms Hwy, Joshua Tree; ⏲11am-3pm Fri & Mon, 10am-3pm Sat & Sun) Great assortment of recycled clothing and accessories, including cowboy shirts and boots, along with some neat old aprons, housewares and vinyl records.

Funky & Darn Near New VINTAGE
(55812 Twentynine Palms Hwy, Yucca Valley) This store just west of the Pioneertown Rd turnoff sells immaculate hand-picked vintage dresses and hand-tailored new clothing at fair prices. It's in a funky block of specialty stores for art and antiques (plus a cool coffee bar).

Information

Joshua Tree National Park (p350) is flanked by I-10 in the south and by Hwy 62 (Twentynine Palms Hwy) in the north. Entry permits ($15 per vehicle) are valid for seven days and come with a map and the seasonally updated *Joshua Tree Guide*.

There are no facilities inside the park other than restrooms, so gas up and bring drinking water and whatever food you need. Potable water is available at the Oasis of Mara, the Black Rock and Cottonwood campgrounds, the West Entrance and the Indian Cove ranger station.

Cell phones don't work in the park, but there's an emergency-only telephone at the Intersection Rock parking lot near the Hidden Valley Campground. Shops around the intersection of Twentynine Palms Hwy and Park Blvd offer internet access.

Pets must be kept on leash and are prohibited on trails.

MEDICAL SERVICES

Hi-Desert Medical Center (☎760-366-3711; 6601 Whitefeather Rd, Joshua Tree; ⏲24hr)

TOURIST INFORMATION

Joshua Tree National Park Visitor Center (6554 Park Blvd, Joshua Tree; ⏲8am-5pm) Just south of Hwy 62.

Black Rock Nature Center (9800 Black Rock Canyon Rd; ⏲8am-4pm Sat-Thu, noon-8pm Fri Oct-May; 👪) National Park visitor center, at the Black Rock Campground.

Cottonwood Visitor Center (Cottonwood Springs, 8 miles north of I-10 Fwy; ⏲9am-3pm)

TURN BACK THE CLOCK AT PIONEERTOWN

Turn north off Hwy 62 onto Pioneertown Rd in Yucca Valley and drive 5 miles straight into the past. Looking like an 1870s frontier town, **Pioneertown** (www.pioneertown.com; admission free; 👪) was actually built in 1946 as a Hollywood Western outdoor movie set. Gene Autry and Roy Rogers were among the original investors, and more than 50 movies and several TV shows were filmed here in the 1940s and '50s. These days the Pioneertown Posse stages mock gunfights on 'Mane St' at 2:30pm on Saturdays and Sundays from April to October.

For local color, toothsome BBQ, cheap beer and kick-ass live music, drop in at **Pappy & Harriet's Pioneertown Palace** (☎760-365-5956; www.pappyandharriets.com; 53688 Pioneertown Rd, Pioneertown; mains $8-29; ⏲11am-2am Thu-Sun, from 5pm Mon), a textbook honky-tonk. Monday's open-mic nights are legendary and often bring out astounding talent.

Within staggering distance is the atmospheric **Pioneertown Motel** (☎760-365-7001; www.pioneertown-motel.com; 5040 Curtis Rd, Pioneertown; r $70-120; ❄📶🐾), where yesteryear's silver-screen stars once slept during filming, and whose rooms are now filled with eccentric Western-themed memorabilia; some have kitchenettes.

About 4.5 miles north of here, **Rimrock Ranch Cabins** (☎760-228-1297; www.rimrockranchcabins.com; 50857 Burns Canyon Rd, Pioneertown; cabins $90-140; ❄🐾) is a cluster of vintage 1940s cabins with kitchens and private patios perfect for stargazing.

National Park visitor center, just inside the park's south entrance.

Joshua Tree Chamber of Commerce (☎760-366-3723; www.joshuatreechamber.org; 6448 Hallee Rd; ⏲10am-4pm Tue, Thu & Sat) Info about hotels, restaurants and shops in the town of Joshua Tree, just north of Hwy 62.

Oasis Park Visitor Center (National Park Blvd, at Utah Trail, Twentynine Palms; ⏲8am-5pm) Outside the north entrance.

Twentynine Palms Chamber of Commerce (☎760-367-3445; www.visit29.org; 73484 Twentynine Palms, Twentynine Palms; ⏲9am-5pm Mon-Fri, 10am-4pm Sat & Sun)

Getting There & Around

Rent a car in Palm Springs or LA. From LA, the trip takes about 2½ to three hours via I-10 and Hwy 62 (Twentynine Palms Hwy). From Palm Springs it takes about an hour to reach the park's west (preferable) or south entrances.

Bus 1, operated by **Morongo Basin Transit Authority** (www.mbtabus.com; one way $2.50, day pass $3.75), runs frequently along Twentynine Palms Hwy. Bus 12 to Palm Springs from Joshua Tree and Yucca Valley (one way/round-trip $10/15) has fewer departures. Many buses are equipped with bicycle racks.

ANZA-BORREGO DESERT STATE PARK

Shaped by an ancient sea and tectonic forces, enormous and little-developed **Anza-Borrego** (☎760-767-4205; www.parks.ca.gov; visitors center 200 Palm Canyon Dr; ⏲park 24hr, visitors center 9am-5pm daily Oct-Apr, Sat, Sun & hol only May-Sep; 👪) covers 640,000 acres, making it the largest state park in the USA outside Alaska. Human history here goes back more than 10,000 years, as recorded by Native American pictographs and petroglyphs. The park is named for Spanish explorer Juan Bautista de Anza, who arrived in 1774, pioneering a colonial trail from Mexico and no doubt running into countless *borregos,* the wild peninsular bighorn sheep that once ranged as far south as Baja California. (Today only a few hundred of these animals survive due to drought, disease, poaching and off-highway driving.) In the 1850s Anza-Borrego became a stop along the Butterfield stagecoach line, which delivered mail between St Louis and San Francisco.

Winter and spring are high seasons. Depending on winter rains, wildflowers bloom brilliantly, albeit briefly, starting in late February. Summers are extremely hot; the daily average temperature in July is 107°F (41°C), but it can reach 125°F (51°C).

Sights & Activities

The park's main town, **Borrego Springs** (population 3429), has a handful of restaurants and lodgings. Nearby are the park visitors center and easy-to-reach sights, such as Borrego Palm Canyon and Fonts Point, that are fairly representative of the park as a whole. The Split Mountain area, east of Ocotillo Wells, is popular with off-highway vehicles (OHVs), but also contains interesting geology and spectacular wind caves. The desert's southernmost region is the least visited and, aside from Blair Valley, has few developed trails and facilities.

Many of the sights are accessible only by dirt roads. To find out which roads require 4WD vehicles, or are currently impassable, check the signboard inside the park visitors center.

Peg Leg Smith Monument — MONUMENT

The pile of rocks by the road northeast of Borrego Springs, where County Rte S22 takes a 90-degree turn east, is actually a monument to Thomas Long 'Peg Leg' Smith – mountain man, fur trapper, horse thief, con artist and Wild West legend. He passed through Borrego Springs in 1829 and allegedly picked up some rocks that were later found to be pure gold. Strangely, when he returned during the Gold Rush era, he was unable to locate the lode. Nevertheless, he told lots of prospectors about it (often in exchange for a few drinks) and many came to search for the 'lost' gold and add to the myths.

Fonts Point — LOOKOUT

East of Borrego Springs, a 4-mile dirt road, sometimes passable without 4WD, diverges south from County Rte S22 out to Fonts Point (1249ft). From up here a spectacular panorama unfolds over the Borrego Valley to the west and the Borrego Badlands to the south. You'll be amazed when the desert seemingly drops from beneath your feet.

Vallecito County Park — HISTORIC SITE

(☎760-765-1188; www.co.san-diego.ca.us/parks; 37349 County Rte S2; admission per car $3; ⏲Sep-May) This pretty little park in a refreshing valley in the southern part of the Anza-Borrego park centers on a replica of a historic **Butterfield Stage Station**. It's 36 miles south of Borrego Springs via County Rte S2.

Agua Caliente County Park SWIMMING
(☎760-765-1188; www.sdcounty.ca.gov/parks/; 39555 Rte S2; entry per car $5; ⏰9:30am-5pm Sep-May) In a lovely park 4 miles from Vallecito, you can take a dip in indoor and outdoor pools fed by hot natural mineral springs.

Hiking

Borrego Palm Canyon Trail HIKING
This popular 3-mile loop trail starts at the top of Borrego Palm Canyon Campground, 1 mile north of the visitors center, and goes past a palm grove and waterfall, a delightful oasis in the dry, rocky countryside. Keep an eye out for bighorn sheep.

Maidenhair Falls Trail HIKING
This plucky trail starts from the Hellhole Canyon Trailhead, 2 miles west of the visitors center on County Rte S22, and climbs for 3 miles past several palm oases to a seasonal waterfall that supports bird life and a variety of plants.

Ghost Mountain Trail HIKING
A steep 2-mile round-trip trail climbs to the remains of the 1930s adobe homestead built by desert recluse Marshall South and his family. Pick it up in Blair Valley, at the Little Pass primitive campground.

Pictograph/Smuggler's Canyon Trail HIKING
In Blair Valley, this 2-mile round-trip trail skirts boulders covered in Native American pictographs and also offers a nice view of the Vallecito Valley. Take the Blair Valley turnoff on County Rte S2, and continue on the dirt road for about 3.8 miles to the turnoff for a parking area reached in another 1.5 miles.

Elephant Tree Trail HIKING
The rare elephant trees get their name from their stubby trunks, which are thought to resemble elephant legs. Unfortunately only one living elephant tree remains along this 1.5-mile loop trail but it's still a nice, easy hike through a rock wash. The turnoff is on Split Mountain Rd, about 6 miles south of Hwy 78 and Ocotillo Wells.

Split Mountain Wind Caves HIKING
Four miles south of the Elephant Tree Trail, on Split Mountain Rd, is the dirt-road turnoff for Fish Creek primitive campground; another 4 miles brings you to Split Mountain, where a popular 4WD road goes right between 600ft-high walls created by earthquakes and erosion. At the southern end of this 2-mile-long gorge, a steep 1-mile trail leads up to delicate **wind caves** carved into sandstone outcrops.

Blair Valley HIKING
In the west of the park, about 5 miles southeast of Scissors Crossing (where County Rte S2 crosses Hwy 78), is Blair Valley, known for its Native American pictographs and *morteros* (hollows in rocks used for grinding seeds). The valley and its hiking trailheads lie a few miles east of County Rte S2, along a dirt road. Over on the north side of the valley, a **monument** at Foot and Walker Pass marks a difficult spot on the Butterfield Overland Stage Route. In **Box Canyon** you can see the marks where wagons had to hack through the rocks to widen the Emigrant Trail.

Cycling

Over 500 miles of the park's dirt and paved roads (but never hiking trails) are open to bikes. Popular routes are Grapevine Canyon off Hwy 78 and Canyon Sin Nombre in the Carrizo Badlands. Flatter areas include Blair

EASY HIKES IN ANZA-BORREGO

Bill Kenyon Overlook This 1-mile loop from Yaqui Pass primitive campground rolls out to a viewpoint over the San Felipe Wash, the Pinyon Mountains and, on clear days, the Salton Sea.

Yaqui Well Trail A 2-mile trail that leads past labeled desert plants and a natural water hole that attracts a rich variety of birds; starts opposite Tamarisk Grove campground.

Narrows Earth Trail Some 4.5 miles east of Tamarisk Grove along Hwy 78, this 0.5-mile path is an amateur geologist's dream walk through a fault zone. Look for low-lying, brilliant-red chuparosa shrubs, which attract hummingbirds.

Cactus Loop Trail A self-guided, 1-mile round-trip past a great variety of cacti; starts across from Tamarisk campground and delivers nice views of San Felipe Wash.

Anza-Borrego State Park

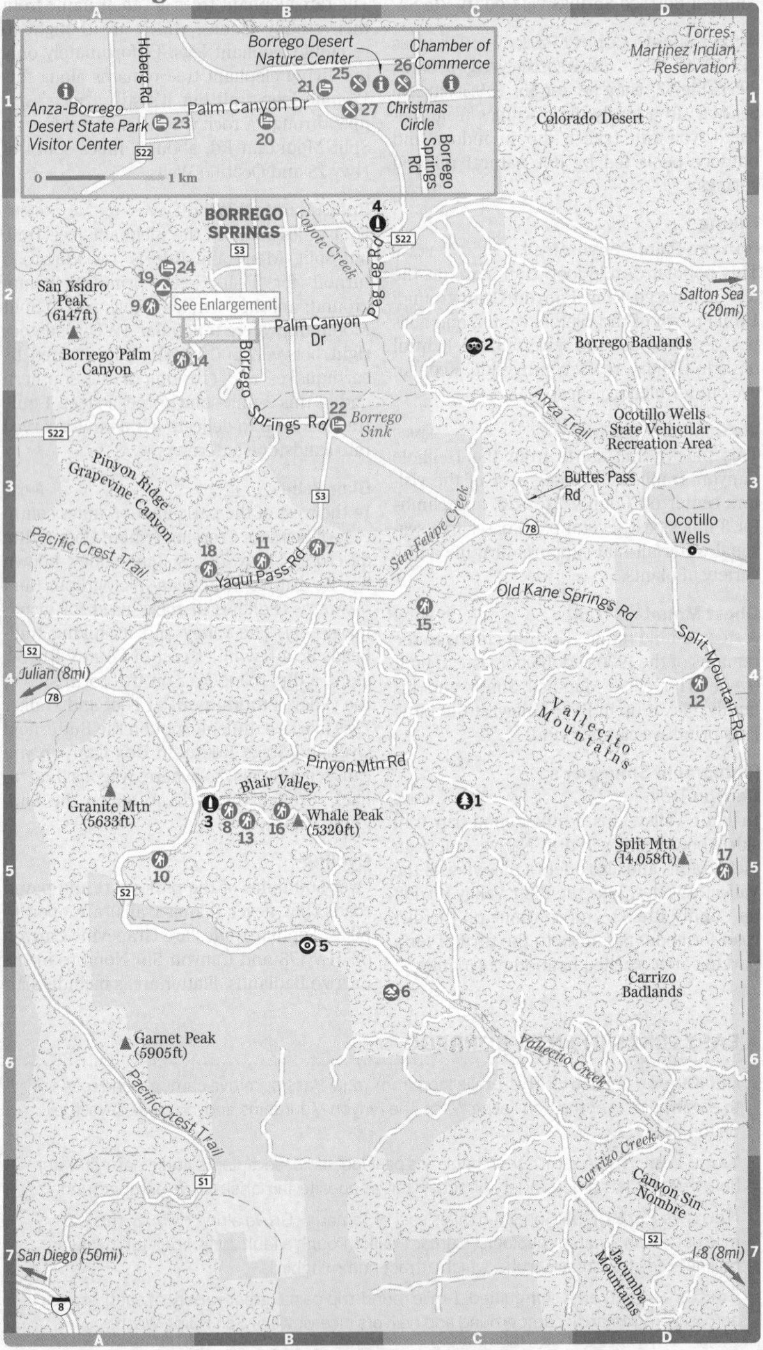

0 10 km
0 5 miles

A B C D
1 2 3 4 5 6 7

Borrego Desert Nature Center
Chamber of Commerce
25
26
21
Hoberg Rd
Anza-Borrego Desert State Park Visitor Center
23
Palm Canyon Dr
20
27
Christmas Circle
Borrego Springs Rd
S22
0 1 km

Torres-Martinez Indian Reservation
Colorado Desert
BORREGO SPRINGS
S3
Coyote Creek
4
Peg Leg Rd
S22
19
24
San Ysidro Peak (6147ft)
9
See Enlargement
Palm Canyon Dr
Salton Sea (20mi)
2
Borrego Badlands
Borrego Palm Canyon
14
Borrego Springs Rd
22
Borrego Sink
Anza Trail
Ocotillo Wells State Vehicular Recreation Area
S22
Pinyon Ridge
Grapevine Canyon
Buttes Pass Rd
S3
San Felipe Creek
78
Ocotillo Wells
Pacific Crest Trail
18
11
7
Yaqui Pass Rd
Old Kane Springs Rd
15
Split Mountain Rd
S2
Julian (8mi)
78
12
Vallecito Mountains
Pinyon Mtn Rd
Blair Valley
Granite Mtn (5633ft)
3
8
13
16
Whale Peak (5320ft)
1
Split Mtn (14,058ft)
17
10
S2
5
6
Carrizo Badlands
Garnet Peak (5905ft)
Vallecito Creek
Pacific Crest Trail
Carrizo Creek
S1
Canyon Sin Nombre
S2
San Diego (50mi)
Jacumba Mountains
I-8 (8mi)
8

Anza-Borrego State Park

Sights
1 Anza-Borrego Desert State Park C5
2 Fonts Point C2
3 Foot and Walker Pass Monument B5
4 Peg Leg Smith Monument B2
5 Vallecito County Park B5

Activities, Courses & Tours
6 Agua Caliente County Park C6
7 Bill Kenyon Overlook B3
8 Blair Valley B5
9 Borrego Palm Canyon Trail A2
10 Box Canyon A5
11 Cactus Loop Trail B3
12 Elephant Tree Trail D4
13 Ghost Mountain Trail B5
14 Maidenhair Falls Trail A2
15 Narrows Earth Trail C4
16 Pictograph/Smuggler's Canyon Trail B5
17 Split Mountain Wind Caves D5
18 Yaqui Well Trail B3

Sleeping
Agua Caliente County Park Campground .... (see 6)
19 Borrego Palm Canyon Campground A2
20 Borrego Valley Inn B1
21 Hacienda del Sol B1
22 La Casa del Zorro B3
23 Palm Canyon Hotel & RV Resort A1
24 Palms at Indian Head A2
Vallecito County Park Campground .... (see 5)

Eating
25 Borrego Springs Center Market B1
26 Carlee's Place C1
Carmelita's Bar & Grill .... (see 27)
27 Kendall's Café B1

Valley and Split Mountain. Get details at the visitors center.

Festivals & Events

Peg Leg Smith Liars Contest CULTURAL
In this hilarious event on the first Saturday of April, amateur liars compete in the Western tradition of telling tall tales. Anyone can enter, so long as the story is about gold and mining in the Southwest, is less than five minutes long and is anything but the truth.

Sleeping

Free backcountry camping is permitted anywhere that's off-road and at least 100ft from water. There are also several free primitive campgrounds with pit toilets but no water in the park. All campfires must be in metal containers. Gathering vegetation (dead or alive) is strictly prohibited.

Room rates drop significantly in summer; some places close altogether.

Hacienda del Sol HOTEL $
(760-767-5442; www.haciendadelsol-borrego.com; 610 Palm Canyon Dr; r/duplex/cottages $80/135/165;) Bask in the retro glow of this small hotel that's been put through some upgrades and now sports new beds and DVD players (free DVD rentals). Choose from hotel rooms, cottages and duplex units. The pool is great for relaxing or socializing.

Borrego Palm Canyon Campground CAMPGROUND $
(800-444-7275; www.reserveamerica.com; tent/RV sites $25/35;) Near the visitors center, this campground has award-winning toilets, close-together campsites and an amphitheater with ranger programs.

Agua Caliente County Park Campground CAMPGROUND $
(reservations 858-565-3600; www.co.san-diego.ca.us/parks; 39555 County Rte S2; tent sites $19, RV sites with partial/full hookups $24/28; Sep-May;) A good choice for sociable RVers, with natural hot-spring pools.

Vallecito County Park Campground CAMPGROUND $
(reservations 858-565-3600; www.co.san-diego.ca.us/parks; 37349 County Rte S2; tent & RV sites $19; Sep-May;) Has tent-friendly sites in a cool, green valley refuge.

Palm Canyon Hotel & RV Resort MOTEL $$
(760-767-5341; www.palmcanyonresort.com; 221 Palm Canyon Dr, Borrego Springs; r $99-179;) For that Old West flair, check into this welcoming motel, but don't be fooled: the place was only built in the '80s! It's about a mile from the park's visitors center and has two pools for unwinding, and a restaurant and saloon for sustenance.

Palms at Indian Head BOUTIQUE HOTEL **$$**
(760-767-7788; www.thepalmsatindianhead.com; 2200 Hoberg Rd; r $139-229;) This former haunt of Cary Grant, Marilyn Monroe and other old-time celebs has been reborn as a chic mid-century modern retreat. Connect with the era over martinis and chicken cordon bleu at the on-site bar and grill (called Red Ocotillo during the day and Krazy Coyote at night) while enjoying mesmerizing desert views.

La Casa del Zorro RESORT **$$$**
(760-767-0100; www.lacasadelzorro.com; 3845 Yaqui Pass Rd; r Sun-Thu from $189, from Fri & Sat $289;) About 5 miles south of central Borrego Springs, San Diego families have been coming to this resort for generations. It had seen hard times and was closed earlier this decade, but it's reopened and is again the region's grandest stay. It has 67 rooms and casitas on 42 landscaped acres with tennis, 26 swimming pools, bocce and croquet courts, as well as a spa and gourmet restaurant.

Borrego Valley Inn INN **$$$**
(800-333-5810, 760-767-0311; www.borregovalleyinn.com; 405 Palm Canyon Dr; r incl breakfast $215-295;) This petite, immaculately kept inn, filled with Southwestern knickknacks and Native American weavings, is an intimate spa-resort, perfect for adults. There's 15 rooms on 10 acres. One pool is clothing-optional. Most rooms have kitchenettes. The grounds are entirely nonsmoking.

Eating & Drinking

In summer many places keep shorter hours or close additional days. Self-caterers can stock up at the **Center Market** (590 Palm Canyon Dr; 8:30am-6:30pm Mon-Sat, to 5pm Sun) in Borrego Springs.

Kendall's Café DINER **$**
(760-767-3491; 587 Palm Canyon Dr, the Mall; mains breakfast $4-12, lunch $6-12, dinner $9-17; 6am-8pm) This coffee shop is a hometown favorite for blueberry pancakes at breakfast and a combination of Mexican (enchiladas, fajitas etc) and straight-down-the-middle American standards the rest of the day.

Carmelita's Bar & Grill MEXICAN **$$**
(760-767-5666; 575 Palm Canyon Dr, the Mall; breakfast $5-9, lunch & dinner $9.50-14; 10am-9pm Mon-Fri, 8am-9pm Sat & Sun;) This lively joint with its cheerful decor serves the best Mexican food in town, including delicious huevos rancheros. The bar staff knows how to whip up a good margarita.

Carlee's Place AMERICAN **$$**
(760-767-3262; 660 Palm Canyon Dr; mains lunch $8-14, dinner $12-27; 11am-9pm) Even though the decor feels like it hasn't been updated since the 1970s, locals pick Carlee's for its burgers, pastas and steak dinners. The pool table, live music and karaoke are big draws, too.

Information

Driving through the park is free but if you camp, hike or picnic, a day fee of $8 per car applies. You'll need a 4WD to tackle the 500 miles of backcountry dirt road.

Borrego Springs has stores, ATMs, banks, gas stations, a post office and a public library with free internet access and wi-fi. Cell phones may work in Borrego Springs but nowhere else.

Borrego Desert Nature Center (760-767-3098; www.california-desert.org; 652 Palm Canyon Dr, Borrego Springs; 9am-5pm daily Sep-Jun, 9am-3pm Fri & Sat Jul & Aug) Excellent bookshop run by the Anza-Borrego Desert Natural History Association, which also organizes tours, lectures, guided hikes and outdoor-skills courses.

Chamber of Commerce (760-767-5555; www.borregospringschamber.com; 786 Palm Canyon Dr, Borrego Springs; 9am-4pm Mon-Sat) Tourist information.

Anza-Borrego Desert State Park Visitor Center (760-767-4205; www.parks.ca.gov; 200 Palm Canyon Dr, Borrego Springs; 9am-5pm Oct-May, Sat & Sun only Jun-Sep) Built partly underground, the stone walls of the park visitors center blend beautifully with the mountain backdrop, while inside are top-notch displays and audiovisual presentations. Two miles west of Borrego Springs.

Wildflower Hotline (760-767-4684).

Getting There & Around

There is no public transport to Anza-Borrego Desert State Park. From Palm Springs (1½ hours) take I-10 to Indio, then Hwy 86 south along the Salton Sea and west onto S22. From LA (three hours) and Orange County (via Temecula) take I-15 south to Hwy 79 to County Rtes S2 and S22. From San Diego (two hours), I-8 to County Rte S2 is easiest, but if you want a more scenic ride, take twisty Hwy 79 from I-8 north through Cuyamaca Rancho State Park and into Julian, then head east on Hwy 78.

AROUND ANZA-BORREGO

Salton Sea

Driving along Hwy 111 southeast of Indio, it's a most unexpected sight: California's largest lake in the middle of its largest desert. The Salton Sea has a fascinating past, complicated present and uncertain future.

Geologists say that the Gulf of California once extended 150 miles north of the present-day Coachella Valley, but millions of years' worth of rich silt flowing through the Colorado River gradually cut it off, leaving a sink behind. By the mid-1800s the sink was the site of salt mines and geologists realized that the mineral-rich soil would make excellent farmland. Colorado River water was diverted into irrigation canals.

In 1905 the Colorado River breached, giving birth to the Salton Sea. It took 18 months, 1500 workers and 500,000 tons of rock to put the river back on course, but with no natural outlet, the water was here to stay. Today, the Salton Sea is about 35 miles long and 15 miles wide and has water that is 30% saltier than the Pacific Ocean.

By mid-century the Salton Sea was stocked with fish and marketed as the 'California Riviera'; vacation homes lined its shores. The fish, in turn, attracted birds, and the sea remains a prime spot for bird-watching, including 400 species of migratory and endangered species such as snow geese, eared grebes, ruddy ducks, white and brown pelicans, bald eagles and peregrine falcons.

These days, if you've heard of the Salton Sea at all, it's probably due to annual fish die-offs, which are caused by phosphorous and nitrogen in agricultural runoff from nearby farmland. The minerals cause algal blooms, and when the algae die they deprive the water – and fish – of oxygen. Even if farming were to stop tomorrow, there are still generations' worth of minerals in the soil, waiting to reach the sink.

One solution would seem to be to cut off the water to the sea and let it die, but that carries its own dilemma. A dry Salton Sea would leave a dust bowl with a potential dust cloud that could widely devastate the local air quality. The debate rages on.

Stop by the visitor center of the **Salton Sea State Recreation Area** (☎760-393-3810; www.parks.ca.gov; ⊙visitor center 10am-4pm Nov-Mar), on the north shore. Further south, **Sonny Bono Salton Sea National Wildlife Refuge** (www.fws.gov/saltonsea; 906 W Sinclair Rd, Calipatria; ⊙sunrise-sunset, visitors center 7am-3:15pm Mon-Fri year-round) is a major migratory stopover along the Pacific Flyway and has a visitors center, a short self-guided trail, an observation tower and a picnic area. It's about 4 miles west of Hwy 111, between Niland and Calipatria.

> OFF THE BEATEN TRACK
>
> **SALVATION MOUNTAIN**
>
> Southeast of the Salton Sea, **Salvation Mountain** (www.salvationmountain.us) is a mighty strange sight indeed: a 100ft-high hill of concrete and hand-mixed adobe slathered in colorful paint and found objects (hay bales, tires, telephone poles) and inscribed with religious messages, surrounded by chapel-like grottoes. The work of Leonard Knight (1931–2014) was 28 years in the making and has become one of the great works of American folk art that's even been recognized as a national treasure in the US Senate. It's in Niland, about 3 miles off Hwy 111, via Main St/Beal Rd and past train tracks and trailer parks.

Julian

The mountain hamlet of Julian, with its three-block main street, is a favorite getaway for city folk who love its quaint 1870s streetscape, gold-mining lore and famous apple pies. Prospectors, including many Confederate veterans, arrived here after the Civil War, but the population did not explode until the discovery of flecks of gold in 1869. Today, apples are the new gold. There are nearly 17,000 trees in the orchards flanking Hwy 178 outside town. The harvest takes place in early fall when some farmers may let you pick your own apples. At any time, at least taste a slice of delicious apple pie, sold at bakeries all over town.

Julian sits at the junction of Hwys 78 and 79. It's about 1¼ hours from San Diego (via I-8 east to Hwy 79 north) and 40 minutes from Borrego Springs Head (south over Yaqui Pass on County Rte S3, then Hwy 78 west).

For more information, contact the **Chamber of Commerce** (☎760-765-1857; www.juliancа.com; 2129 Main St; ⊙10am-4pm).

Sights

Eagle and High Peak Mine HISTORIC SITE
(☎760-765-0036; end of C St; adult/child $10/5; ⏰10am-2pm Mon-Fri, to 3pm Sat & Sun; 👪) Be regaled with tales of the hardscrabble life of the town's early pioneers during an hour-long underground tour through these former gold mines.

Sleeping & Eating

Julian Gold Rush Hotel B&B $$
(☎760-765-0201, 800-734-5854; www.julianhotel.com; 2032 Main St; d incl breakfast $135-210; 📶) At this 1897 antique-filled B&B, lace curtains, claw-foot tubs and other paraphernalia painstakingly evoke a bygone era.

Orchard Hill Country Inn B&B $$$
(☎760-765-1700; www.orchardhill.com; 2502 Washington St; incl breakfast r $195-250, cottage $295-375; @📶) Turn back the clock at this romantic B&B where rooms are spread across a craftsman lodge and a dozen cozy cottages, all furnished with impeccable taste. Each is decorated differently but all feature a fireplace or patio; some also have Jacuzzi tubs.

Julian Pie Company BAKERY $
(www.julianpie.com; 2225 Main St; snacks & pies $3-15; ⏰9am-5pm; 👪) This popular joint churns out apple cider, cinnamon-dusted cider donuts and classic apple-filled pies and pastries.

ROUTE 66

Completed in 1926, iconic Route 66 connected Chicago and Los Angeles across the heartland of America. What novelist John Steinbeck called the 'Mother Road' came into its own during the Depression, when thousands of migrants escaped the Dust Bowl by slogging westward in beat-up old jalopies painted with 'California or Bust' signs, *Grapes of Wrath*-style. After WWII Americans took their newfound wealth and convertible cars on the road to get their kicks on Route 66.

As traffic along the USA's post-WWII interstate highway system boomed, many small towns along Route 66, with their neon-signed motor courts, diners and drive-ins, eventually went out of business.

In California Route 66 mostly follows the National Trails Hwy, prone to potholes and dangerous bumps. From the beach in Santa Monica, it rumbles through the LA basin, crosses over the Cajon Pass to the railroad towns of Barstow and Victorville and runs a gauntlet of Mojave Desert ghost towns, arriving in Needles near the Nevada stateline.

In larger towns, Mother Road relics may require a careful eye amid more contemporary architecture, but as you head toward Nevada, wide open vistas and the occasional landmark remain barely changed from the days of road trippers.

Los Angeles to Barstow

Route 66 kicks off in Santa Monica, at the intersection of Ocean Ave and Santa Monica Blvd. Follow the latter through Beverly Hills and West Hollywood, turn right on Sunset Blvd and pick up the 110 Fwy north to Pasadena. Take exit 31B and drive south on Fair Oaks Ave for an egg cream at the **Fair Oaks Pharmacy** (☎626-799-1414; www.fairoakspharmacy.net; 1526 Mission St; mains $4-8; ⏰9am-9pm Mon-Fri, to 10pm Sat, 10am-7pm Sun; 👪), a nostalgic soda fountain from 1915. Turn around and follow Fair Oaks Ave north, then turn right on Colorado Blvd, where the vintage Saga Motor Hotel (p198) still hands out quaint metal room keys to its guests.

Continue east on Colorado Blvd to Colorado Pl and Santa Anita Park (p197), where the Marx Brothers' *A Day at the Races* was filmed and legendary thoroughbred Seabiscuit ran. During the live-racing season, free tram tours take you behind the scenes into the jockeys' room and training areas; weekends only, reservations required.

Colorado Pl turns into Huntington Dr E, which you'll follow to 2nd Ave, where you turn north, then east on Foothill Blvd. This older alignment of Route 66 follows Foothill Blvd through Monrovia, home of the 1925 Mayan Revival–style architecture of the allegedly haunted **Aztec Hotel** (☎626-358-3231; 311 W Foothill Blvd, Monrovia).

Continue east on W Foothill Blvd, then jog south on S Myrtle Ave and hook a left on E Huntington Dr through Duarte, which puts on a **Route 66 parade** (http://duarteroute66parade.com; ⏰September), with boisterous marching bands, old-fashioned carnival games and a classic-car show. In Azusa, Huntington turns into E Foothill Blvd, which becomes Alosta Blvd in Glendora where **The Hat** (☎626-857-0017; www.thehat.com; 611 W Route 66, Glendora; mains $4-8; ⏰10am-11pm Sun-

Wed, to 1am Thu-Sat;) has made piled-high pastrami sandwiches since 1951.

Continue east on Foothill Blvd, where two campily retro steakhouses await in Rancho Cucamonga. First up is the 1955 **Magic Lamp Inn** (909-981-8659; www.themagiclampinn.com; 8189 Foothill Blvd, Rancho Cucamonga; mains lunch $11-17, dinner $15-42; 11:30am-2:30pm Tue-Fri, 5-11pm Tue-Thu, 5-10:30pm Fri & Sat, 4-9pm Sun), easily recognized by its fabulous neon sign. There's dancing Wednesday through Saturday nights. Up the road, the rustic **Sycamore Inn** (909-982-1104; www.thesycamoreinn.com; 8318 Foothill Blvd, Rancho Cucamonga; mains $22-49; 5-9pm Mon-Thu, to 10pm Fri & Sat, 4-8:30pm Sun) has been dishing up juicy steaks since 1848.

Cruising on through Fontana, birthplace of the notorious Hells Angels biker club, you'll see the now-boarded-up **Giant Orange** (15395 Foothill Blvd, Fontana; no public entry), a 1920s juice stand of the kind that was once a fixture alongside SoCal's citrus groves.

Foothill Blvd continues on to Rialto where you'll find the **Wigwam Motel** (909-875-3005; www.wigwammotel.com; 2728 W Foothill Blvd, Rialto; r $65-80;), whose kooky concrete faux-tepees date from 1949. Continue east, then head north on N East St to the unofficial **First McDonald's Museum** (909-885-6324; 1398 N E St, San Bernardino; admission by donation; 10am-5pm), which has interesting historic Route 66 exhibits. Continue north, then turn left on W Highland Ave and pick up the I-215 Fwy to I-15 and exit at Cleghorn for Cajon Blvd to trundle north on an ancient section of the Mother Road. Get back onto I-15 and drive up to the Cajon Pass. At the top, take the Oak Hill Rd exit (No 138) to the **Summit Inn Cafe** (760-949-8688; 5960 Mariposa Rd, Hesperia; mains $5-10; 6am-8pm Mon-Thu, to 9pm Fri & Sat), a 1950s roadside diner with antique gas pumps, a retro jukebox and a lunch counter that serves ostrich burgers and date shakes.

Get back on I-15 and drive downhill to Victorville, exiting at 7th St and driving past the San Bernardino County Fairgrounds, home of the Route 66 Raceway. Along 7th St in Old Town Victorville, look for landmarks including the bucking bronco sign of the **New Corral Motel**. At D St, turn left for the excellent **California Route 66 Museum** (760-951-0436; www.califrt66museum.org; 16825 D St, Victorville; donations welcome; 10am-4pm Thu-Sat & Mon, 11am-3pm Sun), opposite the Greyhound bus station. Inside a former cafe is a wonderfully eclectic collection including a 1930s teardrop trailer, sparkling red naughahyde booth with tabletop mini-jukebox, advertising signage, vintage photos, and bits and pieces from the Roy Rogers Museum that used to be in Victorville before moving to Branson, Missouri (where it closed in 2010).

Follow South D St north under I-15 where it turns into the National Trails Hwy. Beloved by Harley bikers, this stretch of rolling hills and vast expanses of high desert to Barstow is like a scavenger hunt for Mother Road ruins, such as antique filling stations and tumbledown motor courts.

In Oro Grande, the **Iron Hog Saloon** (20848 National Trails Hwy, Oro Grande; 8am-10pm Mon-Thu & Sun, to 2am Fri & Sat) is an old-time honky-tonk dripping with memorabilia and character(s). It's hugely popular with bikers and serves large portions of rib-stickers, including rattlesnake and ostrich. About 5 miles further north, **Bottle Tree Ranch** (Elmer's Place; 24266 National Trails Hwy, Oro Grande) is a colorful roadside folk-art collection of glass bottles artfully arranged on telephone poles along with weathered railroad signs.

NAVIGATING THE MOTHER ROAD

For Route 66 enthusiasts who want to drive every mile of the old highway, free turn-by-turn driving directions are available online at www.historic66.com. Other useful sites are www.cart66pf.org and www.route66ca.org.

Barstow

At the junction of I-40 and I-15, nearly halfway between LA and Las Vegas, down-and-out Barstow (population 23,000) has been a desert travelers' crossroads for centuries. In 1776 Spanish colonial priest Francisco Garcés caravanned through, and in the mid-19th century the Old Spanish Trail passed nearby, with pioneer settlers on the Mojave River selling supplies to California immigrants. Meanwhile, mines were founded in the hills outside town. Barstow, named after a railway executive, got going as a railroad junction after 1886. After 1926 it became a major rest stop for motorists along Route

66 (Main St). Today it exists to serve nearby military bases and is still a busy pit stop for travelers.

Sights

Barstow is well known for its history-themed **murals** that spruce up often empty and boarded-up downtown buildings, mostly along Main St between 1st and 6th Sts. Pick up a map at the Chamber of Commerce (p367).

Route 66 'Mother Road' Museum MUSEUM
(☎760-255-1890; www.route66museum.org; 681 N 1st St; ⏰10am-4pm Fri & Sat, 11am-4pm Sun, or by appointment) FREE Inside the beautifully restored **Casa del Desierto**, a 1911 Harvey House (architecturally significant railway inns named for their originator Fred Harvey), this museum documents life along the historic highway with some great old black-and-white photographs alongside eclectic relics, including a 1915 Ford Model T, a 1913 telephone switchboard and products made from locally mined minerals. The excellent gift shop stocks Route 66 driving guides, maps and books.

Western America Railroad Museum MUSEUM
(www.barstowrailmuseum.org; 685 N 1st St; ⏰11am-4pm Fri-Sun) FREE Rail buffs make a beeline to the Casa del Desierto to marvel at a century's worth of railroad artifacts, including old timetables, uniforms, china and the Dog Tooth Mountain model railroad. Even when the building's closed, outside you can see historic locomotives, bright-red cabooses and even a car used to ship racehorses.

Desert Discovery Center MUSEUM
(☎760-252-6060; www.desertdiscoverycenter.com; 831 Barstow Rd; ⏰11am-4pm Tue-Sat; 👪) FREE The US Bureau of Land Management operates this kid-oriented, educational center in an adobe building near I-15. Activities include animal-feeding, art club and monthly programs from drums to composting, and you can get info on exploring the local deserts. The star exhibit is the Old Woman Meteorite, the second-largest ever found in the USA, weighing in at a hefty 6070lbs.

Calico Ghost Town THEME PARK
(☎800-862-2542; www.calicotown.com; 36600 Ghost Town Rd, Yermo; adult/child $8/5; ⏰9am-5pm; 👪) This endearingly hokey Old West attraction is a cluster of pioneer-era buildings amid the ruins of a circa 1881 silver mining town, reconstructed nearly a century later by Walter Knott of Knott's Berry Farm (p236). Admission is cheap, but you'll pay extra to go gold panning, tour the Maggie Mine, ride a narrow-gauge railway or see the 'mystery shack.' Old-timey heritage celebrations include Civil War re-enactments and a bluegrass 'hootenanny.' Take the Ghost Town Rd exit off I-15; it's about 3.5 miles uphill. There's also a campground (tent/RV sites with full hookup $30/35).

Sleeping & Eating

Only when the Mojave freezes over will there be no rooms left in Barstow. Just drive along E Main St and take your pick from the string of national chain motels, many with doubles from $40.

Oak Tree Inn MOTEL $
(☎760-254-1148; www.oaktreeinn.com; 35450 Yermo Rd, Yermo; r incl breakfast $53-74; P ⊖ ❄ 📶 🏊 🐾) For class and comfort, steer towards this three-story, 65-room motel near the freeway, where rooms have black-out draperies and triple-paned windows. It's 11 miles east of town (exit Ghost Town Rd off I-15). Breakfast is served at the adjacent 1950s-style diner.

Lola's Kitchen MEXICAN $
(1244 E Main St; mains $5-12; ⏰4am-7:30pm Mon-Fri, to 4:30pm Sat; 👪) Interstate truckers, blue-collar workers and Vegas-bound hipsters all gather at this simple, colorful Mexican *cocina,* tucked away inside a strip mall and run by two sisters who make succulent *carne asada* burritos, *chile verde* enchiladas and more.

Idle Spurs Steakhouse STEAKHOUSE $$
(☎760-256-8888; www.idlespurssteakhouse.com; 690 Hwy 58; mains lunch $10-24, dinner $14-28; ⏰11am-9pm Mon-Fri, from 4pm Sat & Sun; 👪) In the saddle since 1950, this Western-themed spot, ringed around an atrium and a full bar, is a fave with locals and RVers. Surrender to your inner carnivore with slow-roasted prime rib, hand-cut steaks and succulent lobster tail. Kids menu available. It's a couple miles off Rte 66.

Peggy Sue's DINER $$
(☎760-254-3370; www.peggysuesdiner.com; Ghost Town Rd, Yermo; mains $8-13; ⏰6am-10pm; 👪) Built in 1954 as a simple, nine-stool, three-booth diner, Peggy Sue's has since grown into a mini-empire with ice-cream shop, pizza parlor, a park out back with metal sculptures of 'diner-saurs' and a kitschy-awesome gift shop. It's down the street from Oak Tree Inn (p366).

✩ Entertainment

Skyline Drive-In CINEMA
(☎760-256-3333; 31175 Old Hwy 58; adult/child $7/2;) One of the few drive-ins left in California, this 1960s movie theater shows one or two flicks nightly.

Information

Barstow Area Chamber of Commerce (☎760-256-8617; www.barstowchamber.com; 681 N 1st Ave; ⏲8:30am-5:30pm Mon-Fri, 10am-2pm Sat;) At the train station, just north of downtown.

Barstow Community Hospital (☎760-256-1761; 820 E Mountain View St; ⏲emergency room 24hr)

Getting There & Around

You'll need a car to get around Barstow and drive Route 66. A few major car-rental agencies have in-town offices.

Frequent Greyhound buses from LA ($37, 2½ to 5¼ hours), Las Vegas ($32, 2¾ hours) and Palm Springs ($44, 4½ hours) arrive at the main **bus station** (1611 E Main St) east of downtown, near I-15.

Amtrak's *Southwest Chief* runs to/from LA (www.amtrak.com, from $30, 3¾ hours, advance reservations suggested) daily but is often late. There's no staffed ticket office at Barstow's historic **train station** (685 N 1st Ave).

Barstow to Needles

Leave Barstow on I-40 east and exit at Daggett (exit 7), site of the California inspection station once dreaded by Dust Bowl refugees. Drive north on A St, cross the railroad tracks and turn right on Santa Fe St. On your left, just past the general store, you'll see the moodily crumbling, late-19th-century **Daggett Stone Hotel**, where desert adventurers such as Death Valley Scotty (p372) used to stay.

Continue on Santa Fe, take your first right, then turn left to pick up the National Trails Hwy going east.

Shortly after the highway ducks under I-40, you're in Newberry Springs, where the grizzled, 1950s **Bagdad Cafe** (☎760-257-3101; www.bagdadcafethereal.com; 46548 National Trails Hwy, Newberry Springs; mains $6-12; ⏲7am-7pm) was the main filming location of the eponymous 1987 indie flick starring CCH Pounder and Jack Palance, a cult hit in Europe. The interior is chockablock with posters, movie stills and momentos left by fans, while outside, the old water tower and airstream trailer are slowly rusting away.

The National Trails Hwy runs south along the freeway, crosses it at Lavic and continues east along the northern side of I-40. This potholed, crumbling backcountry stretch of Route 66 crawls through ghostly desert towns. In Ludlow turn right on Crucero Rd, cross I-40 again and pick up the highway by turning left.

Beyond Ludlow, Route 66 veers away from the freeway and bumps along past haunting ruins spliced into the majestic landscape. Only a few landmarks interrupt the limitless horizon, most famously the sign of the well-preserved but defunct, 1950s **Roy's Motel & Cafe** (there's a working gas station and small shop). It's east of **Amboy Crater**, an almost perfectly symmetrical volcanic cinder cone that went dormant 600 years ago. You can scramble up its west side (don't attempt it in high winds or summer heat).

Past Essex the Mother Road leaves National Trails Hwy and heads north on Goffs Rd through Fenner, where it once more crosses I-40. In Goffs the one-room, 1914 Mission-style **Goffs Schoolhouse** (☎760-733-4482; www.mdhca.org; 37198 Lanfair Rd; donations welcome; ⏲usually 9am-4pm Sat & Sun) remains part of the best-preserved historic settlement in the Mojave Desert.

Continue on Goffs Rd (US Hwy 95) to I-40 East and follow it to **Needles**. Named after nearby mountain spires, it's the last Route 66 stop before the Arizona border, where the Old Trails Arch Bridge carried the Joad family across the Colorado River in *The Grapes of Wrath*.

Exit at J St and turn left, follow J St to W Broadway, turn right and then left on F St, which runs into Front St, paralleling the railway track. Go past the old mule-train wagon and 1920s Palm Motel to **El Garces**, a 1908 Harvey House that's been undergoing restorations for years.

MOJAVE NATIONAL PRESERVE

If you're on a quest for the 'middle of nowhere,' you'll find it in the wilderness of the **Mojave National Preserve** (☎760-252-6100; www.nps.gov/moja) FREE, a 1.6-million-acre jumble of sand dunes, Joshua trees, volcanic cinder cones, and habitats for bighorn sheep, desert tortoises, jackrabbits and coyotes. Solitude and serenity are the big draws.

SLOW: DESERT TORTOISE X-ING

The Mojave is the home of the desert tortoise, which can live for up to 80 years, munching on wildflowers and grasses. Its canteen-like bladder allows it to go for up to a year without drinking. Using its strong hind legs, it burrows to escape the summer heat and freezing winter temperatures, and also to lay eggs. The sex of the hatchlings is determined by temperature: cooler for males, hotter for females.

Disease and shrinking habitat have decimated the desert tortoise population. They do like to rest in the shade under parked cars (take a quick look around before just driving away), and are often hit by off-road drivers. If you see a tortoise in trouble (eg stranded in the middle of a road), call a ranger.

It's illegal to pick one up or even approach too closely, and for good reason: a frightened tortoise may urinate on a perceived attacker, possibly dying of dehydration before the next rains come.

Daytime temperatures hover above 100°F (37°C) during summer, then hang around 50°F (10°C) in winter, when snowstorms are not unheard of. Strong winds will practically knock you over in spring and fall. No gas is available within the preserve.

Sights & Activities

You can spend an entire day or just a few hours driving around the preserve, taking in its sights and exploring some of them on foot.

Cima Dome MOUNTAIN

Visible to the south from I-15, Cima Dome is a 1500ft hunk of granite spiked with volcanic cinder cones and crusty outcrops of basalt left by lava. Its slopes are smothered in Joshua trees that collectively make up the largest such forest in the world. For close-ups, tackle the 3-mile round-trip hike up **Teutonia Peak** (5755ft), starting on Cima Rd, 6 miles northwest of Cima.

Kelso Dunes DUNES

Rising up to 600ft high, these beautiful 'singing' dunes are the country's third-tallest sand dunes. Under the right conditions they emanate low humming sounds that are caused by shifting sands. Running downhill sometimes jump-starts the effect. The dunes are 3 miles along a graded dirt road west of Kelbaker Rd, 7.5 miles south of Kelso Depot.

Hole-in-the-Wall HIKING, DRIVING

These vertical walls of rhyolite tuff (pronounced toof), which look like Swiss-cheese cliffs made of unpolished marble, are the result of a powerful prehistoric volcanic eruption that blasted rocks across the landscape. On the 0.5-mile **Rings Trail**, metal rings lead down through a narrow slot canyon, once used by Native Americans to escape 19th-century ranchers. **Wild Horse Canyon Rd**, an incredibly scenic 9.5-mile backcountry drive up to Mid Hills, also starts at Hole-in-the-Wall. Ask at the visitors center if it's currently passable. Hole-in-the-Wall is on Black Canyon Rd, east of Kelso-Cima Rd via unpaved Cedar Canyon Rd. Coming from I-40, exit at Essex Rd.

Sleeping & Eating

Baker, north of the Mojave National Preserve along I-15, has plenty of cheap, largely charmless motels and takeout restaurants. Southeast of the preserve, along Route 66, Needles has slightly better options.

Camping

First-come, first-served sites with pit toilets and potable water are available at two small, developed **campgrounds** (tent & RV sites $12): Hole-in-the-Wall, surrounded by rocky desert landscape; and Mid Hills (no RVs), set among pine and juniper trees. Free backcountry and roadside camping is permitted throughout the preserve in areas already used for the purpose, such as the Rainy Day Mine Site and Granite Pass off the Kelbaker Rd, and Sunrise Rock off the Cima Rd. Ask for details and directions at the visitors centers. There's no camping along paved roads, in day-use areas or within 200yd of any water source.

Information

Hole-in-the-Wall Visitor Center (☎760-252-6104; ⌚9am-4pm Wed-Sun Oct-Apr, 10am-4pm Sat May-Sep) Seasonal ranger programs, backcountry information and road-condition updates. It's about 20 miles north of I-40 via Essex Rd.

Kelso Depot Visitor Center (760-252-6108; 9am-5pm Fri-Tue) The preserve's main visitors center is in a gracefully restored, 1920s Spanish-Mission-revival railway depot. It is staffed with knowledgeable rangers who can help you plan your day. There are also excellent natural and cultural history exhibits, as well as an old-fashioned **lunch counter** (dishes $3.50 to $8.50).

Getting There & Away

Mojave National Preserve is hemmed in by I-15 in the north and I-40 in the south. The main entrance off I-15 is at Baker, from where it's about 30 miles south to the central Kelso Depot visitors center via Kelbaker Rd, which links up with I-40 after another 23 miles. Cima Rd and Morning Star Mine Rd near Nipton are two other northern access roads. From I-40, Essex Rd leads to the Black Canyon Rd and Hole-in-the-Wall.

AROUND MOJAVE NATIONAL PRESERVE

Nipton

On the northeastern edge of the preserve, the teensy, remote outpost of **Nipton** (www.nipton.com) got its start in 1900 as a camp for workers in a nearby gold mine. The railway has passed through here since 1905 en route from Salt Lake City to Los Angeles. In 2010 the settlement made news when it opened a solar plant that generates 85% of its electrical needs.

The charismatic **Hotel Nipton** (760-856-2335; http://nipton.com; 107355 Nipton Rd; cabins/r with shared bath from $65/80; reception 8am-6pm;) dates to the first decade of the 20th century. There are five rooms sharing two baths in an adobe hotel with wraparound porch, as well as 'eco-lodges' (tented cabins) equipped with electricity, fans, woodstoves and platform beds. All guests may unwind in the two outdoor hot tubs.

Check-in is at the well-stocked **trading post** (open 8am to 6pm), which has maps, books, groceries, beverages and souvenirs. Next door is the **Whistle Stop Oasis** (760-856-1045; dishes $7-10; 11am-6pm, dinner by reservation;). No alcohol is served, but you're welcome to purchase beer or wine at the trading post and bring it with you.

There's also an **RV park** (sites $25).

Primm

At the Nevada state line, next to an outlet shopping mall off I-15, **Terrible's Primm Valley Casino Resorts** (888-774-6668, 702-386-7867; www.primmvalleyresorts.com; 31900 Las Vegas Blvd S; r from $30;) is a trio of casino hotels linked by a tram. Rooms are basic and long in the tooth, but fine for a night. Family-friendly Buffalo Bill's is best and has its own amusement park, including a white-knuckle roller coaster and a log flume ride, as well as a buffalo-shaped swimming pool. Whiskey Pete's accepts pets ($15 fee). Primm Valley Hotel & Casino, across the freeway, has a spa and updated fitness center. Each has the gamut of casino-style dining options, including fast-food courts, all-you-can-eat buffets and 24-hour coffee shops.

DEATH VALLEY NATIONAL PARK

The very name evokes all that is harsh, hot and hellish – a punishing, barren and lifeless place of Old Testament severity. Yet closer inspection reveals that in **Death Valley** (760-786-3200; www.nps.gov/deva; 7-day entry per car $20) nature is putting on a truly spectacular show: singing sand dunes, water-sculpted canyons, boulders moving across the desert floor, extinct volcanic craters, palm-shaded oases and plenty of endemic wildlife. This is a land of superlatives, holding the US records for hottest temperature (134°F/57°C), lowest point (Badwater, 282ft below sea level) and largest national park outside Alaska (over 5000 sq miles).

Peak seasons are winter and the springtime wildflower bloom. From late February until early April, lodging within a 100-mile radius is usually booked solid and campgrounds fill before noon, especially on weekends. In summer, when the mercury climbs above 120°F (49°C), a car with reliable air-con is essential and outdoor explorations in the valley should be limited to the early morning and late afternoon. Spend the hottest part of the day by a pool or drive up to the higher – and cooler – elevations. Most of the park is served by paved roads, but if your plans include dirt roads, a high clearance vehicle and off-road tires are essential.

Death Valley & Around

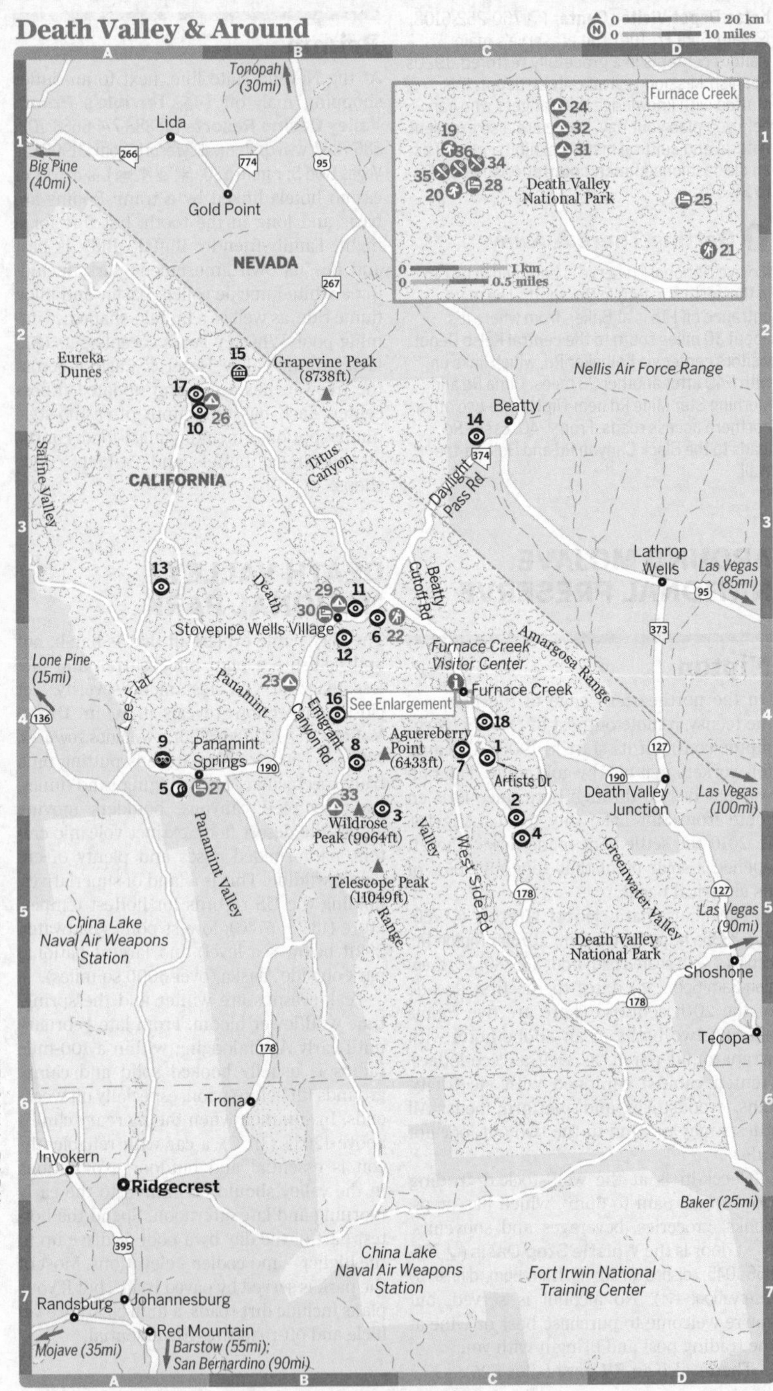

Death Valley & Around

Sights

1 Artists Drive C4
2 Badwater C5
Borax Museum .... (see 28)
3 Charcoal Kilns B4
4 Dante's View C5
5 Darwin Falls A4
6 Devil's Cornfield B3
7 Devil's Golf Course C4
8 Eureka Mines B4
9 Father Crowley Point A4
Goldwell Open Air Museum .... (see 14)
10 Little Hebe Crater A2
11 Mesquite Flat Sand Dunes B3
12 Mosaic Canyon B4
13 Racetrack A3
14 Rhyolite C3
15 Scotty's Castle B2
16 Skidoo B4
17 Ubehebe Crater A2
18 Zabriskie Point C4

Activities, Courses & Tours

19 Furnace Creek Golf Course C1
20 Furnace Creek Stables C1
21 Golden Canyon Interpretive Trail D2
22 Salt Creek Interpretive Trail C3

Sleeping

23 Emigrant Campground B4
24 Furnace Creek Campground C1
25 Inn at Furnace Creek D1
Mahogany Flat Campground .... (see 3)
26 Mesquite Springs Campground B2
27 Panamint Springs Resort A4
28 Ranch at Furnace Creek C1
29 Stovepipe Wells Campground B3
30 Stovepipe Wells Village B3
31 Sunset Campground C1
32 Texas Spring Campground C1
Thorndike Camping .... (see 3)
33 Wildrose Campground B4

Eating

34 49'er Cafe C1
35 Corkscrew Saloon C1
Inn at Furnace Creek .... (see 25)
Panamint Springs Resort .... (see 27)
Toll Road Restaurant & Badwater Saloon .... (see 30)
36 Wrangler Restaurant C1

Sights

Furnace Creek

At 190ft (58m) below sea level, Furnace Creek is Death Valley's commercial hub, with the park's main visitors center, a general store, gas station (super expensive!), post office, ATM, internet access, golf course, lodging and restaurants. Cleverly concealed by a date palm grove is a solar power plant that currently generates one-third of Furnace Creek's energy needs.

Borax Museum MUSEUM

(760-786-2345; 9am-9pm Oct-May, variable in summer) FREE On the grounds of the Ranch at Furnace Creek (p374), this museum explains what all the fuss about borax was about, with alluring samples of local borate minerals and their uses; it's in the 1883 miners' bunkhouse. Out back there's a large collection of pioneer-era stagecoaches and wagons. A short drive north, an interpretive trail follows in the footsteps of late-19th-century Chinese laborers and through the adobe ruins of **Harmony Borax Works**, where you can take a side trip through twisting **Mustard Canyon**.

South of Furnace Creek

If possible start out early in the morning to drive up to **Zabriskie Point** for spectacular valley views across golden badlands eroded into waves, pleats and gullies. Escape the heat by continuing on to **Dante's View** at 5475ft, where you can simultaneously see the highest (Mt Whitney) and lowest (Badwater) points in the contiguous USA. The drive there takes about 1½ to two hours round-trip.

Badwater itself, a foreboding landscape of crinkly salt flats, is a 17-mile drive south of Furnace Creek. Here you can walk out onto a constantly evaporating bed of salty, mineralized water that's otherworldly in its beauty. Along the way, you may want to check out narrow **Golden Canyon**, easily explored on a 2-mile round-trip walk, and **Devil's Golf Course**, where salt has piled up into saw-toothed miniature mountains. About 9 miles south of Furnace Creek, the 9-mile, one-way **Artists Drive** scenic loop offers 'wow' moments around every turn; it's best done in the late afternoon when exposed minerals and volcanic ash make the hills erupt in fireworks of color.

Stovepipe Wells & Around

Stovepipe Wells, about 26 miles northwest of Furnace Creek, was Death Valley's original 1920s tourist resort. Today it has a small store, gas station, ATM, motel, campground and bar. En route, look for the roadside pull-off where you can walk out onto the powdery, Sahara-like **Mesquite Flat sand dunes**. The dunes are at their most photogenic when the sun is low in the sky and are especially magical during a full moon. Across the road, look for the **Devil's Cornfield**, full of arrow weed clumps. Just southwest of Stovepipe Wells, a 3-mile gravel side road leads to **Mosaic Canyon**, where you can hike and scramble along the smooth multihued rock walls. Colors are sharpest at midday.

Along Emigrant Canyon Rd

Some 6 miles southwest of Stovepipe Wells, Emigrant Canyon Rd veers off Hwy 190 and travels south to the park's higher elevations. En route you'll pass the turnoff to **Skidoo**, a mining ghost town where the silent movie *Greed* was filmed in 1923. It's an 8-mile trip on a graded gravel road suitable for high-clearance vehicles only to get to the ruins and jaw-dropping Sierra Nevada views.

Further south, Emigrant Canyon Rd passes the turnoff for the 7-mile dirt road leading past the **Eureka Mines** to the vertiginous **Aguereberry Point** (high-clearance vehicles only), where you'll have fantastic views into the valley and out to the colorful Funeral Mountains from a lofty 6433ft. The best time to visit is in the late afternoon.

Emigrant Canyon Rd now climbs steeply over Emigrant Pass and through Wildrose Canyon to reach the **charcoal kilns**, a line-up of large, stone, beehive-shaped structures historically used by miners to make fuel for smelting silver and lead ore. The landscape is subalpine, with forests of piñon pine and juniper; it can be covered with snow, even in spring.

Panamint Springs

About 30 miles west of Stovepipe Wells, on the edge of the park, Panamint Springs is a tiny enclave with a motel, campground, pricey gas station and small store. Several often overlooked, but wonderful hidden gems are easily accessed from here. **Father Crowley Point**, for instance, peers deep into Rainbow Canyon, created by lava flows and scattered with colorful volcanic cinders. In spring DIY adventurers attempt the 2-mile graded gravel road, followed by a mile-long cross-country hike out to **Darwin Falls**, a spring-fed cascade that plunges into a gorge, embraced by willows that attract migratory birds. You could also take roughshod Saline Valley Rd out to **Lee Flat**, where Joshua trees thrive.

Scotty's Castle & Around

About 55 miles north of Furnace Creek, **Scotty's Castle** (877-444-6777; www.recreation.gov; tours adult/child from $15/7.50; grounds 7am-4:15pm, tour schedules vary) is named for Walter E Scott, alias 'Death Valley Scotty,' a gifted tall-tale teller who captivated people with his fanciful stories of gold. His most lucrative friendship was with Albert and Bessie Johnson, insurance magnates from Chicago. Despite knowing that Scotty was a freeloading liar, they bankrolled the construction of this elaborate Spanish-inspired villa, complete with red-tiled roofs, bell towers and swimming pool (now empty). Restored to its 1930s glory, the historic house has sheepskin drapes, carved California redwood, handmade tiles, elaborately wrought iron, woven Shoshone baskets and a bellowing pipe organ.

There's no charge to enter the grounds, but entrance to the house is by tour only. Costumed guides recount Scotty's apocryphal story in colorful detail on the **Living History Tour** (10am-3pm) and the more technically minded **Underground Tours** (Nov-Apr, as staffing permits). Ranger-guided hiking tours to Scotty's cabin at **Lower Vine Ranch** (adult/child $20/10; as staffing permits) operate on a more limited schedule.

Advance tickets are recommended at least one day before your visit. On tour days, tickets are sold on a first-come, first-served basis at the Scotty's Castle visitors center. Waits of two hours or more for the next available tour are common on high-traffic weekends and holidays.

Three miles west of Scotty's pad, a rough 5-mile road leads to 770ft-deep **Ubehebe Crater**, formed by the explosive meeting of fiery magma and cool groundwater. Hikers can loop around its half-mile-wide rim and over to younger **Little Hebe Crater**.

It's slow going for another 27 miles on a tire-shredding dirt road to the eerie **Racetrack**, where you can ponder the mystery of faint tracks that slow-moving rocks have etched into the dry lakebed. Despite the name, the Racetrack can be accessed only on foot; it's completely off limits when the ground is wet. High-clearance vehicle and off-road tires are required to reach the Racetrack; without them, in the likely event of a flat tire, towing will set you back $1100.

There's a snack bar, but no gas station at Scotty's.

Towards Beatty

Driving north from Furnace Creek, Hwy 374 veers off Hwy 190 and runs 22 miles east to Beatty, across the Nevada state line. About 2 miles outside the park boundary is the turnoff to one-way **Titus Canyon Rd**, one of the most spectacular backcountry roads, leading back toward Scotty's Castle in about 27 miles of unpaved track. The road climbs, dips and winds to a crest in the Grapevine Mountains then slowly descends back to the desert floor past a ghost town, petroglyphs and dramatic canyon narrows. The best light conditions are in the morning. High-clearance vehicles are required. Check road conditions at the visitors center.

Rhyolite (www.rhyolitesite.com; off Hwy 374; sunrise-sunset) FREE, a ghost town a few miles beyond the Titus Canyon turnoff, epitomizes the hurly-burly, boom-and-bust story of Western gold-rush mining towns at the turn of the last century. Amid the skeletal remains of houses, municipal buildings and a three-story bank is the 1906 'bottle house' (built of beer bottles salvaged from town saloons). Also here is the bizarre **Goldwell Open Air Museum** (www.goldwellmuseum.org; off Hwy 374; 24hr) FREE, a trippy art installation conceived by Belgian artist Albert Szukalski.

Activities

Families can pick up fun-for-all-ages **junior ranger program** activity books at the Furnace Creek visitors center, which has info-packed handouts on all kinds of activities, including hiking trails and mountain-biking routes.

Farabee's Jeep Rentals DRIVING TOUR
(760-786-9872; www.farabeesjeeprentals.com; 2-/4-door Jeep incl 200 miles $195/235; mid-Sep–late May) If you don't have a 4WD but would like to explore the park's backcountry, rent a Jeep from this outfit. You must be over 25 years old, have a valid driver's license, credit card and proof of insurance. Rates include water and supplies such as GPS in case of emergency. It's next to Inn at Furnace Creek (p374).

Furnace Creek Bike Rentals MOUNTAIN BIKING
(760-786-3371; bike hire 1/24hr $15/49, Hells Gate Downhill Bike Tour $49; year-round, Hells Gate Downhill Bike Tour 10am & 2pm) The general store at the Ranch at Furnace Creek (p374) rents mountain bikes. Cycling is allowed on all established paved and dirt roads, but never on hiking trails. On demand, staff also organize the 2½-hour **Hells Gate Downhill Bike Tour**, which transports you up to a 2200ft elevation for a 10-mile downhill ride back to the valley floor.

Furnace Creek Golf Course GOLF
(760-786-3373; www.furnacecreekresort.com/activities/golfing; Hwy 190, Furnace Creek; green fees summer/winter $30/60; year-round) For novelty's sake, play a round at the world's lowest-elevation golf course (214ft below sea level, 18 holes, par 70), redesigned by Perry Dye in 1997. It's also been certified by the Audubon Society for its environment-friendly management.

Furnace Creek Stables HORSEBACK RIDING
(760-614-1018; www.furnacecreekstables.net; Hwy 190, Furnace Creek; 1/2hr rides $55/70; mid-Oct–mid-May) Saddle up to see what Death Valley looks like from the back of a horse on these guided rides. The monthly full-moon rides are the most memorable.

CALLING DEATH VALLEY HOME

Timbisha Shoshone tribespeople lived in the Panamint Range for centuries, visiting the valley every winter to gather acorns, hunt waterfowl, catch pupfish in marshes and cultivate small areas of corn, squash and beans. After the federal government created Death Valley National Monument in 1933, the tribe was forced to move several times and was eventually restricted to a 40-acre village site near Furnace Creek, where it still lives. In 2000 President Clinton signed an act transferring 7500 acres of land back to the Timbisha Shoshone tribe, creating the first Native American reservation inside a US national park. Learn more at www.timbisha.com.

Ranch at Furnace Creek Swimming Pool SWIMMING
This huge spring-fed pool is kept at a steady 84°F (29°C) and cleaned with a nifty flow-through system that uses minimal chlorine. It's primarily for Ranch at Furnace Creek (p374) guests, but a limited number of visitor passes are available ($5).

Hiking

Avoid hiking in summer, except on higher-elevation mountain trails, which may be snowed in during winter.

On Hwy 190, just north of Beatty Cutoff Rd, is the half-mile **Salt Creek Interpretive Trail**; in late winter or early spring, rare pupfish splash in the stream alongside the boardwalk. A few miles south of Furnace Creek is Golden Canyon (p371), where a self-guided interpretive trail winds for a mile up to the now-oxidized iron cliffs of **Red Cathedral**. With a good sense of orientation, you can keep going up to Zabriskie Point (p371) for a hardy 4-mile round-trip. Before reaching Badwater, stretch your legs with a 1-mile round-trip walk to the **Natural Bridge**.

Off Wildrose Canyon Rd, starting by the charcoal kilns, **Wildrose Peak** (9064ft) is an 8.4-mile round-trip trail. The elevation gain is 2200ft, but great views start about halfway up.

The park's most demanding summit is **Telescope Peak** (11,049ft), with views that plummet down to the desert floor – which is as far below as two Grand Canyons deep! The 14-mile round-trip climbs 3000ft above Mahogany Flat, off upper Wildrose Canyon Rd. Get full details from the visitors center before setting out.

Festivals & Events

Death Valley '49ers CULTURAL
(www.deathvalley49ers.org) In early or mid-November, Furnace Creek hosts this historical encampment, featuring cowboy poetry, campfire sing-alongs, a gold-panning contest and a Western art show. Show up early to watch the pioneer wagons come thunderin' in.

Sleeping

In-park lodging is pricey and often booked solid in springtime, but there are several gateway towns with cheaper lodging.

Panamint Springs Resort MOTEL, CAMPGROUND $
(☎775-482-7680; www.panamintsprings.com; 40440 Hwy 190, Panamint Springs; tent site $10, RV partial/full hookup $20/35, r $79-129; P ❄ 📶 🏊) Elsewhere 'off the grid' is a state of mind, but it's a statement of fact at this low-key, family-run village of cabins and campgrounds on the park's western border. A generator creates electricity, limited internet access comes via satellite, and phone service is dicey at best (reserve via email or website). At these prices it ain't the Ritz, but rooms, while simple and aging, are clean and decent-sized.

Stovepipe Wells Village MOTEL $$
(☎760-786-2387; www.escapetodeathvalley.com; Hwy 190, Stovepipe Wells; RV sites $33, r $117-176; P ❄ @ 📶 🏊 🐾) The 83 rooms at this sea-level tourist village are newly spruced-up and have quality linens beneath Death Valley-themed artwork, cheerful Native American–patterned bedspreads, coffeemakers and TVs. The small pool is cool and the cowboy-style Toll Road restaurant (p375) serves three squares a day.

Ranch at Furnace Creek RESORT $$
(☎760-786-2345; www.furnacecreekresort.com; Hwy 190, Furnace Creek; cabins $130-162, r $162-213; P ⊖ ❄ 📶 🏊) Tailor-made for families, this rambling resort with multiple, motel-style buildings has received a vigorous facelift, resulting in spiffy rooms swathed in desert colors, updated bathrooms and French doors leading to porches with comfortable patio furniture. The grounds encompass a playground, spring-fed swimming pool, tennis courts, restaurants, shops and the Borax Museum (p371).

Inn at Furnace Creek HOTEL $$$
(☎800-236-7916, 760-786-2345; www.furnacecreekresort.com; Hwy 190; r/ste from $345/450; ⊙mid-Oct–mid-May; P ⊖ ❄ @ 📶 🏊) Roll out of bed and count the colors of the desert as you pull back the curtains in your room at this elegant 1927 Mission-style hotel. After a day of sweaty touring, enjoy languid valley views while lounging by the spring-fed swimming pool, cocktail in hand. The lobby has a 1930s retro look.

Eating & Drinking

Furnace Creek and Stovepipe Wells have general stores stocking basic groceries and camping supplies. Scotty's Castle has a snack bar.

Stovepipe Wells

Toll Road Restaurant & Badwater Saloon AMERICAN $$
(Stovepipe Wells Village, Hwy 190; breakfast buffet $13, lunch $10-17, dinner $13-26; ⏲7am-10am, 11:30am-2pm & 6-10pm;) Above-par cowboy cooking happens at this ranch house, which gets Old West flair from a rustic fireplace and rickety wooden chairs and tables. Many of the mostly meaty mains are made with local ingredients, such as mesquite honey, prickly pear and piñons. Lunch, mid-afternoon drinks and late-night snacks are served next door at **Badwater Saloon** (⏲from 11am), along with cold draft beer and Skynyrd on the jukebox.

Furnace Creek

49'er Cafe AMERICAN $$
(www.furnacecreekresort.com; Ranch at Furnace Creek, Hwy 190; mains breakfast $9-16, lunch $13-20, dinner $10-25; ⏲6am-10am & 11am-9pm Oct-May, 4-9pm only Jun-Sep;) The smallest of the Ranch's main restaurants, this family-friendly stop serves giant omelettes, Benedicts and pancakes for breakfast, plus fish and chips, sandwiches and burgers for lunch. It's always crowded. Portions are huge.

Corkscrew Saloon AMERICAN $$
(Ranch at Furnace Creek, Hwy 190, Furnace Creek; mains $9-19, barbecue $28-36; ⏲11:30am-midnight) This gregarious joint has darts, draft beer and a dynamite barbecue at dinner time, as well as pretty good, but pricey pizzas and pub grub such as onion rings and burgers.

★ **Inn at Furnace Creek** INTERNATIONAL $$$
(☎760-786-2345; mains lunch $13-17, dinner $18-45; ⏲7:30-10:30am, noon-2:30pm & 5:30-9:30pm mid-Oct–mid-May) Views of the Panamint Mountains are stellar from this formal dining room with a dress code (no shorts or T-shirts, jeans ok), where the menu draws inspiration from Continental, Southwestern and Mexican cuisine. Afternoon tea in the lobby lounge and Sunday brunch are hoity-toity affairs. At least have a cocktail on the stone terrace as the sun sets beyond the mountains (and the parking lot, but who's complaining?).

Wrangler Restaurant STEAKHOUSE $$$
(Ranch at Furnace Creek, Hwy 190, Furnace Creek; breakfast/lunch buffet $11/15, dinner mains $27-39; ⏲6-9am, 11am-2pm & 5:30-9pm Oct-May, 6-10am & 6-9:30pm May-Oct) The Ranch at Furnace Creek's main restaurant serves pretty standard but belly-busting buffets at breakfast and lunchtime (when tour bus groups invade) and turns into a pricey steakhouse at night.

CAMPING IN DEATH VALLEY

Of the park's nine campgrounds, only **Furnace Creek** (☎877-444-6777; www.recreation.gov) accepts reservations and only from mid-April to mid-October. All other campgrounds are first-come, first-served. At peak times, such as weekends during the spring wildflower bloom, campsites fill by mid-morning.

Backcountry camping (no campfires) is allowed 2 miles off paved roads and away from developed and day-use areas, and 100yd from any water source; pick up free permits at visitors centers.

Furnace Creek Ranch and Stovepipe Wells Village offer public showers ($5, including swimming-pool access).

CAMPGROUND	SEASON	LOCATION	FEE	CHARACTERISTICS
Furnace Creek	year-round	valley floor	$18	pleasant grounds, some shady sites
Sunset	Oct-Apr	valley floor	$12	huge, RV-oriented
Texas Spring	Oct-Apr	valley floor	$14	good for tents
Stovepipe Wells	Oct-Apr	valley floor	$12	parking-lot style, close to dunes
Mesquite Springs	year-round	1800ft	$12	close to Scotty's Castle
Emigrant	year-round	2100ft	free	tents only
Wildrose	year-round	4100ft	free	seasonal water
Thorndike	Mar-Nov	7400ft	free	may need 4WD, no water
Mahogany Flat	Mar-Nov	8200ft	free	may need 4WD, no water

Panamint

Panamint Springs Resort AMERICAN $$
(Hwy 190, Panamint Springs; dishes from $10; ⏲breakfast, lunch & dinner; 📶) Friendly outback cafe serving pizzas, burgers, salads, steaks and other standards. Toast the panoramic views from the front porch with one of its 100 bottled beers from around the world.

Information

Entry permits ($20 per vehicle) are valid for seven days and are sold at self-service pay stations throughout the park. For a free map and newspaper, show your receipt at the visitors center.

Cell-phone reception is poor to nonexistent in the park; you'll have better luck at Furnace Creek, Stovepipe Wells and Scotty's Castle; get phone cards at general stores in Stovepipe Wells and Furnace Creek.

Furnace Creek Visitor Center (☎760-786-3200; www.nps.gov/deva; ⏲8am-5pm) The park's recently renovated main visitors center has fabulous exhibits on the local ecosystem and the native Timbasha and Shoshone peoples. The gorgeously shot movie *Seeing Death Valley* screens here. Fill up water bottles, and check schedules for ranger-led activities.

Scotty's Castle Visitors Center (☎760-786-2392, ext 231; North Hwy; ⏲8:45am-4:30pm May-Oct, 8:30am-5:30pm Nov-Apr) Has exhibits from the castle's museum-worthy collection.

Getting There & Away

Gas is expensive in the park, so fill up your tank beforehand.

Furnace Creek can be reached via Baker (115 miles, two to 2½ hours), Beatty (45 miles, one to 1½ hours), Las Vegas (via Hwy 160, 120 miles, 2½ to three hours), Lone Pine (105 miles, two hours), Los Angeles (300 miles, five to 5½ hours) and Ridgecrest (via Trona, 120 miles, 2½ to three hours).

AROUND DEATH VALLEY NATIONAL PARK

Beatty, Nevada

Around 45 miles north of Furnace Creek, this historic mining town (population 1154) has certainly seen better days but makes a reasonably inexpensive launch pad for visiting Death Valley. There's an ATM, gas station and library with internet access all along Hwy 95 (Main St).

Sleeping

★**Atomic Inn** MOTEL $
(☎775-553-2250; www.atomic-inn.com; 350 S 1st St; r incl breakfast from $57; ❄📶) 🍃 At this nicely updated, mid-century motel, get a deluxe room to enjoy (somewhat) more contemporary design, flat-screen TVs and DVD players; there's a movie library. Classic movies play in the lobby nightly. Kudos for the solar water-heating system, xeriscaped grounds and little green men out front.

LIFE AT DEATH VALLEY JUNCTION

The spot where Hwys 127 and 190 collide, about 30 miles east of Furnace Creek, is known as Death Valley Junction (population 2, plus a few resident ghosts) and is home to one of California's kookiest roadside attractions: the **Amargosa Opera House** (www.amargosaoperahouse.com; ⏲9am-8pm). Built by the Pacific Borax Company, this 1920s Mexican colonial-style courtyard building was the social hub of Death Valley Junction but fell into disrepair after 1948. In 1967 New York dancer Marta Becket's car broke down nearby. Marta fell in love with the place and decided to inject new life into it by opening an opera house. She entertained the curious with heartbreakingly corny dance-and-mime shows in an auditorium whose walls she personally adorned with fanciful murals showing an audience she imagined attending an opera in the 16th century, including nuns, gypsies and royalty. In 2010 she starred in a 70-minute documentary, *The Ghosts of Death Valley Junction*.

Now in her 80s, Marta's high-stepping days are over, but she still occasionally regales fans with narratives of old times. Tours of the opera house cost $5; enquire at the reception of the attached **motel** (☎775-852-4441; r $70-85). To complete the eccentric experience, spend the night in one of its seriously faded rooms with boudoir lamps and Marta's murals but no TVs or phones. A newer **art gallery** and **train museum** open sporadically, and a **cafe** (mains $9-19, pie per slice $5; ⏲10am-6pm Mon-Thu, 8am-8pm Fri & Sat, 8am-3pm Sun) has delicious homemade pies.

Stagecoach Hotel & Casino CASINO MOTEL $
(775-553-2419, 800-424-4946; www.bestdeathvalleyhotels.com; 900 E Hwy 95 N; r $60-108;) At the edge of town, rooms are pretty bland but large and comfy, while the pool is a nice place to lounge away a dusty day in Death Valley. There's also a small, smoky casino – hello, Nevada! – for slots, blackjack and roulette, and a kids' arcade.

Exchange Club Motel MOTEL $
(775-553-2333; 119 W Main St; s/d $57/62;) The 44 rooms here have had a recent makeover, resulting in new carpets and neutrally hued furniture.

Eating & Drinking

KC's Outpost Eatery & Saloon AMERICAN $
(775-553-9175; 100 Main St; mains $8-9; 10am-10pm Sun-Thu, to 11pm Fri & Sat;) The simple, cinder-block building and formica tables and chairs aren't much to look at, but KC's bulging sandwiches – on homemade bread, no less! – garner raves. The T-bird sandwich is like a mini-Thanksgiving dinner. Potato salad makes a delish side dish. Pizza menu too.

Sourdough Saloon DIVE BAR
(775-553-2266; 106 Main St; 10am-midnight) At the crossroads of town, this classic serves up Jaeger shots, a few American beers on tap, a country-western–heavy jukebox, and locals to mingle with. Every last bit of wall and ceiling space is covered with signed dollar bills. Look for billiards, darts, slot machines and decent pub grub. Downside: main bar is smoky.

Shoshone

Just a blip on the desert map, Shoshone (population 30) is 55 miles from Furnace Creek via Death Valley Junction, though most folks follow the 20-mile-longer, but more scenic, Hwy 178 through Badwater Basin instead. It has a gas station, store, lodging and free public wi-fi access.

Look for a rusted old Chevy parked outside the **Shoshone Museum** (admission by donation; 9am-3pm), which houses quirky and well-meaning exhibits as well the local **visitors center** (760-852-4524; www.deathvalleychamber.org; 10am-4pm;).

Across the street the 1950s **Shoshone Inn** (760-852-4335; www.shoshonevillage.com/shoshone-inn; Hwy 127; d $94-102, cabins $113;) has updated cabins and a dozen basic rooms set around a pine-shaded courtyard, all with satellite TV, that were getting a sprucing up during our visit. Some have a refrigerator and microwave. Bonus: small, warm-springs pool. **Shoshone RV Park** (760-852-4569; RV site with full hookup $25) is just north of town.

Shoshone's only restaurant is **Crow Bar** (760-852-4123; www.shoshonevillage.com/shoshone-crowbar-cafe-saloon; Hwy 127; mains $6-25; 8am-9:30pm), a 1920 road house next to the visitors center. It continues to charm with Mexican dishes with cactus salsa and all-American burgers, sandwiches, steaks and 'rattlesnake' chili (sorry, no actual rattlesnake in it).

Tecopa

Some 8 miles south of Shoshone, the old mining town of Tecopa (population 150) was named after a peace-making Paiute chief and is home to some wonderfully soothing, hot natural mineral springs.

Activities

Delight's Hot Springs Resort HOT SPRINGS
(760-852-4343; www.delightshotspringsresort.com; 368 Tecopa Hot Springs Rd; hot springs 10am-5pm $10, 10am-10pm $15) There are four private hot-springs tubs for splashing around in as well as a handful of 1930s cabins with kitchenette ($89 to $125) and newer motel rooms ($79), in case you want to spend the night.

Tecopa Hot Springs Resort HOT SPRINGS
(760-852-4420; www.tecopahotsprings.org; 860 Tecopa Hot Springs Rd; bathing $8, incl towel $10; call ahead Jun-Sep) Motel lodging ($75 to $95), cabins and campsites (tent/RV $25/35) with spa-pool access included in overnight rates – plus a rock labyrinth and art gallery.

Next door, **Tecopa Hot Springs Campground & Pools** (760-852-4481; hrs vary) has two simple, but clean men's and women's bathhouses (entry $7), where tribal elders, snowbird RVers and curious tourists soak together, plus a private pool for $25 for up to six people.

China Ranch Date Farm FARM
(www.chinaranch.com; 9am-5pm) Just outside Tecopa, this family-run, organic date farm is a lush oasis in the middle of the blistering desert. You can go hiking or bird-watching and, of course, stock up on luscious dates or

try their yummy date nut bread. To get here, follow the Old Spanish Trail Hwy east of Tecopa Hot Springs Rd, turn right on Furnace Creek Rd and look for the signs.

Sleeping & Eating

Cynthia's HOSTEL, INN $$

(760-852-4580; www.discovercynthias.com; 2001 Old Spanish Trail Hwy; dm $22-25, r $75-118, tepee $165-225; check-in 3-8pm;) Match your budget to the bed at this congenial inn helmed by the friendly Cynthia, about three miles from central Tecopa. Your choices: a colorful and eclectically decorated private room in a vintage trailer, a bed in a dorm, or a Native American–style tepee (a short drive away) with thick rugs, fire pits and comfy king-size beds.

Pre-made and freezer-to-grill meals are available with pre-order. Reservations are essential, even if that means just calling ahead from the road.

★ **Pastels Bistro** CALIFORNIAN $$

(860 Tecopa Hot Springs Rd; mains $13-22; noon-9pm Fri-Mon;) This artsy road house sure looks funky-dunky, but the chow is seriously gourmet with lots of healthy, veggie-friendly options (Mediterranean plate, Moroccan eggplant curry, etc.) and charming staff. The California fusion menu, often made with organic ingredients, is always changing. No phone, internet or credit cards.

UPPER MOJAVE DESERT

The Mojave Desert covers a vast region, from urban areas on the northern edge of LA County to the remote, sparsely populated country of the Mojave National Preserve. The upper Mojave is a harsh land, with sporadic mining settlements and vast areas set aside for weapons and aerospace testing. But there are a few things out here worth stopping for, too.

Lancaster-Palmdale

The Antelope Valley is dead flat. It's difficult to see a valley, much less an antelope. But in spring, bright-orange fields of California poppies create a spectacular carpet, like a vision out of *The Wizard of Oz*.

West of Lancaster the **Antelope Valley California Poppy Reserve** (661-724-1180; www.parks.ca.gov; 15101 Lancaster Rd, at 170th St W; per vehicle $10; sunrise-sunset) offers hillside walks among the wildflowers. To get there take Hwy 14 south of Mojave for about 25 miles, exit at Ave I in Lancaster and drive 15 miles west. **Arthur B Ripley Desert Woodland State Park** (Lancaster Rd, at 210th St W; sunrise-sunset), 5 miles west, has an untrammeled interpretive trail leading through precious stands of Joshua trees.

East of Lancaster, **Antelope Valley Indian Museum** (661-942-0662; www.avim.parks.ca.gov; Ave M, btwn 150th & 170th Sts; adult/child under 12yr $3/free; 11am-4pm Sat & Sun) displays Native-American artifacts from around California and the Southwest. There is first-come, first-served camping among Joshua trees and desert-tortoise habitat at nearby **Saddleback Butte State Park** (661-942-0662; www.parks.ca.gov; 170th St E, south of Ave J; tent & RV sites $20), about 17 miles east of Lancaster.

Budget motels line Sierra Hwy, east of downtown Lancaster and Hwy 14. The retro 1950s **Town House Motel** (661-942-1195; www.townhouselancaster.com; 44125 Sierra Hwy; r $60-70;) has clean, simple rooms.

Downtown Lancaster has a quaint, tree-lined main street along Lancaster Ave, lined with plaques commemorating test pilots. **Lemon Leaf Cafe** (661-942-6500; www.lemonleaf.com; 653 W Lancaster Blvd; mains $10-20; 7am-9pm Mon-Thu & Sat, to 10pm Fri) dishes generous portions of market-fresh Mediterranean salads such as the cranberry turkey cobb, grilled panini sandwiches, pastas and pizzas, plus a nicely tangy lemon tart. **Bex** (661-945-2399; www.bexgrill.com; 706 W Lancaster Bl) is a cavernous, all-purpose bar and grill with burgers, pizzas, a music hall and bowling alley.

Mojave

Driving north on Hwy 14, Mojave (population 4238) is the first stop on the 'Aerospace Triangle' that also includes Boron and Ridgecrest. The modest town is home to a huge air-force base as well as the country's first commercial space port, and has witnessed major moments in air- and spaceflight history.

The storied **Edwards Air Force Base** (661-277-3511; www.edwards.af.mil) is a flight-test facility for the US Air Force, NASA and civilian aircraft, and a training school for test pilots with the 'right stuff'. It was from here that Chuck Yeager piloted the world's first supersonic flight, and where the first space shuttles glided in after their missions. Free five-hour tours of the on-base flight museum and NASA flight research center are usually given on the first and third Fridays of the month. Reservations are essential and must be made at least 14 days in advance (30 days for non-US citizens).

The **Mojave Air & Space Port** (www.mojaveairport.com) made history in 2003 with the launch of **SpaceShipOne**, the first privately funded human space flight, thus laying the groundwork for commercial space tourism. Dozens of aerospace companies are hard at work here developing the latest aeronautical technologies, including SpaceShipTwo for Richard Branson's Virgin Galactic.

A replica of SpaceShipOne is on display in the airport's small **Legacy Park**, along with a huge Rotary Rocket, which was an early reusable civilian space vehicle developed here in the late '90s. The **Voyager Cafe** has some great old photographs.

The Air & Space Port is also home to a huge **airplane graveyard** (off-limits to visitors) where retired commercial airplanes roost in the dry desert air waiting to be scavenged for spare parts.

There are national chain motels along Rte 14 in Mojave, but locally owned **Mariah Country Inn & Suites** (☎661-824-4980; www.mariahhotel.com; 1385 Hwy 58, Mojave; r incl breakfast from $89; P ❄ ⓦ ≋ 🐾) is by the entrance to the Air & Space Port. Immaculately kept rooms have early American-style furniture, and there's a pool, small hot tub and a few fitness machines.

Boron

Off Hwy 58, about midway between Mojave and Barstow, this tiny town (population 2253) catapulted onto the map in 1927 with the discovery of one of the world's richest borax deposits. Today, it is home to California's **largest open-pit mine**, operated by the global mining concern Rio Tinto. At 1 mile wide, 2.5 miles long and up to 650ft deep, the mine looks like a man-made Grand Canyon and supplies 40% of the world's demand for this versatile mineral (used in everything from glass to detergents). Historically, Boron was where Death Valley's famous 20-mule teams deposited their huge loads of borax at a dusty desert railway station, hauled from over 165 miles away.

Sights

Borax Visitors Center MUSEUM
(☎760-762-7588; www.borax.com; Borax Rd, off Hwy 58; per car $3; ⏲9am-5pm) On a hilltop on the grounds of the mining complex, this museum reeks 'corporate promo' but also has some fine exhibits and a film explaining the history and process of borax mining, processing, distribution and uses. Views of the mine from up here are stupendous.

Saxon Aerospace Museum MUSEUM
(☎760-762-6600; www.saxonaerospacemuseum.com; 26922 Twenty Mule Team Rd; admission by donation; ⏲10am-4pm) This modest, volunteer-run museum recounts milestones in experimental flight testing in the surrounding desert, including the first breaking of the sound barrier, the first hypersonic flight and the first space-shuttle landing. It has one of America's largest collections of rocket engines, from the X-1 and X-15 to the latest composites

Twenty Mule Team Museum MUSEUM
(☎760-762-5810; www.20muleteammuseum.com; 26962 Twenty Mule Team Rd; admission by donation; ⏲10am-4pm) Next door to Saxon Aerospace Museum, this low-budget museum is a haphazardly organized treasure trove of historic knickknacks: a 1930s beauty shop, products made with locally mined borax, watch fobs, belt buckles and memorabilia of the 2000 movie *Erin Brockovich,* which was filmed nearby and employed many locals as extras; Julia Roberts won an Oscar for the title role.

Eating

Domingo's MEXICAN $$
(☎760-762-6266; 27075 Twenty Mule Team Rd; mains $6-13; ⏲11am-10pm Mon-Sat, 10am-10pm Sun; 👪) Autographed photos of astronauts and air-force test pilots hang on the walls of this festive roadside cantina. Lunchtime crowds from the nearby military base feast on killer homemade salsa with roasted chiles and famous fajitas.

Ridgecrest

Ridgecrest (population 28,325) is a service town where you can find gas, supplies, information and cheap lodging en route to Death Valley or the Eastern Sierra Nevada. Its main raison d'être is the China Lake US Naval Air Weapons Station that sprawls for a million acres (one third the size of Delaware!) north of the town.

US Naval Museum of Armament & Technology (☎760-939-3530; www.chinalakemuseum.org; 10am-4pm Mon-Sat) FREE, right on the base, is an unapologetic celebration of US military might that is likely to fascinate technology, flight, history and military buffs – and perhaps even utter pacifists.

Many of the rockets, guided missiles, torpedoes, guns, bombs, cluster weapons etc on display were developed or tested on this very base before seeing action in wars from WWII to Afghanistan. If you ever wanted to touch a **Tomahawk missile** or have your picture taken with a 'Fat Man' (the atomic bomb that was dropped on Japan, that is), this is the place to do it. A documentary takes you on a helicopter flight of the base for bird's-eye views of the 4-mile-long **supersonic research track** and the anti-missile testing grounds.

To get to the museum, you need to stop at the base's visitors center on China Lake Blvd (near Inyokern Rd), fill out a form and present your driver's license, car registration and vehicle insurance. Foreign visitors must also show their passport.

Trona Pinnacles

What do the movies *Battlestar Galactica*, *Star Trek V: The Final Frontier* and *Planet of the Apes* have in common? Answer: they were all filmed at Trona Pinnacles, an awesome natural landmark where tufa spires rise out of an ancient lakebed in alien fashion. You'll want an off-road vehicle for this trip. Look for the turnoff from Rte 178, about 18 miles east of Ridgecrest. From there it's another 5 miles south along a rutted dirt road to the scenic driving loop and short walking trails. Free primitive campsites are available.

Randsburg

About 20 miles south of Ridgecrest, off US Hwy 395, Randsburg is a 'living ghost town', an abandoned and now (somewhat) re-inhabited mining town circa 1895. You can visit a tiny historical museum, antiques shops, a saloon, general store with lunch counter, and an opera house cafe (where old-timey melodramas are occasionally performed).

LAS VEGAS

It's three in the morning in a smoky casino when you spot an Elvis lookalike sauntering by arm in arm with a glittering showgirl just as a bride in a short white dress shrieks 'Blackjack!'

Vegas, baby: It's the only place in the world you can see ancient hieroglyphics, the Eiffel Tower, the Brooklyn Bridge and the canals of Venice in a few short hours. Sure, they're all reproductions, but in a desert metropolis that has transformed itself into one of the most lavish getaway destinations on the planet, nothing is executed halfway – not even the illusions.

Las Vegas is the ultimate escape. Time is irrelevant here. There are no clocks, just never-ending buffets and ever-flowing drinks. This city has been constantly reinventing herself since the days of the Rat Pack. Today its pull is all-inclusive: Hollywood bigwigs gyrate at A-list ultralounges, while college kids seek cheap debauchery and grandparents whoop it up at the hot, hot penny slots.

Welcome to the dream factory.

Sights

Four miles long, the **Strip** (Las Vegas Blvd) is the center of all the action. The Stratosphere caps the north end of the Strip and Mandalay Bay the south end. Don't be fooled: a walk to what looks like a nearby casino usually takes longer than expected.

Downtown is home to the city's oldest hotels and casinos: expect a retro feel, cheaper drinks and lower table limits. Its main drag is the fun-loving **Fremont Street Experience** (www.vegasexperience.com; Fremont St, btwn Main St & Las Vegas Blvd; hourly dusk-midnight; Deuce, SDX) FREE, a five-block covered pedestrian mall featuring a zip line and a trippy light show hourly after dark.

Major tourist areas are safe. Las Vegas Blvd between downtown and the Strip gets shabby, as does much of downtown off Fremont St.

The Strip

★Bellagio CASINO

(☎702-693-7111; www.bellagio.com; 3600 Las Vegas Blvd S; 24hr) Bellagio dazzles with Tuscan architecture and an 8-acre artificial lake, complete with don't-miss choreographed dancing **fountains** (www.bellagio.com; Bellagio; sh ows every 30min 3-7pm Mon-Fri, noon-7pm Sat & Sun, every 15min 7pm-midnight daily;).

Look up as you enter the lobby: the ceiling is adorned with a backlit glass sculpture composed of 2000 handblown flowers by artist Dale Chihuly. Although small, the **Bellagio Gallery of Fine Art** (☎877-957-9777, 702-693-7871; adult/child under 12yr $16/free; ⏰10am-7pm, last entry 6:30pm) showcases museum-quality paintings. Inside the **Bellagio Conservatory** (Bellagio; ⏰24hr; 👪) FREE, impressive floral exhibits change throughout the year.

★CityCenter LANDMARK

(www.citycenter.com; 3780 Las Vegas Blvd S) This futuristic-feeling complex is a small galaxy of hyper-modern hotels in orbit around glitzy **Crystals** (www.crystalsatcitycenter.com; 3720 Las Vegas Blvd S, CityCenter; ⏰10am-11pm Sun-Thu, to midnight Fri & Sat) shopping mall. The dramatic architectural showpiece is **Aria** (☎702-590-7111; www.aria.com; 3730 Las Vegas Blvd S, CityCenter; ⏰24hr), whose sophisticated casino provides a fitting backdrop for a $40 million public contemporary-art collection. Step inside the hush-hush opulent **Mandarin Oriental** (www.mandarinoriental.com; 3752 Las Vegas Blvd S) hotel for afternoon tea or evening cocktails in the 23-floor 'sky lobby' lounge, which has panoramic Strip views.

★Venetian CASINO

(☎702-414-1000; www.venetian.com; 3355 Las Vegas Blvd S; ⏰24hr) Hand-painted ceiling frescoes, roaming mimes and operatic singers, **gondola rides** (shared ride per person $19, child under 3yr free, private 2-passenger ride $76; ⏰indoor 10am-10:45pm Sun-Thu, 10am-11:45pm Fri & Sat, outdoor rides noon-9:45pm, weather permitting; 👪) and full-scale reproductions of Venice's most famous landmarks are found at this romantic casino hotel. Next door, its sister resort **Palazzo** (☎702-607-7777; www.palazzo.com; 3325 Las Vegas Blvd S; ⏰24hr) puts a more chichi spin on the Italian theme, with even more culinary heavyweights and high-end shopping.

LINQ & High Roller LANDMARK

(☎800-223-7277; www.thelinq.com; 3545 Las Vegas Blvd S; High Roller ride before/after 5:50pm $25/35; ⏰High Roller noon-2am daily) Eclectic shops, buzzing bars and restaurants, live-music venues, a groovy bowling alley and a unique Polaroid photo museum line this new center-Strip pedestrian promenade. Towering above it all and lit by 2000 colorful glowing LEDs, High Roller is the world's tallest observation wheel.

Cosmopolitan CASINO

(☎702-698-7000; www.cosmopolitanlasvegas.com; 3708 Las Vegas Blvd S; ⏰24hr) Hipsters once too cool for Vegas finally have a place to go, with a bevy of eclectic eateries and boutiques. Thankfully, Cosmo avoids utter pretension, despite wink-wink flourishes like Art-o-Mats (vintage cigarette machines hawking original art) and larger-than-life stiletto heel sculptures you can climb into for a photo op.

Stratosphere CASINO

(☎702-380-7777; www.stratospherehotel.com; 2000 Las Vegas Blvd S; tower entry adult/child $18/10, all-day pass incl unlimited thrill rides $34, SkyJump from $110; ⏰casino 24hr, tower & thrill rides 10am-1am Sun-Thu, to 2am Fri & Sat, weather permitting; 👪) Atop the 1149ft-high tapered tripod tower, vertiginous indoor and outdoor viewing decks afford Vegas' best 360-degree panoramas. To get to the top, ride one of America's fastest elevators, lifting you 108 floors in a mere 37 ear-popping seconds,

LAS VEGAS FOR CHILDREN

State law prohibits people under 21 years of age from loitering in casino gaming areas.

Circus Circus (☎702-734-0410; www.circuscircus.com; 2880 Las Vegas Blvd S; ⏰24hr; 👪) casino hotel is all about families. Acrobats, contortionists and magicians perform on a **stage** (⏰shows every 30min, 11am-midnight) suspended above the casino. The **Adventuredome** (www.adventuredome.com; Circus Circus; day pass over/under 48in tall $30/17, per ride $5-8; ⏰10am-6pm daily, later on weekends & May-Sep; 👪) indoor theme park is loaded with more family fun.

Also on the Strip, New York–New York (p384) casino hotel offers a roller coaster, a video-game arcade and Greenwich Village, where cobblestone streets are packed with family-friendly eateries.

East of the Strip, the **Pinball Hall of Fame** (www.pinballmuseum.org; 1610 E Tropicana Ave; per game 25¢-$1; ⏰11am-11pm Sun-Thu, to midnight Fri & Sat; 👪; 🚌201) is an interactive mini museum that's better than any slot machines.

Las Vegas Strip

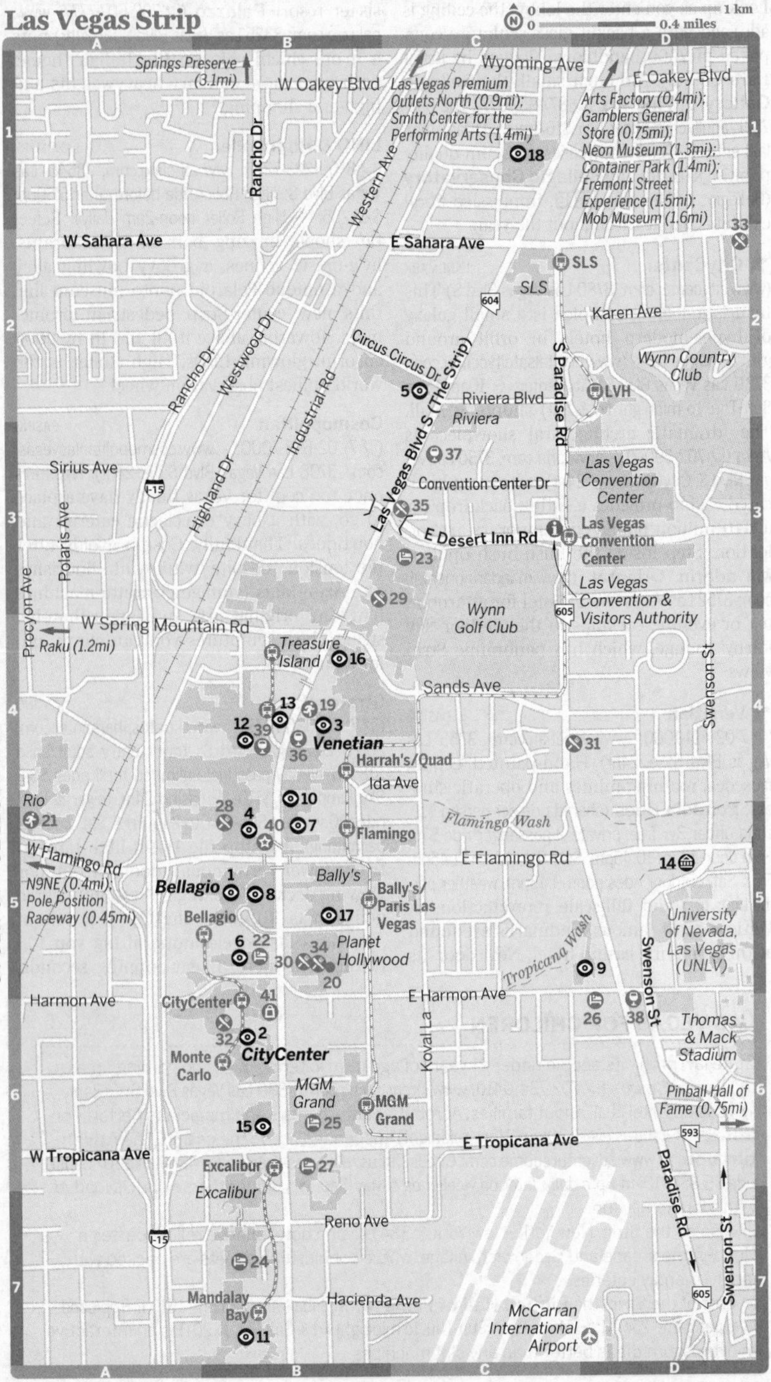

0 — 1 km
0 — 0.4 miles

Springs Preserve (3.1mi)
W Oakey Blvd
Las Vegas Premium Outlets North (0.9mi); Smith Center for the Performing Arts (1.4mi)
Wyoming Ave
E Oakey Blvd
Arts Factory (0.4mi); Gamblers General Store (0.75mi); Neon Museum (1.3mi); Container Park (1.4mi); Fremont Street Experience (1.5mi); Mob Museum (1.6mi)
Rancho Dr
Western Ave
18
33
W Sahara Ave
E Sahara Ave
SLS
SLS
604
Karen Ave
Westwood Dr
Rancho Dr
Industrial Rd
Circus Circus Dr
Las Vegas Blvd S (The Strip)
S Paradise Rd
Wynn Country Club
5
Riviera Blvd
Riviera
LVH
37
Las Vegas Convention Center
Sirius Ave
I-15
Highland Dr
Convention Center Dr
35
Polaris Ave
E Desert Inn Rd
Las Vegas Convention Center
23
Procyon Ave
Las Vegas Convention & Visitors Authority
29
Wynn Golf Club
605
W Spring Mountain Rd
Raku (1.2mi)
Treasure Island
16
Sands Ave
Swenson St
13
19
12
39
3
36
Venetian
Harrah's/Quad
31
Ida Ave
Rio
21
28
4
40
10
7
Flamingo
Flamingo Wash
W Flamingo Rd
N9NE (0.4mi); Pole Position Raceway (0.45mi)
E Flamingo Rd
14
1
Bellagio
8
Bally's
Bally's/ Paris Las Vegas
17
Bellagio
University of Nevada, Las Vegas (UNLV)
6
22
34
30
Planet Hollywood
20
Tropicana Wash
9
Swenson St
Harmon Ave
CityCenter
41
E Harmon Ave
26
38
Thomas & Mack Stadium
32
2
Monte Carlo
CityCenter
Koval La
MGM Grand
MGM Grand
Pinball Hall of Fame (0.75mi)
15
25
593
W Tropicana Ave
E Tropicana Ave
Excalibur
27
Excalibur
Paradise Rd
Reno Ave
I-15
24
Swenson St
Mandalay Bay
Hacienda Ave
605
McCarran International Airport
11

Las Vegas Strip

Top Sights

1 Bellagio B5
2 CityCenter B6
3 Venetian B4

Sights

Aria .... (see 41)
Bellagio Conservatory & Botanical Gardens .... (see 1)
Bellagio Gallery of Fine Art .... (see 1)
Big Apple Roller Coaster .... (see 15)
4 Caesars Palace B5
5 Circus Circus C2
6 Cosmopolitan B5
Eiffel Tower Experience .... (see 17)
7 Flamingo B5
Flamingo Wildlife Habitat .... (see 7)
8 Fountains of Bellagio B5
9 Hard Rock D5
10 LINQ & High Roller B4
11 Mandalay Bay B7
Mandarin Oriental .... (see 2)
12 Mirage B4
13 Mirage Volcano B4
14 National Atomic Testing Museum D5
15 New York–New York B6
16 Palazzo Casino B4
17 Paris Las Vegas B5
Shark Reef Aquarium .... (see 11)
18 Stratosphere C1

Activities, Courses & Tours

Adventuredome .... (see 5)
19 Gondola Ride B4
Qua Baths & Spa .... (see 4)
20 Stripper 101 .... B5
21 VooDoo Zipline A5

Sleeping

22 Cosmopolitan B5
23 Encore C3
Hard Rock .... (see 9)
24 Luxor B7
Mandalay Bay .... (see 11)
25 MGM Grand B6
26 Rumor D6
27 Tropicana B6

Eating

28 Bacchanal B5
29 Buffet at Wynn B3
Culinary Dropout .... (see 9)
30 Earl of Sandwich B5
31 Firefly C4
32 Five50 .... B6
Holsteins .... (see 6)
Jaleo .... (see 6)
Joël Robuchon .... (see 25)
Le Village Buffet .... (see 17)
33 Lotus of Siam D2
34 Spice Market Buffet B5
35 Tacos El Gordo C3
Todd English's Olives .... (see 1)
Wicked Spoon Buffet .... (see 22)

Drinking & Nightlife

36 Carnaval Court B4
Chandelier Bar .... (see 22)
37 Fireside Lounge C3
38 Hofbräuhaus D6
Hyde Bellagio .... (see 1)
Marquee .... (see 22)
Mix Lounge .... (see 11)
39 Rhumbar B4
XS .... (see 23)

Entertainment

40 Absinthe B5
Beatles LOVE .... (see 12)
Circus Acts .... (see 5)
Joint .... (see 9)
Tix 4 Tonight .... (see 7)

Shopping

41 Crystals B6
Forum Shops .... (see 4)
Grand Canal Shoppes at the Venetian .... (see 3)

then queue for high-altitude thrill rides or a 'SkyJump' over the side of the tower.

Paris Las Vegas CASINO

(☎702-946-7000; www.parislasvegas.com; 3655 Las Vegas Blvd S; ⏲24hr) Evoking the gaiety of the City of Light, this pint-sized version of the French capital may not exude the true charm of Paris – it feels like a themed section of Disney World's Epcot – but efforts to emulate famous landmarks, including the Arc de Triomphe and **Eiffel Tower** (☎888-727-4758; adult/child 12yr & under/family $10.50/7.50/32, after 7:15pm $15.50/10.50/47; ⏲9:30am-12:30am Mon-Fri, to 1am Sat & Sun, weather permitting), make it an entertaining stop.

Mirage CASINO

(☎702-791-7111; www.mirage.com; 3400 Las Vegas Blvd S; ⏲24hr) Circling the rainforest atrium is a vast Polynesian-themed casino, including a pro-worthy poker room. In the hotel lobby's 20,000-gallon saltwater **aquarium**, 60 species of critters hailing from Fiji to the Red Sea swim. Out front in a lagoon, a fiery faux **volcano** (⏲shows hourly 6pm, 7pm or

8-11pm or midnight;) FREE erupts after dark, halting Strip traffic.

Caesars Palace CASINO
(702-731-7110; www.caesarspalace.com; 3570 Las Vegas Blvd S; 24hr) Quintessentially kitschy Vegas, Caesars is a Greco-Roman fantasyland featuring marble reproductions of classical statuary, towering fountains, costumed cocktail waitresses, not one but two giant casinos and the fashionable Forum Shops (p389).

Flamingo CASINO
(702-733-3111; www.flamingolasvegas.com; 3555 Las Vegas Blvd S; 24hr) Opened by gangster Bugsy Siegel in 1946, the Flamingo is vintage Vegas. Weave through the slot machines out back to the **wildlife habitat** (702-733-3349; 3555 Las Vegas Blvd S; 8am-dusk, pelican feedings 8am & 2:30pm;) FREE to see Chilean flamingos, African penguins and brown pelicans.

New York–New York CASINO
(702-740-6969; www.newyorknewyork.com; 3790 Las Vegas Blvd S; 24hr) This mini metropolis shows off scaled-down replicas of the Empire State Building, the Statue of Liberty and the Brooklyn Bridge. Wrapping around the flashy facade is the **Big Apple roller coaster** (1 ride/day pass $14/25; 11am-11pm Sun-Thu, 10:30am-midnight Fri & Sat;), with NYC taxi-style cars.

Mandalay Bay CASINO
(702-632-7777; www.mandalaybay.com; 3950 Las Vegas Blvd S; 24hr) Besides its private beach, tropically themed M-Bay has only one standout attraction: the **Shark Reef** (702-632-4555; www.sharkreef.com; adult/child 5-12yr $18/12; 10am-10pm daily late May–early Sep, 10am-8pm Sun-Thu, to 10pm Fri & Sat early Sep–late May, last admission 1hr before closing;), an aquarium home to thousands of submarine beasties, with a shallow pool where kids can pet pint-sized sharks.

Downtown & Off-Strip

★Neon Museum MUSEUM
(702-387-6366; www.neonmuseum.org; 770 Las Vegas Blvd N; 1hr tour adult/child 7-17yr daytime $18/12, after dark $25/22; tours daily, schedules vary) Take a fascinating historical walking tour of the Neon Museum's 'boneyard,' where irreplaceable vintage neon signs – Vegas' original art form – are salvaged. If tours are sold out (book at least a few days ahead), you can stroll the museum's free al-fresco **Urban Gallery** of restored neon signs, including a sparkling genie lamp and retro motel marquees, at the Neonopolis on the Fremont Street Experience and the N 3rd St cul-de-sac just off Fremont St.

★Mob Museum MUSEUM
(702-229-2734; www.themobmuseum.org; 300 Stewart Ave; adult/child 11-17yr $20/14; 10am-7pm Sun-Thu, to 8pm Fri & Sat; Deuce) Inside the historic federal courthouse where mobsters sat for hearings in 1950–51, thoughtfully curated exhibits tell the story of organized crime in America with hands-on FBI equipment, mob-related artifacts and multimedia exhibits featuring interviews with real-life Tony Sopranos. Parking is $5.

Springs Preserve MUSEUM, PARK
(702-822-7700; www.springspreserve.org; 333 S Valley View Blvd; adult/child 5-17yr $19/11; 10am-6pm; ; 104) On the site of the natural springs that fed *las vegas* ('the meadows'), where southern Paiutes and Spanish Trail traders camped, and later Western pioneers settled the valley, this educational museum and gardens complex is an incredible trip through historical, cultural and biological time. The **Desert Living Center** demonstrates sustainable architectural design and everyday eco-conscious living.

Golden Nugget CASINO
(702-385-7111; www.goldennugget.com; 129 E Fremont St; 24hr; Deuce, SDX) Looking like a million bucks, the Nugget has set the downtown benchmark since opening in 1946. No brass or cut glass was spared inside the swanky casino, with a nonsmoking poker room. The 61lb Hand of Faith, the world's largest gold nugget, is displayed around the corner from the hotel lobby.

Hard Rock CASINO
(702-693-5000; www.hardrockhotel.com; 4455 Paradise Rd; 24hr; 108) The original rock 'n' roll casino hotel is home to one of the world's most impressive collections of rock memorabilia, including Jim Morrison's handwritten lyrics to one of the Door's greatest hits, and leather jackets from a who's who of famous rock stars. The **Joint** (888-929-7849; most tickets $40-200; 108) concert hall, **Vinyl** music lounge and **Rehab** pool parties attract a sex-charged crowd.

National Atomic Testing Museum MUSEUM
(☎702-794-5151; www.nationalatomictestingmuseum.org; 755 E Flamingo Rd, Desert Research Institute; adult/child 7-17yr $14/12; ⏲10am-5pm Mon-Sat, noon-5pm Sun; 🚌202) Recalling an era when the word 'atomic' conjured modernity and mystery, this Smithsonian afilliate writes an intriguing testament to the period when nuclear bombs were tested just outside Las Vegas. The deafening **Ground Zero Theater** mimics a concrete test bunker.

Downtown Arts District ARTS CENTER
On the **First Friday** (www.firstfridaylasvegas.com; ⏲5-11pm) of each month, a carnival of 10,000 art-lovers, hipsters, indie musicians and hangers-on descend on Las Vegas' downtown arts district. These giant monthly block parties feature gallery openings, performance art, live bands and food trucks. The action revolves around the **Arts Factory** (☎702-383-3133; www.theartsfactory.com; 107 E Charleston Blvd; ⏲9am-6pm daily, to 10pm 1st Fri of month; 🚌Deuce, SDX).

Activities

Qua Baths & Spa SPA
(☎866-782-0655; Caesars Palace; fitness center day pass $25, incl spa facilities $45; ⏲6am-8pm) Social spa going is encouraged in the tea lounge, herbal steam room and arctic ice room, where dry-ice snowflakes fall.

VooDoo Zipline OUTDOORS
(☎702-777-7776; www.voodoozipline.com; 3700 W flamingo Blvd, Rio; day/night ride $25/37; ⏲noon-midnight Mon-Thu, from 10am Fri-Sun, weather permitting) Suspended between the Rio's two casino-hotel towers, this rooftop zip line slingshots tandem riders over 30mph.

Stripper 101 DANCE
(☎866-932-1818, 702-260-7200; www.stripper101.com; 3663 Las Vegas Blvd S, Miracle Mile Shops, V Theater; tickets from $40; ⏲schedules vary) Ladies, take a (non-nude) pole-dancing class in a cabaret setting completed with strobe lights, cocktails and feather boas.

Pole Position Raceway RACING
(☎702-227-7223; www.polepositionraceway.com; 4175 S Arville St; 1-week membership $6, per race $22-26; ⏲11am-10pm Sun-Thu, to midnight Fri & Sat; 🚌202) Modeled on F1 road courses, this indoor racetrack lets you drive the USA's fastest indoor go-karts (up to 45mph!).

Sleeping

Rates rise and fall dramatically, depending on the season, special events, conventions etc, but weekday rates (Sunday through Thursday nights) are generally lower than weekend rates (Friday and Saturday nights). Check hotel websites, which usually feature calendars listing day-by-day room rates. Book ahead and beware of mandatory resort fees (up to $25 plus tax per night).

The Strip

Luxor CASINO HOTEL $
(☎888-386-4658, 702-262-4000; www.luxor.com; 3900 Las Vegas Blvd S; weekday/weekend r from $45/85; P ❄ @ ≋) As long as you steer clear of noisier, older Pyramid rooms, this less-expensive Strip casino resort is functional enough for a few nights.

★**Mandalay Bay** CASINO HOTEL $$
(☎877-632-7800, 702-632-7777; www.mandalaybay.com; 3950 Las Vegas Blvd S; weekday/weekend r from $105/130; P ❄ @ 📶 ≋) Ornately appointed rooms have a South Seas theme, with floor-to-ceiling windows and luxurious

VEGAS' COOLEST HOTEL POOLS

Mandalay Bay Splash around an artificial surf beach made of California sand, with a wave pool, lazy-river ride and casino games.

Hard Rock (p386) Seasonal swim-up blackjack, wild Rehab weekend pool parties and celeb-spotting at the über-hip Beach Club.

Mirage (p383) Lushly landscaped pools with waterfalls tumbling off cliffs, deep grottoes and palm-tree-studded islands for sunbathing.

Caesars Palace Corinthian columns, fountains, marble-inlaid pools and the topless Venus pool lounge make the Garden of the Gods Oasis divine.

Golden Nugget (p386) At this petite downtown pool, play blackjack or take the waterslide that corkscrews through a shark aquarium.

marble bathrooms. For more luxury, book a room at the Four Seasons or Delano boutique hotels, also at M-Bay. Swimmers will swoon over the sprawling pool complex, which has its own sandy beach.

MGM Grand CASINO HOTEL **$$**
(877-880-0880, 702-891-1111; www.mgmgrand.com; 3799 Las Vegas Blvd S; weekday/weekend r from $70/140; P ❄ @ ≈) Vegas' biggest hotel is a gargantuan place, with over a dozen restaurants and bars and the Strip's most mammoth pool complex. For more space and quiet, nab a condo-style suite next door at the Signature towers.

Tropicana CASINO HOTEL **$$**
(800-462-8767, 702-739-2222; www.troplv.com; 3801 Las Vegas Blvd S; weekday/weekend r from $75/120; P ❄ @ ≈) Keeping the Strip's tropical vibe going since 1953, the Trop's recent multimillion-dollar renovations have brought sunset colors and South Beach–style digs. Tropical gardens and lagoon pools await out back.

★Encore CASINO HOTEL **$$$**
(877-321-9966, 702-770-7100; www.wynnlasvegas.com; 3131 Las Vegas Blvd S; weekday/weekend ste from $199/249; P ❄ @ ≈) Newer than its sister resort Wynn Las Vegas, Encore offers equally opulent, but even more spacious suites amid gorgeous surrounds. Encore's glam nightclubs and DJ-driven pool club are envied hangouts.

Cosmopolitan CASINO HOTEL **$$$**
(855-435-0005, 702-698-7000; www.cosmopolitanlasvegas.com; 3708 Las Vegas Blvd S; r/ste from $160/220; P ❄ @ ≈) Are the luxuriously hip rooms worth the price tag? Style-conscious jetsetters seem to think so. Stumble out of your room at 1am to play some pool in the upper hotel lobby before going on a mission to find the 'secret' pizza joint.

Downtown & Off-Strip

Downtown hotels are generally less expensive than those on the Strip.

Hard Rock CASINO HOTEL **$**
(800-473-7625, 702-693-5000; www.hardrockhotel.com; 4455 Paradise Rd; weekday/weekend r from $45/89; P ❄ @ ≈) Everything about this boutique hotel spells stardom. Brightly colored Euro-minimalist rooms feature souped-up stereos and plasma-screen TVs.

Golden Nugget CASINO HOTEL **$**
(800-634-3454, 702-385-7111; www.goldennugget.com; 129 E Fremont St; weekday/weekend r from $49/89; P ❄ @ ≈) Pretend to relive the fabulous heyday of Vegas in the 1950s at this swank Fremont St address, where upgrades to the Rush Tower are worth every penny.

El Cortez Cabana Suites HOTEL **$**
(800-634-6703, 702-385-5200; http://elcortezhotelcasino.com; 651 E Ogden Ave; weekday/weekend r from $40/80; P ❄ @) Overhauled since its cameo in Scorcese's *Casino,* this downtown hotel has vintage-style suites painted in chartreuse with retro black-and-white tiled bathrooms.

Rumor BOUTIQUE HOTEL **$$**
(877-997-8667, 702-369-5400; www.rumorvegas.com; 455 E Harmon Ave; weekday/weekend ste from $60/120; P ❄ @ ≈) Opposite the Hard Rock, a sultry, nightclub atmosphere infuses these bachelor/ette pad suites, some with Jacuzzi tubs and white leather sofas.

Eating

Sin City is an unmatched eating adventure. Reservations are a must for upscale restaurants, especially on weekends.

The Strip

Along the Strip, cheap eats beyond fast-food joints are tough to find.

Tacos El Gordo MEXICAN **$**
(702-641-8228; http://tacoselgordobc.com; 3049 Las Vegas Blvd S; items $2-10; 9pm-3am Sun-Thu, to 5am Fri & Sat; Deuce, SDX) This Tijuana-style taco shop from SoCal is just the ticket when it's way late, you're almost broke and have a desperate craving for meaty tacos in handmade corn tortillas.

Earl of Sandwich DELI **$**
(www.earlofsandwichusa.com; Planet Hollywood; items $2-7; 24hr) Pennypinchers sing the praises of this popular deli next to the casino that pops out toasted sandwiches, wraps and tossed salads, all with quick service.

Holsteins BURGERS **$$**
(702-698-7940; www.holsteinslv.com; Cosmopolitan; items $6-18; 11am-midnight, to 2am Fri & Sat) Hand-crafted burgers are championship-worthy, as are all-American classic side dishes with unusual twists – deep-fried pick-

les, truffled mac 'n' cheese and milkshakes spiked with chocolate vodka.

Five50 PIZZERIA $$
(Aria, CityCenter; shared plates $9-18, pizzas $22-29; 11am-midnight) At this chef-owned pizza bar, be bewildered by an extra-large menu of artisanal meat and cheese platters, garden-fresh salads, antipasti and more.

★ **Joël Robuchon** FRENCH $$$
(702-891-7925; www.joel-robuchon.com/en; MGM Grand; tasting menu per person $120-425; 5:30-10pm Sun-Thu, to 10:30pm Fri & Sat) A once-in-a-lifetime culinary experience; block off a solid three hours and get ready to eat your way through a multicourse seasonal French menu inside what feels like a 1930s Parisian mansion. Step next door to **L'Atelier de Joël Robuchon** for a marginally more economical meal. Book well in advance.

Jaleo SPANISH, TAPAS $$$
(702-698-7950; www.jaleo.com; Cosmopolitan; shared plates $5-35; noon-midnight;) Pioneering Spanish chef José Andrés' restaurant serves creative modern tapas in a rustic contemporary dining room: recycled wooden tables have mismatched chairs and whimsical glassware. Reservations essential.

Todd English's Olives MEDITERRANEAN $$$
(www.toddenglish.com; Bellagio; mains lunch $17-29, dinner $25-49; restaurant 11am-2:45pm & 5-10:30pm, bar 3-5pm;) East Coast chef Todd English crafts an homage to the life-giving fruit. Flatbread pizzas and housemade pastas get top billing, but the real selling point is patio tables overlooking Lake Como. Book ahead, even for lunch.

Downtown & Off-Strip

Restaurants downtown offer better value than on the Strip. West of the Strip, the pan-Asian restaurants on Chinatown's Spring Mountain Rd are budget-saving options.

★ **Container Park** FAST FOOD $
(702-637-4244; http://downtowncontainerpark.com; 707 E Fremont St; most items $3-9; 11am-11pm Sun-Thu, to 1am Fri & Sat) With food truck menus, outdoor seating and late-night hours, vendors inside downtown's Container Park satisfy all appetites. Over-21s only after 9pm.

★ **Raku** JAPANESE $$
(702-367-3511; www.raku-grill.com; 5030 W Spring Mountain Rd; shared dishes $2-12; 6pm-3am Mon-Sat; 203) LA chefs come to dine when they're in town on this Japanese owner-chef's small plates of *robata*-grilled meats, homemade tofu and more. Book ahead.

Culinary Dropout AMERICAN, FUSION $$
(702-522-8100; www.hardrockhotel.com; 4455 Paradise Rd, Hard Rock; mains brunch $8-14, lunch & dinner $14-32; 11am-11pm Mon-Thu, 11am-midnight Fri, 10am-midnight Sat, 10am-11pm Sun; 108) With nouveau comfort food, a pool-view patio and rockin' live bands, there's no funkier gastropub around. Weekend brunch brings out bacon Bloody Marys.

Lotus of Siam THAI $$
(702-735-3033; www.saipinchutima.com; 953 E Sahara Ave; mains $9-30; 11:30am-2:30pm Mon-Fri, 5:30-10pm daily; ; SDX) It may look like just a strip-mall hole-in-the-wall, but the authentic northern Thai cooking has won almost as many awards as the wine cellar. Make reservations.

Firefly TAPAS $$
(702-369-3971; www.fireflylv.com; 3824 Paradise Rd; shared plates $5-12, mains $15-20; 11:30am-midnight; 108) Twice as fun as an overdone Strip restaurant, but at half the price, is that why it's always hopping? Nosh on traditional Spanish tapas and sip housemade sangria.

★ **N9NE** STEAKHOUSE $$$
(702-933-9900; www.palms.com; 4321 W Flamingo Rd, Palms; mains $28-72; 5:30-10pm Sun-Thu, to 11pm Fri & Sat; 202) At this hip steakhouse heavy with celebs, a dramatically

VEGAS' BEST BUFFETS

Bacchanal (Caesars Palace; buffet per adult $26-54, child 4-10yr $15-27;)

Wicked Spoon Buffet (3708 Las Vegas Blvd S, Cosmopolitan; per person $26-40; brunch 8am-2pm Mon-Fri, to 3pm Sat & Sun, dinner 5-9pm Mon-Thu, 5-10pm Fri, 3-10pm Sat, 3-9pm Sun;)

Le Village Buffet (702-946-7000; Paris Las Vegas; buffet per adult $22-34, child 4-8yr $13-20; 7am-10pm;)

Spice Market Buffet (Planet Hollywood; buffet per adult $22-36, per child 4-12yr $13-20; 7am-11pm;)

Buffet at Wynn (Wynn; per person $22-40; 8am-3pm & 3:30-10pm;)

lit dining room serves up beautifully aged steaks and chops, along with everything else from oysters Rockefeller to Pacific sashimi.

Drinking & Nightlife

Dress to impress at nightclubs, where cover charges vary depending on the door staff, male-to-female ratio, special guests and how crowded it is that night.

The Strip

★XS CLUB
(702-770-0097; www.xslasvegas.com; Encore; cover $20-50; 9:30pm-4am Fri & Sat, from 10:30pm Sun & Mon) XS is *the* hottest nightclub in Vegas – at least for now. Surrounded by extravagantly gold-drenched decor, electronica DJs make the dance floor writhe. High rollers opt for VIP bottle service at poolside cabanas.

Marquee CLUB
(702-333-9000; www.marqueelasvegas.com; Cosmopolitan; 10pm-5am Thu-Sat & Mon) A-list celebrities, famous-name DJs, an outdoor beach club (open seasonally) and an alluring *je ne sais quoi* all make this top-tier club worth waiting in line for.

Hyde Bellagio LOUNGE, NIGHTCLUB
(702-693-8700; www.hydebellagio.com; Bellagio; cover $20-40, usually free before 10pm; lounge 5-11pm daily, nightclub 10pm-4am Tue, Fri & Sat) Sink into a plush loveseat next to an oversized mirror or just stand on the balcony, awestruck, as the Bellagio's fountains dance outside this chic ultralounge.

Mix Lounge LOUNGE
(64th fl, Mandalay Bay; cover after 10pm $20-25; 5pm-midnight Sun-Tue, to 3am Wed-Sat) A posh place to grab sunset cocktails. The glass elevator has amazing views, and that's before you even glimpse the Strip panoramas from the soaring balcony.

Chandelier Bar COCKTAIL BAR
(Cosmopolitan; 24hr) In a city full of lavish casino bars, this triple-decker one pulls out all the stops. Mingle with hipsters and cocktail mixologists in spaces draped with colorful glowing beads.

Rhumbar COCKTAIL BAR
(702-792-7615; www.rhumbarlv.com; Mirage; usually 1pm-midnight Sun-Thu, to 2am Fri & Sat, weather permitting) Caribbean-inspired bar's mojitos and daiquiris are a big step up from the sugary, yard-long frozen drinks sold along the Strip. Cool off on the outdoor patio.

Carnaval Court BAR
(702-369-5000; www.harrahslasvegas.com; 3475 Las Vegas Blvd S, Harrah's; cover charge varies; 11am-3am) Flair bartenders juggling fire and live cover bands keep this open-air bar packed with the kind of party people for whom spring break never ends.

Fireside Lounge LOUNGE
(www.peppermilllasvegas.com; 2985 Las Vegas Blvd S, Peppermill; 24hr) At the Strip's most unlikely romantic hideaway next to a casino coffee shop, couples canoodle with low lighting by a sunken fire pit. Sip a Scorpion with a straw.

Downtown & Off-Strip

Want to chill out with the locals? Head to one of these offbeat favorites.

Beauty Bar BAR
(702-598-3757; www.thebeautybar.com; 517 Fremont St; cover free-$10; 10pm-4am; Deuce) At the salvaged innards of a 1950s New Jersey beauty salon, swill a cocktail or chill out with DJs and live bands in the edgy Fremont East Entertainment District.

★Frankie's Tiki Room BAR
(702-385-3110; www.frankiestikiroom.com; 1712 W Charleston Blvd; 24hr; 206) At the city's only round-the-clock tiki bar, cocktails are rated in strength by skulls and famous tiki designers, sculptors and painters have their work on display all around.

Hofbräuhaus BAR
(www.hofbrauhauslasvegas.com; 4510 Paradise Rd; 11am-11pm Sun-Thu, to midnight Fri & Sat) At this replica Bavarian beer hall and garden, celebrate Oktoberfest year-round with imported suds, fair *fräuleins* and live oompah bands nightly.

Entertainment

Las Vegas has no shortage of entertainment on any given night, with hundreds of production shows to choose from.

Tix 4 Tonight BOOKING SERVICE
(877-849-4868; www.tix4tonight.com; 3200 Las Vegas Blvd S, Fashion Show; 10am-8pm) Offers half-price tix for a limited lineup of same-day shows and small discounts on 'always sold-out' shows. Multiple locations.

★Beatles LOVE
THEATER

(702-792-7777, 800-963-9634; www.cirquedusoleil.com; Mirage; tickets $79-180; 7pm & 9:30pm Thu-Mon;) Those who have seen every acrobatic Cirque production on the Strip say this kaleidoscopic music-and-dance homage to the Fab Four is the best yet.

Smith Center for the Performing Arts
PERFORMING ARTS

(702-749-2000; www.thesmithcenter.com; 361 Symphony Park Ave, Symphony Park; tickets from $20; schedule varies; SDX) Cabaret jazz, classical and contemporary music, dance troupes and comedians all perform at this art deco–inspired center downtown.

Absinthe
THEATER

(800-745-3000; www.absinthevegas.com; Roman Plaza, Caesars Palace; tickets $99-125; 7:30pm & 9:30pm Wed-Sun) Raucous variety show mixes bawdy and surreal comedy with burlesque, cabaret and acrobatics under a big-top tent. No under-18s allowed.

Shopping

Gamblers General Store
SOUVENIRS

(702-382-9903; www.gamblersgeneralstore.com; 800 S Main St; 9am-6pm Mon-Sat, to 5pm Sun; 108, Deuce) Authentic gaming supply shop sells collectible decks of cards used in Vegas casinos.

Grand Canal Shoppes at the Venetian
MALL

(www.grandcanalshoppes.com; Venetian; 10am-11pm Sun-Thu, to midnight Fri & Sat) Italianate luxury with gondolas and international designers, including in the next-door Palazzo.

Forum Shops
MALL

(www.simon.com; Caesars Palace; 10am-11pm Sun-Thu, to midnight Fri & Sat) Fashionista shop in an air-conditioned version of an ancient Roman marketplace.

Container Park
MALL

(702-637-4244; http://downtowncontainerpark.com; 719 E Fremont St; 10am-9pm Mon-Sat, to 8pm Sun) An incubator for up-and-coming local art, clothing and jewelry designers.

Las Vegas Premium Outlets North
MALL

(702-474-7500; www.premiumoutlets.com/vegasnorth; 875 S Grand Central Pkwy; 9am-9pm Mon-Sat, to 8pm Sun; ; SDX) Vegas' biggest-ticket outlet mall features 120 high-end and casual brands.

Information

Wi-fi is available in most hotel rooms ($12 to $15 per 24 hours, sometimes included in the 'resort fee'). Cheaper cybercafes are inside souvenir shops on the Strip. Every casino, shopping mall and bank and most convenience stores have ATMs; casino transaction fees are highest (around $5).

Harmon Medical Center (702-796-1116; www.harmonmedicalcenter.com; 150 E Harmon Ave; 8am-8pm Mon-Fri) Discounts for uninsured patients; limited translation services.

Las Vegas Convention & Visitors Authority (LVCVA; 702-892-7575, 877-847-4858; www.lasvegas.com; 3150 Paradise Rd; 8am-5:30pm Mon-Fri; monorail Las Vegas Convention Center) Small walk-in office near the city's convention center.

Las Vegas Review-Journal (www.lvrj.com) Daily newspaper with Friday's arts-and-entertainment guide, *Neon*.

Las Vegas Weekly (http://lasvegasweekly.com) Free alt-weekly with entertainment, event and restaurant listings.

Lonely Planet (www.lonelyplanet.com/usa/las-vegas) Planning advice, author recommendations, traveler reviews and insider tips.

Police (702-828-3111; www.lvmpd.com).

University Medical Center (UMC; 702-383-2000; www.umcsn.com; 1800 W Charleston Blvd; 24hr) Nevada's advanced trauma center.

Vegas.com (www.vegas.com) Travel info and booking service.

Getting There & Around

Just southeast of the Strip and easily accessible from I-15, **McCarran International Airport** (LAS; 702-261-5211; www.mccarran.com; 5757 Wayne Newton Blvd;) has direct flights from most US cities, and some from Canada and Europe. **Bell Trans** (800-274-7433; www.bell-trans.com) offers airport shuttles to the Strip (one way/round trip $7/13); fares to downtown and off-Strip destinations are slightly higher.

A fast, wheelchair-accessible **monorail** (702-699-8299; www.lvmonorail.com; single-ride $5, 24/48/72hr pass $12/22/28; 7am-midnight Mon, to 2am Tue-Thu, to 3am Fri-Sun) connects the MGM Grand and SLS casino hotels, stopping at some Strip casinos and the city's convention center. **Deuce & SDX** (702-228-7433; www.rtcsnv.com; 2hr/24hr/3-day pass $6/8/20) buses run frequently between the Strip and downtown; double-decker Deuce buses run 24 hours, but SDX buses are faster.

All Strip casinos have taxi stands, free self-parking and also free valet parking (tip at least $2). Many downtown casinos charge a self-parking fee; it's usually refundable with ticket validation inside the casino (no gambling required).

Santa Barbara County

Includes ➡

Santa Barbara...... 392
Santa Barbara Wine Country...... 408
Los Olivos...........414
Solvang...........415
Buellton...........418
Carpinteria........420
Ojai...........421
Ventura...........423
Channel Islands National Park...... 425

Best Places to Eat

- ➡ Lark (p404)
- ➡ Lure Fish House (p424)
- ➡ Santa Barbara Shellfish Company (p403)
- ➡ Succulent Café (p417)
- ➡ Lucky Penny (p402)

Best Places to Stay

- ➡ El Encanto (p401)
- ➡ Inn of the Spanish Garden (p401)
- ➡ Santa Barbara Auto Camp (p400)
- ➡ Blue Iguana Inn (p422)
- ➡ Hamlet Inn (p417)

Why Go?

Frankly put, this area is damn pleasant to putter around. Low-slung between lofty mountains and the shimmering Pacific, chic Santa Barbara's red-tiled roofs, white stucco buildings and Mediterranean vibe give credence to its claim of being the 'American Riviera.' It's a surprisingly bewitching place to loll on the beach, eat and drink extraordinarily well, shop a bit and push all your cares off to another day. The city's car-free campaign has brought electric shuttle buses, urban bike trails and earth-friendly wine tours. Mother Nature returns the love with hiking, biking, surfing, kayaking, scuba diving and camping opportunities galore, from offshore Channel Islands National Park to arty Ojai, surrounded by hot springs. Meanwhile, winemaking is booming in the bucolic Santa Ynez Mountains, where over a hundred wineries vie for your attention. But if all you want to do is relax, no worries – plenty of sunny beaches await.

When to Go

Santa Barbara

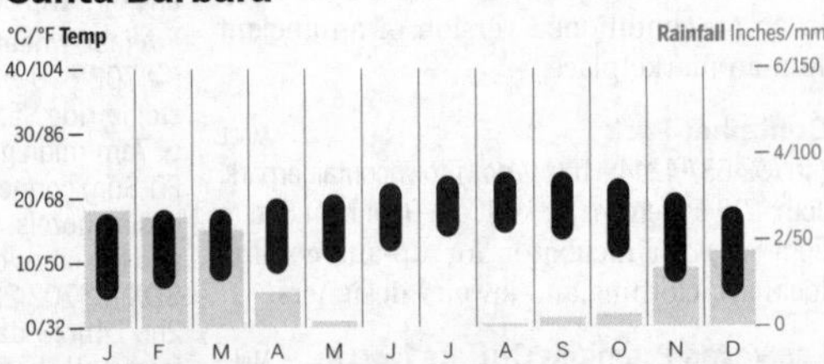

Apr Balmy temperatures, fewer tourists than in summer. Wildflowers bloom on Channel Islands.

Jun Summer vacation and beach season begin. Summer Solstice Celebration parade.

Oct Sunny blue skies and smaller crowds. Wine Country harvest festivities.

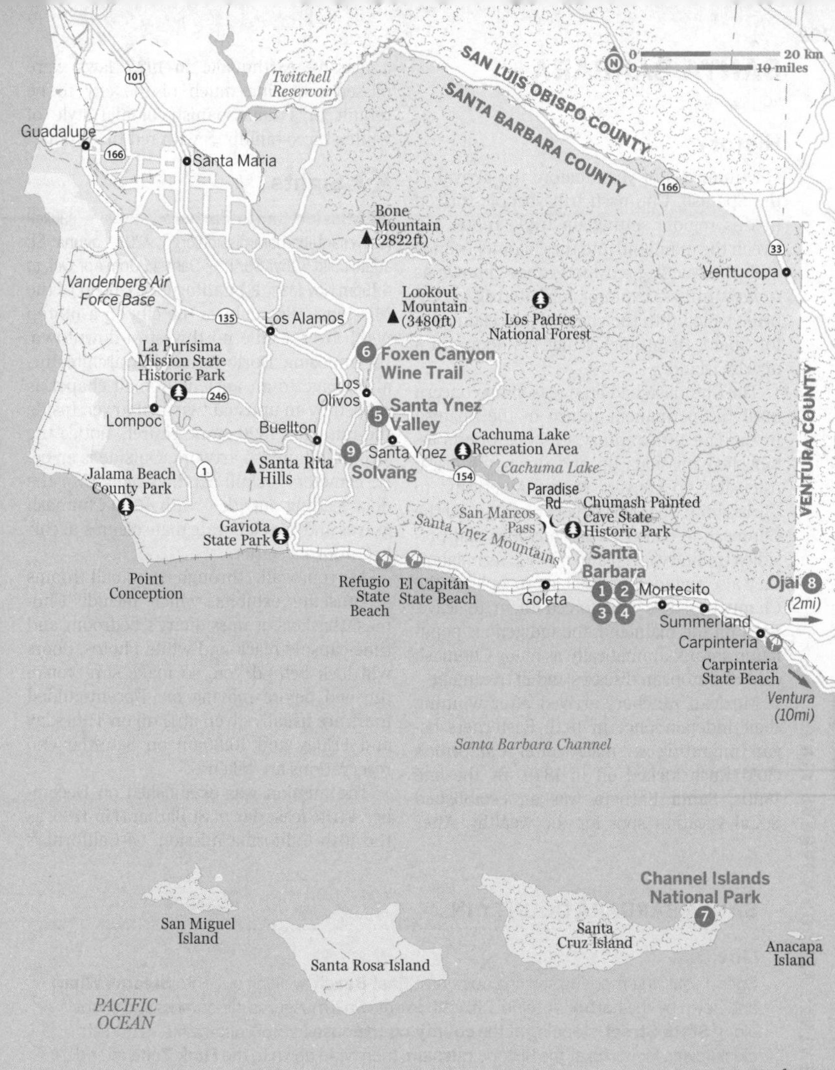

Santa Barbara County Highlights

1 Strolling **Stearns Wharf** (p393), then lazing on Santa Barbara's cinematic **beaches**.

2 Ambling between wine-tasting rooms, hip bars, art galleries and shops in Santa Barbara's **Funk Zone** (p404).

3 Exploring Spanish-colonial historic sites, such as **Mission Santa Barbara** (p392).

4 Eyeing panoramic views atop the *Vertigo*–esque clock tower of the **Santa Barbara County Courthouse** (p393).

5 Pedaling past vineyards and organic farms through the **Santa Ynez Valley** (p413).

6 Following the **Foxen Canyon Wine Trail** (p411) to taste top-rated pinot noir.

7 Kayaking sea caves and watching whales in **Channel Islands National Park** (p425).

8 Rejuvenating your body and soul in new-agey **Ojai** (p421).

9 Eating *ableskivers* (panacke popovers) by a kitschy windmill in the Danish village of **Solvang** (p415).

SANTA BARBARA

POP 89,640

History

For hundreds of years before the arrival of the Spanish, Chumash tribespeople thrived in this region, setting up trade routes between the mainland and the Channel Islands and constructing redwood canoes known as *tomols*. In 1542 explorer Juan Rodríguez Cabrillo sailed into the channel and claimed it for Spain, then quickly met his doom on a nearby island.

The Chumash had little reason for concern until the permanent return of the Spanish in the late 18th century. Catholic priests established missions up and down the coast, ostensibly to convert Native Americans to Christianity. Spanish soldiers often forced the Chumash to construct the missions and presidios (military forts) and provide farm labor; they also rounded up the tribespeople on the Channel Islands and forced them to leave. Back on the mainland, the indigenous population shrank dramatically, as many Chumash died of European diseases and ill treatment.

Mexican ranchers arrived after winning their independence in 1821. Easterners began migrating en masse after California's Gold Rush kicked off in 1849. By the late 1890s, Santa Barbara was an established SoCal vacation spot for the wealthy. After a massive earthquake in 1925, laws were passed requiring much of the city to be rebuilt in a faux-Spanish-colonial style of white-stucco buildings with red-tiled roofs.

Sights

★Mission Santa Barbara CHURCH

(www.santabarbaramission.org; 2201 Laguna St; adult/child 5-15yr $6/1; 9am-4:30pm Apr-Oct, to 4:15pm Nov-Mar; P) California's 'Queen of the Missions' reigns above the city on a hilltop perch over a mile northwest of downtown. Its imposing Doric facade, an architectural homage to an ancient Roman chapel, is topped by an unusual twin bell tower. Inside the mission's 1820 stone church, notice the striking Chumash artwork. Outside is an eerie cemetery – skull carvings hang over the door leading outside – with 4000 Chumash graves and the elaborate mausoleums of early California settlers.

As you walk through 10 small rooms of museum exhibits, which include Chumash baskets, a missionary's bedroom and time-capsule black-and-white photos, doors will lock behind you, so make sure you're finished before moving on. Docent-guided tours are usually given at 11am on Thursday and Friday and 10:30am on Saturday; no reservations are taken.

The mission was established on December 4 (the feast day of St Barbara) in 1786, as the 10th California mission. Of California's

SANTA BARBARA COUNTY IN...

One Day

Spend your first morning soaking up rays at **East Beach**, walking out onto **Stearns Wharf** and down by the **harbor**. After lunch, visit downtown's museums, landmarks and shops along **State Street**, stopping at the **county courthouse** for 360-degree views from its clock tower. Finish up at the historic **mission**, then head down to the **Funk Zone** after dark.

Two Days

Cycle along the coast, go surfing or sea kayaking, or hike in the Santa Ynez foothills. In the afternoon, detour east to posh **Montecito** for shopping and people-watching or hang loose in **Carpinteria**, a retro beach town.

Three Days

Head up to Santa Barbara's Wine Country. Enjoy a do-it-yourself vineyards tour via car, motorcycle or bicycle along a scenic wine trail – **Foxen Canyon** and the **Santa Rita Hills** are exceptionally beautiful. Pack a picnic lunch or grab a bite in charming **Los Olivos** or Danish-esque **Solvang**.

Four Days

On your way back to LA, make time for a detour to arty **Ojai** up in the mountains for its hot springs and spas or book a day trip from **Ventura** by boat to **Anacapa Island** in rugged **Channel Islands National Park**.

original 21 Spanish-colonial missions, it's the only one that escaped secularization under Mexican rule. Continuously occupied by Catholic priests since its founding, the mission is still an active parish church.

From downtown, take MTD bus 22.

Santa Barbara County Courthouse HISTORIC SITE
(☎805-962-6464; www.courthouselegacyfoundation.org; 1100 Anacapa St; ⌚8:30am-4:45pm Mon-Fri, 10am-4:15pm Sat & Sun) FREE Built in Spanish-Moorish Revival style in 1929, the courthouse features hand-painted ceilings, wrought-iron chandeliers, and tiles from Tunisia and Spain. Step inside the hushed mural room depicting Spanish-colonial history on the 2nd floor, then climb El Mirador, the 85ft clock tower, for arch-framed panoramas of the city, ocean and mountains. You're free to explore on your own, but you'll get a lot more out of a free docent-guided tour, usually at 2pm daily and 10:30am on weekdays (except Thursday).

Stearns Wharf HISTORIC SITE
(www.stearnswharf.org; P) FREE The southern end of State St gives way onto Stearns Wharf, a rough wooden pier lined with souvenir shops, snack stands and seafood shacks. Built in 1872, it's the oldest continuously operating wharf on the West Coast, although the actual structure has been rebuilt more than once. During the 1940s it was co-owned by tough-guy actor Jimmy Cagney and his brothers. If you've got kids, tow them inside the Ty Warner Sea Center (p396).

Parking on the wharf costs $2.50 per hour; the first 90 minutes are free with merchant validation. But trust us, you'd rather walk than drive over the wharf's bumpy wooden slats. The wharf entrance is a stop on MTD's downtown and waterfront shuttles.

Santa Barbara Museum of Art MUSEUM
(☎805-963-4364; www.sbma.net; 1130 State St; adult/child 6-17yr $10/6, all free 5-8pm Thu; ⌚11am-5pm Tue-Wed & Fri-Sun, to 8pm Thu) This thoughtfully curated, bite-sized art museum displays European and American masters – think Matisse and Diego Rivera – along with contemporary photography, classical antiquities and though-provoking temporary exhibits. Traipse up to the 2nd floor, where impressive Asian art collections include an intricate, colorful Tibetan sand mandala and the iron-and-leather armor of a Japanese warrior. Guided tours usually start at 1pm daily. There's also an interactive children's space, a museum shop and a cafe.

DON'T MISS

MEETING MONARCHS

If you're here in late fall or winter, ask at the Outdoors Santa Barbara Visitors Center (p406) about the best places to see migratory monarch butterflies roosting in the trees – an extraordinary sight. See p467 for more information on roosting.

Santa Barbara Maritime Museum MUSEUM
(☎805-962-8404; www.sbmm.org; 113 Harbor Way; adult/child 6-17yr $7/4, all free 3rd Thu of each month; ⌚10am-5pm, to 6pm late May–early Sep; P 👪) On the harborfront, this jam-packed, two-story exhibition hall celebrates the town's briny history with nautical artifacts, memorabilia and hands-on exhibits, including a big-game fishing chair from which you can 'reel in' a trophy marlin. Take a virtual trip through the Santa Barbara Channel, stand on a surfboard or watch deep-sea diving documentaries in the theater. There's 90 minutes of free parking in the public lot or take the Lil' Toot water taxi from Stearns Wharf.

Santa Barbara Historical Museum MUSEUM
(☎805-966-1601; www.santabarbaramuseum.com; 136 E De La Guerra St; ⌚10am-5pm Tue-Sat, from noon Sun) FREE Embracing a romantic cloistered adobe courtyard, this peaceful little museum has an endlessly fascinating collection of local memorabilia, ranging from the simply beautiful, such as Chumash woven baskets and Spanish-colonial-era textiles, to the intriguing, such as an intricately carved coffer that once belonged to Junípero Serra. Learn about the city's involvement in toppling the last Chinese monarchy, among other interesting footnotes in local history. Guided tours are usually offered at 2pm on Saturday and Sunday.

Santa Barbara Botanic Garden GARDEN
(☎805-682-4726; www.sbbg.org; 1212 Mission Canyon Rd; adult/child 2-12yr/youth 13-17yr $10/6/8; ⌚9am-6pm Mar-Oct, to 5pm Nov-Feb; P 👪) Take a soul-satisfying jaunt around this 40-acre botanic garden, devoted to California's native flora. More than 5 miles of partly wheelchair-accessible trails meander past cacti, redwoods and wildflowers and by the old mission dam, originally built by Chumash tribespeople to irrigate the

Downtown Santa Barbara

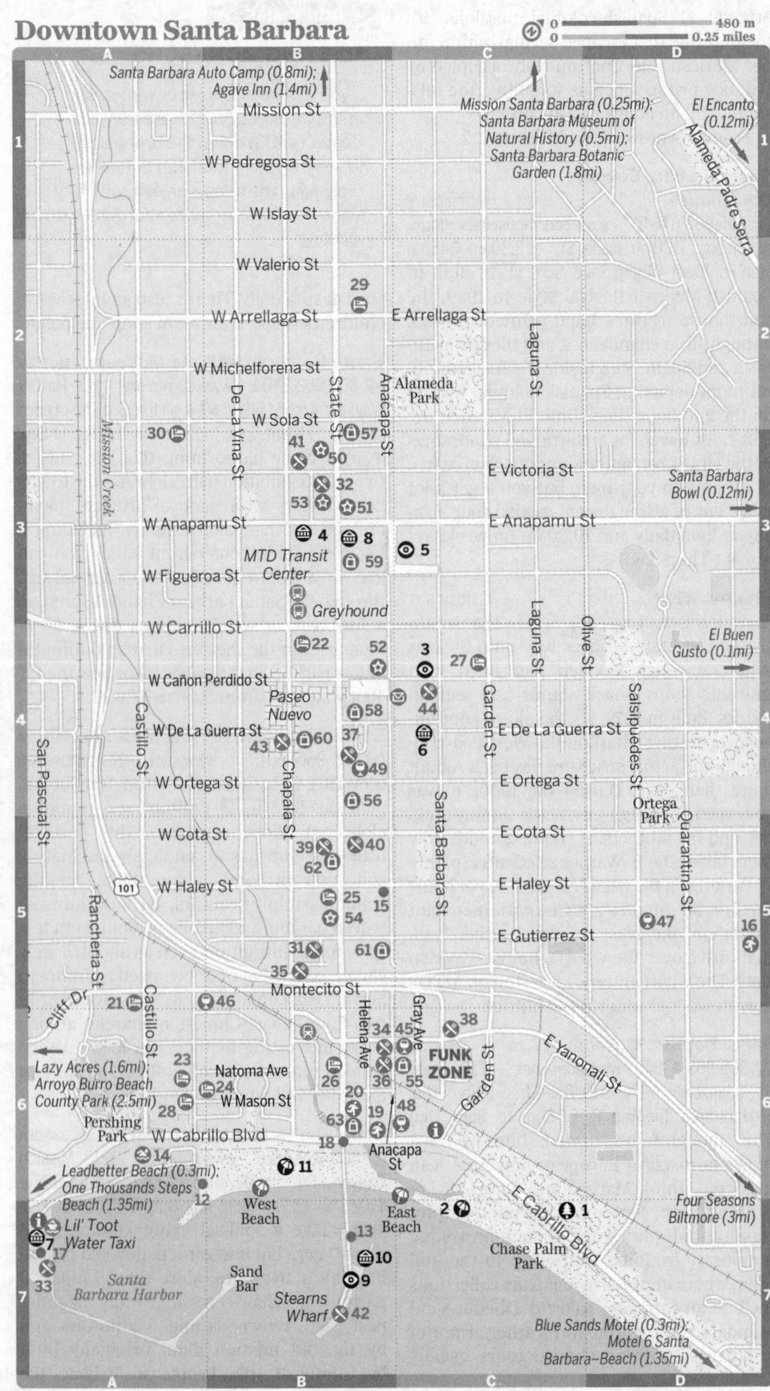

Downtown Santa Barbara

Sights
1 Chase Palm Park C7
2 East Beach C7
3 El Presidio de Santa Barbara State Historic Park C4
4 Karpeles Manuscript Library Museum B3
5 Santa Barbara County Courthouse C3
6 Santa Barbara Historical Museum C4
7 Santa Barbara Maritime Museum A7
8 Santa Barbara Museum of Art B3
9 Stearns Wharf B7
10 Ty Warner Sea Center B7
11 West Beach B6

Activities, Courses & Tours
Channel Islands Outfitters .... (see 17)
12 Condor Express A6
13 Land & Sea Tours B7
14 Los Baños del Mar A6
Paddle Sports Center .... (see 17)
15 Santa Barbara Adventure Company B5
16 Santa Barbara Bikes To-Go D5
17 Santa Barbara Sailing Center A7
18 Santa Barbara Trolley B6
Sunset Kidd's Sailing Cruises .... (see 17)
Surf-n-Wear's Beach House .... (see 63)
Truth Aquatics .... (see 12)
19 Wheel Fun Rentals B6
20 Wheel Fun Rentals B6

Sleeping
21 Brisas del Mar A5
22 Canary Hotel B4
23 Franciscan Inn A6
24 Harbor House Inn B6
25 Holiday Inn Express Santa Barbara B5
26 Hotel Indigo B6
27 Inn of the Spanish Garden C4
28 Marina Beach Motel A6
29 Simpson House Inn B2
30 White Jasmine Inn A3

Eating
31 Backyard Bowls B5
32 Bouchon B3
33 Brophy Brothers A7
34 Lark B6
35 Lilly's Taquería B5
36 Lucky Penny B6
37 McConnell's Fine Ice Creams B4
38 Metropulos C6
39 Olio Pizzeria B5
40 Palace Grill B5
41 Santa Barbara Public Market B3
42 Santa Barbara Shellfish Company B7
43 Silvergreens B4
44 Sojourner Café C4

Drinking & Nightlife
45 AVA Santa Barbara C6
46 Brewhouse B5
47 Carr Winery D5
Cutler's Artisan Spirits .... (see 34)
Figueroa Mountain Brewing Co. .... (see 34)
Handlebar Coffee Roasters .... (see 44)
Marquee .... (see 51)
48 Municipal Winemakers C6
49 Press Room B4
Riverbench Winery Tasting Room .... (see 34)
Telegraph Brewing Company .... (see 47)

Entertainment
50 Arlington Theatre B3
51 Granada Theatre B3
52 Lobero Theatre B4
53 Soho B3
54 Velvet Jones B5

Shopping
55 Channel Islands Surfboards C6
Chocolate Maya .... (see 31)
56 CRSVR Sneaker Boutique B4
57 Diani B3
58 El Paseo B4
59 La Arcada B3
60 Paseo Nuevo B4
61 REI B5
62 Santa Barbara Farmers Market B5
63 Surf-n-Wear's Beach House B6

mission's fields. Leashed, well-behaved dogs are welcome. Guided tours typically depart at 11am and 2pm on Saturday and Sunday, and 2pm on Monday. On weekends, MTD bus 22 from the mission stops at the gardens upon request. If you're driving, head north from the mission to Foothill Blvd (Hwy 192), turn right and then left to continue on Mission Canyon Rd.

El Presidio de Santa Barbara State Historic Park HISTORIC SITE

(☎805-965-0093; www.sbthp.org; 123 E Cañon Perdido St; adult/child under 17yr $5/free; ⏰10:30am-4:30pm) Founded in 1782 to defend the mission, this adobe-walled fort built by Chumash laborers was Spain's last military stronghold in Alta California. But its purpose wasn't solely to protect – the presidio also served as a social and political hub, and as a stopping point for traveling Spanish military. Today this small urban park harbors some of the city's oldest structures. On a self-guided walking tour, be sure to stop at the chapel, its interior radiant with rich hues.

Admission also includes entry to nearby **Casa de La Guerra**, a 19th-century colonial adobe home displaying Spanish, Mexican and California heritage exhibits.

Karpeles Manuscript Library Museum MUSEUM
(☎805-962-5322; www.rain.org/~karpeles; 21 W Anapamu St; ⏰noon-4pm Wed-Sun) FREE Stuffed with a hodgepodge of historical written artifacts, this detour is for history nerds and book and music lovers. One of a dozen Karpeles manuscript museums nationwide, the rotating exhibits at this museum often spotlight literary masterworks, from Shakespeare to Sherlock Holmes.

Activities

Cycling

A paved **recreational path** stretches 3 miles along the waterfront in both directions from Stearns Wharf, west to Leadbetter Beach beyond the harbor and east just past East Beach. For more pedaling routes, **Bike Santa Barbara County** (www.bike-santabarbara.org) offers free downloadable DIY cycling tours of the city, mountains and Wine Country, along with links to bicycle rentals and specialty shops.

Wheel Fun Rentals CYCLING
(☎805-966-2282; www.wheelfunrentals.com) **Cabrillo Blvd** (www.wheelfunrentals.com; 23 E Cabrillo Blvd; ⏰8am-8pm Mar-Oct, to 6pm Nov-Feb; 👪); **State St** (www.wheelfunrentals.com; 22 State St; ⏰8am-8pm Mar-Oct, to 6pm Nov-Feb; 👪) Hourly rentals of beach cruisers ($10), mountain bikes ($11) and two-/four-person surreys ($29/39), with discounted half-day and full-day rates.

Santa Barbara Bikes To-Go CYCLING
(☎805-628-2444; www.sbbikestogo.com; 812 E Gutierrez St) Delivers top-quality road and hybrid mountain bikes to your hotel. Rentals (per day $45 to $105) include helmets and emergency-kit saddle bags. Discounts for multiday, weekly and monthly rentals; reservations essential. Over-18s only.

Kayaking

Paddle the calm waters of Santa Barbara's harbor or the coves of the Gaviota coast, or hitch a ride to the Channel Islands for awesome sea caves.

Paddle Sports Center KAYAKING
(☎805-617-3425; www.channelislandso.com; 117b Harbor Way; single/double kayak rental per

SANTA BARBARA FOR CHILDREN

Santa Barbara abounds with family-friendly fun for kids of all ages, from tots to tweens.

Ty Warner Sea Center (☎805-962-2526; www.sbnature.org; 211 Stearns Wharf; adult/child 2-12yr/youth 13-17yr $10/7/8; ⏰10am-5pm; P 👪) From touch tanks full of tide-pool critters and crawl-through aquariums to whale sing-alongs, it's interactive and educational. Hourly parking on the wharf costs $2.50.

Santa Barbara Museum of Natural History (☎805-682-4711; www.sbnature.org; 2559 Puesta del Sol; adult/child 2-12yr/youth 13-17yr $11/7/8, incl planetarium show $15/11/12; ⏰10am-5pm; P 👪) Giant skeletons, an insect wall and a pitch-dark planetarium captivate kids' imaginations. It's a half-mile drive uphill from the mission.

Santa Barbara Maritime Museum (p393) Peer through a periscope, reel in a virtual fish, watch underwater films or check out the model ships.

Santa Barbara Sailing Center Short, one-hour sails around the harbor ($15) let young 'uns spot sea lions up close.

Lil' Toot water taxi (p408) Take a joyride along the waterfront on this tiny yellow boat.

Chase Palm Park (323 E Cabrillo Blvd; 👪) Antique carousel rides ($2, cash only) plus a shipwreck-themed playground decked out with seashells and a miniature lighthouse.

Arroyo Burro Beach County Park (Hendry's; www.countyofsb.org/parks/; Cliff Dr at Las Positas Rd; ⏰8am-sunset; P 👪) A wide, sandy beach, away from the tourists but not too far from downtown.

hr $25/40, per day $50/65; ⏱usually 8am-6pm) Long-established Channel Islands outfitter also guides harbor and coastal kayaking tours ($75 to $95) for beginner to advanced paddlers. Kayak rentals are available year-round at the harbor and Goleta Beach, and from late May through early September on West Beach. Book ahead online or by phone.

Santa Barbara Adventure Company KAYAKING
(☎877-885-9283, 805-884-9283; www.sbadventureco.com; 32 E Haley St; kayak tours $49-209; 👪) Leads all kinds of guided kayaking trips, from family-friendly harbor excursions and sunset floats to Gaviota coastal paddles and day and overnight trips to the Channel Islands. Some trips require a two- or four-person minimum.

Santa Barbara Sailing Center KAYAKING
(☎805-962-2826; www.sbsail.com; off Harbor Way; single/double kayak rental per hr $10/15, 2hr kayak tour $50; 👪) Just about the cheapest kayak rental and guided tours around, with paddling instruction available by prior arrangement. Call for seasonal hours.

Boating & Whale-Watching

Some tour companies offer year-round whale-watching boat trips, mostly to see grays in winter and spring, and humpbacks and blues in summer.

Condor Express CRUISE
(☎888-779-4253, 805-882-0088; www.condorcruises.com; 301 W Cabrillo Blvd; adult/child 5-12yr 2½hr cruise $50/30, 4½hr cruise from $89/50; 👪) Take a whale-watching excursion aboard the high-speed catamaran *Condor Express*. Whale sightings are guaranteed, so if you miss out the first time, you'll get a free voucher for another cruise.

Santa Barbara Sailing Center CRUISE, SAILING
(☎805-962-2826; www.sbsail.com; off Harbor Way; cruises $15-65, sailing courses from $615; 👪) Climb aboard the *Double Dolphin*, a 50ft sailing catamaran, for a two-hour coastal or sunset cruise. Seasonal whale-watching trips and quick one-hour spins around the harbor to view sea lions are also kid-friendly. If you want to learn to pilot your own sailboat, sign up for a 20-hour instructional course.

Sunset Kidd's Sailing Cruises CRUISE
(☎805-962-8222; www.sunsetkidd.com; 125 Harbor Way; 2hr cruise $40-50) Float in an 18-passenger sailboat on a two-hour whale-watching trip or a morning, afternoon, sunset cocktail or full-moon cruise. Reservations recommended.

> **DIY WALKING TOURS**
>
> Santa Barbara's self-guided 12-block **Red Tile walking tour** is a convenient introduction to downtown's historical highlights. The tour's name comes from the half-moon-shaped red clay tiles covering the roofs of many Spanish Revival-style buildings. You can download a free map of this walking tour, as well as other paths along the waterfront and to the mission, from **Santa Barbara Car Free** (www.santabarbaracarfree.org) 🍃. For a lazy stroll between wine-tasting rooms, follow the city's Urban Wine Trail (p404).

Swimming

Los Baños del Mar SWIMMING
(☎805-966-6110; www.friendsoflosbanos.org; 401 Shoreline Dr; admission $6; ⏱call for public swim schedules; 👪) Beyond the beaches in and around Santa Barbara, you can also swim at this municipal outdoor pool near West Beach that's good for recreational and lap swimming. For kids under eight years old, there's a wading pool with a lifeguard that's open daily in summer, weather permitting.

Surfing

Unless you're a novice, conditions are too mellow in summer – come back in winter when ocean swells kick back up. Santa Barbara's **Leadbetter Point** is best for beginners. Experts-only **Rincon Point** awaits just outside Carpinteria.

Paddle Sports Center SURFING
(☎805-617-3425; www.channelislandso.com; off Harbor Way; rental per 2hr/day wetsuit $5/15, boogie board or surfboard $10/30, SUP set $40/100; ⏱usually 8am-6pm) Rent a boogie board, surfboard or stand-up paddle boarding (SUP) set, along with a wetsuit, conveniently right at the harbor.

Santa Barbara Adventure Company SURFING
(☎877-885-9283, 805-884-9283; www.sbadventureco.com; 32 E Haley St; 2hr surfing or SUP lesson $89, half-/two-day surfing lessons $109/199; 👪) Learn the art of surfing or stand-up paddle boarding (SUP) from this family-friendly outfitter. Two-person minimum; children must be at least 7 years old.

TOP 10 BEACHES AROUND SANTA BARBARA

Although Santa Barbara's beaches are beauty-pageant prize winners, don't expect sunsets over the ocean because most of this coast faces south.

East Beach (E Cabrillo Blvd) Santa Barbara's largest and most popular beach is a long, sandy stretch sprawling east of Stearns Wharf, with volleyball nets for pick-up games, a children's play area and a snack bar. On Sunday afternoons, artists set up booths along the sidewalk, near the bike path.

Butterfly Beach (Channel Dr east of Butterfly Ln) Armani swimsuits and Gucci sunglasses abound at this narrow but chic swimming beach in front of the historic Biltmore hotel. Don't be surprised if you spot a celeb. The beach faces west, so you can catch a sunset here.

West Beach (W Cabrillo Blvd) Between Stearns Wharf and the harbor you'll find calm waters for kayaking, sailing and stand-up paddle boarding (SUP). It's most popular for sunbathing with tourists staying nearby. For lap swimming, head indoors to Los Baños del Mar (p397).

Leadbetter Beach (Shoreline Dr at Loma Alta Dr) Further west of the harbor, this is a fantastic spot for swimming or learning to surf or windsurf. A grassy picnic area atop the cliffs makes it just that much more family friendly.

One Thousand Steps Beach (foot of Santa Cruz Blvd at Shoreline Dr; ⏲ sunrise-10pm) Descend the cliffs on a historic staircase (don't worry, there aren't actually 1000 steps) for some windy beachcombing and tide-pooling (best at low tide), but no swimming. Neighboring **Shoreline Park** has a grassy area with picnic tables and a children's playground.

Arroyo Burro Beach County Park (p396) Near the junction of Cliff Dr and Las Positas Rd, this gem has a picnic area and the family-style Boathouse restaurant. The beach is flat, wide, away from tourists and great for kids, who can go tide-pooling. It's also a popular local surf spot. Look for an off-leash dog area at Douglas Family Preserve, on the cliffs above the beach.

Goleta Beach County Park (www.countyofsb.org/parks; Sandspit Rd, Goleta; ⏲ 8am-sunset) In the western suburbs near the University of California Santa Barbara (UCSB) campus, this beach is a locals' scene. There's a 1500ft-long fishing pier, a bike path and wide, sandy stretches for sunbathing after taking a dip or surfing easy waves. From Hwy 101, take Hwy 217 westbound.

Carpinteria State Beach (p420) About 12 miles east of Santa Barbara off Hwy 101, this mile-long beach has beautifully calm waters that are great for swimming, wading and tide-pooling, especially for younger kids.

El Capitán State Beach (www.parks.ca.gov; El Capitan State Beach Rd, Goleta; per car $10; ⏲ 8am-sunset; P 👪) & **Refugio State Beach** (www.parks.ca.gov; 10 Refugio Beach Rd, Goleta; per car $10; 👪) These twin beauties are worth the trip over 20 miles west of Santa Barbara via Hwy 101. Popular swimming and camping spots, they're connected by a bike path.

Surf-n-Wear's Beach House SURFING
(☎ 805-963-1281; www.surfnwear.com; 10 State St; rental per hr/day wetsuit from $8/12, boogie board $10/16, surfboard $10/35, SUP set per day $50; ⏲ 9am-6pm Sun-Thu, to 7pm Fri & Sat) Not far from Stearns Wharf, rent soft (foam) boards, boogie boards, wetsuits and SUP sets from this 1960s surf shop that also sells collectible vintage boards.

Hiking

Gorgeous day hikes await in the foothills of the Santa Ynez Mountains and elsewhere in the Los Padres National Forest. Most trails cut through rugged chaparral and steep canyons – sweat it out and savor jaw-dropping coastal views. Spring and fall are the best seasons for hiking, when temperatures are moderate. Always carry plenty of extra water and watch out for poison oak (p43).

To find even more local trails to explore, browse **Santa Barbara Hikes** (www.santabarbarahikes.com) online or visit the **Los Padres National Forest Headquarters** (☎805-968-6640; www.fs.usda.gov/lpnf; 6755 Hollister Ave, Goleta; ⏰8:30am-noon & 1-4:30pm Mon-Fri), west of the airport (from Hwy 101, exit Glen Annie Rd southbound onto Storke Rd).

Gliding

For condor's-eye ocean views, **Eagle Paragliding** (☎805-968-0980; www.eagleparagliding.com) and **Fly Above All** (☎805-965-3733; www.flyaboveall.com) offer paragliding lessons (from $200) and tandem flights ($100 to $200). For hang-gliding lessons and tandem flights, talk to Eagle Paragliding or **Fly Away** (☎805-403-8487; www.flyawayhanggliding.com).

Tours

★ Architectural Foundation of Santa Barbara — WALKING TOUR

(☎805-965-6307; www.afsb.org; adult/child under 12yr $10/free; ⏰usually 10am Sat & Sun) Take time out of your weekend morning for a fascinating 90-minute guided walking tour of downtown's art, history and architecture. No reservations required; call or check the website for meet-up times and places.

Land & Sea Tours — GUIDED TOUR

(☎805-683-7600; www.out2seesb.com; adult/child 2-9yr $25/10; ⏰usually noon & 2pm daily year-round, also 4pm daily May-Oct; 👪) If you dig James Bond-style vehicles, take a narrated tour of the city on the *Land Shark*, an amphibious vehicle that drives right into the water. Trips depart from Stearns Wharf; buy tickets before boarding (no reservations).

Santa Barbara Trolley — BUS TOUR

(☎805-965-0353; www.sbtrolley.com; adult/child 3-12yr $18/9; 👪) Biodiesel-fueled trolleys make a narrated 90-minute one-way loop around major tourist attractions, starting from Stearns Wharf (hourly departures 10am to 4pm). Hop-on, hop-off tickets are valid all day; pay the driver directly, or buy discounted tickets online in advance. One child under age 12 rides free with each paid adult ticket.

Santa Barbara Adventure Company — GUIDED TOUR

(☎805-884-9283, 877-885-9283; www.sbadventureco.com; 32 E Haley St) Maximize your outdoors time with a horseback ride on the beach or a Wine Country cycling tour, either costing around $150 per person (two-person minimum).

Festivals & Events

To find out what's happening now, check the events calendars at www.santabarbaraca.com and www.independent.com online.

Santa Barbara International Film Festival — FILM

(http://sbiff.org) Film buffs and Hollywood A-list stars show up for screenings of more than 200 independent US and foreign films in late January and early February.

TOP DAY HIKES AROUND SANTA BARBARA

TRAIL NAME	ROUND-TRIP DISTANCE (MI)	DESCRIPTION	TRAILHEAD	DIRECTIONS
Inspiration Point	3.5	Popular with locals walking their dogs and for daily workouts	Tunnel Rd	Turn left off Mission Canyon Dr before reaching the Santa Barbara Botanic Garden
Rattlesnake Canyon	3.5	Offering shade and waterfalls as you ascend into the canyon; leashed dogs OK	Las Canoas Rd	Turn right off Mission Canyon Dr before reaching the Santa Barbara Botanic Garden
Cold Spring & Montecito Park	up to 9	Steady uphill hike past small cascades with a spur trail to a summit	Mountain Dr	From Montecito, follow Olive Mill Rd north of Hwy 101, continuing past Hwy 192 on Hot Springs Rd, then turn left

SANTA BARBARA ART WALKS

Prime time for downtown gallery hopping is **First Thursday** (www.santabarbaradowntown.com), from 5pm to 8pm on the first Thursday of every month, when art galleries on and off State St throw open their doors for new exhibitions, artists' receptions, wine tastings and live music, all free. Closer to the beach, the **Funk Zone Art Walk** (http://funkzone.net) happens from 1pm to 5pm on the second Saturday of each month, featuring free events and entertainment at offbeat art galleries, bars and restaurants.

I Madonnari Italian Street Painting Festival ART, FOOD
(www.imadonnarifestival.com;) Colorful chalk drawings adorn Mission Santa Barbara's sidewalks over Memorial Day weekend, with Italian food vendors and arts-and-crafts booths too.

★Summer Solstice Celebration FESTIVAL
(www.solsticeparade.com) Kicking off summer in late June, this wildly popular and wacky float parade down State St feels like something out of Burning Man. Live music, kids' activities, food stands, a wine-and-beer garden and an arts-and-craft show happen all weekend long.

French Festival CULTURE, ART
(www.frenchfestival.com) In mid-July, California's biggest Francophile celebration has lots of food and wine, world music and dancing, a mock Eiffel Tower and Moulin Rouge, and even a poodle parade.

Santa Barbara County Fair FAIR
(www.santamariafairpark.com;) In mid-July, this old-fashioned county fair combines agriculture exhibits, carnival rides, and lots of food and wine. The fairgrounds are in Santa Maria, over an hour's drive northwest of Santa Barbara via Hwy 101.

★Old Spanish Days Fiesta CULTURE, ART
(www.oldspanishdays-fiesta.org) The entire city fills up during late July and early August for this long-running – if slightly overblown – festival celebrating Santa Barbara's Spanish and Mexican colonial heritage. Festivities include outdoor bazaars and food markets, live music, flamenco dancing, horseback and rodeo events, and a big ol' parade.

Sleeping

Prepare for sticker shock: basic motel rooms by the beach command over $200 in summer. Don't show up at the last minute without reservations and expect to find any reasonably priced rooms, especially not on weekends. Cheaper motels cluster along upper State St and Hwy 101 northbound to Goleta and southbound to Carpinteria, Ventura and Camarillo.

★Santa Barbara Auto Camp CAMPGROUND $$
(☎888-405-7553; http://autocamp.com/sb; 2717 De La Vina St; d $175-215;) Bed down with vintage style in one of five shiny metal Airstream trailers parked near upper State St, north of downtown. All five architect-designed trailers have unique perks, such as a clawfoot tub or extra twin-size beds for kiddos, as well as a full kitchen and complimentary cruiser bikes to borrow. Book ahead; two-night minimum may apply. Pet fee $25.

Hotel Indigo BOUTIQUE HOTEL $$
(☎805-966-6586, 877-270-1392; www.indigo-santabarbara.com; 121 State St; r from $170;) Poised between downtown and the beach, this petite Euro-chic boutique hotel has all the right touches: curated contemporary-art displays, rooftop patios and ecofriendly green-design elements like a living-plant wall. Peruse local-interest and art history books in the library nook, or retreat to your room and wrap yourself up in a plush bathrobe. Parking $14.

Agave Inn MOTEL $$
(☎805-687-6009; http://agaveinnsb.com; 3222 State St; r incl breakfast from $119;) While it's still just a motel at heart, this boutique-on-a-budget property's 'Mexican pop meets modern' motif livens things up with a color palette from a Frieda Kahlo painting. Flat-screen TVs, microwaves, minifridges and air-con make it a standout option. Family-sized rooms have kitchenettes and pull-out sofa beds. Continental breakfast included.

Harbor House Inn MOTEL $$
(☎888-474-6789, 805-962-9745; www.harborhouseinn.com; 104 Bath St; r from $180;)

Down by the harbor, this converted motel offers brightly lit studios with hardwood floors and a beachy design scheme. A few have full kitchens and fireplaces, but there's no air-con. Rates include a welcome basket of breakfast goodies (with a two-night minimum stay) and beach towels, chairs and umbrellas and three-speed bicycles to borrow. Pet fee $20.

Marina Beach Motel MOTEL **$$**
(805-963-9311, 877-627-4621; www.marinabeachmotel.com; 21 Bath St; r incl breakfast from $155;) Family-owned since 1942, this flower-festooned, one-story motor lodge that wraps around a grassy courtyard is worth a stay just for the location. Right by the beach, tidy remodeled rooms are comfy enough, and some have kitchenettes. Complimentary continental breakfast and beach-cruiser bikes to borrow. Small pets OK (fee $15).

Blue Sands Motel MOTEL **$$**
(805-965-1624; www.thebluesands.com; 421 S Milpas St; r from $120;) With affable owners, this tiny two-story motel may be a bit kitschy, but who cares when you're just steps from East Beach? Book a remodeled room, or for a bigger splurge, one with a fireplace or a full kitchen and ocean views. No air-con. Two-night minimum stay on weekends. Pet fee $10.

Franciscan Inn MOTEL **$$**
(805-963-8845; www.franciscaninn.com; 109 Bath St; r incl breakfast $155-215;) Settle into the relaxing charms of this Spanish-colonial two-story motel just over a block from the beach. Rooms differ in shape and decor, but many have kitchenettes and all evince French-country charm. Embrace the friendly vibe, afternoon cookies and outdoor pool and hot tub. Free continental breakfast. No air-con.

Holiday Inn Express Santa Barbara HOTEL **$$**
(877-834-3613, 805-963-9757; www.hotelvirginia.com; 17 W Haley St; r incl breakfast $185-250;) Formerly the Hotel Virginia, this early-20th-century hotel has heaps of character, starting from the tile-filled lobby with a fountain. Upgraded rooms are serviceable, but its location just off downtown's State St merits a stay. Parking $12.

Motel 6 Santa Barbara–Beach MOTEL **$$**
(805-564-1392, 800-466-8356; www.motel6.com; 443 Corona del Mar; r $100-210;) The very first Motel 6 to 'leave the light on for you' has been remodeled with IKEA-esque contemporary design, flat-screen TVs and multimedia stations. It fills nightly; book ahead. Wi-fi costs $3 extra every 24 hours. Pet fee $10.

★ **El Encanto** LUXURY HOTEL **$$$**
(805-845-5800, 800-393-5315; www.elencanto.com; 800 Alvarado Pl; d from $475;) Triumphantly reborn, this 1920s icon of Santa Barbara style is a hilltop hideaway for travelers who demand the very best of everything. An infinity pool gazes out at the Pacific, while flower-filled gardens, fireplace lounges, a full-service spa and private bungalows with sun-drenched patios concoct the glamorous atmosphere perfectly fitted to SoCal socialites. Grab sunset drinks on the ocean-view terrace. Parking $35.

★ **Inn of the Spanish Garden** BOUTIQUE HOTEL **$$$**
(866-564-4700, 805-564-4700; www.spanishgardeninn.com; 915 Garden St; d incl breakfast from $309;) At this Spanish-colonial-style inn, casual elegance, top-notch service and an impossibly romantic central courtyard will have you lording about like the don of your own private villa. Beds have

CAMPING & CABINS AROUND SANTA BARBARA

You won't find a campground anywhere near downtown Santa Barbara, but less than a half-hour drive west via Hwy 101, right on the ocean, are **El Capitán & Refugio State Beaches** (reservations 800-444-7275; www.reserveamerica.com; off Hwy 101; tent & RV drive-up sites $35-55, hike-and-bike tent sites $10;). Amenities include flush toilets, hot showers, picnic tables and convenience stores; parking costs an additional $10. You'll find family-friendly campgrounds with varying amenities in the mountainous Los Padres National Forest (p409) and at **Cachuma Lake Recreation Area** (info 805-686-5054, reservations 805-686-5055; http://reservations.sbparks.org; 2225 Hwy 154; campsites $28-48, yurts $65-85, cabins $110-210;) off Hwy 154, closer to Santa Barbara's Wine Country.

luxurious linens, bathrooms have oversized bathtubs and concierge service is top-notch. Palms surround a small outdoor pool, or unwind with a massage in your room.

El Capitan Canyon CABIN, CAMPGROUND $$$
(☎805-685-3887, 866-352-2729; www.elcapitan-canyon.com; 11560 Calle Real; safari tent $155, yurt $205, cabins $225-795;) Inland from El Capitán State Beach, this 'glamping' resort is for those who hate to wake up with dirt under their nails. No cars are allowed up-canyon during peak season, making this woodsy resort more peaceful. Safari tents are rustic and share bathrooms, while creekside cabins are more deluxe, some with kitchenettes; all have their own outdoor firepit.

Borrow a bicycle to head over to the beach, or schedule a massage. The property is about 20 miles west of Santa Barbara, off Hwy 101.

Simpson House Inn B&B $$$
(☎805-963-7067, 800-676-1280; www.simpsonhouseinn.com; 121 E Arrellaga St; d incl breakfast $255-610;) Whether you book an elegant suite with a clawfoot bathtub or a sweet cottage with a wood-burning fireplace, you'll be pampered at this Victorian-era estate ensconced in English gardens. From gourmet vegetarian breakfasts through evening wine, hors d'oeuvres and sweets, you'll be well fed. In-room mod cons include streaming internet radio and movies. Complimentary bicycles and beach gear to borrow.

Four Seasons Biltmore RESORT $$$
(☎info 805-969-2261, reservations 805-565-8299; www.fourseasons.com/santabarbara; 1260 Channel Dr; r from $425;) Wear white linen and live like Jay Gatsby at the oh-so-cushy 1927 Biltmore hotel on Butterfly Beach. Every detail is perfect, from bathrooms with Spanish tiles, French-milled soaps, deep soaking tubs and waterfall showers to bedrooms decked out with ultra-high-thread-count sheets. Indulge yourself at the spa or any of the oceanfront bars and restaurants.

Canary Hotel BOUTIQUE HOTEL $$$
(☎805-884-0300, 877-468-3515; www.canary-santabarbara.com; 31 W Carrillo St; r $325-575;) On a busy block downtown, this haute multistory hotel has a rooftop pool and sunset-watching perch for cocktails. Stylish accommodations show off four-poster Spanish-framed beds and all mod cons. In-room spa services, yoga mats and bathroom goodies will soothe away stress, but ambient street noise may leave you sleepless. Complimentary fitness center access and cruiser bicycles. Parking $25.

Hungry? Taste local farm goodness at the hotel's downstairs restaurant, **Finch & Fork**.

White Jasmine Inn B&B $$$
(☎805-966-0589; www.whitejasmineinnsant-abarbara.com; 1327 Bath St; d $160-330;) Tucked behind a rose-entwined wooden fence, this cheery inn stitches together a California bungalow and two quaint cottages. Sound-insulated rooms all have private bathrooms and fireplaces, and some are air-conditioned and come with Jacuzzi tubs. Full breakfast basket delivered daily to your door. No children under 12 years old allowed.

Brisas del Mar HOTEL $$$
(☎800-468-1988, 805-966-2219; www.sbhotels.com; 223 Castillo St; r incl breakfast from $230;) Kudos for all the freebies (DVDs, continental breakfast, afternoon wine and cheese, evening milk and cookies) and the newer Mediterranean-style front section, although some rooms are noisy. It's three blocks north of the beach. The hotel's sister properties, especially those further inland, may charge slightly less.

Eating

Restaurants abound along downtown's State St and by the waterfront, where you'll find a few gems among the touristy claptrap. More creative kitchens are found down in the Funk Zone. East of downtown, Milpas St is lined with Mexicali taco shops.

★Lucky Penny PIZZERIA $
(www.luckypennysb.com; 127 Anacapa St; mains $7-10, pizzas $10-15; ⊙7am-9pm Mon-Sat, from 9am Sun;) With shiny exterior walls covered in copper pennies, this pizzeria next to Lark restaurant is always jam-packed. It's worth the wait for a crispy pizza topped with smoked mozzarella and pork-and-fennel sausage or a wood oven-fired lamb meatball sandwich. Turn up before 11am for crazily inventive breakfast pizzas and farm-fresh egg skillets.

Lilly's Taquería MEXICAN $
(http://lillystacos.com; 310 Chapala St; items from $1.60; ⊙10:30am-9pm Sun-Mon & Wed-Thu, to 10pm Fri & Sat) There's almost always a line roping around this downtown taco shack at lunchtime. But it goes fast, so you'd best be snappy with your order – the *adobada* (mar-

inated pork) and *lengua* (beef tongue) are stand-out choices. Second location in Goleta west of the airport, off Hwy 101.

Backyard Bowls HEALTH FOOD $

(www.backyardbowls.com; 331 Motor Way; items $5-11; 7am-5pm Mon-Fri, from 8am Sat & Sun) This eco-minded little shop serves up real-fruit smoothies and heaping acaí bowls with all kinds of health-conscious add-ons like fresh berries, granola, coconut milk, honey, bee pollen, almonds and loads of other locally sourced, sustainably harvested ingredients.

Metropulos DELI $

(www.metrofinefoods.com; 216 E Yanonali St; dishes $2-10; 8:30am-5:30pm or 6pm Mon-Fri, 10am-4pm Sat) Before a day at the beach, pick up custom-made sandwiches and fresh salads at this gourmet deli in the Funk Zone. Artisan breads, imported cheeses, cured meats, and California olives and wines will be bursting out of your picnic basket.

El Buen Gusto MEXICAN $

(836 N Milpas St; dishes $2-8; 8am-9pm; P) At this red-brick strip-mall joint, order authentic south-of-the-border tacos, tortas, quesadillas and burritos with an *agua fresca* (fruit drink) or cold Pacifico beer. Mexican music videos and soccer games blare from the TVs. *Menudo* (tripe soup) and *birria* (spicy meat stew) are weekend specials.

Silvergreens CALIFORNIAN $

(www.silvergreens.com; 791 Chapala St; items $3-11; 7:30am-10pm;) Who says fast food can't be fresh and tasty? With the tag line 'Eat smart, live well,' this sun-drenched corner cafe makes nutritionally sound salads, soups, sandwiches, burgers, breakfast burritos and more.

★ Santa Barbara Shellfish Company SEAFOOD $$

(www.sbfishhouse.com; 230 Stearns Wharf; dishes $4-19; 11am-9pm; P) 'From sea to skillet to plate' sums up this end-of-the-wharf seafood shack that's more of a buzzing counter joint than a sit-down restaurant. Chase away the seagulls as you chow down on garlic-baked clams, crab cakes and coconut-fried shrimp at wooden picnic tables outside. Awesome lobster bisque, ocean views and the same location for over 25 years.

Olio Pizzeria ITALIAN $$

(805-899-2699; www.oliopizzeria.com; 11 W Victoria St; shared plates $7-24, lunch mains $9-17; usually 11:30am-10pm) Just around the corner from State St, this high-ceilinged pizzeria with a happening wine bar proffers crispy, wood oven-baked pizzas, platters of imported cheeses and meats, garden-fresh *insalate* (salads), savory traditional Italian antipasti and sweet *dolci* (desserts). The entrance is off the parking lot alleyway.

Brophy Brothers SEAFOOD $$

(805-966-4418; www.brophybros.com; 119 Harbor Way; mains $11-25; 11am-10pm; P) A longtime favorite for its fresh-off-the-dock fish and seafood, rowdy atmosphere and salty harborside setting. Slightly less claustrophobic tables on the upstairs deck are worth the long wait – they're quieter and have the best ocean views. Or skip the long lines and start knocking back oyster shooters and Bloody Marys with convivial locals at the bar.

DIY DINING IN SANTA BARBARA

Stock up on fresh fruits and veggies, nuts and honey at the midweek **Santa Barbara Farmers Market** (www.sbfarmersmarket.org; 500 & 600 blocks of State St; 4-7:30pm mid-Mar–early Nov, 3-6:30pm mid-Nov–mid-Mar;), which also happens on Saturday morning from 8:30am until 1pm at the corner of Santa Barbara and Cota Sts. Fill up a Wine Country picnic basket inside the **Santa Barbara Public Market** (http://sbpublicmarket.com; 38 W Victoria St; 7am-10:30pm Mon-Thu, to 11pm Fri & Sat, 11am-8pm Sun), where gourmet food purveyors and quick-fix food stalls are open every day of the week. The best place for healthy, organic groceries is **Lazy Acres** (www.lazyacres.com; 302 Meigs Rd; 7am-11pm Mon-Sat, to 10pm Sun; P), south of Hwy 101 via W Carrillo St. Downtown, **McConnell's Fine Ice Creams** (www.mcconnells.com; 728 State St; noon-9:30pm Sun-Wed, to 10:30pm Thu-Sat;) scoops up premium frozen treats. For more sweet endings, pop sea-salt or passion-fruit truffles from **Chocolate Maya** (www.chocolatemaya.com; 15 W Gutierrez St; 10am-6pm Mon-Fri, to 5pm Sat, to 4pm Sun).

Sojourner Café HEALTH FOOD $$
(www.sojournercafe.com; 134 E Cañon Perdido St; mains $8-13; usually 11am-10pm;) Vegetarians rejoice – the menu is extensive at this cozy, wholesome 1970s-era cafe. While supporting local farms, cooks get fairly creative with vegetables, tofu, tempeh, fish, seeds and other healthy ingredients. Daily desserts including vegan, dairy-free and wheat-free treats. Fair-trade coffee and local beers and wines are poured.

★**Lark** CALIFORNIAN $$$
(805-284-0370; www.thelarksb.com; 131 Anacapa St; shared plates $5-32, mains $24-38; 5-10pm Tue-Sun, bar till midnight) There's no better place in Santa Barbara County to taste the bountiful farm and fishing goodness of this stretch of SoCal coast. Named after an antique Pullman railway car, this chef-run restaurant in the Funk Zone morphs its menu with the seasons, presenting unique flavor combinations like fried olives with chorizo aioli and chile-spiced mussels in lemongrass-lime broth. Make reservations.

Bouchon CALIFORNIAN $$$
(805-730-1160; www.bouchonsantabarbara.com; 9 W Victoria Street; mains $25-36; 5-9pm Sun-Thu, to 10pm Fri & Sat) The perfect, unhurried follow-up to a day in the Wine Country is to feast on the bright, flavorful California cooking at pretty Bouchon (meaning 'wine cork'). A seasonally changing menu spotlights locally grown farm produce and ranched meats that marry beautifully with three dozen regional wines available by the glass. Lovebirds, book a table on the candlelit patio.

Palace Grill CAJUN, CREOLE $$$
(805-963-5000; http://palacegrill.com; 8 E Cota St; mains lunch $10-22, dinner $17-32; 11:30am-3pm daily, 5:30-10pm Sun-Thu, to 11pm Fri & Sat;) With all the exuberance of Mardi Gras, this N'awlins-style grill makes totally addictive baskets of housemade muffins and breads, and ginormous (if so-so) plates of jambalaya, gumbo ya-ya, blackened catfish and pecan chicken. Stiff cocktails and indulgent desserts make the grade. Act unsurprised when the staff lead the crowd in a rousing sing-along.

Drinking & Nightlife

On lower State St, most of the meat-market watering holes have happy hours, tiny dance floors and rowdy college nights. Just south of Hwy 101, the arty Funk Zone's eclectic mix of bars and wine-tasting rooms is a trendy scene.

★**Figueroa Mountain Brewing Co** BAR
(www.figmtnbrew.com; 137 Anacapa St; 11am-11pm) Father and son brewers have brought their gold medal-winning hoppy IPA, Dan-

DON'T MISS

URBAN WINE TRAIL

No wheels to head up to Santa Barbara's Wine Country? No problem. Ramble between over a dozen wine-tasting rooms (and microbreweries, too) downtown and in the Funk Zone near the beach. Pick up the **Urban Wine Trail** (www.urbanwinetrailsb.com) anywhere along its route. Most tasting rooms are open every afternoon or sometimes into the early evening. On weekends, join the beautiful people rubbing shoulders as they sip outstanding glasses of regional wines and listen to free live music.

For a sociable scene, start at **Municipal Winemakers** (www.municipalwinemakers.com; 22 Anacapa St; tastings $12; 11am-6pm;) or **Corks n' Crowns** (corksandcrowns.com; 32 Anacapa St; tastings $7-12; 11am-7pm, last call for tastings 6pm) bottle shop. Then head up to Yanonali St, turning left for **Riverbench Winery Tasting Room** (805-324-4100; www.riverbench.com; 137 Anacapa St; tastings $10; 11am-6pm); **Cutler's Artisan Spirits** (http://cutlersartisan.com; 137 Anacapa St; 1-6pm Thu-Sun) distillery, a storefront where you can sample bourbon whiskey, vodka and apple liqueur; and Figueroa Mountain Brewing Co Walk further west to find more wine-tippling spots, one inside an old tire shop.

Or turn right on Yanonali St and stop at AVA Santa Barbara for a liquid education about Santa Barbara's five distinct wine-growing regions. It's less than a mile's detour to the refined **Carr Winery** (http://carrwinery.com; 414 N Salsipuedes St; tastings $10-12; 11am-6pm Sun-Wed, to 7pm Thu-Sat) barrel room, next door to **Telegraph Brewing Company** (www.telegraphbrewing.com; 416 N Salsipuedes St; 3-9pm Tue-Thu, 2-10pm Fri & Sat, 1-7pm Sun), which makes robust ales and a 'rhinoceros' rye wine.

ish red lager, and double IPA from Santa Barbara's Wine Country to the Funk Zone. Clink pint glasses on the taproom's open-air patio while acoustic acts play. Enter on Yanonali St.

AVA Santa Barbara BAR

(www.avasantabarbara.com; 116 E Yanonali St; ⊙noon-7pm) From the sidewalk, passersby stop just to peek through the floor-to-ceiling glass windows at a wall-sized map of Santa Barbara's Wine Country, all hand-drawn in chalk. Inside, wine lovers lean on the tasting bar while sipping flights of cool-weather Chardonnay or pinot noir and sun-loving sauvignon blanc, grenache, Syrah and cabernet, all grown locally.

Handlebar Coffee Roasters CAFE

(www.handlebarcoffee.com; 128 E Cañon Perdido St; ⊙7am-5pm Mon-Sat, from 8am Sun; 🐾) Bicycle-themed coffee shop brews rich coffee and espresso drinks from small-batch roasted beans. Sit and sip yours on the sunny patio.

Brewhouse BREWERY

(sbbrewhouse.com; 229 W Montecito St; ⊙11am-11pm Sun-Thu, to midnight Fri & Sat; 📶🐾) Down by the railroad tracks, the boisterous Brewhouse crafts its own unique small-batch beer (Saint Barb's Belgian-style ales rule), serves wines by the glass and has cool art and rockin' live music Wednesday to Saturday nights.

Press Room PUB

(http://pressroomsb.com; 15 E Ortega St; ⊙11am-2am) This tiny pub can barely contain the college students and European travelers who cram the place to its seams. Pop in to catch soccer games, stuff the jukebox with quarters and enjoy jovial banter with the British bartender.

Marquee COCKTAIL BAR

(http://marqueesb.com; 1212 State St; ⊙4pm-2am) At downtown's Granada Theatre, flickering candles and glowing lights fill this bar mixing unusual cocktails, pouring wines by the glass and dishing up Mediterranean tapas. Look for jazz, open-mic and comedy nights.

Hollister Brewing Company BREWERY

(www.hollisterbrewco.com; Camino Real Marketplace, 6980 Marketplace Dr, Goleta; ⊙11am-10pm) With over a dozen microbrews on tap, this place draws serious beer geeks out to Goleta, near the UCSB campus, off Hwy 101. IPAs are the permanent attractions, along with nitrogenated stout. Skip the food, though.

☆ Entertainment

Santa Barbara's appreciation of the arts is evidenced not only by the variety of performances available on any given night, but also its gorgeous, often historic venues. For a current calender of live music and special events, check www.independent.com online or pick up Friday's *Scene* guide in the *Santa Barbara News-Press*.

Santa Barbara Bowl MUSIC

(☎805-962-7411; http://sbbowl.com; 1122 N Milpas St; most tickets $35-125) Built by Works Progress Administration (WPA) artisans during the Depression in the 1930s, this naturally beautiful outdoor stone amphitheater has ocean views from the highest cheap seats. Kick back in the sunshine or under the stars for live rock, jazz and folk concerts in summer. Big-name acts like Jack Johnson, Sarah McLachlan and The National have all taken the stage here.

Granada Theatre THEATER, MUSIC

(☎805-899-2222; www.granadasb.org; 1216 State St) This beautifully restored 1930s Spanish Moorish-style theater is home to the city's symphony, ballet and opera, as well as touring Broadway shows and big-name musicians.

Lobero Theatre THEATER, MUSIC

(☎888-456-2376, 805-963-0761; www.lobero.com; 33 E Cañon Perdido St) One of California's oldest theaters presents modern dance, chamber music, jazz and world-music touring acts and stand-up comedy nights.

Arlington Theatre CINEMA

(☎805-963-4408; www.thearlingtontheatre.com; 1317 State St) Harking back to 1931, this Mission Revival–style movie palace has a Spanish courtyard and a star-spangled ceiling. It's a drop-dead gorgeous place to attend a film festival screening.

Soho MUSIC

(☎805-962-7776; www.sohosb.com; ste 205, 1221 State St; most tickets $8-25) One unpretentious brick room plus live music almost nightly equals Soho, upstairs inside a downtown office complex behind McDonald's. Lineups range from indie rock, jazz, folk and funk to world beats. Some all-ages shows.

Velvet Jones MUSIC, COMEDY

(☎805-965-8676; http://velvet-jones.com; 423 State St; most tickets $10-15) Long-running downtown punk and indie dive for rock, hip-hop, comedy and 18-plus DJ nights for the city's college crowd. Many bands stop here between gigs in LA and San Francisco.

Zodo's Bowling & Beyond BOWLING
(☎805-967-0128; www.zodos.com; 5925 Calle Real, Goleta; bowling per game $4-8, shoe rental $4; ⏰8:30am-2am Tue-Sat, to midnight Sun & Mon; 👪) With over 40 beers on tap, pool tables and a video arcade (Skee-Ball!), this bowling alley near UCSB is good ol' family fun. Call ahead to get on the wait list and for schedules of open-play lanes and 'Glow Bowling' blacklight nights with DJs. From Hwy 101 west of downtown, exit Fairview Ave north.

Shopping

Downtown's **State St** is packed with shops of all kinds, and even chain stores conform to the red-roofed architectural style. Cheapskates stick to lower State St, while trust-fund babies should head uptown. For more local art galleries and indie shops, dive into the **Funk Zone**, south of Hwy 101, spreading east of State St.

Paseo Nuevo MALL
(www.paseonuevoshopping.com; 651 Paseo Nuevo; ⏰10am-9pm Mon-Fri, to 8pm Sat, 11am-6pm Sun) This busy open-air mall is anchored by Macy's and Nordstrom department stores and clothing chains. Browse Kitson for cutting-edge styles from LA, Bettie Page Clothing's retro pin-up fashions and the eco-green goddesses' bath, body and beauty shop Lush. First 75 minutes of parking free in the underground garage.

Surf-n-Wear's Beach House CLOTHING
(www.surfnwear.com; 10 State St; ⏰9am-6pm Sun-Thu, to 7pm Fri & Sat) Modern and vintage surfboards dangle from the ceiling at this beach-minded emporium where unique T-shirts and hoodies, colorful bikinis, shades, beachbags and flip-flops jostle for your attention. This shop has been around since before 1967's Summer of Love.

REI OUTDOOR EQUIPMENT
(www.rei.com; 321 Anacapa St; ⏰10am-9pm Mon-Fri, to 7pm Sat, to 6pm Sun) If you forgot your tent or rock-climbing carabiners at home, the West Coast's most popular independent co-op outdoor retailer is the place to pick up outdoor recreation gear, active clothing, sport shoes and topographic maps.

Channel Islands Surfboards OUTDOOR EQUIPMENT
(www.cisurfboards.com; 36 Anacapa St; ⏰10am-7pm Mon-Sat, 11am-5pm Sun) Are you ready to take home a handcrafted, Southern California-born surfboard? Down in the Funk Zone, this surf shack is the place for innovative pro-worthy board designs, as well as surfer threads and beanie hats.

CRSVR Sneaker Boutique SHOES, CLOTHING
(www.crsvr.com; 632 State St; ⏰10am-8pm) Check out this sneaker boutique run by DJs, not just for limited-editions Nikes and other athletic-shoe brands, but also T-shirts, jackets, hats and more urban styles for men.

La Arcada MALL
(www.laarcadasantabarbara.com; 1114 State St; ⏰individual shop hr vary) Filled with specialty boutiques, restaurants and whimsical art galleries, this historic red-tile-roofed passageway was designed by Myron Hunt (builder of Pasadena's Rose Bowl) in the 1920s. Savor handmade French candies from Chocolats du Calibressan as you wander around.

Diani CLOTHING, SHOES
(www.dianiboutique.com; 1324 State St, Arlington Plaza; ⏰10am-6pm Mon, 10am-7pm Tue-Sat, noon-6pm Sun) Carries high-fashion, Euro-inspired designs, with a touch of funky California soul thrown in for good measure. Think Humanoid dresses, Rag & Bone skinny jeans, Stella McCartney sunglasses and Chloé shoes.

El Paseo MALL
(800 block of State St; ⏰individual shop hr vary) A smattering of locally owned boutiques surround a tiny, flower-festooned courtyard, constructed in Spanish-colonial style in the 1920s. It cameoed in the romantic comedy *It's Complicated*.

ℹ Information

FedEx Office (www.fedex.com; 1030 State St; per min 30-40¢; ⏰7am-11pm Mon-Fri, 8am-9pm Sat, 9am-9pm Sun) Self-service online computer workstations.

Outdoors Santa Barbara Visitors Center (☎805-884-1475; 4th fl, 113 Harbor Way; ⏰11am-4pm) Inside the same building as the maritime museum, this volunteer-staffed visitor center offers info on Channel Islands National Park and a harbor-view deck.

Santa Barbara Central Library (☎805-962-7653; www.sbplibrary.org; 40 E Anapamu St; ⏰10am-7pm Mon-Thu, to 5:30pm Fri & Sat, 1-5pm Sun; 📶) Free walk-in internet terminals (photo ID required).

Santa Barbara Cottage Hospital (☎805-682-7111; www.cottagehealthsystem.org; 400 W Pueblo St; ⏲24hr) Emergency room (ER) open 24 hours.

Santa Barbara Independent (www.independent.com) Free alternative weekly tabloid with eating and entertainment listings and reviews, plus an events calendar.

Santa Barbara News-Press (www.newspress.com) Daily newspaper offers an events calendar and Friday's arts-and-entertainment supplement *Scene*.

Santa Barbara Visitors Center (☎805-568-1811, 805-965-3021; www.santabarbaraca.com; 1 Garden St; ⏲9am-5pm Mon-Sat & 10am-5pm Sun Feb-Oct; 9am-4pm Mon-Sat Nov-Jan) Pick up maps and brochures while consulting with the helpful but busy staff. The website offers free downloadable DIY touring maps and itineraries, from famous movie locations to wine trails, art galleries and outdoors fun. Self-pay metered parking lot nearby.

ℹ Getting There & Away

The small Santa Barbara Airport (p480), less than 10 miles west of downtown via Hwy 101, has scheduled flights to/from LA, Las Vegas, San Francisco and other western US cities. A taxi to downtown or the waterfront costs about $30 to $35 plus tip. Car-rental agencies with airport lots include Alamo, Avis, Budget, Enterprise, Hertz and National; reserve in advance.

Santa Barbara Airbus (☎800-423-1618, 805-964-7759; www.sbairbus.com) shuttles between Los Angeles International Airport (LAX) and Santa Barbara ($46/88 one way/round-trip, 2½ hours, eight departures daily). The more people in your party, the cheaper the fare. For more discounts, prepay online.

Amtrak (☎800-872-7245; www.amtrak.com; 209 State St) trains run south to LA ($31, three hours) via Carpinteria, Ventura and Burbank's airport, and north to San Luis Obispo ($27, 2¾ hours) and Oakland ($82, 8¾ hours), with stops in Paso Robles, Salinas and San Jose.

Greyhound (☎800-231-2222, 805-965-7551; www.greyhound.com; 224 Chapala St) operates a few buses daily to LA ($15, three hours), San Luis Obispo ($28, 2¼ hours), Santa Cruz ($53, six hours) and San Francisco ($57, nine hours).

Vista (☎800-438-1112; www.goventura.org) runs frequent daily 'Coastal Express' buses to Carpinteria ($3, 20 to 30 minutes) and Ventura ($3, 40 to 70 minutes); check online or call for schedules.

If you're driving on Hwy 101, take the Garden St or Carrillo St exits for downtown.

GO GREEN IN SANTA BARBARA

Santa Barbara's biggest eco-travel initiative is **Santa Barbara Car Free** (www.santabarbaracarfree.org). Browse the website for tips on seeing the city without your car, plus valuable discounts on accommodations, vacation packages, rail travel and more. Still don't believe it's possible to tour Santa Barbara without a car? Let us show you how to do it.

From LA, hop aboard the *Pacific Surfliner* for a memorably scenic three-hour coastal ride to Santa Barbara's Amtrak station, a few blocks from the beach and downtown. Then hoof it or catch one of the electric shuttles that zips north-south along State St and east-west along the waterfront. Take MTD bus line 22 to reach the famous mission and the botanic gardens. For a DIY cycling tour, Wheel Fun Rentals (p396) is a short walk from the train station.

Even Santa Barbara's Wine Country is getting into the sustainable swing of things. More and more vineyards are implementing biodynamic farming techniques and following organic guidelines. Many vintners and oenophiles are starting to think that the more natural the growing process, the better the wine, too. Sustainable Vine Wine Tours (p414) whisks you around family-owned sustainable vineyards. Minimize your carbon footprint even further by following Santa Barbara's Urban Wine Trail (p404) on foot. If you love both wine and food, **Edible Santa Barbara** (http://ediblecommunities.com/santabarbara/) magazine publishes insightful articles about vineyards and restaurants that are going green. It's available free at many local markets, restaurants and wineries.

Santa Barbara County abounds with ecofriendly outdoor activities, too. Take your pick of hiking trails, cycling routes, ocean kayaking, swimming, surfing or stand-up paddle boarding (SUP). If you're going whale-watching, ask around to see if there are any alternative-fueled tour boats with trained onboard naturalists.

Getting Around

Local buses operated by the **Metropolitan Transit District** (MTD; 805-963-3366; www.sbmtd.gov) cost $1.75 per ride (exact change, cash only). Equipped with front-loading bike racks, these buses travel all over town and to adjacent communities; ask for a free transfer upon boarding. **MTD Transit Center** (1020 Chapala St) has details about routes and schedules.

BUS	DESTINATION	FREQUENCY
5	Arroyo Burro Beach	hourly
11	State St, UCSB campus	every 30 minutes
20	Montecito, Summerland, Carpinteria	hourly
22	Mission, Museum of Natural History and (weekends only) Botanic Garden	seven or eight buses daily

MTD's electric **Downtown Shuttle** buses run along State St down to Stearns Wharf every 10 to 30 minutes from 9am to 6pm daily. A second **Waterfront Shuttle** travels from Stearns Wharf west to the harbor and east to the zoo every 15 to 30 minutes from 9am or 10am to 6pm daily. Between late May and early September, both routes also run every 15 minutes from 6pm to 9pm on Fridays and Saturdays. The fare is 50¢ per ride; transfers between routes are free.

Lil' Toot water taxi (888-316-9363; www.sbwatertaxi.com; 113 Harbor Way; one-way fare adult/child 2-12yr $4/1; usually noon-6pm Apr-Oct, hr vary Nov-Mar;) provides an eco-friendly, biodiesel-fueled ride between Stearns Wharf and the harbor, docking in front of the maritime museum. Look for ticket booths on the waterfront. Trips run every half-hour, weather permitting.

For bicycle rentals, Wheel Fun Rentals (p396) has two locations by Stearns Wharf. Downtown, **Pedego** (805-963-8885; http://pedegosb.com; 436 State St; 9:30am-6:30am Tue-Sun) rents electric bicycles (per hour/day from $16/70) and pedal-it-yourself models (from $10/40).

Taxis are metered around $3 at flagfall, with an additional $3 to $4 for each mile. Call **Yellow Cab** (805-965-5111, 800-549-8294; www.santabarbarayellowcab.com).

Downtown street parking or in any of a dozen municipal lots is free for the first 75 minutes; each additional hour costs $1.50.

SANTA BARBARA WINE COUNTRY

Oak-dotted hillsides, winding country lanes, rows of sweetly heavy grapevines stretching as far as the eye can see – it's hard not to gush about the Santa Ynez and Santa Maria Valleys and the Santa Rita Hills wine regions. From fancy convertibles and Harleys to ecofriendly touring vans and road bikes, you'll find an eclectic, friendly mix of travelers sharing these bucolic back roads.

You may be inspired to visit by the Oscar-winning film *Sideways,* which is like real life in at least one respect: this Wine Country is ideal for do-it-yourself-exploring with friends. Locals here are friendly, from longtime landowners and farmers displaying small-town graciousness to vineyard owners who've fled big cities to follow their passion. Ever more winemakers are showing their passion for the vine in earth-conscious ways, implementing organic practices and biodynamic farming techniques. Many happily share their knowledge and intriguing personal histories, as well as their love of the land, in intimate vineyard tasting rooms.

With more than 100 wineries spread out across the landscape, it can seem daunting at first. But the Santa Ynez Valley's five small towns – Los Olivos, Solvang, Buellton, Santa Ynez and Ballard – are all clustered within 10 miles of one another, so it's easy to stop, shop and eat whenever and wherever you feel like it. Don't worry about sticking to a regimented plan or following prescriptive wine guides. Instead, let yourself be captivated by the scenery and pull over wherever signs looks welcoming.

Wineries

The big-name appellations for Santa Barbara's Wine Country are the Santa Ynez Valley, Santa Maria Valley and Santa Rita Hills, plus smaller Happy Canyon and upstart Ballard Canyon. Wine-tasting rooms abound in Los Olivos and Solvang, handy for anyone with limited time.

The Santa Ynez Valley, where you'll find most of the wineries, lies south of the Santa Maria Valley. Hwy 246 runs east–west, via Solvang, across the bottom of the Santa Ynez Valley, connecting Hwy 101 with Hwy 154.

SCENIC DRIVE: HIGHWAY 154 (SAN MARCOS PASS RD)

What to See

As Hwy 154 climbs from the coast, you'll leave oh-so civilized Santa Barbara behind and enter the rugged Santa Ynez Mountains. You'll notice places where the hillsides have been scarred by wildfires, but don't be alarmed: wildfires are part of the natural process of forest birth and regrowth.

Chumash Painted Cave State Historic Park

This tiny, off-the-beaten path **historic site** (www.parks.ca.gov; dawn-dusk) FREE shelters pictographs painted by Chumash tribespeople over 400 years ago. The sandstone cave is now protected from graffiti and vandalism by a metal screen, so bring a flashlight to get a good look. The turnoff to Painted Cave Rd is off Hwy 154 below San Marcos Summit, about 6 miles from Hwy 101. The two-mile twisting side road to the site is extremely narrow, rough and steep (no RVs). Look for a small signposted pull-off on your left.

Cold Spring Tavern

Cold Spring Tavern (805-967-0066; www.coldspringtavern.com; 5995 Stagecoach Rd; mains breakfast & lunch $9-14, dinner $22-31; 11am-8:30pm Mon-Fri, from 8am Sat & Sun) is an 1860s stagecoach stop that's still a popular watering hole. A rough-hewn plank floor connects a warren of dimly lit rooms decorated with an odd assortment of Western memorabilia. Call ahead to check if the barbecue grill is open, then order the Santa Maria-style tri-tip barbecue sandwich. The tavern's signposted turnoff from Hwy 154 is about a mile downhill beyond the mountain summit, then follow the signs for another 1.5 miles around the loop road.

Los Padres National Forest

The **Los Padres National Forest** (805-967-3481; www.fs.usda.gov/lpnf) stretches over 200 miles from the Carmel Valley to the western edge of LA County. It's a giant playground for hiking, camping, horseback riding and mountain biking.

Several scenic hiking trails lead off Paradise Rd, which crosses Hwy 154 north of San Marcos Pass, over 10 miles from Hwy 101. On the 1-mile round-trip **Red Rock Pools Trail**, the Santa Ynez River deeply pools among rocks and waterfalls, creating a swimming and sunbathing spot; the trailhead is at the end of Paradise Rd.

Stop at the **ranger station** (805-967-3481; 3505 Paradise Rd; 8am-4:30pm Mon-Fri, also 8am-4:30pm Sat late May-early Sep) for posted trail maps and information and a National Forest Adventure Pass (per day $5), which is required for parking (unless you have an 'America the Beautiful' Annual Pass (p472)). Family-friendly **campgrounds** (877-444-6777; www.recreation.gov; campsites $19-35) with drinking water, flush toilets and both first-come, first-served and reservable sites are along Paradise Rd.

Cachuma Lake Recreation Area

This county-run **park** (cruise reservations 805-686-5050/5055; www.countyofsb.org/parks; admission per vehicle $10, 2hr cruise adult/4-12yr $15/7; open daily, seasonal hr vary;) is a haven for anglers and boaters, with wildlife-watching cruises offered year-round. There's also a child-friendly **nature center** (805-693-0691; www.clnaturecenter.org; 10am-4pm Tue-Sat, to 2pm Sun;) and a large campground (p401) with hot showers. First-come, first-served sites fill quickly; book ahead on weekends or for ecofriendly yurts.

The Route

From Hwy 101 west of downtown Santa Barbara, Hwy 154 (San Marcos Pass Rd) heads northwest, winding up through the Los Padres National Forest and passing Cachuma Lake. Beyond the Hwy 246 turnoff west to Solvang, Hwy 154 bisects the Santa Ynez Valley before rejoining Hwy 101 past Los Olivos.

Time & Mileage

It's 35 miles from downtown Santa Barbara to Los Olivos, taking 40 minutes without stops or traffic jams. Returning to Santa Barbara, it's under an hour's trip via Hwy 101.

Santa Barbara Wine Country

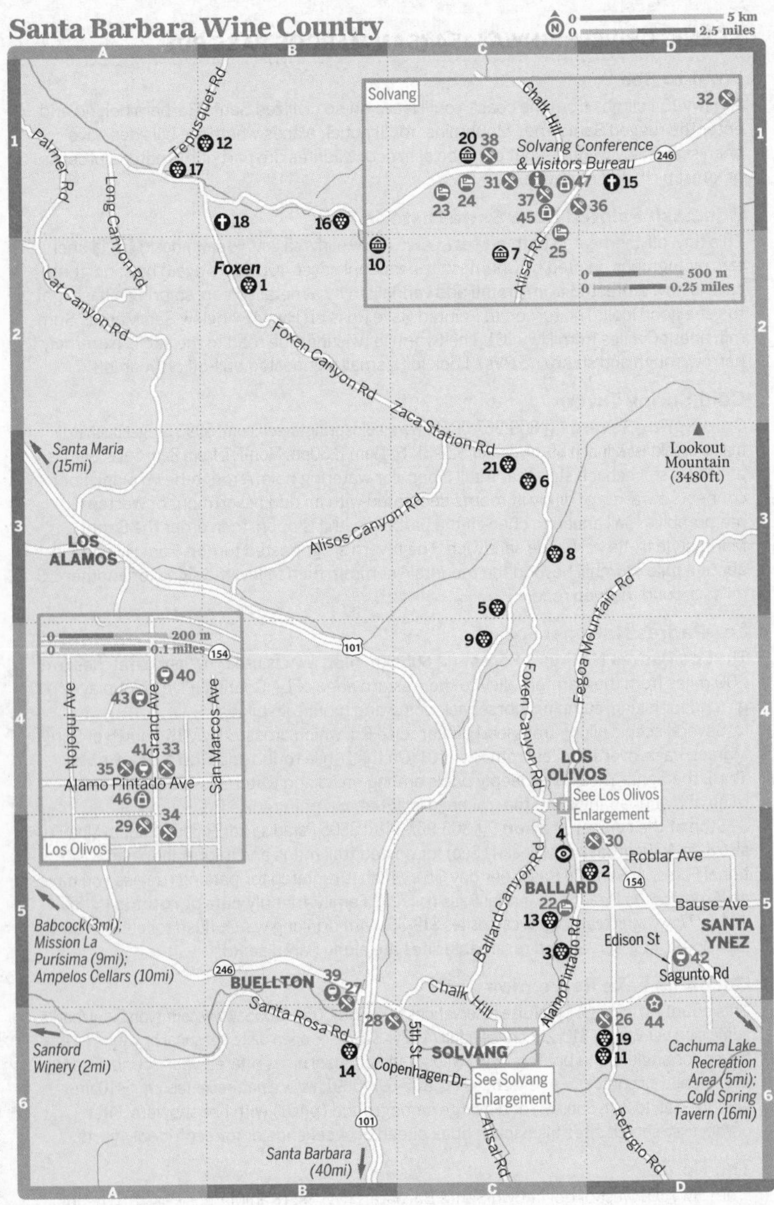

North–south secondary roads bordered by vineyards include Alamo Pintado Rd from Hwy 246 to Los Olivos, and Refugio Rd between Santa Ynez and Ballard.

A half-day trip will allow you to see one winery or tasting room, have lunch and return to Santa Barbara. Otherwise make it a full day and plan to have lunch and possibly dinner before returning to the city.

Santa Barbara Wine Country

Top Sights

1 Foxen B2

Sights

2 Beckmen Vineyards D5
3 Buttonwood Farm Winery & Vineyard C5
4 Clairmont Farms C5
5 Curtis Winery C3
6 Demetria Estate C3
7 Elverhøj Museum C2
8 Fess Parker Winery & Vineyard C3
9 Firestone Vineyards C4
10 Hans Christian Andersen Museum B2
11 Kalyra Winery D6
12 Kenneth Volk Vineyards B1
13 Lincourt Vineyard C5
14 Mosby Winery B6
15 Old Mission Santa Ínes D1
16 Rancho Sisquoc Winery B1
17 Riverbench Vineyard & Winery A1
18 San Ramon Chapel B1
19 Sunstone Vineyards & Winery D6
20 Wildling Museum C1
21 Zaca Mesa Winery C3

Sleeping

22 Ballard Inn & Restaurant C5
23 Hadsten House C1
24 Hamlet Inn C1
25 Hotel Corque C1

Eating

26 El Rancho Market D6
27 Ellen's Danish Pancake House B5
28 Hitching Post II B6
29 Los Olivos Café & Wine Merchant A5
30 Los Olivos Grocery D5
31 Mortensen's Danish Bakery C1
32 New Frontiers Natural Marketplace D1
33 Panino A4
34 Petros A5
Root 246 .... (see 25)
35 Sides Hardware & Shoes A4
36 Solvang Bakery C1
37 Solvang Restaurant C1
38 Succulent Café C1

Drinking & Nightlife

39 Avant Tapas & Wine B5
40 Carhartt Vineyard Tasting Room A4
41 Los Olivos Tasting Room A4
42 Maverick Saloon D5
43 Sarloos + Sons A4

Entertainment

44 Chumash Casino Resort D6

Shopping

Book Loft .... (see 10)
45 Gaveasken C1
46 Jedlicka's Western Wear A4
47 Solvang Antique Center C1

Foxen Canyon Wine Trail

The scenic **Foxen Canyon Wine Trail** (www.foxencanyonwinetrail.com) runs north from Hwy 154, just west of Los Olivos, deep into the heart of the rural Santa Maria Valley. It's a must-see for oenophiles or anyone wanting to get off the beaten path. For the most part, it follows Foxen Canyon Rd.

★ Foxen — WINERY

(☎805-937-4251; www.foxenvineyard.com; 7200 & 7600 Foxen Canyon Rd, Santa Maria; tastings $10; ⏲11am-4pm) On what was once a working cattle ranch, Foxen crafts warm Syrah, steel-cut Chardonnay, full-fruited pinot noir and rich Rhône-style wines, all sourced from standout vineyards. The newer tasting room is solar-powered, while the old 'shack' – a dressed-down space with a corrugated-metal roof, funky-cool decor and leafy patio – pours Bordeaux-style and Cal-Ital varietals under the 'Foxen 7200' label.

Demetria Estate — WINERY

(☎805-686-2345; www.demetriaestate.com; 6701 Foxen Canyon Rd, Los Olivos; tastings $20; ⏲by appt only) This hilltop retreat has the curving arches and thick wooden doors of your hospitable Greek uncle's country house, with epic views of vineyards and rolling hillsides. Tastings are by appointment only, but worth it just to sample the biodynamically farmed Chardonnay, Syrah and viognier, plus rave-worthy Rhône-style red blends.

Zaca Mesa Winery — WINERY

(www.zacamesa.com; 6905 Foxen Canyon Rd, Los Olivos; tastings $10; ⏲10am-4pm daily year-round, to 5pm Fri & Sat late May–early Sep) Stop by this barn-style tasting room for a rustic, sipping-on-the-farm ambience. Santa Barbara's highest-elevation winery, Zaca Mesa is known not only for its estate-grown Rhône varietals and signature Z Cuvée red blend and Z Blanc white blend, but also a life-sized outdoor chessboard, a tree-shaded picnic

WINE COUNTRY CELEBRATIONS

Santa Barbara Vintners (☎805-668-0881; www.sbcountywines.com) publishes a free touring map brochure of the county's vineyards and wine trails, which you can pick up at just about any winery or visitors center, or download their free mobile app. Special events worth planning your trip around include the **Spring Weekend** (www.sbvintnersweekend.com) in mid-April and mid-October's **Celebration of Harvest** (www.celebrationofharvest.com).

area that's dog-friendly and a short, scenic trail overlooking the vineyards.

Firestone Vineyards WINERY

(☎805-688-3940; www.firestonewine.com; 5017 Zaca Station Rd, Los Olivos; tastings $15, incl tour $20; ⏲10am-5pm) Founded in the 1970s, Firestone is Santa Barbara's oldest estate winery. Sweeping views of the vineyard from the sleek, wood-paneled tasting room are nearly as satisfying as the value-priced Chardonnay, sauvignon blanc, merlot and Bordeaux-style blends. Arrive in time for a winery tour, usually offered at 11:15am, 1:15pm and 3:15pm daily (no reservations).

Curtis Winery WINERY

(www.curtiswinery.com; 5249 Foxen Canyon Rd, Los Olivos; tastings $10; ⏲10:30am-5:30pm) Just up the road from Firestone Vineyards, artisan winemaker Andrew Murray specializes in Rhône-style wines, including estate-grown Syrah, Mourvèdre, viognier, grenache blanc and Roussanne. The same wines are poured at Andrew Murray Vineyards' tasting room in downtown Los Olivos.

Kenneth Volk Vineyards WINERY

(☎805-938-7896; www.volkwines.com; 5230 Tepusquet Rd, Santa Maria; tastings $10; ⏲10:30am-4:30pm) Only an established cult winemaker could convince oenophiles to drive so far out of their way to taste rare heritage varietals like floral-scented Malvasia and inky Negrette, as well as standard-bearing pinot noir, Chardonnay, cabernet sauvignon and merlot.

Riverbench Vineyard & Winery WINERY

(www.riverbench.com; 6020 Foxen Canyon Rd, Santa Maria; tastings $10; ⏲10am-4pm) Riverbench has been growing prized pinot noir and Chardonnay grapes since the early 1970s. The rural tasting room is inside a butter-yellow Arts-and-Crafts farmhouse with panoramic views across the Santa Maria Valley. Out back is a picnic ground and bocce ball court. You can also sample their wines on Santa Barbara's Urban Wine Trail.

Fess Parker Winery & Vineyard WINERY

(www.fessparkerwines.com; 6200 Foxen Canyon Rd; tastings $12; ⏲10am-5pm) Besides its on-screen appearance as Frass Canyon in the movie *Sideways,* the winery's other claim to fame is its late founder Fess Parker, best known for playing Davy Crockett on TV. Even though Fess has now passed on, his winery still gives away coonskin-cap-etched souvenir glasses. Savor the pricey, award-winning Chardonnay and pinot noir.

Rancho Sisquoc Winery WINERY

(www.ranchosisquoc.com; 6600 Foxen Canyon Rd, Santa Maria; tastings $10; ⏲10am-4pm Mon-Thu, to 5pm Fri-Sun) This tranquil gem is worth the extra mileage, not necessarily for its hit-and-miss wines, but for the charmingly rustic tasting room surrounded by pastoral views. Turn off Foxen Canyon Rd when you spot **San Ramon Chapel** (www.sanramonchapel.org), a little white church built in 1875. Incidentally, *sisquoc* is the Chumash term for 'gathering place.'

Santa Rita Hills Wine Trail

When it comes to country-road scenery, eco-conscious farming practices and top-notch pinot noir, the less-traveled **Santa Rita Hills** (www.staritahills.com) region holds its own. Almost a dozen tasting rooms line an easy driving loop west of Hwy 101 via Santa Rosa Rd and Hwy 246. Be prepared to share the roads with cyclists and an occasional John Deere tractor. More artisan winemarkers hide out in the industrial warehouses of Buellton near Hwy 101 and farther afield in Lompoc's 'Wine Ghetto' (www.lompoctrail.com).

Alma Rosa Winery & Vineyards WINERY

(☎805-688-9090; www.almarosawinery.com; tastings $5-15; ⏲11am-4:30pm) Richard Sanford left the powerhouse winery bearing his name to start this new winery with his wife, Thekla, using sustainable, organic farming techniques. Cacti and cobblestones welcome you to the ranch, reached via a long, winding gravel driveway. Vineyard-designated pinot noir and fine pinot blanc and pinot gris are what's poured. Call ahead for directions to the new tasting room.

Sanford Winery WINERY
(www.sanfordwinery.com; 5010 Santa Rosa Rd, Lompoc; tastings $15-20, incl tour $25; ⏲11am-4pm Sun-Thu, to 5pm Fri & Sat Mar-Oct, 11am-4pm daily Nov-Feb) Be enchanted by this romantic tasting room built of stone and handmade adobe bricks, all embraced by estate vineyards on the historic Rancho La Rinconda property. Watch the sun sink over the vineyards from the back patio with a glass of silky pinot noir or citrusy Chardonnay in hand. Winery tours are typically given at 11:30am daily (no reservations).

Babcock WINERY
(www.babcockwinery.com; 5175 E Hwy 146, Lompoc; tastings $12-15; ⏲10:30am-5pm) Family-owned vineyards overflow with different grape varietals – Chardonnay, Sauvignon Blanc, Pinot Gris, pinot noir, Syrah, Cabernet Sauvignon, merlot and more – that let innovative small-lot winemaker Bryan Babcock be the star. 'Slice of Heaven' pinot noir alone is worthy of a pilgrimage to this eclectically furnished tasting room with elevated views.

Ampelos Cellars TASTING ROOM
(☎805-736-9957; www.ampeloscellars.com; 312 N 9th Ave, Lompoc; tastings $10; ⏲11am-5pm Thu-Sat, to 4pm Mon) Danish grower Peter Work and wife Rebecca display their passion for the vine through biodynamic farming techniques and encyclopedic knowledge of their lots. Their pinot noir, Syrah and grenache shine. Sample them in Lompoc's Wine Ghetto, an industrial area far from the vineyards, where most of the family-run tasting rooms (Flying Goat Cellars is a fave) are open only on weekends.

Mosby Winery WINERY
(☎805-688-2415; www.mosbywines.com; 9496 Santa Rosa Rd, Buellton; tastings $10; ⏲10am-4pm Mon-Thu, to 4:30pm Fri-Sun) Just west of Hwy 101, by a hillside olive orchard, this casual red carriage house pours unusual Cal-Italian varietals, including a lip-puckering, fruit-forward Dolcetto and a crisp, citrusy estate-grown Cortese. Be forewarned: the 80-proof grappa distilled from estate-grown Traminer grapes is a knock-out punch.

Santa Ynez Valley

Popular wineries cluster between Los Olivos and Solvang along Alamo Pintado Rd and Refugio Rd, south of Roblar Ave and west of Hwy 154. Noisy tour groups, harried staff and stingy pours often disappoint, but thankfully that's not the case at better wine-tasting rooms.

Beckmen Vineyards WINERY
(www.beckmenvineyards.com; 2670 Ontiveros Rd, Solvang; tastings $10-15; ⏲11am-5pm) Bring a picnic to the pondside gazebo at this tranquil winery, where estate-grown Rhône varieties flourish on the unique terroir of Purisima Mountain. Using biodynamic farming principles, natural (not chemical), means are used to prevent pests. To sample superb Syrah and a rare cuvée blend with grenache, Mourvèdre and Counoise, follow Roblar Ave west of Hwy 154 to Ontiveros Rd.

Lincourt Vineyard WINERY
(www.lincourtwines.com; 1711 Alamo Pintado Rd, Solvang; tastings from $10; ⏲10am-5pm) Respected winemaker Bill Foley, who runs Firestone Vineyard on the Foxen Canyon Wine Trail, founded this vineyard first in the late 1990s on a former dairy farm. Today you can still see the original 1926 farmhouse built from a Sears catalog kit. Inside

SANTA BARBARA WINE COUNTRY 101

Although large-scale winemaking has only been happening here since the 1980s, the climate of Santa Barbara's Wine Country has always been perfect for growing grapes. Two parallel, transverse mountain ranges – Santa Ynez and San Rafael – cradle the region and funnel coastal fog eastward off the Pacific into the valleys between. The farther inland you go, the warmer it gets.

To the west, fog and low clouds may hover all day, keeping the weather crisp even in summer, while only a few miles inland, temperatures approach 100°F in July. These delicately balanced microclimates support two major types of grapes. Nearer the coast in the cooler Santa Maria Valley, pinot noir – a particularly fragile grape – and other Burgundian varietals such as Chardonnay thrive. Inland in the hotter Santa Ynez Valley, Rhône-style grapes do best, including Syrah and viognier.

the yellow cottage's tasting room, sip finely crafted Syrah, pinot noir and a dry French-style rosé, all made from grapes grown in the Santa Maria Valley and Santa Rita Hills.

Kalyra Winery WINERY
(www.kalyrawinery.com; 343 N Refugio Rd, Santa Ynez; tastings $10-12; ⏲11am-5pm Mon-Fri, from 10am Sat & Sun) Australian Mike Brown has traveled halfway around the world to combine his two loves: surfing and winemaking. Try one of his full-bodied red blends, unusual white varietals or sweet dessert wines (the orange muscat is a crowd-pleaser), all in bottles with Aboriginal art-inspired labels. Kalyra also pours at a smaller tasting room on Santa Barbara's Urban Wine Trail.

Sunstone Vineyards & Winery WINERY
(www.sunstonewinery.com; 125 N Refugio Rd, Santa Ynez; tastings $10-15; ⏲11am-5pm) Wander inside what looks like an 18th-century stone farmhouse from Provence and into a cool hillside cave housing wine barrels. Sunstone crafts Bordeaux-style wines made from 100% organically grown grapes. Bring a picnic to eat in the courtyard beneath gnarled oaks.

Buttonwood Farm Winery & Vineyard WINERY
(www.buttonwoodwinery.com; 1500 Alamo Pintado Rd, Solvang; tastings $10-15; ⏲11am-5pm; 🐾) Bordeaux and Rhône varieties do well in the sun-dappled limestone soil at this friendly winery, best for wine-tasting neophytes and dog owners. The trellised back patio, bordering a fruit-tree orchard, is a pleasant spot to relax with a bottle of zingy sauvignon blanc.

Tours

Full-day wine-tasting tours average $105 to $160 per person; most leave from Santa Barbara, and some require a minimum number of participants.

Santa Barbara Wine Country Cycling Tours CYCLING
(☎888-557-8687, 805-686-9490; www.winecountrycycling.com; 3630 Sagunto St, Santa Ynez; ⏲8:30am-4:30pm Mon-Sat, by appt Sun) Guided and DIY cycling tours start from the Santa Ynez storefront, which also rents road and hybrid mountain bikes (from $35/45 per half/full day).

Wine Edventures GUIDED TOUR
(☎805-965-9463; www.welovewines.com) Serves up a fun-lovin' side dish of local history and wine education on its shuttle-driven wine-tasting tours, one of which visits a microbrewery, too.

Sustainable Vine Wine Tours GUIDED TOUR
(☎805-698-3911; www.sustainablevine.com) Biodiesel-van tours of wineries implementing organic and sustainable agricultural practices include a local picnic lunch in the vineyards.

Los Olivos

POP 1130

The posh ranching town of Los Olivos is many visitors' first stop when exploring Santa Barbara's Wine Country. Its four-block-long main street is lined with rustic wine-tasting rooms, bistros and boutiques seemingly airlifted straight out of Napa.

Sights

Clairmont Farms FARM
(☎805-688-7505; www.clairmontfarms.com; 2480 Roblar Ave; ⏲usually 10am-6pm Mon-Sat, to 5pm Sun) Natural beauty awaits just outside town at this organic family-owned farm, where purple lavender fields bloom like a Monet masterpiece, usually peaking from mid-June to late July. Peruse lavender honey and sea salt and aromatherapy, bath and body products in the small shop.

WORTH A TRIP

MISSION LA PURÍSIMA

One of the most evocative of Southern California's missions, **La Purísima Mission State Historic Park** (☎805-733-3713; www.lapurisimamission.org; 2295 Purísima Rd, Lompoc; per car $6; ⏲9am-5pm; 👪) was completely restored in the 1930s by the Civilian Conservation Corps (CCC). Today its buildings are furnished just as they were during Spanish-colonial times. The mission's fields still support livestock, while outdoor gardens are planted with medicinal plants and trees once used by Chumash tribespeople. Surrounding the mission are miles of peaceful hiking trails. One-hour guided tours begin at 1pm daily. The mission is about 16 miles west of Hwy 101, via Hwy 146 from Buellton.

Sleeping & Eating

Ballard Inn & Restaurant B&B $$$

(☎805-688-7770, 800-638-2466; www.ballardinn.com; 2436 Baseline Ave, Ballard; r incl breakfast $265-345;) For romantics, this quaint inn awaits in the 19th-century stagecoach town of Ballard, south of Los Olivos heading toward Solvang. Wood-burning fireplaces make en-suite rooms feel even more cozy, though some are dearly in need of updating. Rates include a full hot breakfast and weekend wine tastings. Reservations are essential for rooms and also dinner at the inn's chef-driven Eurasian restaurant.

Los Olivos Grocery MARKET, DELI $

(http://losolivosgrocery.com; 2621 W Hwy 154, Santa Ynez; 7am-9pm) This tiny local market heaps barbecue tri-tip sandwiches, artisan breads, specialty cheeses and everything you'll need for a vineyard picnic, or grab a table on the front porch.

Panino SANDWICHES $$

(http://paninorestaurants.com; 2900 Grand Ave; sandwiches $10-12; 10am-4pm;) Take your pick of gourmet deli sandwiches and salads: curry chicken is a perennial fave, but there are robust vegetarian options too. Order at the counter, then eat outside at an umbrella-covered table.

Los Olivos Café & Wine Merchant CALIFORNIAN, MEDITERRANEAN $$$

(☎805-688-7265; www.losolivoscafe.com; 2879 Grand Ave; mains breakfast $9-12, lunch & dinner $12-29; 11:30am-8:30pm daily, also 8-10:30am Sat & Sun) With white canopies and a wisteria-covered trellis, this wine-country landmark (as seen in *Sideways*) swirls up a casual-chic SoCal ambience. It stays open between lunch and dinner for antipasto platters, hearty salads and crispy pizzas and wine flights at the bar.

Sides Hardware & Shoes AMERICAN $$$

(☎805-688-4820; http://brothersrestaurant.com; 2375 Alamo Pintado Ave; mains lunch $14-18, dinner $26-34; 11am-2:30pm daily, 5-8:30pm Sun-Thu, to 9pm Fri & Sat) Inside a historic storefront, this bistro delivers haute country cooking like 'hammered pig' sandwiches topped by apple slaw, fried chicken with garlicky kale and Colorado lamb sirloin alongside goat-cheese gnocchi. Book ahead for dinner.

Petros GREEK $$$

(☎805-686-5455; www.petrosrestaurant.com; Fess Parker Wine Country Inn & Spa, 2860 Grand Ave; mains lunch $13-20, dinner $16-32; 7am-10pm Sun-Thu, to 11pm Fri & Sat) In a sunny dining room, sophisticated Greek cuisine makes a refreshing change from Italianate wine-country kitsch. Housemade *meze* (appetizers) will satisfy even picky foodies.

Drinking

Grand Ave and Alamo Pintado Rd are lined with wine and beer tasting rooms, which you can amble between all afternoon long.

Los Olivos Tasting Room WINE BAR

(☎805-688-7406; http://site.thelosolivostastingroom.com; 2905 Grand Ave; tastings $10; 11am-5pm) Inside a rickety 19th-century general store, this tasting room stocks rare vintages you won't find anywhere else. Well-oiled servers are by turns loquacious and gruff, but refreshingly blunt in their opinions about local wines, and pours are generous.

Sarloos + Sons WINE BAR

(☎805-688-1200; http://saarloosandsons.com; 2971 Grand Ave; tastings $10; 11am-5pm Wed-Fri & Sun, to 6pm Sat, last pour 30min before closing) Wine snobs are given the boot at this shabby-chic tasting room pouring estate-grown, small-lot Syrah, grenache noir, pinot noir and sauvignon blanc. Pair your wine flight with a 'cupcake flight' ($10, available Thursday through Sunday).

Carhartt Vineyard Tasting Room WINE BAR

(☎805-693-5100; www.carharttvineyard.com; 2990A Grand Ave; tastings $10; 11am-6pm) An unpretentious tasting room inside a red-trimmed wooden shack leads onto a shady garden patio out back, where a fun-loving younger crowd sips unfussy Syrah, sauvignon blanc and 'Chase the Blues Away' rosé.

Shopping

Jedlicka's Western Wear CLOTHING, SHOES

(www.jedlickas.com; 2883 Grand Ave; 9am-5:30pm Mon-Sat, 10am-4:30pm Sun) Wranglers and prairie babes should mosey over to Jedlicka's for name-brand boots – Lucchese, Justin and Tony Lama – as well as genuine cowboy hats, jeans and jackets.

Solvang

POP 5345

My God, cap'n, we've hit a windmill! Which can only mean one thing in Wine Country: Solvang, a Danish village founded in 1911 on what was once a 19th-century

LOCAL KNOWLEDGE

CHRIS BURROUGHS: TASTING ROOM MANAGER

Alma Rosa Winery's tasting-room manager is already familiar to moviegoers for his appearance in the 2004 indie hit *Sideways* as – what else? – a cowboy-hat-wearing tasting-room manager. He shared a few smart wine-tasting tips with us.

Novices Never Fear

Don't let a lack of wine savvy keep you away. Winemakers enjoy sharing their passion and knowledge, and beginners are often their favorite guests.

Travel Light

Most tasting rooms aren't equipped for large crowds. Traveling in small groups means you'll have more time to chat with the staff.

Less is More

Don't keep a scorecard on the number of wineries visited. Spend time at only a handful of tasting rooms on any given day. Wine drinking is a social vehicle (not a mobile party crawl).

Be Open-Minded

At most tasting rooms you'll sample six wines: three whites and three reds. Don't tell the staff you never drink Chardonnay – who knows, the wine you try that day may change your mind.

Nice Guys Finish First

Smoking and heavy perfume? Not so considerate of others, and smoking dulls your wine-tasting senses besides. Be friendly, too. I'd rather drink a mediocre bottle of wine with a cool person than special wine with a jerk.

Spanish-colonial mission and later a Mexican *rancho* land grant. This Santa Ynez Valley town holds tight to its Danish heritage, or at least stereotypical images thereof. With its knickknack stores and cutesy motels, the town is almost as sticky-sweet as the Scandinavian pastries foisted upon the wandering crowds of day trippers. Solvang's kitschy charms make it worth visiting if only to gawk.

Sights

Old Mission Santa Ínes CHURCH

(805-688-4815; www.missionsantaines.org; 1760 Mission Dr; adult/child under 12yr $5/free; 9am-4:30pm) Off Hwy 246 just east of downtown's Alisal Rd, this historic Catholic mission set the stage for a Chumash revolt against Spanish-colonial cruelty in 1824. Ask for a free (albeit historically biased) audioguide tour of the gardens, small museum and restored church, still an active parish today.

Elverhøj Museum MUSEUM

(www.elverhoj.org; 1624 Elverhoy Way; suggested donation adult/child under 12yr $5/free; 11am-4pm Wed-Sun) South of downtown, tucked away on residential side streets, the delightful little museum has modest but thoughtful exhibits on Solvang's Danish heritage, as well as Danish culture, art and history.

Wildling Museum MUSEUM

(805-688-1802; www.wildlingmuseum.org; 1511 Mission Dr; adult/child 6-17yr $5/3; 11am-5pm Mon & Wed-Fri, from 10am Sat & Sun) Need a break from boozing? This petite art museum exhibits wilderness-themed paintings and photography that may inspire you to go hiking in the mountains outside town.

Hans Christian Andersen Museum MUSEUM

(2nd fl, 1680 Mission Dr; 10am-5pm) FREE If you remember childhood fairy tales with fondness, stop by this tiny two-room museum where original letters and first-edition copies of the Danish storyteller's illustrated books are on display.

Activities

Solvang is best known by cyclists for the **Solvang Century** (www.bikescor.com) races in March. For self-guided cycling tours, visit www.solvangusa.com and www.bike-santabarbara.org online and drop by Wheel Fun Rentals (p396), which has a second location in town at 1465 Copenhagen Dr.

Sleeping

Sleeping in Solvang isn't cheap, not even at older motels with faux-Danish exteriors. On weekends, rates skyrocket and rooms fill fast, so book ahead or make it a day trip.

★Hamlet Inn MOTEL $$
(805-688-4413; http://thehamletinn.com; 1532 Mission Dr; r $90-230) This remodeled motel is to wine-country lodging what IKEA is to interior design: a budget-friendly, trendy alternative. Crisp, modern rooms have bright Danish flag bedspreads and iPod docking stations. Free loaner bicycles and a bocce ball court for guests.

Hadsten House BOUTIQUE HOTEL $$
(800-457-5373, 805-688-3210; www.hadstenhouse.com; 1450 Mission Dr; r incl breakfast $165-215) This revamped motel has luxuriously updated just about everything, except for its routine exterior. Inside, rooms are surprisingly plush, with flat-screen TVs, comfy duvets and high-end bath products. Spa suites come with jetted tubs. Rates include a breakfast buffet.

Hotel Corque HOTEL $$$
(805-688-8000, 800-624-5572; www.hotelcorque.com; 400 Alisal Rd; r $169-350) Downtown, this clean-lined hotel is a relief from all things Danish. Overpriced rooms may look anonymous, but they're quite spacious. Amenities include an outdoor swimming pool and hot tub, plus access to the next-door fitness center, where you can work off all those Danish butter rings.

Eating

El Rancho Market SUPERMARKET $
(http://elranchomarket.com; 2886 Mission Dr; 6am-11pm) East of downtown, this upscale supermarket – with a full deli, smokin' barbecued meats and an espresso bar – is the best place to fill your picnic basket before heading out to the wineries.

Solvang Restaurant BAKERY $
(www.solvangrestaurant.com; 1672 Copenhagen Dr; items from $4; 6am-3pm or 4pm Mon-Fri, to 5pm Sat & Sun) Duck around the Danish-inscribed beams with decorative borders to order *ableskivers* – round pancake popovers covered in powdered sugar and raspberry jam. They're so popular, there's even a special take-out window.

Solvang Bakery BAKERY $
(www.solvangbakery.com; 438 Alisal Rd; items from $2; 7am-6pm Sun-Thu, to 7pm Fri & Sat) Tubs of Danish butter cookies and rich almond kringles are popular takeaway treats.

Mortensen's Danish Bakery BAKERY $
(www.mortensensbakery.com; 1588 Mission Dr; 7:30am-5:30pm, to 8pm Jun-Aug) Gobble a custardy Danish butter ring, fruit-filled Danish pastry or apple strudel for breakfast.

New Frontiers Natural Marketplace SUPERMARKET $
(https://newfrontiersmarket.com; 1984 Old Mission Dr; 8am-8pm Mon-Sat, to 7pm Sun) To keep things healthy, organic and local, pick up a tasty variety of deli sandwiches, salads and take-out dishes for picnicking.

★Succulent Café CALIFORNIAN $$
(805-691-9235; www.succulentcafe.com; 1555 Mission Dr; mains breakfast & lunch $9-13, dinner $19-29; breakfast 8:30am-noon Sat & Sun; lunch 11am-3pm Mon & Wed-Fri, to 4pm Sat & Sun; dinner 5:30-9pm Mon & Wed-Sun) An inspired menu allows farm-fresh ingredients to speak for themselves at this family-owned gourmet cafe and market. Fuel up on breakfast biscuits stuffed with cinnamon-cumin pork tenderloin and pineapple chutney with bacon gravy, buttermilk-fried chicken salad and artisan grilled-cheese sandwiches for lunch, or pumpkin seed-crusted lamb for dinner. On sunny days, eat outside on the patio.

Root 246 AMERICAN $$$
(805-686-8681; www.root-246.com; 420 Alisal Rd; dinner mains $19-35, brunch buffet per adult/child 6-12yr $27/11; 5-9pm Tue-Thu, 5-10pm

BEST SANTA BARBARA WINERIES FOR PICNICS

You won't have any problem finding picnic fare in Santa Barbara's Wine Country. The region is chock-full of local markets, delis and bakeries serving up portable sandwiches and salads. When picnicking at a winery, remember it's polite to buy a bottle of wine before spreading out your feast.

- Beckmen Vineyards (p413)
- Sunstone Vineyards & Winery (p414)
- Zaca Mesa Winery (p411)
- Lincourt Vineyard (p413)
- Rancho Sisquoc (p412)

Fri & Sat, 10am-2pm & 5-9pm Sun) Next to the Hotel Corque, chef Bradley Ogden's creative farm-to-table cuisine shows an artful touch. It's hard to beat the pastrami short ribs or Sunday brunch buffet. Make reservations or seat yourself in the sleek fireplace lounge to sip California wines by the glass after 4pm.

Drinking & Entertainment

Sorry, but after dinner this town is deader than an ancient Viking.

Chumash Casino Resort CASINO, LIVE MUSIC
(800-248-6274; www.chumashcasino.com; 3400 E Hwy 246; 24hr) Drive east on Hwy 246 to cutesy Solvang's vice-minded doppelganger, where the slots are plentiful, the cocktails watered-down and the cigarette smoke so thick you could cut it with a Danish butter knife. Get last-minute tickets for concerts by yesterday's pop and rock superstars.

Maverick Saloon BAR
(805-686-4785; www.mavericksaloon.org; 3687 Sagunto St, Santa Ynez; noon-2am Mon-Fri, from 10am Sat & Sun) Off Hwy 246 east of Solvang, the one-horse town of Santa Ynez is home to this Harley-friendly honky-tonk dive bar with live country-and-western and rock bands, dancing and DJs.

Shopping

Downtown Solvang's notoriously kitschy shops cover a half dozen blocks south of Mission Dr (Hwy 246) between Atterdag Rd and Alisal Rd. For Danish cookbooks, handcrafted quilts and other homespun items, visit the Elverhøj Museum (p416).

Gaveasken GIFTS
(433 Alisal Rd; 9:30am-5pm Mon-Sat, from 10am Sun) If decorative Danish plates, elegant silver trays and heart-warming, handmade Christmas ornaments top your shopping list, you'll be crossing off items like mad at 'The Gift Box,' which stocks a primo mix of authentic Scandinavian wares.

Solvang Antique Center ANTIQUES
(http://solvangantiques.com; 1693 Copenhagen Dr; 10am-6pm) For truly fine furnishings, antique clocks and music boxes, decorative art and jewelry from around Europe and America, step inside this museum-like emporium.

Book Loft BOOKS
(www.bookloftsolvang.com; 1680 Mission Dr; 9am-8pm Tue-Thu, to 9pm Fri & Sat, to 6pm Sun & Mon) Downstairs from the Hans Christian Anderson Museum, this independent bookshop carries antiquarian and Scandinavian titles and children's storybooks.

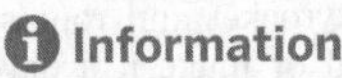

Information

Solvang is the busiest hub for wine-country visitors.

Solvang Coffee Company (1680 Mission Dr, Solvang; 6am-6pm Sun-Tue, to 7pm Wed-Sat;) Enjoy wi-fi with your espresso next to the Book Loft and Hans Christian Anderson Museum.

Solvang Conference & Visitors Bureau (805-688-6144, 800-468-6765; www.solvangusa.com; 1639 Copenhagen Dr, Solvang; 9am-5pm) Pick up free tourist brochures and winery maps at this kiosk in the town center, by the municipal parking lot and public restrooms.

Buellton

POP 4905

A mostly humdrum gateway to Santa Barbara's Wine Country, tiny Buellton is best known for the cartoonish landmark towering over the intersection of Hwys 101 and 246: Anderson's Pea Soup Restaurant, where you can get heaping bowls of the green stuff (though we would advise against it).

Sleeping & Eating

Buellton has slightly less expensive, but more well-worn chain motels and hotels than Solvang, 3 miles further east along Hwy 246.

Ellen's Danish Pancake House BREAKFAST $$
(805-688-5312; www.ellensdanishpancakehouse.com; 272 Ave of Flags; mains $7-12; 6am-8pm Mon-Sat, to 2pm Sun) West of Hwy 101, this old-fashioned, always-busy diner is where locals congregate for the Wine Country's best Danish pancakes, Danish sausages and not-so-Danish Belgian waffles. Breakfast served all day.

Hitching Post II STEAKHOUSE $$$
(805-688-0676; www.hitchingpost2.com; 406 E Hwy 246; mains $23-50; 5-9:30pm;) As seen in the movie *Sideways,* this dark-paneled chophouse offers oak-grilled steaks, pork ribs, smoked duck breast and rack of lamb. Every old-school meal comes with a veggie tray, garlic bread, shrimp cocktail or soup, salad and potatoes. The Hitching Post makes its own pinot noir, and it's damn good (wine tastings at the bar start at 4pm).

Drinking & Nightlife

Avant Tapas & Wine WINE BAR

(805-686-4742; www.avantwines.com; 35 Industrial Way; 11am-9pm) Hidden upstairs in an industrial-chic space, Avant's Enomatic dispensing system pours tastes of over 30 boutique wines barreled in the warehouse – just walk out onto the catwalk and take a look. Happy hour runs 3pm to 5pm on weekdays.

Figueroa Mountain Brewing Co BREWPUB

(805-694-2252; www.figmtnbrew.com; 45 Industrial Way; 4-9pm Mon-Thu, from 11am Fri-Sun) Fig Mountain's original brewpub hosts live-music, comedy and quiz nights. Across the valley in Los Olivos, their cottage taproom also pours tasting samplers of their award-winning brews such as Danish Red Lager and Hoppy Poppy IPA.

Getting There & Around

From Santa Barbara, you can drive to Wine Country in under an hour. Via Hwy 101, it's 45 miles from Santa Barbara to Buellton. Hwy 246 runs east–west from Buellton to Solvang, then across the bottom of the Santa Ynez Valley to Hwy 154. From Santa Barbara, Hwy 154 is a more scenic route; it's fewer miles than taking Hwy 101, but takes longer because the road is often only two lanes wide, with slow-moving traffic. North of Hwy 246, Hwy 154 leads to Los Olivos.

Central Coast Shuttle (805-928-1977, 800-470-8818; www.cclax.com) will bus you from LAX to Buellton for $75/138 one way/round-trip, slightly less if you prepay 24 hours in advance. **Amtrak** (800-872-7245; www.amtrak.com) provides a couple of daily connecting Thruway buses to and from Solvang, but only if you're catching a train (or arriving on one) in Santa Barbara.

Santa Ynez Valley Transit (805-688-5452; www.syvt.com) runs local buses equipped with bike racks on a loop around Buellton, Solvang, Santa Ynez, Ballard and Los Olivos. Buses operate roughly between 7am and 7pm Monday through Saturday; one-way rides cost $1.50 (exact change only).

AROUND SANTA BARBARA

Can't quit your day job to follow your bliss? Don't despair: a long weekend in the mountains, valleys and beaches between Santa Barbara and LA will keep you inspired until you can. In this land of daydreams, perfect waves beckon off Ventura's coast, shady trails wind skyward in the Los Padres National Forest and spiritual Zen awaits you in Ojai Valley. Surf, stroll, seek – if outdoor rejuvenation is your goal, this is the place.

And then there's Channel Islands National Park, a biodiverse chain of islands shimmering just off the coast where you can kayak majestic sea caves, scuba dive in wavy kelp forests, wander fields of wildflower blooms or simply disappear from civilization at a remote wilderness campsite.

Montecito

POP 8965

The well-heeled community of Montecito, just east of Santa Barbara, is like a hitherto-unknown cousin who just inherited the family fortune. This leafy village in the Santa Ynez foothills is not just home to the rich and famous but to the obscenely rich and the uber-famous: it's the type of guarded enclave that would have incited revolutions in eras past.

Though many homes hide behind manicured hedges, a taste of the Montecito lifestyle of yesteryear can be experienced by taking a tour of **Casa del Herrero** (805-565-5653; http://casadelherrero.com; 1387 E Valley

WORTH A TRIP

LOTUSLAND

In 1941 the eccentric opera singer and socialite Madame Ganna Walka bought the 37 acres that make up **Lotusland** (info 805-969-3767, reservations 805-969-9990; www.lotusland.org; 695 Ashley Rd; adult/child 3-18yr $45/20; tours by appt 10am & 1:30pm Wed-Sat mid-Feb–mid-Nov; P) with money from the fortunes she inherited after marrying – and then divorcing – a string of wealthy men. She spent the next four decades tending and expanding this incredible collection of rare and exotic plants from around the world; there are over 120 varieties of aloe alone. Come in summer when the lotuses bloom, typically during July and August. Reservations are required for tours, but the phone is only attended from 9am to 5pm weekdays, 9am to 1pm Saturday.

Rd; 90min tour $20; ⏲10am & 2pm Wed & Sat; P), a gorgeously well-preserved 1920s estate built in Spanish-colonial style and bordered by strolling gardens.

Montecito's cafe and boutique-filled main drag is Coast Village Rd (exit Hwy 101 at Olive Mill Rd). **Dressed & Ready** (805-565-1253; www.dressedonline.com; 1253 Coast Village Rd; ⏲10am-5pm Mon-Sat, 11am-4pm Sun) are twin couture shops that cater to a star-quality crowd with flirty women's fashions by hand-picked designers. For breakfast or weekend brunch, nab a table on the patio at **Jeannine's** (http://jeannines.com; 1253 Coast Village Rd; mains $9-14; ⏲7am-3pm;) bakery and cafe, where from-scratch kitchen goodness includes challah French toast with caramelized bananas in Kahlua sauce.

From Santa Barbara, MTD buses 14 and 20 run to and from Montecito ($1.75, 20 minutes, hourly); bus 20 also connects Montecito with Summerland and Carpinteria.

Summerland

POP 1450

This drowsy seaside community was founded in the 1880s by HL Williams, a real-estate speculator. Williams was also a spiritualist, whose followers believed in the power of mediums to connect the living with the dead. Spiritualists were rumored to keep hidden rooms in their homes for séances with the dearly departed – a practice that earned the town the indelicate nickname of 'Spookville.'

Today, those wanting to connect to the past wander the town's antique shops, where you won't find any bargains, but you can ooh and ahh over beautiful furniture, jewelry and art from decades or even centuries gone by. From Hwy 101 southbound, take exit 91 and turn north, then right onto Lillie Ave. To find the beach, turn south off exit 91 instead and cross the railroad tracks to cliffside **Lookout Park** (www.countyofsb.org/parks; Lookout Park Rd; ⏲8am-sunset;) FREE, with a kids' playground, picnic tables, barbecue grills and access to a wide, relatively quiet stretch of sand (leashed dogs OK).

Grab breakfast or brunch at the Victorian seaside-style **Summerland Beach Café** (805-969-1019; www.summerlandbeachcafe.com; 2294 Lillie Ave; mains $7-14; ⏲7am-3pm Mon-Fri, to 4pm Sat & Sun;), known for its fluffy omelettes, and enjoy the ocean breezes on the patio. Or walk over to **Tinker's** (2275 Ortega Hill Rd; items $5-10; ⏲11am-8pm;), an eat-out-of-a-basket burger shack that delivers seasoned curly fries and old-fashioned milkshakes.

From Santa Barbara, MTD bus 20 runs to Summerland ($1.75, 25 minutes, hourly) via Montecito, continuing to Carpinteria.

Carpinteria

POP 13,230

Lying 11 miles east of Santa Barbara, the time-warped beach of Carpinteria – so named because Chumash tribespeople once built seafaring canoes here – is a laid-back place. You could easily spend an hour or two wandering in and out of antiques shops and beachy boutiques along Linden Ave, downtown's main street. To gawk at the world's largest vat of guacamole, show up for the **California Avocado Festival** (www.avofest.com) in early October.

Sights & Activities

If you're an expert surfer, **Rincon Point** has long, glassy, right point-break waves. It's about 3 miles southeast of downtown, off Hwy 101 (exit Bates Rd)

Carpinteria State Beach BEACH

(805-968-1033; www.parks.ca.gov; end of Linden Ave; per car $10; ⏲7am-sunset;) It's an idyllic, mile-long strand where kids splash around in calm waters and go tide-pooling along the shoreline. In winter, you may spot harbor seals and sea lions hauled out on the sand, especially if you hike over a mile south along the coast to a blufftop overlook.

Surf Happens SURFING

(805-966-3613; http://surfhappens.com; 2hr group/private lesson from $110/160;) Welcoming families, beginners and 'Aloha Surf Sisters,' these highly reviewed classes and weekend camps led by expert staff incorporate the Zen of surfing. In summer, you'll begin your spiritual wave-riding journey off Hwy 101 (exit Santa Claus Ln). Make reservations in advance.

Sleeping

Carpinteria's cookie-cutter chain motels and hotels are unexciting, but usually less expensive than those just up the road in Santa Barbara.

Carpinteria State Beach Campground CAMPGROUND $
(☎800-444-7275; www.reserveamerica.com; tent & RV drive-up sites $35-80, hike-and-bike tent sites $10;) Often crowded, this oceanfront campground offers lots of family-friendly amenities including flush toilets, hot showers, picnic tables and barbecue grills. Book ahead.

Eating & Drinking

Padaro Beach Grill AMERICAN $
(3766 Santa Claus Ln; items $3-11; ⊙usually 10:30am-8pm Mon-Sat, from 11am Sun;) Off Hwy 101 west of downtown, this oceanfront grill makes darn good burgers, grilled fish tacos, sweet-potato fries and thick, hand-mixed milkshakes.

Tacos Don Roge MEXICAN $
(751 Linden Ave; items from $1.50; ⊙10am-9pm) This Mexican taquería stakes its reputation on a rainbow-colored salsa bar with up to a dozen different sauces to drizzle on piquant meat-stuffed, double-rolled corn tortillas – try the jalapeño or pineapple versions.

Corktree Cellars CALIFORNIAN $$
(☎805-684-1400; www.corktreecellars.com; 910 Linden Ave; small plates $5-15; ⊙usually 11:30am-9pm Tue-Thu, to 10pm Fri & Sat, 10am-9pm Sun) Downtown's contemporary wine bar and bistro offers tasty California-style tapas, charcuterie and cheese plates, and a dizzying number of wine flights. Neglectful service can try diners' patience.

Island Brewing Co BREWERY
(www.islandbrewingcompany.com; 5049 6th St, off Linden Ave; ⊙2-9pm Mon-Fri, from 11am Sat & Sun;) Wanna hang loose with beach bums and drink bourbon barrel-aged brews? Find this locals-only, industrial space with an outdoor, dog-friendly patio by the railroad tracks.

Getting There & Away

Carpinteria is 11 miles east of Santa Barbara via Hwy 101 (southbound exit Linden Ave, northbound Casitas Pass Rd). From Santa Barbara, take MTD bus 20 ($1.75, 45 minutes, hourly) via Montecito and Summerland. **Amtrak** (☎800-872-7245; www.amtrak.com; 475 Linden Ave) has an unstaffed platform downtown; buy tickets online or by phone before catching one of five daily *Pacific Surfliner* trains south to Ventura ($11, 25 minutes) or LA ($29, 2¾ hours).

Ojai

POP 7560 / ELEV 745FT

Hollywood director Frank Capra chose the Ojai Valley to represent a mythical Shangri-la in his 1937 movie *Lost Horizon*. Today Ojai ('*oh*-hi', from the Chumash word for 'moon') attracts artists, organic farmers, spiritual seekers and anyone ready to indulge in day-spa pampering. Bring shorts and flip-flops: Shangri-la sure gets hot in summer.

Sights & Activities

Inside downtown's historic firehouse, **Ojai Vineyard** (☎805-798-3947; www.ojaivineyard.com; 109 S Montgomery St; tastings $15; ⊙noon-5pm) pours tastes of its delicate, small-batch wines. It's best known for standard-bearing Chardonnay, pinot noir and Syrah, but the crisp sauvignon blanc, dry Reisling and zippy rosé are also worth sampling. Outside town, take a free guided tour of the olive orchards and sample fruity and herb-infused oils at family-owned **Ojai Olive Oil Company** (☎805-646-5964; www.ojaioliveoil.com; 1811 Ladera Rd; ⊙usually hourly tours 1-4pm Wed & 10am-3pm Sat) FREE.

For the ultimate in relaxation, book a day at top-tier **Spa Ojai** (☎877-597-3731; www.ojairesort.com/spa-ojai/; Ojai Valley Inn & Spa, 905 Country Club Rd), where non-resort guests pay an extra $20 to access two swimming pools, a workout gym and mind/body fitness classes. Or unwind with an aromatherapy or hot-rock massage in a hobbitlike cottage at **Day Spa of Ojai** (☎805-640-1100; www.thedayspa.com; 1434 E Ojai Ave), about a mile east of downtown.

Running beside the highway, the 9-mile **Ojai Valley Trail**, converted from defunct railway tracks, is popular with walkers, runners, cyclists and equestrians. Pick it up downtown two blocks south of Ojai Ave, then pedal west through the valley. Rent bikes downtown at the **Mob Shop** (☎805-272-8102; www.themobshop.com; 110 W Ojai Ave; bicycle rental per day $25-50; ⊙1-6pm Mon, 10am-5pm Tue-Fri, 9am-5pm Sat, 9am-4pm Sun).

Gather camping tips and trail maps for hiking to hot springs, waterfalls and mountaintop viewpoints in the **Los Padres National Forest** at the **Ojai Ranger Station** (☎805-646-4348; http://www.fs.usda.gov/lpnf; 1190 E Ojai Ave; ⊙8am-4:30pm Mon-Fri) or on weekends at **Wheeler Gorge Visitors Center** (http://lpforest.org/wheeler; 17017

WORTH A TRIP

OJAI'S PINK MOMENT

Ojai is famous for the rosy glow that emanates from its mountains at sunset, the so-called 'Pink Moment.' The ideal vantage point for catching the show is the peaceful lookout atop **Meditation Mount** (https://meditationmount.org; 10340 Reeves Rd; 10am-sunset Wed-Sun) FREE. Head east of downtown on Ojai Ave (Hwy 150) for about 2 miles, turn left at Boccali's farm-stand restaurant and drive another 2.5 miles on Reeves Rd until it dead-ends.

Maricopa Hwy; 9am-3pm Sat & Sun), 8 miles north of Hwy 150 via Hwy 33.

Sleeping

★Blue Iguana Inn INN $$
(805-646-5277; www.blueiguanainn.com; 11794 N Ventura Ave; r $129-199, ste from $159, all incl breakfast;) Artsy iguanas lurk everywhere at this funky architect-designed inn – on adobe walls around Mediterranean-tiled fountains and anywhere else that reptilian style could bring out a smile. Roomy bungalow and cottage suites are unique, and the pool is a social scene for LA denizens. Rates include continental breakfast; two-night minimum stay on weekends. Some pets allowed with prior approval only.

For a more romantic atmosphere, try the sister Emerald Iguana Inn, just north of downtown.

Ojai Retreat B&B $$
(805-646-2536; www.ojairetreat.com; 160 Besant Rd; d incl breakfast $99-299;) On a hilltop on the outskirts of town, this peaceful nonprofit inn has a back-to-nature collection of remodeled, country arts-and-crafts-style guest rooms and cottage suites, all perfect for unplugging. Find a quiet nook for reading or writing, ramble through the woods or practice your downward dog in a yoga class. Rates include a healthy breakfast buffet.

Ojai Rancho Inn MOTEL $$
(805-646-1434; http://ojairanchoinn.com; 615 W Ojai Ave; r $120-200;) At this low-slung motel next to the highway, pine-paneled rooms each have a king bed. Cottage rooms come with fireplaces, and some have Jacuzzi tubs and kitchenettes. Besides competitive rates, the biggest bonuses of staying here are a small pool and sauna, shuffleboard, fire pit and bicycles to borrow for the half-mile ride to downtown. Pet fee $20.

Ojai Valley Inn & Spa RESORT $$$
(855-697-8780, 805-646-1111; www.ojairesort.com; 905 Country Club Rd; r from $329;) At the west end of town, this pampering resort has landscaped gardens, tennis courts, swimming pools, a championship golf course and a fabulous spa. Luxurious rooms are outfitted with all mod cons, and some sport a fireplace and balcony. Recreational activities run the gamut from kids' camps and bike rentals to full-moon yoga and astrological readings. Nightly 'service' surcharge $25.

Eating

Ojai Certified Farmers Market MARKET $
(www.ojaicertifiedfarmersmarket.com; 300 E Matilija St; 9am-1pm Sun;) Mingle with Ojai's bohemians at this rain-or-shine farmers market, where you'll find eggs, oils, jams, homemade bread and locally grown, organic-certified fruit, nuts and vegetables.

Farmer & the Cook MEXICAN, VEGETARIAN $$
(http://farmerandcook.com; 339 W Roblar Ave; mains $7-14; 8am-8:30pm;) The flavorful goodness of organic, homemade Mexican cooking bursts out of this tiny roadside market, which has its own farm nearby. Come for the squash and goat cheese tacos with fresh corn tortillas, saucy huevos rancheros or at dinner on weekends, creative pizzas and a salad bar.

Boccali's ITALIAN $$
(805-646-6116; http://boccalis.com; 3277 Ojai-Santa Paula Rd; mains $10-18; 4-9pm Mon & Tue, from noon Wed-Sun;) This roadside farm stand with red-and-white-checkered tablecloths does simple Italian cooking. Much of the produce is grown behind the restaurant, and the fresh tomato salad is often still warm from the garden. The real draw is wood oven-baked pizzas, which take time to make. No credit cards. It's over 2 miles east of downtown via Ojai Ave.

Hip Vegan VEGETARIAN $$
(www.hipvegancafe.com; 928 E Ojai Ave; mains $9-13; ⌚11am-5pm;) Tucked back from the street in a tiny garden, this locals' kitchen stays true to Ojai's granola-crunchy hippie roots with sprout-filled wraps, raw salads, fake-meat Reuben sandwiches and classic SoCal date shakes.

Knead BAKERY, CAFE $$
(http://kneadbakingcompany.com; 469 E Ojai Ave; items $3-16; ⌚8am-4pm Wed-Sun) Family-run artisan bakery mixes batters with the best of Ojai's fresh fruit, herbs, honey and nuts. Get a slice of a sweet tart or savory quiche, or a made-to-order breakfast sandwich. No credit cards.

Shopping

Arcade Plaza, a maze of Mission Revival-style buildings on Ojai Ave (downtown's main drag), is stuffed with gifty boutiques.

Bart's Books BOOKS
(www.bartsbooksojai.com; 302 W Matilija St; ⌚9:30am-sunset) One block north of Ojai Ave, this unique indoor-outdoor space sells new and well-loved tomes. It demands at least a half-hour's browse – just don't step on the lurking but surprisingly nimble cat.

Ojai Clothing CLOTHING
(http://ojaiclothing.com; 325 E Ojai Ave; ⌚noon-5pm Mon & Wed-Thu, noon-5:30pm Fri, 10am-5:30pm Sat, 11am-5pm Sun) Equally comfy for doing an interpretive dance or just hanging out, these earth-toned and vibrantly patterned casual pieces for women and men are made from soft cotton knits and woven fabrics.

Human Arts Gallery ARTS & CRAFTS
(www.humanartsgallery.com; 246 E Ojai Ave; ⌚11am-5pm Mon-Fri, to 6pm Sat, noon-5pm Sun) Browse the colorful handmade jewelry, sculpture, woodcarvings, glassworks, folk-art furnishings and more.

Soul Centered GIFTS, BOOKS
(www.soulcentered.com; 311 N Montgomery St; ⌚10:30am-6pm) A 'metaphysical shoppe' echoes Ojai's hippie-dippie vibe with healing crystals, dream therapy and magic books.

Information

Ojai Valley Chamber of Commerce (☎805-646-8126; www.ojaichamber.org; 206 N Signal St; ⌚9am-4pm Mon-Fri) Pick up free tourist maps and brochures here.

Ojai Library (111 E Ojai Ave; ⌚10am-8pm Mon-Thu, noon-5pm Fri-Sun) Free online computer terminals for public use.

Getting There & Away

Ojai is 33 miles east of Santa Barbara via scenic Hwy 150, or 15 miles inland (north) from Ventura via Hwy 33. On Main St at Ventura Ave in downtown Ventura, catch **Gold Coast Transit** (☎805-487-4222; www.goldcoasttransit.org) bus 16 to downtown Ojai ($1.50, 40 minutes, hourly).

Ventura

POP 107,735

The primary pushing-off point for Channel Island boat trips, the beach town of San Buenaventura may not look to be the most enchanting coastal city, but it has seaside charms, especially on the historic pier and

OFF THE BEATEN TRACK

SANTA PAULA

Now calling itself 'the citrus capital of the world,' the small town of Santa Paula once found its treasure in black gold. If you've seen the movie *There Will Be Blood,* loosely based on the Upton Sinclair novel *Oil!,* then you already know that SoCal's early oil boom was a bloodthirsty business. Today the **California Oil Museum** (☎805-933-0076; www.oilmuseum.net; 1001 E Main St; adult/child 6-17yr $4/1; ⌚10am-4pm Wed-Sun) tells the story of Santa Paula's 'black bonanza' with modest historical exhibits that include an authentic 1890s drilling rig and a collection of vintage gas pumps. Afterward take a walk around downtown Santa Paula's historic district, painted with interesting outdoor murals. Pick up a free self-guided walking tour map inside the museum or one block north at the **chamber of commerce** (☎805-525-5561; www.discoversantapaula.com; 200 N 10th St, Santa Paula; ⌚10am-2pm Mon-Fri, gift shop 10am-noon & 1-4pm Mon-Fri, noon-4pm Sat & Sun). Santa Paula is a 16-mile drive east of Ventura or Ojai, at the intersection of Hwys 126 and 150.

downtown along Main St, north of Hwy 101 via California St.

Sights & Activities

South of Hwy 101 via Harbor Blvd, **Ventura Harbor** is the main departure point for boats to Channel Islands National Park.

San Buenaventura State Beach BEACH
(805-968-1033; www.parks.ca.gov; enter off San Pedro St; per car $10; dawn-dusk;) Along the waterfront off Hwy 101, this long white-sand beach is ideal for swimming, surfing or just lazing on the sand. A recreational cycling path connects to nearby **Emma Wood State Beach**, another popular spot for swimming, surfing and fishing.

Mission San Buenaventura CHURCH
(805-643-4318; www.sanbuenaventuramission.org; 211 E Main St; adult/child under 18yr $4/1; 10am-5pm Mon-Fri, 9am-5pm Sat, 10am-4pm Sun) Ventura's Spanish-colonial roots go back to this last mission founded by Junípero Serra in California. A stroll around the mellow parish church leads you through a garden courtyard and a small museum, past statues of saints, centuries-old religious paintings and unusual wooden bells.

Limoneira FARM
(805-525-5541; www.limoneira.com; 1131 Cummings Rd, Santa Paula; tours $20-40; call for hrs) A 20-minute drive from downtown, this working farm lets you get up close to sniff the fruit Ventura is most famous for growing: lemons. Drop by the historical ranch store and play bocce outside, or book ahead for a guided tour of the modern packing house and sea-view orchards.

Museum of Ventura County MUSEUM
(805-653-0323; http://venturamuseum.org; 100 E Main St; adult/child 6-17yr $5/1; 11am-5pm Tue-Sun) This tiny downtown museum has a mishmash of displays including Chumash baskets, vintage wooden surfboards and a massive stuffed California condor with wings outspread. Temporary exhibits usually spotlight local history and art.

Sleeping & Eating

Midrange motels and high-rise beachfront hotels cluster off Hwy 101 in Ventura. For better deals, keep driving on Hwy 101 southbound about 15 miles to Camarillo, where chain lodgings abound.

In downtown Ventura, Main St is chockablock with Mexicali taco shops, casual cafes and globally flavored kitchens.

Ventura Certified Farmers Market MARKET $
(http://vccfarmersmarkets.com; cnr Santa Clara & Palm Sts; 8:30am-noon Sat;) Over 45 farmers and food vendors show up each week, offering fresh fruits and vegetables, homebaked bread and ready-made meals – Mediterranean, Mexican and more. Another farmers market sets up at midtown's Pacific View Mall from 9am to 1pm on Wednesdays.

Jolly Oyster SEAFOOD $$
(911 San Pedro St; items $5-16; noon-7pm Fri, from 11am Sat & Sun;) At San Buenaventura State Beach, this happy-go-lucky seafood shack vends its own farm-raised Kumamoto and Pacific oysters and Manila clams. Seat yourself at picnic tables to shuck 'em raw or cook 'em yourself on barbecue grills. A short menu of tacos, tostadas, ceviche and salads changes weekly. One-hour parking free.

★**Lure Fish House** SEAFOOD $$$
(805-567-4400; www.lurefishhouse.com; 60 S California St; mains lunch $10-22, dinner $15-33; 11:30am-9pm Sun-Tue, to 10pm Wed-Thu, to 11pm Fri & Sat;) For seafood any fresher, you'd have to catch it yourself off Ventura pier. Go nuts ordering off a stalwart menu of sustainably caught seafood, organic regional farm produce and California wines. Make reservations or turn up at the bar during happy hour (4pm to 6pm Monday to Friday, 11:30am to 6pm Sunday) for strong cocktails, fried calamari and charbroiled oysters.

Drinking & Nightlife

You'll find plenty of rowdy dives down by the harbor.

Surf Brewery BREWERY
(805-644-2739; http://surfbrewery.com; suite A, 4561 Market St; 4-9pm Tue-Thu, from 1pm Fri, noon-9pm Sat, noon-7pm Sun) Ventura's newest microbrewery makes big waves with its hoppy and black IPAs and rye American pale ale. Beer geeks and food trucks gather at the sociable taproom in an industrial area, about 5 miles from downtown (take Hwy 101 southbound, exit Donlon St).

Wine Rack WINE BAR
(805-653-9463; http://thewinerracklounge.com; 14 S California St; 2-10pm Tue-Thu, to midnight Fri, noon-midnight Sat, noon-6pm Sun) At this upbeat wine shop, novices can sidle up to

the bar for a wine flight, loiter over a cheese plate, flatbread pizza or fondue and listen to live music Thursday to Saturday nights.

Shopping

B on Main GIFTS
(www.bonmain.com; 337 E Main St; ⌚10:30am-6pm Mon-Fri, 10am-8pm Sat, 11am-5pm Sun) For coastal living, B sells nifty reproductions of vintage surf posters, shabby-chic furnishings, SoCal landscape art, locally made jewelry and beachy clothing for women.

Ormachea JEWELRY
(www.ormacheajewelry.com; 451 E Main St) Run by a third-generation Peruvian jewelry craftsman, Ormachea skillfullly hammers out one-of-a-kind, handmade rings, pendants and bangles in a downtown studio.

ARC Foundation Thrift Store VINTAGE
(www.arcvc.org; 265 E Main St; ⌚9am-6pm Mon-Sat, 10am-5pm Sun) Loads of thrift stores, antiques malls and secondhand and vintage shops cluster downtown. Most are on Main St, west of California St, where ARC is always jam-packed with bargain hunters.

Rocket Fizz FOOD & DRINK
(www.rocketfizz.com; 105 S Oak St; ⌚10:30am-7pm Sun-Thu, to 9pm Fri & Sat) Retro-style soda pop and old-fashioned candy store is genius for stocking your cooler before a day at the beach.

Camarillo Premium Outlets MALL
(www.premiumoutlets.com/camarillo; 740 E Ventura Blvd, Camarillo; ⌚10am-9pm Mon-Sat, to 8pm Sun) For steeply discounted designer duds, from LA's Kitson to Nike, Neiman Marcus and North Face, drive about 20 minutes from Ventura on Hwy 101 southbound.

Information

Ventura Visitors & Convention Bureau (☎805-648-2075, 800-483-6214; www.ventura-usa.com; 101 S California St; ⌚9-5pm Mon-Sat, 10am-4pm Sun Mar-Oct, till 4pm daily Nov-Feb) Downtown visitor center hands out free maps and tourist brochures.

Getting There & Away

Ventura is about 30 miles southeast of Santa Barbara via Hwy 101. **Amtrak** (☎800-872-7245; www.amtrak.com; Harbor Blvd at Figueroa St) operates five daily trains north to Santa Barbara ($15, 45 minutes) via Carpinteria and south to LA ($24, 2¼ hours). Amtrak's platform station is unstaffed; buy tickets in advance online or by phone. **Vista** (☎800-438-1112; www.goventura.org) runs several daily 'Coastal Express' buses between downtown Ventura and Santa Barbara ($3, 40 to 70 minutes) via Carpinteria; check online or call for schedules.

Channel Islands National Park

Don't let this off-the-beaten-path **national park** (www.nps.gov/chis) FREE loiter for too long on your lifetime to-do list. It's easier to access than you might think, and the payoff is immense. Imagine hiking, kayaking, scuba diving, camping and whale-watching, and doing it all amid a raw, end-of-the-world landscape. Rich in unique species of flora and fauna, tide pools and kelp forests, the islands are home to 145 plant and animal species found nowhere else in the world, earning them the nickname 'California's Galapagos.'

Geographically, the Channel Islands are an eight-island chain off the Southern California coast, stretching from Santa Barbara

CALIFORNIA'S CHANNEL ISLANDS: PARADISE LOST & FOUND

Human beings have left a heavy footprint on the Channel Islands. Livestock overgrazed, causing erosion, and rabbits fed on native plants. The US military even used San Miguel as a practice bombing range. In 1969 an offshore oil spill engulfed the northern islands in an 800-sq-mile slick, killing off uncountable seabirds and mammals. Meanwhile, deep-sea fishing has caused the destruction of three-quarters of the islands' kelp forests, which are key to the marine ecosystem.

Despite past abuses, the future isn't all bleak. Brown pelicans – decimated by the effects of DDT and reduced to one surviving chick on Anacapa Island in 1970 – have rebounded. On San Miguel Island, native vegetation has returned a half century after overgrazing sheep were removed. On Santa Cruz Island, the National Park Service and the Nature Conservancy have implemented multiyear plans to eliminate invasive plants and feral pigs, and hopefully their recovery efforts will meet with success.

ISLAND OF THE BLUE DOLPHINS

For bedtime reading aloud around the campfire, pick up Scott O'Dell's Newberry Medal–winning *Island of the Blue Dolphins*. This children's novel was inspired by the true life story of a Native American girl left behind on San Nicolas Island during the early 19th century, when indigenous people were forced off the Channel Islands. Incredibly the girl survived mostly alone on the island for 18 years, living in a whale-bone hut and sourcing water from a spring, before being rescued in 1853. However, fate was still not on her side: she died just seven weeks after being brought to the mainland. Today her body lies buried in the graveyard at Mission Santa Barbara, where a commemorative plaque is inscribed with her Christian baptismal name, Juana María.

to San Diego. Five of them – San Miguel, Santa Rosa, Santa Cruz, Anacapa and tiny Santa Barbara – comprise Channel Islands National Park. Originally the islands were inhabited by Chumash tribespeople, who were forced to move to mainland Catholic missions by Spanish military forces in the early 1800s. The islands were subsequently taken over by Mexican and American ranchers during the 19th century and the US military in the 20th, until conservation efforts began in the 1970s and '80s.

Sights & Activities

Anacapa and Santa Cruz, the park's most popular islands, are within an hour's boat ride of Ventura. Anacapa is a doable day trip, while Santa Cruz is better suited for overnight camping. Bring plenty of water, because none is available on either island except at Scorpion Ranch Campground on Santa Cruz.

Most visitors arrive during summer, when island conditions are hot, dusty and bone-dry. Better times to visit are during the spring wildflower bloom or in early fall, when the fog clears. Winter can be stormy, but it's also great for wildlife-watching, especially whales.

Before you shove off from the mainland, stop by Ventura Harbor's NPS Visitor Center (p428) for educational natural history exhibits, a free 25-minute nature film and on weekends and holidays, family-friendly activities and ranger talks.

Anacapa Island

Actually three separate islets totaling just over 1 sq mi, Anacapa gives a memorable introduction to the islands' ecology. It's the best option if you're short on time. Boats dock year-round on the East Island and after a short climb, you'll find 2 miles of trails offering fantastic views of island flora, a historic lighthouse, and rocky Middle and West Islands. Kayaking, diving, tide-pooling and watching seals and sea lions are popular activities here. Inside the small museum at the island's visitors center, scuba divers with video cameras occasionally broadcast images to a TV monitor you can watch during spring and summer.

Santa Cruz Island

Santa Cruz, the largest island at 96 sq miles, claims two mountain ranges and the park's tallest peak, Mt Diablo (2450ft). The western three-quarters of Santa Cruz is mostly wilderness owned and managed by the **Nature Conservancy** (www.nature.org) and it can only be accessed with a permit (apply online at www.nature.org/cruzpermit). However, the remaining eastern quarter, managed by the National Park Service (NPS), packs a wallop – ideal for those wanting an action-packed day trip or a more laid-back overnight trip. You can swim, snorkel, scuba dive and kayak. Rangers meet incoming boats at Scorpion Anchorage, a short walk from historic **Scorpion Ranch**.

There are rugged hikes too, which are best not attempted at midday as there's little shade. It's a 1-mile climb to captivating **Cavern Point**. Views don't get much better than from this windy spot. For a longer jaunt, continue 1.5 miles west mostly along scenic bluffs to **Potato Harbor**. From Scorpion Anchorage, the 4.5-mile **Scorpion Canyon Loop** heads uphill to an old oil well for fantastic views, then drops through Scorpion Canyon to the campground. Alternatively, follow Smugglers Rd all the way to the cobblestone beach at **Smugglers Cove**, a strenuous 7.5-mile round-trip from Scorpion Anchorage.

Other Islands

The Chumash called **Santa Rosa** 'Wima' (driftwood) because of the redwood logs that often came ashore here, with which they built plank canoes called *tomols*. This 84-sq-mile island has rare Torrey pines, sandy beaches and hundreds of plant and bird species. Beach, canyon and grasslands hiking trails abound, but high winds can make swimming, diving and kayaking tough for anyone but experts.

While 14-sq-mile **San Miguel** can guarantee solitude and a remote wilderness experience, it's often windy and shrouded in fog. Some sections are off-limits to prevent disruption of the island's fragile ecosystem, which includes a caliche forest (containing hardened calcium-carbonate castings of trees and vegetation) and seasonal colonies of seals and sea lions.

Santa Barbara, only 1 sq mile in size and the smallest of the islands, is a jewel-box for nature lovers. Big, blooming coreopsis, cream cups and chicory are just a few of the island's memorable plant species. You'll also find the humongous northern elephant seal here as well as Scripps's murrelets, a bird that nests in cliff crevices. Get more information from the island's small visitor center.

Tours

Most trips require a minimum number of participants, and may be canceled due to high surf or weather conditions.

Island Packers CRUISE
(805-642-1393; www.islandpackers.com; 1691 Spinnaker Dr, Ventura; 3hr cruise adult/child 3-12yr from $36/26) Offers wildlife cruises year-round, including seasonal whale-watching excursions from late December to mid-April (gray whales) and mid-May through mid-September (blue and humpback whales).

MOVING ON?

For tips, recommendations and reviews, head to shop.lonelyplanet.com to purchase a downloadable PDF of the Central Coast chapter from Lonely Planet's *California* guide.

Santa Barbara Adventure Company KAYAKING
(805-884-9283, 877-885-9283; www.sbadventureco.com; 32 E Haley St, Santa Barbara;) This family-friendly outfitter runs a variety of guided paddling tours, from the sea caves of Santa Cruz to the sea arches of Anacapa. Choose from day trips ($180 to $210) or overnight camping expeditions (from $329).

Channel Islands Outfitters KAYAKING, SNORKELING
(805-899-4925; www.channelislandso.com; 117b Harbor Way, Santa Barbara) Expertly guided kayaking and snorkeling trips visit Anacapa, Santa Cruz or Santa Barbara ($99 to $225, plus ferry tickets); wetsuits are included.

Truth Aquatics DIVING, KAYAKING
(805-962-1127; www.truthaquatics.com; 301 W Cabrillo Blvd, Santa Barbara) Based in Santa Barbara, this long-running outfitter organizes diving, kayaking and hiking day trips and multiday excursions aboard specially designed dive boats. See website for prices.

Raptor Dive Charters DIVING
(805-650-7700; www.raptordive.com; 1559 Spinnaker Dr, Ventura) For certified and experienced divers, boat trips to Anacapa and Santa Cruz, including night dives, cost $110 to $125; equipment rentals available for a surcharge.

Aquasports KAYAKING
(800-773-2309, 805-968-7231; www.islandkayaking.com) Led by naturalist guides, day and

CHANNEL ISLANDS NATIONAL PARK CAMPGROUNDS

CAMPGROUND	NUMBER OF SITES	ACCESS FROM BOAT LANDING	DESCRIPTION
Anacapa	7	0.5-mile walk with over 150 stairs	High, rocky, sun-exposed and isolated
Santa Cruz (Scorpion Ranch)	31	Flat 0.5-mile walk	Popular with groups; often crowded and partly shady
Santa Barbara	10	Steep 0.25-mile walk uphill	Large, grassy and surrounded by trails
San Miguel	9	Steep 1-mile walk uphill	Windy, often foggy with volatile weather
Santa Rosa	15	Flat 1.5-mile walk	Eucalyptus grove in a windy canyon

CHANNEL CROSSINGS

The open seas on the boat ride out to the Channel Islands may feel choppy to landlubbers. To avoid seasickness, sit outside on the upper deck, away from the diesel fumes in back. The outbound trip is typically against the wind and a bit bumpier than the return. Over-the-counter motion-sickness pills (eg Dramamine) can make you drowsy. Staring at the horizon may help. Boats usually brake when dolphins or whales are spotted – always a welcome distraction from any nausea.

overnight kayaking trips to Santa Cruz, Anacapa and Santa Barbara ($125 to $245, plus ferry tickets) leave from Ventura Harbor.

Channel Islands Kayak Center KAYAKING
(805-984-5995; www.cikayak.com; 1691 Spinnaker Dr, Ventura; by appt only) Book ahead to rent kayaks (single/double per day $35/55) or arrange a private guided kayaking tour of Santa Cruz or Anacapa (from $200 per person, two-person minimum).

Sleeping

Each island has a primitive year-round **campground** (reservations 877-444-6777; www.recreation.gov; tent sites $15) with pit toilets and picnic tables. Water is only available on Santa Rosa and Santa Cruz Islands. You must pack everything in and out, including trash. Due to fire danger, campfires aren't allowed, but enclosed gas campstoves are OK. Advance reservations are required for all island campsites.

Information

NPS Visitor Center (805-658-5730; www.nps.gov/chis; 1901 Spinnaker Dr, Ventura; 8:30am-5pm;) Trip-planning information, books and maps are available on the mainland at the far end of Ventura Harbor.

Getting There & Away

You can access the national park by taking a boat from Ventura or Oxnard or a plane from Camarillo. Trips may be canceled anytime due to high surf or weather conditions. Reservations are essential for weekends, holidays and summer trips.

Island Packers (805-642-1393; www.islandpackers.com; 1691 Spinnaker Dr, Ventura; round-trip fare adult/child 3-12yr from $59/41) From Ventura Harbor and Oxnard, Island Packers offers regularly scheduled boat service to all islands. Day trips to Anacapa and Santa Rosa are less expensive than visiting other islands; campers pay an additional surcharge. Be forewarened: if you camp overnight and seas are rough the following day, you could get stuck for an extra night or more.

Channel Islands Aviation (805-987-1301; www.flightstothechannelislands.com; 305 Durley Ave, Camarillo) If you're prone to seasickness, you can take a 25-minute scenic flight to Santa Rosa Island from Camarillo. Half-day packages (per person $160 to $220) include hiking or a guided 4WD tour, while overnight camping excursions (per person $300) are more DIY. Ask about surf-fishing charter trips.

Understand Southern California

SOUTHERN CALIFORNIA TODAY..............430
Growing pains are par for the course on this Pacific coast of dreams, an ongoing social experiment and multicultural mosaic.

HISTORY..................................432
From Native Californians and Spanish missions to water scandals, earthquakes and race riots, here's how SoCal evolved.

THE LIFESTYLE............................441
Find out why people here work so hard – and play even harder.

AS SEEN ON TV (& FILM)...................448
What would SoCal be without 'the Industry'? But it's not just all about Hollywood's A-list.

MUSIC & THE ARTS.........................453
Pop culture? Yes. But modern composers and cutting-edge contemporary arts too. Come see SoCal's creative side.

SOCAL ARCHITECTURE.......................458
It's a New World of architecture, from glamorous art deco to wildly unpredictable postmodern designs.

FLAVORS OF SOCAL.........................461
Eat like an *Iron Chef* judge and tipple sun-kissed wines, then go find fresh seafood shacks and gourmet-food trucks.

WILD THINGS..............................466
Meet some of SoCal's native wildlife and its most famous migratory visitors, from gray whales to monarch butterflies.

Southern California Today

Today's Southern California is the culmination of the efforts of generations of big dreamers. From Los Angeles, the fantasies spun by Hollywood have come to dominate the digital transmissions and cultural trends of the entire planet. Meanwhile, SoCal's iconic images of tanned surfers and golden sands endure, despite the all too real challenges that this densely populated, racially diverse and economically unequal area now faces.

Best in Print

The Tortilla Curtain (TC Boyle) Mexican-American culture clash and chasing the Californian Dream.

My California: Journeys by Great Writers (Angel City Press) Insightful stories by talented chroniclers.

Where I Was From (Joan Didion) California-born essayist shatters palm-fringed fantasies.

Hollywood Babylon (Kenneth Anger) 'Tell-all' about the scandalous lives and times of Hollywood's early stars.

Best on Film

Sunset Boulevard (1950)
Chinatown (1974)
Boyz n the Hood (1991)
LA Story (1991)
The Player (1992)
LA Confidential (1997)
Sideways (2004)

Best Music

California Dreaming (The Mamas and the Papas)
LA Woman (The Doors)
Straight Outta Compton (NWA)
Los Angeles (X)
California Love (2Pac)
California (Phantom Planet)
All I Wanna Do (Sheryl Crow)
California Soul (Fifth Dimension)
Surfin' USA (Beach Boys)

California Dreams vs Reality

Even if you've seen it in movies or on TV, Southern California still comes as a shock to the system. Venice skateboarders, Malibu millionaires, Deepak Chopra-quoting new age yogis and Rodeo Drive-pillaging trophy wives aren't on different channels; they all live together here, a place where at least the pretense of tolerance for other people's beliefs, be they conservative, liberal or just plain wacky, is the essential social glue.

Until recently, the most divisive political hot-potato topic was same-sex marriage, when a state constitutional amendment to ban it was struck down for good in 2013. Still controversial elsewhere in the USA, medical marijuana is old news for Californians, who approved a state proposition allowing its use back in 1996 – although the proliferation of marijuana clubs, Mexican cartel intervention and federal raids are raising eyebrows.

Growing Pains

SoCal is not a finished work. The nightmares faced by the region in the 1990s – race riots, the Northridge earthquake – already belong to a different age. Today's issues revolve around growth: in an area that has an economy bigger than Canada's and is the headquarters for a huge range of industries, from space probes to Disneyland to the movie and TV industry, how to manage an expanding economy and population without sacrificing the environment is the biggest problem.

With burgeoning humanity comes horrific traffic and skyrocketing costs of living and real estate. Although slowly improving, public transport is still woefully inadequate in most places, so everyone hits the tortured freeway systems, which move ever more slowly. Sheer human impact is a palpable force, especially given a recent multi-year drought and prolonged wildfire seasons that drain the state's coffers and natural resources.

Multicultural Mosaic

Both a success story and a victim of its very adaptability, SoCal has found that the human waves of domestic migration and international immigration continue to rise. Every New Year's Day the largest commercial for living here – Pasadena's Rose Parade – snares the imaginations of folks freezing in Wisconsin or struggling to make ends meet in the Rust Belt. Many who heed the 19th-century advice to 'Go West, young man!' wind up on SoCal's sunny shores.

Given the mix of people constantly arriving here, the good news is that it's extremely difficult to envision LA ever returning to the kind of racially charged atmosphere that sparked the 'Zoot Suit Riots' of the 1940s or the uproar that followed the 1992 'all-white jury' verdict in the beating case of Rodney King, an African American, by LA police. You may be surprised to see the amiable multiethnic mix of colleagues and friends walking along boulevards and beaches or gathering for meals at SoCal's plethora of restaurants that deliver authentic global tastes.

Work Smart, Play Hard

Some of the myths surrounding SoCal are true, it has to be admitted. You really *can* surf in the morning, spend the afternoon skiing down pine-forested slopes and end the day with cocktails at a desert hot-springs resort. Who wouldn't want to live here, even with the horrifying commute times? More to the point, who wouldn't want to visit, or even perhaps become part of, such an exciting social experiment?

Time and again, SoCal has proven itself to be resourceful, resilient and innovative. After tourism, major drivers of the economy include international trade (LA and Long Beach form the nation's largest port), technology, finance, film and TV production, health services and design. With climate change threatening, you can bet the bank that Caltech, UCLA and other universities are using their big brains to solve the issues that challenge not just SoCal, but also the rest of the state, the country and the world.

POPULATION: **22 MILLION**

AREA: **45,065 SQ MILES**

GDP: **$900 BILLION**

AVERAGE PER CAPITA INCOME: **$29,550**

UNEMPLOYMENT: **8.1%**

if Los Angeles were 100 people

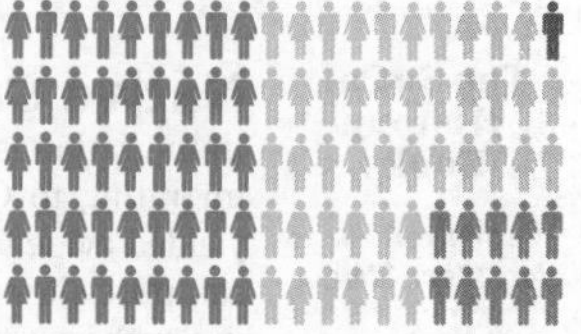

45 would be White
33 would be Latino
11 would be African American
10 would be Asian
1 would be Native American

belief systems

(% of population)

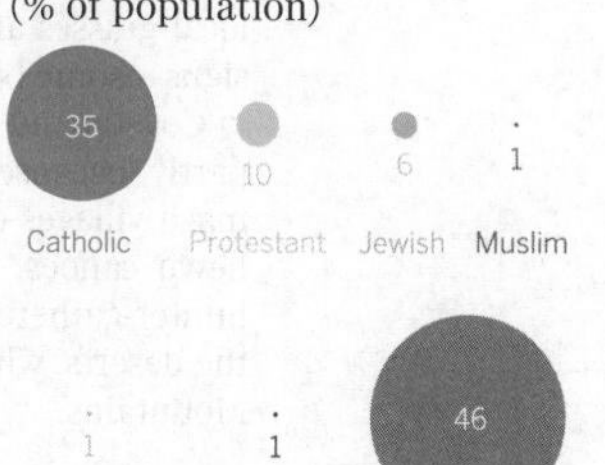

population per sq mile

≈ 80 people

History

When European explorers first arrived in the 16th century, more than 100,000 Native Californians called this land home. Spanish conquistadors marched through in search of a fabled 'city of gold' before establishing Catholic missions and presidios (military forts). After winning independence from Spain, Mexico briefly ruled California, but then got trounced by the fledgling United States just before gold was discovered in 1848. Immigrant waves of star-struck California dreamers haven't stopped washing up on these Pacific shores ever since.

Top SoCal History Books

California: A History (Kevin Starr)

City of Quartz (Mike Davis)

Journey to the Sun: Junípero Serra's Dream and the Founding of California (Gregory Orfalea)

Native Californians

Immigration is hardly a new phenomenon here, since people have been migrating to California for millennia. Many archaeological sites have yielded evidence – from large middens of seashells along the beaches to campfire sites on the Channel Islands – of humans making their homes in Southern California as early as 13,000 years ago.

Traditional Ways of Life

The majority of Native Californians lived in small communities and a few migrated with the seasons. Their diet was largely dependent on acorn meal, supplemented by small game such as rabbits and deer, and fish and shellfish. Native Californians were skilled craftspeople, making earthenware pots, fish nets, bows, arrows and spears with chipped stone points. Many tribes developed a knack for weaving baskets made from local grasses and plant fibers, then decorated them with geometric designs – some baskets were so tightly woven they could hold water.

Coastal and inland peoples traded but generally didn't interact much, partly because they spoke different languages. Kumeyaay and Chumash villages dotted the coast, where people fished and paddled hand-hewn canoes, including out to the Channel Islands. Inland, nomadic hunter-gatherer bands of Cahuilla and Mojave peoples found oases in the deserts, while the Serrano camped seasonally in the San Bernardino Mountains.

TIMELINE

Around 20,000 BC

First people start crossing from Asia into North America via Bering Strait land bridge. The bones of a human found on SoCal's Santa Rosa Island date back 13,000 years.

1542

Portuguese navigator Juan Rodríguez Cabrillo and his Spanish crew become the first Europeans to sight the mainland of New Spain's west coast, anchoring in today's San Diego Bay.

1602

Sebastián Vizcaíno first sets foot on California soil on the feast day of San Diego de Alcalá. In honor of the saint, he names the spot San Diego.

Although there was no concept of private land ownership among Native Californians, the most common cause of conflict between indigenous peoples (that is, until Europeans arrived) was trespassing on another tribe's traditional territory. Natural resources were scarce, especially in the harsh desert, where tribes frequently skirmished.

Find out more about the traditions and lifestyles of Southern California's indigenous tribes with *California Indians and Their Environment*, a readable natural history guide by Kent Lightfoot and Otis Parrish.

From Conquest to Tribal Revival

Starting in the late 18th century, Spanish colonizers virtually enslaved Native Californians. Despite pockets of armed resistance and violent revolts, tribespeople were made to construct the missions and presidios. Spanish soldiers, whose job was ostensibly to protect the missions and deter foreign intruders, became infamous for raping and pillaging. Meanwhile, European diseases such as smallpox and syphilis further decimated indigenous populations.

Native Californians were further dispossessed of tribal lands during the Mexican colonial and early American periods. It wasn't until the 20th century – when the US federal government began recognizing tribes as sovereign nations, including granting Native Americans citizenship and voting rights in 1924 – that California's indigenous population, once driven almost to the point of extinction, began to rebound.

Political activism, including the 'Red Power' protests of the American Indian Movement (AIM) starting in the late 1960s, led not only to a cultural renaissance, but also secured some tribes economic assistance from state and federal agencies, including California's Native American Heritage Commission established in 1978. Deprived of their traditional land base and means of livelihood centuries ago, many contemporary California tribes have turned to casino gaming to relieve unemployment and poverty on their reservations. Today tribal casinos support tens of thousands of jobs in Southern California.

Native California History

- *Indian Canyons (p343)*
- *Tahquitz Canyon (p341)*
- *Autry National Center (p101)*
- *Museum of Man (p280)*
- *Chumash Painted Cave State Historic Park (p409)*

A New World for Europeans

Following the conquest of Mexico in the early 16th century, Spain turned its attention toward exploring the edges of a new empire, fueled by curiosity, lust for power and, above all, greed. Tales of a golden island to the west circulated widely. In 1542 the Spanish crown sent Juan Rodríguez Cabrillo, a Portuguese explorer and retired conquistador, to find it.

The fabled land, of course, proved elusive, but Cabrillo and his crew still made it into the history books as the first Europeans to see mainland California at what is now San Diego. Cabrillo claimed the land for Spain while sitting out a storm in the harbor before sailing northward. Stopping to check out the Channel Islands, the explorer broke a leg, fell ill, died and was buried in 1543 on what is now San Miguel Island.

1769

Spanish captain Gaspar de Portolá leads the first European land expedition north into Alta (Upper) California, establishing colonial forts and missions with the help of priest Junípero Serra.

1781

Spanish governor Felipe de Neve sets out from Mission San Gabriel with a tiny band of settlers, trekking west just 9 miles to establish the future Los Angeles.

1821–46

During Mexico's rule over California, Spanish missions are secularized (except Santa Barbara) and their lands carved up into ranchos. Governor Pio Pico's brother-in-law snaps up San Juan Capistrano.

1826–32

Teenage Kit Carson helps blaze the Santa Fe Trail, which eventually leads to Los Angeles through 900 miles of rattlesnake-filled high desert and plains guarded by Native American tribes.

The Spanish left California alone for the next half century or so, until they decided they needed to secure some ports on the Pacific coast, and sent Sebastián Vizcaíno to find them. Vizcaíno's first expedition was a disaster that didn't get past Baja California, but in his second attempt, in 1602, he rediscovered the harbor at San Diego and became the first European to set foot in what Spaniards called Alta (Upper) California.

The precise etymology of 'California' has never been convincingly established. Many think it derives from a 16th-century Spanish romance novel about a legendary island, fabulously rich in gold and inhabited only by black women warriors ruled by Queen Califia.

The Spanish Mission Period

In the 18th century, everyone wanted a toehold on the western shores of the New World. Around the 1760s, as Russian ships sailed up and down California's coast in search of otter pelts, and British trappers and explorers spread throughout the western continent, King Carlos III finally grew worried that Spain's claim to the territory might be challenged.

Conveniently, the Catholic Church was anxious to start missionary work among Native Californians, so the Church and Spanish crown combined forces and established missions protected by presidios. Native American converts were expected to live in the missions, learn trade and agricultural skills and ultimately establish pueblos, which would be like little Spanish towns. Or so the plan went.

On July 1, 1769, a sorry lot of about 100 missionaries and soldiers, led by the Franciscan priest Junípero Serra and the military commander Gaspar de Portolá, limped ashore at San Diego Bay. They had just spent several weeks at sea sailing from Baja (Lower) California; about half of their cohort had died en route and many of the survivors were sick or near death. It was an inauspicious beginning for Mission San Diego de Alcalá, the first in a chain of 21 Spanish missions in Alta California.

The missions did achieve modest success at farming and just barely managed to become self-sufficient, an essential achievement during the 1810–21 Mexican war for independence from Spain, when supplies from Mexico were cut off completely. As a way of colonizing California and converting the indigenous people to Christianity, however, the mission period was an abject failure. The Spanish population remained small, foreign intruders were not greatly deterred and, ultimately, more Native Californians died than were converted.

SoCal's Standout Missions

San Diego (p287) The oldest

San Juan Capistrano (p268) The most famous

Santa Barbara (p392) The only one never secularized

La Purísima (p414) The most complete

From Mexican Ranchos to Statehood

When Mexico gained its independence from Spain in 1821, many in that new nation looked to California to satisfy their thirst for private land. By the mid-1830s, almost all of the Spanish missions in Alta California had been secularized and divvied up into land grants by Mexican governors. This gave birth to a system of Mexican ranchos, largely raising livestock to supply the hide and tallow trade. The new landowners, called ranche-

1848
Signing the Treaty of Guadalupe Hidalgo on February 2, Mexico turns over one third of its territory, including California, to the US in exchange for $15 million.

1849
Following the discovery of gold at Sutter's Creek in the Sierra Nevada foothills in 1848, the California Gold Rush sees the largest migration in US history.

1850
On September 9, California becomes the 31st state of the US, entering the Union as a free (non-slave-holding) state. Its first constitution is written in Spanish and English.

1869
Gold is discovered in Julian, near San Diego, sparking a mini mining boom. Once the gold runs out, Julian goes back to being a sleepy little town.

ros or Californios, prospered and became the social, cultural and political fulcrums of Alta California under Mexican rule.

Meanwhile, American explorers, trappers, traders, whalers, settlers and opportunists increasingly showed interest in California. Some Americans who started businesses here converted to Catholicism, married local women and assimilated into Californio society. Impressed by California's untapped riches and imbued with Manifest Destiny (an imperialist political doctrine of extending the USA's borders from coast to coast), President Andrew Jackson sent an emissary to offer the financially strapped Mexican government $500,000 for California in 1835.

But Mexico wasn't interested in selling California, and soon a political storm was brewing. In 1836 Texas seceded from Mexico and declared itself an independent republic. When the US annexed Texas in 1845, Mexico broke off diplomatic relations and ordered all foreigners without proper papers to be deported from California. In turn, the US declared war on Mexico and began an invasion. Soon US naval units occupied every port on the California coast, but militarily speaking, California remained a sideshow while the war was mostly fought in Mexico.

The capture of Mexico City by US troops in September 1847 put an end to the fighting and led to the signing of the Treaty of Guadalupe Hidalgo on February 2, 1848, in which the Mexican government ceded much of its northern territory (including Alta California) to the USA, just in time for California's Gold Rush to begin.

The distance between each of California's Spanish colonial missions equaled a day's journey by horseback. Learn more about the missions' historical significance and cultural influence at www.missionscalifornia.com.

Riches of Railroads, Real Estate & Oil

Many Mexican rancheros lost their land when American authorities questioned their title under the 1851 Land Act. During this period of loose government, LA was a Wild West town, filled with saloons, brothels and gambling dens. Added to the mix were thousands of Chinese immigrants who had arrived for the Gold Rush and later railroad construction work. These foreigners were viewed by many with suspicion – the state even enacted a special 'foreign miner's tax' in 1852.

The perception of LA and the rest of the region as a lawless backwater began to change with the arrival of the railroad. Completed in 1869, the transcontinental railroad shortened the trip from New York to San Francisco from two months to less than four days, elevating the latter to California's metropolitan center. SoCal's parched climate, its distance from fresh water and mining resources, and its relatively small population made it unattractive to railroad moguls. Not until the mid-1870s did wheeling and dealing result in a spur line to LA.

During the same period, agriculture diversified, with new crops – especially oranges – being grown in Southern California for markets on the East Coast and abroad. Unlike many fruits, oranges easily survived

1874

US Department of Agriculture ships three seedless navel orange trees to botanists in Riverside. By 1889 citrus orchards cover more than 13,000 acres of SoCal.

1892

Oil is discovered by Edward Doheny in downtown LA, near where Dodger Stadium stands today, sparking a major oil boom. Within five years, 500 wells are operational.

1902

The first Rose Bowl football game takes place in Pasadena, with the University of Michigan defeating Stanford 49-0. The next game isn't held for another 14 years.

1913

The Los Angeles Aqueduct, built under the direction of chief engineer William Mulholland, starts supplying water from the Owens Valley, in the Eastern Sierra.

long-distance rail shipping. As oranges found their way onto New York grocery shelves, a hard-sell California advertising campaign began. Folks back East heeded the self-interested advice of crusading magazine and newspaper editor Horace Greeley to 'Go West, young man.'

A lot of the land granted to the railroads in Southern California was sold in big lots to speculators who also acquired, with the help of corrupt politicians and administrators, much of the farmland that was released for new settlement. A major share of agricultural land thus became consolidated into large holdings in the hands of a few city-based landlords, establishing California's still dominant pattern of industrial-scale 'agribusiness,' rather than small family farms. Never mind that SoCal's supply of fresh water was inadequate and that cheap farm agricultural labor often had to be imported.

Yet LA had other natural resources waiting to be exploited, albeit hidden underground. In 1892 a flat-broke mining prospector and real-estate speculator named Edward Doheny dug a well near downtown LA that would change SoCal forever. Inside of a year, Doheny's well was produc-

CALIFORNIA IMMIGRATION: TAKE IT, THEN LEAVE IT

Southern California has always had a love-hate relationship with its immigrants, yet owes much of its success to its cultural diversity. Newcomers are typically welcomed in periods of rapid growth, only to be rejected when times get tough.

Chinese railroad workers, for instance, were in great demand during the 1860s, but ended up being discriminated against and even violently attacked in LA over the next decade. California's Alien Land Law of 1913 even prevented resident Asians who were ineligible for US citizenship from owning agricultural land. During WWII, around 120,000 people of Japanese heritage – many of them US citizens – were forcibly placed in internment camps. African Americans came to SoCal in large numbers to take jobs during the postwar boom, but suddenly found themselves unemployed when the economy later slowed.

It is estimated that more than three million undocumented immigrants currently work in California, despite continuing efforts to seal the notoriously porous border with Mexico. Mexican and Latin American workers still do most of SoCal's farm labor and domestic work. In 1994, in the face of increasing unemployment and state budget deficits, a majority of Californians voted in favor of Proposition 187, which denied illegal immigrants access to state government services, including schools and hospitals.

Today immigration remains a volatile political topic in Southern California, especially among conservatives, some of whom employ illegal immigrants as nannies and gardeners while simultaneously calling for their expulsion. At the other end of the political spectrum, California passed a law allowing illegal immigrants to get state driver's licenses in 2013. More recently, some state lawmakers have called for undocumented foreigners to be given access to public health care too.

1915

German-born Carl Laemmle builds Universal City Studios on a farm north of Hollywood, selling lunch to curious guests who come to watch the magic of moviemaking.

1923

LA's famous landmark, the 45ft-tall Hollywood Sign, is erected in the Santa Monica Mountains to promote Hollywoodland subdivision. The 'land' drops off in 1949, but the sign remains.

1925

At 6:44am on June 29, a 6.3-magnitude earthquake levels most of downtown Santa Barbara, killing 13 people. The city rebuilds in Spanish Colonial Revival style.

1927

The Jazz Singer premieres at Downtown LA's Million Dollar Theater as the world's first 'talkie' movie, signaling the decline of the silent-film era. Hollywood booms.

ing 40 gallons of 'black gold' (oil) per day. Flowing north from LA into Ventura and Santa Barbara Counties, SoCal's oil industry soon boomed, as fictionally depicted in the 2007 film *There Will Be Blood*.

Los Angeles' Water Wars

The growth of arid Los Angeles into a megalopolis would not have been possible without water. When the city's population surged in the early 20th century, it became clear that groundwater levels would soon be inadequate to meet its needs, let alone sustain further growth. Water had to be imported and Fred Eaton, an ex-mayor of LA, and William Mulholland, the powerful head of the LA Department of Water & Power, knew just how and where to get it: by aqueduct from the Owens Valley, which receives enormous runoff from the Sierra Nevada Mountains.

The fact that the Owens Valley was settled by farmers who needed the water for irrigation purposes bothered neither the two men nor the federal government, which actively supported LA's less-than-ethical maneuvering in acquiring land and securing water rights in the area. Voters gave Mulholland the more than $25 million needed to build the aqueduct. An amazing feat of engineering – crossing barren desert floor as well as rugged mountain terrain for 233 miles – the LA Aqueduct opened to great fanfare in 1913.

The Owens Valley, however, would never be the same. With most of its inflows diverted, Owens Lake quickly shriveled up. A bitter feud between LA and Owens Valley farmers and ranchers grew violent when some opponents to the scheme tried to sabotage the aqueduct by blowing up a section of it. All to no avail. By 1928 LA owned 90% of the water in Owens Valley and agriculture was effectively dead. These early water wars formed the basis for the 1974 noir film *Chinatown*.

These days LA still gets over half of its water supply from this aqueduct, which was extended another 105 miles to Mono Basin in 1940. The remainder of the city's water is siphoned from the Colorado and Feather Rivers; only about 15% comes from groundwater in the San Fernando Valley basin. During periods of extreme drought, water restrictions are put in place for LA residences and businesses – that's why you may have to specifically request drinking water when dining out at restaurants.

SoCal's Top Military Museums & Events

- *USS Midway Museum (p288)*
- *San Diego Air & Space Museum (p281)*
- *Fleet Week & Miramar Air Show (p296)*
- *USS Iowa Battleship (Map p62)*
- *Palm Springs Air Museum (p341)*

Military Might in SoCal

Along with motion pictures, aviation was another major industry to have a significant impact on Southern California beginning in the early 20th century. During and after WWI, the Lockheed brothers and Donald Douglas established aircraft manufacturing plants in LA, while Glenn H Curtiss set up shop in San Diego and San Diego–based Ryan Airlines built the *Spirit of St Louis* for Lindbergh's celebrated transatlantic flight in 1927.

1929

The first Academy Awards ceremony takes place at the Hollywood Roosevelt Hotel, lasting only 15 minutes. Fewer than 300 people fork over $5 each to be part of the crowd.

1942

US Executive Order 9066 banishes 120,000 Japanese Americans to internment camps. The US federal government doesn't make monetary reparations until the 1990s.

1943

Tension between Americans and Mexicans reaches boiling point during the Zoot Suit Riots, which pit US military servicemen against zoot-suit-clad Mexican teens while LA police look on.

1955

Disneyland opens in Anaheim on July 18 after a quick one-year construction period. Temperatures hit 101°F (38°C), high-heeled shoes sink into the soft asphalt and drinking fountains don't work.

In the 1930s, the aviation industry – pumped up by billions of federal dollars for military contracts – helped lift SoCal out of the Great Depression. WWII also had a huge impact on the entire region. After the 1941 bombing of Pearl Harbor, San Diego became the headquarters of the US Pacific Fleet, changing the city forever. Farther north, Camp Pendleton, a huge Marine Corps Base, was established in 1942. Throughout WWII, local aircraft manufacturing plants turned out planes by the thousands.

After WWII, many service people settled in SoCal. The region's military-industrial complex continued to prosper during the Cold War, providing jobs in everything from avionics and missile manufacturing to helicopter and nuclear submarine maintenance. The US Marine Corps still trains recruits and the US Navy holds advanced training for fighter pilots here à la *Top Gun*. There are submarine bases, aircraft testing facilities, air force bases and sprawling gunnery ranges.

Los Angeles once had a wonderfully efficient system of streetcars, until General Motors allegedly conspired to destroy it (search Google for 'GM streetcar conspiracy' and make up your own mind).

Military spending peaked in the 1980s under ex-California governor and then US president Ronald Reagan, but the end of the Cold War spelled economic disaster. Budget cutbacks closed numerous military bases, forcing defense contractors to move on or diversify. Workers who had grown accustomed to regular paychecks from aerospace juggernauts like McDonnell Douglas suddenly got laid off. The USA's current 'war on terror' has once again boosted military manufacturing in the region, however.

Race Riots in Los Angeles

LA's long history of racial strife reached an explosive peak in the 1960s. The city was booming but not everyone was invited to the party. Many ethnic-minority neighborhoods, predominantly African American communities with South Central foremost among them, had for decades been suffering from institutional neglect and lack of opportunity.

On a hot August day in 1965, frustration levels reached a boiling point when an African American motorist being pulled over on suspicion of drink-driving was beaten by police. Six violent days later, when the Watts Riots were over, 34 people were dead and more than 2000 were injured.

As the city licked its wounds, Governor Pat Brown appointed a commission to study the causes of the riots. They identified the problems – an unemployment rate double the LA average, overcrowded and underfunded classrooms, discriminatory housing laws etc – but lacked the vision, money and perhaps motivation to fix them. A generation later there would be a high price to pay for such indifference.

Fast forward to April 29, 1992: 'Not guilty.' The words cut through the stifling air of a hushed Simi Valley courtroom. More than a year earlier – in an eerie déjà vu of 1965 – four LAPD officers had stopped Rodney King, an African American motorist, on suspicion of driving un-

1965

It takes 20,000 National Guards to quell the six-day Watts Riots in LA, which cause death, devastation and over $40 million in property damage. That same year, Rodney King is born.

1966

Ronald Reagan is elected Governor of California, setting a career precedent for fading film stars. He served until 1975, and in 1981 became the 40th president of the United States.

1968

Robert Kennedy is assassinated at the Ambassador Hotel in LA by Palestinian immigrant and anti-Zionist Sirhan Sirhan, who remains in jail today in San Diego County.

1969

UCLA professor Len Kleinrock sends data from a computer in Los Angeles to another at Stanford University, typing just two characters before the system crashes. The internet is born.

der the influence. When King initially resisted arrest, the cops allegedly started to kick, beat and shout at the man as he crouched on the sidewalk. Infamously, the whole incident was caught on videotape.

The cops' acquittal unleashed a replay of the Watts Riots on an even bigger scale, as rioting and looting spread through several neighborhoods. National Guards patrolled the streets with machine guns, businesses and schools were ordered to close, and a dusk curfew was imposed. LA felt like a war zone. The shocking toll: 54 dead, over 2300 injured, 12,000 arrested and nearly $1 billion in property damage.

In LA, charges of police brutality and corruption splash news headlines still today. Given the abyss of distrust between police and some poor and minority communities, it's anybody's guess what the future holds.

Social Movers & Shakers

Unconstrained by the burden of traditions, bankrolled by elite affluence and promoted by film and TV, Southern California has long been a leader in new attitudes and social movements.

In the affluent 1950s, the emerging middle class moved to the suburbs, and no place better defined suburban life than Orange County. The Irvine Company, owner of almost 100,000 acres of private land (a legacy of 19th-century Mexican land grants), built the first 'Master Plan' communities. Strict rules governed their design – hence uniform beige-box architecture. Everybody lived on quiet streets where children could safely play, while shopping centers and strip malls were concentrated along multilane boulevards that made owning a car necessary.

When the postwar Baby Boomers hit their late teens, many rejected their parents' values and heeded LSD guru Timothy Leary's counsel to 'turn on, tune in, drop out.' Though the hippie counterculture was an international phenomenon, SoCal was at the leading edge of its music, psychedelic art and new libertarianism. Sex, drugs and rock 'n' roll ruled the day. LA's Venice Beach was a major hub and hangout for Jim Morrison, Janis Joplin and other luminaries of that era.

In the late 1960s and early '70s, New Left politics, the anti-Vietnam War movement and Black Liberation all forced their way into the political limelight, making flower power and give-peace-a-chance politics seem naive. The 1968 assassination of Robert Kennedy in LA, violent repressions of political demonstrations and the death of a spectator at a Rolling Stones concert at the hands of security guards (Hells Angels had been hired for the occasion) stripped the era of its innocence.

What a difference a few decades make. Since the 1980s, Southern California's new obsession has become the healthy lifestyle, with a mood-altering array of yoga and fitness classes and self-actualization

A literally and symbolically colorful book, *A People's Guide to Los Angeles,* by Laura Pulido, Laura Barraclough and Wendy Cheng, documents milestones and powerful places of struggle over race, class, gender and sexuality.

1984

Los Angeles hosts the Olympic summer games for the second time (the first was in 1932). The USSR doesn't show up, leaving US athletes to win 83 gold medals.

1992

After a 25-year hiatus California resumes executions at San Quentin by killing Robert Alton Harris in the gas chamber for killing two teenage boys in San Diego in 1978.

1994

The 6.7-magnitude Northridge earthquake strikes at 4:31am on January 17, killing 72 and causing $20 billion in property damage – one of the costliest natural disasters in US history.

1994

Orange County, one of the wealthiest municipalities in the US, declares bankruptcy after the county treasurer loses $1.5 billion investing in risky derivatives and pleads guilty to six felony charges.

workshops on offer. Leisure activities like in-line skating, skateboarding, snowboarding and mountain biking all originated in California too. Be careful what you laugh at: from pet rocks to soy burgers, SoCal's flavor of the month is often next year's global trend.

Growing Pains into the 21st Century

In 1997 the Heaven's Gate UFO-millennialist cult brought unwanted publicity to the upscale gated community of Rancho Santa Fe, a San Diego suburb, when leader Marshall Applewhite convinced 38 followers to commit ritual suicide.

The internet revolution, spurred by Silicon Valley up north near San Francisco, rewired California's entire economy and led to a 1990s boom in overspeculated stocks. When the bubble burst in 2000, plunging the entire state's economy into chaos, deregulation of the electricity market led to rolling blackouts and sky-high power bills. In a controversial recall election, Californians voted to give action-movie star Arnold Schwarzenegger (Republican) a shot at fixing things in 2003.

Five years later, the meltdown on Wall Street and the US recession caused another staggering financial crisis that has taken California, led by once-again Governor Jerry Brown (Democrat), several years to recover from. Meanwhile, ballistic population growth, pollution and gridlocked traffic continue to cloud SoCal's sunny skies, the need for public education and prison reform builds, and the conundrum of immigration from Mexico, which fills a critical cheap-labor shortage, remains unsolved.

2003

Arnold Schwarzenegger announces his Republican candidacy for governor on *The Tonight Show with Jay Leno*. In October's recall election, he wins by 1.3 million votes.

2005

Antonio Villaraigosa elected mayor of LA, the first Latino to hold that office since 1872. Born poor in East LA, he says in his victory speech, 'I will never forget where I came from.'

2007

Wildfires sweep across drought-stricken Southern California. One million people evacuate their homes between Santa Barbara and San Diego. Extreme drought returns just three years later.

2013

Proposition 8, a state constitutional ban on same-sex marriage that was narrowly approved by voters in 2008, is struck down after legal wrangling. Same-sex marriages resume in California.

The Lifestyle

In the Southern California of the dream world, you wake up, have your shot of wheatgrass juice and roll down to the beach while the surf's up. Lifeguards wave as they go jogging by in their bathing suits. You skateboard down the boardwalk to your yoga class, where everyone admires your downward dog. A food truck pulls up with your favorite: sustainable fish tacos with organic mango chipotle salsa. But honestly, can you really make that SoCal dream come true?

Regional Identity

Southern California is America at its extremes, with all the good and bad that this entails. Its people are among the nation's richest and poorest, most established and newest arrivals, most refined and roughest, most beautiful and most plain, most erudite and most airheaded. Success here can be spectacular, failure equally so.

What binds the residents of this region together is that they are seekers. Nearly everyone – or their forebears – arrived in Southern California by choice. Whether from across the country, across the border or across the globe, they were drawn here by a dream, be it fame on the silver screen; sand, surf and sun; making a splash in business or research; or earning cash to send home to family. It's as if America's dreamers all rushed west and stopped where the continent ran out of land. They found plenty of company on these sun-kissed shores.

SoCal inventions include the space shuttle, Mickey Mouse, whitening toothpaste, the hula hoop (or at least its trademark), Barbie, skateboard and surfboard technology, the Cobb salad and the fortune cookie.

The Stereotypes

Valley girls snap chewing gum in shopping malls, surfer boys shout 'Dude!' across San Diego beaches, new immigrants gather on street corners in search of day jobs, surgically enhanced babes sip mojitos

LIFE AS AN ANGELENO *AMY BALFOUR*

Just who lives in LA? If you believe the stereotypes, they're a flaky bunch. Liberal. Self-absorbed. Greedy. Botoxed and blow-dried. Though these adjectives may have a hint of truth for certain subgroups, with nearly four million people crammed into the city's 465 sq miles and almost 10 million jostling for space in sprawling LA County, no single label fits all.

How is LA's ethnic diversity playing out in the early 21st century? Simmering issues of distrust linger between various communities but day-to-day life isn't quite as bleak as portrayed in Paul Haggis' 2005 Oscar-winning *Crash*. The main problem? People are quick to demand respect but slow to give it out. The town also runs high on false friendliness and let's-do-lunch superficiality; there's a bit more 'I' and 'me' than 'we' and 'us.'

Angelenos aren't all bad. Optimism, open-mindedness and outside-the-box thinking are the norm (studio execs excluded), and people tend to work hard. From undocumented immigrants on the corner ready for a long day's work to Hollywood assistants holding dreary day jobs while cramming their free hours with indie film projects, everybody's hustling. Griffith Park might be in flames and the ground shaking under our feet, but if it's not blocking traffic, get out of the way. Yes, our reach may sometimes exceed our grasp, but isn't that what LA is for?

poolside, rail-thin Orange County soccer moms in urban assault vehicles flip out in rush-hour traffic, and everyone works in 'the Industry' (film and TV entertainment, that is).

Southern Californians roll their eyes at these stereotypes: they didn't create NASA's Jet Propulsion Lab and almost half the world's movies by slacking off. According to a recent Cambridge University study, creativity, imagination and intellectualism are all defining characteristics of Californians, compared with inhabitants of other US states.

Mike Davis' *City of Quartz* (1990) is an excoriating history of LA and a glimpse into its possible future; in *Ecology of Fear* (1998), he examines the decay of the natural environment in the LA Basin. Davis and collaborators also examined San Diego's underbelly in *Under the Perfect Sun: The San Diego Tourists Never See* (2003).

The Reality

As with everything in SoCal, if you're looking for the stereotype, that's what you'll find. But keep your eyes open and you'll find that reality is a lot more complex and interesting.

In LA the first question you'll often hear from locals is 'What do you do for a living?' This is how people place each other and, unlike many other places in the country, nobody here is very surprised if the answer takes more than a minute. There's nothing unusual about waiting tables, for example, while working toward your dream job as an actor or screenwriter. The second question you might hear is 'Where are you from?' because most people here seem to have come from somewhere else.

Hollywood-esque 'happy talk' trickles down to daily interactions, sometimes to the point that people from other places can have trouble understanding what locals mean. Saying someone has 'issues' is a polite way of implying that the person has problems. 'Let's get together' is often not to be taken literally; it can actually mean 'It was great talking with you, and now I have to go.'

Then there's the car you drive. There's an underlying truth to the stereotype that owning the right car in SoCal is what the right shoes are to Italians. Fancy imports, convertibles and muscle cars still turn heads, but the status symbol *du jour* is an ecofriendly hybrid or electric plug-in car. Angeleno hipsters, even those with means, are increasingly forgoing cars entirely and moving to neighborhoods like Downtown LA and Hollywood that can be accessed by subway, bus and bike. The high-rise condos of downtown San Diego are another burgeoning urban scene.

Beach Life

Some 80% of Californians live near the coast rather than inland, even though most can only afford to rent their housing rather than own. Beach culture colors the region in ways both subtle and in-your-face, but which beach you're at determines exactly which subculture we're talking about.

Riptionary (www.riptionary.com), the world's most definitive online lexicon of surfer slang, will help you translate stuff like 'The big mama is fully mackin' some gnarly grinders!'.

LA's Venice used to be the definitive hippie beach. Despite hippie-unfriendly real estate prices, some of that aesthetic remains on its boardwalk, a mile-and-a-half-long party of street performers, merchants and artists. Neighboring Santa Monica is wealthier, more sanitized and preferred by many families.

For cinematic views, visit the public beaches of Malibu, La Jolla or Santa Barbara, all wealthy enclaves farther afield. For surf culture, hit Orange County's Huntington Beach or San Clemente, and San Diego's Mission Beach, Pacific Beach, Encinitas or Oceanside.

Take note: beachwear is appropriate for Southern California's coastal strip, but not in the rest of LA. 'No shoes, no shirt, no service' signs appear in establishments all over town.

LA vs SoCal

Or rather, SoCal vs LA. Usually LA goes about its business and the rest of the region either depends on or resents it. You can see this in politics, for starters. LA leans to the left – often there is no Republican candidate for mayor – and its politicians carry significant weight in Washington DC. However, much of the rest of SoCal tends to behave more like a 'red' (Republican) state.

Generally speaking, the further from the coast, the more conservative: the city of Santa Barbara votes 'blue' (Democrat), but inland Santa Barbara County votes red. A big exception is Orange County, a largely conservative stronghold with firebrand congressional representatives. In Orange County we've heard progressive views met with 'Well, that's LA talking.' However, things are changing even there, as Democrats take over long-held Republican seats in the US Congress. Conservative politics extend to San Diego and the desert areas, largely because of the high numbers of military personnel and wealthy retirees who live there.

And then there's the rest of California. Angelenos visiting San Francisco are often greeted with 'Ugh!', 'How can you live there?!', 'That place is a hellhole!' and worse, and much of the interior of the state reviles LA for having 'stolen' its water. We wouldn't call any of this a rivalry, though, as these attitudes seem to be one-way. Angelenos generally like the rest of the state (yes, even San Francisco) or are just too busy to notice.

Majorities & Minorities

Even among the settlers who founded LA in 1781, there were different races and nationalities. Today LA is one of only two major metro areas in the nation without a majority ethnic group (the other is Honolulu). Across Southern California, immigrants from over 140 countries have put down roots, creating the largest populations of Mexicans, Koreans, Armenians, Filipinos, Salvadorans, Guatemalans and Vietnamese outside their home countries, as well as America's largest ethnic Cambodian, Japanese and Persian communities.

All this makes LA one of the most tolerant, cosmopolitan and open-minded societies anywhere in the USA. Although there are many monoethnic-dominated neighborhoods, it's not uncommon to interact with people of many ethnicities in a single day in any corner of the city. You might drop off your shirts with a Korean-run dry cleaner, have your nails done by a recent Vietnamese immigrant, pick up groceries from a Mexican grocer and a treat from the Cambodian-run doughnut shop. Dinner might just as easily be sushi, falafel, enchiladas or steak-frites, or maybe you'll be digging into plates of pad Thai while a Thai Elvis impersonator sings 'You Ain't Nothing but a Hound Dog.'

Certainly, LA's explosive race-related incidents have received high-profile exposure, as with the riots of 1965 and again in 1992. Yet day-to-day civility is the norm. Animosity is hard to maintain when you

DAMN THAT TRAFFIC JAM!

Traffic is LA's great leveler. Outsiders often marvel that it's a city without a center. That's less true than it used to be thanks to Downtown LA's redevelopment, but it's also more true in that business districts are widely dispersed. So while you could once count on traffic into Downtown in the morning and outbound in the evening, now traffic jams can happen any time of day or night. Or you might just as easily find the roads mysteriously clear. That same unpredictability applies to most other places in SoCal too.

Subway and light-rail lines have been extended of late, and long-range regional plans call for even more. For now, Angelenos advise to double the time you think it will take to get anywhere (triple at rush hour), take your cell phone (with a hands-free headset – it's the law), and should you get stuck in traffic, try to be Zen about it. Those waiting for you at your destination will understand: you can blame traffic for being late every time.

encounter people of so many different ethnic backgrounds on a daily basis. Interracial couples and families barely raise an eyebrow here.

Latino SoCal

In his column '¡Ask a Mexican!', *OC Weekly* columnist Gustavo Arellano tackles such questions as why Mexicans swim with their clothes on, alongside weighty social issues involving immigrants' rights. Read it at www.ocweekly.com.

One of every four US immigrants lands in California, with the largest segment coming from Mexico, followed by Central America. Almost half of LA County's residents are Latino, according to recent US Census figures, and they are projected to soon become the outright majority.

The collective influence of Latinos on SoCal life is huge. Spanish is the *lingua franca* in many restaurant kitchens, and there are a host of Latino products on the shelves of mainstream supermarkets. Even non-Latino Angelenos can expound on different mole sauces and the advantages of corn versus flour tortillas. From Spanish-language billboards to radio and TV stations, you'll see, hear and experience Latino culture all over SoCal.

Despite their numbers, Latinos had little say in leadership until fairly recently. LA's current mayor has Latino roots, as do members of LA's city council and powerful county board of supervisors, as well as many representatives in the California State Assembly and US Congress from across SoCal. Immigration, both legal and otherwise, is always a hot-button issue, and May Day (May 1) has become the de facto time for an immigration reform rally and deportation protests in Downtown LA.

Perhaps somewhat surprisingly, San Diego is more homogeneous (read: Caucasian) than LA, despite being closer to the border with Mexico. That said, the most recent US census showed the percentage of non-white San Diego County residents now exceeds 50%.

SoCal's Other Ethnic Groups

Historically speaking, Southern California's Chinatowns, Japantowns and other ethnic neighborhoods were often the result of segregationist sentiment, rather than choice. While equal opportunity may now be a shared goal, in practice it's very much still a work in progress. Even racially integrated areas can still be quite segregated by ethnic group in terms of income and language.

CALIFORNIA'S BORDERLAND WITH MEXICO

Estimates put the number of undocumented immigrants in the USA at around 11.5 million people (per Department of Homeland Security estimates for 2011). About a quarter of these unauthorized immigrants live in California, with the majority performing low-paying work such as farm and domestic labor, construction and food service.

The equation is simple: for over a generation, the search for economic opportunity has driven Mexican laborers north to earn money for relatives back home. Remittances from these workers nationwide were about $20 billion in 2013, accounting for almost 2% of Mexico's GDP. On the US side of the border, increasingly vocal opposition has put pressure on lawmakers to do something about immigrants who have entered illegally, leading to hundreds of miles of border fence patrolled by National Guard troops.

Although immigration is under federal control, states have increasingly taken immigration issues into their own hands, with controversial laws preventing undocumented immigrants from obtaining public education and social services, for example. Some of these laws are even more restrictive, such as a 2010 bill in California's neighboring state of Arizona that allowed police to ask for proof of citizenship from anyone suspected of being there illegally.

The recent US recession and laws like these have slowed but hardly stopped immigration. Perhaps the only lasting solution will be for the Mexican economy to reach something like economic parity with the US economy. One visit to Tijuana, a short walk across the border from San Diego County, will tell you there's still a ways to go.

LA's Koreatown is the largest, a vast swath between Hollywood (where you'll find the USA's first Thai Town) and Downtown LA (home of Little Tokyo, one of no fewer than three Japanese neighborhoods in LA). These days Downtown LA's Chinatown offers as much Vietnamese *pho* (soup) as Chinese dim sum, while the real center of contemporary Chinese immigration to SoCal has moved east of LA to the suburban San Gabriel Valley towns of Alhambra, Monterey Park and San Gabriel, where Chinese signage is almost as prevalent as English.

Meanwhile, West LA's Venice Blvd is home to Brazilian cuisine and music, the mayor of Beverly Hills is Swedish American, West Hollywood has a large Russian immigrant contingent, and it's not uncommon to see black-hatted Orthodox Jews walking to synagogue in the Fairfax and Pico-Robertson districts. Armenians form the largest ethnic group in Glendale, Signal Hill near Long Beach is home to a Cambodian community, Cerritos and Artesia (near the border of LA and Orange Counties) are a center for South Asian immigration, and Croatian seafarers made their home in the southern LA port town of San Pedro.

Over 200 different languages are spoken in California, with Spanish, Chinese, Tagalog, Persian and German in the top 10. Almost 40% of state residents speak a language other than English at home.

San Diego honors the heritage of its Portuguese fisherfolk in the Point Loma neighborhood. San Diego also has SoCal's only Little Italy, bursting with cafes and restaurants. Little Saigon, in the inland Orange County towns of Garden Grove and Westminster, has the largest population of ethnic Vietnamese outside Vietnam; many of its residents emigrated around the end of the Vietnam War, and the population tends to be vocally opposed to the current Vietnamese regime. In Anaheim's Little Arabia district, even some non-Muslim restaurants serve halal meat.

Gay & Lesbian SoCal

From Palm Springs to San Diego's bohemian Hillcrest neighborhood, arty Laguna Beach and the hip neighborhoods of Silver Lake and West Hollywood (WeHo) in LA, SoCal's LGBTQ community is out and proud. High-profile gay men, lesbians and transgender people can be found at all levels of society, from government to business and the arts. *Advocate* magazine, PFLAG (Parents, Friends and Family of Lesbians and Gays) and America's first gay church and synagogue all started in LA.

In 2008 the Supreme Court of California ruled that gay and lesbian couples had the same right to marry as heterosexual couples. Over the next several months, some 18,000 same-sex couples were married in the state. The court ruling was overturned in November 2008 when, in a statewide ballot measure known as Proposition 8, the state constitution was amended to specify that marriage had to be between one man and one woman. Prop 8 eventually became the subject of multiple court challenges, whose outcomes, like so much else that originates in California, were expected to have national implications.

So what happened? In 2010 US District Court Judge Vaughn Walker struck down Prop 8 as unconstitutional. A court case challenging that decision eventually reached the US Supreme Court, which on June 26, 2013 decided by a narrow 5-4 margin not to overturn Walker's ruling. Amid celebrations by many, same-sex marriages resumed in California.

Religion: Old & New

Although SoCal residents are less churchgoing than the US mainstream, and one in five professes no religion at all, this region remains one of the world's most religiously diverse. Thanks to SoCal's freewheeling reputation and attitudes, religious tolerance is (mostly) the rule here.

LA is home to the nation's largest Roman Catholic archdiocese and the second-largest Jewish community in North America, with members of almost every Protestant denomination also well represented. The world's second-largest Mormon temple is in the West LA neighborhood

SCIENTOLOGY

The controversial LA-based Church of Scientology follows beliefs articulated by L Ron Hubbard in his book *Dianetics: The Modern Science of Mental Health* (1950). Scientology's celebrity followers include Tom Cruise, John Travolta, Beck, Kirstie Alley, TV host Greta Van Susteren and the late Isaac Hayes.

According to the church's website, following the methods of Dianetics 'increases sanity, intelligence, confidence and well-being' and removes 'unwanted sensations, unpleasant emotions and psychosomatic ills that block one's life and happiness.' The church famously opposes psychiatry and all psychotropic (mind-altering) drugs.

of Westwood, while another spectacular Mormon temple towers over the I-5 Fwy near La Jolla, in San Diego County. SoCal also has the largest community of Buddhists outside of Asia. Some mainstream faiths are also politically powerful, a few controversially so as with the Catholic church's sex-abuse scandal and Mormon support for Proposition 8, which attempted to ban same-sex marriage in California.

Southern California has thousands of believers in Santeria, a fusion of Catholicism and Yoruba beliefs first practiced by West African slaves in the Caribbean and South America. Drop by a *botànica* (herbal folk medicine shop) for charms and candles.

Orange County is famously one of the USA's bastions of ultra conservative, evangelical Christianity, with well-known televangelists Pastor Rick Warren of Saddleback Church and the Schuller family of the *Hour of Power* show formerly broadcast from the Crystal Cathedral, which was sold to the Catholic church in 2012.

Other offshoots of mainstream religions include the yogic Self-Realization Fellowship, with large centers in Pacific Palisades and the San Diego County beach town of Encinitas. Despite a federal government investigation into its financial accounting practices, West LA's Kabbalah Centre has seen many celebrity practitioners of its version of Jewish mysticism.

Southern California has also long been a breeding ground for religious cults, which have sometimes become violent and taken over news headlines. Most infamously, the UFO-millennialist cult Heaven's Gate was based in a mansion in northern San Diego County, where 38 members committed mass suicide in 1997.

Sports & Fitness

Southern California's outdoor lifestyle has made it a mecca for fitness buffs since early days. Starting with Muscle Beach in Venice, SoCal residents visit the gym with almost religious fervor. Marathons in LA and San Diego are major civic events. No matter where you are in SoCal, you'll never be too far of a drive from mountains for hiking, biking, climbing or horseback riding.

SoCal's Spectator Sports

LA's sports teams have long and often successful histories, but they're also known as much for their celebrity quotient on and off the court or field as for their undeniable athletic prowess.

The Los Angeles Lakers basketball team plays at Downtown LA's Staples Center, where you can watch the game alongside such famous fans as Jack Nicholson, Penny Marshall and Leonardo DiCaprio. On the court, the Lakers' roster of fabled players has included household names such as Kareem Abdul-Jabbar, Magic Johnson, Shaquille O'Neal and current star Kobe Bryant. The NBA's Los Angeles Clippers, who have been on quite a winning streak recently, also play at the Staples Center, as do the Los Angeles Kings, who have won two National Hockey League (NHL) Stanley Cup championships in the last few years.

The Brooklyn Dodgers baseball team became the Los Angeles Dodgers in 1958, and New Yorkers have never quite forgiven LA for that. Ringed by hills, Dodger Stadium is one of the most beautiful in baseball, even if the team's most recent news headlines include an ugly, tabloid-fodder divorce between its former owners and occasionally violent confrontations between fans. San Diego's Petco Park is the gorgeous home of the San Diego Padres. In Orange County, you can watch the awkwardly named Los Angeles Angels of Anaheim, as well as the equally oddly named Anaheim Ducks of the NHL.

SoCal's only professional football team is the San Diego Chargers. In LA, the big tickets are for college sports, particularly crosstown rivals the UCLA Bruins and the recently scandal-plagued USC Trojans. LA's long-neglected Major League Soccer (MLS) team, the Galaxy, got a boost with the 2007 arrival of icon David Beckham and his $250 million price tag, but his on-and-off Galaxy career through 2012 was less than stellar.

Fans of the Los Angeles Dodgers are (in)famous for leaving during the 8th inning in order to beat traffic exiting Dodger Stadium.

Del Mar Racetrack in northern San Diego County is the ritziest of SoCal's horse-racing tracks, while LA County's historic Santa Anita Racetrack featured in the classic Marx Brothers movie *A Day at the Races* (1937) and the short-lived HBO series *Luck*. The roaring Grand Prix, a Formula 1 race, takes over the streets of Long Beach every April.

Surfing, Skating & Extreme Sports

Surfing first hit the US mainland in 1914, when Irish-Hawaiian surfer George Freeth gave demonstrations at Huntington Beach in Orange County. It has been Surf City USA ever since, with professional wave-riding competitions taking place every year, including the US Open of Surfing in July. Other surf competitions take place in Carlsbad and Oceanside in northern San Diego County, and at Trestles (San Clemente) and San Onofre State Beach in southern Orange County.

Back on the sand, beach volleyball, which originated in Santa Monica during the 1920s, has become an Olympic sport. Pro beach volleyball tournaments happen every summer in LA's South Bay, as well as at beaches in Orange County and San Diego.

Extreme sports in SoCal go back to the 1970s when skateboarders on the Santa Monica–Venice border honed their craft by breaking into dry swimming pools in the backyards of mansions (the 2005 film *Lords of Dogtown* chronicles the rise of the Z-Boys). Extreme sports deities Tony Hawk and Shaun White, both professional skateboarders and X Games champs, hail from San Diego County.

As Seen on TV (& Film)

Imagine living in a world without Orson Welles whispering 'Rosebud,' Judy Garland clicking her sparkly red heels three times or the Terminator threatening 'I'll be back.' LA is where iconic images like these are hatched onto the big screen. But Tinseltown is about more than just movies. Every other car commercial seems to be shot in Downtown LA, and county-wide locations have become backdrops for TV series. The upshot: few people come to LA without seeing something – or someone – they recognize.

The Industry in LA & Beyond

Palm Springs became a favorite getaway of Hollywood stars in the mid-20th century partly because its distance from LA (just under 100 miles) was as far as they could travel under their restrictive studio contracts.

From almost the very moment that film – and later TV – became the USA's dominant entertainment medium, LA took center stage in the world of popular culture and has stood there ever since. It's also been the best (and sometimes the worst) ambassador for Southern California and the rest of the USA to the world.

You might know it as TV and movie entertainment, but to Angelenos it's simply the 'Industry.' It all began in the humble orchards of Hollywoodland, where entrepreneurial moviemakers – most of them European immigrants – established studios in the first decade of the 20th century. German-born Carl Laemmle opened Universal City Studios in 1915; Polish immigrant Samuel Goldwyn joined with Cecil B DeMille a year earlier to form Paramount Studios; and Jack Warner and his brothers arrived a few years later from Poland via Canada.

SoCal's sunny weather (over 315 days of sunshine per year) meant that most outdoor scenes could be easily shot here, and moviemaking flourished. What's more, the proximity of the Mexican border enabled filmmakers to rush their equipment to safety when challenged by the collection agents of patent holders such as Thomas Edison. Fans loved early resident LA film stars such as Charlie Chaplin and Harold Lloyd, and the first big Hollywood wedding occurred in 1920 when Douglas Fairbanks wed Mary Pickford.

Although Hollywood became the cultural and financial hub of the movie industry by the 1920s, it's a myth that most production ever took place there. Of the major studios, only Paramount Pictures is in Hollywood proper, albeit surrounded by block after block of production-related businesses including lighting and post-production. The first big

RUNAWAY FILM & TV PRODUCTION

Entertainment is big business in LA County, lassoing $47 billion in revenue and ranking third in employment behind tourism and international trade. But the high cost of filming in SoCal has sent location scouts looking elsewhere too. States such as New Mexico, North Carolina, Louisiana and Connecticut temptingly offer production credits, tax incentives, state-of-the-art facilities and, in some cases, nonunionized workforces. In Canada, film production is welcomed with open arms – and pocketbooks – from Vancouver to Toronto, Montréal and beyond.

movie palaces were not located on Hollywood Blvd, but on Broadway in Downtown LA.

Most movie studios shot elsewhere around LA, in Culver City (MGM, now Sony Pictures), Studio City (Universal Studios) and Burbank (Disney and Warner Bros). Moviemaking hasn't been limited to LA either. Founded in 1910, the American Film Company (aka Flying 'A' Studios) filmed first in San Diego and then Santa Barbara, pushing out box-office hits. Balboa Studios in Long Beach was another major silent-film-era dream factory.

Although LA sometimes feels like a company town, the Los Angeles Economic Development Council reports that in 2012 only some 162,000 people in LA County were employed directly in film, TV and radio production. That doesn't tell the whole story, though, because the Industry indirectly supports over a half million jobs across LA County, from high-powered attorneys to cater-waiters.

For stargazers or movie buffs, LA is still *the* place for a pilgrimage. You can tour major movie studios, line up alongside the red carpet for an awards ceremony, be part of a live studio audience, attend a high-wattage film festival, shop at boutiques favored by today's hottest stars and see where celebs live, eat, drink and party in real life.

SoCal on the Silver Screen

Critics and cinephiles have written volumes about Hollywood movies, and at any time of the day or night in SoCal you can just turn on the TV for the latest entertainment news and celeb gossip. To put you in an LA mood, here's a rundown of movies featuring the City of Angels – in some cases almost as a character in itself.

Classic LA Movies

Perhaps the greatest film set in LA is Roman Polanski's *Chinatown* (1974), about the city's early-20th-century water wars. *The Bad and the Beautiful* (1952) takes a hard look at film biz, with Lana Turner recalling the exploits of an aggressive, egotistic film producer played by Kirk Douglas. In David O Selznick's *A Star Is Born* (1937), Janet Gaynor plays a woman rising to stardom as her movie-star husband declines in popularity; later remakes starred Judy Garland and Barbra Streisand.

The most memorable of James Dean's scenes in *Rebel Without a Cause* (1955) takes place above LA in Griffith Park. In *The Graduate* (1967), Dustin Hoffman and Anne Bancroft play a game of nihilism, floundering and seduction in 1960s Pasadena. Based on James Ellroy's neo-noir novel, *LA Confidential* (1997) deftly portrays the violent world of deals, sexual betrayal and double-crossing by cops during the crime-ridden 1950s.

MILESTONES IN SOCAL FILM HISTORY

1913

The first full-length feature Hollywood movie, a silent Western drama called *The Squaw Man,* is shot by director Cecil B DeMille.

1915

Universal City Studios (now Universal Studios Hollywood) opens, charging visitors 25¢ including lunch to watch movies being made.

1927

The first talkie, *The Jazz Singer,* ends the silent-film era. Sid Grauman opens his Chinese Theatre in Hollywood, where stars have been leaving their handprints ever since.

1928

The first Academy Awards ceremony takes place. A cartoonist named Walt Disney releases *Steamboat Willie,* the first animated short with fully synchronized sound, starring a mouse named Mickey.

1939

The Wizard of Oz is the first wide-release movie to be shown in full color. Nonetheless, it loses the Oscar for Best Picture to *Gone with the Wind*. Both were filmed in Culver City.

1950s

On a witch hunt for Communists, the federal House Un-American Activities Committee investigates and blacklists many Hollywood actors, directors and screenwriters, some of whom leave for Europe.

Contemporary Films about LA

Robert Altman's *Short Cuts* (1993) weaves together several stories by Raymond Carver, showing a sadly depraved Los Angeles. Another dispiriting, multistory tale told by an award-winning ensemble is the drama *Crash* (2005). In Joel Schumacher's *Falling Down* (1993), Michael Douglas plays an unemployed defense worker for whom a traffic jam triggers a war with the world. Quentin Tarantino, in Chandleresque fashion, creates a surreal Los Angeles from the bottom up in *Pulp Fiction* (1994).

During the 1930s, '40s and '50s, many famous literary figures (including F Scott Fitzgerald, Dorothy Parker, Truman Capote and William Faulkner) did stints as Hollywood screenwriters.

Gritty city tales include *Stand and Deliver* (1988), based on a true story, about a take-no-prisoners LA high-school teacher who successfully teaches college-level calculus to Latino gang members. John Singleton's tragic *Boyz n the Hood* (1991) stars Cuba Gooding Jr and offers a major reality check on coming-of-age as a black teenager in the inner city. In *Freedom Writers* (2007), Hilary Swank plays a Long Beach high-school teacher whose students work out their feelings about race and their personal hardships through writing.

In David Lynch's surrealist *Mulholland Drive* (2001), an amnesiac woman (played by Naomi Watts) tries to put her life back together through encounters with weird and terrifying people on various edges of dark LA mindscapes. *Laurel Canyon* (2002) shows another strange view of life in LA: a young psychiatrist (Christian Bale) and his fiancée return to live with his pot-smoking mother (Frances McDormand), who's producing her latest boy toy's rock-and-roll record.

Three of Paul Thomas Anderson's films have come to be called the 'Valley Trilogy' for their San Fernando Valley locations: *Boogie Nights* (1997) starred Mark Wahlberg as prodigiously endowed porn star Dirk Diggler; *Magnolia* (1999) brought together mega-stars including Tom Cruise, Julianne Moore and Philip Seymour Hoffman in a tale of interwoven family dramas; and the darkly romantic *Punch-Drunk Love* (2002)followed Adam Sandler's character overcoming anger management issues.

SOCAL'S TOP FILM FESTIVALS

Besides churning out blockbuster movies, SoCal hosts dozens of high-powered film festivals every year. The following faves are worth planning your trip around (check online for schedules and ticket info):

AFI Fest (www.afi.com/afifest) One of the most influential festivals in the country presents top-notch films by newbies and masters from around the world in November. *Monster*, Steven Spielberg's *Lincoln* and other Academy Award winners premiered here.

Los Angeles Film Festival (www.lafilmfest.com) This June festival corrals the best indie movies from around the world – from shorts and music videos to full-length features and documentaries.

Outfest (www.outfest.org) The largest continuous film fest in SoCal, this 30-year-old celluloid celebration in July screens more than 200 shorts, films and videos by and about the LGBTQ community.

Palm Springs International Film Festival (www.psfilmfest.org) Founded in 1990 by then-mayor Sonny Bono, this balmy January festival is getting more glam every year. It's an intimate yet star-studded affair with almost 200 films from 60 countries.

Newport Beach Film Festival (www.newportbeachfilmfest.com; ⊙mid-Apr) The buzz surrounding this competition, with 400 films over eight days in late April and early May, has been increasing steadily since Oscar-winner *Crash* premiered here in 2005.

Santa Barbara International Film Festival (http://sbiff.org) For almost three decades, this festival has featured independent films from around the US and abroad, with stars such as Martin Scorsese and Leonardo DiCaprio walking the red carpet.

LA Comedies

Tony Richardson's outrageously sardonic *The Loved One* (1965), based on an Evelyn Waugh novel about the funeral industry, stars Sir John Gielgud and Liberace (the latter as a huckstering mortician). Cameron Crowe wrote *Fast Times at Ridgemont High* (1982), which launched the careers of Sean Penn, Jennifer Jason Leigh, Nicolas Cage and Forest Whitaker among others, about students at a fictional San Fernando Valley high school. *Bill & Ted's Excellent Adventure* (1989) turned Keanu Reeves and Alex Winter into time-traveling San Gabriel Valley teen slackers.

The '90s produced some classic LA comedies. Steve Martin's *LA Story* (1991) hilariously parodiesaspects of LA life, from lattes to colonics. Julia Roberts became a screen queen for playing the definitive LA hooker with a heart of gold in Garry Marshall's rom-com (romantic comedy) *Pretty Woman* (1990). *Clueless* (1995) starred Alicia Silverstone as a spoiled Beverly Hills teenager in an update of the novel *Emma* by Jane Austen. *Swingers* (1996) was Vince Vaughn's breakout film as a Hollywood hipster, coining the word 'money' as a compliment and bringing 'Vegas, baby, Vegas!' into the lexicon.

More recently, LA has been the backdrop for the merry band of comedic actors led by director Judd Apatow in *The 40-Year-Old Virgin* (2005), starring Steve Carrell, and *Knocked Up* (2007) with Seth Rogen and Katherine Heigl. Directed by Marc Webb, *(500) Days of Summer* (2009), pairing Joseph Gordon-Levitt and Zooey Deschanel, is not a love story but a funny story about love – and architecture – in Downtown LA.

SoCal Movies Beyond LA

In *Orange County* (2002), screenwriter Mike White gives a humorous snapshot of SoCal pop culture: a surfer tries to get into Stanford University and escape his oddball family, including his brother (played by Jack Black). In Nancy Meyers' comedy *It's Complicated* (2009), Meryl Streep, Alec Baldwin and Steve Martin get up to romantic shenanigans in the ritzy Santa Barbara suburb of Montecito. Ask any oenophile about the wacky indie flick *Sideways* (2004), and you'll get an earful about Santa Barbara's wine country and Paul Giamatti.

The most famous film shot in San Diego was *Some Like it Hot* (1959), starring Marilyn Monroe, Jack Lemmon and Tony Curtis, in which the iconic Hotel del Coronado served as a stand-in for Florida. In addition to classics such as Tony Scott's *Top Gun* (1986), starring a young Tom Cruise, Val Kilmer and Kelly McGillis, modern box-office hits shot in San Diego include *Almost Famous* (2000), Steven Soderbergh's *Traffic* (2000), *Bring it On* (2000) with Kirsten Dunst and *Bruce Almighty* (2003) starring Jim Carrey.

1960

The Hollywood Walk of Fame debuts on Hollywood Blvd. Among the first celebs to be inaugurated with a pink star are Joanne Woodward and Burt Lancaster.

1970s

The San Fernando Valley (aka 'Silicone Valley') becomes home base to the USA's adult-film industry, eventually producing almost 90% of the USA's legal pornographic movies.

1975

The age of the modern blockbuster begins with the thriller *Jaws*, directed by a young filmmaker named Steven Spielberg whose string of box-office hits include *E.T.* and *Jurassic Park*.

1999

Independent, low-budget horror film *The Blair Witch Project* inaugurates the era of viral internet marketing, successfully racking up almost $250 million dollars in profit worldwide.

2001

In the Hollywood & Highland high-rise complex on revitalized Hollywood Blvd, the Kodak (now Dolby) Theatre becomes the permanent home of the Academy Awards ceremony.

2009

Sci-fi fantasy *Avatar* becomes the highest grossing movie of all time, making close to $3 billion and beating out the previous record holder, *Titanic* (1997), also directed by James Cameron.

HOLLYWOOD ON HOLLYWOOD

Hollywood likes nothing better than to turn the camera around and make movies about itself. Self-indulgent? Maybe, but often very entertaining.

Sunset Boulevard (1950) Gloria Swanson plays Norma Desmond, a washed-up silent film star pining for her return, and William Holden plays the screenwriter she hires to make that happen.

Singin' in the Rain (1952) An exuberant musical fairy tale about love in the time of talkies, starring Gene Kelly, Debbie Reynolds and Donald O'Connor.

Silent Movie (1976) Mel Brooks' screwball comedy imagines a director trying to revive a movie studio by producing the first silent film in decades.

Postcards from the Edge (1990) Mike Nichols directs Shirley MacLaine and Meryl Streep as a mother-daughter pair dealing with stardom's seedy underbelly.

Barton Fink (1991) John Turturro and John Goodman engage in a battle of wits over how to write a screenplay in this dark comedy by the Coen Brothers.

The Player (1992) In one of the most accessible films by legendary director Robert Altman, Tim Robbins plays a studio executive who takes his power too far.

Ed Wood (1994) Tim Burton directs Johnny Depp as perhaps the worst director in Hollywood history, who was famous for wearing pink angora sweaters.

Get Shorty (1995) Based on the Elmore Leonard novel, this comedy stars John Travolta as a mafioso who gets entangled in Hollywood and wonders which industry has fewer scruples.

Television

Ever since the first TV station began broadcasting in LA in 1931, iconic images of the city have been beamed into living rooms across America in shows such as *Dragnet* (1950s), *The Beverly Hillbillies* (1960s), *The Brady Bunch* (1970s), *LA Law* (1980s), *Baywatch* and *Melrose Place* (1990s). The teen 'dramedy' (drama comedy) *Beverly Hills 90210* (1990s) made that LA zip code into a status symbol and *The OC* (2000s) glamorized Newport Beach.

SoCal is also a versatile backdrop for edgy cable dramas, starting with HBO's *Six Feet Under,* which examined contemporary LA through the eyes of an eccentric family running a funeral home. Showtime's *Weeds* fictionalized a pot-growing SoCal widow with ties to Mexican drug cartels, while FX's *The Shield* riffed on police corruption in the City of Angels. HBO's *Entourage* portrayed the highs, the lows and the intrigues of the Industry by following a rising young star and his posse. Showtime's *Californication* shows what happens when a successful New York novelist goes Hollywood. For more biting social satire, check out early LA-based seasons of HBO's *Curb Your Enthusiasm* by *Seinfeld* co-creator Larry David, who got Hollywood celebrities to play themselves.

Easily the most famous piece of footage ever shot in Orange County is the opening of the classic *Gilligan's Island* TV series, filmed at Newport Harbor.

If you're a fan of reality TV, you'll glimpse SoCal in an endless variety of shows from *Top Chef* to *The Real Housewives of Orange County,* as well as in MTV's drama-reality hybrid series *Laguna Beach* and *The Hills.*

Music & the Arts

Go ahead: mock. But when Californians thank their lucky stars – or good karma, or the goddess – that they don't live in NYC, they're not only talking about beach weather. Anyone who thinks that LA is all about pop culture hasn't been paying attention. It's one of the country's most prolific – and progressive – generators of music, art and literature of all kinds. What's even better is that SoCal's contemporary arts scene isn't afraid to be completely independent, or even outlandish at times.

Music

The history of music in LA might as well be the history of American music, at least for the last 75 years. Much of the recording industry is based in LA, and the film and TV industries have proven powerful talent incubators. Today's pop princess troublemakers and airbrushed boy bands only rose to stardom thanks to the tuneful revolutions of decades past.

LA Music Radio Stations

KCRW (89.9FM) – eclectic indie music mix

KROQ (106.7FM) – the latest contemporary rock

KRTH (101.1FM) – all-American oldies soundtrack

KPWR (105.9FM) – hip-hop, R&B and club hits

KSCA (101.9FM) – popular regional Mexican tunes

Folk, Swing, Jazz, Blues & Soul

Chronologically speaking, Mexican folk music arrived first in Southern California during the rancho era. But the next big musical thing didn't come along for over a century: swing music. During the 1930s and '40s, big bands sparked a lindy-hopping craze in LA.

California's African American community grew with the 'Great Migration' during WWII's shipping and manufacturing boom, and so the West Coast blues sound was born. Texas-born bluesman T-Bone Walker worked in LA's Central Ave clubs before making hit records of his electric guitar stylings for Capitol Records.

With Beat poets riffing over improvised bass lines and audiences finger-snapping their approval, cool West Coast jazz emerged in the 1950s, including on the Sunset Strip. In the African American cultural hub along LA's Central Ave, the hard bop of Charlie Parker and Charles Mingus kept the jazz scene alive and swinging.

In the 1950s and '60s, doo-wop, rhythm and blues, and soul music were all in steady rotation at nightclubs in South Central LA, considered the 'Harlem of the West.' Soulful singer Sam Cooke ran his own hit-making record label here, attracting soul and gospel talent to LA.

Rock, Pop & Punk

The first homegrown rock-and-roll talent to make it big in the 1950s was Ritchie Valens, born in the San Fernando Valley, whose 'La Bamba' was a rockified version of a Mexican folk song. Dick Dale (aka 'King of the Surf Guitar') started experimenting with reverb effects in Orange County in the 1950s, then topped the charts with his band the Del-Tones in the early '60s, influencing everyone from the Beach Boys to Jimi Hendrix. Dale's recording of 'Miserlou' featured in Tarantino's movie *Pulp Fiction*.

It's hard to say which LA band is the most emblematic of the 1960s: The Doors, the Beach Boys, the Mamas and The Papas, Joni Mitchell, the Byrds or Crosby, Stills & Nash. The epicenter of the 1960s rock movement was LA's Laurel Canyon neighborhood, just uphill from the Sunset Strip and legendary Whisky a Go-Go nightclub, ground zero for the psychedelic rock scene.

The country-influenced pop of Eagles, Jackson Browne and Linda Ronstadt became America's soundtrack for the early 1970s, joined by the Mexican-fusion sounds of Santana and iconic funk bands War, founded in Long Beach, and Sly and the Family Stone, which got their groove on in San Francisco before moving to LA.

The 1980s saw the rise of such influential LA punk and crossover bands as X and Bad Religion (punk), Black Flag (punk/hardcore) and Suicidal Tendencies (hardcore/thrash), while more mainstream all-female bands the Bangles and the Go-Gos, new-wavers Oingo Boingo, and rockers Jane's Addiction and funky Red Hot Chili Peppers took the world by storm. Bangin' out of Hollywood, Guns N' Roses was the '80s hard-rock band of choice. On avant-garde rocker Frank Zappa's 1982 single *Valley Girl,* his 14-year-old daughter Moon Unit taught the rest of America to say 'Omigo-o-od!'.

Waiting for the Sun: A Rock & Roll History of Los Angeles, by Barney Hoskyns, follows the twists and turns of the SoCal music scene from the Beach Boys to Black Flag.

Rap, Hip-Hop & Indie Sounds

Since the 1980s, LA has been a hotbed for West Coast rap and hip-hop. Eazy E, Ice Cube and Dr Dre released the seminal NWA (Niggaz With Attitude) album, *Straight Outta Compton,* in 1989. Death Row Records, cofounded by Dr Dre, has launched megawatt rap talents including Long Beach bad boys Snoop Dog and Warren G. LA rapper Game's 2009 *R.E.D Album* featured an all-star line-up including Dr Dre and Snoop Dogg.

In the 1990s, LA's Linkin Park combined hip-hop with metal and popularized nu metal while alternative rock acts such as Beck and Weezer gained national attention. Another key '90s band was the ska-punk-alt-rock No Doubt, of Orange County (which later launched the solo career of lead singer Gwen Stefani). From East LA, Los Lobos was the king of Chicano (Mexican American) bands, an honor that has since passed to Ozomatli.

SoCal rock stars of the new millennium included the approachable hip-hop of LA's Black Eyed Peas, San Diego alt-rockers Stone Temple Pilots and pop-punksters Blink-182, Orange County's punk band The Offspring and, for better or for worse, whoever wins the season's *American Idol,* the finals of which are held in Downtown LA's Nokia Theatre.

SOCAL MUSIC FESTIVALS

All over SoCal, annual music festivals host a mix of big-name and local acts. Buy tickets early for radio station–sponsored shows. Festivals worth planning a trip around include the following:

Coachella Valley Music & Arts Festival (p345) Sweat it out in the desert in Indio, with indie bands, up-and-comers and the occasional blockbuster star over two weekends in April.

KROQ Almost Acoustic Christmas (www.kroq.com) Winter punk and modern rock event happens every December, currently at the Shrine Auditorium near Expo Park.

KROQ Weenie Roast (www.kroq.com) Alt-rock bands like the the Black Keys, 30 Seconds to Mars and Vampire Weekend perform in Irvine, Orange County, in May or June.

Stagecoach Festival (p345) All things country and western, from Shelby Lynne and Asleep at the Wheel to BBQ, on the weekend after Coachella in Indio.

San Diego IndieFest (www.sandiegoindiefest.com) Three days of independent music and films in mid-August. Acts run the gamut from surf pop, hip-hop and metal to country, folk, jazz and blues.

'THE DUDE' OF THE LA PHIL

In 2009 Gustavo Dudamel, not yet 30 years old, took over as conductor of the Los Angeles Philharmonic from the iconic Finnish conductor-composer Esa-Pekka Salonen, and the city has taken to him *con gusto*. The Venezuelan Dudamel came up musically through El Sistema, that nation's program for creating youth orchestras, culminating with his conducting the Simón Bolívar Youth Orchestra. With his shock of wild, black curls, prodigious energy on the podium and youthful enthusiasm, 'the Dude' has energized LA in a way few thought possible. Just as importantly, he has brought techniques from El Sistema to this city where youth could no doubt use the outlet as much as – if not more than – those in Dudamel's homeland.

Film & TV Scores

John Williams, a frequent collaborator with Steven Spielberg, is perhaps the best known of legions of Hollywood film composers, having created music for *Jaws, Star Wars, Raiders of the Lost Ark, Schindler's List* and *Lincoln,* to name just a few.

The 1950s through 1980s were a golden age for film scores, including works by Elmer Bernstein *(The Magnificent Seven, Ghostbusters),* Bernard Herrmann (*Citizen Kane, Vertigo, Psycho,* the *Twilight Zone* TV series) and Ennio Morricone *(The Good, the Bad & the Ugly, A Fistful of Dollars).*

Present-day soundtrack composers include Randy Newman *(The Natural, Seabiscuit, Toy Story, Cars),* Oingo Boingo cofounder Danny Elfman (*Pee-wee's Big Adventure, Dick Tracy, Edward Scissorhands, Men in Black, The Simpsons* theme) and Marco Beltrami *(The Scream, 3:10 to Yuma, The Hurt Locker).*

You can hear historical and contemporary film music played during the Hollywood Bowl's annual movie night, when a live orchestra accompanies movie clips projected onto a giant screen.

Classical Music

First stop for fans of 'serious music' should be Downtown LA's Walt Disney Concert Hall. It's the home of one of the USA's top symphony orchestras, the LA Philharmonic, under the baton of the young Venezuelan phenom Gustavo Dudamel. The LA Phil's summer home is the Hollywood Bowl, an outdoor venue for classical, jazz and pop performances.

Not to be outdone, Orange County boasts the Segerstrom Center for the Arts in Costa Mesa, with two state-of-the-art concert halls. The San Diego Symphony performs at Copley Symphony Hall and at Embarcadero Marina Park South in summer. In Palm Springs, check the calendar for the Annenberg Theater at the Palm Springs Art Museum.

The Los Angeles Opera, under the artistic direction of Placido Domingo, plays at Music Center in the Dorothy Chandler Pavilion. San Diego also has an active opera company, while the risk-taking Long Beach Opera company stages new and rare works.

The cover of Eagles' album *Hotel California* (1976) shows LA's Beverly Hills Hotel, but the group won't say which hotel actually inspired the title.

Theater

In your Southern California dream you're discovered by a movie talent scout, but most actors actually get their start in theater. Home to about 25% of the nation's professional actors, LA is the second-most influential city in America for theater after NYC.

Spaces to watch around LA include the Geffen Playhouse close to UCLA, the Ahmanson Theatre and Mark Taper Forum in Downtown LA, and the Actors' Gang Theatre, cofounded by actor Tim Robbins, in Culver City. Small theaters flourish in West Hollywood (WeHo) and North

LATINO MURALS IN SOCAL

Beginning in the 1930s, when the federal Works Progress Administration (WPA) sponsored schemes to uplift and beautify cities across the country, murals came to define California cityscapes. Mexican muralists Diego Rivera, David Alfaro Siqueiros and José Clemente Orozco sparked an outpouring of murals across LA that today number in the thousands. Murals gave voice to Chicano pride and protests over US Central American policies since the 1970s, notably in San Diego's Chicano Park and East LA murals by collectives such as East Los Streetscapers, still active today.

For an online directory of contemporary LA murals, including panoramic photos and directions to the sites, visit www.muralconservancy.org.

Hollywood (NoHo), the West Coast's answers to off- and off-off-Broadway. Influential multicultural theaters include Little Tokyo's East West Players. Critically acclaimed outlying companies include Orange County's South Coast Repertory in Costa Mesa.

Visual Arts

A 2006 exhibition at Paris' Pompidou Center called LA an 'Art Capital,' a designation that only surprised folks who haven't spent time here. NYC may be the nation's largest art market, but much of that art is made in LA. Cofounded by Walt Disney in 1961, the California Institute of Arts (CalArts), in the northern LA County suburb of Valencia, is one of the art world's premier schools. Heavy-hitting artists who have taught there include Laurie Anderson, John Baldessari, Jonathan Borofsky, Judy Chicago and Roy Lichtenstein.

To find art museums, art galleries, fine-art exhibition spaces and calendars of upcoming art shows throughout SoCal, check out *ArtScene* (www.artscenecal.com) and *Artweek LA* (www.artweek.la) magazines.

SoCal's contemporary art scene brings together muralist-led social commentary, an obsessive dedication to craft and a new-media milieu pierced by cutting-edge technology. LA's Museum of Contemporary Art (LACMA) puts on provocative and avant-garde shows, as does LA's Broad Contemporary Art Museum, the Museum of Contemporary Art San Diego, Costa Mesa's Orange County Museum of Art and the Santa Barbara Museum of Art. More specialized art museums worth detouring for include Long Beach's Museum of Latin American Art and West LA's Hammer Museum.

To see California-made art at its most experimental, browse the burgeoning gallery scenes in Downtown LA and Culver City. San Diego's Little Italy neighborhood also hosts a growing number of galleries. In Orange County, there are vibrant art scenes in Santa Ana, home of the Bowers Museum, and in the historic artists' colony of Laguna Beach. The latter's annual Festival of Arts is capped by a Pageant of the Masters, in which actors re-create world-famous paintings on stage.

Literature

The entire state has long attracted novelists, poets and storytellers, and today SoCal's literary community is stronger than ever. You've probably already read books by Southern Californians without knowing it: some of the best-known titles by resident writers aren't set in their home state, for example, Ray Bradbury's 1950s dystopian classic *Fahrenheit 451.*

Early 20th-Century Literature

LA sheltered many illustrious foreign writers in the first half of the 20th century, among them British immigrant Aldous Huxley and German authors Bertolt Brecht and Thomas Mann, who resided here after being exiled from their homeland during WWII. Meanwhile, much of the local writing talent always seems to be harnessed to the film industry – even literary luminaries such as F Scott Fitzgerald, William Faulkner, Dorothy Parker and Truman Capote came to LA temporarily to make a living by writing screenplays.

Starting in the 1920s, many novelists looked at LA in political terms, often viewing it unfavorably as the ultimate metaphor for capitalism. Classics in this vein include Upton Sinclair's *Oil!* (1927), a muckraking work of historical fiction with socialist overtones. Aldous Huxley's *After Many A Summer* (1939) is an ironic work based on the life of publisher William Randolph Hearst (also an inspiration for Orson Welles' film *Citizen Kane*). F Scott Fitzgerald's unfinished final novel, *The Last Tycoon* (1940), makes scathing observations about Hollywood's early years by following the life of a movie producer who is slowly working himself to death.

In the 1930s San Francisco and Los Angeles became the capitals of the pulp detective novel, examples of which were often made into noir crime films. The king of hard-boiled crime writers was Raymond Chandler, who thinly disguised his hometown Santa Monica as Bay City.

To learn more about LA's literary scene, listen to the weekly 'Bookworm' talk show on Santa Monica–based radio station KCRW (88.9FM). Download it as a free podcast or listen online at www.kcrw.com.

Late 20th-Century Literature & Beyond

LA fiction's banner year was 1970. Terry Southern's *Blue Movie* dived into the seedy, pornographic side of Hollywood. Joan Didion's *Play It as It Lays* depicted Angelenos with a dry, not-too-kind wit. *Post Office,* by poet-novelist Charles Bukowski, captured the down-and-out side of Downtown LA (Bukowski himself worked at the US Postal Service's Terminal Annex.) *Chicano,* by Richard Vasquez, took a dramatic look at the Latino barrio of East LA.

The 1980s brought the startling revelations of Bret Easton Ellis' *Less Than Zero,* about the cocaine-addled lives of wealthy Beverly Hills teenagers. For a more comedic insight into LA during the go-go '80s, pick up Richard Rayner's *Los Angeles Without a Map,* which follows a British man who gets lost in his Hollywood fantasies while chasing an aspiring actress. Kate Braverman's *Palm Latitudes* traces the intersecting lives of a flamboyant prostitute, a murderous housewife and a worn-out matriarch who maintain their strength and dignity against the backdrop of the violence and machismo of LA's Mexican barrio.

In 1991 Peter Lefcourt chronicled insider Hollywood in his novel *The Deal.* Pulp noir fiction made a comeback in LA in the 1990s. Walter Mosley's famed *Devil in a Blue Dress,* set in the Watts neighborhood of South Central LA, places its hero in impossible situations that test his desire to remain an honest man. James Ellroy's *LA Confidential,* set during the 1950s, delves into sex scandals and police corruption. Elmore Leonard's *Get Shorty* follows a Florida loan shark who moves to SoCal and gets mixed up in the movie industry. All three novels – like many of the neo-noir genre – have translated brilliantly into films.

Contemporary LA novelists to look for include USC English professor TC Boyle, who has written prolifically about the region in novels and short stories, including *The Tortilla Curtain* (1995) and *San Miguel* (2012). Lisa See's *Shanghai Girls* (2009) is set in LA's Chinatown in the 1950s, when anti-communist sentiment was prominent in US politics.

Few writers nail SoCal's culture as well as Joan Didion. In *Where I Was From* (2003) she contrasts California's mythology and reality. Her perceptive essays in *Slouching Toward Bethlehem* (1968) and *The White Album* (1979) narrate the social upheavals of 1960s California with an autobiographical slant.

UCI: SOCAL'S LITERARY INCUBATOR

The writers' programs at the University of California, Irvine in Orange County are consistently rated among the top in the nation. Counted among its graduates are dozens of leading American novelists, including Michael Chabon *(The Amazing Adventures of Kavalier & Klay),* Richard Ford *(Independence Day)* and Alice Sebold *(The Lovely Bones).*

SoCal Architecture

There's more to Southern California's architecture than beach houses and boardwalks. SoCal may also have a reputation for the urban sprawl by which all other sprawl is measured, but look closer and you'll discover – particularly in LA – one of the country's most architecturally dynamic regions. Freely adapting and being inspired by architectural periods and styles from around the world for centuries, SoCal architecture today reveals the element of the unexpected. It was postmodern before the word even existed.

Spanish Missions & Victorian Mansions

The first Spanish missions were built around courtyards, using materials that were at hand: adobe, limestone and grass. Many missions crumbled into disrepair as the church's influence waned and under Mexican rule, but the style remained practical for SoCal's climate. Early American settlers adapted it later into the rancho adobe style, as seen at El Pueblo de Los Angeles in Downtown LA and in San Diego's Old Town.

Once California's mid-19th-century gold rush began, nouveau riche residents built grand mansions marked by ornamental excess in imitation of upper-class East Coast architectural fashions, in turn imported from Europe during the reign of England's Queen Victoria. One of SoCal's finest examples of Victorian whimsy is San Diego's Hotel del Coronado. San Diego's Gaslamp Quarter is also filled with more modest Victorian buildings, as is the Old West mining town of Julian.

California architecture has always had a contrarian streak. Many turn-of-the-20th-century architects rejected the frilly Victorian style and returned to the simpler, classical lines of Spanish designs. Spanish Colonial Revival architecture, also known as Mission Revival style, hearkened back to early California missions with arched doors and windows, long covered porches, fountain courtyards and red-tile roofs. Santa Barbara showcases this style, as do some stately buildings in San Diego's Balboa Park and many SoCal train depots, including in Downtown LA, San Diego and San Juan Capistrano.

Oddball SoCal Architecture

- *Theme Building – LAX Airport*
- *Chiat/Day Building – Venice*
- *Watts Towers – South Central LA*
- *Christ (Crystal) Cathedral – Orange County*
- *Integratron – Near Joshua Tree*
- *Salvation Mountain – By the Salton Sea*

Arts and Crafts & Art Deco Styles

Simplicity and harmony were hallmarks of California's early-20th-century Arts and Crafts style, influenced by Japanese design principles and England's Arts and Crafts Movement. The style's handmade touches marked a deliberate departure from the Industrial Revolution's mechanized design. SoCal architects Charles and Henry Greene popularized this style with their single-story bungalows in Pasadena. Overhanging eaves, airy terraces and sleeping porches formed transitions between, and extensions of, warm wooden interiors into the natural environment.

California was cosmopolitan from the start, and by the early 1920s, the emerging international art deco style made it fashionable to copy earlier architectural periods from around the globe. No style was off-limits: neoclassical, baroque, Moorish, Mayan, Aztec or Egyptian. Downtown LA's Central Library is a prime example of this mishmash of motifs.

When it came to skyscrapers, art deco's vertical lines and symmetry created a soaring effect, often culminating in a stepped pattern toward the top, as in LA's City Hall. Heavy ornamentation, especially above doors and windows, featured flowers, sunbursts and zigzags, as seen in Downtown LA's Eastern Columbia building and West Hollywood's Sunset Tower Hotel.

Streamline moderne, a derivative of art deco, sought to incorporate the machine aesthetic, in particular the aerodynamic look of airplanes and ocean liners. Outstanding examples of this style include the Coca-Cola Building in Downtown LA, the Cross Roads of the World building in Hollywood and the Hotel Shangri-La in Santa Monica.

When Downtown LA's Walt Disney Concert Hall was first built, some of its stainless-steel exterior panels reflected the sun so brightly that drivers were blinded by glare and nearby condos heated up. The offending panels had to be sanded to dull their shiny finish.

SoCal Modernism

Clothing-optional California has never been shy about showcasing its assets. Starting in the 1960s, California embraced the stripped-down, glass-wall aesthetics of the International Style championed by Bauhaus architects Walter Gropius, Ludwig Mies van der Rohe and Le Corbusier. Its characteristics included boxlike building shapes, open floorplans, minimalist facades and abundant glass.

Austrian-born Rudolph Schindler and Richard Neutra brought modernism to LA and Palm Springs, where Swiss-born Albert Frey also worked. Their midcentury modern residential homes aimed for seamlessness between indoor and outdoor spaces with floor-to-ceiling windows perfectly suited to SoCal's see-and-be-seen culture. Neutra and Schindler were also influenced by the earlier work of Frank Lloyd Wright, who designed LA's Hollyhock House in a style he dubbed 'California Romanza.'

DOWNTOWN LA'S GLAMOUR BUILDINGS

Check out some of these gems, mostly built in the early 20th century.

Central Library (☎213-228-7000; www.lapl.org/central; 630 W Fifth St; ⊙10am-8pm Mon-Thu, to 5:30 Fri & Sat, 1-5pm Sun) Bertram Goodhue, inspired by the discovery of King Tut's tomb, incorporated numerous Egyptian motifs into this public building. An eight-story glass atrium hung with 2000lb bronze chandeliers was added in 1993.

US Bank Tower (633 W 5th St) The tallest building west of Chicago has 73 floors and juts over 1000ft into the air. Designed by Henry Cobb, an architect from the New York firm cofounded by IM Pei, the US Bank Tower was attacked by an alien spaceship in the 1996 movie *Independence Day*. Some still call it by its original name, Library Tower.

One Bunker Hill (601 W 5th St) Above the entrance to this 12-story art deco office tower, reliefs depicting energy, light and power recall the building's former occupant, the Southern California Edison company. Inside, the lobby is adorned with over a dozen kinds of marble, gold-leaf ceilings and a mural by Hugo Ballin, a set designer for director Cecil B DeMille.

Millennium Biltmore Hotel (☎213-624-1011; www.thebiltmore.com; 506 S Grand Ave) One of LA's grandest and oldest hotels was designed by the team that also created New York's Waldorf-Astoria and Miami's Biltmore hotels. It has hosted US presidents, political conventions and eight Academy Awards ceremonies. The hotel's sumptuous interior boasts carved and gilded ceilings, marble floors, grand staircases and palatial ballrooms, while the exterior merges Spanish Colonial Revival and Beaux Arts styles.

Oviatt Building (617 S Olive St) On the National Register of Historic Places, this 1928 art deco gem was conceived by the mildly eccentric James Oviatt, owner of the men's clothing store previously on the premises. Oviatt fell in love with art deco on a visit to Paris and had carpets, draperies and fixtures shipped over from France, including the purportedly largest shipment of decorative glass by René Lalique ever to cross the Atlantic.

Fine Arts Building (811 W 7th St) This 12-story Romanesque Revival building is a visual feast inside and out. Its facade is awash in floral and animal ornamentation, with human figures peering down from arcaded upstairs windows. Above the cathedral-like lobby, large sculptures representing the arts gaze down from a galleried mezzanine.

His son Lloyd Wright later built the Wayfarers Chapel atop the cliffs overlooking the Pacific in Palos Verdes.

Together with Charles and Ray Eames, Neutra also contributed to the experimental Case Study Houses, several of which still jut out of the LA landscape and are often used as filming locations, as seen in *LA Confidential.* The Los Angeles Conservancy's Modern Committee aims to preserve several Case Study Houses, as well as other significant modernist structures. The Palm Springs Modern Committee celebrates that desert resort's signature architectural, design and fashion style each spring during **Modernism Week** (www.modernismweek.com).

Postmodern Evolutions

Postmodernism was partly a response to the starkness of modernism's International Style, and sought to re-emphasize the structural form of the building and the space around it. And true to its mythos, SoCal couldn't help wanting to embellish the facts a little anyway, veering away from strict modernism to add unlikely postmodern shapes to the local landscape, starting as early as 1965 with La Jolla's monumental Salk Institute designed by San Diego architect Louis I Kahn.

Fans of the mid-century modern tiki style will want to head to San Diego's Point Loma district, where Shelter Island feels like palmy Polynesia. Show up in August for the Tiki Oasis festival of art, design, music and more (www.tikioasis.com).

Richard Meier perfected and transcended the postmodernist vision in 1997 at the Getty Center, a cresting white wave of a building atop a sunburned West LA hilltop, which can only be approached by tram. Santa Monica resident 'starchitect' Frank Gehry is known for his deconstructivist buildings with sculptural forms and distinctive facade materials such as stainless steel. Since opening in 2003, Gehry's Walt Disney Concert Hall has become an emblem of Downtown LA's reemergence. Look closely: the ship-shaped building's exterior metal 'sails' wink cheekily at streamline moderne.

Also in Downtown LA, the Cathedral of Our Lady of the Angels, designed by Spanish architect Rafael Moneo in 2002, echoes the grand churches of Mexico and Europe, albeit from a controversially postmodern and deconstructivist angle. Maverick architect Thom Mayne of LA's Morphosis firm has also made his mark, winning the 2005 Pritzker Prize for his futuristic, energy-efficient design of Downtown LA's Caltrans District 7 Headquarters, which is covered in a mechanical 'skin.'

Italian architect Renzo Piano's signature inside-out 'high-tech' postmodern style can be glimpsed in the sawtooth roof and red-veined exterior escalators and stairways of the Broad Contemporary Art Museum at the Los Angeles County Museum of Art. Meanwhile, Downtown LA's Grand Ave will soon be transformed by another postmodern Broad Contemporary Art Museum building, designed by the NYC firm of Diller Scofidio + Renfro, as well as a hotel, retail and residential complex opposite Walt Disney Concert Hall and masterminded by Frank Gehry.

LA'S BACK-TO-SCHOOL ARCHITECTURE

Among the most noteworthy new buildings in Downtown LA are educational institutions.

Ramón C Cortines High School for the Visual and Performing Arts (450 N Grand Ave) The metal-clad exterior – by Austrian architectural firm Coop Himmelb(l)au – echoes the Walt Disney Concert Hall a few blocks away, as if to inspire students. Look for the ramp spiraling out of the main building up toward the sky.

Southern California Institute of Architecture (Sci-Arc; www.sciarc.edu; 960 E 3rd St; gallery admission free; ⏲gallery 10am-6pm) Faculty member Gary Paige transformed this 'found object' – a 1907 Santa Fe freight depot in an unloved corner of Downtown LA – into the home base for Sci-Arc, one of the world's most avant-garde architecture schools. The building is as long as the Empire State Building is tall (about 0.25 miles).

Flavors of SoCal

While Los Angeles is known for chichi restaurants run by celebrity chefs, you don't have to drop a Benjamin to eat well here, especially with Little Tokyo and Thai Town just around the edible corner. Southern California's culinary scene is diverse and cutting edge, and many foodie trends have started in its coastal kitchens, from fusion sushi to Nuevo Latino fare. Best of all, the region's cuisine keeps redefining and refining itself – and along with it, the way the rest of America eats.

California Cuisine

The cardinal rule of California cuisine is that the ingredients should be extremely fresh, minimally processed and prepared so that the flavors speak for themselves. Locally grown and organic foods are favored. Chefs generally rely on flavor-packed reduction sauces rather than fatty gravies. Apart from that, there are few rules, and influences may come from Europe, Asia and Latin America.

Californians adore culinary trends. Some crazes are silly and doomed to failure (eg chocolate pasta), others are good but overused (eg foams), while still others get integrated from foreign countries and become a popular part of the California repertoire. Perhaps no one has done as much to popularize California's healthy-minded, fusion-style cuisine nationwide peripatetic Austrian-born chef Wolfgang Puck, who began his career as a celebrity restaurateur in Beverly Hills.

Apart from LA's mobile food truck revolution and hipster underground supper clubs, one of the hottest and most accessible trends these days is 'small plate' dining. That is, a group will order several appetizer-sized dishes of food, letting everyone at the table share. It's not unlike Spanish tapas, but in SoCal you're just as likely to find small-plate menus at French, Middle Eastern, Japanese and Chinese restaurants.

Trendy Menu Ingredients

Meyer lemon – Sweet local citrus

Heirloom tomatoes – In a rainbow of colors

Huitlacoche – Corn fungus, a Mexican delicacy

Bronze fennel – Mild anise flavor and golden foliage

SOCAL COOKING COURSES

Bring a taste of SoCal back to your table at home with these cooking classes.

California Sushi Academy (☎310-231-4499; www.sushi-academy.com; 11310 Nebraska Ave; 3hr class $80-85) Learn the art of finessing raw fish or sake tasting in West LA.

New School of Cooking (☎310-842-9702; www.newschoolofcooking.com; 8690 Washington Blvd, Culver City; recreational classes $45-95) Globally inspired classes built around a technique, ingredient and/or country (eg Italian pasta, Asian dumplings, French macarons).

Hipcooks (www.hipcooks.com; 3hr classes $60-65) Small-group, hands-on cooking classes with light hearted international or cocktail-party themes in West LA, East LA and San Diego.

Pascale's Kitchen (☎805-965-5112; www.pascaleskitchen.com; tasting events & classes $35-90) Seasonal gourmet menus with global spices and epicurean wine-country influences around Santa Barbara.

It's All Fruits & Nuts, Honey

Make all the jokes you want about this being the land of fruits, nuts and flakes. It's true, and locals couldn't be prouder. You name it, Southern California grows it. Avocado, citrus, dates, berries and all manner of vegetables are just a sampling of the crops that flourish between Santa Barbara County and the Mexican border.

In salads, forget iceberg lettuce (although that too is grown here): a SoCal salad is likely to include endive, radicchio, arugula and other greens that may not pass your smartphone's spell-checker. Other classics: the Cobb salad (invented in Hollywood), the Caesar salad (invented in Tijuana, Mexico) and the Chinese chicken salad (popularized in LA during the health-conscious 1970s) made with sliced Napa cabbage, slivered carrot, green onion, grilled chicken, toasted sesame seeds and a tangy soy-based dressing.

LA Times food writer Jonathan Gold won the Pulitzer Prize for criticism in 2007, the first time a restaurant critic won this award. To find out where Gold is eating these days, visit www.latimes.com or follow him on Twitter (@thejgold).

An Omnivore's Feast

You may associate SoCal with vegetarianism, but locals ardently love meat too. Trendy new steakhouses open all the time, many proudly printing on the menu the names of local ranches supplying grass-fed, free-range and hormone-free beef, pork, lamb, chicken, duck and even heritage-breed turkeys. When it comes to comfort-food classics, downtown LA's Phillipe the Original claims to have invented the French-dip roast beef sandwich way back in 1908.

With hundreds of miles of coastline, fishing is not only a huge industry in SoCal, but also a popular sport. As you travel between Santa Barbara and San Diego, you'll often see halibut, rockfish, sablefish (black cod) and sand dabs on restaurant menus, much of it locally caught. A rare and pricey treat is farm-raised abalone, which has a delicate flavor and texture similar to squid.

Small World, Big Tastes

No less than Ruth Reichl, the one-time California chef, food writer and former *New York Times* restaurant critic, has said that LA's real culinary treasure is its ethnic restaurants. With 140 nationalities in LA County alone, you will only be scratching the surface with the next great Korean BBQ truck, Japanese ramen shop or Persian ice-cream parlor.

You'll find Mexican restaurants all over SoCal. Japanese eateries are concentrated in LA neighborhoods such as Downtown's Little Tokyo and Torrance, which is inland from the South Bay. Downtown LA's Chinatown and communities in the San Gabriel Valley are the epicenter of Chinese cooking. LA's Koreatown and Orange County's Little Saigon are each the largest respective ethnic expat communities outside their home countries, while Anaheim's Little Arabia is best for Middle Eastern fare. San Diego has a thriving Little Italy too.

If you want to taste all of SoCal in just one place, Downtown LA's Grand Central Market is stuffed with energetic vendors dishing up street food from around the globe, from Latin American *pupusas* (filled corn tortillas) and fresh-squeezed fruit *jugos* (juices) to Hawaiian barbecue and Japanese *bentō* boxes.

In *Spanglish* (2004), Adam Sandler plays a chef in a top LA restaurant, who learns a thing or two about life from Flor, the family maid. Top chef Thomas Keller, of Napa Valley's celebrated French Laundry restaurant, consulted on the food scenes.

Mexican

Mexican food is iconic here, and not exclusively among people of Latino heritage. Until you've sampled *carnitas* (braised pork), *al pastor* (marinated and grilled pork) or San Diego–style fish tacos washed down with a cold beer or a margarita, you haven't experienced SoCal culture.

Virtually any Cal-Mex meal starts with tortillas (flatbread made of wheat or corn flour). Small ones are wrapped around meat, cheeses and vegetables and called tacos; larger, rolled versions are enchiladas (traditionally pan-fried and covered in sauce then baked), while burritos are huge tortillas, stuffed with the same, well, stuff, plus rice and beans. Rather than slushy supermarket brands, locally made salsa is a finely diced mix of fresh tomatoes, onions, cilantro and jalapeños.

Japanese

Angelenos were enthusiastically chowing down sushi and sashimi when most of America still considered it foreign fare not to be trusted. The quickest way to start a hot debate in LA? Ask locals who they think the city's best sushi-bar chef is, then stand back and watch the verbal punches fly.

But SoCal's Japanese food scene goes far beyond raw piscine treats. Many a good meal starts with *edamame* (boiled soybeans in the pod) and continues with *yakitori* (grilled skewers of chicken or vegetables), tempura (lightly battered and fried vegetables or fish) and an endless variety of artful hot and cold appetizers, most often shared by groups of friends at an *izakaya* (gastropub).

Other Japanese restaurants might specialize in just one dish, such as ramen (noodle soup), cook-it-yourself *sukiyaki* and *shabu-shabu* hot pots, or *okonomiyaki* – vegetable, seafood and pork-filled pancakes topped with a savory, barbecue-like sauce, Japanese mayonnaise and crispy seaweed flakes.

Many seafood species – especially what's dished up at many sushi bars – are being overfished, some to the point of extinction. To find out what's good to eat (and what's not), consult the Monterey Bay Aquarium's Seafood Watch List (www.seafoodwatch.org), also available as a free mobile app or as a printable pocket guide.

Chinese

Sure, you'll find familiar take-out favorites like *kung pao* this and General Tso's that. But if you can, gobble up Cantonese dim sum. A small army of servers stroll around cavernous rooms for hundreds of diners filled with circular tables, pushing carts loaded with dumplings such as *har gao* (shrimp) and *shu mai* (pork). Other regional cuisines, including Hunan and Szechuan, abound, especially around LA.

Korean

The signature dish is beef ribs *(kalbi)*, marinated in soy, sesame oil, green onion and garlic, then grilled at your table, above which vents whisk away the smoke. *Bibimbap* is a large bowl of mixed Korean vegetables, sliced meat (usually beef) and a fried egg topped with hot chili sauce over a mini mountain of rice. All of these are served with a variety of healthy side dishes including *kimchi* (spicy pickled cabbage).

Vietnamese

Vietnam's national dish is *pho* (pronounced 'fuh'): white rice noodles in clear beef broth, topped with sliced meat (usually beef) and served with a plate of bean sprouts and Thai basil, which you add into the soup along with sliced chilies and maybe hoisin sauce or fresh-squeezed lime juice.

FISH TACOS, SAN DIEGO–STYLE

San Diego may not have an official food, but the whole city obsesses over where to get the best fish tacos. The fish used can vary, but a firm fish like mahimahi works well. It's cut bite-sized, then seasoned and grilled, or – for 'Baja-style' tacos – battered and deep-fried. The cooked fish is placed inside a tortilla (purists say it must be made of corn) and drizzled in a creamy white sauce seasoned with jalapeños, capers, cayenne pepper and other spices. On top of that goes shredded cabbage and fresh *pico de gallo* (chopped tomato, onion and chili) salsa. Squeeze a little lime, take a bite. It's addictive.

THE LEGEND OF TWO-BUCK CHUCK

When Southern Californians say 'TJ,' they're talking about Tijuana, Mexico. But when they say 'TJ's,' they mean beloved **Trader Joe's** (www.traderjoes.com). Many locals count this bargain-priced, global-cuisine supermarket as one of life's essentials, alongside sunshine and the beach.

TJ's, which started life in Pasadena in 1967, offers an amazing, budget-priced selection of California wines. College students and penny-pinching artists swear by 'Two-buck Chuck,' the nickname for Charles Shaw private-brand wines sold at TJ's. Chuck's varietal wines cost an unbelievably cheap $2.49 per bottle, but they've won numerous awards in wine competitions. Believe it, dude – the checkout staff in Hawaiian shirts wouldn't lie to you, would they?

The original chopped Cobb salad – romaine lettuce, tomatoes, avocado, chicken breast, blue cheese, watercress, chives, a hard-boiled egg and old-fashioned French dressing – was invented in 1937 by Bob Cobb, owner of Hollywood's Brown Derby restaurant.

Wine, Beer & Beyond

Made in SoCal: Wine & Beer

Californians love wine. In fact, each year California bottles more than 660 million gallons of wine – enough to fill over 1000 Olympic-sized swimming pools.

Excellent wines are produced up and down the length of the Golden State, but the largest SoCal growing regions are Santa Barbara County (known for pinot noir and Rhône varietals such as Syrah and viognier) and upstart Temecula, a wild West frontier town on the edge of the desert outside San Diego.

Many SoCal winemakers are implementing their passion for the vine in earth-conscious ways, using organic practices and biodynamic farming techniques, which they'll enthusiastically share their knowledge of in winery tasting rooms and on guided vineyard tours.

Beer drinkers should seek out SoCal's award-winning microbreweries, especially in San Diego and other coastal beach towns. If you're hungry, brewpubs usually serve good grub too.

SoCal Cocktails, Old & New

The margarita (traditionally made with tequila, triple sec and lemon or lime juice, either frozen and blended or served straight up 'on the rocks' with ice) is the drink of choice with Mexican cuisine. Go ahead, splurge on higher-grade tequilas – they say it'll help avoid hangovers.

In recent years, there has been a growing thirst for classic and new artisanal cocktails, especially in LA and San Diego. These days bartenders are judged not by flashy tricks, but by their knowledge of a drink's history and boutique liquors from California's burgeoning microdistilleries, as well as handmade herbal and fruit infusions, often using seasonal and organic local ingredients. Don't be surprised if your cocktail comes served in a Mason jar instead of a highball or martini glass.

The outlandish film *Sideways* (2004) captures the folly and passion of California's wine snobbery. pinot noir, a highly sensitive grape, becomes a metaphor for the beleaguered, middle-aged main character, Miles, brilliantly played by Paul Giamatti.

Coffee, Tea & Other Drinks

No alcohol? No problem. Fruit smoothies are a SoCal staple: fresh fruit blended with ice, frozen yogurt, sorbet, vitamins or 'energy boosters' and other (mostly) healthful goodies. Fresh-pressed juices made from vegetables such as kale and carrots, sometimes blended with non-dairy substitutes including almond, rice or soy milk or coconut water, have also become popular.

A treat that originated in Asian neighborhoods but can now be found in almost every SoCal strip mall is boba tea – sweetened milk tea with tapioca 'pearls' at the bottom, sipped through a super-thick straw.

For java jonesing, LA-based chain Coffee Bean & Tea Leaf offer frozen ice-coffee blended drinks. For stronger, more interesting coffee and espresso drinks, look for local gourmet roasters and specialty coffee bars, such as Intelligentsia Coffee or Handsome Coffee Roasters in LA.

Vegetarians, Vegans & Locavores

California cuisine is all about being local, organic and seasonal, so eating green like a slow food–loving 'locavore' isn't a tall order. Certified farmers markets abound, as do natural and organic food stores. Many top chefs make a point of using organic produce whenever possible and only order fish, seafood or meat that's from local, sustainable sources. Southern California is so vegetarian-friendly that it's a cliché. While strictly vegetarian, vegan or raw-food restaurants are rare outside bigger cities, almost every restaurant offers at least a handful of vegetarian choices. And bottled water shipped over from Fiji or France? No thank you, filtered tap will be fine (and cheaper).

Starring Meryl Streep, the drama *Julie & Julia* (2009) in part dramatizes the real-life adventures of TV chef and French cookbook author extraordinaire Julia Child, who was born in Pasadena, an LA suburb.

SoCal's Farmers Markets

Cities throughout the Southland have farmers markets on certain days of the week, where farmers and small producers of foodstuffs such as honey and cheese come to sell their best, often trucking it in themselves from the fields. Prices are higher than at supermarkets, but quality is excellent and much of what's on offer is organic. Most vendors offer free samples too. Some farmers markets feature live entertainment and appearances by local chefs. Be sure to keep an eye out for specialty items that are available only seasonally.

TOP 10 SOCAL FOOD & DRINK EVENTS

California Avocado Festival (p420) Curious to see the world's largest vat of guacamole? Come to Carpinteria, just south of Santa Barbara, in early October.

California Strawberry Festival (www.strawberry-fest.org) Oxnard's family-fun festival features recipe cook-offs and chefs' demos in mid-May.

dineLA Restaurant Week (www.discoverlosangeles.com) Take advantage of bargain-priced multicourse menus from some of LA's hottest chefs in late January.

LA Street Food Festival (http://lastreetfoodfest.com) Let the food trucks come to you at Pasadena's Rose Bowl in late June.

Little Italy Festa (p296) Over 100,000 hungry folks turn out for San Diego's Italian food and cultural celebration in mid-October.

National Date Festival (www.datefest.org) Save the date (get it?) for Indio's February celebration of its prime local product. Bonus: camel races!

San Diego Bay Wine & Food Festival (www.sandiegowineclassic.com) Winemakers' tastings and dinners and top chefs' classes and competitions in mid-November.

San Diego Beer Week (http://sdbw.org) Taste stellar craft brews from all around SD, SoCal and the country, plus local food-truck fare, in early November.

Santa Barbara Vintners' & Harvest Festival Weekends (www.sbcountywines.com) SoCal's premier wine country hosts weekend bashes in April and October.

San Diego Restaurant Week (www.sandiegorestaurantweek.com) Special deals on prix-fixe menus at nearly 200 restaurants across the county in mid-September.

Wild Things

Much of Southern California's coast is blessed by a Mediterranean climate, with warm, dry summers and mild, wet winters. This ecological 'island' is a haven for diverse plants and animals, from SoCal hillsides covered in golden poppies to majestic migratory gray whales and monarch butterflies. Although the staggering numbers of animals that greeted the first Europeans are now a thing of the past, keep your peepers open and you'll be surprised by just how many critters still call this area home.

Animals

Marine Mammals

Spend even one day along Southern California's coast and you may spot pods of bottle-nosed dolphins and porpoises swimming and doing acrobatics in the ocean. Playful sea otters and harbor seals typically stick closer to shore, especially around public piers and protected bays. To see pinnipeds such as barking sea lions and elephant seals, in the wild rather than at SeaWorld, hop aboard a boat to Channel Islands National Park

When it comes to SoCal's superstar marine wildlife, think big. School-bus big. Gray whales make cameo appearances every year between December and April. That's when they migrate along the Pacific coast, traveling from their summertime feeding grounds in the arctic Bering Sea, down to southern breeding grounds off Baja California – and then all the way back up again. Pregnant gray whales give birth to calves weighing up to 1500lb; if lucky, those newborn whales will live up to 60 years, some growing 50ft long and weighing up to 40 tons.

You can occasionally see migrating whales spout and breach from shoreline lookouts, such as San Diego's Point Loma and Torrey Pines in La Jolla or Point Vicente on LA's Palos Verdes Peninsula. Better yet, head out to meet the cetaceans on their own own turf by going on a whale-watching tour, with departures from LA's Long Beach, San Pedro and Marina Del Rey; San Diego; Dana Point and Newport Beach in Orange County; and Ventura and Santa Barbara, northwest of LA.

SoCal for the Birds

- *Ballona Wetlands (p170)*
- *Bolsa Chica State Ecological Reserve (p248)*
- *Malibu Lagoon State Beach (p146)*
- *Sonny Bono Salton Sea National Wildlife Refuge (p363)*
- *San Elijo Lagoon (p327)*
- *Upper Newport Bay Nature Preserve (p256)*

Feathered Friends

Out on a boat, or just standing on a SoCal beach, you'll spot plenty of winged creatures, including hefty pelicans darting for lunch like top-gun pilots and skinny sandpipers foraging for invertebrates in the wet sand.

SoCal is an essential stop on the migratory Pacific Flyway between Alaska and Mexico. Almost half the bird species in North America use wildlife refuges and nature preserves for rest and refueling, peaking during the wetter winter season. Grab a pair of binoculars and scan the skies over SoCal's coast and inland by the Salton Sea.

Some beaches may be closed between March and September to protect endangered western snowy plovers, who lay their eggs in exposed ground scrapes in the sand. Give these easily frightened birds plenty of space, as the presence of humans – and especially dogs – can cause them to fatally abandon their young.

The Audubon Society's California chapter website (http://ca.audubon.org) offers birding checklists, photos and videos, conservation news and a Pacific Flyway blog.

Also keep an eye out for bald eagles, which soared off the endangered species list in 2007. These birds of prey have regained a foothold on the Channel Islands, and some spend their winters at Big Bear Lake near LA.

Mountain Kings

Mountain lions – also called cougars or pumas – inhabit forests and mountains throughout SoCal, especially in areas teeming with deer. Reaching up to 8ft in length and weighing as much as 175lb, this solitary animal is a formidable predator. Only a few attacks on humans have occurred, mostly where encroachment has pushed hungry lions to their limits – for example, at the borders of wilderness and rapidly developing suburbs.

Although an estimated 25,000 to 30,000 black bears roam around California, the possibilities of close encounters with bears in SoCal are extremely unlikely and limited to the San Gabriel Mountains and the San Bernardino Mountains east of LA. The only place you'll possibly see a grizzly bear these days is on the state flag, since this species was extirpated from California during the 1920s.

The California condor is the largest flying bird in North America. In 1987 there were only two dozen or so birds left in the wild. Thanks to captive breeding and release programs, there are about 240 flying free today.

Desert Critters

The desert is far from deserted, but most animals are too smart to hang out in the daytime heat, coming out only at night. Roadrunners, those black-and-white mottled ground cuckoos with long tails and punk-style mohawks, can often be spotted on roadsides. Other desert inhabitants include burrowing kit foxes, tree-climbing grey foxes, hopping jackrabbits and kangaroo rats, slow-moving desert tortoises, and a variety of snakes, lizards and spiders. Desert bighorn sheep and myriad birds flock to watering holes in SoCal's native fan-palm oases.

Plants

Native Trees & Shrubs

You've seen them on film, you've seen them on TV: the swaying palm trees with trunks as slender as a giraffe's neck that are so evocative of Southern California. Well, those guys are like most locals: they're not really from here. In fact, the only native species is the fan palm, found naturally in SoCal's desert oases.

Oak trees are a different story. California has 20 native species of oak. Live, or evergreen, oaks with holly-like leaves and scaly acorns especially

AN AUDIENCE WITH A MONARCH BUTTERFLY

Monarch butterflies are delicate-looking orange creatures that follow remarkably lengthy migration patterns to spend their winters in California and Mexico. Walt Sakai, biology professor at Santa Monica College and a recognized authority on monarch butterflies, shares with us his favorite SoCal viewing spots:

- SoCal's premier site is **Ellwood Main** in Goleta, west of Santa Barbara. From Hwy 101, take the Hollister Ave exit south, then turn right at the stoplight by Ellwood School. Park at the end of the road, then walk a half-mile along a signposted path. Late November and early December are the best times to see the butterflies here.
- In Ventura, head to **Camino Real Park** in December and January. Look for monarchs in the eucalyptus grove above the creek near the tennis courts. From Hwy 101, go north on Victoria Ave, left on Telegraph Rd, left on S Bryn Mawr St and right on Aurora Dr.
- In Malibu's Point Mugu State Park, **Big Sycamore Canyon** also hosts monarch butterflies, especially in sycamore trees by the hike-and-bike camping area. October is the best month to see them – they're often gone by mid-November.

thrive. You'll traipse past them while exploring the Santa Monica Mountains and other coastal ranges. Other common plants include the aromatic California bay laurel tree, whose long slender leaves turn purple, and manzanita shrubs with intensely red bark and small berries.

SoCal's Wildlife-Watching Hot Spots

Channel Islands National Park (p425)

Death Valley National Park (p369)

Joshua Tree National Park (p350)

Mt San Jacinto Wilderness State Park (www.msjnha.org)

Santa Monica Mountains (p161)

Coastal Beauties & Beyond

The gnarled Torrey pine tree has adapted to sparse rainfall and sandy, stony soils. It only grows at Torrey Pines State Reserve near San Diego and on Santa Rosa Island in Channel Islands National Park, which is home to dozens more endemic plant species. The same is true of Catalina Island, where you'll find the Catalina ironwood and Catalina mahogany trees, flowering Santa Catalina bedstraw and succulent Catalina live-forever, all displayed at the Wrigley Memorial & Botanical Gardens.

Except in the deserts and high mountains, the hills of SoCal turn green in winter, not summer. As soon as winter rains arrive, dried-out brown grasses spring to life. As early as February, wildflowers pop up, notably the bright-orange California poppy, the state flower, which blooms into May. Resist the temptation to pick one – it's illegal (and incurs a $500 fine) and besides, they wilt almost instantly when plucked from the ground.

Desert Cacti & Their Cousins

Cacti and other desert plants have adapted to the arid climate of SoCal's deserts with thin, spiny leaves that resist moisture loss (and deter grazing animals), and seed and flowering mechanisms that kick into gear during brief rains. With enough winter rainfall, wildflowers can bloom spectacularly in spring (roughly from February through April), carpeting valleys and drawing thousands of onlookers and shutterbugs.

The sheer variety of cacti found in SoCal is astonishing. Among the most common and easy to identify is cholla, which appears so furry that it's nicknamed 'teddy-bear cactus.' But it's far from cuddly and instead will bury extremely sharp, barbed spines in your skin at the slightest touch. Also watch out for catclaw acacia, nicknamed 'wait-a-minute bush' because its small, sharp, hooked thorny spikes can snatch your clothing and skin as you brush past.

A colorful photographic survey of more than 2300 of SoCal's varied wildflowers, from desert cacti to alpine blooms, awaits at www.calflora.net/bloomingplants/.

Almost as widespread is prickly pear, a flat, fleshy-padded cacti that produces showy flowers in shades of red, yellow and purple, and whose juice is traditionally used as medicine by Native Americans. Then there's cactus-like creosote (actually a small evergreen bush with a distinctive smell) and spiky ocotillo, which grows up to 20ft tall and has cane-like branches hung with blood-red flowers.

Like whimsical figments from a Dr Seuss book, Joshua trees are the largest type of yucca and are related to agave plants. Allegedly, they were named by migrant Mormons, who thought the crooked branches resembled the outstretched arms of a biblical prophet. Joshua trees grow throughout the Mojave Desert, although their habitat and long-term survival is seriously threatened by global warming. Their heavy, creamy greenish-white flowers erupt in spring.

Survival Guide

DIRECTORY A–Z 470
- Accommodations 470
- Courses 472
- Customs Regulations 472
- Discount Cards 472
- Electricity 473
- Food 473
- Gay & Lesbian Travelers 473
- Health 473
- Insurance 474
- Internet Access 474
- Legal Matters 474
- Maps 476
- Money 476
- Opening Hours 477
- Public Holidays 477
- Safe Travel 477
- Tourist Information 477
- Travelers With Disabilities 478
- Visas 478

TRANSPORTATION . . 479
- GETTING THERE & AWAY 479
- Entering the Region 479
- Air 479
- Land 480
- GETTING AROUND 481
- Air 481
- Bicycle 481
- Bus 481
- Car, Motorcycle & RV 482
- Tours 484
- Train 484

Directory A–Z

Accommodations

Amenities

➡ Budget-conscious accommodations include campgrounds, hostels and motels. Because midrange properties generally offer better value for money, most of the accommodations we recommend fall into that category.

➡ At midrange motels and hotels, expect clean, comfortable and decent-sized rooms with at least a private bathroom and standard amenities such as cable TV, direct-dial telephone, a coffeemaker and perhaps a microwave and a mini fridge.

➡ Top-end lodgings offer more and better amenities and perhaps a scenic location, edgy decor or historical ambience. Pools, fitness rooms, business centers, full-service restaurants and bars and other convenience facilities are all standard.

➡ Air-conditioning is a standard amenity except at some beachfront properties, where only fans may be provided.

➡ Accommodations offering online computer terminals for guests are designated with the internet icon (@). A fee may apply (eg at full-service business centers inside hotels).

➡ There may be a fee for wireless internet (wi-fi icon), especially in-room access. Look for free wi-fi hot spots in hotel public areas (eg lobby, poolside).

SLEEPING PRICE RANGES

The following price ranges refer to a private room with bathroom during high season, unless otherwise specified. Taxes and breakfast are not normally included in the price.

$ less than $100

$$ $100 to $200

$$$ more than $200

Rates & Discounts

➡ Generally, midweek rates are lower except at urban hotels geared to business travelers, which lure leisure travelers with weekend deals.

➡ Discount cards (eg AAA, AARP) may get you about 10% off standard rates at participating hotels and motels.

➡ Look for motel and hotel discount coupons in freebie ad magazines at gas stations, highway rest areas, tourist information offices and online at **HotelCoupons** (http://hotelcoupons.com).

➡ Bargaining may be possible for walk-in guests without reservations, especially at off-peak times.

Seasons & Reservations

➡ High season is from June to August everywhere, except the deserts and mountain ski areas, where December to April are the busiest months.

➡ Demand (and prices) spike around major holidays and special events, when some properties may impose multi-day minimum stays.

➡ Reservations are recommended for weekend and holiday travel year-round, and any day of the week during high season.

➡ If you walk up without reservations, request to see a room before paying for it, especially at motels.

Smoking

➡ Some hotels are now entirely smokefree, meaning you're not allowed to smoke anywhere on the property, or even outdoors within a certain distance of entryways.

➡ Where smoking rooms still exist at hotels, they're often left unrenovated and in less desirable locations.

➡ Expect to pay a hefty 'cleaning fee' ($100 or more) if you light up in designated nonsmoking rooms.

B&Bs

If you want an atmospheric or perhaps romantic alternative to impersonal motels and hotels, bed-and-breakfast inns typically inhabit fine old Victorian houses or other heritage buildings, bedecked with floral wallpaper and antique furnishings. Travelers who prefer privacy may find B&Bs too intimate.

Rates often include breakfast, but occasionally do not (never mind what the name 'B&B' suggests). Amenities vary widely, but rooms with TV and telephone are the exception; the cheapest units share bathrooms. Standards are high at places certified by the **California Association of Boutique & Breakfast Inns** (www.cabbi.com).

Most B&Bs require advance reservations; only a few will accommodate drop-in guests. Smoking is generally prohibited and children are usually not welcome. Multi-night stays may be required, especially on weekends and in high season.

Camping

Camping in Southern California is a lot more than just a cheap way to spend the night. The best campsites have you waking up to ocean views, under a canopy of pine trees or next to desert rock formations. Many campgrounds are open year-round, and the most popular ones (eg near the beach) fill up in high season, so make reservations or arrive early.

Basic campsites with firepits, picnic tables and access to drinking water and pit toilets are common in national forests and on Bureau of Land Management (BLM) land. Campgrounds in state and national parks usually have flush toilets and sometimes hot showers and recreational vehicle (RV) hookups. Private campgrounds are often located closer to towns and cater more to the RV crowd.

GREEN HOTELS & MOTELS

Surprisingly, many of SoCal's hotels and motels haven't yet jumped on the environmental bandwagon. Apart from offering you the option of reusing your towels and sheets, even such simple eco-initiatives as providing recycling bins, switching to bulk soap dispensers or replacing plastic and Styrofoam cups and dropping pre-packaged items from the breakfast buffet are pretty rare. The **California Green Lodging Program** (www.calrecycle.ca.gov/epp/greenlodging/) is a voluntary state-run certification program – in the online directory, search for properties that have achieved the 'Environmentalist Level,' denoted by three palm trees.

Many public and almost all private campgrounds accept both online and phone reservations for all or at least some of their campsites through one or both of the following agencies:

Recreation.gov (☎877-444-6777, 518-885-3639; www.recreation.gov; most campsites $10-25) Camping reservations in national parks, national forests (USFS) and other federal recreation lands (eg BLM).

Reserve America (☎800-444-7275, 916-638-5883; www.reserveamerica.com; campsites $10-70, cabins $40-100) For California state park campgrounds and cabins that accept reservations.

Hostels

SoCal has five hostels affiliated with **Hostelling International USA** (HI-USA; ☎888-464-4872; www.hiusa.org). There are two each in San Diego and LA, and one in Fullerton near Disneyland. Dorms in HI hostels are typically gender-segregated and alcohol and smoking are prohibited. HI-USA membership cards ($28 per year) get you $3 off per night.

Independent hostels are most common in Hollywood and Venice in LA and in San Diego. They generally have more relaxed rules, with frequent guest parties and activities. Some include a light breakfast in their rates, arrange local tours or pick up guests at transportation hubs. No two hostels are alike but typical facilities include mixed dorms, semi-private rooms with shared bathrooms, communal kitchens, lockers, internet access, laundry and TV lounges.

Some hostels say they accept only international visitors (basically to keep out homeless locals), but US citizens who look like travelers (eg you're in possession of an international plane ticket) may be admitted, especially during slow periods.

Dorm-bed rates cost $25 to $55, including tax. Reservations are always a good idea, especially in high season. Most hostels take reservations online or over the phone. Booking services like www.hostels.com, www.hostelz.com and www.hostelworld.com sometimes offer lower rates than the hostels directly.

BOOK YOUR STAY ONLINE

For more accommodations reviews by Lonely Planet authors, check out http://lonelyplanet.com/hotels/. You'll find independent reviews, as well as recommendations on the best places to stay. Best of all, you can book online.

Hotels & Motels

Hotel and motel rooms are often priced by the size and number of beds in a room, rather than the number of occupants. A room with one double or queen-size bed usually costs the same for one or two people, while a room with a king-size bed or two double beds costs more.

There is often a small surcharge for the third and fourth person, but children under a certain age (this varies) may stay free. Cribs or rollaway cots usually incur an extra fee. Beware that suites or 'junior suites' may be simply oversized rooms; ask about the layout when booking.

Recently renovated or larger rooms, or those with a view, are likely to cost more. Descriptors like 'oceanfront' and 'oceanview' are often too liberally used, and may require a periscope to spot the surf.

Rates may include breakfast, which could be just a stale doughnut and wimpy coffee, an all-you-can-eat hot and cold buffet, or anything in between.

You can make reservations at chains by calling their central reservation lines, but to learn about specific amenities and local promotions, call the property directly.

Courses

New York Film Academy (Map p100; ☎818-333-3558; www.nyfa.com; 3300 Riverside Dr, Burbank) NYFA's West Coast branch is located adjacent to Universal Studios' backlot. Learn about acting, filmmaking, screenwriting and music videos in workshops or degree programs lasting from one week to two years. Courses start at $1100.

Robert McKee's Story Seminar (☎888-676-2533; www.mckeestory.com) Even seasoned writers come to pick up tips and inspiration from McKee's four-day seminar featured in the movie *Adaptation*. Former students include the screenwriters of *Lord of the Rings* and *Boardwalk Empire*. Offered in LA at least once a year for $865.

Upright Citizens Brigade Training Center (☎323-908-8702; http://losangeles.ucbtheatre.com) Learn the improv basics or delve into sketch writing during eight-week, three-hour classes run by the improv theater co-founded by Amy Poehler. Alumni have gone on to write for *The Daily Show*, Conan O'Brien and sit-coms such as *30 Rock*. Tuition from $400.

Customs Regulations

Currently, non-US citizens and permanent residents may import:

- 1L of alcohol (if you're over 21 years old)
- 200 cigarettes (one carton) or 100 (non-Cuban) cigars (if you're over 18 years old)
- $100 worth of gifts

Amounts higher than $10,000 in cash, traveler's checks, money orders and other cash equivalents must be declared. Don't even think about bringing in illegal drugs.

For more complete, up-to-date information, check with **US Customs and Border Protection** (www.cbp.gov).

Discount Cards

'America the Beautiful' Annual Pass (☎888-275-8747; http://store.usgs.gov/pass; pass $80) Admits four adults and all children under 16 years for free to all national parks and federal recreational lands (eg USFS, BLM) for 12 months from the date of purchase. US citizens and permanent residents 62 years and older are eligible for a lifetime Senior Pass ($10) that grants free entry and 50% off some recreational-use fees such as camping, as does the lifetime Access Pass (free for US citizens or permanent residents with a permanent disability).

American Association of Retired Persons (AARP; ☎800-566-0242; www.aarp.org; annual membership $16) Advocacy group for Americans 50 years and older offers member discounts (usually 10%) on hotels, car rentals and more.

American Automobile Association (AAA; ☎877-428-2277; www.aaa.com; annual membership from $48) Members of AAA and its foreign affiliates (eg CAA) qualify for small discounts (usually 10%) on Amtrak trains, car rentals, motels and hotels, chain restaurants and shopping, tours and theme parks.

Go Los Angeles & San Diego Cards (www.smartdestinations.com; 1-day pass adult/child 3-12yr from $70/63) The Go Los Angeles Card and the pricier Go San Diego Card both include admission to major SoCal theme parks (but not Disney); for the best deals, buy online.

International Student Identity & Youth Travel Cards (www.isic.org; 1-year card $25) Offers savings on airline fares, travel insurance and local attractions for full-time students (ISIC) and for nonstudents under 26 years of age (IYTC). Cards are issued by student unions, hostelling organizations and youth-oriented budget travel agencies.

Senior Discounts People over the age of 65 (sometimes 55, 60 or 62) often qualify for the same discounts as students; any ID showing your birthdate should suffice as proof.

Southern California CityPass (www.citypass.com/southern-california; adult/child 3-9yr from $328/284) If you're visiting SoCal theme parks, CityPass covers three-day admission to Disneyland and Disney California Adventure and one-day admission each to Universal Studios and SeaWorld, with add-ons available for Legoland and the San Diego Zoo or Safari Park. Passes are valid for 14 days from the first day of use. It's cheapest to buy them online in advance.

Student Advantage Card (☎800-333-2920; www.studentadvantage.com; 1-year card $22.50) For international and US students, offers 15% savings on Amtrak trains and 20% on Greyhound buses, plus discounts of 10% to 20% on some rental cars and shopping.

Electricity

120V/60Hz

120V/60Hz

Food

Check out the Flavors of SoCal chapter for more information on food and drink (p461).

Gay & Lesbian Travelers

SoCal is a magnet for LGBTQ travelers. Hot spots include West Hollywood (WeHo), Silver Lake and Long Beach around LA, San Diego's Hillcrest neighborhood and the desert resort of Palm Springs. Some scenes are predominantly male-oriented, although women usually won't feel too left out.

Same-sex marriage is legal in California. Despite widespread tolerance, homophobic bigotry has not been completely rooted out in SoCal, especially in rural areas.

Helpful Resources

Advocate (www.advocate.com/travel) Online news, gay travel features and destination guides.

Damron (www.damron.com) Classic, advertiser-driven gay travel guides and 'Gay Scout' mobile app.

Gay & Lesbian National Hotline (☎888-843-4564; www.glnh.org; ⏲1-9pm Mon-Fri, 9am-2pm Sat) For counseling and referrals of any kind.

Gay.net Travel (www.gay.net/travel) City guides, travel news and pride events coverage.

Out Traveler (www.outtraveler.com) Free online magazine with travel tips, destination guides and hotel reviews.

Purple Roofs (www.purpleroofs.com) Online directory of LGBTQ accommodations.

Health

Healthcare & Insurance

Many healthcare professionals demand payment at the time of service, especially from out-of-towners. Except for medical emergencies (in which case call ☎911 or go to the nearest 24-hour hospital emergency room, or ER), phone around to find a walk-in clinic or doctor who will accept your insurance.

Keep all receipts and documentation. Some insurance policies require you to get pre-authorization for medical treatment before seeking help. Overseas visitors with travel health-insurance policies may need to contact a call center for an over-the-phone assessment before seeking medical treatment.

Dehydration, Heat Exhaustion & Heatstroke

➡ Take it easy as you acclimatize to SoCal's high temperatures. Always drink plenty of water. A minimum of 3L per person per day is recommended when you're active outdoors. Be sure to eat a salty snack too, as sodium is necessary for rehydration.

➡ Dehydration (lack of water) or salt deficiency can cause heat exhaustion, often characterized by heavy sweating, fatigue, lethargy, headaches, nausea, vomiting, dizziness and muscle cramps.

➡ Long, continuous exposure to high temperatures can lead to possibly fatal heatstroke, when body temperature rises to dangerous levels. Warning signs include altered mental status, hyperventilation and flushed, hot and dry skin (ie sweating stops). Immediate hospitalization is essential.

Hypothermia

➡ Skiers and hikers will find temperatures in the mountains and desert can quickly drop below freezing, especially during winter. Even a sudden spring shower or high winds can lower your body temperature rapidly.

EATING PRICE RANGES

The following price ranges refer to an average main course at dinner, unless otherwise specified. These prices don't include taxes or tip.

$ less than $10

$$ $10 to $20

$$$ more than $20

- Instead of cotton, wear synthetic or wool clothing that retains warmth even when wet. Carry waterproof layers (eg Gore-Tex jacket, plastic poncho, rain pants) and high-energy, easily digestible snacks like chocolate, nuts and dried fruit.
- Symptoms of hypothermia include exhaustion, numbness, shivering, stumbling, slurred speech, dizzy spells, muscle cramps and irrational or even violent behavior.
- To treat mild hypothermia, get out of bad weather and change into dry, warm clothing. Drink hot liquids (no caffeine or alcohol) and snack on high-calorie food.
- For more advanced hypothermia, seek immediate medical attention.

Insurance

See p473 for health insurance and p482 for car insurance.

Travel Insurance

Getting travel insurance to cover theft, loss and medical problems is highly recommended. Some policies do not cover 'risky' activities such as scuba diving, motorcycling and skiing, so read the fine print. Make sure the policy at least covers hospital stays and an emergency flight home.

Paying for your airline ticket or rental car with a credit card may provide limited travel accident insurance. If you already have private US health insurance or a homeowners or renters policy, find out what those policies cover and only get supplemental insurance. If you have prepaid a large portion of your vacation, trip cancellation insurance may be a worthwhile expense.

Worldwide travel insurance is available at www.lonelyplanet.com/travel-insurance. You can buy, extend and claim online anytime, even if you're already on the road.

Internet Access

- Cybercafes typically charge $6 to $12 per hour for online access.
- With branches in most SoCal cities and towns, **FedEx Office** (☎800-463-3339; www.fedex.com/us) offers internet access at self-service computer workstations (30¢ to 40¢ per minute) and sometimes free wi-fi, plus digital-photo printing and CD-burning stations.
- Accommodations, cafes, restaurants, bars etc that provide guest computer terminals for going online are identified by the internet icon(@); the wi-fi icon (wi-fi) indicates that wireless access is available. There may be a fee for either service.
- Free or fee-based wi-fi hot spots can be found at major airports; many hotels, motels and coffee shops (eg Starbucks); and some tourist information centers, museums, campgrounds (eg KOA), stores (eg Apple), bars and restaurants (including fast-food chains such as McDonald's).
- Free public wi-fi is proliferating (for a list, click to http://ca.gov/WiFi/) and even some state parks are now wi-fi-enabled (get more details at www.parks.ca.gov).
- Public libraries have internet terminals (online time may be limited, advance sign-up required and a nominal fee charged for out-of-network visitors) and increasingly, free wi-fi.

Legal Matters

Drugs & Alcohol

- Possession of under 1oz of marijuana is a misdemeanor in California. Possession of any other drug or more than an ounce of weed is a felony punishable by lengthy jail time. For foreigners, conviction of any drug-related offense is grounds for deportation.
- Police can give roadside sobriety checks to assess if you've been drinking or using drugs. If you fail, they'll require you to take a breath, urine or blood test to determine if your blood-alcohol level is over the legal limit (0.08%). Refusing to be tested is treated the same as if you had taken and failed the test.
- Penalties for driving under the influence (DUI) of drugs or alcohol range from license suspension and fines to jail.
- It's illegal to carry open containers of alcohol inside a vehicle, even if they're empty. Unless they're full and sealed, put them in the trunk.
- Consuming alcohol anywhere other than at a private residence or licensed premises is a no-no, which puts parks and beaches off-limits.

INTERNATIONAL VISITORS

See Customs Regulations (p472), Entering the Region (p479), Passports (p479) and Visas (p478).

Embassies & Consulates

Most foreign embassies are in Washington, DC, but some countries have consular offices in Los Angeles, including the following:

Australian Consulate (☎310-229-2300; www.losangeles.consulate.gov.au; 2029 Century Park E, Suite 3150) Century City.

Canadian Consulate (☎213-346-2700; http://can-am.gc.ca/los-angeles; 550 S Hope St, 9th fl) Downtown LA.

French Consulate (☎310-235-3200; www.consulfrance-losangeles.org; 10390 Santa Monica Blvd, Suite 410) Near Century City.

German Consulate (☎323-930-2703; www.germany.info/losangeles; 6222 Wilshire Blvd, Suite 500) Mid-City.

Japanese Consulate (☎213-617-6700; www.la.us.emb-japan.go.jp; 350 S Grand Ave, Suite 1700) Downtown LA.

New Zealand Consulate (☎310-566-6555; www.nzcgla.com; 2425 Olympic Blvd, Suite 600E) Santa Monica.

UK Consulate (☎310-789-0031; www.gov.uk/government/world/organisations/british-consulate-general-los-angeles; 2029 Century Park E, Suite 1350) Century City.

For countries not listed here, visit www.state.gov/s/cpr/rls/fco/.

Post

The **US Postal Service** (USPS; ☎800-275-8777; www.usps.com) is inexpensive and reliable. For sending important documents or packages overseas, try **FedEx** (FedEx; ☎800-463-3339; www.fedex.com) or **UPS** (UPS; ☎800-742-5877; www.ups.com).

Cell (Mobile) Phones

You'll need a multiband GSM phone in order to make calls in the US. Popping in a US prepaid rechargeable SIM card is usually cheaper than using your own network; they're sold at any major telecommunications or electronics store. If your phone doesn't work in the USA, these stores also sell inexpensive prepaid phones, including some airtime.

For short stays, you could rent a cell phone, for example, from **TripTel** (☎310-645-3500; www.triptel.com; Tom Bradley International Terminal; ⏲7am-10pm) at Los Angeles International Airport (LAX) in the international terminal arrivals area. Rentals cost from $3 per day ($15/45 per week/month) plus at least 49¢ per minute for incoming/outgoing US calls (much more for international calls).

DIALING CODES

- US phone numbers consist of a three-letter area code and a seven-digit local number.
- When dialing a number within the same area code, use the seven-digit number (if that doesn't work, try all 10 digits).
- For long-distance calls, dial ☎1 plus the area code plus the local number.
- Toll-free numbers begin with ☎800, ☎855, ☎866, ☎877 or ☎888 and must be preceded by ☎1.
- For direct international calls, dial ☎011 plus the country code plus the area code (usually without the initial '0') plus the local phone number.
- If you're calling from abroad, the country code for the US is ☎1 (the same as for Canada, but beware international rates apply between the two countries).

PAYPHONES & PHONECARDS

Where payphones still exist, they're usually coin-operated, although some accept credit cards. Local calls usually cost 50¢ minimum. For long-distance calls, you're usually better off buying a prepaid phonecard.

PRACTICALITIES

DVDs Coded for region 1 (USA and Canada only)

Electricity 110/120V AC, 50/60Hz

Newspapers Major dailies: center-left *Los Angeles Times* (www.latimes.com), conservative *San Diego Union-Tribune* (www.utsandiego.com), right-leaning *Orange County Register* (www.ocregister.com); alternative tabloids: *LA Weekly* (www.laweekly.com), *San Diego Reader* (www.sandiegoreader.com), *OC Weekly* (www.ocweekly.com)

Radio National Public Radio (NPR), lower end of FM dial

Time California is on Pacific Standard Time (UTC-8). During Daylight Saving Time (DST), from the second Sunday in March until the first Sunday in November, clocks are set one hour ahead.

TV PBS (public broadcasting); cable: CNN (news), ESPN (sports), HBO (movies), Weather Channel

Weights & Measures Imperial (except 1 US gallon = 0.83 imperial gallons)

➡ Bars, clubs, restaurants and liquor stores often ask for photo ID to prove you are of legal drinking age (21 years old). Being 'carded' is standard practice, so don't take it personally.

Police & Security

➡ For police, fire and ambulance emergencies, dial ☎911. For nonemergency police assistance, contact the nearest local police station (dial ☎411 for directory assistance).

➡ If you are stopped by the police, be courteous. Don't get out of the car unless asked. Keep your hands where the officer can see them (eg on the steering wheel) at all times.

➡ There is no system of paying fines on the spot. Attempting to pay the fine to the officer may lead to a charge of attempted bribery.

➡ For traffic violations, the officer will explain your options. There is usually a 30-day period to pay a fine; most matters can be handled by mail.

➡ If you are arrested, you have the right to remain silent and are presumed innocent until proven guilty. Everyone has the right to make one phone call. If you don't have a lawyer, one will be appointed free of charge.

➡ Due to security concerns about terrorism, never leave your bags unattended, especially not at airports or bus and train stations.

Smoking

➡ Smoking is generally prohibited inside all public buildings, including airports, shopping malls and train and bus stations.

➡ There is no smoking allowed inside restaurants, although lighting up may be tolerated at patio or sidewalk tables.

➡ At hotels, you must specifically request a smoking room; some properties are entirely nonsmoking by law.

➡ In some cities and towns, smoking outdoors within a certain distance of any public business is illegal.

Maps

Visitors centers distribute free (but often very basic) maps. If you're doing a lot of driving, you'll need a more detailed road map or map atlas. Members of the **American Automobile Association** (AAA; ☎800-453-9125; www.aaa.com) or its international affiliates (eg CAA) can get free driving maps from any local AAA office. Benchmark Maps' comprehensive *California Road & Recreation Atlas* ($25) shows campgrounds, recreational areas and topographical features, although it's less useful for navigating urban areas.

Money

ATMs

ATMs are available 24/7 at most banks, shopping malls, airports and grocery and convenience stores. Expect a minimum surcharge of $2.50 per transaction, in addition to any fees charged by your home bank. Most ATMs are connected to international networks and offer decent foreign-exchange rates.

Cash

Most people do not carry large amounts of cash for everyday use, relying instead on credit and debit cards. Some businesses refuse to accept bills over $20.

Credit Cards

Credit cards are almost universally accepted. In fact, it's almost impossible to rent a car, book a hotel room or buy tickets without one. Visa, MasterCard and American Express are widely accepted.

Moneychangers

You can exchange money at major airports, some banks and all currency-exchange offices such as American Express or Travelex. Always enquire about rates and fees. Outside big cities, exchanging money may be a problem, so make sure you have a credit card and sufficient cash.

Tipping

Tipping is *not* optional. Only withhold tips in cases of outrageously bad service.

Airport skycaps and hotel bellhops $2 per bag, minimum per cart $5

Bartenders 15% per round, minimum $1 per drink

Concierges No tips required for simple information, up to $10 for securing last-minute restaurant reservations, sold-out show tickets etc

Housekeeping staff $2 to $4 daily, left under the card provided; more if you're messy

Parking valets At least $2 when handed back your car keys

Restaurant servers and room service 18% to 20%, unless a gratuity is already charged (common for groups of six or more)

Taxi drivers 10% to 15% of metered fare, rounded up to the next dollar

Traveler's Checks

Traveler's checks have pretty much fallen out of use. Big-city restaurants, hotels and larger stores often will accept traveler's checks (in US dollars only), but smaller businesses and fast-food chains may refuse them.

Opening Hours

Standard opening hours are as follows:

Banks 9am-5pm Mon-Thu, to 6pm Fri, some 9am-1:30pm Sat

Bars 5am-2am daily

Business hours (general) 9am-5pm Mon-Fri

Post offices 8:30am-4:30pm Mon-Fri, some 9am-noon Sat

Restaurants 7:30am-10:30am, 11:30am-2:30pm & 5:30-10pm daily

Shops 10am-6pm Mon-Sat, noon-5pm Sun (malls open later)

Supermarkets 8am-9pm daily

Public Holidays

On the following national holidays, banks, schools and government offices (including post offices) close, and transportation, museums and other services operate on a Sunday schedule. Holidays falling on a weekend are usually observed the following Monday.

New Year's Day January 1

Martin Luther King Jr Day Third Monday in January

Presidents' Day Third Monday in February

Good Friday Friday before Easter (March/April)

Memorial Day Last Monday in May

Independence Day July 4

Labor Day First Monday in September

Columbus Day Second Monday in October

Veterans Day November 11

Thanksgiving Day Fourth Thursday in November

Christmas Day December 25

School Holidays

Colleges take a one- or two-week 'spring break' around Easter, sometime in March or April. Some hotels and resorts, especially by beaches, near theme parks and in the deserts, may raise their rates during this time. School summer vacations make July and August the busiest times.

Safe Travel

Earthquakes

Earthquakes happen all the time but most are so tiny they are detectable only by sensitive seismological instruments. If you're caught in a serious shaker:

➡ If indoors, get under a desk or table or stand in a doorway.

➡ Protect your head and stay clear of windows, mirrors or anything that might fall.

➡ Don't head for elevators or go running into the street.

➡ If you're in a shopping mall or large public building, expect the alarm and/or sprinkler systems to come on.

➡ If outdoors, get away from buildings, trees and power lines.

➡ If you're driving, pull over to the side of the road away from bridges, overpasses and power lines. Stay inside the car until the shaking stops.

➡ If you're on a sidewalk near buildings, duck into a doorway to protect yourself from falling bricks, glass and debris.

➡ Prepare for aftershocks.

➡ Turn on the radio and listen for bulletins.

➡ Use the telephone only if absolutely necessary.

Riptides

If you find yourself being carried offshore by a dangerous ocean current called a riptide, the important thing is to just keep afloat. Don't panic or try to swim against the current, as this will quickly exhaust you and you may drown. Instead, try to swim parallel to the shoreline and once the current stops pulling you out, swim back toward shore.

Tourist Information

For pretrip planning, peruse the information-packed website of the **California Travel & Tourism Commission** (www.visitcalifornia.com). This state-run agency also operates several **California Welcome Centers** (www.visitcwc.com), where staff dispense maps and brochures and may be able to help find accommodations.

Travelers With Disabilities

Southern California is reasonably well-equipped for travelers with disabilities. Disneyland is a shining example when it comes to catering to visitors with special needs.

Communications

- Telephone companies provide relay operators (dial ☎711) for the hearing impaired.
- Many banks provide ATM instructions in Braille.

Helpful Resources

A Wheelchair Rider's Guide to the California Coast (www.wheelingcalscoast.org) Free online directory and downloadable PDF guide for LA and Orange County coasts covers wheelchair access at beaches, parks and more.

Accessible San Diego (http://access-sandiego.org) Free online city guide (downloadable/print version $4/5) that's updated annually.

California State Parks (http://access.parks.ca.gov) Online searchable map and database for finding accessible features at parks statewide.

Los Angeles for Disabled Visitors (www.discoverlosangeles.com/search/site/disabled) Tips for accessible sightseeing, entertainment, museums and transportation.

MossRehab Resource Net (www.mossresourcenet.org/travel.htm) Useful links and general advice for accessible travel.

Theme Park Access Guide (www.mouseplanet.com/tag) An insider's view of Disneyland and other SoCal theme parks 'on wheels.'

Mobility & Accessibility

- Most intersections have dropped curbs; some have audible crossing signals.
- The Americans with Disabilities Act (ADA) requires public buildings built after 1993 to be wheelchair-accessible, including restrooms.
- Motels and hotels built after 1993 must have at least one ADA–compliant accessible room; state your specific needs when making reservations.
- For nonpublic buildings and those built prior to 1993, including hotels, restaurants, museums and theaters, there are no accessibility guarantees; call ahead to find out what to expect.
- Most national and many state parks and some other outdoor recreation areas offer paved or boardwalk-style nature trails accessible by wheelchairs.

Transportation

- All major airlines, Greyhound buses and Amtrak trains can accommodate people with disabilities, usually with 48 hours of advance notice required.
- Major car-rental agencies offer hand-controlled vehicles and vans with wheelchair lifts at no extra charge, but you must reserve these well in advance.
- For wheelchair-accessible van rentals, also try **Wheelchair Getaways** (☎800-642-2042; www.wheelchairgetaways.com) in LA or **Mobility Works** (☎877-275-4915; www.mobilityworks.com) in Pasadena.
- Local buses, trains and subway lines usually have wheelchair lifts.
- Seeing-eye dogs are permitted to accompany passengers traveling on public transportation.
- Taxi companies have at least one wheelchair-accessible van, but you'll usually need to call first.

Visas

- Depending on your country of origin, the rules for entering the USA keep changing. Double-check current visa and passport requirements *before* coming to the USA.
- Currently, under the US Visa Waiver Program (VWP), visas are not required for citizens of 38 countries for stays up to 90 days (no extensions) as long as you have a machine-readable passport (MRP) that's valid for six months beyond your intended stay.
- Citizens of VWP countries must still register online with the Electronic System for Travel Authorization (https://esta.cbp.dhs.gov/) at least 72 hours before travel. Once approved, ESTA registration ($14) is valid for up to two years or until your passport expires, whichever comes first.
- For most Canadian citizens traveling with Canadian passports that meet current US standards, a visa for short-term visits (usually up to six months) and ESTA registration aren't required.
- Citizens from all other countries or whose passports don't meet current US standards need to apply for a temporary visitor visa. Best done in your home country, the process costs a nonrefundable fee (minimum $160), involves a personal interview and can take several weeks, so apply as early as possible.
- For up-to-date information about entry requirements and eligibility, check the visa section of the **US Department of State website** (http://usvisas.state.gov) or contact the nearest US embassy or consulate in your home country (for a complete list, visit www.usembassy.gov).

Transportation

GETTING THERE & AWAY

Flights, cars and tours can be booked online at lonelyplanet.com/bookings.

Entering the Region

California is an important agricultural state. To prevent the spread of pests and diseases, certain food items (including meats, fresh fruit and vegetables) may not be brought into the state. Bakery items, chocolates and hard-cured cheeses are admissible. If you drive into California across the border from Mexico or from the neighboring states of Oregon, Nevada or Arizona, you may have to stop for a quick questioning and inspection by California Department of Food and Agriculture agents.

Under the US Department of Homeland Security's Orwellian-sounding Office of Biometric Identity Management, almost all foreign visitors to the USA (excluding, for now, many Canadians, some Mexican citizens, children under age 14 and seniors over age 79) will be digitally photographed and have their electronic (inkless) fingerprints scanned upon arrival.

For more information about entering the USA, visit www.cbp.gov online.

Passports

- Under the Western Hemisphere Travel Initiative (WHTI), all travelers must have a valid machine-readable passport (MRP) when entering the US by air, land or sea.
- The only exceptions are for some US, Canadian and Mexican citizens traveling *by land* who can present another WHTI-compliant document (eg pre-approved 'trusted traveler' cards). For details, visit www.cbp.gov/travel online.
- All foreign passports must meet current US standards and be valid for six months longer than your intended stay in the USA.
- MRP passports issued or renewed after October 26, 2006 must be e-passports (ie have a digital photo and integrated chip with biometric data).

Air

Southern California's primary international airport is LAX. Regional hubs have mostly domestic flights and are often served by low-cost carriers, such as Southwest Airlines, JetBlue, Alaska Airlines and Frontier Airlines.

Los Angeles International Airport (LAX; Map p62; www.lawa.org/lax; 1 World Way) California's largest and busiest airport, 20 miles southwest of Downtown LA, near the beaches.

CLIMATE CHANGE & TRAVEL

Every form of transport that relies on carbon-based fuel generates CO_2, the main cause of human-induced climate change. Modern travel is dependent on airplanes, which might use less fuel per mile per person than most cars but travel much greater distances. The altitude at which aircraft emit gases (including CO_2) and particles also contributes to their climate change impact. Many websites offer 'carbon calculators' that allow people to estimate the carbon emissions generated by their journey and, for those who wish to do so, to offset the impact of the greenhouse gases emitted with contributions to portfolios of climate-friendly initiatives throughout the world. Lonely Planet offsets the carbon footprint of all staff and author travel.

WARNING

In early 2014, the **US State Department** (http://travel.state.gov) issued a travel warning about increased Mexican drug-cartel violence and crime along the US–Mexico border. Travelers should exercise extreme caution in Tijuana, avoid large-scale gatherings and not venture out after dark, especially in cars with US license plates.

Bob Hope Airport (BUR; Map p62; www.burbankairport.com; 2627 N Hollywood Way, Burbank) About 14 miles northwest of Downtown LA, close to Universal Studios.

John Wayne Airport (SNA; www.ocair.com; 18601 Airport Way, Santa Ana) Off the I-405 Fwy in inland Orange County.

LA/Ontario International Airport (ONT; www.lawa.org/ont; 2500 E Airport Dr) In Riverside County, east of LA, closer to some desert destinations.

Long Beach Airport (LGB; www.lgb.org; 4100 Donald Douglas Dr, Long Beach) Easy access to LA and Orange County.

Palm Springs International Airport (PSP; Map p340; www.palmspringsairport.com; 3400 E Tahquitz Canyon Way) In the desert, east of LA.

San Diego International Airport (SAN; www.san.org; 3325 N Harbor Dr) Just 4 miles from downtown San Diego.

Santa Barbara Airport (SBA; www.flysba.com; 500 Fowler Rd, Goleta; Wi-Fi) Nine miles west of downtown Santa Barbara, off Hwy 101.

Land

Border Crossings

On the US–Mexico border between San Diego and Tijuana, San Ysidro is the world's busiest border crossing. Entering Mexico is usually not a problem, but coming back into the USA almost always entails a long wait, especially if you're driving. The website http://apps.cbp.gov/bwt shows current border wait times.

US citizens do not require a visa for stays of 72 hours or less within the border zone (ie from Tijuana south to Ensenada). To get back into the USA:

- US citizens will need to present a valid US passport or another WHTI–compliant document (see www.cbp.gov/travel). A regular US driver's license is no longer sufficient as proof.
- Non-US citizens may be subject to a full immigration inspection upon returning to the US, so bring your passport and US visa if required. For current passport and visa requirements, consult http://travel.state.gov.

Bus

Greyhound (☎800-231-2222; www.greyhound.com) operates a nationwide route system serving dozens of destinations in Southern California. Some cross-border routes connect with **Greyhound México** (☎01-800-710-8819; www.greyhound.com.mx) and **Greyhound Canada** (☎800-661-8747; www.greyhound.ca). Northbound buses from Mexico can take some time to cross the US border, as US immigration authorities may insist on checking every person on board.

Car & Motorcycle

If you're driving into the USA from Canada or Mexico, bring your vehicle's registration papers, liability insurance and driver's license. Many rental agencies prohibit their vehicles from being driven across international borders.

Unless you're planning an extended stay in Mexico, driving a car from the USA across the border to Tijuana is more hassle than it's worth. Instead take the trolley from downtown San Diego, or park on the US side and walk across the border instead. If you do decide to drive, you must buy Mexican car insurance beforehand or near the border crossing.

Train

Amtrak (☎800-872-7245; www.amtrak.com) operates a fairly extensive rail system throughout the USA. Trains are comfortable, if slow, and are equipped with dining cars on long-distance routes. Fares vary according to the type of seating (eg coach or business class, sleeping compartments).

Major long-distance routes to/from Southern California:

Coast Starlight Travels the West Coast daily from Seattle to LA (from $92, 35 hours) via Portland, Sacramento, Oakland, Santa Barbara and Burbank.

Southwest Chief Daily departures between Chicago and LA (from $135, 43 hours) via Kansas City, Albuquerque and Flagstaff.

Sunset Limited Thrice-weekly service between New Orleans and LA (from $130, 47 hours) via Houston, San Antonio, Tucson and northern Palm Springs.

TRAIN PASSES

Amtrak's USA Rail Pass is valid for coach-class train travel only (not Thruway buses) for 15 ($449), 30 ($679) or 45 ($879) days; children aged two to 15 pay half-price. Travel is limited to eight, 12 or 18 one-way 'segments,' respectively. A segment is not the same as a one-way trip. If reaching your destination requires riding more than one train, you'll use multiple pass segments. Purchase passes online, then make advance reservations for each trip segment.

GETTING AROUND

Air

Although it is possible to fly from, say, LA to San Diego or Palm Springs, the time and cost involved don't make planes a sensible way to get around SoCal.

Bicycle

Although cycling around SoCal is a nonpolluting way to travel, the distances involved make it hard to cover much ground. You must be able to cope with high temperatures, especially in summer.

Adventure Cycling Association (www.adventurecycling.org) Online resource for purchasing bicycle-friendly maps and long-distance route guides.

Better World Club (☎866-238-1137; www.betterworldclub.com) Annual membership (from $40) gets you two 24-hour emergency roadside pickups and transport within a 30-mile radius.

Rental & Purchase

➡ You can rent bicycles by the hour, day or week in most cities and tourist towns.

➡ Rates start at $10 per hour for beach cruisers up to $45 or more per day for mountain bikes; ask about multiday and weekly discounts. A credit-card security deposit may be required.

➡ Buy new models from specialty bike shops and sporting-goods stores, or used from notice boards at hostels, cafes etc.

➡ To buy or sell used bicycles, check online bulletin boards like **Craigslist** (www.craigslist.org).

Road Rules

➡ Cycling is allowed on all roads and highways – even along freeways if there's no suitable alternative, such as a smaller parallel road; all mandatory exits are marked.

➡ Some cities have designated bicycle lanes, but keep your wits about you when riding in heavy traffic.

➡ Cyclists must follow the same rules of the road as vehicles. Don't expect drivers to always respect your right of way.

➡ Wearing a bicycle helmet is mandatory for riders under 18 years old.

Transporting Bicycles

➡ Some local buses and trains are equipped with bicycle racks. Other local trains allow bicycles on board, though possibly not during peak hours.

➡ Greyhound transports bicycles as luggage (surcharge typically $30 to $40), provided the bike is disassembled and placed in a rigid container ($10 box available at some terminals).

➡ Amtrak's *Pacific Surfliner* trains feature special bicycle racks, but be sure to reserve a spot when making your ticket reservation. On Amtrak trains without bicycle racks, bikes must be put into a box ($15 at most staffed terminals) then checked as luggage (fee $10).

Bus

Southern California cities served by **Greyhound** (☎800-231-2222; www.greyhound.com) include LA, Anaheim, Long Beach, Santa Barbara, San Diego, Oceanside, Temecula and northern Palm Springs. Frequency of service varies from 'rarely' to 'constantly,' but main routes operate every hour or so, sometimes around the clock.

Greyhound buses are usually clean, comfortable and reliable. The best seats are typically toward the front and away from the bathroom. Limited on-board amenities include freezing air-con (bring a sweater) and slightly reclining seats. Smoking on board is prohibited.

Bus stations are typically dreary, often in dodgy areas; this is especially true of Downtown LA and Palm Springs. If you arrive at night, take a taxi into town or directly to your hotel.

Costs

It's easy to buy tickets online with a credit card, then pick them up (bring photo ID) at the bus terminal. You can also buy tickets over the phone or in person from a ticket agent. Ticket agents also accept debit cards, traveler's checks (in US dollars) and cash.

You may save a few dollars by purchasing tickets at least seven days in advance and by traveling between Monday and Thursday. Other promotions, including companion fares (50% off), are often available, though they may have restrictions or blackout periods. Check the website

SAMPLE GREYHOUND FARES

ROUTE	ADULT FARE	DURATION	FREQUENCY
LA–Anaheim	$10-16	¾-1¼hr	7 per day
LA–Palm Springs	$19-33	2½-3½hr	4 per day
LA–San Diego	$11-22	2¼-3¼hr	20 per day
LA–Santa Barbara	$9-19	2¼-2¾hr	4 per day

for current fare specials or ask when buying tickets.

Discounts are regularly available – on unrestricted fares only – for seniors aged over 62 (5% discount), students with a Student Advantage Card (20%) and children aged two to 11 (25%). Children under two years old ride free.

Reservations

➡ Most boarding is done on a first-come, first-served basis.

➡ Buying tickets in advance does not guarantee you a seat on any particular bus, unless you also purchase priority boarding (add $5).

➡ Arrive at least one hour prior to the scheduled departure time to secure a seat. Allow extra time on weekends and during holidays.

Car, Motorcycle & RV

Automobile Associations

For 24-hour emergency roadside assistance, free maps and discounts on lodging, attractions, car rentals and more:

American Automobile Association (AAA; ☎877-428-2277; www.aaa.com) Walk-in offices throughout California, add-on coverage for RVs and motorcycles, and reciprocal agreements with some international auto clubs (eg CAA in Canada, AA in the UK) – bring your membership card from home.

Better World Club (☎866-238-1137; www.betterworldclub.com) Ecofriendly alternative auto club supports environmental causes and offers add-on emergency roadside assistance for cyclists.

Driver's Licenses

➡ Visitors may legally drive a car in California for up to 12 months with their home driver's license.

➡ If you're from overseas, an International Driving Permit (IDP) will have more credibility with traffic police and also simplify the car-rental process, especially if your license doesn't have a photo or isn't written in English.

➡ To drive a motorcycle, you'll need a valid US state motorcycle license or a specially endorsed IDP.

➡ International automobile associations can issue IDPs, valid for one year, for a fee. Always carry your home license together with the IDP.

Fuel

➡ Gas stations in California, nearly all of which are self-service, are ubiquitous, except in national parks and some sparsely populated desert and mountain areas.

➡ Gas is sold in gallons (one US gallon equals 3.78L). At press time, the average cost for mid-grade fuel in California was $4.25.

Insurance

California law requires liability insurance for all vehicles. When renting a car, check your auto-insurance policy from home or your travel insurance policy to see if you're already covered. If you're not, expect to pay about $20 per day.

Insurance against damage to the car itself, called Collision Damage Waiver (CDW) or Loss Damage Waiver (LDW), costs another $10 or more per day. The deductible (excess) may require you to pay the first $100 to $500 for any repairs.

Some credit cards will cover CDW/LDW, provided you charge the entire cost of the car rental to the card. If there's an accident, you may have to pay the car-rental company first, then seek reimbursement from the credit-card company.

Rental

CARS

To rent a car, you'll typically need to be at least 25 years old, hold a valid driver's license and have a major credit card (not a check or debit card). A few companies may rent to drivers under 25 but over 21 for a hefty surcharge. If you don't have a credit card, you may occasionally be able to make a large cash deposit instead.

With advance reservations, you can often get an

ROAD DISTANCES (Miles)

	Anaheim	Big Bear Lake	Death Valley	Las Vegas	Los Angeles	Newport Beach	Palm Springs	San Diego	San Francisco
Big Bear Lake	90								
Death Valley	285	235							
Las Vegas	270	220	130						
Los Angeles	30	95	290	280					
Newport Beach	20	100	300	290	45				
Palm Springs	95	80	300	285	105	115			
San Diego	95	145	350	340	120	90	125		
San Francisco	410	470	530	580	385	425	485	525	
Santa Barbara	120	185	340	355	95	140	205	220	325

economy-size vehicle from about $30 per day, plus insurance, taxes and fees. Rates usually include unlimited mileage, but expect surcharges for additional drivers and one-way rentals. Airport rental locations may offer lower rates, but have higher fees; if you buy a fly-drive package, local taxes may be extra.

Child or infant safety seats are legally required; reserve them (around $10 per day) when booking your car. If you'd like to minimize your contribution to SoCal's polluted air, some major car-rental companies offer 'green' fleets of hybrid or bio-fueled rental cars. Expect to pay significantly more for those models and reserve them well in advance.

To find and compare independent car-rental agencies, as well as to search for cheaper long-term rentals, try **Car Rental Express** (www.carrentalexpress.com).

Alamo (☎877-222-9075; www.alamo.com)

Avis (☎800-633-3469; www.avis.com)

Budget (☎800-218-7992; www.budget.com)

Dollar (☎800-800-4000; www.dollar.com)

Enterprise (☎800-261-7331; www.enterprise.com)

Fox (☎800-225-4369, 310-641-3838; www.foxrentacar.com) Locations near LA, San Diego, Orange County, Burbank and Ontario airports.

Hertz (☎800-654-3131; www.hertz.com)

National (☎877-222-9058; www.nationalcar.com)

Rent-a-Wreck (☎877-877-0700; www.rentawreck.com) Minimum rental age and under-25 driver surcharges vary by location. SoCal branches include LAX, West LA, North Hollywood and Pasadena.

Simply Hybrid (☎888-359-0055, 323-653-0011; www.simplyhybrid.com) Rents hybrid, electric and flex-fuel vehicles in LA; ask about free delivery and pickup.

Super Cheap! Car Rental (www.supercheapcar.com) Near LAX and in Irvine, Orange County. No surcharge for drivers aged 21 to 24 years; nominal daily fee for drivers under age 21 with full-coverage insurance.

Thrifty (☎800-847-4389; www.thrifty.com)

Zipcar (☎866-494-7227; www.zipcar.com) Currently in LA and San Diego, this car-sharing club charges usage fees (per hour or daily) including free gas, insurance (a damage fee up to $750 may apply) and limited mileage. Apply online (foreign drivers OK); application fee $25.

DO I NEED A CAR IN SOCAL?

Southern California is practically synonymous with car culture but, with time and patience, you can get around using public transportation. Focus your itinerary and do in-depth explorations of smaller areas rather than a big, sweeping loop. Even if you have a car, consider ditching it for at least part of the time.

Amtrak and Metrolink trains and Greyhound buses link major coastal cities, as well as some inland destinations. Many cities and towns have local bus, train and/or trolley systems, and beach towns are usually compact enough to explore by bicycle. Even in LA you'll be OK as long as you limit yourself to seeing just one or two neighborhoods a day.

MOTORCYCLES

Motorcycle rentals and insurance are not cheap, especially if you've got your eye on a Harley. Depending on the model, it costs $100 to $250 per day plus taxes and fees, including helmets, unlimited miles and liability insurance; one-way rentals and CDW cost extra. Discounts may be available for multi-day and weekly rentals. Security deposits cost up to $2000 (credit card required).

Eagle Rider (☎888-900-9901, 310-321-3180; www.eaglerider.com) SoCal rentals in LA, San Diego, Newport Beach and Palm Springs.

Route 66 Riders (☎888-434-4473, 310-578-0112; www.route66riders.com; 4161 Lincoln Blvd, Marina del Rey; ⏲10am-6pm Tue-Sat, 11am-5pm Sun) Harley-Davidson rentals in LA's South Bay.

RECREATIONAL VEHICLES

In big cities, RVs are a nuisance, since there are few places to park or plug them in. RVs are cumbersome to navigate and burn fuel at an alarming rate, but they do solve transportation, accommodation and cooking needs in one fell swoop. Outside of urban areas, it's easy to find RV campgrounds with electricity and water hookups.

Book RV rentals far in advance. Rental costs vary by size and model; expect to pay at least $100 per day, excluding mileage, vehicle prep fees and bedding and kitchen kits. If pets are allowed, a surcharge may apply.

Cruise America (☎800-671-8042, 480-464-7300; www.cruiseamerica.com) RV rentals in LA, Burbank, San Diego, Oceanside and Costa Mesa.

El Monte (☎888-337-2214, 562-483-4956; www.elmonterv.com) RV rentals in LA, San Diego, Newport Beach and Van Nuys (San Fernando Valley).

Escape Campervans (☎877-270-8267, 310-672-9909; www.escapecampervans.com) Awesomely painted campervans at economical rates in LA and San Francisco.

Happy Travel Campers (☎310-929-5666, 855-754-6555; www.camperusa.com) Campervan rentals in the San Francisco Bay Area, LA and Las Vegas, Nevada

Jucy Rentals (☎800-650-4180; www.jucyrentals.com) Campervan rentals in San Francisco, LA and Las Vegas, Nevada.

Vintage Surfari Wagons (☎714-585-7565, 949-716-3135; www.vwsurfari.com) VW campervan rentals in Orange County.

Road Rules

- Drive on the right-hand side of the road.
- Talking or texting on a cell phone without a hands-free device while driving is illegal.
- The use of seat belts is required for drivers, front-seat passengers and children under age 16.
- Infant and child safety seats are required for children under six years old or weighing less than 60lbs.
- All motorcyclists must wear a helmet.
- High-occupancy (HOV) lanes marked with a diamond symbol are reserved for cars with multiple occupants, sometimes only during signposted hours.
- Unless otherwise posted, the speed limit is 65mph on freeways, 55mph on two-lane undivided highways, 35mph on major city streets, and 25mph in business and residential districts and near schools.
- Except where indicated, turning right at a red stoplight after coming to a full stop is permitted, although intersecting traffic still has the right of way.
- At four-way stop signs, cars proceed in the order in which they arrived. If two cars arrive simultaneously, the one on the right has the right of way. When in doubt, wave the other driver ahead.
- When emergency vehicles (ie police, fire or ambulance) approach from either direction, cautiously pull over to the side of the road.
- When parking, read all posted regulations and pay close attention to any colored curbs and parking meters, or you may be ticketed and/or towed.
- Driving under the influence of alcohol or drugs is illegal. It's also illegal to carry open containers of alcohol, even partly full or empty ones, inside a vehicle (store them in the trunk instead).

Tours

Adventure Bus (☎888-737-5263, 909-633-7225; www.adventurebus.com) Offers springtime camping and sleeping-bus tours of Death Valley and Joshua Tree National Parks, departing from Las Vegas, Nevada. All ages welcome.

California Motorcycle Tours (☎888-408-7631, 858-677-9892; www.ca-motorcycle-tours.com) San Diego–based outfitter offers guided trips on Harley Davidsons, including to beaches, mountains, deserts and Mexico's Baja California.

Green Tortoise (☎800-867-8647, 415-956-7500; www.greentortoise.com) Youthful budget-backpacker trips utilize converted sleeping-bunk buses. The three-day 'Mojave Desert Loop' route visits Joshua Tree National Park and Las Vegas, departing from LA.

Road Scholar (☎800-454-5768; www.roadscholar.org) Formerly Elderhostel, this nonprofit organization offers educational trips – including bus and walking tours and outdoor activities like hiking and birding – for older adults.

Train

Amtrak

Amtrak (☎800-872-7245; www.amtrak.com) runs comfortable, occasionally tardy trains throughout California. At some stations, Thruway buses provide onward connections to smaller destinations. Smoking is prohibited aboard trains and buses.

Hugging the coast for much of its route, the memorably scenic *Pacific Surfliner* is Amtrak's main rail service in SoCal. Double-decker trains have on-board bicycle and surfboard racks and a cafe car. Business-class seats feature slightly more legroom, electrical outlets and sometimes wi-fi.

Up to 12 trains daily ply the *Surfliner* route between San Diego and LA, making stops at Oceanside (for Legoland), San Juan Capistrano and Anaheim (for Disney-

SAMPLE AMTRAK FARES

ROUTE	COACH	BUSINESS CLASS	DURATION
LA–Anaheim	$15	$25	¾hr
LA–San Diego	$37	$56	2¾hr
LA–Santa Barbara	$32	$47	2¾hr
San Diego–Anaheim	$28	$42	2¼hr
San Diego–Oceanside	$18	$28	1hr
San Diego–San Juan Capistrano	$22	$33	1½hr

land), among others. Some trains continue north to Santa Barbara via Burbank's Bob Hope Airport, Ventura and Carpinteria, and two go all the way to San Luis Obispo.

Among Amtrak's long-distance trains, which have dining and sleeping cars, the *Coast Starlight* stops in Santa Barbara, Burbank and LA, while the *Sunset Limited* travels to LA and northern Palm Springs.

COSTS

Purchase tickets at train stations, by phone or online (in advance for the best discounts). Fares depend on the day of travel, the route, the type of seating etc. Fares may be slightly higher during peak travel times (eg summer). Round-trip tickets typically cost the same as two one-way tickets.

Usually seniors over 62 years and students with an ISIC or Student Advantage Card receive a 15% discount, while up to two children, aged two to 15 and accompanied by an adult, get 50% off. Children under two years of age ride free. AAA members save 10%. Special promotions can become available anytime, so check the website or ask when making reservations.

RESERVATIONS

Amtrak reservations can be made up to 11 months prior to departure. In summer and around holidays, trains sell out quickly, so book tickets as early as possible. The cheapest coach fares are usually for unreserved seats; business-class fares come with guaranteed seats.

TRAIN PASSES

Amtrak's California Rail Pass costs $159 ($80 for children aged two to 15) and is valid on all trains (except certain long-distance routes) and most connecting Thruway buses for seven days of travel within a 21-day period. Passholders must reserve each leg of travel in advance and obtain hard-copy tickets prior to boarding.

Regional Trains

Major SoCal population centers are linked to LA by a commuter-train network called **Metrolink** (☎800-371-5465; www.metrolinktrains.com). Seven lines connect Downtown LA's Union Station with the surrounding counties – Orange, Riverside, San Bernardino and Ventura – as well as northern San Diego County.

The most useful Metrolink line for visitors is the Orange County Line, stopping in Anaheim, Orange, Santa Ana, San Juan Capistrano, San Clemente and Oceanside. From Oceanside, **Coaster** (☎760-966-6500; www.gonctd.com/coaster) trains run to Downtown San Diego via Carlsbad, Encinitas, Solana Beach and Old Town.

Most trains depart during weekday morning and afternoon rush hours, with only one or two services during the day or late evening. Some lines offer limited weekend services. Tickets are available from station vending machines; fares are zone-based.

Behind the Scenes

SEND US YOUR FEEDBACK

We love to hear from travelers – your comments keep us on our toes and help make our books better. Our well-traveled team reads every word on what you loved or loathed about this book. Although we cannot reply individually to your submissions, we always guarantee that your feedback goes straight to the appropriate authors, in time for the next edition. Each person who sends us information is thanked in the next edition – the most useful submissions are rewarded with a selection of digital PDF chapters.

Visit **lonelyplanet.com/contact** to submit your updates and suggestions or to ask for help. Our award-winning website also features inspirational travel stories, news and discussions.

Note: We may edit, reproduce and incorporate your comments in Lonely Planet products such as guidebooks, websites and digital products, so let us know if you don't want your comments reproduced or your name acknowledged. For a copy of our privacy policy visit lonelyplanet.com/privacy.

AUTHOR THANKS

Andrew Bender

Suki Gear, Cliff Wilkinson, Alison Lyall, Hilary Angel, Juan Flores, Joe Timko, Sarah Weinberg, Suzi Dennett and the good folks at the SPP Help Desk.

Adam Skolnick

Los Angeles is a city I love, full of people I love. LA is home. Still, it's never easy to dissect your own backyard, mostly because you usually don't know what you're missing. So thanks to Alma Lauer, Trisha Cole, Jessica Ritz, Nina Gregory, Burton Breznick, Tchaiko Omawale, Dan Cohn, Angel Payne, Christine Lazzaro, Liebe Geft, the folks at the Wende Museum, Michael McDowell, Alex Capriotti, and John Moore. Thanks also to all those wild seals, sea lions, dolphins and whales that keep us entertained in the water, and to the Lonely Planet staff and my cohorts Sara Benson and Andy Bender.

ACKNOWLEDGEMENTS

Climate map data adapted from Peel MC, Finlayson BL & McMahon TA (2007) 'Updated World Map of the Köppen-Geiger Climate Classification', *Hydrology and Earth System Sciences*, 11, 163344.

Cover photograph: Manhattan beach and pier at sunset, Rick Frohne Landscape Photographer/Getty

THIS BOOK

The 4th edition of Lonely Planet's *Los Angeles, San Diego & Southern California* guidebook was researched and written by Sara Benson, Andrew Bender and Adam Skolnick. All three authors also worked on the 3rd edition. The 2nd edition was written by Andrea Schulte-Peevers, Amy C Balfour and Andrew Bender. This guidebook was commissioned in Lonely Planet's Oakland office, and produced by the following:

Commissioning Editor Suki Gear

Destination Editors MaSovaida Morgan, Clifton Wilkinson

Product Editor Penny Cordner

Senior Cartographer Alison Lyall

Book Designer Jessica Rose

Assisting Editors Bruce Evans, Paul Harding, Kate Mathews, Anne Mulvaney, Lauren O'Connell, Kristin Odijk, Monique Perrin

Assisting Cartographers Anita Banh, David Kemp, Corey Hutchison, Valentina Kremenchutskaya

Cover Researcher Naomi Parker

Thanks to Imogen Bannister, Ryan Evans, Larissa Frost, Charlotte Harpin, Jouve India, Zak Lamon, Anne Mason, Wayne Murphy, Claire Naylor, Karyn Noble, Katie O'Connell, Semin Poonja, Oliver Pullent, Alison Ridgway, Samantha Russell-Tulip, Lyahna Spencer, Samantha Tyson

Index

A

Abalone Cove Shoreline Park 183
Academy Awards 25, 64, 449, 451
accommodations 470-2, *see also individual locations*
activities 37-45, *see also* cycling, diving, fishing, hang-gliding, hiking, kayaking, kiteboarding, rock climbing, skiing, snorkeling, surfing, swimming, windsurfing
air travel 479-80, 481
airports 21, 479-80, *see also* Los Angeles International Airport (LAX)
amusement parks, *see* theme parks
Anacapa Island 426
Anaheim 219-36, **220**
- accommodations 228-9
- drinking & nightlife 232-3
- entertainment 233
- food 231-2
- itineraries 225
- travel to/from 235-6

animals 368, 466-7
Anza-Borrego Desert State Park 17, **360**, **17**
architecture 24, 458-60
area codes 21, 475
art galleries, *see* galleries, museums
arts 453-7, *see also* literature, music, visual arts
ATMs 476

B

Backbone Trail 161
Balboa Island 253

Map Pages **000**
Photo Pages **000**

Balboa Park 11, 275-82, **278**
Balboa Peninsula 249
Barstow 365-7
baseball 105-6, 107-8, 233, 283, 313, 447
beaches 33-6, **34**
- Balboa Peninsula 249
- Bolsa Chica State Beach 248
- Butterfly Beach 398
- Cardiff State Beach 327
- Carlsbad Coast 330
- Carpinteria State Beach 420, **163**
- Corona del Mar 259
- Coronado Municipal Beach 290, **163**
- Crystal Cove State Park 259-60, **163**
- Dana Point 269-70
- Doheny State Beach 269
- East Beach 398, **163**
- El Capitán State Beach 398
- El Matador State Beach, 144, 158, **95**
- Goleta Beach County Park 398
- Hermosa Beach 158
- Huntington Beach 244-9, **162**
- La Jolla Beaches 320
- Laguna Beach 260-7
- Leadbetter Beach 398
- Leo Carrillo 158
- Los Angeles 158
- Malaga Cove 158
- Malibu 144, **163**
- Malibu Lagoon State Beach 146
- Manhattan Beach 158
- Mission Beach 291-3, **162**
- Mothers Beach 249
- Newport Beach 249-57, **250-1**
- Ocean Beach 291, 301, 308, 311, **292**
- OEX Sunset Beach 243
- One Thousand Steps Beach 398
- Pacific Beach 291-3, 301-2, 308, 312, **294**
- Paradise Cove 158
- Refugio State Beach 398
- Salt Creek Beach 269
- San Buenaventura State Beach 424
- San Clemente 271
- San Diego 290
- San Elijo State Beach 327
- Santa Barbara 398
- Santa Monica 158, **162**
- Seal Beach 241-3
- Silicon Beach 175
- Silver Strand State Beach 290
- Solana Beach 326-7
- Sunset Beach 243-4
- Surfrider Beach 145
- Trestles 271
- Venice Beach 94, 158, **94**
- Westward Beach 144-5, 158
- White Point Park 186
- Windansea Beach 320
- Zuma 144-5, 158

Beatty, Nevada 376-7
beer 309, 464
Bel Air 94, 131-43, **134**, **94**
- accommodations 138-9
- drinking & nightlife 141-2
- entertainment 142
- food 139-41
- shopping 142-3
- sights 131-7

Beverly Hills 131-43, **132-3**
- accommodations 138-9
- activities 138
- drinking & nightlife 141-2
- entertainment 142
- food 139-41
- shopping 142-3
- sights 131-7

bicycle travel, *see* cycling
Big Bear Lake 12, 216-17, **12**
Bolsa Chica State Beach 248
books, *see* literature
border crossings 298, 480
Boron 379
Borrego Springs 358
Bowers Museum 238
Boyle Heights 202-3
Brentwood 94, 131-43, **94**
- accommodations 138-9
- drinking & nightlife 141-2
- entertainment 142
- food 139-41
- shopping 142-3
- sights 131-7

budget 21
Buellton 418-19
Burbank 94, 189-93, **95**
bus travel 480, 481-2
bushwalking, *see* hiking
business hours 21, 477
butterflies 393

C

Cachuma Lake Recreation Area 409
car travel 21, 480, 482-4, *see also* scenic drives
Cardiff-by-the-Sea 327
Carlsbad 329-32
Carpinteria 420-1
Catalina Island 213-15
celebrity spotting 24
cell phones 20
Channel Islands National Park 15, 425-8, **15**
children, travel with 50-2, *see also* theme parks
- beaches 35
- Disneyland 48-9
- Huntington Beach 246, **162**
- Las Vegas 381
- Los Angeles 69
- San Diego 289

Santa Barbara 396
Christ Cathedral 240
Chumash Painted Cave State Historic Park 409
Cinco de Mayo 25
climate 20, 25-6, *see also individual locations*
Coachella Music & Arts Festival 25, 345
Coachella Valley 339-41, **340**
Corona del Mar 259
Coronado 17, 289-90
Costa Mesa 257-9
costs, *see* budget
courses 461, 472
credit cards 476
Crescent Bay 260, **11**
Crystal Cove State Park 259-60, **163**
culture 430-1, 441-7
Culver City 94, 127-31, **95**
currency 20
customs regulations 472
cycling 44-5, 481
Anza-Borrego Desert State Park 359-61
Death Valley National Park 373
Joshua Tree National Park 350-8, **352-3**, **15**
Newport Beach 252-3
Santa Barbara 396
Santa Monica 156

D

Dana Point 269-70
dangers, *see* safety
day spas, *see* hot springs & day spas
Death Valley Junction 376
Death Valley National Park 13, 369-76, **370**
Del Mar 323-6
disabilities, travelers with 478
Disneyland 49
Discovery Science Center 238
Disney California Adventure 225-7
Disneyland 11, 46-9, 219-36, **219**, **220**, **222**, **10**
accommodations 49, 218, 227-8
children, travel with 228, 229
climate 218
drinking & nightlife 232-3
entertainment 232, 233
Fastpass 226
food 49, 218, 230-1
highlights 219
information 234-5
itineraries 225
shopping 233-4
sights 221-36
tickets 47-8
travel seasons 46-7, 218
travel to/from 235-6
diving 37-8, 253, 261, 320
Dodger Stadium 105-6
Downtown Los Angeles 68-87, 94, **70-1**, **94**
accommodations 79-80
activities 79
drinking & nightlife 83-4
entertainment 84-5
food 80-3
shopping 85-7
sights 68-79
drinking & nightlife, *see individual locations*
drinks, *see* beer, wineries
driving, *see* car travel, scenic drives

E

Eagle Rock 201-2
Echo Park 105-8, 94
economy 430-1
electricity 473, 476
El Matador 144, 158, **95**
emergencies 21
entertainment, *see individual locations*
Encinitas 327-9, **16**, **19**
events 25-6
exchange rates 21
Exposition Park 205-13

F

family activities, *see* children, travel with
festivals & events 25-6
film 450
food 465
Los Angeles 64-8
music 454
films 191, 430, 448-52
fishing 44, 181, 187, 294-5
Fonts Point 358
food 22, 461-5, *see also individual locations*
Foxen Canyon Wine Trail 13, 411-12
free attractions 22-3
Fryman Canyon 157
Furnace Creek 371

G

galleries, *see also* museums
Ace Gallery 135-6
Arts District (Culver City) 127
Barnsdall Art Park 100-1
Bo Bridges Photography & Spit Studio 177
LA Louver 169
Laguna Beach 264
Santa Barbara 400
Streetcraft LA 155
Gaslamp Quarter 14, **14**
gay travelers 445, 473
Los Angeles 122-3
Palm Springs 348
San Diego 311
Getty Center 131-3, **94**
golf 45
Carlsbad 330
Furnace Creek 373
Los Angeles 103
Palm Springs 344
Griffith Observatory 99-100, **66-7**
Griffith Park 94, 99-105, **100-1**
activities 103
drinking & nightlife 104
entertainment 104-5
food 103-4
shopping 105
sights 99-103

H

hang-gliding 44, 321, 399
health 473-4
Hermosa Beach 158, 179-81
Highland Park 201-2
Highway 1 9, **8-9**
Highway 154 (San Marcos Pass Rd) 409
hiking 40-3
Anza-Borrego Desert State Park 359
Backbone Trail 161
Death Valley National Park 374
Hidden Valley Trail 351-89
Indian Canyons 343
Joshua Tree National Park 354
Keys View Trail 351
Laguna Beach 263
Los Angeles 161
Malibu Creek State Park 149
Mishe Mokwa Trail & Sandstone Peak 148
Mt San Jacinto State Park 343-89
Pt Mugu State Park 149
Runyon Canyon 115
San Gabriel range 161
Santa Barbara 398-9
Santa Monica Mountains 19, 161, **19**
Tahquitz Canyon 341-3
Topanga Canyon State Park 148-9
history 24, 432-40
Desert Queen Ranch 351
Mexican ranchos 434-5
native Californians 432-3
racial riots 438-9
social movements 439-40
Spanish Mission 434
holidays 477
Hollywood 87-93, 94, 96-9, **88**, **28**, **95**
accommodations 92-3
activities 92
drinking & nightlife 96-7
entertainment 97-8
food 93-6
shopping 99
sights 87-92
Hollywood Bowl 87
Hollywood Bowl Overlook 157
Hollywood Sign 87-9, **95**
Hollywood Walk of Fame 89, **28**
horseback riding 44
hot springs & day spas 38
Club Mud 238
Palm Springs 344
Tecopa 377
hot-air ballooning 44
Hotel Del Coronado 289, **17**
Huntington Beach 244-9, **162**
Hurricane Harbor 215

I

immigration 443-5
Indian Canyons 343
insurance 474, 482
international visitors 475
internet access 474
internet resources 21, 57
itineraries 27-32, **27-32**, *see also individual locations*

J

Joshua Tree National Park 15, 350-8, **352-3**, **15**
Julian 18, 363-4, **18**

K

kayaking 38-9, 262, 396-7, 427-8
Kidseum 238
kiteboarding 40-5
Knott's Berry Farm 236-7
Koreatown 203-5

L

La Jolla 14, 317-23, **318**, **14**
Laguna Beach 11, 260-7, **262**, **11**
Lancaster-Palmdale 378
language 20
Las Vegas 380-9, **382**
  accommodations 385
  activities 385
  drinking & nightlife 388
  entertainment 388-9
  food 386-8
  shopping 389
  sights 380-5
legal matters 474-6
Leo Carrillo 158
lesbian travelers 445, 473
  Los Angeles 122-3
  Palm Springs 348
  San Diego 311
Lincoln Heights 201-2
literature 430, 456-7
Little Osaka 153
Little Saigon 242
Long Beach 183-9, **184**
  accommodations 187
  activities 187
  drinking 189
  entertainment 189
  food 188-9
  sights 185-7
Los Angeles 9, 56-217, **58-9**, **62-3**, **70-1**, *see also individual suburbs for accommodations, activities, drinking & nightlife, entertainment, food, shopping & sights listings*
  activities 79
  Bel Air 94, 131-43, **134**, **94**
  Beverly Hills 131-43, **132-3**
  Boyle Heights 202-3
  Brentwood 94, 131-43, **94**
  Burbank 94, 189-93, **94**
  climate 56
  Culver City 94, 127-31, **95**
  Downtown 68-87, 94, **70-1**, **94**
  Eagle Rock 201-2
  Echo Park 94, 105-8
  Exposition Park 205-13
  festivals & events 64-8, 84
  Griffith Park 94, 99-105, **100-1**
  Hermosa Beach 179-81
  Highland Park 201-2
  highlights 58-9
  history 60
  Hollywood 87-93, 94, 96-9, **88**, **28**, **95**
  itineraries 61
  Koreatown 203-5
  Lincoln Heights 201-2
  Little Osaka 153
  Long Beach 183-9, **184**
  Los Feliz 94, 99-105, **102**, **95**
  Malibu 94, 144-52, **146-7**, **163**
  Manhattan Beach 158, 177-9
  Mar Vista 94, 127-31, **95**
  Marina del Rey 94, 168-77
  medical services 209
  Mid-City 94, 108-27, **110-11**
  Mt Washington 201-2
  Pacific Palisades 94, 144-52, **146-7**
  Palos Verdes Peninsula 182-3
  Pasadena 193-201, **194**
  Redondo Beach 181-2
  San Fernano Valley 94, 189-93
  San Gabriel Valley, the 193-201
  Santa Monica 94, 152-68, **154**, **95**
  Silver Lake 94, 105-8, **66**
  South Central LA 205-13
  Torrance 181-2
  tourist information 209-10
  tours 60-4
  travel seasons 56
  travel to/within 210-13
  Universal City 94, 189-93
  Venice 94, 168-77, **170**, **94**
  walking tour 77
  websites 57, 210
  West Hollywood 94, 108-27, **110-11**
  Westlake 203-5
  Westwood 94, 131-43, **134**
Los Angeles County Museum of Art (LACMA) 109, **66**
Los Angeles International Airport (LAX) 21, 210, 211, 479-80
Los Feliz 94, 99-105, **102**, **95**
  activities 103
  drinking & nightlife 104
  entertainment 104-5
  food 103-4
  shopping 105
  sights 99-103
Los Olivos 414-15
Los Padres National Forest 409
Lotusland 419

M

Malaga Cove 158
Malibu 144-52, 94, **146-7**, **163**
  accommodations 149-50
  activities 148-9
  drinking & nightlife 151
  entertainment 151
  food 150-1
  shopping 151-2
  sights 144-8
Malibu Bluffs Park 144
Malibu Canyon 148
Manhattan Beach 158, 177-9
maps 476
Mar Vista 94, 127-31, **95**
Marina del Rey 94, 168-77
markets
  Farmers Market (Los Angeles) 109
  flea markets (Los Angeles) 200
  Pasadena 200
  Santa Monica Farmers Markets 160
measures 476
medical services 473-4
Medieval Times Dinner & Tournament 237-8
Meditation Mount 422
Mesquite Flat sand dunes 372, **13**
Mexican border 298, 444, 480
Mid-City (Los Angeles) 94, 108-27, **110-11**
  accommodations 115-16
  activities 114-15
  drinking & nightlife 120-1
  entertainment 121-4
  food 116-20
  shopping 124-7
  sights 109-14
Miramar Air Show & Fleet Week 26
Mission Bay 293, 302
Mission Beach 162, 293, 312, **294**, **162**
missions
  La Purísima Mission State Historic Park 414
  Mission Basilica San Diego de Alcalá 287
  Mission San Buenaventura 424
  Mission San Fernando Rey de España 202
  Mission San Juan Capistrano 17, 268, **17**
  Mission San Luis Rey de Francia 333
  Mission Santa Barbara 392-3, **13**
mobile phones 20
Modernism Week 25
Mojave 378-9
Mojave National Preserve 367-9
money 20, 472-3, 476-7
Montecito 419-20
motorcycle travel 480, 482-4
mountain biking 44-5
Mt San Jacinto State Park 343
Mt Washington 201-2
museums 24
  Anne Frank Exhibit 137
  Bowers Museum 238
  Broad 75
  California Oil Museum 423
  California Science Center 206
  California Surf Museum 332
  Getty Center 131-3, **94**
  Getty Villa 145
  Griffith Observatory 99-100, **66-7**
  Huntington Library 195

Map Pages **000**
Photo Pages **000**

International Surfing Museum 245
Laguna Art Museum 260
Los Angeles County Museum of Art (LACMA) 109, **66**
Maritime Museum 288
Mingei International Museum 280
Mob Museum (Las Vegas) 384
Museum of Contemporary Art 69
Natural History Museum of Los Angeles 206
Neon Museum (Las Vegas) 384
New Children's Museum 282
Ocean Institute 269
Orange County Museum of Art 250
Palm Springs Art Museum 341
Richard Nixon Library & Museum 240
Ronald Reagan Library & Museum 214
Route 66 'Mother Road' Museum 366
USS Midway Museum 288-9
Wende Museum 128
music 430, 453-5
festivals 454

N

Naples 185-6
national parks & reserves
Abalone Cove Shoreline Park 183
Angeles National Forest 195-6
Antelope Valley California Poppy Reserve 378
Anza-Borrego Desert State Park 17, 358-62, **17**
Cachuma Lake Recreation Area 409
Channel Islands National Park 15, 425-8, **15**
Chumash Painted Cave State Historic Park 409
Crystal Cove State Park 162, 259-60, **163**
Death Valley National Park 369-76
Griffith Park 94, 99, 105, **100-1**
Joshua Tree National Park 15, 350-8, **352-3**, **15**
Los Padres National Forest 409
Mt San Jacinto State Park 343
Pt Mugu State Park 149
Salt Creek Beach 269
Topanga Canyon State Park 148-9
Will Rogers State Historic Park 147
Needles 367
Newport Bay Ecological Reserve 256
Newport Beach 249-57, **250-1**
nightlife, *see individual locations*
Nipton 369

O

Ocean Beach 291, 301, 308, 311, **292**
Oceanside 332-4
Ojai 18, 421-3, **18**
Old Towne Orange 239-40
opening hours 21, 477
Orange County 218, 240-71, **219**
climate 218
highlights 219
Oscars, *see* Academy Awards

P

Pacific Beach 291-3, 301-2, 308, 312, **294**
Pacific Coast Highway 9, **8-9**
Pacific Palisades 94, 144-52, **146-7**
Palm Springs 12, **338**, **12**
accommodations 337, 345-6
climate 337
drinking & nightlife 347-9
entertainment 349
festivals & events 344-5
food 337, 346-7
highlights 338
shopping 349
sights 339-41
tourist information 349-50
travel seasons 337
travel to/around 350
Palm Springs Aerial Tramway 339
Palms to Pines Scenic Byway 216
Palomar Mountain 335
Palomar Observatory 335
Palos Verdes Peninsula 182-3
Panamint Springs 372
Paradise Cove 158
paragliding, *see* hang-gliding
parks & gardens
Balboa Park 11, 275-82, **278**
Barnsdall Art Park 100
Echo Park Lake 106
Huntington Library 195
Living Desert Zoo & Gardens 341
Los Angeles Zoo & Botanical Gardens 101
Malibu Bluffs Park 144
Moorten Botanical Gardens 341
Pasadena 193-201, **194**
accommodations 198
activities 198
drinking & nightlife 200
entertainment 200-1
food 199-200
shopping 201
sights 193-8
passports 479
Pioneertown 357
planning 6-54
budgeting 21
calendar of events 25-6
children, travel with 50-2
Disneyland 46-9
itineraries 27-32
regions 53-4
travel seasons 20
websites 21
plants 467-8
Point Loma 290-1
poison oak 43
politics 430
population 431
Primm 369
public holidays 477

R

radio 476
Randsburg 380
Redondo Beach 181-2
religion 431, 445-6
Richard Nixon Library & Museum 240
Ridgecrest 379-80
road trips, *see* scenic drives
rock climbing 44, 354-5
Ronald Reagan Library & Museum 214
Rose Bowl & Parade 25
Route 66 16, 364-7, **16**

S

safety 477
Salton Sea 363
Salvation Mountain 363
San Clemente 271
San Diego 16, 272-316, **273**, **274**, **277**, **284-5**
accommodations 272, 296-302
Balboa Park 11, 275-82, **278**
Bankers Hill 285-6
climate 272
Downtown 282-3
drinking & nightlife 308-12
Embarcadero 288-9
entertainment 312-13
festivals & events 296
food 272, 302-8
highlights 273
Hillcrest 285-6, **278**
itineraries 281
Little Italy 286-7
Mission Bay 293, 302
Mission Beach 162, 293, **294**, **162**
North Park 285-6
Ocean Beach 291, **292**
Old Town 287-8
Pacific Beach 293, **294**
Point Loma 290-1
San Diego Zoo 11, 275-82, **10**
shopping 313-14
tourist information 314-15
travel seasons 272
travel to/from 315-16
Waterfront, the 288-9
San Diego County 317-334, **324**
San Diego Zoo 11, 275-82, **10**
San Diego Zoo Safari Park 331
San Fernando Valley 94, 189-93
San Gabriel Mountains 157, 161
San Gabriel Valley 193-201
San Jacinto Mountains 216, **12**
San Juan Capistrano 268-9
San Miguel 427

Santa Barbara 13, 392-408, **394**
accommodations 400
drinking & nightlife 404-5
entertainment 405-6
food 402-4
highlights 391
itineraries 392
shopping 406
tourist information 406-7
travel to/within 407-8
walking tour 397
Santa Barbara County 390-428, **391**
accommodations 390
climate 390
food 390
travel seasons 390
Santa Barbara Island 427
Santa Barbara Wine Country 408-19, **410**
Santa Cruz Island 426
Santa Monica 94, 152-68, **154**, **95**, **162**
accommodations 158-60
activities 156-8
drinking & nightlife 164-5
entertainment 165-6
food 160-4
shopping 166-8
sights 152-6
Santa Monica Mountains 19, 161, **19**
Santa Monica Pier 152, **95**
Santa Paula 423
Santa Rita Hills Wine Trail 412-14
Santa Ynez Valley 413-26
scenic drives 23
Big Bear Lake 217
Joshua Tree National Park 353-4
Malibu 148
Mulholland Drive 157
Palms to Pines Scenic Byway 216
Route 66 16, **16**
Scotty's Castle 372
scuba-diving, *see* diving
Seal Beach 241-3
seasickness 39
shopping 23, *see also individual locations*
Shoshone 377
Silicon Beach 175
Silver Lake 94, 105-8, **66**, **94**
Six Flags Magic Mountain 215
Skidoo 372
skiing 44, 344
snorkeling 37-8, 213, 261, 294, 320
Soak City OC 237
Solana Beach 326-7
Solvang 415-18
South Bay 177-83
Hermosa Beach 179-81
Manhattan Beach 177-9
Palos Verdes Peninsula 182-3
Redondo Beach 181-2
Torrance 181-2
South Central Los Angeles 205-13
spas, *see* hot springs & day spas
Split Mountain wind caves 359, **17**
sports 446-7, *see also* baseball, swimming, surfing
Stovepipe Wells 372
Summerland 420
Sunnylands 347
Sunset Beach 243-4
surfing 19, 35-6
Encinitas 327-9, **19**
Huntington Beach 245, **162**
La Jolla 320
Malibu 149
Newport Beach 251
San Diego 293-7
Santa Barbara 397-8
Trestles 271
swimming 33-5, *see also* beaches

T

Tahquitz Canyon 341-3
taquerías 14, **14**
Tecopa 377-8
telephone services 20
television 91, 452, 476
Temecula 18, 334
Temecula area 334-6
theater 455-6
theme parks 22
Balboa Fun Zone 250
Belmont Park 293
Calico Ghost Town 366
Disney California Adventure 225-36
Disneyland 11, 46-9, 219-36, **219**, **220**, **222**, **10**
Knott's Berry Farm 236-7
Legoland 329-30
Puzzle Zoo 167
SeaWorld San Diego 291-3
Six Flags Magic Mountain 215
Soak City OC 237
Terrible's Primm Valley Casino Resorts 369
Universal Studios Hollywood 190, **95**
Wet 'n' Wild Palm Springs 344
Tijuana (Mexico) 298
time 476
tipping 477
Topanga Canyon 148
Torrance 181-2
tourist information 477, *see also individual locations*
tours 484, *see also* walking tours
train travel 480, 484-5
transportation 479-85
travel seasons 20, 25-6, *see also individual locations*
travel to/from SoCal 479-80
travel within SoCal 481-5
Trestles 271
Trona Pinnacles 380

U

Universal City 94, 189-93
Universal Studios Hollywood 190, **95**
Urban Wine Trail 404

V

vacations 477
vegetarian & vegan travelers 465
Venice 94, 168-77, **170**, **94**
accommodations 172-3
activities 171-2
drinking & nightlife 175-6
food 173-5
sights 168-71
Venice Beach 94, 158, **94**
Venice Beach Freakshow 172
Venice Boardwalk 168-9
Ventura 423-5
Victorville 365
visas 20, 478
visual arts 456

W

walking, *see* hiking
walking tours
Laguna Beach Art Walk 265
Santa Barbara Art Walks 400
Venice Art Walk 169
Walt Disney Concert Hall 68, **9**
weather 20, 25-6, *see also individual locations*
websites, *see* internet resources
weights 476
West Hollywood 94, 108-27, **110-11**
accommodations 115-16
activities 114-15
drinking & nightlife 120-1
entertainment 121-4
food 116-20
shopping 124-7
sights 109-14
Westlake 203-5
Westward Beach 158
Westwood 94, 131-43, **134**
accommodations 138-9
drinking & nightlife 141-2
entertainment 142
food 139-41
shopping 142-3
sights 131-7
whale-watching 39-45
San Diego 295
Santa Barbara 397
windsurfing 40
wineries 22, 464, **13**, **18**
Foxen 411
Foxen Canyon Wine Trail 13, 411-12
Santa Barbara 408-414, 417, **410**
Santa Rita Hills Wine Trail 412-14
Temecula 334-6
Urban Wine Trail 404

Y

yoga 44

Z

zoos
Living Desert Zoo & Gardens 341
Los Angeles Zoo & Botanical Gardens 101
San Diego Zoo 276
San Diego Zoo Safari Park 331
Zuma 158

Map Legend

Sights

- Beach
- Bird Sanctuary
- Buddhist
- Castle/Palace
- Christian
- Confucian
- Hindu
- Islamic
- Jain
- Jewish
- Monument
- Museum/Gallery/Historic Building
- Ruin
- Sento Hot Baths/Onsen
- Shinto
- Sikh
- Taoist
- Winery/Vineyard
- Zoo/Wildlife Sanctuary
- Other Sight

Activities, Courses & Tours

- Bodysurfing
- Diving
- Canoeing/Kayaking
- Course/Tour
- Skiing
- Snorkeling
- Surfing
- Swimming/Pool
- Walking
- Windsurfing
- Other Activity

Sleeping

- Sleeping
- Camping

Eating

- Eating

Drinking & Nightlife

- Drinking & Nightlife
- Cafe

Entertainment

- Entertainment

Shopping

- Shopping

Information

- Bank
- Embassy/Consulate
- Hospital/Medical
- Internet
- Police
- Post Office
- Telephone
- Toilet
- Tourist Information
- Other Information

Geographic

- Beach
- Hut/Shelter
- Lighthouse
- Lookout
- Mountain/Volcano
- Oasis
- Park
- Pass
- Picnic Area
- Waterfall

Population

- Capital (National)
- Capital (State/Province)
- City/Large Town
- Town/Village

Transport

- Airport
- BART station
- Border crossing
- Boston T station
- Bus
- Cable car/Funicular
- Cycling
- Ferry
- Metro/Muni station
- Monorail
- Parking
- Petrol station
- Subway/SkyTrain station
- Taxi
- Train station/Railway
- Tram
- Underground station
- Other Transport

Note: Not all symbols displayed above appear on the maps in this book

Routes

- Tollway
- Freeway
- Primary
- Secondary
- Tertiary
- Lane
- Unsealed road
- Road under construction
- Plaza/Mall
- Steps
- Tunnel
- Pedestrian overpass
- Walking Tour
- Walking Tour detour
- Path/Walking Trail

Boundaries

- International
- State/Province
- Disputed
- Regional/Suburb
- Marine Park
- Cliff
- Wall

Hydrography

- River, Creek
- Intermittent River
- Canal
- Water
- Dry/Salt/Intermittent Lake
- Reef

Areas

- Airport/Runway
- Beach/Desert
- Cemetery (Christian)
- Cemetery (Other)
- Glacier
- Mudflat
- Park/Forest
- Sight (Building)
- Sportsground
- Swamp/Mangrove

OUR STORY

A beat-up old car, a few dollars in the pocket and a sense of adventure. In 1972 that's all Tony and Maureen Wheeler needed for the trip of a lifetime – across Europe and Asia overland to Australia. It took several months, and at the end – broke but inspired – they sat at their kitchen table writing and stapling together their first travel guide, *Across Asia on the Cheap*. Within a week they'd sold 1500 copies. Lonely Planet was born.

Today, Lonely Planet has offices in Franklin, London, Melbourne, Oakland, Beijing and Delhi, with more than 600 staff and writers. We share Tony's belief that 'a great guidebook should do three things: inform, educate and amuse'.

OUR WRITERS

Sara Benson

Coordinating Author, Santa Barbara County After graduating from college Sara jumped on a plane to California with just one suitcase and $100 in her pocket. After driving tens of thousands of miles, to every corner of the state, she decided to settle down in a little beach town on the Southern California coast. She's an avid hiker, backpacker, cyclist and all-seasons outdoor enthusiast who has also worked for the National Park Service in California. Already the author of more than 55 travel and nonfiction books, Sara is the lead writer for Lonely Planet's *California*, *California's Best Trips* and *Discover Las Vegas* guides. Follow her latest adventures online at www.indietraveler.blogspot.com, www.indietraveler.net, @indie_traveler on Twitter and indietraveler on Instagram. Sara also wrote the Las Vegas content of the Palm Springs & the Deserts chapter as well as the Plan Your Trip, Understand and Survival Guide chapters. Read more about Sara at lonelyplanet.com/members/Sara_Benson

Andrew Bender

Disneyland & Orange County, San Diego, Palm Springs & the Deserts Andy is a true Angeleno, not because he was born in Los Angeles but because he's made it his own. This native New Englander drove cross-country to work in film production, and eventually realized that the joy was in the journey (and writing about it). He writes the Seat 1A travel site for Forbes, and his writing has also appeared in the *Los Angeles Times*, in-flight magazines and over three dozen Lonely Planet titles. Current obsessions: discovering SoCal's next great ethnic enclave and photographing winter sunsets over the Pacific. Andrew also wrote the Disneyland Trip Planner chapter.

Adam Skolnick

Los Angeles Adam Skolnick has written about travel, culture, health, sports, human rights and the environment, for Lonely Planet, *New York Times*, *Outside*, *Men's Health*, *Travel & Leisure*, Salon.com, BBC.com and ESPN.com. He has authored or coauthored 25 Lonely Planet guidebooks. His debut novel, *Middle of Somewhere*, is set to publish in 2014. You can read more of his work at www.adamskolnick.com. Find him on Twitter and Instagram (@adamskolnick).

Published by Lonely Planet Publications Pty Ltd
ABN 36 005 607 983
4th edition – December 2014
ISBN 978 1 74220 298 3

10 9 8 7 6 5 4 3 2 1
Printed in China